Original text:
Steindór Steindórsson frá Hlöðum

Editor:
Eva Hálfdanardóttir
Hálfdan Örlygsson
Örlygur Hálfdanarson

Supervision of maps and the Atlas:
Þórdís Guðrún Arthursdóttir

Advertisements:
Eva Hálfdanardóttir
Óttar Sveinsson

VEGAHANDBÓKIN EHF.

TABLE OF

Important reading

CONTENT

Iceland Road Guide – 13th edition.
– Former title: *The Visitor´s Key to Iceland*
– Former title: *Iceland Road Atlas*

This book was published under the title Iceland Road Guide 1975, 1978, 1981 and 1988.
Revised 1996, 1999, 2001 and 2003 under the title The Visitor´s Key to Iceland.
Revised 2005, 2007 and 2009 under the title Iceland Road Atlas.
Revised 2011 and 2013 under the title Iceland Road Guide.

All plans in this book are based on maps prepared by the Icelandic Geodetic Survey and the original maps produced by Geodætisk Institut in Copenhagen. This book is published by special agreement with Icelandic Geodetic Survey.

Original design: Jakob Hálfdanarson, engineer.

Map drawing: Narfi Þorsteinsson directed the original drawing of the maps which form the basis of the maps in this edition and have been converted into machine-readable form. Sigurgeir Skúlason was in charge of the text on the maps. Ólafur Valsson produced the maps.

English version: Einar Guðjohnsen and Pétur Kidson Karlsson (based on the original Icelandic editions 1973 and 1974) with additional material 1988 by Leo Munro and Helgi Magnússon.
Revision of the 1996 edition (based on additional material by Örlygur Hálfdanarson): Wincie Jóhannsdóttir.
Revision of the 1999, 2001, 2003, 2005, 2007, 2009 and 2011 edition Örlygur Hálfdanarson/ Eva Hálfdanardóttir

Lay-out: Vegahandbókin ehf. / Þríbrot ehf.
Printing and bound by: Prentmiðlun ehf., Poland

ISBN 978-9979-9992-6-3

HOW TO USE THIS BOOK

Please spend a few minutes reading these pages before you start using and enjoying the Iceland Road Guide.

Information is arranged according to the Public Roads Administration's regional numbering system, which is also used on road signs throughout the country. Roads are listed in numerical order. **The Ring Road, Highway 1,** is covered in **pages 51-151.** It is followed by roads in Regions 2 to 9, and finally by the mountain roads, which are prefixed by a letter F. Almost all roads have both numbers and names.

There are eight regions. The regional boundaries are shown on the map on page 5.

All roads in each region are identified on the regional maps, next to these is a list of the roads (both their names and numbers) with their corresponding page(s) in the guide.

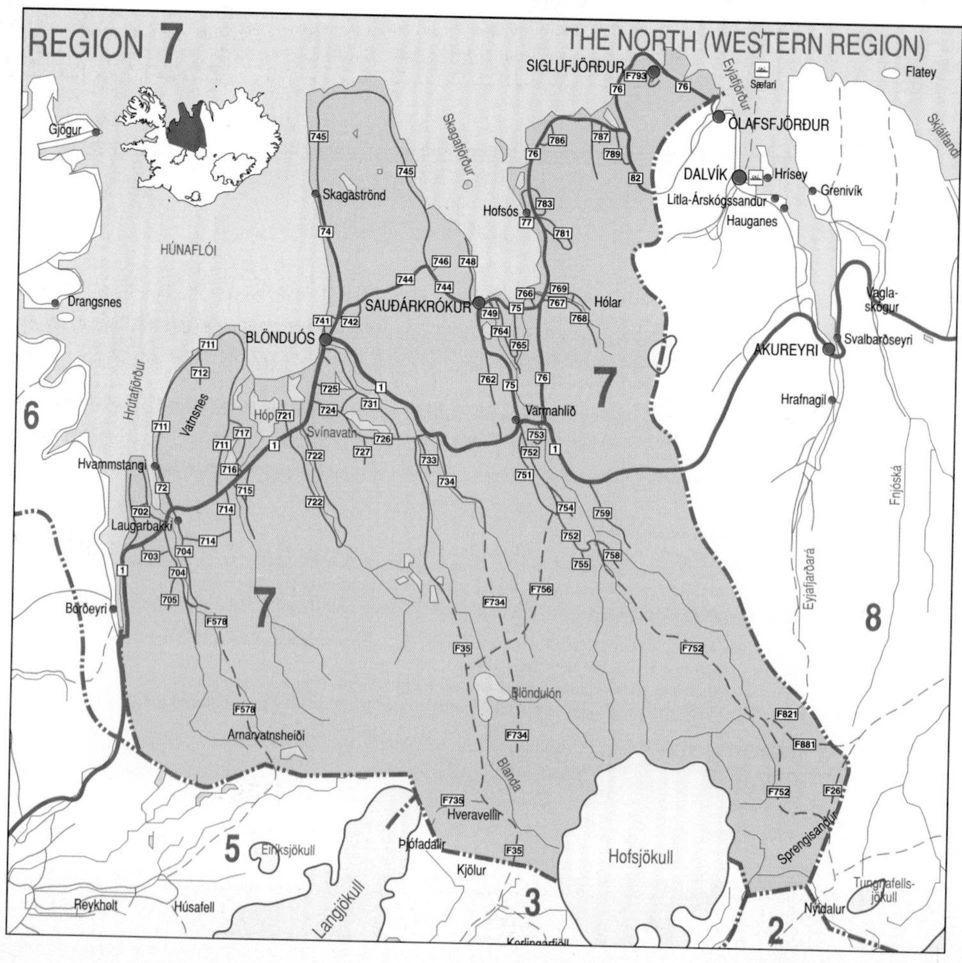

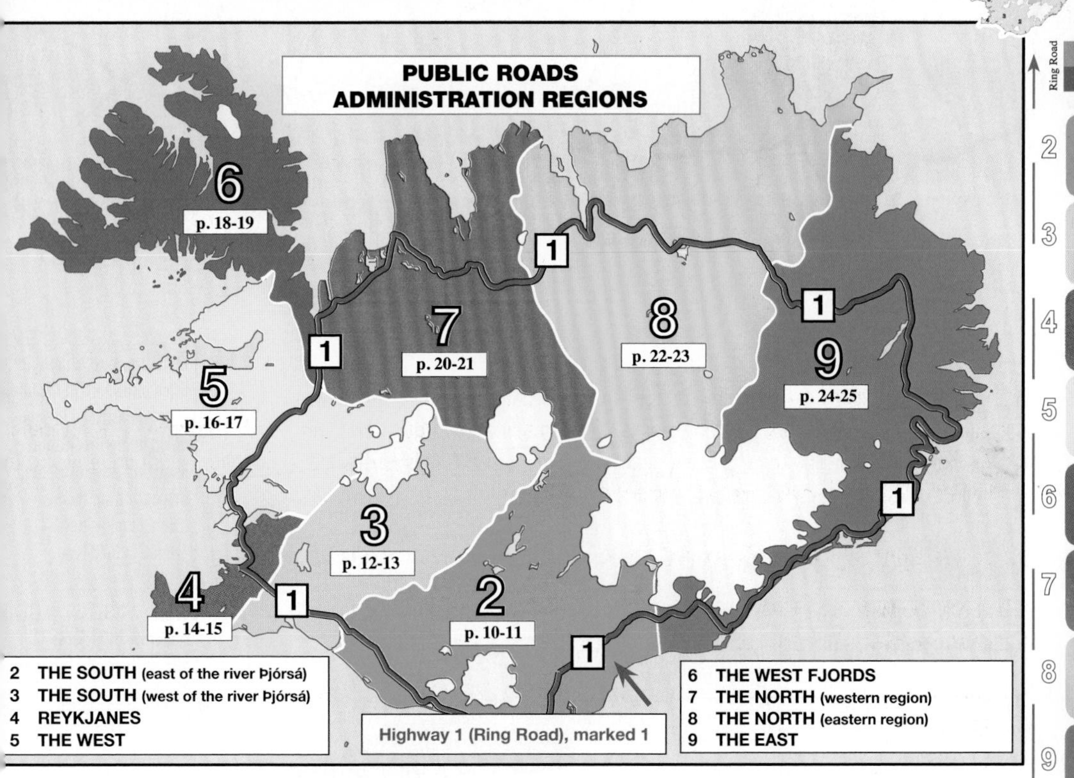

Ring Road
2
3
4
5
6
7
8
9

Iceland is divided into eight regions, numbered from 2 to 9.
There is no region 1.

'his map shows the regions, and also Highway 1 (the Ring Road), which passes through ll regions. The numbers of all roads in each area (with the exception of Highway 1) egin with the relevant regional number. For example, all roads in Region 2 have umbers beginning with 2. The roads within each region are listed in numerical, rather ıan alphabetical, order. For example, the first road in Region 3, Skeiða- og Irunamannavegur, is no. 30, and the last, Arnarbælisvegur, is no. 375.

Use the colour bars on the side to find each new section easily.

Use the region color chart for quick region reference.

If you are taking the Ring Road from Reykjavík to the west and the north, start at page 51. If you are travelling east from Reykjavík, begin instead at page 151 and follow the pages in reverse order until you get to Reykjavík via Hvalfjörður and Kjalarnes.

Key locations and the distances between them are listed at the top and bottom of the map. This makes it easy to use for travel in either direction.

The numer in the triangle (1-24) is a refernece to an Atlas (p. 562-587) so you can orient yourself within a bigger region.

Every region has its own colour code.

The road-map includes symbols which indicate various services available in the area.

Advertisements detail various services available in the area.

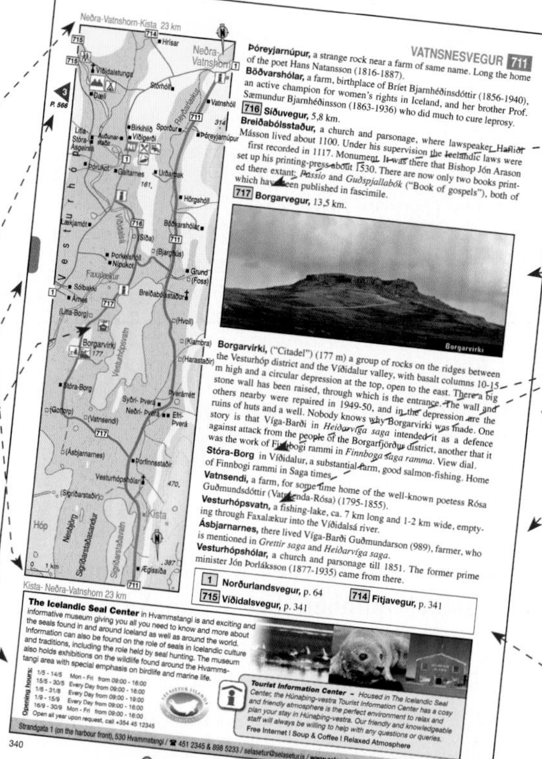

VATNSNESVEGUR 711

Þóreyjarnúpur, a strange rock near a farm of same name. Long the home of the poet Hans Natansson (1816-1887).
Böðvarshólar, a farm, birthplace of Bríet Bjarnhéðinsdóttir (1856-1940), an active champion for women's rights in Iceland, and her brother Prof. Sæmundur Bjarnhéðinsson (1863-1936) who did much to cure leprosy.
716 **Síðuvegur,** 5,8 km.
Breiðabólsstaður, a church and parsonage, where lawspeaker Hafliði Másson lived about 1100. Under his supervision the Icelandic laws were first recorded in 1117. Monument. It was there that Bishop Jón Arason set up his printing-press about 1530. There are now only two books printed there extant: *Passio* and *Guðspjallabók* ("Book of gospels"), both of which have been published in fascimile.
717 **Borgarvegur,** 13,5 km.

Borgarvirki

Borgarvirki, ("Citadel") (177 m) a group of rocks on the ridges between the Vesturhóp district and the Víðidalur valley, with basalt columns 10-15 m high and a circular depression at the top, open to the east. There a big stone wall has been raised, through which is the entrance. The wall and others nearby were repaired in 1949-50, and in the depression are the ruins of huts and a well. Nobody knows why Borgarvirki was made. One story is that Víga-Barði in *Heiðarvíga saga* intended it as a defence against attack from the people of the Borgarfjörður district, another that it was the work of Finnbogi rammi in *Finnboga saga ramma*. View dial.
Stóra-Borg in Víðidalur, a substantial farm, good salmon-fishing. Home of Finnbogi rammi in Saga times.
Vatnsendi, a farm, for some time home of the well-known poetess Rósa Guðmundsdóttir (Vatnsenda-Rósa) (1795-1855).
Vesturhópsvatn, a fishing-lake, ca. 7 km long and 1-2 km wide, emptying through Faxalækur into the Víðidalsá river.
Ásbjarnarnes, there lived Víga-Barði Guðmundarson (989), farmer, who is mentioned in *Grettir saga* and *Heiðarvíga saga*.
Vesturhópshólar, a church and parsonage till 1851. The former prime minister Jón Þorláksson (1877-1935) came from there.

1 **Norðurlandsvegur,** p. 64
715 **Víðidalsvegur,** p. 341
714 **Fitjavegur,** p. 341

The Icelandic Seal Center in Hvammstangi is and exciting and informative museum giving you all you need to know and more about the seals found in and around Iceland as well as around the world. Information can also be found on the role of seals in Icelandic culture and traditions, including the role held by seal hunting. The museum also holds exhibitions on the wildlife found around the Hvammstangi area with special emphasis on birdlife and marine life.

Opening hours:
1/5 - 14/5 Mon - Fri from 09:00 - 16:00
15/5 - 30/5 Every Day from 09:00 - 16:00
1/6 - 31/8 Every Day from 09:00 - 19:00
1/9 - 15/9 Every Day from 09:00 - 16:00
16/9 - 30/9 Mon - Fri from 09:00 - 16:00
Open all year upon request, call +354 45 12345

Tourist Information Center – Housed in The Icelandic Seal Center, the Húnaþing-vestra Tourist Information Center has a cosy and friendly atmosphere is the perfect environment to relax and plan your stay in Húnaþing-vestra. Our friendly and knowledgeable staff will always be willing to help with any questions or queries.
Free Internet | Soup & Coffee | Relaxed Atmosphere

Strandgata 1 (on the harbour front), 530 Hvammstangi / ☎ 451 2345 & 898 5233 / selasetur@selasetur.is / www.selasetur.is / GPS: 65°23,709N 20°56,634W

340

ÚTVARPIÐ FM 89,1/93,0 LW 189/207 · RÁS FM 95,5/98,0 · BYLGJAN FM 98,9 · FM 94,3

Minor roads which are not listed elsewhere in the book may be described in some detail in the text of the page. In these cases, the number of the road is framed and its name printed in bold type.

Hundreds of pictures and photographs bring to life the information accompanying the maps.

Words in bold type are listed in the index at the back of the book.

Each map is accompanied by interesting information on the history and natural features of the area.

The relevant page number(s) for information on other roads is listed at the bottom of the text.

Frequencies for the National Radio, Bylgjan and FM957 are listed at the bottom of each page.

New in this edition!

This edition now includes a detailed 24-page Atlas, on pages **p. 562-587**.
On a scale of **1:500,000**, you can get a clear **overview** of all of the Icelandic regions and refer quickly back and forth to place descriptions by page number. For instance, if you are reading **p. 281** as you travel towards Búðardalur, you can orient yourself within a bigger region by noting the arrow referring you to Map 3 (P. 566) in the Atlas, on **p. 566**.

READ THIS
SO YOU DON'T GET LOST!

One of the advantages of this Guide is that it is equally easy to use when **travelling in either direction** on any road.

The road descriptions begin with Highway 1 (the Ring Road), starting from Reykjavík and continuing clockwise round the country through the West, North, East and South Regions and reaching Reykjavík again by Suðurlandsvegur.

It may seem odd to have to read the map and the corresponding information upwards and not from the top down as you are probably used to doing. There is a natural reason for this, which you will soon understand and get used to immediately.

Of course, it is also possible to follow Highway 1 in an **anti-clockwise** direction from Reykjavík. To do this, begin your journey at **Rauðavatn** on page 151 and follow each page from top to bottom, and in reverse order (i.e. going from **page 151 to 150** and so on until you returned to Reykjavík via Hvalfjörður and Kjalarnes).

There are street maps of all main towns and villages in the country, with symbols showing services offered by advertisers in this Guide.

If you are taking the Ring Road from Reykjavík to the west and the north, start at page 51.
If you are travelling east from Reykjavík, begin instead at page 151 and follow the pages in reverse order until you get to Reykjavík via Hvalfjörður and Kjalarnes.

KEY TO MAP SYMBOLS

- Hospital / Clinic
- Police station
- Chemist
- Rescue hut
- Emergency phone
- Fire extinguiser
- Clinic
- Information
- Information centre
- Telephone
- Public toilets
- Earth closet
- Town centre
- Place of interest
- Walking routes
- Picnic spot
- View dial
- Garbage containers
- Petrol station
- Auto mechanic
- Tyre service
- 4W bike rental
- Car rental
- Restaurant
- Home cooking

- Licensed premises
- Guesthouse
- Sleeping bag accommodation
- Meeting facilities
- Icelandic farm holidays
- Breakfast
- Youth hostel
- Summerhouse rental
- Summerhouse colony
- Tourist hut
- Campsite
- Waste tank dischange
- Caravan park
- Cooking facilities
- Shower
- Hot tub
- Washing machine
- Swimming pool
- Gymnasium
- Sports area
- Seal view
- **Playground**
- Farmyard animal zoo
- Tourist cowshed
- Dog hotel
- Horse rental

- Stable area
- Race track
- Veterinarian
- Fishing permits
- Sea angling
- Whale watching
- Snowcat trips
- Ski slopes
- Shooting arena
- Cross-country skiing area
- Ski slopes
- Golf course
- Jet ski rental
- Bicycle rental
- Boat rental
- River rafting
- Water skiing
- Glacier tours
- Bus tours
- Jeep tours
- Shark fishing
- Open all year
- Greenhouse
- Church
- Graveyard
- Bank

- ATM
- Post office
- Tourist shop
- Grocery store
- Bakery
- Roadhouse
- Museum
- Internet connection
- Live music
- Library
- Aquarium
- Bird view
- Rubbish container
- Handicrafts
- Ice-cream shop
- Book store
- Gallery
- Cinema
- Coffee house
- Photographic equipments
- Travel bureau
- Solarium / gym
- Billiards
- Car ferry
- Boat trips
- Airport

- Airport
- Tunnel
- Factory
- Hydroelectric station
- Lighthouse
- School
- Community centre
- Radio
- N1 station
- Olís station
- Shell station
- ÓB gas station
- Orkan gas station
- Ego gas station
- **Bónus Groceries**
- Landsbanki Bank
- Open Forest
- Golf course
- National Museum of Iceland
- 1 61 702 F622 Road numbers

Above and below each map are the names of the distance points, and normally the distance between them. Some place names are also printed in red on the maps themselves. On p. 62, for example, the distance points are Grænumýrartunga - Reykjaskóli and Reykjaskóli - Grænumýrartunga. Grænumýrartunga is printed in red, but in parentheses. The parentheses, together with the open square ■ which is also printed in red, show that the farm is abandoned. If farming had been discontinued but the buildings were still maintained, then the square would be filled in: ■ At the top of the page, Reykjaskóli is printed in red, and also with a filled square, since the school is in operation. On p. 168, the distance points are Hvolsvöllur - Hlíðarendi; the name Hvolsvöllur is printed in red at the bottom of the map, with the symbol for a built-up area also in red. At the top of the map, Hlíðarendi is printed in red, but instead of the farm symbol there is the symbol for a church, in red. If the farm Hlíðarendi were abandoned then the name would be in parentheses, but not around the symbol for the church, since it is in use.

■	Farm
(Farm name) ■	Farm and distance point
■	Farm; uninhabited, but buildings maintained
(Farm name) ■	Farm, uninhabited, distance point
□	Abandoned farm
□	Abandoned farm, distance point
†	Church
†	Church and distance point
	Built-up area

The Meaning of Icelandic Place Names

Most Icelandic place names, both of towns, villages, and natural features in the landscape, mean something. This can help the reader to identify and understand them. For instance, words containing the compounds *hver, laug,* and *reyk(ja)* indicate the proximity of hot springs. It should be noted that words or compounds in declension sometimes appear rather different from the nominative.

The last part of a place name is usually the name of the geographical feature, e.g. Þing*vellir* (*vellir* is the plural of völlur = plain), Þjórs*á* (*á* = river), Akra*fjall* (*fjall* = mountain), Sel*foss* (*foss* = falls).

The following list is intended primarily as an aid to map-reading.

alda = hilly ridge (plural: *öldur)*
á = river
ás = small hill, ridge
bær = farm, township
bakki = river bank
bjarg = cliff, rock
borg = city; crag
botn = bottom, head of valley or fiord
brekka = slope
brú = bridge
bunga = rounded peak
dalur = valley
djúp = long inlet; deep
drag = watercourse (plural: *drög*)
drangur = isolated column of rock
dyngja = dome
eiði = isthmus
ey = island (plural: *eyjar*)
eyri = sandspit, delta
fell = mountain; hill
fjall = mountain (plural: *fjöll*)
fjörður = fiord; broad inlet; valley (plural: *firðir*)
fljót = large river
foss = waterfall
gígur = crater
gil = gorge, ravine
gjá = chasm, fissure
grunn = shoal, shallow
háls = ridge, isthmus
hamar = crag
heiði = heath, moor
hlíð = mountain side
hnjúkur/*hnúkur* = peak
höfði = promontory
höfn = harbour
hóll = rounded hill (plural: *hólar*)
hólmur = islet
holt = stony hill
hraun = lava-field, lava
hryggur = ridge
hver = hot spring
hvoll = hill
jökull = glacier
jökulsá = glacial river
kirkja = church
klettur = rock, cliff
kot = small farm
kvísl = river; branch of river
lækur = brook
laug = warm spring
lón = lagoon
melur = gravel; barren plain
múli = headland, spur
mynni = mouth
mýri = swamp
nes = headland, ness
núpur = spur, peak
oddi = point, tongue of land
öræfi = desert
ós = estuary
reykur = smoke, steam
rif = reef
sandur = sand(s)
skagi = peninsula
skarð = mountain pass
sker = skerry
skógur = wood, shrubland
slétta = plain
staður = place; parsonage (plural: *staðir*)
stapi = bluff , crag
súlur = (mountain) peaks
tangi = narrow peninsula
tindur = summit
tjörn = small lake; pond
tunga = tongue (of land)
vað = ford (plural: *vöð*)
varða = cairn (plural: *vörður*)
vatn = lake; water (plural: *vötn*)
vegur = road; track
ver = grassy spot
vík = inlet; small bay
vogur = inlet; creek
völlur = plain (plural: *vellir*)

Conversion table

Temperature

0°C = 32°F
10°C = 50°F
20°C = 68°F
-5°C = 23°F
-10°C = 14°F

To convert Centigrade into Fahrenheit:
Multiply by 9, divide by 5, and add 32.

To convert Fahrenheit into Centigrade:
Subtract 32, multiply by 5, and divide by 9.

Length

1 metre = 1.094 yards
1 yard = 0.914 metre
1 kilometre = 0.6214 mile
1 mile = 1.609 kilometres

Area

1 square metre = 1.196 square yards
1 square yard = 0.836 square metre
1 square kilometre = 0.386 square mile
1 square mile = 2.59 square kilometres

Volume

1 litre = 1.76 pints (2.1 US pints)
1 pint = 0.568 litre
1 litre = 0.22 gallon (0.263 US gallons)
10 litres = 2.2 gallons (2.63 Us gallons)
1 gallon = 4.546 litres

Weight

1 kilogram = 2.205 pounds
1 pound (lb) = 0.454 kilogram
1 tonne (metric ton) = 1 kilogram = 0.984 long ton
1 ton = 1016.04 kilograms

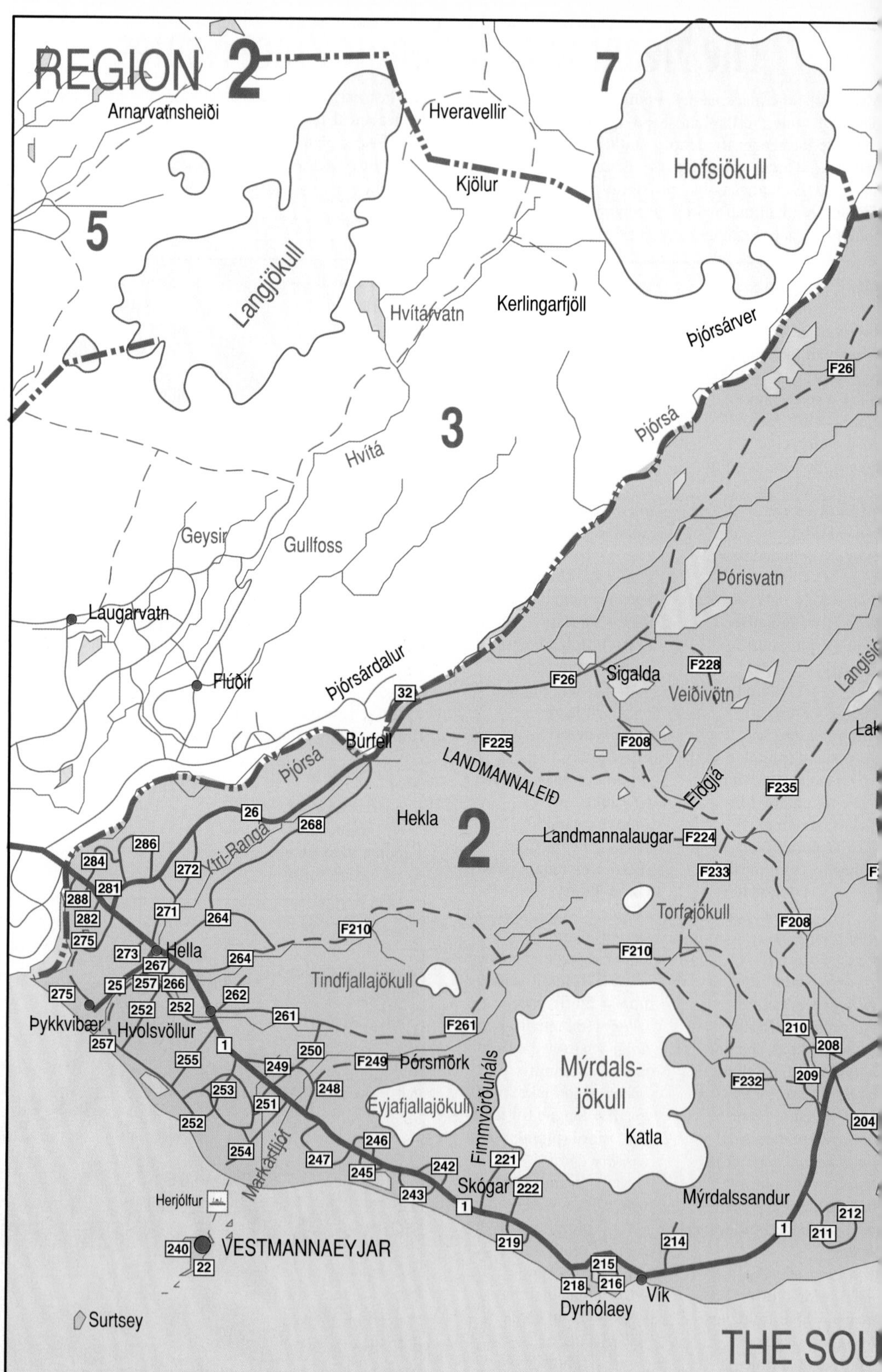
REGION 2
Arnarvatnsheiði
Hveravellir
7
Kjölur
Hofsjökull
5
Langjökull
Hvítárvatn
Kerlingarfjöll
Þjórsárver
F26
3
Þjórsá
Hvítá
Geysir
Gullfoss
Þórisvatn
Laugarvatn
Flúðir
Þjórsárdalur
32
F26
Sigalda
F228
Veiðivötn
Búrfell
F225
F208
Þjórsá
LANDMANNALEIÐ
Eldgjá
F235
26
268
Hekla
2
Landmannalaugar
F224
286
284
272
Ytri-Rangá
F233
281
288
271
264
Torfajökull
282
F210
F208
275
273
Hella
264
F210
267
Tindfjallajökull
275
25
257
266
262
252
252
261
F261
210
208
Þykkvibær
Hvolsvöllur
257
1
250
255
249
F249
Þórsmörk
Fimmvörðuháls
Mýrdals-
jökull
F232
209
253
248
251
Eyjafjallajökull
252
204
Katla
246
Markarfljót
254
247
221
242
245
Skógar
222
243
Mýrdalssandur
Herjólfur
1
212
1
211
219
214
240
VESTMANNAEYJAR
22
215
218
216
Vík
Dyrhólaey
Surtsey
THE SOU

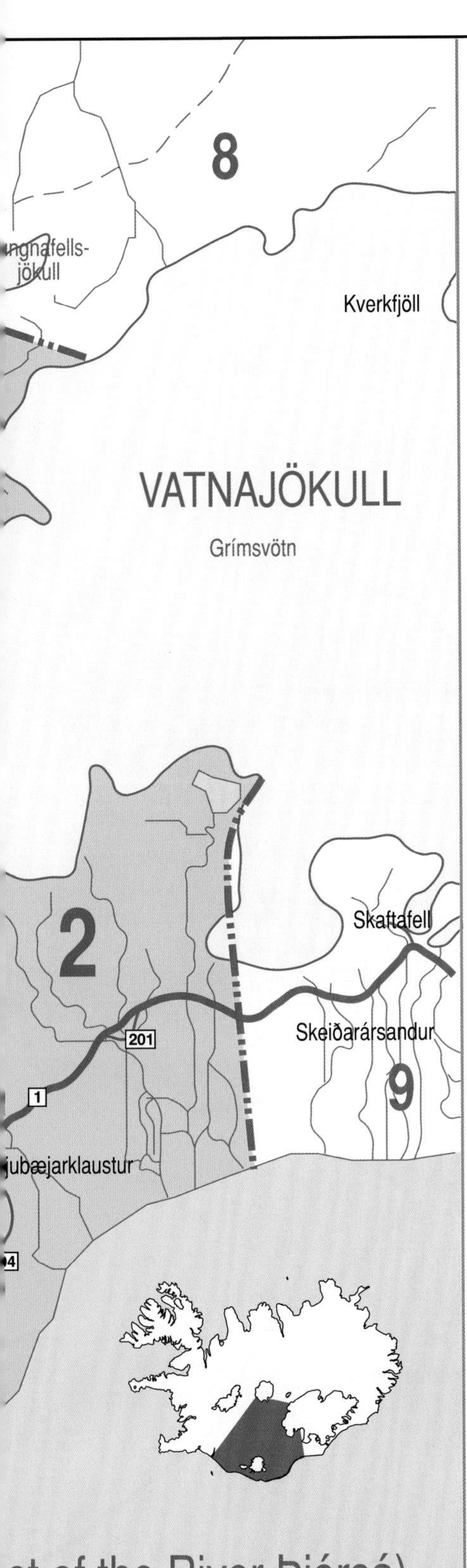
8
Kverkfjöll
VATNAJÖKULL
Grímsvötn
2
Skaftafell
Skeiðarársandur
9
201
1
st of the River Þjórsá)

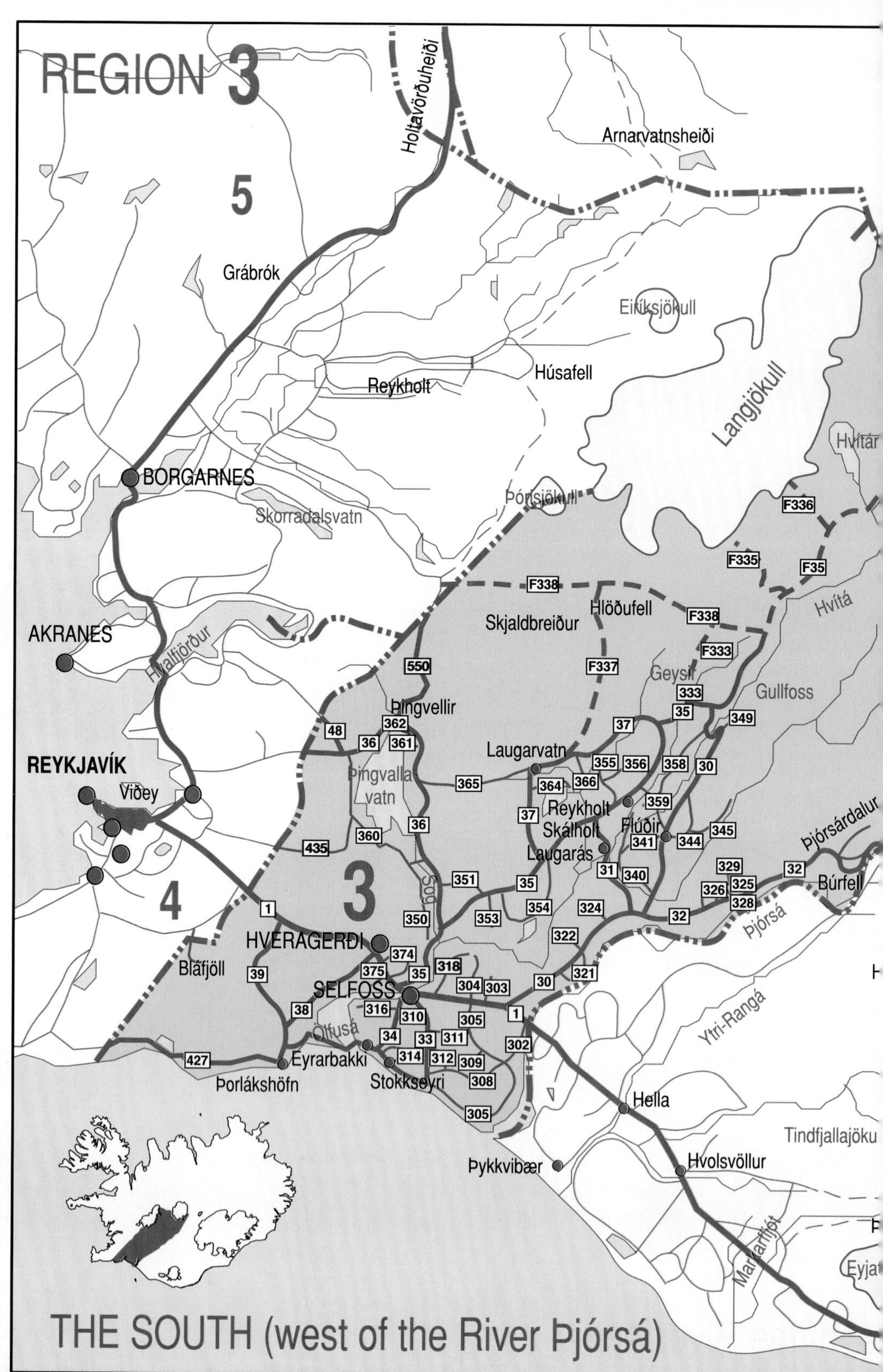
REGION 3
THE SOUTH (west of the River Þjórsá)
5
3
4
Holtavörðuheiði
Arnarvatnsheiði
Grábrók
Eiríksjökull
Húsafell
Reykholt
Langjökull
Hvítár
BORGARNES
Skorradalsvatn
Þórisjökull
F336
F335
F35
F338
Hlöðufell
Skjaldbreiður
Hvítá
AKRANES
Hvalfjörður
550
F337
F333
Geysir
333
Gullfoss
Þingvellir
362
35
349
48
36
361
37
Laugarvatn
355
356
358
30
REYKJAVÍK
Þingvallavatn
365
364
366
Viðey
Reykholt
359
Skálholt
Flúðir
345
Þjórsárdalur
36
341
344
360
Laugarás
435
329
31
340
351
35
32
Búrfell
326
325
328
354
324
1
353
32
Þjórsá
350
HVERAGERÐI
322
374
Bláfjöll
39
375
35
318
321
SELFOSS
304
303
30
38
316
310
1
305
Ytri-Rangá
Ölfusá
34
33
311
302
427
Eyrarbakki
314
312
309
Þorlákshöfn
Stokkseyri
308
Hella
305
Tindfjallajöku
Þykkvibær
Hvolsvöllur
Markarfljót
Eyja

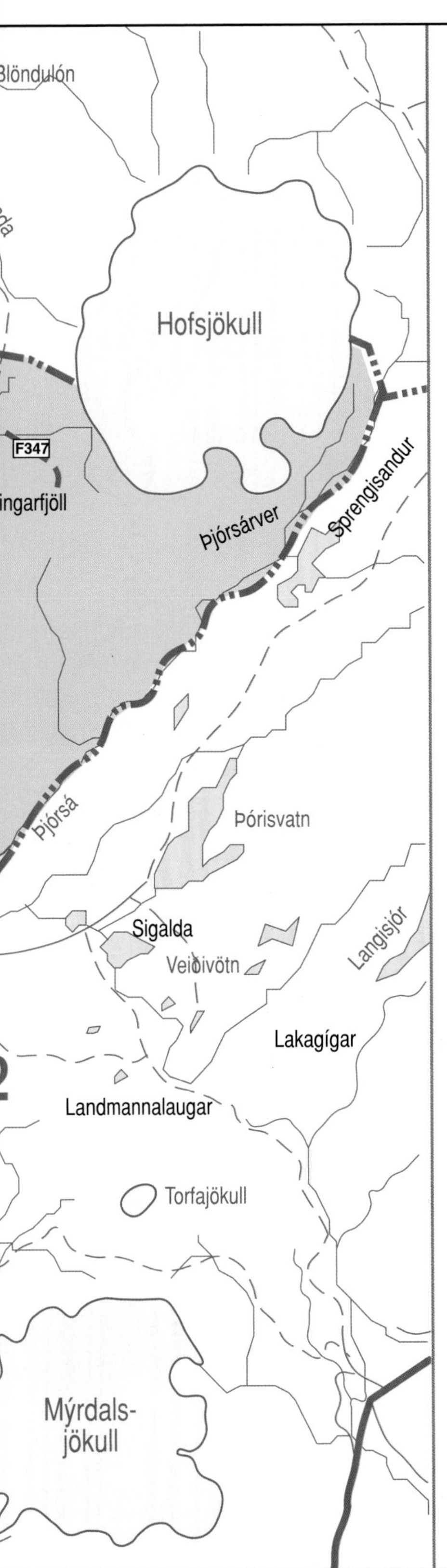
Blöndulón
Hofsjökull
F347
ingarfjöll
Þjórsárver
Sprengisandur
Þjórsá
Þórisvatn
Sigalda
Veiðivötn
Langisjór
Lakagígar
Landmannalaugar
Torfajökull
Mýrdals-
jökull

REGION 4
FAXAFLÓI
BORGARNES
Borgarfjörður
5
Akrafjall
AKRANES
47
460
Hvalfjörður
1
Esja
458
Grundarhverfi
Kollafjörður
REYKJAVÍK
SELTJARNARNES
Viðey
MO
1
Bessastaðir
Álftanes
KÓPAVOGUR
40
41
415
GARÐABÆR
HAFNARFJÖRÐUR
Straumsvík
Garðskagi
45
Garður
45
SANDGERÐI
429
423
45
41
KEFLAVÍK
Keflavík Airport
420
41
Vogar
46
421
NJARÐVÍK
417
42
407
Hafnir
Kleifar-
vatn
Bláfjöll
425
43
428
4
Bláa lónið
426
427
Reykjanes
425
427
427
GRINDAVÍK
REYKJANES

alsvatn
Kaldidalur
Uxahryggir
47
4
Þingvellir
Þingvalla-
vatn
Lyngdalsheiði
ÆR
3
Þrastaskógur
HVERAGERÐI
SELFOSS
Ölfusá
Eyrarbakki
Stokkseyri

REGION 5

THE WEST

Brjánslækur
Vatnsfjörður
Skálmarfjörður
Flatey
Baldur
BREIÐAFJÖRÐUR
STYKKISHÓLMUR
Rif
Hellissandur
ÓLAFSVÍK
Fróðár-heiði
Grundarfjörður
Snæfellsnes
Vatnaheiði
Kerlingar-skarð
Snæfellsjökull
Vegamót
Búðir
Arnarstapi
FAXAFLÓI
577 58 576 54 558 575 574 570 56 571 572 568 567

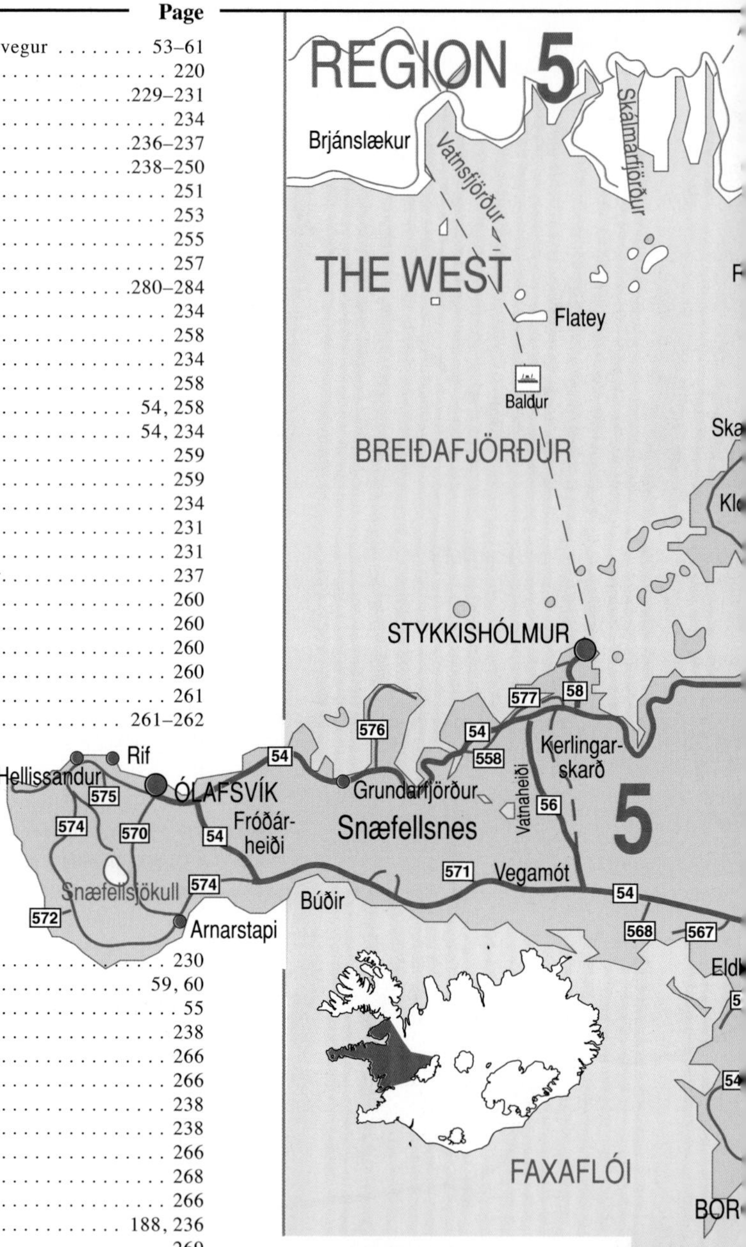

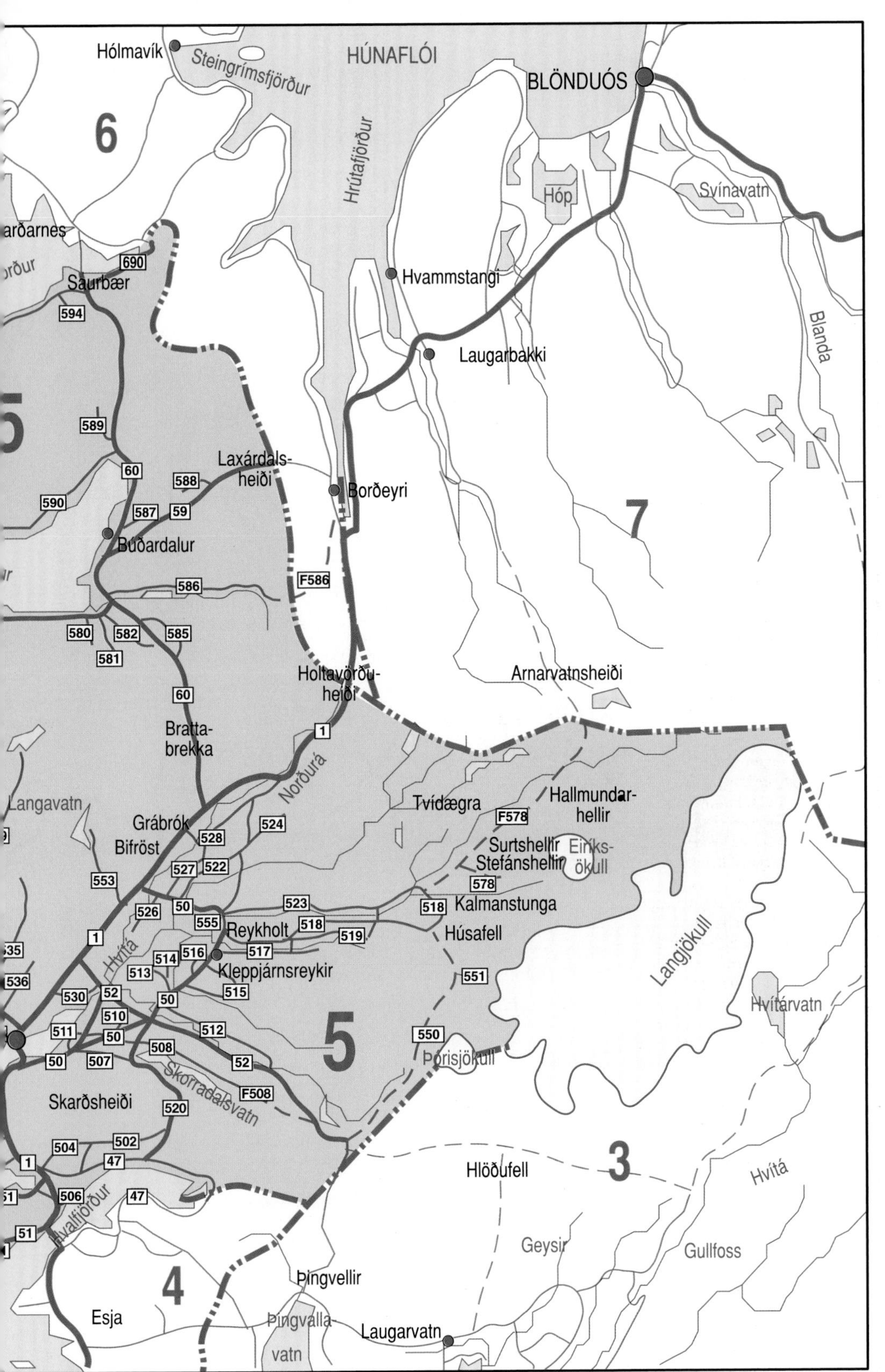
Hólmavík
Steingrímsfjörður
HÚNAFLÓI
BLÖNDUÓS
6
Hrútafjörður
Hóp
Svínavatn
Hvammstangi
Laugarbakki
Blanda
Saurbær
Laxárdals-
heiði
Borðeyri
Búðardalur
7
Holtavörðu-
heiði
Arnarvatnsheiði
Bratta-
brekka
Norðurá
Langavatn
Grábrók
Bifröst
Tvídægra
Hallmundar-
hellir
Surtshellir
Stefánshellir
Eiríks-
jökull
Kalmanstunga
Reykholt
Húsafell
Hvítá
Kleppjárnsreykir
Langjökull
Hvítárvatn
5
Þórisjökull
Skorradalsvatn
Skarðsheiði
Hlöðufell
3
Hvítá
Hvalfjörður
Geysir
Gullfoss
4
Þingvellir
Esja
Þingvalla-
vatn
Laugarvatn

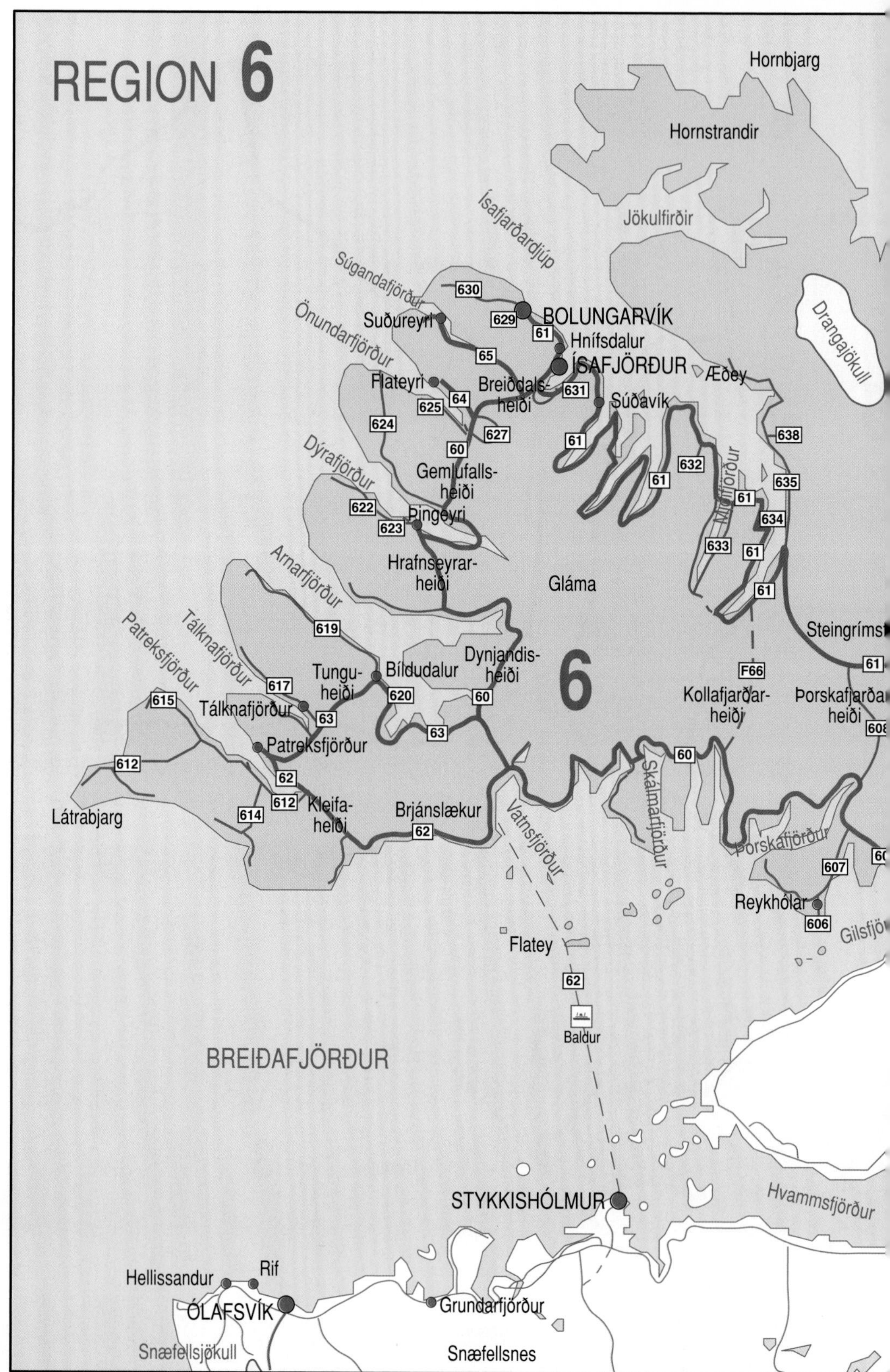
REGION 6
Hornbjarg
Hornstrandir
Ísafjarðardjúp
Jökulfirðir
Súgandafjörður
Drangajökull
630
629
BOLUNGARVÍK
Suðureyri
Önundarfjörður
61
Hnífsdalur
65
ÍSAFJÖRÐUR
Æðey
Flateyri
Breiðdals-
heiði
64
631
625
Súðavík
624
627
638
Dýrafjörður
60
61
632
Gemlufalls-
heiði
61
635
622
61
623
Þingeyri
634
633
61
Arnarfjörður
Hrafnseyrar-
heiði
Gláma
61
619
Steingríms
Tálknafjörður
Dynjandis-
heiði
61
Patreksfjörður
617
Tungu-
heiði
Bíldudalur
F66
620
60
6
Kollafjarðar-
heiði
Þorskafjarðar-
heiði
615
Tálknafjörður
63
63
60
612
Patreksfjörður
62
Skálmarfjörður
Látrabjarg
612
Kleifa-
heiði
614
Brjánslækur
Vatnsfjörður
62
Þorskafjörður
607
Reykhólar
606
Gilsfjö
Flatey
62
Baldur
BREIÐAFJÖRÐUR
STYKKISHÓLMUR
Hvammsfjörður
Hellissandur
Rif
ÓLAFSVÍK
Grundarfjörður
Snæfellsjökull
Snæfellsnes

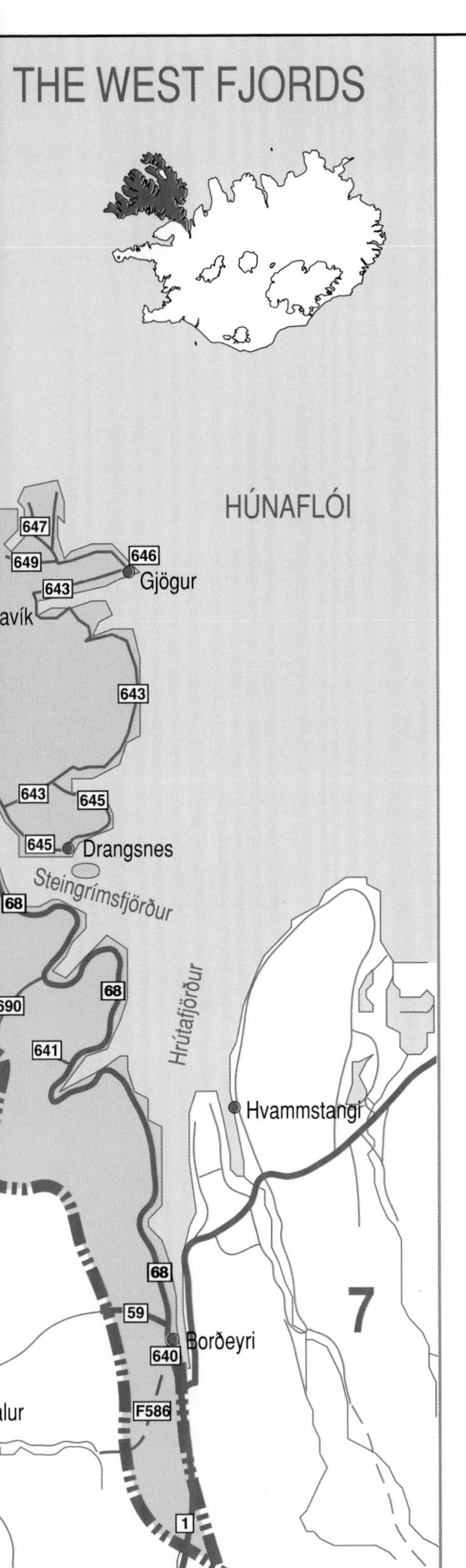

Road no.		Page
1	Ring Road/Norðurlandsvegur	59–60
59	Laxárdalsvegur	257
60	Vestfjarðavegur	280–292
61	Djúpvegur	292–303
62	Barðastrandarvegur	305–306
63	Bíldudalsvegur	307
64	Flateyrarvegur	290
65	Súgandafjarðarvegur	308
67	Hólmavíkurvegur	311
68	Innstrandavegur	309-311
602	Garpsdalsvegur	282
606	Karlseyjarvegur	312
607	Reykhólasveitarvegur	312
608	Þorskafjarðarvegur	313
611	Siglunesvegur	306
612	Örlygshafnarvegur	315
614	Rauðasandsvegur	315
615	Kollsvíkurvegur	315
617	Tálknafjarðarvegur	307
619	Ketildalavegur	317
622	Svalvogavegur	289
623	Flugvallarvegur Dýrafirði	289
624	Ingjaldssandsvegur	290
625	Valþjófsdalsvegur	290
627	Önundarfjarðarvegur	290
628	Hjarðardalsvegur	290
629	Syðradalsvegur	293
630	Skálavíkurvegur	293
631	Flugvallarvegur Ísafirði	292, 299
632	Laugardalsvegur	301
633	Mjóafjarðarvegur	301
634	Reykjanesvegur	301
635	Snæfjallastrandarvegur	318
638	Laugalandsvegur	318
640	Borðeyrarvegur	62, 309
641	Krossárdalsvegur	310
643	Strandavegur	319–321
645	Drangsnesvegur	319
646	Flugvallarvegur Gjögri	321
647	Munaðarnesvegur	321
649	Ófeigsfjarðarvegur	321
690	Steinadalsvegur	283, 310

Road no.		Page
1	Ring Road/Norðurlandsvegur	62–73
72	Hvammstangavegur	338
74	Skagastrandarvegur	322
75	Sauðárkróksbraut	323–326
76	Siglufjarðarvegur	327–332
77	Hofsósbraut	328
82	Ólafsfjarðarvegur	332
702	Heggstaðanesvegur	334
703	Hálsbæjavegur	334
704	Miðfjarðarvegur	335
705	Vesturárdalsvegur	335
711	Vatnsnesvegur	338–340
712	Þorgrímsstaðavegur	339
714	Fitjavegur	341
715	Víðidalsvegur	341
716	Síðuvegur	340
717	Borgarvegur	340
721	Þingeyravegur	342
722	Vatnsdalsvegur	343
724	Reykjabraut	344
725	Miðásavegur	67
726	Auðkúluvegur	344
727	Svínadalsvegur	344
731	Svínvetningabraut	345–346
733	Blöndudalsvegur	346
734	Svartárdalsvegur	347
741	Neðribyggðarvegur	322
742	Mýravegur	348
744	Þverárfjallsvegur	348
745	Skagavegur	349–351
748	Reykjastrandarvegur	352
749	Flugvallarvegur Sauðárkróki	326
751	Efribyggðarvegur	353
752	Skagafjarðarvegur	353–354
753	Vindheimavegur	70, 353
754	Héraðsdalsvegur	353
755	Svartárdalsvegur	354
757	Villinganesvegur	354
758	Austurdalsvegur	354
759	Kjálkavegur	354
762	Sæmundarhlíðarvegur	323
764	Hegranesvegur	326
766	Bakkavegur	327
767	Hólavegur	355
768	Hjaltadalsvegur	355
769	Ásavegur	355
781	Deildardalsvegur	328
783	Höfðastrandarvegur	328
786	Sléttuhlíðarvegur	329
787	Flókadalsvegur	330
789	Sléttuvegur	363
792	Langeyrarvegur	330
793	Skarðsvegur	330

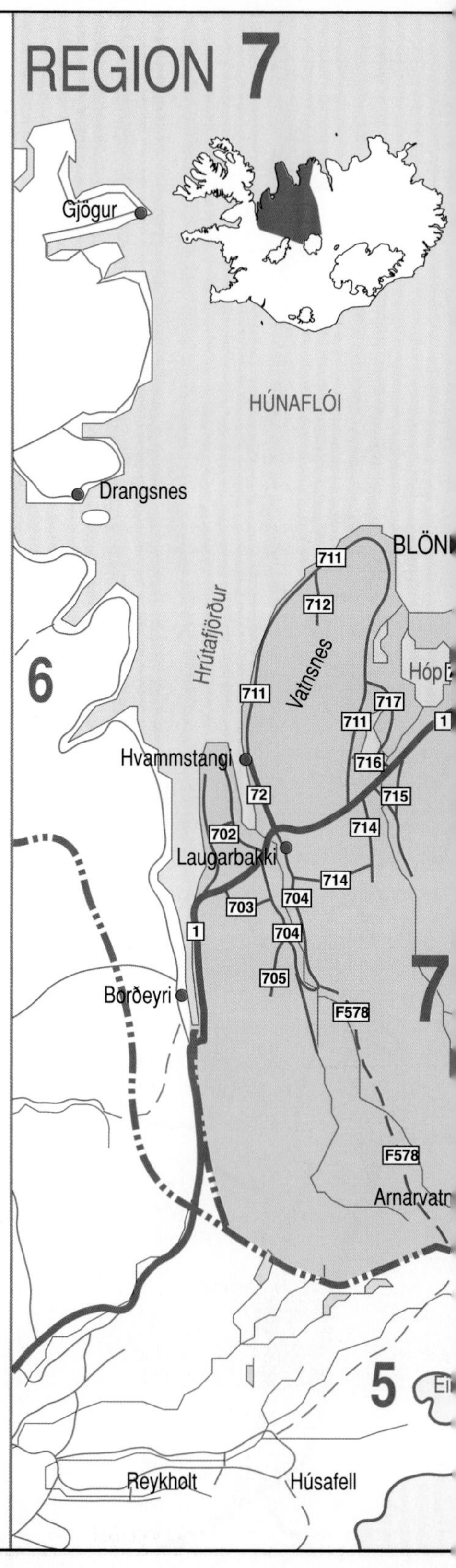

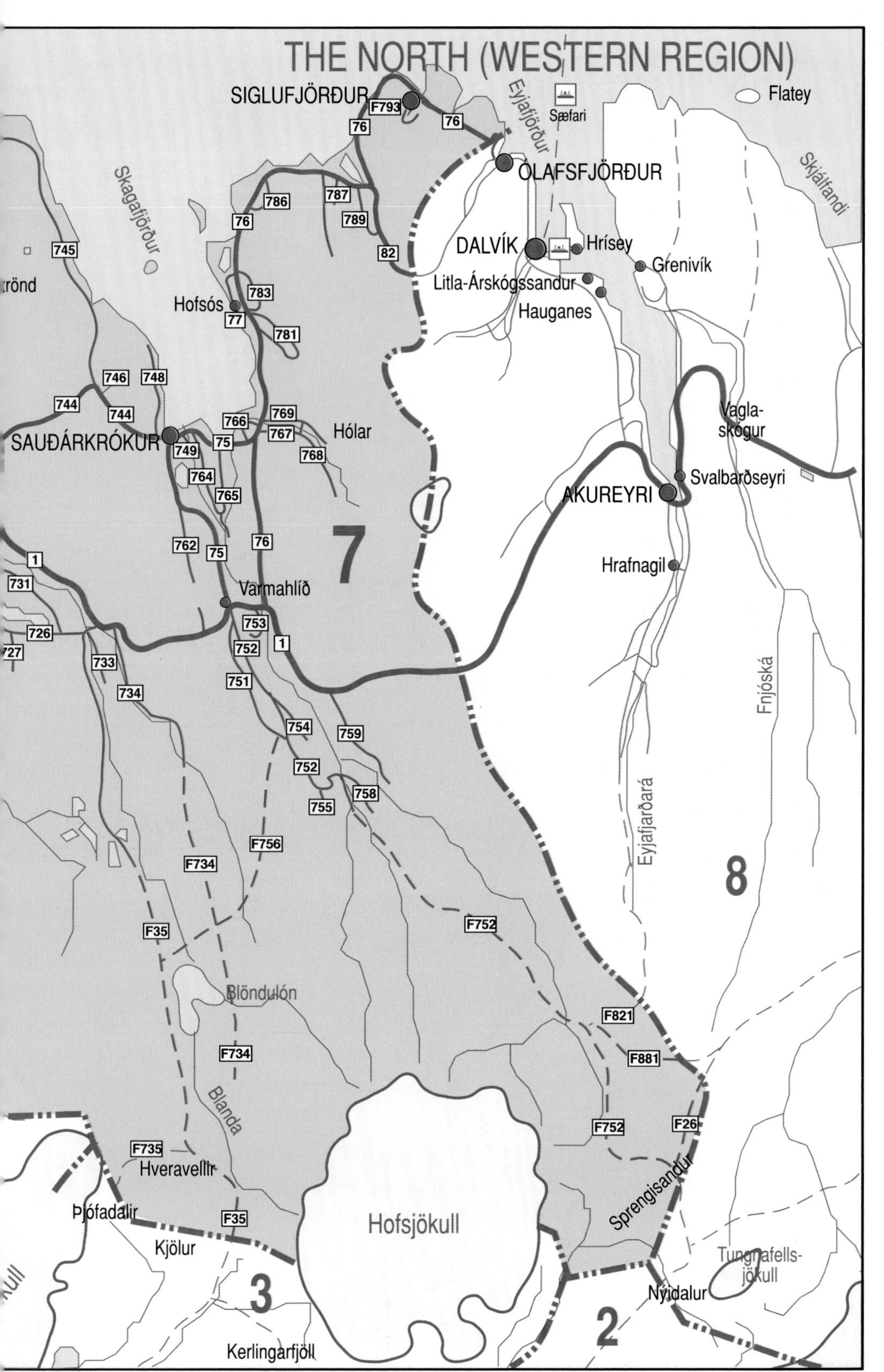
THE NORTH (WESTERN REGION)
SIGLUFJÖRÐUR
ÓLAFSFJÖRÐUR
DALVÍK
Hrísey
Grenivík
Litla-Árskógssandur
Hauganes
Sæfari
Flatey
Eyjafjörður
Skjálfandi
Skagafjörður
Hofsós
Hólar
SAUÐÁRKRÓKUR
Varmahlíð
AKUREYRI
Svalbarðseyri
Vagla-
skógur
Hrafnagil
Fnjóská
Eyjafjarðará
Blöndulón
Blanda
Hveravellir
Þjófadalir
Kjölur
Kerlingarfjöll
Hofsjökull
Sprengisandur
Nýidalur
Tungnafells-
jökull
7
8
3
2

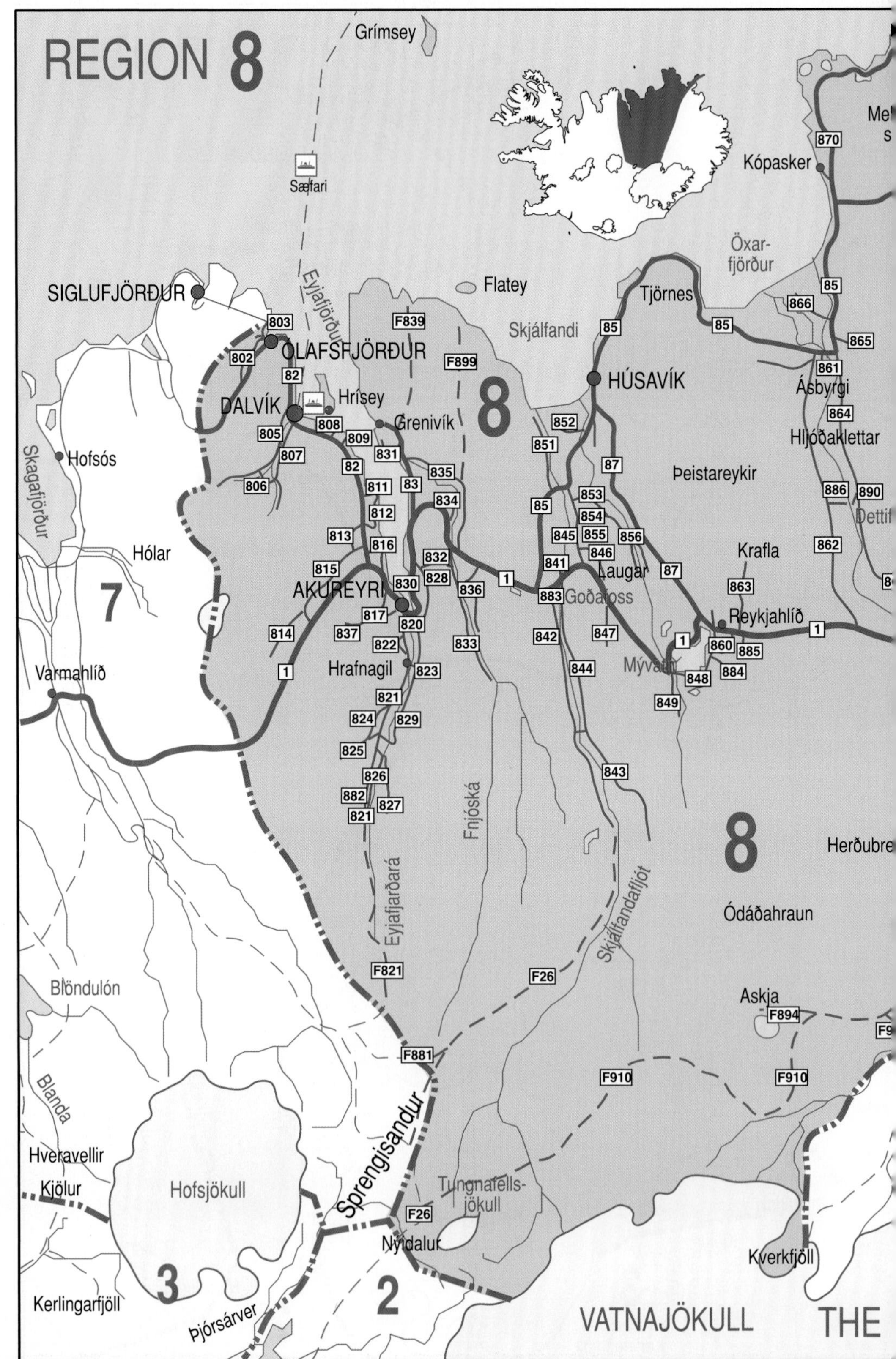
REGION 8
Grímsey
Sæfari
SIGLUFJÖRÐUR
ÓLAFSFJÖRÐUR
DALVÍK
Hrísey
Grenivík
Eyjafjörður
Flatey
Skjálfandi
HÚSAVÍK
Tjörnes
Öxarfjörður
Kópasker
Ásbyrgi
Hljóðaklettar
Þeistareykir
Krafla
Laugar
Goðafoss
Reykjahlíð
Mývatn
AKUREYRI
Hrafnagil
Hofsós
Skagafjörður
Hólar
Varmahlíð
Fnjóská
Eyjafjarðará
Skjálfandafljót
Ódáðahraun
Herðubreið
Askja
Blöndulón
Blanda
Hveravellir
Kjölur
Hofsjökull
Kerlingarfjöll
Þjórsárver
Sprengisandur
Nýidalur
Tungnafellsjökull
Kverkfjöll
VATNAJÖKULL
8
7
3
2

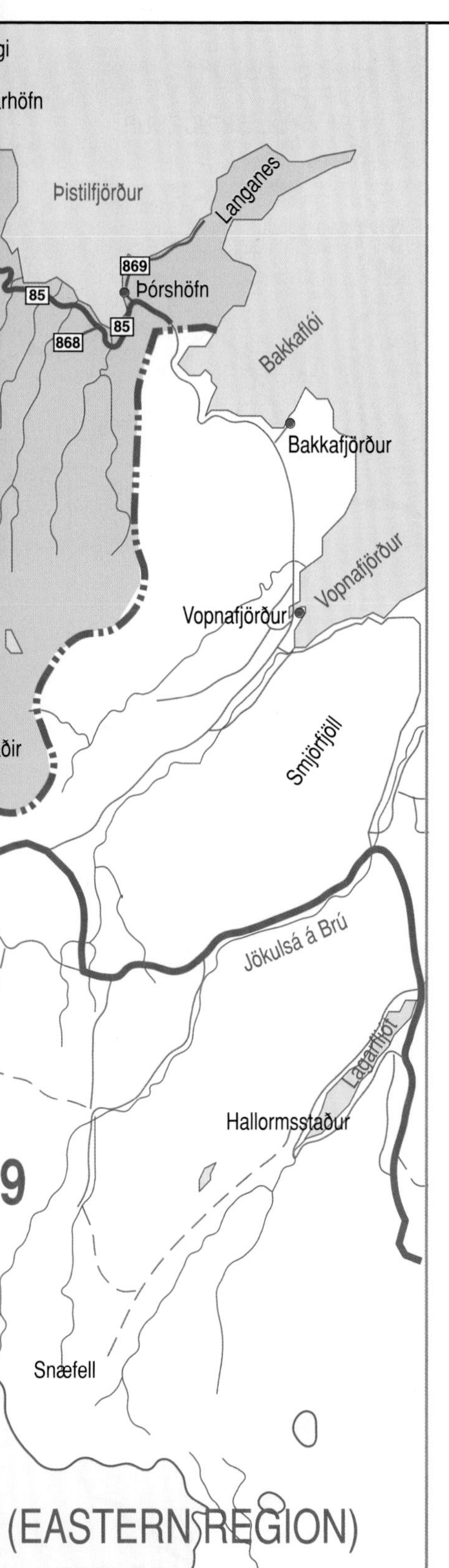

Road no.		Page
1	Ring Road/Norðurlandsvegur	73–95
82	Ólafsfjarðarvegur	357–363
83	Grenivíkurvegur	365
85	Norðausturvegur	366–378
87	Kísilvegur	386
802	Garðsvegur	362
803	Kleifavegur	362
805	Svarfaðardalsvegur	387
806	Tunguvegur	388
807	Skíðadalsvegur	388
808	Árskógssandsvegur	358
809	Hauganesvegur	358
811	Hjalteyrarvegur	357
812	Bakkavegur	357
813	Möðruvallavegur	357
814	Staðarbakkavegur	390
815	Hörgárdalsvegur	389, 390
816	Dagverðareyrarvegur	389
817	Blómsturvallavegur	76
818	Hlíðarvegur	76
820	Flugvallarvegur Akureyri	391
821	Eyjafjarðarbraut vestri	391–392
822	Kristnesvegur	391
823	Miðbraut	391
824	Finnastaðavegur	391
825	Dalsvegur	392
826	Hólavegur	393
827	Sölvadalsvegur	393
828	Veigastaðavegur	394
829	Eyjafjarðarbraut eystri	394–395
830	Svalbarðseyrarvegur	86
831	Höfðavegur	365
832	Vaðlaheiðarvegur	87, 396
833	Illugastaðavegur	396
834	Fnjóskadalsvegur vestri	397
835	Fnjóskadalsvegur eystri	397
836	Vaglaskógarvegur	396
837	Hlíðarfjallsvegur	76
841	Fremstafellsvegur	398
842	Bárðardalsvegur vestri	398–399
843	Lundarbrekkuvegur	399
844	Bárðardalsvegur eystri	398–399
845	Aðaldalsvegur	400
846	Austurhlíðarvegur	400
847	Stafnsvegur	89
848	Mývatnsvegur	92
849	Baldursheimsvegur	92
851	Út-Kinnarvegur	403
852	Sandsvegur	367
853	Hvammavegur	400
854	Staðarbraut	400
855	Fagranesvegur	400
856	Laxárdalsvegur	400
860	Grjótagjárvegur	92
861	Ásbyrgisvegur	373, 405
862	Dettifossvegur	480
863	Kröfluvegur	92
864	Hólsfjallavegur	404–405
865	Gilsbakkavegur	373
866	Austursandsvegur	373
868	Laxárdalsvegur	381
869	Langanesvegur	408
870	Sléttuvegur	374, 376
874	Raufarhafnarvegur	376, 378
875	Hálsavegur	376, 378
882	Leyningshólavegur	392, 393
883	Goðafossvegur	88, 398
884	Dimmuborgavegur	92
885	Námaskarðsvegur	92
886	Dettifossvegur vestri	404
890	Dettifossvegur eystri	404

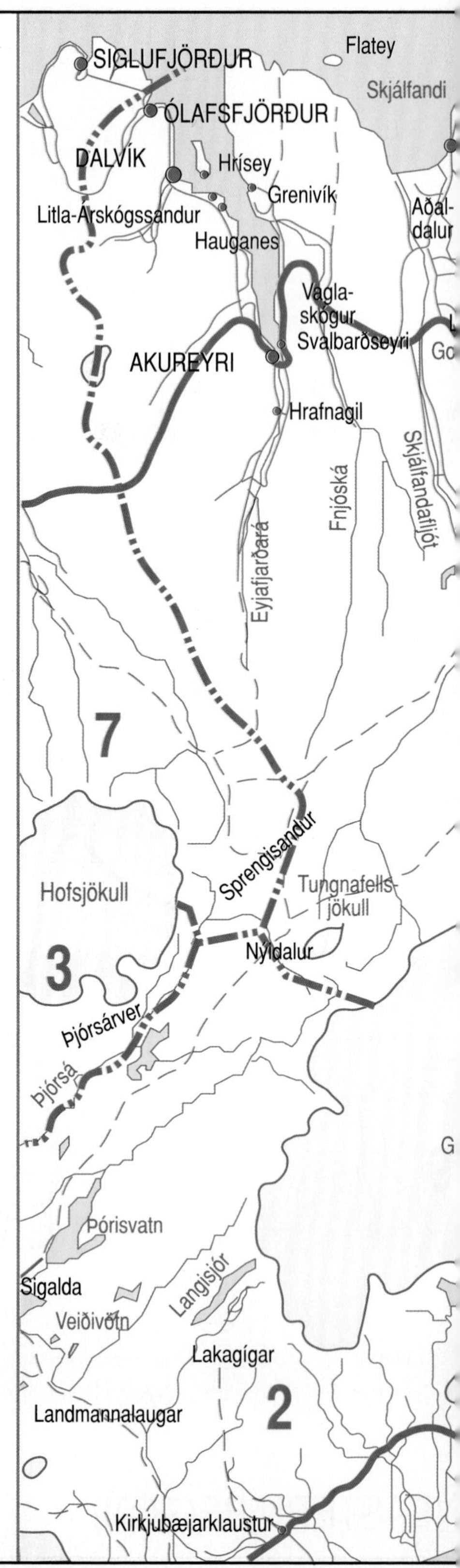

SIGLUFJÖRÐUR
Flatey
Skjálfandi
ÓLAFSFJÖRÐUR
DALVÍK
Hrísey
Grenivík
Litla-Árskógssandur
Hauganes
Aðal-
dalur
Vagla-
skógur
Svalbarðseyri
AKUREYRI
Hrafnagil
Skjálfandafljót
Fnjóská
Eyjafjarðará
7
Sprengisandur
Hofsjökull
Tungnafells-
jökull
3
Nýidalur
Þjórsárver
Þjórsá
Þórisvatn
Sigalda
Langisjór
Veiðivötn
Lakagígar
Landmannalaugar
2
Kirkjubæjarklaustur

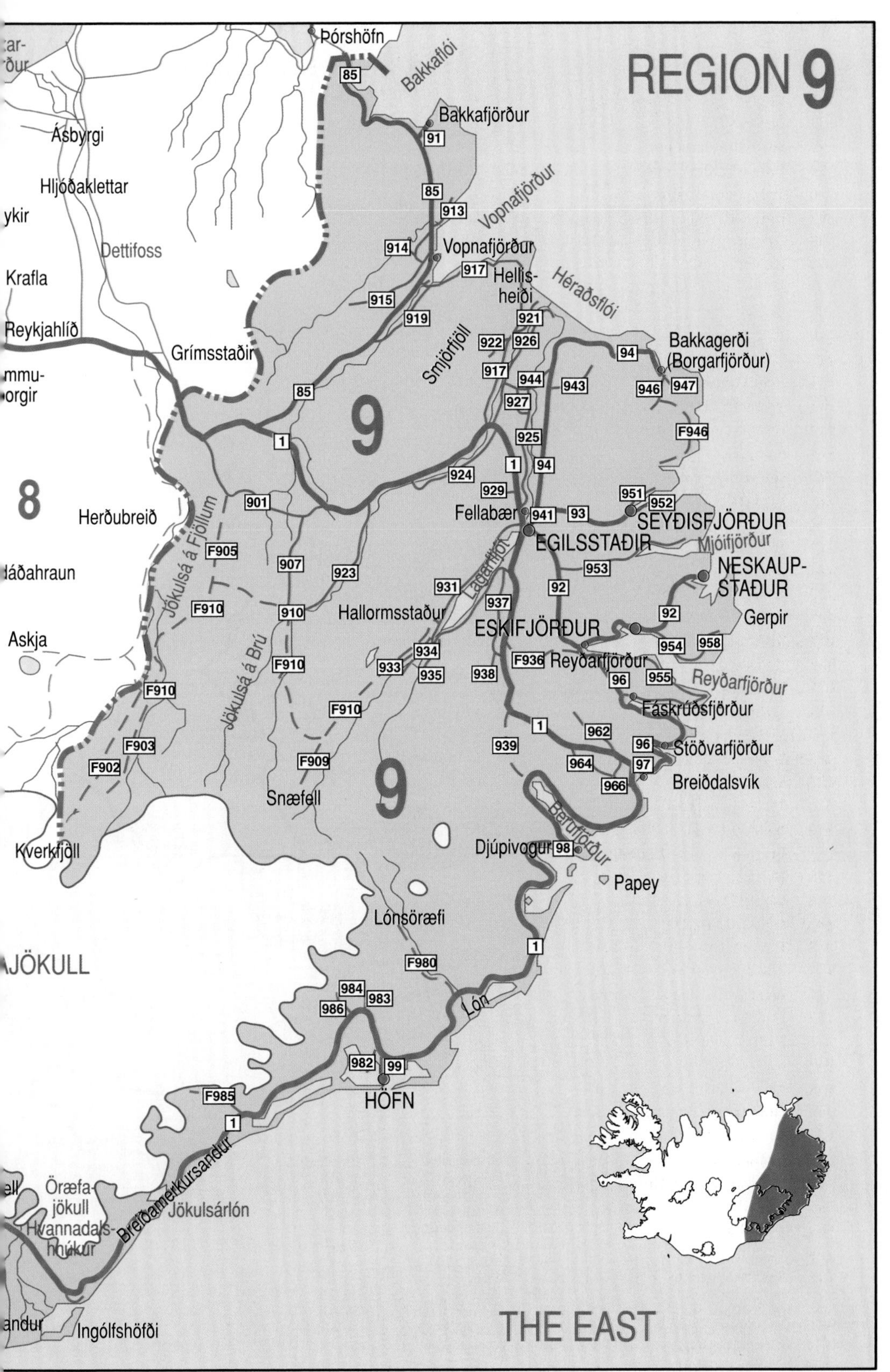
REGION 9
THE EAST
Þórshöfn
Bakkaflói
Bakkafjörður
Vopnafjörður
Héraðsflói
Hellis-
heiði
Smjörfjöll
Bakkagerði
(Borgarfjörður)
Ásbyrgi
Hljóðaklettar
Dettifoss
Krafla
Reykjahlíð
Grímsstaðir
Herðubreið
Jökulsá á Fjöllum
Askja
Jökulsá á Brú
Snæfell
Kverkfjöll
Hallormsstaður
Lagarfljót
Fellabær
EGILSSTAÐIR
SEYÐISFJÖRÐUR
Mjóifjörður
NESKAUP-
STAÐUR
Gerpir
ESKIFJÖRÐUR
Reyðarfjörður
Fáskrúðsfjörður
Stöðvarfjörður
Breiðdalsvík
Berufjörður
Djúpivogur
Papey
Lónsöræfi
Lón
HÖFN
Breiðamerkursandur
Jökulsárlón
Öræfa-
jökull
Hvannadals-
hnúkur
Ingólfshöfði
8
9

Mountain Roads

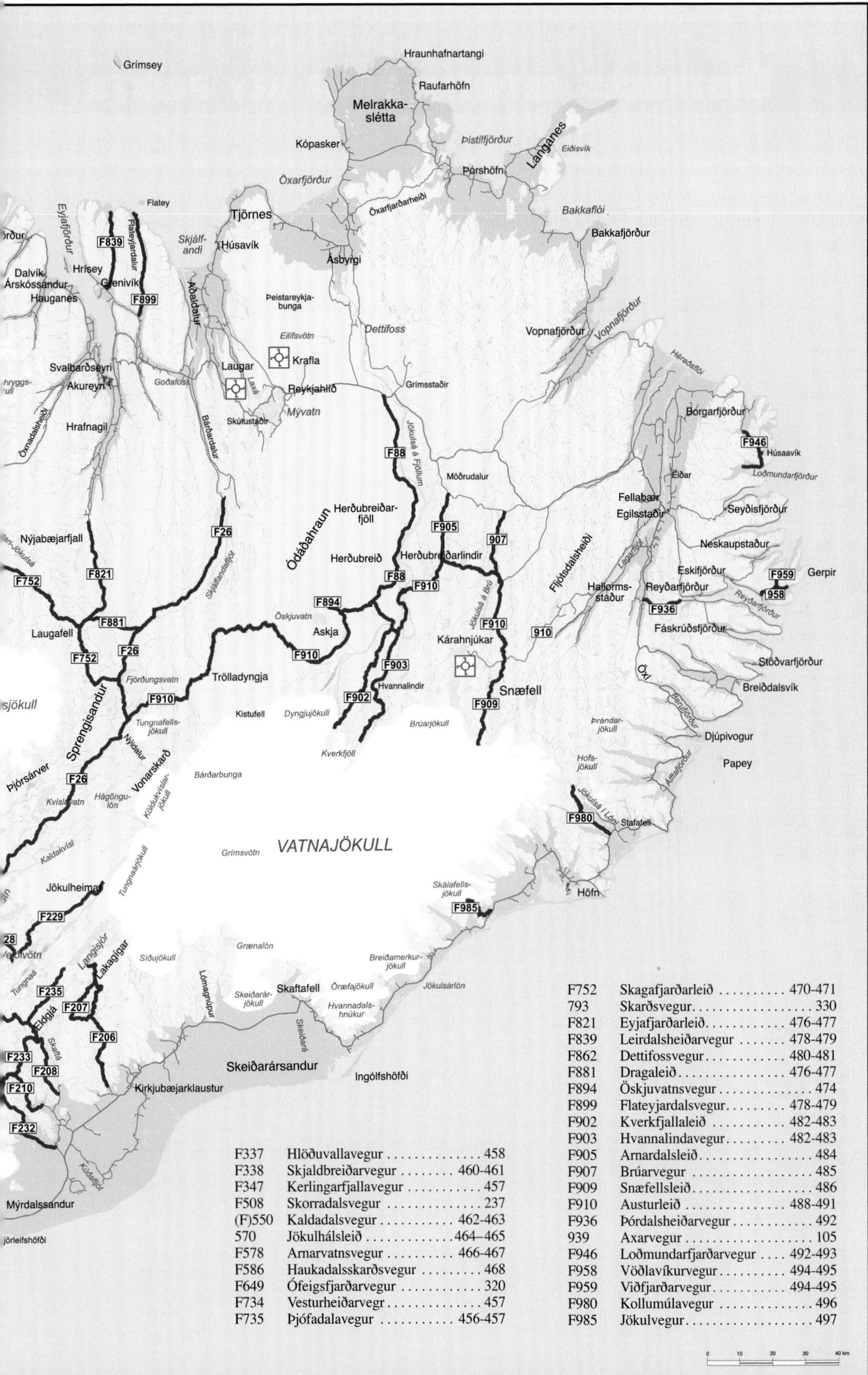
Grímsey
Hraunhafnartangi
Raufarhöfn
Melrakka-
slétta
Kópasker
Þistilfjörður
Langanes
Eiðisvík
Þórshöfn
Öxarfjörður
Öxarfjarðarheiði
Bakkaflói
Bakkafjörður
Flatey
Tjörnes
Eyjafjörður
Flateyjardalur
Skjálf-
andi
Húsavík
F839
Dalvík
Hrísey
Grenivík
Árskógssandur
Hauganes
F899
Aðaldalur
Ásbyrgi
Þeistareykja-
bunga
Eilífsvötn
Dettifoss
Vopnafjörður
Krafla
Laugar
Svalbarðseyri
Akureyri
Goðafoss
Reykjahlíð
Grímsstaðir
Héraðsflói
Mývatn
Skútustaðir
Bárðardalur
Hrafnagil
Öxnadalsheiði
Jökulsá á Fjöllum
Borgarfjörður
F946
Húsavík
F88
Möðrudalur
Eiðar
Loðmundarfjörður
Fellabær
Egilsstaðir
Seyðisfjörður
Herðubreiðar-
fjöll
Ódáðahraun
F905
907
F26
Nýjabæjarfjall
Neskaupstaður
Fljótsdalsheiði
Herðubreið
Herðubreiðarlindir
Eskifjörður
F959
Gerpir
F821
F752
F88
F910
Hallorms-
staður
Reyðarfjörður
958
Skjálfandafljót
F894
Jökulsá á Brú
Lagarfljót
Öskjuvatn
F936
F881
Askja
F910
910
Fáskrúðsfjörður
Laugafell
Kárahnjúkar
F26
F752
F910
F903
Stöðvarfjörður
Fjórðungsvatn
Tröllladyngja
Öxi
Breiðdalsvík
Hvannalindir
F910
F902
Snæfell
F909
Kistufell
Dyngjujökull
Brúarjökull
Berufjörður
Tungnafells-
jökull
Sprengisandur
Þrándar-
jökull
Djúpivogur
Nýidalur
Vonarskarð
Kverkfjöll
Hofs-
jökull
Papey
Þjórsárver
F26
Bárðarbunga
Álftafjörður
Kvíslavatn
Hágöngu-
lón
Köldukvíslar-
jökull
Jökulsá í Lóni
F980
Stafafell
VATNAJÖKULL
Grímsvötn
Kaldakvísl
Tungnaárjökull
Skálafells-
jökull
Höfn
Jökulheimar
F985
F229
Grænalón
Langisjór
Lakagígar
Síðujökull
Breiðamerkur-
jökull
Tungnaá
F235
Lómagnúpur
Skaftafell
Öræfajökull
Jökulsárlón
F207
Skeiðarár-
jökull
Hvannadals-
hnúkur
Eldgjá
Skeiðará
F206
Skaftá
F233
F208
Skeiðarársandur
Ingólfshöfði
F210
Kirkjubæjarklaustur
F232
Kúðafljót
Mýrdalssandur
0 10 20 30 40 km

Distances between some key points

These distances are based on using Highway 1, the "Ring Road" around the country, which is 1332 km long. Distances in red are via Skeiðarársandur (on the south coast). Highway 1 lies about 8 km from the long-distance bus station (Umferðarmiðstöðin, BSÍ) in central Reykjavík and about 4 km from Höfn in Hornafjörður. Highway 1 runs through the Hvalfjörður Tunnel. Driving round Hvalfjörður instead adds another 42 km to distances.

	Vík	Selfoss	Rvík	Borgarnes	Ísafjörður	Akureyri	Egilsstaðir	Höfn	Notes
Akranes	219	90	49	38	419	352	616	491	
Akureyri	558	429	388	314	558		264	510	
Arnarstapi	362	233	193	119	444	410	674	635	via Laxárdalsheiði
Ásbyrgi	701	584	544	470	714	155	191	438	via Hólsfjallavegur
Bakkagerði	581	710	723	649	893	335	71	317	
Bíldudalur	597	468	427	354	205	547	810	870	via Suðurfirðir
Bjarkalundur	385	256	215	141	240	334	598	657	via Laxárdalsheiði
Blönduós	414	285	244	170	414	144	408	654	
Borgarnes	244	115	74		381	314	578	516	
Breiðdalsvík	429	558	614	660	904	346	82	165	
Búðardalur	323	194	153	80	302	272	536	595	via Laxárdalsheiði
Dalvík	582	453	412	338	582	44	307	554	
Djúpivogur	367	496	553	612	968	410	146	104	
Egilsstaðir	510	639	652	578	822	264		246	
Eskifjörður	507	636	692	627	871	313	49	243	via Sunnfirðir
Eyrarbakki	142	13	59	118	499	432	652	414	via Óseyrarbrú
Fáskrúðsfjörður	475	604	660	628	872	314	50	211	via Sunnfirðir
Flateyri	617	488	447	374	22	566	830	889	
Flókalundur	509	380	339	265	116	458	722	781	via Laxárdalsheiði
Grenivík	596	467	426	353	597	38	262	509	via Fnjóskadalur
Grindavík	213	84	50	119	500	433	697	485	via Reykjanesbraut
Grundarfjörður	347	218	177	103	408	374	637	619	via Laxárdalsheiði
Gullfoss	176	71	115	156	537	471	681	443	via Skeið
Hallormsstaður	514	643	678	604	848	290	26	250	
Hella	93	36	93	151	533	466	603	365	
Hellissandur	374	245	204	130	442	409	672	646	via Laxárdalsheiði
Herðubreiðarlindir	701	620	579	505	749	191	191	438	via Austurland
Hofsós	497	368	327	253	497	132	396	642	via Út-Blönduhlíð
Hólmavík	403	274	233	159	225	336	600	675	
Húsafell	301	172	132	62	404	337	601	574	
Húsavík	649	520	479	405	649	91	219	465	via Kísilvegur
Hvammstangi	367	238	197	123	367	203	466	639	
Hveravellir	266	161	206	247	522	204	468	534	
Hvolsvöllur	80	49	106	164	546	479	590	352	
Höfn in Hornafjörður	272	401	458	516	898	510	246		
Ísafjörður	625	496	455	381		558	822	897	
Keflavík	223	94	46	114	496	429	693	496	via Reykjanesbraut
Kirkjubæjarklaustur	73	202	258	317	698	631	439	201	
Kópasker	728	617	576	502	746	188	218	464	via Hólssandur
Króksfjarðarnes	369	240	199	125	257	318	582	641	
Landeyjahöfn	73	138	136	195	635	509	583	345	
Landmannalaugar	122	79	195	254	576	568	537	300	
Laugarvatn	167	39	77	118	499	432	675	437	via Grímsnes
Mýri / Bárðardalur	645	516	475	401	645	87	252	499	

	Vík	Selfoss	Rvík	Borgarnes	Ísafjörður	Akureyri	Egilsstaðir	Höfn	Notes
eskaupstaður	530	659	715	650	894	336	72	266	via Suðurfirðir
orðurfjörður / Westfjords	506	377	336	263	307	439	703	778	
ýidalur	251	207	264	323	603	132	349	429	via fjallaslóðir
lafsfjörður	572	443	403	329	573	61	325	571	
lafsvík	364	235	194	121	433	399	663	637	via Laxárdalsheiði
atreksfjörður	570	441	400	326	178	519	783	842	via Suðurfirðir
aufarhöfn	762	651	610	536	780	222	252	498	
eyðarfjörður	491	620	677	611	855	297	33	228	via Sunnfirðir
eykholt / Borgarfjörður	278	149	108	39	385	318	581	550	
eykjahlíð / Mývatn	657	528	487	413	657	99	165	411	
eykjavík	186	57		74	455	388	652	458	
andgerði	232	103	54	123	504	437	701	504	via Reykjanesbraut
auðárkrókur	460	331	291	217	461	120	384	630	
elfoss	129		57	115	497	430	639	401	
eyðisfjörður	537	666	679	606	849	291	28	274	
glufjörður	556	427	386	312	556	77	341	587	
kaftafell	140	269	326	385	766	637	373	136	
kagaströnd	436	307	266	193	436	163	427	673	
kógar (by Eyjafjöll)	33	98	154	213	594	527	543	305	
taðarskáli	333	204	163	89	334	225	489	605	via Steingrímsfjarðarheiði
ykkishólmur	342	213	172	98	388	354	618	614	via Laxárdalsheiði
töðvarfjörður	447	576	633	651	895	337	73	183	
uðureyri / Súgandafjörður	632	503	462	388	23	575	838	904	
álknafjörður	585	456	415	341	192	534	798	857	via Bíldudalur
naðsdalskirkja	489	360	320	246	216	423	686	762	viaSteingrímsfjarðarheiði
armahlíð	464	335	294	220	464	94	358	604	
ík í Mýrdal		129	186	244	626	559	510	272	
opnafjörður	640	660	619	546	790	231	130	376	
ingeyri	578	449	408	334	49	527	791	850	
ingvellir (Service Centre)	174	45	50	90	472	405	669	446	
orlákshöfn	157	28	51	110	491	425	667	429	via Þrengsli
órshöfn	vv	679	638	564	808	250	197	444	
órsmörk; Básar	91	101	157	216	597	531	601	363	

Length of day & night

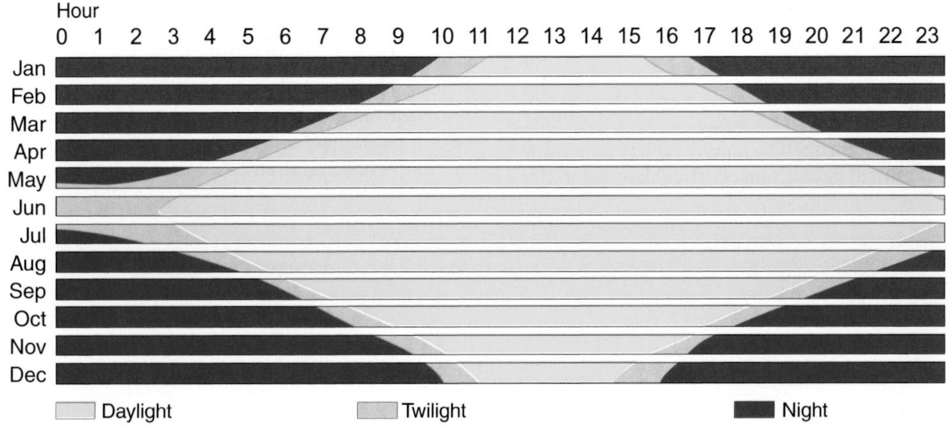

MOUNTAIN ROADS

Road Number	Place	Height in meters
1	Reynisfjall	119
1	Hellisheiði	374
1	Holtavörðuheiði	407
1	Vatnsskarð	420
1	Öxnadalsheiði	540
1	Víkurskarð	325
1	Fljótsheiði	247
1	Mývatnsheiði	335
1	Námaskarð	410
1	Vegaskarð	500
1	Langidalur	600
1	Breiðdalsheiði	470
1	Almannaskarð	153
26	Sigalda	500
32	Skeljafell	300
36	Mosfellsheiði	260
39	Þrengsli	288
365	Gjábakkahraun	300
42	Vatnsskarð	180
48	Kjósarskarð	260
50	Ferstikluháls	170
50	Geldingadragi	217
52	Uxahryggir	410
54	Fróðárheiði	361
55	Heydalur	165
59	Laxárdalsheiði	200
60	Brattabrekka	402
60	Svínadalur	220
60	Hjallaháls	335
60	Ódrjúgsháls	160
60	Klettsháls	332
60	Helluskarð	468
60	Dynjandisheiði	500
60	Hrafnseyrarheiði	552
60	Gemlufallsheiði	270
60	Vestfjarðargöng, tunnel - Breiðdalsleggur	199
61	Steingrímsfjarðarheiði.	439
62	Kleifaheiði	404
63	Miklidalur	369
63	Hálfdán	500
65	Vestfjarðargöng, tunnel - Súgandafjarðarleggur	177
68	Stikuháls	165
68	Ennisháls	290
690	Steinadalsheiði	330
605	Tröllatunguheiði	420
608	Þorskafjarðarheiði	490
612	Hafnarfjall	330
615	Hænuvíkurháls	320
624	Sandsheiði	530
643	Bjarnarfjarðarháls	180
643	Veiðileysuháls	220
744	Þverárfjall	322
82	Lágheiði	409
85	Brekknaheiði	160
85	Sandvíkurheiði	275
92	Fagridalur	350
92	Oddsskarð (tunnel)	632
93	Fjarðarheiði	620
94	Vatnsskarð	431
901	Möðrudalsleið	660
917	Hellisheiði eystri	655
939	Öxi	532
953	Mjóafjarðarheiði	578
F26	By Jökuldalur	820
F208	By Grænafjall	700
F208	Frostastaðaháls	625
F35	Kjalvegur - Bláfellsháls	600
F35	Kjalvegur - Fjórðungsalda	672
(F)550	Kaldidalur	720
F66	Kollafjarðarheiði	460
F821	Nýjabæjarafrétt	940

SOME FUN FACTS ABOUT ICELAND

Country	km^2
Iceland	103000
Terra Firma	23805
Glaciers	11922
Lakes	2757
Wastelands	64538
Ring Road	1332 km
All roads	12955 km
Coastline	4970 km
Population	321857

Largest islands	km^2
Flatey	2,8
Grímsey	5,3
Heimaey	13,4
Hjörsey (Faxaflói)	5,5
Hrísey	8,0
Málmey	2,4
Papey	2

Highest mountains	m
Bárðarbunga	2000
Eiríksjökull	1675
Eyjafjallajökull	1666
Hekla	1491
Herðubreið	1682
Hofsjökull	1765
Hvannadalsjökull	2109
Kerling	1538
Kverkfjöll	1920
Snæfell	1833
Tungnafellsjökull	1540
Þorvaldsfell (Askja)	1510

Highest Falls	m
Dettifoss	44
Glymur	190
Goðafoss	12
Gullfoss	32
Háifoss	122
Hengifoss	128
Hrauneyjafoss	29
Seljalandsfoss	65
Skógafoss	62

Largest Glaciers	km^2
Drangajökull	160
Hofsjökull	925
Langjökull	953
Mýrdalsjökull	596
Vatnajökull	8300

Largest Lakes	km^2
Hvítárvatn	30
Lögurinn	53
Mývatn	37
Þingvallavatn	82
Þórisvatn	83-88

Deepest Lakes	m
Hvalvatn	160
Þingvallavatn	114
Þórisvatn	113
Öskjuvatn	217
Jökulsárlón	248

Longest Rivers	km
Hvítá/Ölfusá	185
Jökulsá á Dal	150
Jökulsá á Fjöllum	206
Lagarfljót	140
Skjálfandafljót	178
Þjórsá	230

Longest Bridges	m
Skeiðará	880
Borgarfjörður	520
Súla	420
Ölfusarós	360
Gígjukvísl	336
Kúðafljót	302
Lagarfljót	301
Hornafjarðarfljót	254
Markarfljót	250
Jökulsá í Lóni	247

Brúará in Biskupstungur

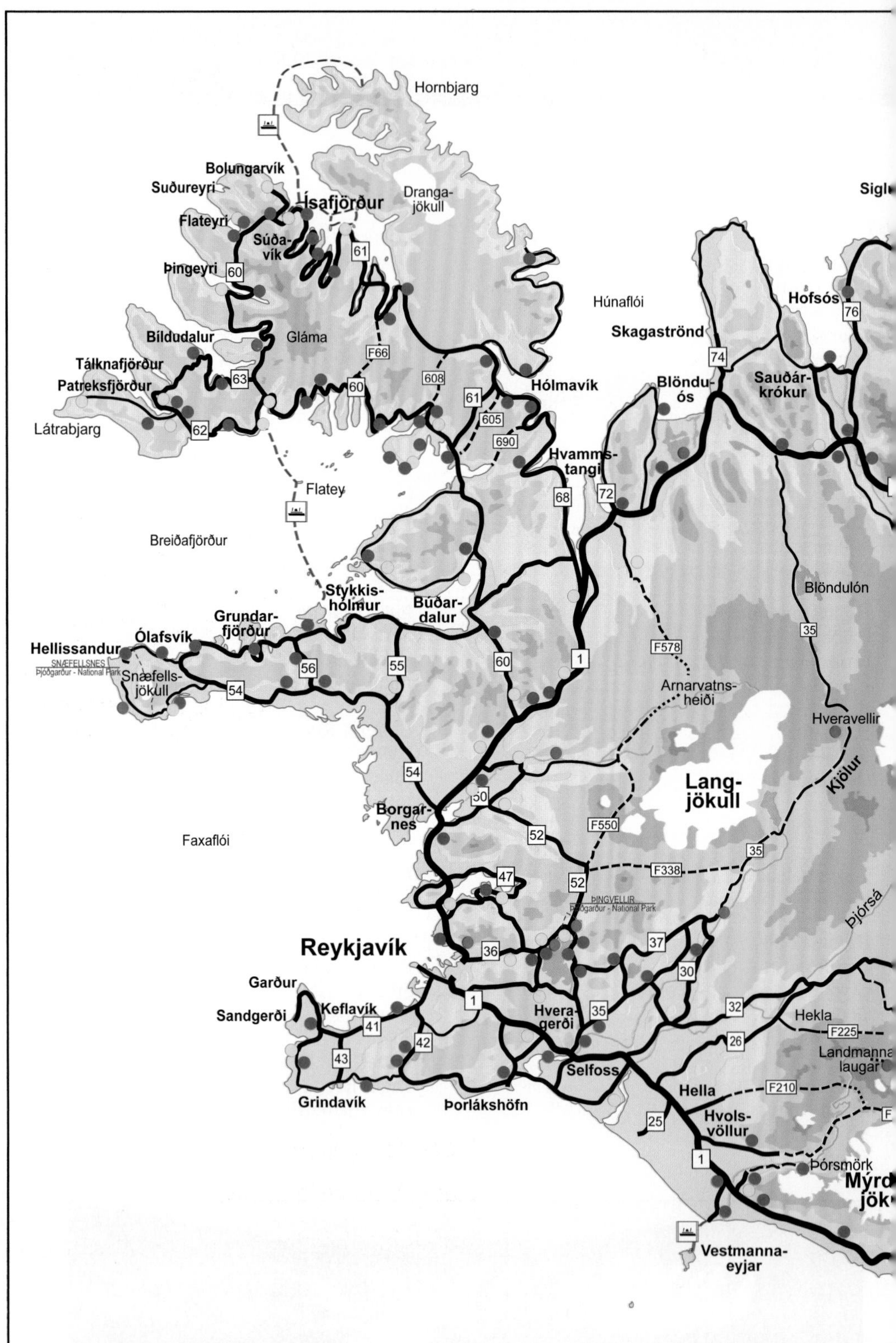
Hornbjarg
Bolungarvík
Suðureyri
Ísafjörður
Drangajökull
Flateyri
Súðavík
Þingeyri
Bíldudalur
Gláma
Tálknafjörður
Patreksfjörður
Látrabjarg
Húnaflói
Skagaströnd
Hofsós
Hólmavík
Blönduós
Sauðárkrókur
Hvammstangi
Flatey
Breiðafjörður
Blöndulón
Stykkishólmur
Búðardalur
Grundarfjörður
Ólafsvík
Hellissandur
SNÆFELLSNES
Þjóðgarður - National Park
Snæfellsjökull
Arnarvatnsheiði
Hveravellir
Kjölur
Langjökull
Borgarnes
Faxaflói
ÞINGVELLIR
Þjóðgarður - National Park
Þjórsá
Reykjavík
Garður
Sandgerði
Keflavík
Hveragerði
Hekla
Landmannalaugar
Selfoss
Grindavík
Þorlákshöfn
Hella
Hvolsvöllur
Þórsmörk
Vestmannaeyjar
60
61
F66
608
63
62
605
690
68
72
74
76
F578
35
56
55
60
1
54
54
50
F550
52
F338
47
52
37
36
30
1
41
35
32
42
43
26
F225
F210
25
1

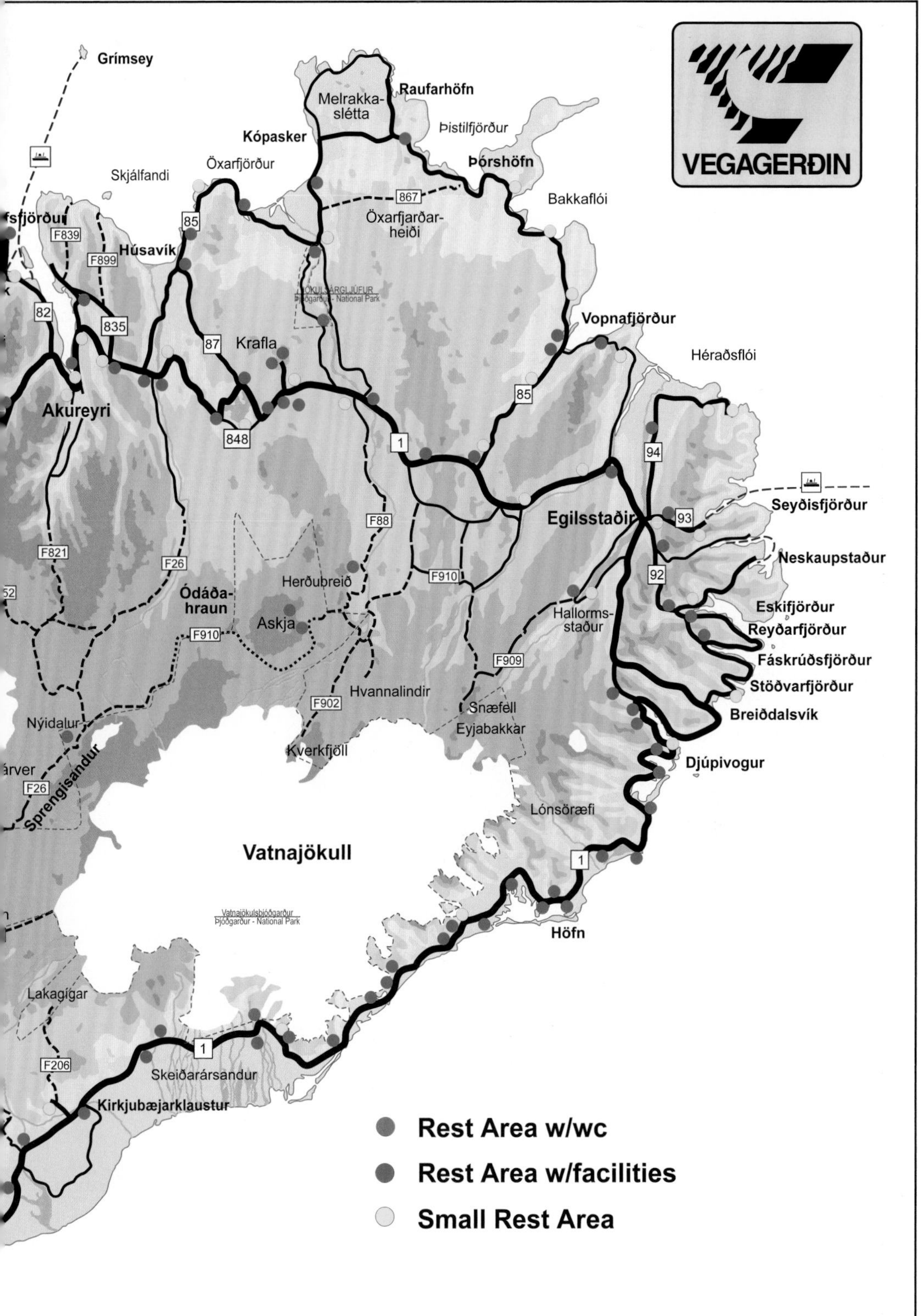
VEGAGERÐIN
Grímsey
Raufarhöfn
Melrakka-
slétta
Þistilfjörður
Kópasker
Öxarfjörður
Skjálfandi
Þórshöfn
Bakkaflói
Öxarfjarðar-
heiði
Húsavík
Vopnafjörður
Héraðsflói
Krafla
Akureyri
Egilsstaðir
Seyðisfjörður
Neskaupstaður
Herðubreið
Ódáða-
hraun
Askja
Hallorms-
staður
Eskifjörður
Reyðarfjörður
Fáskrúðsfjörður
Stöðvarfjörður
Breiðdalsvík
Hvannalindir
Snæfell
Eyjabakkar
Nýidalur
Kverkfjöll
Djúpivogur
Sprengisandur
Lónsöræfi
Vatnajökull
Höfn
Lakagígar
Skeiðarársandur
Kirkjubæjarklaustur
Rest Area w/wc
Rest Area w/facilities
Small Rest Area

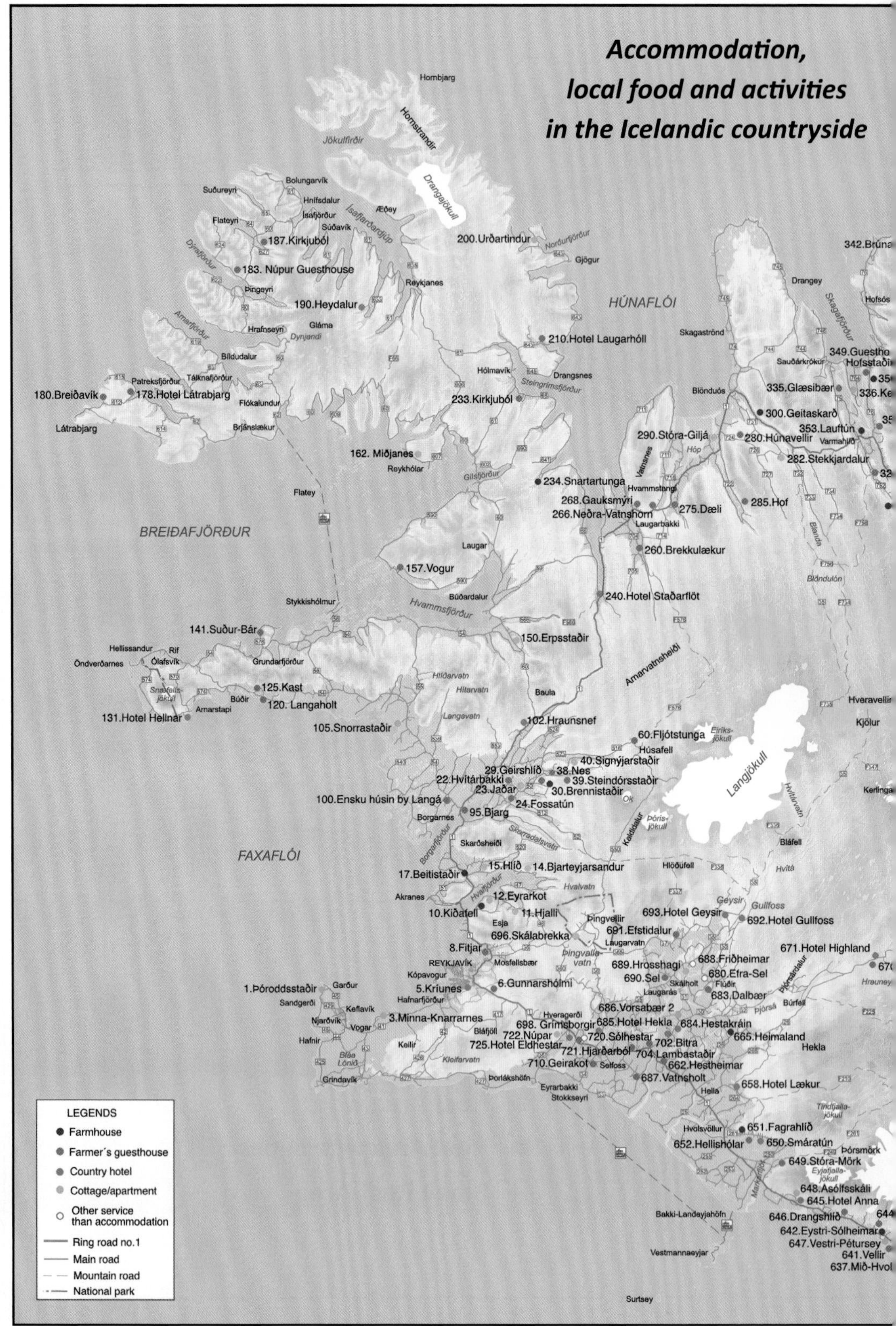
Accommodation,
local food and activities
in the Icelandic countryside
Hornbjarg
Hornstrandir
Jökulfirðir
Drangajökull
Bolungarvík
Suðureyri
Hnífsdalur
Ísafjörður
Súðavík
Æðey
Ísafjarðardjúp
Flateyri
187.Kirkjuból
Dýrafjörður
200.Urðartindur
Norðurfjörður
Gjögur
183. Núpur Guesthouse
Þingeyri
Reykjanes
190.Heydalur
Arnarfjörður
Gláma
Hrafnseyri
Dynjandi
HÚNAFLÓI
210.Hotel Laugarhóll
Bíldudalur
Hólmavík
Drangsnes
Patreksfjörður
Tálknafjörður
Steingrímsfjörður
180.Breiðavík
178.Hotel Látrabjarg
Flókalundur
233.Kirkjuból
Látrabjarg
Brjánslækur
162. Miðjanes
Reykhólar
Gilsfjörður
234.Snartartunga
Flatey
BREIÐAFJÖRÐUR
Laugar
157.Vogur
Búðardalur
Stykkishólmur
Hvammsfjörður
141.Suður-Bár
150.Erpsstaðir
Hellissandur
Rif
Öndverðarnes
Ólafsvík
Grundarfjörður
Snæfellsjökull
125.Kast
Búðir
120. Langaholt
Arnarstapi
131.Hotel Hellnar
Hlíðarvatn
Hítarvatn
Langavatn
105.Snorrastaðir
Baula
102.Hraunsnef
342.Brúna
Drangey
Skagafjörður
Hofsós
Skagaströnd
349.Guestho
Hofsstaði
Sauðárkrókur
Blönduós
335.Glæsibær
336.Ke
300.Geitaskarð
290.Stóra-Giljá
280.Húnavellir
353.Lauftún
Varmahlíð
Hóp
Vatnsnes
282.Stekkjardalur
Hvammstangi
268.Gauksmýri
266.Neðra-Vatnshorn
275.Dæli
285.Hof
Laugarbakki
260.Brekkulækur
Blanda
Blöndulón
240.Hotel Staðarflöt
Arnarvatnsheiði
Hveravellir
Kjölur
60.Fljótstunga
Eiríksjökull
Húsafell
40.Signýjarstaðir
Langjökull
29.Geirshlíð
38.Nes
22.Hvítárbakki
39.Steindórsstaðir
23.Jaðar
30.Brennistaðir
100.Ensku húsin by Langá
24.Fossatún
Ok
Kerlinga
Borgarnes
95.Bjarg
Kaldidalur
Þórisjökull
Skorradalsvatn
Skarðsheiði
Bláfell
FAXAFLÓI
Borgarfjörður
15.Hlíð
14.Bjarteyjarsandur
Hlöðufell
Hvítá
17.Beitistaðir
Akranes
Hvalfjörður
12.Eyrarkot
Hvalvatn
Geysir
Gullfoss
10.Kiðafell
11.Hjalli
Þingvellir
693.Hotel Geysir
692.Hotel Gullfoss
Esja
691.Efstidalur
696.Skálabrekka
Laugarvatn
671.Hotel Highland
8.Fitjar
REYKJAVÍK
Mosfellsbær
Þingvallavatn
689.Hrosshagi
688.Friðheimar
Kópavogur
680.Efra-Sel
Þjórsárdalur
Hrauney
1.Þóroddsstaðir
Garður
6.Gunnarshólmi
690.Sel
Skálholt
Flúðir
5.Kríunes
Laugarás
683.Dalbær
Sandgerði
Hafnarfjörður
Keflavík
686.Vorsabær 2
Þjórsá
Búrfell
Njarðvík
3.Minna-Knarrarnes
Hveragerði
Vogar
698. Grímsborgir
685.Hotel Hekla
684.Hestakráin
Hafnir
Bláfjöll
722.Núpar
720.Sólhestar
665.Heimaland
Keilir
725.Hotel Eldhestar
702.Bitra
Bláa Lónið
721.Hjarðarból
704.Lambastaðir
Hekla
Kleifarvatn
710.Geirakot
Selfoss
662.Hestheimar
Grindavík
Þorlákshöfn
687.Vatnsholt
Eyrarbakki
Hella
658.Hotel Lækur
Stokkseyri
Tindfjallajökull
Hvolsvöllur
651.Fagrahlíð
652.Hellishólar
650.Smáratún
Þórsmörk
649.Stóra-Mörk
Eyjafjallajökull
648.Ásólfsskáli
645.Hotel Anna
Bakki-Landeyjahöfn
646.Drangshlíð
642.Eystri-Sólheimar
647.Vestri-Pétursey
Vestmannaeyjar
641.Vellir
637.Mið-Hvol
Surtsey
LEGENDS
Farmhouse
Farmer´s guesthouse
Country hotel
Cottage/apartment
Other service than accommodation
Ring road no.1
Main road
Mountain road
National park

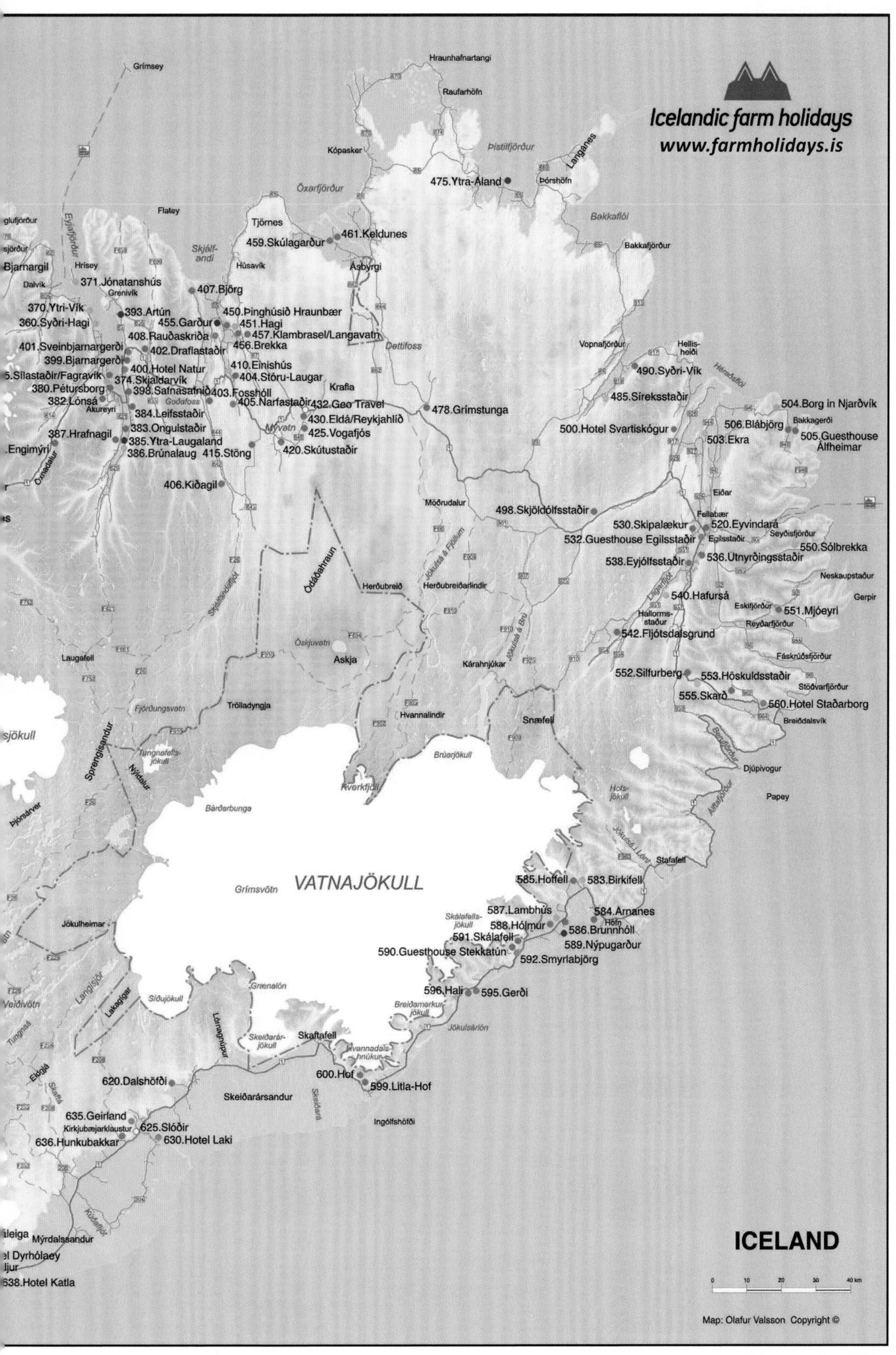
Icelandic farm holidays
www.farmholidays.is
ICELAND
VATNAJÖKULL
475.Ytra-Áland
461.Keldunes
459.Skúlagarður
371.Jónatanshús
370.Ytri-Vík
360.Syðri-Hagi
407.Björg
393.Artún
455.Garður
450.Þinghúsið Hraunbær
451.Hagi
457.Klambrasel/Langavatn
456.Brekka
408.Rauðaskriða
402.Draflastaðir
401.Sveinbjarnargerði
399.Bjarnargerði
400.Hotel Natur
410.Einishús
404.Stóru-Laugar
374.Skjaldarvík
398.Safnasafnið
403.Fosshóll
380.Pétursborg
382.Lónsá
405.Narfastaðir
432.Geo Travel
384.Leifsstaðir
430.Eldá/Reykjahlíð
425.Vogafjós
383.Ongulstaðir
387.Hrafnagil
385.Ytra-Laugaland
386.Brúnalaug
415.Stöng
420.Skútustaðir
406.Kiðagil
478.Grímstunga
490.Syðri-Vík
485.Síreksstaðir
500.Hotel Svartiskógur
504.Borg in Njarðvík
506.Blábjörg
503.Ekra
505.Guesthouse Álfheimar
498.Skjöldólfsstaðir
530.Skipalækur
520.Eyvindará
532.Guesthouse Egilsstaðir
550.Sólbrekka
538.Eyjólfsstaðir
536.Útnyrðingsstaðir
540.Hafursá
551.Mjóeyri
542.Fljótsdalsgrund
552.Silfurberg
553.Höskuldsstaðir
555.Skarð
560.Hotel Staðarborg
585.Hoffell
583.Birkifell
587.Lambhús
584.Arnanes
588.Hólmur
586.Brunnhóll
591.Skálafell
589.Nýpugarður
590.Guesthouse Stekkatún
592.Smyrlabjörg
596.Hali
595.Gerði
600.Hof
599.Litla-Hof
620.Dalshöfði
635.Geirland
625.Slóðir
636.Hunkubakkar
630.Hotel Laki
638.Hotel Katla
Map: Olafur Valsson Copyright ©

ITA Huts in

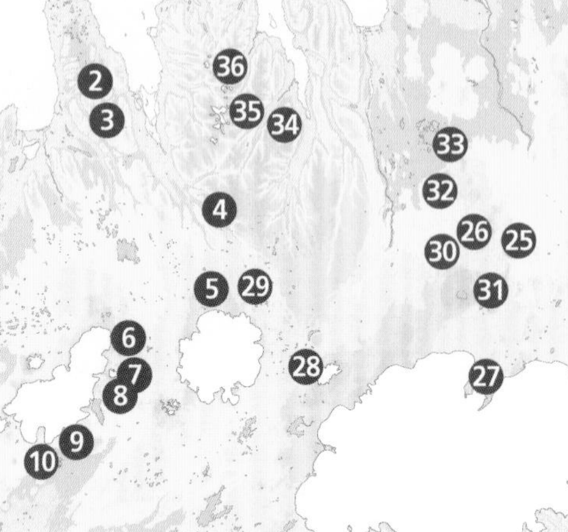

Iceland Touri Associatio
www.fi.is

1 

Norðurfjörður Valgeirsstaðir (p. 591)
Sleeps: 20
Service:
GPS Co-ordinates: 66°03.080 21°33.970

2 

Trölli í Tröllabotnum (p. 57
Sleeps: 16
Service:
GPS Co-ordinates: 65°42.603 19°53.163

3 

Þúfnavellir í Víðidal (p. 579)
Sleeps: 12
Service:
GPS Co-ordinates: 65°38.330 19°49.480

4 

Hildarsel í Austurdal (p. 59
Sleeps: 36
Service:
GPS Co-ordinates: **65°15.330 18°43.91**

5 

Ingólfsskáli í Lambahrauni (p. 597)
Sleeps: 28
Service:
GPS Co-ordinates: 65°00.470 18°53.790

6 

Þjófadalir (p. 59
Sleeps: 12
Service:
GPS Co-ordinates: 64°48.900 19°42.510

7 

Þverbrekknamúli (p. 596)
Sleeps: 20
Service:
GPS Co-ordinates: 64°43.100 19°36.860

8 

Hvítárnes (p. 59
Sleeps: 30
Service:
GPS Co-ordinates: 64°37.007 19°45.394

9 

Hagavatn (p. 596)
Sleeps: 12
Service:
GPS Co-ordinates: 64°27.760 20°14.700

10 

Hlöðuvellir (p. 57
Sleeps: 15
Service:
GPS Co-ordinates: 64°23.911 20°33.387

11 

Landmannalaugar (p. 589)
Sleeps: 78
Service:
GPS Co-ordinates: 63°59.600 19°03.660

12 

Hrafntinnusker Höskuldsskáli (p. 58
Sleeps: 52
Service:
GPS Co-ordinates: 63°56.014 19°10.109

Iceland (highland)

13

Álftavatn (p. 589)
Sleeps: 70
Service:
GPS Co-ordinates: 63°51.470 19°13.640

14

Hvanngil (p. 589)
Sleeps: 60
Service:
GPS Co-ordinates: 63°50.026 19°12.507

15
Emstrur (p. 589)
Sleeps: 60
Service:
GPS Co-ordinates: 63°45.980 19°22.450

16
Þórsmörk Skagfjörðsskáli (p. 599)
Sleeps: 75
Service:
GPS Co-ordinates: 63°40.960 19°30.890

17

Leirás í Múladal (p. 585)
Sleeps: 6
Service:
GPS Co-ordinates: 64°39.053 14°57.772

18

Múlaskáli á Lónsöræfum (p. 599)
Sleeps: 25
Service:
GPS Co-ordinates: 64°33.199 15°09.077

19

Kollumúlavatn (p. 599) (p. 599)
Sleeps: 22
Service:
GPS Co-ordinates: 64°36.680 15°08.750

20

Geldingafell (p. 585)
Sleeps: 16
Service:
GPS Co-ordinates: 64°41.690 15°21.690

21

Snæfell (p. 584)
Sleeps: 62
Service:
GPS Co-ordinates: 64°48.250 15°38.600

22

Karlsstaðir í Vöðlavík (p. 584)
Sleeps: 33
Service:
GPS Co-ordinates: 65°01.803 13°40.354

23

Húsavík (p. 598, 588)
Sleeps: 33
Service:
GPS Co-ordinates: 65°23.716 13°44.160

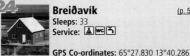

24

Breiðavík (p. 598)
Sleeps: 33
Service:
GPS Co-ordinates: 65°27.830 13°40.286

25

Herðubreiðarlindir Þorsteinsskáli
Sleeps: 30 (p. 598)
Service:
GPS Co-ordinates: 65°11.560 16°13.390

26
Bræðrafell í Ódáðahrauni (p. 597)
Sleeps: 12
Service:
GPS Co-ordinates: 65°11.310 16°32.290

27

Sigurðarskáli í Kverkfjöllum
Sleeps: 82 (p. 597)
Service:
GPS Co-ordinates: 64°44.850 16°37.890

28
Nýidalur (p. 598)
Sleeps: 90
Service:
GPS Co-ordinates: 64°44.130 18°04.350

29

Laugafell (p. 598)
Sleeps: 35
Service:
GPS Co-ordinates: 65°01.630 18°19.950

30

Dyngjufell í Dyngjufjalladal (p. 598)
Sleeps: 16
Service:
GPS Co-ordinates: 65°07.480 16°55.280

31
Dreki í Dyngjufjöllum (p. 581)
Sleeps: 60
Service:
GPS Co-ordinates: 65°02.520 16°35.720

32

Botni í Suðurárbotnum (p. 582)
Sleeps: 16
Service:
GPS Co-ordinates: 65°16.180 17°04.100

33

Heilagsdalur (p. 582)
Sleeps: 18
Service:
GPS Co-ordinates: 65°27.334 16°47.514

34

Lambi á Glerárdal (p. 582)
Sleeps: 6
Service:
GPS Co-ordinates: 65°34.880 18°17.770

35

Baugasel í Barkárdal (p. 589)
Sleeps: 10
Service:
GPS Co-ordinates: 65°39.400 18°36.700

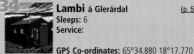

36

Á Tungnahrygg
Sleeps: 10
Service:
GPS Co-ordinates: 65°41.340 18°50.820

ÚTIVIST HUTS

Skælingar

Útivist's mountain hut at Stóragil in Skælingar was rebuilt by members in 1996-1997. An old hut for the annual sheep round-up that the local farmers had stopped using was previously located on the site. The surrounding countryside is magnificent, with large lava formations reminiscent of a landscaped park. There is a short hike to Hólaskjól from the hut, and ideal day tours include hikes to Uxatindar or Gjátindur. A rough vehicle track extends from the road leading to Gjátindur, to the hut. The hut is heated with a small oil stove and has mattresses and gas for cooking, but no tableware. Water is fetched from a brook nearby. The hut is not insulated and is therefore not suitable for winter stays. It can accommodate 16 people.
GPS coordinate is N 63°58.849′ W 18°31.319′

Álftavötn

A good jeep track leads most of the way to the house, although the last 2-300 m must be traversed on foot. Consequently the area is very quiet and peaceful, as well as extremely beautiful. A popular riding trail passes in front of the hut and a fence has been erected to the north so that riders can rest their horses. There is much vegetation near the hut and excellent camping facilities with running water and a water toilet. Lodging is available indoors for up to 24 people. Numerous hikes may be taken in the vicinity, including a day hike to Strútslaug or Gjátindur.
Hólaskjól is a short walk away.
GPS coordinate: N 63° 53.890′ W 18°41.467′

Dalakofinn

The location of Dalakofinn hut is excellent for all kinds of tours in the Fjallabak area and other mountain huts are within reach for ongoing hikers. It's ideal for access to nearby natural wonders, i.e. the colourful geothermal areas and rhyolite mountains. The location is also great for for snow scooter og cross country skiers during winter. The hut is easily accessible from farm Keldur without any river fording.
GPS coordinate: N 63° 57.048′ W 19°21.584′

Básar in Goðaland

The huts can accommodate 80-90 people and are occupied by wardens from early May until October. In summer there is running water and water toilets near the huts and on many of the campsites. The huts are heated with oil stoves and the electrical station Básabína uses water from a nearby brook to generate electricity for lighting. Útivist has published a hiking map with descriptions of paths around Þórsmörk and Goðaland. It is safe to say that the heart of Útivist beats at Básar.
GPS coordinate: N 63°40.559′ W 19°29.014′

Fimmvörðuskáli

Fimmvörðuhálsskáli hut is located on the highest part of the hill, just west of the marked path between Skógar and Þórsmörk. The hut is heated with an oil stove and provides the most necessary cooking utensils and tableware. Special arrangements have been made regarding toilets, as it is not possible to insert a septic tank on the site; hence travellers are asked to follow set rules. It should be pointed out that running water in the area cannot be counted on and in late summer it is difficult to find snow for melting. The hut can accommodate 20 people.
GPS coordinate: N 63°37.320′ W 19°27.093′

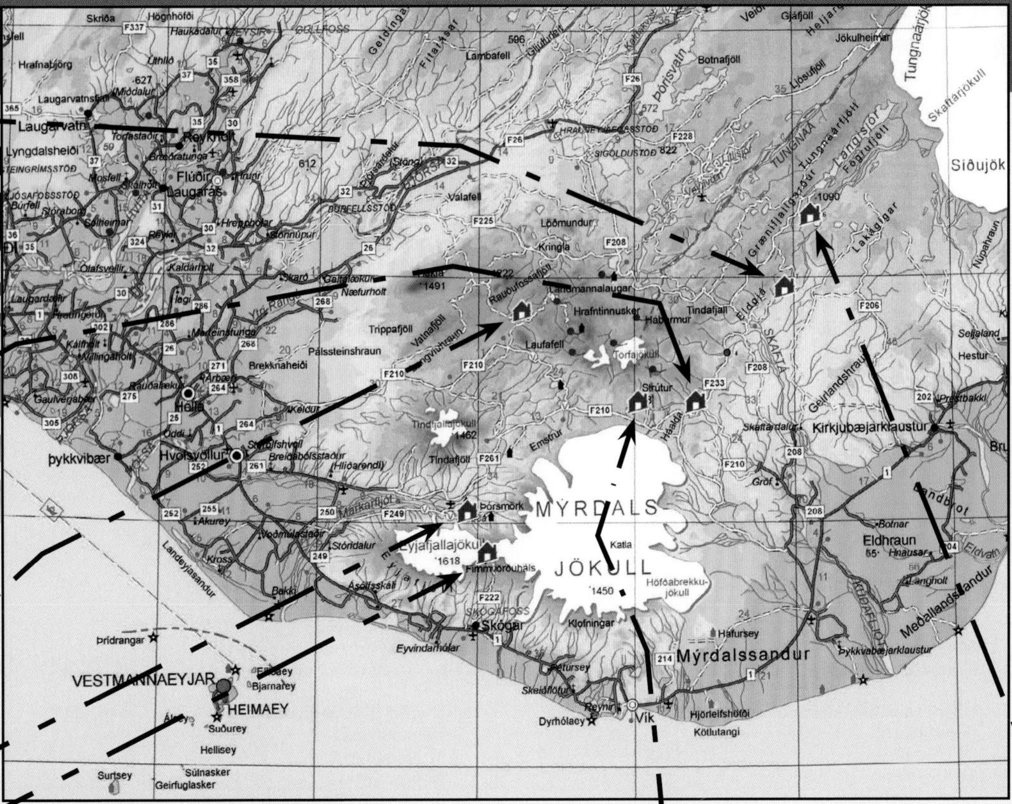

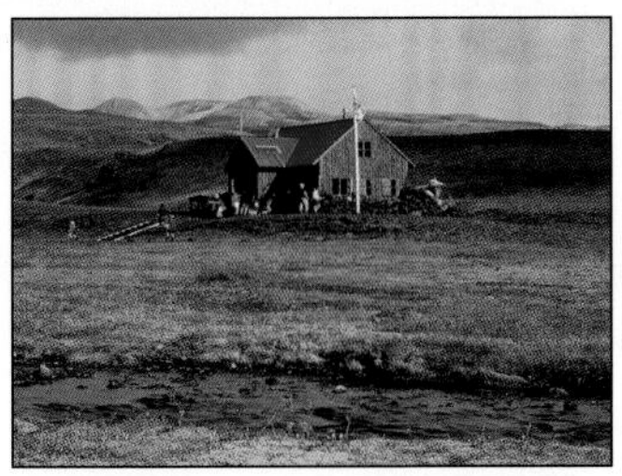

Strútur on Mælifellssandur

The hut was built in autumn 2002 and is fully-equipped, with oil heating, cooking facilities and a water toilet. Vehicles access the hut from Mælifellssandur via a jeep track that leads north from Syðri-Fjallabaksleið to the western part of Mælifell. Day hikes to fantastic locations may be taken from the hut, including Rauðibotn, Hólmsárlón, Strútslaug and Torfajökull. The hut is an ideal rest stop for hikers from Álftavötn en route to Hvanngil or Emstrur. The hut sleeps 26.
GPS coordinate: N 63°50.330′ W 18°58.477′

Sveinstindur

The hut at Mt. Sveinstindur is to the south-east of the mountain. Vehicle access is via tracks leading to Langisjór lake, and a marked trail used by hydrographers is followed to the east until the hut is reached. In early summer the trail may have patches of wet sand. A hiking path has been marked out from the tracks leading to Langisjór to the hut, and a marked path also extends to the top of the mountain from the southwest. The hut is heated with a small oil stove and gas for cooking is provided, along with necessary utensils. Drinking water is piped into the hut in summer.
The hut sleeps 20.
GPS coordinate: N 64°05.176′ W 18°24.946′

ÚTIVIST
Ferðafélagið Útivist
Laugavegur 178 – 105 Reykjavík
Tel.: 562 1000 – Fax: 562 1001
utivist@utivist.is – www.utivist.is

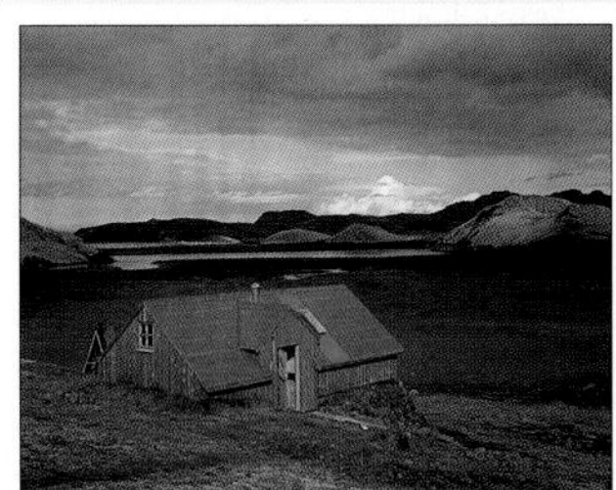

Information Centres in ICELAND

1. Tourist Information Centre (p. 510)
Aðalstrætii 2
101 Reykjavík
☎ 590-1550
info@visitreykjavik.is • www. visitreykjavik.is

2. District Tourist Information Centre (p. 207)
Strandgata 6
220 Hafnarfjörður
☎ 585-5500
hafnarfjordur@hafnarfjordur.is • www.hafnarfjordur.is

3. Tourist Information Centre (p. 209)
Keflavík Interantional Airport
235 Reykjanesbær
☎ 570-7790
airport@ita.is • www.visitreykjanes.is

4. District Tourist Information Centre (p. 221)
Kjósarstofa / Ásgarður
276 Mosfellsbær
☎ 857 0100
kjosarstofa@kjos.is • www.westiceland.is

5. District Tourist Information Centre (p. 232)
Suðurgata 57
300 Akranes
☎ 433-1065
info@visitakranes.is • www.visitakranes.is

6. Regional Tourist Information Centre (p. 56)
Hyrnutorg, Borgarbraut 58-60
310 Borgarnes
☎ 437-2214
info@ westiceland.is • www.westiceland.is

7. District Tourist Information Centre (p. 261)
Snorrastofa
320 Reykholt
☎ 433-8000
gestastofa@snorrastofa.is • www.westiceland.is

8. District Tourist Information Centre (p. 254)
Aðalgata 29
340 Stykkishólmur
☎ 433-8120
travelinfo@stykkisholmur.is • www.westiceland.is

9. District Tourist Information Centre (p. 248)
The Heritage Centre
350 Grundarfjörður
☎ 438-1881
info@sagan.is • www.westiceland.is

10. District Tourist Information Centre (p. 276)
Kirkjutún 2
355 Snæfellsbær
☎ 433-9930
info@snb.is • www.westiceland.is

11. Visitor Centre - Snæfellsjökull National Park (p. 276)
Hellnar
360 Hellissandur
☎ 436-6888
snaefellsjokull@ust.is • www.ust.is/snaefellsjokull.is

12. District Tourist Information Centre (p. 282)
Leifsbúð
370 Búðardalur
☎ 434-1441
info@dalir.is • www.westiceland.is

13. District Tourist Information Centre (p. 285)
Maríutröð
380 Reykhólahreppur
☎ 894-1011
info@reykholar.is • www.westiceland.is

14. Regional Tourist Information Centre (p. 294)
Aðalstrætii 7
400 Ísafjörður
☎ 450-8060
info@vestfirdir.is • www.westfjords.is

15. District Tourist Information Centre (p. 293)
Vitastígur 1
415 Bolungarvík
☎ 450-7010
touristinfo@bolungarvik.is • www.westfjords.is

16. District Tourist Information Centre (p. 288)
Hafnarstræti 5
470 Þingeyri
☎ 456-8304
thingeyri@thingeyri.is • www.westfjords.is

17. District Tourist Information Centre (p. 311)
Höfðagata 8 - 10
510 Hólmavík
☎ 451-3111
info@holmavik.is • www.westfjords.is

18. District Tourist Information Centre (p. 338)
Strandgata 1
530 Hvammstangi
☎ 451-2345
selasetur@selasetur.is • www.northiceland.is

19. District Tourist Information Centre (p. 70)
Varmahlíð
560 Varmahlíð
☎ 455-6161
info@skagafjordur.is • www.visitskagafjordur.is

20. District Tourist Information Centre (p. 331)
Gránugata 24
580 Siglufjörður
☎ 464-9120
info@fjallabyggd.is • www.northiceland.is

21. Regional Tourist Information Centre (p. 81)
Hof Menningarhús, Strandgata 12
600 Akureyri
☎ 450-1050
info@visitakureyri. • www.northiceland.is

22. District Tourist Information Centre (p. 371)
Húsavíkurstofa, Hafnarstétt 1
640 Húsavík
☎ 464-4300
info@visithusavik.is • www.visithusavik.is

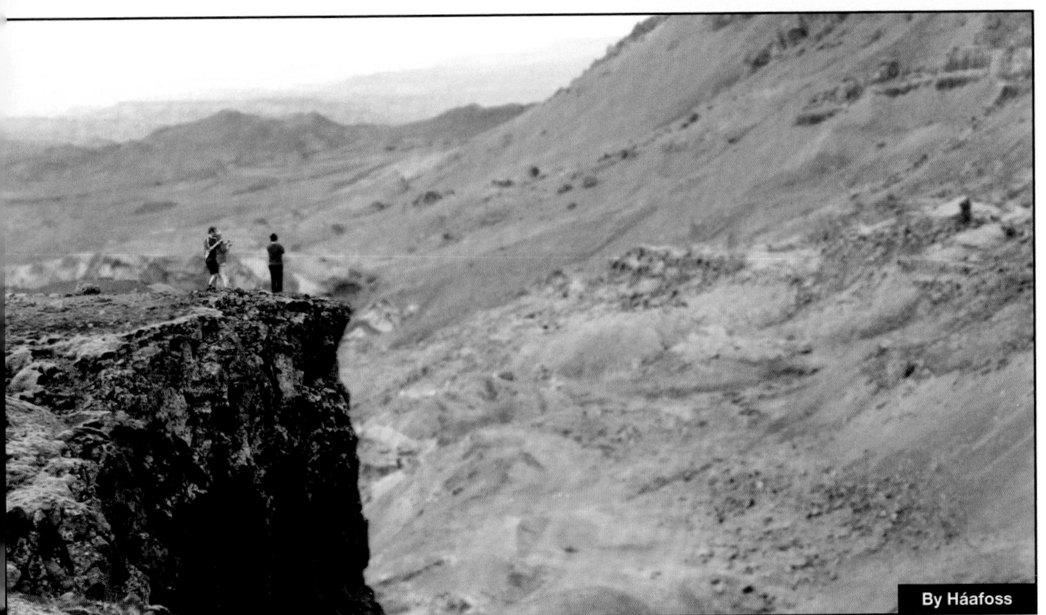

23. District Tourist Information Centre (p. 91)
Mývatnsstofa, Hraunvegur 8
660 Mývatn
☎ 464-4390
info@visitmyvatn.is • www.visitmyvatn.is

24. Vatnajökull National Park - Ásbyrgi (p. 405)
Gljúfrastofa, Ásbyrgi
671 Kópasker
☎ 470-7100
asbyrgi@vjp.is • www.vjp.is

25. District Tourist Information Centre (p. 380)
Langanesvegur 18b
680 Þórshöfn
☎ 468-1515
sund@langanesbyggd.is • www.northiceland.is

26. Regional Tourist Information Centre (p. 102)
Miðvangur 1-3
700 Egilsstaðir
☎ 471-2320
east@east.is • www.east.is

27. District Tourist Information Centre (p. 428)
Snæfellsstofa, Skriðuklaustur
701 Egilsstaðir
☎ 470-0840
snaefellsstofa@vjp.is • www.vjp.is

28. Regional Tourist Information Centre (p. 415)
Ferjuleira 1
710 Seyðisfjörður
☎ 472-1551
ferdamenning@sfk.is • ww.visitseydisfjordur.com

29. District Tourist Information Centre (p. 109)
Langabúð
765 Djúpivogur
☎ 478-8228
ugnius@djupivogur.is • www.east.is

30. Vatnajökull National Park - Skaftafelli
Skaftafellsstofa (p. 121)
785 Öræfi
☎ 470-8300
skaftafell@vjp.is • www.vjp.is

31. District Tourist Information Centre (p. 144)
Austurvegur 2
800 Selfoss
☎ 480-1990
tourinfo@arborg.is • www.south.is

32. District Tourist Information Centre (p. 175)
Þjórsárstofa, Árnesi
801 Selfoss
☎ 486-6115
thjorsarstofa@skeidgnup.is • www.south.is

33. Regional Tourist Information Centre (p. 146)
Sunnumörk 2-4
810 Hveragerði
☎ 483-4601
tourinfo@hveragerdi.is • www.south.is

34. District Tourist Information Centre (p. 140)
Austurvegur 8
860 Hvolsvöllur
☎ 487-8043
tourinfo@hvolsvollur.is • www.south.is

35. District Tourist Information Centre (p. 132)
Víkurbraut 28
870 Vík
☎ 487-1395
info@vik.is • www.visitvik.is

36. District Tourist Information Centre (p. 124)
Skaftárstofa, Klausturvegur 10
880 Kirkjubæjarklaustur
☎ 487-4620
info@klaustur.is • www.south.is

37. District Tourist Information Centre (p. 154)
Safnahúsið við Ráðhúströð
900 Vestmannaeyjar
☎ 481-3555
tourinfo@vestmannaeyjar.is • www.south.is

See more map p. 42-43

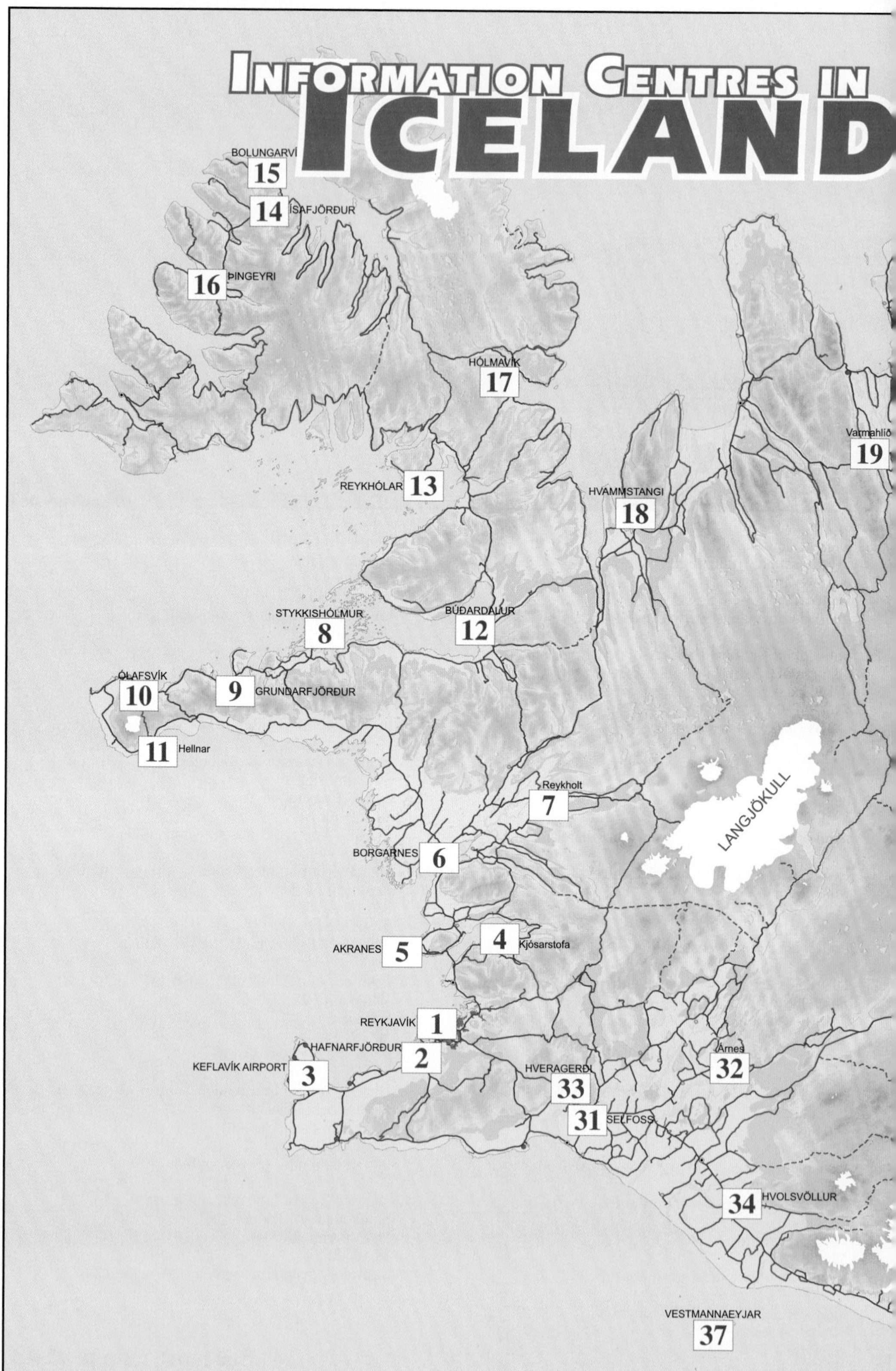
INFORMATION CENTRES IN
ICELAND
BOLUNGARVÍ
15
14 ÍSAFJÖRÐUR
16 ÞINGEYRI
HÓLMAVÍK
17
Varmahlíð
19
REYKHÓLAR 13
HVAMMSTANGI
18
STYKKISHÓLMUR
8
BÚÐARDALUR
12
ÓLAFSVÍK
10
9 GRUNDARFJÖRÐUR
11 Hellnar
Reykholt
7
LANGJÖKULL
BORGARNES 6
4 Kjósarstofa
AKRANES 5
REYKJAVÍK 1
HAFNARFJÖRÐUR 2
KEFLAVÍK AIRPORT 3
Árnes
32
HVERAGERÐI
33
31 SELFOSS
34 HVOLSVÖLLUR
VESTMANNAEYJAR
37

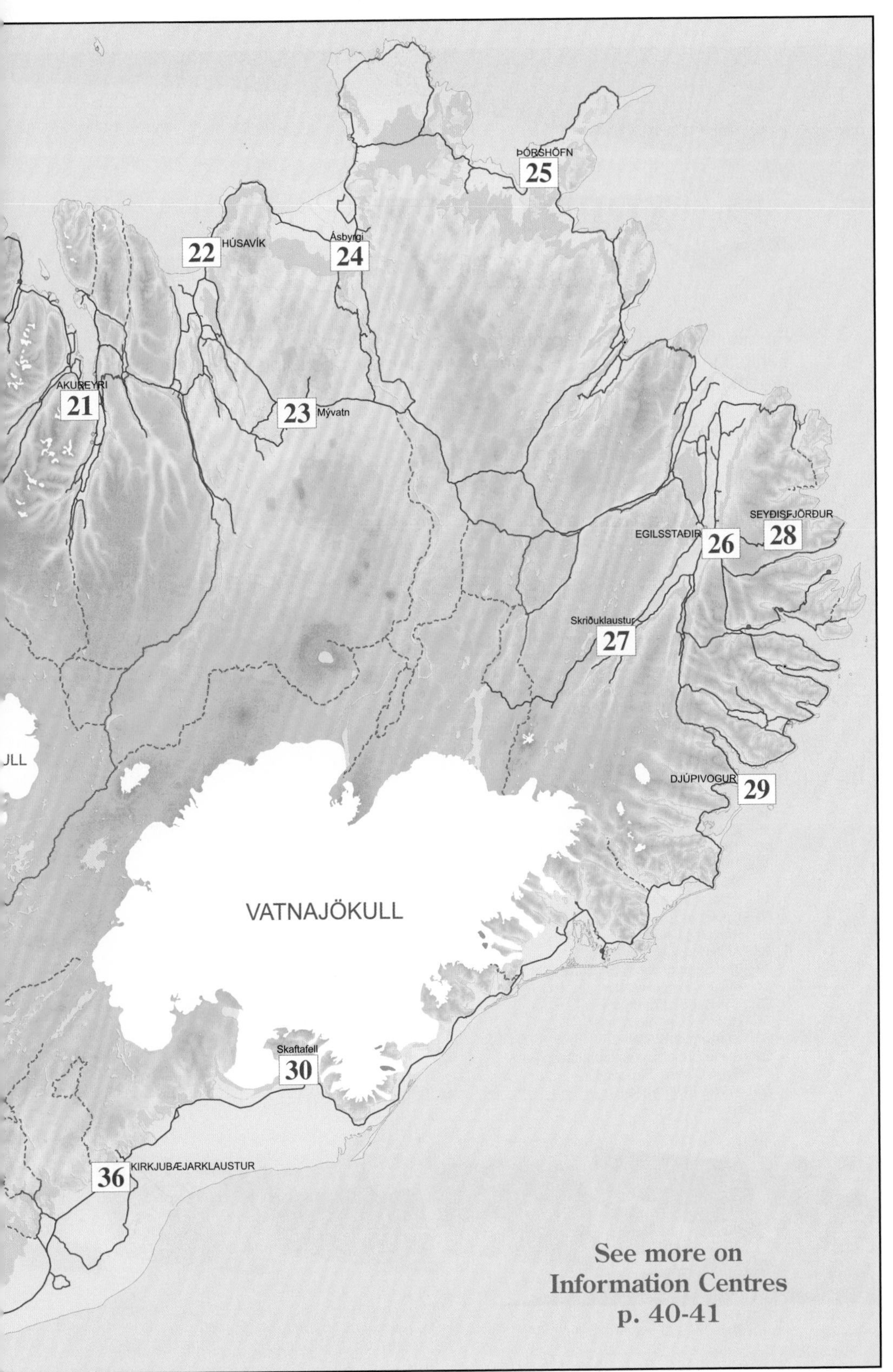

See more on
Information Centres
p. 40-41

Experience Iceland´s History

Follow the Saga Trails to historic places, saga sites, museums, parks and exhibitions all over Iceland, where the country's rich and eventful history is brought to life.

Visit our website or pick up a Saga Trails Association booklets.

Welcome to the Icelandic Saga Trails!

1 Viking World
2 Viking Village
3 Hofsstaðir Historic Park
4 National Museum of Iceland
5 Manuscripts at the Culture House
6 Saga Museum
7 Reykjavík 871+/-2 Settlement Exhibition
8 Lets Talk... Comedy Show
9 Þingvellir National Park
10 The Settlement Centre in Borgarnes
11 Reykholt
12 Eiríkisstaðir
13 The Saga of Gísli Súrsson
14 Vatnsfjörður
15 The Saga of Grettir the Strong
16 The Saga of the People of Vatnsdalur
17 Museum of Prophecies
18 Sturlung Trail
19 Hólar in Hjaltadalur
20 Gásir
21 Þorgeir's Church
22 Arctic Henge
23 The Saga of the Vopnafjörður People
24 Kloster Skriðuklaustur
25 The Saga of Hrafnkell
26 History in the Southeast
27 Convent at Kirkjubær
28 Stave Church, Westman Islands
29 Saga Centre, Hvolsvöllur
30 Þjórsá River Valley
31 Skálholt

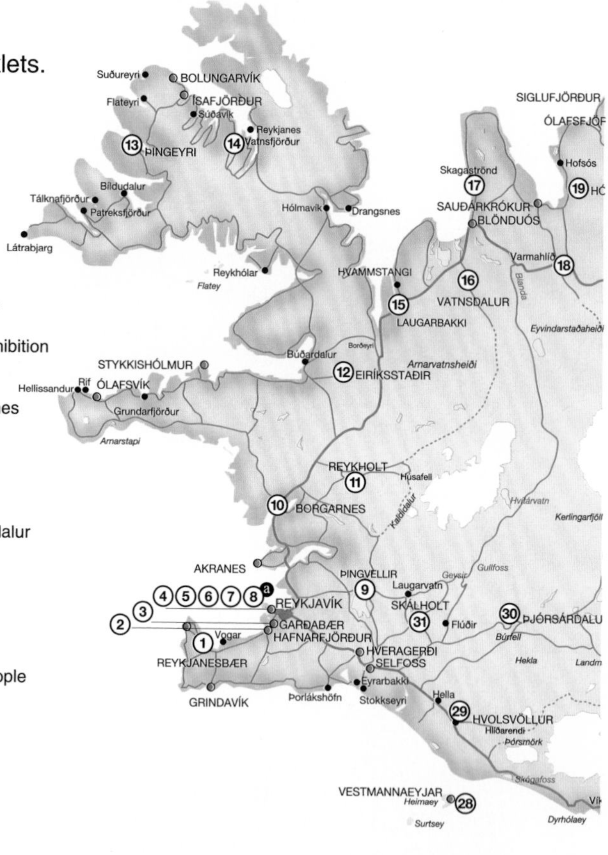

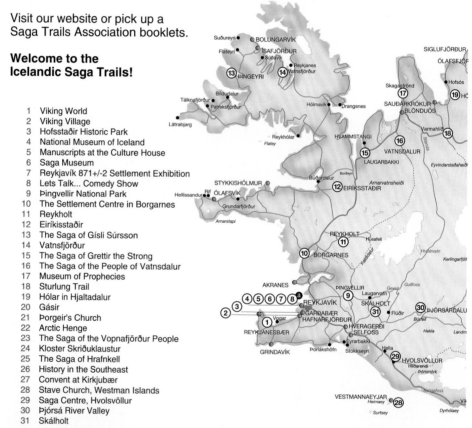

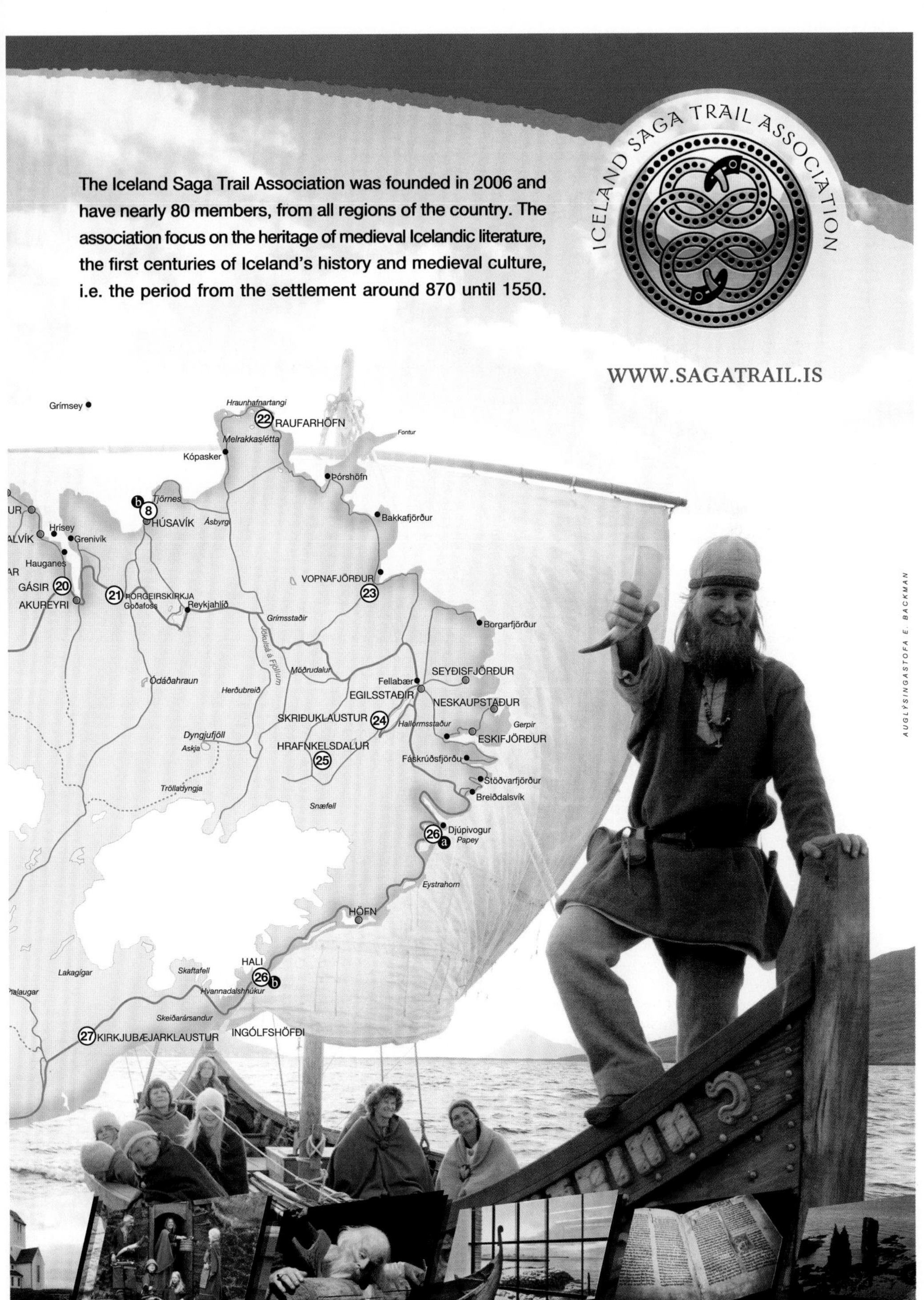
ICELAND SAGA TRAIL ASSOCIATION
The Iceland Saga Trail Association was founded in 2006 and have nearly 80 members, from all regions of the country. The association focus on the heritage of medieval Icelandic literature, the first centuries of Iceland's history and medieval culture, i.e. the period from the settlement around 870 until 1550.
WWW.SAGATRAIL.IS
Grímsey
Hraunhafnartangi
22 RAUFARHÖFN
Melrakkaslétta
Fontur
Kópasker
Þórshöfn
Tjörnes
8 HÚSAVÍK
Ásbyrgi
Bakkafjörður
Hrísey
Grenivík
Hauganes
GÁSIR 20
AKUREYRI
21 ÞORGEIRSKIRKJA
Goðafoss
Reykjahlíð
VOPNAFJÖRÐUR
23
Grímsstaðir
Borgarfjörður
Jökulsá á Fjöllum
Möðrudalur
Ódáðahraun
Herðubreið
SEYÐISFJÖRÐUR
Fellabær
EGILSSTAÐIR
NESKAUPSTAÐUR
SKRIÐUKLAUSTUR 24
Hallormsstaður
Gerpir
ESKIFJÖRÐUR
Dyngjufjöll
Askja
HRAFNKELSDALUR
25
Fáskrúðsfjörður
Stöðvarfjörður
Tröllladyngja
Breiðdalsvík
Snæfell
26 Djúpivogur
Papey
Eystrahorn
HÖFN
HALI
Lakagígar
Skaftafell
26
Hvannadalshnúkur
Skeiðarársandur
27 KIRKJUBÆJARKLAUSTUR
INGÓLFSHÖFÐI
AUGLÝSINGASTOFA E. BACKMAN

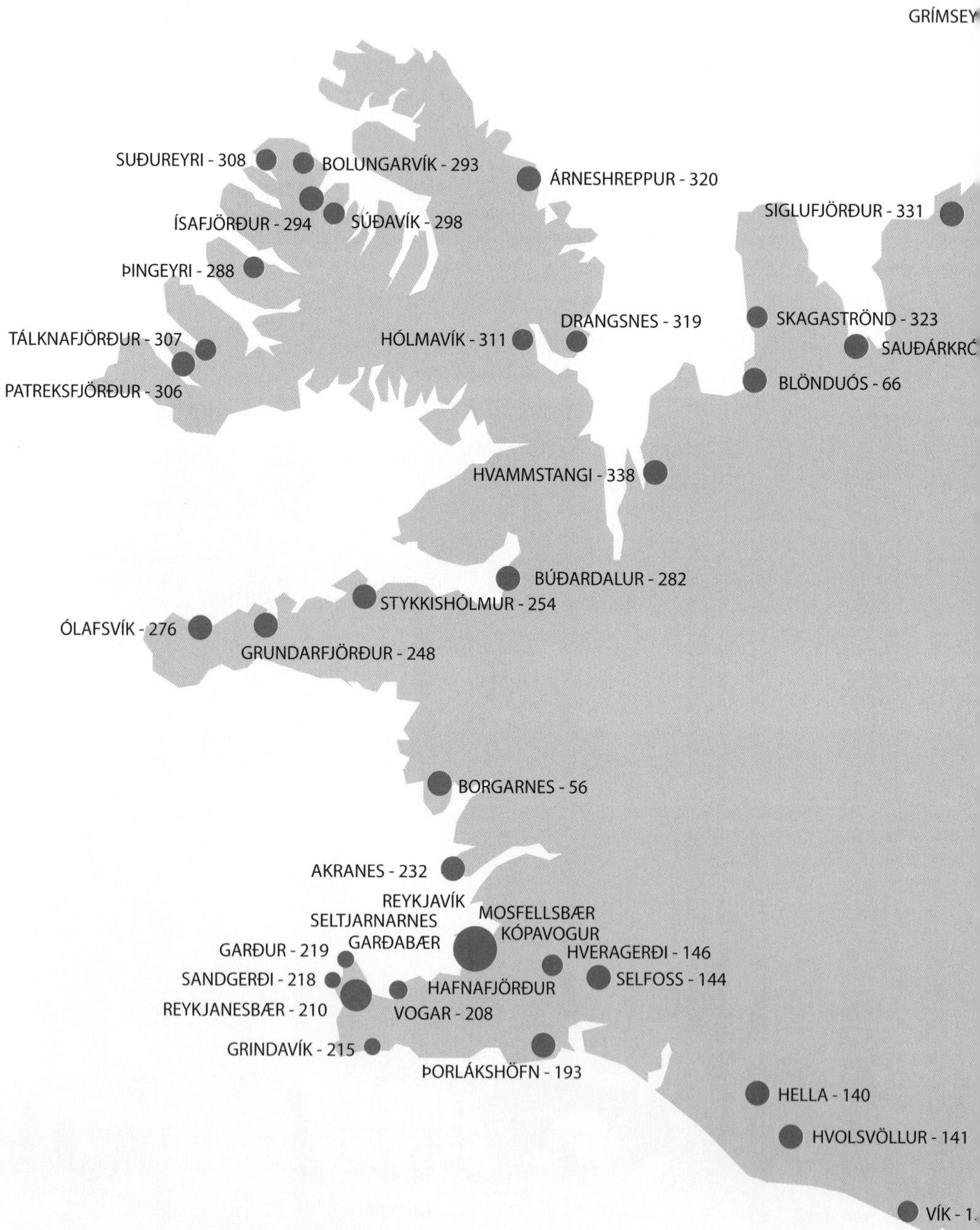

GRÍMSEY

SUÐUREYRI - 308
BOLUNGARVÍK - 293
ÁRNESHREPPUR - 320
ÍSAFJÖRÐUR - 294
SÚÐAVÍK - 298
SIGLUFJÖRÐUR - 331
ÞINGEYRI - 288
TÁLKNAFJÖRÐUR - 307
HÓLMAVÍK - 311
DRANGSNES - 319
SKAGASTRÖND - 323
SAUÐÁRKR
PATREKSFJÖRÐUR - 306
BLÖNDUÓS - 66
HVAMMSTANGI - 338
BÚÐARDALUR - 282
STYKKISHÓLMUR - 254
ÓLAFSVÍK - 276
GRUNDARFJÖRÐUR - 248
BORGARNES - 56
AKRANES - 232
REYKJAVÍK
SELTJARNARNES
MOSFELLSBÆR
KÓPAVOGUR
GARÐABÆR
GARÐUR - 219
HVERAGERÐI - 146
SANDGERÐI - 218
HAFNAFJÖRÐUR
SELFOSS - 144
REYKJANESBÆR - 210
VOGAR - 208
GRINDAVÍK - 215
ÞORLÁKSHÖFN - 193
HELLA - 140
HVOLSVÖLLUR - 141
VÍK - 1
VESTMANNAEYJAR - 154

A map with locations of Post offices arround Iceland along with the Road Guide page number.

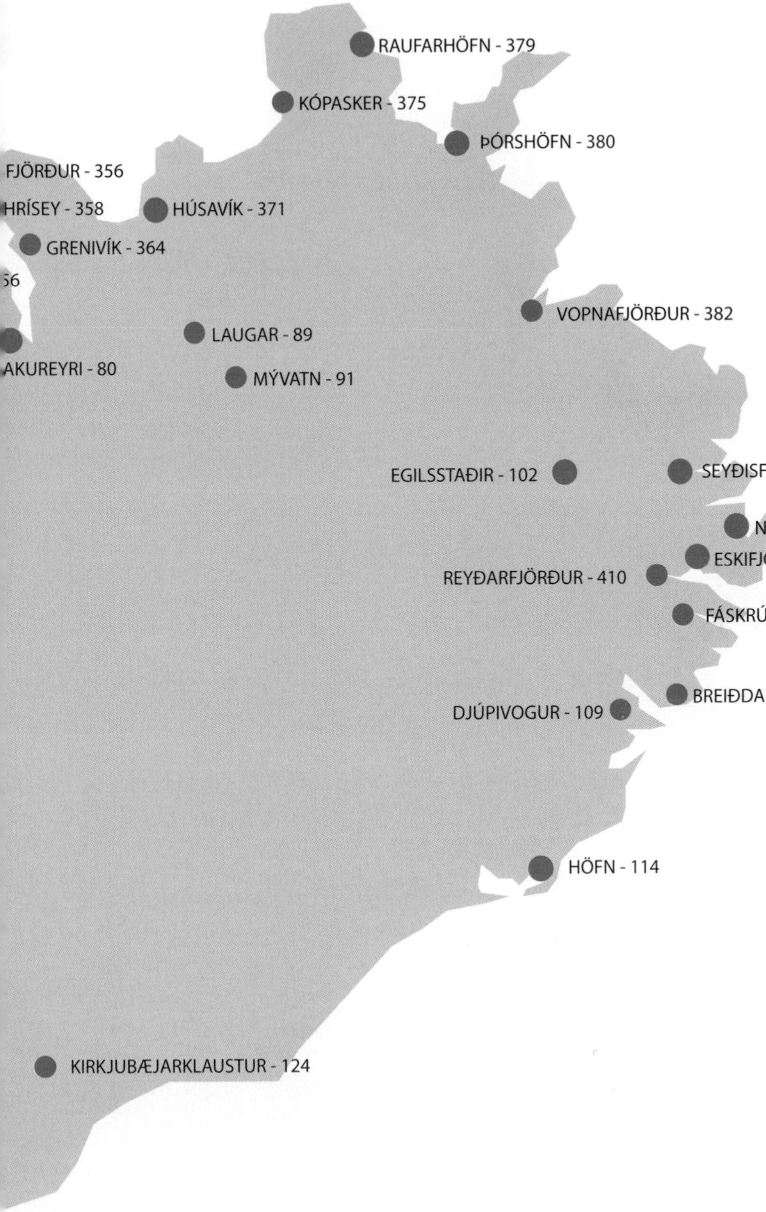

www.postur.is

NATIONAL MUSEUM OF

National Museum Historic Buildings Collection
Towns and Villages
Roads

ICELAND

HISTORIC BUILDING COLLECTION OF THE NATIONAL MUSEUM

Your trip starts here

If you are taking the Ring Road from Reykjavík to the west and the north, start at page 51. If you are travelling east from Reykjavík, begin instead at page 151 and follow the pages in reverse order until you get to Reykjavík via Hvalfjörður and Kjalarnes.

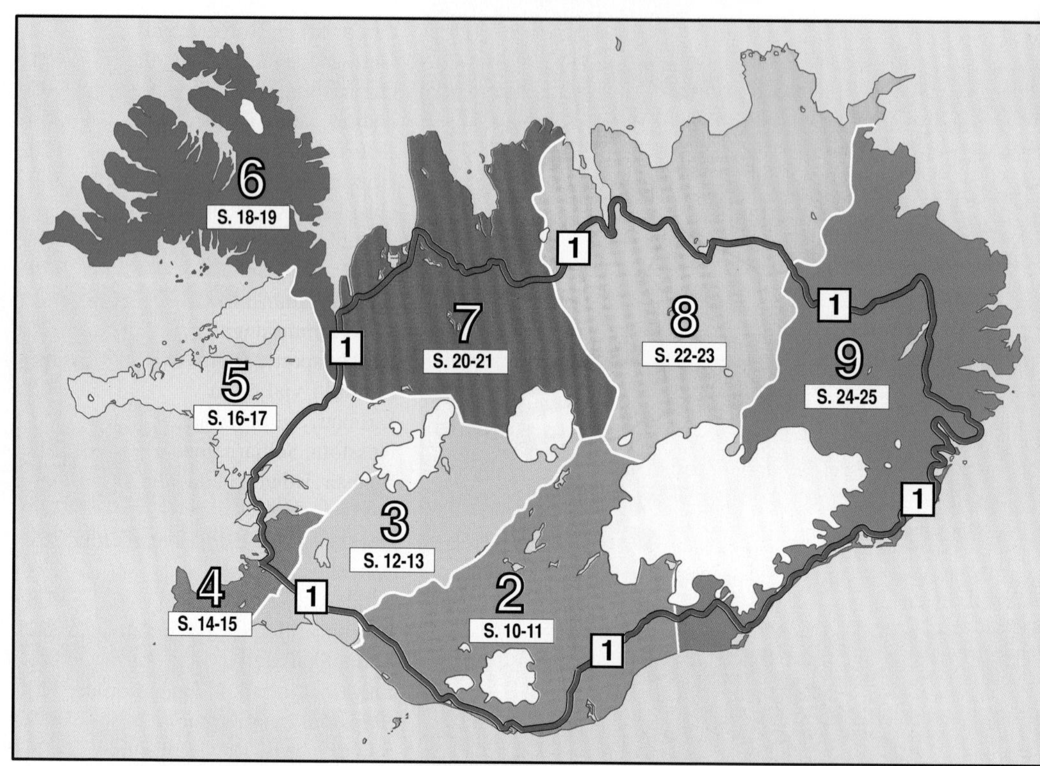

Iceland is divided into eight regions, numbered from 2 to 9.

There is no Region 1.

This map shows the regions, and also Highway 1 (the Ring Road), which passes through all regions. The numbers of all roads in each area (with the exception of Highway 1) begin with the relevant regional number. For example, all roads in Region 2 have numbers beginning with 2. The roads within each region are listed in numerical, rather than alphabetical, order. For example, the first road in Region 3, Skeiða- og Hrunamannavegur, is no. 30, and the last, Arnarbælisvegur, is no. 375.

See more detailed information on how to use this book on p. 4-7

1 VESTURLANDSVEGUR

Esja, (914 m) For many citizens of Reykjavík this mountain is virtually a part of the city, and indeed it often protects it from the full fury of the north-east winds in winter. Good viewing points are **Kerhólakambur** (850 m), **Kistufell** (830 m) and **Þverfell** (guest book). There are many routes up the mountain, the most popular being from Mógilsá and Esjuberg.

Mógilsá, a mixed forest in the Alps-like surroundings of Mt. Esja, one of Reykjavík's most popular areas for outdoor recreation. The Mógilsá Research Station's clonal archives, a wide variety of paths and a path network leading from the research station. An excellent variation on the traditional Mt. Esja hike – sort of like a 'mini' Mt. Esja hike!

Mosfellskirkja, a church in Mosfellsdalur. In front of the church is a monument of Ólafía Jóhannsdóttir often called „Mother Teresa of the North". She was born in Mosfell in 1863 and was a womens rights activist.

Álafoss, a village by Varmá, built around a woollen mill of the same name which was founded in 1896. The mill buildings are now artists' studios.

Reykjalundur, a sanatorium and workshop, built 1945, originally for TB patients. Now a general rehabilitation centre.

Mosfellsbær, (pop. 8,651) a town and surrounding community with the usual services. Some light industry. The satellite commnication receiver Skyggnir is nearby.

Lágafell, once a farm and often the residen of priests. There is a church built in 1889, it is a wooden church with a concrete foundation. Extensions and renovations have been made to the original building.

Úlfarsfell, (295 m) a mountain and a farm of the same name. The cliffs on west the mountain are now called **Hamrahlíð**, formerly **Lágafellshamrar**. On the east side of Úlfasfell is Skyggnir a satellite communication base for phone, television and air control.

Korpúlfsstaðir, a farm built after 1922 by Thor Jensen (1863-1947). He took over a cottage farm and made it one of the largest and richest farms in the country. The large farm building which, among other things, housed 300 cows, still stands. The Thors family are descended from him; among them Ólafur Thors (1892-1964) a prominent politician and former prime minister, and the author Thor Vilhjálmsson (1925-2011). There is a golf course there now.

Keldnaholt, a group of research laboratories for farming, building and industry.

Keldur, a research institute for diseases and bacteriology.

Gufunes, a farm. Since 1935 the site of a telecommunication centre, both for domestic and foreign communication. The sculpture garden of Hallsteinn Sigurðsson is on a slope above the plant.

Grafarholt, one of Reykjavík´s suburbian districts. There is also the golf course of Reykjavík Golf Club. Near the road is a large split rock, thought to be inhabited by the "hidden people". The rock has been move twice. The first time it was moved it split in two. One piece weighs 15 tons and the other 35.

Grafarvogur, one of Reykjavík´s suburbian districts.

Esjuberg-Ártúnshöfði 18 km

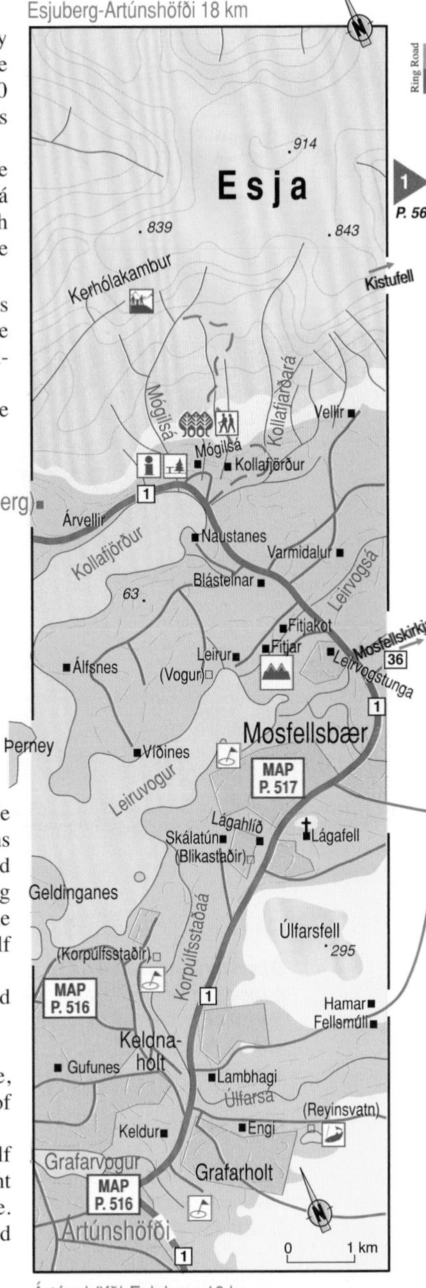

Ártúnshöfði-Esjuberg 18 km

36 Þingvallavegur, p. 187

Hlésey, a small farm and a place of Viking culture. It is the private home of Jóhanna Harðardóttir an artist and a heathen priestess of Ásatrú, the religion of the settlers of Iceland. As a skilled Rune reader she uses the wisdom of the god Óðin to channel a path from past to future. There are no set opening hours, but if you are interested in a rune reading or in Jóhanna's artwork, you can make an advance appointment.

Kúludalsá, a farm and a river of the same name. The river runs just east of the farm.

Hvalfjörður Tunnel (Whale Fjord). Built in 1996–1998, the tunnel is 5650 m. This first underwater tunnel in Iceland shortened the journey north and west from Reykjavík by 47 km. It is the only road for which payment is collected of vehicle owners.

Ártún, an abandoned farm on the banks of Blikadalá river.

Saurbær, a farm and church. In 1424 English pirates raided the farm.

Kjalarnes, the district to the west of Esja between the fjords Kollafjörður and Hvalfjörður. Became a part of Reykjavík in 1998.

Andríðsey, an island. It is said that a farmer from the time of settlement was buried there.

458 Brautarholtsvegur, 2 km.

Brautarholt, church and farm. There the poet Bjarni Thorarensen (1786–1841) was born.

Hof, a farm where the second largest heathen temple is supposed to have been, though no ruins are visible.

Grundarhverfi, a community of 528 inhabitants.

Fólkvangur, a community centre in Grundarhverfi.

Móar, a farm and formerly a parsonage. First parish of the poet and priest Matthías Jochumsson, who translated *Hamlet* and other Shakespeare plays while serving there as well as writing Iceland's national anthem.

Esjuberg, a farm where the first church in Iceland is said to have been built by the Hebridean Örlygur Hrappsson.

47 Hvalfjarðarvegur, p. 220 **51 Akrafjallsvegur,** p. 234
460 Eyrarfjallsvegur, p. 224 **506 Grundartangavegur,** p. 54, 234

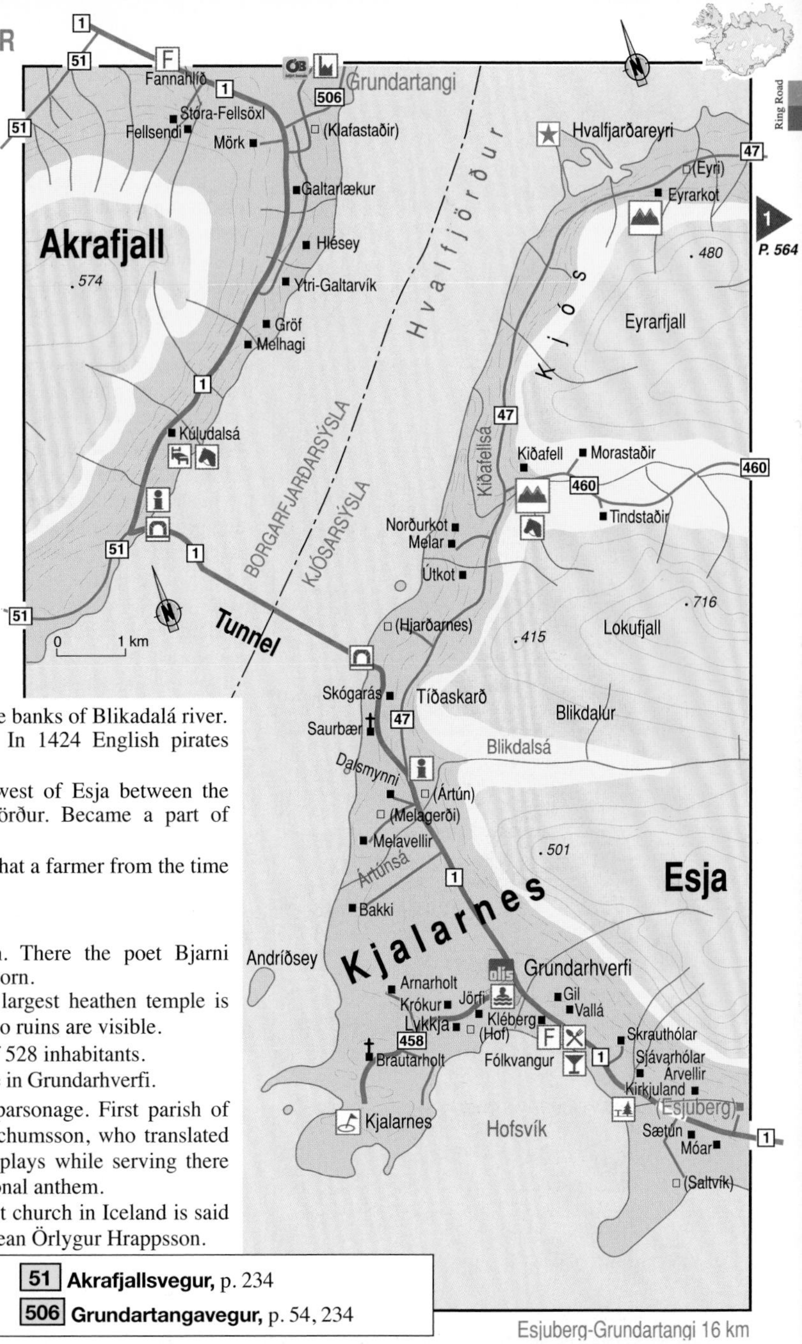

1 P. 564

Esjuberg-Grundartangi 16 km

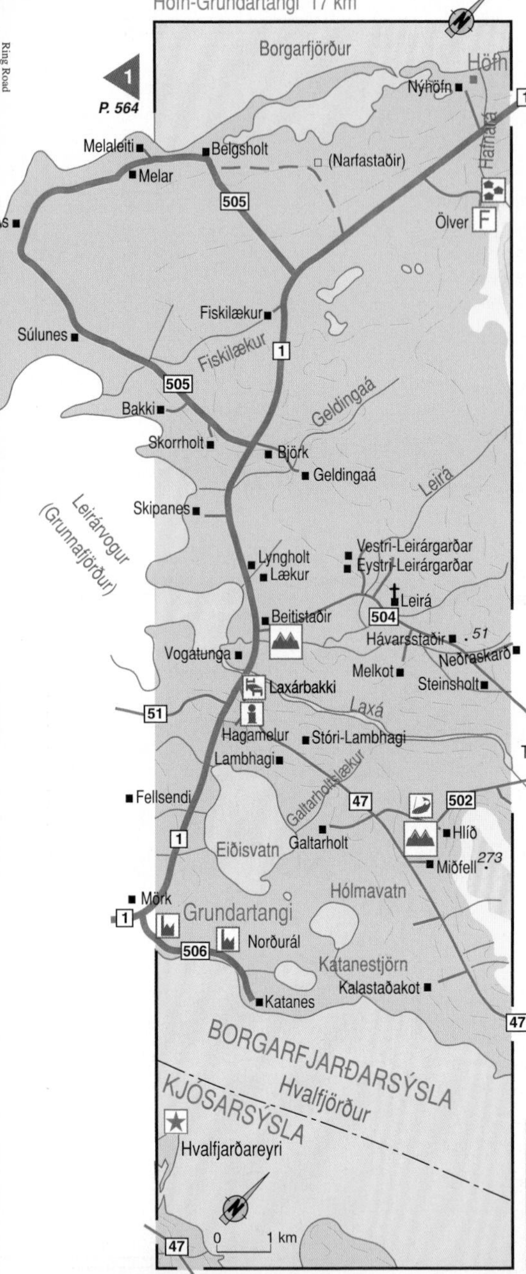

Belgsholt, there a windmill was installed in 2011. It was the first windmill in Iceland, producing upto 30kW, providing the farm most of the electricity it needs.

Höfn, a farm and in earlier times the seat of chieftains. In the 17th century the home of Steinunn Finnsdóttir, the first known Icelandic poetess.

Ölver, (602 m) in the birch woods below this mountain there is a community centre and summer cottages.

Melar, a farm and, until 1855, a church but the site is now much eroded by the sea. Served by Helgi Sigurðsson 1815 (1808-88), who was the major force in the establishment of the National Museum and the first Icelander to study photography, which he did in Copenhagen alongside his academic studies 1842-45.

505 Melasveitarvegur, 11,68 km.

Leirá, ("Clay river") a farm and church, from earliest times the home of influential men. Chief Justice Magnús Stephensen put up a printing press at a nearby farm, **Leirárgarðar**, and later moved it to Beitistaðir. Good salmon fishing in the river. Hot springs, swimming pool, school and community centre.

Beitistaðir, a farm where there was a printing press which was brought there from Leirárgarðar in 1814 and was moved in 1819 to Viðey, then the only printing-house in the country.

Galtarholtslækur, a small stream flowing into Eiðisvatn. This is where the executioner drowned, in the novel *Íslandsklukkan* by Nobel prize-winning author Halldór Laxness.

Grundartangi, (on Rd. 506), ferrosilicon plant built 1977-80 belonging to Icelandic Alloys Ltd. New aluminium plant commenced production 1998.

Katanes, a farm by the sea. During the last century a monster was said to have come from the sea and found a hiding-place in the small lake Katanestjörn. Extensive preparations were made to kill the monster but the story turned out to be a hoax.

506 Grundartangavegur, 2,46 km.

47 Hvalfjarðarvegur, p. 220
51 Akrafjallsvegur, p. 234
502 Svínadalsvegur, p. 258
504 Leirársveitarvegur, p. 258

1 VESTURLANDSVEGUR

530 Ferjubakkavegur, 5 km.

Brennistaðir, a community centre.

Einkunnir, a 265 ha park, protected for recreational use and the preservation of the typical landscape of the area since 2006. The main characteristics for this area are rocky islands or bluffs that rise from the vast flat wetlands.

Borg á Mýrum**,** church and parsonage. Originally settled by Skallagrímur Kveldúlfsson father of the poet Egill Skallagrímsson of *Egils saga*. Many of his relatives and descendants lived there, including Snorri Sturluson for a time. Tradition has it that Kjartan Ólafsson, one of the main characters of *Laxdæla saga*, is buried there.

Borgarnes, (pop. 1,759) a small town on Borgarfjörður. One of the very few costal towns in Iceland not dependent on fishing. Engaged mainly in commerce, service and industry. Sheriff and health centre. The first building know to have been built in Borgarnes was built by a Scot in 1858 for salmon-canning. Rivers and lakes are rich of salmons and trout's. The settler Skallagrímur Kveldúlfsson is buried in Borgarnes, his burial mound now being the central feature in a beautiful public garden, Skallagrímsgarður. Landnámssetið, the Icelandic Settlement Centre, is situated in the picturesque township of Borgarnes. The Borgarfjordur area is the setting for Egils Saga, one of the most graphic of the settlement sagas, and this historical context combined with the charming natural beauty of the site make it an ideal location for the Centre. Over a thousand years ago, Viking adventurers discovered a large untouched island in the north Atlantic and claimed the land for their own. A rapid period of settlement ensued and thus the Icelandic nation was born. The prime objective of the Icelandic Settlement Centre at Borgarnes is to dramatically recreate the fascinating sagas surrounding the birth of this island nation.

Brákarsund, ("Brák's channel") between the town and the island Brákarey ("Brák's island"), both named for Brák, a slave of Skallagrímur's. Fleeing her master's anger, she tried to swim out to the island but he threw a boulder which hit her between the shoulders and killed her. A memorial in her remembrance is there.

Borgarfjarðarbrú, second longest bridge in Iceland at 520 m, opened to traffic in 1980.

Seleyri, a spit of land. Through there lies a water pipe to Borgarnes from Hafnarfjall. A good spot for fishing sea trout and sea char.

Hafnarfjall, (844 m) a basalt mountain, barren and with big screes on the slopes. Some light-coloured granophyre crags in the screes, called **Flyðrur**. Landgræðsla ríkisins has revegetated extensive land areas in this region.

50 Borgarfjarðarbraut, p. 231
505 Melasveitarvegur, p. 54, 258
508 Skorradalsvegur, p. 259
511 Hvanneyrarvegur, p. 231
54 Snæfellsnesvegur, p. 238
507 Mófellsstaðavegur, p. 259
510 Hvítárvallavegur, p. 231

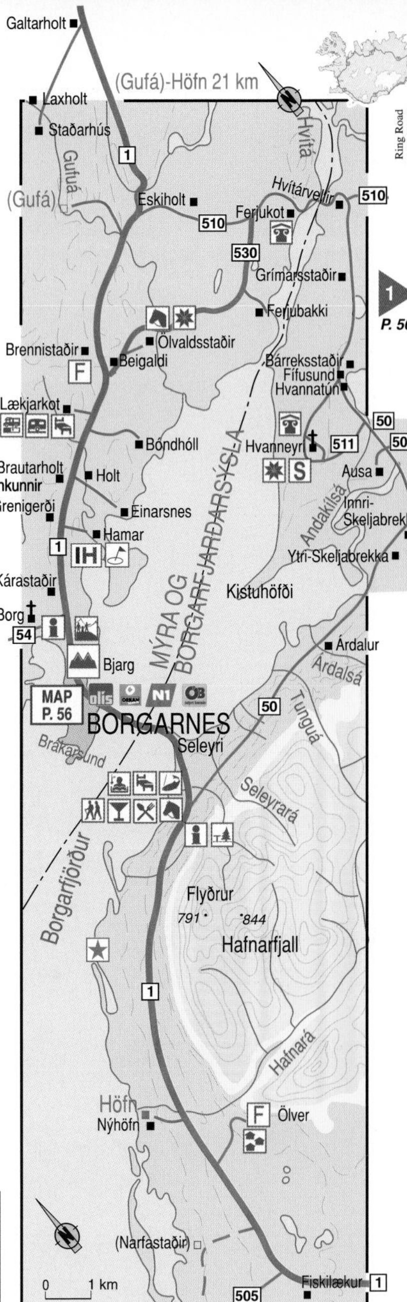

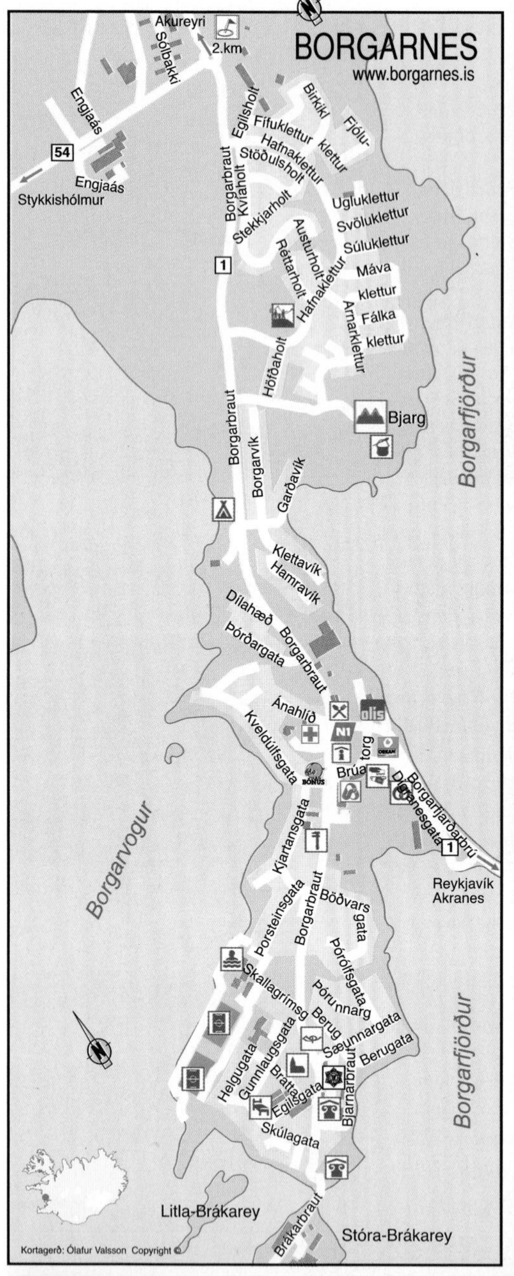

BORGARBYGGÐ

Office - Borgarbraut 14
Tel. 433 7100 • Fax 433 7101
www.borgarbyggd.is

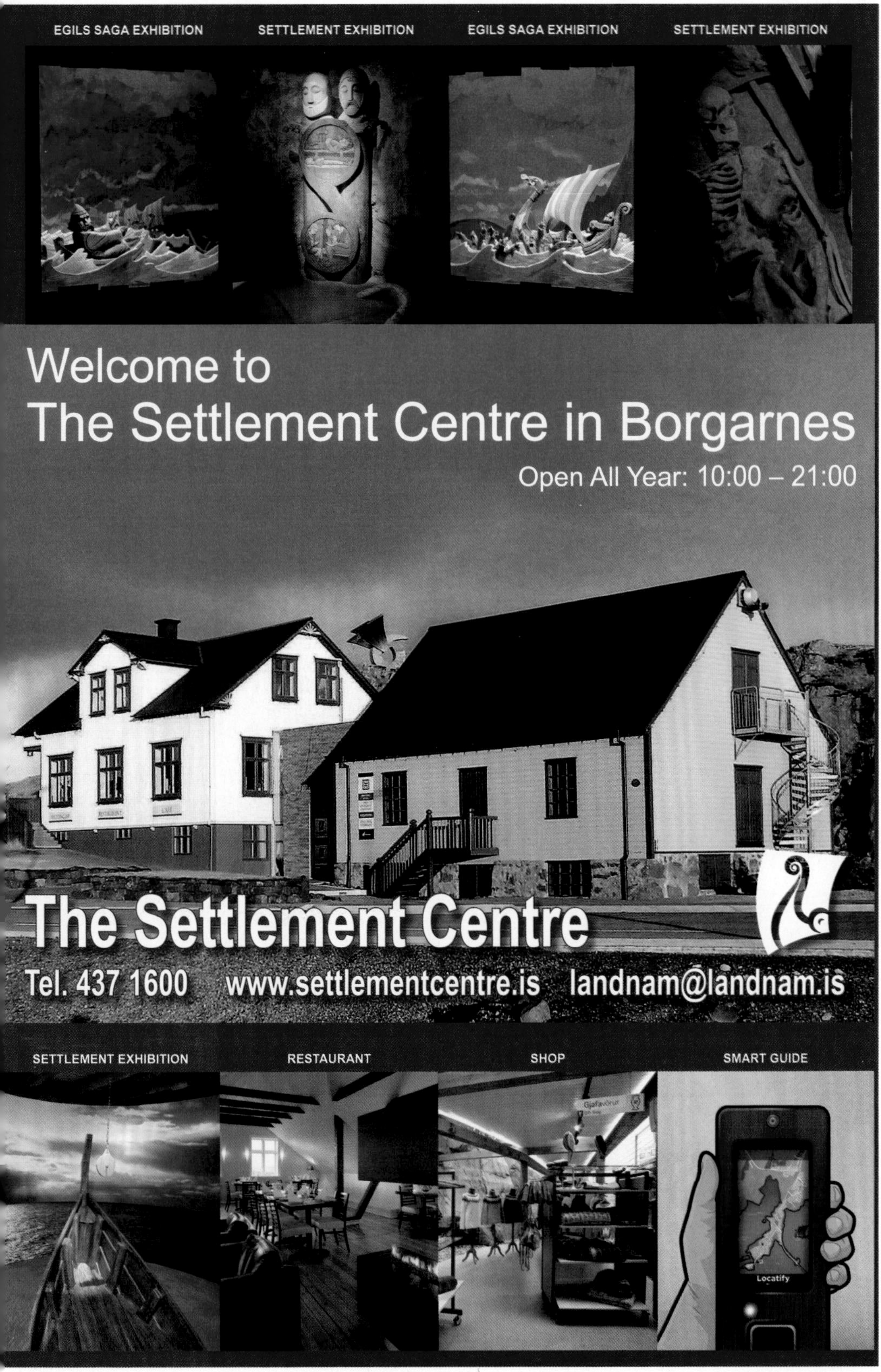

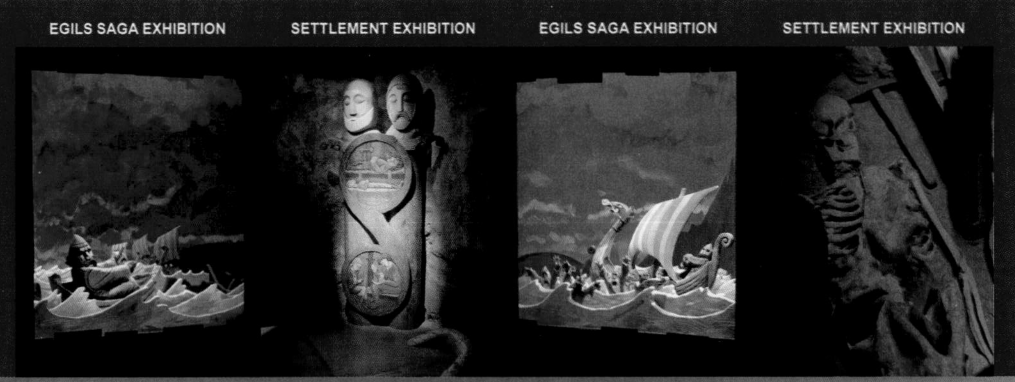

EGILS SAGA EXHIBITION
SETTLEMENT EXHIBITION
EGILS SAGA EXHIBITION
SETTLEMENT EXHIBITION
Welcome to
The Settlement Centre in Borgarnes
Open All Year: 10:00 – 21:00
The Settlement Centre
Tel. 437 1600 www.settlementcentre.is landnam@landnam.is
SETTLEMENT EXHIBITION
RESTAURANT
SHOP
SMART GUIDE
Locatify

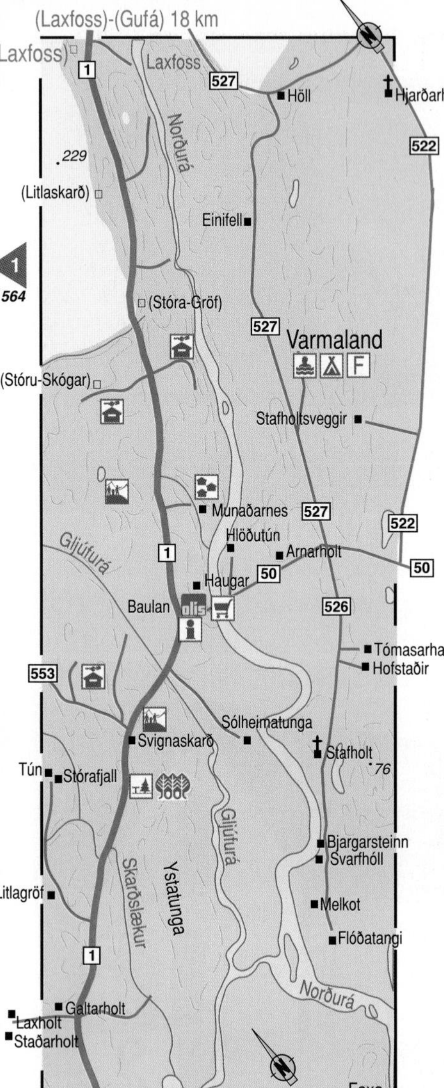

The Glanni waterfalls in Norðurá river.

Laxfoss, waterfall in the river Norðurá and a farm of the same name Good salmon-fishing below the falls. Plant fossils found nearby.

Munaðarnes, a farm on whose land a great many summer house have been built for the Union of state and municipal employees.

Varmaland, (on Rd. 527) a school centre built near a large ho spring. Greenhouses, shops and swimming pool. There is walking path through the woods to a cliff called Hnjúkurinn.

Gljúfurá, a branch of Langá and tributary of Norðurá it flow through an impressive long, straight canyon.

Svignaskarð, a substantial farm since early times, where many men of consequences have lived. Snorri Sturluson owned i for some time. The view from the view-dial on the crags, **Kastali** just north of the farm is extremely good on clear days, with the glaciers Eiríksjökull, Geitlandsjökull, Þórisjökull and Ok to the east Skarðsheiði and Hafnarfjall to the south and Baula to the north.

Ferjukot, a farm by the bridge on Hvítá with good salmon-fishing At Ferjukot is a salmon and history museum. Once sport tournament were held on the banks of the river Hvítá and later hourse tournament by a place now known as **Faxaborg**.

Hvítá, ("White river") the biggest river in western Iceland, dividing the counties Borgarfjarðarsýsla and Mýrasýsla. Like other rivers o the same name, it is a glacial river, coming from the western foot o Eiríksjökull. Along with its tributary Norðurá, however, which is 11 km long and has its source at the north-eastern end of Langjökull. In 1648 a Dutchman built a salmon-fishing lodge by the mouth of the river.

50	**Borgarfjarðarbraut,** p. 230	510	**Hvítárvallavegur,** p. 231
522	**Þverárhlíðarvegur,** p. 265	526	**Stafholtsvegur,** p. 230
527	**Varmalandsvegur,** p. 230	530	**Ferjubakkavegur,** p. 55
553	**Langavatnsvegur,** p. 269		

1 VESTURLANDSVEGUR

Grábrók.

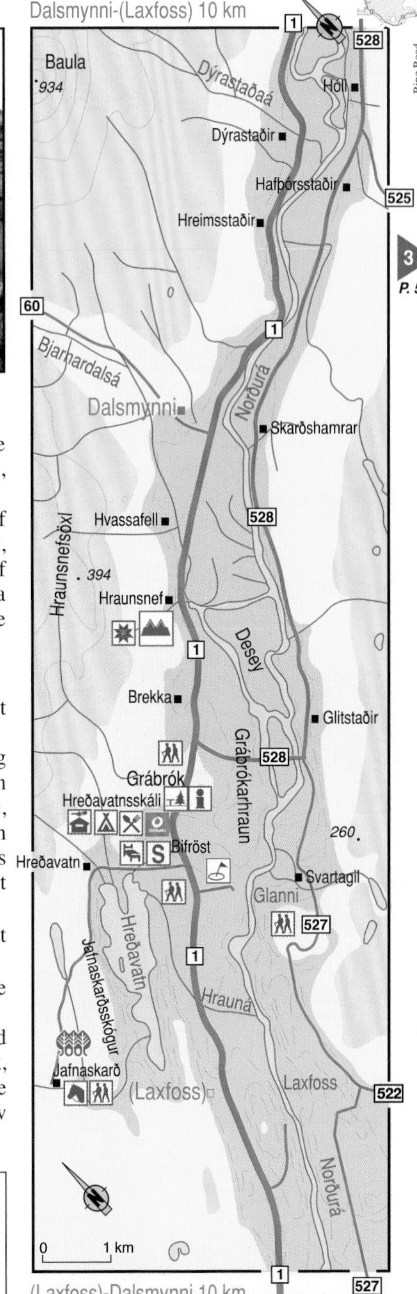

Dalsmynni, ("Mouth of the valley") has been a farm site since the original settlement. The settler was Rauða-Björn ("Iron-oxide-Björn"), who was the first to work iron from the moors.

Hraunsnefsöxl, a mountain ridge, half of which is said to have split off and fallen down into the valley shortly before the original settlement, leaving a 100 m high cliff face on the mountain and another 100 m of gravel and rock scree below it. At Hraunsnef is a guesthouse and a restaurant. There you can get a map with information about where the local fairies, hidden people, gnomes, dwarves and trolls live.

528 Norðurárdalsvegur, 16 km.

Bifröst, a business college first operated by the co-operative movement in Iceland. Now a university.

Hreðavatn, a lake and farm of the same name. There is trout-fishing in the lake and several small islands covered with the rich vegetation which is a feature of the immediate area. Lignite, mined at one time, is found a little above the farm, also plant fossils from the warm interval of the Tertiary period. Some distance west of the lake there is a lone pyramid-shaped peak, **Vikrafell** (539 m). By the lake is a forrest **Jafnaskarðsskógur**.

Hreðavatnsskáli, probably Icelands oldest restaurant by the road. First built in 1933 but moved in 1946 to its current location.

Glanni, waterfall in the river Norðurá. The river bank has interesting lave formation and a magical landscape. Well worth a visit.

Grábrókarhraun, a rough lava-field about 3,000 years old, covered with moss and birch bushes. The lava came from three craters, **Grábrók**, which is the largest, **Grábrókarfell**, and a small crater that has been more or less dug up and used as gravel for the road. There is an excellent view from the top of Grábrók.

Jafnaskarðsskógur, an expansive forest with delightful walking paths and routes shown on a walking map published by the Stafholtstungur Youth Association. Great views from the forest.

60 Vestfjarðavegur, p. 280

522 Þverárhlíðarvegur, p. 265

527 Varmalandsvegur, p. 230

3 P. 566

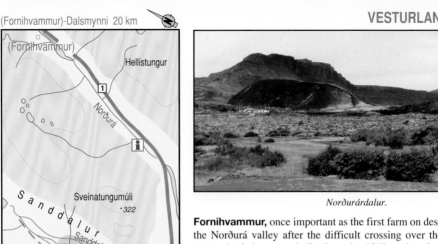

(Fornihvammur)-Dalsmynni 20 km

(Fornihvammur)
Hellistungur
1
Norðurá
Sanddalur
Sveinatungumúli
322
Sanddalsá
(Sveinatunga)
(Krókur)
Hvammsmúli
305
1
Litlaá
Háreksstaðir
Skildingafell
Hvammur
528
Hóll
Dýrastaðaá
Dýrastaðir
Baula
Hafþórsstaðir
525
1
316
Norðurá
Hreimsstaðir
60
Bjarnardalsá
Dalsmynni
Skarðshamrar
0 1 km
1
528

Dalsmynni-(Fornihvammur) 20 km

Norðurárdalur.

Fornihvammur, once important as the first farm on descending south into the Norðurá valley after the difficult crossing over the Holtavörðuheiði moor. A shelter was built there in 1840 and a farm in 1853. Now abandoned.

Sveinatunga, once a farm. There is the oldest concrete building in Iceland, built 1895.

528 Norðurárdalsvegur, 16 km.

Háreksstaðir, a farm on the southern side opposite Hvammur. The farm of the settler Örn the Old, who laid claim to the valley from Sveinatunga down to Arnarbæli or Bæli. Bæli is a rigde that goes across the valley to **Klettstía**, now the river **Norðurá** has carved its way through there.

Hvammur, church.

Baula, (934 m) a rhyolite mountain, most likely a lava bulge from the ice age. The mountain is cone-shaped and steep, with screes and boulders on all sides. There are no particular obstacles for climbers but care should be taken because of falling rocks. On the top there is a small rock shelter and the view from there is excellent in all directions. In a rock shelter is a guest book, there is also a cairn. To the west and north of Baula is **Litla-Baula** ("Little-Baula") and **Skildingafell**. All of these mountains were formed over 3 million years ago. The river **Dýrastaðaá** runs from a lovely little valley, **Sátudalur**, through a deep canyon with many waterfalls, to join **Norðurá** between the farms **Hóll** and **Hafþórsstaðir**.

Hafþórsstaðir, a farm on the southern side of Norðurá, opposite Dýrastaðir. From Hafþórsstaðir Grjóthálsvegur goes across Grjótháls ridge to Grjót in Þverárhlíð, 8 km.

60 Vestfjarðavegur, p. 280
525 Grjóthálsvegur, p. 265
528 Norðurárdalsvegur, p. 59

Grænumýrartunga, an abandoned farm at the northern descent off the moor Holtavörðuheiði. Once a resting place and inn.

Miklagil, a river whose source is along the Tröllakirkja mountain; flows north from Holtavörðuheiði. Formerly an obstacle to travellers.

Konungsvarða, ("The king's cairn") a cemented cairn built at the northern end of Grunnavatnshæð ("Shallow lake hill") in 1936 to commemorate the trip of King Christian X, of Denmark and Iceland, and his queen Alexandrine across Holtavörðuheiði moor that year. The king's initials are carved on the cairn.

Konungsvarða.

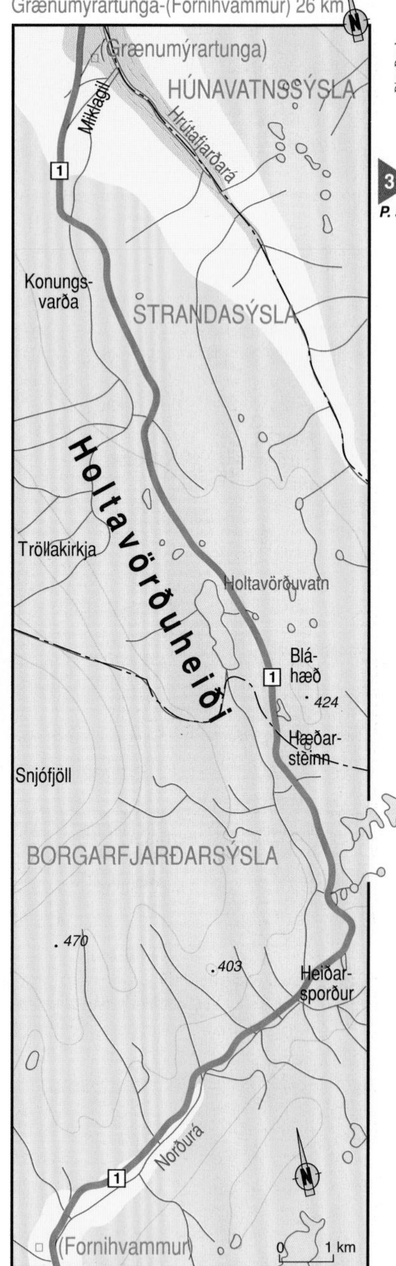

Ring Road
3
P. 566

Holtavörðuvatn, a fair-sized lake in a hollow west of the road. Trout-fishing. Swans and diving birds often seen there in summertime.

Hæðarsteinn, a big rock at the southern end of the high ridge; boundary between the counties Mýrasýsla and Strandasýsla.

Haukadalsskarð, north of Tröllakirkja and Klambrafells and south of Geldingafell was once a much travelled route between the North and the West. It was used if the weather was bad at Holtavörðuheiði.

Tröllakirkja, ("Giants' church") (1,001 m) a mountain to the north of Snjófjöll. The highest mountain in this area, with a good deal of permanent snow and ice.

Snjófjöll, ("Snow mountains") (808 m) a wide mountain ridge to the southwest of Holtavörðuheiði.

Holtavörðuheiði, moors with extensive and rather flat hills and mountains between Norðurárdalur and Hrútafjörður, quite marshy and with many lakes, maximum altitude about 400 m. The road across Holtavörðuheiði has long been the main route between the north and south of Iceland. Once considered to be haunted. Good view towards Eiríksjökull and Langjökull.

Never drive off roads

3
P. 566

Hrútey
Eyjanes
Sæberg
Reykjaskóli
Reykjatangi
Reykir
Hrútafjarðarháls
Borðeyrarbær
Akurbrekka
Þóroddsstaðir
287
Laugarholt
Borðeyri
(Lyngholt)
(Gilsstaðir)
172.
Brautarholt
Oddsstaðir
Valdasteinsstaðir
Hvalshöfði
HRÚTAFJÖRÐUR
HÚNAVATNSSÝSLA
STRANDASÝSLA
Brandagil
Markhöfði
Fjarðarhorn
Smáragil
Staðarskáli
Staður
Fagrabrekka
Staðarflöt
Bálkastaðir
Hrútatungurétt
Hrútatunga
Melar
Síká
(Foss)
Ormsá
Óspaksstaðir
Hrútafjarðará
Hrútatunga
(Grænumýrartunga)
0 1 km

In Miðfjörður.

Reykjatangi, the small peninsula which one can see tidemarks showin changes in the sea-level through the ages. There is also a folk museur which houses among other things the old shark-fishing boat Ófeigur.

Þóroddsstaðir, a farm since the original settlement. According to *Gretti saga* Þorbjörn öxnamegin was killed there by Grettir Ásmundarson th strong, as the name Spjótsmýri ("Spear-marsh"), still reminds us.

Gilsstaðir, a farm on the shore, formerly a point for the ferry to Borðeyri

Borðeyri, a village and a trading place since 1846.

640 Borðeyrarvegur, 0,64 km.

Brandagil, a farm from where a jeep-track goes over to Hnúkur i Miðfjörður. The track can be difficult. By the lakes on the ridge are larg collonies og the Great Northern Loon.

Staður, a farm, church and former parsonage. It was long a dispatc centre for overland postmen and a resting place for all travellers, as th **Staðarskáli** roadhouse. Memorial to overland postmen by the roadside.

Melar, a substantial farm for many centuries, see p. 309.

Brú, once a telephone exchange and post office built in 1950, when th service was moved from Borðeyri.

Hrútafjarðará, a long river with many tributaries, originating in the lake of the Holtavörðuheiði and Tvídægra moors. Forms the boundar between the counties Vestur-Húnavatnssýsla to the east and Strandasýsl and Mýrasýsla to the west and south. A well-known salmon river.

59 **Laxárdalsvegur,** p. 257 | 68 **Innstrandavegur,** p. 309
702 **Heggstaðanesvegur,** p. 334 | F586 **Haukadalsskarðsvegur,** p. 46

tóri-Ós, a farm, in Saga times the home of Þórður hreða, a well-known arrior and craftsman.

eykir, a farm above Laugarbakki. In Saga times the home of Miðfjarðar-keggi, famed for taking the sword Sköfnungur from the burial mound of rólfur kraki.

augarbakki, (pop. 48) a village south of the bridge across Miðfjarðará. was previously called Langafit, and horse fights were held there, as ld in the Saga of Grettir the strong. The first house was built there in 933. Community centre Ásbyrgi, sport centre, swimming pool, hot ıbs, campsite, grocery store, handcraft market, organic greenhouse, krúðvangur, and a hotel. At Grettisból is a farmers market in the sumıer time. Laugarbakki is a geothermal site, which sustains this village nd also that of Hvammstangi.

elstaður, a farm since Saga times, a church and parsonage. The ome of the poet Kormákur and later Oddur Ófeigsson of *Bandamanna ıga*. After the country had been Christianized in the year 1000, it ecame still more important and was considered the second-richest arish in the north, the present church indeed containing a number of ıteresting old objects. From 1598 to 1648 Arngrímur Jónsson lærði 'the learned"), lived there and wrote many of his books about celandic history and culture. His books, giving accurate information bout the country and its people, were written in Latin and were of interational interest at the time. Among them are: *Crymogæa, Anatome lefkeniana, Brevis Commentarius de Islandiae, Specimen Islandiae hisıricum* and *Gronlandia*.

annastaðir, a farm and the birthplace of Björn Gunnlaugsson (1788-876) mathematician, surveyor and the first person to make an exact map of Iceland.

68 **Innstrandavegur,** p. 309
72 **Hvammstangavegur,** p. 338
702 **Heggstaðanesvegur,** p. 334
703 **Hálsbæjarvegur,** p. 334
704 **Miðfjarðarvegur,** p. 335
711 **Vatnsnesvegur,** p. 338

Hrútafjarðarháls, the long range of hills between Hrútafjörður and Miðfjörður, wet and marshy. Where it continues to the north it is called **Heggsstaðanes** or **Bálkastaðanes**. There is Europes biggest Great Northern Loon collony. More info Brandagil p. 62.

Reykjaskóli, a centre for school field trips, formerly a boarding school, heated by water from the Reykjahver hot spring. Interesting museum of shark fishing.

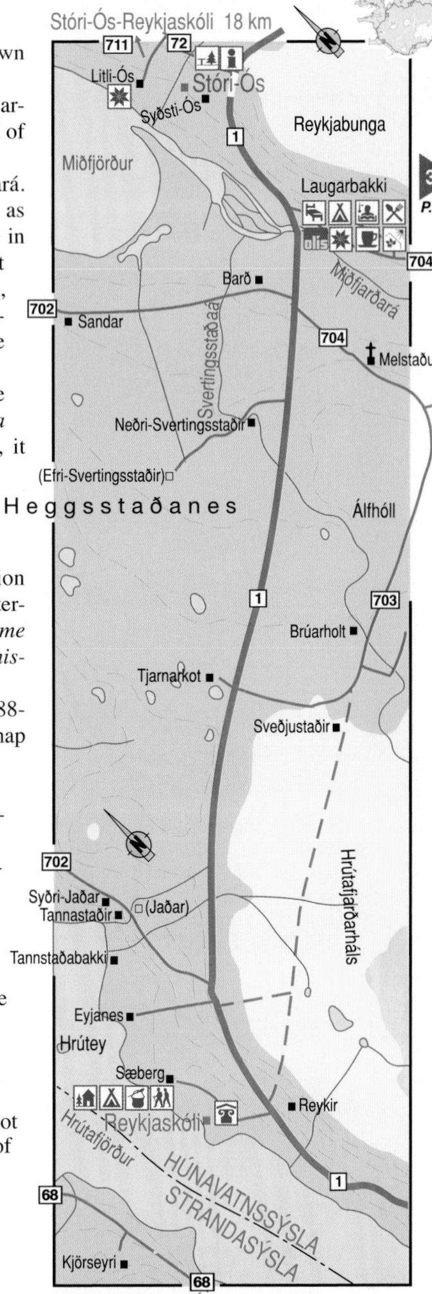

Lækjamót-Stóri-Ós 17 km

3 P. 566

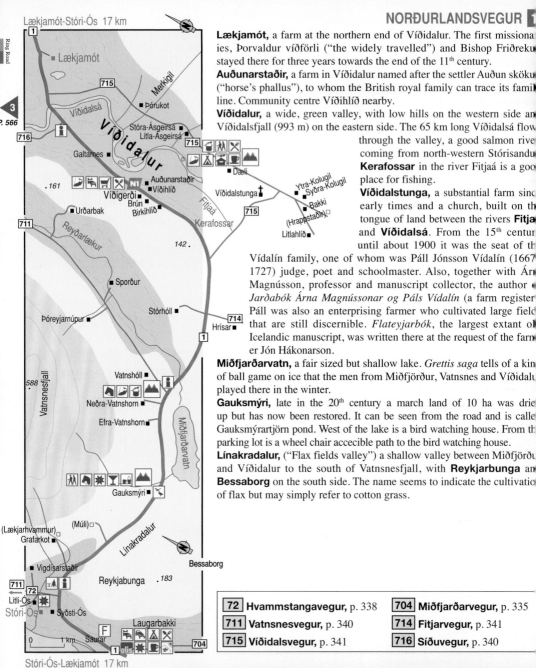

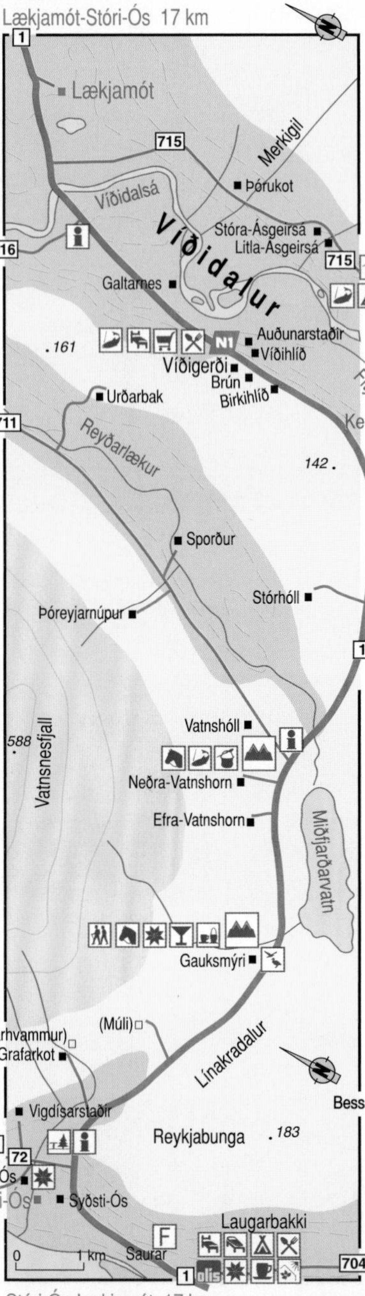

Lækjamót, a farm at the northern end of Víðidalur. The first missiona ies, Þorvaldur víðförli ("the widely travelled") and Bishop Friðreku stayed there for three years towards the end of the 11th century.

Auðunarstaðir, a farm in Víðidalur named after the settler Auðun sköku ("horse's phallus"), to whom the British royal family can trace its famil line. Community centre Víðihlíð nearby.

Víðidalur, a wide, green valley, with low hills on the western side an Víðidalsfjall (993 m) on the eastern side. The 65 km long Víðidalsá flow through the valley, a good salmon rive coming from north-western Stórisandu **Kerafossar** in the river Fitjaá is a goo place for fishing.

Víðidalstunga, a substantial farm sinc early times and a church, built on th tongue of land between the rivers **Fitja** and **Víðidalsá**. From the 15th centu until about 1900 it was the seat of th Vídalín family, one of whom was Páll Jónsson Vídalín (1667 1727) judge, poet and schoolmaster. Also, together with Árn Magnússon, professor and manuscript collector, the author *Jarðabók Árna Magnússonar og Páls Vídalín* (a farm register Páll was also an enterprising farmer who cultivated large field that are still discernible. *Flateyjarbók*, the largest extant o Icelandic manuscript, was written there at the request of the farm er Jón Hákonarson.

Miðfjarðarvatn, a fair sized but shallow lake. *Grettis saga* tells of a kin of ball game on ice that the men from Miðfjörður, Vatnsnes and Víðidalu played there in the winter.

Gauksmýri, late in the 20th century a march land of 10 ha was drie up but has now been restored. It can be seen from the road and is calle Gauksmýrartjörn pond. West of the lake is a bird watching house. From th parking lot is a wheel chair accecible path to the bird watching house.

Línakradalur, ("Flax fields valley") a shallow valley between Miðfjörðu and Víðidalur to the south of Vatnsnesfjall, with **Reykjarbunga** an **Bessaborg** on the south side. The name seems to indicate the cultivatio of flax but may simply refer to cotton grass.

Stóri-Ós-Lækjamót 17 km

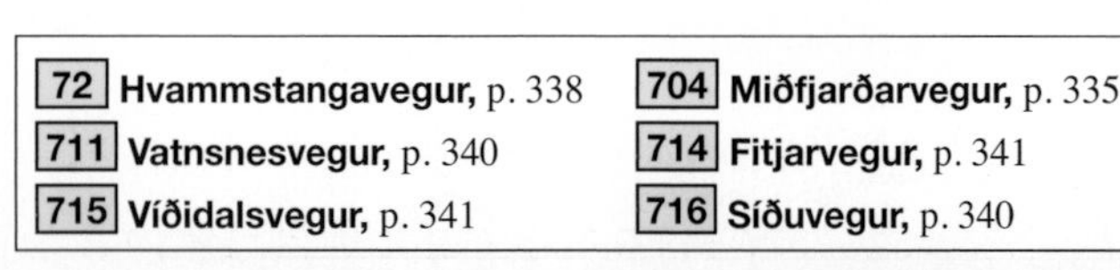

72 **Hvammstangavegur,** p. 338
711 **Vatnsnesvegur,** p. 340
715 **Víðidalsvegur,** p. 341
704 **Miðfjarðarvegur,** p. 335
714 **Fitjarvegur,** p. 341
716 **Síðuvegur,** p. 340

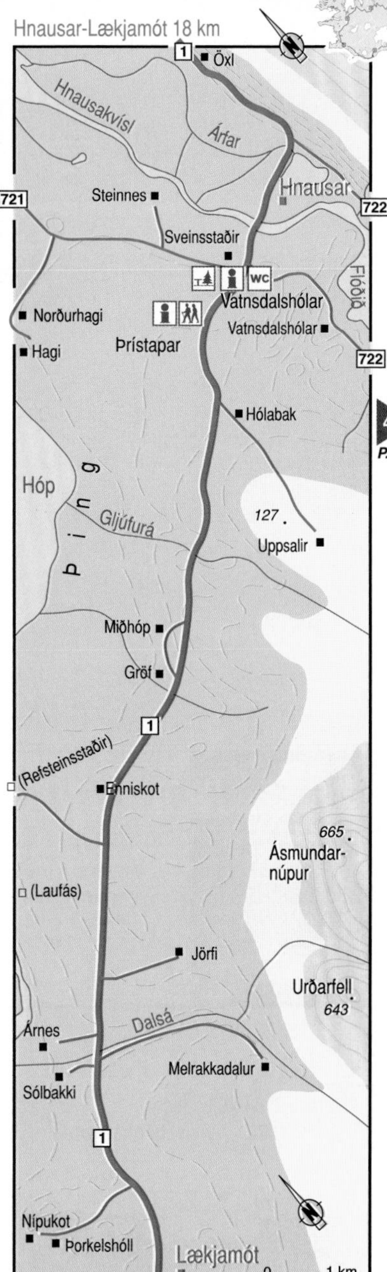

4 P. 567

Inausar, a farm built on the debris of a landslide that fell from /atnsdalsfjall in 1545, called Skíðastaðaskriða. The slide destroyed the arm Skíðastaðir and killed 14 people. The lake **Hnausatjörn** was ormed by the slide.

Inausakvísl, the river between the lakes Flóðið and Húnavatn. Calm nd deep, it is a good fishing river.

Sveinsstaðir, a substantial farm by Vatnsdalshólar where, in 1522, there vas a battle between the Catholic bishop Jón Arason and Teitur Þorleifsson.

Vatnsdalshólar, a cluster of small hills at the mouth of Vatnsdalur, supposedly uncountable, the debris of a tremendous landslide from /atnsdalsfjall. About 4 km^2 in area. Other geographical features in celand considered to be uncountable are the islands of Breiðafjörður and he lakes on Arnarvatnsheiði moor.

Þrístapar, a group of three small hills on the north side of the road, the ite of the last execution in Iceland, January 12th 1830, when Natan Ketilsson' murderers, Agnes and Friðrik, were beheaded. See p. 339.

Þing, the district between the rivers Gljúfurá and Giljá, flat and fertile.

Hóp, the fifth largest lake in Iceland, 29-44 km^2 depending on the tide vhich affects the water level. Fed by Víðidalsá and Gljúfurá, it empties out through Bjargaós.

Gljúfurá, a river in a narrow canyon dividing the counties Austur- and Vestur-Húnavatnssýsla.

Ásmundarnúpur, (665 m) the northern tip of Víðidalsfjall, a steep peak with loose screes.

Dalsá, a river flowing from Melrakkadalur.

721 **Þingeyrarvegur,** p. 342
722 **Vatnsdalsvegur,** p. 343

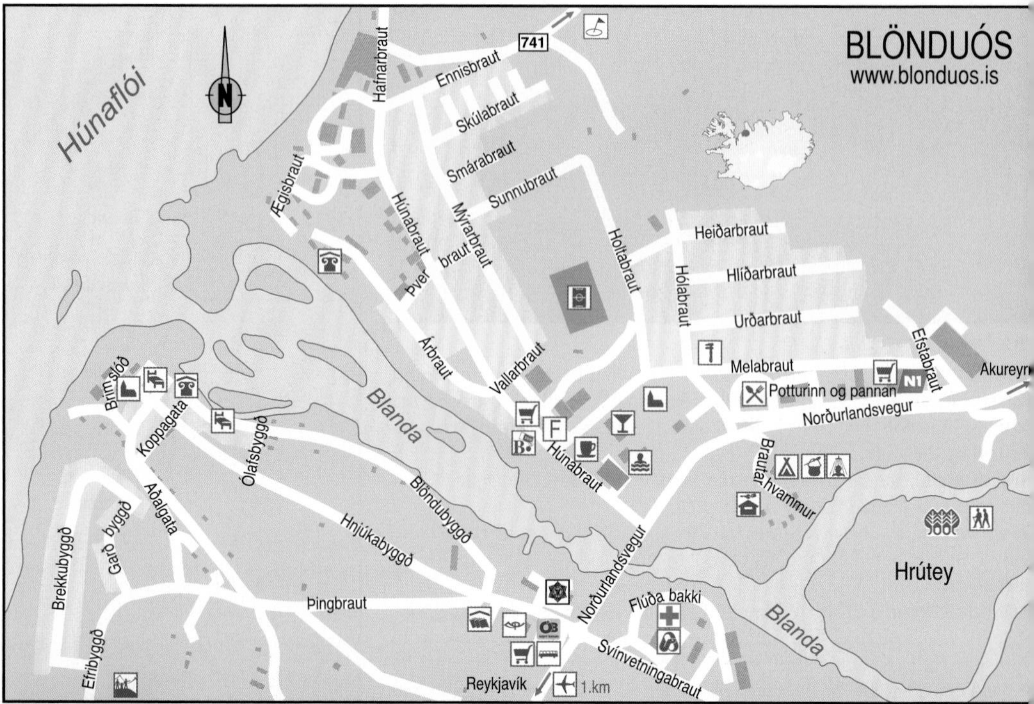

BLÖNDUÓS

www.blonduos.is

Húnaflói
741
Hafnarbraut
Ennisbraut
Skúlabraut
Smárabraut
Sunnubraut
Ægisbraut
Húnabraut
Mýrarbraut
Þverbraut
Holtabraut
Heiðarbraut
Hlíðarbraut
Hólabraut
Urðarbraut
Melabraut
Efstabraut
Akureyri
Árbraut
Vallarbraut
Potturinn og pannan
Norðurlandsvegur
Brautarhvammur
Blanda
Brimslóð
Koppagata
Aðalgata
Ólafsbyggð
Blöndubyggð
Hnjúkabyggð
Brekkubyggð
Garðbyggð
Efribyggð
Þingbraut
Húnabraut
Norðurlandsvegur
Flúðabakki
Svínvetningabraut
Hrútey
Reykjavík
1.km

Eyvindarstofa

Special food and exhibition.

Open every day from 11:00 to 22.

Norðurlandsvegur 4, 540 Blönduós
Tel.: 453 5060 & 898 4685
info@eyvindarstofa.is
www.eyvindarstofa.is

Eyvindarstofa dedicated to the outlaw Fjalla-Eyvindur and his wife Halla. The dining room's design is inspired by Eyvindur's cave, and there guests can experience the home Fjalla-Eyvindur had in Hveravellir. Come and experience this unique atmosphere with sounds that remind you of the highlands, the geysers and of fire. Stories of Fjalla-Eyvindur are told through pictures and texts, and a special kind of food is served on plates and in bowls according to the crafts of Fjalla-Eyvindur.

Guesthouse Kiljan

Aðalgata 2, 540 Blönduós
Tel. 452-4500 **www.booking.com**

GLAÐHEIMAR

Melabraut 21, 540 Blönduós
Tel. 820-1300 & 690-3130
gladheimar@simnet.is
www.gladheimar.is

Phone: 580 1200
www.postur.is

Potturinn Restaurant Blönduós

www.pot.is

A comfortable restaurant by the ring road in North - West Iceland, offering a broad selection of tasty food at reasonable prices.

Family friendly and fresh

Norðurlandsvegur 4
540 Blönduós
Tel.: +354 453-5060
pot@pot.is
Open: 11:00 - 22:00

Blönduós, (pop. 813) a town at the mouth of the river Blanda, built on both sides of the river. A harbour and trading post since 1875. Industry connected with agriculture, trading and transport services. District judge, hospital, hotel, guesthouse, campsite, swimming pool, community centre, restaurant, café, the Textile Museum and the Sea Ice Exhibition Centre. Forestry research on **Hrútey**, an island in the river just east of town which is also a public park. Good salmon-fishing. See town map.

725 Miðásavegur, 3,47 km.

Hjaltabakki, a farm, church and parsonage until 1895.

Laxá á Ásum, one of the best salmon river in Iceland, in which is the waterfall Mánafoss, flowing from Laxárvatn to Húnavatn. Harnessed for electricity in 1933.

Torfalækur, a farm with fertile grasslands.

Stígandahróf, the place on the Búðartangi peninsula on **Húnavatn,** between the church at Þingeyrar and the farm **Akur**, where the settler Ingimundur the Old beached his ships after sailing from Norway. He named the lake Húnavatn ("Cup Lake") after finding a mama bear with two cups there.

Ásar, the district between the rivers Gilljá and Blanda. Its ancient name was Kolkumýrar.

Stóra-Giljá, a farm where Þorvaldur Koðránsson víðförli ("widely travelled") lived. He was a Christian missionary in Iceland who travelled around with the bishop Friðrekur, from Sachen. Þorvaldur later founded a monastery in Constantinople (Mikligarður, in Icelandic) and died there. There is a memorial to these missionaries at the nearby stone **Gullsteinn,** ("Golden stone") which was revered by the heathens. When Friðrekur wanted to exorcise it, the stone split.

721 Þingeyravegur, p. 342
722 Vatnsdalsvegur, p. 343
724 Reykjabraut, p. 344
731 Svínvetningabraut, p. 345

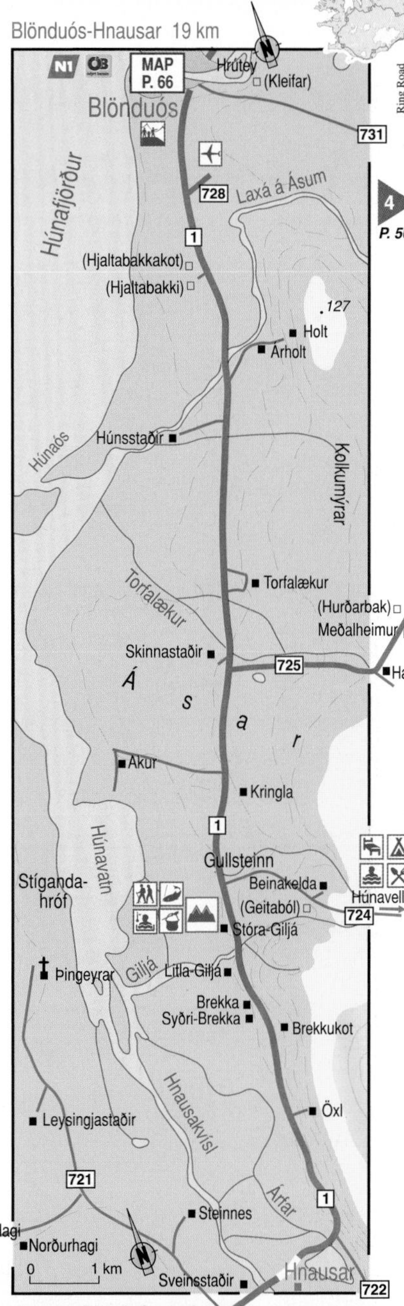

Auðólfsstaðir-Blönduós 23 km

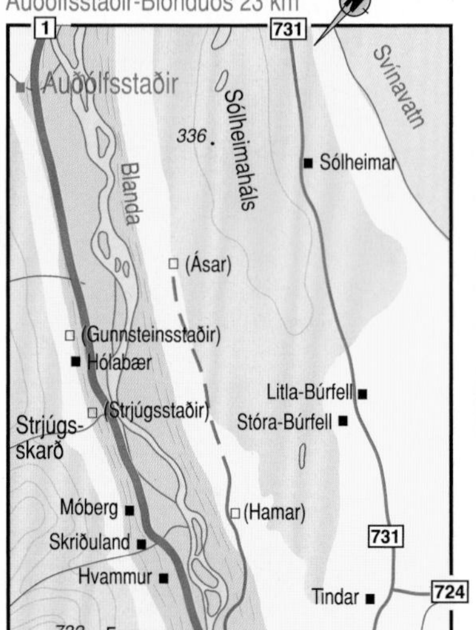

4 P. 567

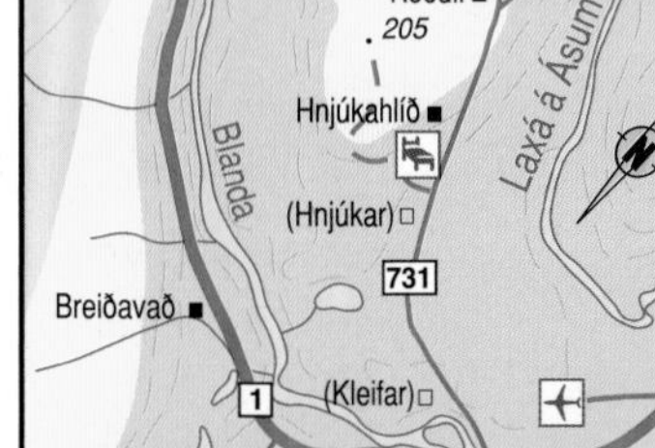

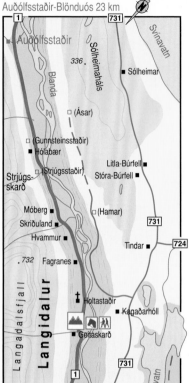

Blönduós-Auðólfsstaðir 23 km

The church in Blönduós.

Langidalur, ("Long valley") the district along the east side of Blanda from Breiðavað to the junction of Svartá and Blanda, green and fertile with many big farms. To the east of it is the 25 km long mountain **Langadalsfjall**, 700-800 m high, steep with many peaks and three deep passes over to Laxárdalur in the east. There have been many big landslides on this mountain, such as those from Illveðurshnjúkur ("Foul weather peak") north of Geitaskarð pass and from Móbergsfjall ("Tuff mountain"), which left bare a vertical rockface called Móbergsstofur or Stofur.

Auðólfsstaðir, a farm since the time of the settlement. A jeep-track from there across Auðólfsstaðaskarð pass to Laxárdalur.

Strjúgur, there lived one of Icelands greatest poets in the 16th century Þórður Magnússon.

Hvammur, from there are the brothers Guðmundur (1903–1989) and Jóhann Frímann poet (1906–1990).

Holtastaðir, a substantial farm and a church. Formerly a ferry point.

Geitaskarð, a substantial farm of historical note, built below a pass of the same name. Farmers there have often been district judges and outstanding men of the district. The home of Kolfinna, the sweetheart of the poet Hallfreður vandræðaskáld of Saga times.

Blanda, glacial river about 125 km long, with a large hydroelectric plant flowing from the western sides of Hofsjökull. Two bridges, one by Blönduós and the other by Langamýri in Blöndudalur. The magnificent canyon Blöndugil is south of the head of Blöndudalur. Good fishing.

74 **Skagastrandarvegur,** p. 322 | 724 **Reykjabraut,** p. 344
731 **Svínvetningabraut,** p. 346 | 741 **Neðribyggðarvegur,** p. 322

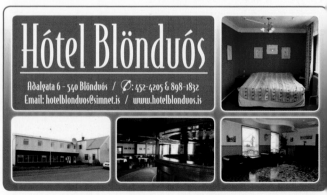

tóra-Vatnsskarð, a farm at the eastern end of the Vatnsskarð pass.

atnshlíð, the easternmost farm in Húnavatnssýsla. Good fishing in the earby lake, Vatnshlíðarvatn, which along with Krókagil canyon between e mountains Vatnshlíðarhnjúkur and Grísafell acts as a boundary etween the counties Skagafjarðarsýsla and Húnavatnssýsla.

atnsskarð, (ca. 440 m) a mountain pass between the districts of únaflói and Skagafjörður. Good views in the western part from axhöfði, on the south side of the road and Víðivörðuháls, on the north de. From Botnastaðabrún farthest west in the pass there is also a fine ew over the Svartárdalur valley below.

verárdalur, a pass, actually a valley open at both ends, connecting vartárdalur and Laxárdalur. The river Hlíðará flows along this short valy originating in the Hólsvötn lakes way up in the mountains to the ortheast.

únaver, a community centre to the south of the river Hlíðará.

ólstaðarhlíð, a church and substantial farm for centuries. For 300 ears, 1528-1825, the home of successive generations of the same family, hich produced numerous children, many of whom have been famous or fluential people in their time. Descendants are still known as the ólstaðarhlíð family.

:sustaðaskriður, steep screes by Æsustaðir.

:sustaðir, the southernmost farm in Langidalur, at one time a arsonage.

731 **Svínvetningabraut,** p. 346   734 **Svartárdalsvegur,** p. 347

The church at Bólstaðahlíð

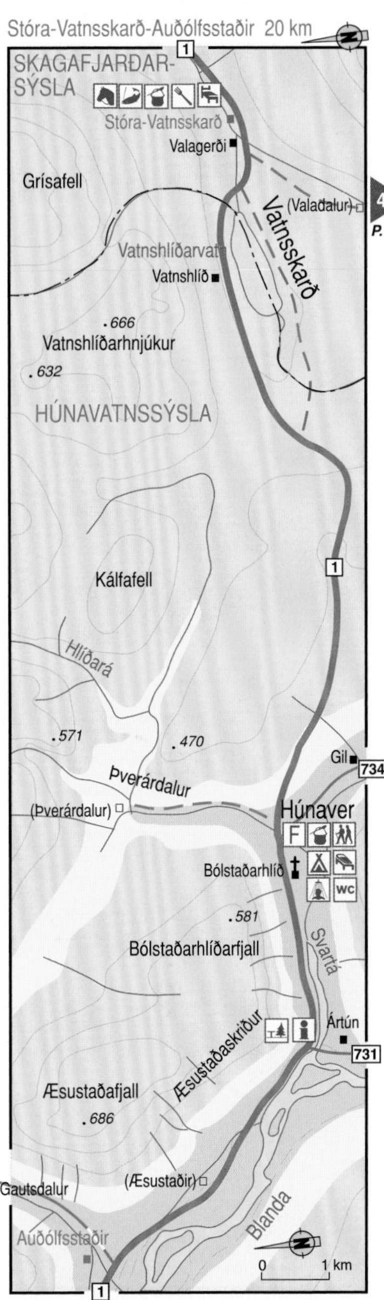

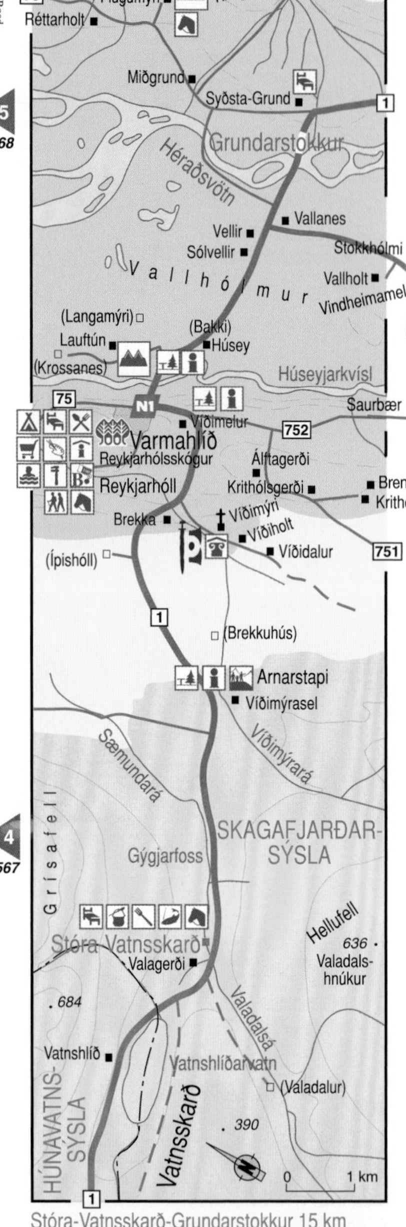

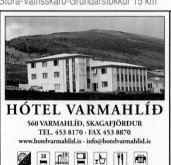

5 P. 568

4 P. 567

Grundarstokkur, the bridged part of the many-armed river Héraðsvötn. It was bridged in 1937. A new bridge by Vellir took over in 1981, it is 188m long.

Vellir, a farm in Hólmur. The birthplace of the historian Gísli Konráðsson (1787–1877).

753 Vindheimavegur, 6,88 km to road 752.

Vallhólmur, (or Hólmur) the flat area between the rivers Héraðsvötn and Húseyjarkvísl.

Langamýri, a farm and a holiday home run by the state church. Birthplace of the grammarian Konráð Gíslason (1808-91). He was one of a group of writers and poets who led the national awakening to the importance of maintaining the Icelandic language and gaining sovereignty.

Húseyjarkvísl, a clear river formed by many smaller rivers originating on distant Eyvindarstaðaheiði moor.

Varmahlíð, (pop. 128) a community that has been built up at the crossroads during recent years. Geothermal heat, swimming pool, sport cenre, hotel, information centre, grocery store and a gas station. A very good view from the hill **Reykjarhóll** (111 m) a short distance above Varmahlíð in Reykjarhólsskógur.

Reykjarhólsskógur, a forest rich in diversity, linked to a larger outdoor recreation area in Varmahlíð.

Víðimýri, a farm and church. A place of historical importance for centuries, and frequently the home of outstanding leaders, among them Kolbeinn ungi Arnórsson and Kolbeinn Tumason. The church was built 1834 and is one of the most precious gems of Icelandic architecture. In the keeping of the National Museum since 1936. The church is open for guests in the summer.

Brekka, from there came the poet Andrés Björnsson (1883–1916).

Brekkuhús, formerly sheep-cots belonging to the nearby farm Brekka. The poet Bólu-Hjálmar (1796-1875) died there.

Arnarstapi, ("Eagle crag") a hill at the eastern end of Vatnsskarð and a very good viewpoint. A memorial to the poet Stephan G. Stephansson (1853-1927) has been erected on the hill. Stephan lived for a while in nearby **Víðimýrarsel** and later emigrated to Canada; he is now often called Klettafjallaskáldið or "The poet of the Rocky Mountains".

Valadalsá, a river flowing from the valley Valadalur. It becomes the river **Sæmundará**, in which is the waterfall **Gýgjarfoss.**

75 Sauðárkróksbraut, p. 323
76 Siglufjarðarvegur, p. 327
751 Efribyggðarvegur, p. 353
752 Skagafjarðarvegur, p. 353

Miklibær, a farm, church and parsonage, often mentioned in the Sagas and the stage for various dramas through the ages. In 1786, for instance, Rev. Oddur Gíslason (1740-1786) disappeared when travelling from one farm to another and was never seen again. The female ghost Solveig was blamed. She had been a maid in his household, fallen in love with him, been rejected, gone mad and finally cut her own throat, after which she haunted Oddur wherever he went, especially in the dark. Solveig's remains were found in the churchyard wall in 1937 and given a Christian burial at Glaumbær. The grave of the poet Bólu-Hjálmar is at Miklibær, marked with a stone monument.

Stóru-Akrar and **Minni-Akrar,** two farms. Remnants of a farmhouse built in the mid 18th century for Skúli Magnússon, later Treasurer, known as the father of Reykjavík. The living room, entrance building and corridors are of a late type of stave construction. In the keeping of the National Museum since 1954. The poet Bólu-Hjálmar lived at Minni-Akrar for 27 years. Formerly a ferry point. Community centre Héðinsminni.

Haugsnes, an abandoned farm on the south banks of the river Djúpá. In 1246 this was the site of the battle Haugsnesbardagi, where Þórður kakali and Brandur Kolbeinsson fought, with the loss of Brandur and 105 of his men, the greatest loss of life in any battle ever fought in Iceland.

Djúpidalur, a substantial farm for centuries, in a valley of the same name. Owned by the same family since 1733. The river, Djúpadalsá, coming from the valley used to be a bad obstacle until the bridge was built.

Glóðafeykir, (990 m) an impressive mountain, steep and rocky, above Flugumýri. The story goes that Helga Sigurðardóttir, mistress of the catholic bishop Jón Arason, hid out on this mountain while Danish warships were in the north in 1551, the summer after Jón was beheaded in the struggles of the Reformation.

Flugumýri, a farm and a church, an important place since early times. For a while the home of Earl Gissur Þorvaldsson, the only Icelander to have been titled "Earl". In 1253 the farm was burned down (Flugumýrarbrenna, "The burning of Flugumýri"), when his opponents tried to take his life. Formerly the official meeting-place for the priests of the diocese of Hólar. Above the farm is **Virkishóll** ("Fort Hill"), a name probably given to the hill in the time of Earl Gissur. At Flugumýri is a horse breeding farm from where the well known stead Ófeigur 882 is from.

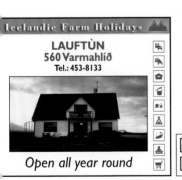

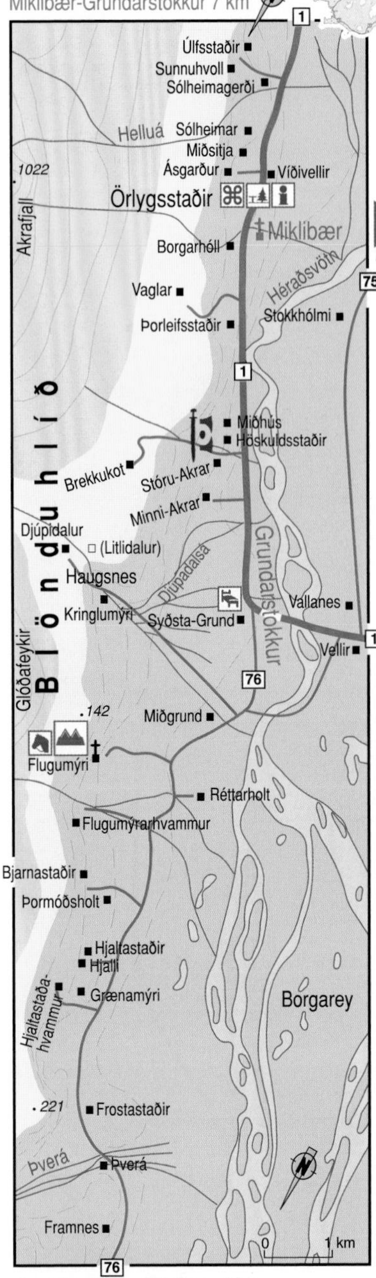

Silfrastaðir-Miklibær 10 km

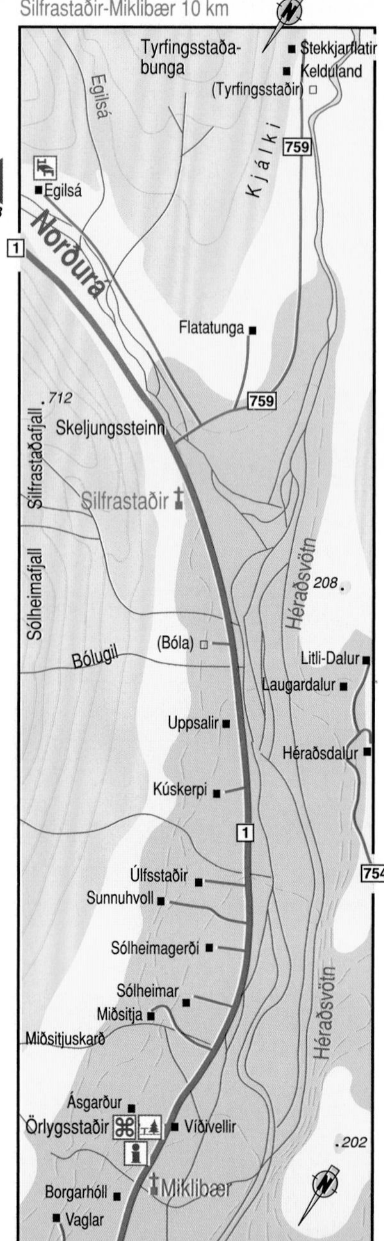

Miklibær-Silfrastaðir 10 km

5 P. 568

Ring Road

The church at Miklibær.

Silfrastaðir, a church and a substantial farm. The turf-roofed churc which was formerly at Silfrastaðir is now located in Reykjavík (local his tory) Museum. The present church at Silfrastaðir is a curiously construc ed octagonal timber building dating from about 1900. Below the road, n far from the farm, there is a big stone, **Skeljungssteinn**. According t folktales the ghost Skeljungur was tied to it, two holes through the ston being the proof of this.

Bóla, a farm where the poet Hjálmar Jónsson (1796-1875), lived for som time and from which he got his name, Bólu-Hjálmar. A memorial to hi has been erected by the road. The farm is named for the slave-woma possibly a giantess, Bóla from Silfrastaðir, who escaped and hid in th rocky canyon Bólugil above the farm, from where she made forays t steal farmers' crops and cattle until she was finally killed by Skeljungu the shepherd (and later ghost, see above) at Silfrastaðir. The canyon i very rugged with many waterfalls, some of which can be seen from th road.

Örlygsstaðir, an important historical site with some ruins a short dis tance above the home-field of Víðivellir. This was the scene of one of th most fateful battles of old, Örlygsstaðabardagi, in 1238, when Sturl Sighvatsson was killed together with his father and brothers and about 6 others. Memorial to the battle.

Víðivellir, an old manor farm, often a parsonage, the seat of district judge and other magistrates. The home of the Rev. Pétur Pétusson (1754-1842 who was the first person to grow potatoes in Skagafjörður. Birthplace o Gottskálk, father of the famous sculptor Bertel Thorvaldsen who was hal Danish and lived in Denmark.

754 **Héraðsdalsvegur,** p. 353 759 **Kjálkavegur,** p. 354

Egilsá.

rjótá, a small river on Öxnadalsheiði, dividing the counties Eyja-jarðarsýsla and Skagafjarðarsýsla. Sæluhús (shelter) not far from there.
xnadalsheiði, the moor and valley connecting Norðurárdalur and)xnadalur. The highest point of the road is about 540 m.
örgárdalsheiði, a moor and valley connecting Norðurárdalur and lörgárdalur. There is an old mountain trail over Hörgárdalsheiði.
álfdanartungur, an abandoned farm in Norðurárdalur, said to be aunted.
alagilsá, a small river that emerges from a narrow and deep canyon, not ar from Fremri-Kot. In 1954, when there were landslides and rivers were n spate, the river broke down the bridge.
remri-Kot, a farm in Norðurárdalur and now the only farm on the north ide of the river. Ytri-Kot, abandoned after a big landslide in 1954, is elieved to be the Þorbrandsstaðir mentioned in *Landnámabók* ("The ook of Settlements"), a farm where food was free for all travellers.
lorðurárdalur, a narrow mountain valley east of Silfrastaðir. Trout-ishing in the river.
otagil, one of the most magnificent canyons by the road between eykjavík and Akureyri.
gilsá, the only farm on the south side of the river.
jálki, the district on the east side of Héraðsvötn, from the River Norðurá o Merkigil in Austurdalur.
latatunga, a farm in the Kjálki district. Some very old wood carvings reserved there considered to be a detail from *The Last Judgement* carved n the 11th century in Byzantine style. Now in the National Museum.

759 **Kjálkavegur,** p. 354

5 P. 568

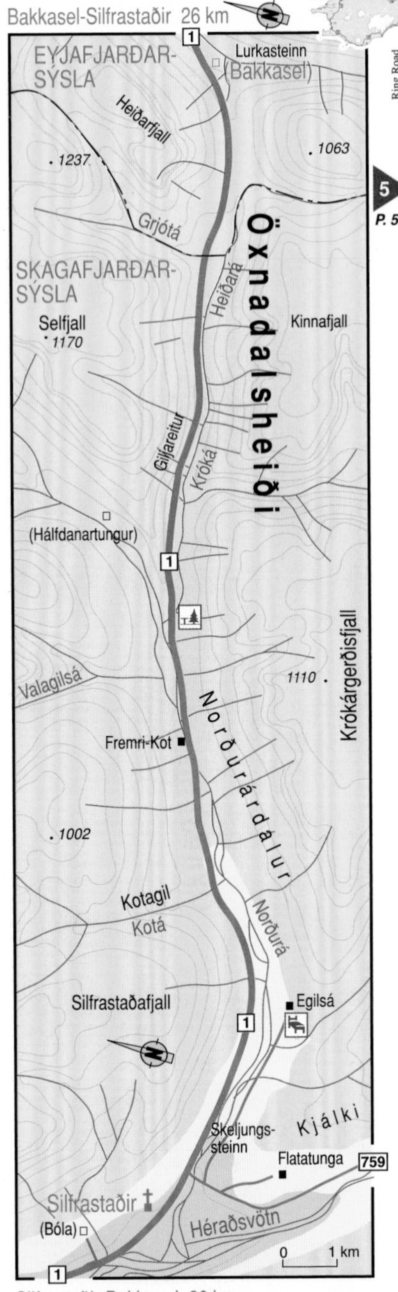

P. 568

Steinsstaðir-Bakkasel 18 km

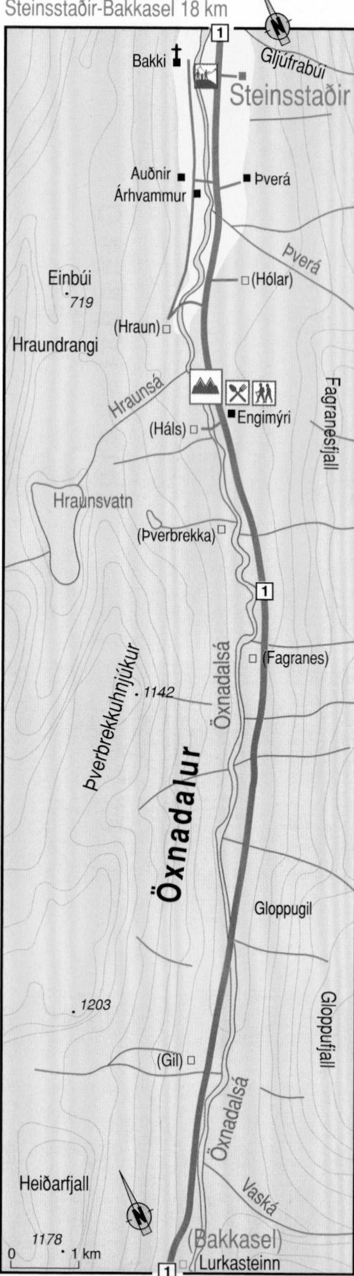

Bakkasel-Steinsstaðir 18 km

Hraundrangi

Öxnadalur, a deep and narrow valley about 35 km long with high mountains on both sides. Around the middle of the valley are numerous mounds, the debris from old landslides.

Bakki, a farm and a church on the west side of the river. Around 1200 the home of Guðmundur dýri, well-known for both his quarrels and his great enterprise. The church, built in 1843, is the oldest in the Eyjafjörður ditrict.

Steinsstaðir, a farm where the 19th century poet and naturalist Jónas Hallgrímsson lived as a young man. Trees have been planted there in his memory. View dial. The waterfall **Gljúfrabúi** ("Canyon dweller") in the gully nearby.

Þverá, a farm and a river of the same name. From there leads an old riding trail over Kambsskarð to Skjóldalur.

Hraundrangi, (1,075 m) a pinnacle on the rocky mountain ridge between Öxnadalur and Hörgárdalur. According to legend a treasure chest was hidden there waiting for the first climber to fetch it. Hraundrangi was first climbed in 1956 by a party of three, an American and two Icelanders, but none of them appeared to be richer after the ascent. The flat area on top of it turned out to be less than 0.5 m^2.

Hraun, a farm in the hills on the west side of the river, birthplace of Jónas Hallgrímsson (1807-45), naturalist and one of the most important Romantic poets in Iceland. **Hraunsvatn**, a good trout-fishing lake 50-60 m deep, is in the valley behind the hills. Hallgrímur, father of Jónas, drowned in it.

Þverbrekka, abandoned farm on the west side of the river, once the home of Víga-Glúmur of Saga times. **Þverbrekkuhnjúkur** (1,142 m), one of the highest and most rugged mountains in the vicinity is above the farm. There is a guest book in a cairn at the top of the peak. Above some small hills on the side of the mountain is a small lake **Þverbrekkuvatn**.

Lurkasteinn, a rock not far from Bakkasel, where Þórður hreða killed Sörli sterki in Saga times. It is said that travellers who are passing the rock for the first time should through a stone in its direction and say a prayer before heading on the Öxnadalsheiði moor.

Bakkasel, formerly a farm and an inn, now abandoned.

Laugaland, a farm which is mentioned in the Sagas. Geothermal heat. Swimming pool named after the poet Jónas Hallgrímsson.

Vaglir, self-sowing birch and willows have spread after being protected. Also a planted forest of larch, pine and spruce. National Forest.

Vindheimaöxl, an impressive rocky ridge above the farm Vindheimar ("Home of the wind"). A small glacier, **Vindheimajökull**, south of there, its highest points **Strýta** (1,451 m) and **Kista** (1,447 m). The rivers Húsá and Fossá flow from the glacier, the two separate valleys derive their names from the rivers. Good mountaineering country.

Ytri-Bægisá, a farm, church and parsonage until 1941. Among the clergymen who served there were Jón Þorláksson (1744-1819) and Arnljótur Ólafsson (1823-1904). Jón was an outstanding poet and the translator of many works, among them *Paradise Lost* by Milton and *Messias* by Klopstock.

Hörgárdalur, a valley about 50 km long on the west side of Eyjafjörður, high mountains with small glaciers on both sides. Good fishing in the river Hörgá, which usually has some glacial water in it.

Bægisá, a river joining Öxnadalsá between the farms Ytri-and Syðri-Bægisá. Bægisá flows from the glacier **Bægisárjökull** at the end of Bægisárdalur, a valley surrounded by majestic mountains: **Landafjall**, a narrow ridge between the valleys Bægisárdalur and Öxnadalur on the west, and on the east, the mountain **Tröllafjall** ("Giants' mountain") (1,471 m), which also dominates Glerárdalur above Akureyri on the east side. This is magnificent mountaineering country.

Miðhálsstaðir, an abandoned farm, now used for experiments in forestry by the Forestry Association of Eyjafjörður.

814 **Staðarbakkavegur,** p. 390 815 **Hörgárdalsvegur,** p. 390

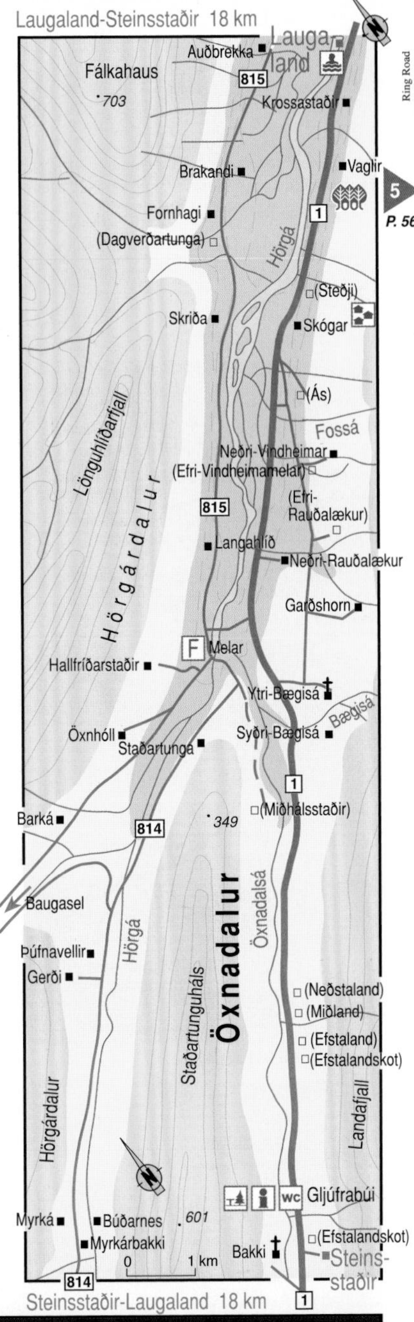

5 P. 568

Akureyri-Laugaland 13 km

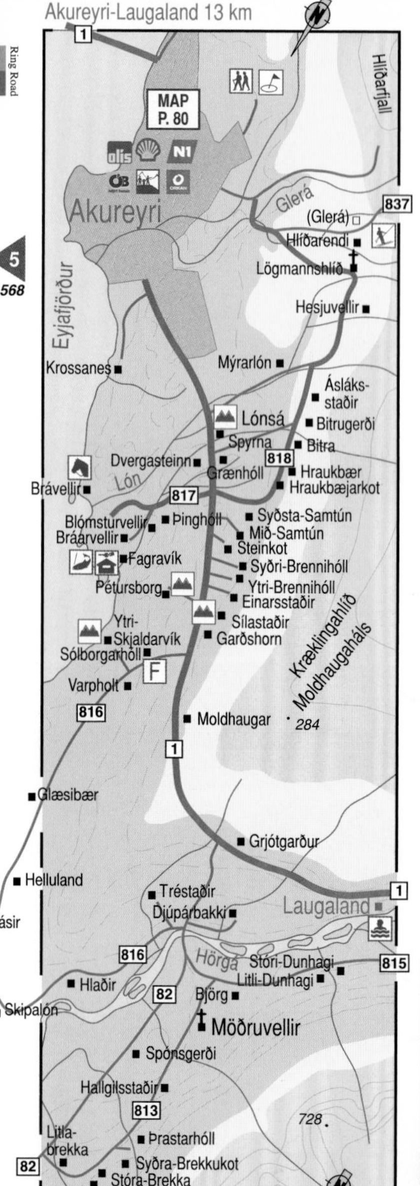

The church at Möðruvellir

Glerárdalur, a long uninhabited valley above Lögmannshlíð, surrounded by the highest mountains in the north of Iceland, the highest being **Kerling** (1,538 m), **Tröllafjall** and **Vindheimajökull** from 1,100 to 1,400 m high. Magnificent outdoor area both in summer and winter. The Akureyri Ski Resort is on the lower slopes of the mountain **Hlíðarfjall**. Fossils have been found in the valley. The river Glerá emerges from the valley and flows through the northern outskirts of Akureyri.

837 Hlíðarfjallsvegur, 7,5 km. Leads to Hlíðarfjall Ski Resort which is open November - April. Good view of the town Akureyri.

Lögmannshlíð, a farm and a church with an interesting 17th century altar-piece.

817 Blómsturvallavegur, 1,65 km. **818 Hlíðarvegur,** 2,5 km.

Sólborgarhóll, a community centre, Hlíðarbær.

Kræklingahlíð, a mountain side from Hörgárósar to Glerá. On top of it lies **Hlíðarfjall** and **Stórihnjúkur,** 912 m.

Moldhaugnaháls, ("Heaps-of-earth ridge") a low mountain ridge between Hörgárdalur and Kræklingahlíð. Coming from the west, the view opens towards Akureyri. A war memorial was erected there by British soldiers in 1942 to commemorate their stay in Iceland.

Möðruvellir, a substantial farm of great historical importance for many centuries. Church and parsonage. See p. 357.

82 Ólafsfjarðarvegur, p. 357
813 Möðruvallarvegur, p. 357
815 Hörgárdalsvegur, p. 389
816 Dagverðareyrarv., p. 389

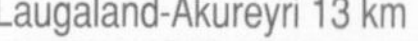
Laugaland-Akureyri 13 km

THE TOWN OF
Akureyri
www.akureyri.is

Minjasafn

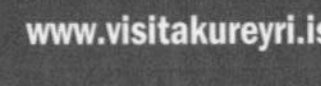
www.visitakureyri.is

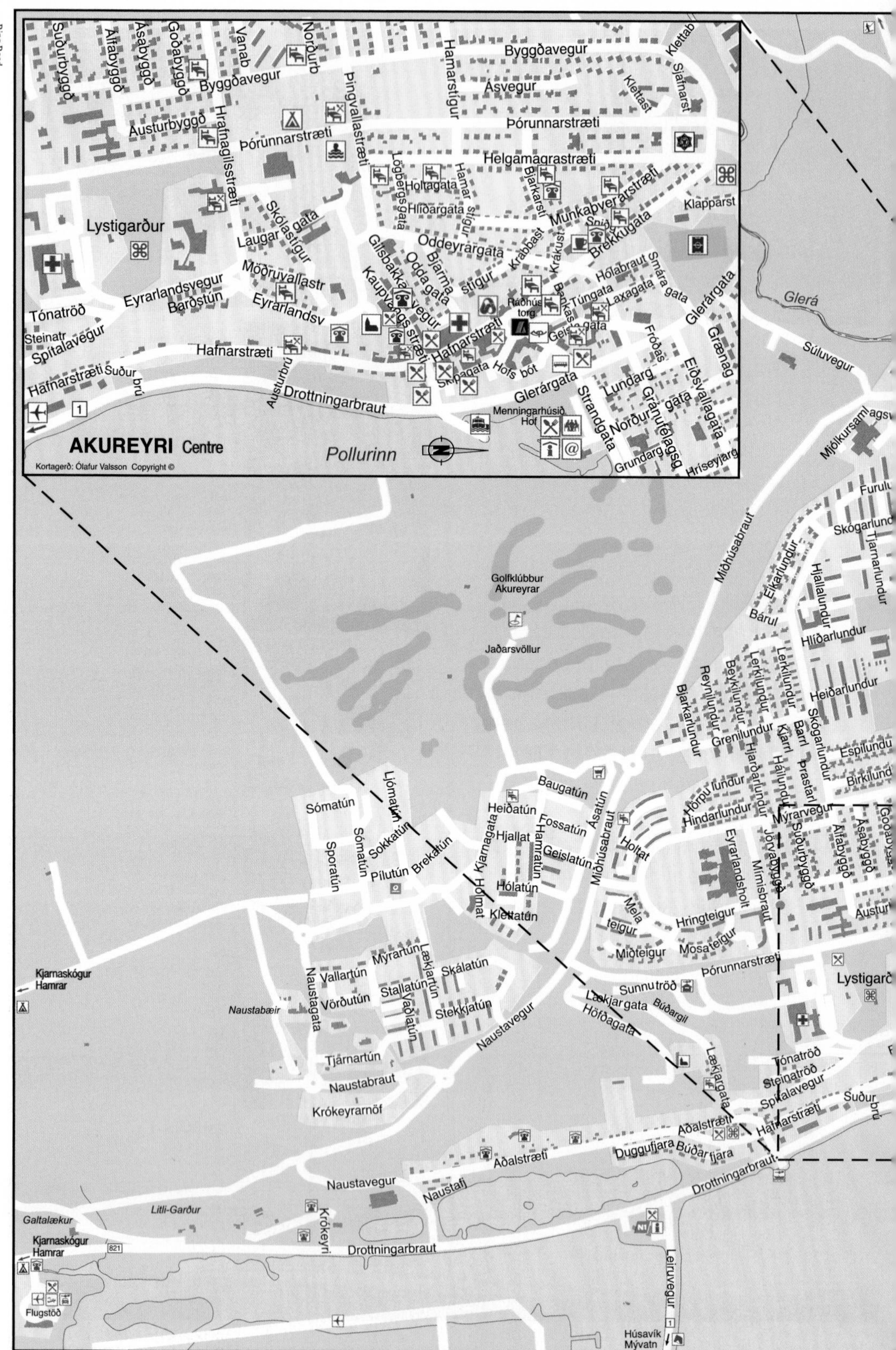
AKUREYRI Centre
Kortagerð: Ólafur Valsson Copyright ©
Pollurinn
Lystigarður
Golfklúbbur Akureyrar
Jaðarsvöllur
Glerá
Kjarnaskógur Hamrar
Naustabæir
Litli-Garður
Galtalækur
Flugstöð
Húsavík Mývatn

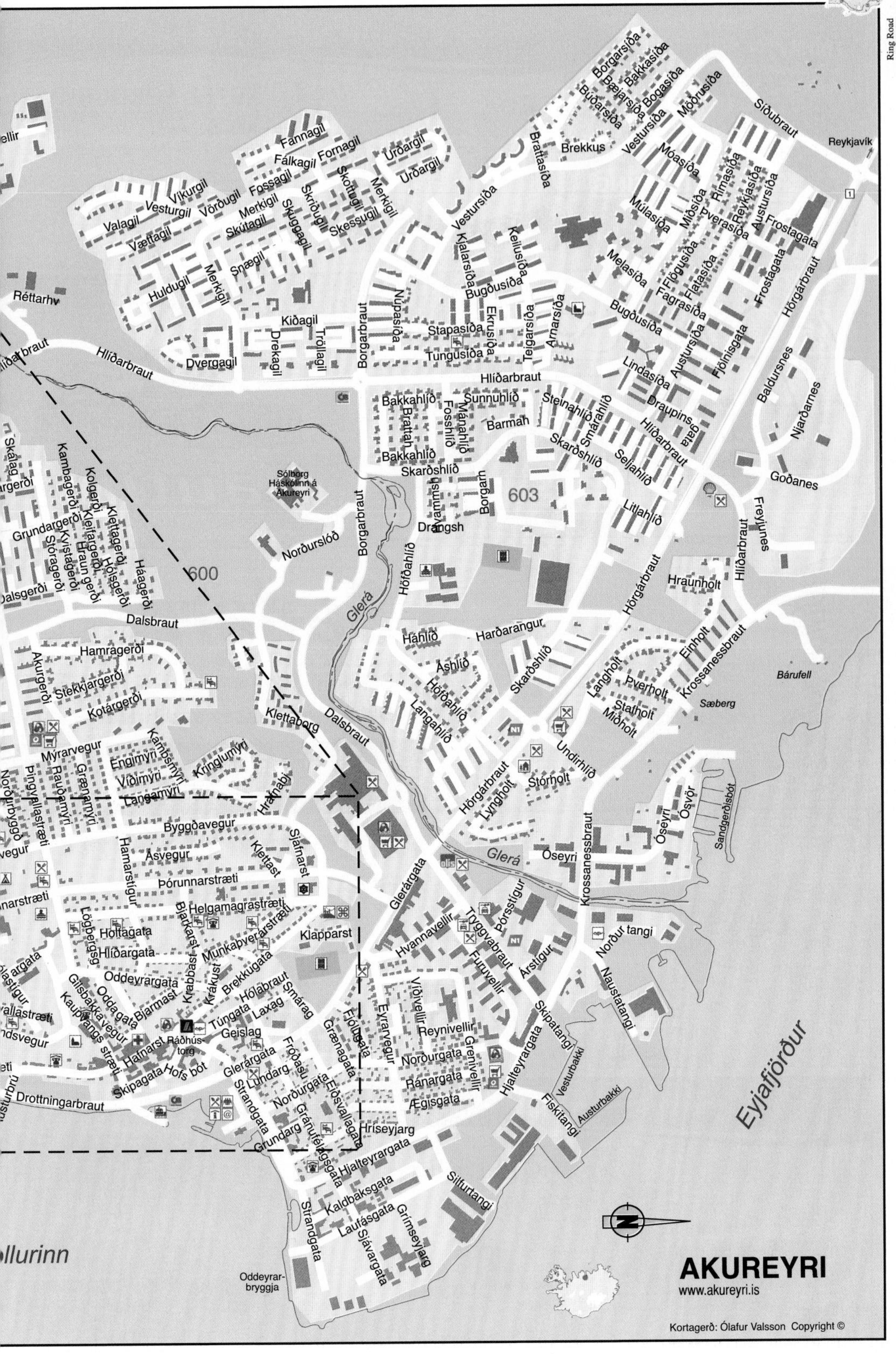
AKUREYRI
www.akureyri.is
Kortagerð: Ólafur Valsson Copyright ©
Reykjavík
Eyjafjörður
Bárufell
Sæberg
Glerá
600
603
Sólborg Háskólinn á Akureyri
Oddeyrarbryggja
Borgarsíða
Bakkasíða
Bæjarsíða
Búðarsíða
Bogasíða
Móðusíða
Vestursíða
Brekkus
Brattasíða
Síðubraut
Móasíða
Rimasíða
Múlasíða
Miðsíða
Reykjasíða
Austursíða
Þverasíða
Frostagata
Melasíða
Fögusíða
Flatasíða
Fagrasíða
Frostagata
Hörgárbraut
Bugðusíða
Lindasíða
Austursíða
Fjölnisgata
Baldursnes
Njarðarnes
Draupinsgata
Goðanes
Freyjunes
Fannagil
Fálkagil
Fornagil
Urðargil
Víkurgil
Valagil
Vesturgil
Vörðugil
Fossagil
Merkigil
Skriðugil
Skútagil
Skessugil
Skottugil
Vættagil
Skuggagil
Snægil
Huldugil
Merkigil
Kiðagil
Drekagil
Tröllagil
Dvergagil
Réttarhv
Hlíðarbraut
Borgarbraut
Núpasíða
Kjalarsíða
Keilusíða
Stapasíða
Ekrusíða
Teigarsíða
Arnarsíða
Tungusíða
Bakkahlíð
Brattah
Fosshlíð
Mánahlíð
Sunnuhlíð
Barmah
Steinahlíð
Smárahlíð
Skarðshlíð
Seljahlíð
Hlíðarbraut
Litlahlíð
Drangsh
Borgarh
Norðurslóð
Höfðahlíð
Hraunholt
Hlíðarbraut
Hahlíð
Harðarangur
Áshlíð
Langahlíð
Skarðshlíð
Langholt
Þverholt
Einholt
Krossanessbraut
Stafholt
Miðholt
Undirhlíð
Hörgárbraut
Lyngholt
Stórholt
Óseyri
Ósvör
Sandgerðisbót
Krossanessbraut
Norður tangi
Naustatangi
Skipatangi
Vesturbakki
Austurbakki
Fiskitangi
Hjalteyrargata
Silfurtangi
Skálag
Kambagerði
Kolgerði
Grundargerði
Kleifargerði
Klettagerði
Stóragerði
Kvistagerði
Hraungerði
Hólsgerði
Háagerði
Dalsgerði
Dalsbraut
Hamragerði
Akurgerði
Stekkjargerði
Kotárgerði
Klettaborg
Dalsbraut
Mýrarvegur
Kambsmýri
Engimýri
Kringlumýri
Grænamýri
Rauðamýri
Víðimýri
Langamýri
Hrafnabj
Þingvallastræti
Byggðavegur
Ásvegur
Hamarstígur
Sjafnarst
Klettast
Þórunnarstræti
Helgamagrastræti
Bjarkarst
Lögbergsg
Holtagata
Hlíðargata
Munkaþverárstræti
Klapparst
Krabbast
Krákust
Brekkugata
Oddeyrargata
Hólabraut
Smárag
Gilsbakkavegur
Oddagata
Bjarmast
Kaupvangsstræti
Túngata
Laxag
Geislag
Ráðhústorg
Hafnarst
Skipagata
Hofsbót
Glerárgata
Lundarg
Fróðasu
Grænagata
Fjólugata
Eyrarvegur
Víðivellir
Reynivellir
Norðurgata
Grenivellir
Ránargata
Ægisgata
Drottningarbraut
Strandgata
Norðurgata
Eiðsvallagata
Gránufélagsgata
Grundarg
Hríseyjarg
Hjalteyrargata
Kaldbaksgata
Laufásgata
Grímseyjarg
Sjávargata
Strandgata
Glerárgata
Hvannavellir
Tryggvabraut
Þórsstígur
Furuvellir
Árstígur
Gilsbakkavegur
Pollurinn

2 Outdoor Swimming Pools • Indoor Swimming Pool
4 Hot Pots • Steambath • Solarium • Playground

For the best of times!

The Akureyri Swimming Pool

Summer: Monday - Friday 06[45] - 21[00] • Weekends 8[00] - 19[30]
Winter: Monday - Friday 06[45] - 21[00] • Weekends 9[00] - 18[00]

Tel.: 461 4455 • www.akureyri.is • www.visitakureyri.is

1 NORÐURLANDSVEGUR

Vaðlaskógur, woodland on the east shore of Pollurinn.

Hallland, the southernmost farm along Svalbarðsströnd. The poet Hjálmar Jónsson (Bólu-Hjálmar) was born there in 1796, when his mother sought shelter for one night.

Akureyri, (pop. 17,693) is the second largest urban area, after the capital area of Reykjavík, and the centre of trade and services in northern Iceland. It is also a town of culture and education, often called a school town as it boasts many educational estabishments, including a university. Fishing and fish processing centres also make their mark on the town. The original "Akureyri" is a small gravel bank below Búðargil formed from the deposits of a creek flowing through the gulley. The market town's first settlement was built there, and the town's oldest house, Laxdalshús at Hafnarstræti 11, can still be found at this location. The house was built in 1795. There are records of trade in Akureyri going as far back as 1602. In 1787 the town gained municipal rights, and it obtained its municipal charter in 1862, since then it has had its own town council. Akureyri is heated with geothermal water coming from Laugaland and Hjalteyri in Eyjafjörður. There is contiguous open area around Akureyri where the biosphere and landscape are extremely diverse, and vegetation in many places is especially lush. In the urban area there are also interesting natural features, and on the hills of Akureyri there are many intriguing plants. Within the Akureyri town limits there are many interesting recreation areas and hiking paths. The Akureyri Botanical Garden is known far and wide for its beautiful walking paths and luxuriant flora. One of Akureyri's gems, it was founded in 1912, and it contains nearly every plant found in Iceland ca. 450 and nearly 7,000 foreign plants. The town has many museums, e.g. notable museums like Akureyri Museum, Aviation Museum, Industrial Museum, Motorcycle Museum, Art Museum, Nonni Museum, Memorial Museums Sigurhæð and Davíðshús commemoration the life's of two of Iceland's most loved poets. There are also galleries and exhibitions who offers insight in the diversity of the culture and the nation as a whole. Visitors can choose between varied accommodation and excellent range of restaurants, some of which specialise in local food. Akureyri also boasts one of Iceland's most popular swimming facilities, 18-hole golf course, the best skiing area in the country and free city bus. The town is a good base for many of Iceland's most beautiful natural wonders as waterfalls, volcanic areas and canyons. Selection of exciting activities as river rafting, hiking, fishing, whale watching and horse riding as well as tours to local villages and national parks, northern light tours and visits to the small island in the fjord. Akureyri and the surrounding area offers a number of annual events as well as many occasional concerts, exhibitions, theatre ect. For more details visit the event calender at **www.visitakureyri.is/en**.

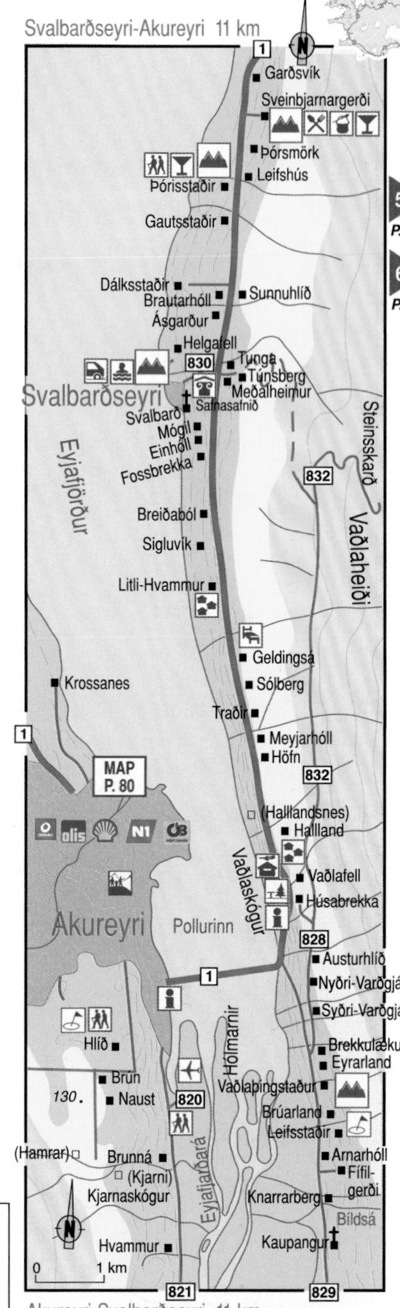

820 **Flugvallarvegur,** p. 391
821 **Eyjafj. braut vestri,** p. 391
828 **Veigastaðavegur,** p. 394
829 **Eyjafj. braut eystri,** p. 394
830 **Svalbarðseyrarvegur,** p. 86
832 **Vaðlaheiðarvegur,** p. 86, 396

Ring Road
5 p. 568
6 p. 569

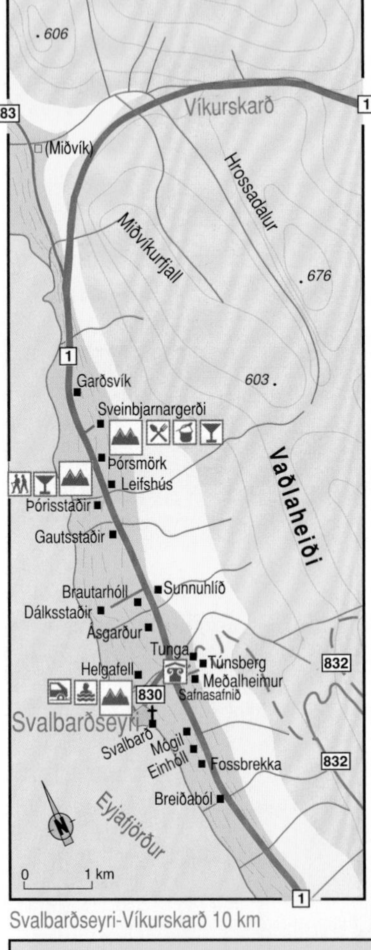

Svalbarðseyri-Víkurskarð 10 km

Víkurskarð, (325 m) a fairly wide pass in the mountain range between the Svalbarðsströnd coast and Fnjóskadalur.

Svalbarðsströnd, a coast and mountainside east of Eyjafjörður, below Vaðlaheiði, between the farms Varðgjá and Miðvík at Víkurskarð. The northernmost part of it is commonly called Kjálki. Very little lowland though there are some broad terraces in the mountainside, providing a good deal of space for cultivation in the southern parts. Grassy areas along the coast, many farms.

Vaðlaheiði, (600-700 m) the mountain range on the east side of Eyjafjörður between the passes Víkurskarð to the north and Bíldsárskarð to the south. Mostly quite grassy. The view from Vaðlaheiði across the fjord towards Akureyri with its backdrop of majestic mountains is renowned.

Svalbarðseyri, (pop. 271) a village. A former trading place and a herring-salting station. At Svalbarðseyri you will find a meat processing plant, a base for contractors, public service, a guesthouses, an elementary school, a swimming pool and sports facilities. There is a beautiful forest grove at the turn-off to Svalbarðseyri as well as Safnasafnið, an interesting folk art gallery, housed in the old local assembly building displaying folk art and special collections like embroidery, models souvenirs, books, dolls, toys and tools. The museum is open during the summer.

Svalbarð, church and ancient manor farm. Geothermal heat.

832 Vaðlaheiðarvegur, the old road over Vaðlaheiði, to Fnjóskadalur.

830 Svalbarðseyrarvegur, 1 km.

83 Grenivíkurvegur, p. 365
835 Fnjóskad.v. eystri, p. 397

1 NORÐURLANDSVEGUR

Stórutjarnir, ("Big ponds") a farm in the eastern section of Ljósavatns-karð. Geothermal heat, swimming pool, school and a summer hotel.

Ljósavatnsskarð, ("Lake of lights pass") a wide valley open at both ends, connecting Fnjóskadalur and Bárðardalur. Widespread birch bushes on the mountain slopes.

Sigríðarstaðaskógur, on the land of **Sigríðarstaðir** with extensive birchwoods, which are now protected by the Forestry Service. National forest.

Háls, farm, church and parsonage. Above the farm is the mountain **Hálshnjúkur** (682 m).

Vaglaskógur, one of two major birchwood forests in Iceland, about 300 hectares or 750 acres, highest trees 12-13 m. Centre of the Forestry Service. Summer outings and gatherings are held there. Campsites. Marked walking routes. National forest.

Fnjóskárbrú, the old concrete arch bridge on the river Fnjóská built 1908, at that time the longest bridge of its type in Scandinavia. Now a footbridge. The new bridge near Nes was opened in 1969.

Fnjóskadalur, a long and narrow valley with steep scree mountains on the east side. Long gravel ridges along the slopes, old tidemarks from the ice age, when there was a lake in the valley. Many farms have been abandoned during the last years and the three valleys that continue to the south, **Bleiksmýrardalur**, **Hjaltadalur** and **Timburvalladalur**, now have no functioning farms. The river Fnjóská is a good fishing river.

The Fnjóskárbrú bridge, built 1908.

83 Grenivíkurvegur, p. 365	**832 Vaðlaheiðarvegur,** p. 86, 396
833 Illugastaðavegur, p. 396	**834 Fnjóskadalsv. vestri,** p. 397
835 Fnjóskadalsvegur eystri, p. 397	**836 Vaglaskógarvegur,** p. 396

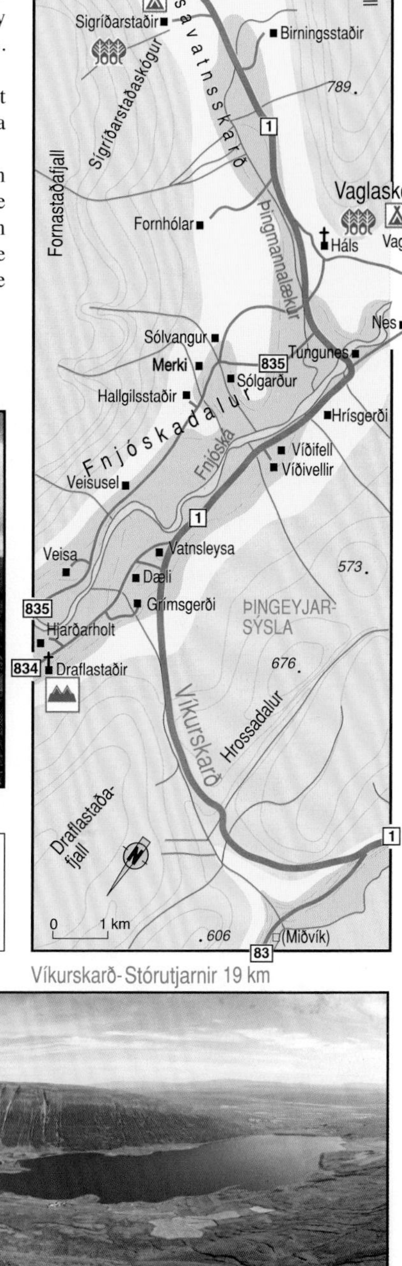

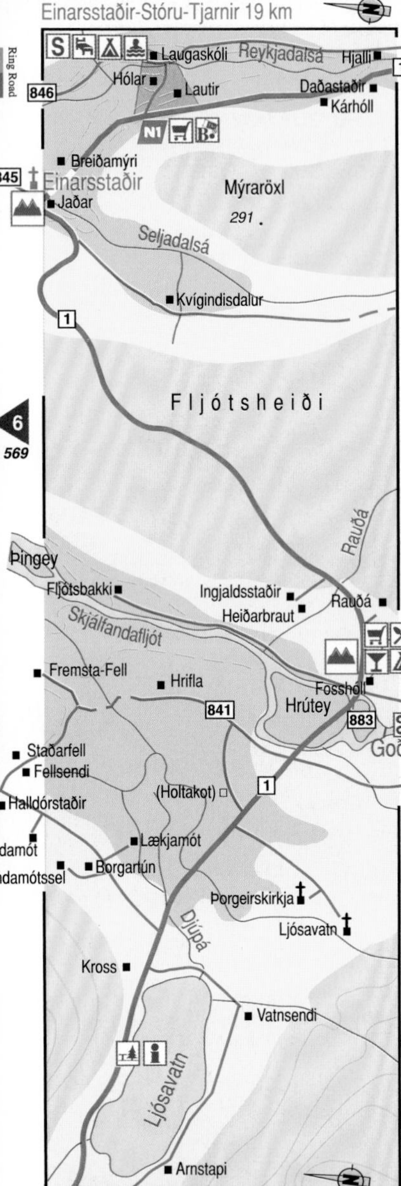

Stóru-Tjarnir-Einarsstaðir 19 km

Fljótsheiði, (280 m) an extensive and long but low mountain range, green and wet in places with many small lakes. There used to be many farms in this area, now all abandoned.

Fosssel, an abandoned farm on Fljótsheiði, quite far to the north of the road. Extensive birchwoods, now protected by the Forestry Service. The view from there is good especially across to the island **Þingey**, used of old for official gatherings, in the Skjálfandafljót river on the west side. According to the Sagas the settler Bárður towed his ships up the Skjálfandafljót river to **Skipapollur** ("Boat pool") below Þingey.

Fosshóll, a farm since 1930 and a trading place. Fosshóll is a small commerce community at Goðafoss waterfall. There one can find a shop, a gas station, a restaurant, a handcrafts market and an information center for tourists as well as accommodations. This is a nice spot to stop while travelling on the highway, observe Goðafoss in the Skjálfandi River and enjoy the scenery at Ljósavatnsskarð Passage where there are several historical sites, such as Ljósavatn Lake and Þorgeirskirkja, but this church is named after Þorgeir goði, who was the one who decided that Icelanders should switch from being heathens and become Christians. In the Skjálfandi River, a little to the north of Fosshóll, one can visit Þingey which this county and district are named after. There is an effort being made to refine the availability of information about the remarkable historical heritage which the region has to offer and there is an instructor at Þorgeirskirkja to welcome tourists and offer them information about the district.

883 Goðafossvegur, 0,34 km.

Goðafoss, ("Falls of the gods") among the finest in the country, not very high but cut into two horseshoe-shaped falls, Not far above the falls the river Skjálfandafljót divides in two, forming the island **Hrútey**. According to the Sagas Þorgeir of Ljósavatn threw his statues of the gods into the falls when Iceland converted to Christianity in the year 1000, hence the name. The lavafield by the falls, Bárðardalshraun, came from Trölladyngja north of Vatnajökull more than 7,000 years ago and reached as far as 100 km from the crater.

Hrifla, a farm on the banks of Skjálfandafljót. The birthplace of Jónas Jónsson (1885-1968), one of the most influential politicians of the 20th century, and a great social innovator. He founded the Progressive Party.

Djúpá, a river, runs from Ljósavatn in Skjálfandafljót.

Ljósavatn, ("Lake of lights") a deep lake, 3.28 km², good fishing. Farm of the same name. In the year 1000 the home of the lawspeaker and chieftain Þorgeir, who threw his idols into Goðafoss after having converted to Christianity. A new church, **Þorgeirskirkja**, was consecrated there in summer 2000, marking the 1000th anniversary of the conversion of Iceland.

Arnstapi, a farm, birthplace of Guðmundur Finnbogason (1873-1944) state librarian and renowned author.

85 Norðausturvegur, p. 366	**841 Fremstafellsvegur,** p. 398
842 Bárðardalsvegur vestri, p. 398	**844 Bárðardalsvegur eystri,** p. 398
845 Aðaldalsvegur, p. 400	**846 Austurhlíðarvegur,** s. 400

Goðafoss

1 NORÐURLANDSVEGUR

Arnarvatn, a farm and a lake of the same name. Fishing permits for the **Arnarvatnsá** river can be got there.

Helluvað, one of the first farms in the Mývatn district when approaching from the west. Long the home of the poet Jón Hinriksson (1829-1921).

Hofsstaðir, a farm by Laxá and belonging to the Mývatn district. Ruins found there in 1908 believed to be a farm from the 10th or the 11th century.

Laxá, one of the best known and most popular fishing rivers in Iceland. Considered the fairest of rivers with its many grassy or wooded islands, deep pools and swift currents. Comes from Lake Mývatn and runs through Laxárdalur and Aðaldalur. Hydroelectric plant at Brúar.

Laxárdalur, a shallow but fairly narrow valley, 26 km long from Brúar to Helluvað. Laxá runs along it on a lava bed. Luxuriant vegetation.

Másvatn, a lake with good fishing above Reykjadalur, its outlet, **Máslækur**, runs into the river Reykjadalsá.

Narfastaðir, in 1995 a church bell believed to date from before 1200 was dug up there. It is made of copper and is 14,5 cm high, with the same diameter. There are very few bells of this age existing.

847 Stafnsvegur, 5,68 km.

Laugar, (pop. 111) a small school and commerce community in the eastern part of the Þingeyjar region. A public school was built there in 1924 which is still running. The schools dorms are used as a hotel in summer. Geothermal heat. Heating distribution The first indoor swimming pool in the country was built there in 1925. A new outdoor swimming pool with large hot tub was built in 2005. At Laugar one can find among other things a repair shop, a gasoline station, a market, a restaurant, a savings bank and a post office. A fish drying factory is also found there which specializes in drying fish heads and other produce that are exported to Nigeria. Beautiful and peaceful surroundings.

Breiðamýri, a farm and community centre beside which is a grove of trees planted before 1920.

Einarsstaðir, a substantial farm and a church by the crossroads of Norðurlandsvegur (Road no. 1) and Aðaldalsvegur (Road no. 845). The birthplace of the Rev. Bergur Guðsteinsson, a 12th century translator of the story of Archbishop Thomas of Canterbury. Long the home of Einar Jónsson (1915-87), a well known medium and healer.

845 Aðaldalsvegur, p. 400 | **846 Austurhlíðarvegur,** p. 400

848 Mývatnsvegur, p. 92

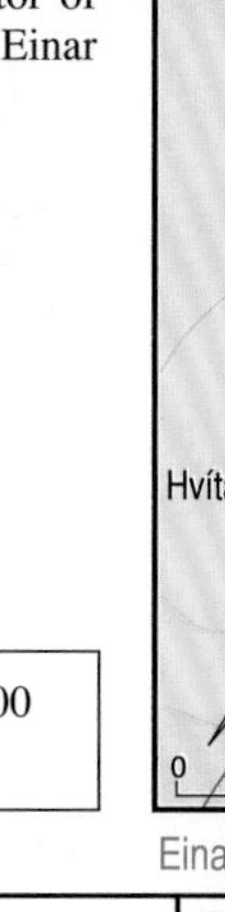

Reykjahlíð, (pop. 153 in the town, 378 in the district) the "capital" of the Mývatn district, on the land of a farm claiming about 6,000 km² of land, more than any other farm in Iceland, its land reaching from the Gæsafjöll mountains and Dettifoss falls all the way to the Vatnajökull glacier. A church and formerly a parsonage. Diatomite plant. Not far from the home field of Reykjahlíð is the rift Stóragjá which has warm water in it and was a popular place for bathing, it is not suited for bathing now. One of the longest series of eruptions in the history of Iceland, Mývatnseldar ("The Lake Mývatn fires") took place near there in 1724-29. There were eruptions of lava in many places, the greatest quantity of lava coming from a crater-row associated with the mountain **Leirhnjúkur**. Lava surrounded the old church in 1729, a new church being built beyond the lava field. From 1975-84 there was a series of tremors and eruptions originating in the old volcano Kröfluaskja to the north of the lake, but no lava to speak of reached the Mývatn area.

Mývatn, ("Midge lake") among the largest lakes in Iceland, 36.5 km², altitude 277 m, with a very indented shoreline, almost cut into two halves by a long peninsula and islands. Rather shallow, the average depth being 2.5 m, 4.5 m at its deepest, with lots of diatomite (kieselguhr) in the lake bed. Many islands, islets and pseudo craters, rich plant life in the lake and around it. A greater variety of birds, especially ducks, than anywhere else in Iceland, or even a large part of the world. The lake abounds in trout and there is very good trout fishing. Lots of midges and hence the name. The surrounding area is extremely beautiful with many interesting lava fields, geothermal heat in caves and canyons and steep mountains in the background. In October 1999 three men were killed when they were hit by a storm while laying a fiber optic cable across the lake.

Lofthellir, a cave located in the lava fields of Laxárhraun. The cave is 370m long and more than 3500 years old. It has beautiful natural ice sculptures all year long. Guided tours every day all year long from Mývatn and Akureyri.

The entire Mývatn area along with the river Laxá and its banks all the way to the sea, is protected by law.

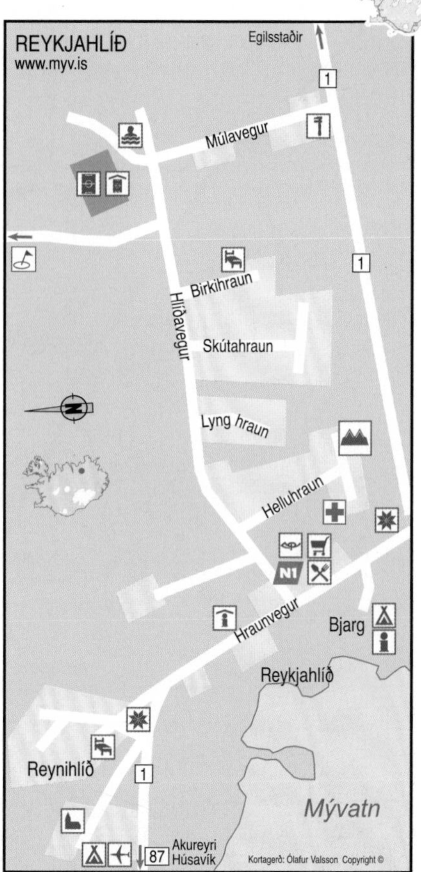

Ring Road

6
P. 569

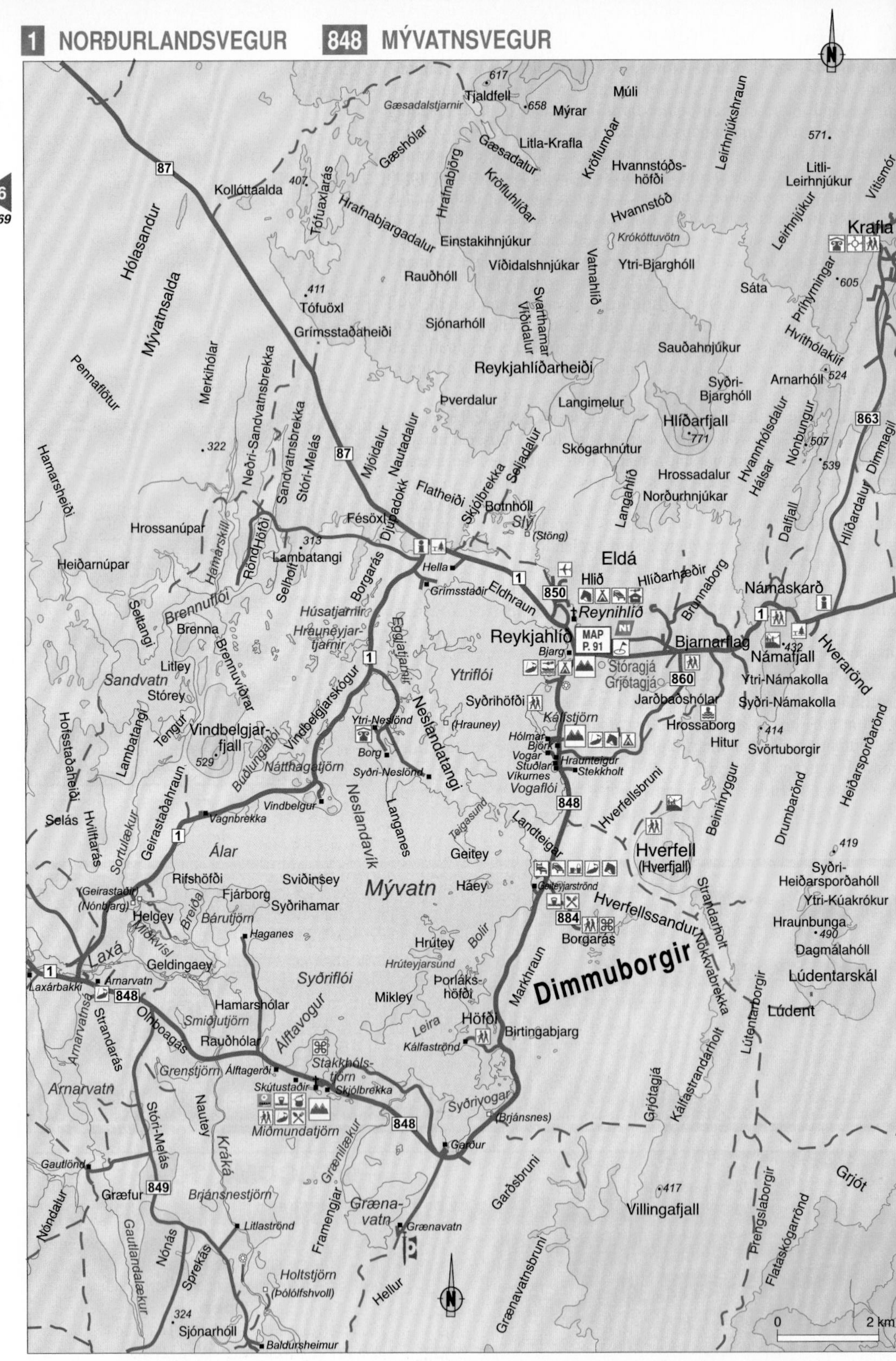

87 **Kísilvegur,** p. 386

rænavatn, ("Green lake") a farm by lake of the same ame, out of which flows Grænilækur into Mývatn. The ıme family in the direct male line has lived at there nce 1818. Large turf farmhouse from about 1913, of a ıte type. In the keeping of the National Museum since 000. Jeep-track south to Suðurárbotnar and Dyngjufjöll.

kútustaðir, church, parsonage, the Skjólbrekka ommunity centre. Numerous craters, **Skútustaðagígar** nd pseudocraters in the area which are a protected atural feature. Marked walking routes.

eilagsdalur, shallow dale below Bláfjall. Grass, bushes nd pretty streams. Lavafield to the east. It is likely that ıis was formerly a resting-place for travellers riding own from Ódáðahraun. Some traces of old tracks and airns visible.

áfjall, (1,222 m) an old volcano.

dáðahraun, the largest lava-field in Iceland, extending etween the glaciers Mývatnsjökull and Vatnajökull etween the rivers Jökulsá and Skjálfandafljót, covering 440 km². The plateau covers 800 m at its highest point nd has many mountains, the highest being **Herðubreið** ,682 m) and **Dyngjufjöll** (1,510 m).

49 Baldursheimsvegur, 8 km.

aldursheimur, a farm where in 1860 an interesting agan grave was found. This discovery was an important ıcentive to the founding of the National Museum.

itlaströnd, home of the poet Jón Stefánsson (Þorgils jallandi) (1851-1915).

autlönd, a farm since the original settlement. Since 818 the same family has lived there, many of its ıembers having been prominent politicians and local aders.

útnes, a small island well-known for rich plant life nd numerous birds.

ogar, a farm from which came Benedikt Jónsson röndal, writer and Chief Justice (1762–1825).

verfjall, (312 m) a roundish crater about 140 m deep nd 1,300 m diameter. Said to be one of the largest such aters in the world.

immuborgir, ("Dark crags") a magnificent lava ındscape with strange formations, columns, caves, ches, etc. It seems this was formed from a lava-lake, out f which molten lave flowed, causing much upheaval. ne of the strangest spots is **Kirkjan** ("The Church"), an ıormous arch. Some rich vegetation, including birch-ushes, now protected. It is easy to get lost if the marked aths are not followed. Dimmuborgir is under threat of lting up with windblown sand from the highlands, in ıe past parts have been totally submerged. To counteract ıis a conservation program was initiated and ownership anded over to the Soil Conservation Service in 1942.

údentsborgir, a row of craters east of Mývatn. They e a continuation of Þrengslaborgir, having erupted at ıe same time. Named for the explosion crater Lúdent to e southwest, which has a diameter of 600–800 m and epth of 60–70 m. The crater rims rise about 100 m ove the surrounding terrain. In 1968 Lúdentsborgir as the training area for Neil Armstrong and other stronauts before the moon landing.

rengslaborgir, a very impressive row of craters, north f the mountain Bláfjall, from which lava, known as Laxárhraun, flowed over the centre of the Mývatn district continued down Laxárdalur valley and north along Aðaldalur, covering a total area of 170 km². Believed to be 2,000 years old and Mývatn in its present form of a similar age.

Höfði, a public park on Hafurshöfði point opposite Kálfaströnd, given to the people of Mývatn by the desendents of Héðinn Valdimarsson (18921948), a leader of the Icelandic labour movement. Beautiful trees and garden. Magnificent views.

Kálfaströnd, a farm on a peninsula of the same name which provides some of the prettiest and most varied scenery on the Lake Mývatn shore. Many rock islands in the lake. Marked walking routes.

Krafla, (818 m) a tuff mountain north of Námafjall. Considerable geothermal heat on the west side of Krafla with fumaroles and mud-springs (solfataras). At the northwest side is **Víti,** ("Hell") an explosion crater, 300 m in diameter with green water in the bottom. **Leirhnjúkur** ("Clay peak"), is west of Krafla and on the southeast side is **Hrafntinnuhryggur,** ("Raven flint (i.e. obsidian) ridge") where pure obsidian is to be found. Construction of a geothermally powered electric plant started in 1974. Its first stage has been completed and provides 30 MW. From 1975-84 there was a series of tremors and eruptions in the area, 9 eruptions altogether along a 7,5 km long fissure. These originated in the old volcano Kröfluaskja.

Námafjall, the mountain south of Námaskarð, with geothermal heat all over the east side of the mountain, which looks light yellow from a distance. Sulphur was mined there for centuries from the Hlíðarnámur mines and exported. **Great care must be taken and all warnings observed as there have been many accidents.**

Námaskarð, a narrow pass between the mountains Námafjall and Dalfjall.

863 Kröfluv., 7,5 km. **885 Námaskarðsv.,** 1,3 km.

860 Grjótagjárv., 4 km. **884 Dimmuborgav.,** 1,3 km.

Bjarnarflag, the area west of Námafjall. The water from the drill hole at Bjarnarflag is piped into bathing lagoons at Lake Mývatns Earth Baths.

Jarðbaðshólar, crater hills south of the road. Steam vents there have long been used for steam baths, which are considered beneficial for rheumatism. Southeast from Jarðbaðshólar, about 1km from the main road in Bjarnarflag are the Earth Baths at Lake Mývatn. The lagoons are man-made structures with bottoms containing sand and gravel. The nature of the water is in some aspects very unique. It contains a large amount of minerals, alkaline and is therefore very suitable for bathing. Because of the mineral content, undesirable bacteria and vegetation do not thrive in the lagoon which makes the use of chlorine or other disinfectant unnecessary.

Grjótagjá, a rift with hot water south of Jarðbaðshólar. Formerly a popular bathing place, but in the disturbances 1975-84 the water became too hot for bathing. **The water is now over 50°C (122°F) and bathing is strictly forbidden.**

Stóragjá, a rift near Reykjahlíð. Used to be a popular bathing place but is not suited for bathing now.

7 P. 570

The Sæluhús shelter by the Jökulsá river.

Grímsstaðir á Fjöllum, ("Grímsstaðir in the mountains") a farm at a crossroads in the district Fjöll ("Mountains"), or Hólsfjöll, long an importan resting place for travellers in this area. Before the bridge was built ove Jökulsá there was a ferry point on the river, supervised from Grímsstaðir.
Jökulsá á Fjöllum, a large glacial river, the largest in the north o Iceland, coming from the Vatnajökull glacier and Kverkfjöll mountains. A big tributary, Kreppa, joins Jökulsá by Herðubreiðarlindir. Many falls i the river, the greatest being Dettifoss.
Sæluhús, a shelter built in 1881 near the ferry point on Jökulsá. Thi building was in many ways better than such shelters used to be, made o stones cemented together and having three floors: the basement for th horses and the upper ones for accommodation for travellers. However, th place soon got the reputation of being haunted and there are some ghos stories and folktales connected with the shelter. In the keeping of th National Museum since 1988.
Hrossaborg, an old crater, elliptical, about 500 m long. From there a jeep track leads to Herðubreiðarlindir (about 60 km) and Askja (about 100 km).
Pétursskirkja, ("Pétur's church") a shelter for sheep herders, built by th farmer Pétur Jónsson in 1925. Gunnar Gunnarsson´s novel *Aðventa* (Th Good Shepherd) takes place in this area, telling the story of Benedik Sigurjónsson (Fjalla-Bensi, or "Mountain-Benny") searching for sheep i late December. He spent Christmas Eve in the old shelter besid Pétursskirkja.
Nýjahraun, a lava-field that came from the 30 km long Sveinagjá rift i 1875. The road crosses the northern tip of this lava-field.
Sveinar, craters on the Sveinagjá rift, both north and south of the road. I direct line and south of Sveinar are **Rauðuborgir**.
Skógarmannafjöll, ("Outlaw mountains") (400 m) two parallel tuff mountains
Búrfell, (953 m) an impressive table mountain.
Kræðuborgir, a crater row several km long, the highest craters bein 50-60 m. A considerable lavafield has its origins in these craters.
Austaribrekka, the east side of a wide but shallow subsided valley. Jeep tracks from there to Dettifoss, Hólmatungur, Hljóðaklettar and Keldu hverfi.

862 **Dettifossvegur,** p. 480 864 **Hólsfjallavegur,** p. 404 - 405
F88 **Öskjuleið**, p. 451

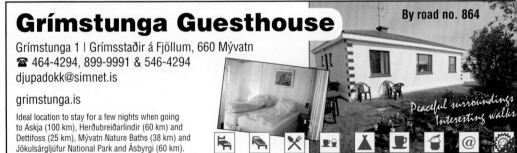

In the Vegaskarð area.

ɘgaskarð, a pass between the mountains **Vegahnjúkur** (783 m) to the ›uth and **Sauðahnjúkur** (641 m) to the north.

íðidalur, a valley and the westernmost farm in Norður-Múlasýsla. One the most isolated farms in Iceland.

iskupsháls, ("Bishops' ridge") a tuff mountain ridge between Gríms-aðir and Víðidalur, the boundary between the counties Suður-Þingeyjar-ʼsla and Norður-Múlasýsla. In earlier days it is said the bishops of Hólar the north and Skálholt in the south were to meet there when visiting ıd travelling through their districts. According to folktales the bishops d not quite agree on the limits of their districts and therefore decided to ɛct a cairn on Biskupsháls to mark the agreed eastern border. Then each them was to ride all the way round his bishopric and they would set the ɛstern boundary where they met again. They both set off, the bishop of ‹álholt riding as fast as he could and the bishop of Hólar taking it easy ıd enjoying himself en route. They met in Hrútafjörður (V-Hún), the shop of Skálholt obviously having travelled much farther and the estern boundary was set there. In the light of this story, the two cairns ı Biskupsháls, which are called **Biskupavörður** ("The bishops' cairns"), ight have been built about the year 1200 or even earlier.

ólsfjöll, a small and isolated district east of Jökulsá á Fjöllum, 300-400 above sea level and the highest inhabited district in Iceland. Sandy in aces and subject to erosion, yet having good grasslands and pastures for eep. The smoked lamb (hangikjöt) from Hólsfjöll is renowned. Low ff mountains on the east side, the highest points being **Grímsstaða-ɹrling** (859 m) and **Hólskerling** (801 m). Formerly there were eight ɾms in the district but now there are only two left, **Grímsstaðir** and **ýhóll**. A church at Víðirhóll and formerly a parsonage.

864 **Hólsfjallavegur,** p. 404

Vegaskarð-Jökulsá á Fjöllum 16 km

Vegahnjúkur, Sauðahnjúkur, Vegaskarð, Skarðsá, .656, Hádegistindur .828, Sótaskarð .807, Víðidalsfjöll, Víðidalsá, Rauðinúpur, (Víðidalur), .644, Fremri-Grímsstaðanúpur, .644 Rauðafell, NORÐUR-MÚLASÝSLA, Biskupsháls, Biskupavörður, Ytri-Grímsstaðanúpur, ÞINGEYJAR-SÝSLA, Jökulsá á Fjöllum, Hólsfjöll, (Gömlu-Grímsstaðir), Syðri-Vatnsleysa, Grímsstaðir, Grímstunga, 864, .387, 0 1 km

Jökulsá á Fjöllum-Vegaskarð 16 km

7 P. 570

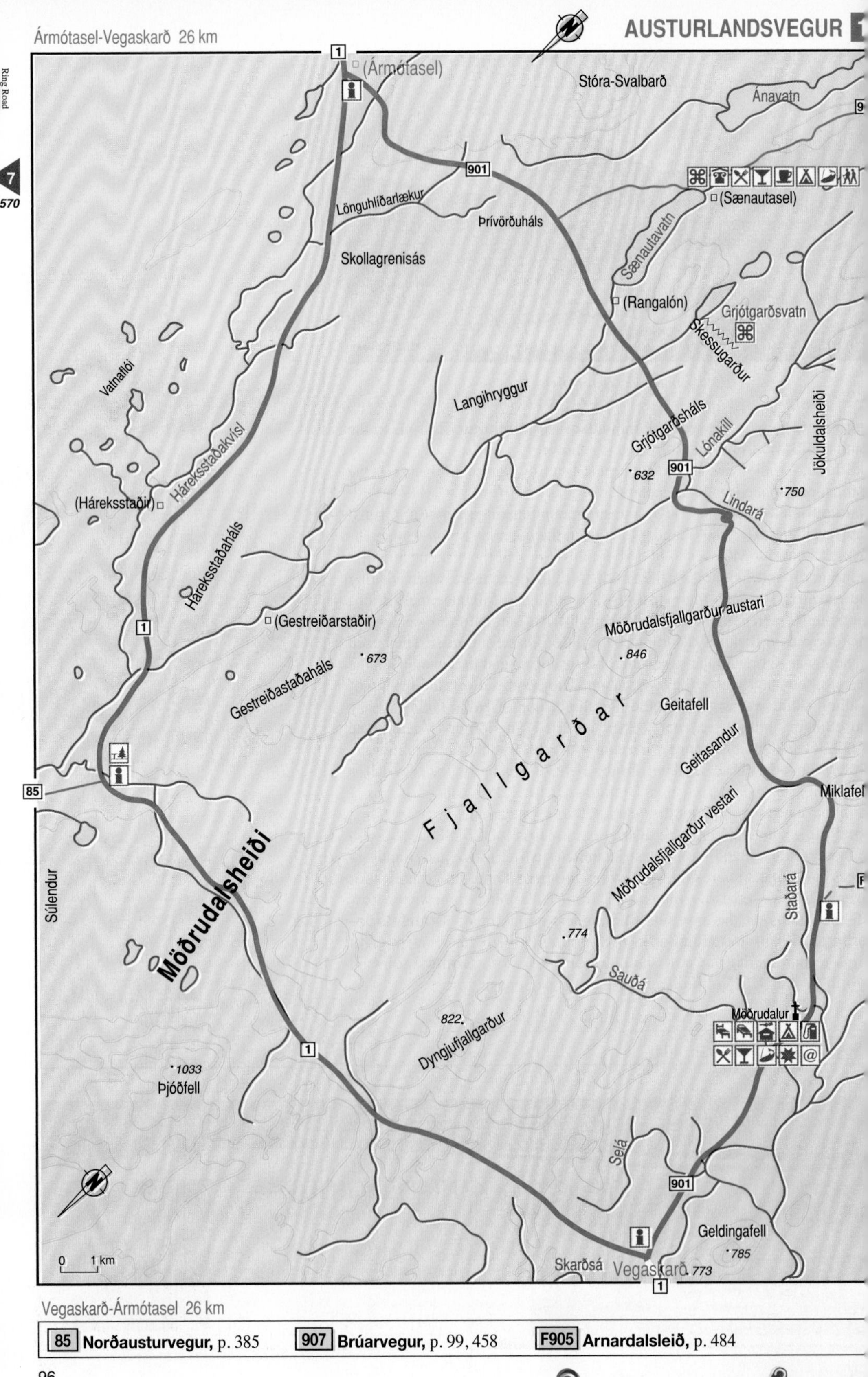

85 **Norðausturvegur,** p. 385 · 907 **Brúarvegur,** p. 99, 458 · F905 **Arnardalsleið,** p. 484

The church at Möðrudalur

Möðrudalur

láreksstaðir, an abandoned farm on Jökuldalsheiði vhich was first built in 1841 by Jón Sölvason (1803-864). Prior to that time the place was the site of nedieval farm ruins. Háreksstaðir was the first farm built n this area in the 20th century and among the most uccsessfull ones before it was abandoned in 1925. everal tales exist about the people who lived in the area ɔng ago. There is a sheep pen used by the people of 'opnafjörður to sort out their sheep.

iestreiðarstaðir, an abandoned farm on Jökuldalsheiði. 'he name may indicate that this farm dates back to the niddle ages, as do names of places in the area that are in ne way or the other connected with the name of the farm.

ökuldalsheiði, a vast moor covered with low hills and nountains southwest of Vopnafjörður and along the ökuldalur valley, with higher mountains on both sides. Aostly grassy and wet with many lakes, good fishing in ll of them. About 100 years ago there were many farms n this region but during the great eruption of Askja in 875 large quantities of ashes and pumice fell there so nat most of the inhabitants moved away, a number of nem emigrating to North America. The last inhabitants ft the area in 1946.

jóðfell, a tuff mountain, easily accessible from the ighway at 500 - 600 meters. Splendid view.

01 Möðrudalsleið, 40 km.

angalón, a farm in the middle of Jökuldalsheiði moor, y the northern end of **Sænautavatn**, which has good out-fishing. Abandoned in 1923.

Skessugarður, ("Giantess' rampart") an ancient end morrain lying at right angles across the Grjótgarðsháls ridge, just to the west of the mountain Sænautafell about 2 km south of the road. One of the most magnificent natural formations in Iceland, forming a 5 m high wall made of gigantic boulders of porphorytic basalt.

Möðrudalsfjallgarður, (750-950m) western and eastern, two mountain ranges of tuff, with steep sides, barren. Between them lies a flat plain, **Geitasandur** ("Goat sands"). Very good view from the western ridge across Möðrudalur and towards Vatnajökull and Ódáðahraun with the majestic Herðubreið, often called the queen of the northern mountains, in the middle.

Möðrudalur, a farm on Efra-Fjall (469 m) situated at a higher altitude than any other farm in Iceland; also one of the most isolated. Möðrudalur has extensive lands considered very well suited for sheep-farming and has thus been a substantial farm for centuries. Formerly a parsonage. The present church was built by the farmer Jón Stefánsson, who painted the altar-piece himself. From Möðrudalur there is a very good view of the surrounding mountains, especially the majestic **Herðubreið**, 1682 m in heigth, is one of the most beautiful mountains in Iceland and from there one can also see Dyrafjöll mountains, part of Vatnajökull glacier and **Kverkfjöll** on its northern fringe. An indication of the isolated character of the farm is the tale of a traveller who stayed there overnight in 1814. According to him, the farmer had six grown-up children who had never been to another farm even though the oldest of them was married and a parent of three children. Now a travel service is run at Mörðudalur as well a goat- and sheep farm.

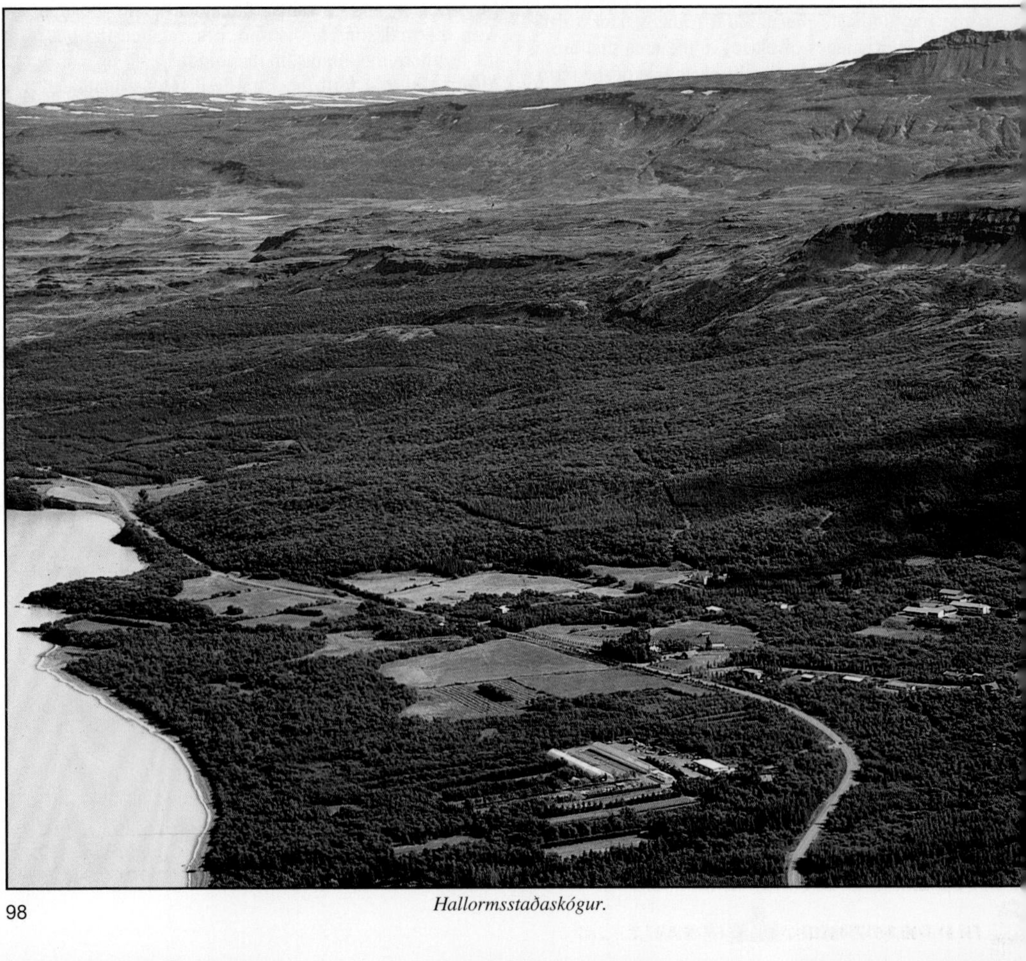

Hallormsstaðaskógur.

kjöldólfsstaðir, a substantial farm since the original settlement. uesthouse, campsite, restaurant, gas station and a swimming pool.

ökulsá á Brú or **Jökulsá á Dal**, a glacial river, at 150 km the longest ver in eastern Iceland.Considered the muddiest of Icelandic rivers, it ırried about 112 tons of clay and sand to the ocean daily. The river is duced in volume, both water and deposits, when the generators of the árahnjúkar Hydroelectric Power Station started to revolve. The deposits will remain behind the gigantic dam in the river's canyons and the mainstay of the water will be diverted to river Lagarfljót.There are five bridges over the river.

Dimmugljúfur.

Jökuldalur, a long valley going up from Fljótsdalshérað, mostly with low mountains on both sides. Narrow, especially far inland where there is little or no flat land, though the opes are grassy and provide good grazing. Scattered population.

ilsá, a swift river that comes down the valley almost parallel to the road ıd joins Jökulsá. The bridge was built in 1972.

navatn, a good fishing lake about 7 km long. There were two farms by e lake, **Veturhús** on the north and Heiðarsel on the south, the latter eing the last farm to be abandoned in the region of Jökuldalsheiði in the ear 1941.

ænautasel, an abandoned farm (occupied 1843–1943) at the outhern end of the lake Sænautavatn ("Sea-monster lake"). It chieved notoriety through the Halldór Laxness' account *A Midwinter ight on Jökuldalsheiði Moor*. It was renovated in 1992-3 and is onsidered well worth a visit. Land reclamation and revegetation.

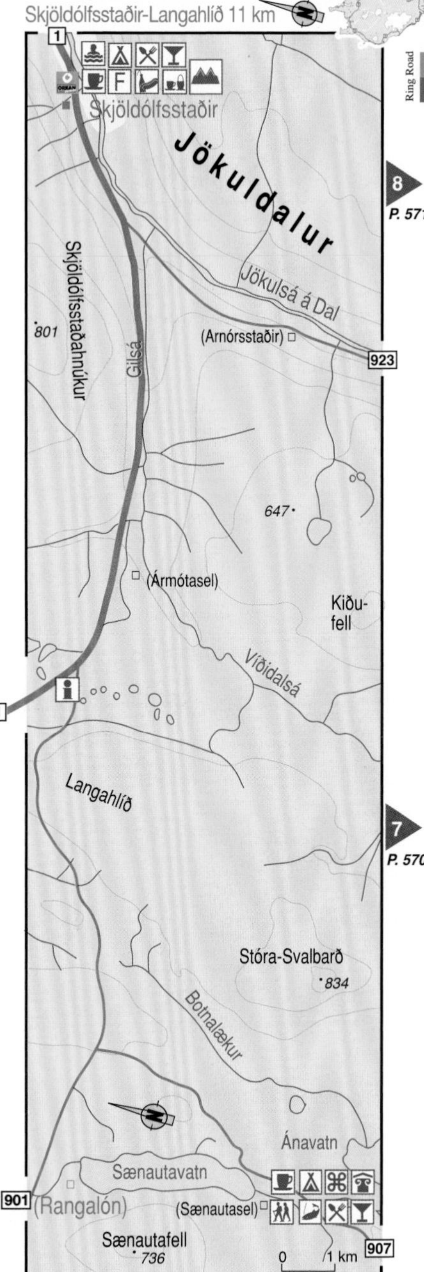

901 **Möðruvallarvegur,** p. 96
907 **Brúarvegur,** p. 485
923 **Jökuldalsvegur,** p. 424

Ring Road
8
P. 571

Jökulsárbrú-Skjöldólfsstaðir 31 km

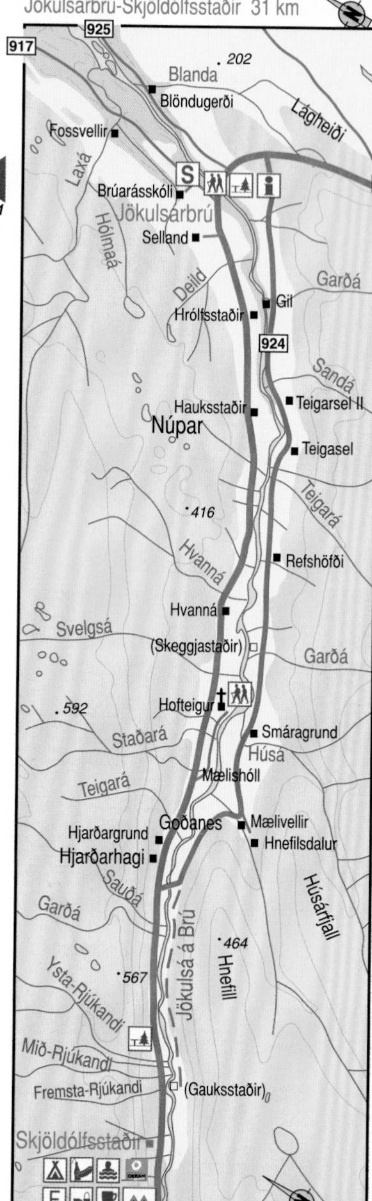

Skjöldólfsstaðir-Jökulsárbrú 31 km

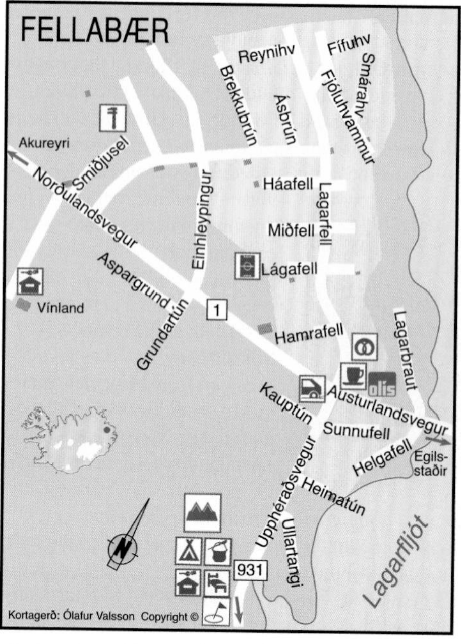

Jökulsárbrú, the present bridge was built in 1994, about 1 km south of that built in 1931. The river runs through a fairly deep, narrow (17-18 m) gorge at this point. The new bridge is the highest in Iceland, 40 m above the river. The first bridge, sponsored by German merchants, was built before 1564. According to the folktales of Jón Árnason, a monster, said to have been somewhat bigger than a horse, was seen in the river above the bridge and was also seen from several farms swimming upstream. At one place it stranded on shallows but nobody dared to go and take a closer look.

Brúarás, an elementery school since 1979. Now also a music school, preschool and a gymnasium.

Hvanná, a farm by a river of the same name, built close to the big river, Jökulsá. Birthplace of the composer Jón Jónsson from Hvanná (1910-63).

Hofteigur, a manor-farm and church, parsonage until 1925.

Mælishóll, which is said to be the home of "hidden people", exceptionally ornate and beautiful. According to legend, if three women with the name Ingibjörg happen to own the farm **Hnefilsdalur** nearby, one at a time, each will be bewitched and disappear into Mælishóll. This has supposedly already happened to two such Ingibjörgs.

Goðanes, a promontory by Jökulsá downstream from the river Teigará. A temple of Thor was built there in Saga times and some ruins can still be seen on the promontory. A spring which comes up not far from the ruins is reddish because of iron compounds. The name of the spring is Blótkelda ("The spring of sacrifices") or Blóðkelda ("The spring of blood"), it being believed that the colour and taste of the water derived from the blood of sacrificial animals (or even people).

924 Jökuldalsv. eystri, 23 km.

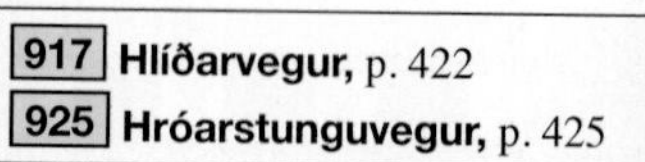

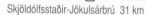

917 Hlíðarvegur, p. 422
925 Hróarstunguvegur, p. 425

yvindará, a river and farm of the same name.
gilsstaðabær (Egilsstaðir), located in the heart of East-Iceland in the road valley of Fljótsdalshérað. Dense population can be found in Eiðar nd Hallormsstaður but the largest rural district is Egilsstaðir/Fellabær, e only full scale town in Fljótsdalshérað. Together they form the core of e valley with the population of about 3,434 inhabitants. This core is the ommunication- and service center of East Iceland. The main occupations clude light industry, various services, supermarkets and stores, tourism, nd agriculture, while handcraft shops of the area are widely known. A iverse educational service is available in the area in musical schools, ursery schools, elementary- and high schools and college. Egilsstaðir upports an attractive swimming pool, well-equipped gymnasium, modrn outdoor sports field and a nine hole golf course. Regular sightseeing xcursions are available, as well as hiking tours on marked trails. The skig area in Stafdalur is open during the winter. A local drama club, jazz lub and many choires are example of the fertile cultural life in Egilsaðir. The Museum Center reflect the history of the area. A first class otel, summertime lodging, farm accommodation, and coffee and guest ouses make the traveller's stay comfortable. An important attraction is e glacially hollowed Lake Lögurinn, which empties into the wide bay éraðsflói through Lagarfljót River. Through the area flows the Lagarfljót ke which is home to Iceland's most renowned water monster, agarfljótsormur (The Lagarfljóts wyrm), considered to be the sister of e Loch Ness monster. Whether hunting for reindeer, geese or ptarmigan, e chances are high. Trout fishing is widely possible, and salmon fishing available in several rivers in the neighbourhood. The transportation onnections are optimal and frequent service by high capacity vehicles arries goods in all directions all year round and scheduled passenger trafc is available during the high season of tourism in summer. A domestic irport and substitute airport for international flight is located in gilsstaðir with only one hour's flight from Reykjavík and a mere two ours flight from Europe.
gilsstaðir, a substantial farm. A centre of communications after the bridge as built on Lagarfljót. Hotel, grain farming and the principal airfield in astern Iceland nearby. Wild aspen grows in the woods of Egilsstaðir.

41 Flugvallarvegur, 0,55 km. **929 Hafrafellsvegur,** 7,3 km.

elskógur, a small forest on the outskirts of Egilsstaðir. Hiking trails rough the forest.
agarfljótsbrú, (301 m) this was for years the longest bridge in Iceland.
ellabær, (pop. 403) a village across the bridge from Egilsstaðir. Main ctivities trading, service and industry.
afrafell, (216 m) a rocky mountain by the road. **Grímstorfa** ("Grímur´s rf"), a wooded ledge on its eastern side very difficult to reach whether om above or below, was for a while the hiding place of Grímur Dropugarson, according to the Sagas.
róarstunga, the district north of Rangá between the big rivers Jökulsá nd Lagarfljót, the southernmost part being Lágheiði moor, across which e road goes. Long and low hills with wet ground, fens and marshes in etween, many lakes.

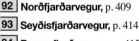

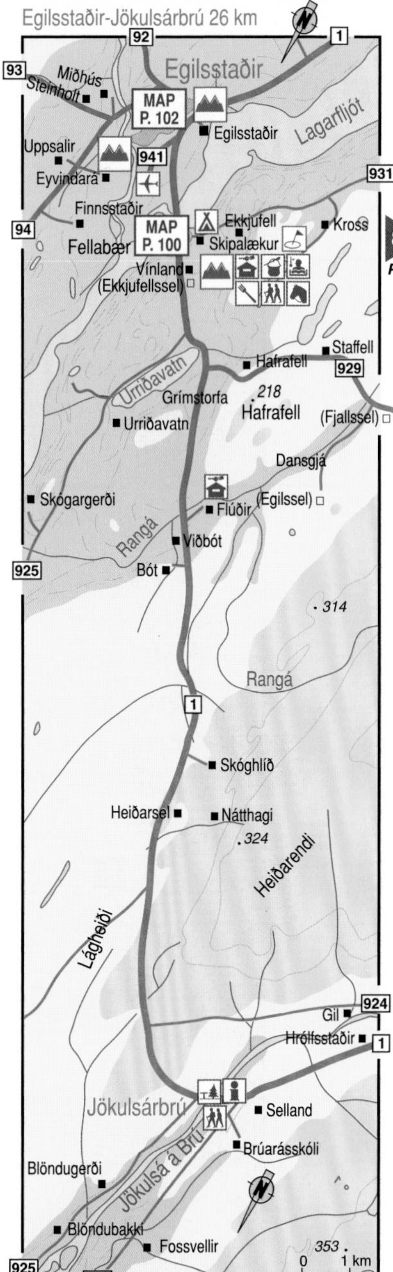

92 Norðfjarðarvegur, p. 409
93 Seyðisfjarðarvegur, p. 414
94 Borgarfjarðarvegur, p. 415
917 Hlíðarvegur, p. 422
924 Jökuldalsvegur eystri, p. 100
925 Hróarstunguvegur, p. 425
931 Upphéraðsvegur, p. 426

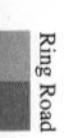

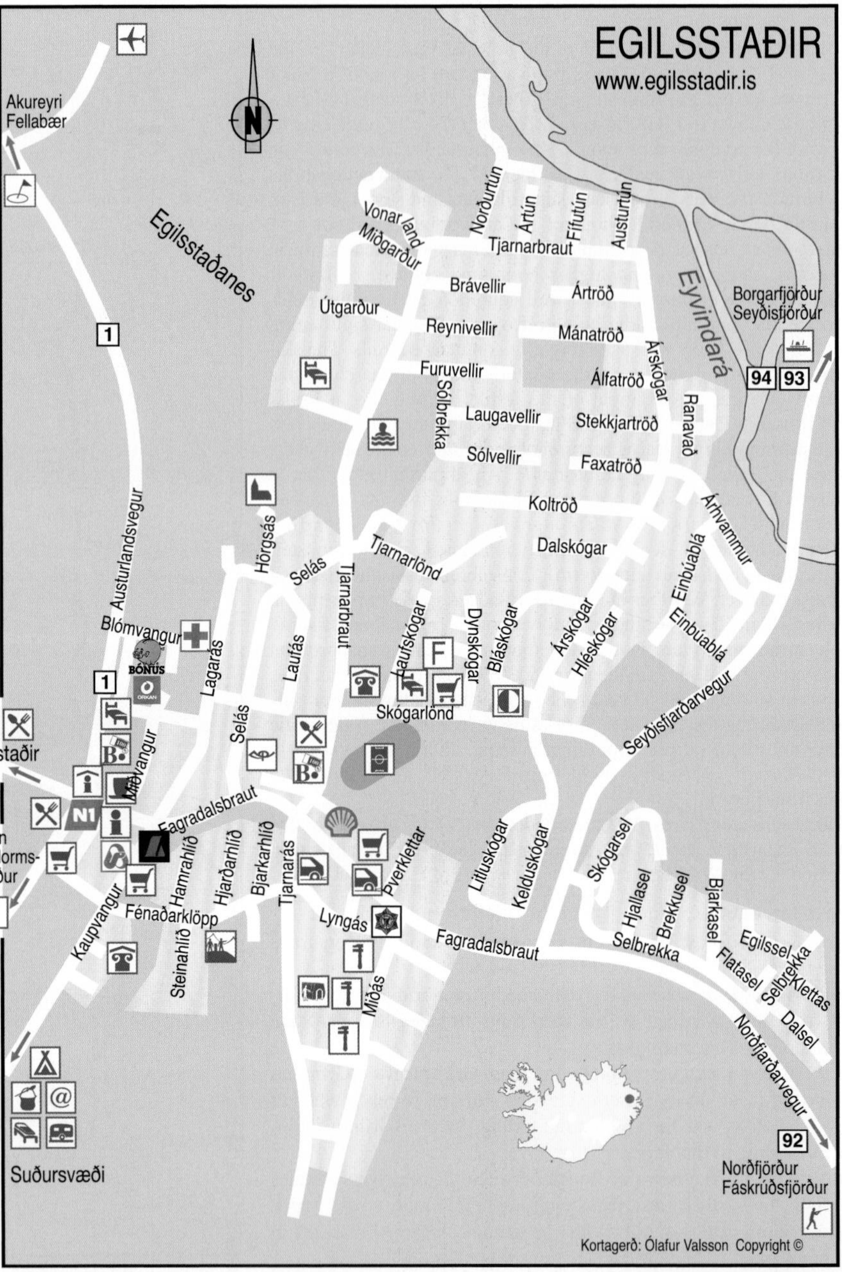

EGILSSTAÐIR

www.egilsstadir.is

Akureyri
Fellabær
Egilsstaðanes
1
Vonarland
Miðgarður
Norðurtún
Ártún
Fífutún
Austurtún
Tjarnarbraut
Útgarður
Brávellir
Ártröð
Reynivellir
Mánatröð
Furuvellir
Sólbrekka
Álfatröð
Árskógar
Laugavellir
Stekkjartröð
Ranavað
Sólvellir
Faxatröð
Eyvindará
Borgarfjörður
Seyðisfjörður
94
93
Koltröð
Dalskógar
Árhvammur
Hörgsás
Selás
Tjarnarlönd
Tjarnarbraut
Austurlandsvegur
Einbúablá
Blómvangur
Laugarás
Laufás
Laufskógar
F
Dynskógar
Bláskógar
Árskógar
Hléskógar
Einbúablá
BÓNUS
ORKAN
1
Skógarlönd
Seyðisfjarðarvegur
Egilsstaðir
Selás
Miðvangur
N1
Fagradalsbraut
Höfn
Hallormsstaður
Hamrahlíð
Hjarðarhlíð
Bjarkarhlíð
Tjarnarás
Þverklettar
Litluskógar
Kelduskógar
Skógarsel
Hjallasel
Brekkusel
Bjarkasel
Fénaðarklöpp
Kaupvangur
Steinahlíð
Lyngás
Fagradalsbraut
Selbrekka
Egilssel
Flatasel
Selbrekka
Klettas
Dalsel
Miðás
Norðfjarðarvegur
92
Suðursvæði
Norðfjörður
Fáskrúðsfjörður
Kortagerð: Ólafur Valsson Copyright ©

Egilsstaðir

Ring Road
9 P. 572

Litla-Sandfell-Egilsstaðir 21 km

1 937 Litla-Sandfell Sandfell Vað Sauðhagi Stóra-Sandfell I Stóra-Sandfell Gilsá Hjálpleysa Grófargerði Grímsárvirkjun Lundur Höttur Uxalækur Arnkelsgerði Grímsá 937 Ásgarður (Tunghagi) Gíslastaðir Víkingsstaðir Hvammur Gíslastaðagerði 931 Úlfsstaðir (Vallaneshjáleiga) Einarsstaðir Eyjólfsstaðir Vallanes 1 Jaðar Kaldá Sólskógar Beinárgerði 474 Ketilsstaðir Langahlíð Kelduhólar Unalækur Stangarás Útnyrðingsstaðir 189 Höfði Lagarfljót (Lögurinn) 1 931 92 N1 Egilsstaðir MAP P. 102 Egilsstaðir 0 1 km 93 Skipalækur 931

Egilsstaðir-Litla-Sandfell 21 km

Grímsárvirkjun, a hydro-electric power plant built in 1958.

Hjálpleysa, ("Lack of help") a pass or a side valley often used by hikin travellers to and from Reyðarfjörður. There is **Valtýshellir** cave.

Höttur, (1,106 m) a rhyolite mountain by Hjálpleysa.

Vallanes, a farm and church. See more p. 427.

Grímsá, a river formed by the two rivers Geitdalsá coming from lakes in th highlands east of Hornbrynja through Norðurdalur, and Múlaá coming fro the Ódáðavötn lakes. Until it reaches the lake Skriðuvatn in Suðurdalur Múla is called Öxará.

Eyjólfsstaðir, formerly a substantial farm, has extensive birchwood fores that are now protected and in the care of the district's Forestry Association. bible school has been run there since 1989. There are some hiking trails in th forrest and two waterfalls, one which can be accessed from behind.

Einarsstaðir, a summerhouse colony.

Ketilsstaðir, a farm, formerly the seat of district judges, also formerly church and a free church. Now a horse farm. New farms are being built nea by. One of several noted judges from Ketilsstaðir was Pétur Þorsteinsso (1720-95). He was among those who imported reindeer and he had a numb of books written and printed, especially religious works, hymns etc. His so was Sigurður Pétursson (1759-1827), a poet and playwright whose plays we the first to be printed in Iceland (1844 and later).

Útnyrðingsstaðir, a farm, birthplace of Þorsteinn M. Jónsson (1885-1977), member of parliament, headmaster and publisher, owner of one of the largest private collections of Icelandic books, now in the Árni Magnússon Institute. Now a horse farm.

Höfði, now a forest farm owned by Iceland Forest Service.

The Vallanes church.

92 **Norðfjarðarvegur,** p. 409
93 **Seyðisfjarðarvegur,** p. 414
931 **Upphéraðsvegur,** p. 426
937 **Skriðdalsvegur,** p. 105

Breiðdalsheiði.

Breiðdalsheiði, (470 m) a mountain road across the moor between Skriðdalur and Breiðdalur, steep at the Breiðdalur end. A small lake, Heiðarvatn, not far from the road, where trout has been introduced and seems to thrive well. Between the road and the lake is Tjarnarflöt, where legend has it the men of Vopnafjörður and Breiðdalur fought in the old days. Reindeer may be seen along the road on Breiðdalsheiði.

Ódáðavötn, two lakes above the Skriðdalur valley. Formerly a frequented route between Fljótsdalur and Djúpivogur. In 1964 dams were built by the lakes in order to maintain an even flow of water for the Grímsárvirkjun hydroelectric plant.

939 Axarvegur, 18,6 km between Skriðdalur og Berufjörður, highest point 532 m. Rather steep in Berufjörður, many beautiful waterfalls. The road is open for all cars in the summer time.

Skriðdalur, a long valley between Hérað and Breiðdalsheiði, wide at its mouth and dividing into two valleys, Norðurdalur and Suðurdalur. The eastern mountains are mostly of multi-coloured rhyolite.

Haugahólar, a group of hills, most likely the debris from an old landslide. The farm **Haugar** by the hills and the 3 km long lake **Skriðuvatn** nearby.

Arnhólsstaðir, a farm by the river Jóka which runs out of the valley Þórudalur. There is a jeep track along the east bank of Jóka to Reyðarfjörður. Formerly the main horse track from the Upphérað district.

Múlakollur (Þingmúli), 508 m, a tuff mountain, splitting Skriðdalur in to two valleys. Some fosiles have been found there.

Þingmúli, ("Meeting mountain") a farm, church and parsonage until 1890, formerly an official meeting place and hence the name of the two counties, Suður-Múlasýsla og Norður-Múlasýsla. Some ruins from earlier times are still to be seen. Place-names indicate that there was a heathen temple there. A mountain (508 m) of the same name between the valleys. Some fossils found there.

938 Múlavegur syðri, 6 km.

937 Skriðdalsvegur, 19 km.

Þórisá, a river in the land of the farm Eyrarteigur. In 1995 a heathen tomb was found there, thought to be from the time of settlement. It was lined with horse skins, unusual in this country, richly furnished with weapons and other objects, containing among other things a fragment of a silver coin thought to be from the time of Athelstan, King of England 925–940. It also contained the skeletons of a man, a horse and a dog. This is one of the most remarkable archeological finds in Iceland.

Skúmhöttur, (1,229 m) a rhyolite mountain between Skriðdalur and the head of Reyðarfjörður, one of the highest mountains in this region.

936 Þórdalsheiðarvegur, p. 492

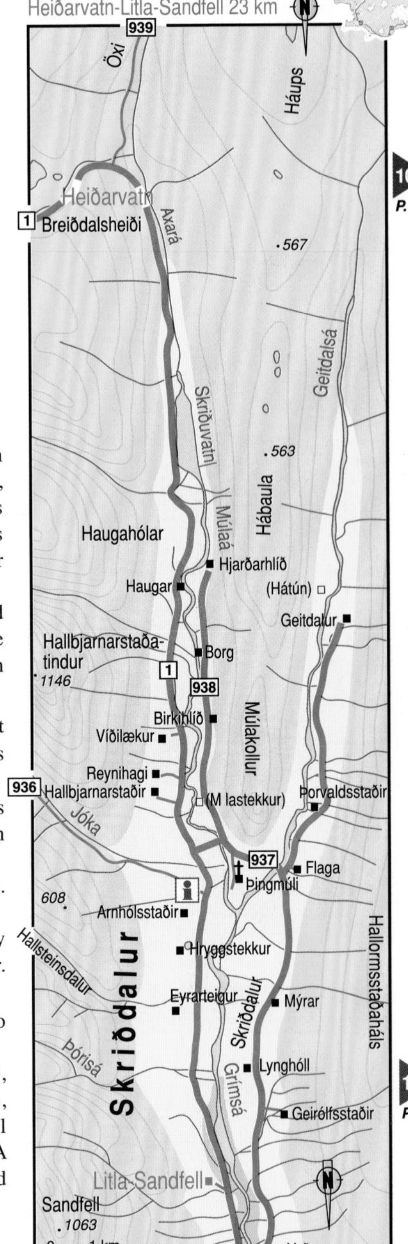

Streitishvarf-Heiðarvatn 44 km

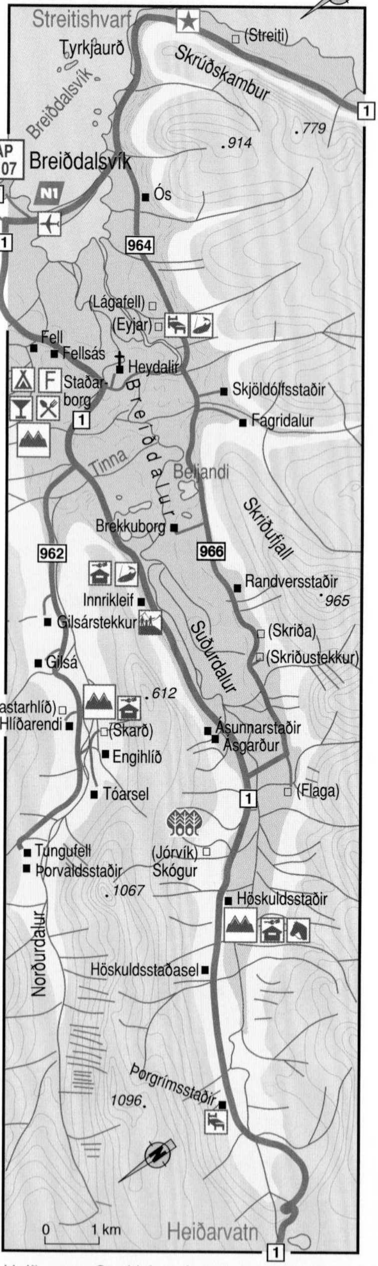

MAP P. 107

10 P. 573

Heiðarvatn-Streitishvarf 44 km

Skrúðskambur, a rock-wall by the road, where a giant was supposed to have lived. His two brothers lived on the islands Papey and Skrúður.

Streitishvarf, the peninsula on the south side of the Breiðdalsvík bay. Streiti has great natural hiking trails and view points out to the islands. A lighthouse has been there since 1922.

Tyrkjaurð, ("Turks' scree") above Streitishvarf, where legend has it that a farmer killed 18 Algerian pirates when he found them asleep.

Breiðdalseyjar, several islands in the south of Breiðdalsvík. The islands are home to seals, eider ducks, and many other seabirds.

Breiðdalsvík, ("Broad valley bay") a short, wide bay with a wide beach of black sand across the end of the bay. A town of the same name (pop. 130). The small town lies at the entrance to the valley between the headlands of Kambanes and Streitishvarf. The first house was built in 1883 by the Gránufélagið association. The community developed slowly at first, but grew rapidly when major harbour improvements were made in the mid 20th century. Nothing is known for sure about the settlement until about 1880 when the Gránufélagið built a warehouse. Yet full-time settlement did not begin until 1896, when the Brynesverslun store in Seyðisfjörður built a branch store at the top of Selnes at the eastern corner of Selnesbót. In the spring of 1906 the store burned down and the same year a new store was built to the west of the inlet. That building still exists today, making it the oldest building in Breiðdalsvík. The old co-op has been rebuilt as a geology centre, which is fitting as Breiðdalur is East Iceland's volcanic region, as indicated by the colours of the mountains.

964 Breiðdalsvegur, 9 km. **966 Suðurbyggðarvegur,** 14 km.

Heydalir, often called Eydalir, a farm, church and parsonage, formerly considered one of the richest parishes in Iceland. Among the best known clergymen of Heydalir was the poet Einar Sigurðsson (1538-1626) who wrote one of the most popular of all Icelandic Christmas hymns. Above the road is **Staðarborg** the first community centre in Breiðdalur. Beautiful walking trails connect Heydalir and Staðarborg.

Hafnarey, a good harbour for small boats, belongs to Heydalir.

Flaga, a river which runs down from Flögutindur and Smátindur peaks, in cliff steps ending in a 60 m fall through a hole in the cliff making an eye or an arch around the tip of a waterfall **Flögufoss.**

Tinna, a river running through Tinnudalur from the peaks Njáll and Bera. The peaks are named after a giant couple that lived in the mountains and were eventually turned into stone. A wonderful walking trail leads up the valley alongside the river.

Breiðdalur, the biggest of the valleys cutting into the eastern mountains, wide towards the sea but dividing into two valleys, Norðurdalur and Suðurdalur, further inland. The highway goes through the latter. The valley is surrounded by mountains 1,100-1,200m high and extremely colourful because of rhyolite which came from the Breiðdalseldstöð volcano in the tertiary period. Big gravel beds in the middle of the valley are gravel plains, seashores from when the ocean reached further inland. These are quite common in the eastern fjords and their height above the present sea level varies markedly. At the farm Þorgrímsstaðir at the head of the valley there is a small electrical power station for home use, harnessing a stream where the water falls 255m.

962 Norðurdalsvegur í Breiðdal, 12 km.

Breiðdalsá, one of the most beautiful salmon fishing rivers in Iceland.

Beljandi, ("The roarer") a waterfall in Breiðdalsá, one of most beautiful waterfalls in Breiðdalur. It is accessible by jeep or in walking distance from the road (964).

Jórvík, a perfect place for a picnic, hiking and nature exploring. Walking path from Jórvík to Norðurdalur. The land was given to the National Forest Association for cultivation, 600 ha of forest. A small ravine runs up the slope towards the mountain. The forest contains traditional Icelandic tree types such as natural aspen and birch combined with cultivated areas and remains of forest cultivation experience of the first half of the 19th century. National Forest.

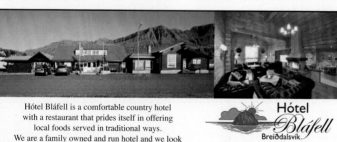

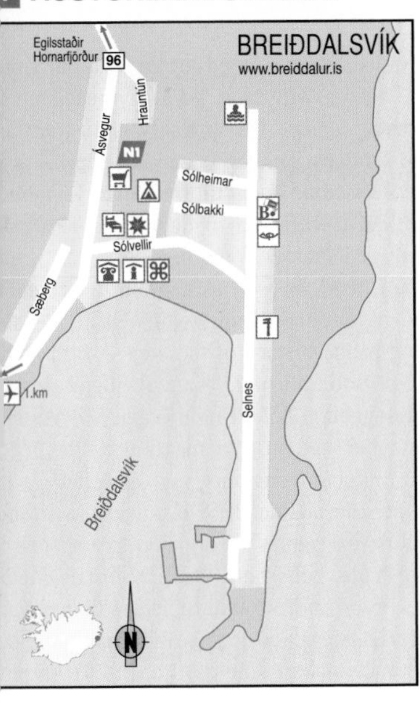

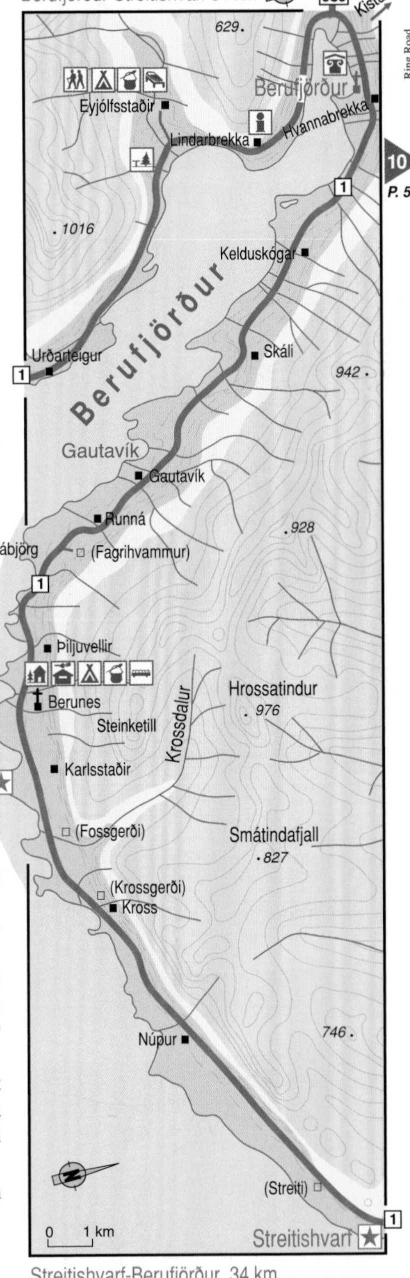

Berufjörður, a long, fairly wide fjord with many islets and reefs, and high and beautiful mountains on both sides, the highest being Búlandstindur to the south. Many interesting peaks and pinnacles, particularly around the head of the fjord. Very little flat land, especially on the south side. Rhyolite is common in the mountains and ignimbrite is found on the Berufjarðarströnd shore.

Berufjörður, a farm, church and parsonage until 1906. The birthplace of Professor Eiríkur Magnússon (1833-1913), librarian in Cambridge. There is a museum Nönnusafn. From Berufjörður an old trail, now improved for jeeps, goes across Öxi to Skriðdalur. When the Algerian pirates attacked the Westman Islands in 1627 they also attacked many places on the eastern fjords, among others Berufjörður where they burned the farm, killed many of the animals and took whatever valuables they could get their hands on.

Kistufell, (1,111 m) the highest mountain in this area, rising gradually up from Öxi but with steep rocky faces on the other sides.

939 Öxi to Skriðdalur, see p.105.

Berufjarðarskarð, (700 m) a mountain pass and trail between the head of Berufjörður and Breiðdalur, formerly frequently travelled, steep at both ends but not too difficult.

Skáli, a farm of the original settlement. The home of the ghost Skála-Brandur, well-known from the folk tales of Sigfús Sigfússon.

Gautavík, a farm and trading post until the 17th century, at that time one of the main harbours in eastern Iceland. The landing place of the missionary Þangbrandur when he came to convert Iceland in the 11th century. Old ruins still to be seen. A protected site.

Berunes, a church and a substantial farm, often the seat of district judges. Local place names indicate official gatherings. There is a lighthouse on Gíslatangi point, as many islets and skerries in the fjord make navigation quite dangerous.

Blábjörg, blue green cliff on the shore, a short distance from the farm Fagrihvammur, formed in a massive volcanic eruption.

Djúpivogur-Berufjörður 23 km

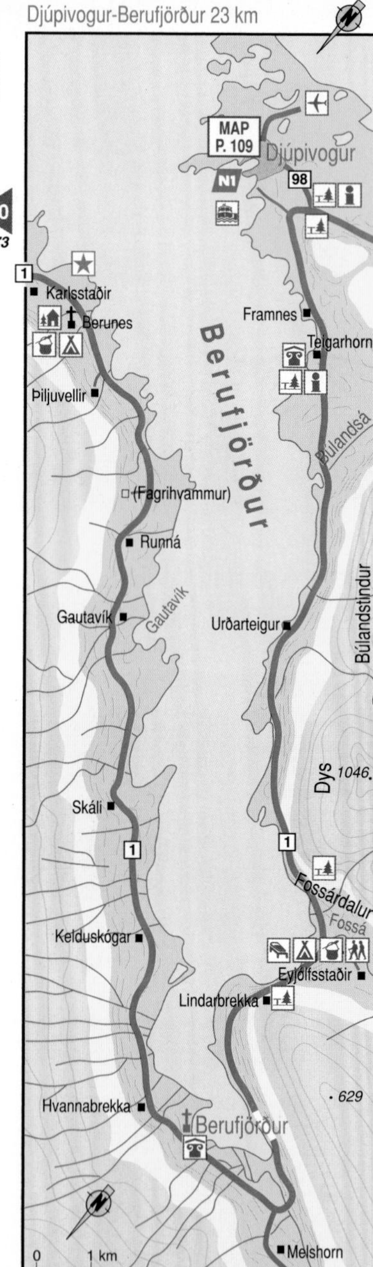

Berufjörður-Djúpivogur 23 km

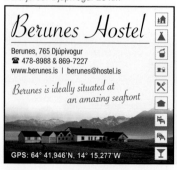

98 **Djúpavogsvegur,** 2,5 km.

Djúpivogur, (pop. 348) a town situated at the mouth of Berufjörður fjord on the south coast. There is a hotel, swimming pool, gymnasium, an elementary school and the district doctor. The primary industries are fishing, fish processing, trade and services. Trading began in Djúpivogur in the 17th century and an old store, Langabúð, can still be found. Langabúð was built by Danish merchants and is believed to date from 1790. An exhibition about the life and work of Ríkarður Jónsson, (1888-1977), tree carver and sculptor, may be found there, as well as a room dedicated to Eysteinn Jónsson (1906-93) and his wife Sólveig Eyjólfsdóttir. The top floor has various artefacts relating to the history of the area. A bird and hand craft collection is in a house next to Langabúð. A map with 52 marked walking trails can be bought in Langabúð, Hótel Framtíð and Við Voginn. Djúpivogur is rich of local handcraft and just to mention a few Jón in Bergholti is a local craftsman, making souvenirs and jewellery with Icelandic stones and wood under the name JFS Handverk. Arfleifð, heritage, from Iceland design is a new designer's workshop that opened in 2010. A young designer making bags, belts and clothes from Icelandic materials and skins such as cod, salmon, redfish and the Icelandic reindeer. Guests can monitor the production process and receive information about the complete procedure process, materials and the design. In 2010 a new mineral stone museum opened in the village, Steinasafn Auðuns. Guests can view variety of mineral stones from the area, get to know their history as well as study about the stage of processing. In the local souvenir shop, Bakkabúð, guests can view variety of souvenirs from the area. Don't miss the outdoor sculpture, Eggin í Gleðivík, by the world famous Icelandic artist Sigurður Guðmundsson, consisting of 34 eggs. The artwork is on the coast, about 1 km from the centre of the village, in a convenient walking distance. Djúpivogur and its environs are ideal for bird watching, as bird life in the region is highly diverse. The Djúpavogur forestry effort is one of the area's delights.

Teigarhorn, a farm about 5 km from Djúpivogur. Timber house built in 1880-82. A photographic studio was operated there around 1900. In the keeping of the National Museum since 1992. Zeolites found there are said to be the most beautiful and varied anywhere in the world. A protected natural feature.

Búlandstindur, (1,068 m) one of the highest and most majestic mountains in the east of Iceland. In continuation west of Búlandstindur is **Goðaborg** ("Crag of the gods"), where it is said the idols of the heathen gods were carried up and thrown off the cliffs when Iceland converted to Christianity in the year 1000.

Urðarteigur, a farm.

Fossárdalur, a valley. Fossá waterfall falls from a high cliff by Fossárvík. The river runs from **Líkárvatn** ("Lake of the dead"). It is said that it got its name when two men died when they went fishing there.

939 **Axarvegur,** 20 km across Öxi between Berufjörður and Skriðdalur. See p. 105.

Beruhóll, a small hill below the farm of Berufjörður, said to be the burial mound of Bera who lived there with her husband Sóti. The story goes that once when Bera and Sóti were returning with a group of people from a visit to Breiðdalur they ran into bad weather on the mountain and lost their way. All of them died at **Mannabeinahjalli** exept Sóti who walked over a cliff on the mountain in Sótabotn where he was buried. And Bera who kept going, letting her horse and dog find the way, but didn´t notice where she was until the horse went galloping into the stable so she was knocked out of the saddle and broke her neck.

Djúpivogur

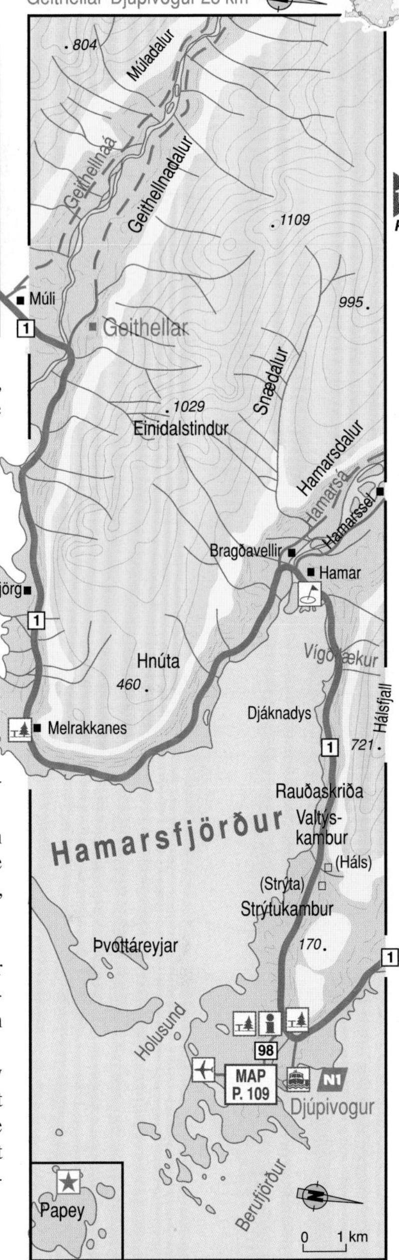

10 P. 573

Bragðavellir, a farm. In 1952 two ancient Roman coins were found there, which might indicate that Roman seafarers visited Iceland long before the settlement.

Hamar, once the site of a prayer house. A "sibyl's grave" mound in the home field.

Hamarsá, among the longest and biggest rivers of the eastern mountains, getting some glacial colour from the glacier Þrándarjökull.

Hamarsdalur, a long valley with birch bushes. The glacier **Þrándarjökull** (1,248 m) near the head of the valley.

Vígðilækur, a spring 2–3 km north of Hamar. Consecrated by Bishop Guðmundur the Good around the year 1200.

Djáknadys, ("Deacon's cairn") a heap of rocks by the road on the north side of Hamarsfjörður, between the farms Strýta and Hamar. According to folktales the priest of Háls and deacon of Hamar quarrelled there and killed each other. All travellers passing there for the first time were to throw three stones in the heap in order to prevent mishaps during the trip. The cairn is a protected site.

Valtýskambur, a cliff east of Rauðuskriður. The cliff got its name when a menn called Valtýr saved his live after he had committed a crime. He gave himself by standing on his head on the cliff during a mess at Háls, after that he went free.

Háls, an abandoned farm, formerly a church and parsonage until 1816.

Strýta, a farm where two famous artists were born: the sculptor Ríkarður Jónsson (1888-1977) and his brother, the painter Finnur Jónsson (1892-1993). A rock in the home field is believed to be a church of the "hidden people".

Papey, a large island opposite Búland and Hamarsfjörður, surrounded by islets. Formerly a substantial farm but now deserted. The name indicates that Irish monks lived there before the settlement. A popular tourist attraction, church and lighthouse.

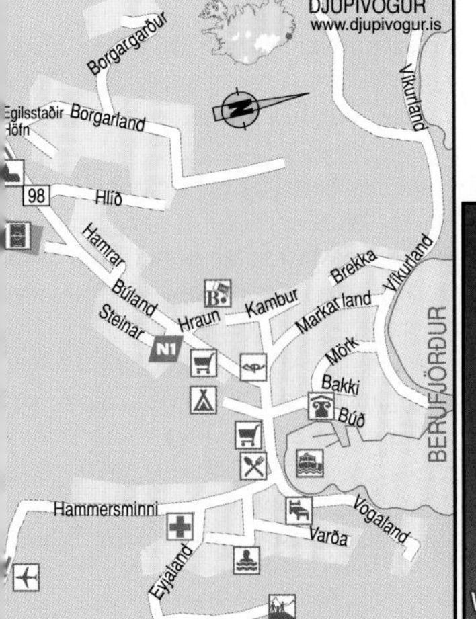

Geithellar-Djúpivogur 28 km

Ring Road
10
P. 573

Hvalnesskriður and **Þvottárskriður** lie between **Lón** and **Álftafjörða ur**. The road was moved there from **Lónsheiði**.

Lónsheiði, (389 m) the mountain track and road between Álftafjörðu and Lón, 18 km long. A rock, Sýslusteinn, marks the boundary of th counties Suður-Múlasýsla and Austur-Skaftafellssýsla. This road is n longer in use.

Þvottá, ("Ablution River") a farm and the home of Síðu-Hallur in Sag times after he moved from Hof. The 10th century Norwegian priest an missionary Þangbrandur stayed there one winter, converted Síðu-Hallu and his folk to Christianity and baptized them in the river, hence its name Many place-names connected with him, such as Þangbrandsbrunnur, well still in use, and Þangbrandstóft, protected ruins. A monument in th memory of Síðu-Hallur was unveiled in 1999; it is located close to th highway. A church until 1754 and a parsonage a little longer. The birth place of Jón Bjarnason (1845-1914), a clergyman and leader among thos Icelanders who emigrated to Canada.

Starmýri, ("Sedge marsh") a farm north of Lónsheiði, a chapel in earl times. The name is said to be from Stari the settler, but more likely it i derived from an extensive sedge-grown meadow.

Þangbrandsbryggja, a cliff 50 m above the road, 2–3km from Starmýr Named after the priest Þangbrandur a missonary who came to Iceland i the year 997.

Hof, a farm and a place of settlement, for a while the home of Síðu Hallur, a chieftain of the 10th century. His son, Þiðrandur was killed i the field at Hof, now called **Þiðrandalág**. A church and parsonage unt 1905. Birthplace of the brothers Eysteinn Jónsson (1906-93), member c parliament, minister of state and chairman of the Progressive Party, an the Rev. Jakob Jónsson (1904-89), well-known cleric and author.

Hof in Álftafjörður 1902. Goðaborg to the left.

Hofsdalur, a valley off southern Álftafjörður, with a side-valley Flugu staðadalur, mostly uninhabited. Through it runs the glacial river Hofsá which comes from **Hofsjökull** and other smaller glaciers. Birch bushes especially in Tunga between the valleys.

Geithellnadalur, a long and narrow valley between high mountains. Th river Geithellnaá comes from the glacier Þrándarjökull. It once had man farms, now mostly deserted. Formerly the easiest route to the valley **Víði dalur**, to the west of Hofsjökull, while it was inhabited. The rive Geithellnaá has many waterfalls and gorges.

Geithellnar, long a manor farm where the first settlers of Iceland Ingólfur Arnarson and Hjörleifur Hróðmarsson, are believed to have spen the winter when they visited Iceland the first time. There is a "sibyl' grave" mound in the home field.

Álftafjörður, the southernmost of the eastern fjords, actually a shallow and wide lagoon closed by a sand reef called **Starmýrarfjörur**, with a outlet through **Melrakkanesós**.

Djúpivogur-Geithellar 28 km

The farm Stafafell in the Lón district, 1902.

Stafafell, a manor farm, church and a parsonage until 1920. An old pulpit and altar piece are preserved in the church. A jeep track to the colourful Lónsöræfi goes south of Jökulsá, fording Skyndidalsá, and over Kjarrdalsheiði moor to **Illikambur**. From there on a selection of hiking tours can be made, for example to Sauðhamarstindur (1,319 m) and to the eastern section of Vatnajökull, or across Jökulsá by a footbridge and across Kollumúli to the valley Víðidalur, populated in the 19th century, or to the impressive **Tröllakrókar** with wind-eroded needles and pinnacles. This whole area, known as **Lónsöræfi** ("The lón (lagoon) wilderness"), is particularly attractive and varied walking country, giving fairly easy access to the eastern peaks of the Vatnajökull glacier, e.g. Grendill. Hiking tours of various lengths are organized from Stafafell.

Jökulgilstindur, (1313 m) the highest mountain in the area. A considerable glacier on the north side of the mountain with an outlet through the Jökulgil canyon to the valley Flugustaðadalur in the district of Álftafjörður. Very interesting country for mountain lovers.

Bær, a farm near the sea, in settlement times the home of Úlfljótur, the first lawspeaker, to whom a monument was set up 1985.

Svínhólar, a farm near the road to the south of Lónsheiði. Metal ores (e.g. copper) have been found there. View dial.

Lón, the easternmost district of Austur-Skaftafellssýsla, a wide area between the two capes, Eystrahorn and Vesturhorn. Two long sand-reefs enclose the two lagoons Lón, whose outlet is Bæjarós, and Papafjörður, with its outlet through Papós. Majestic mountains all around the district, which is rather barren and thinly populated.

Hvalnes, the easternmost farm, now abandoned, in the district of Lón, impressively situated under the rock-walls of **Eystra-Horn**, also called Hvalneshorn. These mountains are batholites mostly made of gabbro and granophyre, and very interesting from the geological point of view. Hvalneskrókur formerly a point place for fishermen. Lighthouse. Turf houses were built there for the film *Paradísarheimt* based on a novel by Halldór Laxness.

F980 **Kollumúlavegur,** p. 496

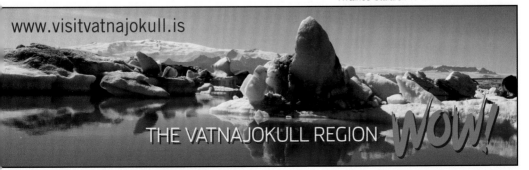

Stafafell-Hvalnes 17 km

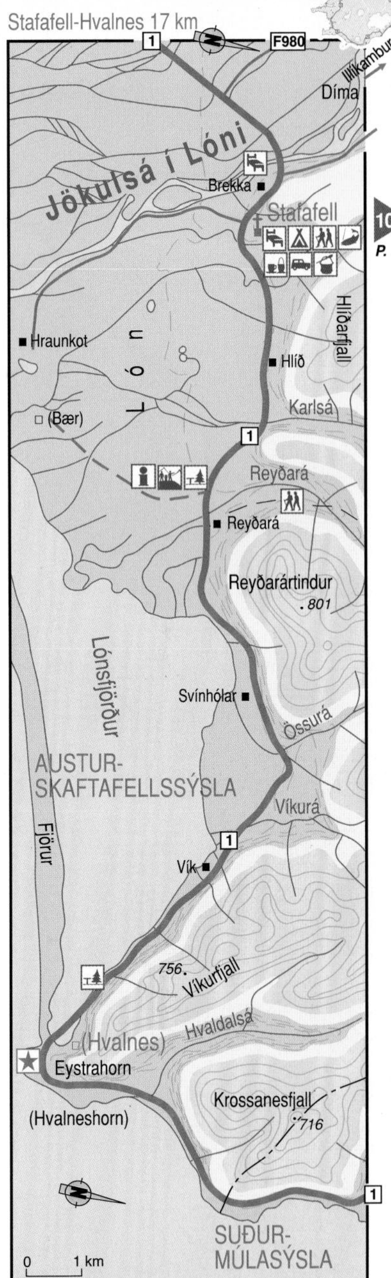

Hvalnes-Stafafell 17 km

Ring Road
10
P. 573

Ring Road
12 P. 575
10 P. 573

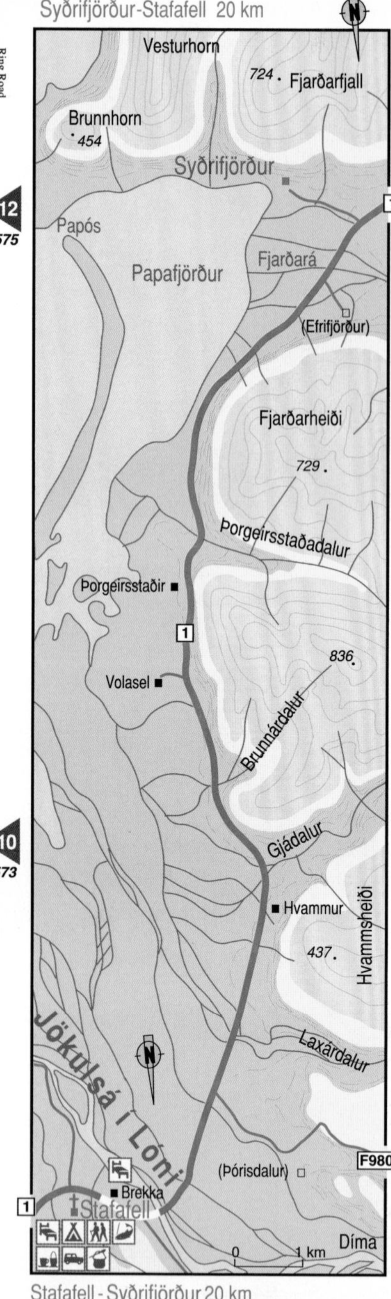

Vesturhorn, (454 m) the mountain jutting out between Lón and Hornafjörður, a bat ho lite made of gabbro, with high cliffs and steep screes Brunnhorn (683 m) a separate peak near Papós to the east of Vesturhorn.

Papós, the outlet from Papafjörður in the land of Syðri-Fjörður. Formerly a fishing station and a trading place 1860-97. There was a boarding school there from 1898 to 1899. South of the ruins of this village are older ruins, Papatættur, said to be the remains of the buildings of Irish hermits from before the settlement.

Syðrifjörður, the sunrise can´t be seen there from September 29th till early march.

Endalausidalur, ("Endless valley") a narrow, uninhabited valley between Laxárdalur and Efri-Fjörður, open at both ends with rivers flowing in both directions. Within this valley are two others **Loklausidalur** and **Slaufrudalur**. There is a big batholite (10 km^2) made of gabbro at Slaufrudalur. There is Bleikitindur, 615m.

Jökulsá í Lóni, a big river coming from the eastern side of Vatnajökull. A major tributary is Skyndidalsá, coming from the glacier Lambatungujökull. Formerly difficult to ford, now bridged by one of the longer bridges of Iceland (247m). **Díma,** a cliff skerry in the river bed a little above the road, is a protected natural feature.

Þórisdalur, a farm in the district of Lón. Once the home of Þórður Þorkelsson Vídalín (1661-1742) a rector at Skálholt, clergyman, doctor, natuarlist etc. He wrote an important work on the nature of glaciers which was published in 1754 in German in the *Hamburgisches Magazin*, translated into Icelandic and published in 1965. The story goes that Þórður was so cunning that he could force ghosts to return to those who sent them, and so skilled that from Þórisdalur he could detect a ghost coming up through Almannaskarð on its way to Stafafell. He took his horse, arrived at Stafafell ahead of the ghost and turned it back. Yet Þórður was so good and kind that he would not even hurt a fly with his magic. From Þórisdalur the jeep-track goes across the river Skyndidalsá and up over Kjarrdalsheiði moor to Illikambur, this route being preferable to that starting from Stafafell because of Jökulsá.

An old sheep fold in Þórisdalur in the Lón district.

F980 **Kollumúlavegur,** p. 496

Hornafjörður, a big lagoon with an outlet through Hornafjarðarós. Very deep, the current is so strong that it was a big hindrance to navigation until the advent of the motorboat. The current also carries sand and mud, building up deposits on navigation routes, so a great deal of work is necessary to ensure that vessels can come in and out at all times.

99 Hafnarvegur, 5,36 km.

Höfn, (pop. 1,690) a town situated on the coast of Hornafjörður fjord, belonged to the municipality of Nesjahreppur until the town became its own municipality with some 300 inhabitants in 1946. It was granted town status on December 31st 1988. The municipality merged with Nesjahreppur and Mýrahreppur in 1994, and four years later all the district municipalities merged into a single Municipality of Hornafjörður. Höfn is situated by the mouth of Hornafjörður fjord and major structures have been erected to safeguard the passing of ships. The primary industries are fishing, tourism, trade and manufacturing. The town has a district commissioner's office, a health care centre, the site of the Hornafjörður Cultural Centre, a university centre, a new ventures centre and the Austur Skaftafellssýsla Upper Secondary School, a swimming pool and a nature reserve at Ósland. There is also a folk museum and a tourist information desk by the harbour. The majority of migrating birds to Iceland first reach land in the Hornafjörður region; hence a bird research centre has been set up at Höfn. Trade was moved from Papós to Höfn in 1897. At the Höfn harbour there is a memorial to the arrival of first settler Ingólfur Arnarson to Iceland, a gift from Norwegian seafarers in 1997.

Mígandisfoss, a small beautifull waterfall. It is possible to walk on a ledge behind it.

Nes, the easternmost district of the Hornafjörður area, reaching from Hornafjörður and the river Hornafjarðarfljót on the west side to Skarðsfjörður on the east. Quite fertile and good farming country, being mostly flat land with small hills and wet areas in between. The coastline is particularly interesting with its innumerable inlets, small peninsulas and islets.

Skarðsfjörður, a wide and shallow lagoon reaching in to Almannaskarð.

Horn, formerly a church, point place for fishermen and seal hunters. A former NATO radar station on the nearby **Stokksnes** peninsula.

Almannaskarð, (153 m) a narrow mountain pass between Hornafjörður and Lón. Steep scree mountains on both sides, **Skarðstindur** (488 m) on the north, **Hádegistindur** ("Midday peak") (724 m) and **Klifatindur** (890 m) on the south. There is a fine view to the west from Almannaskarð.

99 Hafnarvegur-Syðrifjörður 16 km

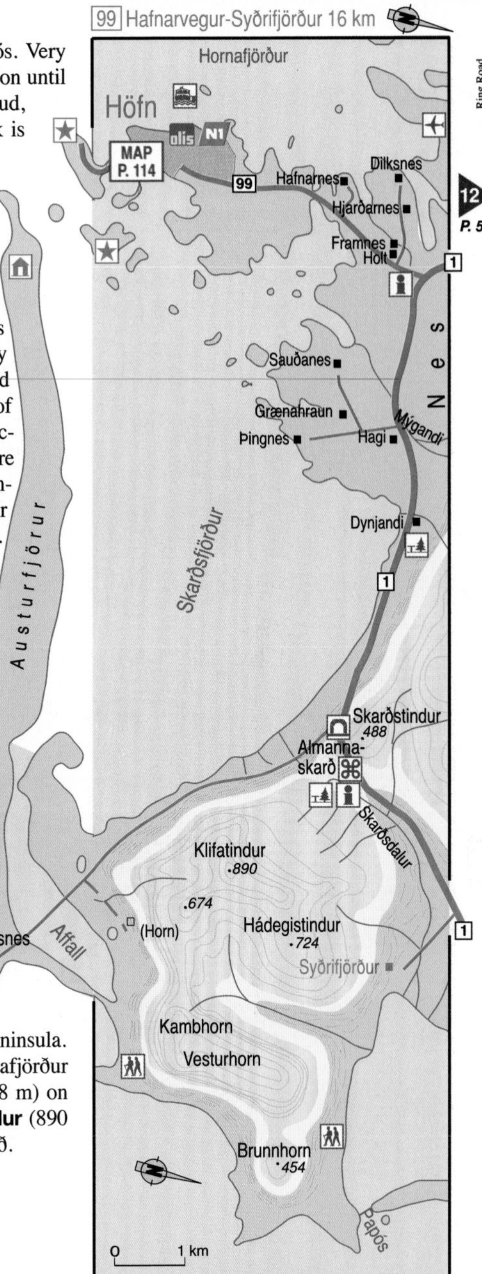

12 P. 575

Syðrifjörður- 99 Hafnarvegur 16 km

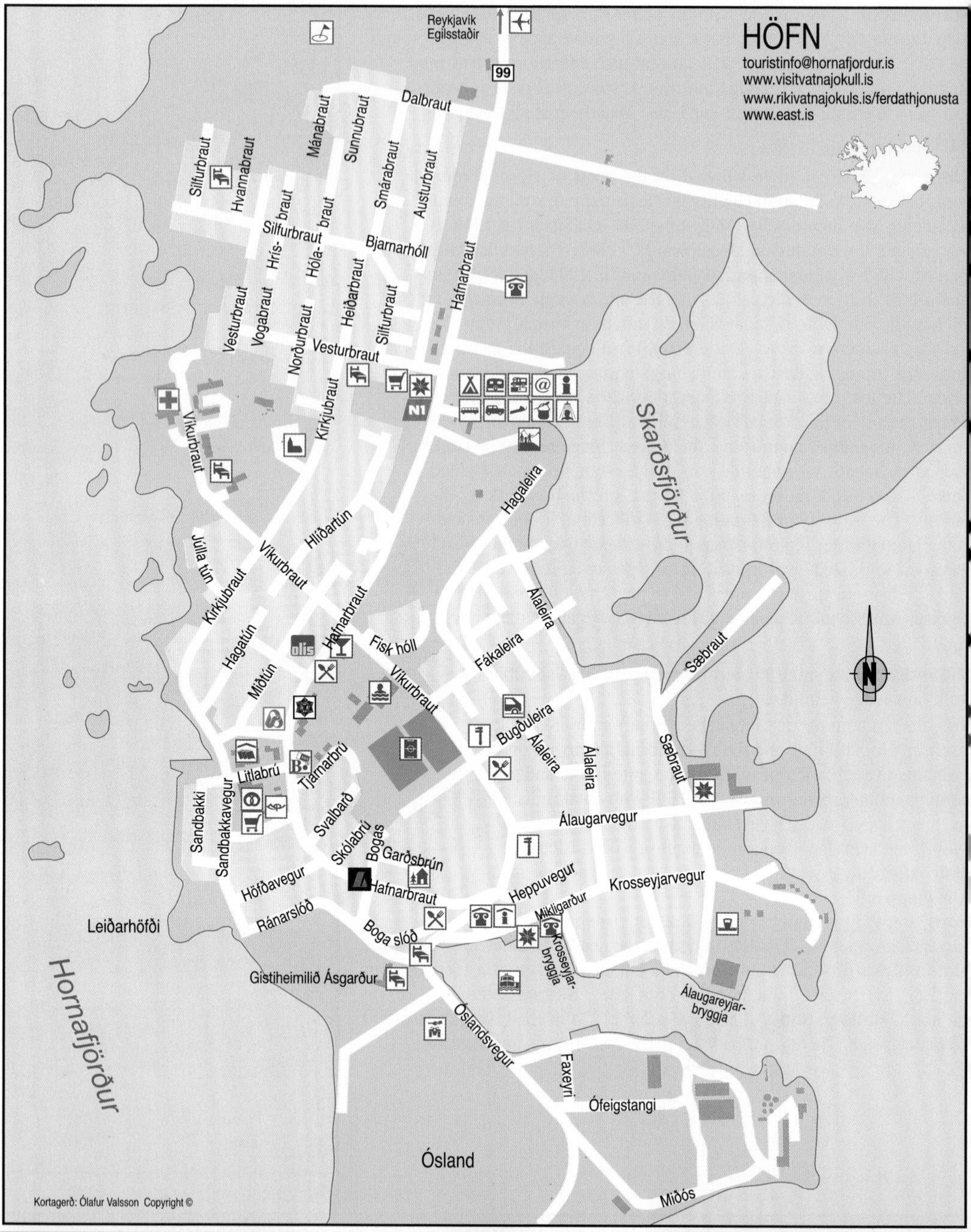

HÖFN

touristinfo@hornafjordur.is
www.visitvatnajokull.is
www.rikivatnajokuls.is/ferdathjonusta
www.east.is

Reykjavík
Egilsstaðir
99

Dalbraut, Mánabraut, Sunnubraut, Smárabraut, Austurbraut, Silfurbraut, Hvannabraut, Hrís-braut, Hóla-braut, Bjarnarhóll, Hafnarbraut, Vesturbraut, Vogabraut, Norðurbraut, Heiðarbraut, Kirkjubraut, Víkurbraut, Hlíðartún, Júlla tún, Hagatún, Miðtún, Fisk hóll, Hagaleira, Álaleira, Fákaleira, Bugðuleira, Sæbraut, Litlabrú, Tjarnarbrú, Sandbakki, Sandbakkavegur, Svalbarð, Skólabrú, Bogas, Garðsbrún, Höfðavegur, Ránarslóð, Boga slóð, Heppuvegur, Krosseyjarvegur, Álaugarvegur, Mikligarður, Krosseyjar-bryggja, Álaugareyjar-bryggja, Óslandsvegur, Faxeyri, Ófeigstangi, Miðós

Skarðsfjörður
Hornafjörður
Leiðarhöfði
Gistiheimilið Ásgarður
Ósland

Kortagerð: Ólafur Valsson Copyright ©

Golf

WELCOME TO HORNAFJÖRÐUR

Glacier hiking

Höfn swimming pool.

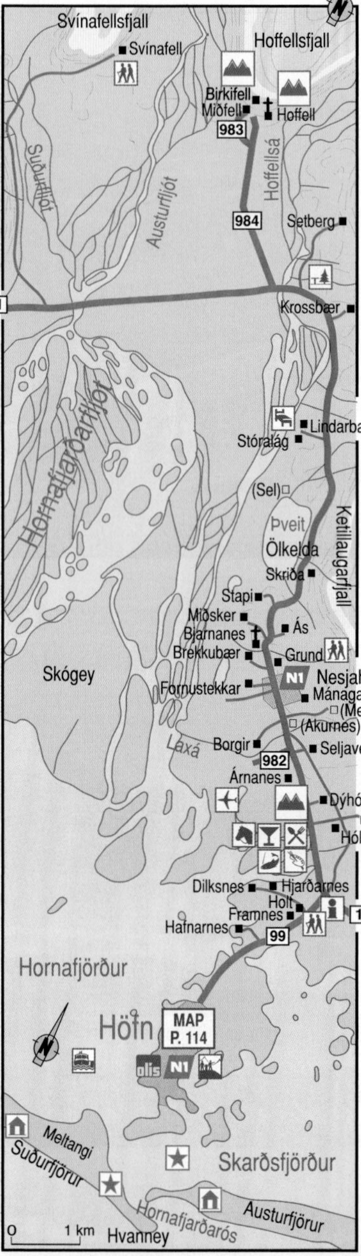

Ring Road

12 P. 575

Skógey, revegetation and soil conservation area.

983 Miðfellsvegur, 1,1 km. **984 Hoffellsvegur,** 3,5 km.

Hoffell, a farm since the time of the settlement, beautifully situated amidst mountains, glaciers, rivers and gravel beds. **Goðaborg** ("Crag of the gods") (1,425 m), the highest point on the mountain range reaching into the glacier, was once believed to be a house built by gods or spirits even though it looked like a rock. A shepherd is said to have strayed there when looking for sheep and found a big, grey, ferocious-looking bull standing in a huge open doorway. It seemed to the shepherd that he was wading through leaves, but he did not pay any attention to this until he came down to Setbergsheiði moor where his shoe came off and he found that the leaves that fell out of it were in fact gold coins. It is said that Judge Jón Helgason of Hoffell fetched gold from **Goðaborg** every year. A vein of Iceland spar is in the land of Hoffell and was worked for a while. Jasper, opal, marble and other stones are also found.

Ketillaugarfjall, (668 m) a colourful batholite mountain. According to legend, a woman named Ketillaug disappeared into the mountain carrying a kettle full of gold. Walking route up the mountain, beautiful view.

Þveit, the largest lake in Austur-Skaftafellssýsla, thought to be haunted.

Bjarnanes, a manor farm since ancient times and a historical place, church and parsonage. In the 15th century this was the home of Teitur Gunnlaugsson the rich, a lawman responsible for the execution of the aggressive and unpopular bishop Jón Gerreksson, by having him drowned in Brúará in Árnessýsla. In the 16th century there were great disputes about the ownership of Bjarnanes, which finally was placed under the bishopric of Skálholt.

Nesjahverfi, (pop. 71) a community belonging to the township of Hornafjarðarbær, built up around the community centre Mánagarður. By the farm **Hólmur** at the top of Laxárdalur, in 1996, an old grave was discovered and excavations carried out near the ruins of a farm from the Viking age. This has given rise to theories that the site also contains the ruins of a temple or house of sacrifice; however, scholars differ in their opinions regarding this. Should the theory prove correct this would be the first time that a place of sacrifice from the Viking age is found in Iceland and indeed in the entire Nordic Region.

Laxá, a river flowing from Laxárdalur, which turns into **Endalausidalur** reaching east into the Lón district.

982 Airport Road, 0,68 km.

Árnanes, airport for Hornafjörður.

Hólar, a substantial farm, birthplace of the painter Jón Þorleifsson (1891-1961).

Dilksnes, a site of a small archaelogical find.

99 Hafnarvegur, p. 113

1 AUSTURLANDSVEGUR

kálafell, the easternmost farm in the district of Suðursveit. Birthplace of Jón iríksson (1728-87), councillor to the King of Denmark and one of the most nfluential advocates of Iceland in Denmark, hence the memorial to him by the oadside. Nearby the river **Kolgríma** comes rushing out of its narrow canyon.

kinneyjarhöfði, a skerry or low cape on the coast, the only elevated land n a long stretch. Formerly a point place for fishermen, but always difficult. kinney used to be among the bigger farms of the Mýrar district but was bandoned because of floods.

runnhóll, a church, before there were churches at Holt and inholt.

ýrar, the district between the rivers Hornafjarðarfljót and Kolríma, flat, wet, with many low rock-hills and extensive gravel-eds. The coast is characterised by long, wide sand-bars with nudflats and lagoons. Vatnajökull dominates the background vith many glaciertongues in between high and majestic mounains. Glacial rivers, counting from the east: Hólmsá, Heinaergsvötn and Kolgríma, spread all over, continually changng their courses. The streams of Heinabergsvötn, for nstance, were bridged in 1947 but the following year they hanged their course and started running into Kolgríma, so he bridge has stood on dry land ever since. The glacierongues Fláajökull and Heinabergsjökull stretch far down into he district. It is possible to drive to Fláajökull along Hólmsá.

einabergsjökull divides into two arms around the mountain afrafell, north of which there is another mountain, **Snjófjall,** vith a peculiar glacier hollow on the south side. The valley Vatnsdalur "Water (or lake) valley") on the western side of Heinabergsjökull often colects large quantities of water dammed up by the glacier, **Heinabergsvötn.** Once in a while this water forces its way out under the glacier, causing big loods in the rivers. The low mountain **Jökulfell** (150 m) in front of Fláajökull vas hidden by ice at the beginning of the century, but began to come into view round 1920.

986 Rauðabergsvegur, 4,1 km.

aukafell, 2,5 km west of the farm Rauðaberg.

ornafjarðarfljót, a big glacial river flowing mostly from Hoffellsjökull nd emptying into Hornafjörður. Very wide but shallow, dividing into two nain rivers: Austurfljót and Suðurfljót ("East and south rivers"). The bridge 225 m) built in 1961 was the second longest in the country until 1973.

Skálafell-Hornafjarðarfljót 21 km

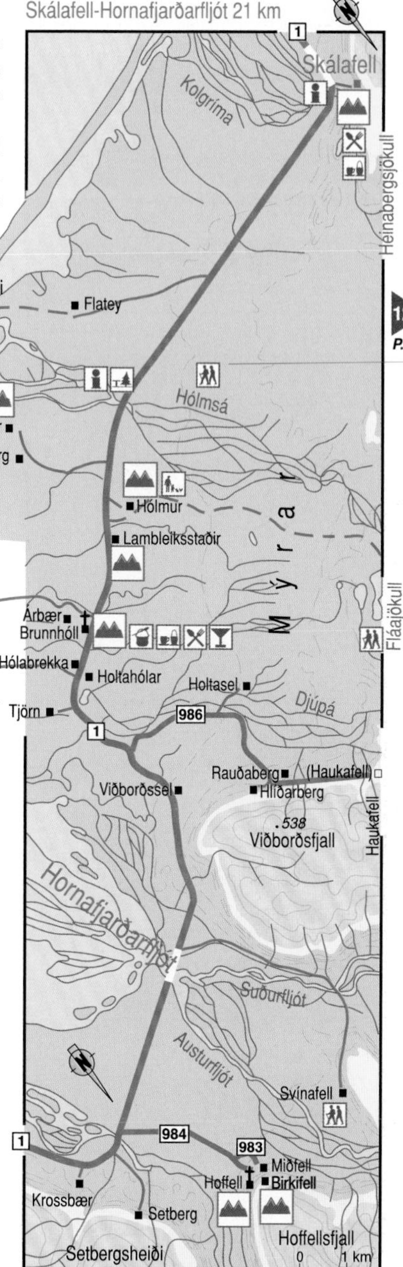

Hornafjarðarfljót-Skálafell 21 km

12 P. 575

983 **Miðfellsvegur,** p. 116   984 **Hoffellsvegur,** p. 116

12
P. 575

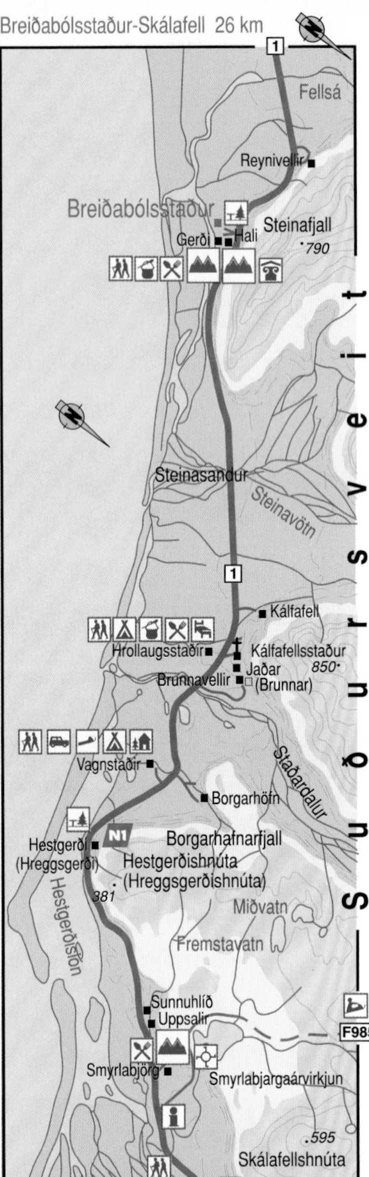

Breiðabólsstaður, a group of farms below the mountain Breiðabólsstaðarfjall, originally settled by Hrollaugur, son of Earl Rögnvaldur of the Möre district in Norway. One of the farms is **Hali**, birthplace of the author Þórbergur Þórðarson (1889-1974), there is a monument in his and his brothers honour. There is a walking path leading from the monument with 13 signs that have quotes from his books. The walk takes about an hour if all the signs are visited. There is also a museum at Hali dedicated to Þórbergur, **Þórbergssetur**. Guided tours are available.

Steinafjall, (789 m) an impressive rock-wall rising up from the flatlands.

Steinasandur, mud flats, once the bed of the various streams of the river Steinavötn which were formerly more extensive.

Kálfafellsstaður, a group of farms, a church and parsonage, community centre. It is said that an old route used to go up from Kálfafellsstaður through the valley Staðardalur and north across the Vatnajökull glacier. The birthplace of the writer Torfhildur Þ. Hólm (1845-1918), the first woman novelist in Iceland. Below the home field is a "sibyl's grave" mound and they say that any person that attends to it will have good luck.

Suðursveit, the district between the river Kolgríma and the Breiðamerkursandur sands, mostly narrow flatlands between the mountains and the sea. Very impressive mountains in the background, giving good shelter from the glacier and destructive rivers. Lagoons and sand-reefs along the sea. The three big valleys Staðardalur, Kálfafellsdalur and Steinadalur cut into the mountains. The bottom of **Kálfafellsdalur** is very steep with a glacier-tongue, **Brókarjökull** ("Breeches glacier"), dividing around the rock Brók, and hence the name. The area provides some of the most majestic mountaineering country in Iceland.

Borgarhöfn, a group of farms in the eastern section of the Suðursveit district.

Hestgerði, or Hreggsgerði, a farm by the mountain Borgarhafnarfjall where the lagoons almost reach the mountains. Fishermen sailed from the nearby **Kambstún**, but this was discontinued after a serious shipwreck around 1570 when 53 men were lost. Many local names and remains point to the activities of fishermen.

F985 Jökulvegur, to the glacier Vatnajökul, 16 km. From there are pick-ups for jeep and skidoo tours on Skálafellsjökull glacier.

Smyrlabjörg, a farm which harnessed a nearby waterfall 1969, to provide 1,200 kW. Since then the falls have disappeared, except in torrential rain.

F985 **Jökulvegur,** p. 497

.vísker, the easternmost farm in the Öræfi district, formerly very impor-ınt for travellers seeking guidance across the sands and treacherous big vers. Beautiful view and good sheep-farming country. Glaucous dog-ɔse (*Rosa dumalis*) (glitrós) found in the birch bushes nearby and owhere else in Iceland. The first ascent of Öræfajökull was made from ;vísker in 1794 by Sveinn Pálsson. Home of the so-called "Kvísker rothers" Flosi (1906–1993), Hálfdan and Sigurður Björnsson, self-taught aturalists of great erudition.

reiðamerkurfjall, (774 m) mountain on the western edge of Breiða-ıerkurjökull. In about 1700 the glaciers on both sides united in front of ıe mountain, and it remained a glacier island until 1946. Since then the laciers have retreated.

reiðamerkursandur, extensive sand area created by glaciers and gla-ial rivers. The principal breeding grounds of the Great Skua in Iceland. here used to be several farms in the western section of the sands, but ıey were destroyed by advancing glaciers in the 17th century. One of the ırms was Breiðá, home of Kári Sölmundarson of *Njáls saga*.

ökulsá á Breiðamerkursandi, the biggest river on the sands, though very hort, only about 1,500 m. Comes from a 248 m deep lake, or lagoon, **ökulsárlón**, the deepest lake in Iceland, at the foot of the glacier. There re usually icebergs floating on the lake. The river, which used to seri-usly hinder travel, was bridged 1966-67, but the bridge is now in danger ue to the encroachment of the sea. Boat trips are available.

reiðamerkurjökull, a wide glacier-tongue coming down to the Breiða-ıerkursandur sands, flat and relatively free of crevasses. It almost eached the sea in 1891-92, but has retreated considerably since then. ong moraine lines descend from Mávabyggðir and Esjufjöll, two exten-ive glacier islands or nunataks.

verártindsegg, (1,554 m) an impressive mountain ridge by the glacier.

'ell, once one of the biggest farms of the district but destroyed by a big ood in the river Veðurá in 1869.

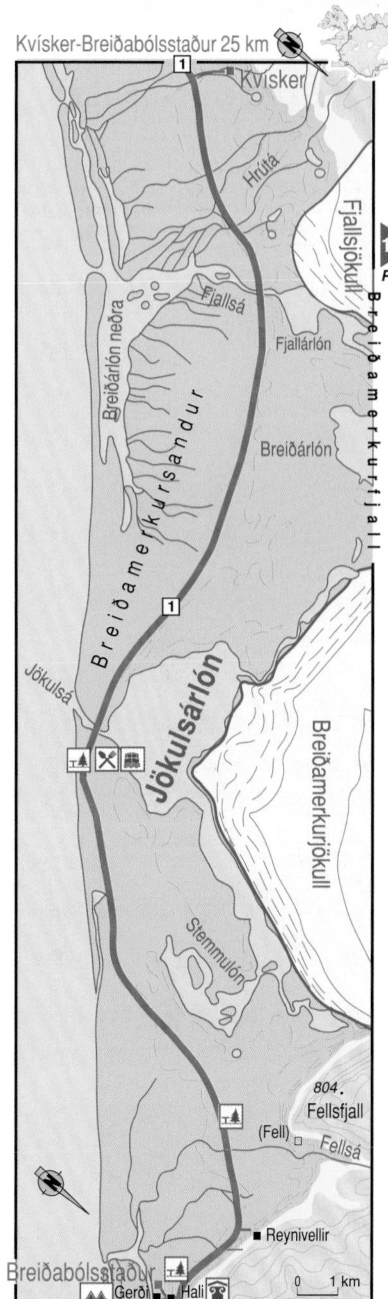

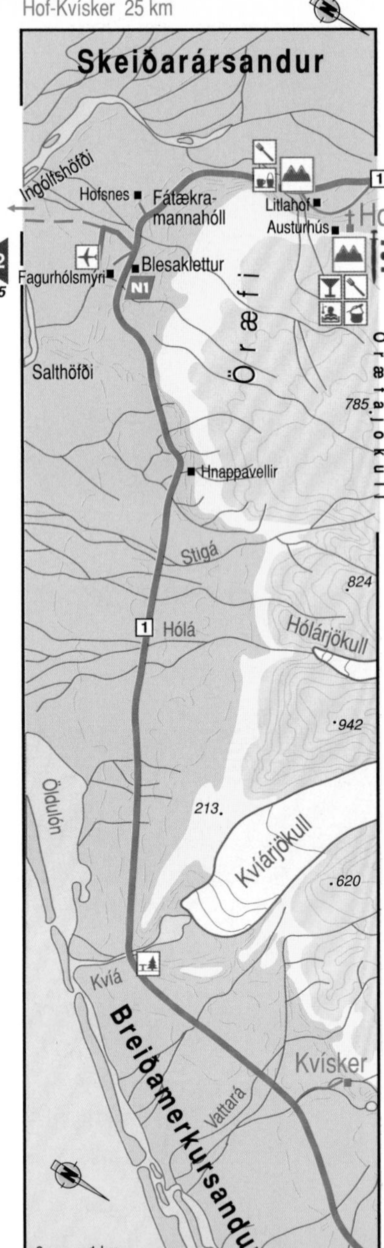

The church at Hof

Hof, a group of farms and a church of turf, built in 1883. The youngest turf church in the country. In the keeping of the National Museum since 1951. Ruins of the nearby farm **Gröf**, which was buried in ashes and pumice in the eruption of 1362, have been excavated.

Ingólfshöfði, a cape on the coast 9-10 km south of Fagurhólsmýri, 76 m high, 1,200 m long and 750 m wide, birdcliffs, a shelter and a lighthouse. Hay wagon trips to the cape for tourists. A jeep-trail goes to it across sands, mud-flats and many rivers. Formerly a point-place for fishermen though always difficult and dangerous. Named after the first settler Ingólfur Arnarson, who spent his first winter there in 874, commemorated by a monument raised there in 1974.

Fagurhólsmýri, a farm and weather station. The farm is built on formerly coastal cliffs, beautiful view.

Hnappavellir, a group of farms where the old building style of the Öræfi district has lasted longer than in other places. This is one of the most popular climbing area in the country, many routes. Glacier Guides at Skaftafell offer trips to the area for both beginners and more experienced climbers.

Öræfi, the westernmost district of Austur-Skaftafellssýsla between the sands Skeiðarársandur and Breiðamerkursandur, a semi-circle around the base of Öræfajökull. For long one of the most isolated districts of Iceland with no harbours on the coast, Vatnajökull to the north and dangerous rivers to east and west. Until 1962 mice, rats and cats were unknown in the district. Magnificent views and great variety in landscape and nature. Only seven farms or groups of farms along the 43 km road between the farms Skaftafell and Kvísker.

Öræfajökull, a great glacier-covered mountain range connected to the Vatnajökull massif. Its highest point, **Hvannadalshnúkur** (2,110 m), is also the highest point in Iceland. It is a volcano which has erupted twice in historical times, 1362 and 1727. Many farms were destroyed in these eruptions, the earlier one being more destructive. Older names were Hnappafell mountain and Hnappafellsjökull glacier. Glacier Guides at Skaftafell offer guided trips to Hvannadalshnjúkur peak with all technical equipment that is needed (crampons, harness, ice axe and ropes). The trip takes 10-15 hours going over challenging terrain.

1 AUSTURLANDSVEGUR

Skaftafell, the westernmost estate in Öræfi built high on the southern slopes of Skaftafellsheiði moor because of the destructive forces of Skeiðará. Extensive birchwoods, rich vegetation (*Saxifraga cotyledon*, *Campanula rotundifolia* etc. etc.), gullies, canyons, waterfalls, glaciers and valleys. Extensive and varied view from the view-dial at Sjónarsker. In 1967 the land of Skaftafell was purchased by the state and made into a National Park because of the great variety of natural beauty. Skaftafellsstofa is an information and education centre where visitors can find answers to their questions about the Skaftafell area, along with information about hiking trails, accommodation and nearby recreational options. Skaftafellstofa has an exhibition room where the story of fire and ice is told; the way in which volcanoes and glaciers have struggled to form the surrounding region and the effects of eruptions and glacial outburst floods on daily lives of people. Park Wardens operate in the Park, assisted by Park Rangers during the summer months. Visitors are encouraged to seek information and advice from Park staff. Hiking trips led by rangers give visitors the opportunity to get to know the magnificent Skaftafell area and find out about the history and natural phenomena of the area, in the company of a well-informed guide. The hikes follow a variety of routes, and everyone should be able to find a suitable outing. Also on offer are short trips walking on glacier, 2 and a half hour and 5 hours, that explore the peculiar landscape on the glacier tongues. The Guides educate on the nature of glaciers, as well as the geological history and human settlement in the region. More sporty orientated are Climbing tours and the ascension of Iceland's highest peak Hvannadalshnjúkur 2110 m. Glacier equipment is provided for all tours.

See information on Vatnajökull National Park on p. 122.

Sel, a small turf farmhouse of the southern type built in 1912. The baðstofa (communal living space) is built over the cowshed for warmth. Nearby barns are of ancient type of construction. In the keeping of the National Museum since 1972.

998 Skaftafellsvegur, 1,86 km.

Svínafell, a manor farm since early days and once one of the most important farms in the eastern region of Iceland. The home of Flosi Þórðarson well known from *Njáls saga* and of his family, known as Svínfellingar, who played an important role in the events of the 12th and 13th century. Beautiful surroundings, good weather, birch bushes and the longest tongue of the glacier Svínafellsjökull almost in the home field. Swimming pool **Flosalaug**.

Falljökull, a glacier tongue, steep and fissured, descending like a waterfall from the mountain.

Sandfell, an abandoned farm, a church until 1914 and a parsonage until 1931, one of the oldest farms in the Öræfi district. The easiest and most-travelled route to Öræfajökull and Hvannadalshnjúkur starts from Sandfell. The traveller goes first up Sandfellsheiði moor where it is possible to ascend to about 1,300 m before stepping onto the glacier, where there are 400-500 m of rather steep glacier, usually with many big crevasses, to be covered before reaching the 4 km wide plateau to the north of the mountain Rótarfjallshnjúkur (1,848 m). This has to be crossed to get to the 2,110 m high Hvannadalshnjúkur, rising about 200 m from the northwest edge of the plateau. This final peak is usually icy and greatly fissured. The whole climb is quite strenuous and takes 15-20 hours. Standard glacier-climbing techniques should be applied. Ice-axes, crampons and lines are essential, and inexperienced people must have guides.

Skaftafell-Hof 18 km

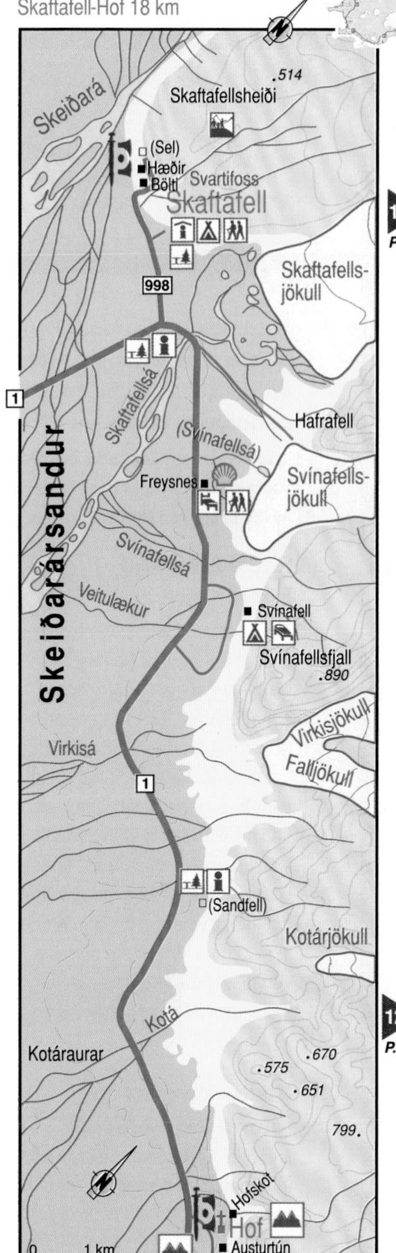

Hof-Skaftafell 18 km 1

Vatnajökull National Park, established in 2008, takes in not only all of Vatnajökull glacier but extensive surrounding areas. These include the former national parks at Skaftafell in the southwest and Jökulsárgljúfur to the north, so that today's national park covers 13% of Iceland.

In general, national parks are protected areas considered unique for their nature or cultural heritage. Vatnajökull National Park is above all unique through the great variety of landscape features created by the combined forces of rivers, glacial ice, and volcanic and geothermal activity.

Recreation and interpretive activities

Travellers can enjoy and experience the nature of Vatnajökull National Park in various ways, either on their own or through park ranger programs. Skaftafell and Jökulsárgljúfur offer large camp sites and numerous hiking trails, and provide along with Skriðuklaustur various services for guests. Less service is to be found in the highlands where accommodation in mountain huts is the primary service. There are however excellent hiking opportunities nearby all of these huts.

Visitor centres and information offices

National park visitor centres provide information and services for the park and its immediate environs. Through exhibits and lectures, such centres also provide visitors with education on nature, culture and history. Vatnajökull National Park has three visitor centres:

Skaftafell Visitor Centre
- open all year

Snæfellsstofa Visitor Centre
- open May 1 – Sept. 30

Ásbyrgi Visitor Centre
- open May 1 – Sept. 30

A visitor and information office is located at Gamlabúð in Höfn. Other information offices are in Kirkjubæjarklaustur and at the guesthouses in Hoffell, Hólmur and Skálafell, all of which are located in southeast Iceland.

Highland ranger stations

During the summer, national park rangers conduct patrols and educational services in the park's highland areas. Station opening times vary from area to area, with the first rangers arriving around the days when their roads are opened, soon after the middle of June, and the last rangers leaving at the end of September. The highland ranger stations are located in Drekagil by Askja, Kverkfjöll, Hvannalindir, Snæfell, Lónsöræfi, Lakagígar, Eldgjá and Nýidalur.

Travelling in the highlands

There are number of roads within the highlands of Vatnajökull National Park that provide access to the national park's primary attractions. These roads are of various qualities and some of them only passable for well-equipped 4x4 vehicles. Travellers are encouraged to seek information about routes prior to their travels. A brochure including a road map for Vatnajökull National Park is available in visitor centres, information centres and from park rangers. The map shows all roads within the national park that are open for public use. The map also indicates quality of roads. Those unfamiliar with travelling in the highlands of Iceland are also encouraged to seek information about weather outlook, road conditions and fords, since circumstances in the highlands can change swiftly and without notice.

Further information about Vatnajökull National Park, event schedule, campsites, hiking routes, recreation and activities are available on www.vjp.is, in visitor centres, information offices and from park rangers.

WELCOME TO VATNAJÖKULL NATIONAL PARK!

Laki - West

Morsárdalur og Svínafellsjökull – South

Dettifoss – North

Snæfellsstofa Visitor Centre – East

Skaftafell Visitor Centre – South

Photos: ©Guðmundur Ögmundsson

Further information about Vatnajökull National Park, event schedule, campsites, hiking routes, recreation and activities are available on www.vjp.is, in visitor centres, information offices and from park rangers.

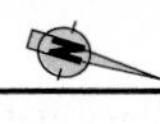

Ring Road

11 P. 574

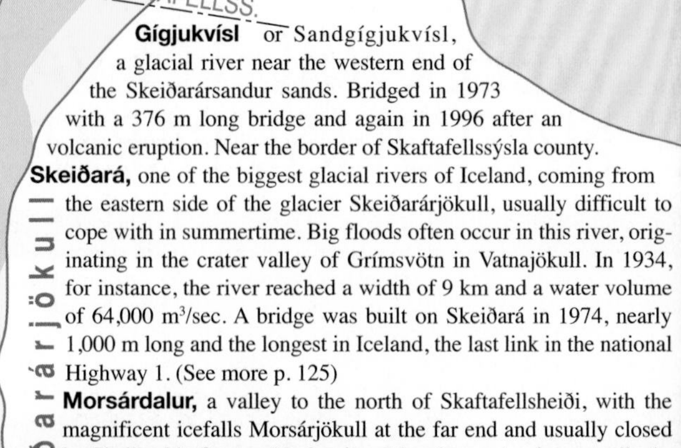

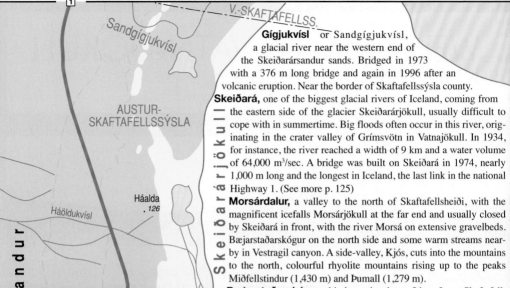

Gígjukvísl or Sandgígjukvísl, a glacial river near the western end of the Skeiðarársandur sands. Bridged in 1973 with a 376 m long bridge and again in 1996 after an volcanic eruption. Near the border of Skaftafellssýsla county.

Skeiðará, one of the biggest glacial rivers of Iceland, coming from the eastern side of the glacier Skeiðarárjökull, usually difficult to cope with in summertime. Big floods often occur in this river, originating in the crater valley of Grímsvötn in Vatnajökull. In 1934, for instance, the river reached a width of 9 km and a water volume of 64,000 m^3/sec. A bridge was built on Skeiðará in 1974, nearly 1,000 m long and the longest in Iceland, the last link in the national Highway 1. (See more p. 125)

Morsárdalur, a valley to the north of Skaftafellsheiði, with the magnificent icefalls Morsárjökull at the far end and usually closed by Skeiðará in front, with the river Morsá on extensive gravelbeds. Bæjarstaðarskógur on the north side and some warm streams nearby in Vestragil canyon. A side-valley, Kjós, cuts into the mountains to the north, colourful rhyolite mountains rising up to the peaks Miðfellstindur (1,430 m) and Þumall (1,279 m).

Bæjarstaðarskógur, birchwoods about 5 km from Skaftafell, with straight-trunked trees up to 12 m in height. Birch trees from Bæjarstaðarskógur stock are considered the best in Iceland. The 22 hectare wood has been protected since 1935, in the care of the Forestry Service. Geothermal heat. Glacier Guides, based in Skaftafell, offer guided tours in the woods.

998 Skaftafellsvegur, 1,86 km.

álfafell, farm, church. Parsonage until 1880. Served by the Rev. Páll álsson (1836-90), the first Icelander to teach the deaf. He first started aching in 1867, publishing two textbooks for the deaf the same year, *ible Stories* and *Luther's Theology*. It was almost 130 years before a new xtbook for the deaf was published in 1995.

júpá, ("Deep river") a sizeable glacial river. A short walk along the astern bank north of the bridge over the main road takes one to where e waterfall Gufufoss ("Steam falls") tumbles over the edge of a deep nd impressive canyon. Canyon and waterfall are spectacular.

úpsstaður, the first farm west of Skeiðarársandur. A restored chapel om around 1850 and farmhouses from around 1900 in the care of the ational Museum. It was extremely difficult to make one's way across e sands before the rivers were bridged, horseback being the only feasi-le mode of travel. The most skilled and experienced travellers in the area ere known, respectfully, as "water men" and the best horses as "water orses". Núpsstaðir was the home of the last such water man, the well-nown Hannes Jónsson (1880-1968) who carried the post between Síða nd Hornafjörður.

ómagnúpur, (668 m) a headland which once rose from the sea, now sing from the sands. One of Iceland's highest perpendicular inland cliffs. 1 July 1789 a large part of the south-western side of the cliff collapsed nd evidence of this may be seen in the rock to this day. An avalanche fell n the east side of Lómagnúpur, west of Hellisflái and to the east of óragil, in June 1998. This avalanche was on a much smaller scale then e one in 1789.

úpsvötn, a wide and many-streamed glacial river on the western side of keiðarársandur, joined by the river **Súla** some distance upstream. This ver often rises considerably, causing big floods when the lake **irænalón** by the edge of Skeiðarárjökull forces its way out under the lacier. The whole valley between Lómagnúpur and Skeiðarársandur is ery interesting for the tourist but difficult to reach because of the rivers. he rivers Núpsá and Hvítá join in two falls into a beautiful canyon and om then on they are called Núpsvötn. It is possible to make one's way long the eastern side of the canyon with the help of an iron chain which as been bolted to the rock. A fine day's hike from the valley across **ystrafjall** to **Núpsstaðarskógar** and Eggjar to Grænalón or to the npressive Súlutindar by the western edge of Skeiðarárjökull.

keiðarársandur, a vast sand desert about 20 by 30 km between the dis-icts Fljótshverfi in the west and Öræfi in the east. It is said that there were nce many farms in this area, but these were destroyed by tremendous oods from Grímsvötn in Vatnajökull breaking their way under the glacier. he largest of these Skeiðarárhlaup, as the floods are called, have been ompared with the Amazon river. In 1974 bridges were built across the riv-rs Núpsvötn, Sandgígjukvísl and Skeiðará thus completing the main high-ay round Iceland. Considerable volcanic activity in Vatnajökull glacier in 996 destroyed one bridge and damaged another. Much quagmire remains nd travellers are warned that great care should be taken and no attempt ade to drive off the main road in this area.

Kálfafell-Sandgígjukvísl 19 km

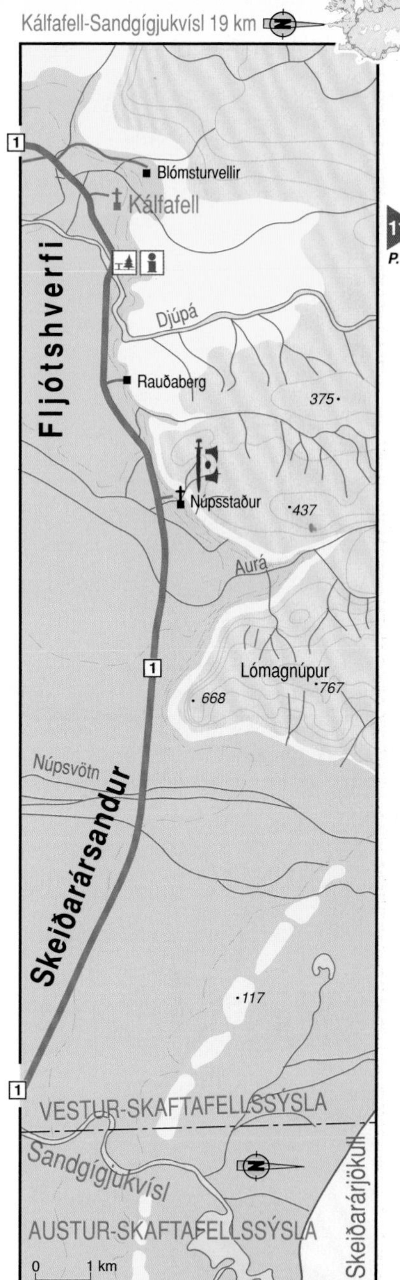

Sandgígjukvísl-Kálfafell 19 km

11 P. 574

At Núpsstaður

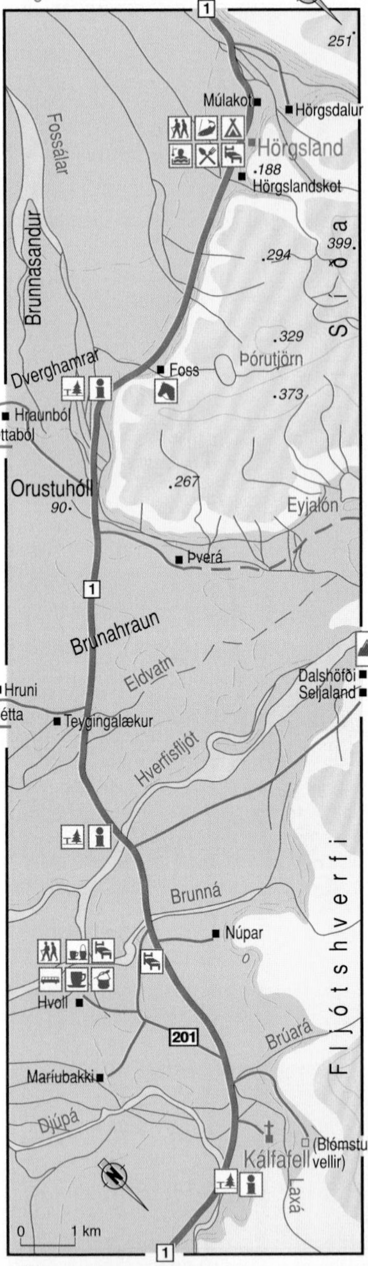

11 P. 574

Hörgsland-Kálfafell 20 km

Múlakot, a schoolhouse built 1909. One of many such houses, now rare built after the new school laws were enacted in 1907. Renovated and pro tected.

Hörgsdalur, a farm and a former parsonage.

Hörgsland, a farm. Often a parsonage. One clergyman, Magnú Pétursson, who lived there in the 17th century, was a poet and said to b skilled in black magic, one of his feats being to divert a fleet of Turkis pirate ships away from the shores of the country. He was also skilled a slaying ghosts. A hospital in the 17th and 18th century.

Brunasandur, a green area along the edge of Brunahraun, which starte to grow after the eruption of 1783-44. The first farm was built there i 1822.

Foss, a farm taking its name from an unusual waterfall coming off th cliffs on the mountainside.

Þverá, a jeeptrack leeds from Þverá to road F206 Lakavegur through a amazing world of waterfalls, lavaformations and caves.

Dverghamrar, ("Dwarf crags") rocks with hexagonal columns by th roadside. Such columns are often found where lava has flowed into wate and been abruptly cooled.

Brunahraun, the eastern part of the Skaftáreldahraun lava of 1783-4 coming from the Lakagígar craters and following the river Hverfisfljót An interesting walk to the old **Hverfisfljótsgljúfur** canyon.

Orustuhóll, ("Battle hill") a tuff cliff-sided hill (90 m) south of the high way. A grand view from the top.

Eldvatn, ("Fire water") (on Brunasandur), a clear river flowing fron under the lava-field and eventually into Hvalsíki.

Hverfisfljót, a glacial river coming from the southwest part o Vatnajökull, Síðujökull. Divides the districts Fljótshverfi to the east an Síða to the west and flows into Hvalsíki.

Fljótshverfi, the district between the rivers Hverfisfljót and Núpsvötn the easternmost district of Vestur-Skaftafellssýsla.

Núpar, a farm formerly called Gnúpar, where the settler Gnúpa-Bárðu settled after having moved from Bárðardalur in the north across the inte rior through Vonarskarð and down to Fljótshverfi. The Sagas say tha Bárður had each of his animals carry its own food across the desert.

201 Vallavegur, 3,59 km.

Kálfafell-Hörgsland 20 km

kaftá, a glacial river and one of the big rivers of Iceland. Comes from ıe glacier Skaftárjökull in Vatnajökull, divides the districts Skaftártunga ıd Síða, then turns eastward along Síða and thence southward along andbrot.

ólmur, a farm. The home of Bjarni Runólfsson (1891-1938), a self-ught electrical engineer, who built many power-stations throughout eland. This was the side of a carpentery school from 1945 to 1963.

íða, the district from Skaftá to Þverá. Lies on the south side of some w mountains.

05 Klausturvegur, 1,35 km. **202 Prestbakkavegur,** 4,6 km.

irkjubæjarklaustur, ("The church farm convent") (pop. 119) for long ne of the biggest farms of the county Skaftafellssýsla. Now a village ith the community centre Kirkjuhvoll, a Vatnajökull National Park formation centre, a weather station, elementary school, sport centre and swimming pool. Christian Irishmen are supposed to have lived there efore the Norse settlement, and after Ketill the foolish settled there no eathen people were allowed to live at this spot. A convent was situated ere from 1186 until the Reformation the 15th century. Many place-names mind us of the convent, such as **ystrastapi** ("The sisters' crag"), **ystrafoss** ("The sisters' falls"), **ystravatn** ("The sisters' lake") and **önghóll** ("Hill of chanting") to the uth of the river Skaftá, where the onks of Þykkvibær on their way to isit the nuns of Kirkjubæjarklaustur ould start their chanting as irkjubæjarklaustur came into sight. West of Systrastapi is **Eld-essutangi** ("Fire sermon point") where, in the eruption of 783, the advancing lava miraculously stopped before it reached e church where Rev. Jón Steingrímsson was delivering his famous ldmessa" ("Fire sermon"). It was common belief that it was due to s prayers that the lava-stream stopped. National Forest.

The crag Systrastapi.

irkjugólf, ("Church floor") curious basaltic rock formation just east of irkjubæjarklaustur. Resembles the tiled floor of an ancient cathedral.

tjórn, a clear river running across the Stjórnarsandur sands where the nd has been effectively recultivated. On a sunny day the water, which ns down over dark rocks, can warm up enough for bathing.

restbakki, a farm. Church built in 1859.

eldunúpur, a farm and a mountain of the same name. There is a cave **unnarshellir**, named after Gunnar Keldugnúpsfífl. In the year 1948 eople found a big cross carved in to the wall of the cave.

03 Geirlandsvegur, 2,66 km.

204 Meðallandsvegur, p. 162 **206 Holtsvegur,** p. 128, 163
F206 Lakavegur, p. 434

Hunkubakkar-Hörgsland 14km

Hörgsland-Hunkubakkar 14 km

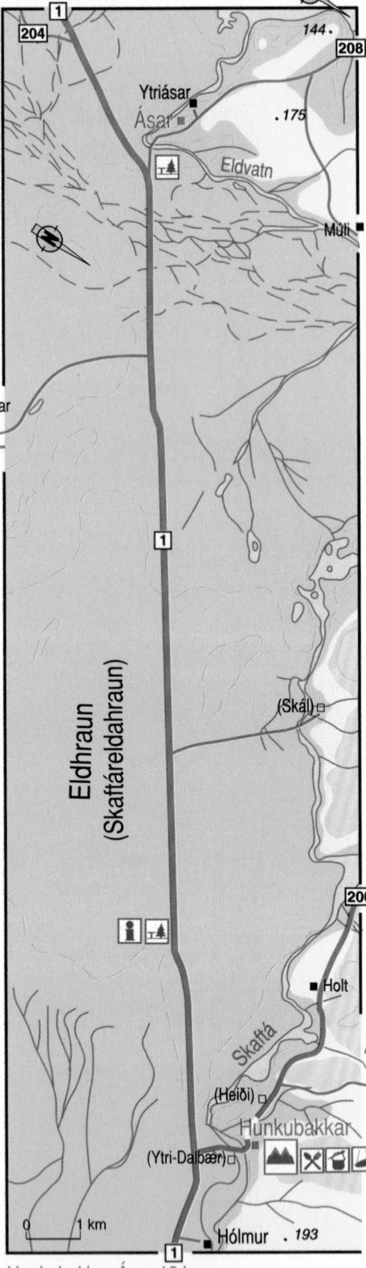

Ásar-Hunkubakkar 18 km

14 P. 577

11 P. 574

Hunkubakkar-Ásar 18 km

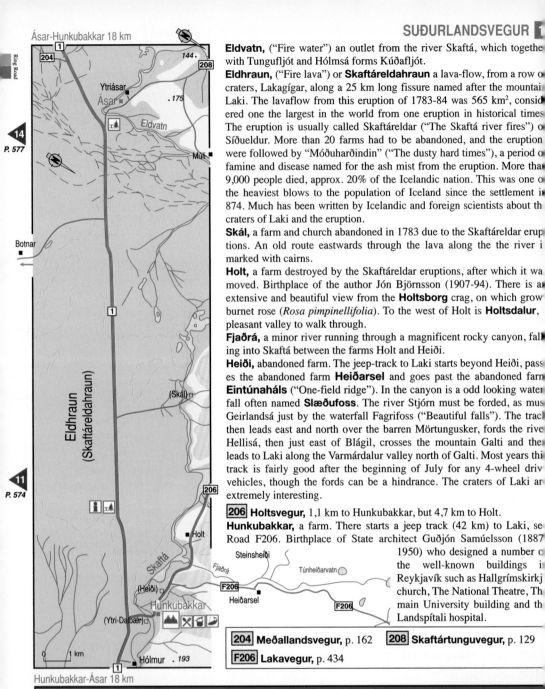

Eldvatn, ("Fire water") an outlet from the river Skaftá, which togethe with Tungufljót and Hólmsá forms Kúðafljót.

Eldhraun, ("Fire lava") or **Skaftáreldahraun** a lava-flow, from a row o craters, Lakagígar, along a 25 km long fissure named after the mountai Laki. The lavaflow from this eruption of 1783-84 was 565 km^2, consid ered one the largest in the world from one eruption in historical times The eruption is usually called Skaftáreldar ("The Skaftá river fires") o Síðueldur. More than 20 farms had to be abandoned, and the eruption were followed by "Móðuharðindin" ("The dusty hard times"), a period o famine and disease named for the ash mist from the eruption. More tha 9,000 people died, approx. 20% of the Icelandic nation. This was one o the heaviest blows to the population of Iceland since the settlement i 874. Much has been written by Icelandic and foreign scientists about th craters of Laki and the eruption.

Skál, a farm and church abandoned in 1783 due to the Skaftáreldar erup tions. An old route eastwards through the lava along the the river i marked with cairns.

Holt, a farm destroyed by the Skaftáreldar eruptions, after which it wa moved. Birthplace of the author Jón Björnsson (1907-94). There is a extensive and beautiful view from the **Holtsborg** crag, on which grow burnet rose (*Rosa pimpinellifolia*). To the west of Holt is **Holtsdalur**, pleasant valley to walk through.

Fjaðrá, a minor river running through a magnificent rocky canyon, fall ing into Skaftá between the farms Holt and Heiði.

Heiði, abandoned farm. The jeep-track to Laki starts beyond Heiði, pass es the abandoned farm **Heiðarsel** and goes past the abandoned farn **Eintúnaháls** ("One-field ridge"). In the canyon is a odd looking water fall often named **Slæðufoss**. The river Stjórn must be forded, as mus Geirlandsá just by the waterfall Fagrifoss ("Beautiful falls"). The trac then leads east and north over the barren Mörtungusker, fords the rive Hellisá, then just east of Blágil, crosses the mountain Galti and the leads to Laki along the Varmárdalur valley north of Galti. Most years thi track is fairly good after the beginning of July for any 4-wheel driv vehicles, though the fords can be a hindrance. The craters of Laki ar extremely interesting.

206 Holtsvegur, 1,1 km to Hunkubakkar, but 4,7 km to Holt.

Hunkubakkar, a farm. There starts a jeep track (42 km) to Laki, se Road F206. Birthplace of State architect Guðjón Samúelsson (1887 1950) who designed a number c the well-known buildings i Reykjavík such as Hallgrímskirkj church, The National Theatre, Th main University building and th Landspítali hospital.

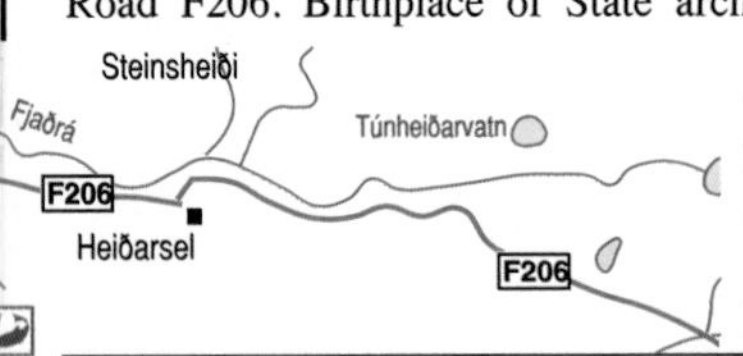

204 Meðallandsvegur, p. 162 **208 Skaftártunguvegur,** p. 129
F206 Lakavegur, p. 434

Kirkjugólf, p. 127.

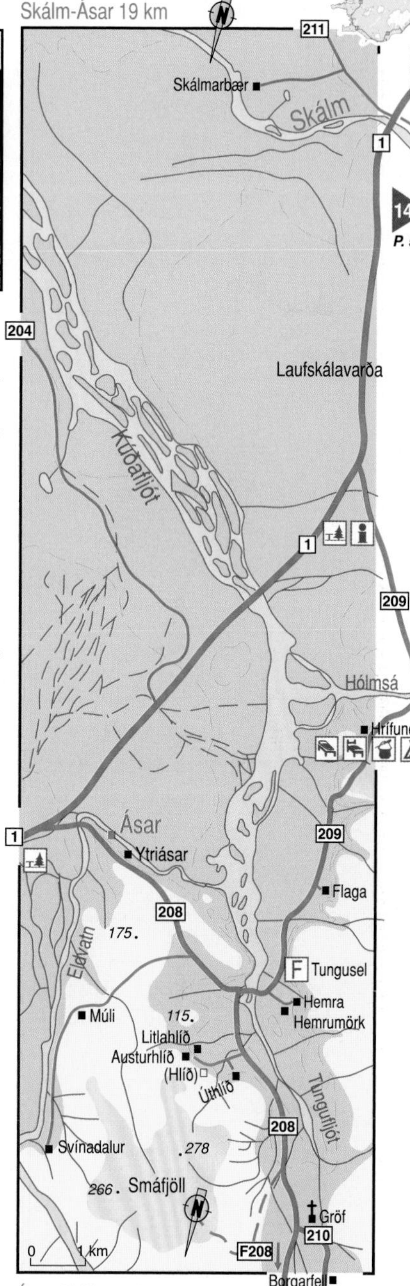

aufskálavarða, a low gravel ridge with many small cairns. Every traveller who passed for the first time was supposed to build a cairn for good ıck. An information board is located by the cairns.

úðafljót, a big glacial river formed by the rivers **Eldvatn**, Tungufljót, ólmsá and Skálm. About 4 km wide and difficult to ford before it was ridged, because of quicksands. Seals and trout in the river mouth. The ish settler Vilbaldi had a boat named Kúði, from which the river gets its ame. It is thought the boat may have been an Irish coracle.

ólmsá, a glacial river drawing its water from the north and east of the ýrdalsjökull glacier, and often getting a good share of the floods when ıe volcano Katla erupts. Many outlets from the north of Mýrdalsjökull ombine to form the river Brennivínskvísl ("The schnaps branch"), which ıins Hólmsá after this has emerged from Rauðibotn, the southern end of ıe Eldgjá canyon, in many falls and rapids.

kaftártunga, a settlement between the river Hólmsá and the river kaftá.

rífunes or Hrísnes, the southernmost farm in the Skaftártunga area, here an extensive wood has been largely destroyed by sandstorms.

09 Hrífunesvegur, 12,4 km.

sar, a farm and parsonage. For a time the home of Hróar Tungugoði nason (920).

laga, a farm and formerly a popular resting place for travellers.

ungufljót, a clear river that comes from the mountains Svartahnúksfjöll ıd Bláfjall.

08 Skaftártunguvegur, 15 km.

10 Ljótarstaðavegur, 6 km.

röf, a farm and church.

204 Meðallandsvegur, p. 162
211 Álftaversvegur, p. 130
F208 Fjallabaksleið nyrðri, p. 436

Ring Road
14
P. 577

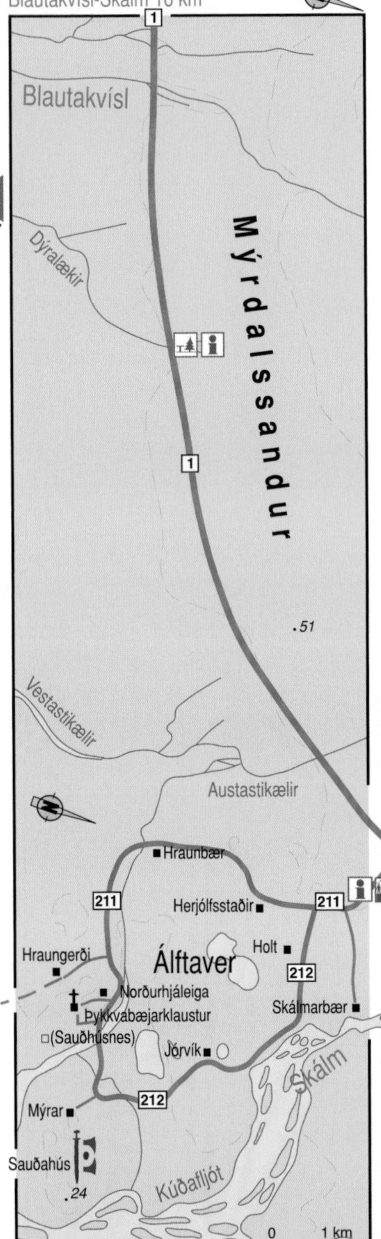

Vík

Hafursey, (582 m) a rugged tuff mountain with gorges, gullies and peculia rock formations. A nesting place for fulmars

Mýrdalssandur, a 700 km² desert southeast of Mýrdalsjökull, created b floods from Katla and changing glacial rivers. Landgræðsla ríkisins, th Soil Conservation Service of Iceland has revegetated areas along the roa to minimize the effect of drifting sand on road traffic.

Mýrdalsjökull, (1,480 m) the fourth largest glacier in Iceland, about 70 km². Many glacier tongues protrude from the main glacier towards Mýrdals sandur, such as **Kötlujökull**, Öldufellsjökull, Sandfellsjökull and Höfða brekkujökull. Under Mýrdalsjökull above Höfðabrekkujökull is the volcan **Katla** , which has erupted 16 times in the past 1,100 years, about once eve 70 years or so. The interval between eruptions varies from 40 to 80 year The first recorded eruption was in 894 and the last one in 1918. The eruptio usually start quite abruptly, sending torrents of melted glacier down acros Mýrdalssandur, so huge they sweep away everything in their path. Man farms have been destroyed and many lives lost in some of these floods.

211 Álftaversvegur, 8 km. **212 Hryggjavegur,** 8,5 km.

Álftaver, a small district between Mýrdalssandur and Kúðafljót. Some hil and pseudo-craters on the north side have provided considerable protectio from many of the floods from Katla. The craters are a protected natural fe ture. A view dial is located on Álftaver Road, near the crossroads at the Rin Road, a board with information about Þykkvabæjarklaustur nearby.

Þykkvabæjarklaustur, farm, church and a monastery from 1168 un the Reformation in the 17th century. Its first abbot was Þorlák Þórhallsson the Holy, the only Icelander to have been canonized by th Roman Catholic church, which was confirmed by the Pope in 198 The 23rd of December is Þorláksmessa, his saints day. Plaque commemora ing the monastery can be seen where the altar once was. In the sands abov the farm a very big medieval farmstead which was buried in a flood from **Katla** has been dug up. About 6 km distance south of Þykkvabæjarklaustur on an almost impassable path are two sheep-houses of turf from about 1900. One of them has lymegrass between rafters and turf roofing and a unique type of timber frame. In the keeping of the National Museum since 1974.

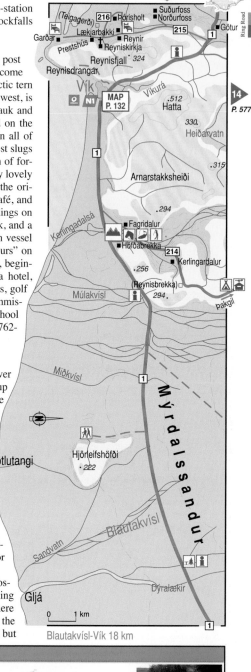

eynisfjall, (324 m) a steep mountain, with a discontinued loran-station n top and a difficult jeep-track leading to there from Vík. Big rockfalls ave occurred. A nesting-place for fulmars and puffins.

eynisdrangar, 66 m high rocks and needles in the sea.

ík, a town with approximately 280 inhabitants, an official trading post nce 1887. Vík attracts a great number of tourists year-round, who come experience its famed natural beauty and mild climate. A large arctic tern esting colony is located east of Vík, while Mt. Reynisfjall, to the west, is ome to a vast number of bird species, including puffin, fulmar, auk and ttiwake. A great diversity of flowers and grasses may be found on the astern side of Mt. Reynisfjall, the most extensive in one place in all of eland. This is also where the most robust field mice and the largest slugs the country are found, something that has captured the attention of forgn scientists. The entire area is perfect for nature lovers and many lovely king paths exist in Vík and its surrounding regions. Brydebúð, the orins of which date from 1831, contains an information centre, a café, and khibitions about living conditions, nature, climate and ship strandings on e southern coast. There is a memorial to German seafarers in Vík, and a orehouse opposite Brydebúð contains the Skaftfellingur, a 60-ton vessel ilt in 1916-1917, which sailed with people and goods to "harbours" on e harbourless coast of Vestur-Skaftafellssýsla for some 20 years, beginng in 1918. Various services are available in Vík, including a hotel, iesthouse, hostel and campground. There is also a field for sports, golf ourse, gymnasium and a swimming pool, as well as a district commisoner's office, bank, health care centre, preschool, elementary school ıd a music school. Vík was the home of Sveinn Pálsson, MD (1762-340), the first Icelandic natural historian.

14 Kerlingardalsvegur, 2,4 km.

erlingardalur, a valley and farm of the same name. The river erlingardalsá flows past the mouth of the valley. A road runs up ong Kerlingardalur, over Höfðabrekkuheiðar heaths to the bridge Selfjall. A lovely route, with unique rock formations in ambaskörð and a magnificent view from Léreftshöfði.

akgil, ("Roof Canyon") draws its name from the good shelter gives. Now there is a campsite and some cabins, open during e summer. Beautiful walking routes. The road to Þakgil is 14 n and is passable for all cars.

öfðabrekka, a farm and formerly a church. The farm was ıce situated at the foot of the mountain, but was moved higher after the Katla eruption of 1660 and then down again in 1964. ome centuries ago Jóka was the lady of the house. It was said at she got so angry at one of the farmhands for making her daugher pregnant that after her death she haunted him and the farm for ars. This notorious ghost was known as Höfðabrekku-Jóka.

jörleifshöfði, (221 m) a headland named after Hjörleifur, the fosr-brother of Ingólfur Arnarson, the first settler in Iceland. According *Landnámabók* ("The Book of Settlements") Hjörleifur stayed there r a while and was killed there. There is a large fulmar colony in the iffs and there was a farm there until 1937. Formerly on the coast but ow several km inland. Shelter.

ötlutangi, the southernmost pointv Iceland. Formed by floods from ýrdalsjökull. In the Katla eruption 1918 the land increased for 2 km the south, but the sea has since orn much of the increase away.

15 Reynishverfisvegur, 4km.

16 Þórisholtsvegur, 1 km.

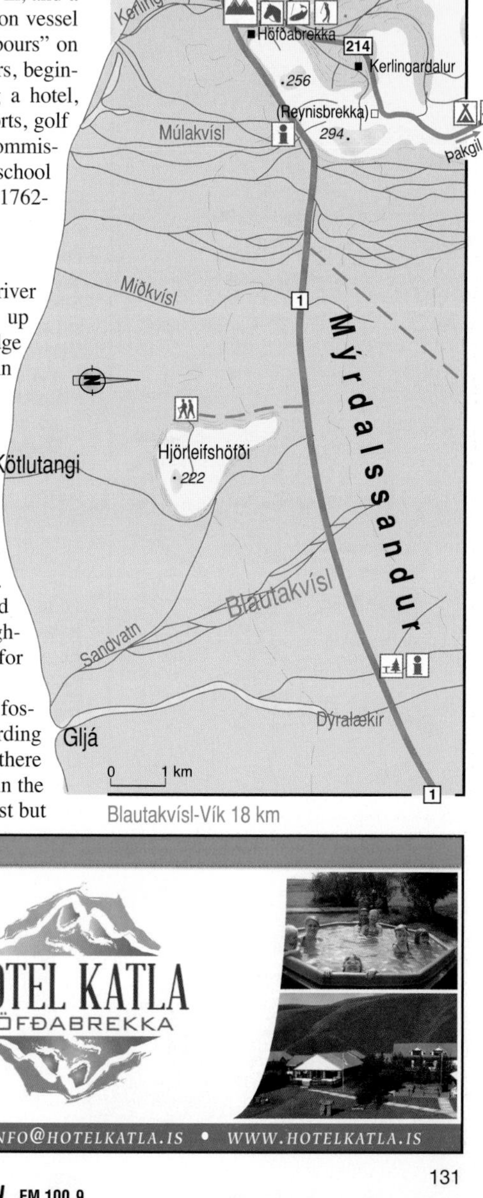

14 P. 577

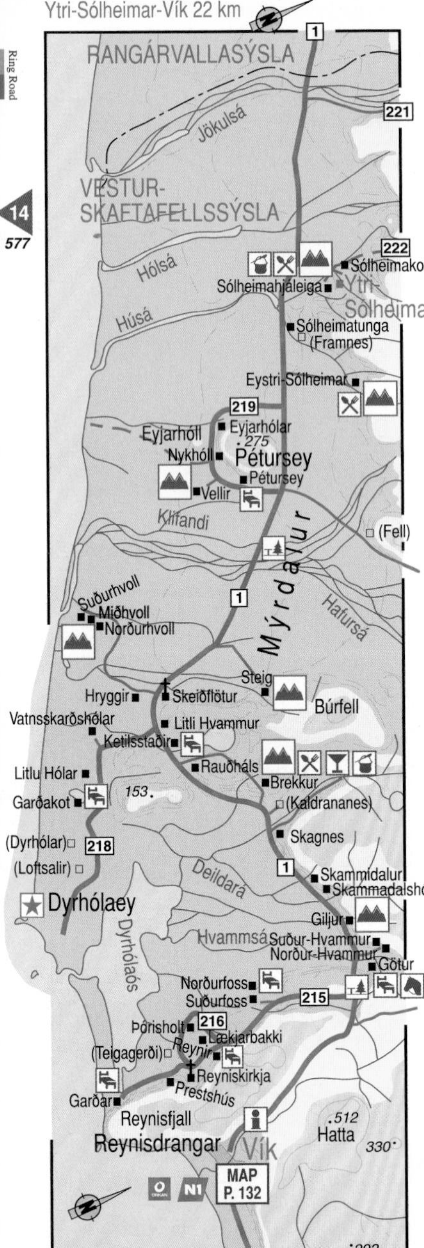

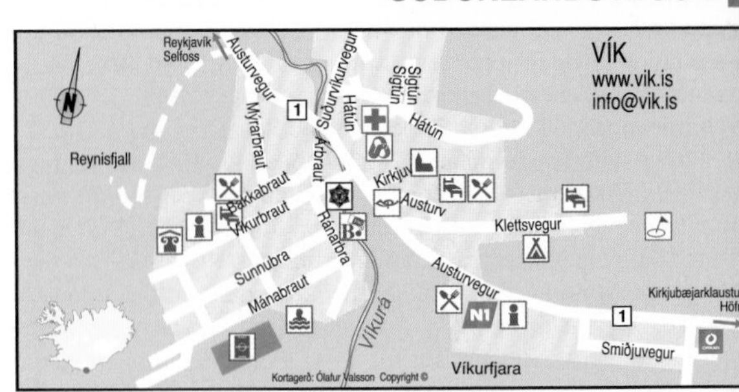

Sólheimar, westernmost farms in Mýrdalur. The home of the settl Loðmundur the Old. **Sólheimajökull,** a glacier tongue coming from th southwest of the glacier Mýrdalsjökull, is named for the farm. The spec tacular surroundings of the glacier are marked by rugged and majest rock formations thoroughly shaped by the glacier. This is an easy walk o crampons up onto the ice field where a wonderland of ice sculpture ridges and deep crevasses await your discovery. Glacier Guieds off guided tours on the glacier and at the beginning of the tour an exper enced glacier guide will teach you how to use basic ice equipment, cram pons and ice axe required for your trip into this magical frozen world.

Mýrdalur, the district between the deserts Sólheimasandur and Mýrdal sandur. Immensely varied landscape: green pastures and fields wi valleys, gullies and canyons, and the glacier Mýrdalsjökull in th background.

218 Dyrhólavegur, 6 km. **219 Péturseyjarvegur,** 4 km.

Pétursey, (277 m) a solitary mountain.

Fell, an abandoned farm and formerly a parsonage. Now summer hous and forestry.

Skeiðflöt, a church. In a hill on the south side of the farm is a five-poi ted star.

Dyrhólahverfi, a cluster of farms, which includes Dyrhólar, home *Njáls saga*'s Kári Sölmundarson.

Loftsalir, a farm. The cave Loftsalahellir, which was used for offici gatherings up to the turn of the century is in the mountain Geitafjall.

Dyrhólaey, ("Doorway hill island") a cape or headland 110-120 high, with perpendicular cliffs on the southern and western sides and narrow rock rim with an arch-shaped opening through it protruding in the sea. Boats and even small planes can pass through the arch, hence th name Dyrhólaey, or Portland as it has been called. **Dyrhólahöfn** west Dyrhólaey used to be a point place for fishermen. Cliffs and pillars off th coast, one of them, Háidrangur (56 m), climbed by Hjalti Jónsson 1893. Dyrhólaey is a nature sanctuary.

Dyrhólaós, a lagoon.

Skammidalur, a farm where interesting fossils have been found.

215 Reynishverfisvegur, 4 km. **216 Þórisholtsvegur,** 1 km.

Reynir, a church untill 1987.

Garðar, the southernmost farm in Iceland. Some interesting caves a hexagonal pillar rocks near by at the sea end of the mountain Reynisfjal

221 Sólheimajökulsvegur, p. 442 **222 Mýrdalsjökulsvegur,** p. 442

‹ógar, formerly the site of a regional secondary school and a major farm. ıere was also a church here until the year 1890. Skógar is the location of the .ógar Museum, the largest Folk Museum outside the Reykjavík area. It pre- rves among other things old tools, implements, a church and farm houses lly furnished, showing the living conditions of the gone past. The chief :raction of the Skógar Museum, and no doubt its most historically valuable set, is the eight-oar fishing boat Pétursey, Icelands best-kown boat of its nd. The legendary ring from Thrasi's treasure chest, once hidden behind the :ógafoss waterfall, is also on display. The latest addition to the Skógar useum is the Museum of Transport (est. 2002) which explores the history of ınsport, communications and technology in Iceland.

‹ógafoss, (60 m) a waterfall in the river **Skógá**, one of the highest in eland. There are many other waterfalls further up in the river. Legend ıs it that the settler Þrasi hid his chest of gold behind Skógafoss.

mmvörðuháls, ("Five cairn ridge") (1,000 m) a ridge between the aciers Eyjafjallajökull and Mýrdalsjökull, itself formerly covered by acier. From Skógar one can take a jeep track to Fimmvörðuháls from here there is a good hiking track to Goðaland and Þórsmörk. However, is even more interesting to get there along the marked hiking path up side the river Skógá with its many waterfalls which can not be seen om the jeep track. There is a good hike to the peak of the glacier jafjallajökull from Fimmvörðuháls, though this is not the shortest ute. On Fimmvörðuháls there are two huts, a new one belonging to the uring club Útivist and an older one just south of Fimmvörðuháls longing to the touring club Ferðafélag Íslands (FÍ). In the spring of 10 a volcanic eruption started on the hiking path in Goðaland. It lasted proximately 2 weeks and now one can walk on new mountains and see w alive the Icelandic nature is. An exciting new experience with or thout a local guide. Estimated hiking time from Skógar to Þórsmörk 10 hours. See more info on Fimmvörðuháls on p. 164.

‹ógasandur, a large part this sandy area has been revegetated with pine and extensive grassfields have been developed on the sand.

ıkulsá á Sólheimasandi, a short but swift glacial river coming from e glacier Sólheimajökull. Also known as **Fúlilækur** ("Foul river") on account of the strong sulphur smell. This river used to be a serious obstacle to travel. A bridge was built over it in 1921 and another in 1967.

Sólheimasandur, a sand desert east of Jökulsá, the eastern continuation Skógasandur on the other side of the river.

219 **Péturseyjarvegur,** p. 132

221 **Sólaheimajökulsvegur,** p. 442

222 **Mýrdalsjökulsvegur,** p. 442

Drangshlíð - Ytri-Sólheimar 13 km

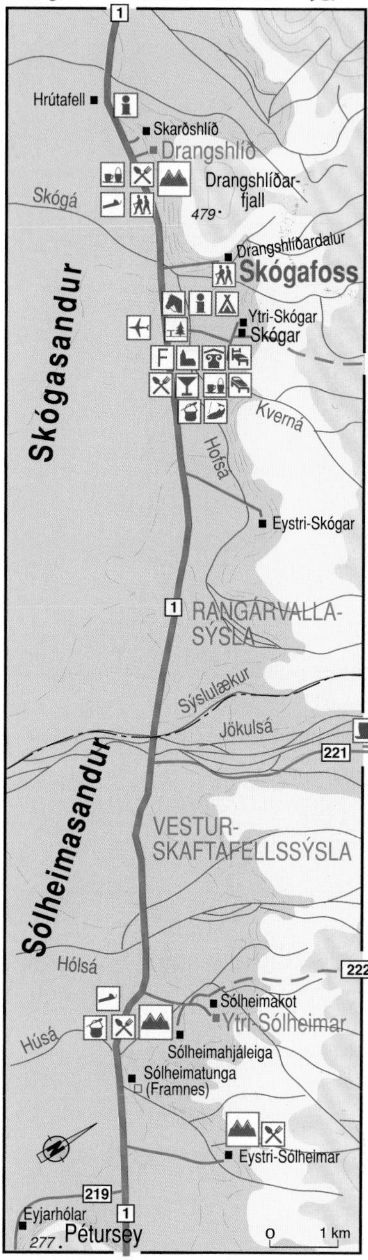

Ytri-Sólheimar-Drangshlíð 13 km

Ystiskáli-Drangshlíð 15 km

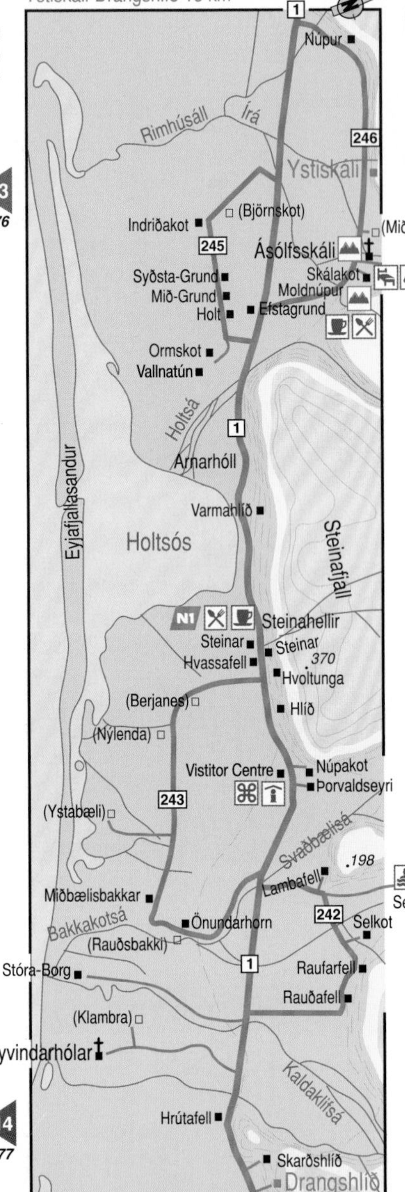

Drangshlíð-Ystiskáli 15 km

13
P. 576
14
P. 577

246 **Skálavegur,** 5,4 km. **245** **Hverfisvegur,** 3,6 km.

Steinahellir, a cave used for official gatherings until the second half c the 19th century.

Steinar, ("Rocks") a farm previously with a church. Has been move many times because of rockfalls.

242 **Raufarfellsvegur,** 4,4 km. **243** **Leirnavegur,** 6,4 km.

Þorvaldseyri, a substantial farm, the leader in grain cultivation eve since this was reintroduced in Iceland, which includes a speci Icelandic grain.

Visitor Centre, an information centre dedicated to the dramat eruption in Eyjafjallajökull volcano in 2011.

Seljavellir, there a swimming pool was built in the mountain side i 1923 by the Youth movement, making use of natural hot water on the spo One of the shortest climbing routes to the glacier Eyjafjallajökull starts i the vicinity. This route is quite steep and some crevasses may be expecte en route.

Stóra-Borg, a farm to the east of Bakkakotsá, quite well-known in Iceland because of the semi-historical novel, *Anna of Stóra-Borg*, by Jón Trausti. Digs in an ancient cemetery and farmhouses have revealed a number of important remains.

Eyvindarhólar, a farm and a church. Parsonage until 1904.

Hrútafell, a farm. In a rock just east of the farm there is the cave **Rút hellir**, probably the first man-made dwelling in Iceland. Recent researc has revealed that there was a forge there of an ancient type, so Rútshellir the site of remains of great importance.

Skarðshlíð, a farm. Interesting caves shaped by ocean waves in the hom field.

Drangshlíð, takes its name from a unique cliff in the middle of a fie called **Drangurinn**. Ledgend says that Grettir Ásmundsson "*the strong* pushed this cliff from the mountain Hrútafell leaving a scar in th mountain. Under this cliff are caves which have been used through th ages. A protected natural feature.

yjafjöll, the district between the rivers Álar and Jökulsá on Sólheima-
ındur. Most of the district is flat land, wet and sandy, between the ocean
ıd steep mountain slopes which, though rocky, are often very grassy.
umerous streams and falls coming off the 300-400 m high mountain-
de, cut in many places by valleys through which fall glacial rivers from
e glacier Eyjafjallajökull which towers in the background.

yjafjallajökull, (1,666 m) a volcano covered by about 100 km² of glaci-
. Three eruptions in historical times, in 1612, 1821-22 and 2010. It is
ımparatively easy to climb this glacier and there is a choice of routes.
ne of the easiest and safest is from Langanes on the road to Þórsmörk,
/ Grýtutindur and Sker. See more info p. 164.

tóri-Dalur, a farm and a church, often mentioned in *Njáls saga*. In Saga
nes the home of Runólfur Úlfsson, one of the chief opponents of
hristianity when it was made legal in the year 1000.

attarnef, ("Cat's nose"), a rocky point protruding towards
ıarkarfljót, previously an obstacle to travellers when the river
as high.

amragarðar, an abandoned farm. Many streams and waterılls nearby, among them one of the most unusual small waterılls in the country, **Gljúfrabúi** ("Canyon dweller"), half hidden
 a gorge. A great variety of flora on the slopes by the falls.

eljalandsfoss, one of the higher waterfalls in Iceland, though
 has little water. A path at the bottom of the cliff makes it possi-
e to walk behind the fall. The waterfall and its surroundings are
oodlit at night.

eljaland, a farm where many small caves are to be found, one of
em **Kverkarhellir**, previously used for official gatherings. Above
e farm is the cave **Seljalandshellir**, sometimes called **Papa-
ellir**, where there are many ancient remains and cross marks in the
ff walls, near the highway.

47 Sandhólmavegur, 10,6 km.

aradísarhellir, ("Paradise cave") a cave up in the cliff-wall west of the
rm **Fit**, an easy climb. According to folktales the outlaw Hjalti Magn-
son, lover of Anna of Stóra-Borg, had his hideout there in the 16th cen-
ry. A path leads to it from sheep pens above the main road.

eimaland, a community centre. **Drífandi**, a high waterfall but with very
tle water, falls of the cliffs behind the house. If the wind is strong it
ows the waterfall back up on the cliff.

stiskáli, a farm where the doctor Sveinn Pálsson (1772-1840) lived and
rote a work on the flora of the district. He was the first person to make
ıportant discoveries about the movements of glaciers.

sólfsskáli, a farm and church. The original settler was Ásólfur the
ıristian, driven from his home by heathens. The story goes that wherever
 came to stay, barren rivers would suddenly teem with fish.

olt, a church till 1888 and a parsonage.

oltsós, a sea lagoon, which the river Holtsá runs into.

45 Hverfisvegur, 3,6 km. **246 Skálavegur,** 5,4 km.

249 Þórsmerkurvegur, p. 138, 166

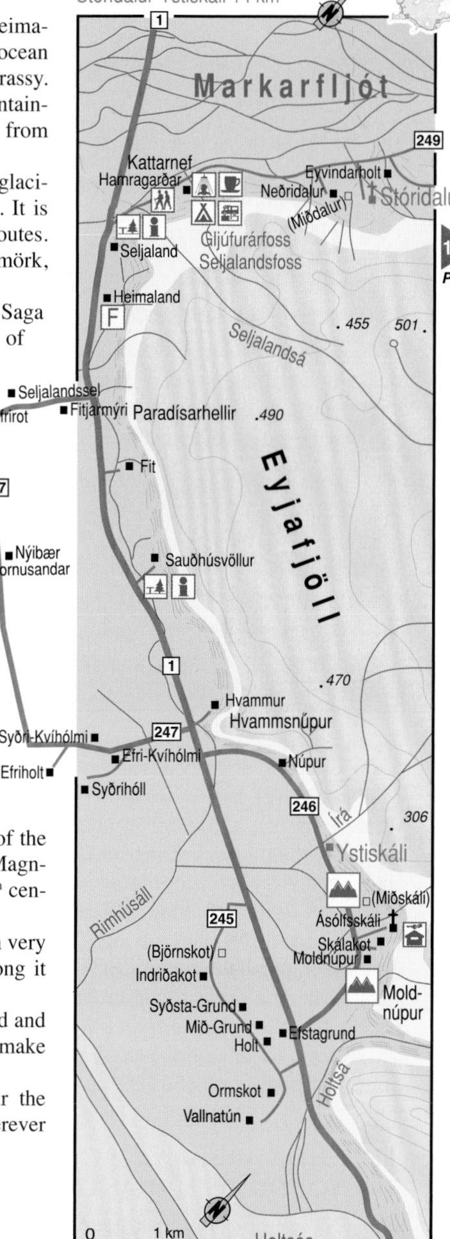

WHAT IS A GEOPARK?

The Global Geopark Network was established in response to an increasing need for comprehensive protection, development and management of many of the world´s most significant natural sites of geological, archaeological and esthetic value. The international network, endorsed by UNESCO, has now expanded to include 89 members in 27 countries around the globe.

ICELAND'S FIRST AND ONLY GEOPARK

In September 2011 Iceland gained membership to both the European Geoparks Network and the UNESCO-assisted Global Network of National Geoparks with the creation of Katla Geopark, Iceland´s first and only existing geopark.

ATTRACTION

Geology & Culture

1 Alviðruhamrar
2 Drangurinn í Drangshlíð
3 Dyrhólaey
4 Dyrhólaós, Loftsalahellir
5 Eyjarhóll, Pétursey
6 Hjörleifshöfði
7 Hrafnar, Svartinúpur
8 Hvammsmúli, Kálfhamar, Pöstin og
9 Hverfisfljót við Eldvatnstanga
10 Katla, Mýrdalsjökull, Mýrdalssandu
11 Kirkjugólf
12 Kúðafljót
13 Lómagnúpur
14 Meðallandssandur
15 Mögugilshellir, Þórólfsfell
16 Nauthúsagil
17 Skaftáreldahraun
18 Skaftárós
19 Skógafoss
20 Steinahellir
21 Stóra-Dímon, Litla-Dímon
22 Systrastapi, Systrafoss, Klausturhe
Systravatn, Sönghellir
23 Vatnsdalshellir
24 Þórsmörk
25 Efra-Hvolshellar
26 Eldmessutangi
27 Hrútafell, Hrútshellir
28 Höfðabrekka /Höfðabrekkuheiði
29 Laufskálavarða
30 Orrustuhóll
31 Paradísarhellir
32 Seljavallalaug
33 Þríhyrningur

Katla Geopark encompasses an area of 9542 sq.km², spanning roughly 9% of the country, from Hvolsvöllur on its western border, to Skeiðarársandur in the east. A corner of the mighty Vatnajökull Glacier forms the northernmost perimeter and long section of the south coast´s black sand beaches form the park's southern rim. The main population centers include Hvolsvöllur, the service center for the region, the charming village of Vik and the historic Kirkubæjarklaustur, with a combined population of 2700.

THE HILLS ARE ALIVE WITH THE SOUND OF FIRE AND ICE

It can be safely said that Katla Geopark is one of the most dynamic, diverse and geologically exciting regions of the world, ranging from landforms created millions of years ago to freshly minted lava that came with the eruption of Eyjafjallajökull in 2010. There is practically nowhere else on earth where fire and ice collide so dramatically, where the ebb and flow of the landscape is in such constant motion and all of this happening, as it were, in our own backyard. With over 150 volcanic eruptions recorded here since record keeping began in the 9th century, it is the most volcanically active area of Iceland.

WHAT IS GEOHERIT AND HOW IS THIS

Geoheritage can be describe as the intertwining of geology with culture- its effects on the history, culture, traditions and folklore of the local populatior It refers to the cultural significance of the eruptions Katla and Laki volcanoes, bot

ıly Geology

.lftaversgígar
leiksárgljúfur
ijúpá
rumbabót
verghamrar
ýralækjasker
ldgjá, Ófærufoss
ldgjárhraun
mstrur, Fjallabak
yjafjallajökull, Gígjökull, Steinsholtsjökull
agrifoss
immvörðuháls, Magni & Móði
laðrárgljúfur
oss á Síðu
lafursey
ólmsárfoss
vernugil
akagígar
andbrotshólar
anganes, Djúpidalur, Eystri-Rangá
angisjór, Fögrufjöll, Skuggafjöll, Grænifjallgarður
eiðólfsfell
jarnir, Tjarnarnes
larkarfljótsgljúfur, Markarfljótsaurar
lerkjárfoss
eynisfjall, Reynisdrangar, Reynisfjara
ljúpnafell, Atley
eljalandsfoss, Gljúfrabúi
kaftá
kammadalskambar
ólheimajökull, Sólheimasandur, Sólheimaheiði
tjórnarfoss
indfjallajökull, Tindfjöll
röllshylur, Grenlækur

Mainly Geology

69 Bjarnargarður
70 Fellsheiði
71 Granahaugur
72 Hellur (Jón Steingrímsson)
73 Kálkháls
74 Kirkjubæjarklaustur
75 Kúabót
76 Núpstaður
77 Sauðahús í Álftaveri
78 Skálmarbær
79 Tólfahringur
80 Vík (older part of the village)
81 Þykkvabæjarklaustur

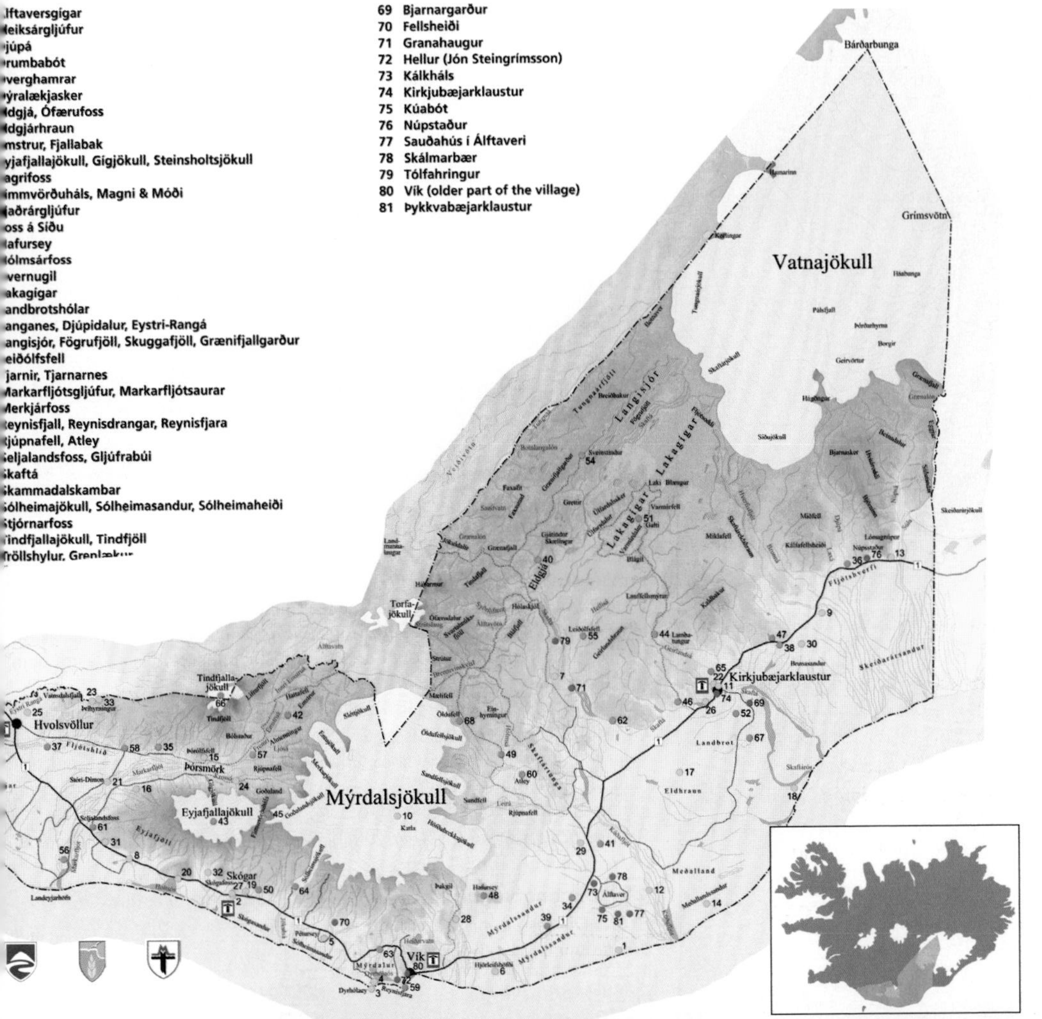

) GEODIVERSITY TED IN ICELAND?

ɔf which had an enormous impact ɔn life in Iceland, resulting in years ɔf hardship and famine. The ɾolcanic ash plume from the ɜruption of Laki caused the ɫeaths of 1/5th of the population ɑnd was called the eruption that ɔhanged Iceland forever.

THE BEDROCK OF BIODIVERSITY STARTS WITH GEODIVERSITY

Geodiversity refers to the soil, rocks, minerals, landforms and various processes such as earthquakes, volcanoes that have shaped these elements over time. Mountains, caves, beaches, deserts, rivers, oceans and even the weather are all elements of geo-diversity. Geological diversity is in fact the foundation of life, giving support to the ecosystems as well as providing places to live, resources for industry, soils from which we grow our food, areas for recreation, places of healing, places of worship, learning and inspiration. We look to Katla geopark´s magnificent geo diversity for inspiration, for peace, for healing, and as a way to refresh our souls, without which the world would be a dreary place to live indeed.

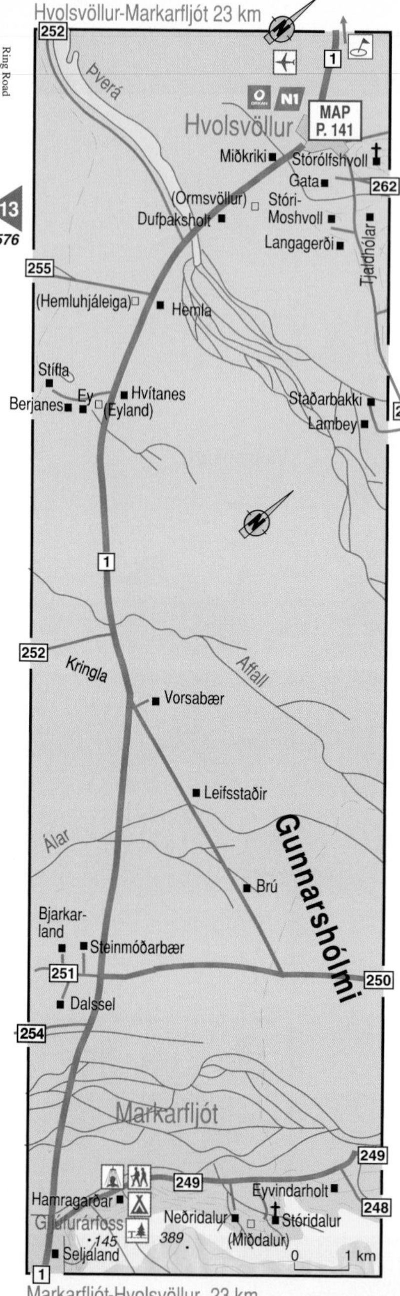

Hvolsvöllur, (pop. 902) the main town in Rangárþing eystra district, municipality formed in 2002 through the merging of six municipalitie between the rivers Eystri-Rangá and Jökulsá á Sólheimasandi. Centre c trade and travel, built up since 1930. Sheriff, doctor, veterinarian, healt service, swimming pool, sport centre and the community centre Hvoll. Th Sögusetrið historical centre is the site of two museums, one depicting Njál Saga and the other – the Kaupfélagasafn – focusing on the history of trad in South Iceland. There Njáls Saga is also being sewed in *refill*, which is special form of viking tapestry (**www.njalurefill.is**) Primary industries ar trade, tourism, service and manufacturing, eg. a knitter wear procutio with wool products and a processing plant of the major butcher and meat packing company Sláturfélag Suðurlands, founded in 1907 making it th oldest firm of its kind in Iceland. In summer there is a Farmers Market a Hvolsvöllur on weekends with local products.

Hvolsvöllur.

Þverá, a clear river into which all the streams from Fljótshlíð flow Previously this river got a good share of glacial water from Markarfljót which would turn Þverá into a menace that often broke down the fertil land of the district. A series of protective rock barriers was built in orde to keep Markarfljót in its own course and since then grasslands are being recultivated.

Vorsabær, a farm where Höskuldur Hvítanesgoði of *Njáls saga* lived.

Gunnarshólmi, grasslands near the rivers Álar and Markarfljót. *Njáls saga* tells us that this is where Gunnar from Hlíðarendi turned and wen back to Hlíðarendi, where he was eventually killed, instead of going int exile as he had been sentenced to.

Steinmóðarbær, in the year 2004 some scenes from the film *A little trip to Heaven* were filmed there.

250 Dímonarvegur, 12 km. **249 Þórsmerkurvegur,** 16,4 km.

Stóra-Dímon, a lone mountain near the river Markarfljót. In *Njáls saga* this mountain is called Rauðuskriður.

248 Merkurvegur, p. 166
251 Hólmabæjarvegur, p. 166
252 Landeyjavegur, p. 166
254 Landeyjahafnrvegur, p. 166
255 Akureyjavegur, p. 166
261 Fljótshlíðarvegur, p. 168
262 Vallarvegur, p. 168
F249 Þórsmerkurvegur, p. 450

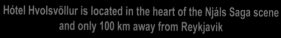

1 SUÐURLANDSVEGUR

267 Selalækjarvegur, 2,5 km.

Selalækur, there lived congressman Gunnar Sigurðsson (1888–1962) .

Rangárvellir, the district between the two rivers Ytri-Rangá and Eystri-Rangá. The upper parts covered by lava fields and sands, the middle flat and sandy and the lowest part wet.

266 Oddavegur, 4,3 km.

Oddi.

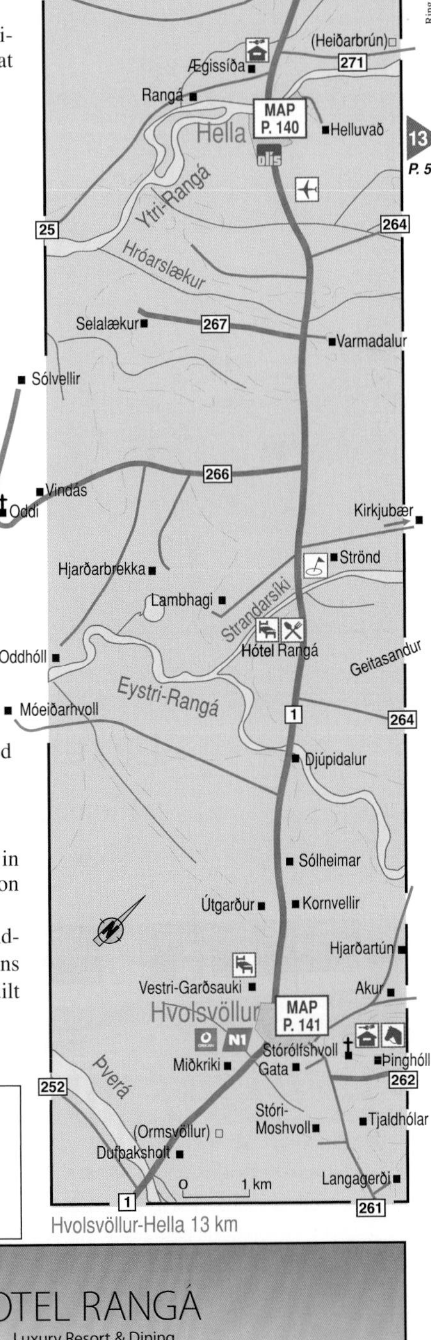

Oddi, a farm, church and parsonage. A major historic site. It first became famous around the middle of the 12th Century, when a church was built there, and thus is one of the oldest church sites in Iceland. In the year 1078, Sæmundur the Learned became priest of Oddi. He had studied for the clergy in France (at the Sorbonne). Sæmundur established a school at Oddi, which is believed to have stood for two centuries.

Oddhóll, there live one of Icelands best riders Sigurbjörn Bárðarson.

Strönd, once an elementery school, now a golf course.

Geitasandur, a sandy plain. The area has been used for experiments in soil reclamation, re-vegetation and forestry by the Soil Conservation Service of Iceland.

Eystri-Rangá, a river that comes from Rangárbotnar north of Tindfjallajökull. Mostly clear, though there is a small glacial tributary. It joins Þverá and later Ytri-Rangá to form the river Hólsá. First bridge built 1914, the second bridge 1969. Good salmon river.

Djúpidalur, once a slaughter house.

25 Þykkvabæjarvegur, p. 156	**252 Landeyjavegur,** p. 166
261 Fljótshlíðarvegur, p. 168-169	**262 Vallarvegur,** p. 168
264 Rangárvallavegur, p. 170	**271 Árbæjarvegur,** p. 158
273 Bugavegur, p. 156	

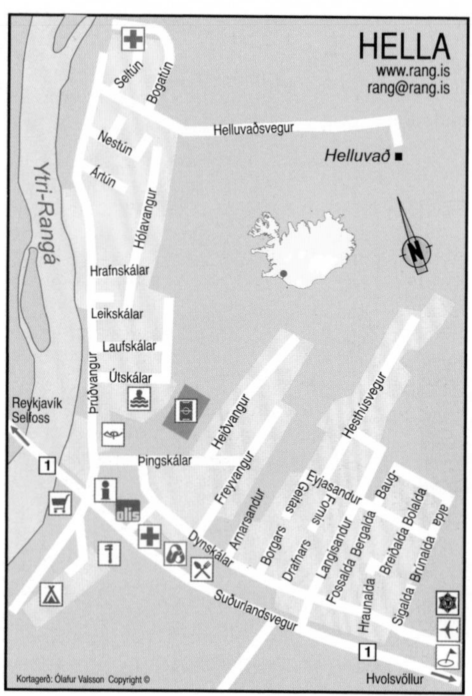
HELLA
www.rang.is
rang@rang.is
Seltún
Bogatún
Nestún
Ártún
Helluvaðsvegur
Helluvað
Hólavangur
Ytri-Rangá
Hrafnskálar
Leikskálar
Laufskálar
Útskálar
Þrúðvangur
Reykjavík
Selfoss
Þingskálar
Heiðvangur
Freyvangur
Hesthúsvegur
Eyjasandur
Geitas
Fornis
Baug-
Bolalda
alda
Arnarsandur
Borgars
Drafnars
Langisandur
Fossalda
Bergalda
Breiðalda
Brúnalda
Dynskálar
Suðurlandsvegur
Hraunalda
Sigalda
olís
1
Kortagerð: Ólafur Valsson Copyright ©
Hvolsvöllur

Hella, p. 142.

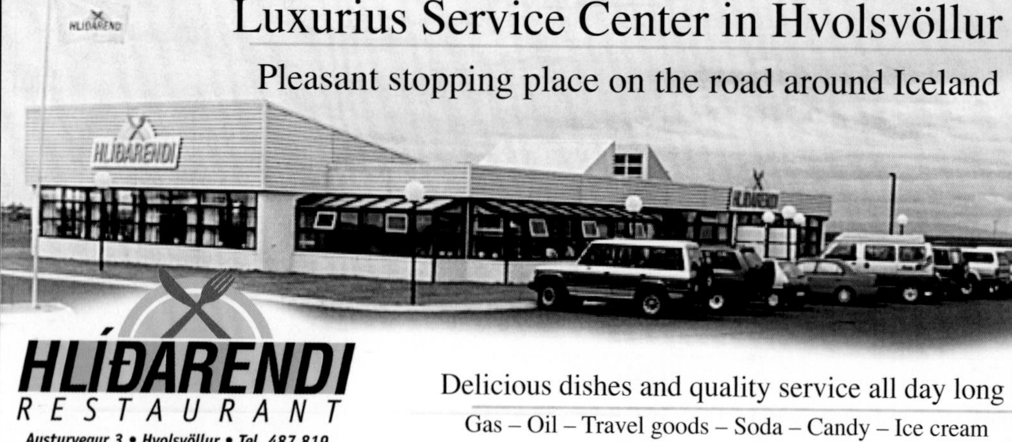
Luxurius Service Center in Hvolsvöllur
Pleasant stopping place on the road around Iceland
HLÍÐARENDI
HLÍÐARENDI
RESTAURANT
Austurvegur 3 • Hvolsvöllur • Tel. 487 819
Delicious dishes and quality service all day long
Gas – Oil – Travel goods – Soda – Candy – Ice cream

Photos from Iceland
www.vignirmar.com

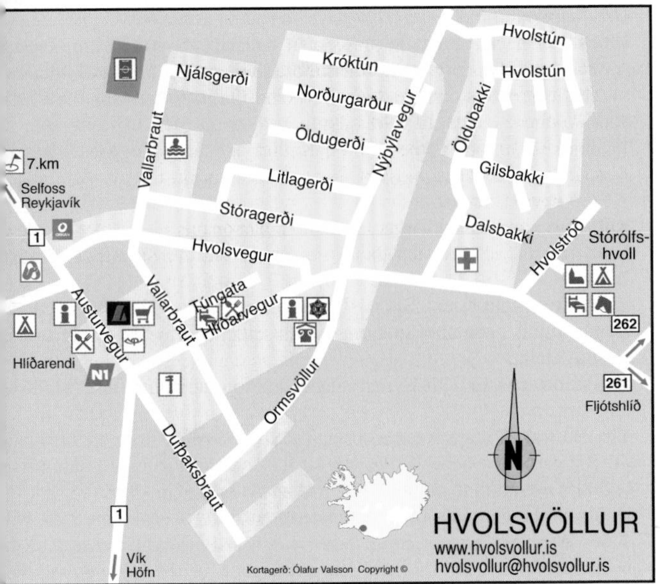

Hvolsvöllur, p. 138.

Eastern Rangárþing

Eastern Rangárþing, (pop. 1735) is a new name given to a municipality which was formed in 2002 when small municipalities merged into one. This new municipality lies between two great rivers, the Eystri-Rangá to the west and the Jökulsá á Sólheimasandi to the east. Many beautiful nature sites are located in this area, for example, Þórsmörk, the Tindfjöll mountains, the Eyjafjallajökull glacier, black beaches and the waterfalls Skógafoss and Seljalandsfoss. Various kinds of recreation are available, such as visits to museums, swimming pools, a sport centre, a community centre, horse rentals, golf courses, galleries, fishing sites, guided hiking and adventure tours etc. The local government of East Rangárþing is at Hvolsvöllur.

13 P. 576

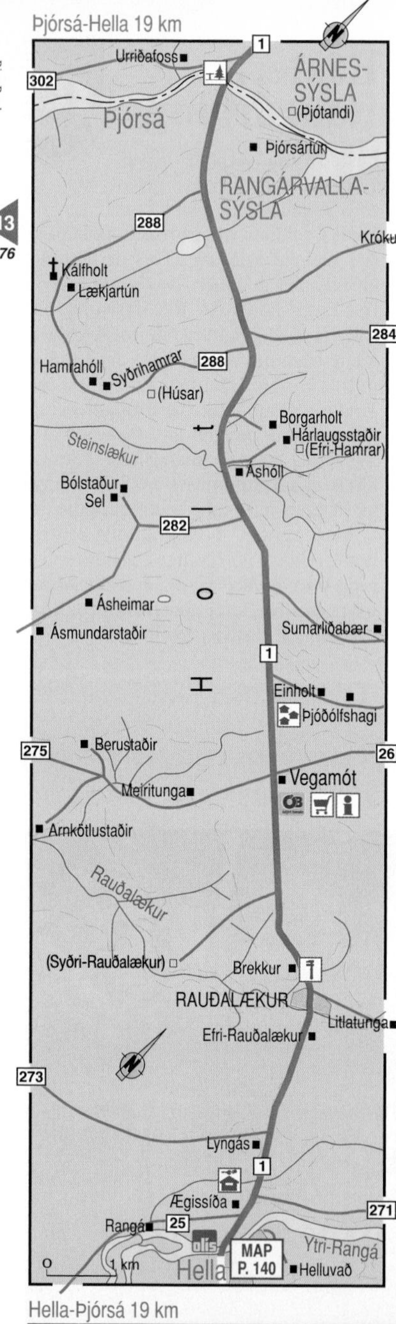

Hella-Þjórsá 19 km

Urriðafoss, a farm and falls of the same name in the river Þjórsá.

Þjórsá, a glacial river, the longest in Iceland, about 230 km, averag flow about 400m^3/sec. Its northernmost source is on Sprengisandur ea of the glacier Hofsjökull and it collects most of its water from the easter and southern sides of Hofsjökull and from the western side c Vatnajökull through the rivers Kaldakvísl and Tungnaá. Severa waterfalls in the river, most of them in the interior. First bridge built i 1895 near Þjótandi.

Kálfholt, a farm and church. Formerly a parsonage.

Holt, the district between the rivers Þjórsá and Ytri-Rangá (see Roa 26).

Efri-Rauðalækur and **Syðri-Rauðalækur,** farms taking their name from a reddish-coloured stream. A small settlement by the main road jus west of Hella.

Ægissíða, a farm with 11 man-made caves in the home-field (see Roa 25).

Ytri-Rangá, (Rangá West) a spring fed river coming from the lavafield off Rangárbotnar beneath Mt. Hekla. Icelands best salmon fishing rive in 2006. First bridge built in 1912 and a new bridge in 1960.

Hella, is the district´s most populated area and its economic hub, wit about 790 inhabitants. Hella´s industry is based primarily on serving th needs associated with agricultural production in the surrounding are and on services to inhabitants and tourists. Hella boasts a grocery store bakery, bank, post office, tourist information, hotel, guesthouse, summe houses, campsite, restaurants, shops, pharmacy, surgery, sports area pool, primary school, riding area, rescue team, veterinary clinic, abattoi garage, tyre centre and petrol station as well as various other businesse and public services.

25 **Þykkvabæjarvegur,** p. 156	26 **Landvegur,** p. 158
271 **Árbæjarvegur,** p. 158	273 **Bugavegur,** p. 156
275 **Ásvegur,** p. 156	282 **Ásmundarstaðavegur,** p. 156
284 **Heiðarvegur,** p. 158	288 **Kálfholtsvegur,** p. 156
302 **Urriðafossvegur,** p. 178	

Urriðafoss

1 SUÐURLANDSVEGUR

Ölfusá-Hvítá, one of the biggest rivers in Iceland, 185 km long. It has many tributaries, the last and greatest being the river Sog, and it is after the clear Sog has joined the glacial Hvítá ("White river") that the river is named Ölfusá.

Selfoss, (pop. 6,510) is a part of the Municipality of Árborg. A town situated by the bridge of the river Ölfusá. In 1891 a bridge, which used to be the biggest construction in Iceland, was built across Ölfusá, after which the town began to grow. A new bridge was built in 1945. Selfoss is the largest town in South Iceland and the main service centre of trade and industry. The Tourist Information Centre is located in the public library. Various accommodation options can be found in the town for example a hotel, a few guesthouses and a campsite. Many interesting restaurants and cafés are situated in Selfoss. At Svarfhóll, on the outskirt of Selfoss, there is an attractive 9 hole golf course on the bank of the Ölfusá river. Furthermore the town has an outdoor and an indoor swimming pool with steam bath and hot tubs, galleries and a bus terminal. Like all good service centres Selfoss has a sheriff, a hospital, great variety of shops, two comprehensive schools and a college. The largest dairy company in Iceland is in Selfoss. The National Circular Highway no. 1 leads through the town. Many scheduled trips go from Selfoss to, for example, Gullfoss waterfall and Geysir and to the wilderness of Þórsmörk. North of Selfoss is Hellisskógur with nice hiking paths by the Ölfusá river and a view over the golf course. The distance from the capital is 57 km.

Laugardælir, the site of a church. Bobby Fisher (1948-2008) the Grand Chessmaster is buried there. Selfoss gets its hot water supply from nearby Þorleifskot.

304 Oddgeirshólavegur, 13 km. **303 Ölvisholtsvegur,** 4,2 km.

Stóra-Ármót, a research sheep and dairy farm.

Oddgeirshólar, a substantial farm and formerly the site of a church, beautifully situated near the river Hvítá.

Flói, the agricultural area between the rivers Ölfusá-Hvítá and Þjórsá, reaching inland to the Merkurhraun lavafield. Flat country with the occasional hill, the Þjórsárhraun lava field being the "bedrock" under the soil. In 1927 a remarkable irrigation project was undertaken, using the river Hvítá and constructing the Flóaáveita system of 300 km of ditches and 450 km of dykes to irrigate an area of 12 thousand hectares.

Þingborg, a school and community centre near the farm Skeggjastaðir. The main ditch of the irrigation system Flóaáveita is just west of Þingborg.

Brúnastaðir, a farm near Hvítá, where the irrigation water of Flóaáveita is taken from Hvítá at the rate of 19 m³/sec.

30 Skeiða- og Hrunamannav, p. 172
33 Gaulverjabæjarv., p. 178
34 Eyrarbakkavegur, p. 178
35 Biskupstungnabraut, p. 180
302 Urriðafossvegur, p. 178
305 Villingaholtsvegur, p. 178
310 Votmúlavegur, p. 178

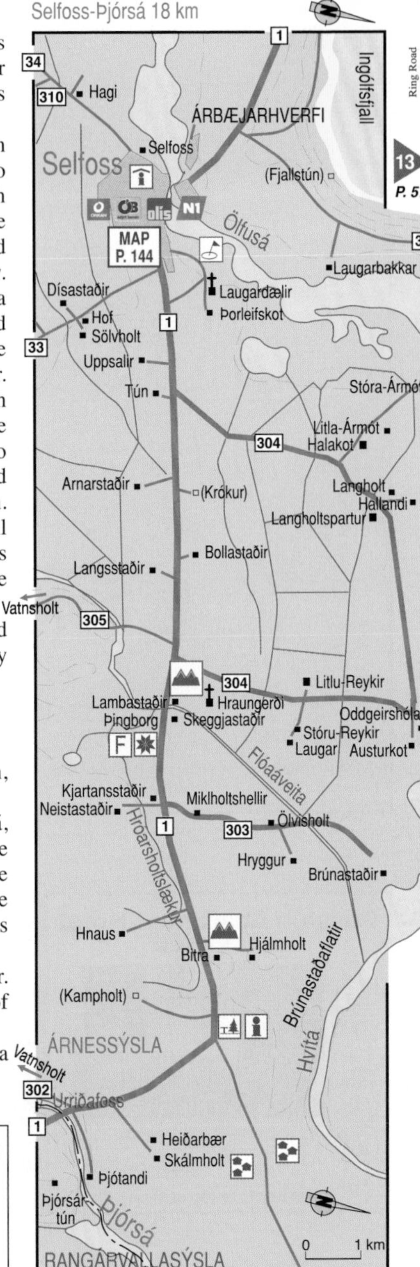

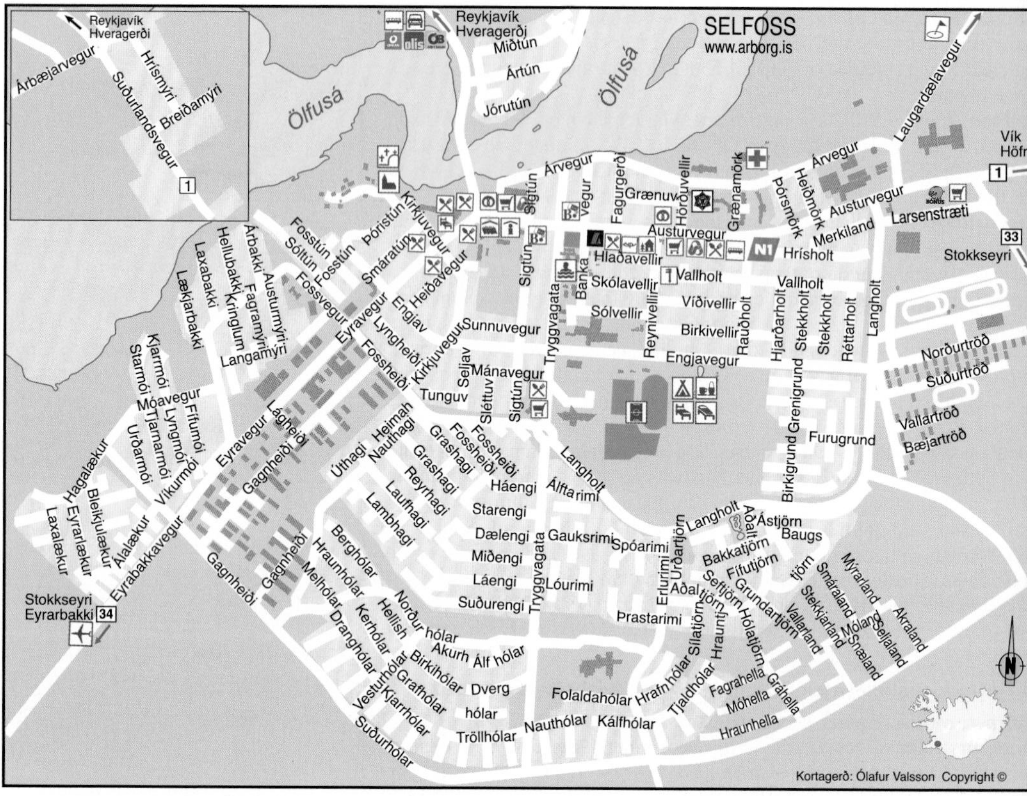

SELFOSS
www.arborg.is

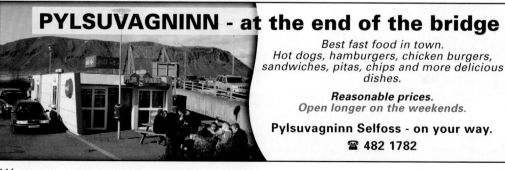

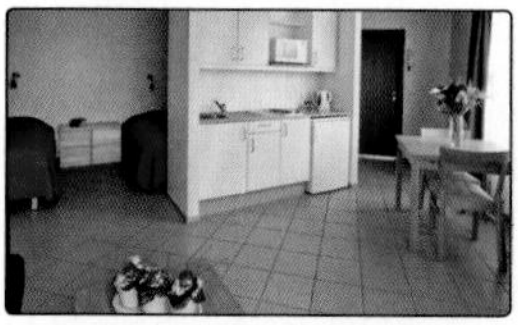

Kortagerð: Ólafur Valsson Copyright ©

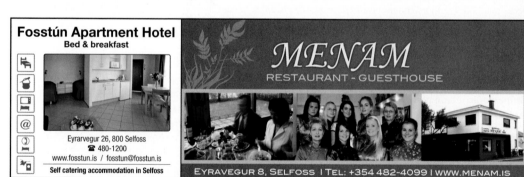

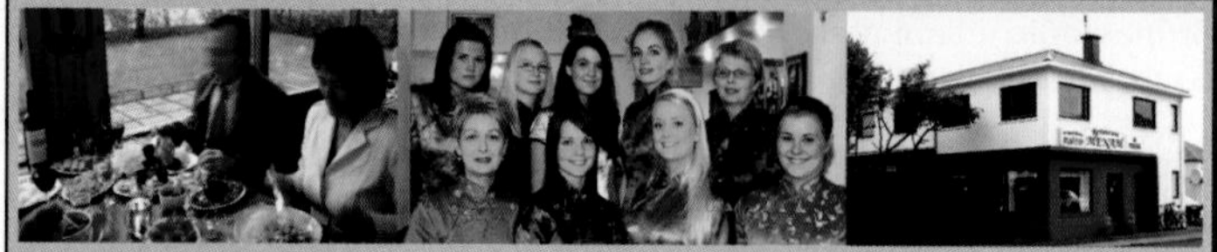

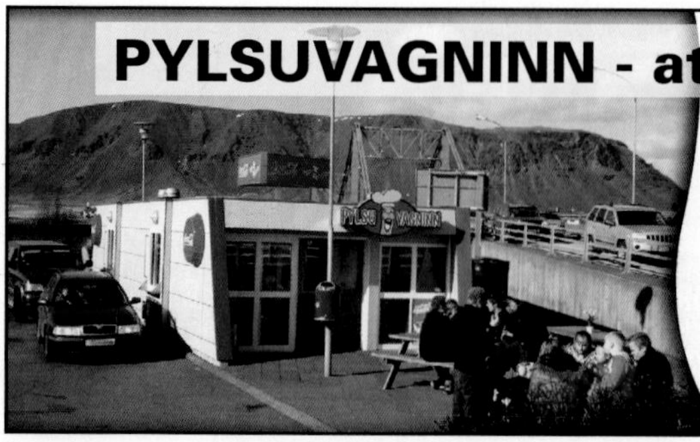

Welcome to the Swimming Pools in Árborg

Free of charge for children under 18 years old

Selfoss Swimming Pool

Open all year

Monday too Friday: 06:30 – 21:30

Saturaday – Sunday: 09:00 – 19:00

Stokkseyri Swimming Pool

Opening hours 18. Aug. 2012 – 31. May 2013:

Monday too Friday: 16:30 – 20:30

Saturaday: 10:00 – 15:00

Sunday: Closed

Opening hours 1. Jun. 2013 – 18. Aug. 2013:

Monday too Friday: 13:00 – 21:00

Saturaday: 10:00 – 17:00

Sunday: 10:00 – 17:00

Prices

Adult (18-66 years old)

One ticket	550 kr.
10 tickets	3.400 kr.
30 tickets	7.400 kr.
Open ticket for one year	25.900 kr.

Admission is free of charge for people older then 67 years upon presenting an ID card. Admission is free of charge for disabled people upon presenting a Disabled Person Card.

Sundhöll Kobbi kútur Selfoss

Sundlaug Fribbi froskur Stokkseyrar

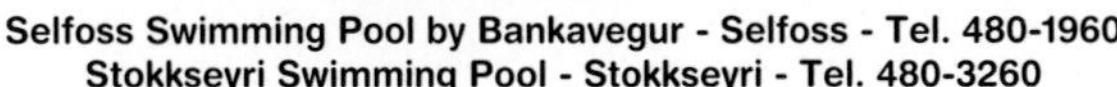

Selfoss Swimming Pool by Bankavegur - Selfoss - Tel. 480-1960
Stokkseyri Swimming Pool - Stokkseyri - Tel. 480-3260

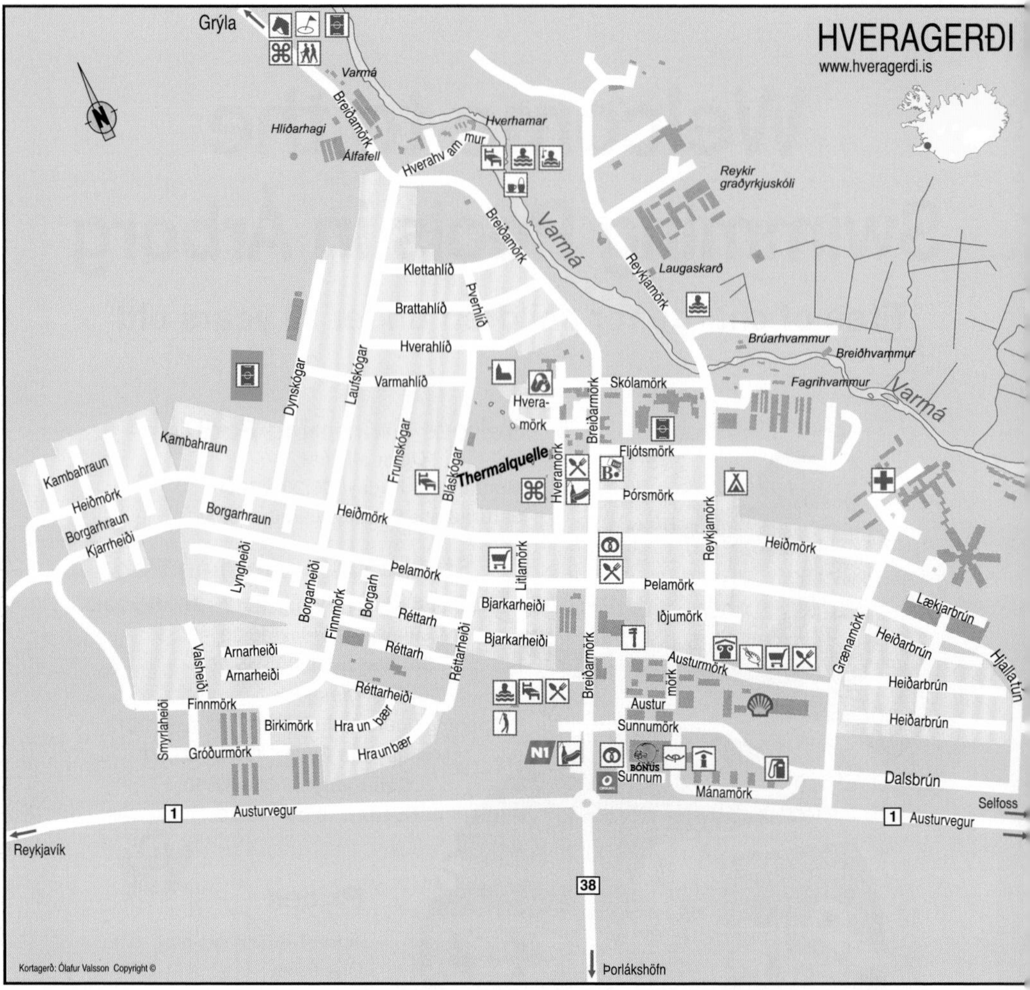

HVERAGERÐI

www.hveragerdi.is

Grýla
Varmá
Breiðamörk
Hlíðarhagi
Álfafell
Hverahvammur
Hverhamar
Reykir garðyrkjuskóli
Laugaskarð
Reykjamörk
Klettahlíð
Þverhlíð
Brattahlíð
Hverahlíð
Varmahlíð
Dynskógar
Laufskógar
Frumskógar
Bláskógar
Thermalquelle
Hveramörk
Skólamörk
Brúarhvammur
Breiðhvammur
Fagrihvammur
Fljótsmörk
Þórsmörk
Kambahraun
Heiðmörk
Borgarhraun
Kjarrheiði
Lyngheiði
Borgarheiði
Finnmörk
Borgarh
Þelamörk
Réttarh
Réttarheiði
Litlamörk
Bjarkarheiði
Iðjumörk
Austurmörk
Austurmörk
Grænamörk
Lækjarbrún
Heiðarbrún
Hjallatún
Valsheiði
Arnarheiði
Finnmörk
Smyrlaheiði
Birkimörk
Hraunbær
Gróðurmörk
Sunnumörk
Mánamörk
Dalsbrún
Selfoss
Austurvegur
Reykjavík
38
Þorlákshöfn

Kortagerð: Ólafur Valsson Copyright ©

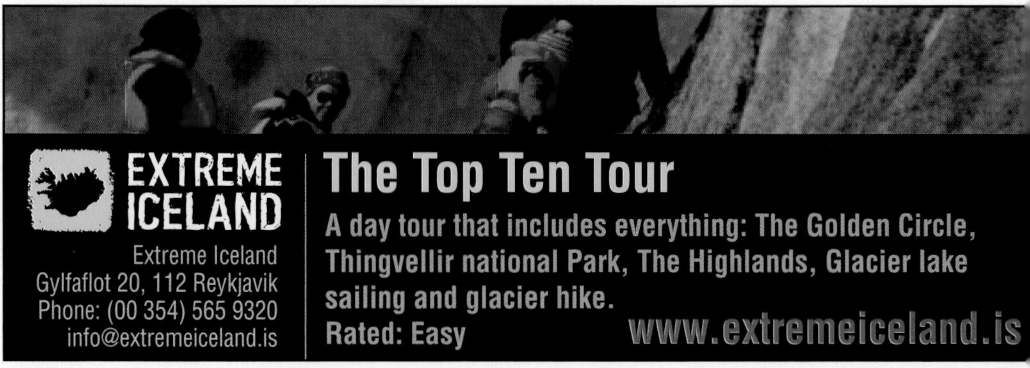

Welcome to Hveragerði

A blossoming town

Tourist Information Centre
Sunnumörk
810 Hveragerði
Tel. 483 4601. Fax: 483 4604
tourinfo@hveragerdi.is

Laugaskarð Swimming Pool
810 Hveragerði
Tel. 483 4113

Geothermal Park
Hveramörk 13
810 Hveragerði
Tel. 483 5062, 660 3905.
tourinfo@hveragerdi.is
hveragerdi.is

Reykjamörk Campsite
810 Hveragerði
Tel. 483 4605, 660 9280.

www.hveragerdi.is

2 P. 565

Hellisheiði-Selfoss 22 km

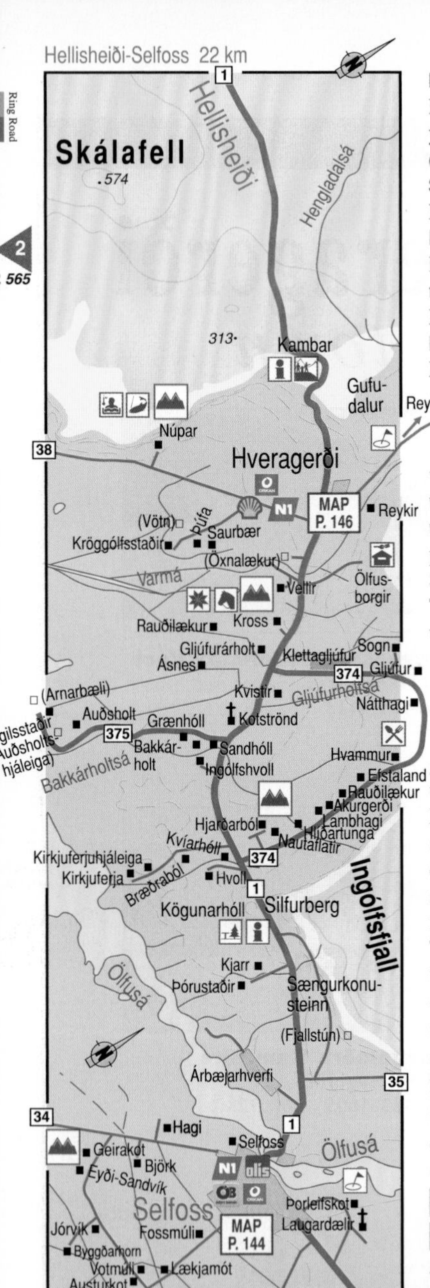

Selfoss-Hellisheiði 22 km

Hellisheiði, a plateau to the south of Hengill. Covered with man lavafields old and new. The most recent, from the year 1000, the sam year Iceland converted to Christianity, is called Kristnitökuhrau ("Conversion lava").

Skálafell, (574 m) mountain providing one of the best views in souther Iceland, an easy climb.

Kambar, the eastern slope of Hellisheiði. The road lies along the path o lava that flowed down the slope. From Kambabrún ("Kambar's edge" there is a fine view across the southern lowlands, all the way to the glacie Eyjafjallajökull, the Westman Islands and Surtsey.

Hveragerði, (pop. 2,316) a small town that has been built up since 193(Main activities are tourism, health care, greenhouses and trading. One o the biggest assets of the town is the Geothermal park in the centr of the town. Such a natural wonder in the middle of a residentia area is extremely rare in the world. There are interesting hiking trail within the town. The Poets´Trail winds its way through historical parts o the town visiting three streets that made up the "artists´ quarters" betwee the years 1940-1965. These are Bláskógar(Blue woods), the street o painters; Frumskógar (Jungles), the street of poets, formerly known a Skáldagata, and Laufskógar (Leaf Woods), the street of the musicians The Geothermal Trail visits the principal geothermal areas in and aroun town. Hveragerði is the home of the Horticultural College of Iceland. Th regions art gallery is located in Hveragerði with its changing exhibitions A vegetarian rehabilitation and Health Clinic in located here with e.g clay baths, inand outdoor swimming pools and various treatments. Th Hveragerði surroundings are a paradise for outdoors people. There ar good hiking trails within the town that link up with a network of trails o the land belonging to the Agricultural University of Iceland at the foot o Reykjafjall Mountain and in Ölfusborgir. After an earthquake struc southern Iceland on May 29th, 2008 a new hot springs area appeare directly above the town. The area demonstrates how the forces of natur shape the land, as the hot springs are quite diverse and constantly chang ing. The earthquake measured 6.3 on the Richter scale. South Icelan Tourist Information Centre located in Hveragerði, has an earthquake sim ulator, a lite up earthquake rift under the floor and various informatio about the earthquake.

Reykir, once the home of Gissur jarl ("Earl") Þorvaldsson (1208-1268).

Ölfusborgir, summer houses.

Klettagljúfur, settlement.

Kotströnd, church site. The cemetery is walled off with an exquisitel constructed wall of lava rock.

Grænhóll, a horse breeding farm.

374 Hvammsvegur, 7,6 km.

375 Arnarbælisvegur, 4,3 km.

Arnarbæli, an old manor farm, church until 1909 and a parsonage unti 1940, now a group of farms. The farm was badly hit by the earthquake of 1706 and 1896. The area around the farm is called **Arnarbælisforir**.

Ingólfsfjall, (551 m) a tuff mountain named after Ingólfur Arnarson, th first settler in Iceland. Legend has it that Ingólfur is buried in Inghóll, small hill on the mountain. South of the mountain are some gray coloure rocks called **Silfurberg** ("Silver rocks").

Kögunarhóll, a single cone under the mountain Ingólfsfjall.

Fjallstún, a deserted farm. Ingólfur Arnarsson wintered there in his thir year in Iceland. (See Road 35.)

33 Gaulverjabæjarvegur, p. 178
34 Eyrarbakkavegur, p. 178
35 Biskupstungnabraut, p. 180
38 Þorlákshafnarvegur, p. 192
310 Votmúlavegur, p. 178

Vífilsfell, (655 m) a steep tuff mountain named after Vífill, a freed slave of Ingólfur Arnarson's.

Jósepsdalur, a narrow valley east and south of Vífilsfell.

Svínahraun, a 5,000 year old lava-flow between Sandskeið and Kolviðarhóll. Lava from eruptions around the year 1000 lies on top of it, as can be seen quite clearly on approaching from the west.

Hellisheiði Power Plant, there is a Geothermal Energy Exhibition on how geothermal energy is harnessed. Experienced guides are provide informative presentations backed by multimedia shows about sustainable green energy as a global energy source. Geothermal resources can be found worldwide. Some refreshments are available at Kaffi Kolviðarhóll.

Bolavellir, ("Bull meadows") grasslands to the north of Svínahraun (see **Hengill**, below).

Kolviðarhóll, formerly a popular resting place for travellers across Hellisheiði, first with a primitive shelter and later an inn. Still later Kolviðarhóll became a popular ski lodge, but it is now deserted. From the road bend by Kolviðarhóll a rock formation resembling a well-known Icelandic poet, Matthías Jochumsson the author of the national anthem, can be seen in the mountainside to the south.

Hveradalir, a valley in the southern slopes of the mountain Reykjafell, where considerable geothermal heat is to be found.

Hengill, a tuff mountain or a mountain range, with widespread geothermal heat some of which has been harnessed. Good hiking in summertime and skiing in wintertime, especially in **Innstidalur**, the westernmost valley of Hengladalir. Highest point 803 m, **Skeggi**, a rocky point on the northwest side, overlooking a small valley, **Marardalur**, a fairly large, grassy plain closed in by cliffs and screes on all sides, with a narrow canyon leading out of it to the west. The valley is easily closed off, and bulls were often kept there. They often managed to escape, however, and roamed the moors, e.g. the **Bolavellir** meadows (see above). The bulls were fierce and a danger to travellers, other dangers including ghosts, as place names such as Draugahlíð ("Ghosts' hillside") and Draugatjörn ("Ghosts' pond") indicate.

Kristnitökuhraun, ("Conversion lava") a lava-field on Hellisheiði that came from a 6.5 km long fissure east of the mountain Reykjafell. According to the Sagas, the eruption started in the year 1000 while Icelanders were discussing at the Althing at Þingvellir whether to convert from paganism to Christianity. Hence the name.

Hellukofinn ("flat-stone hut"), on the Hellisheiði uplands, was built in 1830 by re-stacking rocks taken from a centuries-old cairn that had stood on the same bedrock. Measuring 1.85 m on each side and 2 m high, the hut can shelter 4-5 persons in a blizzard.

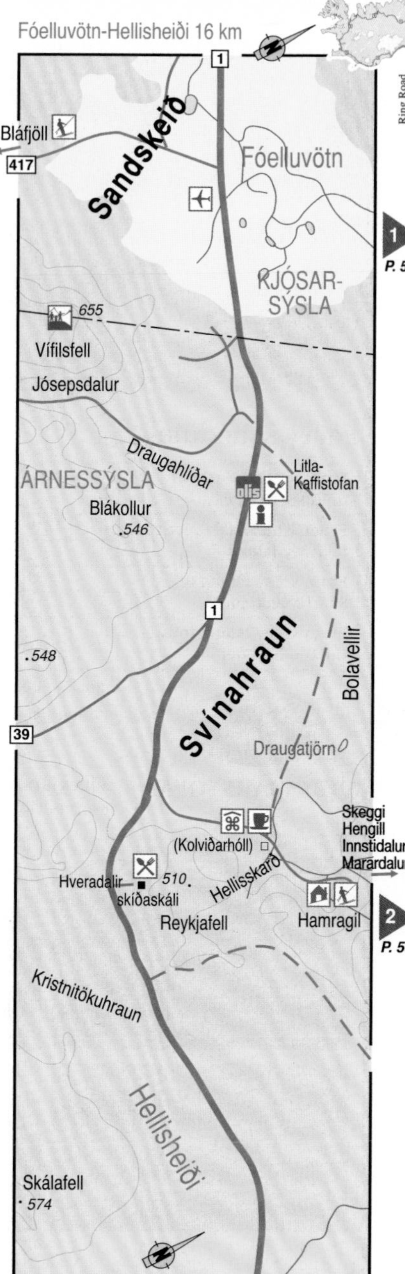

1 P. 564

2 P. 565

39 **Þrengslavegur,** p. 194 417 **Bláfjallavegur,** p. 225

Viðey

Island

Ferry schedule

From the Old Harbour to Viðey Island	Summer		12:00						
	Winter								
From Skarfabakki pier to Viðey Island	Summer	11:15	12:15	13:15	14:15	15:15	16:15	17:15	
	Winter			13:15	14:15	15:15			
From Viðey Island to Skarfabakki pier	Summer		12:30	13:30	14:30	15:30	16:30	17:30	18:30
	Winter			13:30	14:30	15:30	16:30		
From Viðey Island to the Old harbour	Summer					15:30			
	Winter								

Summer (daily from 15 May to 30 September

Winter (on weekends) from 1 October to 14 May

VIÐEYJARSTOFA
Restaurant

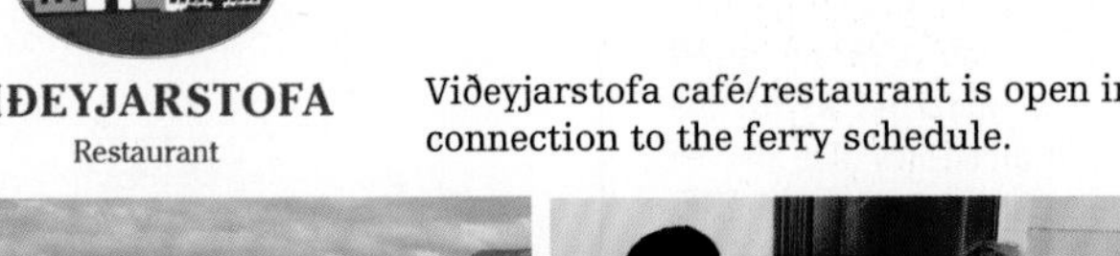

Viðeyjarstofa café/restaurant is open in connection to the ferry schedule.

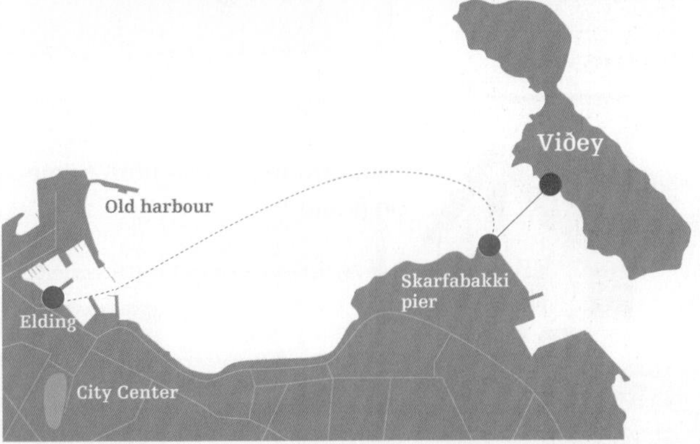

- History, nature, art
- Restaurant / Café
- Horse rental
- Bike rental

Tel. +354 533 5055
Web. www.videy.com

Rauðavatn, a small lake on the eastern outskirts of Reykjavík. East of the lake is a grove where mountain pines were planted in the beginnig of last century.

Rauðhólar, a group of red hills, pseudocraters. Great quantities of pumice have been taken from them and used to build roads and the runways of Reykjavík Airport. The pseudocraters have thus been to a great extent spoiled but are now protected.

Elliðavatn, the largest lake in the vicinity of Reykjavík. Also a farm of the same name, where in the 18th century a Swedish-German baron, by the name of Hastfer, started a sheep-breeding station. On the Þinganes point and surrounding area by the lake remains have been found which confirm that the Kjalarnesþing meetings were held there of old, for a period at least. It might even have been there that they prepared to establish the Althing at Þingvellir in the year 930. Archeological digs there have brought to light important relics from as far back as the settlement.

Heiðmörk, a recreation and forestry area belonging to Reykjavík and the neighbouring communities, a nature reserve since 1948. Millions of trees have been planted there. Good walking routes and a view-dial. Arctic Adventures offers moutain bike tours in Heiðmörk.

Gunnarshólmi, a farm. South of the road is **Silungapollur,** a former kindergarten.

Tröllabörnin, ("The giants' children") a group of small pseudocraters by the road. Portected since 1983.

Gvendarbrunnar, named after Guðmundur bishop Arason (1160–1237) from there the people of Reykjavík get its drinking water4.

Lækjarbotnar, formerly a farm and a popular resting-place for travellers.

Bláfjöll, a mountain range south of Vífilsfell, a skiing and outdoor-sports area a few km from the main road. Good skiing area, both Alpine and cross-country in Bláfjöll and Heiðin há, especially in late winter and springtime. Skilifts, lodge etc. The lava-fields west of Bláfjöll can be very dangerous, however, because of cracks, subsidence and open-roofed caves where the fall down to the rough floor may be as much as 10 m.

Lyklafell, a small mountain on the north side of the road in Fóellu vötn. Where 3 counties meet Árnessýsla, Gullbringusýsla and Kjósarsýsla.

Sandskeið, a fairly large sandy plateau, the bed of an old lake, now partly cultivated. Airstrip and headquarters of the Icelandic Gliding Association. On a low, rocky hill to the west of Sandskeið are the remains of an old mountain hut. The road used to lie over Sandskeið, south of the airstrip. It has now been moved north across the **Fóelluvötn** area, where considerable lakes are formed in the spring melts. They empty down over the Fossvellir plains into the river Hólmsá. In Fossvallaklif pass there is a stone marked 1887 showing when the first road for vehicles was laid.

41 **Reykjanesbraut,** p. 204 | 413 **Breiðholtsbraut,** p. 202
417 **Bláfjallavegur,** p. 225 | 435 **Nesjavallaleið,** p. 187

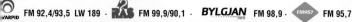

Ártúnshöfði-Fóelluvötn 25 km

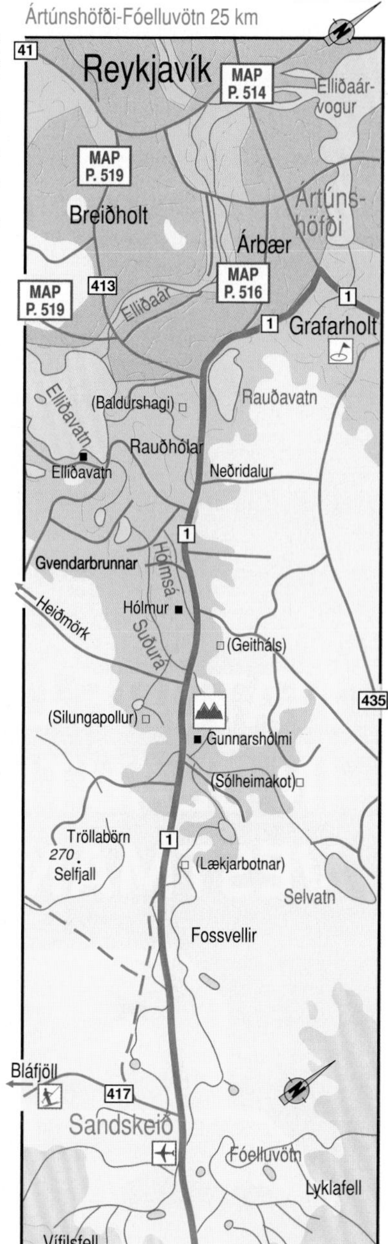

Fóelluvötn-Ártúnshöfði 25 km

1 P. 564

NATURE UP CLOSE IN BEAUTIFUL VESTMANNAEYJAR

The ferry Herjólfur sails from Landeyjahöfn to the islands, a comfortable and economic trip that only takes 40 minutes. About 2 hrs. drive from Reykjavík.

Schedule, bookings and further information on **herjolfur.is**

HERJÓLFUR

Tel. +354 481 2800 | www.herjolfur.is

FÍTON / SÍA F1045467

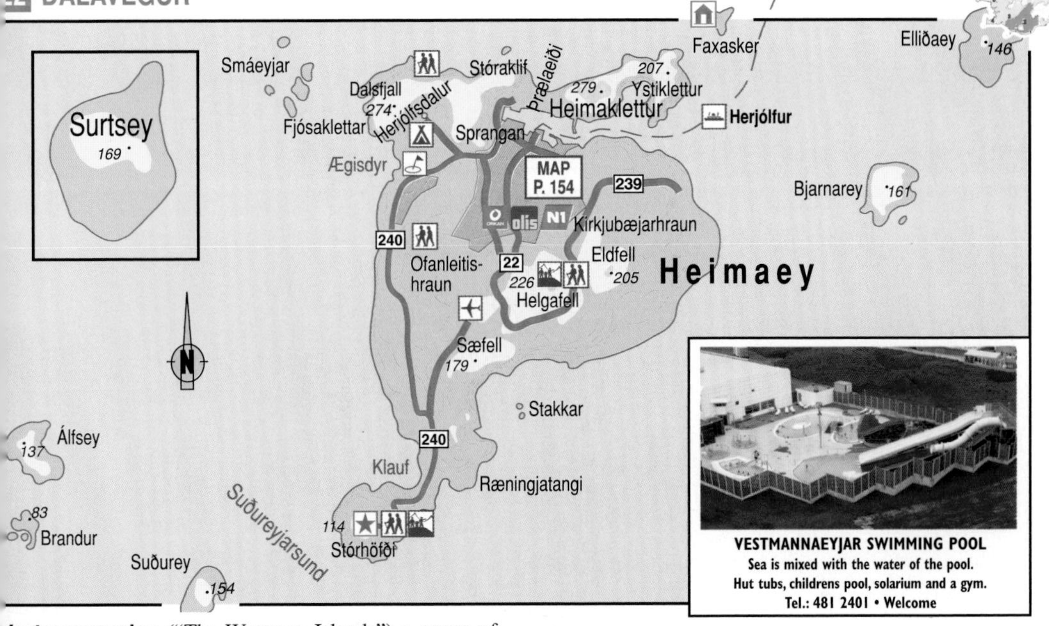

Vestmannaeyjar, ("The Westman Islands") a group of 15-18 steep and rocky islands, with green mountain sides and ridges. All the islands come from submarine eruptions, the oldest from about 10,000 years ago and others from 5,000 years ago when the mountain Helgafell erupted and the Ofanleitishraun lava field was formed. In 1963 there was a submarine eruption which went on for almost 5 years and eventually formed the island Surtsey. Then, in 1973, there was an eruption on the only inhabited island of the group, Heimaey. No lives were lost, though almost 400 of the 1,200 houses of the town were buried under lava from the new volcano **Eldfell** ("Fire mountain"). Before the town was evacuated in the 1973 eruption the population was 5,300, now it's 4,219. The islands of Vestmannaeyjar are famous for the millions of birds in puffin and other sea bird colonies there. The hunting of puffins is widely practiced throughout the islands and each year thousands of fulmar and guillemot eggs are collected from the cliffs by locals who lower each other on long ropes to get at them. Since 1900 Heimaey has been one of the most important fishing towns in Iceland. A very good aquarium is located there, an historical museum and a library. A replica of a 11th century wooden church has been build in the Islands as a gift from Norway on a occation of the 1000th anniversary of the adoption of Christianity in the year 2000 to commemorate the arrival of Hjalti Skeggjason and Gissur the White in Iceland in 1000 AD, whose mission was to convert Icelanders to the new faith. The church was to be built in the place where the two first landed on their way to Þingvellir. A special Vestmannaeyjar activity is Sprangan at Skiphellar ("Ship caves") where children and teenagers practice lowering each other and swinging along the cliffs on ropes. Informtion Centre in the Museum building by City Hall. Ferry connections between Vestmannaeyjar and Bakki.

239 Eldfellsvegur.

240 Stórhöfðavegur, 7 km to the lighthouse.

Ræningjatangi, ("Pirate point") near Stórhöfði. In 1627 sea rovers from Algeria landed there and killed scores of people. A number escaped by hiding in caves and the lava fields, but about 240 people were taken to Algeria and sold there as slaves. A few were rescued about ten years later. One of the most famous of these was Guðríður Símonardóttir, known as Tyrkja-Gudda ("Turk-Guðríður"), who later married the priest and poet Hallgrímur Pétursson, author of the *Passíusálmar* ("Passion Hymns").

Stórhöfði, a good spot to watch the puffin colonies.

Helgafell, (226 m) the elder of the volcanos on Heimaey. View dial.

Herjólfsdalur, an open valley in the outskirts of town where, since 1874, the people of Vestmannaeyar have celebrated their annual festival (known as their "national" holiday) over the 3-day weekend in the beginning of August.

Fjósaklettar, in Herjólfsdalur is the site where man-made caves were discovered in 1999. It is speculated that these caves were once used to house cattle.

Pompei of the North, is a name given to an excavation of houses that were lost in an volcanic eruption in 1973.

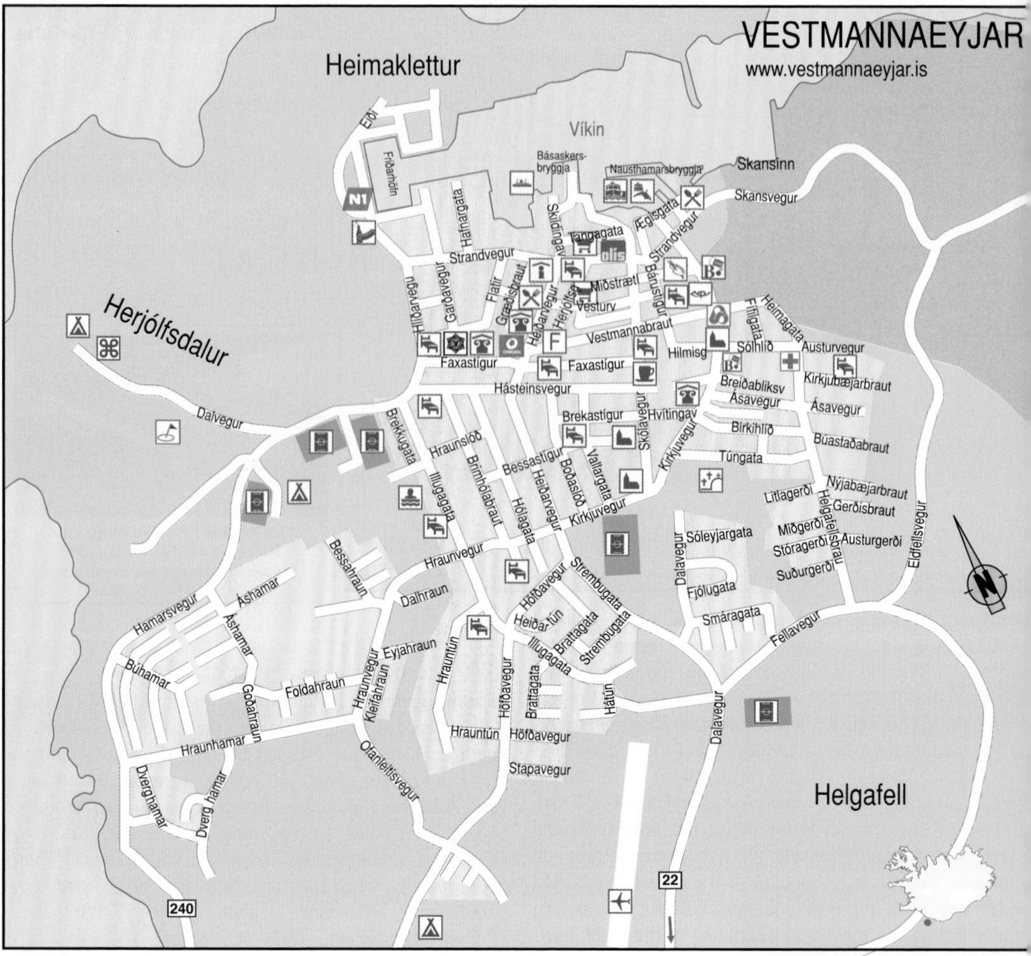

VESTMANNAEYJAR

www.vestmannaeyjar.is

Heimaklettur
Víkin
Skansinn
Skansvegur
Básaskersbryggja
Nausthamarsbryggja
Herjólfsdalur
Dalvegur
Friðarhöfn
Eiði
Hafnargata
Strandvegur
Tangagata
Ægisgata
Skildingav
Hlíðarvegur
Garðavegur
Flatir
Græðisbraut
Heiðarvegur
Herjólfsg
Miðstræti
Vesturv
Bárustígur
Vestmannabraut
Heimagata
Fífilgata
Hilmisg
Sólhlíð
Austurvegur
Kirkjubæjarbraut
Faxastígur
Hásteinsvegur
Breiðabliksv
Ásavegur
Brekastígur
Hvítingav
Skólavegur
Birkihlíð
Búastaðabraut
Túngata
Brekkugata
Hraunslóð
Bessastígur
Boðaslóð
Vallargata
Kirkjuvegur
Illugagata
Brimhólabraut
Heiðarvegur
Hólagata
Nýjabæjarbraut
Litlagerði
Helgafellsbraut
Gerðisbraut
Miðgerði
Stóragerði
Austurgerði
Suðurgerði
Sóleyjargata
Eldfellsvegur
Dalavegur
Fjólugata
Smáragata
Fellavegur
Hraunvegur
Bessahraun
Dalhraun
Hamarsvegur
Áshamar
Búhamar
Goðahraun
Foldahraun
Hraunvegur
Kleifahraun
Eyjahraun
Hrauntún
Höfðavegur
Heiðartún
Brattagata
Strembugata
Hátún
Hraunhamar
Ofanleitisvegur
Stapavegur
Dverghamar
Dverg hamar
Helgafell
240
22

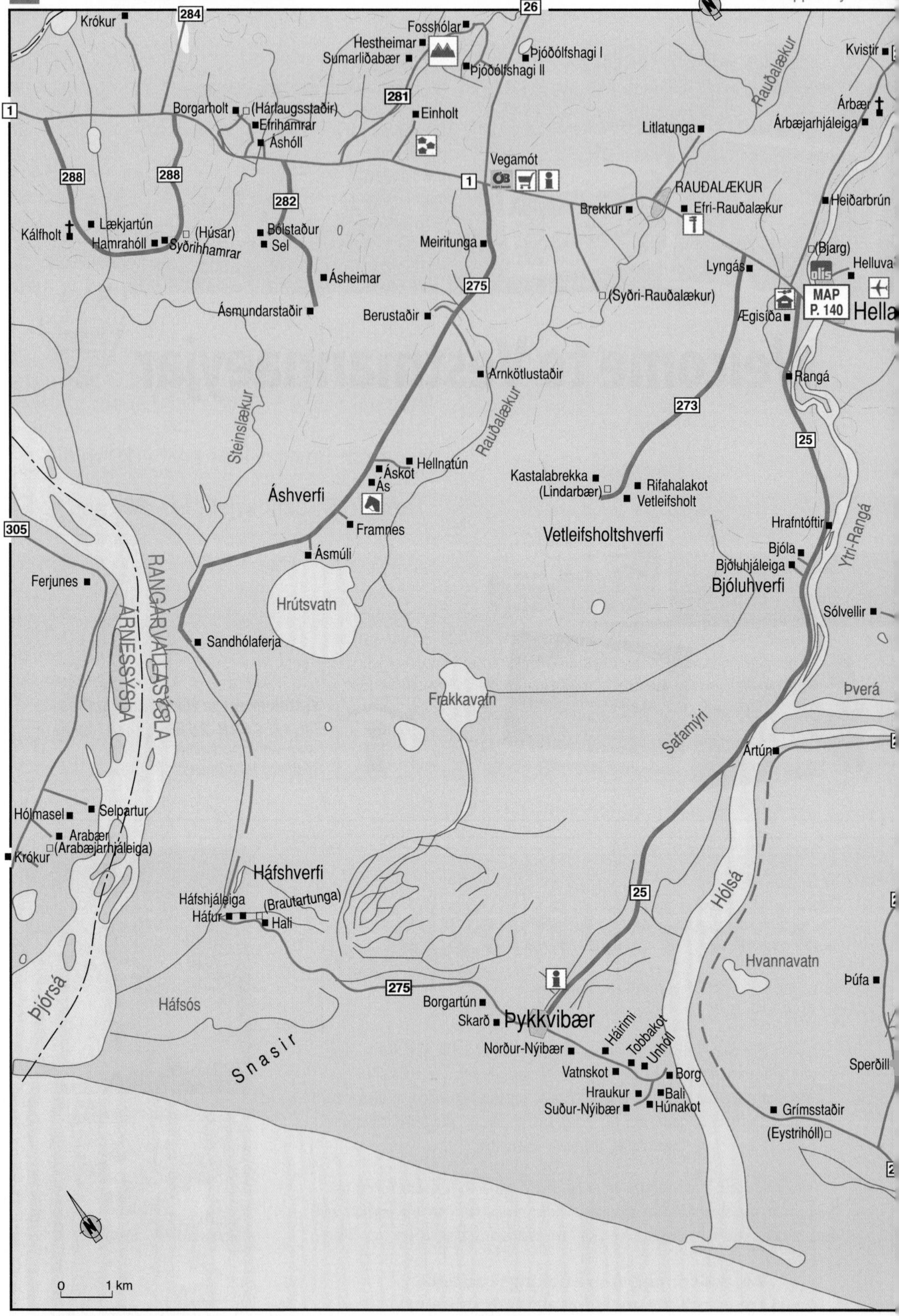

13 P. 576

1 Suðurlandsvegur, p. 142 | 26 Landvegur, p. 128 | 252 Landeyjavegur, p. 166
271 Árbæjarvegur, p. 158 | 284 Heiðarvegur, p. 158 | 305 Villingaholtsvegur, p. 178

:gissíða, a farm on the western banks of the Rangá ver. There are 11 man-made caves in the home-field, ne of them large and used for storing hay up until 1980. ome of the caves have peculiar carvings on the walls, lieved by some to have been made by Irish hermits efore the settlement in the 9th century. There was a ford n the Rangá near Ægissíða, and this used to be a much-avelled route.

tri-Rangá, a clear river originating on the sands etween Hekla and Þjórsá. Good fishing.

ióluhverfi, a group of farms near Rangá, one of them eing **Hrafntóftir**, dwelling-place of the settler Ketill engur during his first winter in Iceland, and the rthplace of his son Hrafn Hængsson, who was the first w-speaker after the enactment of the laws of Úlfljótur.

afamýri, formerly extensive marshes, extremely grassy. as now mostly been drained after dykes were built ong the rivers on the east side.

'5 Þykkvabæjarvegur, 16 km.

ykkvibær, a district to the south of Safamýri, formerly urrounded by rivers with the ocean on the south side, robably the oldest country-village in Iceland. A church **Hábær**. Formerly the rivers threatened this district but ykes have changed this. One of the main potato-growing istricts in Iceland. Potato processing plant.

73 Bugavegur, 5,4 km.

etleifsholt, a farm and the settling place of Ráðormur. small hill, Kollhóll, below the farm, said to be a home f the "hidden people" and not to be spoiled in any way, therwise bad luck will follow.

yðri-Rauðalækur, an abandoned farm where two aves were made in 1896-97 and 1916, possibly the most ecent man-made caves in Iceland.

:75 Ásvegur, 12 km.

Ás, a substantial farm, the main one of a group of farms known together as **Áshverfi**. The birthplace of Gísli Bjarnason (1678-1707), who died at sea from smallpox, the disease then being brought to Iceland with his belongings. It became the worst epidemic since the Plague, killing 12,000 in the diocese of Skálholt and 6,000 in the north.

Hrútsvatn, ("Ram's lake") southwest of Ás, the biggest lake in the district of Holt, 2,4 km^2. A monster resembling a brown ram is said to live in the lake, hence the name.

Sandhólaferja, a farm by Þjórsá, one of the principal ferry points east of the river until the bridge was built. In early Saga times some historical killings took place at Sandhólaferja when Sigmundur and Steinn came from Eyrarbakki and both of them wanted to be first across the river.

Háfshverfi, a group of farms, and a church until 1914 when it was moved to **Hábær** in Þykkvibær. The land there is so flat that the two lakes, Hrútsvatn and **Frakkavatn**, are only 5 m above sea level. It is easiest to get to Háfshverfi via Þykkvibær. Háfur was the settling place of Þorkell bjálfi.

Þjórsárós, the Þjórsá estuary, becoming 3-4 km wide below Sandhólaferja. Half-closed on the sea side by a long sandreef forming a lake or lagoon. Seals are common there. In the Sagas it said that ships often landed in Þjórsárós.

281 Sumarliðabæjarvegur, 5,6 km.

282 Ásmundarstaðavegur, 3,2 km.

288 Kálfholtsvegur, a 7 km long circle.

Kálfholt, a farm and a church, formerly a parsonage.

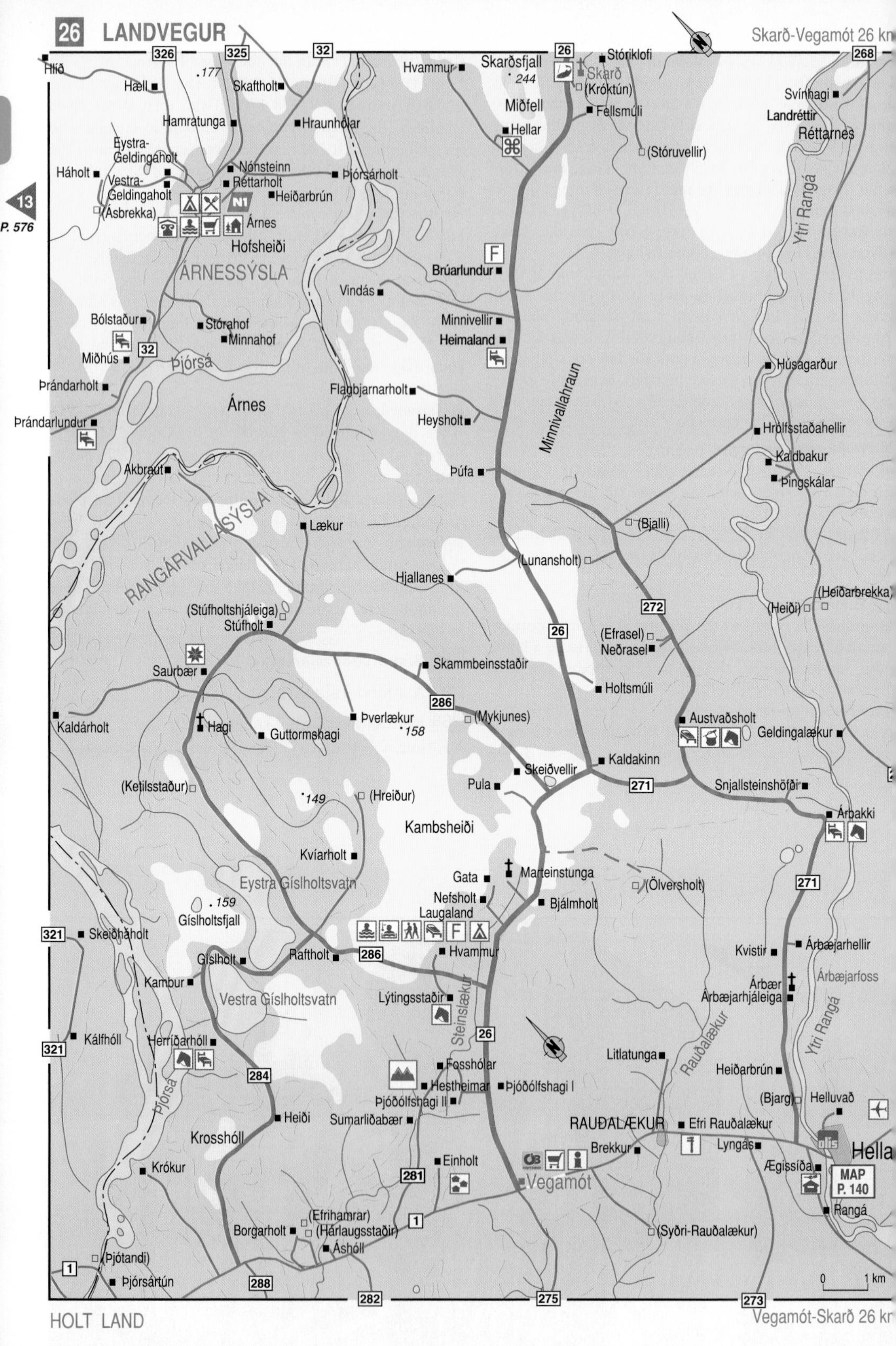
Hlíð
Hæll
Skaftholt
Hamratunga
Hraunhólar
Eystra-Geldingaholt
Háholt
Vestra-Geldingaholt
(Ásbrekka)
Nónsteinn
Réttarholt
Heiðarbrún
Þjórsárholt
Árnes
Hofsheiði
ÁRNESSÝSLA
Hvammur
Skarðsfjall
244
Stóriklofi
Skarð
(Króktún)
Miðfell
Fellsmúli
Hellar
(Stóruvellir)
Svínhagi
Landréttir
Réttarnes
Ytri Rangá
Brúarlundur
Vindás
Bólstaður
Stórahof
Minnahof
Miðhús
Þjórsá
Þrándarholt
Árnes
Þrándarlundur
Minnivellir
Heimaland
Flagbjarnarholt
Heysholt
Minnivallahraun
Húsagarður
Hrólfsstaðahellir
Kaldbakur
Þingskálar
Akbraut
Þúfa
Lækur
RANGÁRVALLASÝSLA
(Bjalli)
(Lunansholt)
Hjallanes
(Heiðarbrekka)
(Heiði)
(Stúfholtshjáleiga)
Stúfholt
(Efrasel)
Neðrasel
Saurbær
Skammbeinsstaðir
Holtsmúli
Kaldárholt
Hagi
Guttormshagi
Þverlækur
158
(Mykjunes)
Austvaðsholt
Geldingalækur
Skeiðvellir
Kaldakinn
(Ketilsstaður)
149
(Hreiður)
Pula
Snjallsteinshöfði
Árbakki
Kambsheiði
Kvíarholt
Gata
Marteinstunga
(Ölversholt)
Eystra Gíslholtsvatn
159
Gíslholtsfjall
Nefsholt
Laugaland
Bjálmholt
Skeiðháholt
Gíslholt
Raftholt
Hvammur
Kvistir
Árbæjarhellir
Árbæjarfoss
Kambur
Vestra Gíslholtsvatn
Lýtingsstaðir
Steinslækur
Árbær
Árbæjarhjáleiga
Kálfhóll
Herríðarhóll
Fosshólar
Litlatunga
Rauðalækur
Heiðarbrún
Hestheimar
Þjóðólfshagi I
Þjóðólfshagi II
(Bjarg)
Helluvað
Heiði
Sumarliðabær
RAUÐALÆKUR
Efri Rauðalækur
Krosshóll
Brekkur
Lyngás
Hella
Einholt
Ægissíða
MAP P. 140
Krókur
Vegamót
(Efrihamrar)
Borgarholt
(Hárlaugsstaðir)
Áshóll
(Syðri-Rauðalækur)
Rangá
(Þjótandi)
Þjórsártún
0 1 km
326
325
32
26
268
272
286
271
321
284
281
1
288
282
275
273
P. 576
13

‹arð, a farm and church, long a manor farm. Much of land, like that of many farms in the Landsveit district, as destroyed by sand erosion. The farmhouse was rmerly at the foot of the **Skarðsfjall** mountain, where ere are now several-meter-high sand dunes. Good view om the mountain.

ellsmúli, a farm and parsonage since 1912.

vammur, a farm, long the home of Eyjólfur Guðundsson (1857-1940), a leader in his district and in the ght against the sand erosion that threatened the grassnds of the upper Landsveit district.

ellar, ("Caves") a farm where some man-made caves e used as hay-barns. The Bishop of Iceland celebrated ass in the cave in 2000 to mark the 1000th anniversary the conversion of Iceland.

rúarlundur, the community centre of the Landsveit strict, built near the now deserted church-farm of **tóruvellir**, formerly a parsonage and manor farm.

agbjarnarholt, a farm. Not far from there is Þinghóll Meeting hill") where some ruins, excavated in 1883, dicate that official gatherings were held there, though is is not mentioned in old records.

rnes, ("River peninsula") an island in the Þjórsá river, at e time the official meeting place for Árnessýsla, and nce the name of the county. Some ruins can still be seen, d place names like Þinghóll (see above). There are more ins on the west side of the river. It is believed that the ver was formerly all to the east of Árnes, and later broke rough on the west side where the main channel is now. vo waterfalls in the river by Árnes, Búðafoss in the west annel and Hestafoss in the east channel.

72 Bjallavegur, 8,65 km.

and or **Landsveit,** the district north of Holt between órsá and Rangá. Most of the land is old, dry lava-fields vered with soil and vegetation. Much has been done to op the sand erosion and recultivate the lava-fields.

arteinstunga, a farm and church.

augaland, a school and community centre. Geothermal at. This heat has been harnessed to provide central ating to much of the district. A primary school is run ere.

óðólfshagi, a farm with a man-made cave.

Holt, the district between the rivers Þjórsá and Rangá, mostly rolling hills with marshes in between. The soil is very thick and the district green and grassy.

271 Árbæjarvegur, 12,5 km.

Lækjarbotnar, a farm where once lived Gissur, whom the giantesses were going to catch. From the mountain Búrfell he heard a voice say, "Sister, lend me a pot", and from the mountain Bjólfell came the answer, "What do you want it for?" From Búrfell, "Cook a man in it." From Bjólfell, "Who is he?" and from Búrfell, "Gissur from Botnar, Gissur from Lækjarbotnar". He escaped (see **Tröllkonuhlaup**).

Landréttir, sheep-folds by Rangá.

Hrólfsstaðahellir, a farm, birthplace of the poet Guðmundur Guðmundsson (1874-1919). In a hill in the home field are some man-made caves, among them **Hrútshellir**("Ram´s cave"), named for a ghost ram that has often been seen there.

Snjallsteinshöfði, a farm, in Saga times the home of Steinn hinn snjalli ("the clever"), a relative of Gunnar from Hlíðarendi of *Njáls saga*. Formerly a church. Some ancient runic writings on the cliff east of the farm.

Árbær, a farm and church by Ytri-Rangá.

286 Hagabraut, a 20 km long circle.

Skeiðvellir, a horse breeding farm.

Akbrautarholt, a small hill near the farm Akbraut, where ruins of an old church and a graveyard are to be found, interesting columnar rocks.

Hagi, a farm and church. In the church there is a carved font by the artist Ríkarður Jónsson given to the church on its 100th birthday.

Kaldárholt, a farm by the river Þjórsá west of Hagi. Geothermal heat.

284 Heiðarvegur, 11 km.

Gíslholt, a farm between two lakes both named after the farm. The mountain Gíslholtsfjall (159 m) north of the farm is the highest point in the district of Holt. A small lake on top of the mountain.

Herríðarhóll, a traditional farm with horse breeding, sheep and milking cows, situated between river Þjórsá and lake Gíslholt.

281 Sumarliðabæjarvegur, 5,6 km.

1 **Suðurlandsvegur,** p. 142
25 **Þykkvabæjarvegur,** p. 156
32 **Þjórsárdalsvegur,** p. 175
268 **Þingskálavegur,** p. 171
273 **Bugavegur,** p. 156
275 **Ásvegur,** p. 156
282 **Ásmundarstaðavegur,** p. 156
288 **Kálfholtsvegur,** p. 156
321 **Skeiðháholtsvegur,** p. 172
325 **Gnúpverjavegur,** p. 175
326 **Hælsvegur,** p. 175

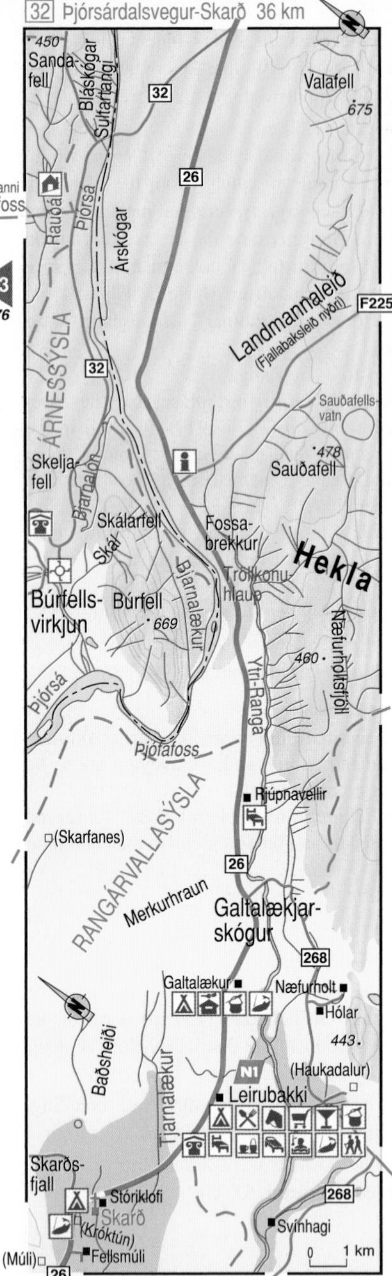

Þjófafoss.

Fossabrekkur, ("Waterfall slopes") an interesting place by the river Rang an oasis in the pumice desert, falls and rich vegetation (angelica etc.).

Tröllkonuhlaup, ("Giantess' leap") a waterfall in Þjórsá. Giantess believed to live in Búrfell and Bjólfell used the rocks in the river as steppi stones when they tried to catch Gissur of Lækjarbotnar.

Hekla, (1,491 m) the most famous volcano in Iceland, a ridge more th 4 km long. There have been at least 18 eruptions in recorded history, t first in 1104 and the latest in 2000, when scientists were able to predi the eruption half an hour in advance using the alarm system of t Icelandic Meteorological Office. In the eruption of 1947 the peak rose m. The easiest climbing route is along the northern ridge. The first know ascent was made by the explorers Eggert Ólafsson and Bjarni Pálsson June 20th 1750.

Þjófafoss, a waterfall in the Þjórsá river south of Búrfell; a 5 km lo jeep-track leads there, very difficult to drive.

Þjórsárhraun, a great lava-field that came about 8,000 years ago fro cracks near the Veiðivötn lakes and flowed along Þjórsárdalur, Landsve Skeið and Flói to reach the sea between the rivers Ölfusá and Þjórsá, distance of 130 km and covering some 800 km². One of the largest know lava-flows anywhere on Earth.

Skarfanes, a deserted farm now belonging to the Forestry Servic Extensive birchwoods protected since 1941. Can be reached via jee tracks from Þjófafoss and Skarð.

Galtalækjarskógur, some birch-woods north of Galtalækur, a favori meeting place of the temperance movement, which sponsors an annu festival held in the first weekend in August.

Galtalækur, the northernmost farm in the Landsveit district. The o mountain tracks Fjallabaksvegur nyrðri and Sprengisandsvegur st there. Formerly a popular stopping place for those who climbed Hekla.

Baðsheiði, ("Bath moor") the area north of Skarð, geothermal he where there was once a steam-bath.

Leirubakki, there is the Hekla Museum.

Stóriklofi, a farm and formerly a church. Best known from judge To Jónsson of the 15th century. The Klofi farmhouse went under sand dun and was rebuilt across from Skarð.

32 **Þjórsárdalsvegur,** p. 176
268 **Þingskálavegur,** p. 171
F225 **Landmannaleið,** p. 444

ɔrisvatn, the second largest lake in Iceland, 70 km^2, 109 m deep. This ke is regulated and may rise by as much as 5 meters, reaching 80 km^2. . upper end is cut in two by the mountain Útigönguhöfði, forming two ıys. The shores are mostly steep and desolate. Formerly the outlet was **ɔrisós**, but there is now a regulated outlet down to the power station of galda.

galda, (543 m) low mountain ridges on both sides of Tungnaá. The galda power station was opened in 1977, power 150,000 kW.

Sigölduvirkjun Power Station.

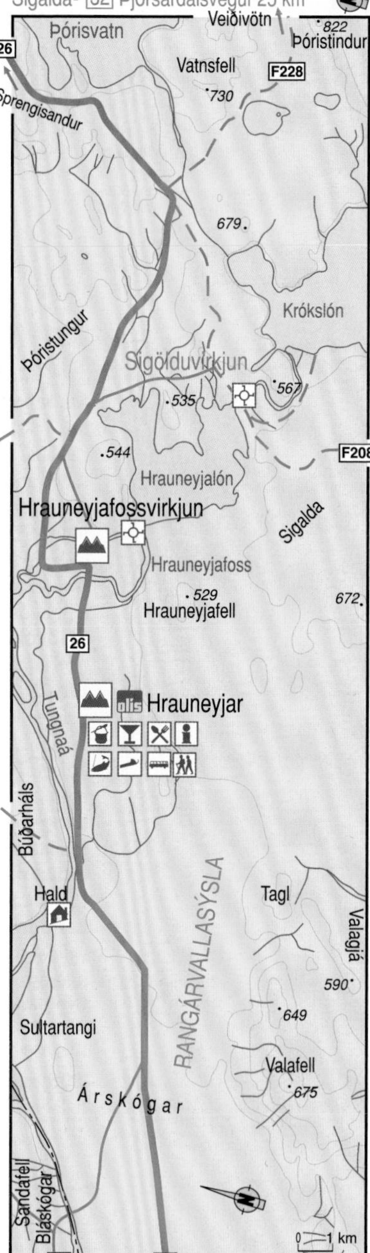

ɔristungur, the triangle between the rivers Kaldakvísl and Tungnaá ɪrth of Hrauneyjafoss.

rauneyjafoss, a 29 m high waterfall in the river Tungnaá where a new 0,000 kW power station was built in 1981.

ıðarháls, a long ridge, 600-700 m above sea level, between the rivs Þjórsá and Kaldakvísl, mostly desolate and bare. Jeep-traffic was once ɛquent along this ridge.

ıngnaá, a glacial river coming from the west side of Vatnajökull. ɪrmerly a serious obstacle for travellers, which could only be crossed by ɪrry at **Hald** and **Bjallavað** and forded at **Hófsvað**. Two power stations .ve been built on Tungnaá at Sigalda and Hrauneyjafoss.

ıltartangi, a former isthums at the crossing of the rivers Tungnaá and órsá. A 6 km wide dam has been constructed there and given the name ıltartangastífla. Sultartangastífla was built there to provide a reservoir r the Búrfellsvirkjun Power Statation. A tunnel goes out of the reservoir the south-west through Sandfell to the Sultartangi Power Plant (120 W), inaugurated in October 1999. The tunnel is 12 m high and 3,4 km ıg.

'skógar, desolate and sandy lava fields on the east of Þjórsá up to ıngnaá. Landgræðsla ríkisins, the Soil Conservation Service of Iceland, .s revegetated extensive land areas in this region.

32 **Þjórsárdalsvegur,** p. 176 | F208 **Fjallabaksleið,** p. 436

F26 **Sprengisandsleið,** p. 430 | F228 **Veiðivatnaleið,** p. 446

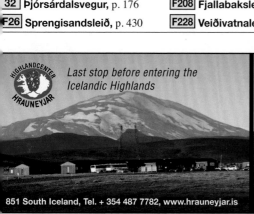

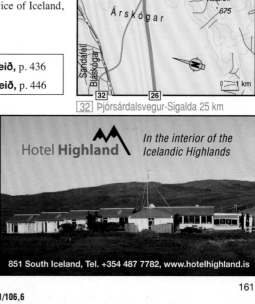

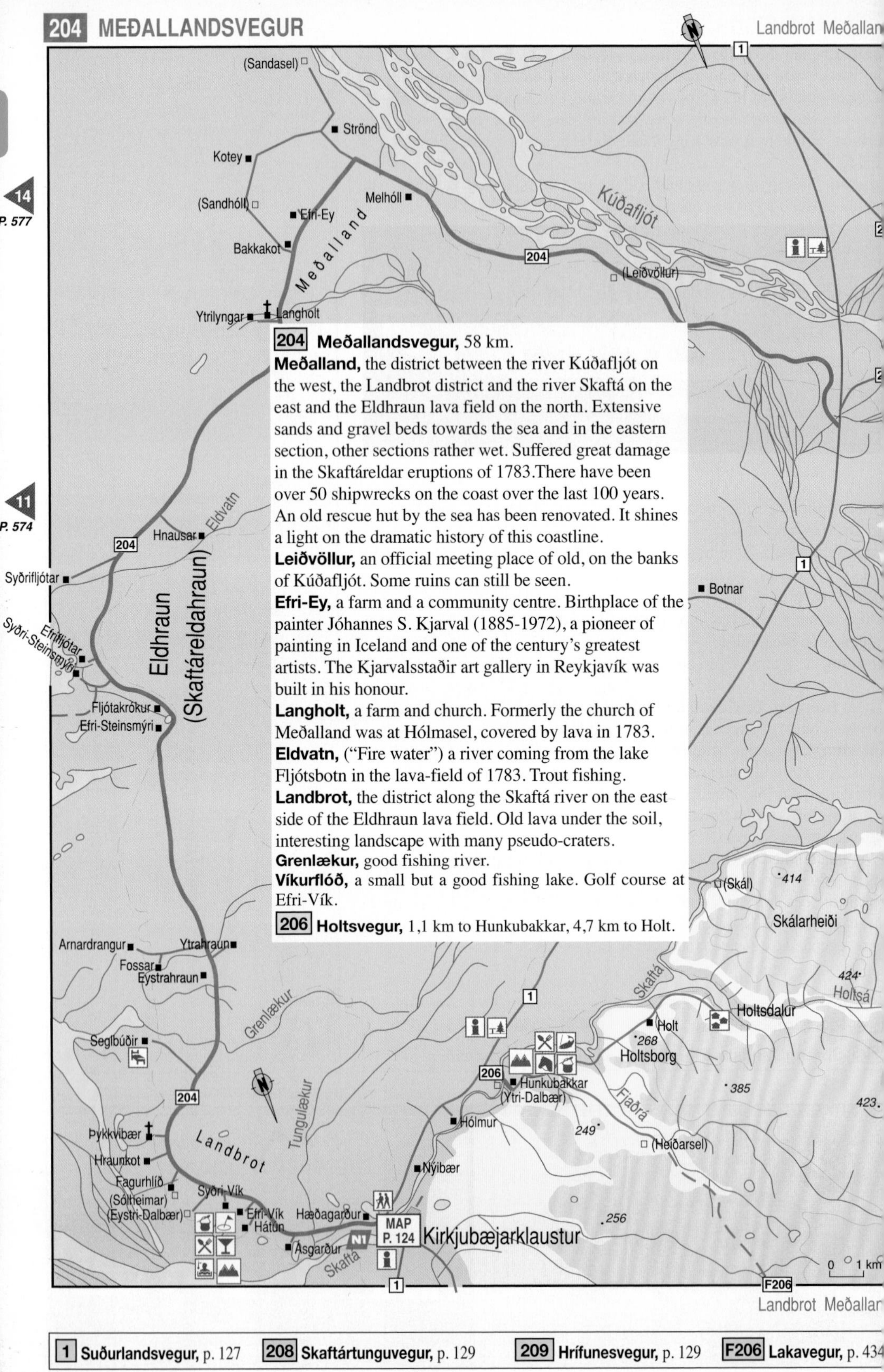

204 Meðallandsvegur, 58 km.

Meðalland, the district between the river Kúðafljót on the west, the Landbrot district and the river Skaftá on the east and the Eldhraun lava field on the north. Extensive sands and gravel beds towards the sea and in the eastern section, other sections rather wet. Suffered great damage in the Skaftáreldar eruptions of 1783.There have been over 50 shipwrecks on the coast over the last 100 years. An old rescue hut by the sea has been renovated. It shines a light on the dramatic history of this coastline.

Leiðvöllur, an official meeting place of old, on the banks of Kúðafljót. Some ruins can still be seen.

Efri-Ey, a farm and a community centre. Birthplace of the painter Jóhannes S. Kjarval (1885-1972), a pioneer of painting in Iceland and one of the century's greatest artists. The Kjarvalsstaðir art gallery in Reykjavík was built in his honour.

Langholt, a farm and church. Formerly the church of Meðalland was at Hólmasel, covered by lava in 1783.

Eldvatn, ("Fire water") a river coming from the lake Fljótsbotn in the lava-field of 1783. Trout fishing.

Landbrot, the district along the Skaftá river on the east side of the Eldhraun lava field. Old lava under the soil, interesting landscape with many pseudo-craters.

Grenlækur, good fishing river.

Víkurflóð, a small but a good fishing lake. Golf course at Efri-Vík.

206 Holtsvegur, 1,1 km to Hunkubakkar, 4,7 km to Holt.

1 **Suðurlandsvegur,** p. 127 | 208 **Skaftártunguvegur,** p. 129 | 209 **Hrífunesvegur,** p. 129 | F206 **Lakavegur,** p. 434

Vatnajökull National Park

Europe's Greatest Outdoor Playground!

nerly a national park in itself, **ftafell** lies at the foot of the sive icecap that gives **Vatnajökull ional** Park its name. The ajökull massif is not only the est glacier in the world outside of olar regions, but together with urrounding mountain ranges has ially become Europe's largest onal park. A vast land where ndless glacial tongues stretch to horizon in all directions, flanked gged peaks and lush greenery, re iceberg-packed lagoons feed ng rivers, there are few places arth that can compare in sheer scale or awe-inspiring beauty. For this reason, as well as its proximity to endless hiking, climbing, and adventure options, Skaftafell has become the hub of glacier and mountain operations in Iceland, and you can find Glacier Guides in the heart of it all!

For those with a passion for nature at its purest or a thirst for outdoor adventure, Skaftafell promises to be the ultimate destination! With a range of activities from mild to wild, Glacier Guides has developed a menu of outdoor activities that caters to everyone.

Our **easy glacier walks** follow the path of least resistance through glacier and mountain landscapes, while our longer hikes take a more adventurous approach into the world of deep blue crevasses and towering ice falls. For those craving a serious challenge, consider a guided multi-day summit trip to Iceland's highest peak, **Hvannadalshnúkur**, at 2110m, or put your nerves and skills to the wall for some vertical **ice climbing**!

If glaciers are an interest but not quite the same obsession they are to us, get into something totally different like **mountain biking** or **rock climbing**, or jump on a **combo tour** for a chang of scenery after an introduction to the ice! Check out puffins and other sea birds at the **Ingólfshöfði Cape**, o relax on the decks of a cruise boat as it meanders through a maze of curiou seals and towering icebergs on the famous **Jökulsárlón** glacial lagoon!

Whatever your passion, you'll find plenty of it in Vatnajökull National Park!

Eyjafjallajökull

The Eyjafjallajökull central volcano (1,660 m) is less than a million years old and therefore still considered as young. No high-temperature area appears on the surface, probably because the volcano's magma chamber is small and lies at great depth. The jökull part of the name means glacier; this one is 80 km2 in size and the seventh largest in Iceland. Its ice generally fills the 2.5-km2 caldera on top of the volcano, from where the outlet glacier Gígjökull flows downwards to the lowlands. During most of the volcano's existence, it has been covered by either

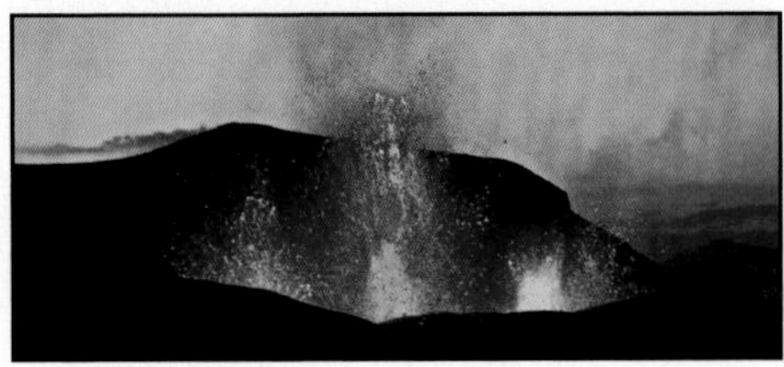

this glacial ice or that of Ice Age glaciations, so that uncounted eruptions under ice have largely produced hyaloclastite material and gradually piled it up to form the mountain.
One recorded eruption occurred in 1612, while another started on the evening of 19 December 1821 and lasted, including short periods of inactivity, until January 1823.

The Fimmvörðuháls volcanic eruption

In 1994, scientists noticed magma flowing under Eyjafjallajökull central volcano, with accompanying earthquakes. A similar event occurred in 2000. In the following years, measurements indicated that fissures around the glacier peak were beginning to enlarge, with clear signs of increasing geothermal heat below. In mid-2009, a magma influx began once more, accompanied by earthquakes. In the first three months of 2010, the seismic activity inside the volcano was nearly constant. Everyone wondered whether the magma would ever reach the surface, since the source of these earthquakes generally lay at a depth of about 10 km.

Around 11 p.m. on 20 March, a small eruption finally began in the northern part of Fimmvörðuháls pass. The lava from this eruption flowed north, towards Þórsmörk, but there was never much seismic activity and the eruption ended on 12 April.

The Eyjafjallajökull volcanic eruption

About 11 p.m. on 13 April, an earthquake measuring 2.5 occurred, located approximately 6 km beneath Eyjafjallajökull. About 7 a.m. the next morning, apparently after volcanic activity had been melting ice at the summit for several hours, the volume of water emerging from under Gígjökull outlet glacier started increasing fast. Two major jökulhlaups, or glacial floods, gushed down from their source in the caldera on 14 April, although little damage was caused by these, while additional, minor jökulhlaups flowed from the caldera over the next few days. As long as the rising lava still contacted water in the caldera, steam explosions resulted that threw the lava up in bits, creating an ash cloud and seriously affecting Europe's air traffic. However, just over a week after the eruption began, the lava no longer encountered water and began running north under the Gígjökull ice, thereby producing much less ash. By Day 10 of the eruption, the amount of fresh lava had stabilised and was much less than at the beginning.

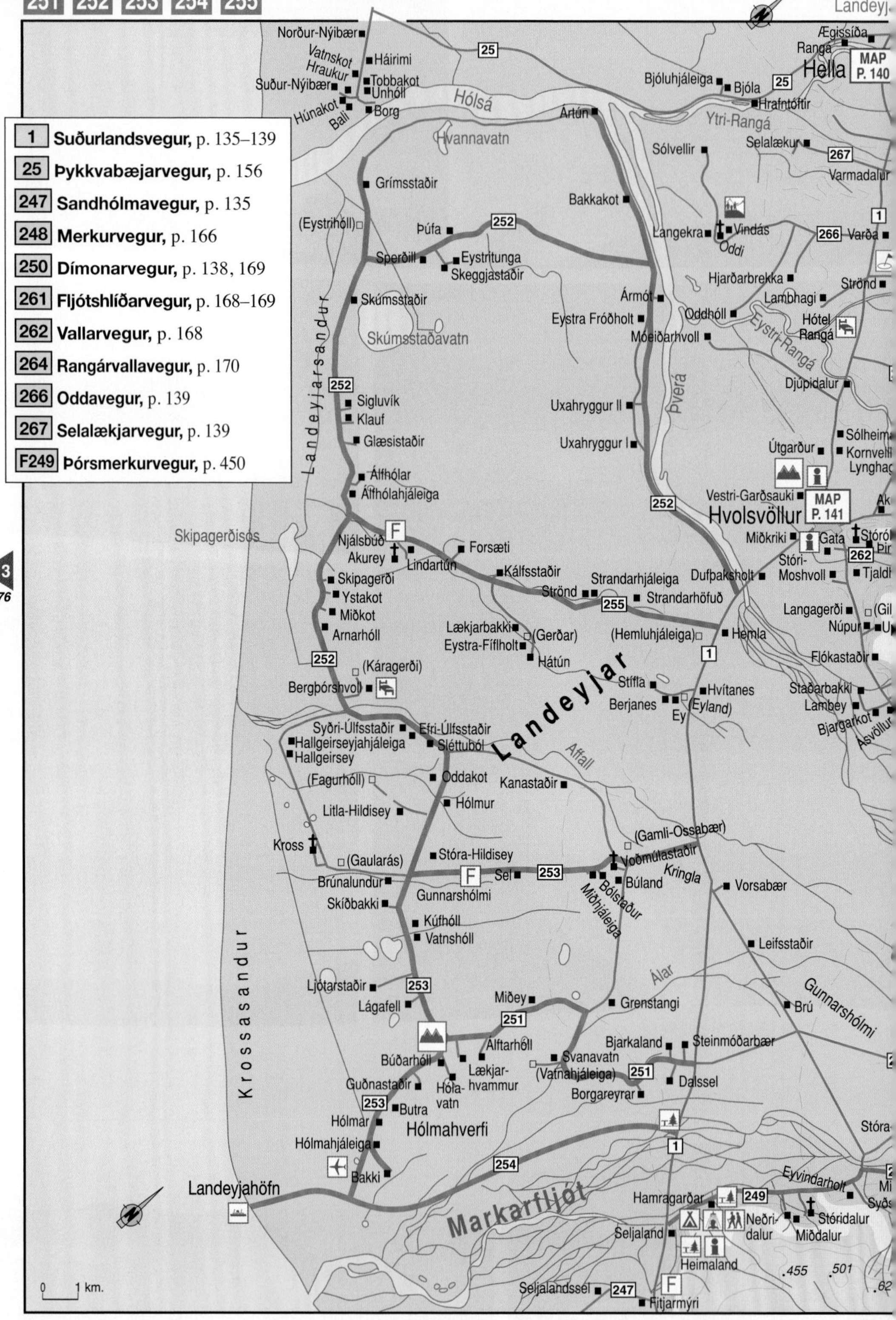

1	**Suðurlandsvegur,** p. 135–139
25	**Þykkvabæjarvegur,** p. 156
247	**Sandhólmavegur,** p. 135
248	**Merkurvegur,** p. 166
250	**Dímonarvegur,** p. 138, 169
261	**Fljótshlíðarvegur,** p. 168–169
262	**Vallarvegur,** p. 168
264	**Rangárvallavegur,** p. 170
266	**Oddavegur,** p. 139
267	**Selalækjarvegur,** p. 139
F249	**Þórsmerkurvegur,** p. 450

Landeyjar
Landeyjarsandur
Krossasandur
Markarfljót
Hólmahverfi
Hvolsvöllur
MAP P. 141
Hella
MAP P. 140
Landeyjahöfn
Hólsá
Ytri-Rangá
Eystri-Rangá
Þverá
Affall
Álar
Gunnarshólmi
Skúmsstaðavatn
Hvannavatn
Skipagerðisós
0 1 km.

13
P. 576

The farm Bergþórshvoll 1899.

andeyjar, ("Land islands") the district bordered by the vers Þverá to the north and Hólsá and Álar to the west nd east. Mostly flat country, wet and sandy towards the ea. Divided by the river **Affall** into Austur- and Vestur-andeyjar.

52 Landeyjavegur, 55 km circuit.

251 Hólmabæjavegur, 10,5 km.

ergþórshvoll, a farm on the western banks of Affall, parsonage. This was the home of Njáll Þorgeirsson of *jáls saga*. Many place-names remind us of the Saga, uch as Flosalág, Káragerði (a farm), Káragróf, Línakrar tc. *Njáls saga* tells of the burning of Bergþórshvoll in 011, and archeological studies verify that the house did ndeed burn in the early 11th century.

allgeirsey, a farm by the mouth of the river Affall. For while a cooperative store was located there, and goods vere landed from the sea.

ross, a farm and church, and a parsonage until 1920.

oðmúlastaðir, a farm and church.

amli-Ossabær, ruins 1 km from Voðmúlastaðir and 3 m from Vorsabær, believed to have been the farm of löskuldur Hvítanesgoði of *Njáls saga*.

255 Akureyjavegur, 11 km.

kurey, farm, church, community centre.

jálsbúð, community centre.

253 Bakkavegur.

254 Landeyjahafnarvegur, 11 km.

unnarshólmi, community centre.

ólmar, or Hólmahverfi, a group of farms. From there a eep-track goes down to the coast.

Krosssandur, this is the nearest point to Vestmanna-eyjar, which are about 10 km away.

Bakki, ferry point and an airport for Vestmannaeyjar (Westman Islands). Electricity, telephone and water are led from there to Vestmannaeyjar.

Markarfljót, a glacial river with its main source on the Mýrdalsjökull glacier and another on the Eyjafjallajökull glacier, but its longest branch comes from Reykjadalir west of the Torfajökull glacier. It carries a good deal of stones and gravel. It has often overflowed its banks in the lowlands causing great damage to farming country, but recently-built dykes have given good protection. The Markarfljót is 100 km long with a total drainage area of ca. 1,070 km^2 and an average flow of 85 m^3 per sec. The 242 m bridge over Markarfljót was opened in 1934. A new bridge to the west of the farm Seljaland was opened in 1992, and a bridge was built at Emstrur (see Road F210) in 1978. The river was formerly widely believed to harbour monsters, and there is a modern account of people who claim to have seen a strange creature 12-15 m long in it. According to folk-tales the monster originated from a large skate, or ray-fish, thrown into the river by a local farmer after it had been hung up to dry. The farmer hoped to protect the people of the Fljótshlíð district from glacial floods, especially those in Markarfljót. The skate came to life and turned into a monster. It is said that when fording Markarfljót or Þverá on horseback there is a danger of "skidding on the skate".

249 Þórsmerkurvegur, from Road 1 by Seljalandsmúli east of Markarfljót to Road F29 Merkurvegur.

248 Merkurvegur, 3,46 km to Stóra-Mörk.

13 P. 576

Grjótá, a farm, the home of Þráinn Sigfússon of *Njá saga*.

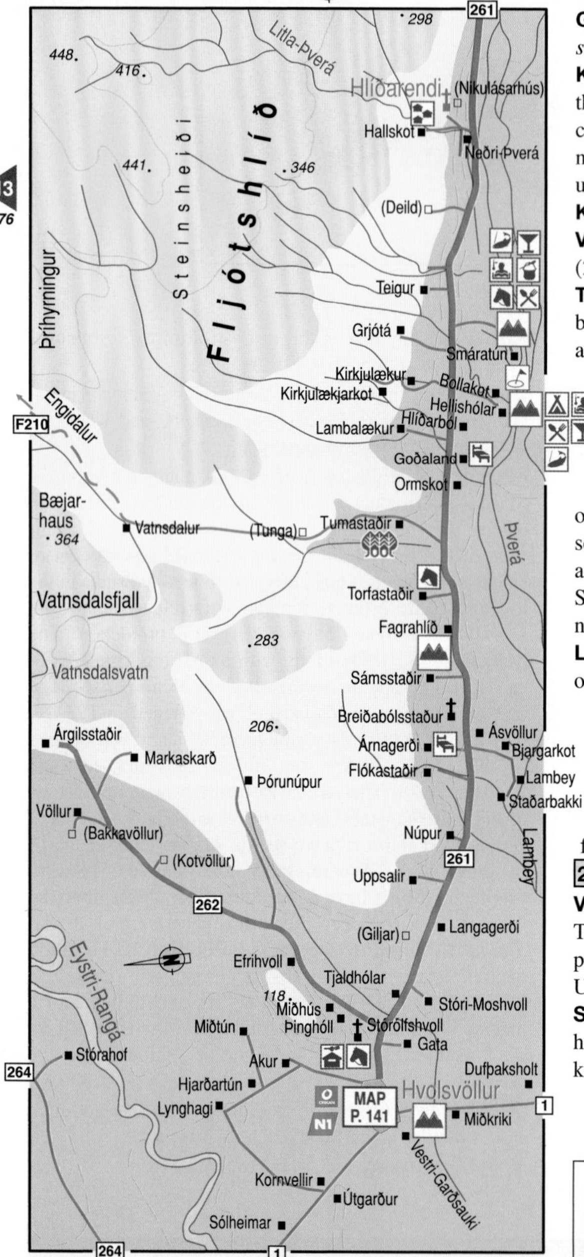

Kirkjulækur and Kirkjulækjarkot, farms on the west the Grjótá river, usually called Kirkjulækjartorfan. centre for Pentecostals. A small cave by the strea northwest of the farm was used for official gatherin until 1894.

Kvoslækur, a school by the river Kvoslækjará.

Vatnsdalsvatn, a lake on the mountain Vatnsdalsfja (279 m). A monster is said to live in the lake.

Tumastaðir, a farm, since 1935 a forestry cent belonging to the Forestry Service. Good access to path and trails. The 'Republic Grove' and tree collectio with numerous species. National Forest.

Sámsstaðir, a farm where experiments in grai farming (primarily oats, barley and rye) have bee made since before 1930. State-operated.

Breiðabólsstaður, a farm, church and parsonag often mentioned in historical records. Jón Ögmundssc served there before he became the first catholic bisho at Hólar. The burial place of the Rev. Tóma Sæmundsson (1807-41), a well-known writer an nationalist, friend and colleague of Jónas Hallgrímsso

Lambey, an island in the river Þverá, formerly a official meeting place, a farm and church, abandone about 1702.

Fljótshlíð, the slope along the river Þverá, ea from Hvolhreppur. Densely populated, we cultivated, with many rivers and waterfalls, a goo view and many beautiful spots. The westernmo farm is **Núpur**.

262 Vallarvegur, 6,8 km.

Völlur, a farm, the home of Mörður gígja of *Njáls sag*. The birthplace of Halldór Hermannsson (1878-1958 professor and curator of the Fiske Collection at Corne University in New York state.

Stórólfshvoll, a farm and church. In Saga times th home of Stórólfur Hængsson and his son Ormur, well known for his exceptional strength.

1 Suðurlandsvegur, p. 138–139

264 Rangárvallavegur, p. 170

F210 Fjallabaksleið syðri, p. 438

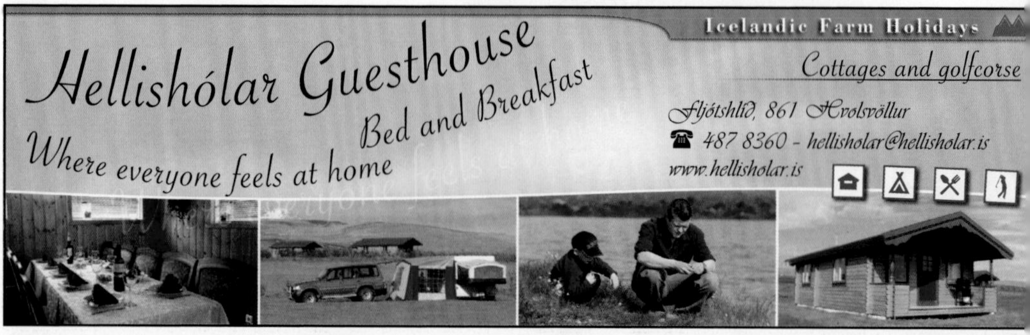

órólfsfell, (574 m) a tuff mountain, named after the settler Þórólfur skssonur, he was the great grandfather of Njáll in Njáls saga. In *Njáls ga* it says that Njáll had a farm in Þórólfsfell, yet no remains are now to e seen. On the southwest side is an interesting cave, **Mögugilshellir,** ow spoiled by the river.

ljótsdalur, a farm and a Youth Hostel. Emstruleið ("The Emstra route"), difficult summer road, often hardly passable because of unbridged vers, leads from there to Fjallabaksleið syðri ("The southern behind-the-ountains route") at Hvanngil.

leiksárgljúfur, a deep and narrow canyon, in places so narrow that it ems feasible to jump across but is in fact much too dangerous to tempt, and several deaths have occurred there. The first acted movie enes to be taken in Iceland were taken there in 1923, for the film *Hadda adda* by Guðmundur Kamban.

50 Dímonarvegur, 12,1 km .

lúlakot, a farm formerly widely known in Iceland for beautiful tree ardens. A fine view from the farm. Home of the painter Ólafur Túbals 897-1964). The Iceland Forest Service's first tree planting station, from 935. The tallest trees in Iceland, some 24 m high, were found in Múlakot 2005 – black cottonwood that grew out of sucker shoots in 1963. ational Forest.

lerkjá, a river falling off the cliffs in a beautiful waterfall, Merkjárfoss r Gluggafoss ("Window falls"). Þórðarfoss waterfall just west of there.

líðarendakot, a farm where the poet Þorsteinn Erlingsson (1858-1914) as brought up. Near the farm is his memorial, a bust by the sculptor ína Sæmundsson (1892-1965). Memorial to her at Hlíðarendi church. he waterfall **Drífandi** in the background.

ikulásarhús, an abandoned farm were Jónína Sæmundsdóttir was born 1892–1965) better know as Nína Sæmundsson sculptor. She studied in in openhagen and Rome but lived in Hollywood for the longest time and as well know for her art.

líðarendi, a farm and church, long a manor farm, one of the most amous in Iceland. It was the home of Gunnar Hámundarson of *Njáls aga*. Also the birthplace of Bishop Þorlákur helgi (St. Thorlak), and the hildhood home of the poet Bjarni Thorarensen (1786-1841). In the 17th entury it was the home of Gísli Magnússon (1621-96), who experiment-d with gardening and grain-farming, and imported and planted Caraway Carum carvi) which now grows wild in many parts of Iceland.

verá, now a clear river formed by the numerous streams of Fljótshlíð nd flowing along the whole length of Fljótshlíð. Formerly a large part of ne glacial river Markarfljót joined Þverá, and in those days it was a nenace, breaking down large areas of good farming land. Eventually mbankments were built along Markarfljót, the furthest inland being at the nountain Þórólfsfell. Vegetation is increasing on the former floodlands.

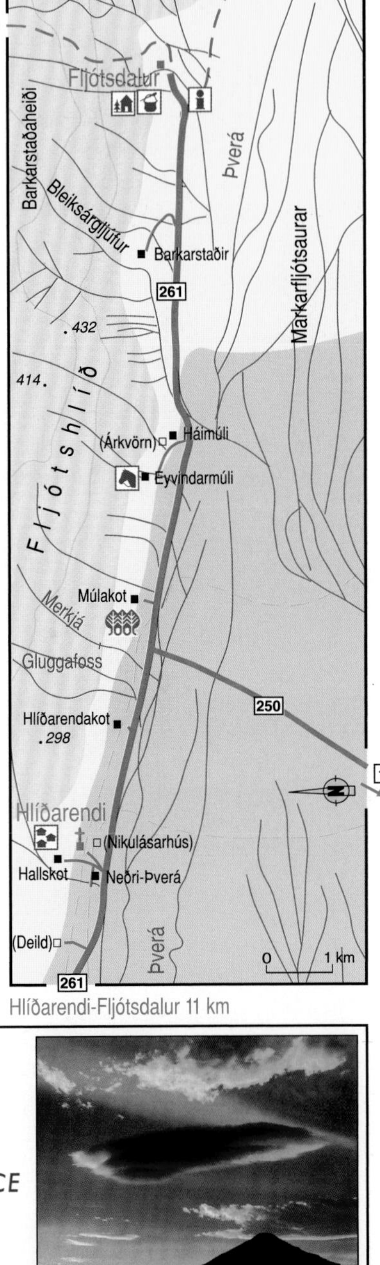

13 P. 576

1 **Suðurlandsvegur,** p. 138 F261 **Emstruleið,** p. 452

13 P. 576

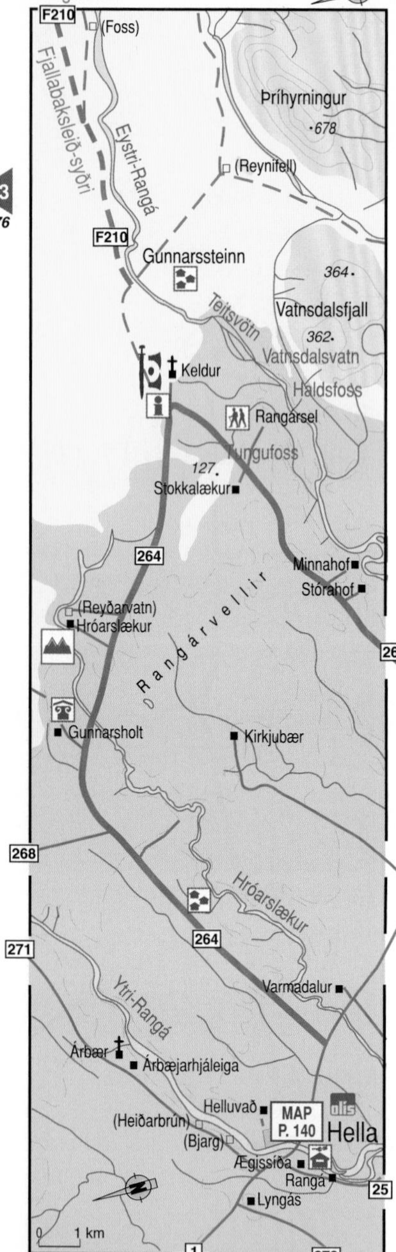

Þríhyrningur, (678 m) a tuff mountain, dominating the surroundings. Th hiding place of Flosi of *Njáls saga* and his men after they set fire t Bergþórshvoll, burning Njáll inside.

Gunnarssteinn, where Gunnar of Hlíðarendi of *Njáls saga* and hi brothers fought some 30 men after being ambushed at **Knafahólar**. Som bones etc. have been found to verify this.

Keldur.

Keldur, a manor farm since Saga times, mentioned in *Njáls saga* as on of the main farms of the family of Oddi. Over 20 houses are preserved including the primary living quarters and the accommo dation for livestock. The farmhouses are of ancient typ of turf houses. The hall, probably dating from the 16th cen tury, is of so called stave construction with Romanesque style ornament. The date 1641 is carved on a ledge in the hall but it is likely that the hall is much older. Beneath the hall is a tunnel believed to date from the 11th -13th century, probably fo escape in times of conflict. In the keeping of the National Museum since 1947.

Stóra-Hof, a farm since the original settlement. The settler was Ketil hængur, a man of noble family who had many outstanding descendants After him it was the home of Valgarður hinn grái (the grey) and his sor Mörður, frequently mentioned in *Njáls saga*, the latter being one of the main opponents of his relative, Gunnar of Hlíðarendi.

Kirkjubær, long a substantial farm, in the middle of the Rangárvellir area the only farm in a great area of grass between the sands. Often mentioned in *Njáls saga*, being the home of Otkell Skarfson. Now a horse-breeding farm.

Rangárvellir

1 **Suðurlandsvegur,** p. 139 | 25 **Þykkvabæjarvegur,** p. 156
268 **Þingskálavegur,** p. 171 | 271 **Árbæjarvegur,** p. 158
273 **Bugavegur,** p. 156 | F210 **Fjallabaksvegur syðri,** p. 438

Hekla, (1,491 m) the most famous volcano in Iceland and one of the best-known volcanoes in the world and has been active for thousands of years. The mountain is a long ridge with a 4 km long crack along the top. There have been 20 eruptions in recorded history, the first in 1104 and the latest in February 2000, when scientists were able to predict the eruption half an hour in advanse using the alarm system of the Icelandic Meteorological Office. Folk tales tell us the souls of the damned were once believed to pass through the crater of Hekla on their way to Hell. First ascent of Hekla was made June 20th 1750 by the explorers Eggert Ólafsson and Bjarni Pálsson. It is easiest to climb the mountain from the northwest side or following the north ridge. The climb takes about 8 hours.

Næfurholt, a farm closest to Hekla. The farm has been moved many times because of volcanic eruptions and other natural disasters.

Hraunteigur, birch-woods along the river Rangá across from Galtalækur. A bridge over Rangá not far upstream from there, only 2,6 m wide.

Bjólfell, (443 m) a mountain to the southwest of Hekla. The farms Næfurholt, Hólar and Haukadalur on the north and west of the mountain. Once believed to be the home of a giantess, the sister of the giantess at Búrfell (see road 26).

Selsund, a farm to the south of Hekla, where the first ascent of Hekla in 1750 was begun. In the earthquakes of 1912 a crack opened nearby and one side of the crack subsided all of four metres.

Bolholt, a farm. The area is being cultivated and many trees have been planted there through the years.

Víkingslækur, an anabandoned farm because of sand erosion, once a manor farm.

Þingskálar, an ancient official meeting-place with some protected ruins.

Gunnarsholt, Gunnarsholt, formerly a substantial farm and a church, abandoned in 1925. A monument in memory of the church built there around 1200 and abandoned in 1837 when it was engulfed by sand. Now a growing settlement. It houses the headquarters of the Soil Conservation Service of Iceland which runs a big seed processing station. A team of scientists and executives and are working to improve and restore land quality throughout the country. A new Visitor Centre Telling the Story of Restoring the Land is now open. Learn about the unique story of Iceland´s environmental history: A 1000 years of devastation by nature and human activity and 100 years of restoring of the land.

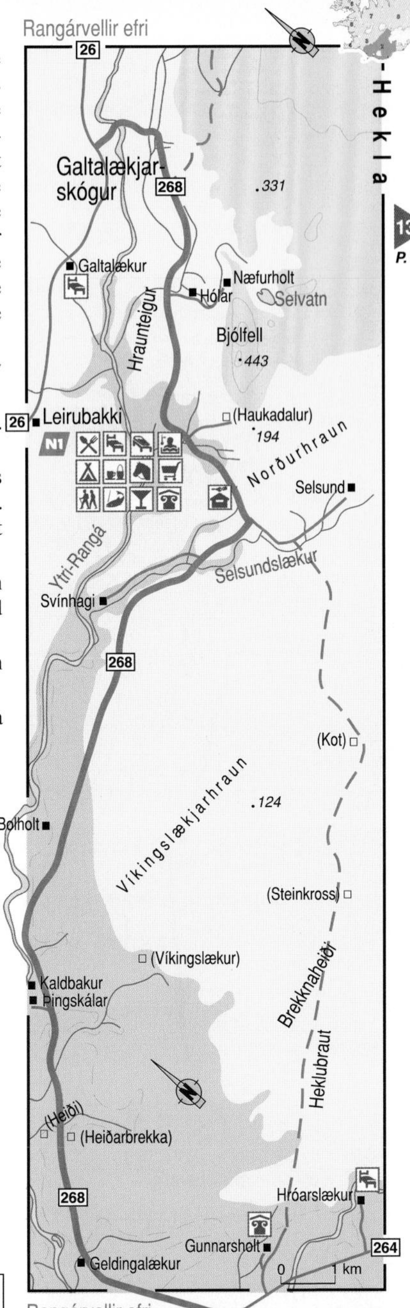

26 **Landvegur,** p. 160 264 **Rangárvallavegur,** p. 170

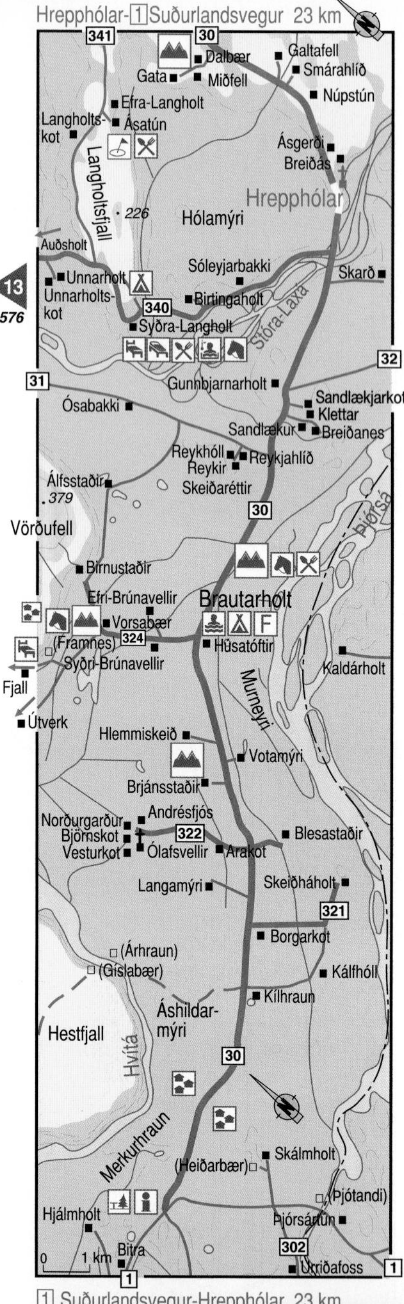

340 Auðsholtsvegur, 11 km.

324 Vorsabæjarvegur, 7,8 km.

Birtingaholt, a farm, long the home of Ágúst Helgason (1862-1948 outstanding among farmers. His three brothers, all ministers, we Guðmundur (1853-1922) of Reykholt, Kjartan (1865-1931) of Hruni an Magnús (1857-1940), the first rector of the teachers' school in Reykjavík

Álfaskeið, a small valley on the south side of the mountain Langholts fjall.

Laxárholt, by the bridge across Laxá, ancient place of official meetings.

Stóra-Laxá, a clear river that starts on the south of Kerlingarfjöll an flows through impressive canyons in the interior. Good salmon river. jeep track goes along the canyon.

Hreppar, the northernmost districts of Árnessýsla, between Hvítá an Þjórsá, Ytrihreppur or Hrunamannahreppur to the west and Eystrihreppu or Gnúpverjahreppur to the east. Uneven land with many ridges an mountains but green and grassy, good farming country.

Húsatóftir, there is Hestakráin, restaurant and guesthouse.

Brautarholt, (pop. 54) a school, swimming pool and a community centr Geothermal heat.

322 Ólafsvallavegur, 3 km.

321 Skeiðháholtsvegur, 6 km.

Ólafsvellir, a farm, church and parsonage until 1925.

Áshildarmýri, a hollow in the old **Merkurhraun** lava-field. A memori has been erected there to commemorate the Áshildarmýri agreemen (Áshildarmýrarsamþykkt) of 1496 when the people gathered to protes against bad government and demand improvements.

Skeið, the district between the rivers Hvítá and Þjórsá, from Flói to Stóra-Laxá and Sandlækjarós. Flat and wet in many places, lava under the soil. The irrigation system, Skeiðaáveita, is from 1924.

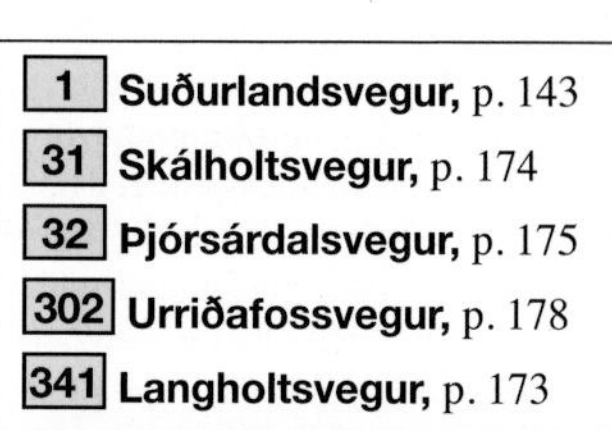

1 **Suðurlandsvegur,** p. 143
31 **Skálholtsvegur,** p. 174
32 **Þjórsárdalsvegur,** p. 175
302 **Urriðafossvegur,** p. 178
341 **Langholtsvegur,** p. 173

rúarhlöð, narrows and rapids of the river Hvítá. Interesting rock ›rmations. Birch bushes on the banks. Arctic Rafting offer tours down (vítá river with a relay at Brúrarhlöð. There rafters are invited to jump f the cliffs into the river.

49 Tungufellsvegur, 2,7 km.

ungufell, a farm and church. Towerless wooden church built in 1856. In ıe keeping of the National Museum since 1987. The farm furthest from ıe sea in southern Iceland, 58 km from the head of Hvalfjörður. From ungufell a jeep-track continues northward to Svínárnes and the .erlingarfjöll mountains. A walking route to Gullfoss, starts 5,5 km from 'ungufell.

líð, formerly a farm. Birthplace of the famous outlaw Eyvindur Jónsson 1714-1782), known as Fjalla-Eyvindur ("Eyvindur of the mountains").

44 Hrunavegur, 7,7 km.

45 Kaldbaksvegur, 8,38 km.

eykjadalur, a farm. A church and a parsonage until 1819.

runi, a farm, church and a parsonage. The birthplace of Earl Gissur orvaldsson (1208-1268). A well-known folktale, the Dance in Hruni, is onnected with this place. The church once stood on a cliff above the resent farm, and people would dance, drink and play cards in the church n Christmas night. One Christmas the Devil appeared and dragged the hurch building and all the people down into the underworld.

vítárholt, a farm near the river Hvítá where Saga age ruins have been xcavated, showing the oldest building style of Iceland. A Roman copper oin dating from 275-276 AD was found there.

41 Langholtsvegur, 7,7 km.

lúðir, (pop. 420) a village in the geothermal area of Hellisholt. ìreenhouses, community centre, swimming pool, hotel, restaurant, rocery and liquor store. Good walking routes in the area.

lellisholt, a farm south of Flúðir where in 1899, Dr. Helgi Pjeturss discovered ıoraines which yielded important information about the Ice Age in Iceland.

ìaltafell, a farm and the birthplace of the sculptor Einar Jónsson (1873–954), whose works can be seen in a special gallery in Reykjavík, the :inar Jónsson Museum. One can see the influence of the surrounding ındscape in some of his works.

repphólar, a farm and a place of settlement, a church and parsonage ntil 1880. One of the clergymen was Jón Egilsson (1548-1636), who egan a new age of historical writings in Iceland when he wrote *3iskupsannálar* ("The annals of the bishops").

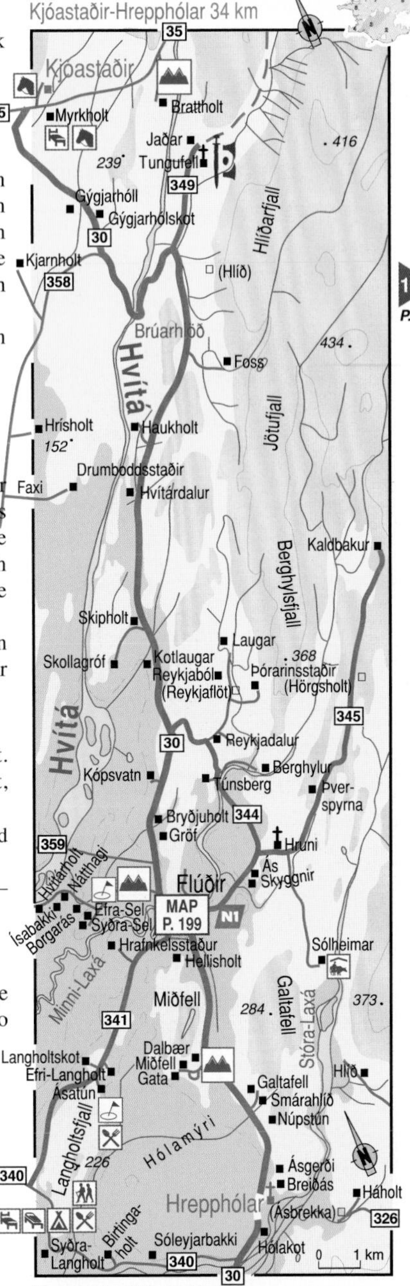

35	**Biskupstungnabraut,** p. 183	326	**Hælsvegur,** p. 175
340	**Auðsholtsvegur,** p. 172	341	**Langholtsvegur,** p. 173
358	**Einholtsvegur,** p. 183	359	**Bræðratunguvegur,** p. 198

Spóastaðir-Reykir 15 km

13 P. 576

Spóastaðir, a farm near the bridge on Brúará, formerly a ferry point.

Biskupstungur, ("Bishop's tongues") a tongue of land between the rive Brúará and Hvítá, divided into two tongues by the Tungufljót river. Th western sections are wet in places, the eastern and northern sections drie

Skálholt, a farm and a church, the seat of bishops 1056-1796, a school after the Reformation and intermittently in Catholic times. A printing press was operated there for several years. Many historical events are connected with Skálholt, such as the execution of the last Catholic bishop, Jón Arason, along with two of his sons in 1550. A memorial ha been erected on the spot where Jón Arason was beheaded. A ne cathedral has been built and decorated with important works by Icelandi artists. A tomb of the bishops and a related museum is there, and a larg collection of books is preserved in the tower. Concerts every week-end i summer. The first settler at Skálholt was Teitur Ketilbjarnarson, the fathe of Gissur hvíti. A Visitor Centre.

The cathedral at Skálholt.

Laugarás, (pop. 119) a village by Hvítá, medical centre, many greer houses, animal park.

Iðubrú, a suspension bridge over the river Hvítá built in 1957. The was formerly a busy ferry-point there. The farm **Iða** on the south sid of the bridge.

Vörðufell, (391 m) a mountain with the lake **Úlfljótsvatn** on tc which has its outlet through the gorge Úlfsgil.

Reykir, a group of farms, geothermal heat. Near Reykir ar the sheep-folds **Skeiðaréttir**, among the largest in Icelan and noted for merry-making at round-up times. They wer built in 1881 with lave blocks from the area and renovated in 198 Landgræðsla ríkisins, the Soil Conservation Service of Iceland, ha revegetated extensive land areas in this region. The first soil conservatio area in Iceland was established at Reykir when in 1908 an area wa fenced off to provide protection from grazing.

30 **Skeiða- og Hrunamannavegur,** p. 172
32 **Þjórsárdalsvegur,** p. 175
35 **Biskupstungnabraut,** p. 182
324 **Vorsabæjarvegur,** p. 172
340 **Auðsholtsvegur,** p. 172

Reykir-Spóastaðir 15 km

32 ÞJÓRSÁRDALSVEGUR

aukshöfði, a rocky bluff by the river Þjórsá near the mouth of the jórsárdalur valley. In the 19th century old bones and a spearhead were ound, believed to have belonged to Gaukur Trandilsson, who was killed ere. His home was at Stöng in Þjórsárdalur. Excellent viewing point, specially towards Hekla.

agi, a substantial farm under the mountain, Hagafjall. Nearby is Hagaey, large island in the Þjórsá river

29 Mástunguvegur, 8 km.

káldabúðir, a farm by Mástunguvegur. From there a jeep-track leads lland on the east side of the river Stóra-Laxá, to Sultarfit and on to Fossrdrög. Upstream from the abandoned farm, Grímsstaðir, Stóra-Laxá goes rough long and majestic canyons.

28 Stóra-Núpsvegur, 2,4 km.

tóri-Núpur, a farm and a church. The home of Hjalti Skeggjason, a ieftain well-known for his part in the conversion of Iceland Christianity in year 1000. Birthplace of contemporary painter Jóhann Briem (1907–91) and long the home of his grandfaer, minister and hymn-writer Valdimar Briem (1848–1930).

kaftholtréttir sheep-folds, by Skaftholt. Considered to be the oldest in eland, from the 12th century. They were built from lava blocks from jórsárdalshraun lavafields.

jórsárholt, a farm where hot steam coming from rifts was ormerly used for baths.

25 Gnúpverjavegur, 10,4 km.

26 Hælsvegur, 3,3 km.

sar, a farm.

teinsholt, a farm and formerly a church and parsonage, or until 1789, hen they were moved to Stóri-Núpur.

rnes, a community centre and also a Visitor Centre.

rándarholt, a farm with the rocky mountain **Þrándur** above. According the Sagas, Þórður Andrésson, the last member of the Oddi clan, was illed there by Gissur Þorvaldsson. Nearby is **Árnes** ("River point") hich used to be a place of official meetings. It is now an island in the jórsá river but was formerly connected to the west bank. On the west ide is a the waterfall **Búðafoss**, on the east side is the waterfall Hestaoss.

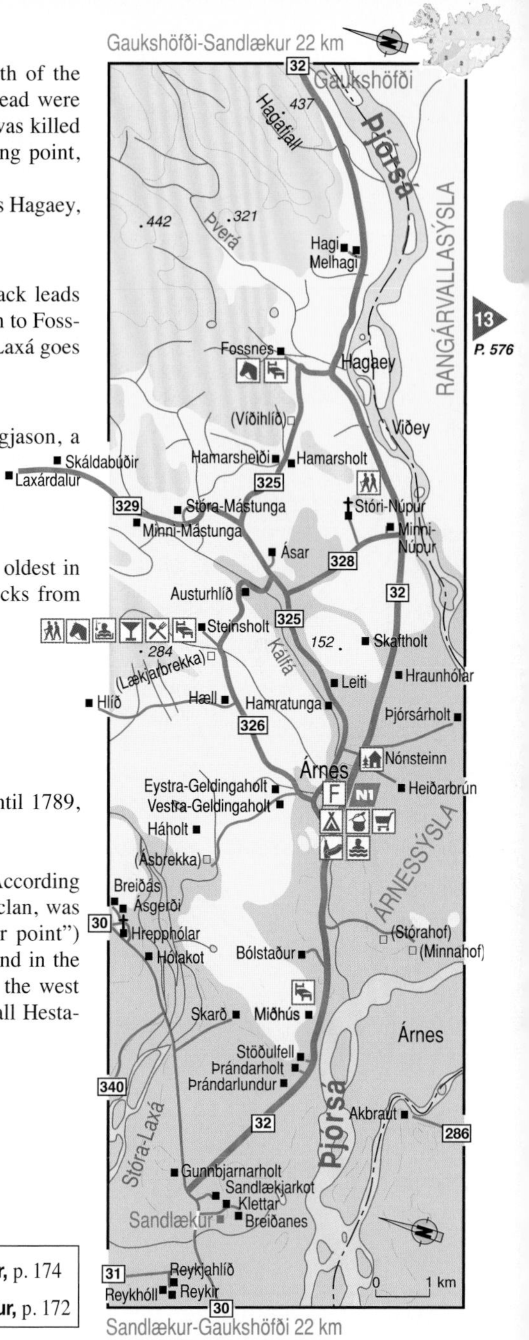

Gaukshöfði-Sandlækur 22 km

13 P. 576

Sandlækur-Gaukshöfði 22 km

30 Skeiða- og Hrunamannavegur, p. 172
31 Skálholtsvegur, p. 174
286 Hagabraut, p. 158
340 Auðsholtsvegur, p. 172

13 P. 576

26 Landvegur-Gaukshöfði 32 km

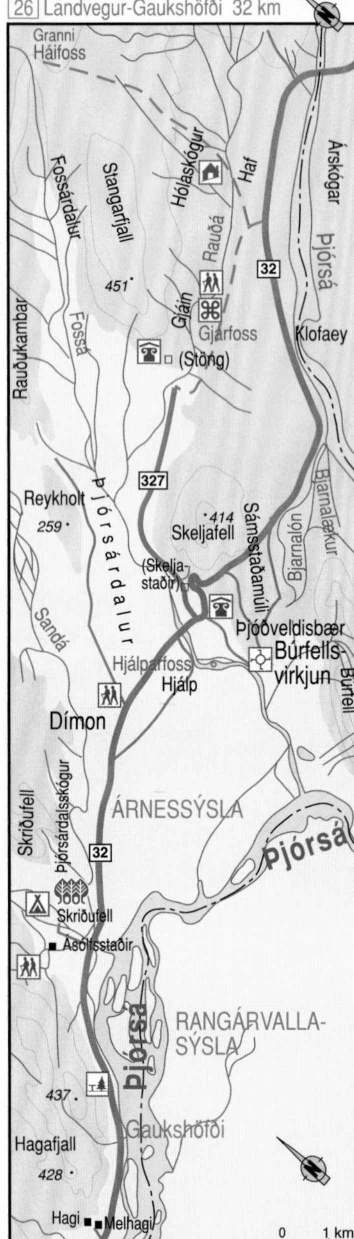

Gaukshöfði- 26 Landvegur 32 km

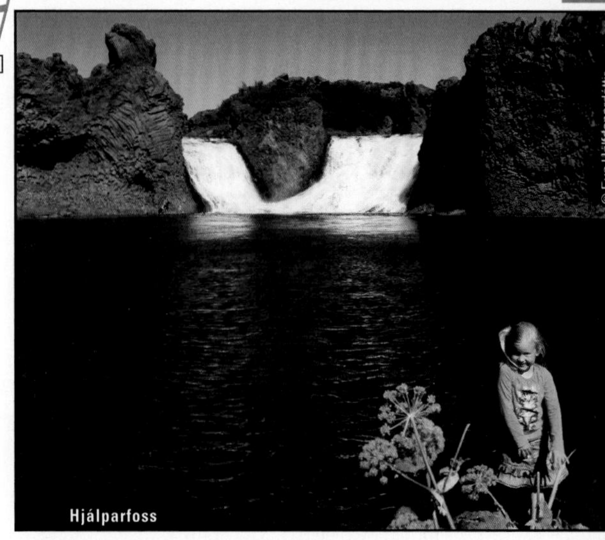
Hjálparfoss

26 Landvegur, p. 160

Þjórsá, a glacial river, the longest river in Iceland, 230 km, with an average flow of 360 m³/sec. Gathers most of its water from the glaciers Vatnajökull and Hofsjökull, but its northernmost origin is on the Sprengisandur sands. Several waterfalls, especially in the interior. In 1973 a 185 m bridge was built north of Búrfell.

Háifoss, ("High falls") a 122 m high waterfall, the second highest in Iceland, in the river Fossá in the **Fossárdalur** valley. Another waterfall Granni, nearby. About 2 hours' walk from Stöng, but it is easier to reach by a road called Línuvegur ("Lines road"), the access road for repair and maintenance of electricity lines.

Rauðukambar, ("Red crests") multi-coloured rhyolite mountain, geothermal heat.

Gjáin, a gorge with beautiful rock formations and waterfalls like **Gjárfoss** in the river Rauðá ("Red river").

Hólaskógur, a piece of land just inside the boundaries of Þjórsárdalur. An emergency hut was built there in 1970, and in 1998 a guest lodge was constructed.

327 Stangarvegur, 11 km.

Stöng, protected ruins of a farm, excavated in 1939, believed to have been buried under pumice and ashes from the Hekla eruption of 1104.

Skeljastaðir, the ruins of the church farm that served Þjórsárdalur of old. A great many skeletons have been excavated from the churchyard giving much information about the people.

Þjóðveldisbær, ("Farm of the republic") a farm building below the spur **Sámsstaðamúli,** constructed in the medieval style in commemoration of the 1,100 years of settlement in Iceland in 1974. A small stave church enclosed with turf, has been built next to the farmhouse replica. The design is conjectural, based on ruins of a church found in excavations at Stöng.

Búrfellsvirkjun, a power-station, 210,000 kW, built in 1969 on the river Þjórsá. A big dam was built to the northeast of **Búrfell** and the water diverted through tunnels to the generators under Sámsstaðamúli.

Hjálparfoss, ("The help falls") a beautiful waterfall in the river Fossá opposite the power-station.

Dímon, remarkable strata has been found there.

Þjórsárdalur, the easternmost valley of Árnessýsla. There are now only two farms in this valley, Ásólfsstaðir and Skriðufell, but ruins of 20 farms have been found. It is believed that the valley was deserted after heavy pumice rain from the eruption of Hekla in 1104. The valley of Þjórsárdalur has been partly revegetated by Landgræðsla ríkisins the Soil Conservation Service of Iceland, **Þjórsárdalsskógur**. Extensive birchwoods in many places. Two rivers Sandá and Fossá flow through the valley, and the Þjórsá river closes it to the south. National Forest.

Þríbrot ehf. · www.3brot.is

Quality and hospitality

Árnes / Borg / Brautarholt / Flúðir
Laugarás / Laugarvatn / Reykholt / Sólheimar

www.sveitir.is

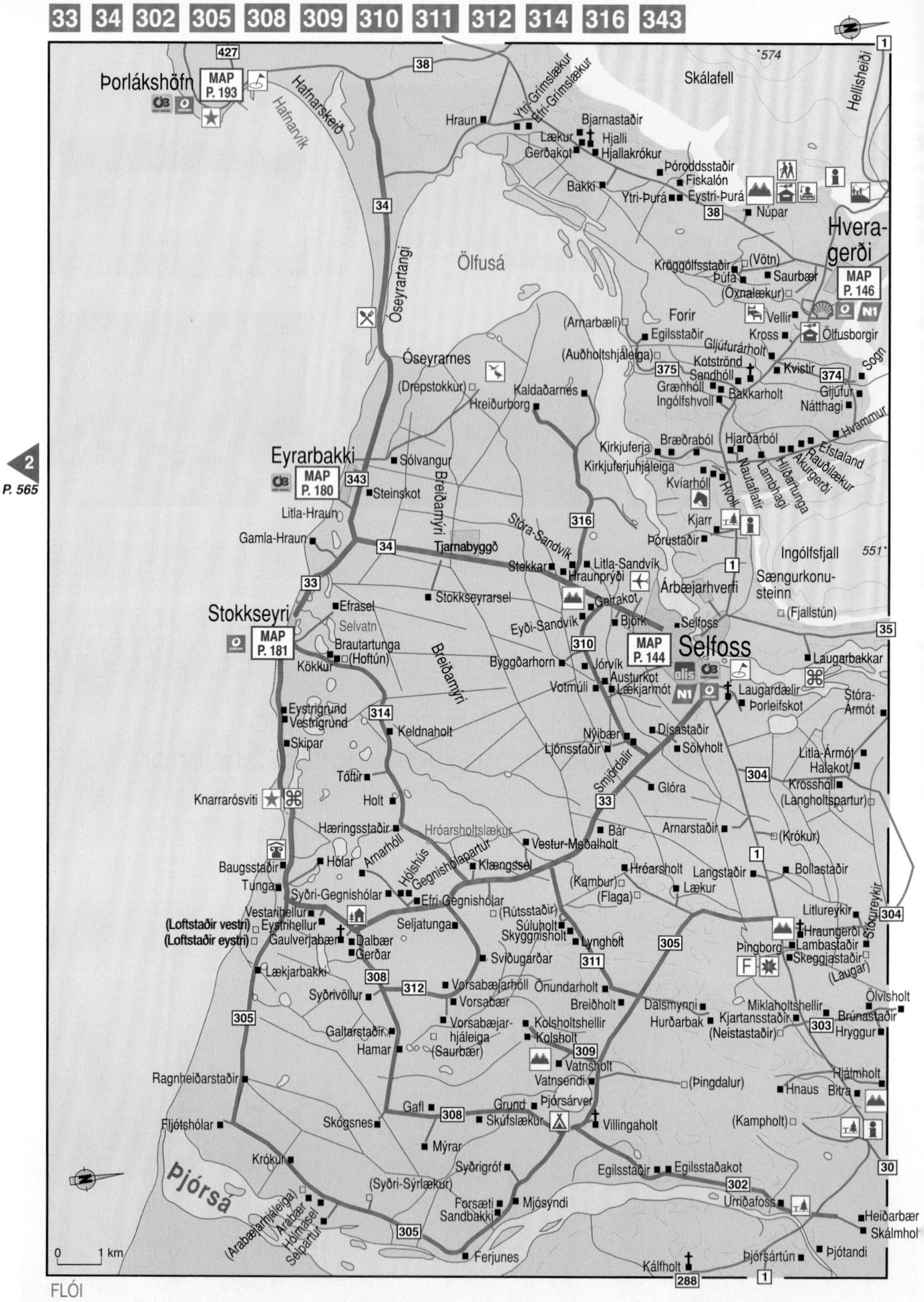

2 P. 565

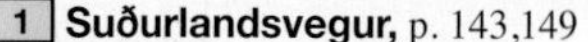

FLÓI

1 **Suðurlandsvegur,** p. 143,149	30 **Skeiða- og Hrunamannavegur,** p. 172	
35 **Biskupstungnabraut,** p. 180	38 **Þorlákshafnarvegur,** p. 192	288 **Kálfholtsvegur,** p. 156
303 **Ölvisholtsvegur,** p. 143	304 **Oddgeirshólavegur,** p. 143	374 **Hvammsvegur,** p. 148
375 **Arnarbælisvegur,** p. 148	427 **Suðurstrandarvegur,** p. 227	

34 **Eyrarbakkavegur,** 24 km.

316 **Kaldaðarnesvegur,** 6 km. **343** **Álfsstétt,** 2 km.

Flói, the district between the rivers Ölfusá and Þjórsá up to the old lava field Merkurhraun.

Ölfusá, one of the biggest rivers in Iceland. With its source river, Hvítá, which comes from the Hvítárvatn lake near the Langjökull glacier, it is 185 km long.

Eyrarbakki, (pop. 531) is a part of the Municipality of Árborg. The village was once the largest commercial community and the main harbour on the South Coast of Iceland. A large number of houses from the period 1890-1920 are preserved in Eyrarbakki, which gives it a unique position among towns in South-Iceland. Iceland's oldest school for children, founded in 1852, is in Eyrarbakki. To complete this historical atmosphere, there are two museums to visit; the Eyrarbakki Maritime Museum and the Árnessýsla Folk Museum, located at **Húsið** „The House" in Eyrarbakki, built in 1765 and one of the oldest surviving buildings in Iceland. Húsið and Assistentahúsið, two connected buildings: the House is a type of log building, brought in kit form to Iceland and erected in 1765 for the local merchant. The Assistants' House is a timber-frame structure, added in 1881. In the keeping of the National Museum since 1992. Modern services for example a gas station, a camping place, guesthouse, Tourist Information at Staður, Women's Library and a restaurant, are also in Eyrarbakki. To the west of the village is Óseyrarnes, an old ferry point on the Ölfusá river, where once stood the farm Refstokkur, home of Bjarni Herjólfsson, one of Iceland's first permanent settlers and a great seafarer. On his way to Greenland he got lost in a fog, sailed in a different direction and discovered a land to the west, which he didn't explore. This led to Leifur Eiríksson expedition to Vineland (North America). The seashore at Eyrarbakki is popular for hiking and bird watching. The Flói Bird Reserve lies northwest of Eyrarbakki. The reserve covers an area of about 5 sq km (1.93 sq miles). The land is low, only about 2 m above sea level. It is an important nesting area, especially for wetland birds, and listed by the Bird Life International Association.

Litla-Hraun, a state penitentiary.

Kaldaðarnes, a substantial farm and often the home of local leaders, formerly a church. During Catholic times there was a holy cross at Kaldaðarnes and people made long pilgrimages to see it. Immediately after the Reformation in 1550 the cross was taken to the Bishop´s house at Skálholt, where it was chopped up and burned on the orders of the Bishop, who died shortly thereafter. His death was commonly accounted God's revenge. There was a leprosy hospital in Kaldaðarnes in the 18th century. During World War II the British forces had big camps there and built an airfield for warplanes. A monument honouring the presence of the RAF in Kaldaðarnes was unveiled at Selfoss Airport in 1999 in the presence of British pilots who were stationed in Kaldaðarnes during the war.

Stóra-Sandvík and **Litla-Sandvík,** one of the biggest farms in the Flói district.

33 **Gaulverjabæjarvegur,** 27 km.

310 **Votmúlavegur,** 5 km. **311** **Önundarholtsvegur,** 5 km.

Rútsstaðir, a cluster of farms now deserted. The birthplace of the painter Ásgrímur Jónsson (1876-1958). An art gallery in Reykjavík is devoted to his works.

314 **Holtsvegur,** 10 km. **308** **Hamarsvegur,** 11 km.

312 **Vorsabæjarvegur í Flóa,** 5,3 km.

Stokkseyri, (pop. 465) is a part of the Municipality of Árborg. The village is located on the Þjórsárhraun lava field, which extends offshore outside Stokkseyri and Eyrarbakki to form skerries up to 400 – 700 m from the coast. The lava is the largest lava field on earth since the end of the last ice-age. The seashore at Stokkseyri is known for its beauty – skerries, breaking waves and bird life, and thus popular for hiking. The village has a rich art and cultural life. Paintings- and glass galleries, Ghost Centre and a Museum of Icelandic Wonders along with artist's workshop and gallerys which are all situated in the Cultural centre, an old fish processing factory that has found a new role due to changes in the fishing industry. In Stokkseyri there is also a Hunting Museum with a large collection of mounted animals and firearms. Culture is not the only thing the town has to offer. It also has a seafood restaurant, an outdoor swimming pool, kayak sailing tours and a camping place. Þuríðarbúð is a bunkhouse that shows the conditions fishermen had to live with in the past. It is named after Þuríður Einarsdóttir (1777-1863), famous as a woman foreman, or captain, on one of the large rowing boats used for fishing at the time. Further east from Stokkseyri is the Baugsstaðir creamery and Knarrarósviti lighthouse, whose design is an interesting blend of functionalism and art nouveau (jugenstil) schools in architecture.

Baugsstaðir, one of Iceland's oldest dairies, preserved largely unchanged as a museum.

Loftsstaðir, by the farm is a cone like hill with a grand view.

305 **Villingaholtsvegur,** 30 km.

Hróarsholt, Hróarsholt, an old manor farm, stands beneath a cliff ridge, Hróarsholtsklettar. A monument was erected there in 1999 in honour of Freystein Gunnarsson (1892–1976), principal who was born at **Voli**, a farm not far away, now deserted.

Villingaholt, a church and parsonage till 1856. An elementery school and community centre, Þjórsárver. A campsite.

Fljótshólar, a farm with a spectacular view of the mountains and its surroundings.

302 **Urriðafossvegur,** 8 km. A view deck by Urriðafoss waterfall.

309 **Kolsholtsvegur,** 2,1 km.

Minni-Borg- 1 Suðurlandsvegur 20 km

Borg, a farm, community centre, not far from there are some old craters, **Borgarhólar**.

Stóra-Borg, a farm and church, moved from Klausturhólar in 1932.

351 Búrfellsvegur, 9,3 km, see Road 36.

Klausturhólar, a farm from the original settlement, a church and parsonage till 1887.

Seyðishólar, a group of craters from which much of the lava of Grímsnes has come. Much gravel and pumice, which is red there, has been taken from the hills for building so they have been spoiled. Good view from the hills.

Kerið, a 55 m deep explosion crater about 3,000 years old, in **Tjarnarhólar**, a group of crater-hills. A must for sightseers. The story goes that when the water level rises in Kerið, it falls to an equal extent in the small lake on the mountain Búrfell in the Grímsnes district, and vice versa. A protected natural feature.

Snæfoksstaðir, formerly a farm and church, and a parsonage until 1801.**Öndverðarnes,** a farm from the original settlement, formerly a church. Ruins of this and the graveyard can still be seen.

Þrastaskógur, woodlands along the river Sog, donated to the The Icelandic Youth Association and protected since then under their supervision.

Alviðra, a farm. The last farmer who lived there, Magnús Jóhannesson, donated the farms Alviðra and Öndverðarnes II to Árnessýsla county and the Icelandic Enviroment Association in 1973.

Grímsnes, the district marked by the rivers Sog on the south and Hvítá-Brúará on the east. The southern parts mostly flat and covered by old lava-fields with extensive birch-bushes. The upper parts wet in places, with an interesting mountain region furthest inland. A very popular area for summer houses.

Fjallstún, a place name below the mountain Ingólfsfjall, where legend has it that the first settler Ingólfur Arnarson had one of his first winter quarters in Iceland. Protected ruins. There have been many rock slides in the mountain above the site. One of the rocks is **Sængurkonusteinn,** ("Childbed stone") and it is said a pregnant travelling woman who was turned away at the farm gave birth to her child there. The farm was buried in a landslide the same night.

1 **Suðurlandsvegur,** p. 143
304 **Oddgeirshólavegur,** p. 143
351 **Búrfellsvegur,** p. 189
354 **Sólheimavegur,** p. 196
36 **Þingvallavegur,** p. 189
350 **Grafningsv. neðri,** p. 189
353 **Kiðjabergsvegur,** p. 196

1 Suðurlandsvegur-Minni-Borg 20 km

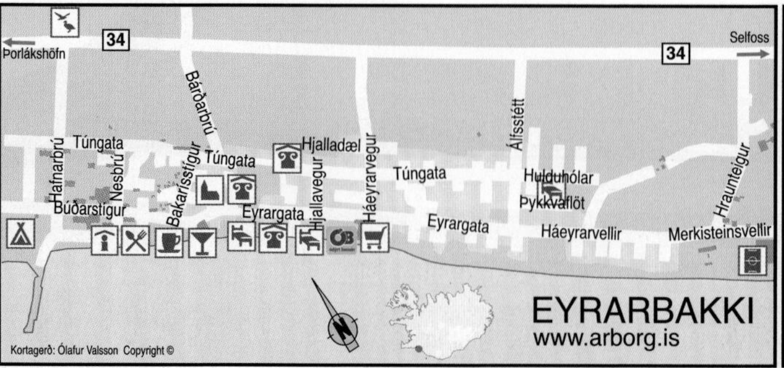

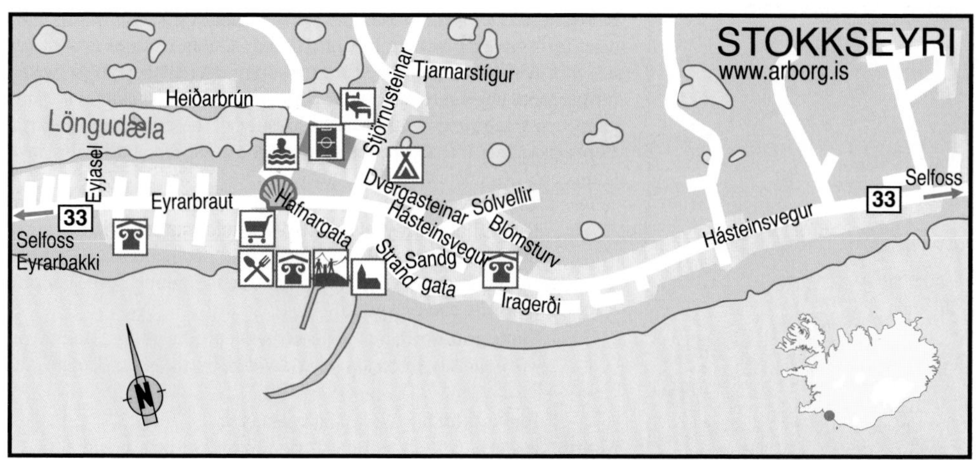

The beach at Stokkseyri

ÞURÍÐARBÚÐ „ÞURÍÐUR'S BUNKHOUSE"

A memorial to the conditions fishermen had to put up with in times past. The bunkhouse was named for the famous woman foreman Þuríður Einarsdóttir (1777–1863). **Open daily all year.**

STOKKSEYRI SWIMMING POOL

is open June 1st to August 31st: Weekdays 13–21, weekends 10–17. ***Swimming pool, hot-tubs, jakuzi.***

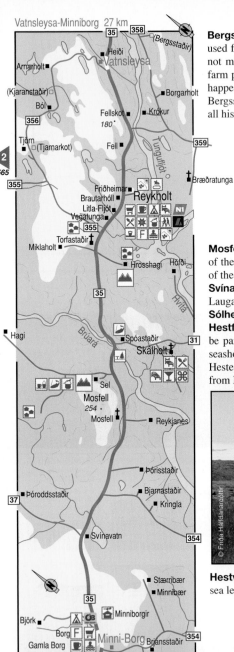

Vatnsleysa-Minniborg 27 km

Bergsstaðir, an abandoned farm where a hollowed rock was at one time used for keeping whey in. It is enchanted, so that if water gets in, it does not mix with the whey nor does the whey ever freeze. If, however, the farm people neglect to keep whey in it, they will have bad luck. This has happened three times within living memory. The first time the farmer at Bergsstaðir lost 150 sheep, the second time 40 sheep and finally, in 1960, all his cows (see Road 35, Haukadalur).

Vatnsleysa, ("Lack of water") a farm. The waterfall **Faxi** in Tungufljót nearby, also called **Vatnsleysufoss**.

Reykholt, (pop. 206) a village in a geothermal area with many greenhouses. A community centre, swimming pool, guesthouse, campsite and restaurant.

Biskupstungur, the district between the rivers Brúará on the west and Hvítá on the east divided by the river Tungufljót (see Road 31).

Torfastaðir, a church and parsonage.

Mosfell, a farm, church and parsonage, built below a mountain (254 m) of the same name. The settling place of Ketilbjörn the old, the forefather of the Haukdælir, a powerful and influential family for many centuries.

Svínavatn, ("Pig lake") a farm by a lake of the same name. Road 37 to Laugarvatn nearby.

Sólheimar, see p. 197.

Hestfjall, ("Horse mountain") (317 m) a mountain by Hvítá, believed to be part of an old shield-volcano made of tuff with a cap of basalt. Old seashore lines found 120 m up in the mountainsides. Highest point called Hesteyru ("Horse ears"), probably part of the crater rim. Very good view from Hestfjall, which is a gentle climb.

© Fríða Hálfdanardóttir

Hestvatn, a lake of 6 km², 60 m deep, the bottom thus being 12 m below sea level. Good trout-fishing. Sometimes Hvítá flows into the lake.

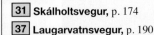

Minniborg-Vatnsleysa 27 km

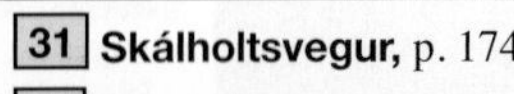
31 **Skálholtsvegur,** p. 174
37 **Laugarvatnsvegur,** p. 190
354 **Sólheimavegur,** p. 196
355 **Reykjavegur,** p. 190
356 **Tjarnarvegur,** p. 190
358 **Einholtsvegur,** p. 183
359 **Bræðratunguvegur,** p. 198

Gullfoss.

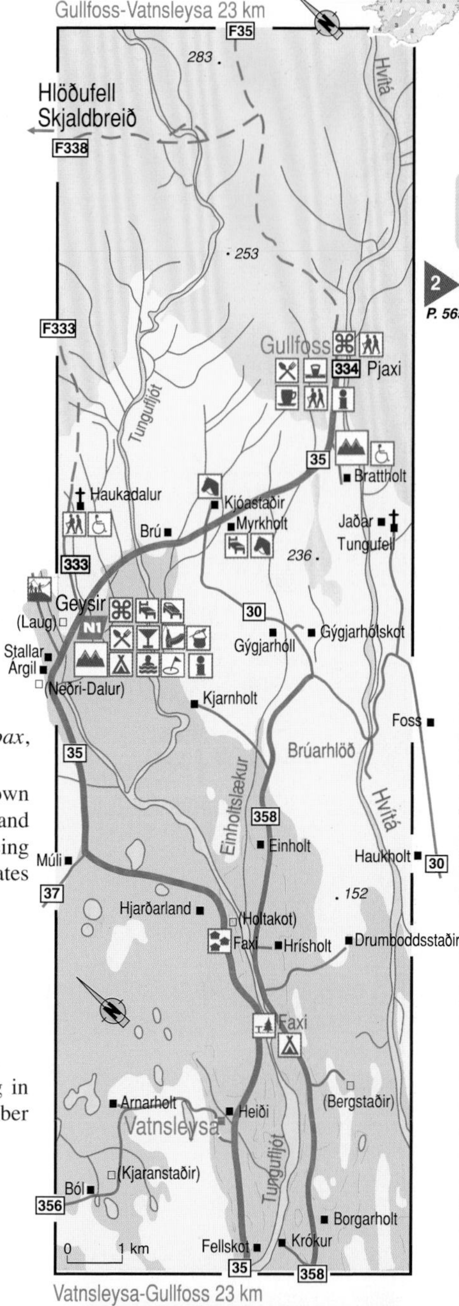

ullfoss, ("Golden falls") in the river Hvítá, one of the most beau-ful waterfalls in Iceland and a favourite with tourists. It falls 32 m n two cascades. The canyon below the falls is 2,500 m long and 0 m deep, a magnificent sight. Gullfoss is state property. A tourist ore is located near the falls. See also **Brattholt.**

jaxi, a dell in the canyon not far below Gullfoss. Birch-bushes and ich vegetation. The name is probably derived from the Latin word *pax*, neaning peace.

rattholt, a farm to which part of **Gullfoss** used to belong. Well-known ecause of the struggle of the farmer Tómas Tómasson (1845-1926) and is daughter Sigríður Tómasdóttir (1871-1957) to prevent Gullfoss being old to foreign buyers. A statue of Sigríður by Gullfoss commemorates er victory.

aukadalur, see special map on next page.

eysir, see next page.

jarnarfell, (727 m) a mountain west of Geysir, good viewing point

58 Einholtsvegur, 7,5 km.

34 Gullfossvegur, 0,72 km.

rumbosstaðir, there is Arctic Raftings base camp for river rafting in outh Iceland. They offer daily departures from May 15th to September 1th of September at 10:00 and 14:00.

30 Skeiða- og Hrunamannavegur, p. 173
F35 Kjalvegur, p. 454
37 Laugarvatnsvegur, p. 190
333 Haukadalsvegur, p. 184
356 Tjarnarvegur, p. 190
F333 Haukadalsvegur, p. 454, 461
F338 Skjaldbreiðarvegur, p. 460

Haukadalur, a church and formerly a substantial farm and historically important home of local leaders. Now a local headquarters of the Forestry Service and the State Soil Conservation Service. The land of Haukadalur had been badly damaged by erosion when in 1938 a Dane, Kristian Kirk, bought the farm to give it to the Forestry Service to be protected and re-forested. Much has been done since then and a memorial to Kirk has been erected there. National Forest, **Haukadalsskógur**. In Saga times the family of Haukadalur, Haukdælir as they were called, was one of the most important and powerful families in the country. Teitur Ísleifsson founded a school in Haukadalur in the 10th century and many learned men got their education there, the best-known being Ari Þorgilsson (1067-1148), who wrote the oldest extant book in Iceland, *Íslendingabók* (The Book of Icelanders). According to folktales the giant Bergþór of Bláfell is buried near the church of Haukadalur. The iron ring on the church door is said to be from Bergþór's walking-stick and the iron spike from the stick, 1.4 m long, is said to be kept there and was recorded as one of the belongings of the church in the 15th century. The whey stone at **Bergsstaðir** (see p. 182) was supposedly made by Bergþór, also. There is much geothermal heat in the land of Haukadalur. From Haukadalur there is a reasonably good road over the heath as far as road F338 which is a mountain track.

Haukadalsheiði, a land reclamation area.

Laugarfell, a small mountain by Geysir.

Geysir, one of the most famous spouting hot springs of the world, its name the source of the English word "geyser". It is believed that Geysir started spouting in the 13th century. However, at the beginning of last century it stopped altogether, possibly because it was half choked by visitors throwing rocks and turf into the spring in order to activate it. In 1935 it was re-awakened by lowering the water level and at its best spouted to a height of 60 m. The nearby **Strokkur** spouts with great frequency and Geysir itself spouts once in a while. The centre Geysistofa houses a multimedia exhibition on the forces of nature in Iceland, a restaurant, facilities for research and education, exhibitions on old farming methods and the history of the Geysir area, and a shop.

Konungssteinar, ("The king's stones") three stones on the slope west of the hot spring area. Their name derives from the fact that three Danish kings on official visits to Iceland, Christian IX in 1874, Frederick VIII in 1907 and Christian X in 1922, used them as seats while waiting for Geysir to spout.

333 Haukadalsvegur, 2,11 km.

Geysir

Á Hvítá

Geysir

Kárastaðir, the first farm in the Þingvallasveit district when approaching from Mosfellsheiði moor.

Vinaskógur, ("Friends' wood") a grove of trees on the land of Kárastaðir. Trees planted there are all associated with the President of Iceland and are the gifts of foreign friends. It is customary for foreign heads of state who visit Iceland to plant a tree there. Vinaskógur was started on the 60th birthday of President Vigdís Finnbogadóttir when the foreign embassies in Iceland, under the leadership of the German Ambassador, together gave Iceland a birch grove in honour of the President.

Skálafell, (771 m) a mountain with a telecommunications station on top, for both telephone and television. Very good skiing country, with ski-lifts and two ski-cabins.

Mosfellsheiði, an extensive moorland area between the Mosfellssveit district and the lake Þingvallavatn. A shield-volcano from a warm period of the ice age, covered by basalt lava, some of which also reached the Reykjavík area. The highest point, **Borgarhólar** (410 m), remnants of the crater.

434 Skálafellsvegur, 4 km.

Móskarðshnúkar, rhyolite mountains between Skálafell and Esja, several cone-shaped, light-coloured peaks, the highest 807 m.

Skeggjastaðir, a farm in the Mosfellssveit district. An interesting waterfall, **Tröllafoss** ("Giants' falls"), not far from there in the river Leirvogsá. Popular with tourist.

Gljúfrasteinn, was the home and workplace of Halldór Laxness (winner of the Nobel Prize for Literature in 1955) and his family for more than half a century. It has now been opened to the public as a museum, unchanged from when Laxness lived there.

Laxnes, a farm where Halldór Laxness was brought up.

Reykjahlíð, a community in the Mosfellsdalur valley with many greenhouses. Geothermal water is piped from there to Reykjavík, a distance of 20 km.

Mosfell, a farm, church and a parsonage, on the slopes of a mountain of the same name. In Saga times Egill Skallagrímsson of *Egils saga* spent his last days at Mosfell and the story goes that he buried two chests of silver coins in the area.

Hrísbrú, a farm by Mosfell. A church was already there when Iceland became Christian in the year 1000 but was moved to Mosfell in the years 1130-60. Some excavation have been done there.

Mosfellsdalur, a wide, green valley between the mountains Mosfell and Helgafell. Much geothermal heat.

Grímmannsfell, (454 m) a small mountain on the north side of the road.

Hengill, (803 m) a mountain to the south of the road, its highest point being **Skeggi** at the northwestern edge. From there, and elsewhere along the mountains edge there are spectacular views, particularly over the Faxaflói bay and Lake Þingvallavatn. Hengill is a central volcano and acid rocks are found in Sleggja on the southwestern side. There are volcanic rifts to the north and south of Hengill, the most recent eruptions having been about 2,000 years ago. On the western slopes is **Marardalur**, a fairly large, grassy plain closed in by cliffs and scree on all sides, with a narrow canyon leading out of it to the west. The valley is easily closed off, and bulls were often kept there, signs of walls can still be found. Bulls used to be pastured on many moors, from Bolavellir by Kolviðarhóll up to Hofmannaflöt on Bláskógaheiði moor. The bulls became quite fierce and there are many stories of travellers' encounters with them. The enormous loss of cattle in the Móðuharðindi period 1783-85 put an end to the highland pasturing of bulls. Reindeer frequented the area near Marardalur up until 1925. They were the last reindeer on the Reykjanes peninsula.

Dyrafjöll, one of the tuff ridges on the way to Nesjavellir.

Nesjavellir, a geothermal power station, owned by the Reykjavík Heating Service (Orkuveita Reykjavíkur). There is a great deal of geothermal heat under the northern and northeastern slopes of the mountain Hengill.

435 Nesjavallaleið, 27 km. A beautiful route, many marked walking routes on the way.

Kárastaðir- 1 Vesturlandsvegur 30 km — Nesjavallavegur-Dalland-Nesjavellir 20 km

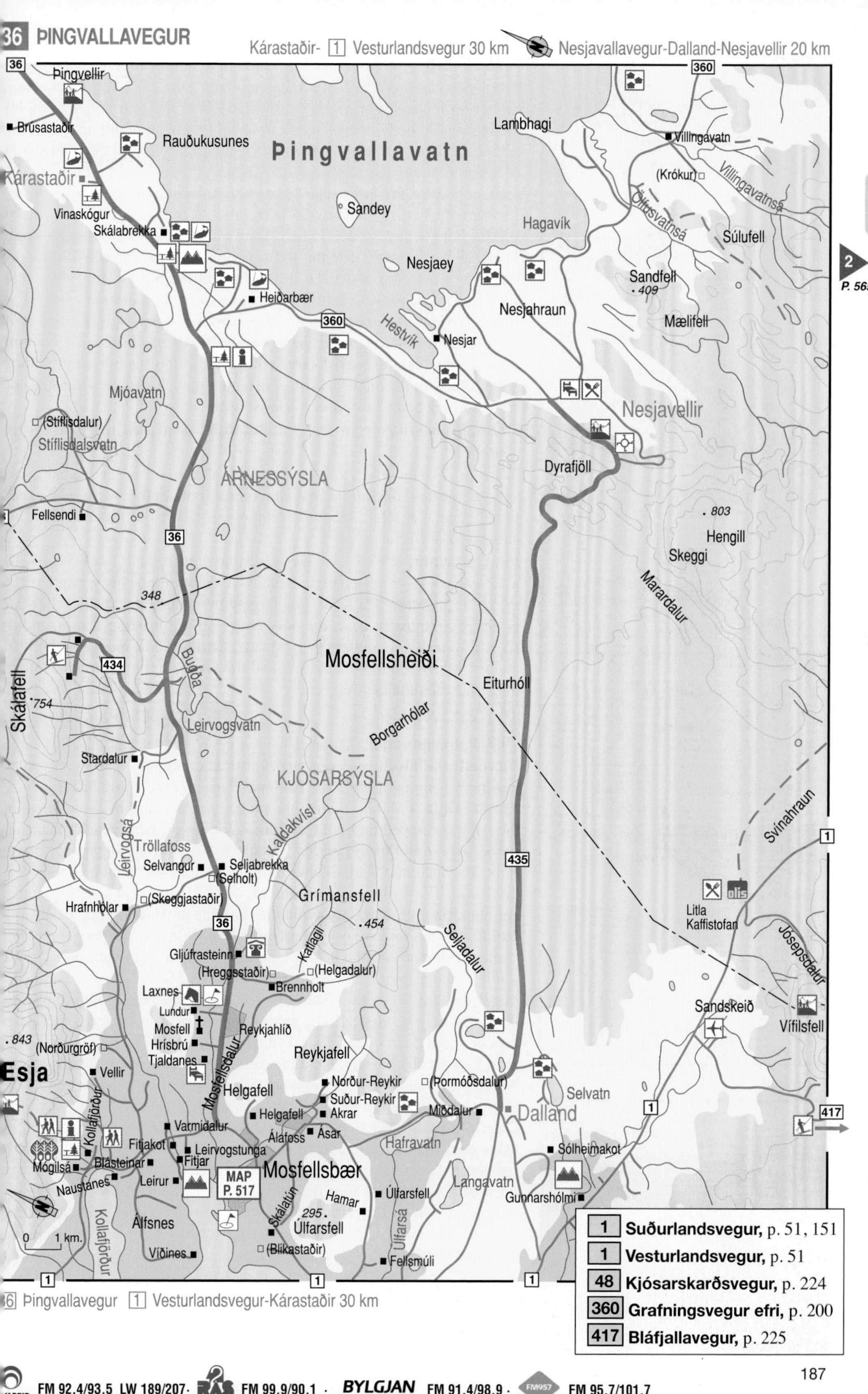

36 Þingvallavegur 1 Vesturlandsvegur-Kárastaðir 30 km

1	**Suðurlandsvegur,** p. 51, 151
1	**Vesturlandsvegur,** p. 51
48	**Kjósarskarðsvegur,** p. 224
360	**Grafningsvegur efri,** p. 200
417	**Bláfjallavegur,** p. 225

FM 92,4/93,5 LW 189/207 · RÁS 2 FM 99,9/90,1 · BYLGJAN FM 91,4/98,9 · FM957 FM 95,7/101,7

2
P. 565

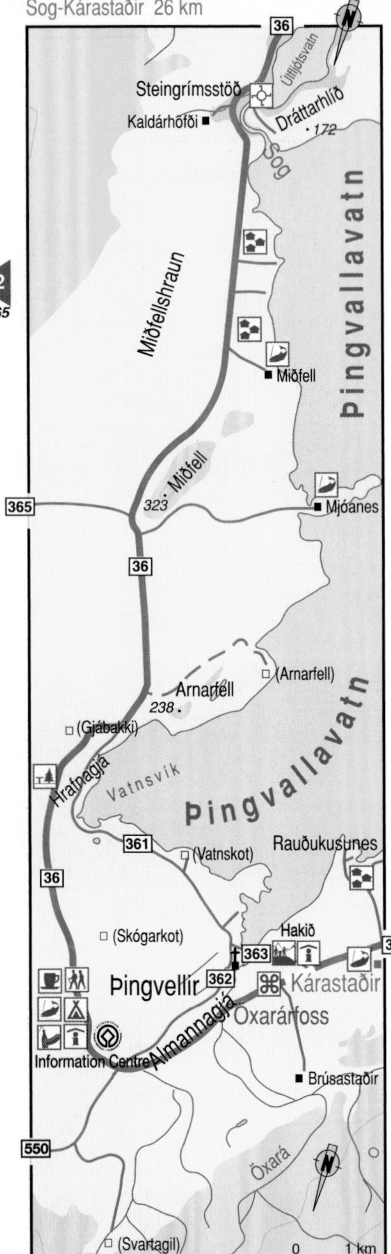

Kárastaðir-Sog 26 km

Hrafnabjörg, (765 m) a rocky tuff mountain dominating the area.

Þingvellir National Park ("Parliament plains") the most important histori cal site in Iceland. For nearly 9 centuries, from the year 930 the Althing the legislative body of Icelanders, was held there annually near the nort end of the lake. Some marked ruins there and in the canyon Almannagjá A flagpole marks the likely site of Lögberg ("Law cliff") where the law speaker recited the laws. The plains and surrounding area were made National Park in 1928. The area is mostly covered with birch and willow and has many lava fissures, some filled with icy cold, crystal-clear wate There is a parsonage, church and a national graveyard where the poet Einar Benediktsson and Jónas Hallgrímsson are buried. Þingvellir we added to the UNESCO World Heritage List in the summer of 2004. A Hakið, a viewspot where tourists may walk down into Almannagjá faul a tourist information centre has been built for the Þingvellir Nationa Park. In this centre, tourists are introduced to the history and nature c Þingvellir with the aid of multimedia techniques. Þingvellir is a very pop ular camping place in summer. Tourist centre.

Flosagjá, **Nikulásárgjá** and **Peningagjá** waterfilled rifts, east of th church.

Silfra, a rift that leads to Þingvallavatn lake. It is one of Iceland's be kept secrets and one of the best snorkeling spots in the world with excep tionally clear waters. Arctic Adventures offer trips to this amazing, hic den world of Silfra.

Þingvallavatn, at 83,7 km^2, the largest lake in Iceland. Its surface is 10 m above sea level, its average depth 34,1 m, but it reaches a depth of 11 m, i.e. 11 m below sea level. Fed largely by underwater springs the wate is always extremely cold, the only river feeding it being Öxará, and th river Sog being its outlet. Two islands, **Sandey** and **Nesjaey**, both o craters. Many summer houses around the lake. Angling permits availab in the information centre.

361 Vallavegur, 9 km. **362 Efrivallavegur,** 1,5 km.

363 Valhallarvegur, 0,5 km.

Þjónustumiðstöð, a service and information centre visitors can get a general information about the National Park, its nature and history.

Almannagjá, ("Public ravine")in ancient times many of those attendin the Alþing camped on the level grassy bottom of the ravine. Almannagj is the largest and most famous tectonic fissure in the Þingvellir Nationa Park. Its western edge is higher than the eastern one which is considera bly lower. The entire piece of land between Almannagjá and Hrafnagjá a graben (fault trough). View-dial on the edge of Almannagjá.

Hakið, the interpretive centre at Hakið is at the top of Almannagjá. Ther visitors can discover the history and nature of the area with the help of multimedia program. The history and nature of Þingvellir is described i detail on large screens where diverse and interesting photographs an drawings may be viewed. The exhibition visitors can choose either narra tion or subtitles in one of four different languages (Danish, English, Ge man or French) besides Icelandic and control by use of touch-screen which topics they view and in what order. Lavatories can also be found i the interpretive centre and are open 24/7 all year round.

Öxará, a clear river flowing into Almannagjá in a lovely waterfall. Th story goes that our forefathers changed the course of the river in order get better access to water. **Drekkingarhylur** ("The drowning pool"), deep pool in the river near the bridge in Almannagjá, formerly a place c execution. Up to the early 18th century women found guilty of crime such as adultery, incest and murdering infants were tied in sacks an drowned there.

365 Lyngdalsheiðarvegur, p. 201 **550 Kaldadalsvegur,** p. 236

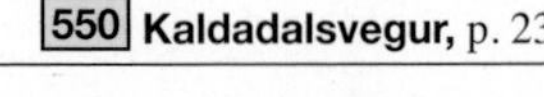

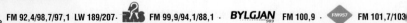

lftavatn, a shallow lake through which flows the river Sog. The Sog is o wide and slow-moving below the lake that a rise in the level of Ölfusá iver, beyond Sog, can cause it to back up and raise the level of the lake. xtensive birchwoods near the lake make it a popular area for summer ouses.

51 Búrfellsvegur, 9,3 km to road 35.

lausturhólar, a farm and a place of settlement, a church and a parsonge until 1887. A leprosy hospital was operated there for a while.

úrfell, (536 m) a mountain with a farm and church of the same name at s foot. A lake on top of the mountain. It is said that the water level rises nd falls there in relation to its fall and rise in the explosion crater Kerið, nd vice versa.

350 Grafningsvegur neðri, 12,2 km.

jósifoss, a waterfall in the river Sog by Efri-Brú. Two power stations in ne Sog are associated with it, Ljósifoss, harnessed in 1935-37 and 1934-4, total power 15 MW and Írafoss-Kistufoss, harnessed in 1950-53, ower 48 MW. A community which has grown up around the stations and as its own school takes its name from the falls.

fri-Brú, a farm, birthplace of the poet Tómas Guðmundsson (1901-83).

aldárhöfði, a farm by the river Sog, between the lakes Þingvallavatn nd **Úlfljótsvatn**. In an islet in Úlfljótsvatn called Torfnes a heathen rave from the 10th century was found in 1946. A man and a hild had been buried there in a boat, together with weapons nd other objects.

ráttarhlíð, the hill to the south of Lake Þingvallavatn by the river og. In 1956-59 a tunnel was dug through there and the power station **teingrímsstöð** built on the lower side with a drop of 22 m, power 6,400 kW.

og, the largest clear river in Iceland, the outlet from Þingvallavatn and unning into the river Hvítá, now running through the Steingrímsstöð ower station. Total length 19 km with a volume of 114 m³/sec. A very ood salmon-river.

35 Biskupstungnabraut, p. 180 **360 Grafningsvegur efri,** p. 200

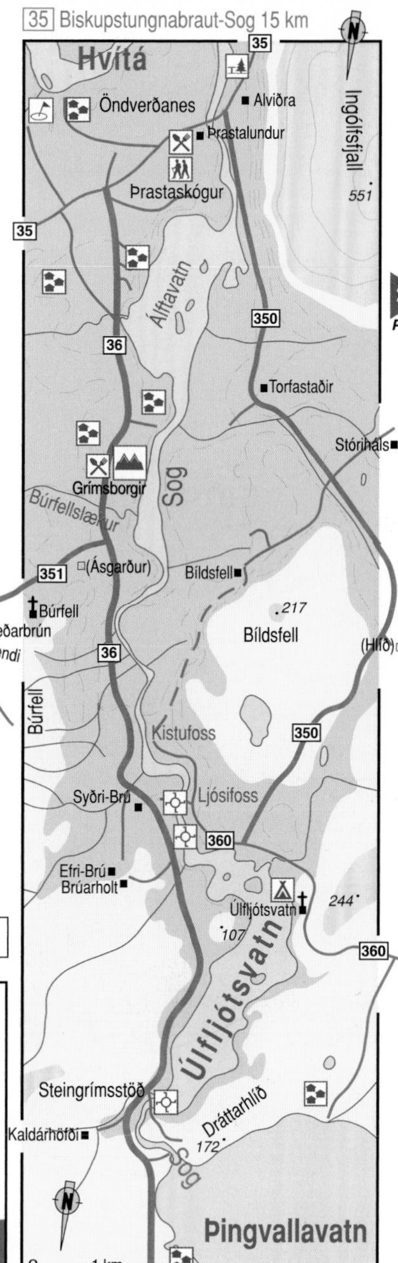

Þingvellir

© Fríða Hálfdanardóttir

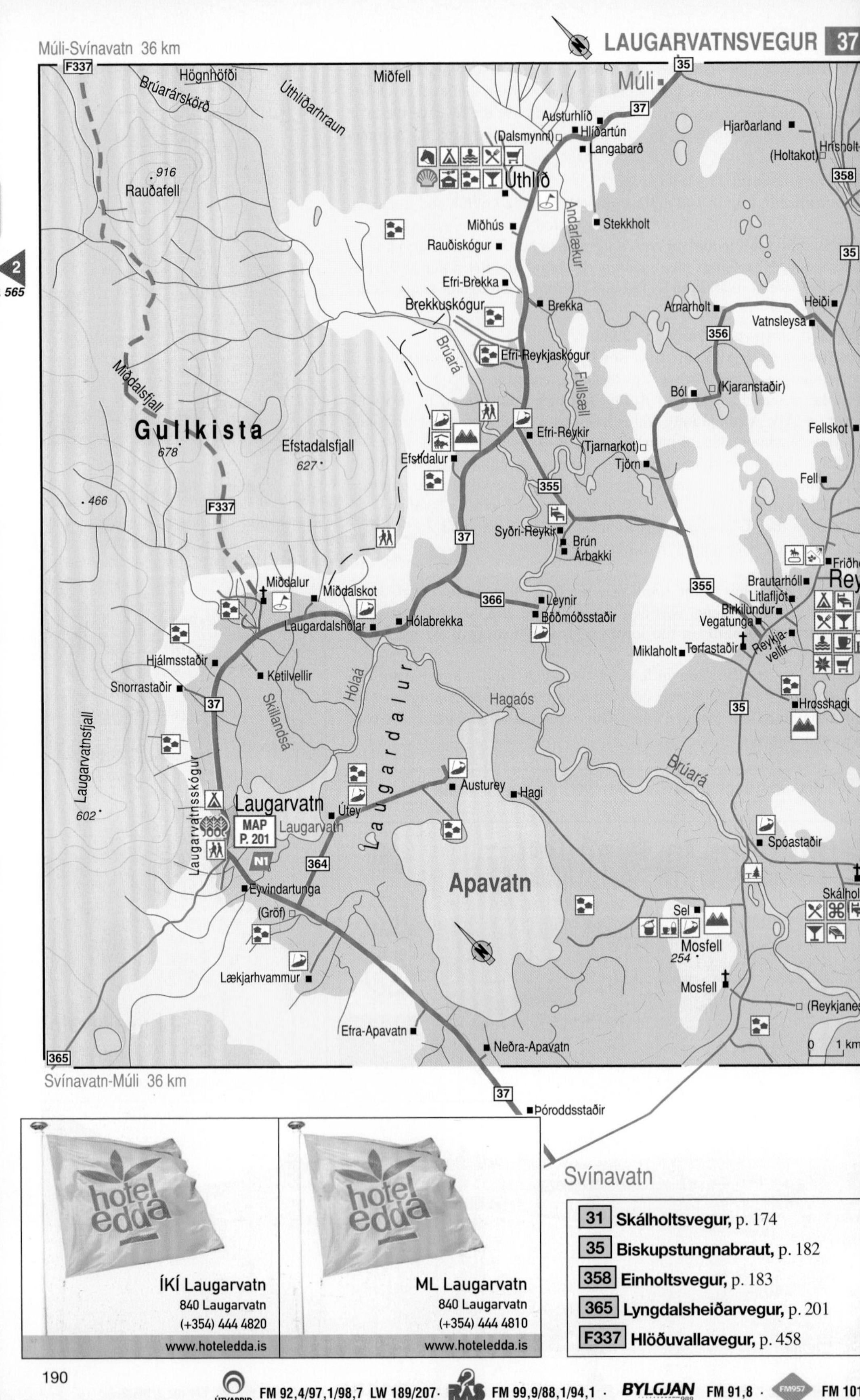
Múli-Svínavatn 36 km
F337
Högnhöfði
Brúarárskörð
Úthlíðarhraun
Miðfell
Múli
35
37
Austurhlíð
(Dalsmynni)
Hlíðartún
Langabarð
Hjarðarland
(Holtakot)
Hrísholt
358
Úthlíð
916
Rauðafell
Miðhús
Rauðiskógur
Andarlækur
Stekkholt
2
P. 565
Efri-Brekka
Brekkuskógur
Brekka
Arnarholt
Heiði
Vatnsleysa
356
Brúará
Efri-Reykjaskógur
Fullsæll
Ból
(Kjaranstaðir)
Miðdalsfjall
Gullkista
678
Efstadalsfjall
627
Efstidalur
Efri-Reykir
(Tjarnarkot)
Tjörn
Fellskot
Fell
466
F337
355
Syðri-Reykir
Brún
Árbakki
Friðheimar
Rey
Miðdalur
Miðdalskot
366
Leynir
Böðmóðsstaðir
Brautarhóll
Litlafljót
Birkilundur
Vegatunga
Laugardalshólar
Hólabrekka
Miklaholt
Torfastaðir
Reykjavellir
Hjálmsstaðir
Snorrastaðir
Ketilvellir
Hólaá
Laugardalur
Hagaós
37
Skillandsá
Hrosshagi
Laugarvatnsfjall
Laugarvatnsskógur
Austurey
Hagi
Laugarvatn
Útey
MAP P. 201
Laugarvatn
602
N1
364
Spóastaðir
Eyvindartunga
Apavatn
Skálholt
(Gröf)
Sel
Mosfell
254
Lækjarhvammur
Mosfell
(Reykjanes)
Efra-Apavatn
Neðra-Apavatn
0 1 km
365
Svínavatn-Múli 36 km
37
Þóroddsstaðir
Svínavatn
31 Skálholtsvegur, p. 174
35 Biskupstungnabraut, p. 182
358 Einholtsvegur, p. 183
365 Lyngdalsheiðarvegur, p. 201
F337 Hlöðuvallavegur, p. 458
hotel edda
ÍKÍ Laugarvatn
840 Laugarvatn
(+354) 444 4820
www.hoteledda.is
hotel edda
ML Laugarvatn
840 Laugarvatn
(+354) 444 4810
www.hoteledda.is
ÚTVARPIÐ FM 92,4/97,1/98,7 LW 189/207 · RÁS 2 FM 99,9/88,1/94,1 · BYLGJAN FM 91,8 · FM957 FM 101

thlíð, a farm since the original settlement, a church until recently. Extensive lavafield, Úthlíðarhraun, idely grown with birch bushes north of there. Some ins of the heathen temple of Geir goði can be seen in e homefield, e.g. a sacrificial blood bowl, also what is lieved to be his burial mound.

rekkuskógur, an area covered with birch bushes, in e land of the farm Brekka. In recent years a great many mmer houses have been built there, e.g. by the Association of Academics.

ri-Reykir, a farm by Brúará. It provides hot water for farms and 500 summer houses in the area.

55 Reykjavegur, 8 km. **356 Tjarnarvegur,** 9 km.

rúará, a clear river originating on the **Rótarsandur** nds and falling through impressive canyons, **Brúarárskörð**, between the mountains Rauðafell and Högnhöfði. he most impressive canyons of Árnessýsla, 3-4 km ng, dug by Brúará through layers of loose sediments of nglomerate. On the flat land Brúará flows into a long, rrow rift in the middle of the river bed. There is a footidge there, but there was once a natural bridge, which is said the cook at the bishopric of Skálholt had stroyed in 1602, when the country was suffering hard nes. He wanted to stop travellers from getting to Skálolt and begging for food, but was himself drowned in e river a short while later.

stidalur, the innermost farm in the Laugardalur valley. ow there is a guesthouse, restaurant and a café.

lfhóll ("Fairies' hill") is behind the farm, a fine viewg point towards the mountains behind and the districts low. Extensive birch bushes in the neighbourhood.

66 Böðmóðsstaðavegur, 2,4 km.

öðmóðsstaðir, once a ferry point. Geothermal heat, een houses.

Laugardalur, a valley or depression under the slopes of the mountains Laugarvatnsfjall and Efstadalsfjall, with two large lakes, Laugarvatn and Apavatn.

Gullkista, ("Chest of gold") an interesting little box-shaped peak on the mountain Miðdalsfjall (678 m).

Miðdalur, a farm, church and a golf course.

Laugarvatn, (pop. 147) a village that has grown around a number of schools: a junior college, an intermediate school, The College of Physical Education and an elementary school. This is a geothermal area, and it is said that when Christianity was legalized in the year 1000, the chieftains from the north refused to be baptised in the cold waters of Þingvellir, and were brought to Laugarvatn to be baptised in the warm spring, **Vígðalaug** ("Consecrated spring"). The bodies of the last Catholic bishop, Jón Arason, and his sons were washed there after they had been beheaded at Skálholt in 1550, and were later taken to Hólar in Skagafjörður for burial. Three children were baptised in Vígðalaug at the celebrations in 2000 commemorating the conversion of Iceland. A natural steambath reopen in June 2011 with sandy beaches by the lake. At Laugarvatn you will also find a gas station, grocery store, restaurants, hotels and a gallery. A popular camping area in summer. Beautiful walking routes in the area.

Laugarvatn, a lake, 2,14 km², with geothermal heat on the banks and the bottom, mostly shallow and rich in plant-life.

Laugarvatnsskógur, expansive forest, combination of birch and planted species. Declared protected in early 20th century. National Forest.

364 Eyjavegur, 4,9 km.

Apavatn, ("Ape lake") a lake of 14 km², good trout-fishing. Two farms, Efra-Apavatn and Neðra-Apavatn, south of the lake. In the 11th century the home of the poet Sighvatur Þórðarson.

Þorlákshöfn-Hveragerði 20 km

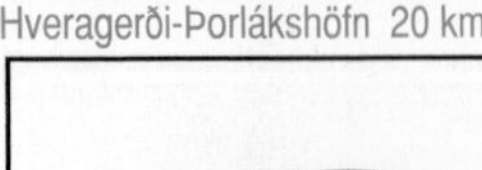

Hveragerði-Þorlákshöfn 20 km

Þorlákshöfn, (pop. 1,489) a young but rapidly growing village, nam after Iceland's only saint, St. Þorlákur, Bishop of Skálholt (1133-1193). Ju outside of the town is a challenging 18 hole golf course and in town is large sports hall with excellent outdoor and indoor swimming pools, a s and a gym. For those who want to get to know the history of this old fishi village there is a path, guided with signs, through some of the town's sit of interest. The town library and folk museum is situated in the town ha where there is an exhibition of stuffed fish and sea animals and a small ga lery. Services offered to visitors are expanding and improving every ye and now include a campsite and an art gallery. Fishing boats have put to s from Þorlákshöfn for hundreds of years. During the days when fisherm rowed out to sea, a fleet of 20-30 boats was common, and the populati swelled to three or four hundred during the fishing season. The mode town grew up around the successful Meitill hf. fisheries company in t middle of the last century. The population increased again in the 1970s af an eruption on the island of Heimaey. Þorlákshöfn is one of many icelan communities that owes its present existance to soil conservation work. T area was threatened by drift sand and sandstorms, and an 7500 ha ar around Þorlákshöfn was fenced off in 1935. Initiating extensive soil cons vation and restoration work that is still ongoing today. Þorlákshöfn is als great place for surfing both for beginners and more advanced surfers. Arc Surfers offer tours in the area.

Hafið Bláa, a restaurant located at the coast with a great view over t sand coast and the Atlantic Ocean.

Ölfus, a municipality, the most westerly district in Árnessýsla. It covers total area of 750 km^2 and has a population of over 2,000 people. The mo important industries are fishing, fish processing, retail services, agricult and light industries.

Vindheimar, a farm where Adventist have built and earlier run a interm diate school, **Hlíðardalsskóli**.

Hraun, a farm where judge Lénharður was killed in 1502.

Hjalli, a substantial farm and church. In Saga times the home of la speaker Skafti Þóroddsson. Bishop Ögmundur Pálsson, the last Catho bishop at Skálholt, was captured there by Danish soldiers in 1541.

Þurá, ("Dry river") a farm where part of the lava flow of Krist tökuhraun ("Conversion lava") came down from Hellisheiði moor in t year 1000, now called **Þurárhraun**.

1 **Suðurlandsvegur,** p. 149 | 34 **Eyrarbakkavegur,** p. 178
39 **Þrengslavegur,** p. 194 | 427 **Suðurstrandarvegur,** p. 22

© Styrmir Kári

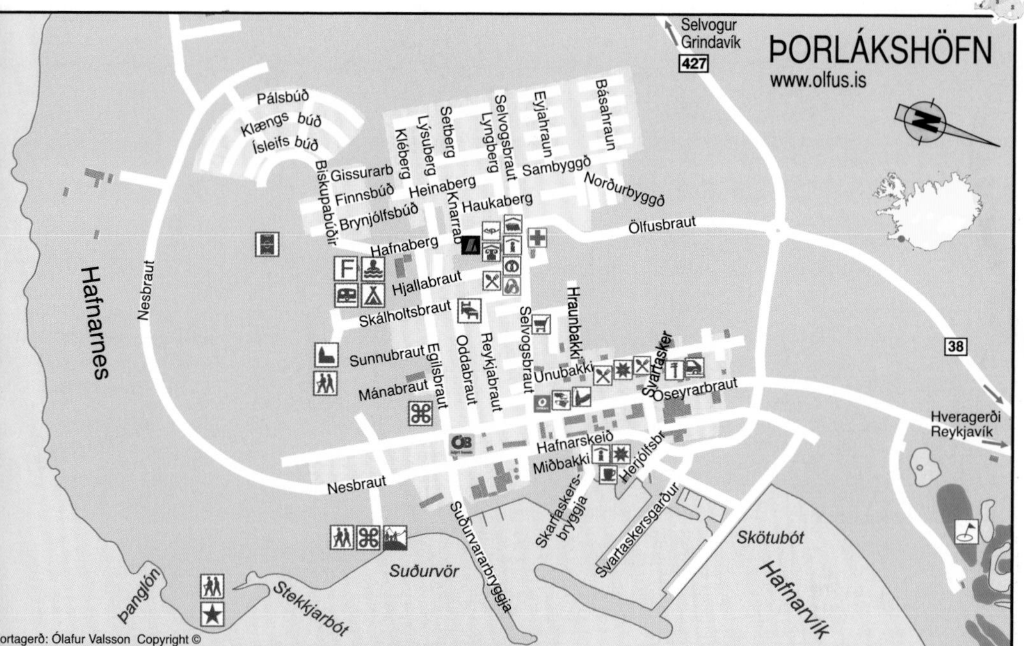

The Þorlákshöfn Pier Concert.

On a beautiful summer day at Skötubót just east of Þorlákshöfn.

1 Suðurlandsvegur-38 Þorlákshafnarvegur 14 k

1
1
Litla-Kaffistofan
Rauðuhnúkar
655
Vífilsfell
Draugahlíðar
417
Svínahraun
Blákollur
546
KJÓSARSÝSLA
417
Jósepsdalur
586
Ólafsskarð
Drottning
407
(Kolviðarhóll)
Bruni

1
P. 564

Bláfjöll
Leiti
546
Lambafell
Stóra-Reykjafell
510
Hveradalir
Þrengsli
Hellisheiði
39
Stórimeitill
521
ÁRNESSÝSLA
Lambafellshraun
Stóra-Sandfell
Litlimeitill
Heiðin há
Votaberg
Litla-Sandfell
Eldborgarhraun
509
Hrossagjá
Geitafell
39
Krossfjöll
Hjallafjall
Þúfnavellir
Raufarhólshellir
Búrfell
Hlíðardalsskóli
Breiðabólsstaður
Efri-Grímslækur
Litlaland
Ytri-Grímslækur
(Hlíðarendi)
Hraun
Selvogsheiði
Þorlákshöfn
38
0 1 km

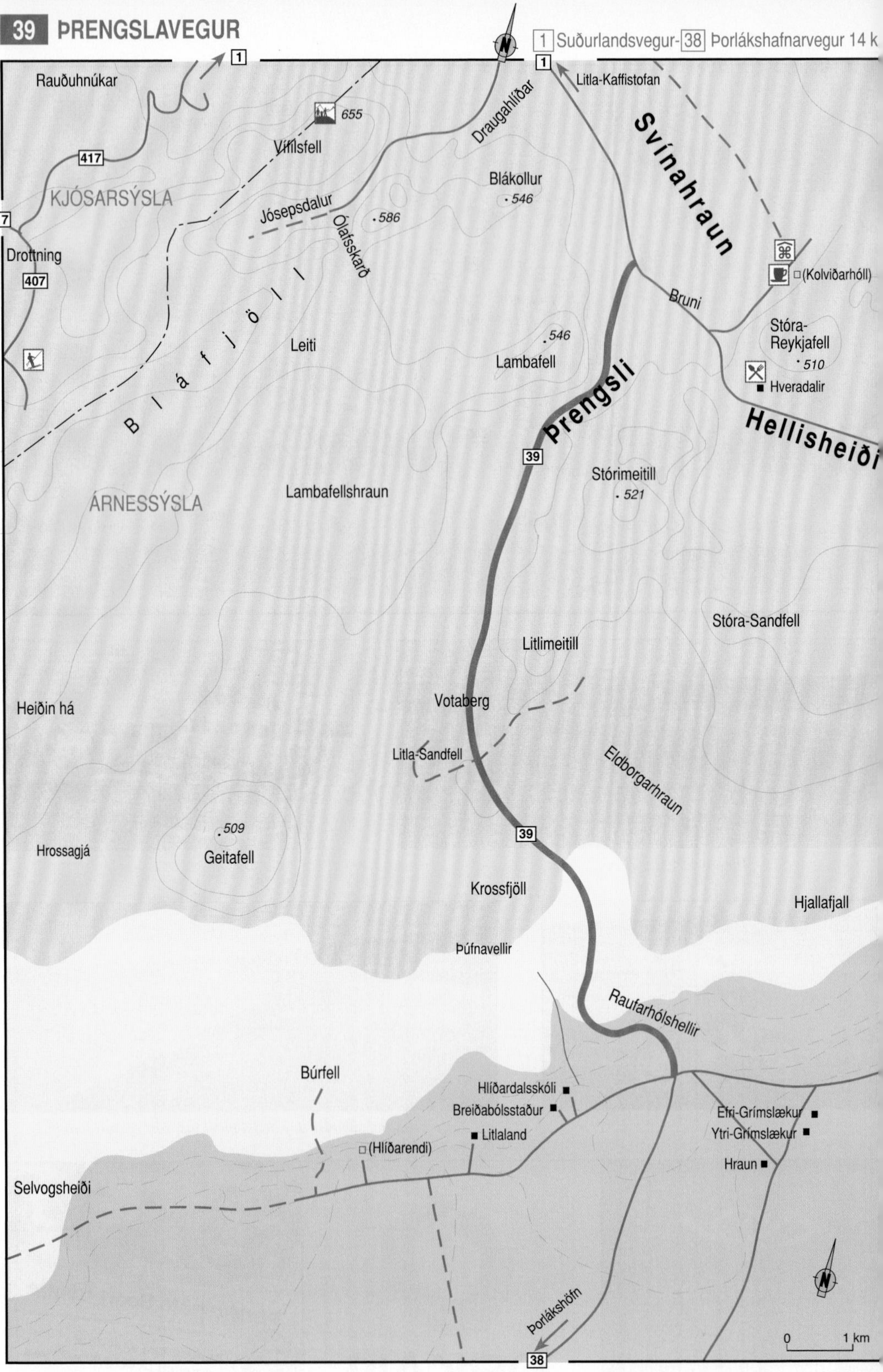

17 **Bláfjallavegur,** 4,3km from Bláfjallavegur Road by auðuhnúkar to the skiing area.

eiti, craters by the eastern slopes of the Bláfjöll ountains, not far south of Ólafsskarð pass. About 5,000 ears ago great masses of lava came from there and read across an extensive area. The Lambahraun lava eld on the moors east of Bláfjöll, over Hraunsheiði to e sea by Þorlákshöfn, the Svínahraun and Elliðaárhraun va fields as well as Rauðhólar and the cave **aufarhólshellir** are all part of this lava field. Highway crosses part of it, from the river Elliðaár to the Drauga-íðar slopes. The Þrengslavegur road goes across this lava south of Þrengsli. Two younger lava flows, Svínahraunsbrunar, from the middle of the 14th century, coming from two small craters called Eldborg east of Leiti.

Raufarhólshellir, about 1 km long cave, one of the largest caves in Iceland. Difficult to traverse due to piles of loose rocks that have fallen from the roof. Beautiful in the bottom. Good lights are essential. The road passes over the cave.

Stalagmites and stalactites in the caves are a protected natural feature!

1 **Suðurlandsvegur,** p. 148, 151 | 38 **Þorlákshafnarvegur,** p. 192 | 417 **Bláfjallavegur,** p. 225

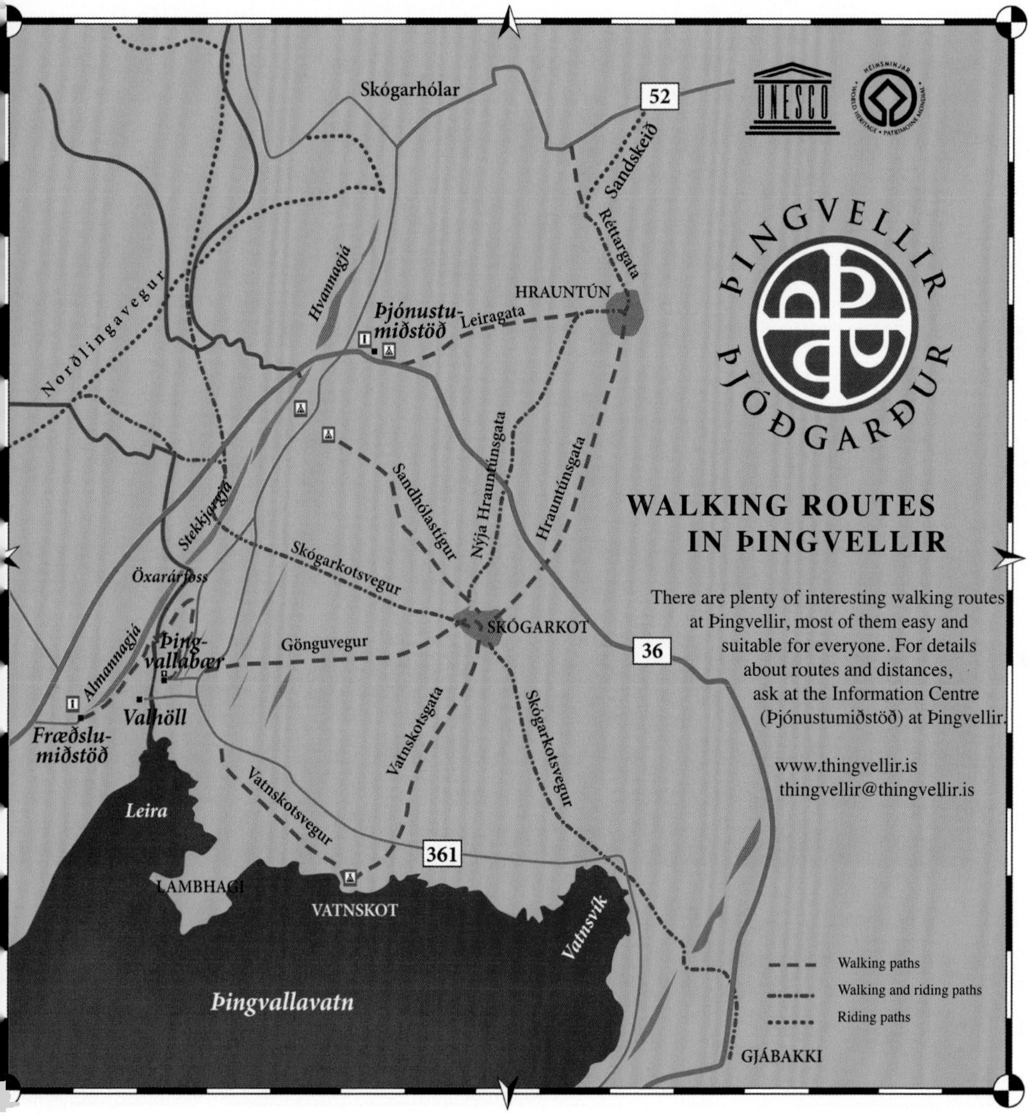

WALKING ROUTES IN ÞINGVELLIR

There are plenty of interesting walking routes at Þingvellir, most of them easy and suitable for everyone. For details about routes and distances, ask at the Information Centre (Þjónustumiðstöð) at Þingvellir.

www.thingvellir.is
thingvellir@thingvellir.is

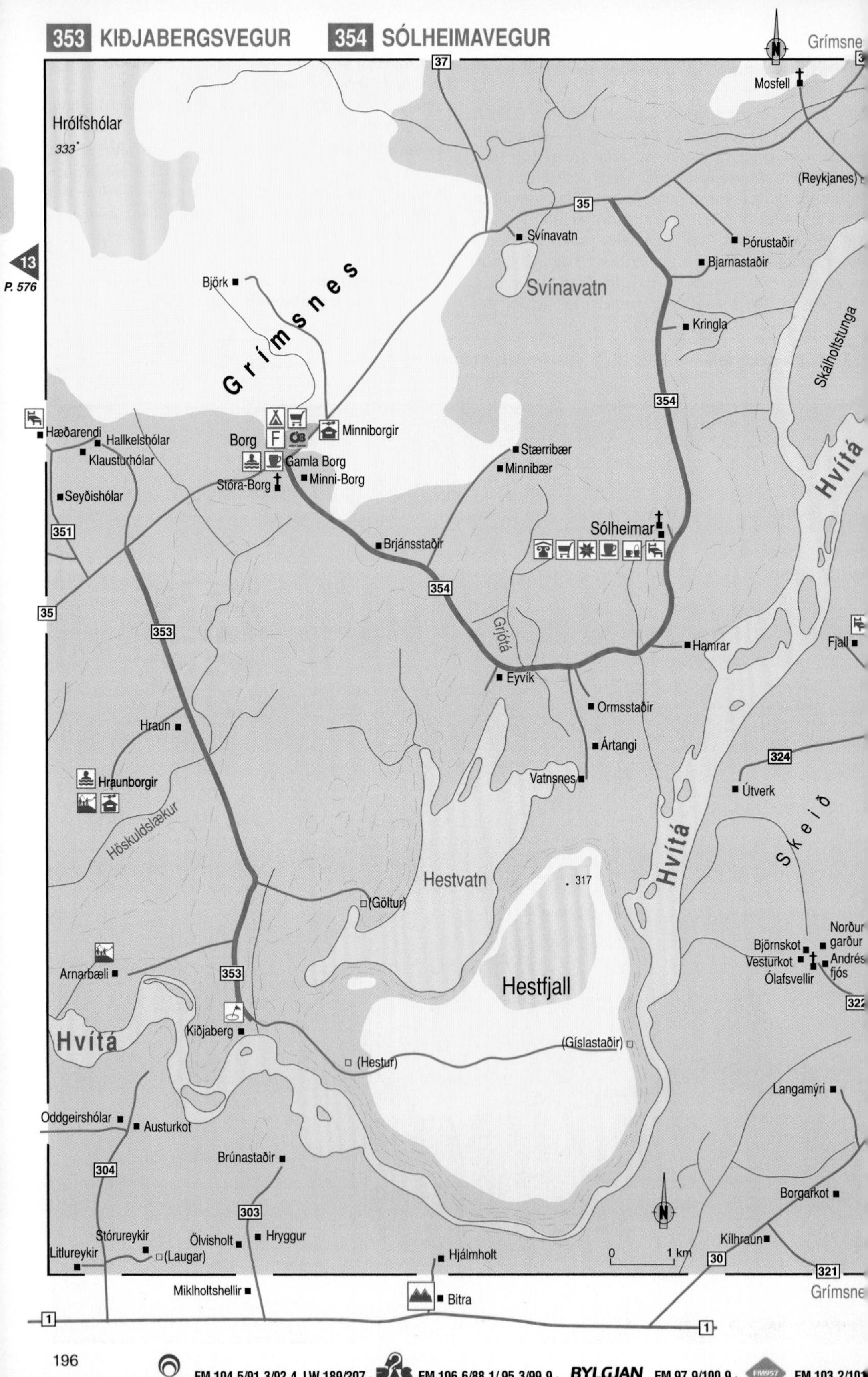

Grímsnes
Mosfell
Hrólfshólar
333
(Reykjanes)
35
37
Svínavatn
Þórustaðir
Bjarnastaðir
Svínavatn
13
P. 576
Björk
Grímsnes
Kringla
Skálholtstunga
354
Hæðarendi
Hallkelshólar
Klausturhólar
Borg
Minniborgir
Gamla Borg
Minni-Borg
Stóra-Borg
Stærribær
Minnibær
Hvítá
Seyðishólar
351
Sólheimar
Brjánsstaðir
354
35
353
Grjótá
Hamrar
Fjall
Eyvík
Ormsstaðir
Hraun
Ártangi
324
Hraunborgir
Vatnsnes
Útverk
Höskuldslækur
Skeið
Hvítá
Hestvatn
317
(Göltur)
Norðurgarður
Björnskot
Vesturkot
Andrésfjós
Ólafsvellir
Arnarbæli
353
Hestfjall
322
Hvítá
Kiðjaberg
(Gíslastaðir)
(Hestur)
Langamýri
Oddgeirshólar
Austurkot
Brúnastaðir
304
Borgarkot
303
Stórureykir
Ölvisholt
Hryggur
Kílhraun
Litlureykir
(Laugar)
Hjálmholt
0
1 km
30
321
Miklholtshellir
Bitra
Grímsnes
1
1

At Stóragil above the campsite at Laugarvatn.

rímsnes, the district marked by the rivers Sog on the uth and Hvítá-Brúará on the east. Named after the setr Grímur who settled there. The southern parts mostly at and covered by old lava-fields with extensive birchshes. The upper parts wet in places, with an interesting ountain region furthest inland. A very popular area for mmer houses.

lausturhólar, a farm and a place of settlement, a urch and a parsonage until 1887. A leprosy hospital as operated there for a while.

losfell, a farm, church and parsonage, built below a ountain (254 m) of the same name. The settling place Ketilbjörn the old, the forefather of the Haukdælir, a owerful and influential family for many centuries.

vínavatn, ("Pig lake") a farm by a lake of the same me. Road 37 to Laugarvatn nearby.

estvatn, a lake of 6 km^2, 60 m deep, the bottom thus ing 12 m below sea level. Good trout-fishing. Somenes Hvítá flows into the lake.

Hestfjall, ("Horse mountain") (317 m) a mountain by Hvítá, believed to be part of an old shield-volcano made of tuff with a cap of basalt. Old seashore lines found 120 m up in the mountainsides. Highest point called Hesteyru ("Horse ears"), probably part of the crater rim. Very good view from Hestfjall, which is a gentle climb. In the year 2000 two big earthquakes shook South Iceland, one who originated in Hestfjall.

354 Sólheimavegur, 15 km.

Sólheimar, a world renowned sustainable community known for its artistic and ecological atmosphere where about 100 people live and work together. It was founded in 1930 by Sesselja Hreindís Sigmundsdóttir (1902-1974). It is a small village set out in the countryside, characterized by vegetation, open common spaces and buildings that nicely co-exist with the landscape. Sólheimar is blessed with enough space for residential and common housing and there are ideal conditions for outdoor activities in the village, which play a big part in the residents' health and wellbeing. The Sólheimar community focuses on the growth and development of man and nature. The social emphasis is that different individuals are offered variable opportunities to work, live, and socialize.

353 Kiðjabergsvegur, 8 km.

Kiðjaberg, a farm from the time of the settlement, interesting surroundings.

Hvítá, ("White river") comes out of the lake Hvítárvatn. Once it reaches the low land it flows to the southwest, between the Biskupstungur and Hrunamannahreppur districts. Lower down it runs between the districts Grímsnes and Skeið, then bends south of the mountain Hestfjall to flow west above the Flói district until the river Sog joins it below the mountain Ingólfsfjall. From this confluence to the river mouth it is called Ölfusá, which has more water in it than any other Icelandic river, with a flow of 371 cubic meters/minute at Selfoss and a drainage basin of 6,100 km^2. Hvítá, Ölfusá and a number of their tributaries all offer good salmon fishing.

1 Suðurlandsvegur, p. 143
30 Skeiða- og Hrunamannavegur, p. 172
35 Biskupstungnabraut, p. 182
37 Laugarvatnsvegur, p. 190
303 Ölvisholtsvegur, p. 143
304 Oddgeirshólavegur, p. 143
321 Skeiðháholtsvegur, p. 172
322 Ólafsvallavegur, p. 172
324 Vorsabæjarvegur, p. 172
351 Búrfellsvegur, p. 180, 189

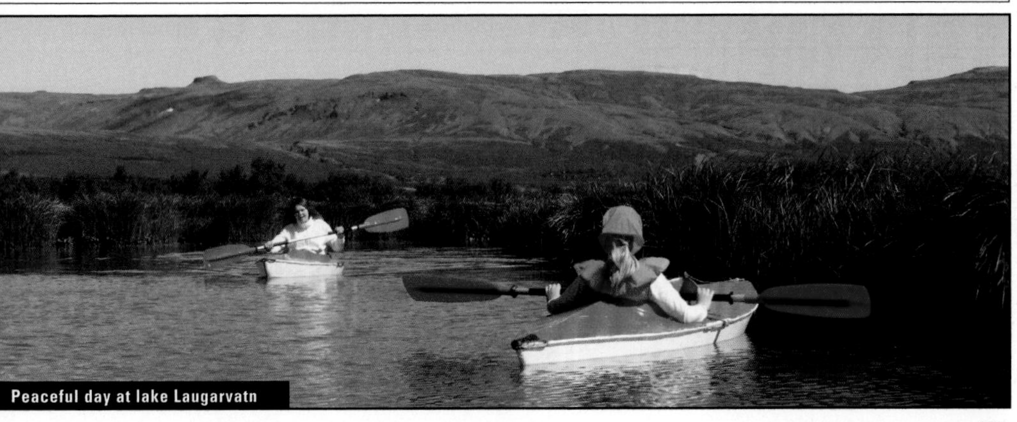

Peaceful day at lake Laugarvatn

13 P. 576

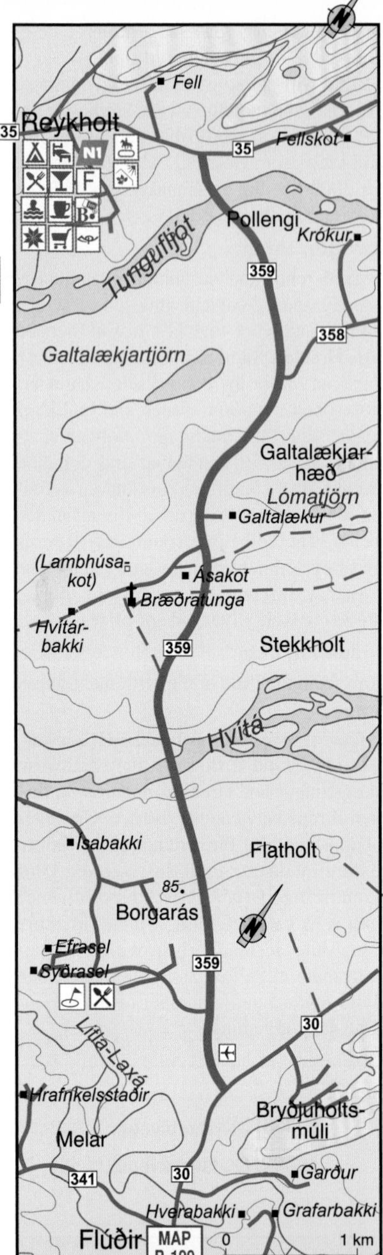

Tungufljót, formerly a glacial river coming from the lake **Sandva** and joining Hvítá. There used to be large mud-flats around Sandva and in dry periods these caused much sand erosion down in the farr ing country. To prevent this the water level of Sandvatn was raised 1994 by closing the two outlets, Sandá and Ásbrandsá and creati a new outlet in the Sandá river flowing east into Hvítá. Ásbrandsá now a clear river and along with small streams from Haukadalshei moor forms Tungufljót, which has become good for salmon-raisi after the salmon-ladder was made in the Faxi (or Tungufoss) waterfa

Bræðratunga, a farm and church, often the home of chieftains a outstanding men, such as Ásgrímur Elliðagrímson in *Njáls saga,* Ea Gissur Þorvaldsson, and the lawyers Gísli Hákonarson (1583-163 and later Magnús Sigurðsson (1651-1707) known for his cases agair Professor Árni Magnússon of Copenhagen, cf. *Íslandsklukkan* b Halldór Laxness.

Hvítá, ("White river") comes out of the lake Hvítárvatn. Once it reac es the low land it flows to the southwest, between the Biskupstung and Hrunamannahreppur districts. Lower down it runs between the di tricts Grímsnes and Skeið, then bends south of the mountain Hestfj to flow west above the Flói district until the river Sog joins it below t mountain Ingólfsfjall. From this confluence to the river mouth it called Ölfusá, which has more water in it than any other Icelandic riv with a flow of 371 cubic meters/minute at Selfoss and a drainage bas of 6,100 km^2. Hvítá, Ölfusá and a number of their tributaries all off good salmon fishing.

At Flúðir

30 **Skeiða- og Hrunamannavegur,** p. 173
35 **Biskupstungnabraut,** p. 182
341 **Langholtsvegur,** p. 173
358 **Einholtsvegur,** p. 183

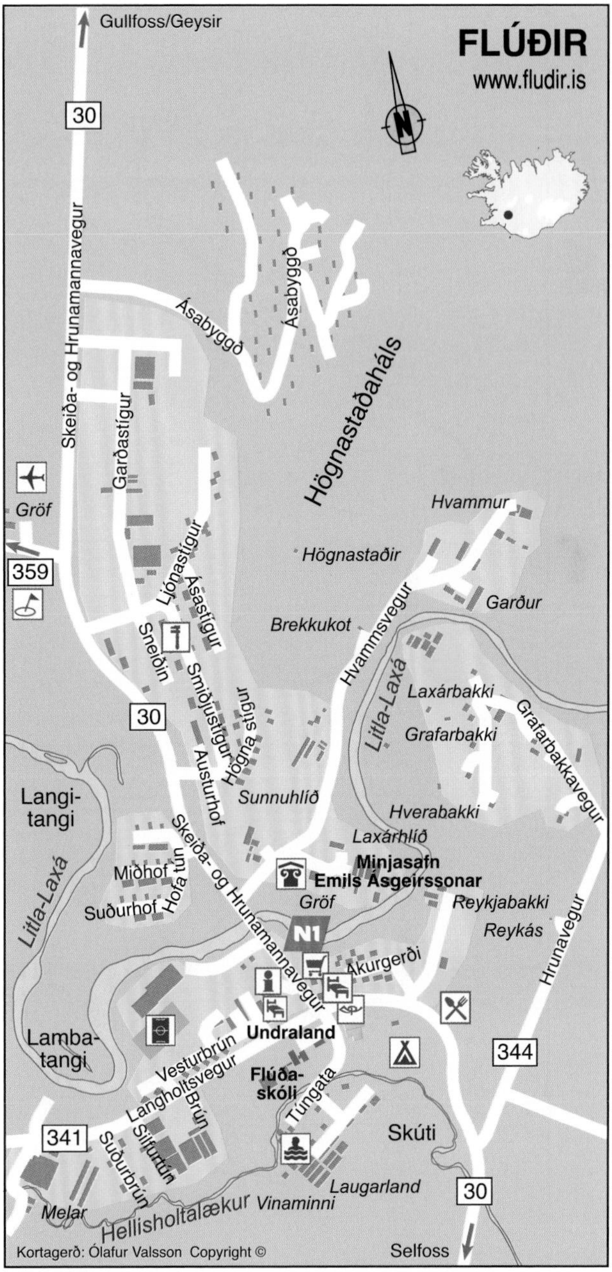

FLÚÐIR

www.fludir.is

Gullfoss/Geysir
30
Skeiða- og Hrunamannavegur
Ásabyggð
Ásabyggð
Högnastaðaháls
Garðastígur
Gröf
359
Ljónastígur
Ásastígur
Sneiðin
Smiðjustígur
Högna stígur
Austurhof
Hvammur
Högnastaðir
Garður
Brekkukot
Hvammsvegur
Litla-Laxá
Laxárbakki
Grafarbakki
Grafarbakkavegur
Hverabakki
Sunnuhlíð
Langi-tangi
Skeiða- og Hrunamannavegur
Laxárhlíð
Minjasafn Emils Ásgeirssonar
Gröf
Reykjabakki
Reykás
Miðhof
Hofa tún
Suðurhof
Litla-Laxá
Akurgerði
Hrunavegur
N1
Undraland
Lamba-tangi
Vesturbrún
Langholtsvegur
Flúða-skóli
Brún
Túngata
344
341
Silfurtún
Suðurbrún
Skúti
Laugarland
Melar
Hellisholtalækur
Vinaminni
30
Kortagerð: Ólafur Valsson Copyright ©
Selfoss

PARADISE ALL YEAR ROUND

FLÚÐIR IS CENTRALLY SITUATED IN THE SOUTH OF ICELAND, CLOSE TO MANY OF THE MOST BEAUTIFUL AND HISTORICAL PLACES IN THE COUNTRY

Serivce in the area:

Hótel Flúðir. Tel. 486-6630, fax 486-6530
Flúðir Gymnasium. Tel. 486-6544
Flúðir Swimming pool. Tel. 486-6790
Flúðir Campsite. Tel. 486-6535
Efra-Sel Golf Course. Tel. 486-6690
Ásatún Golf Course. Tel. 486-6601
Syðra-Langholt Guesthouse. Tel. 486-6574
Syðra-Langholt Horse rental. Tel. 486-6774

Strax Grocery store. Tel. 486-6633
Grund Guesthouse. Tel. 552 6962
Álfaskeið Campsite. Tel. 486-6674
Flúðir Community Centre. Tel. 486-6620
Útlaginn Coffe house. Tel. 486-6425
Gröf Folk Museum. Tel. 486-6634
Guesthouse Dalbær and Glas Workshop. Tel. 486-6770
Sólheimar open farm, museum. Tel. 486-6590

www.fludir.is

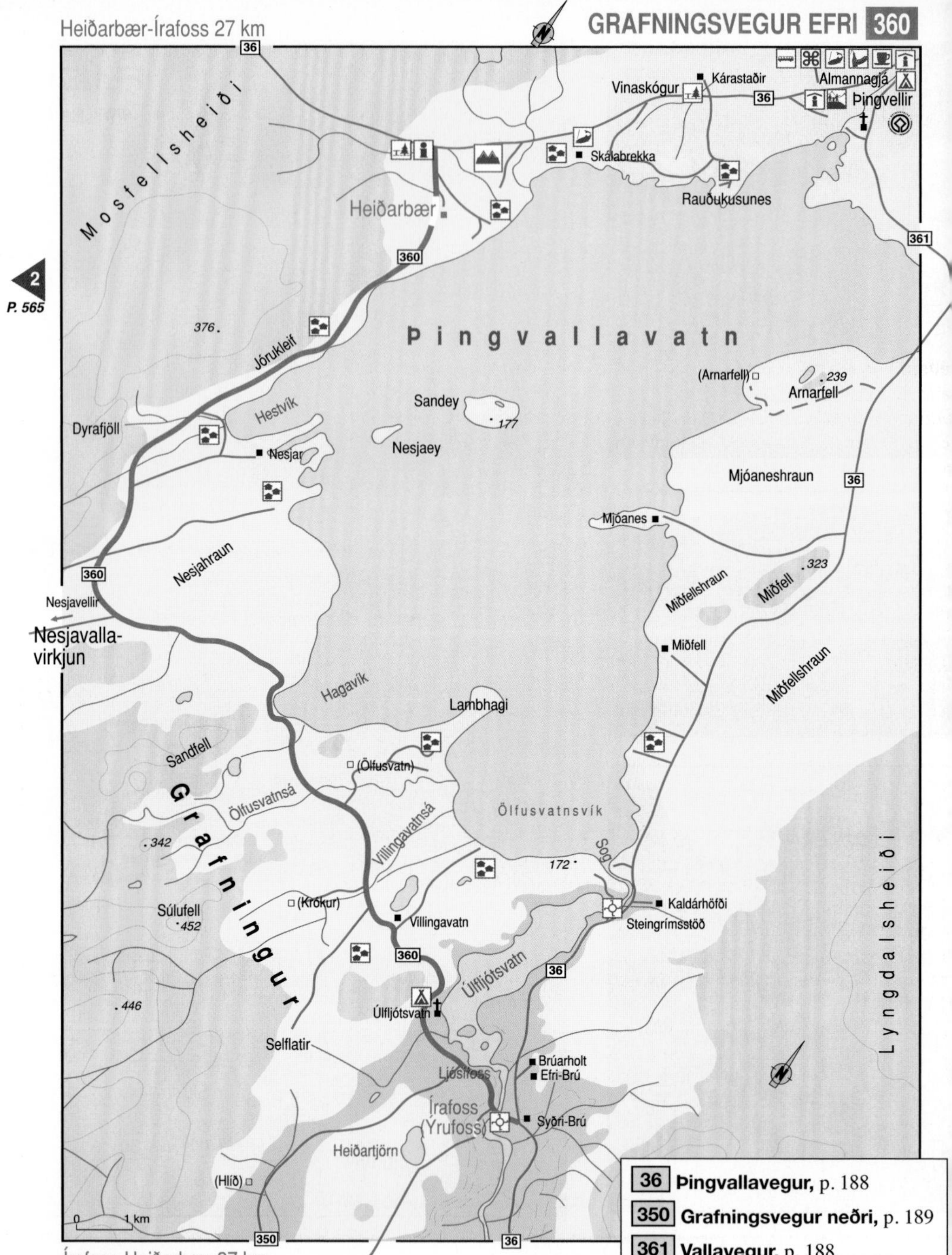

Jórukleif, a rocky wall above the **Hestvík** inlet.
Nesjavellir, a farm belonging to the City of Reykjavík. Much geothermal heat, harnessed for Reykjavík (see Road 36).
Dyrafjöll, (442 m) an interesting tuff mountain range where a recreation area has been organised, with marked footpaths. Forestation has been started.
Hagavík, a deserted farm where Dr. Helgi Tómasson (1896– 1958) planted more trees than any other individual in Iceland. A large lavafield, Hagavíkurhraun, to the north of the mountain Hengill, now densely covered by birch-bushes etc.
Grafningur, the district to the west of Lake Þingvallavatn and the river Sog, with Mosfellsheiði and Dyrafjöl and several low mountain ridges, Grafningsfjöll, to the west, with the mountain Hengill beyond them. Many va leys, often wooded, between the mountains and ridges.
Úlfljótsvatn, a churh, farm and a lake of the same nam

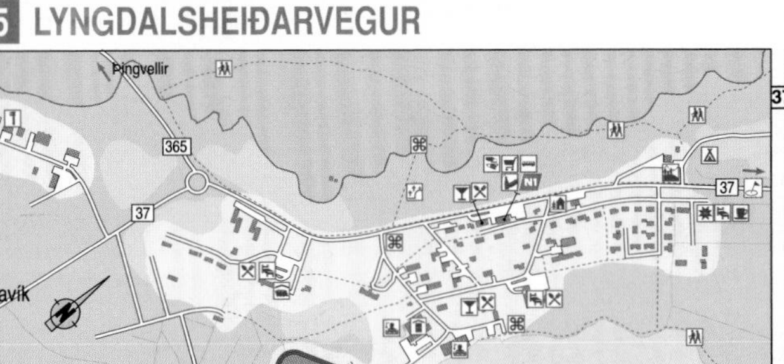

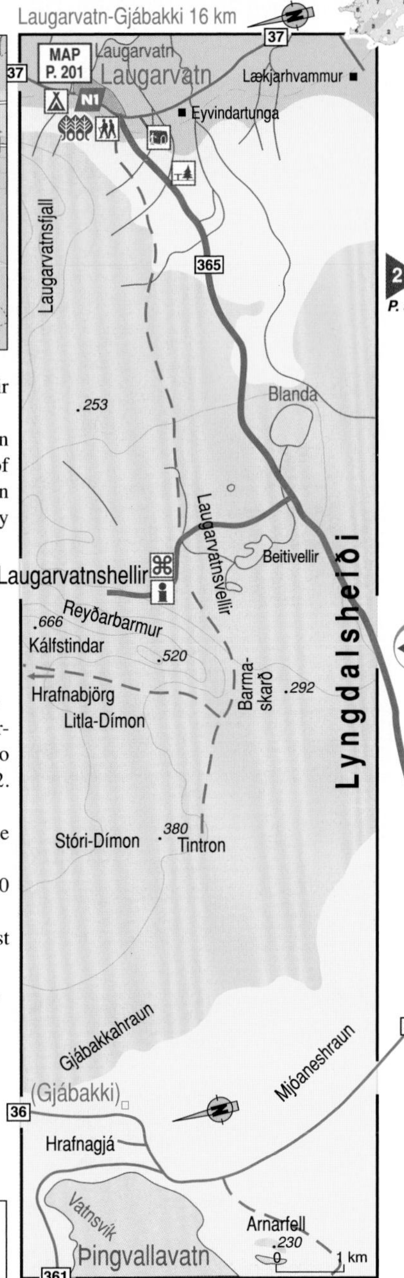

2 P. 565

álfstindar, (826 m) a row of tuff peaks to the north of the Laugarvatnsvellir ains.

augarvatnsvellir, dry flatlands to the east of Reyðarbarmur. Two caves on e west side of the flats were often used to house sheep but were the home of ople during the first decades of this century. A young couple lived there in 10-11 and had an "inn" in a tent near by. It was again inhabited in 1918 by single man who lived there for a year and a married couple who stayed til 1922. During that time they had a daughter and the husband delivered e baby himself. Afterwards he had to travel far, through deep snow that osed all paths, to fetch the midwife. Everything went well and the daughr is the only living Icelander to have been born and lived in a cave. South Laugarvatnsvellir are **Beitivellir**, an old resting place.

opnalág, ("Weapons hollow") and **Kárahella,** ("Kári's slab") place mes to the east of Reyðarbarmur where the road comes down from Baraskarð pass. It is said that Kári Sölmundarson in *Njáls saga* waited there to nbush Flosi and his men when they came from Alþingi in the spring of 1012. osi realised they were there and turned north.

eyðarbarmur, a tuff ridge with a pass through it, Barmaskarð, where the ad lies.

tóra-Dímon and **Litla-Dímon,** two small tuff mountains, 347 m and 380 high respectively.

intron, an old steam vent in the lava, very deep and dark at the bottom, just uth of Stóra-Dímon; a side track leads to there.

yngdalsheiði, an old, flat shield-volcano. The road passes to the north, ross the Gjábakkahraun lava field.

rafnagjá, a long lava rift marking the eastern edge of the plain of Þingellir.

jábakkahellir, a 364m long lava tube cave that was formed during an uption 9000 years ago. Arctic Adventures and Extreme Iceland are among ose who offer guided tours to this extraordinary cave.

36 **Þingvallavegur,** p. 188 | 37 **Laugarvatnsvegur,** p. 190
361 **Vallavegur,** p. 188

1
P. 564

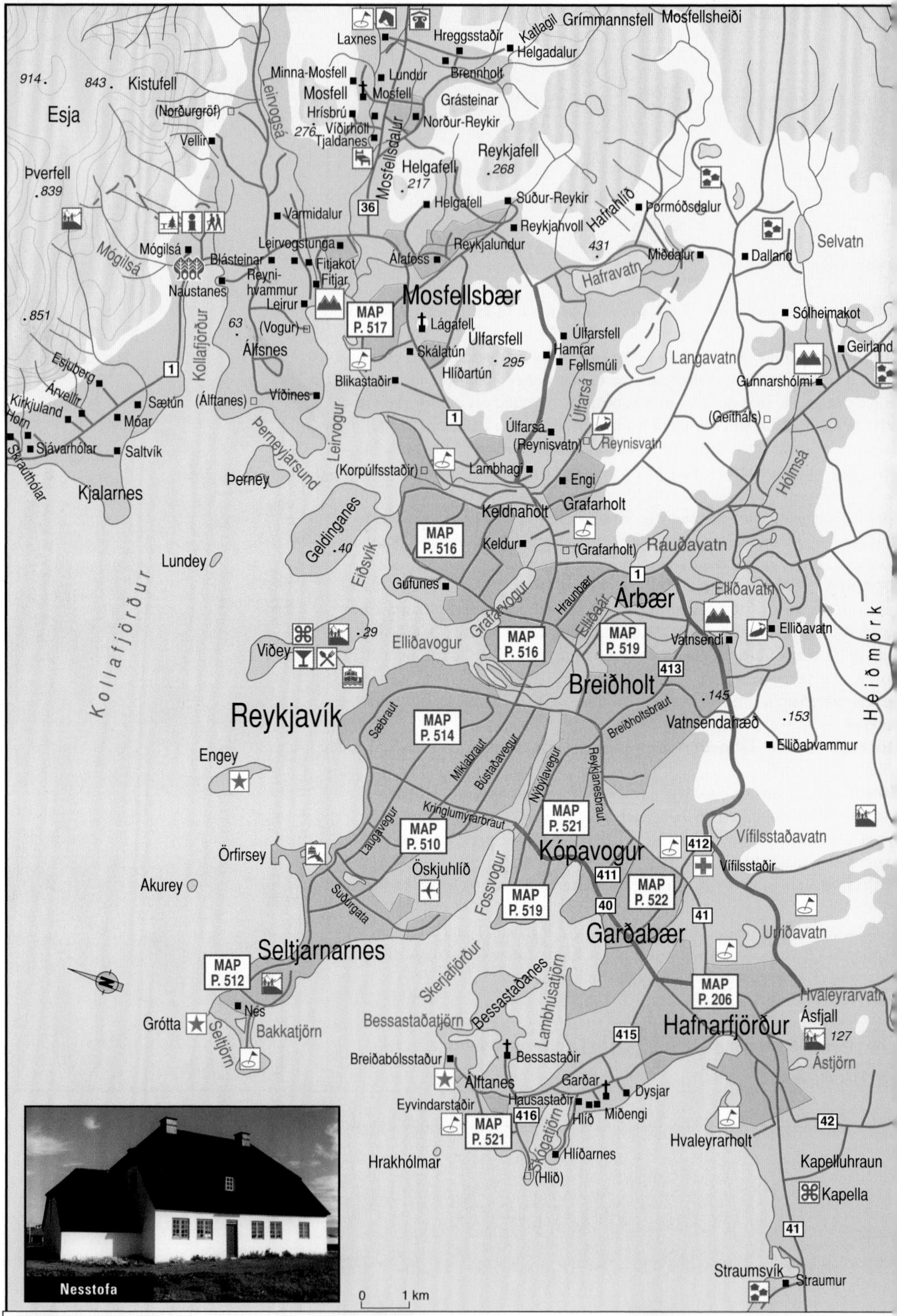

Laxnes
Hreggsstaðir
Katlagil
Grímmannsfell
Mosfellsheiði
Helgadalur
Minna-Mosfell
Lundur
Brennholt
914
843
Kistufell
Mosfell
Mosfell
Grásteinar
Esja
(Norðurgröf)
Hrísbrú
Norður-Reykir
Leirvogsá
276
Víðirholt
Tjaldanes
Vellir
Mosfellsdalur
Reykjafell
Helgafell
268
Þverfell
839
217
36
Helgafell
Suður-Reykir
Hafrahlíð
Þormóðsdalur
Varmidalur
Reykjahvoll
Selvatn
Mógilsá
Leirvogstunga
Reykjalundur
431
Miðdalur
Dalland
Mógilsá
Blásteinar
Fitjakot
Álafoss
Reyni-
hvammur
Fitjar
Hafravatn
Naustanes
Leirur
Mosfellsbær
Sólheimakot
851
MAP P. 517
63
(Vogur)
Lágafell
Úlfarsfell
Úlfarsfell
Geirland
Álfsnes
Kollafjörður
Skálatún
Hamrar
Langavatn
Esjuberg
1
Hlíðartún
295
Fellsmúli
Gunnarshólmi
Árvellir
Blikastaðir
Kirkjuland
Sætún
(Álftanes)
Víðines
Horn
Móar
Úlfarsá
(Geithals)
Sjávarhólar
Saltvík
Þerneyjarsund
1
Úlfarsá
(Reynisvatn)
Reynisvatn
Skrauthólar
Leirvogur
Kjalarnes
Þerney
(Korpúlfsstaðir)
Lambhagi
Engi
Hólmsá
Geldinganes
Keldnaholt
Grafarholt
MAP P. 516
40
Keldur
(Grafarholt)
Rauðavatn
Lundey
Eiðsvík
Gufunes
1
Hraunbær
Elliðavatn
Árbær
Grafarvogur
Elliðaár
Viðey
29
Elliðavogur
MAP P. 516
MAP P. 519
Vatnsendi
Elliðavatn
Heiðmörk
Kollafjörður
413
Breiðholt
145
Reykjavík
Sæbraut
MAP P. 514
Breiðholtsbraut
Vatnsendahæð
153
Elliðahvammur
Engey
Miklabraut
Bústaðavegur
Nýbýlavegur
Reykjanesbraut
MAP P. 521
Kringlumýrarbraut
Laugavegur
MAP P. 510
Vífilsstaðavatn
Örfirsey
Kópavogur
412
Vífilsstaðir
Öskjuhlíð
411
Akurey
Fossvogur
MAP P. 519
MAP P. 522
Suðurgata
40
41
Garðabær
Urriðavatn
Seltjarnarnes
Skerjafjörður
MAP P. 512
Bessastaðanes
Lambhúsatjörn
MAP P. 206
Hvaleyrarvatn
Nes
Ásfjall
Grótta
Seltjörn
Bakkatjörn
Bessastaðatjörn
415
Hafnarfjörður
127
Bessastaðir
Ástjörn
Breiðabólsstaður
Álftanes
Garðar
Dysjar
Eyvindarstaðir
Hausastaðir
416
Hlíð
Miðengi
42
MAP P. 521
Skógtjörn
Hvaleyrarholt
Hrakhólmar
Hlíðarnes
Kapelluhraun
(Hlíð)
Kapella
41
Nesstofa
0 1 km
Straumsvík
Straumur

1	**Vesturlandsvegur,** p. 51	1	**Suðurlandvegur,** p. 151	36	**Þingvallavegur,** p. 186
41	**Reykjanesbraut,** p. 204	42	**Krýsuvíkurvegur,** p. 213	411	**Arnarnesvegur,** p. 204
412	**Vífilsstaðavegur,** p. 204	415	**Álftanesvegur,** p. 204	416	**Bessastaðavegur,** p. 204

Hafnarfjörður Museum

Welcome to Hafnarfjörður

;uður-Reykir, a geothermal area providing Reykjavík ;ith hot water for heating.

/liðdalur, the home of the painter, sculptor and graphic rtist Guðmundur Einarsson (1895-1963).

;eltjarnarnes, (pop. 4,322) a town on a peninsula west of ;eykjavík which gained municipal rights in 1974. On the ill Valhúsahæð the falcon farm of the King of Denmark ;as once located, exporting some 200-300 bird per annum, ach of them worth four horses. The first view-dial to be ut up in Iceland is on Valhúsahæð. **Nesstofa,** a stone built ouse from 1761-63, at the request of the Danish governnent, for the newly appointed Director of Public Health, ;jarni Pálsson. The house was designed by Jacob Fortling, nason to the Danish court. It was built close to the old armhouse. The stone in the house is Icelandic dolerite and ;as carved by a Danish stonemason. The stones were emented with chalk imported from Denmark. In the house ;as a flat and an office for the Director, and also a pharmay which was the first in the country. In the keeping of the ;ational Museum since 1979 and now houses a Medical /luseum. The birthplace of Sveinbjörn Sveinbjörnsson 1847-1926), composer of the Icelandic national anthem. 'he northernmost part of Seltjarnarnes peninsula, including he lighthouse, is a nature reserve and public park. The sland **Grótta**, with its lighthouse, can be reached dry-foot-d at low tide, but care must be taken as the tide can rise uite swiftly and cover the causeway in less than the time it akes to walk across it. Medical centre, swimming pool. See town map under Reykjavík.)

Hafnarfjörður, its name simply means 'harbour fjord' and efers to the excellent natural harbour, which has Iceland's ongest history of continuous port trade - since the 1300s. Hafnarfjörður is Iceland's third-largest town, with just ver 26,800 residents. And yet that number is open to lebate, since legend has it that some of Iceland's elves and idden people live in Hafnarfjörður's lava cliffs and rocks, in peaceful coexistence with the town's human residents. In fact, it is possible to tour the elf lands, and those with second sight may even be lucky enough to spot one or two! Naturally the town also offers plenty of more conventional outdoor activities, from golf and swimming to horse riding and scenic walking routes. Museums and galleries turn the spotlight on history, music and visual arts. Free admision in museums. And every summer hordes of Norsemen invade the town for the annual Viking Festival, held this year from 8-16 June. So relax and enjoy your favourite activity. The staff of the Tourist Information Centre is always ready to welcome you and is happy to provide any advice or information you may need during your stay. Hafnarfjörður nestles comfortably among the lava, and the splendour of the great outdoors is everywhere. One need go no further than the beautiful Hellisgerði park, which has been ingeniously landscaped amongst the lava. Founded in 1922, the park has recently been given the addition of about 150 miniature bonsai trees - the northernmost bonsai collection in the world. Birdwatchers are sure to enjoy the Ástjörn nature reserve, and for walkers there are many lovely routes in and around the town. For those who wish to venture a little further afield, many places of outstanding natural beauty may be found within an easy distance of Hafnarfjörður, although a car is required for visitors planning their own itinerary. Inland from Mt. Ásfjall is a lovely area with lava and mountain scenery containing various walking routes. Enjoy the peaceful surroundings of Hvaleyrarvatn lake, or climb Mt. Helgafell (338m) for stunning panoramic views. Hafnarfjörður is famous for having one of Iceland's largest settlements of elves, dwarves and other mystical beings, which (translating from the Icelandic) are collectively called 'Hidden Folk.' Centuries-old folklore has it that whole clans of such beings reside in the rocks that make up part of the town's centre. We do not doubt this at all.

1 P. 564

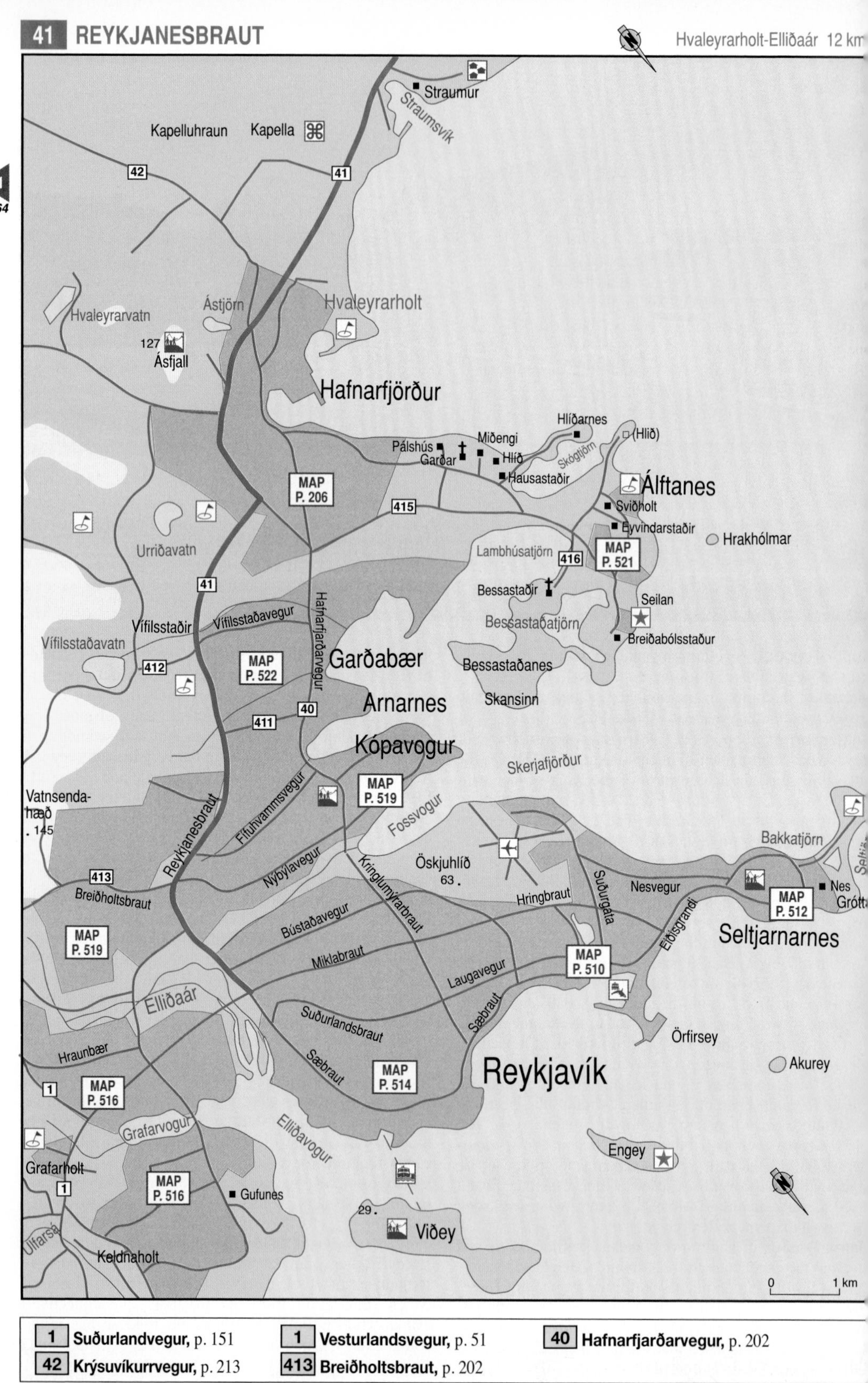

1 **Suðurlandvegur,** p. 151
42 **Krýsuvíkurrvegur,** p. 213
1 **Vesturlandsvegur,** p. 51
413 **Breiðholtsbraut,** p. 202
40 **Hafnarfjarðarvegur,** p. 202

afnarfjörður, see p. 203.

arðabær, (pop. 11,421) a town between Kópavogur and afnarfjörður, gained municipal rights in 1976. Within the wn's boundaries there is a variety of natural features, ktraordinary lava formations, caves etc., as well as ancient mains, now protected. Farming used to be the main occuation in Garðabær along with some fishing from the lftanes peninsula, not far away from the fishing banks. oday industry is growing rapidly in Garðabær. An elemenry school was founded at Hausastaðir in Garðabær in 1791, arking the inception of public education in Iceland. On rnarnes, near the junction of the roads Arnarnesvegur and egranesvegur, there is a concrete column, a restoration of ne built by the German geophysicist Alfred Wegener in 930 to test his theory of continental drift, which he origilly advanced in the years 1908-12. See more p. 522.

lftanes, (pop. 2,392) known for its beautiful nature, with a ariety of flora and fauna. Ingólfur Arnarson, known as the rst settler of Iceland, claimed Álftanes as part of his possessns, so that its history extends back to the very beginning of e country's settlement.

ópavogur, (pop. 31,719) a town between Reykjavík and afnarfjörður, the second largest town in Iceland. The first habitants of today's Kópavogur settled there in 1936. In 945 the population was 521, in 1955, when Kópavogur gaied municipal rights, it was 3,783. Kópavogur is an old site of e official meeting Kópavogsþing, one of four such assemies in Gullbringusýsla. A fateful event in the history of ópavogsþing was when the Icelanders were forced to ackowledge Fredrik III, King of Denmark, as absolute monarch 1662. A monument commemorating these events was erecd at the actual site of Kópavogsþing in 1962. At the same ace there are also traces of old ruins, believed to be the rmer assembly house. A view-dial on the hill Víghóll.

eykjavík, see p. 500.

15 Álftanesvegur, 5,25 km.

16 Bessastaðavegur, 0,82 km.

Eyvindarstaðir, a farm on the Álftanes peninsula. Residence of Sveinbjörn Egilsson (1791-1852), rector of Lærði skólinn (see below) in Reykjavík and author of *Lexicon Poëticum*, a dictionary of poetic language. The childhood home of his son, the poet and naturalist Benedikt Gröndal (1826-1907).

Bessastaðir, an ancient manor farm, official residence of the President of Iceland. First mention of Bessastaðir is in *Íslendinga saga* (The Saga of the Icelanders) by Sturla Þórðarson; the place then belonged to Snorri Sturluson. Later it became the first royal estate in Iceland, being in the possession of the King of Norway. From 1805 Bessastaðir was the site of the highest educational institution in Iceland, Lærði skólinn ("The learned school"), for 40 years. The eminent poet Grímur Thomsen (1820-96) was born at Bessastaðir and lived there from 1867. Upon his death, Bessastaðir became a private estate and remained so until 1941, since when it has been the official residence of the President of the Republic: Sveinn Björnsson (1881-1952) lived there from 1941 to 1952, first as governor then (from 1944) as president, Ásgeir Ásgeirsson (1894–1972) from 1952 to 1968, Kristján Eldjárn (1916-82) from 1968 to 1980, Vigdís Finnbogadóttir (b. 1930) from 1980 to 1996 and Ólafur Ragnar Grímsson (b. 1943) from 1996. The main building is among the oldest houses in Iceland, built in 1761–66. It has since been added to and renovated. Further renovations were made in 1987 in Bessastaðastofa, revealing some relics of major importance under the floorboards. The church at Bessastaðir was built 1777–1823. Ruins of a fort from the 17th century at Skansinn.

412 Vífilsstaðavegur, 3 km.

411 Arnarnesvegur, 2 km.

Vífilsstaðir, the home of Vífill, freed slave of the first settler, Ingólfur Arnarson, and the one who found Ingólfur's pillars when they drifted ashore at Reykjavík. Vífilsstaðir was formerly a TB sanatorium and a hospital for respiratory diseases.

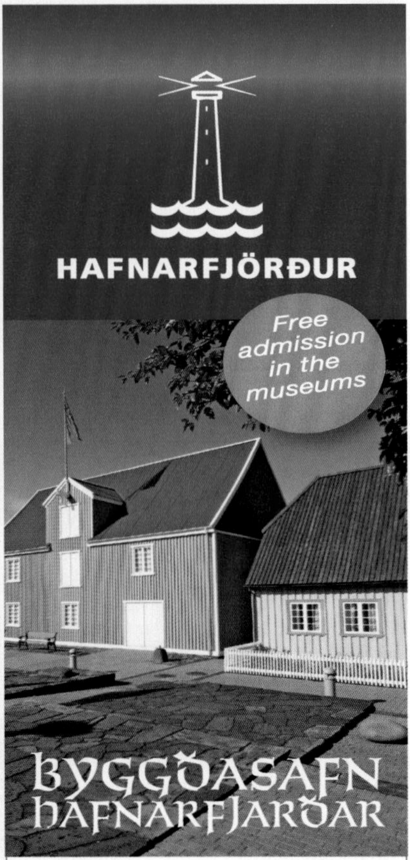

HAFNARFJÖRÐUR

www.hafnarfjordur.is

Hvaleyrarhöfði
Hvaleyri
Golfklúbburinn Keilir
Hvaleyrarholt
Hvaleyrarhraun
Reykjanesbraut
41
Hellnahraun
Kortagerð: Ólafur Valsson Copyright ©
Hringhella
Álfhella
Gjáhella
Breiðhella
Einhella
Dranghella
Dverghella
Jötnahella
Straumhella
Tunguhella
Krýsuvíkurvegur
Norðurhella
Suðurhella
Dofrahella
Berghella

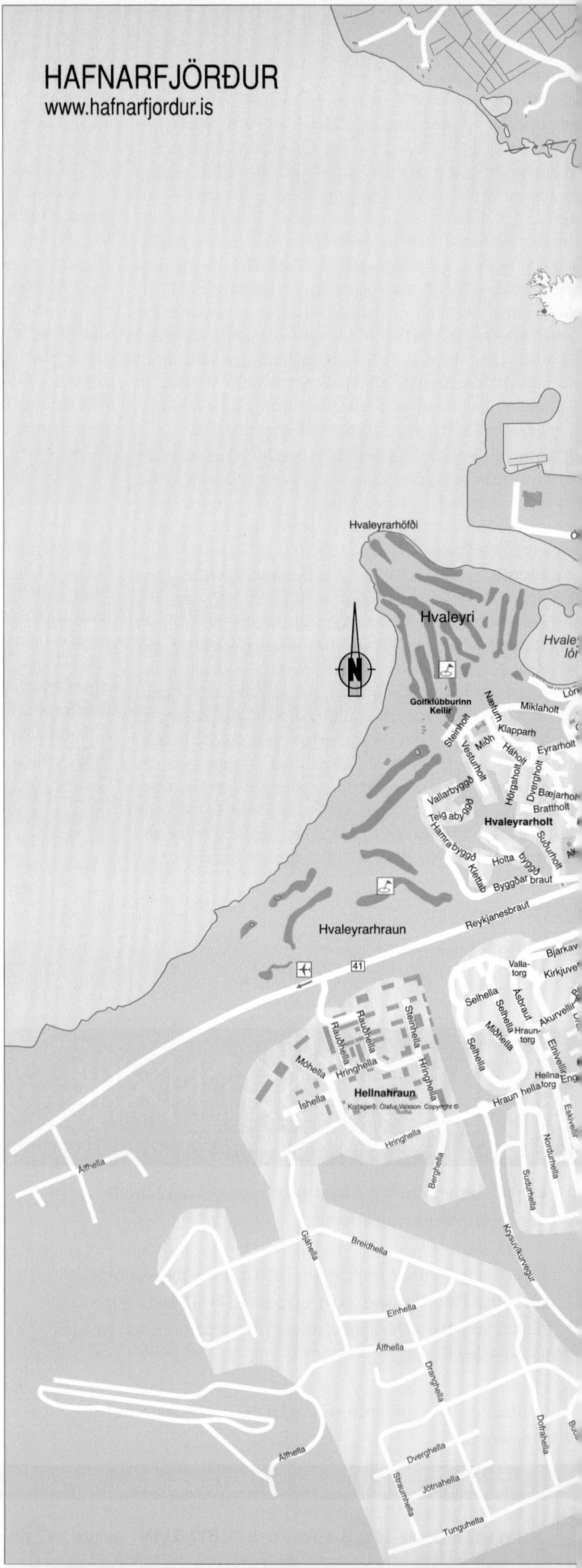

Flatir
Sunnuflöt
Hraunsholtslækur
Hafnarfjarðarhraun
Hleinar
Nausta hlein
Boðahlein
Garðavegur
Hraunavangur
Sjávarbraut
Norðurvangur
Heiðvangur
Breiðvangur
Miðvangur
Þrúðvangur
Blómvangur
Glitvangur
Laufvangur
Hjallabraut
Vesturvangur
Skjólvangur
Herjólfsbraut
Sævangur
Norðurbær
Víðivangur
Suðurvangur
Reykjavíkurvegur
Dalshraun
Stakkahraun
Trönuhraun
Hjallahraun
Hólshraun
Bæjarhraun
Fjarðarhraun
Kaplahraun
Skútahraun
Drangahraun
Stapahraun
Flatahraun
Vesturhraun
Norður hraun
Suðurhraun
Miðhraun
Garðahraun
Molduhraun
Urriðaholtsstræti
Austurhraun
Reykjanesbraut
Álftanesvegur
Kaplakriki
Víðistaða-kirkja
Vesturbær
Hjallabraut
Hrauntunga
Herjólfsgata
Drangagata
Klettagata
Víðistaða-tún
Garðavegur
Hraunbrún
Tunguv
Slétt ahraun
Haukahraun
Máva hraun
Álfaskeið
Svölu hraun
Vörðuberg
Tinnuberg
Víðib
Lyngberg
Reynib
Kvistaberg
Hraun
Hafnarfjörður
Hellisgata
Kirkjuv
Vesturgata
Norðurbakki
Miðbær
Fríkirkjan
Álfaskeið
Hverfisgata
Mánastígur
Sólvangur
Sólvangsvegur
Reykjanesbraut
Grenib
Furuberg
Einiberg
Glitberg
Fagraberg
Hólsberg
Urriðakots-vatn
Golfklúbburinn Setberg
Sunnuvegur
Tjarnarbraut
Skólabraut
Lækjargata
Hafnarfjarðar-kirkja
Hamarinn
Suðurbær
Hvaleyrarbakki
Suðurbakki
Óseyrarbraut
Suðurhöfn
Cuxhavengata
Fornubúðir
Óseyrarbryggja
Flensborgar-höfn
Lónsbraut
Stapagata
Hvaleyrar-lón
Álfaberg
Hlíðarberg
Setberg
Setbergsholt
Klukkuberg
Mosahlíð
Stekkjarhraun
Hádegisholt
Lindarberg
Hlíðarberg
Lækjarberg
St. Jósepsspítali
Hringbraut
Selvogsgata
Holtsgata
Öldugata
Kaldakinn
Hvammabraut
Hvaleyrarbraut
Skipalón
Hólabraut
Ásbúðartröð
Miklaholt
Grandatröð
Eyrartröð
Melabraut
Suðurbraut
Brekkuhvammur
Lækjarhvammur
Hvammabraut
Fjóluhv
Fagrihv
Stekkjarhv
Reykjanesbraut
Ásbraut
Goðatorg
Nóringaháls
Oddsmýrardalur
Skálab
Furuhlíð
Kaldárselsvegur
Eilliðavatnsvegur
Ásland
Hvaleyrarholt
Bæjarholt
Bratthholt
Háholt
Áslandsholt
Blikaás
Álftaás
Lóuás
Spóaás
Erluás
Vörðutorg
Prastarás
Gauksás
Ásar
Kríuás
Fjóluás
Furuás
Hlíðarás
Brekkuás
Hlíðarendi
Svínaholt
Lækjarbotnar
Ástorg
Tjarnarvellir
Ásvellir
Vellir
Krókar
Ástjörn
Ásfjall
Hlíðarþúfur
Gráhelluhraun
Kaldárselsvegur
Sörlastaðir
Grísanes
Myntuvellir
Mosavellir
Línvellir
Laufvellir
Lerkivellir
Möðruvellir
Liljuvellir
Rósavellir
Sóleyjarvellir
Lindarvellir
Lækjarvellir
Smáravellir
Ásvallabraut
Burknavellir
Akurvellir
Daggarvellir
Drekavellir
Eskivellir
Fífuvellir
Furuvellir
Fléttuvellir
Glitvellir
Fjóluvellir
Hafravellir
Hvannavellir
Klukkuvellir
Hnoðravellir
Kvistarvellir
Norðurhella
Suðurhella
Krýsuvíkurvegur
Ásbraut
Borgarhella
Dofrahella
Búðarhella

Vogar-Hvaleyrarholt 20 km

1 P. 564

Vogar, (pop. 1,029) a village at the extreme south of Vatnsleysuströnc with a harbour and lighthouse, fishing and fish processing, industria mechanics, pork and poultry farming. Preschool, elementary school sports centre, swimming pool, community centre, campsite and motel. B the elementary school there is a memorial to Jón Daníelsson the stron (1771-1855), made of a stone weighing 450 kg, which Jón is said to hav picked up and carried.

420 Vatnsleysustrandarvegur, 11,3 km.

Vatnsleysuströnd, a community along the coast southwest of Straums vík to Vogastapi sea cliffs, the farms being close to sea. Little grass excep around the farms, otherwise mostly lava all the way to the Reykjane mountains. Fish hatcheries.

Kálfatjörn, a church and parsonage until 1907. The church is one of larg est country churches in Iceland. 2-3 km to **Staðarborg**, a several hun dred year old stone-built sheep fold.

Keilir, (379 m) a cone-shaped tuff mountain with fine views. It is usuall possible to drive to Höskuldarvellir just east of Keilir.

Kúagerði, west of the Afstapahraun lava field, which probably flowe after the settlement of Iceland. Was the site of one of the few fresh-wate springs in this area.

Hraun, the name for the area west and south of Straumsvík. The bay wa formed between Lambhagatjarnir to the east and Hraun to the west. I Hraun there are many ruins and remains of old farms and outhouses There is evidence of fishing being conducted from the shore, c fishermen´s lodgings, storage rooms, walls and areas for processing fish Scattered in the lava plains there are many freshwater ponds that com and go with the tide. Some of these ponds are home to dwarf trout tha life on the freshwater-seawater boundary.

Brunntjörn, the biggest freshwater pond in the area.

Straumur, the farmer of Kikjuból in Garðskagi was executed there by th Danes for allowing Kristján skrifara to be killed, but he allow the execu tion of Jón Arason bishop in Skálholt 1550.

Straumsvík, site of an aluminium smelting plant, with a good harbou Located in the Kapella lava field, which is named for a chapel, the ruin of which are opposite the factory. In 1950 a small statue of St. Barbar was found there, indicating that the chapel dated from Catholic times.

Búrfellshraun, lava ca. 7,000 years old, from an eruption in the Búrfel crater, that flowed into the sea near Hafnarfjörður.

Hafnarfjörður, see p. 203.

42 Krýsuvíkurvegur, p. 213
415 Álftanesvegur, p. 204
421 Vogavegur, p. 209

Hvaleyrarholt-Vogar 20 km

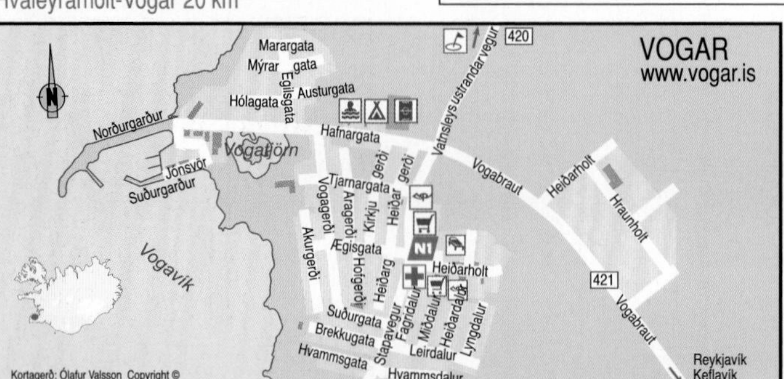

ıvalsnes, ("Whale point") a church, formerly also a farm. The present hurch building built of hewn stone in 1887. Hallgrímur Pétursson 1614-74), the author of the *Passion Hymns*, served there before moving ɔ Saurbær in Hvalfjörður. The church Hallgrímskirkja in Reykjavík is amed after him.

˂eflavík Airport, international airport on Miðnesheiði moor, built by Americans during and after the Second World War, later handed over to celanders. Outside the terminal building are the sculptures *Þotuhreiður* "Jet Nest") by Magnús Tómasson and *Regnboginn* ("Rainbow") by Rúrí.

ʀeykjanesbær, (pop. 14,153) was at one time a fishing town, but this is ot the case any longer. There is now more emphasis on industry, servic-s connected to the airport and the commercial harbor at Helguvík, and arnessing energy and natural resources on the Reykjanes peninsula. ʀeykjanesbær was incorporated in 1994, although one of its forerunners, ˂eflavík, was previously incorporated in 1949. The downtown area has ndergone a number of improvements. The Duusverslun and ischersverslun storefronts form the old commercial centre of the town, vhile the docks in front of them were previously the heart of Keflavík. he marina at Gróf is particularly attractive. According the Herdís gilsdóttir's story about Sigga and the mountain ogress, this is where the gress slept in a small cave. At the marina you can also see Baldur KE 7 or "the Golden Nugget" (1961), which was the first Icelandic boat to se stern tow. The town's major activities are fishing, fish processing, ndustry, retail shops and travel services. In Reykjanesbær you'll find hurches, a hospital, a health clinic, a secondary school, a sports training enter, Vatnaveröld water park, the Viking ship Icelander and Viking xhibition, the Power Plant Earth educational exhibit on Reykjanes eninsula, the Hljómahöllin music centre, and the Duushús Cultural Centre in Reykjanesbær, which houses the Reykjanes Art Museum, the rímur Karlsson Boat Museum, exhibitions for the Reykjavík Heritage Auseum and restaurant Ráin that can fit up to 300 persons in their 2 eautiful dining halls. At Ásbrú, the former NATO base on Reykjanes eninsula, you'll find Keilir – Atlantic Centre for Excellence, the Eldey entre for new business ventures, and the Research Centre for Energy ciences. Public art is displayed through the town, including a statue of celandic Prime Minister Ólafur Thors by Áki Granz, a memorial to fish-rmen lost at sea by Ásmundur Sveinsson, and a memorial to legendary ailor Stjáni blái by Erlingur Jónsson. There are a number of hiking paths nd outdoor activities at Bergin. Hiking maps are available from the nformation office. Ljósanótt (or "The Night of Lights"), an annual cul-ural festival for families, is held at the beginning of September.

421 **Vogavegur,** 2,24 km.
423 **Miðnesheiðarvegur,** 1,66 km.
424 **Keflavíkurvegur,** 2,5 km.
429 **Sandgerðisvegur,** 6,4 km.

Stekkjarkot, by Fitjar. The home of non-farming fishermen from about 1850. It has now been rebuilt as a folk museum and is also used for gath-rings of various kinds.

Vogastapi, or Stapi, an 80 m high sheer sea cliff, below which there ised to be good fishing grounds. Said to be haunted. In recent years ome travellers have thought they saw a man walking there, with his ıead under his arm. He has been ˂nown to take a seat in the cars of hose driving past, especially if they re alone in their cars. View-dial at rímshóll.

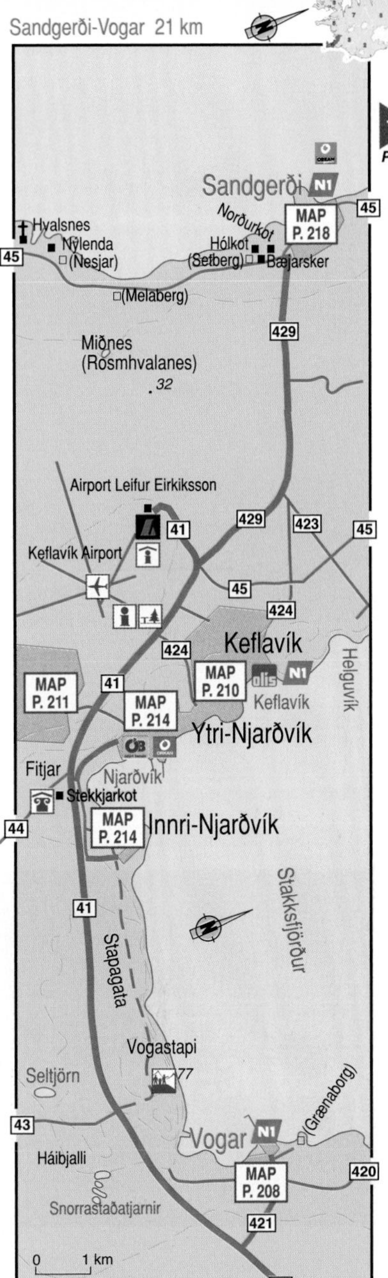

1 P. 564

43 **Grindavíkurvegur,** p. 218
44 **Hafnavegur,** p. 219
45 **Garðskagavegur,** p. 219
420 **Vatnsleysustrvegur,** p. 208

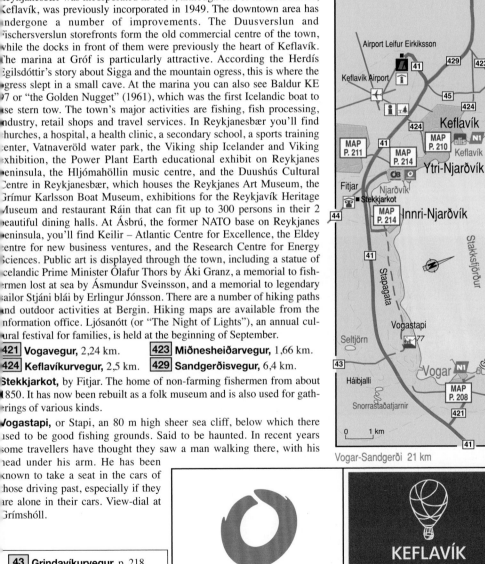

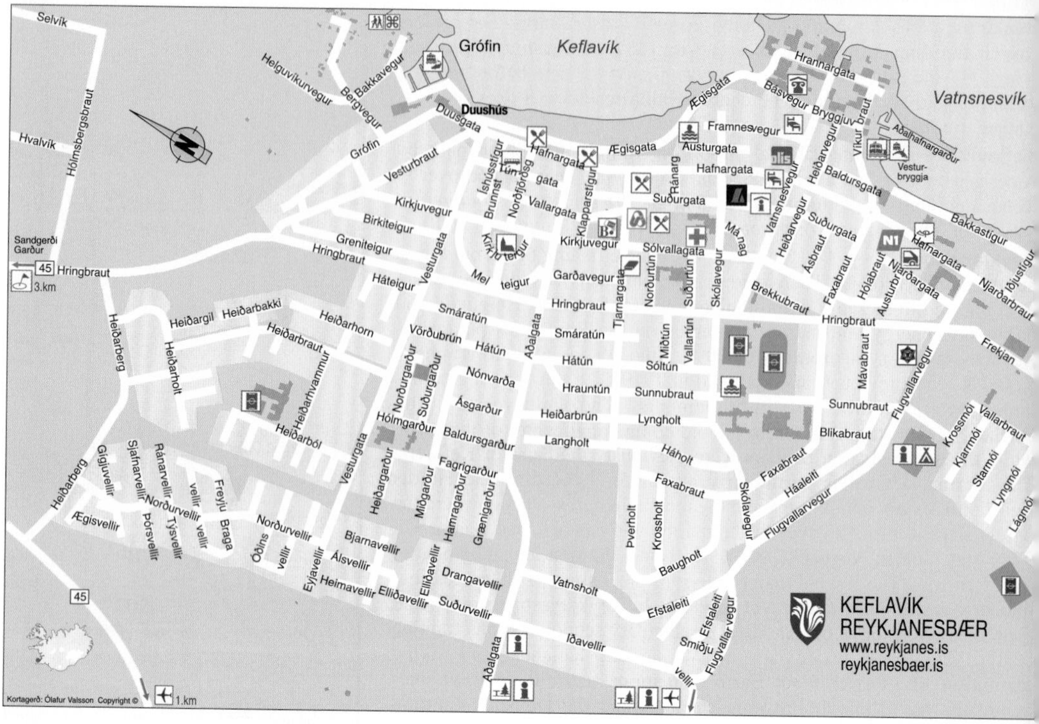

KEFLAVÍK
REYKJANESBÆR
www.reykjanes.is
reykjanesbaer.is

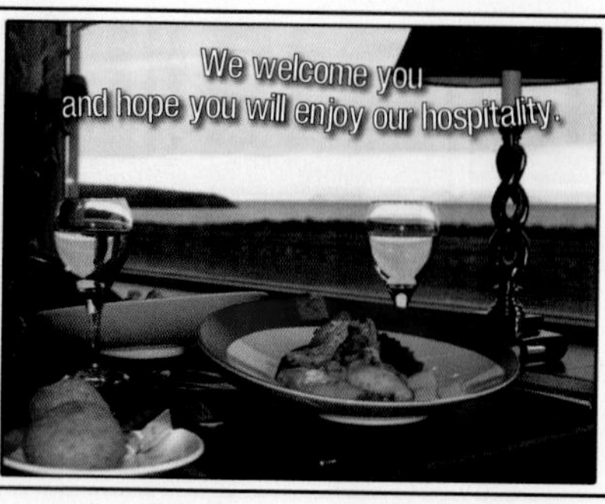

Kortagerð: Ólafur Valsson Copyright ©

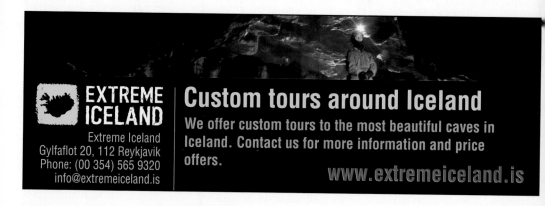

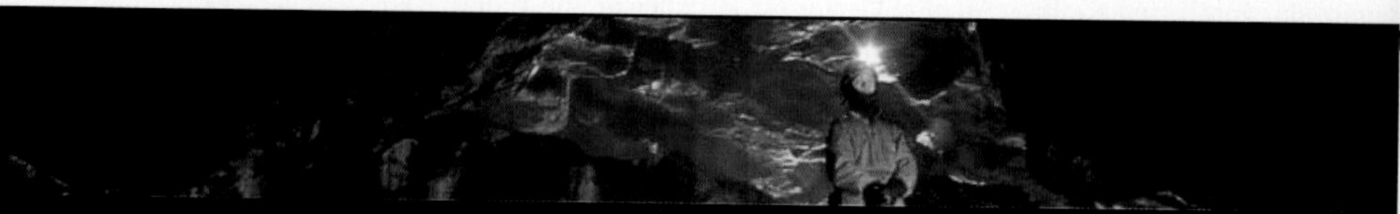

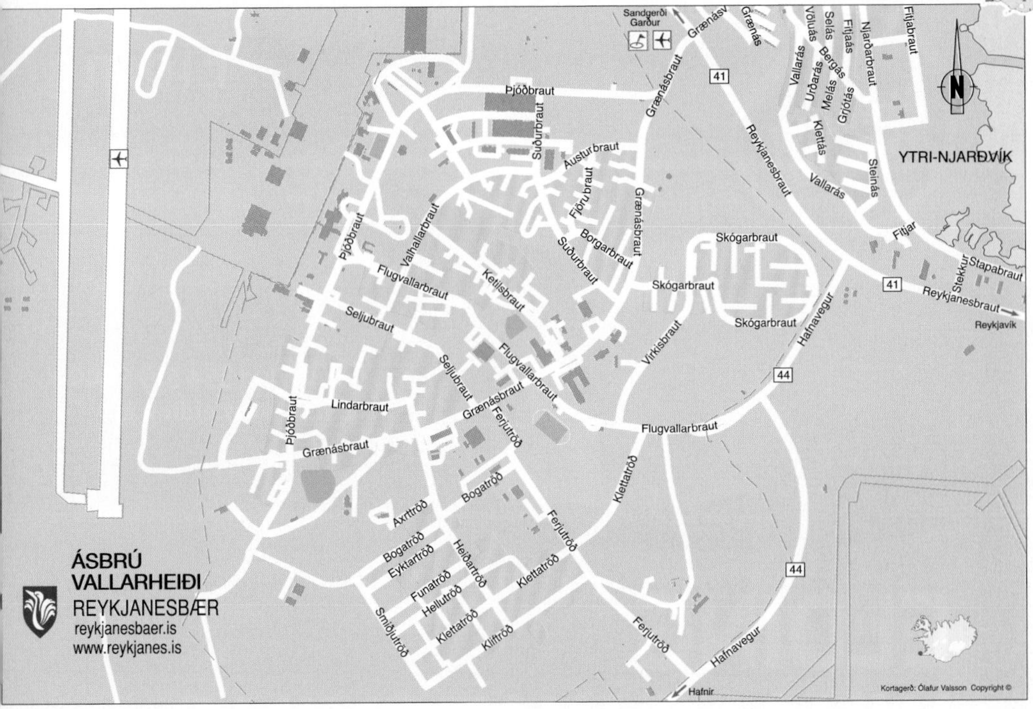

ÁSBRÚ
VALLARHEIÐI
REYKJANESBÆR
reykjanesbaer.is
www.reykjanes.is

YTRI-NJARÐVÍK

Kortagerð: Ólafur Valsson Copyright ©

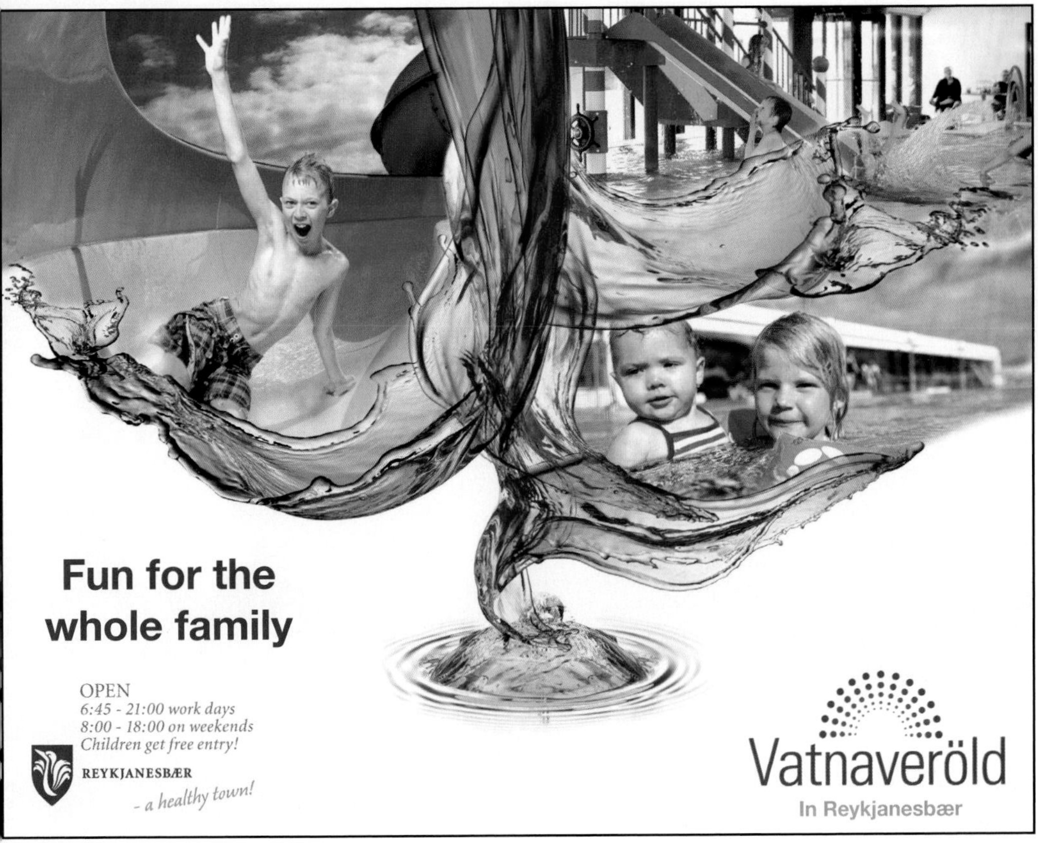

Fjallið eina, ("The lone mountain") a single tuff mountain (223 m) with surprisingly panoramic views from the top.

428 Vigdísarvallavegur, 21 km.

Sveifluháls, a tuff ridge with a maximum height of 395 m. Descends in steep cliffs to the lake Kleifarvatn. The old route from Krýsuvík to Hafnarfjörður and Reykjavík went over Sveifluháls along the path Ketilstígur. At the south end of the ridge is a single mountain **Mælifell,** 228 m.

Kleifarvatn, nearly 10 km^2 and up to 97 m deep, the third largest lake in southern Iceland. The water level rises and falls at intervals according to precipitation. Formerly a dead lake, but some trout have been imported and are prospering. At the crag Innri-Stapi on the shore there is a bronze plaque commemorating the guide Stefán Stefánsson, whose ashes were scattered in the lake, as he requested.

Djúpavatn, ("Deep Lake") a small lake west of the Sveifluháls ridge. A side-track goes to it from the Krýsuvík road west of the Vatnsskarð pass and south along Sveifluháls. Trout have been imported into this and other nearby lakes.

Austurengjahver, a big steam hot spring south of the Kleifarvatn lake, east of road. It grew very much larger after an earthquake in 1924.

Seltún, a geothermal area in Krýsuvík. **Walk only on marked paths.**

Krýsuvík, ancient manor farm and church now abandoned along with other nearby farms. Much geothermal heat, with drill-holes for possible exploitation. The church was lost in a fire in the year 2010. A special school for young people, a treatment community for the upbringing and education of drug addicts. The land belongs to Hafnarfjörður. To the south, on the coast, are the Krýsuvíkur bird cliffs. The only place possible to climb the cliff is at **Ræningjastígur**.

Grænavatn, ("Green Lake") a lake in an explosion crater, 44 m deep. Another old crater also with water, Gestsstaðavatn, on the other side of the road.

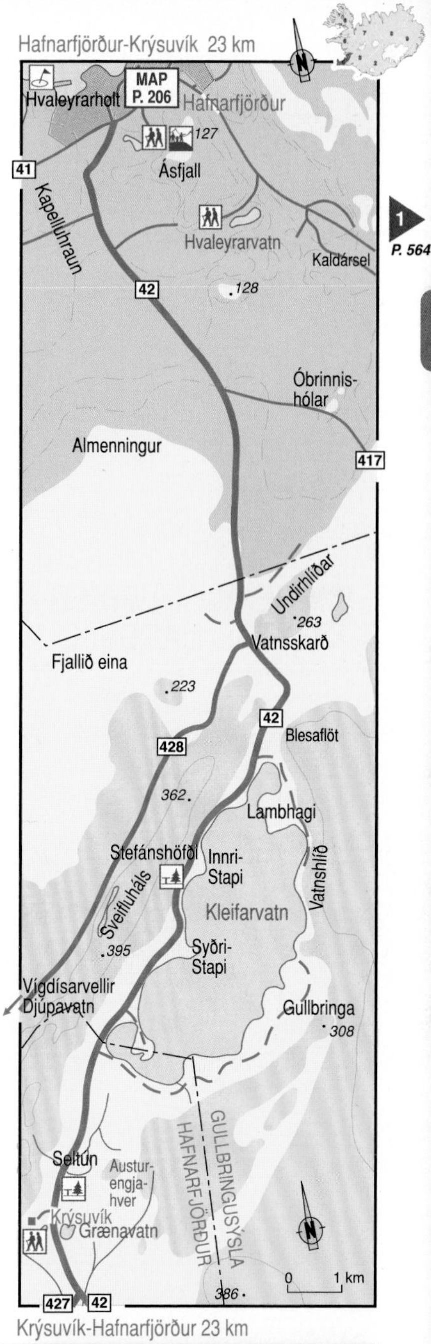

Hafnarfjörður-Krýsuvík 23 km

Hvaleyrarholt
MAP P. 206
Hafnarfjörður
127
Ásfjall
41
Kapelluhraun
Hvaleyrarvatn
Kaldársel
1 P. 564
42
.128
Óbrinnis-hólar
Almenningur
417
Undirhlíðar
.263
Vatnsskarð
Fjallið eina
.223
42
Blesaflöt
428
362.
Lambhagi
Stefánshöfði
Innri-Stapi
Vatnshlíð
Kleifarvatn
Sveifluháls
.395
Syðri-Stapi
Vígdísarvellir
Djúpavatn
Gullbringa
.308
GULLBRINGUSÝSLA
HAFNARFJÖRÐUR
Seltún
Austur-engja-hver
Krýsuvík
Grænavatn
0 1 km
386.
427 42

Krýsuvík-Hafnarfjörður 23 km

41 Reykjanesbraut, p. 208
417 Bláfjallavegur, p. 225
427 Suðurstrandarvegur, p. 228

REYKJANESBÆR
INNRI-NJARVÍK
www.reykjanes.is
Thorkilligata
Kópubraut
Kirkjubraut
Guðnýjarbraut
Tjarnargata
Stapagata
Njarðvíkurbraut
Lágseyla
Háseyla
Akurbraut
Skólabraut
Tjarnarbraut
Spóatjörn
Svölutjörn
Brekadalur
Dalsbraut
Mosdalur
Mardalur
Unardalur
Seljudalur
Víðidalur
Reynidalur
Bjarkardalur
Dalsbraut
Sædalur
Prastartjörn
Urðarbraut
Laufdalur
Mýrdalur
Vikingabraut
Álftatjörn
Blikatjörn
Erlutjörn
Lómatjörn
Mávatjörn
Sölutjörn
Tjarnabakki
Stapabraut
Fífudalur
Hamradalur
Hraundalur
Leirdalur
Trönudalur
Engjadalur
Aspardalur
Birkidalur
Eikardalur
Einidalur
Furudalur
Lerkidalur
Geirdalur
Grenidalur
Beykidalur
Njarðvíkurvegur
Keflavík
Ytri-Njarðvík
Reykjanesbraut
41
Reykjavík
Kortagerð: Ólafur Valsson Copyright ©

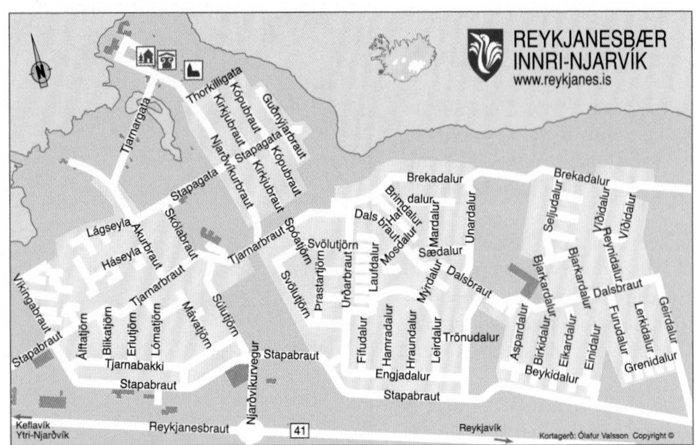

Innri-Njarðvík, p. 209.

REYKJANESBÆR
HAFNIR
www.reykjanes.is
Hafnargata
Seljavogur
Kirkjuvegur
Djúpivogur
Nesvegur
44
Kefla
425
Grindavík
Reykjanesviti
Kortagerð: Ólafur Valsson Copyright ©

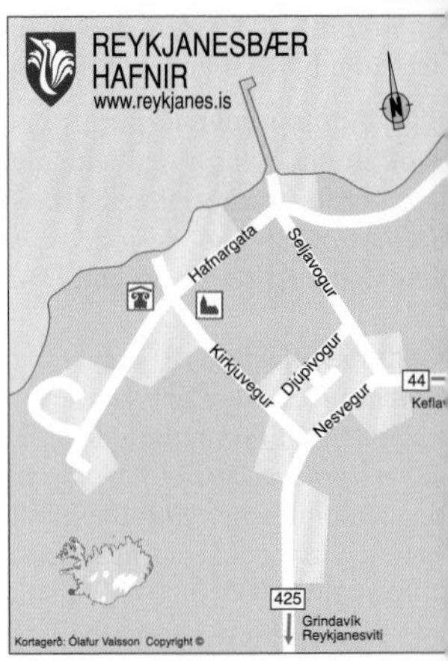

Hafnir, p. 219.

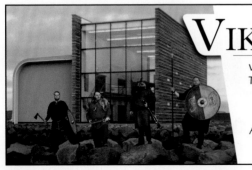

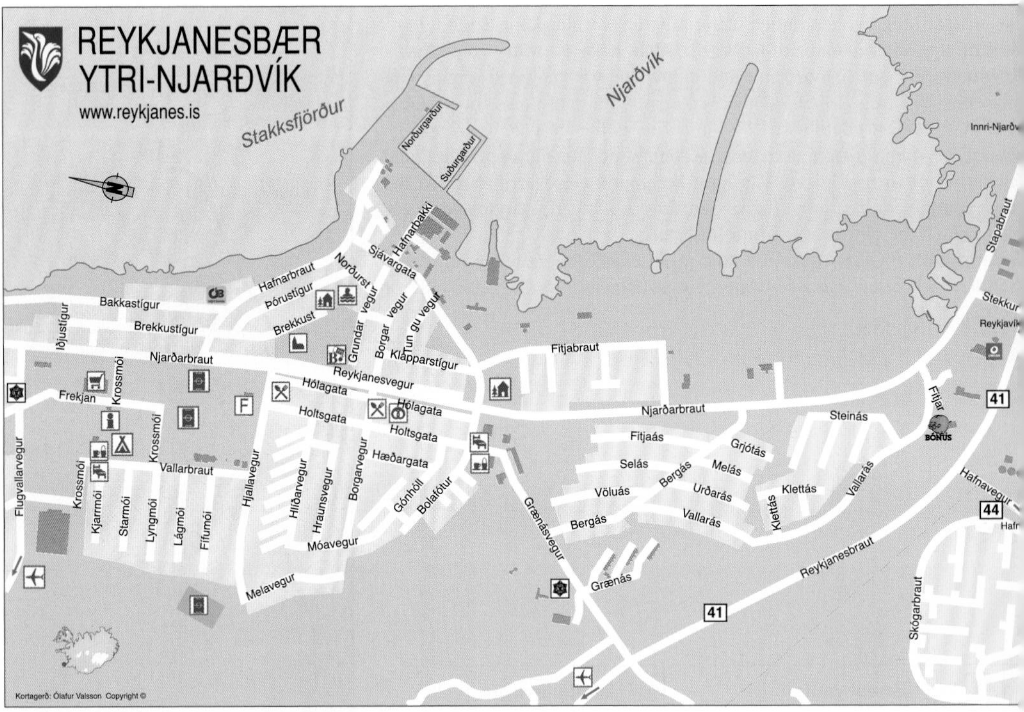

REYKJANESBÆR
YTRI-NJARÐVÍK
www.reykjanes.is
Stakksfjörður
Njarðvík
Norðurgarður
Suðurgarður
Hafnarbakki
Sjávargata
Norðurstígur
Hafnarbraut
Þórustígur
Bakkastígur
Brekkustígur
Iðjustígur
Njarðarbraut
Grundarvegur
Borgarvegur
Tunguvegur
Klapparstígur
Reykjanesvegur
Hólagata
Holtsgata
Hæðargata
Frekjan
Krossmói
Vallarbraut
Flugvallarvegur
Kjarrmói
Starmói
Lyngmói
Lágmói
Fífumói
Hjallavegur
Hlíðarvegur
Hraunsvegur
Borgarvegur
Grænásvegur
Gónhóll
Bolafótur
Móavegur
Melavegur
Fitjabraut
Njarðarbraut
Fitjaás
Selás
Völuás
Bergás
Grjótás
Melás
Urðarás
Vallarás
Klettás
Steinás
Fitjar
BÓNUS
Grænás
Reykjanesbraut
Stapabraut
Stekkur
Reykjavík
Innri-Njarðv
Hafnavegur
Hafn
Skógarbraut
41
44
Kortagerð: Ólafur Valsson Copyright ©

Ytri-Njarðvík, p. 209.

GRINDAVÍK

www.grindavik.is

Kortagerð: Ólafur Valsson Copyright ©

Grindavík, p. 228.

Aurora Borealis

Olgeir Andrésson

Olgeir (Olie) Andrésson is an Icelander living on the Reykjanes peninsula in southwest Iceland, in the town of Keflavík.

His desire to take pictures developed via a great interest in movies and film-making. He has held one-man shows, participated in group exhibitions, and won a number of awards, e.g. as Danish photography magazine Zoom's Photographer of the Year, and one of his pictures was displayed by Kodak on Times Square, New York.

The Northern Lights (Aurora Borealis) are one of the leading themes of my photography.

www.olgeir.zenfolio.com

As the effects of solar wind are greatest in the belts around the magnetic poles, the aurora (Northern and Southern Lights) are most visible at those locations. In Iceland we are lucky enough to be within the North Polar belt during the nights, in normal conditions. Changes in solar winds cause the belt to grow or shrink, so the Lights are seen at varying latitudes. An example of this kind of variation can be seen when solar flares send massive emissions of material into space. When the material reaches the earth, the northern and southern belts can stretch a long way towards the equator, and there are examples of aurora having been seen at the equator itself."

When are the Aurora Borealis visible

The Aurora Borealis or Northern Lights can be seen in all parts of Iceland from September through to March – as long as the "Aurora Belt" is over Iceland, the skies are clear and it is dark. Just as for stargazing, it is best to get away from the light pollution of urban areas in order to enjoy the Aurora Borealis in all their glory. Ideally, choose a sheltered place as your observation point, as clear winter nights in Iceland tend to be cold, especially if a wind is blowing.

The best time to observe the Aurora is between about 9 pm and 2 am, although they can, of course, often be seen both earlier and later. In Iceland the Midnight Sun means that the Northern Lights cannot be seen in summer, although they are still there.

Source - www.visindavefur.is

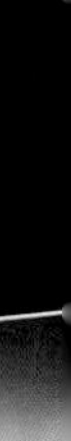

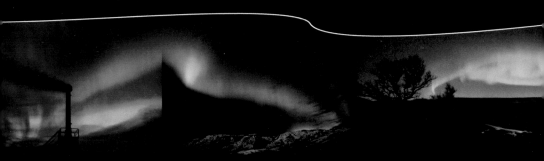

Grindavík-Vogastapi 14 km

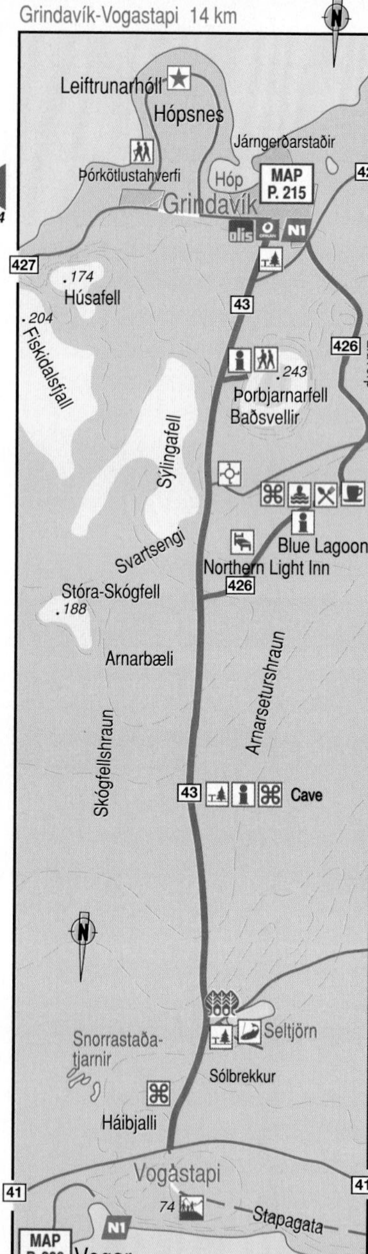

Vogastapi-Grindavík 14 km

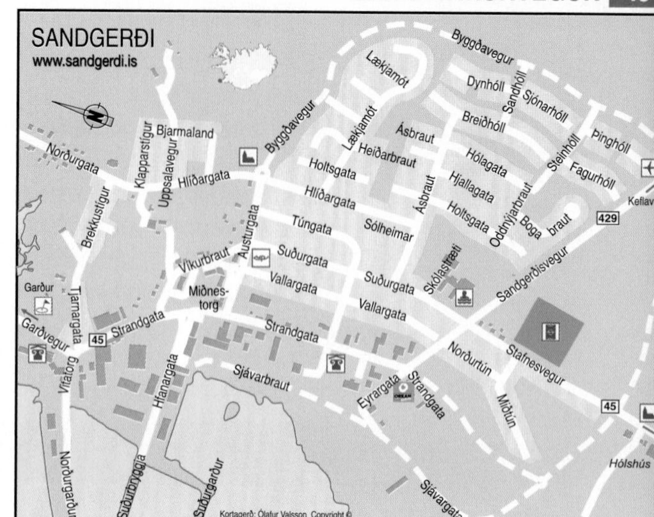

Grindavík, see p. 228.

Staður, now abandoned, west of Grindavík. Former parsonage and church. One of best-known clergymen there was the Rev. Oddur V. Gíslason (1836-1911), a pioneer in the prevention of accidents at sea. He was known for having kidnapped his bride and also for winning a foreign prize for the production of medicinal cod liver oil.

Arnarsetushæð, a good view point and rest stop. By the rest stop is a cave entrance.

Eldvörp, a crater row northwest of Grindavík. Geothermal heat in one crater, with steam emission, temperature 80°C.

Þorbjarnarfell, (243 m) a tuff mountain, a volcano from the Ice Age, grassy and easy to climb, fine views. In a ravine there, **Þjófagjá** ("Thieves' ravine"), between eight and fifteen thieves are said to have had their hide-out at one time. A good walking route.

Baðsvellir, marshland at the foot of Þorbjarnarfell mountain. The name might suggest that earth baths were there once.

Svartsengi, grassy area north of the mountain Sýlingafell to the north of Grindavík. The geothermal power plant at Svartsengi is located at the northern edge of the postglacial Illahraun lava field. It produced electricity by means of steam turbines for the surrounding districts.

426 Bláalónsvegur, 7 km.

Bláa lónið, ("The Blue Lagoon") an internationally popular recreational and therapeutic pool of deliciously warm and mineral rich geothermal water carved out of the Svartsengi lava field. The tectonically supercharged brine flows from Svartsengi power plant, and its beautiful blue color comes from light refracting micro-organisms that thrive in this unusual ecosystem. Arctic Adventures offers mountain biking tours around the peninsula that ends in the Blue Lagoon.

Seltjörn and **Sólbrekkur**, outdoor recreation areas near the town of Reykjanesbær. Trout has been released into Seltjörn and fishing licences are sold. Sólbrekkur has an outdoor barbecue and play equipment for children. One of the planned outdoor recreation areas at Vogar is at **Háabjalli** and **Snorrastaðatjarnir**. All the ponds are in grabens and the woods are sheltered beneath tall fault walls.

41 Reykjanesbraut, p. 209
425 Nesvegur, p. 226
427 Suðurstrandavegur, p. 228

44 HAFNAVEGUR 45 GARÐSKAGAVEGUR

44 Hafnavegur, 8,7 km. **45 Garðskagavegur,** 24 km.

afnir, (pop. 76) a community with big farms and much sea fishing. hurch at Kirkjuvogur. From the nearby mountain Stapafell a great deal f material has been taken for use on construction work at Keflavík irport. In Hafnir Lúðubankinn ("The halibut bank") runs the only arine zoo on the mainland. Nearby is the anchor of the ship *Jamestown* hich drifted ashore, unmanned, at Ósabotnar by Hafnir in 1870.

ásendar, or Bátsendar, former trading place and fishing centre just outh of the Stafnes lighthouse. A record high tide on January 9th 1799 estroyed most buildings but all the people bar one managed to escape.

tafnes, formerly an ancient manor farm with many smaller farms round it. Lighthouse. This coast has proved very dangerous for shipping.

valnes, a church built out of stone in 1887. One of Iceland's most cherhed poets served there as a priest from 1644-1651. Inside the church is a mbstone made made by him for his daughter which he lost at an young age.

429 Sandgerðisvegur, 6,38 km.

andgerðisbær, (pop. 1,546) a town where there is much fishing and sh processing, rapid growth in the last 20-30 years, good harbour, sport enter with swimming pool. The Nature Centre is an environmental travel nd learning centre based on the local Icelandic reality. It relates to the a, the shore, the fish, the birds and the fresh-water ecology in the immeiate environment. There you can also find the unique Suðurnes Science nd Learning Center, a research center that offers high quality research cilities and accommodation for researchers. There are two exhibitions the Center: a natural history museum and the magnificent exhibition ttraction of the Poleson the work, life and death of the French medical octor and polar scientist Jean-Baptiste Charcot. His research ship, *ourquoi-Pas?*, was perished by the coast of Iceland in 1936.

arðskagi, the outermost point of the Miðnes peninsula, the northointing "toe" of the Reykjanes peninsula. Quite densely populated. Old nd new lighthouses, birdwatching station. In the old lighthouse, built in 897, there is a map of the Garðskagi reef showing where ships have randed, and other information about the coast. In earlier times there was ore cultivation of land in this area than in most other parts of Iceland. hales can be seen swimming in the sea at Garðskagi.

tskálar, a church and parsonage.

arður, (pop. 1,430) a village focusing on fish processing and service. he art project Fresh Breeze at Garður is an Art Festival which puts its ark on the village with all the art work. There is also a Folk museum ith various interesting artifacts from the story of Garður and machine ollection by Garðskagaviti lighthouse with restaurant Flösin is on the econd floor. At Garður there is also a good campsite, walking routes, wimming pool and hot tubs. It is also possible to go sea angling, all the ost common species found in Iceland can be caught there.

41 **Reykjanesbraut,** p. 209 423 **Miðnesheiðarvegur,** p. 209
425 **Nesvegur,** p. 226

1 P. 564

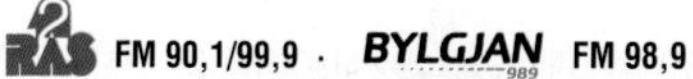

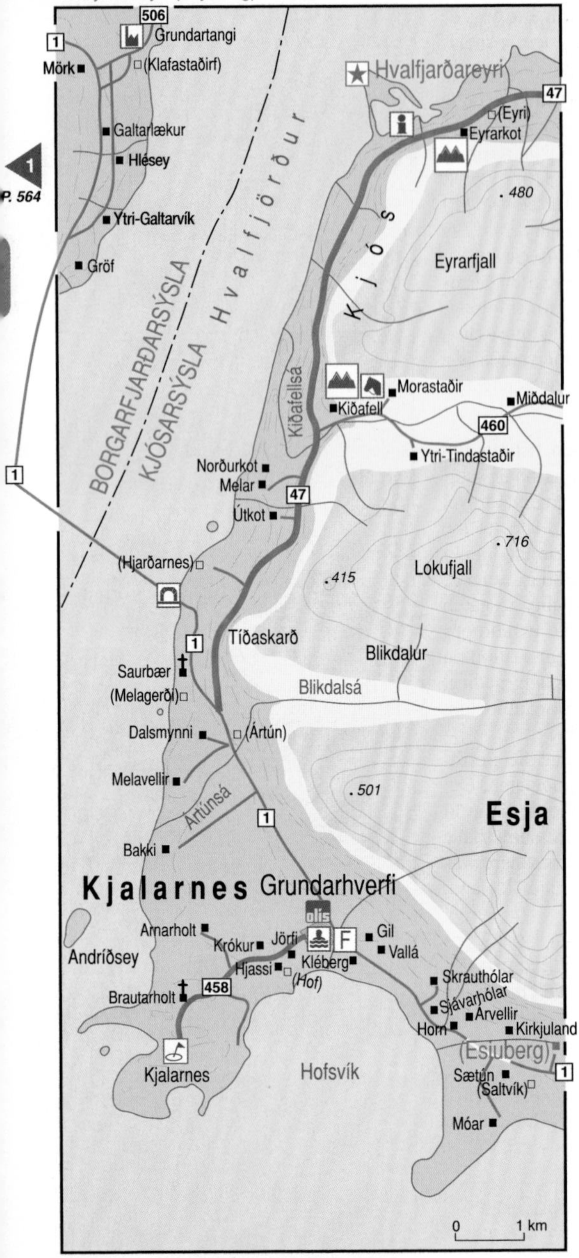

1 P. 564

Hvalfjarðareyri, once a ferry point to Kalastaðakot Many beautiful stones can be found there.

Tíðaskarð, a small pass above the farm Saurbær.

Hvalfjarðargöng, a tunnel see p. 53.

Saurbær, a farm and church. In 1424 English pirate raided the farm.

Ártún, abandoned farm.

458 Brautarholtsvegur, 2,5 km.

Andríðsey, an island. It is said that a farmer from th time of settlement was buried there.

Brautarholt, church and a manor farm.

Hof, a farm where the second largest heathen temple i supposed to have been, though no ruins are visible.

Kjalarnes, the district to the west of Esja between th fjords Kollafjörður and Hvalfjörður. Became a part o Reykjavík in 1998.

Grundarhverfi, a community of 528 inhabitants

Fólkvangur, a community centre in Grundarhverfi.

Esjuberg, a farm where the first church in Iceland i said to have been built by the Hebridean Örlygu Hrappsson.

Saltvík, training area for the police.

Móar, a farm and formerly a parsonage. First parish o the poet and priest Matthías Jochumsson, who translate *Hamlet* and other Shakespeare plays while serving ther as well as writing Iceland's national anthem.

1 Vesturlandsvegur, p. 53

460 Eyrarfjallsvegur, p. 224

506 Grundartangavegur, p. 54, 234

47 HVALFJARÐARVEGUR

lvalfjörður, ("Whale fjord") the longest fjord in the southwest of Ice-
ınd, about 30 km long and up to 84 m deep. Formerly a good harbour, ıd during the Second World War a big naval base run by the Allied Forc-;, where convoys often used to gather. In 1402 the plague was brought to lvalfjörður and from there it spread around the island. Fishing often used) be good and great quantities of herring have been caught there.

otnssúlur, (1,095 m) a group of high mountains with five peaks rising t the head of the fjord, the remnant of an old volcano. A fine viewing oint.

laðhamar, cliffs on the shore, once a loading place for ships.

lúlafjall, (391 m) a steep mountain with many cliff-faces between otnsdalur and Brynjudalur.

rynjudalur, the valley to the south of Múlafjall. Falls in the river near ıe road were spectacular until salmon-ladders were blasted in the cliff to y-pass them.

The view from Hvítanes. The mountain Þyrill in the middle of the picture.

lvítanes, an abandoned farm where the British Navy had its ıeadquarters during the war. Some ruins remain.

arlinn í Skeiðhóli, ("The old man of Skeiðhóll") also known as **taupasteinn** ("Dram rock"), **Prestasteinn** ("Priests' rock") or **Steðji**. goblet-like rock by the old road. Formerly a popular resting place for avellers. A protected natural feature.

lvammur or **Hvammsvík,** beautiful area and many walking routes. ome forestry at **Hvammsmörk.** Arctic Adventures offers kayaking trips the summer in Hvammsvík. The route follows the beautiful coastline ıd is great for beginners.

eynivallaháls, (415 m) a long mountain ridge between Hvalfjörður and jós, with steep slopes and cliffs on the seaward side.

eðri-Háls, an organic dairy farm in the Kjós district.

laríuhöfn, ("Mary's harbour") in Laxárvogur inlet. Iceland's major entre of commerce in the 14th century.

axá, a well-known salmon river.

ugða, a short river flowing from Meðalfellsvatn into Laxá. Good shing.

jós, the district from Kiðafellsá to the head of Hvalfjörður, most of it eing a wide valley between the mountains Eyrarfjall and Reynivallaháls ith a single mountain, Meðalfell, in the centre. A well-cultivated area ith trout and salmon rivers.

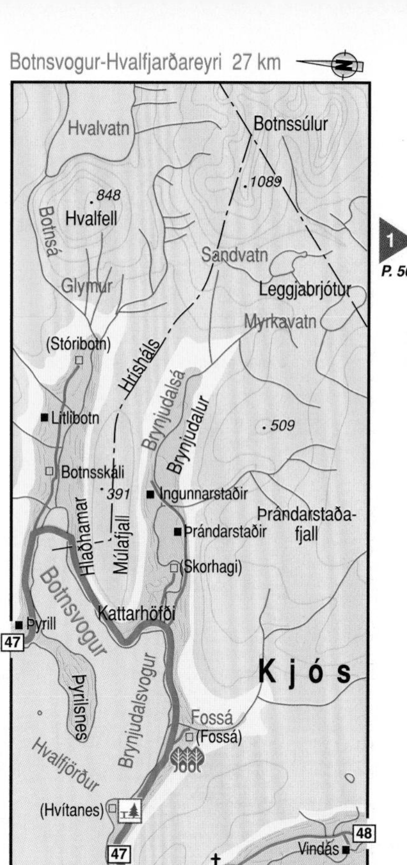

1 P. 564

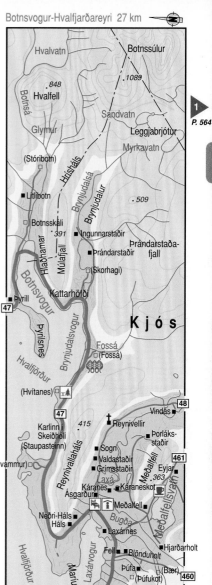

48 **Kjósarskarðsvegur,** p. 224 460 **Eyrarfjallsvegur,** p. 224
461 **Meðalfellsvegur,** p. 224

1 P. 564

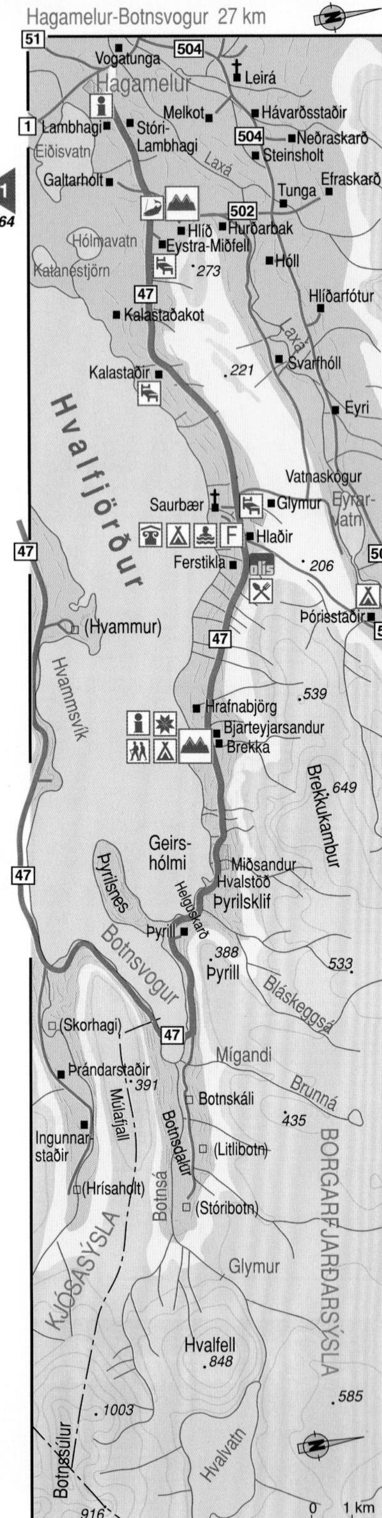

Saurbær, a farm, church and parsonage. Hallgrímur Pétursson (1614-74), the author of the *Passíusálmar* ("Passion Hymns"), served there 1651-69 and is buried there. Many local features bear his name, such as Hallgrímslind ("Hallgrímur's fountain") and Hallgrímssteinn ("Hallgrímur's rock"), against which he is said to have sat when composing the *Passíusálmar.* Like Hallgrímskirkja in Reykjavík this church was built in his memory. It is decorated with stained glass windows by the artist Gerður Helgadóttir.

Ferstikla, a roadhouse and a museum.

Miðsandur, formerly a farm which began to grow into a village afte the U.S. Navy made its headquarters there during the last war. Many oi tanks. A nearby whaling station has not been in use since 1989.

Geirshólmur, a small steep-sided island where, according to the Sagas a large band of outlaws hid out under the leadership of Hörður Grímkelsson.

Þyrill, (388 m) a basalt mountain with cliffs on three sides. Some rare kinds of zeolites are found there. Above the farm of the same name ther is a steep gully through the cliffs called **Helguskarð** ("Helga's pass") where the Sagas say Helga, daughter of a Norwegian Earl and mistres of the outlaw Hörður Grímkelsson, made her escape along with her tw young sons. She climbed up there after swimming with them fror Geirshólmur after her lover had been hunted down and killed alon with his band of outlaws.

Botnsá, a river in which is the waterfall **Glymur** ("Clamour"), th highest falls in Iceland at 200 m. The river divides the countie Kjósarsýsla and Borgarfjarðarsýsla.

Botnsdalur, a short valley with widespread birch bushes two abandone farms **Stóribotn** and **Litlibotn**. An old track called Leggjabrjótur ("Leg breaker") leads from there across to Þingvellir.

Hvalfell, (848 m) tuff mountain. On the east side of Hvalfell is the lak **Hvalvatn** ("Whale lake"), 160 m deep and the second deepest lak in Iceland. There are folktales about a man who betrayed a woman o the "hidden people" by refusing to have their child christened. He wa changed into a terrible whale that killed many fishermen, including tw brothers whose father was a priest and a "poet of power". He place poetry spells on the whale forcing it to swim into Hvalfjörður, along th river at its head, up the waterfall Glymur - which brought roars of protes from the whale, and into the lake. It is said that whale bones have bee found in the lake.

This cairn shows where the Síldarmannagötur at Botnsvogur, Hvalfjörður begin.

1 **Vesturlandsvegur,** p. 54
51 **Akrafjallsvegur,** p. 234
502 **Svínadalsvegur,** p. 258
504 **Leirársveitarvegur,** p. 258
520 **Dragavegur,** p. 264

1 P. 564

Kjósarskarð, a pass between the districts of Kjós and Þingvallasveit. 2 km between Vesturlandsvegur (Highway 1) and Þingvallavegur (Road 36).

Írafell, a farm near the top end of the Kjós district, for which was name Írafells-Móri, a famous ghost of olden times said to be still in evidenc now and again, though he was most active at the nearby farm, Möðruvell in Kjós.

Vindáshlíð, a church site below the mountain Sandfell. YMCA summe camp.

Reynivellir, a church and parsonage.

461 Meðalfellsvegur, 10,7 km.

Meðalfell, ("Middle mountain") a farm since the settlement and a manc farm of old at the foot of a mountain of same name. Summer house Fishing in Meðalfell lake.

460 Eyrarfjallsvegur, 11 km.

Kiðafell, a farm since it was originally settled by Svartkell hinn katnesk who later moved to Eyri.

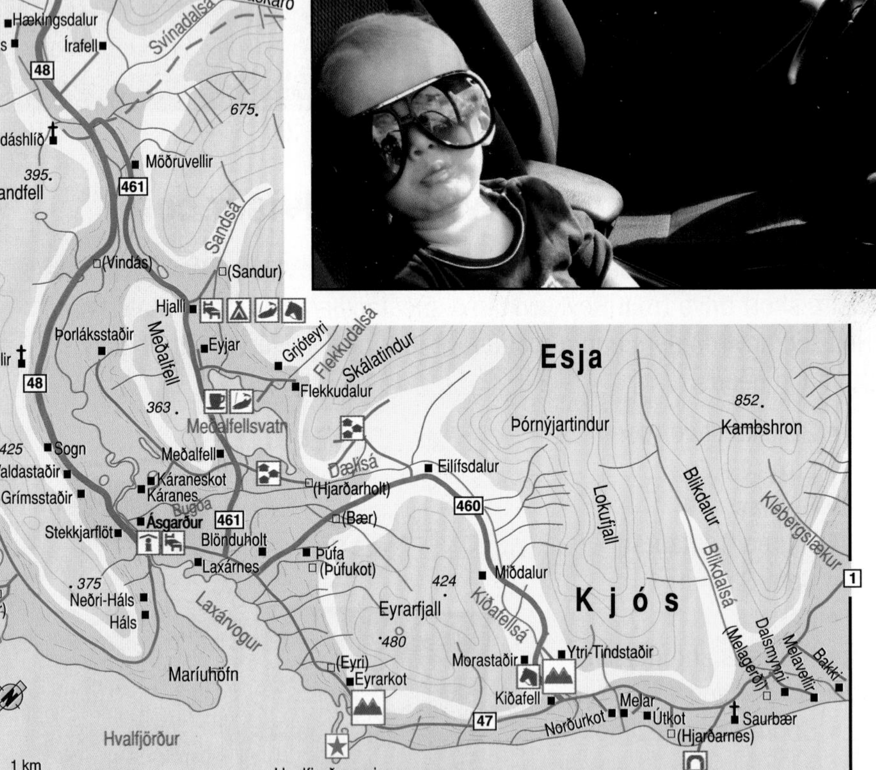

Kjós **1 Vesturlandsvegur,** p. 53 **36 Þingvallavegur,** p. 187 **47 Hvalfjarðarvegur,** p. 221

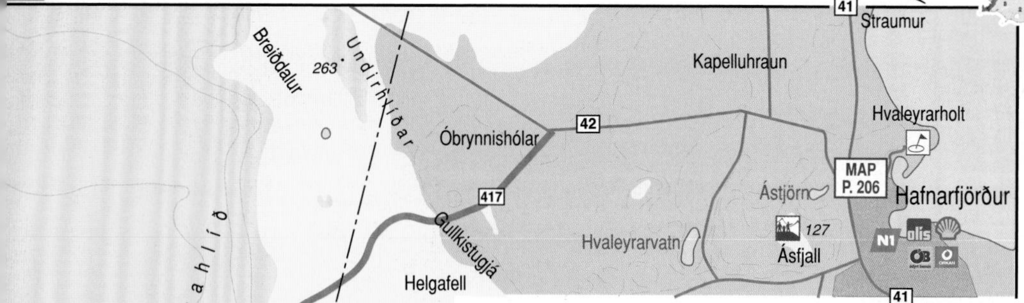

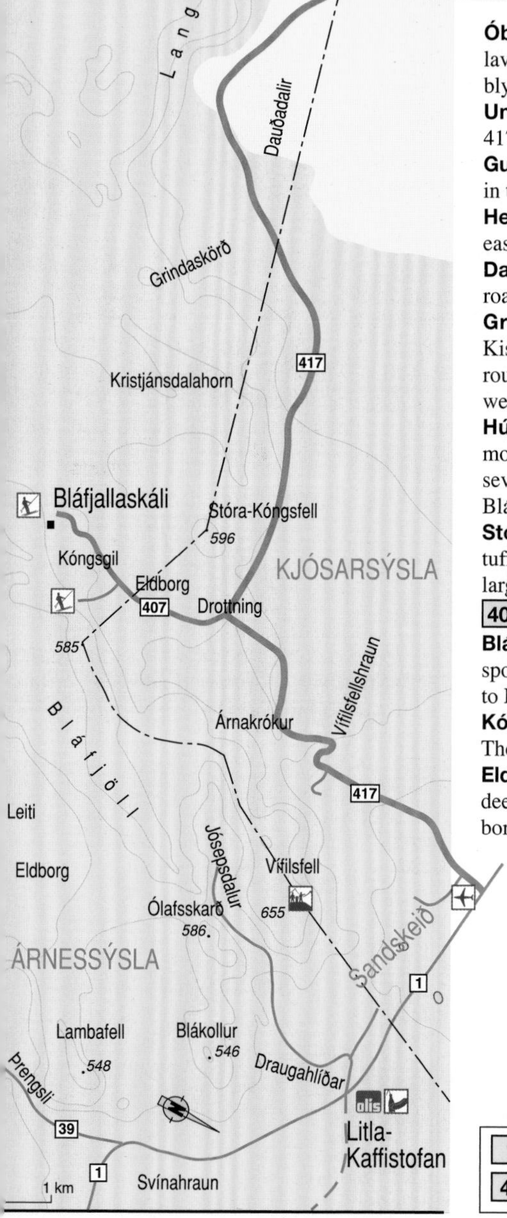

Óbrynnishólar or **Óbrinnishólar,** a volcano from which lava flowed into the sea by Straumsvík (see Road 41), probably about 200 B.C.

Undirhlíðar, slopes stretching from Bláfjallavegur (Road 417) to Krýsuvíkurvegur (Road 42).

Gullkistugjá, ("Chest of gold canyon") a remarkable fissure in the lava.

Helgafell, ("Holy mountain") a tuff mountain (338 m). An easy climb offering a great view over Hafnarfjörður.

Dauðadalir, ("Death valleys") hollows in the lava near the road with some interesting caves.

Grindaskörð, a wide pass between the mountains Kistjánsdalahorn and Langahlíð. A formerly much-travelled route from Hafnarfjörður to Selvogur, called **Selvogsgata**, went through the pass.

Húsfellsbruni, a lava field stretching from the Bláfjöll mountains towards Lækjarbotnar in the north, consisting of several lava flows, all of which originated in volcanoes near Bláfjöll.

Stóra-Kóngsfell, ("King's mountain the big") the highest tuff mountain in the area (596 m), surrounded by craters, the largest being on the west side.

407 Bláfjallaleið, 4,3 km.

Bláfjallaskáli, a ski-hut in **Bláfjöll**, the Reykjavík winter-sports centre. From there it is 11 km to Highway 1 and 21 km to Krýsuvíkurvegur (see Road 42).

Kóngsgil, ("King's canyon") the main skiing area of Bláfjöll. The name is a reference to the mountain Stóra-Kóngsfell.

Eldborg, a circular crater, ca. 200 m in diameter and 30 m deep. A protected natural feature. Lava has flowed from Eldborg to the north as far as Lækjarbotnar.

Drottning, ("The queen") a tuff mountain (513 m).

Rauðuhnúkar, a tuff ridge west of Bláfjöll, 2 km long. Near the middle on the northern side there is a tiny row of very old craters.

Sandskeið, headquarters of the Reykjavík Gliding Club.

1	**Suðurlandsvegur,** p. 149	39	**Þrengslavegur,** p. 194
41	**Reykjanesbraut,** p. 208	42	**Krýsuvíkurvegur,** p. 213

ndskeið-42 Krýsuvíkurvegur 25 km

1 P. 564

Hafnaberg, sea-cliffs with many seabirds. South of the cliffs, the New World meets the Old World, geologically speaking. The European and American plates come together there, and the line of their meeting "comes ashore" at this point, and there are many signs of geological disturbance through the ages.

Reykjanes, the south-western point of the Reykjanes peninsula, barren, with lava and a much-indented coast-line. The shield-volcanoes Skálafell and Háleyjarbunga and the volcanic rifts Stampar. The tuff mountain Valahnúkur where many species of birds nest. Much geothermal heat, sulphur and mud springs, the best known hot spring being **Gunna**. Drilling has been done there by a local sea chemical plant. The first lighthouse in Iceland was built there in 1878. Just off the coast is a tuff pinnacle rock, **Karl** (51 m) part of which fell away in the winter of 1969-70.

Eldey, a rock, or island, 77 m high, ca. 14 km off Reykjanes. Home of the biggest gannet colony in the world, protected. First climbed in 1894 by three Icelanders, Hjalti Jónsson (Eldeyjar-Hjalti) (1869-1949) and his two companions.

Staðarberg, from there lies a path to Brimketill, an interesting rock formation.

Staður, a former church and parsonage, the church was moved from there in 1909. The westernmost settlement in Grindavík, now mostly abandoned.

426 Bláalónsvegur, 7 km.

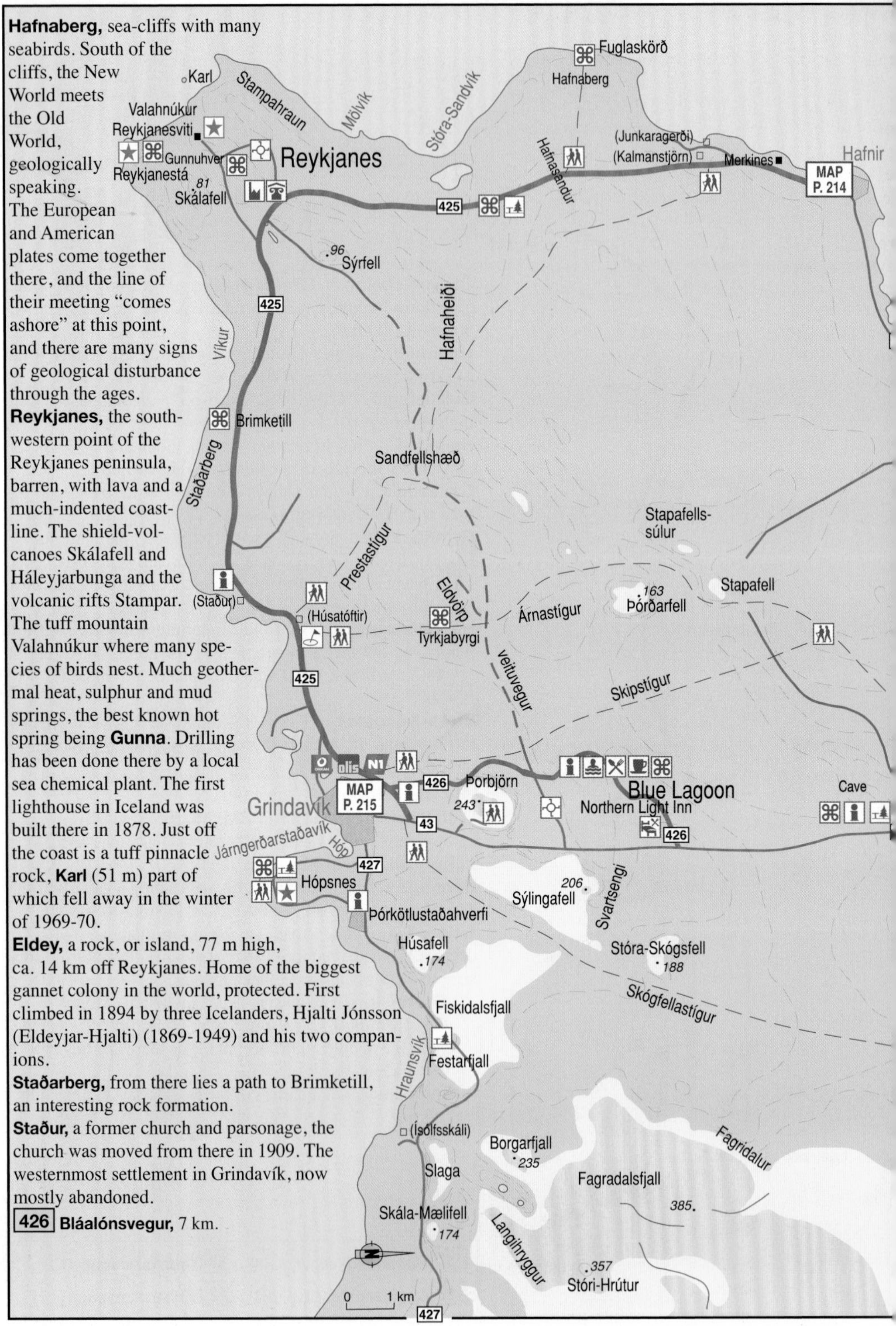

Grindavík-Hafnir 28 km

43 Grindavíkurvegur, p. 218 **44 Hafnavegur,** p. 219 **427 Suðurstrandarvegur,** p. 228

rýsuvíkurberg, a cliff by the sea where thousands of sea birds nest. A ıck leads to the cliff.

tóra-Eldborg and **Litla-Eldborg,** two nicely shaped craters off the ghway to the south of the mountain **Geitahlíð**. There is also a large cra- r on Geitahlíð. Eldborg is a protected natural feature.

erdísarvík, formerly a substantial farm with much seafishing. The crag- ' mountain Herdísarvíkurfjall, from which much lava has flowed, above e farm. The poet Einar Benediktsson (1864-1940) lived there in later 'e, and died there. He is buried in the national graveyard at Þingvellir. ərdísarvík is now owned by the University of Iceland.

rennisteinsfjöll, ("Sulphur mountains") a mountain ridge in the eykjanes range, whence much lava has flowed all the way into the sea at ərdísarvík. It poured down from high ground, forming rocky cascades. ɔrmerly this lava was thought to have flowed before the settlement of eland, but riding-trails have since been found that continue under the va, so some of it must be younger than that. In the late 19th century the :ot W.G. Spence Paterson, for a time teacher at the Möðruvellir school ıd later British consul at Hafnarfjörður, started sulphur-mining east of e mountains but this never paid. The popular route between afnarfjörður and Selvogur once went via **Grindaskörð** and east of the ountains.

líðarvatn, a good fishing lake.

ɔgsósar, near Hlíðarvatn in Selvogur. Formerly a parsonage. Best ıown for the clergyman-sorcerer Eiríkur Magnússon (1638-1715).

trandarkirkja, ("Coast church") a church in Selvogur, now far from rms and the only remains of the once flourishing community Strönd Coast"), at one time the home of some of the richest and most powerful en in Iceland. It is popularly believed that this church has a special ɔwer to aid success or good luck. Many gifts are therefore donated to it connection with people's hopes and fears. It is one of the richest ıurches in the country.

əlvogur, the westernmost settlement in Árnessýsla. Formerly a thriving ;hing centre, now much eroded by sand.

venngönguhólar, ("Women walk hills") at Kaldraðanes, p. 179, there ıs a holy cross there which people came from all over to see and touch. hen the women at Selvogur couldn´t go to the cross the walked to venngönguhólar to look over to Kaldraðanes, hence the name.

38 **Þorlákshafnarvegur,** p. 192 | 42 **Krýsuvíkurvegur,** p. 213

Krýsuvík-Hlíðardalsskólii 42 km

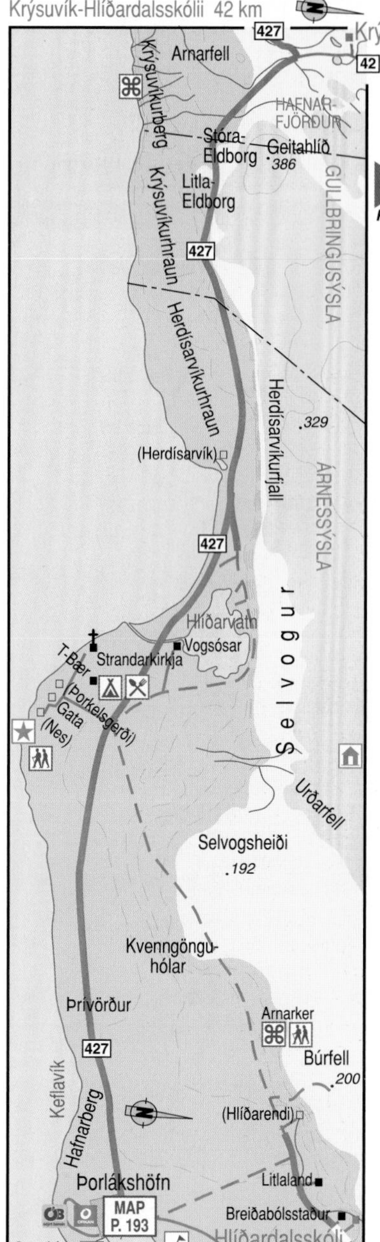

Hlíðardalsskóli-Krýsuvík 42 km

Strandarkirkja

1 P. 564

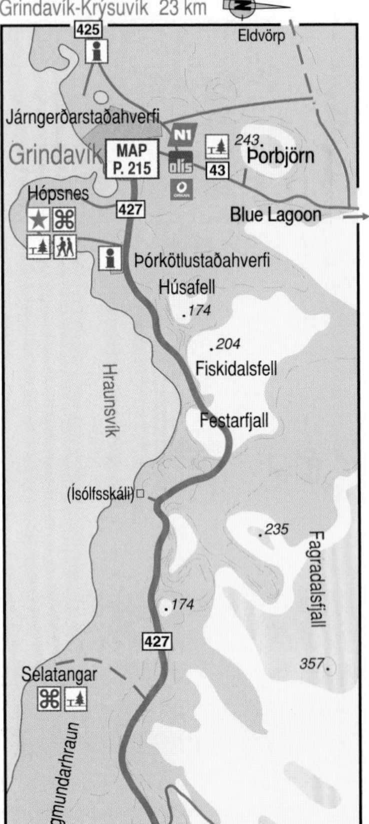

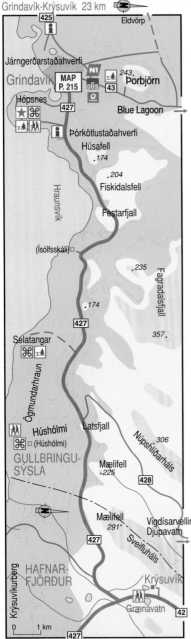

Grindavík, (pop. 2,856) a fishing village that became a market tow in 1974. The town consists of three main areas: **Þórkötlustaðahverfi** **Járngerðarstaðahverfi**, now the main part of town; and **Staðarhverfi** to the far west, which today is mostly deserted. Information signs i each area document its history. Entering the harbour remains a challeng for sailors, despite extensive improvements there. Nonetheless, thi harbour has been used for fishing for centuries, and contributed great ly to the wealth of the bishop at Skálholt. The peninsula of Reykjane was so important for fishing and trade that the English and German fought there over the most sheltered places for boats. This struggle cli maxed on June 11th 1532, when the Germans allied with some native and killed about 20 Englishmen. This event marked a turning point i Iceland's commercial history, ending an era of English dominance. Mai industries: fishing and fish processing. The town has a church, com pulsory school, community centre, health centre and swimming pool There is a monument to drowned sailors by Ragnar Kjartansson, whil glass art by Einar Lárusson depicts the historical raid here by Muslin pirates. A local thistle, Cirsium arvense, is otherwise rare in Iceland; i is said that it first appeared when the blood of the Muslim pirates mixe with that of the Christians. The French trawler Cap Fragnet stranded b Þórkötlustaðahverfi in 1931. For the first time in history, a line throwe was used in order to reach the crew and rescue 38 people.

Festarfjall, (190 m) the remains of an old volcano, taking its name fror **Festi**, a basalt column that goes through the mountain.

Fagradalsfjall, there Frank M. Andrew, commander of US troops i Europe, along with 13 others was killed when his airplain crashed int the mountain.

Selatangar, protected remains of an old fishing-station on the coas south of the Núpshlíðarháls ridge. The ghost Tanga-Tómas, or Tumi, wa said to haunt the place.

Ögmundarhraun, a lava field believed to have flowed in 1151 from row of craters between the ridges Núpshlíðarháls and Sveifluháls.

Húshólmi and Óbrennishólmi, situated in the Ögmundarhraun lava fielc above Hólmasund strait, in the westernmost section of th Krýsuvíkurbjarg cliffs, just west of Selatangi point. The Húshólmi an Óbrennishólmi sites exhibit ancient ruins, houses and gardens, some times called Old Krýsuvík. There are indications that there once was church on the site as well. The ruins are thought to be from the earlie years of Iceland's settlement. The Ögmundarhraun lava field flooded th area in the 12th century, covering the settlement. Today one can still se the remnants of three houses and a church, as well as large gardens, stone sheep enclosure and a shepherd's hut. Access to Húsahólmi is goo for hikers. It is also possible to drive to the location in off-road vehicle The hike from Ísólfsskálavegur road begins at the signpost fc Húsahólmi, continuing down along the edge of the lava field until th Húshólmastígur hiking path is reached, then continuing about 1.1 kr east through the lava field. The entire hike from Ísólfsskálavegur roa takes about one hour.

Krýsuvík, ancient manor farm see p. 213.

Grænavatn, ("Green lake") a lake in an explosion crater, 44 m dee Another old crater also with water, Gestsstaðavatn, on other side of th road.

Sveifluháls, a tuff ridge, maximum height 397 m, which drops in stee cliffs down to the Kleifarvatn lake. At the south end of Sveifluháls is lone peak, **Mælifell** (225 m).

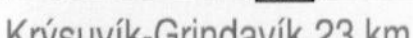

42 Krýsuvíkurvegur, p. 213 | **43 Grindavíkurvegur,** p. 218
425 Nesvegur, p. 226 | **428 Vigdísarvallavegur,** p. 21

ljáfoss, a waterfall in the river Hvítá. A bridge. There are records of a ridge there from the Sturlunga age in the 13th century.
eildartunga, a manor farm, now and in ages past.
555 Deildartunguvegur, 0,6 km.
eildartunguhver, this hot water spring is protected by conservation aws and is the most powerful hot spring in Iceland, with 200 l/sec. f 100°C hot water, supplying the towns of Borgarnes and Akranes ith hot water. The only place in Iceland where a variety of hard ern (*Blechnum spicant* var. *fallax*) is found. Many hothouses.
eykjadalsá, a calm, winding river flowing through the Reykoltsdalur valley.
leppjárnsreykir, (pop. 51) a community where there is hothouse ultivation using heat from one of Borgarfjörður's bigger hot prings, 70 l/sec.
tóri-Kroppur, a farm below Kroppsmúli spur. Airstrip.
lókadalur, a broad, grassy valley, actually two, down which ow the rivers **Flóka** and **Geirsá**.
lókadalsá, or Flóka, a river flowing out of Flókadalur.
armalækur, the settlement land of Óleifur hjalti. For a me the home of Hallgerður langbrók ("long-breeches") nd her husband Glúmur (*Njáls saga*).
armalækjarmúli, a steep spur at the end of the Lundarháls ridge.
lundsvatn, a rather big lake, though shallow, in the Bæjarsveit district.
æjarsveit, flatlands between the rivers Grímsá and Flóka. Marshy but rassy with low ridges.
ossatún, a restaurant and a 5 tar campsite. Beautiful walking outes and views.
rímsá, a sizeable river flowing own the Lundarreykjadalur valey into Hvítá. Good fishing. ome low waterfalls.
estur, a former church and arsonage. Now an experimental heep breeding station.
estfjall, (221 m) a jagged ountain above Hestur.

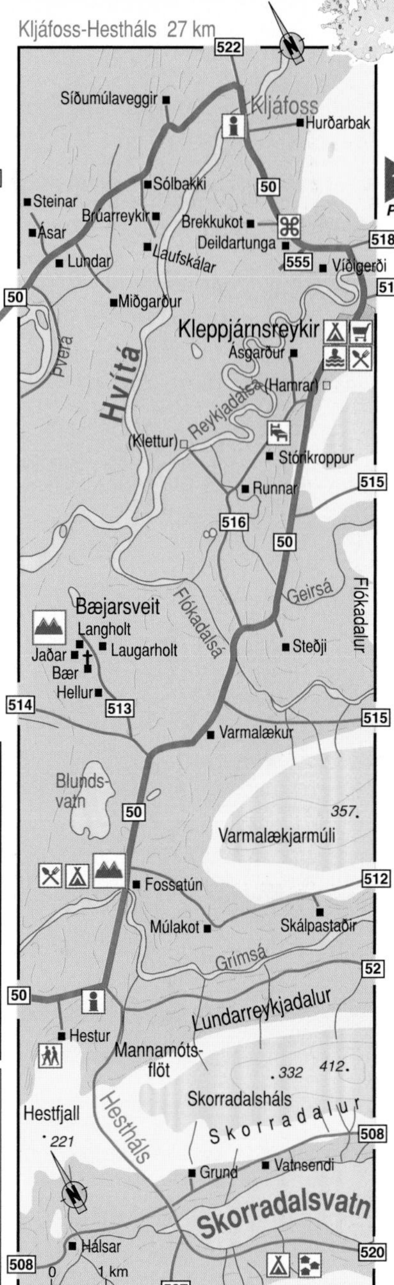

1 **Vesturlandsvegur,** p. 58
52 **Uxahryggjavegur,** p. 237
507 **Mófellsstaðavegur,** p. 259
508 **Skorradalsvegur,** p. 259
512 **Lundareykjadalsvegur,** p. 237
513 **Bæjarsveitarvegur,** p. 260
514 **Laugarholtsvegur,** p. 260
515 **Flókadalsvegur,** p. 260
516 **Stóra-Kroppsvegur,** p. 260
517 **Reykdælavegur,** p. 261
518 **Hálsasveitarvegur,** p. 261
520 **Dragavegur,** p. 264
522 **Þverárhlíðarvegur,** p. 265

1 P. 564

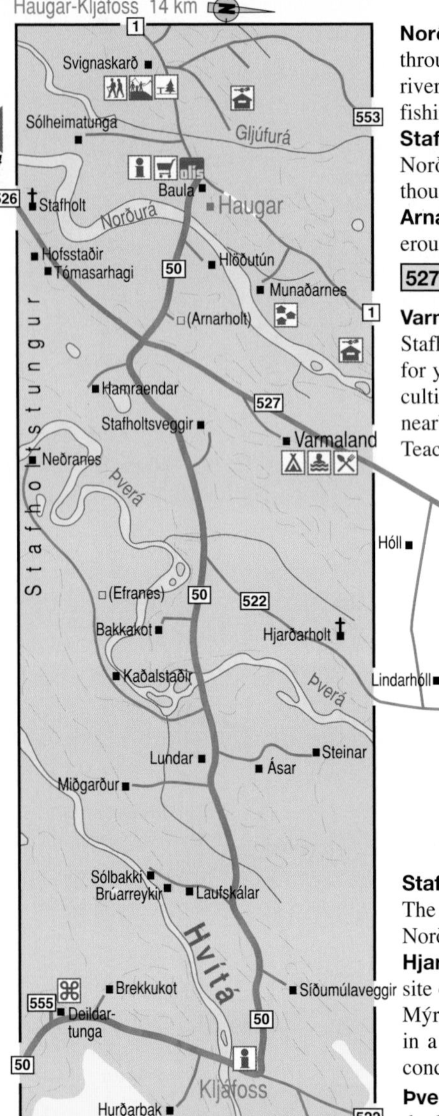

Norðurá, a river originating up on Holtavörðuheiði moor and flowin through the Norðurárdalur valley and the Stafholtstungur district into th river Hvítá. It is smooth, deep and navigable lower down. Good salmo fishing. In Norðurá are the waterfalls **Laxfoss** and **Glanni**.

Stafholtstungur, three tongues of land between the rivers Gljúfurá Norðurá, Þverá and Hvítá. Stony ridges, mostly marshy in betweer though the westernmost tongue has a lot of birch bushes.

Arnarholt, a farm in the Stafholtstungur district. A nearby grove of coniferous trees was planted around 1910.

527 Varmalandsvegur, 13,9 km.

Varmaland, a school centre built by the big hot spring at the farr Stafholtsveggir. The Borgarfjörður school of domestic science was ther for years, the building now housing a middle school. Extensive hothous cultivation. Mushroom production was first started in Iceland at th nearby farm, **Laugaland**, whose buildings now belong to the Icelandi Teacher's Training College.

526 Stafholtsvegur, 6 km.

Stafholt.

Stafholt, a church and parsonage in the lower Stafholtstungur distric The church was built 1875-77. Lignite is found at Stafholtskastali by th Norðurá river.

Hjarðarholt, a farm and church, long the home of men of influence and site of official gatherings. For a time it was the residence of the county c Mýrasýsla sheriffs, one of whom died of exposure right by the farmstea in a dreadful winter storm. At a church conference in 1684 a man wa condemned and burnt at the stake (1685) for blasphemy.

Þverá, a clear river formed from several rivers and streams coming fror the lakes on the Tvídægra moors. Considered to be one of the best salm on-fishing rivers in Iceland.

555 Deildartunguvegur, 0,6 km.

1 Vesturlandvegur, p. 58
522 Þverárhlíðarvegur, p. 265
523 Hvítársíðuvegur, p. 265
553 Langavatnsvegur, p. 269

The bridge on the river Hvítá.

vítárbrú, the bridge across Hvítá built in 1928.

vítárvellir, a manor farm now and of old, having the best salmon-shing in Borgarfjörður. Often the home of men of influence. At ie beginning of the 20th century the home of the French baron oilleau, one street in Reykjavík, Barónsstígur, being called after im. In 1859 James Ritchie, a Scotsman, established a cannery at vítárvellir and operated it for several years. In the old days mar-ets were held at Hvítárvellir, as ships could be sailed that far pstream.

ndakíll, a settlement.

11 Hvanneyrarvegur, 2,5 km. **510 Hvítárvallavegur,** 10 km.

vanneyri, (pop. 251) a substantial farm and a farming school nce 1889. Also a parsonage, agricultural college and a vet-rinarian's surgery. Also the Agricultural Museum of Iceland. he Agricultural University of Iceland from 2005. Some of the est grass-land in Iceland is there, especially in the so-called vanneyrarfit. When the college was started many small farms in e surrounding area were taken under Hvanneyri. The first settler Hvanneyri was Grímur háleyski.

ndakílsárvirkjun, a power station built in 1947 when falls in the ver **Andakílsá** were harnessed. Water reservoir in Skorradalsvatn.

karðsheiði, a high mountain range dominating the Borgarfjörður area n the south side. Highest point **Heiðarhorn**, (1,053 m). **Skessuhorn** 'Giantess' peak") (963 m) is a particularly impressive and outstanding eak when the range is viewed from the north.

nri-Skeljabrekka and **Ytri-Skeljabrekka,** farms at the foot of Brekku-all mountain.

rekkufjall, (409 m) a solid basalt mountain, considered to be the vol-anic plug of what was once a volcano.

1 Vesturlandsvegur, p. 55	**507 Mófellsstaðavegur,** p. 259
508 Skorradalsvegur, p. 259	**514 Laugarholtsvegur,** p. 260
526 Stafholtsvegur, p. 230	**530 Ferjubakkavegur,** p. 55

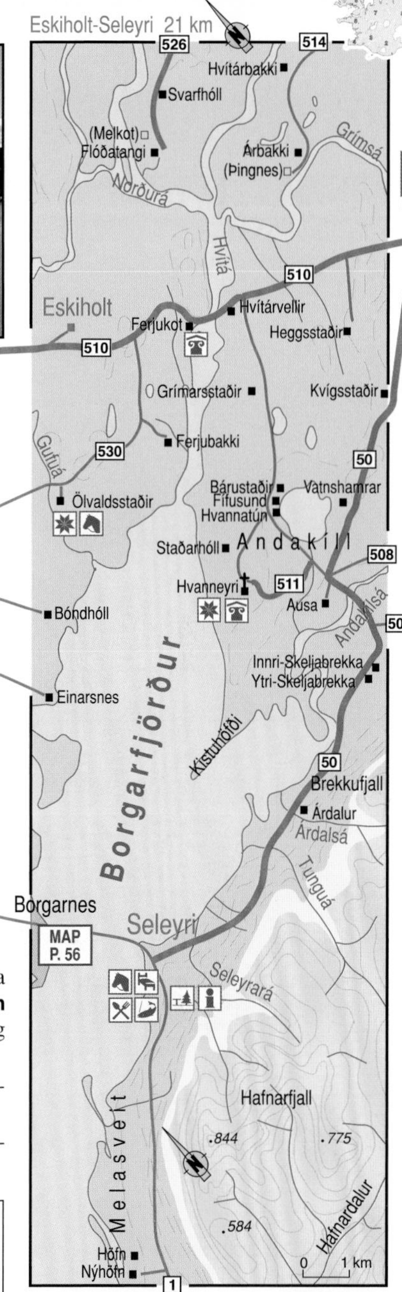

1 P. 564

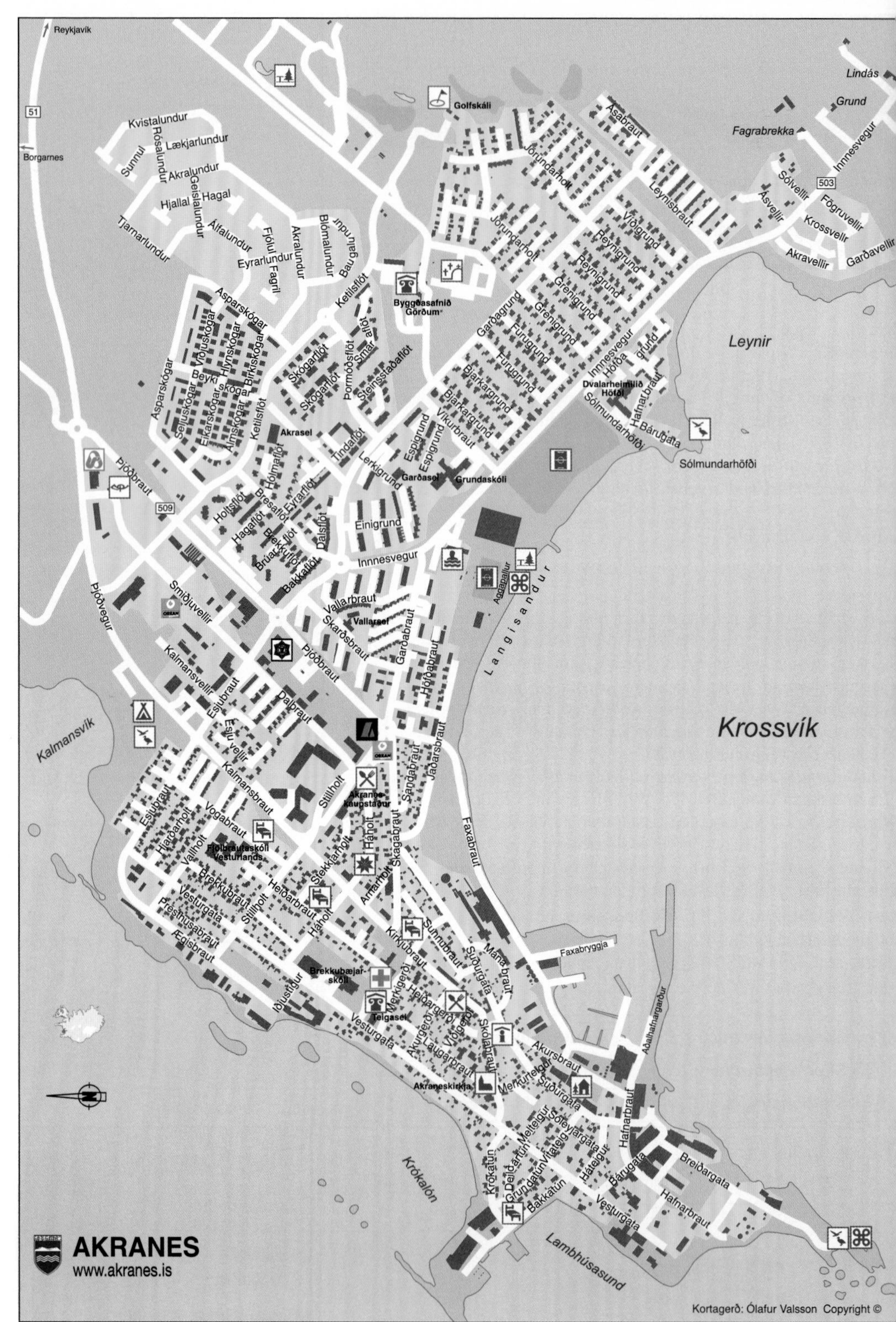

AKRANES
www.akranes.is
Krossvík
Leynir
Kalmansvík
Krókalón
Lambhúsasund
Langisandur
Sólmundarhöfði
Kortagerð: Ólafur Valsson Copyright ©

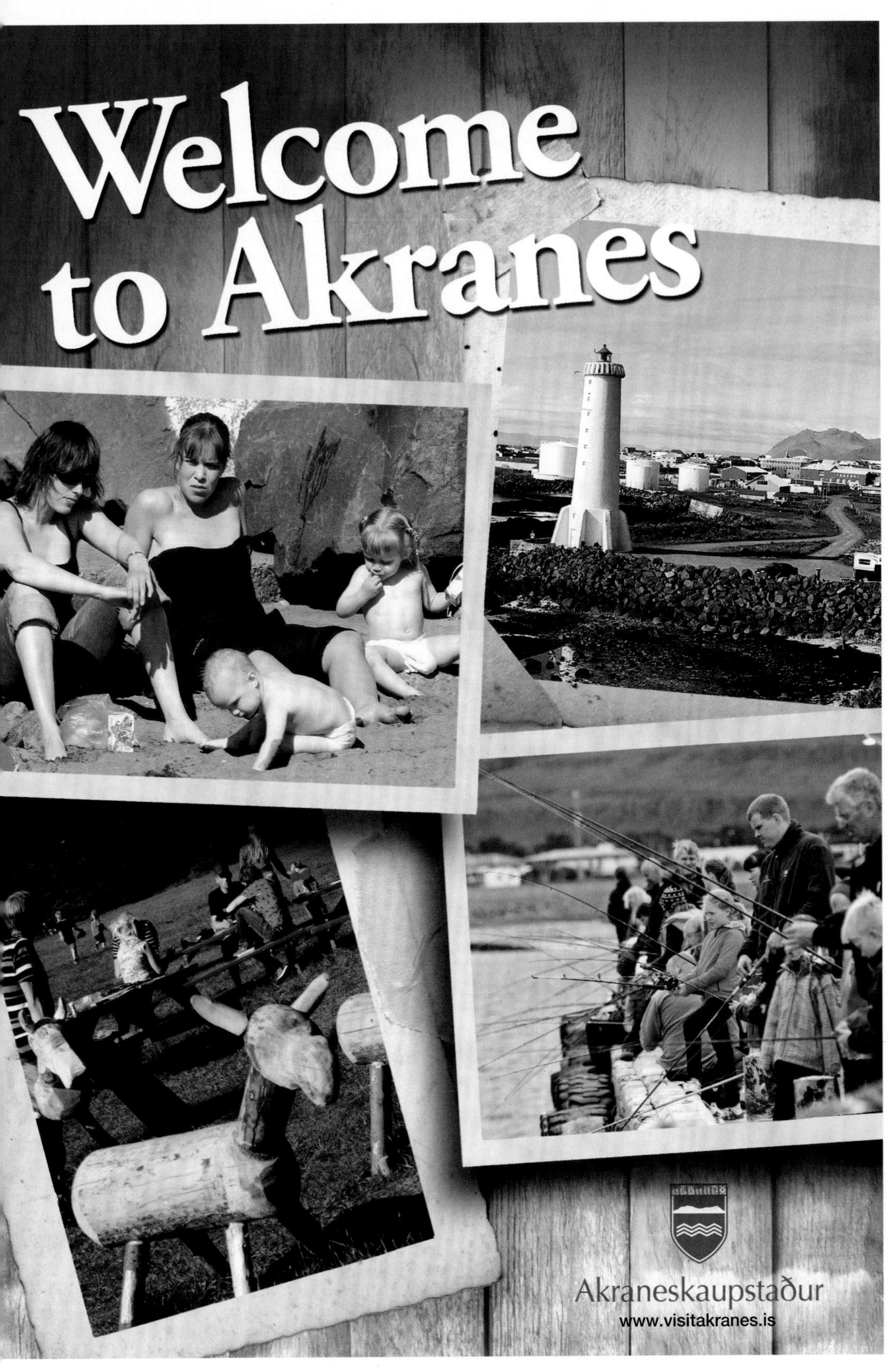

Welcome to Akranes
Akraneskaupstaður
www.visitakranes.is

Akranes- 1 Vesturlandsvegur 14 km

1 P. 564

MAP P. 232

Akranes, (pop. 6,636) a town, gained municipal rights in 1942. The mai activities are fishing, fish processing, commerce and industry, e.g. cement factory. Extensive harbour facilities and a lighthouse. Hospita secondary school, trade school, sports stadium. As well as being a important fisheries centre, has repeatedly made its name in sports, bot nationally and even internationally, and has outdoor and indoo swimming pools, football grounds, a sports stadium, a busy 18-hole gol course, riding trails, a bowling alley, an outdoor shooting range, gol course and a popular outdoor recreation area. On Akratorg square is th sculpture *Memorial to sailors*, by Marteinn Guðmundsson and in front c the old people's home, *Grettir's challenge* by Magnús Tómasson. Rov boat fishing started there centuries ago and there was some sort of villag already in the 17th century.

Akrafjall, (643 m) a mountain between Hvalfjörður and Grunnafjörðu the nesting place of huge numbers of gulls. An outlawed thief spent th summer on the mountain in 1756. Farmers formed a search party to loo for him in the autumn, but he sneaked himself into the search party an helped them search, thus avoiding capture.

503 Innnesvegur, 4,9 km.

Garðar, former parsonage, church and manor farm. Now part of Akranes The Akranes Museum Centre in Gardar comprises the unique Iceland's Mineral Kingdom, the highly interesting Iceland´s Museum of Sports, th informative Exhibition of the National Land Survey of Iceland, and th Akranes Folk Museum with innumerable items of very great interest The Centre has been much acclaimed by both Icelanders and foreig visitors since it was opened to the public recently. The local folk muse um is housed in the former parsonage which was built in 1871, of con crete blocks and cement, the first house in Iceland built by this method Sigurfari, a typical fishing vessel from around the turn of last century, an the only such cutter left in Iceland, is on display there.

Reynir, a farm, the home of farmer Jón Hreggviðsson, made famous by Halldór Laxness in the novel *Íslandsklukkan*.

Innri-Hólmur, a parsonage and substantial farm. For a time home of th Governor Ólafur Stefánsson and his son, Chief Justice Magnús Steph ensen, who later moved to Viðey.

509 Akranesvegur, 2,5 km. **501 Innrahólmsvegur,** 3,1 km.

506 Grundartangavegur, 2,5 km.

Grundartangi, a ferrosilicon plant belonging to the Icelandic Alloy Co The plant started production in 1979, for export only. An aluminium plan commenced production 1998.

1 Vesturlandsvegur, p. 53 **47 Hvalfjarðarvegur,** p. 220
502 Svínadalsvegur, p. 258

1 Vesturlandsvegur-Akranes 14 km

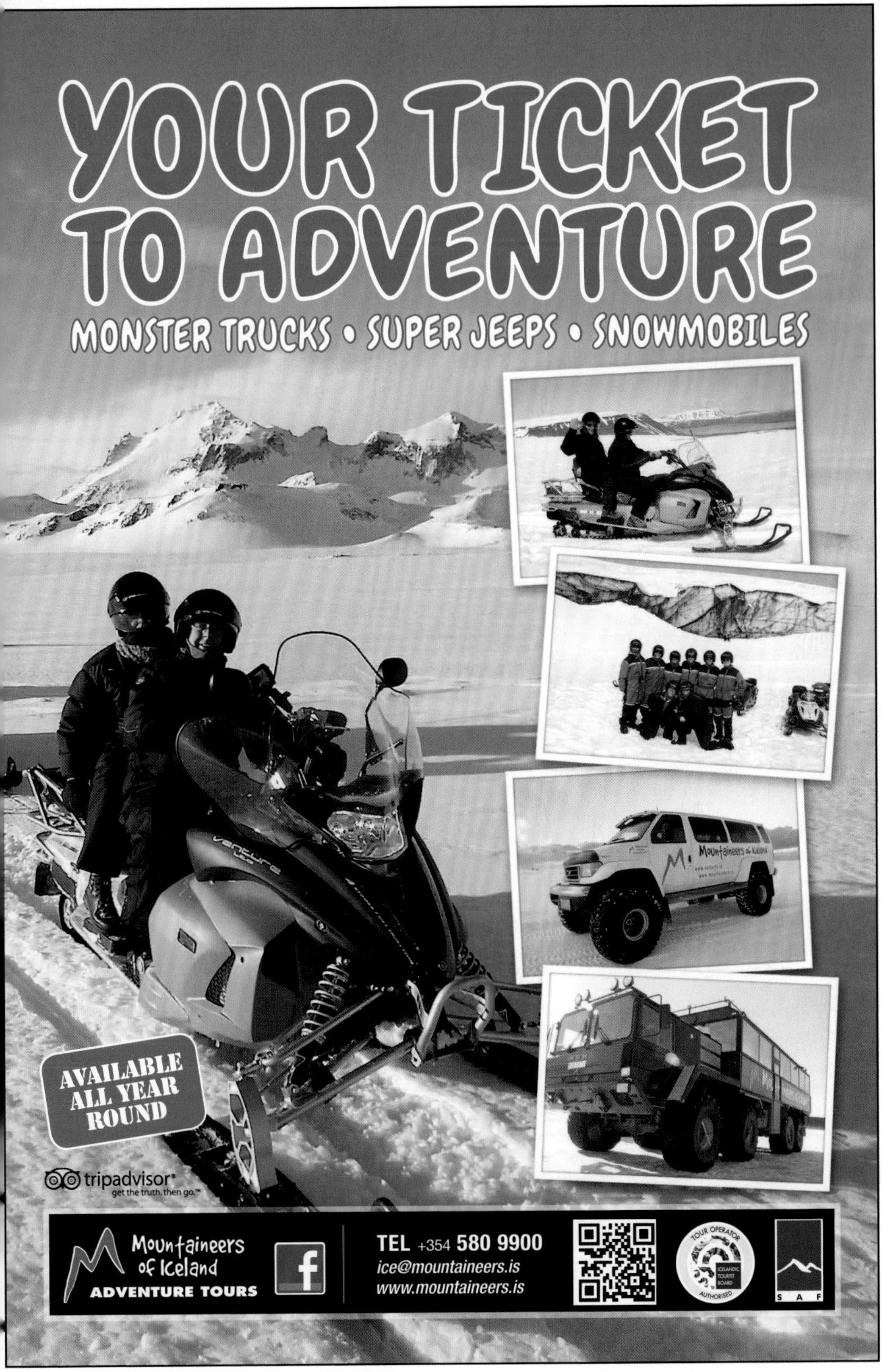

2
P. 565

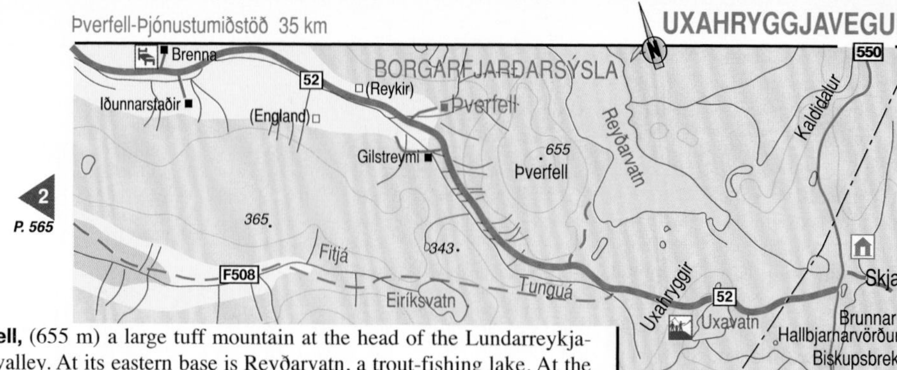

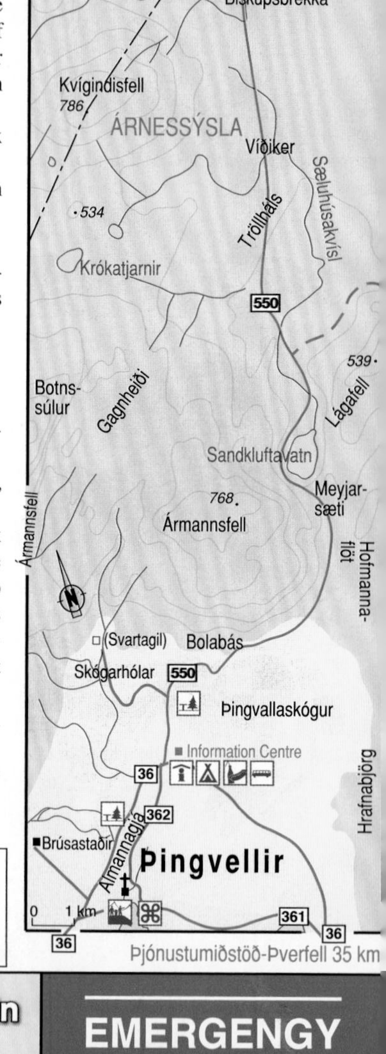

Þverfell, (655 m) a large tuff mountain at the head of the Lundarreykjadalur valley. At its eastern base is Reyðarvatn, a trout-fishing lake. At the foot of the mountain is a farm of the same name, the birthplace of Kristmann Guðmundsson (1901-83), novelist. He lived in Norway for years and wrote a great many novels in Norwegian. His books have been translated into many languages.

Uxahryggjaleið, the route along the stony ridge, Uxahryggir ("Ox ridge"), alongside the Uxavatn lake. View dial.

Kvígindisfell, (786 m) an easy mountain to climb, rewarded with an impressive panoramic view.

Brunnar, an old resting place.

Hallbjarnarvörður, stony mounds with cairns on them, on the Sæluhúshæðir hills. *Landnámabók* ("The Book of Settlements") mentions battles there.

Biskupsbrekka, ("Bishop's slope") a grassy slope beside the road where there is a memorial to Bishop Jón Vídalín, who died there in 1720 on his way to a funeral.

Víðiker, a natural hollow north and west of the Tröllháls ridge. A jeep-track goes west from there to the Hvalvatn lake.

Skjaldbreiður, (1,060 m) an evenly-shaped shield volcano with a large, deep crater, about 300 m in diameter.

Hofmannaflöt, a grassy area east of the mountain Ármannsfell. A track leads from there east through the Goðaskarð pass and north of the Tindaskagi mountains to the mountain Skriða (1,005 m) and to Hlöðuvellir fields. From **Hlöðuvellir** there is also a track south across Rótarsandur sands and the mountain Miðdalsfjall to the Laugardalur valley (see Road 37). It is possible to drive round Hlöðufell. Tourist hut at Hlöðuvellir.

Meyjarsæti, a cone shaped hill by Hofmannaflöt, the passes on both sides are of the brand are Sandkluftir.

Ármannsfell, (768 m) a tuff mountain north of Þingvellir. Below it to the south is **Bolabás,** ("Bulls' stall") where horse races took place.

550 **Kaldadalsvegur,** a road between Þingvellir and Húsafell.

36 **Þingvallavegur,** p. 188
361 **Vallarvegur,** p. 188
362 **Efrivallavegur,** p. 188
550 **Kaldadalsvegur,** p. 462-463
F508 **Skorradalsv.,** p. 237
F338 **Skjaldbreiðarvegur,** p. 460-461

Þjónustumiðstöð-Þverfell 35 km

ötuás, there is the junction of Uxahryggjavegur.

undarreykjadalur, a valley, ca. 28 km long, rather narrow, between e ridges Skorradalsháls and Lundarháls. It splits at its head to either de of the mountain Tungufell. Grassy but marshy.

korradalsháls, a ca. 28 km long ridge from the Kýrmúli spur and in s far as Eiríksvatn. Mostly over 300 m high. Not an old place-name, but ections of it are derived from the names of local farms. For example, rossöxl ("Cross shoulder") above the farm Kross and Kistufell a little rther on. Above Skarð is Skarðshnöttur with two side-valleys: Skarðs-alur and Tötradalur.

rímsá, a river flowing from the Reyðarvatn lake down the Lundar-eykjadalur valley in numerous falls and rapids. Farthest down river are e waterfalls Hrísbrekknafoss and Jötnabrúarfoss, which is as far as almon goes. Higher up are the waterfalls Kleppagilsfoss, Selmýrafoss, leppafoss, Kerlingafoss, Kálfsgilsfoss and many others.

12 Lundarreykjadalsvegur, 15 km.

undur, a church and former parsonage. Site of an ancient heathen emple. In the winter of 1981 a landslide did some damage to the farm.

ullberastaðir, a farm originally settled by Björn gullberi ("Gold-arrier").

rosslaug, ("Cross spring") by the road below Reykir. Men from west-rn Iceland were baptized there in the year 1000, when Iceland converted Christianity. After that it was a holy place, reputed to have healing owers.

rautartunga, a farm, community centre, ancient assembly site. eothermal heat and hothouse cultivation.

ngland, a farm, hot springs. Formerly a swimming pool. The story goes at a farmer there used to say that Copenhagen wasn´t the only place here there was an England! This was during the time that Iceland was overned from Copenhagen, and Denmark was the foreign country most amiliar to Icelanders.

eykir, a farm and hot spring area. There was a swimming pool by the ot spring where they taught swimming in the mid-19th century.

F508 Skorradalsvegur, 9,3 km. A beautiful route but only accessible y jeeps.

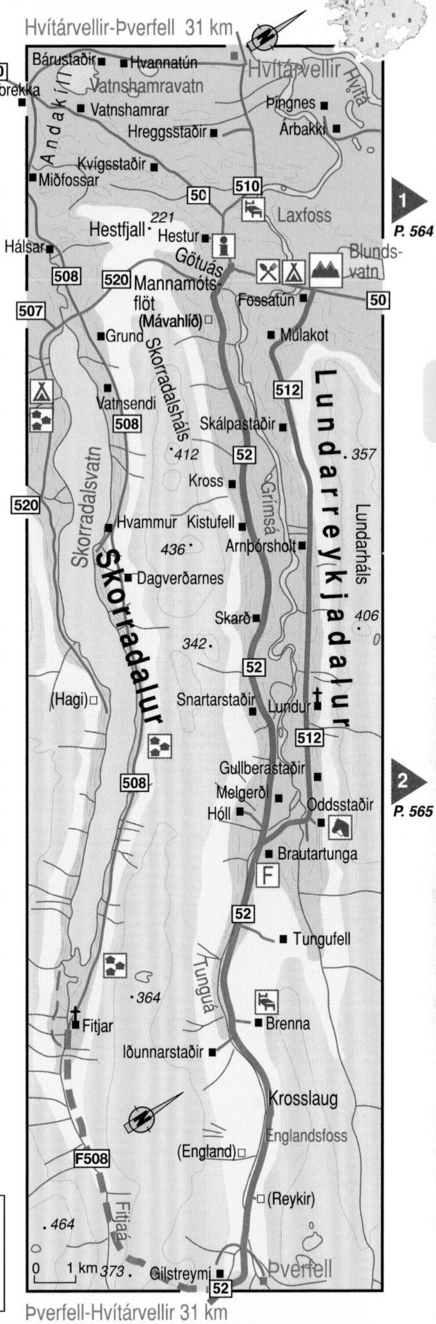

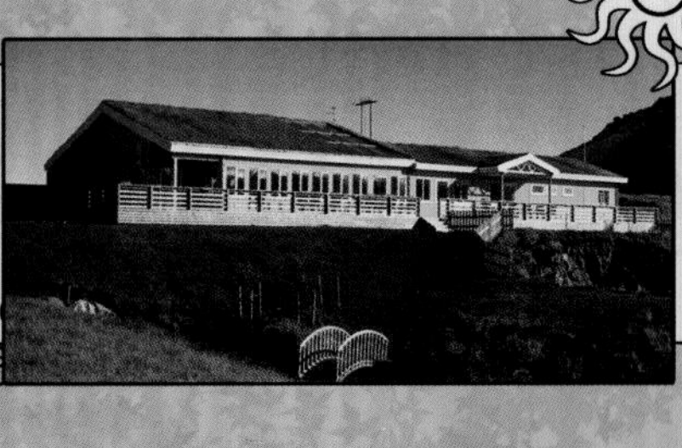

Hvítárvellir-Þverfell 31 km
P. 564
P. 565
Þverfell-Hvítárvellir 31 km

Álftá-Borgarnes 13 km

P. 564

Borgarnes

Álftártunga, farm and church.

Arnarstapi, community centre.

535 Grímsstaðavegur, 12 km. **532 Þursstaðavegur,** 4,8 km.

Grímsstaðir, a farm and birth place of Haraldur Níelsson (1863–1928 professor.

Langárfoss, a farm on the northern bank of the Langá river. Waterfal and rapids in the river. Good salmon-fishing.

Langá, a salmon river, flowing from the Langavatn lake through th Grenjadalur valley. A large salmon-ladder has been installed near th waterfall Sveðjufoss.

Rauðanes, where Skallagrímur had his smithy. He needed a har smooth rock to use as an anvil, so he rowed out into the fjord, dived dow and found a large boulder, heaved it into the boat and rowed ashor where he put the boulder outside the door to the smithy. That stone is st in the same place, quite unlike other rocks at Rauðanes, and is thoug to need four men to move it.

Borg á Mýrum**,** a church and parsonage. Originally settled by Skall grímur Kveldúlfsson father of the poet Egill Skallagrímsson of *Egi saga*. Many of his relatives and descendants lived there, including Snor Sturluson for a time. Tradition has it that Kjartan Ólafsson, one of th main characters of *Laxdæla saga*, is buried there. The sculpture *Son torrek* ("Irretrievable Loss of Sons") by Ásmundur Sveinsson (189 1982), based on the incident in *Egils saga* when Egill Skallagrímsso loses both his sons and eventually composes the long poem, *Sonatorre* as a way of dealing with his grief.

536 Stangarholtsvegur, 5,87 km.

1 Vesturlandsvegur, p. 55 **533 Álftaneshreppsvegur,** p. 266
537 Skíðholtsvegur, p. 266 **539 Hítardalssvegur,** p. 268

Borgarnes-Álftá 13 km

olbeinsstaðir, an old manor farm, residence of chieftains and law-
)eakers. Church, community centre. **Kolbeinsstaðafjall** (862 m) a
ıountain above the farm. Its southernmost peak is called Tröllakirkja
'Giants' church").

arnaborgarhraun, a lavafield west of the river Hvítá. The **Barnaborg**
·ater rises quite high above the lavafield.

agraskógarfjall, ("Fair forest mountain") an impressive mountain (644
ı) west of the Hítardalur valley. From its western side extends a tuff
dge, **Grettisbæli** ("Grettir's hide-out") where according to the Saga
rettir the strong stayed for a time in a cleft that he roofed over with
omespun cloth.

rúarfoss, ("Bridge falls") a farm on the south bank of the
ítará river, by the main road. A waterfall of the same
ame nearby. There is a bridge over the river there, a
shermen's hut and a summer house. The wrestler and
otellier Jóhannes Jósefsson (1883–1967), called
)hannes in Borg, who built the Hótel Borg in the
entre of Reykjavík, spent many summers there. The
ory goes that there was once a natural bridge there, a
one arch. A man who had been sentenced to death escaped
om his place of execution and ran over the arch, which col-
ıpsed into the river as soon as he had reached the other side. This
as considered proof of his innocence. There are some unusual
ot-holes in the river by Brúarfoss. Grettisstillur, a number of rocks
oth large and small that lie nearly in single file over the river, can
e seen a short distance upstream. According to Grettis Saga, these rocks
ere put there by the saga strongmen Grettir and Björn Hítadælakappi.

taðarhraun, a farm, church and once a parsonage. The church contains
ome old relics, brought there from the church at Hítardalur. A little to the
est of Staðarhraun is Grettisoddi ("Grettir's point") where Grettir the
rong fought alone against great numbers, eventually driving them off
fter killing 10, mortally wounding 5 and injuring others. He had been on
is way to his hide-out on Fagraskógarfjall mountain with stolen cattle.

lelur, birthplace of the Rev. Bjarni Þorsteinsson, composer (1861–
938), famous for collecting Icelandic folk songs and publishing them in
ıe collection *Íslensk Þjóðlög*.

lftá, ("Swan river") a small clear river, its main source in the Hraundalur
alley, running into the Faxaflói bay. Salmon river. Five nearby farms are
amed for the river.

rriðaá, ("Sea-trout river") shallow river with its source in Gríms-
aðamúli and running into the Langá river.

66 Hítarnesvegur, 7 km.

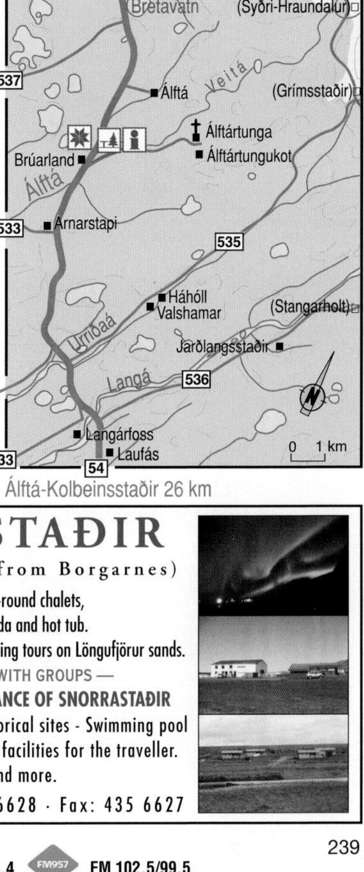

15 P. 578
1 P. 564

55 **Heydalsvegur,** p. 251
535 **Grímsstaðavegur,** p. 238
537 **Skíðholtsvegur,** p. 266
540 **Hraunhreppsvegur,** p. 266
533 **Álftaneshreppsvegur,** p. 266
536 **Stangarholtsvegur,** p. 238
539 **Hítardalsvegur,** p. 268

15
P. 578

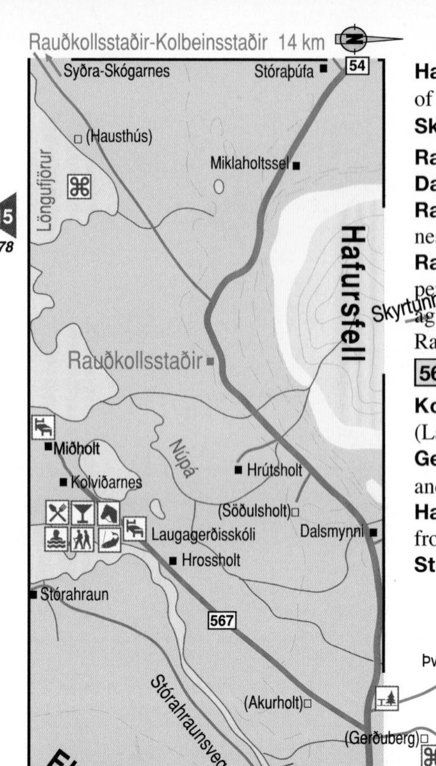

Kolbeinsstaðir-Rauðkollsstaðir 14 km

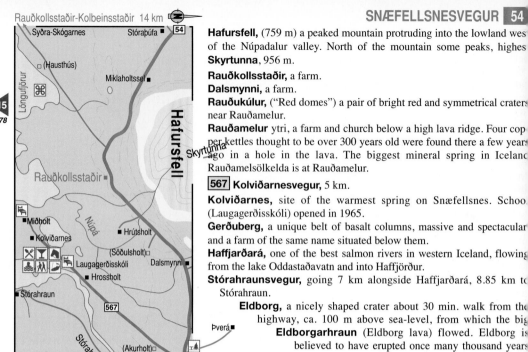

Hafursfell, (759 m) a peaked mountain protruding into the lowland wes of the Núpadalur valley. North of the mountain some peaks, highes **Skyrtunna**, 956 m.

Rauðkollsstaðir, a farm.

Dalsmynni, a farm.

Rauðukúlur, ("Red domes") a pair of bright red and symmetrical craters near Rauðamelur.

Rauðamelur ytri, a farm and church below a high lava ridge. Four copper kettles thought to be over 300 years old were found there a few years ago in a hole in the lava. The biggest mineral spring in Icelanc Rauðamelsölkelda is at Rauðamelur.

567 Kolviðarnesvegur, 5 km.

Kolviðarnes, site of the warmest spring on Snæfellsnes. Schoo (Laugagerðisskóli) opened in 1965.

Gerðuberg, a unique belt of basalt columns, massive and spectacular and a farm of the same name situated below them.

Haffjarðará, one of the best salmon rivers in western Iceland, flowing from the lake Oddastaðavatn and into Haffjörður.

Stórahraunsvegur, going 7 km alongside Haffjarðará, 8.85 km to Stórahraun.

Eldborg, a nicely shaped crater about 30 min. walk from the highway, ca. 100 m above sea-level, from which the big **Eldborgarhraun** (Eldborg lava) flowed. Eldborg is believed to have erupted once many thousand years ago and again in settlement times, as mentioned in *Landnámabók* ("The Book of Settlements"). It is a protected natural feature.

Follow the marked paths on the slopes of Eldborg!

Hnappadalur, a broad valley below the Snæfellsnes mountain range with a great lava field, Gullborgarhraun, from the Gullborg crater Unusual large caves in the lava.

55 Heydalsvegur, p. 251

Eldborg

One of the crater domes at Rauðamelur.

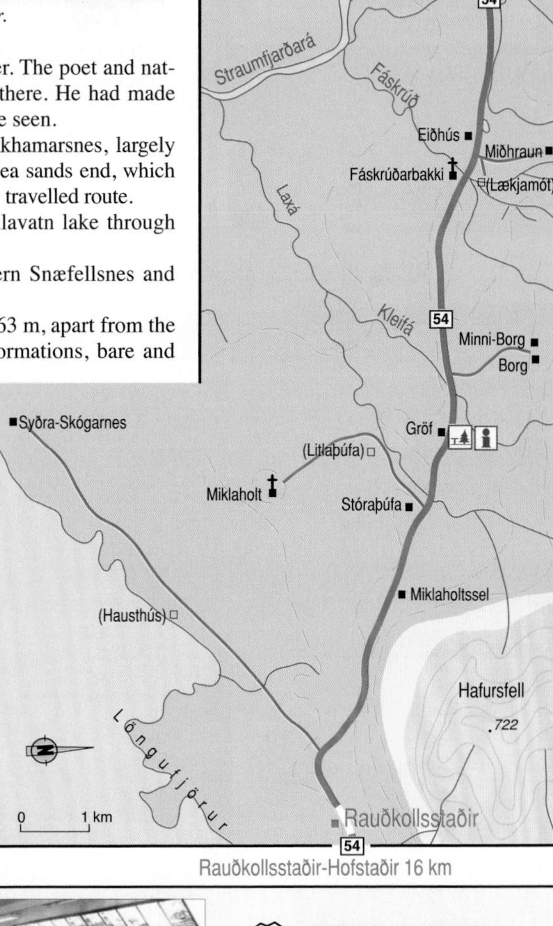

lofstaðir, a farm just west of the Straumfjarðará river. The poet and nat-ıralist Eggert Ólafsson (1726-68) had meant to live there. He had made mprovements to the land, signs of which could still be seen.

ıtakkhamar, a farm on the coast. A long reef, Stakkhamarsnes, largely ncloses a big lagoon. This is where the Löngufjörur sea sands end, which each all the way from Hítarnes. Previously a frequently travelled route.

ıtraumfjarðará, a river flowing from the Baulárvallavatn lake through ne valley Dökkólfsdalur. Fishing-river.

'egamót, ("Crossroads") where the routes to western Snæfellsnes and orth across the Kerlingarskarð pass meet.

.jósufjöll, the highest mountains on Snæfellsnes, 1,063 m, apart from the lacier, formed of rhyolite. Three pyramid-shaped formations, bare and nowfree on their south side, but with permanent now on the north.

'áskrúðarbakki, a church and community centre. he river Fáskrúð nearby.

Iiklaholt, a former church and parsonage that was noved to Fáskrúðarbakki. Now a chapel, consecra-ed in 1946. The oldest existing record of Miklaholt hurch dates from 1181.

ıkógarnes, a farm on the coast. Former trading entre. It was off this coast that the postal steamer *'hönix* stranded in 1881. Strong ebbtide.

.öngufjörur, ("Long beach") sands and mud-flats ll along the coast of Hnappadalssýsla from Hítarnes vest to Stakkhamar. Light-coloured sand, with low eadlands here and there. Shallow and rocky.

56 **Vatnaleið,** p. 253

www.olgeir.zenfolio.com

15
P. 578

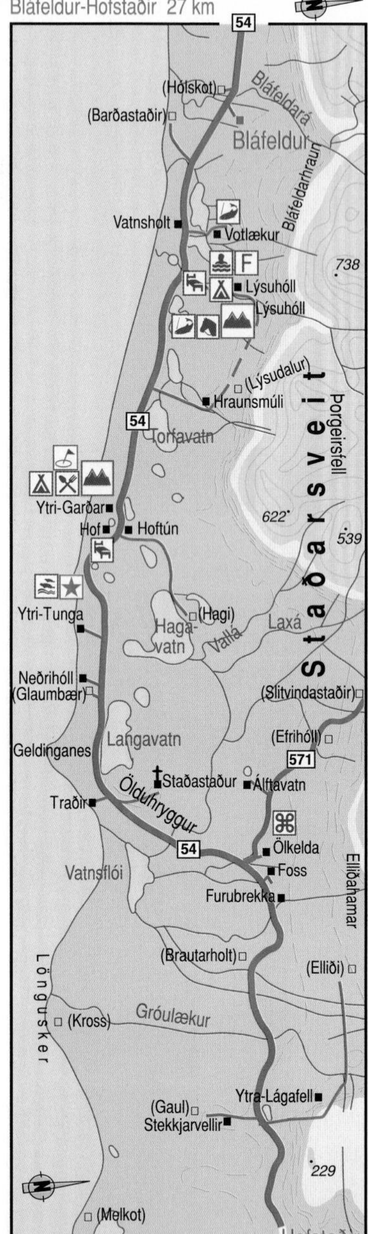

Hofstaðir-Bláfeldur 27 km

Bláfeldarhraun, a lava field that flowed from the crater Rauðkúla, on th edge of the mountains.

Lýsuhóll, a farm in the Staðarsveit district where there is a warm minera spring, one of few in the world.

Þorgeirsfell, (622 m) a mountain protruding southwards. Gabbro in thi mountain.

Staðarsveit, a flat, grassy and marshy lowland district from the Hof staðaháls ridge west to the mountain Axlarhyrna. A string of farm between the mountains and the shore. Many lakes above the Ölduhryggu ridge, Langavatn being the nearest one to Staðastaður. Nesting islets an trout-fishing in many of the lakes.

Ölduhryggur, a flat gravel ridge, a former shoreline, extending more o less continuously from the Miklaholt area far to the west. The road run along this ridge.

Staðarstaður, a parsonage, church - one of the most famous Saga farm on Snæfellsnes. Ari fróði (the Wise), the pioneer of Saga writing, i believed to have lived there. Many well-known clergymen have live there, four of whom became bishops. A fifth bishop was brought up there The folktale about Galdra-Loftur, a student at the school at Hólar wh dabbled in the black arts, ends at Staðarstaður, where he is dragged int the sea by a shaggy grey paw.

571 Ölkelduvegur, 0,5 km.

Ölkelda, a farm in the Staðarsveit district, taking its name from a minera spring in the homefield which provides good drinking water – eas access.

Elliðahamar, a sheer, overhanging crag with steep sides. To the north the peaks **Elliðatindar** (864 m) and **Tröllatindar** (930 m). Halfway up the mountain are caves, supposedly connected to a tunnel reaching all the way to Öxarhamar. Iron rungs are said to have been driven into the rock in the old days to provide access to the caves.

Lágfell, a farm. Above the farm, the peak **Lágafellshyrna** (230 m) is the nearest one on the ridge named Hofstaðaháls.

The mineral spring at the farm Ölkelda.

lafsvík, (pop. 1,010) a town forming part of Snæfellsbær Community. ood harbour. Main activities fishing and trading. As evidence of early usiness activity, there is still standing a warehouse dating from 1841, of istinctive architecture. It now houses a part of the Snæfell rural museum nd a store. Jónshús, another old house that has been restored, occupies a rominent place in the town. Building materials for the original construc-on are believed to have been imported in 1892. Near the town is an npressive mountain, Enni.

róðá, formerly a church. Nearby is the abandoned farm Forna Fróðá, here the "Fróðá marvels" recounted in the *Eyrbyggja Saga* took place. hey involved a long period during which the place was plagued with alking dead, rains of blood etc., the most hair-raising ghost story on cord in Iceland.

róðárheiði, (361 m) a mountain pass and road across the Snæfellsnes nge.

nörr, there lived Bjarni „ghost buster" Jónsson (1709–1790) a man of agic and sorcery.

úðahraun, a lava field near Búðir that came from the crater **Búða-lettur** (88 m). There is a cave in Búðaklettur, said to reach all the way to e cave Surtshellir (see Road 518) and be paved with gold. Great variety plants and ferns, some of which are very rare.

úðir, an old anchorage, later a trading centre. The 19th century church is nusual, not only in its setting, but also because it was raised by a woman ho did not have the support of the church authorities, but special per-ission from the king in Denmark. This can be seen on a ring on the nurch door. Fine views. One of the best sand and shingle beaches in Ice-nd, good for sea and sun bathing.

ælifell, (566 m) a rhyolite mountain near Búðir.

iarnarfoss, a high but fairly meager waterfall coming off the edge of e plateau. When the wind is from the south, the water is blown back owards and never reaches the bottom. There are many rare grasses on opes.

úðaós, formerly called Hraunhöfn ("Lava harbour"). Boats can enter at gh tide but there is a strong ebb. The Hraunhafnará river flows into this let.

Fróðá-Bláfeldur 18 km

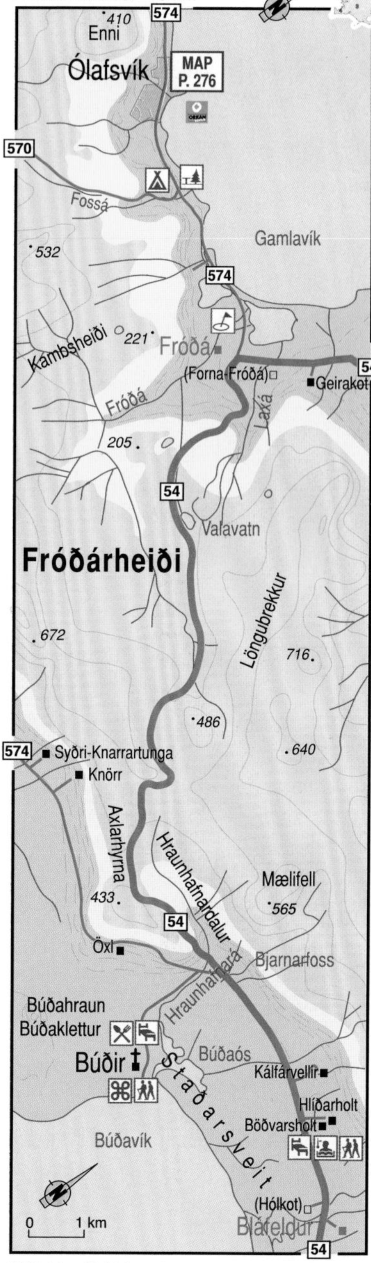

Bláfeldur-Fróðá 18 km

15 P. 578

574 **Útnesvegur,** p. 270 570 **Jökulhálsleið,** p. 464-465

P. 578

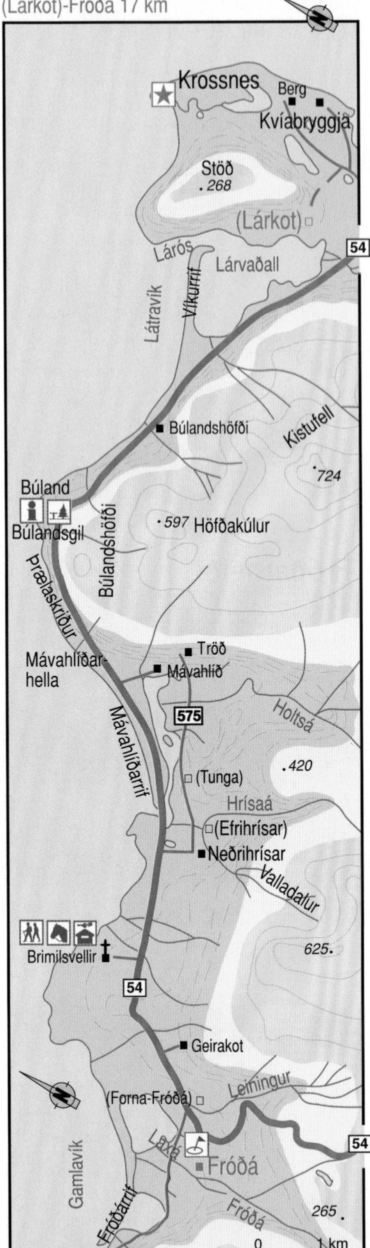

Eyrarsveit, the district reaching across the fjords beyond Búlandshöfð Grundarfjörður, Kolgrafarfjörður and Hraunsfjörður. Narrow areas of fl land between the sea and high mountains. Impressive scenery.

Kvíabryggja, a prison.

Stöð, (268 m) a single, low, elongated mountain, on the peninsula east o the Lárvaðall lagoon. Formerly called "Coffin" by the Danes.

Lárvaðall, a shallow lagoon off Látravík bay, east of the Búlandshöfð headland.

Búlandshöfði, a headland descending sheer into the sea, with rock bel at its top and base, and scree in between. Formerly a great obstacle travel because of its steepness, **Þrælaskriða** being the most notoriou scree. In Búlandshöfði Dr. Helgi Pjeturss (1872-1949) found interestin strata of sea-shells and remains from the Ice Age 135-180 m above se level. This is an important contribution to the knowledge of climat changes during the Ice Age in Iceland. Similar strata have since bee found in other mountains nearby, e.g. Stöð, Kirkjufell, Mýrarhyrna.

Mávahlíð, an old manor below Búlandshöfði. Frequently mentioned i *Eyrbyggja Saga*. Mávahlíð and Brimilsvellir were formerly considere extremely attractive properties. A well-known quatrain on the happines of marrying Margrét, the daughter of the family at Ingjaldshóll, who wa going to inherit them, is evidence of this.

575 Tunguvegur.

Brimilsvellir, formerly a substantial farm and rowing boat fishing-statio Until about 1930 fourteen farmers lived there and the total population wa about 100.

Forna-Fróðá, a farm and the site of the Fróðá marvels mentioned in *Ey byggja saga*, the most hair-raising ghost story on record in Iceland (se Road 54 Fróðá).

574 Útnesvegur, p. 270

raunsfjörður, a narrow fjord, the first fjord in Iceland to have been ridged - at Mjósund. At the head of the fjord are the abandoned farms **rnabotn**, Fjarðarhorn and Þórólfsstaðir. There are two fine, high waterılls there, and an old track over Tröllaháls ridge to Eyrarbotn in Kolrafarfjörður.

raunsfjarðarvatn, a good fishing lake.

olgrafarfjörður, now the fjord has been bridged.

76 Framsveitarvegur, 10 km.

allbjarnareyri, the home of the champion Steinþór á Eyri, menoned in *Eyrbyggja Saga*. Eyrarfjall is named after this place. Forerly a leprosy hospital.

lelrakkaey, an island in the mouth of Grundarfjörður. Known for its eming birdlife. Nature reserve.

etberg, a farm, church and parsonage. A fine view of Grundarfjörður ıd the Helgrindur mountains. omparable to the views from úðir, Mávahlíð or Helgafell.

rund, a farm at the head of rundarfjörður. Nearby waterfall, rundarfoss in the river Grundará.

elgrindur, (988 m) impressive ıd majestic mountains south of rundarfjörður. Permanent snow.

rundarfjörður, (pop. 852) a townıip in a fjord of the same name. as prospered in recent decades: shing and fish processing. There as formerly a trading-post at the ıstern end of the head of the fjord. hurch.

irkjufell, ("Church mountain") 63 m) an impressive mountain, imbable but difficult and tiring ecause of rocks. One of the most eautiful mountains on Snæfellsnes. alled "Sugarloaf" by the Danes.

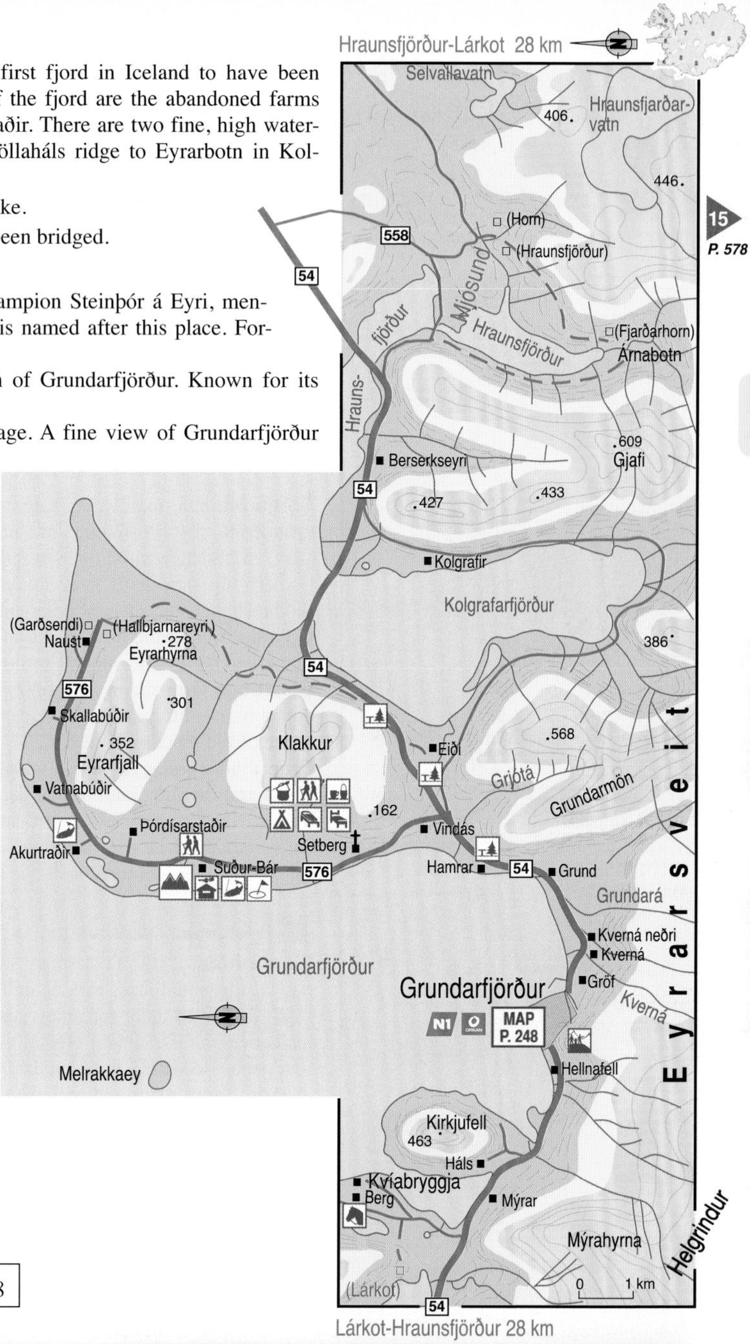

Hraunsfjörður-Lárkot 28 km

15 P. 578

Lárkot-Hraunsfjörður 28 km

558 **Berserkjahraunsvegur,** p. 248

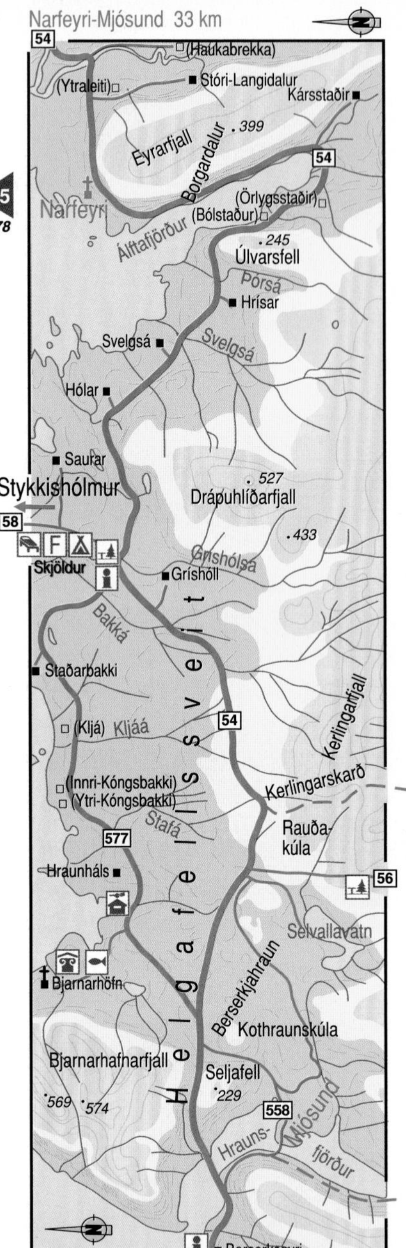

15 P. 578

Borgardalur, a small valley halfway between Narfeyri and Kárastaðir.

Ljósufjöll, rhyolite mountains south of Álftafjörður, maximum heigh 1,063 m, the highest on the Snæfellsnes peninsula, apart from the glacie Usually big snowdrifts even in summer. To the east is Hestur (864 m saddle-shaped and sheer at both ends.

Örlygsstaðir, at the head of Álftafjörður. The Sagas tell us Arnkell goð was killed there. The mineral spring Glæsikelda nearby.

Bólstaður, farm site in Álftafjörður, former home of Arnkell goði, aban doned before the year 1000. Excavations made in 1929 uncovered som of the oldest remains in Iceland.

Drápuhlíðarfjall, (527 m) an unusual and colourful mountain containin basalt and rhyolite, with lignite between basalt layers and fossilised tre trunks. Sulphur pebbles, jasper and other stones. It was long believe there was gold in the mountain, but only very small quantities wer found. The most colourful and one of the most beautiful mountains in Ice land.

577 Helgafellssveitarvegur, 11,5 km. **558 Berserkjahraunsvegu**

Bjarnarhöfn, ("Björn's harbour") the farm of the settler Björn austræn now a substantial farm with church. The homeopath Þorleifur Þorleifsso (1801-77) lived there for many years; he was probably the most psychi Icelander ever. Dr. Oddur Hjaltalín (1819-62) also lived there; he was th first person to write a book on the botany of Iceland. The church was bui in 1856. It has many old and historically valable artefacs. The alterpiec is believed to have been painted in 1640, there are two cassocks, one o which is more than 500 years old and the other was made in 1762. Th church also possesses a chalice from 1286 and a pulpit from 1694. A sig recounting the history of Bjarnarhöfn is located near the higway.

Berserkjahraun, ("Berserkers' lava field") lava from a small row of cra ters below Kerlingarskarð pass, the largest crater being Rauðakúla. Th name is derived from Víga-Styr's berserkers. He got them to cut a pat through the lava, then betrayed and killed them. The path is still visible and beside it the burial mound of the berserkers.

Helgafellssveit, the district between Hraunsfjörður an Álftafjörður. Indented coast with many islands and ske ries, inlets and peninsulas.

Bjarnarhöfn

56 Vatnaleið, p. 253
58 Stykkishólmsvegur, p. 255

kógarströnd, the coast along Hvammsfjörður from Álftafjörður to the ver Gljúfurá, where Dalasýsla county begins. Some small rivers, fishing most of them. One valley leading into the mountain range is Heydalur, rough which goes Road 55 to the Hnappadalur valley. Birch-bushes.

reiðabólsstaður, a church and long a parsonage. Sveinn Kristján jarnason (1887-1960) was born there, but later moved with his parents Canada and changed his name to Holger Cahill. In 1932, following education in art history, he became acting director of the Museum f Modern Art in New York. During the presidency of Franklin D. oosevelt, Cahill worked closely with him and became one of the most fluential people in the American art world.

rangar, a farm near which Eric the Red killed two men, for which he as outlawed and fled to Greenland.

rokey, the biggest island in Breiðafjörður, off Skógarströnd, offering any advantages to the farmer. A flour mill was built there and driven by e tides, its remains still visible. One farmer, Jón Pétursson, falcon-hunt- (1584-1667), had sailed the seven seas in his youth and was versed in nglish, German and Danish, rare in a farmer in those days. He encour- ged an eider duck colony on Brokey, and was the first to clean eider own. He had 30 children, the last when over 80 years old. Another farm- was the Dane Hans Becker, made governor of North and West Iceland the early 18th century.

tóri-Langidalur, a valley east of Eyrarfjall. Pretty and grassy with the lmon-fishing river Langá. Towards its mouth is **Klungurbrekka** slope, amed for the wild rose growing there, whose old Icelandic name was lungur. The parents of Sir William Stephenson (1896-1989) lived at lungurbrekka before they moved to Canada. William was considerd to the inspiration for the character of James Bond 007.

arfeyri, a farm and church north of the Eyrarfjall mountain, the west- nmost farm on Skógarströnd. Home of Oddur Sigurðsson 681-1741), local governor and the farmer Vilhjálmur gmundsson (1897-1965), who was famous for his mathe- atical observations.

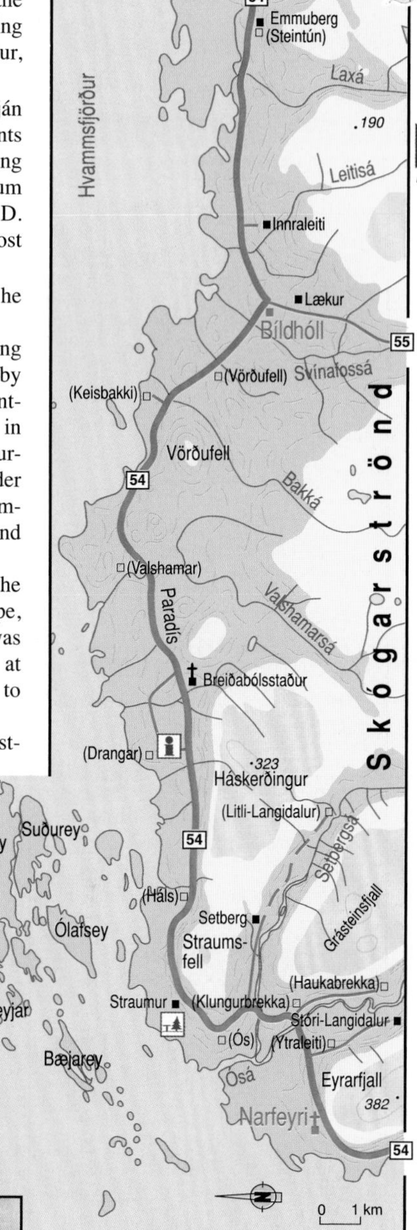

55 **Heydalsvegur,** p. 251

Bjarnarhafnarfjall

Respect the tranquillity of the countryside

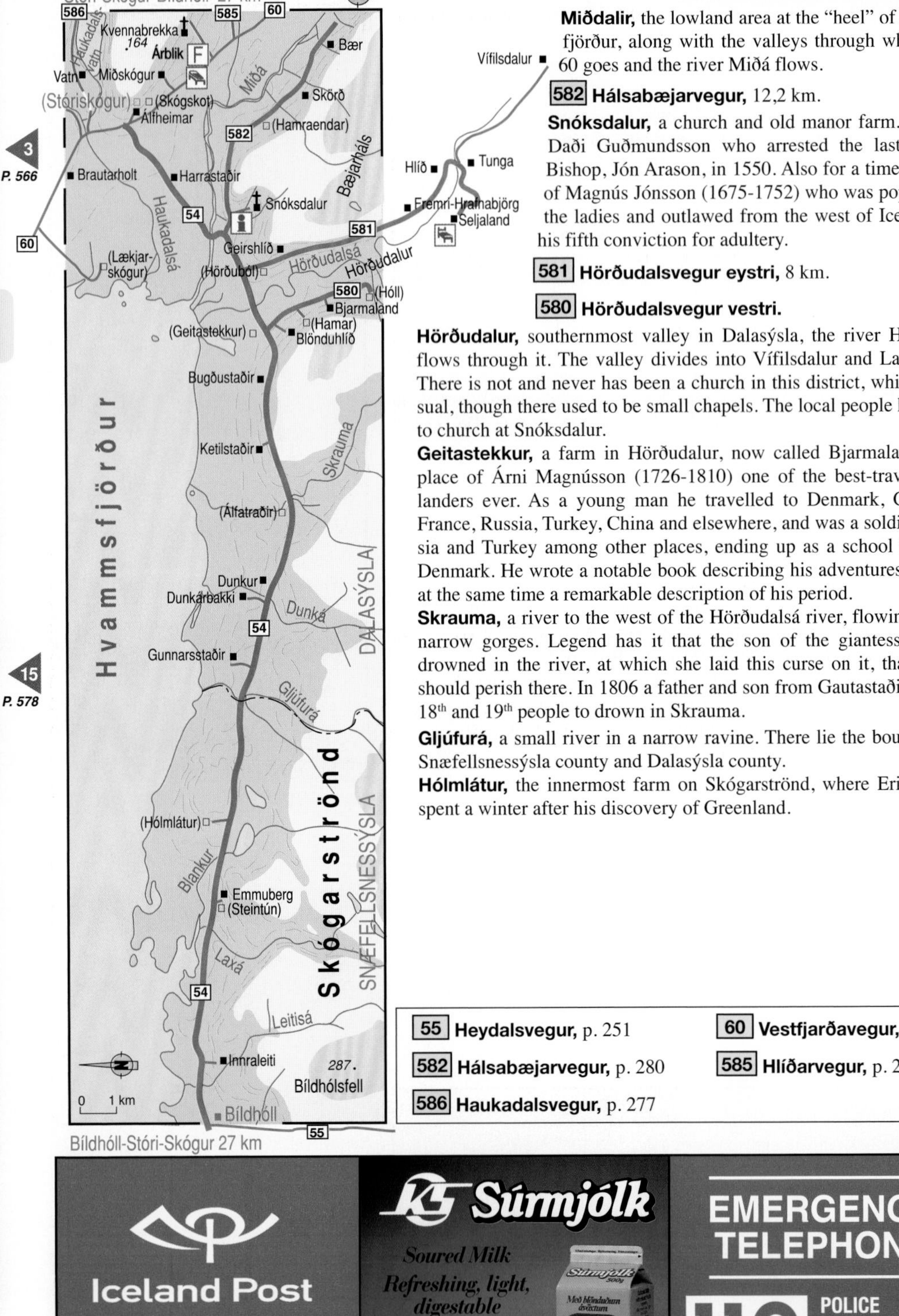

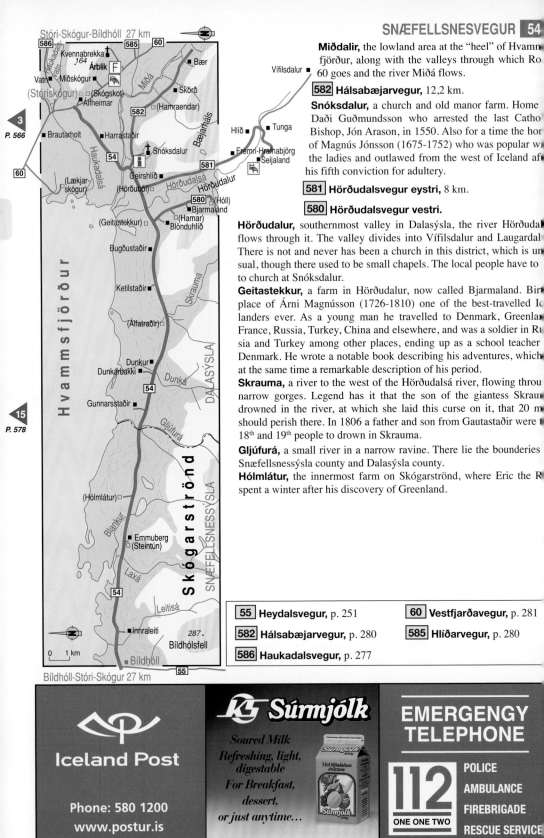

Miðdalir, the lowland area at the "heel" of Hvamm fjörður, along with the valleys through which Ro 60 goes and the river Miðá flows.

582 Hálsabæjarvegur, 12,2 km.

Snóksdalur, a church and old manor farm. Home Daði Guðmundsson who arrested the last Catho Bishop, Jón Arason, in 1550. Also for a time the hor of Magnús Jónsson (1675-1752) who was popular wi the ladies and outlawed from the west of Iceland af his fifth conviction for adultery.

581 Hörðudalsvegur eystri, 8 km.

580 Hörðudalsvegur vestri.

Hörðudalur, southernmost valley in Dalasýsla, the river Hörðuda flows through it. The valley divides into Vífilsdalur and Laugardal There is not and never has been a church in this district, which is un sual, though there used to be small chapels. The local people have to to church at Snóksdalur.

Geitastekkur, a farm in Hörðudalur, now called Bjarmaland. Bir place of Árni Magnússon (1726-1810) one of the best-travelled Ic landers ever. As a young man he travelled to Denmark, Greenla France, Russia, Turkey, China and elsewhere, and was a soldier in Ru sia and Turkey among other places, ending up as a school teacher Denmark. He wrote a notable book describing his adventures, which at the same time a remarkable description of his period.

Skrauma, a river to the west of the Hörðudalsá river, flowing throu narrow gorges. Legend has it that the son of the giantess Skrau drowned in the river, at which she laid this curse on it, that 20 m should perish there. In 1806 a father and son from Gautastaðir were t 18th and 19th people to drown in Skrauma.

Gljúfurá, a small river in a narrow ravine. There lie the bounderies Snæfellsnessýsla county and Dalasýsla county.

Hólmlátur, the innermost farm on Skógarströnd, where Eric the R spent a winter after his discovery of Greenland.

55 Heydalsvegur, p. 251
582 Hálsabæjarvegur, p. 280
586 Haukadalsvegur, p. 277
60 Vestfjarðavegur, p. 281
585 Hlíðarvegur, p. 280

55 HEYDALSVEGUR

eydalur, a shallow valley on Rauðamelsheiði moor south of the hill ílduhóll on the Skógarströnd coast. The road along it joins the Ólafsvík ad near Kolbeinsstaðir. This is the lowest and least snowy road across e Snæfellsnes range.

The lake Hlíðarvatn.

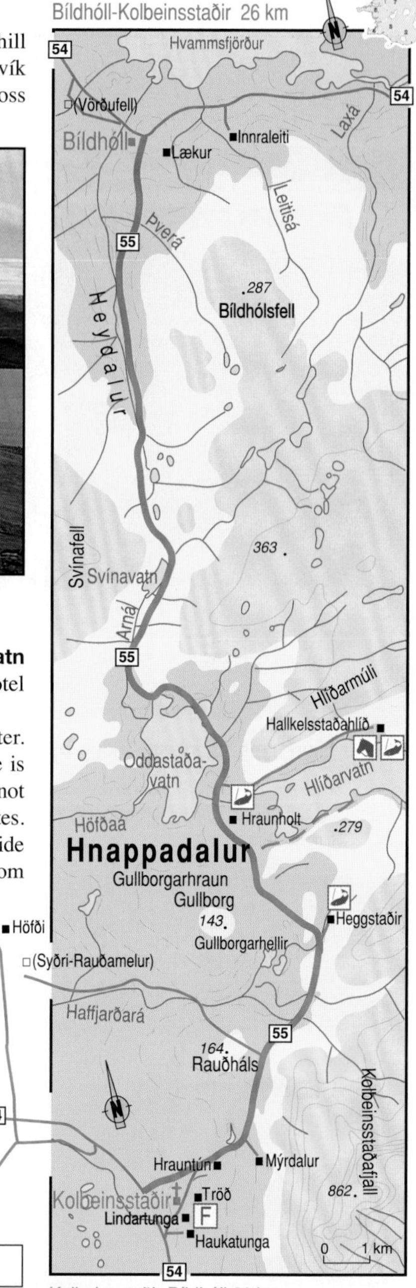

15 P. 578

nappadalur, a broad valley, full of lava. Two large lakes, **Hlíðarvatn** d **Oddastaðavatn**, with good trout-fishing. In 1964 a floating hotel aped like a Viking ship was put on Hlíðarvatn but was not a success.

ullborgarhraun, a lava field in Hnappadalur from the **Gullborg** crater. here are some large and unusual caves in the lava field. One of these is **ullborgarhellir**, considered one of the loveliest lava caves in Iceland, not ast because of the unusual number of beautiful stalagmites and stalactites. ne cave is a protected natural feature and can only be visited with a guide om the farm **Heggstaðir**. Some ruins nearby are believed to date from e Sturlunga age in the 13th century, when Aron Hjörleifsson had a de-out in the lava field. It is said that his main hide-out was in a ve called Aronshellir. In 1979 one more cave was found in this lava eld.

auðháls, craters in the Rauðhólshraun lava field.

ýrdalur, a farm at the foot of the mountain Kolbeinsstaðafjall. ehind the farm is Mýrdalsgjá, an unusual ravine.

ndartunga, a community centre.

olbeinsstaðir, an old manor farm, and the home of many influen- al men. Church, community centre. The highest peak on the moun- in **Kolbeinsstaðafjall** above the farm is called **Tröllakirkja** Giants' church") (862 m). Another peak is Hrútaborg, with steep ags. A challenging mountain for climbers.

54 Snæfellsnesvegur, p. 238-250

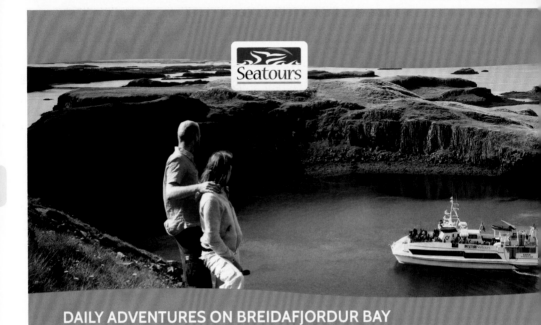

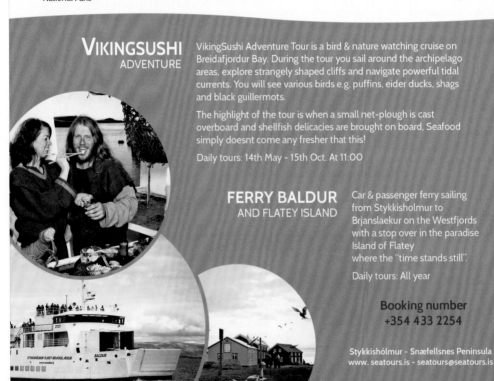

Þrápuhlíðarfjall, (527 m) an unusual and olourful mountain containing basalt and hyolite, with lignite between basalt lay-rs and fossilised tree-trunks. Sulphur ebbles, jasper and other stones. It was ong believed there was gold in the moun-ain, but only very small quantities were ound. The most colourful and one of the nost beautiful mountains in Iceland.

Grettistak, ("Grettir's challenge") a arge tuff boulder that has fallen down rom Kerlingafjall. Formerly a resting lace for travellers, fine views.

Kerlingarfjall, (585 m) a mountain on he east side of the Kerlingarskarð pass. Vatnaheiði forms a deep depression in the nountain range a short way west of Kerlingarskarð. There are three angling akes on the heath: Baulárvallavatn, Hraunsfjarðarvatn and Selvallavatn.

Baulárvallavatn, a good fishing lake otorious for its monsters, as many as 5 aving supposedly been seen at once, unning themselves on the shore and eturning to the water at dusk. There was ormerly a farm, Baulárvellir, near the ake. One midwinter day in the 19th cen-ury the farmer went off, leaving his wife lone with the children. She heard a loud oise as if the farm were being pulled own, and an icy blast filled the room, ut she dared not move. The next day everal outbuildings were found to have een destroyed, and the huge tracks of an nknown creature could be traced to a ole in the ice on the lake. Just north of here are the lakes Hraunsfjarðarvatn and elvallavatn.

Kerlingarskarð, ("Old woman pass") a ass (311 m) over the Snæfellsnes moun-ain range. The pass is named after a rock amed **Kerling.** A folktale tells of a iantess of the troll type who was on her vay home with her catch after a good ights fishing in the lake when she was aught by the sun and turned to stone. She can still be seen, her line of trout ver her shoulder, on a ridge of the moun-ain Kerlingarfjall opposite the mountain Hafrafell, at the north end of the pass. here is also a fine view from that nd of the pass. Burial mounds.

Vegamót, ("Crossroads") where the outes west out onto Snæfellsnes and orth across the Kerlingarskarð pass neet.

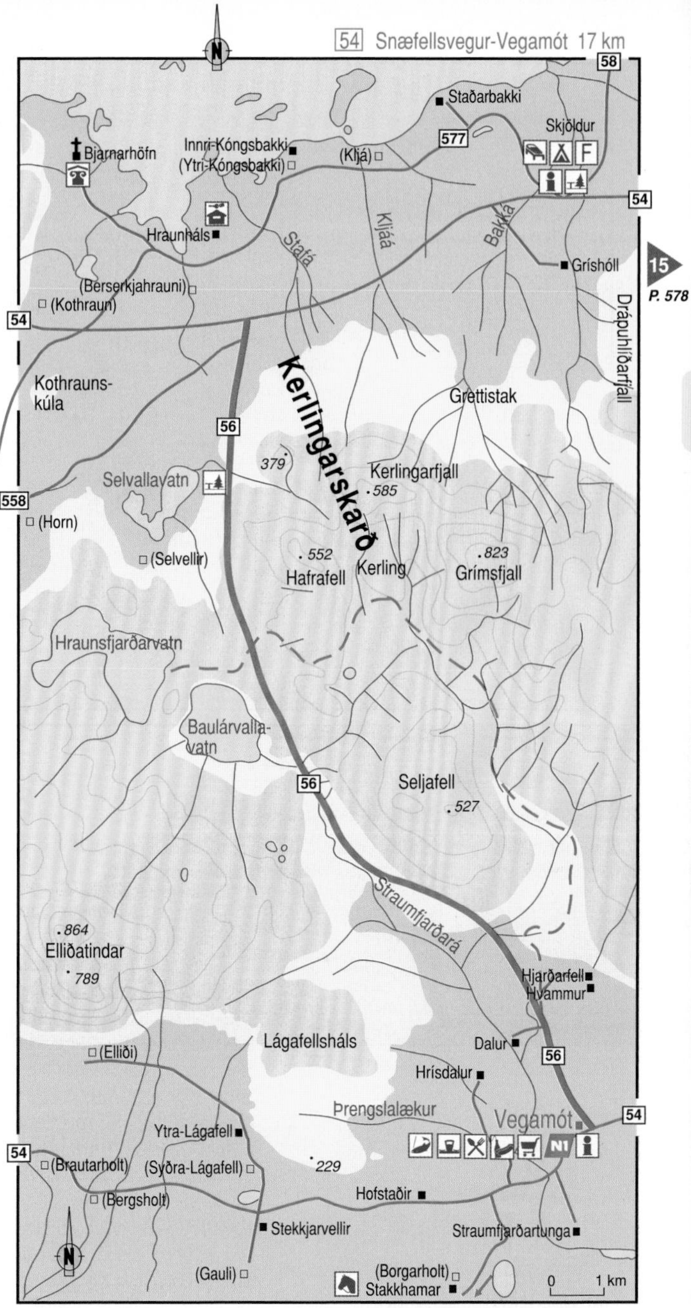

54 **Snæfellsnesvegur,** p. 238-250
58 **Stykkishólmsvegur,** p. 255
558 **Berserkjahraunsvegur,** p. 248
577 **Helgafellssveitarvegur,** p. 248

54 Snæfellsvegur-Vegamót 17 km

Staðarbakki
Skjöldur
Bjarnarhöfn
Innri-Kóngsbakki
(Ytri-Kóngsbakki)
(Kljá)
Hraunháls
Stafá
Kljáá
Bakká
Gríshóll
(Berserkjahrauni)
(Kothraun)
Kerlingarskarð
Kothraunskúla
Grettistak
Drápuhlíðarfjall
379
Kerlingarfjall
585
Selvallavatn
(Horn)
(Selvellir)
552
Hafrafell
Kerling
823
Grímsfjall
Hraunsfjarðarvatn
Baulárvallavatn
Seljafell
527
Straumfjarðará
864
Elliðatindar
789
Hjarðarfell
Hvammur
Lágafellsháls
Dalur
(Elliði)
Hrísdalur
Þrengslalækur
Vegamót
Ytra-Lágafell
(Brautarholt)
(Syðra-Lágafell)
229
(Bergsholt)
Hofstaðir
Stekkjarvellir
Straumfjarðartunga
(Gauli)
(Borgarholt)
Stakkhamar
0 1 km

P. 578

Vegamót – 54 Snæfellsnesvegur 17 km

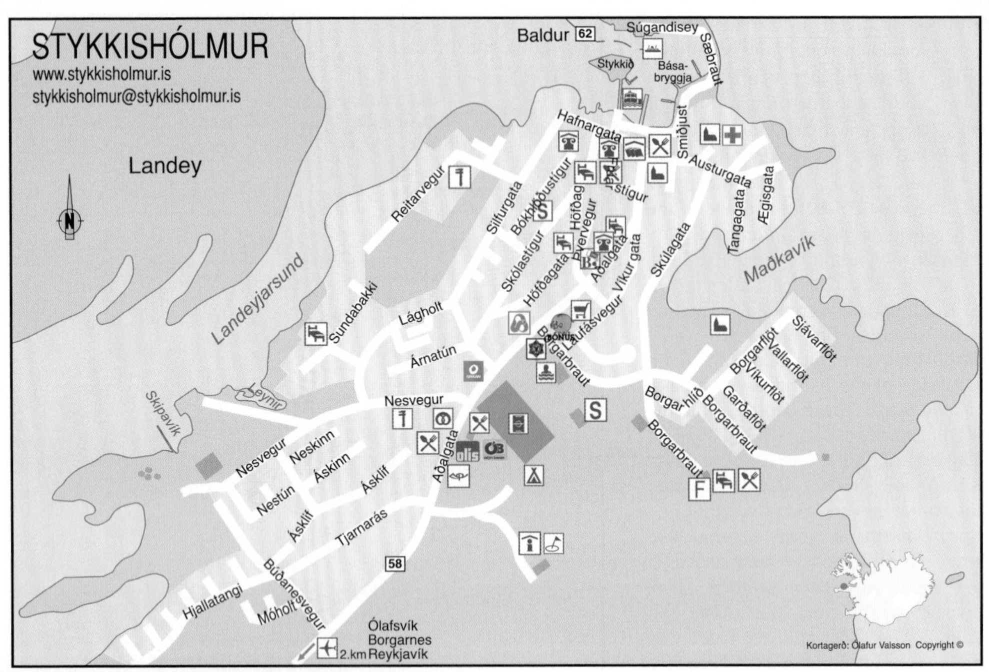
STYKKISHÓLMUR
www.stykkisholmur.is
stykkisholmur@stykkisholmur.is
Landey
Baldur 62
Súgandisey
Stykkið
Bása-bryggja
Sæbraut
Hafnargata
Smiðjust
Austurgata
Tangagata
Ægisgata
Maðkavík
Reitarvegur
Silfurgata
Skólastígur
Höfðagata
Aðalgata
Víkurgata
Skúlagata
Landeyjarsund
Sundabakki
Lágholt
Árnatún
Laufásvegur
Borgarbraut
Sjávarflöt
Vallarflöt
Borgarflöt
Víkurflöt
Garðaflöt
Borgarhlíð
Skipavík
Nesvegur
Neskinn
Áskinn
Ásklif
Nestún
Tjarnarás
Búðanesvegur
Hjallatangi
Móholt
58
Ólafsvík
Borgarnes
2.km Reykjavík
Kortagerð: Ólafur Valsson Copyright ©

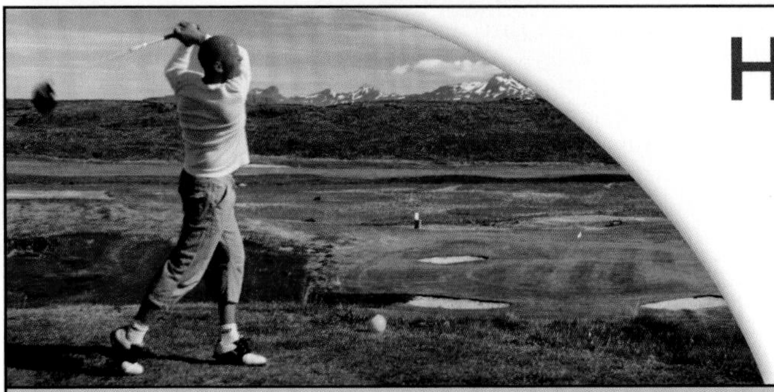

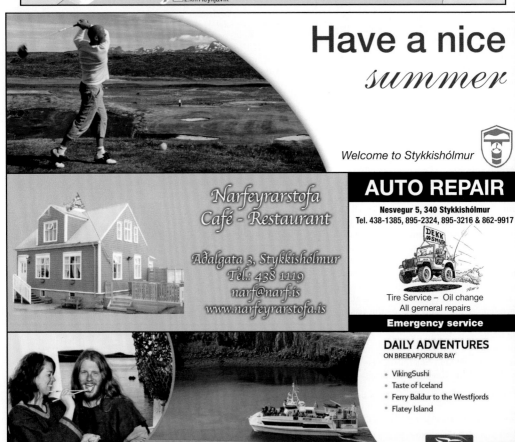

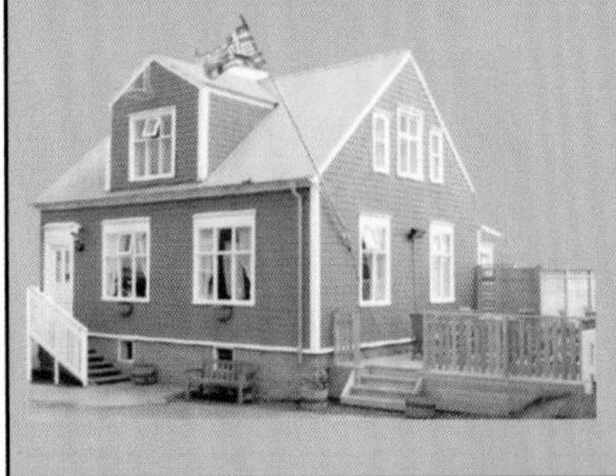

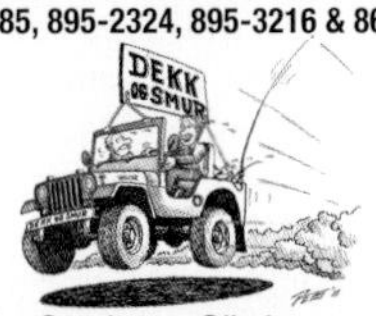

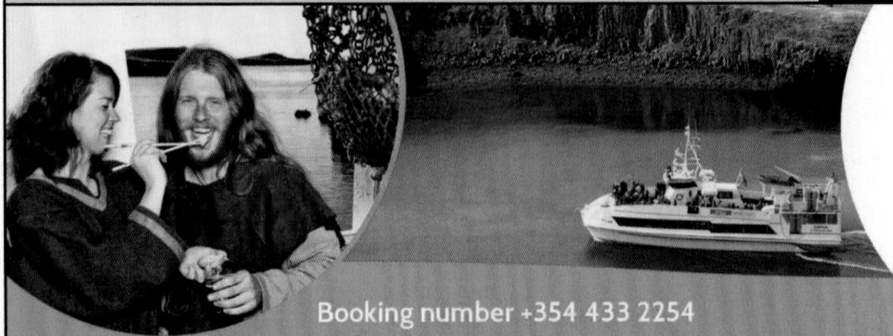

58 STYKKISHÓLMSVEGUR

tykkishólmur, (pop. 1,108) a town with municipal rights since May 2nd 1987. It is named after a large skerry in the harbour, which is pro- :cted by the rock island Súgandisey. Stykkishólmur has been a centre f fishing, trading and transportation for the Breiðafjörður settlements or centuries. The town is still an ideal destination for those whose who /ish to experience diversity of nature, services and life on Breiðafjörður. 1 summer, daily sightseeing trips go out in the fjord on the Seatours Sæferðir) boats, while the ferry Baldur connects Snæfellsnes with the Vest Fjords with daily sailings to Brjánslækur making a stop at Flatey. great deal of effort has been put into preserving the town's old houses, nd old buildings thus have a great influence on the appearance of owntown Stykkishólmur. The oldest house, Norska húsið ("The Nor- /egian house"), so called because the building materials were imported rom Norway, was built by the merchant Árni Thorlacius about 1832. rni began regular meteorological observations in Stykkishólmur in 845 and they have continued uninterrupted to this day, the oldest con- nuous meteorological observations in Iceland. Now souvenirs and andicrafts are sold there and often special exhibitions are put on by the Museum or artists. Many craftspeople live in Stykkishólmur, and a rafts market there is open in summer. The Danish days festival is held nnually on the third weekend of August, when town residents and visi- ors celebrate with dance, song and various artistic events. In 1879 a hurch was built in Stykkishólmur. It is one of the old houses that have ow been renovated. Now there is also a new at Borg. It is a striking andmark from the sea as well as the land. It is open to tourists . Besides ormal church services there are concerts at least fortnightly over the ummer. At Stykkishólmur there is the Library of Water, situated at a lace with one of the most beautiful views. An American artist Roni Iorn created and shaped the Library of Water. It is open daily in sum- ner. There is also the Volcano Museum, a unique exhibition of interna- onal art and objects related to volcanic eruptions and their impact. Res- aurants, coffee shops, a bakery and a grocery store can be found in tykkishólmur, as can hotels and other types of accommodation. There s a very good campsite next to a 9 hole golf course and a swimming ool that contains an enjoyable chute for children, as well as hot pots /ith certificated pure water that comes straight from the borehole. The /ater is famed for its healing powers, as it is full of minerals and works /ell for all sorts of skin problems. Besides the football field and athlet- cs track, a tarmac basketball field and playing field can be found on the rounds of the primary school and are open to all. Beautiful walking outes through town and to the beaches and view points. See town map.

Iofsstaðir, the farm of Þórólfur Mostraskegg, who originally settled the órsnes peninsula. The first known Þing or official meeting place, in Iceland.

ingvellir, plains on the peninsula south of the Nesvogur inlet. The Þing /as moved there from Hofsstaðir and some ruins can still be seen, as /ell as a sacrificial stone, where people were condemned to be sacri- iced. Inside the ring is Þór´s stone, on which the sacrificial victims /ere broken. Blood stains can still be seen on the stone.

Ielgafell, (73 m) this small mountain, though not high, is conspicuous 1 the plain. It was sacred to people of the Saga age, and they hoped to ie on it. The story goes that if you start from the grave of Guðrún Ósví- ursdóttir and climb to the Tótt (remains of a chapel) without speaking a ingle word or looking back on the way, you can have three wishes. Iowever, the wishes must be pure-hearted, told to no one, and made hile facing east by the chapel ruins. At the southern foot of Helgafell re a farm of the same name, famous in the Sagas, and a church (former arsonage). The farm was in its time the residence of Snorri goði and ater of Guðrún Ósvífursdóttir of *Laxdæla saga*. Her grave can be seen nere. From 1184 until the Reformation there was a wealthy monastery earby. Books and manuscripts from there were burned after the refor- nation.

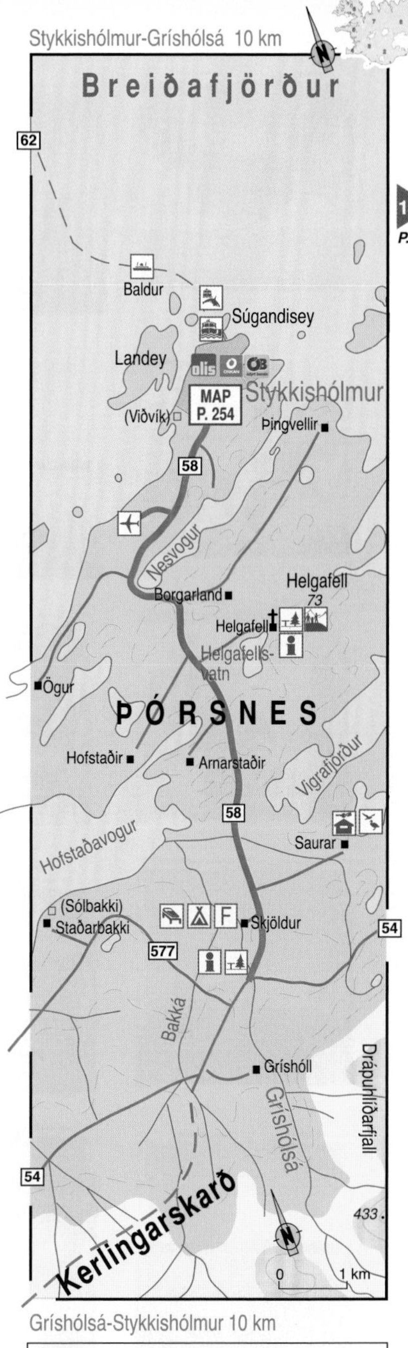

54 Snæfellsnesvegur, p. 248

62 Barðastrandarvegur, p. 306

577 Helgafellssveitarvegur, p. 248

59 LAXÁRDALSVEGUR

xárdalur, a long, narrow valley between low grassy ridges, not spec- cular though the river Laxá, that flows through it, is a good fishing river. e setting for the *Laxdæla saga* ("Saga of the people of Laxárdalur"). the old bridge there is a pool called Papi.

xárdalsheiði, (200 m), a moor, traversed by Laxárdalsvegur (Road 59) tween the villages Búðardalur and Borðeyri. Two Laxá rivers flow wn from there, one to Hvammsfjörður, the other to Hrútafjörður. attish with many lakes, the biggest being Laxárvatn.

lheimar, the innermost farm in Laxárdalur, home of the ghost Sólhei- a-Móri. The place was so severly haunted at one time that one farmhand er the other died suddenly in the space of a few years. Many horses re killed as well as other livestock. The ghost also enticed people into ers, pits and gullies.

8 Gillastaðavegur, 1,88 km.

7 Hjarðarholtsvegur, 9 km.

iðólfsstaðir, a farm which *Laxdæla saga* tells us was the home of a n and wife who had such magic powers that they could strike people ad. Their son was no less powerful, for when he looked out through a le in the sack in which he had been trapped, all the grass there withered d has never grown since. Another son was drowned in Hvammsfjörður er which there were no fish in the fjord.

skuldsstaðir, home of Höskuldur Dala-Kollsson, father of Ólafur pá 'eacock"). Ólafur's mother was Irish and of royal blood. Old remains l visible.

arðarholt, a church and manor farm since Saga times. Home of Ólafur , birthplace of Kjartan Ólafsson, the main character of *Laxdæla saga*. rmer parsonage.

appsstaðir, home of Hrappur who after his death was one of the worst osts of the Saga age.

0 **Vestfjarðavegur,** p. 281 | 68 **Innstrandavegur,** p. 309

Borðeyri-Búðardalur 36 km

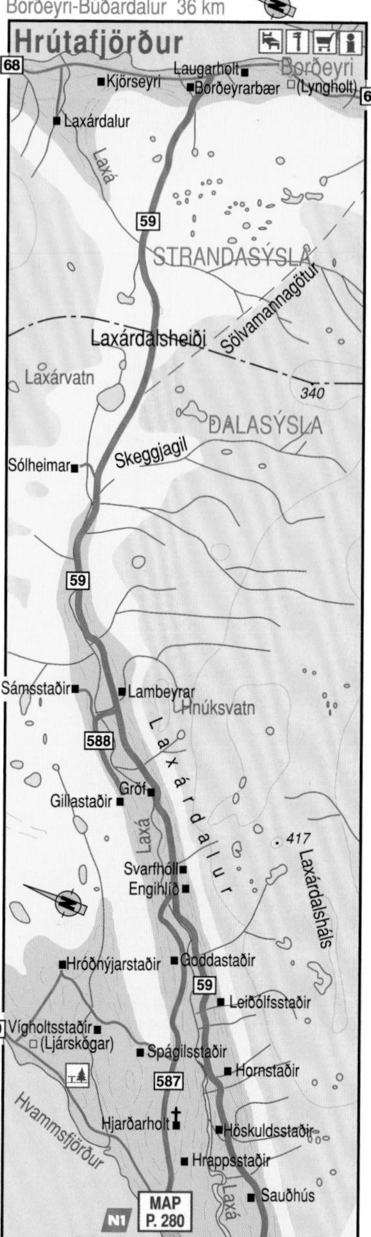

3 P. 566

Búðardalur-Borðeyri 36 km

Hjarðarholt 1898

1 P. 564

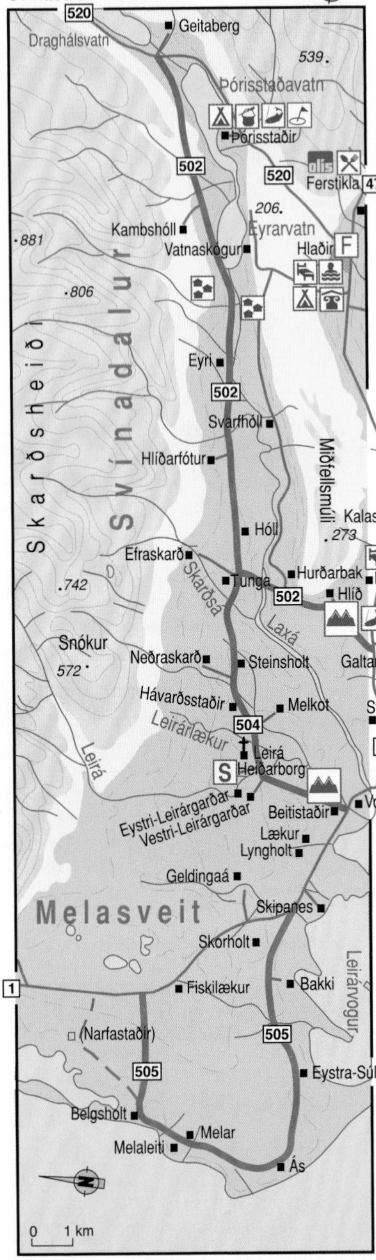

502 Svínadalsvegur, 15 km.

Svínadalur, a valley above Ferstikluháls ridge, in which there are thr quite big lakes: **Eyrarvatn** (or Kambhólsvatn), from which the La flows, **Þórisstaðavatn** and **Draghálsvatn**, the road going along narrow isthmus between the latter two. Trout-fishing in the lakes.

Vatnaskógur, woods alongside the lakes in the valley Svínadalur, a pr tected area since 1914. The YMCA has a boys' summer camp the Lindarrjóður.

Laxá, a river flowing from Eyrarvatn and emptying into Leirárvogur. A good salmon river.

Skarðsheiði, a high mountain range dominating the Borgarfjörður ar on the south side. Highest point Heiðarhorn, (1,053 m). Skessuho ("Giantess' peak") (963 m) is a particularly impressive and outstandi peak when the range is viewed from the north. It is easy to climb fro Svínadalur, the best approach being from the outerm valley facing south, or up beside the Skarðsá river.

504 Leirársveitarvegur, 6,7 km.

Beitistaðir, a farm where there was a printing press whi was brought there from Leirárgarðar in 1814 and was mov in 1819 to Viðey, then the only printing-house in the countr

Leirá, ("Clay river") a farm and church occupied by men influence from earliest times. Chief Justice Magn Stephensen put up a printing press at a nearby farm, Leir garðar, and later (1795) moved it to Beitistaðir. Good salm fishing in the river. Hot springs. A bathing place of old.

505 Melasveitarvegur, 11,7 km.

Melar, a farm and, until 1855, a church but the site is n much eroded by the sea. Served by Helgi Sigurðsson (181 88), who was the major force in the establishment of t National Museum and the first Icelander to study photog phy, which he did in Copenhagen alongside his acade studies 1842-45.

1 **Vesturlandsvegur,** p. 54
47 **Hvalfjarðarvegur,** p. 22
51 **Akrafjallsvegur,** p. 234
520 **Dragavegur,** p. 264

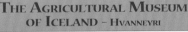

)8 Skorradalsvegur, 24 km.

.orradalur, the southernmost of the Borgarfjörður valleys, 28 km long t narrow. Widespread birch-bushes. In recent years the Forestry Service s done extensive forestation there, developing a quite luxuriant conifer ›ods. The settler Skorri is buried at Skorrahólar a good way up the val-/. Skorradalsskógur is a natural delight with large, old, dense birch es. Substantial vegetation on the forest floor. Bird life at the river estu-/. Fitjaár rivers very diverse. Rare vegetation. Protection of site ınned. Difficult to reach by jeep. National Forest.

.orradalsvatn, a 16 km long lake going right down the valley. Area .7 km^2, maximum depth 48 m. The bed of the lake was formed by a ıcier, which left a ridge closing the mouth of the valley. The Andakílsá er flows out of the lake, its waters being used in the Andakílsá power tion. Trout-fishing.

austurskógur (Vatnshornsskógur), a national forrest.

jar, a substantial farm and church, fertile land. Some waterfalls in the jaá river, the biggest being **Hvítserkur**.

ıafell, farm adjacent to Stálpastaðir. Coniferous trees were planted ıong the low birch bushes there as early as 1938.

álpastaðaskógur, popular hiking paths in a forest with numerous ›pes. Some 30 tree species from 70 locations around the globe. Labelled e collection and picnic table. Many of the country's largest Christmas es originate there. National Forest.

lsskógur, very pleasant campground among the birch trees. Hiking :hs through the forest in many places. Conifer trees are common, as are ›rway spruce and Sitka spruce. Located south of Skorradalsvatn, north Skarðsheiði. National Forest.

ınd, a substantial farm. Bishop Brynjólfur Sveinsson (1605-1675) ilt a house there which he intended his wife to live in if she would ever :ome a widow. For long the main farm of the district. Roads from there Andakíll on both sides of the river Andakílsá, across the Hestháls ridge, wn into the valleys Lundarreykjadalur and Skorradalur.

ssar, there is a power station Andakílsárvirkjun. Built in 1947, power MW. Reservoir at lake Skorradalsvatn.

7 Mófellsstaðavegur, 6,7 km.

ihreppur, there is a swimming pool called Hreppslaug.

stur, formerly a church and parsonage. Now an experimental sheep-eding station.

ıdakíll, a settlement.

i0 **Borgarfjarðarbraut,** p. 237
10 **Hvítárvallavegur,** p. 231
20 **Dragavegur,** p. 264
52 **Uxahryggjavegur,** p. 237
511 **Hvanneyrarvegur,** p. 231
F508 **Skorradalsvegur,** p. 237

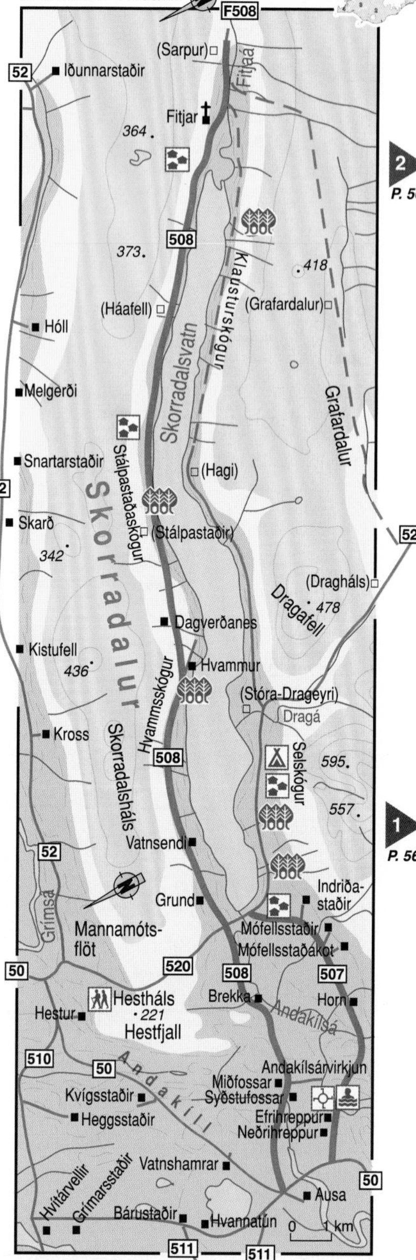

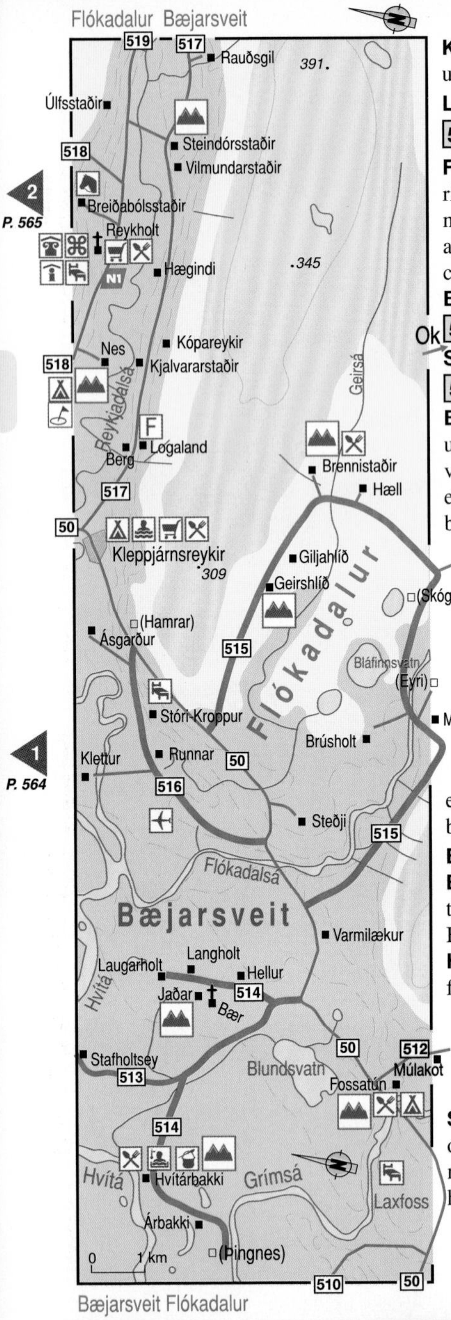

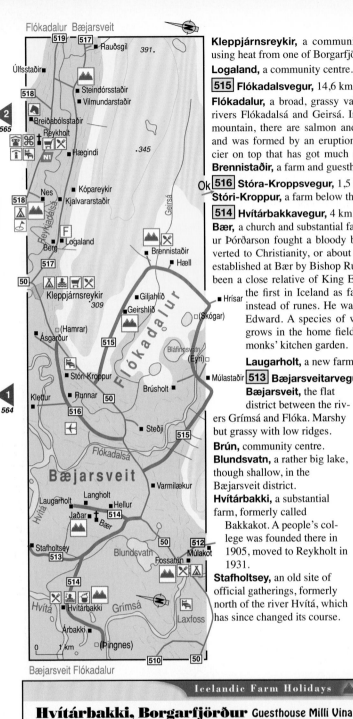

Kleppjárnsreykir, a community where there is hothouse cultivati using heat from one of Borgarfjörður's bigger hot springs, 70 l/sec.

Logaland, a community centre.

515 Flókadalsvegur, 14,6 km.

Flókadalur, a broad, grassy valley, actually two, down which flow t rivers Flókadalsá and Geirsá. In Flókadalsá, which comes from the C mountain, there are salmon and trout. **Ok** (1,198 m) is made of bas and was formed by an eruption late in the Ice Age. It has a small gl cier on top that has got much smaller recently, leaving the crater ba

Brennistaðir, a farm and guesthouse.

516 Stóra-Kroppsvegur, 1,5 km.

Stóri-Kroppur, a farm below the Kroppsmúli spur. Airstrip.

514 Hvítárbakkavegur, 4 km.

Bær, a church and substantial farm, where Sturla Sighvatsson and Þorle ur Þórðarson fought a bloody battle in 1237. Shortly after Iceland co verted to Christianity, or about 1030, the first monastery in Iceland w established at Bær by Bishop Rúðólfur (Rudolph), who is thought to ha been a close relative of King Edward of Britain. Rúðólfur ran a scho the first in Iceland as far as is known, and he introduced lette instead of runes. He was later made Abbot of Abington by Ki Edward. A species of wild onion, exceedingly rare in Icelan grows in the home field at Bær. They may be a left-over of t monks' kitchen garden.

Laugarholt, a new farm near geothermal heat.

513 Bæjarsveitarvegur, 2,4 km.

Bæjarsveit, the flat district between the rivers Grímsá and Flóka. Marshy but grassy with low ridges.

Brún, community centre.

Blundsvatn, a rather big lake, though shallow, in the Bæjarsveit district.

Hvítárbakki, a substantial farm, formerly called Bakkakot. A people's college was founded there in 1905, moved to Reykholt in 1931.

Stafholtsey, an old site of official gatherings, formerly north of the river Hvítá, which has since changed its course.

50 Borgarfjarðarbraut, p. 230

510 Hvítárvallavegur, p. 231

512 Lundarreykjadalsvegur, p. 237

517 Reykdælavegur, p. 261

518 Hálsasveitarvegur, p. 261

519 Reykholtsdalsvegur, p. 261

P. 565

P. 564

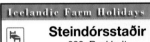

óri-Ás, a church where Miðfjarðar-Skeggi, who took the sword öfnungur from the burial mound of Hrólfur kraki in *Hrólfs saga*, is said be buried.

19 Reykholtsdalsvegur, 13,3 km. **517 Reykdælavegur,** 8,4 km.

eiðabólstaður, a farm in Reykholtsdalur. Site of a Saga-age tragedy, en Hallbjörn from Kiðjaberg chopped off the head of his wife, llgerður, when she refused to move away with him.

ykholt, a church, parsonage, a medieval institution and a hotel in one the most famous places in Iceland's history, the home of Snorri rluson (1179–1241), who was murdered there. Snorri was a writer, ieftain and law speaker, the best-known Icelandic medieval writer. nong many famous clergymen to serve Reykholt was Finnur Jónsson 704–89), later a bishop of Skálholt. Attached to the church is Snorra-fa, a medieval research centre, established to do research and provide ormation on the works of Snorri, medieval literature and history in gen-l, also the area of Reykholt and Borgarfjörður. A statue of Snorri by stav Vigeland presented by Norway was unveiled 1947. Snorralaug norri's pool"), an outdoor bathing pool with piped warm water and a nel leading to it from under the old farmhouse are considered to be ong the oldest extant constructions in the country. Graves of the rlungas, the powerful family to which Snorri belonged, are in the irchyard. Much geothermal heat is in the area. The main hot spring, rifla, supplies the Snorralaug pool and the local buildings with hot ter. The building of the old district school with its beautiful architecture a part of the National Library of Iceland. Excavations have been made er the past years by the National museum of Iceland on the old farm-use site, the passage between the houses and the pool, and on the old irchyard. The old timber-church in Reykholt was built 1886-87 and irs a certain resemblance to Reykjavík Cathredal. In the keeping of the tional Museum since 2001.

áneyjarbunga, (260 m) the mountain above the farm Skáney, with ne view.

áney, a farm in the Reykholtsdalur valley, the residence in the 16th cen-y of a German doctor, Lazarus Mattheusson, called in to cure syphilis. ld onions grow there, as at Bær.

hver, a hot spring in the Reykjadalsá river. It spouted regularly at one time, up to 12 m, but now only spouts if soap is thrown into it. Another name for the spring is **Vellir**.

50 Borgarfjarðarbraut, p. 229
23 Hvítársíðuvegur, p. 265

Sturlureykir, a farm in Reykholtsdalur. The first hot spring to be harnessed for domestic heating in Iceland, in 1908.

Reykholtsdalur, a wide, grassy, valley between low ridges. Geothermal heat in many places.

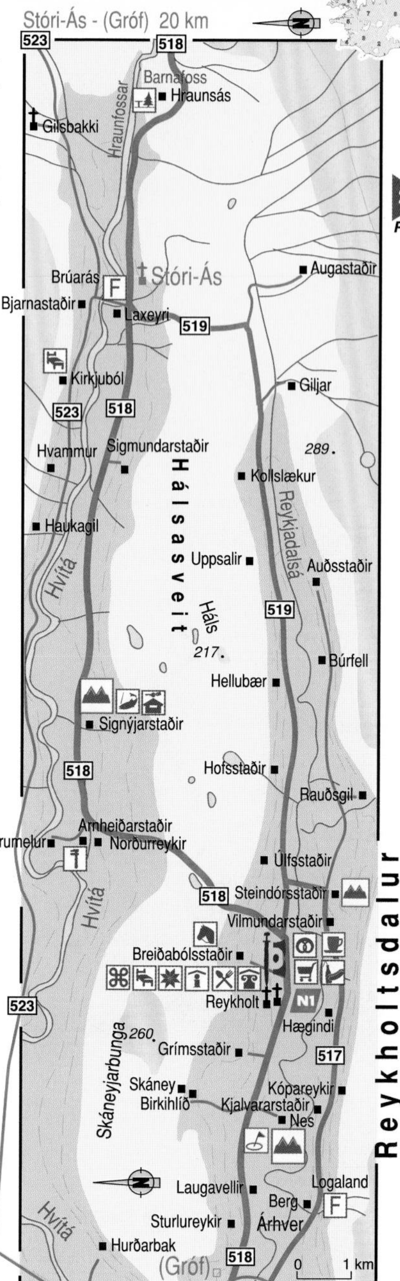

Kalmanstunga-Stóri-Ás 11 km

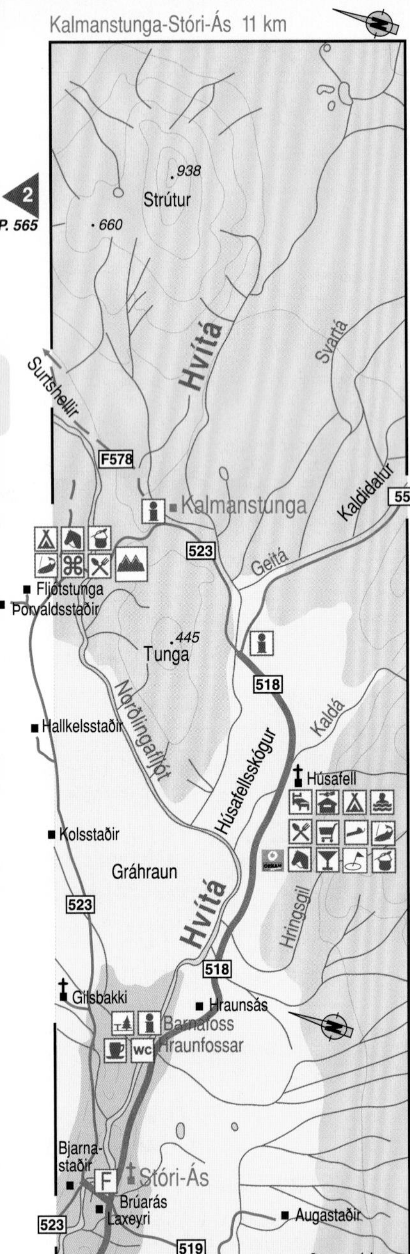

Stóri-Ás-Kalmanstunga 11 km

Kvíar and the Kvíahella at Húsafell.

550 **Eiríksjökull,** (1,675 m) a tuff mountain with a glacier, one of the m beautiful in Iceland. Road accessible by jeeps to the west side, from whe it is an easy 3 hour climb onto the glacier. Excellent view from the top.

Strútur, (938 m) a pyramid-shaped mountain above the far Kalmanstunga. A very difficult jeep-track to the top.

Húsafell, the innermost farm in the Hálsasveit district. Formerly parsonage and church, now a chapel. Made famous among other thin by Snorri Björnsson (1710-1803), versifier, poet and strong man, w tried his strength on the boulder **Kvíahella** (180 kg) which still stands the cemetery. Woods and geothermal heat. An ancient farm has be excavated west of Húsafell. Páll Guðmundsson (b. 1959) a know Icelandic sculptor and artist was born and raised at Húsafell and in fact still lives there. Some is artwork can be found all around Húsafell as sculptures faces on rocks he finds there.

Barnafoss, ("Children's falls") waterfalls in the river Hvítá. Two childr are said to have once fallen off a natural rock bridge over the river a drowned, hence the name. There is now a footbridge over the fal Interesting ravine.

Hraunfossar, ("Lava falls") along the northern bank of the Hvítá riv gorge. Springwater flows from under the lava for about 1 km, cascadi in numerous waterfalls between rocks and trees into the river. A beauti and unusual sight.

Augastaðir, where research into the northern lights has been going since 1984, financed by the Japanese government. This station is simi to those at Mánárbakki and Æðey, but being the headquarters of t research it is larger.

519 **Reykholtsdalsvegur,** p. 261 — 523 **Hvítársíðuvegur,** p. 265
F550 **Kaldadalsvegur,** p. 462 — F578 **Arnarvatnsvegur,** p. 466

The burial cairn Erfingi at Ferstikluháls.

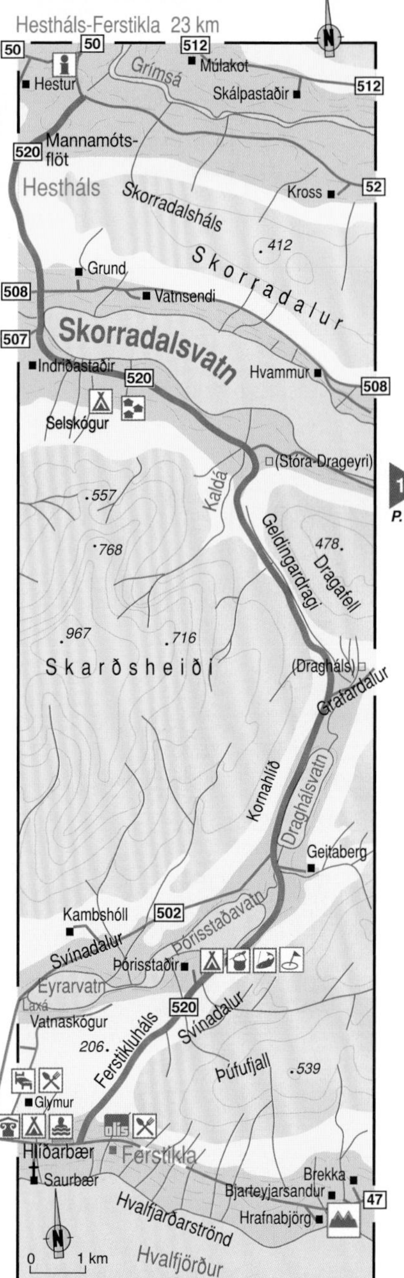

esthals, low bush-covered ridges between the mountain Hestfjall and e Skorradalsháls ridge. Main route from Grund in Skorradalur. The ad is flanked by grasslands where people would hold social gatherings.

rund, a farm. Bishop Brynjólfur Sveinsson (1605-1675) built a house ere which he intended his wife to live in if she was ever widowed.

korradalur, the southernmost of the Borgarfjörður valleys, 28 km long ıt narrow. Widespread birch-bushes. In recent years the Forestry rvice has done extensive forestation there, developing a quite luxuriant nifer woods.

korradalsvatn, a 16 km long lake going right down the valley. Area .3 km², maximum depth 60 m. The bed of the lake was formed by a acier, which left a ridge closing the mouth of the valley. The Andakílsá ver flows out of the lake, its waters being used in the Andakílsá power ation. Trout-fishing.

eldingadragi, ("Gelding trail") now usually called Dragi, a pass 43 m) between the valleys Svínadalur and Skorradalur on the main ghway, with the mountain **Dragafell** (478 m) to the east. The name is rived from the Saga *Harðar saga og Hólmverja*, in which Hörður and s men stole some geldings which had trouble getting across the pass in ep snow. Geldingadragi forms the eastern boundary of Skarðsheiði.

raghals, the uppermost farm in Svínadalur, a crossroads, with tracks to e Grafardalur valley. Four brothers and sisters, poets and writers, were ought up there, one of them, Sveinbjörn Beinteinsson (1924-93), havg been High Priest of the followers of the pagan Nordic religion until s death. There is a statue of Thor at Dragháls, where the pagan ceremoes were performed.

rafardalur, a farm an a home of Sveinbjörn Beinteinson (1924–1993) sherjargoði.

eitaberg, a farm at the southern end of the lake Geitabergsvatn. ormerly a well-known stopping place for travellers.

ínadalur, a valley above Ferstikluháls ridge, in which there are three ite big lakes: **Eyrarvatn,** (or Kambhólsvatn) from which the river ıxá flows, **Þórisstaðavatn** and **Draghálsvatn**, the road going along a rrow isthmus between the latter two. Trout-fishing in the lakes.

erstikluháls, a ridge between the Svínadalur valley and Hvalfjörður. n its northern edge there is a pile of stones by the road, topped by a oss. This is usually called **Erfingi** ("Heir") and is said to be the burial irn of a man whose request to be buried there was refused by the ıthorities. However, when his body was being taken across the ridge, e horses stopped at this point and refused to move another step.

47 **Hvalfjarðarvegur,** p. 222 | 50 **Borgarfjarðarbraut,** p. 229
52 **Uxahryggjavegur,** p. 237 | 502 **Svínadalsvegur,** p. 258
507 **Mófellsstaðavegur,** p. 259 | 508 **Skorradalsvegur,** p. 259
512 **Lundarreykjadalsvegur,** p. 237

Bjarnastaðir-Kalmanstunga 14 km

519 518 523 Kirkjuból Laxeyri Stóriás Bjarnastaðir F Brúarás Hvítá
2 P. 565
Barnafoss Hraunfossar Hraunsás 518 Gilsbakki .376 523 Húsafell (Kolsstaðir) Gráhraun Norðlingafljót 518 Hallkelsstaðir .445 Tunga Þorvaldsstaðir 425. Fljótstunga 523 Kalmanstunga Víðgelmir .438 F578 938. Strútur Kleppavatn Surtshellir Stefánshellir Hallmundarhraun Fiskivatn 0 1 km Hallmundarhellir Eiríksjökull

Kalmanstunga-Bjarnastaðir 14 km

Gilsbakki, a church and manor farm, formerly a parsonage, famous poems and Sagas. Gunnlaugur Ormstunga ("Serpent-tongue"), a hero the Sagas, came from there. The farm's land is rich in salmon and tro and formerly it had swan hunting as well. Fine views.

Kalmanstunga, the easternmost and furthest inland farm in th Borgarfjörður district, over 40 km from the sea. It has always been a su stantial farm, its land extending over the whole of the Arnarvatnshei moor and the Hallmundarhraun lava field. Many trees. It was once on th main horseback route to the north via Kaldidalur, Stórisandur an Arnarvatnsheiði.

Víðgelmir, one of the biggest lava-caves in Iceland, ca. 1 km southeast Fljótstunga, the uppermost farm in the Hvítársíða district. Many stala mites and stalacites, some evidence of ancient dwellings there.

Hallmundarhraun, a lava field from craters at the northwestern edge the Langjökull glacier, reaching north of the Eiríksjökull glacier along th Norðlingafljót river valley to the river Hvítá near Gilsbakki. Parts of it a known as Skógarhraun and Gráhraun. Not difficult to cross in most pla es. Big caves Kalmanshellir, the biggest known cave in Icelan Víðgelmir, Surtshellir and Stefánshellir, and other smaller ones.

Surtshellir, in the Hallmundarhraun lava field about 7 km from the far Kalmanstunga along a road (F578) that is slow but passable for all cars far as the caves. One of Iceland's longest and best-known caves, it is 19 m long, or 3500 m along with the cave Stefánshellir, which connects to it. There are many stories connected with Surtshellir, and clear trac of people having lived there.

Arnarvatnsheiði, extensive moors with many fishing-lakes. Accessib by jeep but very difficult in places. The track runs east between the lak Arnarvatn and Réttarvatn on the Stórisandur sands, whence there are tw routes, one to the valleys Víðidalur and Vatnsdalur, the other east to th Kjalvegur (Road F35) north of the mountain Sandkúlufell.

518 **Hálsasveitarvegur,** p. 262 519 **Reykholtsdalsvegur,** p. 261
F578 **Arnarvatnsvegur,** p. 466

Hraunfossa

523 **Hvítársíðuvegur,** 19 km.

vítársíða, a farming district along the Hvítá river north of Síðumúla-ggir, Hálsasveit to the south.

irkjuból, a farm in the Hvítársíða district, from which come the poets uðmundur Böðvarsson (1904-1974) and his son Böðvar Guðmundsson . 1939).

iðumúli, a farm and church in the lower part of Hvítársíða.

522 **Þverárhlíðarvegur,** 20 km.

verárhlíð, a farming area above the Stafholtstungur district, separated om the Norðurárdalur valley by the Grjótháls ridge. Broad lowlands ith marshes and birch-bushes.

orðtunga, a church. Nice woods, fenced in and put under the protecon of the Forestry Service in 1929.

orðtunguskógur, a forest planted mostly in straight lines – an example "Danish-style" planning from the early 20th century. National Forest.

jarðarholt, a farm and church. Often the home of sheriffs and wealthy ırmers.

verá, a clear river formed from several rivers and streams coming from e lakes on the Tvídægra moors. Considered one of the best salmon-fishg rivers in eland.

524 **Þverárvegur,** 2,6 km.

Hvítársíða Þverárhlíð

P. 565

P. 566

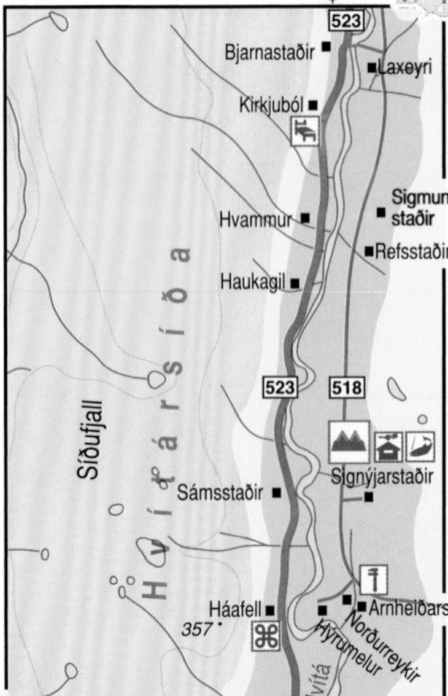

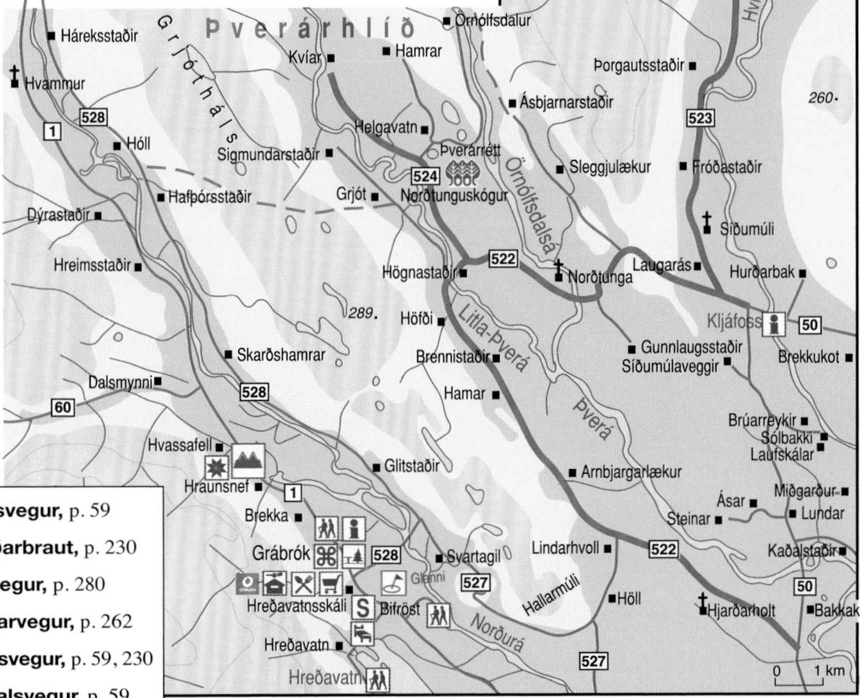

1 **Vesturlandsvegur,** p. 59
50 **Borgarfjarðarbraut,** p. 230
60 **Vestfjarðavegur,** p. 280
518 **Hálsasveitarvegur,** p. 262
527 **Varmalandsvegur,** p. 59, 230
528 **Norðurárdalsvegur,** p. 59

Þverárhlíð Hvítársíða

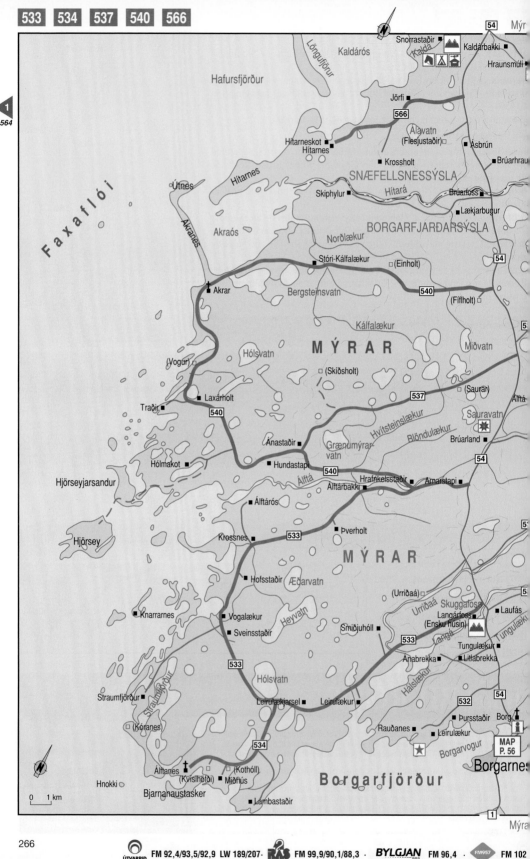

1
P. 564

54 Mýr
Snorrastaðir
Kaldárbakki
Kaldá
Hraunsmúli
Kaldárós
Löngufjörur
Hafursfjörður
Jörfi
566
Álavatn
(Flesjustaðir)
Ásbrún
Hítarneskot
Hítarnes
Krossholt
Brúarhrau
Hítarnes
SNÆFELLSNESSÝSLA
Útnes
Skiphylur
Hítará
Brúarfoss
Faxaflói
Lækjarbugur
Akranes
Akraós
BORGARFJARÐARSÝSLA
Norðlækur
Stóri-Kálfalækur
(Einholt)
54
Akrar
Bergsteinsvatn
540
(Fíflholt)
Kálfalækur
MÝRAR
Hólsvatn
Miðvatn
(Vogur)
(Skíðsholt)
Laxárholt
(Saurar)
537
Álftá
Traðir
540
Sauravatn
Hvítsteinslækur
Blöndulækur
Ánastaðir
Brúarland
Grænumýrarvatn
54
Hólmakot
Hundastapi
540
Hjörseyjarsandur
Álftá
Hrafnkelsstaðir
Arnarstapi
Álftárbakki
Álftárós
Þverholt
533
Krossnes
Hjörsey
MÝRAR
Hofsstaðir
Æðarvatn
(Urriðaá)
Urriðaá
Skuggafoss
Laufás
Knarrarnes
Langárfoss
(Ensku húsin)
Vogalækur
Heyvatn
Smiðjuhóll
Sveinsstaðir
533
Langá
Tungulækur
Tungulækur
Ánabrekka
Litlabrekka
533
Hólsvatn
Hálslækur
Straumfjörður
Straumfjörður
54
Leirulækjarsel
Leirulækur
532
Þursstaðir
Borg
(Kóranes)
Rauðanes
Leirulækur
534
Borgarvogur
MAP P. 56
Borgarnes
Álftanes
(Kothóll)
(Kvíslhöfði)
Miðhús
Borgarfjörður
Hnokki
Bjarnanaustasker
0 1 km
Lambastaðir
1
Mýra

norrastaðir, birthplace of Ólafur Egilsson (1564-;39), pastor, who was taken captive by Algerian pirates hen they attacked the Westman Islands. When he later turned to Iceland he wrote a remarkable account of his periences.

66 Hítarnesvegur, 7,15 km.

órfi, a farm where Víga-Styr was killed, according to e Sagas. He was an aggressive and violent man, a killer ho boasted that he had slain 33 men without making paration for any of them. Finally he slew the farmer at rfi, whose son, a small man and a weakling, killed íga-Styr, dealing him such a blow that the ax stuck in s brain.

ítarnes, formerly a parsonage and church. The home Þórður Kolbeinsson, poet, arch-enemy of Björn ítdælakappi in *Bjarnar saga Hítdælakappa*. Þórður duced Björn's wife and eventually killed Björn, but at lost him the woman's love.

ítará, a good salmon river flowing out of the Hítarvatn ke and into the Akraós estuary. Not far from its mouth the pool Þangbrandshylur and an old ship anchorage.

kiphylur, ("Ship's pool") a farm taking its name from a ool in Hítará now called Þangbrandshylur, where it is id the missionary Þangbrandur moored his boat after ifting into the mouth of Hítará when he came to Iceland 997. Near this pool is the rock **Klukkusteinn** ("Bell ock") which he used as a mooring. A bell-sounding echo heard when this stone is struck with another stone.

40 Hraunhreppsvegur, 33,69 km.

krar, a church and old manor farm where Skallagrímur, ather of Egill in *Egils saga*, is said to have tilled his elds. West of the farm is a 5 km long peninsula, kranes, which with Hítarnes separates the **Akraós** estu-y from the sea.

ogur, a farm. There stayed the first doctors for the ounty of Mýrarsýslu. **Hjörsey,** the largest island off this oast. Was a substantial farm, and a church until 1896, ith rich land and fishing, but has been much damaged y the sea and sand. This was the home of Oddný, the oman Þórður Kolbeinsson and Björn Hítdælakappi ought over.

lftá, a fishing river that separates to counties, Álftanes-reppur and Hraunhreppur.

33 Álftaneshreppsvegur, 31 km.

rnarstapi, a community centre.

Knarrarnes, an island with rich farming land, eider ducks and seals. The sea has broken through the isthmus that connected it with the shore.

537 Skíðholtsvegur, 11,36 km.

Straumfjörður, the next farm to the west of Álftanes, named after the inlet by which it stands. Up until the 20th century there was off and on a trading and rowing-boat fishing centre. Very rocky coast with many skerries. The French research ship *Pourquoi pas?* foundered on the Hnokki skerry in 1936, only one of the 39 men on board surviving. Among those drowned was the French scientist Jean-Baptiste Charcot (1867-1936), the leader of the expedition. In the15th century this was the home of Straumfjarðar-Halla, notorious for sorcery, and the local place-names Höllubjarg ("Halla's crag") and Höllubrunnur ("Halla's well") are named for her. An Icelandic movie deals with both the *Pourqui pas?* disaster and Straumfjarðar-Halla.

Kóranes, formerly a general store run by the father of Ásgeir Ásgeirsson (1894-1972), the 2nd president of Iceland, who was born and raised there.

Leirulækur, a farm, the home of Vigfús Jónsson (1648-1728), best known as Leirulækjar-Fúsi. He was a talented poet, famous for his satirical verse, considered to be a "poet of power". Some of his poems have survived to the present day.

Langárfoss, a farm on north bank of the river Langá. Falls and rapids in the river, good salmon-fishing.

Langá, a salmon river flowing from the Langavatn lake through the valley Grenjadalur. There is a big salmon-ladder near the waterfall Sveðjufoss.

534 Álftanesvegur, 6,31 km.

Álftanes, a church and substantial farm at the end of the Álftanes peninsula, much eroded by the sea. The manor farm for the district since earliest times. Skallagrímur Kveldúlfsson of *Egils saga* lived there his first years as a farmer. Very rich land. Good view from Virki, a small hill in the home-field.

1 Vesturlandsvegur, p. 55
54 Snæfellsnesvegur, p. 238
532 Þursstaðavegur, p. 238
535 Grímsstaðavegur, p. 238
536 Stangarholtsvegur, p. 238
539 Hítardalsvegur, p. 268

(Hólmur)-Hítardalur 10 km

Þröskuldardalur
Svín-
bjúgur
Ok
Tjaldbrekka
BORGARFJARÐARSÝSLA
SNÆFELLSNESSÝSLA
Vatnshlíð
Hítarvatn
Foxufell
Bjarnarhellir
Grafheiði
Hrauntangar
(Hólmur)
Hólmur
Hólmshraun
Klifs-
sandur
Fossabjörg
Rauðakúla
Hítará
Svörtutindar
Valfell
Hítardalur
Bæjarfell
Hróbjörg
(Hróbjargarstaðir)
Hítardalsrétt
Hítardalur
Hítará
(Vellir)

Hítardalur-(Hólmur) 10 km

15
P. 578

Hítarvatn, a big fishing lake, one of the largest in the lowlands of t county, 8 km². In it are several islets where lovely flowering plants gro Out of the lake runs the river Hítará. East of Hítarvatn is the mounta Foxufell (419 m) in which is the cave Bjarnarhellir. There are carvings the cave and a seat has been hewn in the rock.

Hítará, a river flowing out of the Hítarvatn lake and into the Akraós est ary. A good salmon river. The Brúarfoss and Kattarfoss waterfalls are Hítará, opposite Grettisbæli. A bit above Brúarfoss are the Grettisstill stepping stones, where large and small stones lie in an almost straight li across the river. Not far from the mouth of Hítará is the pool Þangbrand hylur and an old ship anchorage where it is said the 10th century missio ary Þangbrandur moored his ship when he was forced to land again aft setting set sail to foreign countries. In a rock by the pool is a moorin ring, called Klukkusteinn ("Bell rock") because of the reverberations th are set up when it is struck. The pool was formerly called Skiphyl ("Ship's pool"), and a nearby farm bears that name.

Hítardalur, a rather broad valley between the mountains Múlaselsm and Fagraskógarfjall. Lava in many places. The valley is closed by a tu fell, Hólmur (334 m), below which was a farm of the same name, t home of Björn Hítdælakappi ("The hero of Hítardalur"). Björn Arngeir son Hítdælakappi, a great hero and poet, lived at Hólmur in the early 1 century. There was a feud between him and another poet, Þórður Kc beinsson of Hítarnes, over the beautiful Oddný eykyndill ("torch of t island") Þorkelsdóttir from Hjörsey, who was engaged to marry Björn b was stolen from him by Þórður. Þórður eventually attacked Björn's hor with a force of 24 and killed him. Oddný became ill at the news and *Bjarnar saga Hítdælakappa* it says that "Þórður would have preferred it Björn were still alive, were that possible, and he himself might reclai the love of his wife."

Hítardalur, an old manor farm and a parsonage and church until 189 Bishop Magnús Einarsson of Skálholt died there in a fire in 1148 alo with 70-80 other people, the greatest loss of life in a fire in Icelandic hi tory. In the home field is Nafnaklettur("Name cliff"), a tuff rock-fa where many people have carved their names, including Ebenez Henderson, the well-known traveller and founder of the Icelandic Bib Society. In the mountain Bæjarfell are two caves, Fjárhellir ("She cave") and Sönghellir ("Song cave"), and in the Drangar cliffs there a clear forms of faces. They are said to be Bárður Snæfellsás and the giar ess Hít, who was said to have lived in Hítardalur, which is named for he An old cornerstone in the Hítardalur church has a carving which the cor mon people considered to be a picture of the giantess Hít, though the cle ics said it was an icon. This stone is in the Hítardalur home field, and cast of it in the National Museum in Reykjavík.

Tthere are 15 km to the Hítardalur farm from Road 54 and 25 km to the lake Hítarvatn.

In Hítardalur valley

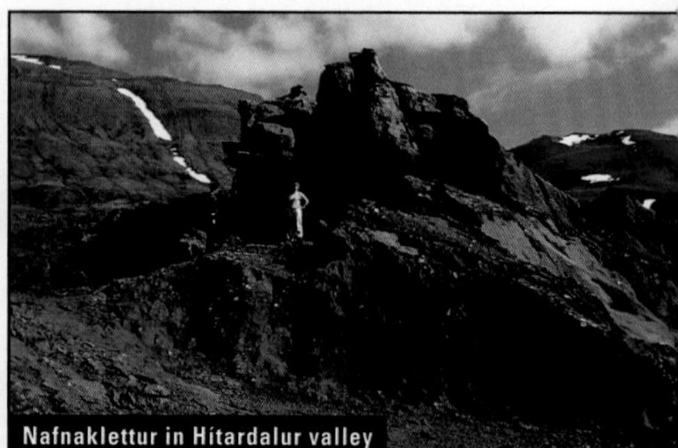
Nafnaklettur in Hítardalur valley

553 LANGAVATNSVEGUR

angavatnsdalur, the valley north of Langavatn. There were farms there settlement times, after which it was grazing land for sheep and bulls ntil the mid-19th century, when the bulls all drowned in the lake. A farm as built there in the early 19th century but the attempt came to tragic end hen first, the farmer got lost and died of exposure when he had gone to e nearest farm to fetch fire, and then the daughter was caught stealing a orse, for food, from Hörðudalur (see Roads 57 and 581). There used to e a track up the valley, over Sópandaskarð pass and along the augardalur valley to Hörðudalur. It was much-travelled in early times, g. in the 13th century, the time of the Sturlungas.

angavatn, a lake, 5 km long and up to 36 m deep, formed by lava hich has dammed the river at the Langá River end. Good fishing. round the turn of last century the fishing rights belonged to that same rench baron C.G. Boilleau that had a salmon canning factory at vítárvellir (see Road 53), and for whom the street Barónstígur in eykjavík is named.

rísatunga, an abandoned farm above Þinghóll, a crossroads of the ajor horseback trails of old. One trail went up the Langavatnsdalur valy, the other up along the Gljúfurá river, behind the mountains and down Hraundalur in the Hraunhreppur district. Before the roads were laid e latter way was often chosen so as to avoid the marshes in the Mýrar istrict. These bogs and marshes were so notorious that farmers from the pper reaches of the Borgarfjörður lands would make their pack-horse ips to the market town very early in the spring, while the ground was ill frozen, travelling as much as two months earlier than most people.

inghóll, ("Assembly hill") north and east of the ford in the river Gljúfrá, below the abandoned farm Grísatunga. It is thought that the spring ssembly of the Þverárþing west of the river Hvítá was held there for a me, probably from the beginning of the land-quarter assemblies (about 65) until they started having assemblies at Faxið by the river Þverá.

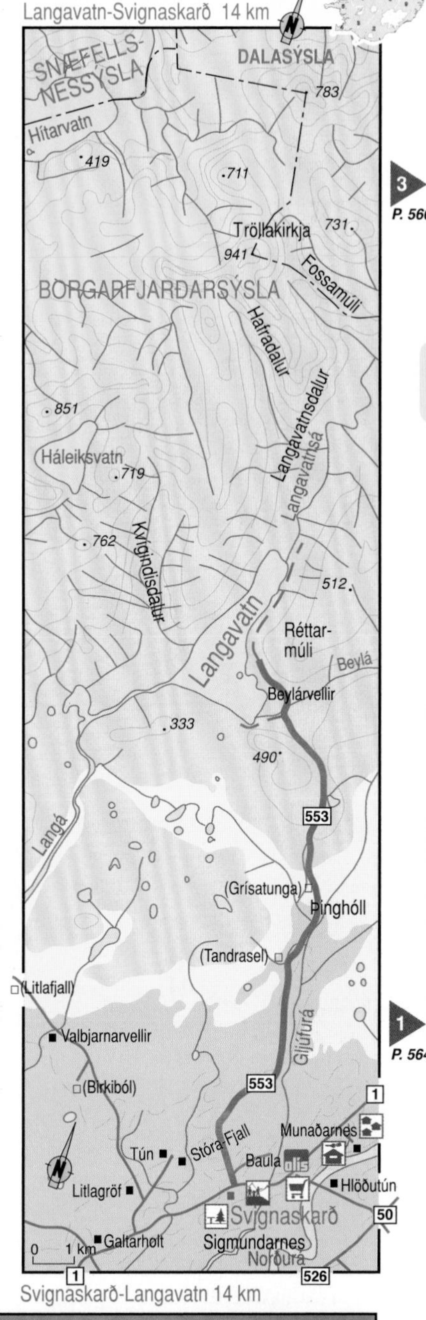

1 Vesturlandsvegur, p. 58
50 Borgarfjarðarbraut, p. 230
526 Stafholtsvegur, p. 230

The old corner stone in Hítardalur church

The portrait of Bárður Snæfellsás and the giantess Hít

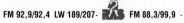

15 P. 578

At Snæfellsjökll.

Stapafell, (526 m) an elongated tuff mountain with much scree, extendir south from the lower slopes of the Snæfellsjökull glacier. On top is a roc **Fellskross**, supposedly the dwelling of the "hidden people" or elves. T the north of Stapafell is the **Sönghellir** ("Singing cave"), known for i echoes. Many names are carved in the rock, including those of Egge Ólafsson and Bjarni Pálsson who travelled the country in the 18th century **Klifahraun,** a lava-field north and east of Stapafell, ending in the sha crags **Sölvahamar,** along the top of which the old travel route la Through the lava runs the river Sandalækur, north of which the riv Grísafossá comes pouring out of the mountain Botnsfjall, to flow into t sea near Sölvahamar. Near the spring source of this river is a popul campsite, where one of the shortest routes onto the Snæfellsjökull glaci starts.

Sleggjubeina, a small stream towards the west end of the Breiðavík ba falling down the mountain **Botnafjall** into a deep, narrow, almost circul gorge, **Rauðfeldargjá**, which is near-invisible from the road. It is poss ble to get quite far up the gorge once the snows have melted, though we lington boots and rainwear are recommended because of spray from t stream. Though the gorge is so narrow, there is sufficient light fro above. On the eastern bank of the stream are the overgrown ruins of t farm Grímsstaðir, where the poet Sigurður Breiðfjörð (1798-1846) live for a time.

Stóri-Kambur, a farm in Breiðavík, often mentioned in *Eyrbyggja sag* the home of Björn Breiðvíkingakappi, "who was friendlier with the mi tress of the house at Fróðá than with her brother, the chieftain Helgafell", the latter being Snorri goði, who eventually drove Björn aw from Iceland. He is thought to have gone west to Vínland (Nor America) where Icelandic travellers said they had met him.

Breiðavík, the pretty little district between the Búðahraun lava field a the village Arnarstapi, along a bay of the same name. Grassy and she tered. A long, yellow sand reef, Hraunlandarif, creates the Miðhúsava lagoon. Above is the rocky mountain **Knarrarklettar**, where many a tra eller has fallen to his death after losing his way on the Fróðárheiði moor **Öxl,** a farm above Búðir below the steep scree mountain **Axlarhyrr** (433 m) where Axlar-Björn ("Bjö from Öxl") lived in the 16th centur He was Iceland's most notorio murderer, said to have killed 18 pe ple, mostly travellers to whom offered hospitality. At Öxl **Ásmundarleiði**, where the settl Ásmundur is said to be buried. Fi view of Faxaflói.

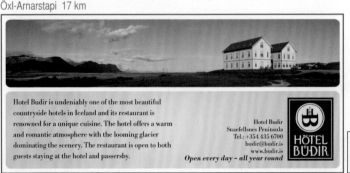

54 Snæfellsnesvegur, p. 245
570 Jökulhálsleið, p. 464-465

572 **Dritvíkurvegur,** 2 km.

Ialarrif, ("Pebble reef") the southern extremity of this coastline, light-ouse. Large, smooth, black pebbles on the beach. A path to Lóndrangar ·om there, 30 minutes walk.

'atnshellir, a 200 m long lava cave on the south slopes of Purkhólahraun ıva flow, considered to be 5-8000 years old. A spiral staircase has been ut into the cave to enable access but entrance is only allowed with guides ·rom the National Park.

óndrangar, two pillar rocks by the sea 15 minutes walk from road, the ıller one being 75 m. The remains of a volcano, scoria with basalt averns. The higher one to the east has been climbed. Seabirds nest there.

valþúfa, on a ridge east of Lóndrangar, probably the remains of a crater. ·elow it is the rock Þúfubjarg, where according to a folktale the poet Kolbeinn jöklaskáld ("the glacier poet") had an encounter with the Devil nd beat him in a verse-making contest.

Iellnar, a village on a pretty coastline with strange rock formations. The ave **Baðstofa** is there, known for the strange light in it. A church, for-ıerly at **Laugarbrekka**, where the cemetery is. Hellnar is the birthplace f Guðríður Þorbjarnardóttir, the wife of Þorfinnur karlsefni. They ttempted to settle in Vínland in the year 1004 and Guðríður gave birth › the first white child to be born in America, Snorri Þorfinnsson. Guðríður was one of the greatest travellers of medieval times, walking ıl the way to Rome, among other things. She eventually settled down at Glaumbær in Skagafjörður (see Road 75). Most Icelanders are thought to e able to trace their ancestry to her. By Gróuhóll in Hellnar there is a pring that goes by the name of **Lífslind Hellnamanna** ("Spring of life"), ut has in recent times been called **Maríulind** ("Spring of Mary") after an nage of the Virgin Mary was put up by the spring. It is belived that the pring has healing powers and it is said that it will never dry up. According › legend, Bishop Guðmundur the Good came to this place in 1230 and long with his fellow travellers had a vision of a woman accompanied by ıree angels. She bade him consecrate the spring, and he did so. Walking oute to Arnarstapi. Just below the main road, to the west of Laugarvatn bove Þinghamar and the ruins of the farm and church at Laugarbrekka, is memorial to Guðríður, and a statue of her by Ásmundur Sveinson.

ınæfellsjökull, (1,446 m) an ancient cone volcano, one of finest moun-ıins in Iceland. An impressive sight from as far away as Reykjavík, from vhere it can be seen in clear weather, seeming to rise from the sea. Many rehistoric eruptions took place in the glacier-covered crater at its peak, nd its slopes are covered with lava. Arctic Adventures are one of those vho offer guided trips to the glacier, with all the neccessary equippment. he walk to the highest peak of the glacier, Þúfur, takes 5-7 hours and is hysically demanding. At the eastern base is a Tourist Association hut, ow in ruins. The glacier dominates the area, the western part of which is overed with lava and known as "under the glacier". In Jules Verne's ovel, *A Journey to the Centre of the Earth*, the entrance to the under-round way was through the crater of Snæfellsjökull. In the eyes of both traditional" believers in the supernatural and new agers Snæfellsjökull as more hidden power than any other mountain.

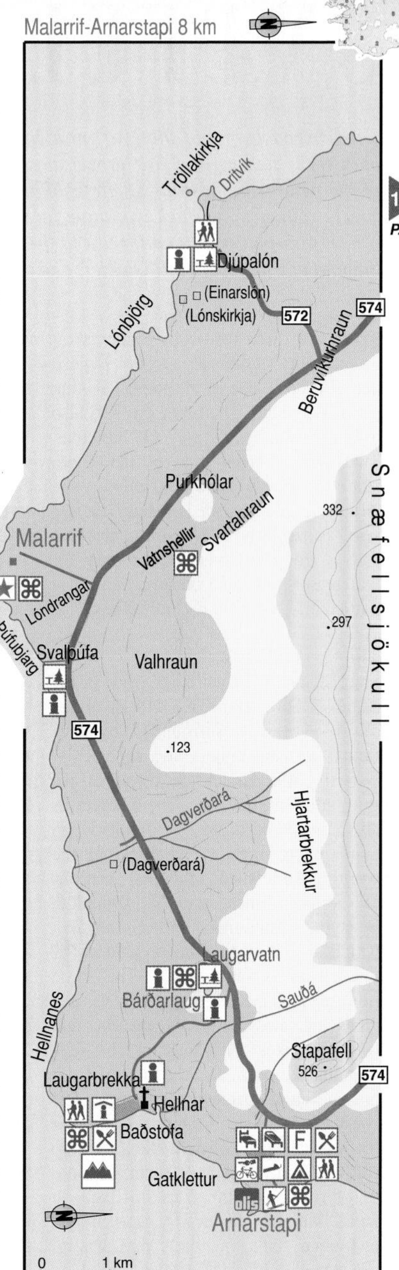

15 P. 578

ırnarstapi, a fishing village in very interest-ıg natural surroundings, with weird basalt olumns, gorges and caves by the coast, in ıost of which there are populous sea-bird olonies. The most famous cliff is **Gatklettur** 'Hole cliff'), through which the sea spouts in tormy weather. The path to the caves is eached through the harbour and goes along ıe top of the cliffs so one sees the caves, and ıe nesting birds, from above. Walking route › Hellnar.

Lóndrangar

SNÆFELLSBÆR

Snæfellsbær is one of the four municipalities on Snæfellsnes Peninsula, with about 1720 inhabitants. The mai industry is fishing and fish processing, but the tourism industry is growing rapidly. Snæfellsbær covers 680 km of the peninsula, hosting Snæfellsjökull Glacier at its centre, as part of The Snæfellsjökull National Park whic covers 160km². The Park is unique for being the only National Park in Iceland with boundaries to the ocean, an is rich with places that connect it to the Icelandic fishing heritage. The Park's Visitor Centre is at Hellnar, right the foot of Snæfellsjökull Glacier, and is open daily during the summer months.

There are three towns in Snæfellsbær municipality. Ólafsvík is the largest, and also hosts one of the largest fishing ports in Iceland. The other are Rif, also a big fishing port, and Hellissandur. Two tiny villages are on the south side of the peninsula, Hellnar and Arnarstapi. Arnarstapi is a busy fishing port, particularly in the summer time, and is frequently visited not only for that reason, but also because it is in a particularly beautiful natural setting.

The National Park:
Snæfellsjökull Glacier is the pride of the National Park. It rises 1.446 m above sea level and is surrounded by lava fields, dormant craters and spectacular coastal cliffs. Under the cover of ice is a dormant volcano. The Glacier is also considered to be one of the seven major energy centres (chakras) of the world. Renowned fishing stations of former times are at Djúpalón, Beruvík, Lóndrangar and Gufuskálar, which are all within the boundaries of Snæfellsjökull National Park. The Arctic flora and fauna is rich with various types of moss, low vegetation and flowers. Foxes can sometimes be seen roaming the park, and the coastal cliffs host different species of sea birds. The coast opens to the Atlantic Ocean and the waves have polished the lava into soft and shiny stones or formed it into rough rocks with the shapes of faces in them. Many hiking trails, marked and unmarked, fantastic view, and several beaches with black or golden sand. One can drive around Snæfellsjökull Glacier by using road 574, and the snowline of the Glacier can also be accessed by road 570, which is a gravel road. Along the road is Sönghellir cave, whose name dates back to the first settlers in this area, who probably settled here in the early nine hundreds.

Tours to remember:
Snjófell at Arnarstapi offers tours on snowmobiles or snow-cats to the top of Snæfellsjökull Glacier on daily basis. Tours are however subject to weather and conditions on the ice. The National Park has scheduled guided hiking tours and guided tours in to Vatnshellir cave during the summer time. The cave Vatnshellir is a 100m long lava cave, which is believed to be approximately 5-8000 years old. Further information can at The National parks visitors centre at Hellnar.

Healing water:
Lýsuhólslaug is a geothermal mineral water pool on the southern part of Snæfellsnes Peninsula, and it is the only one of its kind in Iceland. A soak there is both healing and relaxing.

Hiking trails:
There are many marked and unmarked hiking trails in Snæfellsbær. One of the most popular ones is the hiking trail from Arnarstapi to Hellnar. It takes you along a very special coastal area, with pot-holes, basalt columns and natural stone arches. The cliffs host kittiwakes, fulmars and seagulls and the grounds, the aggressive arctic tern. Keep your hat on!

Fishing trips and sea bird hunting:
Nesvargar Hunting offers amazing sea fishing trips, cruising, adventurous seabird hunting and more. The company operats from Ólafsvík

Bird watching:
The area between Hellissandur and Rif hosts one of the largest breeding ground in the world for the arctic tern. The tern is not the only bird to choose this area for breeding. Eider ducks and other species of birds can be found there as well. A large sign with names of all the birds is situated by the access road to Rif.

Whale watching:
Trips from Ólafsvík with Láki Tours which offer ocean adventures on a beautiful oak fishing vessel, specially modified for tourists.

Golf – Horse trekking:
Two golf courses are in Snæfellsbæ One is located at Langaholt i Staðarsveit, and the other near Ólafsvík The farms at Lýsuhóll, and Brimilsvelli offer horse trekking tours.

Heritage, historical and informatio centres:
For a small rural municipality Snæfellsbær has taken good care c its heritage and visitors can learn lot about the people who live ther today, and have lived there in the pas The Snæfellsjökull National Park' Visitor Centre is at Hellnar with a ver special and informative exhibitior The Sjóminjasafnið heritage centre a Hellissandur shows how life used to b in the old fishing stations. If you want t view some of the fish that the fisherme go out to catch on daily basis, you ca visit Sjávarsafnið in Ólafsvík.
Pakkhúsið in Ólafsvík has preserve the heritage from the 19th and 20t century, and also craft market. Th tourist information centre is locate in Átthagastofa in Ólafsvík (close t Pakkhúsið) tel: **00 354 433 6929** o **info@snb.is**

Accommodation/restaurants:
Many hotels and guesthouses offe various types of accommodation i Snæfellsbær, anywhere from B&B to luxury hotels. There a quite a fev cafes and restaurants in Snæfellsbæ that offers many different types c food, some of which offer local se food. Further information abou accommodation or restaurants can b found at **www.west.is** and the touris information centre in Átthagastofa tel: **00 354 433 6929** or **info@snb.is**

A sustainable destination:
Snæfellsbær municipality, along with th other four municipalities on Snæfellsne Peninsula, joined GREEN GLOBE i 2003, today know as EARTH CHECK EARTH CHECK is an internationa organization that certifies sustainabl tourism and communities worldwide.

15 P. 578

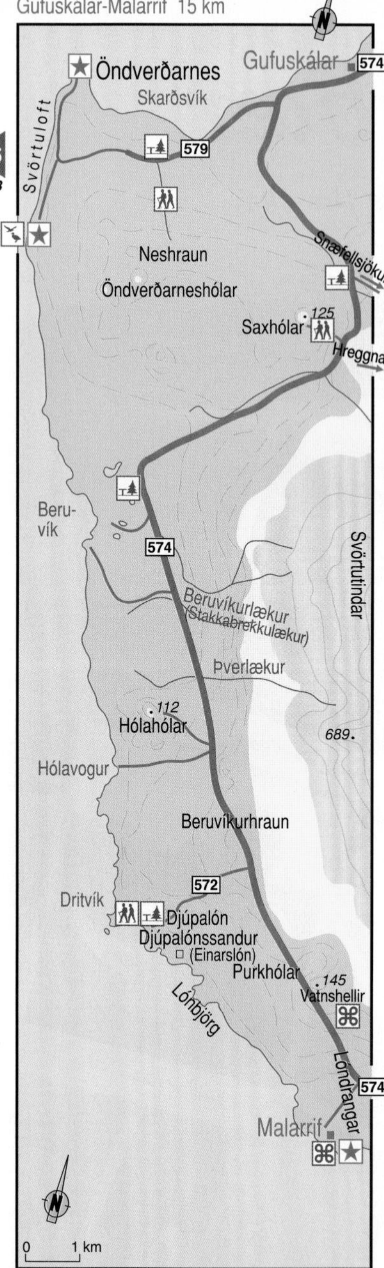

Malarrif-Gufuskálar 15 km

Svörtuloft

Móðulækur, a small stream which legend has it was once a big river bu sank into the ground.

Hreggnasi, (469 m) a peak at the end of a tuff ridge sticking north from th glacier. The highest peak on the ridge, **Bárðarkista** ("Bárður's chest") (66 m), is said to be where Bárður Snæfellsás' treasure is hidden.

Saxhóll, a crater. Easy climb and a great view at the top.

Öndverðarnes, the extreme tip of the Snæfellsnes peninsula. The are between Öndverðarnes and Rif is a great place for bird watching. Formerly substantial farm with a chapel, now a lighthouse. Deep in the ground is th old well, **Fálki**, with 18 steps leading down to it. South of Öndverðarnes ar cliffs known as **Svörtuloft** ("Black skies"), where ships have been wrecked Nearby is the big Neshraun lava field, with many old craters such a Öndverðarneshólar, Saxhóll etc.

Beruvík, an area where there once were many farms, now abandoned. Som remains of the old fishing-station and settlement.

Hólahólar, old craters, one of which, Berudalur, is like a beautiful, natura amphitheatre, open on one side and with a grassy bottom.

Dritvík, for centuries on of the best and busiest fishing-stations in Iceland often as many as 60 boats with 300-400 fishermen rowing from there. Rescu hut. To the east is a large rock, Tröllakirkja ("Giants' church"), and in the middle of the inlet another, known as Bárðarskip (Bárður's ship"). A **Djúpalónssandur** between Dritvík and Einarslón are four well-known lifting-stones, on which the fishermen tested their strength. The biggest is know as Fullsterkur ("Fully-strong"), weighs 154 kg and is very difficult to lift Hálfsterkur ("Half-strong") is 100 kg, Hálfdrættingur ("Weakling"), 54 kg an Amlóði ("Useless"), 23 kg. Men who could not lift Hálfdrættingur were no accepted on the fishing boats. There is a road to Djúpalónssandur.

Einarslón, an abandoned farm, once a church.

579 Öndverðanesvegur, 6,99 km.

574 ÚTNESVEGUR

)lafsvík, (pop. 1,010) a fishing town below the mountain Enni. There is a retty waterfall in the mountainside above it, beyond which is the steep peak Irói.

:nni, (410 m) a mountain falling sheer to the sea, with cliffs. The travel route sed to be along the foot of the cliffs, passable when the tides were right, and angerous because of falling rocks and surf. The mountain was thought to be aunted.

svöðufoss, a waterfall in the river Hólmkelsá, visible from the road.

Rif, (pop. 163) a village which was once the most important fishing and trading centre on the Snæfellsnes peninsula. It is again gaining importance with the ecent building of a new harbour and the resultant growth in the fishing industry. In 1467 English buccaneers killed the local governor, Björn Þorleifsson, ut his widow Ólöf took dreadful revenge. This supposedly included getting he King of Denmark to wage war on England, making her the only Icelander o be responsible for a war between nations. Björnssteinn, the stone where Björn was slain, can still be seen. Near by there is a monument with information about the landing place at Rif which was used by fishermen in medieval imes. There is also an airport.

ngjaldshóll, a church, ancient manor farm and the main setting of *Víglundar aga*. Often the residence of sheriffs and other important officials. The church s believed to be the oldest concrete church in the world, built in 1903. A painting in the church by Áki Gränz shows Christopher Columbus conversing with the local clergyman in 1477 about the voyages of celanders to the west (Vinland – now America). Life stories of Columbus indicate that he visited this part of Iceland in the company of English merchants at Rif in order to get information about the earlier Viking voyages to the west. View dial.

Keflavíkurbjarg, a cliff between Hellissandur and Rif. On its west side s **Balalind**, a water source which is claimed to have healing powers. A ign by the road leads to the cliff.

Hellissandur, (pop. 389) Icelands oldest fishing village. A trading and community centre. Hotel, maritime museum and a small park. There is a oad leading to Snæfellsjökull, great view.

Gufuskálar, formerly the site of a U.S. loran station with a 420 m high mast, he highest construction in Iceland and at one time (1963) the highest in Europe. It is now to used for long-wave broadcasts of the Icelandic National Radio and is also a training center for the Icelandic Lifesaving Association. Many remains of the old fish-drying installations from the time when there was a great deal of rowing-boat fishing there.

rskra brunnur, ("Well of the Irishmen") a well from the time of the settlement, in the fields near Gufuskálar, Írskra kirkja ("Church of the Irishmen") uins on the shore and Írskra búðir ("Irishmen's booth") ruins at the edge of the ava field. At **Gufuskálavör** (vör = landing) one can see grooves worn in the ock over the ages where the rowingboats were pulled ashore. Memorial to Elínborg Þorbjarnardóttir, the last person to make her home there, unveiled in 1987.

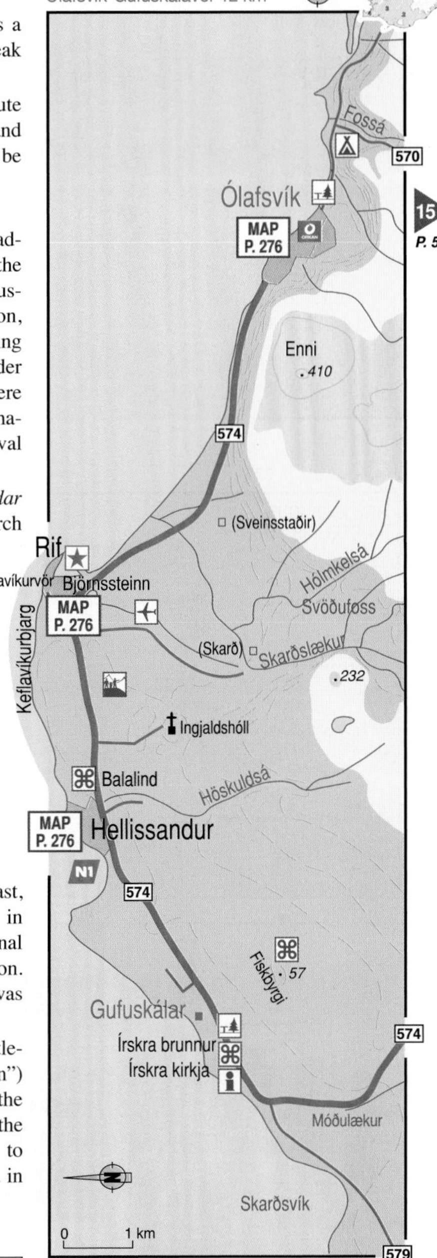

54 **Snæfellsnesvegur,** p. 245 570 **Jökulhálsleið** p. 465-465
579 **Öndverðanesvegur** p. 274

Amlóði, Hálfdrættingur, Hálfsterkur and Fullsterkur

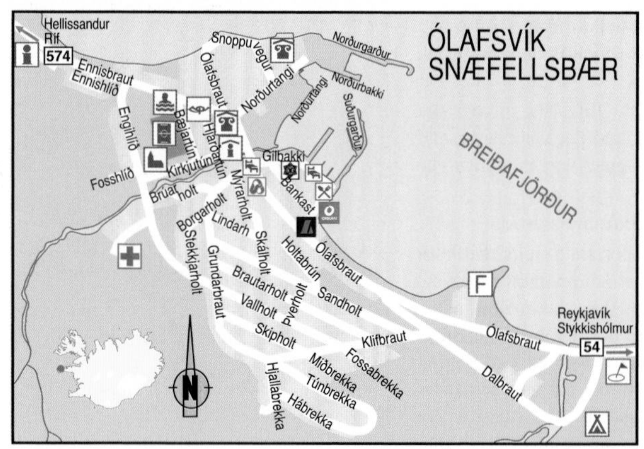

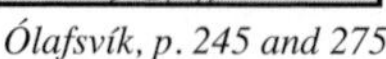
Ólafsvík, p. 245 and 275

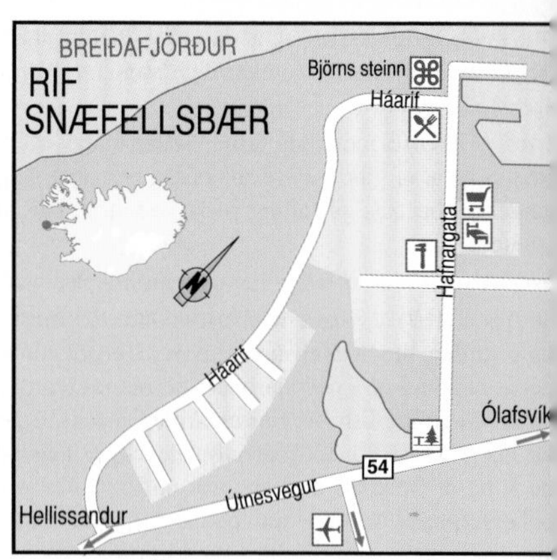

Rif, p. 27

Hellissandur, p. 275.

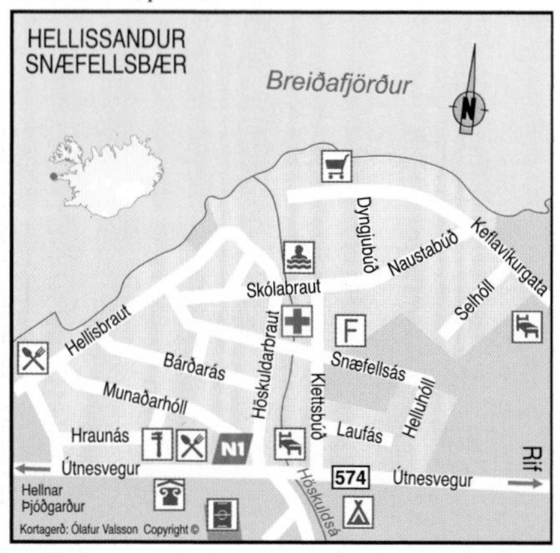

586 HAUKADALSVEGUR

Haukadalsskarð, a pass that was once an important route from the Haukadalur valley over to Hrútafjörður in the north. Little used now but passable for jeeps in summer.

Jörfi, a farm below the peak **Jörfahnúkur** (714 m). Notorious festivities (Jörfagleði) were held there at one time, but the debauchery is said to have been so great that they were abolished early in the 18th century and have never been revived. It is said that 19 illegitimate children were conceived at the last Jörfagleði, which was the last straw for the authorities. A folktale states that one winter a traveller asked for lodging at Jörfi for himself and his horses, but was refused. This enraged the visitor who said the local farmer would lose some of his own horses. At about the same time the following year the farmer's horses became terrified without a reason, rushed up the nearby peak and fell to their deaths on the slippery ice slopes.

Leikskálar, a farm where the same family, in a direct male line, lived for two centuries, being named alternately Bergþór and Þorvarður.

Eiríksstaðir in Haukadalur.

Eiríksstaðir, an abandoned farm on the land of Stóra-Vatnshorn, where Eric the Red lived before he went to Greenland. It is believed that his son Leifur the Lucky Eiríksson was born there. Archaeological research has been conducted in the area recently, showing that the timeline described in the sagas can be verified to a considerable extent. The excavations will be made accessible to the public, and nearby a so-called "theoretical house" has been built. Guides in Viking Age costume describe the lifestyle of the Viking settlers and serve samples of traditional food. Some ruins of the house and smithy still visible - now protected. This is an attempt to show what the farm Eiríksstaðir may have looked like when it was inhabited. Open from June 1st until September 1st from 9:00 to 18:00 every day.

Stóra-Vatnshorn, a church. The same family has lived there since 1658.

Haukadalur, a fairly long, fertile valley going east. At its lower end is **Haukadalsvatn**, a 4 km long fishing-lake, from which flows Haukadalsá, a good salmon river. Formerly well wooded but now hardly any trees.

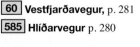

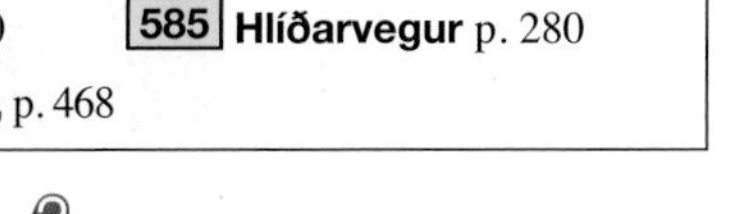

54 **Snæfellsnesvegur,** p. 250 — 60 **Vestfjarðavegur,** p. 281

582 **Hálsabæjarvegur** p. 280 — 585 **Hlíðarvegur** p. 280

F586 **Haukadalsskarðsvegur,** p. 468

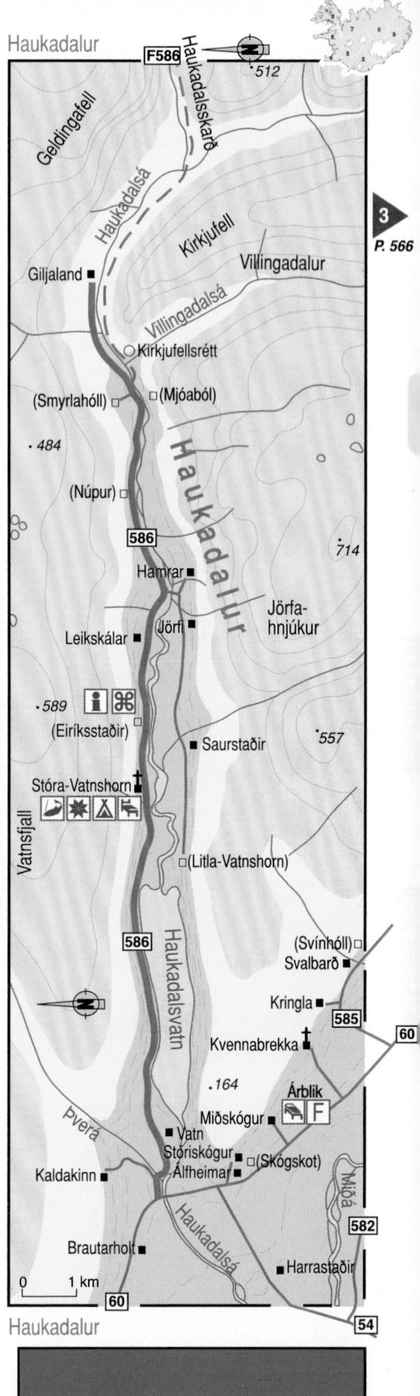

3
P. 566

Fellsströnd

Klakkeyjar
Dagverðarnes
590
Kvennahóll
(Arnarbæli) (Stakkaberg)
Ormsstaðir
(Víghólsstaðir)
Vogur
Klofningsfjall
Hvammsfjörður
FELLSSTRÖND
(Ytrafell)
(Stóra-Tunga)
(Galtartunga)
(Harrastaðir)
(Galtardalur)
593
Galtardalur
(Orrahóll)
Lyngbrekka
.249
Tungumúli
(Svínaskógur)
Staðarfell
Hallsstaðir
Flekkudalsá
.640
(Skógar)
590
Valbúfa
(Skorravík)
Breiðabólsstaður
175 .
(Hafursstaðir)
(Hóll)
Hólsá
Rauðbarðaholt
(Ketilsstaðir)
613 .
(Teigur)
(Knarrarhöfn)
(Kýrunnarstaðir)
(Skafsstaðir)
590
Hvammur
Hofakur
Hvammsfjörður
Skerðingsstaðir
60
Hólar
Krosshólar
Laxá
0 1 km
60

15 P. 578

3 P. 566

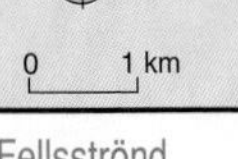

Fellsströnd

Klakkeyjar, two high, cone-shaped islands. Eric the Red equipped his ship there before setting off to discover Greenland.

Hrappsey, the most famous island in the county of Dalasýsla. Formerly a substantial farm, now abandoned. From 1773-95 there was a printing-press there.

Dagverðarnes, a church on a peninsula of the same name, which is deeply indented with many outlying islands.

Vogur, there is a memorial to Bjarni Jónsson (1863–1926), poet at Vogur.

593 Efribyggðarvegur, 15 km.

Galtardalur, an abandoned farm. Birthplace of the grammarians Dr Guðbrandur Vigfússon (1827-89), who worked in Copenhagen and Oxford and completed an Icelandic-English Dictionary often associated with Cleasby, and Björn Guðfinnsson (1905-50), an effective and influential grammarian who wrote text-books on his subject.

Staðarfell, a manor farm through the ages, on very good land. Church. Trading place and small harbour. There was a school of domestic science there 1927-76 which is now a rehabilitation centre for alcoholics.

Fellsströnd, the coast along Hvammsfjörður. Just above the shore is a steep elongated mountain, beyond which is some settled lowland named Efribyggð.

Hvammur, a church and famous Saga-place. The land settled by Auður djúpúðga ("the wise") and long occupied by her descendants. Auður was the daughter of Ketill Suðureyjajarl ("Earl of the Hebrides") and married king Ólafur hvíti of Dublin. After their son Þorsteinn died in battle in Scotland Auður came to Iceland with her children and grand-children around the year 890, bringing with her a large number of Scots and Irishmen. Hvammur was also the home of Hvamm-Sturla, forebear of the Sturlunga family, and the birthplace of the writer and law-speaker Snorri Sturluson and his brothers (see Road 518, Reykholt). In the churchyard there is a memorial in honour of Snorri Sturluson, built by the people of Borgarfjörður in 1979 on the 800th anniversary of his birth.

Krosshólar, large crags. *Landnámabók* ("The Book of Settlements") states that Auður djúpúðga had a cross raised there, where she went to pray. The remains of her first farm, Auðartóttir, nearby. A stone cross was erected on the crags in 1965. Auður's descendants considered Krosshólar a holy place.

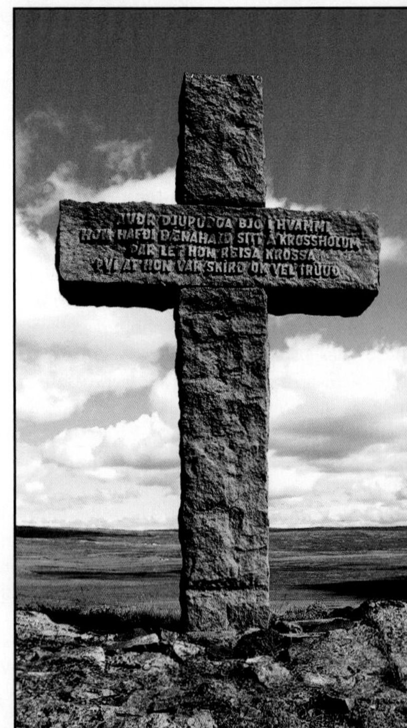

The stone cross at Krosshólar

60 **Vestfjarðavegur,** p. 282

Klofningur.

594 Staðarhólsvegur, 3,34 km.

Staðarhóll, formerly a very big manor farm where the Saga writer and district governor Sturla Þórðarson lived.

Salthólmavík, ("Salty islet bay") formerly a trading centre in Saurbær. No harbour but a strong ebbtide. The name indicates salt production at some time.

Akureyjar, a farm.

Tindar, an abandoned farm where lignite was mined, last ca. 1960.

Búðardalur, a farm and former church, occupied by many local leaders. Late in the 18th century Magnús Ketilsson (1732-1803), sheriff and prolific writer, lived there. He experimented with land cultivation.

Skarð, a historic manor farm which has been in the possession of the same family since the 11th century, and probably from the first settlement days. Original settler Geirmundur heljarskinn, the noblest of the original settlers. Skarð was best know when Björn Þorleifsson, sub-governor, and his wife Ólöf Loftsdóttir lived there in the 15th century. In the church is an altarpiece together with other valuable objects believed to have been donated by Ólöf. Two famous vellum manuscripts come from Skarð, both called *Skarðsbók*, the Law-book and the Sagas of Saints. A small harbour nearby where there was once a trading post, also a lignite mine.

Skarðsströnd, the coast between Klofningur and Saurbær. Little lowland but small valleys and many islands.

Klofningsfjall, ("Cloven mountain") (496 m) the outermost mountain in the range. View dial. Great view over the islands in Breiðafjörður fjord.

Klofningur, a belt of rock west of the mountain Klofningsfjall, cleft by a deep chasm through which the highroad goes. Klofningsvegur (Road 590) is 83 km long.

60 Vestfjarðavegur, p. 282

3 P. 566

15 P. 578

For further information:

A unique event occurred in the summer of 1879 when an eagle seized a two-year-old girl named Ragnheiður Eyjólfsdóttir (1877-1959) in the field by the farm Skarð, soared to a great height and flew towards the mountain Krossfjall where it had made a nest. The people of the farm were bringing in the hay when the abduction took place and at first it seemed that little could be done to save the child. One of the locals, Bogi Kristjánsson (1851-1937), was an impulsive and quick-thinking man who was also a good shot. Shooting the eagle crossed his mind but he realised this could only be done as a last result, as he might hit the child by accident and anyway she would plummet to earth if the bird was killed. He therefore grabbed a long pole, mounted a fleet horse and set out in the direction of Krossfjall and the eagle's nest. The girl was big for her age and it soon became obvious that the eagle had taken on more than it could handle, for as it drew near the mountain it tired and lost sufficient altitude for Bogi to hit it in one wing with the pole and force it down. The bird promptly released its burden and flew off. It had grabbed the child's clothes so she had hardly any wounds to speak of; it had also grabbed her hair with its beak. The girl was unconscious when she was rescued. For the first few days after the incident she was gloomy and distracted but she suffered no permanent damage from this unexpected flight.

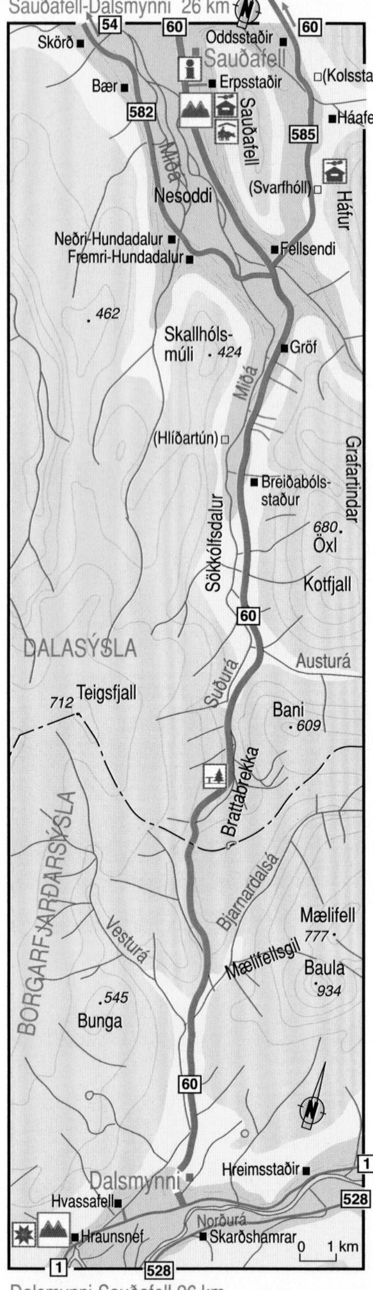

3 P. 566

585 **Hlíðarvegur,** 8,6 km.

Sauðafell, a farm at the foot of a mountain of the same name, a manor farm through the ages. The home of Sturla Sighvatsson when the men of Vatnsfjörður attacked it in January 1229, committing gross atrocities against the place and its people, as related in *Sturlunga saga*. Sturla himself escaped as he happened to be away from home that day, and he took revenge by killing the Vatnsfjörður brothers when they were passing Sauðafell three years later. Governor Hrafn Oddsson (1226-1289) lived at Sauðafell. He was made Governor over Iceland, and thus the most powerful man in the country, in 1279. He is best known for his firm opposition to the episcopal powers. It was at Sauðafell that Daði Guðmundsson from Snóksdalur took captive Jón Arason, the last Catholic Bishop, and his sons, later sending them to Skálholt (see Road 31) where they were executed November 7, 1550. Birthplace of Jakob Jóhannesson Smári (1889-1972), well-known poet, grammarian and translator.

Erpsstaðir, a farm, originally settled by Erpur, son of a Scottish earl and an Irish princess. Now a comprehensive tourist services are offered there, while the farm also makes cheeses, ice cream and the Icelandic milk product skyr and sells these directly to the consumer. Visitors can also get information about agriculture and the local community.

Nesoddi, a grassy area by the Miðá river. There is a horse-racing course.

Fellsendi, a substantial farm at the southern end of Sauðafell. An old people's home there was built with money bequeathed to the county by the son of a local farmer.

582 **Hálsabæjarvegur,** 12,2 km to road 54, p. 250.

Bær, home of Jón Sigurðsson (ca. 1685-1720), lawwriter and poet.

Hlíðartún, an abandoned farm in Sökkólfsdalur valley.

Breiðabólsstaður, in the valley Sökkólfsdalur, long a substantial farm, the innermost farm north of Brattabrekka.

Bani, ("Death") (609 m) a high rocky mountain, on the slopes of which is a grassy patch called Grettisbæli, where Grettir the strong is said to have dwelt. Bani is said to be so called because 18 people once died on its slopes.

Brattabrekka, ("Steep slope") the road from Highway 1 in the Norðurárdalur valley west to the Dalir district, max. height 402 m. The actual Brattabrekka is the slope down into the Dalir district, where the former post-route lay. The road goes up Bjarnardalur through Miðdalur and down to Suðurárdalur.

Dalsmynni, p. 59.

1 **Vesturlandsvegur,** p. 59

528 **Norðurárdalsvegur,** p. 59

54 **Snæfellsnesvegur,** p. 250

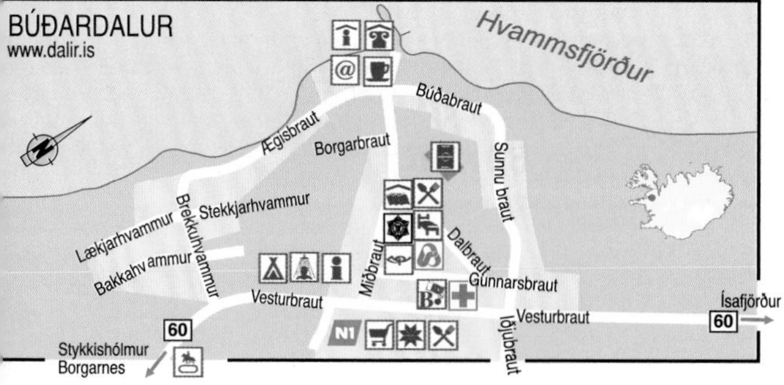

Ásgarður-Sauðafell 33 km

.sgarður, a substantial farm, formerly also a church. In the land of \sgarður there is a cone-shaped cliff which is said to be inhabited by lves. Old legend has it that if a group of people walk to the top of the liff in order of age without looking back, their wishes will be helped long if spoken on top of the cliff.

'áskrúð, a salmon river, its source on distant Gaflfellsheiði moor.

.járskógar, ("The woods of the river Ljá") the largest farm in Dalasýsla ounty. Birthplace of Jón Jónsson (1914-45), poet and singer, a memorial ɔ him by the road. At now abandoned **Ljárskógasel**, nearby, the poet óhannes úr Kötlum (1899-1972) was brought up. In Búðardalur, a monunent was erected in memory of Jóhannes in 1999. Many farms in)alasýsla are named after woods, though there are now few trees. On the ınd of Ljárskógar, beside the highway, are the so-called **Klofasteinar** "Cleft stones"), considered by some to be the residence of "hidden peo›le". The stones have twice been moved during roadworks, being replaced 1 their original position the second time, in 1995. At that time the ontractors ran into a number of difficulties, sometimes said to e due to the "hidden people's" being displeased.

.já, a small river flowing through the small valley Ljárdalur.

'úðardalur, (pop. 252) a village in Dalabyggð county on the hores of Hvammsfjörður fjord. It has always been easy to reach ıe village from other regions. Throughout the area, history is vident in numerous place names, not least those of the Laxdæla Saga.)f the 686 inhabitants of Dalabyggð municipality, 249 live in the vilıge, which offers all basic services such as a compulsory school, ealth centre, the veterinarian and district commissioner, a commuity centre and a dairy which produces the popular Höfðingi, Dala'rja and Dala-Brie cheeses. Bogi Sigurðsson (1858-1930), honured as Father of the Village, opened the first store in Búðardalur 1 1899. A former county sheriff, Þorsteinn Þorsteinsson, used to ve here; he was one of Iceland's leading book collectors, though his brary has now been transferred to Skálholt in South Iceland. Down y the small-craft harbour, Leifsbúð houses a tourist information centre, restaurant and exhibits from the local art and heritage museums.

'aurar, once the home of Saura-Gísli (1820-94), a trouble-maker and ›orn in the flesh of the authorities.

.ambsnes, ("Comb peninsula") where the *Laxdæla saga* says the settler ıuður djúpúðga lost her comb, hence the name.

'vennabrekka, a parsonage and church. Birthplace of Árni Magnússon, rofessor and manuscript collector (1663-1730). The Árni Magnússon ıstitute in Reykjavík is based on his collection and bears his name.

Sauðafell-Ásgarður 33 km

3 P. 566

54 **Snæfellsnesvegur,** p. 250
582 **Hálsabæjarvegur,** p. 280
586 **Haukadalsvegur,** p. 277
590 **Klofningsvegur,** p. 278
59 **Laxárdalsvegur,** p. 257
585 **Hlíðavegur,** p. 280
587 **Hjarðarholtsvegur,** p. 257

3 P. 566

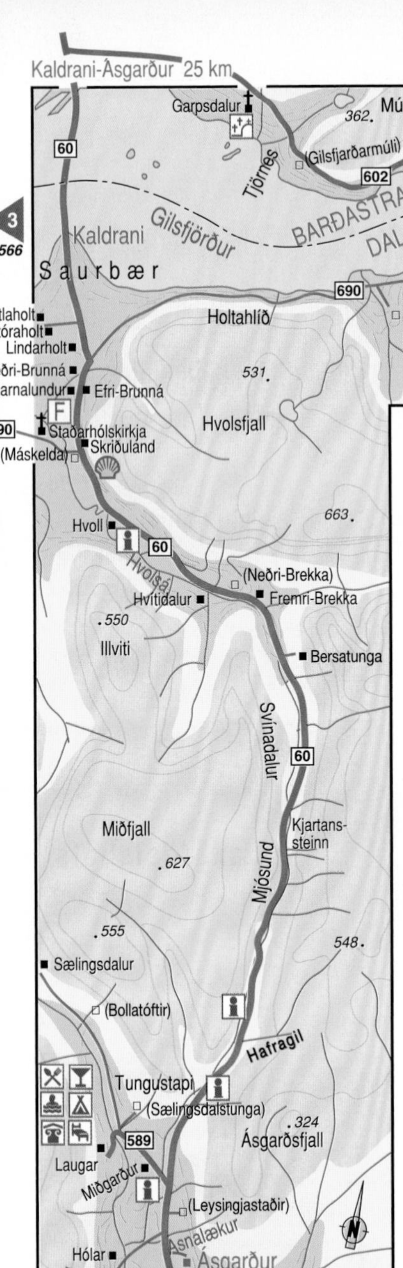

602 **Garpsdalsvegur,** 12,75 km going off Road 60 at the northern end of the bridge across Gilsfjörður, as far as the junction with Road 690 to Steinadalsheiði.

Garpsdalur, a church, a parsonage until 1890. Early in the 19th century a female ghost terrified the local inhabitants. The buildings shook, doors and a boat were broken up and all loose objects were thrown back and forth.

Gilsfjarðarbrekka, the easternmost farm in Barðastrandarsýsla county.

Gilsfjörður, the bridge over this fjord has shortened Road 60 by about 17 km.

Stóraholt, a farm having some of the best land in the area. A good beach for gathering edible seaweed, several churches, including Hólar cathedral, having gathering rights. Airstrip.

Kirkjuhvoll, in the centre of the Saurbær district. Church built in 1900 when two parishes (Staðarhóll and Hvoll) were united. Community centre **Tjarnarlundur**.

Skriðuland, grocery store.

Hvoll, a farm and parsonage. The farm has more meadows than any other in the district. A good deal of falling rock from the mountainside.

Illviti, (550 m) a mountain above the farm Hvítidalur.

Saurbær, the northernmost district in the Dalasýsla county, surrounded by high peaks, grassy but marshy. Many small valleys and two bigger ones: Staðarhólsdalur and Hvolsdalur, the road going through the latter.

Bersatunga, the uppermost farm in Hvolsdalur, where he poet Stefán frá Hvítadal ended his days. The name comes from Hólmgöngu-Bersi ("Bersi of the islet-duels") in the Sagas.

Kjartanssteinn, a big stone in the Svínadalur valley, where it is said Kjartan Ólafsson of *Laxdæla saga* was killed.

Hafragil, it was there were Bolli and Guðrún Ósvífursdóttir´s brothers waited for Kjartan Ólafsson an then slaid him.

Svínadalur, a deep, narrow valley.

589 **Sælingsdalsvegur,** 2,5 km.

Gilsfjörður. The inset photograph shows Tungustapi.

'ungustapi, a big crag below the farm Sælingsdals-ınga. It is connected to one of the most beautiful and npressive Icelandic folk tales connected with elves or hidden people". It was believed that the cathedral and ishopric of the elves was in the crag.

;ælingsdalstunga, an abandoned farm in the valley ;ælingsdalur. Snorri goði lived there after moving from Ielgafell.

.augar, a farmstead in the valley Sælingsdalur. Home of)svífur, father of Guðrún in *Laxdæla saga*. Now a chool. Geothermal heat and an old spring, Sælingsdals-aug, which was an official meeting place of old. Folk nuseum.

;ælingsdalur, a farm in a valley of the same name, with ne **Bollatóftir** ruins, where Bolli Þorleifsson of *Laxdæla aga* was slain in revenge for the murder of Kjartan)lafsson.

690 **Steinadalsvegur,** over **Steinadalsheiði**, a route etween Gilsfjörður and Kollafjörður, highest point is 30 m.

Kleifar, the northernmost farm in Dalasýsla county at the head of Gilsfjörður. Above is a high but narrow waterfall, Gullfoss. As the crow flies, it is only 7 km over to Bitrufjörður in Strandasýsla. The river Brekkuá forms the boundary between Dalasýsla and Barðastrandarsýsla counties.

Holtahlíð, a very steep mountainside along Gilsfjörður with no flat land below it, so that the road formerly went along the shore in many places, making travellers dependent on the tides.

Ólafsdalur, a small valley south of Gilsfjörður. A farm of the same name, where Torfi Bjarnason (1838-1915) founded the first agricultural school in Iceland, which he ran 1880-1907, marking a milestone in the history of Icelandic farming. The building still stands. In 1955 a monument was raised to the memory of Torfi and his wife Guðlaug Zakaríasdóttir. www.olafsdalur.is

68 **Innstrandavegur,** p. 310

590 **Klofningsvegur,** p. 279

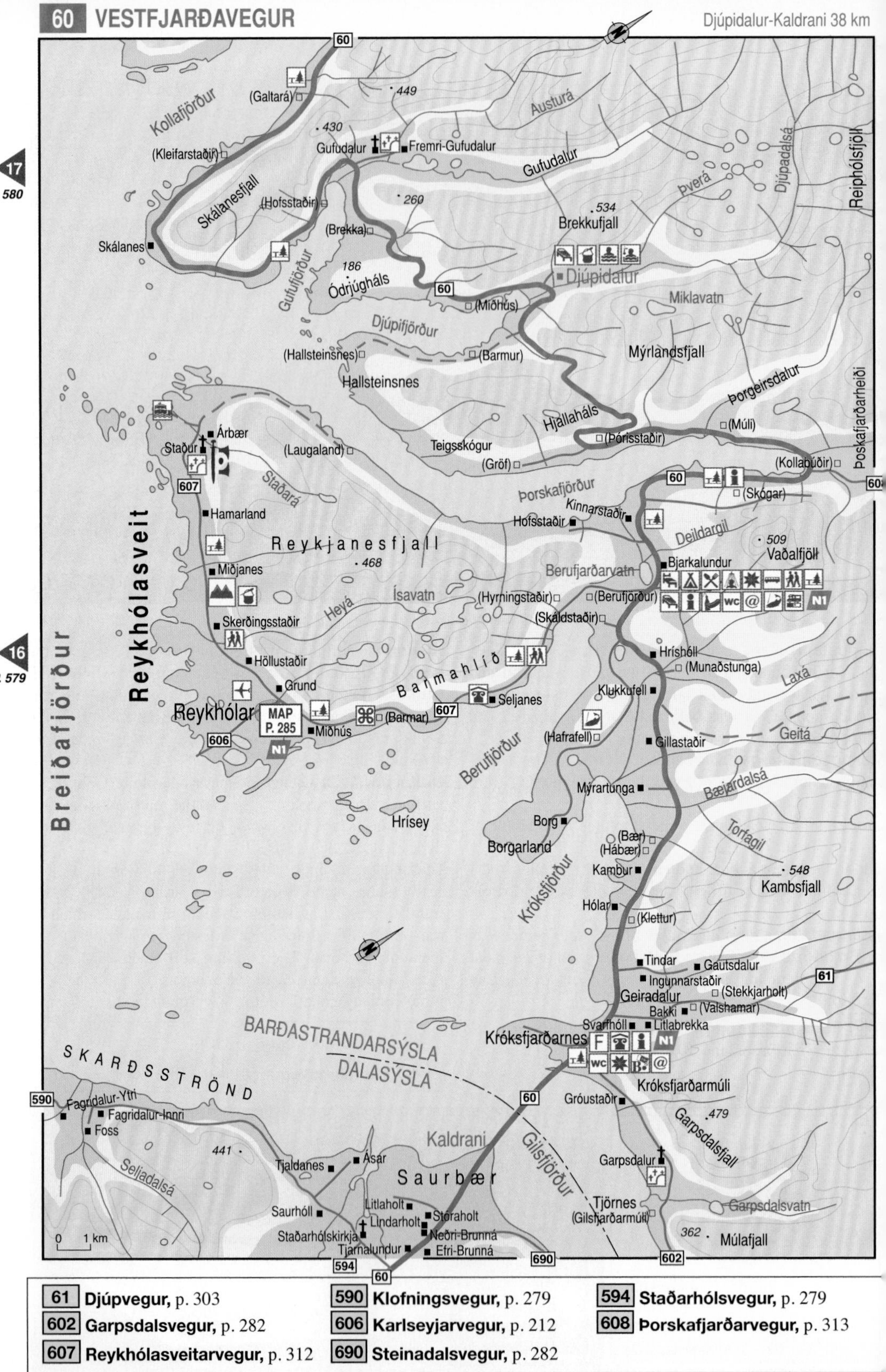

17 P. 580

16 P. 579

61 **Djúpvegur,** p. 303
602 **Garpsdalsvegur,** p. 282
607 **Reykhólasveitarvegur,** p. 312
590 **Klofningsvegur,** p. 279
606 **Karlseyjarvegur,** p. 212
690 **Steinadalsvegur,** p. 282
594 **Staðarhólsvegur,** p. 279
608 **Þorskafjarðarvegur,** p. 313

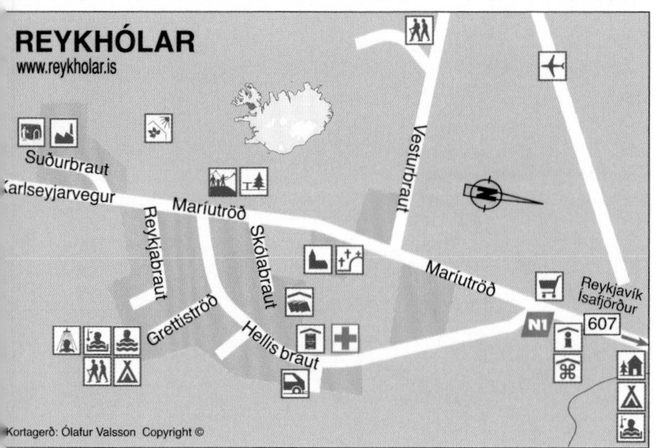

Berufjarðarvatn, south of Bjarkalundur, a lake into which runs the stream Alifiskalækur ("Fed-fish stream"). Trout were introduced into the stream centuries ago, making it the first known fish-breeding station in Iceland.

Berufjörður, a short fjord between the Borgarnes and Reykjanes peninsulas, in which there are many islets with eider duck colonies, Hrísey being the biggest. A farm of the same name at the head of the fjord.

Reykhólasveit, a district, reaching over Króksfjörður, Borgarland, Berufjörður and Reykjanes to Múlaá in Þorskafjörður. The farmhouse at Barmar was rebuilt in 1971–1974, then the only original farmhouse in the Westfjords still standing.

Barmahlíð, the mountainside along the western side of Berufjörður. The poet Jón Thoroddsen (1818-68) wrote a well-known romantic poem about its beauty.

Borgarland, the south end of the Borgarnes peninsula, where there are some unusual rock formations.

Gillastaðir, an abandoned farm, where the leader Þorvaldur Vatnsfirðingur was burnt to death in 1228.

Mýrartunga, a farm, home of the writer Gestur Pálsson (1852-91). Memorial to Gestur Pálsson on Road 607 above Reykhólar.

Bær, an abandoned farm at the head of Króksfjörður.

Tindar, peaks containing rhyolite, normally scarce in the Western fjords.

Geiradalur, a small, grassy valley, marshy and often snowy.

Króksfjarðarnes, a trading post between Gilsfjörður and Króksfjörður. An old assembly site and now a community centre, Vogaland. Land settled by Þórarinn krókur ("hook") from whom the fjord takes its name.

allsteinsnes, the land of a settlement farm at the outhern end of a peninsula of the same name, on which the wood **Teigaskógur**, the biggest in the eastern part f the district.

jallaháls, a ridge where jasper, zeolites and other unuıal stones are to be found.

ollabúðir, ("Crown bothies") an abandoned farm at the ead of Þorskafjörður. Some trace the name to Irish seters who were Christian and shaved the crown of their eads. By the Músará river was the ancient Þorskafjörður ssembly site, where in the latter half of the 19th century e Kollabúðir meetings for freedom and progress were eld. See statue at road side. Road 608 goes from there nto Þorskafjarðarheiði moor.

kógar, ("Woods") a small farm, birthplace of the pastor nd poet Matthías Jochumsson (1835-1920), one of the ost important poets of the romantic movement in celand and writer of the national anthem. A monument his honour is lacated on a cliff overlooking the road. here is a monument to him on the rocks above the road.

orskafjörður, ca. 16 km long, narrow, fjord with strong ɔb tides. Little flat land, many flats that can be crossed low tide.

aðalfjöll, two isolated peaks, 6–7 km north of Bjarkaındur, easy to climb. Good view.

jarkalundur, a summer hotel, built 1945-47. Jeep track Vaðalfjöll.

17
P. 580

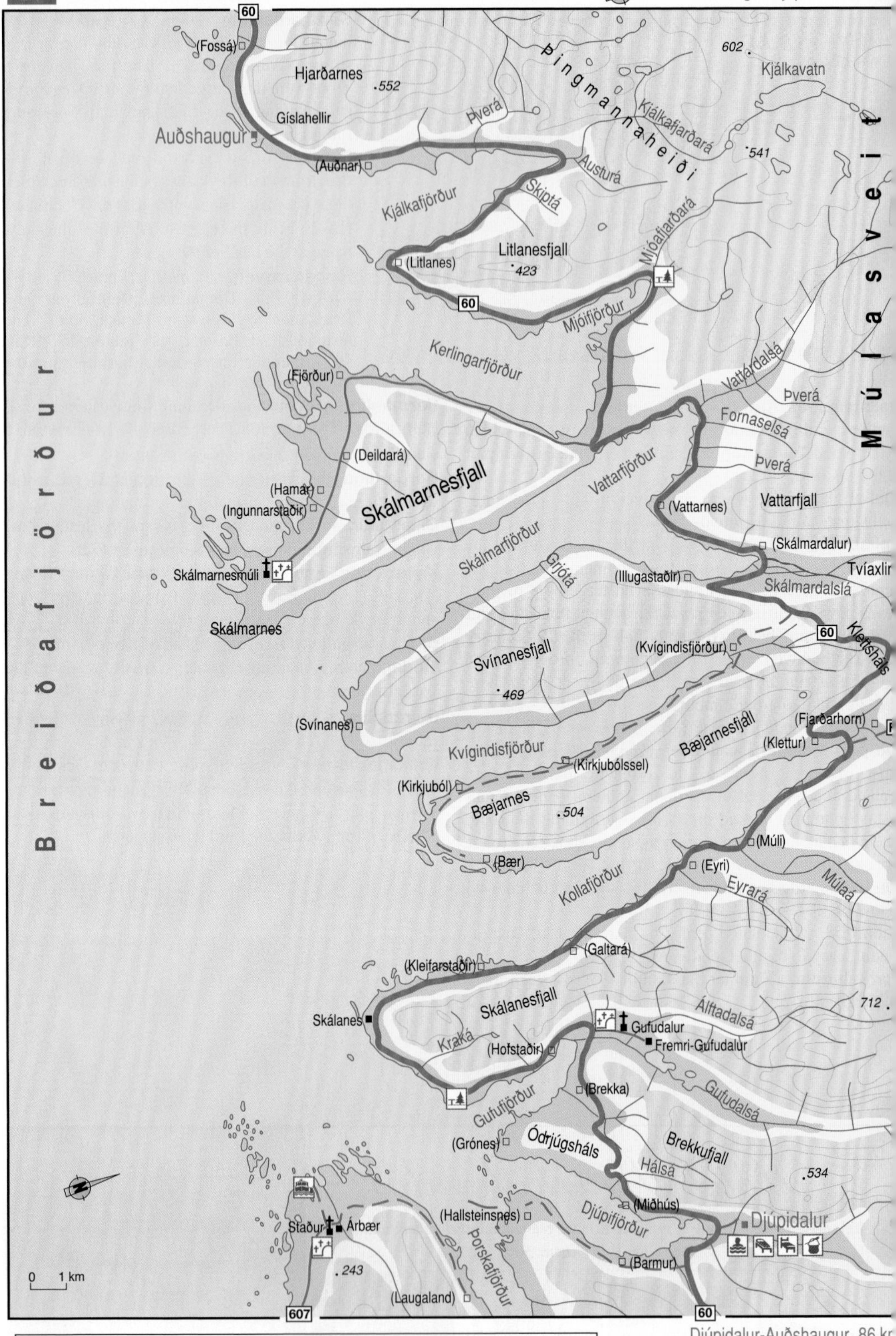

60
(Fossá)
Hjarðarnes
.552
Gíslahellir
Auðshaugur
(Auðnar)
Þverá
Þingmannaheiði
602
Kjálkavatn
Kjálkafjarðará
.541
Austurá
Skiptá
Kjálkafjörður
Mjóafjarðará
(Litlanes)
Litlanesfjall
.423
60
Mjóifjörður
Múlasveit
Kerlingarfjörður
(Fjörður)
Vattardalsá
Þverá
Fornaselsá
(Deildará)
Þverá
Vattarfjörður
(Hamar)
Skálmarnesfjall
(Ingunnarstaðir)
(Vattarnes)
Vattarfjall
(Skálmardalur)
Breiðafjörður
Skálmarfjörður
Skálmarnesmúli
Grjótá
(Illugastaðir)
Tvíaxlir
Skálmardalsá
Skálmarnes
60
Klettsháls
Svínanesfjall
(Kvígindisfjörður)
.469
(Svínanes)
(Fjarðarhorn)
Bæjarnesfjall
(Klettur)
Kvígindisfjörður
(Kirkjubólssel)
(Kirkjuból)
Bæjarnes
.504
(Múli)
(Bær)
(Eyri)
Kollafjörður
Eyrará
Múlaá
(Galtará)
(Kleifarstaðir)
712
Skálanesfjall
Álftadalsá
Skálanes
Gufudalur
Kraká
Fremri-Gufudalur
(Hofstaðir)
(Brekka)
Gufudalsá
Gufufjörður
Brekkufjall
(Grónes)
Óðrjúgsháls
Hálsá
.534
(Miðhús)
(Hallsteinsnes)
Djúpifjörður
Djúpidalur
Staður
Árbær
Þorskafjörður
.243
(Barmur)
0 1 km
(Laugaland)
607
60

F66 **Kollafjarðarheiði,** p. 313 607 **Reykhólasveitarvegur,** p. 312

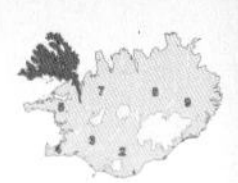

Dynjandi, see p. 288.

Kjálkafjörður, between the peninsulas Hjarðarnes and .itlanes, ca. 6 km long, rocky and sometimes dangerous or sheep, which can by trapped by high tides, as is the ase in most fjords in the area.

Skiptá, a river marking the boundary between the coun-ies Vestur- and Austur-Barðastrandarsýsla.

.itlanes, the peninsula between Kjálkafjörður and Kerlingarfjörður, with the mountain Litlanesfjall (424 m). t is 4-5 km long and 0.5 km wide at its broadest part, ery rocky. Now uninhabited.

Kerlingarfjörður, ca. 9 km long, between the Litlanes nd Skálmarnes peninsulas, with the inlet Mjóifjörður.

Þingmannaheiði, (400 m) a moor across which there is mountain road between Vattarfjörður and Vatnsfjörður, a. 25 km. Stony, bare, often blocked by snow in winter. ts western end goes down the Þingmannadalur valley.

Skálmarnes, mountainous, triangular peninsula between Kerlingarfjörður and Skálmarfjörður, joined by a low sthmus to the southern end of Þingmannaheiði moor. About 300 m high, cliffs on all sides, the only flat land eing on the southern side.

Skálmarnesmúli, the main farm on Skálmarnes, church.

Vattarnes, a point of land and a farm of the same name, ow abandoned. Formerly the last stopping place before raversing Þingmannaheiði. Local place-names indicate ne site of an ancient assembly.

Skálmarfjörður, ca. 15 km long, between the Skálmar-es and Svínanes peninsulas. Splits at Vattarnes, west of vhich it is known as Vattarfjörður, where the route onto Þingmannaheiði started. From the valley Skálmardalur nere is a route via Skálmardalsheiði moor north to Ísa-farðardjúp.

Svínanes, ("Swine ness") between Skálmarfjörður and Kvígindisfjörður, going steeply down to the sea, but with rees in places. No road. There was a farm of the same ame, now abandoned, at the end of the peninsula.

Kvígindisfjörður, a fjord, ca. 15 km long and very nar-ow. The mountain Svínafellsfjall to the west is very teep, with rocks and scree, but some trees. It is said that ne settler Geirmundur heljarskinn kept his pigs on Svínanes, hence the name.

Bæjarnesvegur, the road along the western shore of Kvígindisfjörður to the abandoned farm Bær.

Bæjarnesfjall, (504 m) the mountain forming the Bæjarnes peninsula, very rocky, especially along Klettshlíð.

Múlasveit, the westernmost district in Austur-Barðastrandarsýsla county. Reaching from Bæjarnes, Kvígindisfjörður, Svínanes, Skálmarfjörður, Múlanes, Kerlingarfjörður, Litlanes and Kjálkafjörður.

Klettsháls, a ridge (330 m) between the heads of the valleys in Kollafjörður and Kvígindisfjörður. **The area between Múli in Kollafjörður and Auðshaugur in Kjálkafjörður is totally uninhabited.**

Fjarðarhorn, the innermost farm in Kollafjörður, now deserted. A jeep-track goes from there up to Kollafjarðarheiði moor and down into the valley Laugarbólsdalur in Ísafjörður, 25 km.

Kollafjörður, the westernmost fjord in the Gufudalssveit district, ca. 16 km long, with many fords. Many flats that can be crossed at low tide.

Skálanes, the southernmost farm on the peninsula of the same name. Trading post. Formerly a centre for the islanders of Breiðafjörður, when they brought their sheep to the mainland.

Gufudalur, a church and parsonage until the turn of last century.

Gufufjörður, a small fjord, so shallow that it becomes nothing but mud-flats at low tide. They are, however, impassable because of quicksand.

Djúpifjörður, ("Deep fjord") between the peninsulas Grónes and Hallsteinsnes, short and narrow and - despite its name - shallow, almost drying up at low tide, though there is a channel down the middle.

Djúpidalur, a farm in a valley of the same name, off Djúpifjörður. Birthplace of Björn Jónsson editor and Minister of State (1846-1912), father of Sveinn Björnsson (1881-1952), first president of the republic. There are chalk layers in the earth there, and Iceland spar was mined for a time. Geothermal heat.

Mjólkárvirkjun-Auðshaugur 54 km

17 P. 580

Auðshaugur-Mjólkárvirkjun 54 km

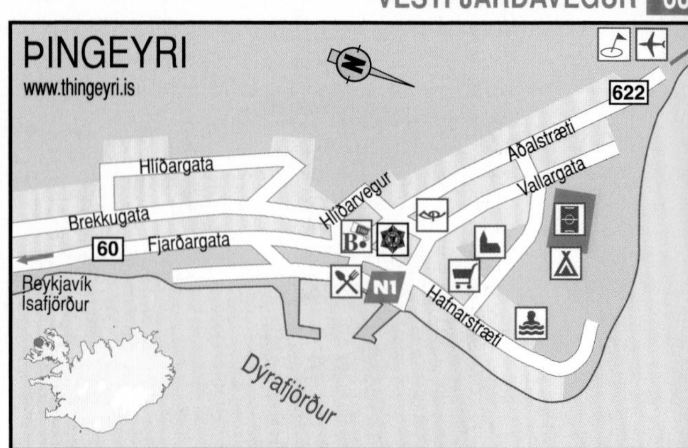

Gljúfurá, an abandoned farm by a river of the same name. Ownership this farm ensured Jón forseti the right to vote in 1845 (see Road 6 Hrafnseyri).

Mjólkárvirkjun, hydro-electric power station for the Westfjords, bui 1958, 8.1 MW.

Dynjandi, an abandoned farm. Above it is the biggest waterfall in th Western fjords and one of finest in Iceland, also named **Dynjan** ("Resounding"), also known as Fjallfoss, itself 100 m high and ve broad. There are five more falls immediately below it: Háifoss, Úðafos Göngufoss, Hundafoss and Bæjarfoss. It is possible to walk behi Göngufoss. All six falls can be seen from the shore.

Dynjandisheiði, (500 m) the moor between Geirþjófsfjörður ar Dynjandisvogur on Arnarfjörður. The boundary between the counti Barðastrandar- and Vestur-Ísafjarðarsýsla is on these moors.

Langibotn, at the head of Geirþjófsfjörður. Some woods protected by th Forestry Service. The rock **Einhamar**, where Gísli Súrsson of *Gísla sa Súrssonar* was slain, a silhouette of him has been carved into it. His hi ing-place is still visible.

Helluskarð, (468 m) the pass where in 1959 the road system for th northern part of the Western fjords was joined to the main Icelandic ne work. Bíldudalsvegur junction close by.

Hornatær, (700 m and more) several peaks on one of which Hrafn Flóki is thought to have stood when he named Iceland (see Road 6 Brjánslækur).

Flókalundur, ("Flóki's grove") a wooded area near the crossroads. So services, summer hotel, summer house area and swimming pool nearby.

Vatnsfjörður, the westernmost fjord of the district, short and broad, wi wooded slopes.

Vatnsdalur, a short, well-wooded valley. Vatnsdalsvatn lake, 4 km lon 1.5 km wide, good trout-fishing. The river Vatnsdalsá, only 1 km lon flows out of it.

Smiðjukleifar, ("Smithy rocks") at the mouth of Þingmannadalur, rocky but wooded slope. The name is derived from an iron ore smith said to have belonged to Gestur Oddleifsson the wise of Saga times, b probably more recent.

Hjarðarnes, a mountainous (552 m) peninsula, with wooded slope stony and bare higher up. There are three farms on it.

Fossá, there begins the Öskjudalur valley. **Gíslahellir** small cave west Fossá. It is said that the outlaw Gísli Súrsson dwelled there for a while.

Auðshaugur, there lived Refur and Álfdís, people who helped Gís Súrsson the outlaw.

62 **Barðastrandarvegur,** p. 305 63 **Bíldudalsvegur,** p. 307

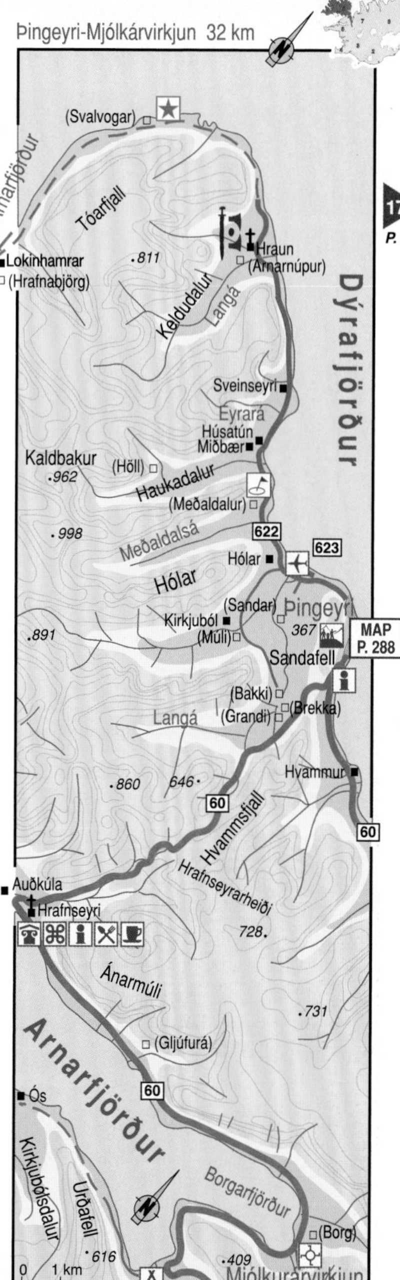

22 Svalvogavegur, 30,5 km.

eldudalur, a short valley. The newly repaired church at Hraun is of der towerless type, built in 1885 and is the only building in Iceland with of- shingles. The church was deconsecrated in 1971 and has been in the eping of The National Museum since 1980.

aukadalur, a short valley. Site of the first fish-freezing plant in the strict, later moved to Þingeyri. Grave of French seamen. Site of the ain action in *Gísla saga Súrssonar*, one of Iceland´s most famous tlaws. It was off Haukadalur that sheriff Hannes Hafstein was almost owned in 1899, when British trawlermen he was trying to arrest for shing in Icelandic waters overturned his boat. Three of his men owned.

23 Flugvallarvegur, 0,04 km.

andafell, (367 m) a mountain above the village Þingeyri, named after e ancient manor farm Sandar, often mentioned in records from the time the Sturlungas in the 13th century. It was long a parsonage, now abanned, but the cemetery is still there. It is possible to drive up the mountain a view-dial.

ingeyri, (pop. 260) a village which is the oldest trading place in the Ísaarðarsýsla county. Service station, medical centre, store, excellent campte and very interesting iron foundry museum.

ftamýri, a church and parsonage until 1880.

uðkúla, a farm and trading place. In the mountain above it is the bigst rhyolite area in the Western fjords. Also gabbro.

rafnseyri, a church and parsonage with a long history. In 1977-78 an cheological dig uncovered the farm site of Án rauðfeldur, the first ttler there. His wife was Grélöð Bjartmarsdóttir, and the ruins that were covered have been named for her, **Grélutóttir**. The farm was named r Hrafn Sveinbjarnarson, an influential man in the 12th-13th century, obably the first trained doctor in Iceland. It is the birthplace of Jón Sigðsson (1811-1879), who contributed more than anyone towards Icend's regaining independence. He was often called Jón forseti ("present") because he was president of the Icelandic Literary Society and ng the leader of the house in Parliament. His birthday, the 17th of June, as chosen to be the Icelandic national holiday when the Republic was tablished in 1944. A chapel was consecrated and a museum about Jón ened in 1981. Jón Sigurðsson's grandfather built a new farmhouse at afnseyri towards the end of the 18th century, almost certainly according plans drawn up by the Rev. Guðlaugur Sveinsson, dean, of Vatnsfjörður Ísafjarðardjúp (see Road 61). The farmhouse was one of the first of the bled farmhouses in Iceland. Around the turn of the century the buildgs, which were collapsing, were torn down, all but one wall which is ll standing. The gabled farmhouse has now been re-built in accordance ith careful on-site measurements and a model built to the specifications people who had actually seen the old farmhouse (see Road 61).

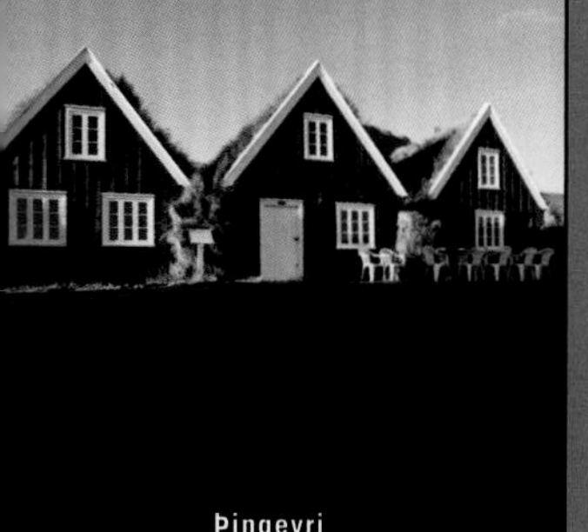
Þingeyri

18 P. 581

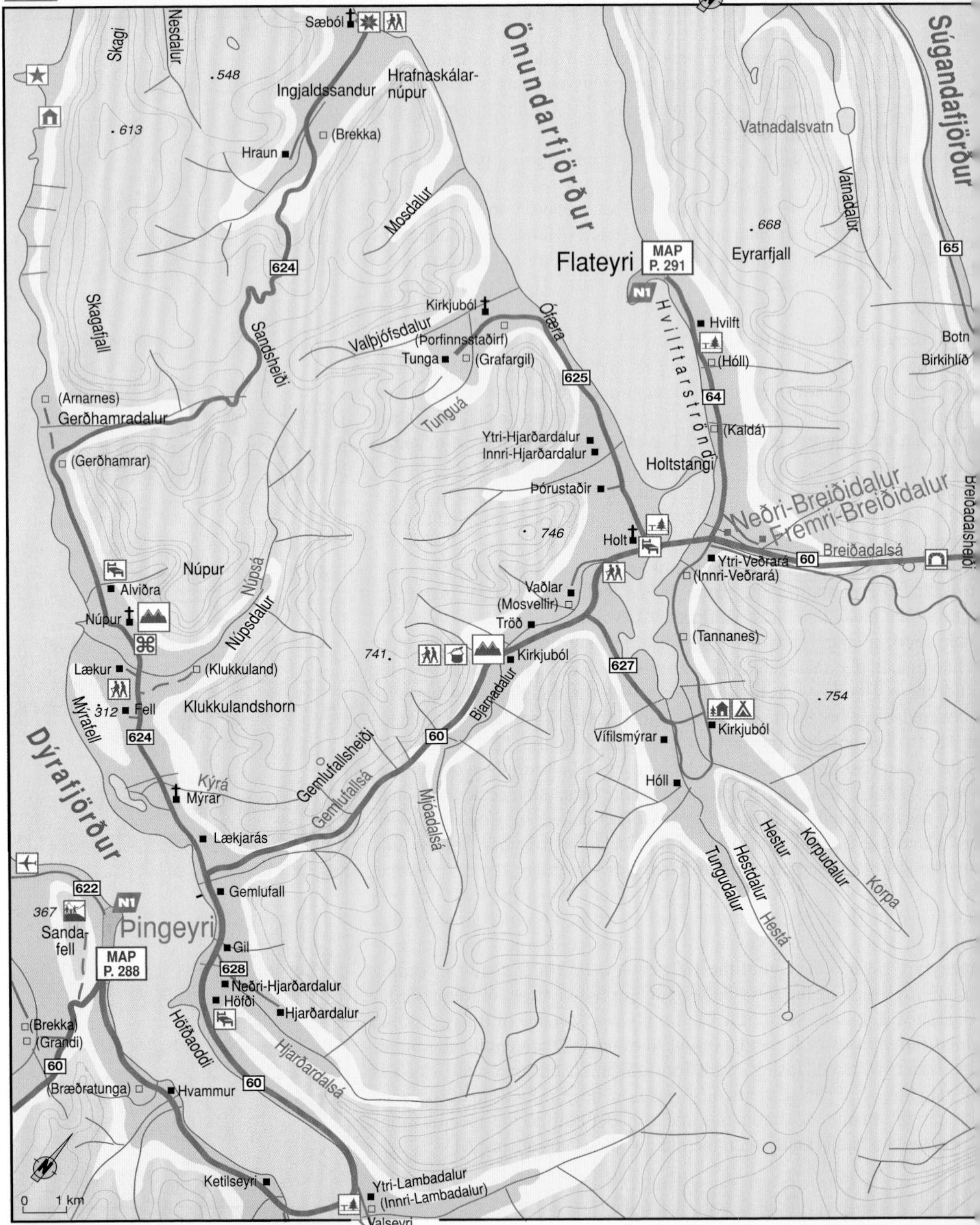

Sæból
Skagi
Nesdalur
. 548
Ingjaldssandur
Hrafnaskálarnúpur
Önundarfjörður
Súgandafjörður
. 613
(Brekka)
Hraun
Vatnadalsvatn
Vatnadalur
Mosdalur
. 668
624
Flateyri
MAP P. 291
Eyrarfjall
65
Skagafjall
Kirkjuból
Hvilft
Sandsheiði
Valþjófsdalur
(Þorfinnsstaðirf)
Tunga
(Grafargil)
Ófæra
(Hóll)
Botn
Birkihlíð
625
Hvilftarströnd
64
(Arnarnes)
Gerðhamradalur
Tunguá
(Kaldá)
Ytri-Hjarðardalur
Innri-Hjarðardalur
(Gerðhamrar)
Holtstangi
Þórustaðir
Neðri-Breiðidalur
Fremri-Breiðidalur
Breiðadalsheiði
. 746
Holt
Breiðadalsá
Ytri-Veðrará
60
(Innri-Veðrará)
Núpur
Alviðra
Núpsá
Vaðlar
(Mosvellir)
Núpur
Núpsdalur
Tröð
(Tannanes)
741.
Kirkjuból
Lækur
(Klukkuland)
627
Klukkulandshorn
. 754
Mýrafell
312
Fell
Bjarnadalur
Kirkjuból
624
60
Vífilsmýrar
Dýrafjörður
Gemlufallsheiði
Hóll
Kýrá
Mýrar
Gemlufallsá
Mjóadalsá
Hestur
Korpudalur
Lækjarás
Tungudalur
Hestdalur
Korpa
622
Gemlufall
367
Þingeyri
Sandafell
Hestá
MAP P. 288
Gil
628
Neðri-Hjarðardalur
Höfði
Hjarðardalur
(Brekka)
(Grandi)
Höfðaoddi
60
Hjarðardalsá
(Bræðratunga)
Hvammur
60
Ketilseyri
Ytri-Lambadalur
(Innri-Lambadalur)
0 1 km
Valseyri
Botnsdalur

24 Ingjaldssandsvegur, 28 km.

gjaldssandur, a valley with one or two farms between : mountains Hrafnaskálanúpur (584 m) to the east and ırði (548 m) to the west. Church at Sæból.

ıpur, a manor farm through the ages, a church and for while a boarding school founded by Rev. Sigtryggur ıðlaugsson. He and his wife Hjaltlína Guðjónsdóttir so created Skrúður, the oldest botanical garden in eland that has been rebuilt.

ri-Hús, Rögnvaldur Ólafsson (1874–1917) was born ere. He is considered to be the first Icelandic architect hough poor healt cut his education short.

ekur, an eiderdown farm.

ýrar, a farm and church near the mountain Mýrafell 12 m). An historical place. Birthplace of Þórdís, moth- of President Jón Sigurðsson (see Hrafnseyri). Now one the biggest eider duck breeding grounds in Iceland.

emlufall, an old ferry point to Þingeyri.

emlufallsheiði, (283 m) a mountain road between ýrafjörður and Önundarfjörður.

28 Hjarðardalsvegur, 2 km.

lseyri, an ancient assembly site, mentioned in *Gísla ga Súrssonar*. Remains of booths.

tnsdalur, a valley at the head of Dýrafjörður, named r the farm Botn, abandoned in 1925 after damage by an alanche. It is said there once were seven big farms in s valley. A prominent hill, Dýrahaugur, where some y the settler Dýri is buried. Many trees and a local ıntation.

rafjörður, the largest of the fjords in Vestur-Ísafjarð- sýsla county, with the most varied scenery. About 39 ı long, mostly narrow. Near the mouth of the fjord are eer, barren cliffs down to sea, but there is more flat ıd and grass further in. Two isolated mountains, Mýra- l (312 m) to the north and Sandafell (367 m) to the uth, are conspicuous landmarks.

Kirkjuból í Bjarnardal, a farm. A memorial to Hallór Kristjánsson a famer and a poet who used to live there.

64 Flateyrarvegur, 3 km.

Flateyri, (pop. 199) a village and authorised trading place, where trading actually started soon after 1790, swimming pool, camping site. Fishing and fish-processing are now the main industries. In 1889 the Norwegian Hans Ellefsen started a whaling station near Flateyri, called Sólbakki, which was burned down in 1901 and then closed. The official reception house of the Icelandic Government, by the lake in Reykjavík, was formerly Ellefsen's residence, presented by him in 1904 to the government minister Hannes Hafstein and moved from Flateyri. There is said to have been a pagan temple on the hill Goðahóll above Flateyri. In the early hours of the 26th of October 1995 an avalanche fell on nineteen houses in Flateyri. Of the 45 people in the houses, 20 died. Population now 237. Before this tragic event the population of Flateyri was 380. A protective wall against avalanches has now been built above the town. The wall has a tower that provides an excellent view.

625 Valþjófsdalsvegur, 7 km.

Valþjófsdalur, a valley with several farms. Church at **Kirkjubóli**.

Holt, a church and parsonage, fertile fields, earlier considered one of the wealthiest benefices in Iceland. Birthplace of Bishop Brynjólfur Sveinsson (1605-75). There is a monument to him. Sand-castle building competition have been held there during the first weekend in august.

Önundarfjörður, a fjord between the headlands Barði and Sauðanes, with steep cliffs, opening out towards the mouth, but very narrow at the head, where there is a good deal of flat land. Bridged in 1980.

627 Önundarfjarðarvegur, 9 km.

65 Súgandafjarðarvegur, p. 308

22 Svalvogavegur, p. 289

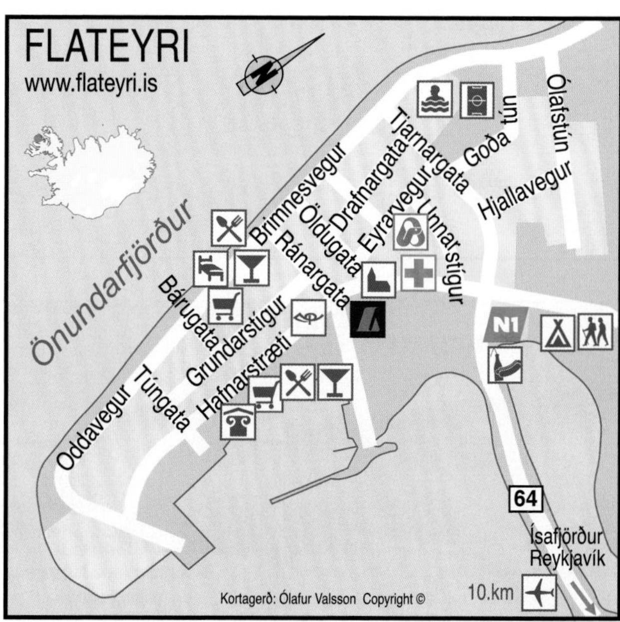

61 Djúpveg

18 P. 581

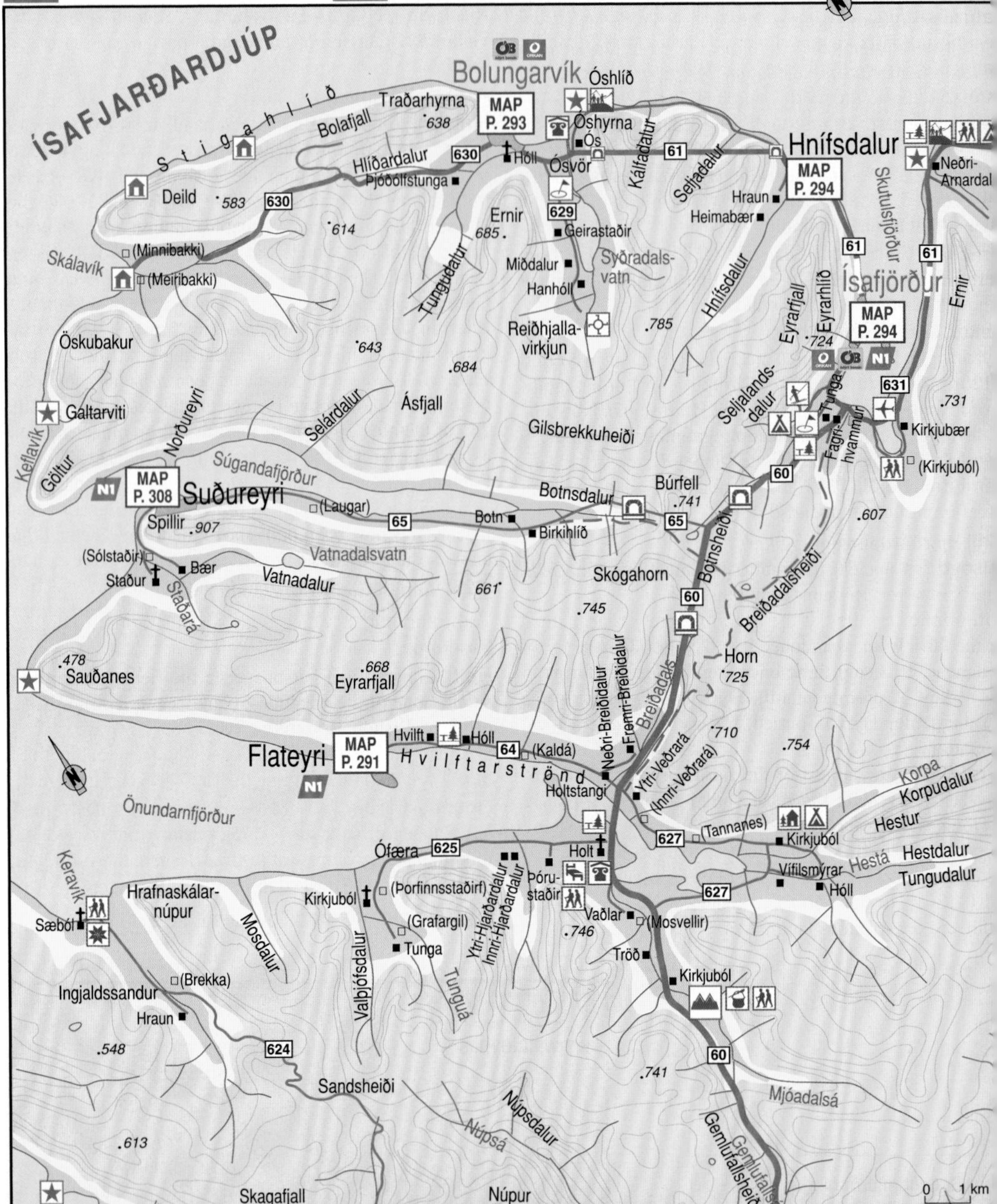

ÍSAFJARÐARDJÚP
Bolungarvík Óshlíð
Stigahlíð
Traðarhyrna .638
MAP P. 293
Bolafjall
Óshyrna
Ós
Hlíðardalur 630
Höll
Ósvör
Kálfadalur
61
Seljadalur
Hnífsdalur
MAP P. 294
Neðri-Arnardal
Deild .583 630
Þjóðólfstunga
Ernir 629
685.
Geirastaðir
Hraun
Heimabær
Skutulsfjörður
.614
(Minnibakki)
Skálavík
(Meiribakki)
Tungudalur
Miðdalur
Hanhóll
Syðradals-vatn
Hnífsdalur
Eyrarfjall
Eyrarhlíð
61
61
Ísafjörður
Ernir
MAP P. 294
Reiðhjalla-virkjun
.785
.724
Öskubakur
.643
.684
631
Selárdalur
Ásfjall
Seljalands-dalur
Tunga
.731
Galtarviti
Norðureyri
Gilsbrekkuheiði
Fagri-hvammur
Kirkjubær
Keflavík
Göltur
Súgandafjörður
(Kirkjuból)
MAP P. 308
Suðureyri
Búrfell
60
Botnsdalur .741
(Laugar)
65
Botn
65
.607
Spillir .907
Birkihlíð
(Sólstaðir)
Bær
Vatnadalsvatn
Staður
Vatnadalur
Staðará
Skógahorn
Botnsheiði
Breiðadalsheiði
661
60
.745
.478
Sauðanes
.668
Eyrarfjall
Neðri-Breiðidalur
Fremri-Breiðidalur
Breiðadalsá
Horn
.725
.710
.754
MAP P. 291
Flateyri
Hvilft
Höll
64 (Kaldá)
Hvilftarströnd
Holtstangi
Ytri-Veðrará
(Innri-Veðrará)
Korpa
Korpudalur
Önundarfjörður
(Tannanes)
Kirkjuból
Hestur
Ófæra 625
Holt
627
Hestá
Hestdalur
Keravík
Hrafnaskálar-núpur
Kirkjuból
(Þorfinnsstaðirf)
Ytri-Hjarðardalur
Innri-Hjarðardalur
Þóru-staðir
Vífilsmýrar
Höll
Tungudalur
627
Sæból
Mosdalur
(Grafargil)
Vaðlar
(Mosvellir)
.746
Tunga
Valþjófsdalur
Tunguá
Tröð
Kirkjuból
Ingjaldssandur
(Brekka)
Hraun
.548
624
60
Sandsheiði
.741
Mjóadalsá
Núpsdalur
Núpsá
Gemlufallsheiði
Gemlufallsá
.613
Skagafjall
Núpur
0 1 km

61 Djúpveg

ıfjarðardjúp, the greatest of the Western fjords. veral smaller fjords open into it.

ıfjörður, (pop. 2,624) the biggest settlement in the ɜstern Fjords and their only market town, municipal arter since 28th January 1866. Built on a spit reaching ›st of the way across Skutulsfjörður, inside which is an cellent harbour. In the oldest part of town, **Neðsti-upstaður**, there are four of the oldest houses in Ice-ıd, one of which houses the maritime museum. They ›re built in the mid-18th century. Fishing has been the ıin industry for centuries and trade has always been ;nificant. Site of the old parsonage Eyri, famous cause of *Píslarsaga síra Jóns Magnússonar* ("The suf-ings of Rev. Jón Magnússon"). See more p. 296

ngudalur, a valley close to the town of Ísafjörður, ge areas of birchwood. Many inhabitants of Ísafjörður d summer cottages there but in April 1994 an avalanche stroyed about 40 cottages, sweeping away large tracts birchwood and costing one man his life. Higher up is : popular skiing area in Seljalandsdalur, along with ski-ges. The 1994 avalanche destroyed ski-lifts and other nstructions but these have been rebuilt and additional i-facilities put up in Tungudalur itself. Summer camp :ilities for scouts and schools. Campsite.

29 **Syðradalsvegur,** 3 km.

tnsheiði, (516 m) a heath.

eiðadalsheiði, (610 m), possible to drive in a 4x4 car.

stfjarðagöng, tunnels built in the 1990's under both eiðadalsheiði and Botnsheiði moors have completely nsformed communications in the area. Two kilometers ›m the tunnel entrance in Tungudalur valley outside ıfjörður there is a fork in the road, right under Botns-iði. From the junctions one arm leads to Súganda-›rður (3 km), the other to Önundarfjörður (4 km).

30 **Skálavíkurvegur,** 11 km.

álavík, a small cove, once settled but now abandoned.

Stigahlíð, the mountainside west of Bolungarvík, sheer and rocky with much scree, contains lignite. The mountain itself, Deild, (585 m). Road up to a radar station from where there are splendid views.

Bolungarvík, (pop. 894) a town and fishing centre on a bay of the same name. Off the inlet are two valleys, Tungudalur and Syðridalur, between which is the mountain Ernir (685 m). Wild but beautiful scenery. Bolungarvík is one of the oldest fishing stations in Iceland, being close to the banks, but landing was often difficult. Now a good harbour and prosperous place, with a fish-processing industry. Good fishing at the end of the pier. In front of the community centre is a memorial to Einar Guðfinnsson (1898-1985) and his wife Elísabet Hjaltadóttir (1900-1981). Einar was a prominent businessman and the driving force behind much of the town´s development. The cairn was built by Jón Sigurpálsson, using stone from Litli-Bær in Skötufjörður, Einar´s birthplace. The bas-relief is by Ríkey Ingimundardóttir.

Hóll, church, formerly a substantial farm and home of local leaders, near Bolungarvík.

Syðradalsvatn, a good fishing lake.

Óshlíð, the mountainside between Hnífsdalur and Bolungarvík, very steep and with much scree. There have often been avalanches and landslides there.

Ósvör, a maritime museum in fisherman's booths that have been rebuilt on old ruins at Óshólar.

Hnífsdalur, (pop. 216) a village in a small valley, enclosed by big mountains. Community centre. A danger area for avalanches, the worst having occurred February 18th 1910, when 20 lives were lost.

64 **Flateyrarvegur,** p. 290 | **65** **Súgandafjarðarvegur,** p. 308 | **624** **Ingjaldssandsvegur,** p. 290

625 **Valþjófsdalsvegur,** p. 290 | **627** **Önundarfjarðarvegur,** p. 290

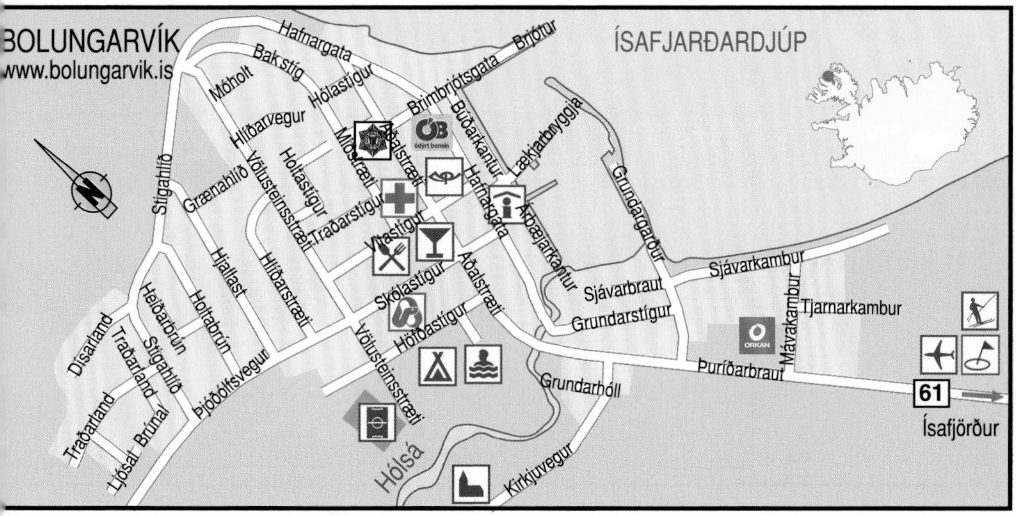

BOLUNGARVÍK
www.bolungarvik.is

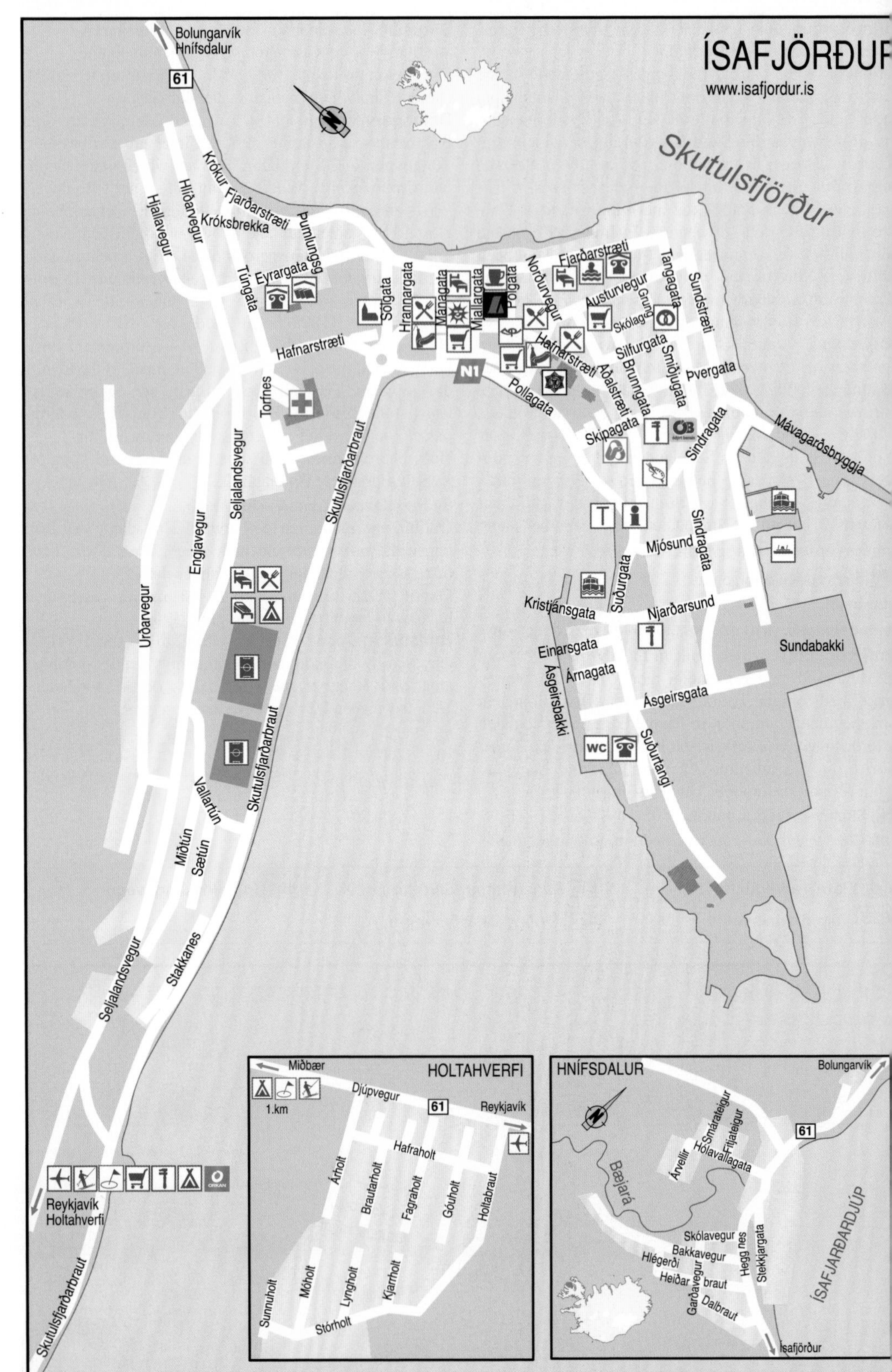

ÍSAFJÖRÐUR
www.isafjordur.is
Skutulsfjörður
Bolungarvík
Hnífsdalur
61
Krókur
Fjarðarstræti
Króksbrekka
Pumlungsg
Hlíðarvegur
Hjallavegur
Túngata
Eyrargata
Sólgata
Hrannargata
Mánagata
Mjallargata
Pólgata
Norðurvegur
Fjarðarstræti
Tangagata
Sundstræti
Austurvegur
Grunng
Skólag
Silfurgata
Smiðjugata
Brunngata
Þvergata
Hafnarstræti
Aðalstræti
Pollagata
N1
Torfnes
Skipagata
Sindragata
Mávagarðsbryggja
Seljalandsvegur
Engjavegur
Skutulsfjarðarbraut
Úrðarvegur
Mjósund
Sindragata
Suðurgata
Kristjánsgata
Njarðarsund
Einarsgata
Árnagata
Ásgeirsbakki
Ásgeirsgata
Sundabakki
Suðurtangi
Vallartún
Miðtún
Sætún
Stakkanes
Seljalandsvegur
Reykjavík
Holtahverfi
Skutulsfjarðarbraut
HOLTAHVERFI
Miðbær
1.km
Djúpvegur
61
Reykjavík
Hafraholt
Árholt
Brautarholt
Fagraholt
Góuholt
Holtabraut
Sunnuholt
Móholt
Lyngholt
Kjarrholt
Stórholt
HNÍFSDALUR
Bolungarvík
61
Smárateigur
Fitjateigur
Árvellir
Hólavallagata
Bæjará
ÍSAFJARÐARDJÚP
Skólavegur
Bakkavegur
Hlégerði
Heiðar
Garðavegur
braut
Hegg nes
Stekkjargata
Dalbraut
Ísafjörður

Myndir: © Gústaf Gústafsson

Ísafjörður, (pop. 2,624) the biggest settlement in the Westfjords, gained municipal status in 28th January 1866. Skutulsfjörður ("Harpoon fjord") is the westernmost south-reaching fjord off Ísafjarðardjúp, surrounded by high, sheer mountains. Near the middle of the fjord, under the mountain Eyrarfjall, a long, flat hook-shaped gravel spit reaches out into the fjord. Inside it is *Pollurinn* ("The puddle"), one of the best natural harbours in Iceland. Between the spit and the mountainside opposite is a narrow channel known as *Sundin*. The community in Skutulsfjörður used to be called Eyrarhreppur, named for the parsonage Eyri that stood at the land-end of the spit. *Landnámabók* ("The Book of Settlements") tells of two settlers in Skutulsfjörður, Helgi Hrólfsson, who built his farm at Eyri and Þórólfur brækir, who settled in Skálavík. Helgi is said to have found a harpoon washed up on the beach and named the fjord for it. In 1786 a royal decree abolished the trade monopoly in Iceland, and six trading centres were established, Ísafjörður being one. In the spring of 1788 Norwegian merchants came to Ísafjörður, which is what the new trading centre was named, settled just below the parsonage at Eyri and built their stores there. One of these buildings is still there, Aðalstræti 42 in the area known as Hæstikaupstaður ("The highest trading place"). In 1816 Ísafjörður lost its trading centre status, but trade continued and there was a lot of growth around mid-century. Ísafjörður again became a legal trading centre by royal decree in 1866. The basis for Ísafjörður's prosperity was the fishing on so-called *þilskip* ("boats with decks") instead of the open rowing boats that were still common at the time. Merchants owned and operated the fishing boats which fished for both cod and shark. From abo 1900-1930 there was also a good deal of herring fishin There was a steady increase in population, reachi 1,085 by 1901. One of the largest companies in Icela at the time, Ásgeirsverslun, operated in Ísafjörður. T company was by far the biggest producer of the country most valuable export product, saltfish. In 1996 the tov of Ísafjörður was amalgamated with the villages Suðureyri, Þingeyri and Flateyri to form Ísafjarðarb (Ísafjörður municipality). Borea Adventures offers ka aking for both beginners and experienced kayakers Ísafjarðardjúp fjord. The serene beauty of the fjord sy tem is well known by locals but unfamiliar to the outsi world. The coast of Snæfjallaströnd really gives you t feeling that you are close to the Arctic Circle with snow covered hills and the fifth largest glacier in Icela just around the corner. Folafótur a small peninsu between the sheltered fjords of Seyðisfjörður a Hestfjörður, is a beautiful place to paddle around in long day, enjoying the marine wildlife and the coastli from a unique angle.

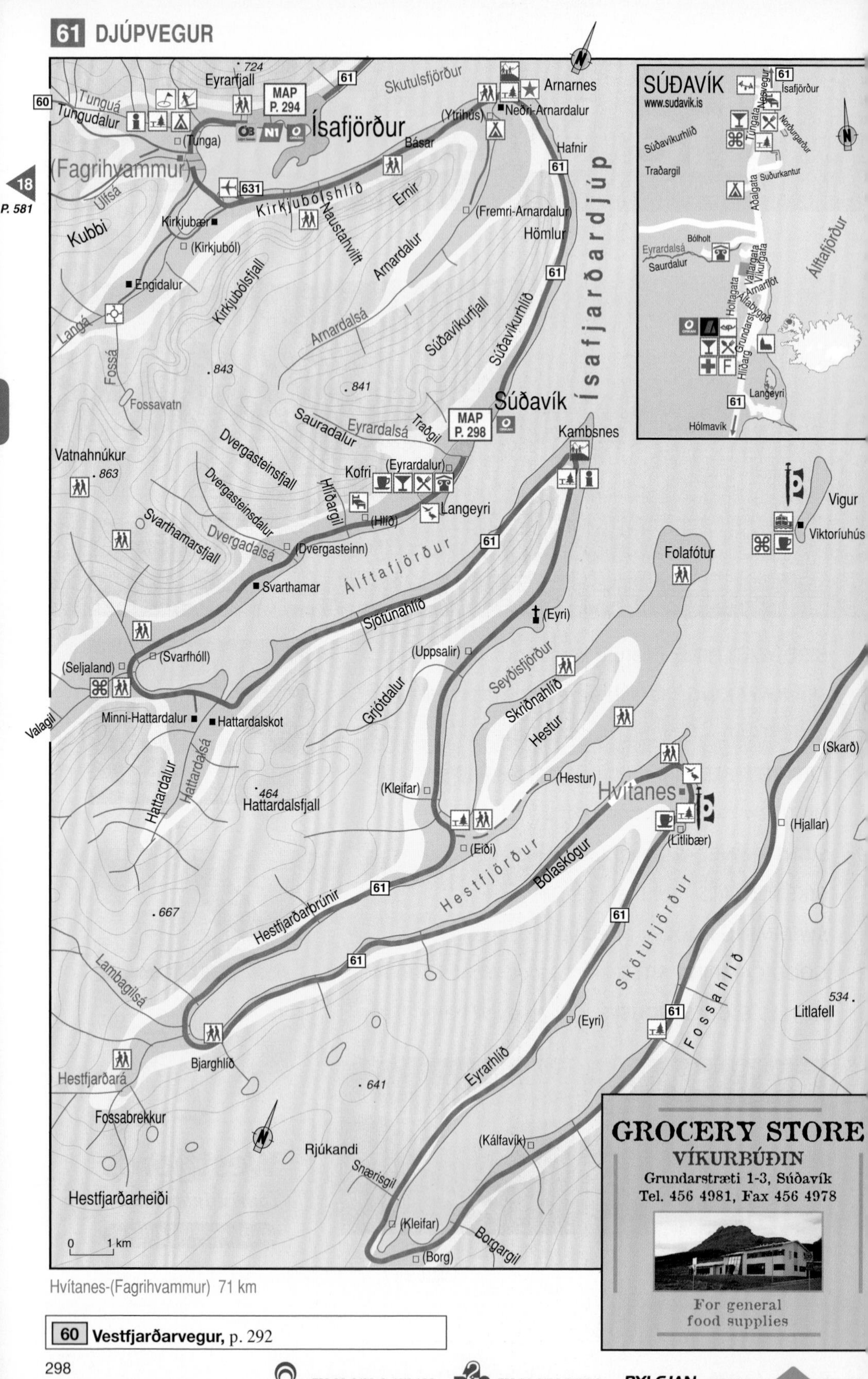

Hvítanes-(Fagrihvammur) 71 km

60 **Vestfjarðarvegur,** p. 292

kutulsfjörður, the westernmost and shortest fjord off afjarðardjúp. Little flat land, but short valleys at its head.
ungudalur, a valley close to the town of Ísafjörður, rge areas of birch wood. Many inhabitants of Ísafjörður ad summer cottages there but in April 1994 an avalanche estroyed about 40 cottages, sweeping away large tracts birchwood and costing one man his life. Higher up is e popular skiing area in Seljalandsdalur, along with ski-dges. The 1994 avalanche destroyed ski-lifts and other onstructions but these have been rebuilt and additional i-facilities put up in Tungudalur itself. Summer camp cilities for scouts and schools. Campsite.
irkjuból, a farm and formerly a church in Skutuls-örður where in the 17th century the Rev. Jón Magnússon ad a father and son burnt for sorcery.

31 Airport road.

rnir, a narrow mountain ridge with a good viewpoint at austahvilft.
rnardalur, a valley at the end of Arnarnes. The mountain the west is called Ernir, and that to the east Hömlur. The rm Neðri-Arnardalur was the home of Þorbjörg Kolbrún, hom the poet Þormóður kolbrúnarskáld ("The poet of olbrún") praised in verse, as mentioned in *Fóstbræðra ga*. The farm Fremri-Arnardalur was the birthplace of annibal Valdimarsson (1903-1991) long a member of arliament, Minister of State and President of ASÍ (The elandic Federation of Labour).
rnarnes, the outermost point of land on Skutulsfjörður. o the east is **Arnarneshamar**, a basalt cape, through hich the first road tunnel in Iceland was made in 1948 nd remained the only one until the Strákagöng tunnel near iglufjörður in 1967 (see Road 76). Length c. 35 m. The ritish trawler *Cæsar* stranded off Arnarnes in April 1971 ausing considerable oil pollution which killed many birds.
úðavíkurhlíð, th slopes from Arnarnes to Súðavík.
úðavík, (pop. 145) town. Primary industries are fish rocessing and fishing, with tourism also a growing sector, ostly sea angling. According to the Book of Settlements, yvindur kné and his wife Þuríður rymgylta arrived in eland at Álftafjörður and Seyðisfjörður in the 10th centu-, from Agder, Norway. A town began forming in Álftafjörður in the mid-19th century and Súðavík was first mentioned as a village in the 1880 census. In 1883, a group of Norwegians opened a whaling river. In April 30th 1995, ground was broken for the new residential area in Súðavík. By winter 1996 51 new buildings had been completed and 8 houses moved from the older residential area to the new one. A memorial grove to those who were lost was made the avalanche fell. There are numerous marked hiking paths in the Súðavík area, including an old mail route leading from the bottom of Álftafjörður fjord, over to Önundafjörður fjord. There is also a good campsite and a family park Raggagarður, with recreational equipments and a barbecue. The Arctic Fox Centre opened in 2010, a research and exhibition centre, focusing on the arctic fox, the only native terrestrial mammal in Iceland. At the Centre is also a coffee house, a souvenir shop and internet access. The Eyrardalur farm is the oldest house in Súðavík, recently renovated. The farm is a Norwegian timber house and is connected to the whaling history at Langeyri. It is said the Jón Indíafari (1593-1679) lived at Eyrardalur the last years of his life.
Langeyri, a spit of land where Norwegians built a quay and the first whaling station in Iceland in 1883, the famous whaler Svend Foyn being one of the founders. He was a pioneer in Norwegian seal hunting and whale fishing and invented the explosive harpoon which was a revolution in whaling. This station was operated until the early 20th century.
Kofri, (635 m) an unusual mountain above Langeyri. Can be climbed via Hlíðargil canyon.
Dvergasteinn, á Dvergasteinseyri reistu Norðmenn hvalstöð 1896. Síðar var þar síldarsöltun.
Svarthamar, a farm, the home of Jón Ólafsson Indíafari ("who visited India") (1593-1679), one of the most widely travelled Icelanders in the 17th century. A book he wrote about his travels has been translated into many languages.
Valagil, a beautiful ravine with a spectacular and awesome landscape. There is a great variety of lava flow strata that indicate an ancient central volcano under Lambadalsfjall. A marked hiking trail leads from the highway to the ravine.
Hattardalur, a valley with two farms. At Hattareyri there was a herring-salting station for a time.
Eyri, a church and old manor farm, home of Magnús Magnússon (1630-1704), sheriff and writer. The neighbouring farm Tröð, now abandoned, was the birthplace of Magnús Hj. Magnússon (1873-1916), the poet of Þröm, who was the model for Nobel Prize-winning novelist H. Laxness's Ólafur Ljósvíkingur in *Heimsljós*.
Hestur, a peculiar mountain.
Folafótur, ("Colt's foot") the promontory below the mountain Hestur. Formerly a substantial farm of the same name, now abandoned. Was a lively fishing-station earlier.
Hestfjörður, the first shrimp banks to be found off Iceland were discovered off-shore in 1927.

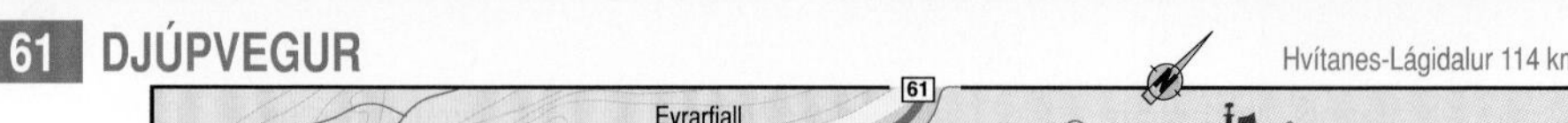

Hvítanes-Lágidalur 114 km

18 P. 581

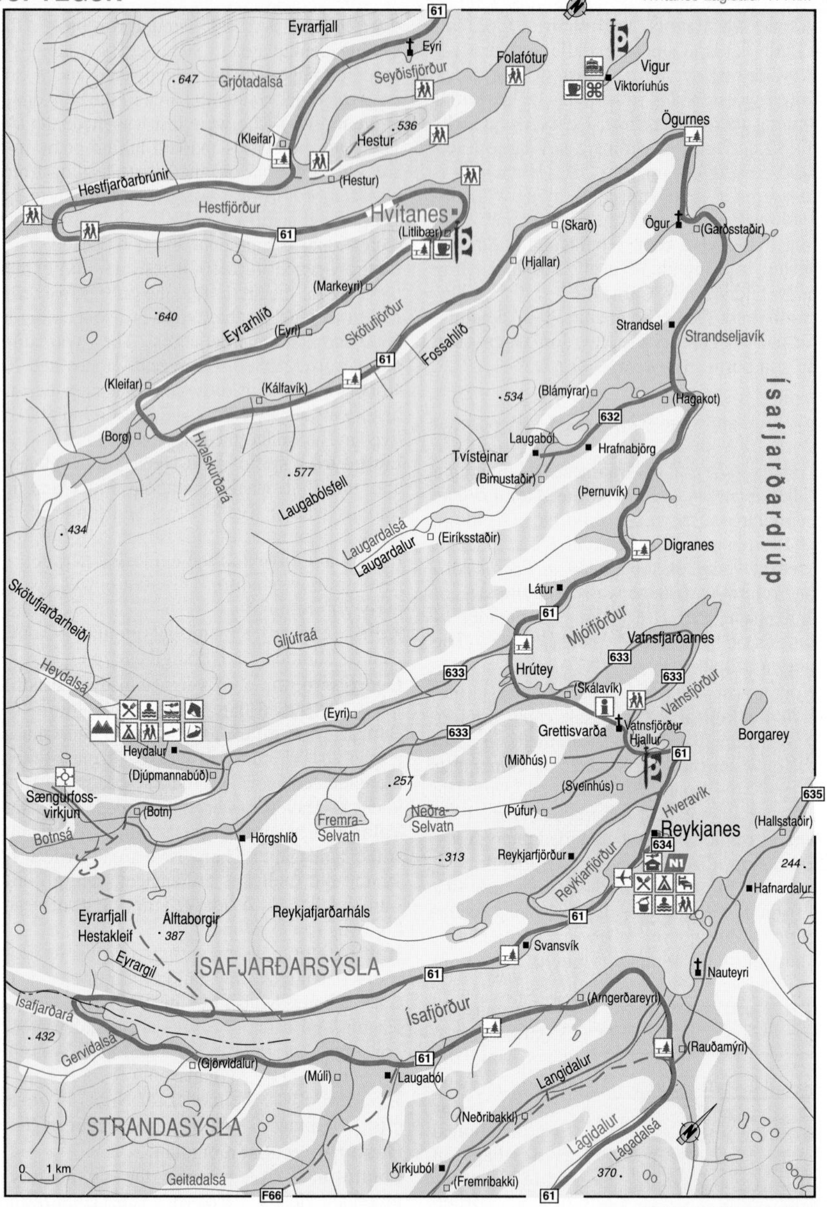

Lágidalur-Hvítanes 114 km

635 **Snæfjallastrandarvegur,** p. 318 F66 **Kollafjarðarheiði,** p. 313

itlibær, now deserted, was inhabited until 1969. /ooden house from 1895 with outer walls of stone, and ırf roof. It originally housed two families. In the keep-ıg of the National Museum since 1999.

igur, a lovely island west of the Ögurnes peninsula, .59 km², rich in eider duck and puffin, formerly a fish-ıg-station. Some relics of old farming methods are pre-erved on Vigur, including Viktoríuhús and Iceland's nly protected windmill, belived to have been built in 860. In the keeping of the National Museum since 1992. here is also the country's oldest 8-oar rowing boat, hich is in fact still in use. Popular tourist place.

gur, a substantial farm and church, occupied through ıe ages by men of influence. Some old relics in the hurch. About the middle of the 19th century one of the iggest dwelling-houses in rural Iceland was built there nd is still standing. The first electric generator on a farm ı the Ísafjarðardjúp district was built at Ögur in 1930. ormerly a fishing-station.

arðsstaðir, an abandoned farm, once the home of oet and sorcerer Þorleifur Þórðarson (1570-1647), best nown as Galdra-Leifi ("Leifi the sorcerer") about whom ıere are many tales. He was for instance said to have got old of the head of a drowned man, sprinkled it with onsecrated wine and bread, and then used it for augery nd other magic.

trandsel, a farm on the shallow bay Strandseljavík. irthplace of Jón Baldvinsson (1882-1938), member of arliament, one of the pioneers of the trade union move-ıent in Iceland.

32 Laugardalsvegur, 5,1 km.

augardalur, a shallow valley.

ljóifjörður, some forest and geothermal heat.

33 Vatnsfjarðarvegur, 42,6 km.

34 Reykjanesvegur, 4,3 km.

orgarey, an island with many eider duck and puffins

atnsfjörður, an ancient manor farm and setting f Sagas, on a fjord of the same name. Church and arsonage. Many clergymen there became wealthy. mong noted farmers was Björn Einarsson Jórsalafari ("who visited Jerusalem") (d.1415) who travelled widely, to Jerusalem among other places. He also went once to Greenland and three times to Rome, travelling like a king with a large retinue. His daughter Kristín was the mother of governor Björn ríki ("the rich") Þorleifsson (1408?-1467) who was killed by Englishmen at Rif (see Skarð). The Rev. Hjalti Þorsteinsson (1665-1754) was the best painter in Iceland in his day. Three Vatnsfjörð-ur pastors in a row wrote annals, the most recent being the Rev. Guðlaugur Sveinsson (1731-1807). In 1791 he published an essay together with sketches which were to cause a revolution in the placing of farmhouses and their appearance, being the first known conception of the Icelandic gabled farmhouse (see Hrafnseyri). Above the farm is the hollow cairn **Grettisvarða**, once thought to have been made by Grettir the strong as a hide-out but more probably a watch tower of some sort, perhaps from the stormy time of the Sturlungas (1220-1262). **Hjallur,** large shack for drying stockfish, with stone walls and turf roof, built around 1880. In the keeping of the National Museum since 1975.

Reykjanes, a narrow peninsula between Ísafjörður and Reykjafjörður. There is a hotel, open all year, in which was once a district school founded in 1934 and renovated around 1960. There is a swimming pool, originally built 1889, green houses and hot springs. From 1774 till the end of the 19th century there was salt-processing by the hot spring. It was operated again in 2008 and is the only place in the world where salt is produced in an environ-mentally sustainable way. Good walking routes and rich birdlife in the area.

Laugaból, a substantial farm on Ísafjörður, well-wood-ed. Considered by some to have been the farm of Þorbjörn Þjóðreksson of *Hávarðar saga Ísfirðings*. Long the residence of the poetess Halla Eyjólfsdóttir (1866-1937). A jeep track from there across Kollafjarðarheiði moor to the farm Fjarðarhorn in Kollafjörður and Road 60.

Arngerðareyri, formerly a trading centre, now a land-ing stage for the Fagranes ferry boat from Ísafjörður.

Steingrímsfjarðarheiði, (440 m) moors with many lakes and brook The moors are very flat on top and in the old days many people got lo there in foggy weather. A refuge hut at Þrívörðuholt.

Þorskafjarðarheiði, (490 m) a moor providing the shortest rou between Breiðafjörður and Ísafjarðardjúp and the most-travelled rou between Breiðafjörður and Ísafjarðardjúp for centuries. Stony ar barren with many small lakes. A Highway Department refuge hut.

Staðará, a river flowing from Steingrímsfjarðarheiði moor dow through the valley Staðardalur. Fairly calm and deep at its lower end, good fishing river.

Staður, a church in the Staðardalur valley, built in 1855, a former pa sonage. Staður was considered one of the richest benefices in the enti country. Among the best-known clergymen there was Jón Árnasc (1665-1743), Bishop of Skálholt. In the church there is a remarkab pulpit painted with figures of Christ and his disciples, dating back to th year 1731.

68 **Innstrandavegur,** p. 311
608 **Þorskafjarðarvegur,** p. 313
643 **Strandavegur,** p. 319

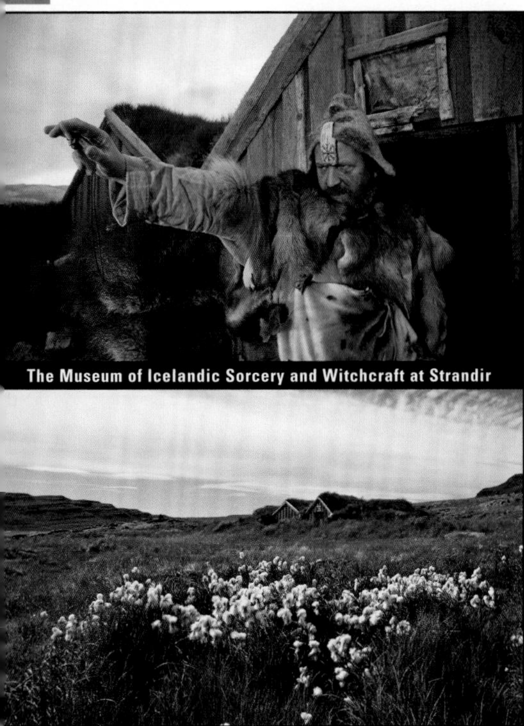

The Museum of Icelandic Sorcery and Witchcraft at Strandir

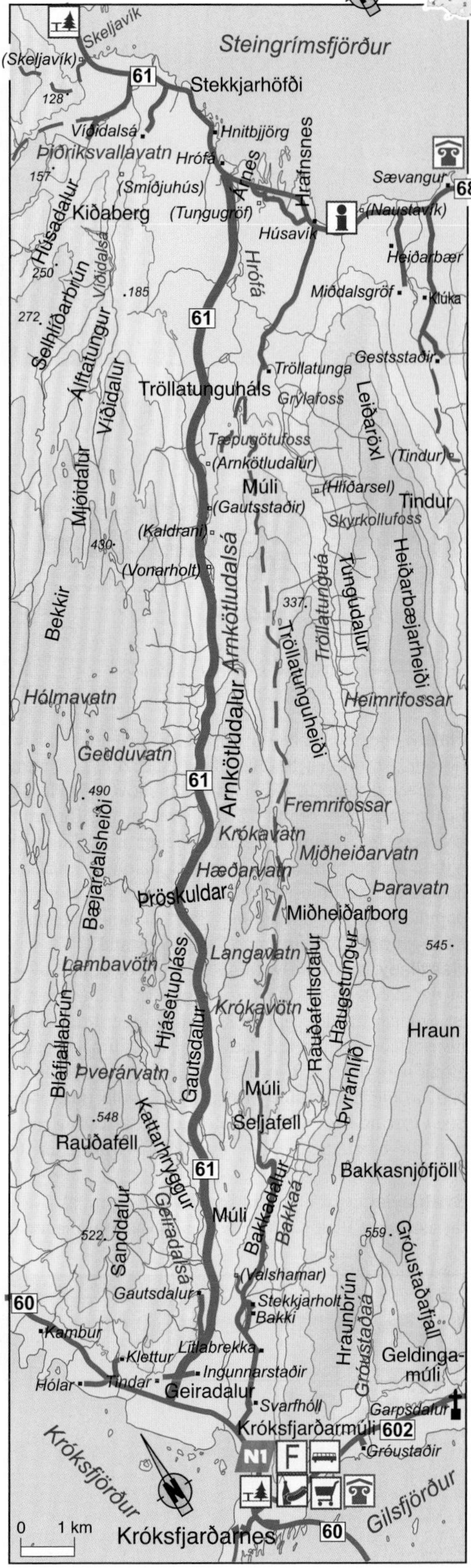

keljavík, there is a memorial to Hermann Jónasson 1896–1976) a member of parliament 1934–67 and prime ninister.

röllatunga, a church, and a parsonage until 1906. Lignite nd plant fossils in places. It used to be said metals and easure were hidden in the ground, so some Danes obtained fficial permission to dig, but they found nothing but stones 1 **Gullhóll** ("Gold hill"). In Tröllatungukirkja church there vas an ancient church bell, in the National Museum of celand since 1988.

úsavík, a farm on Steingrímsfjörður. Close by is lúsavíkurkleif where lignite and fossils from the Tertiary eriod have been found. A stream flows through a gorge ıere in a small waterfall. Some iron ore is also found there.

teingrímsfjörður, the biggest fjord in Strandasýsla coun-, 28 km long and 7 km wide at the mouth. Lowish, round-d mountains descending to the sea in ledges and terraces. ome flat land and many valleys.

60 **Vestfjarðavegur,** p. 284
68 **Innstrandavegur,** p. 311
602 **Garpdalsvegur,** p. 282

16 P. 579

Flatey

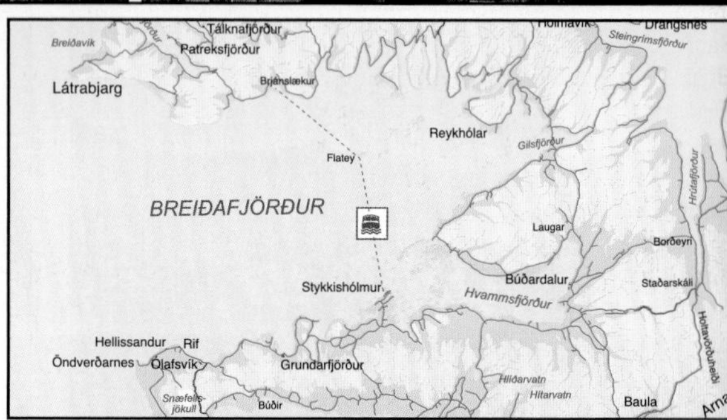

Flatey, the most notable of all the islands in Breiðafjörður. An official trading place since 1777. A monastery erected there in 1172 was later moved to Helgafell. In the early 19th century Flatey was in the forefront of progress and culture in Iceland. There is a church there with a fresco by the contemporary painter Baltasar. Old houses are well preserved on the island, which is now a popular tourist attraction. The famous manuscript *Flateyjarbók* takes its name from the island.

Hergilsey, an island with geothermal heat, site of some of the events of *Gísla saga Súrssonar*. In the year 1910 an English trawler captain kidnapped the director of the district council in Hergilsey and took him to England, along with the sheriff of Barðastrandasýsla-county. They had, in the line of duty, rowed out to the trawler in an open rowing boat with the intention of arresting the captain for breaking the law by fishing within territorial waters.

Svefneyjar, a group of 52 islands, 2-3 nautical miles off the island of Flatey. There was a substantial manor farm there at one time. Eggert Ólafsson (1726-68) naturalis poet and cultural leader, one of the most remarkable me in Iceland in the 18th century, was born in Svefneyjar. Hi best known work is the *Ferðabók* which he wrote wit Bjarni Pálsson (1719–1779), later the first Surgeo General of Iceland, after their travels and research i Iceland from 1752-57. (*Travels in Iceland* by Egger Ólafsson and Bjarni Pálsson 1752-1757, first printe by Barnard & Sultzer, Water Lane, Fleet Street, 1805 It contains observations on the manners and customs c the inhabitants, descriptions of the lakes, rivers, glaciers hot-springs and volcanoes, various kinds of earth stones, fossils and petrifactions, as well as description of animals, insects, fishes, etc.) Eggert and his wife, the newly-wed, were drowned in Breiðafjörður along wit all the crew, when they were crossing the fjord on thei way to his farm Hofstaðir on the Snæfellsnes peninsula Eggert is said to have had with him on board the halber of Gunnar from Hlíðarendi of *Njáls saga* (see Road 54 Hofsstaðir).

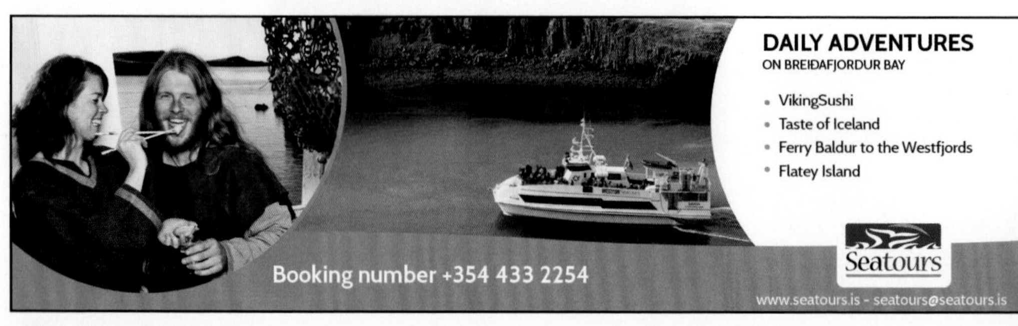

Iagatafla, (603 m) a picturesque mountain west of Hagi.

Iagi, a big manor farm and church. For long the office of a sheriff, the ast of whom was the poet Jón Thoroddsen. In Saga times the home of Gestur Oddleifsson the wise. He was one of the wisest men in the land in is time and appears in *Laxdæla saga* among others. He was thought to ave the power of foresight.

Mórudalur, a small valley through which flows the fishing-river Móra. Geothermal heat. A swimming pool, fallen into disuse.

Kross, a community at the mouth of Mórudalur.

Reiðskörð, jagged crags where the criminal Sveinn skotti, the son of the otorious 16th century murderer Björn from Öxl (see Road 574, Öxl), was anged, after which the place was said to be haunted.

Barðaströnd, the coastline from Vatnsfjörður to the farm Siglunes. Continuous flat land with steep cliffs above and some small valleys, ndented by the shallow inlet Hagavaðall, that almost dries up at low tide. Sandy and grassy, with birch-bushes, farms.

Brjánslækur, an ancient manor farm, church, parsonage. Nearby are the **Flókatóttir** remains, said to be ruins of the booth built by Flóki Vilgerðarson or Hrafna Flóki ("Raven-Flóki"), for his first winter's stay in celand in the 9th century. He got his nickname because he used ravens to elp him find Iceland when he first came there, and is responsible for aming the country Iceland. If they were indeed his booth, these are the ldest ruins of a man-made structure in Iceland. Above the farm is the **Surtarbrandsgil** ravine where there is lignite. It is one of the best places or finding fossils from the Tertiary period, first noticed by the explorers Eggert Ólafsson and Bjarni Pálsson. Car ferry to Stykkishólmur, road 58.

Flókalundur, ("Flóki's grove") a wooded area near the crossroads. Some ervices, summer hotel, summer house area and swimming pool nearby.

58 **Stykkishólmsvegur,** p. 255
60 **Vestfjarðavegur,** p. 288
611 **Siglunesvegur,** p. 306

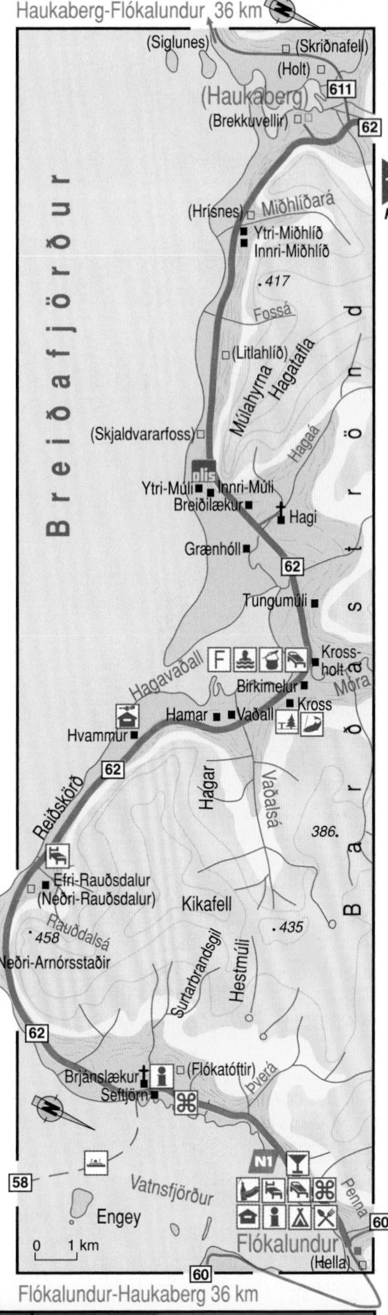

Patreksfjörður-Haukaberg 25 km

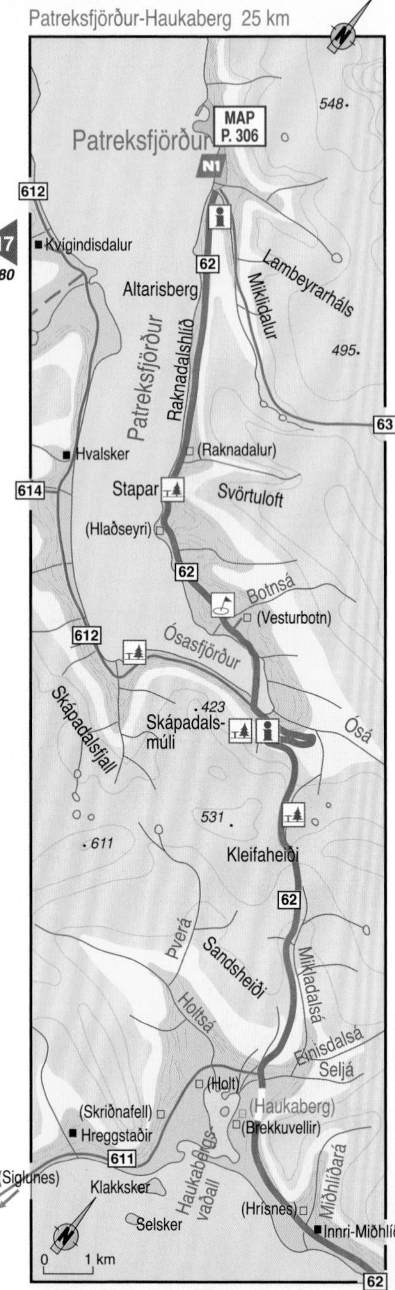

Haukaberg-Patreksfjörður 25 km

Patreksfjörður, (pop. 651), a town on a fjord of same name, built on th two sandspits Vatneyri and Geirseyri. A very old trading place. The har bour, dug in shallow water on Vatneyri in 1946, is called Patrekshöfn Main industries fishing and fish-processing. A snow avalanche in 198 killed 4 people and destroyed many homes. There is a memorial to tha event. There is also a memorial honouring British seamen in Icelandi waters and those who died there. This memorial was a joint venture b the citizens of Aberdeen, Hull and Grimsby in the United Kingdom.

Raknadalshlíð, steep, stony cliffs along the fjord east of Patreksfjörðu town.

Skápadalur, on the shore is Garðar, Icelands oldest steel boat, constructe in Norway 1912. As the boat is very rusty it is not recommended to go o board.

Kleifaheiði, (404 m) a mountain road from the Barðaströnd coast to th head of Patreksfjörður. On the top of the moors, at their western edge, is the Kleifabúi cairn in the shape of a man, raised by road workers. It is said the it resembles Hákon J. Kristófersson (1877-1967) a farmer and a congress man from the farm Hagi at Barðaströnd.

Stálfjall, ("Steel mountain") a mountain (650 m) between the Rauðisandur sands and the Barðaströnd coast. Lignite deposits, and during First World War there was some mining there, now discontinued.

611 Siglunesvegur, 7,3 km.

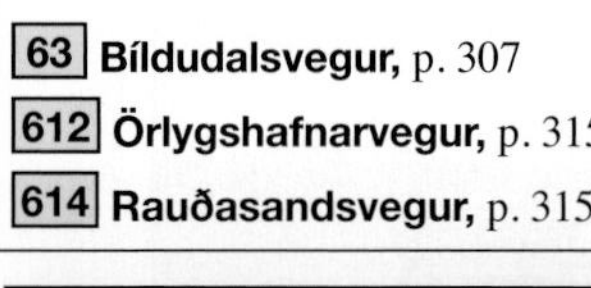

63 Bíldudalsvegur, p. 307
612 Örlygshafnarvegur, p. 315
614 Rauðasandsvegur, p. 315

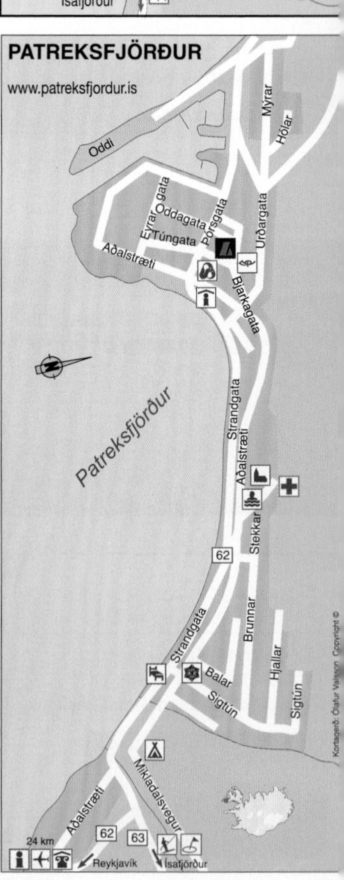

Sjóræningjahúsið

617 **Tálknafjarðarvegur,** 11,6 km.

:tóri-Laugardalur, a church built in 1907. There is also an old pool that vas once used for washing called Djáknalaug.

.itli-Laugardalur, geothermal heat. The hot water is used to heat ıp a swiming pool and to a hut tub which is open around the ·lock all year round.

:veinseyri, farm, community centre and school, swimming pool .nd forestry.

'álknafjörður, (pop. 275) The village at Tálknafjörður ·egan forming around 1945 vhen the Tálknafjörður reezing plant was opened. Jntil that point there was ıot much of a community ·uilt up, although Bakki was ·eginning to become a com-ıunity, as it was home to ·ne of the region's two ·chools and was used as a ·ase for some fishing outfits. Tálknafjörður is actually one ·f the younger settlements n the West Fjords, which is no doubt because of the amount of ice that ormed at Hópið, making it difficult for timber boats to break though. Iowever, this changed with the dawn of metal boats, and not long after, he new settlement appeared. Fisherman's huts had previously been used ·ut at the end of the fjord as it was shorter to the fishing grounds and the ce didn't obstruct the path. Fishing is still the main industry. The village ncludes an elementary school, swimming pool, community centre and hurch, Tálknafjörður Church, consecrated in 2002.

Tálknafjörður swimming pool

3íldudalur, (pop. 170) a village in a small inlet of Arnarfjörður. As a well ituated for fishing and trading, it was once one of the most important ishing stations in Iceland. Bíldudalur was at its height at the turn of the ast century, at the time of Pétur Thorseinsson the father of the present rillage and a pioneer in fishing and processing, way ahead of his time. Main Occupation today still is fishing but also processing of calcified lgae. Main attractions: Bird life and nature. The Sea Monster Museum, ;ymnasium, hostel, restaurant and a natural hot spring in Reykjarfjörður. The music museum Melodies and memories contains many exhibits relat-·d to Icelands's musical history. Monument to drowned seamen. 3irthplace of the artist Guðmundur Thorsteinsson (Muggur 1891-1924) he son of Pétur Thorsteinsson.

60 **Vestfjarðavegur,** p. 288 62 **Barðastrandarvegur,** p. 306
619 **Ketildalavegur,** p. 317

Patreksfjörður-Helluskarð 63 km

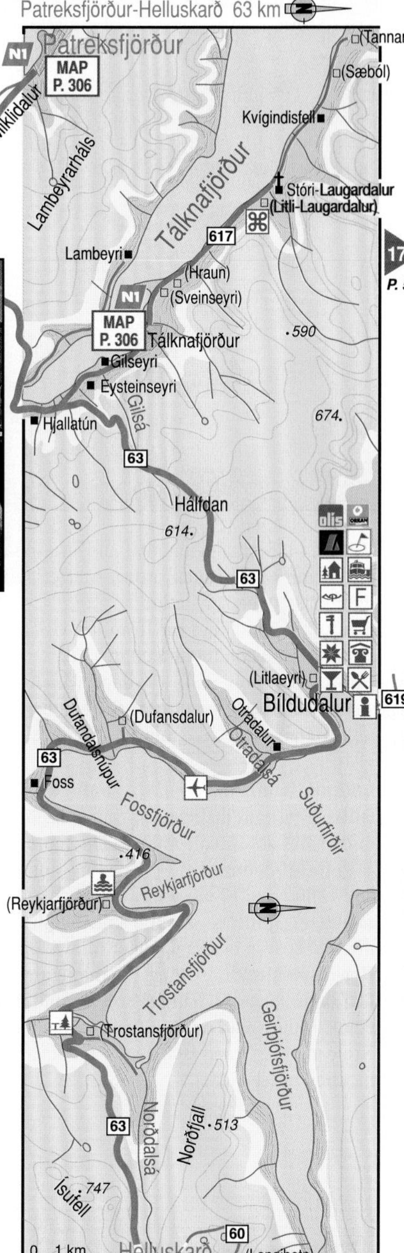

Helluskarð-Patreksfjörður 63 km

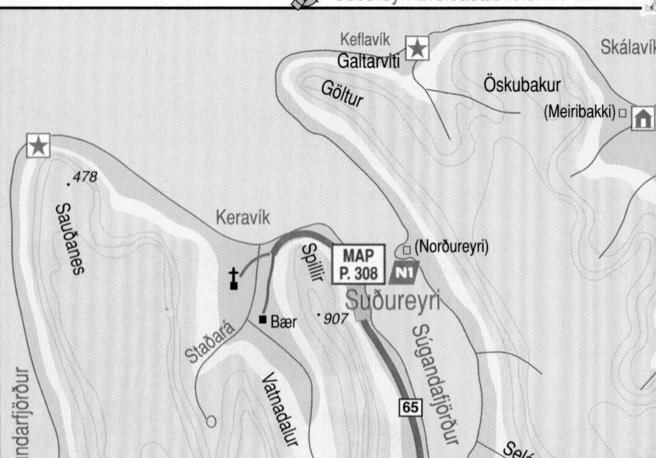

Göltur, (445 m) a distinctive and striking mountain on the northern side of the mouth of Súgandafjörður. At Keflavík below Göltur is the Galtarviti lighthouse. Weather station.

Staður, a church not far from the village. Nearby is Sauðanes, where the steamer *Talisman* foundered in 1922.

Suðureyri, (pop. 264) a village which has been an official trading place since just before the turn of the century. Now much fishing, fish-processing. Memorial to Magnús Hj. Magnússon, "the poet from Þröm" (1873-1916).

Laugar, swimming pool, first built in 1933.

Botn, a farm at the head of Súgandafjörður, where lignite was sometimes mined, but not since 1940-42. The lignite was used for fuel.

Súgandafjörður, a fjord opening out between the mountains Sauðanes and Göltur, ca. 12 km long. Broadish at the mouth, but narrowing near the mountain Spillir to about 1 km. Shallow, steep cliffs, birch-bushes, geothermal heat in places. Danger of avalanches.

Breiðadalsheiði, (610 m) the mountain road between Önundarfjörður and Ísafjörður, one of the highest in Iceland. Formerly frequent avalanche accidents. Motor-road opened in 1936. Tunnels that have been made under the Breiðadalsheiði and Botnsheiði moors are a great improvement to communication in the area.

60 **Vestfjarðavegur,** p. 292

Prestbakki, a church and parsonage.

Bær, a farm, often the seat of the local sheriff. In the 17th century the sub-governor Þorleifur Kortsson lived there. He was notorious for the number of people he had burnt for witchcraft. His son Hannes was historian to the King, and was sent to Iceland to collect sagas and manuscripts. He was lost at sea in 1682 along with all the manuscripts.

The farm Bær in Hrútafjörður.

Kjörseyri, a farm, for 40 years the home of the scholar Finnur Jónsson (1842-1924), who wrote about Icelandic national customs and sagas.

Laxárdalsheiði, (200 m), a moor, traversed by Laxárdalsvegur (Road 59) between the villages Búðardalur and Borðeyri. Two Laxá rivers flow down from there, one to Hvammsfjörður, the other to Hrútafjörður. Flattish with many lakes, the biggest being Laxárvatn.

640 Borðeyrarvegur, 0,64 km.

Borðeyri, a trading place, authorised in 1846. For a time the seat of the sheriff's office.

Fjarðarhorn, a farm from where a disused moorland track, **Sölvamannagötur** ("Sea-weed men's road"), goes up onto Laxárdalsheiði moor. The name indicates that men from North Iceland used to go that way to buy the edible sea-weed dulse at Saurbær.

Melar, an old substantial farm and home of local leaders. The same family has lived there since 1530, and all the farmers have been christened Jón, except for one Jósep.

Brú, once a telephone exchange and post office opened about 1950, moved from Borðeyri. Connects North, South and West Iceland.

1 **Norðurlandsvegur,** p. 62
59 **Laxárdalsvegur,** p. 257
702 **Heggstaðanesvegur,** p. 334
F586 **Haukadalsskarðsvegur,** p. 468

Prestbakki-Brú 25 km

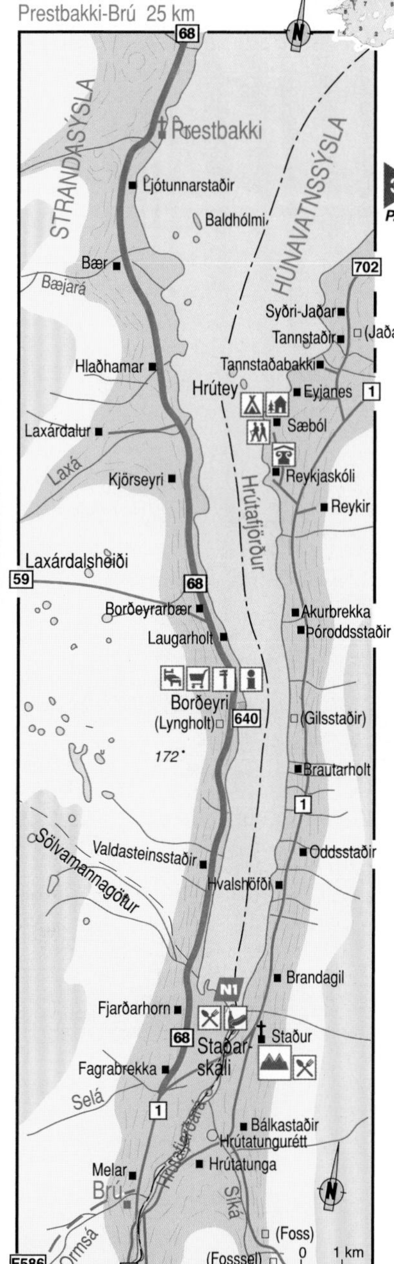

3 P. 566

Brú-Prestbakki 25 km

Kollafjarðarnes-Prestbakki 68 km

Kollafjarðarnes · Broddanes · Broddadalsá · Ljúfustaðir · (Litla-Fjarðarhorn) · Steinadalur · Miðhús · Fell · (Undraland) · Stóra-Fjarðarhorn · Ennishöfði · Svartifoss · Skriðnesenni · Ennisá · Bræðrabrekka · Einfætingsgil · Árdalur · Gröf · Hvítarhlíð · Bitrufjörður · Óspakseyri · Stikuháls · Snartartunga · Þambárvellir · Þambá · Skálholtsvík · Guðlaugsvík · Kattará · Víkurá · Sandfell · Kolbeinsá · Borgir · (Stóra-Hvalsá) · (Litla-Hvalsá) · Hvalsá · Kollsá · Hrafnadalsfjall · Prestbakki

3 P. 566

Prestbakki-Kollafjarðarnes 68 km

Kollafjörður, a small fjord about 8 km long. Skerries and shoals in the middle known as Skottar, dangerous for boats.

690 Steinadalsvegur, 29 km.

Steinadalsheiði, (330 m) the mountain road between Kollafjörður and Gilsfjörður, 17 km long. The small lake **Heiðarvatn** by the road. Three cairns show the boundary of three counties: Strandasýsla, Austur-Barðastrandarsýsla and Dalasýsla. Available to most cars during the summer.

Fell, an ancient manor farm and church until 1909. Nearby is the waterfall **Svartifoss**, behind which is a cave where the outlaw Fjalla-Eyvindur ("Mountain-Eyvindur") is said to have stayed and which is a good landmark for ships. One of best-known farmers was sheriff Halldór Jakobsson (1736-1810). Among his writings is the history of volcanoes, published in Danish in 1757 and for long a popular reference book abroad. Fell was also the home for a time of the Rev. Oddur Þorsteinsson (ca. 1600), who is said to have been a powerful sorcerer and about whom there are many folk tales.

Broddanes, a farm with many natural advantages, such as seals, eider ducks, driftwood. Some crags in the sea nearby, called Broddar ("Spikes").

Skriðnesenni, the outermost farm on Bitrufjörður, where the same family has lived for 200 years. Nearby is a very steep headland, Ennishöfði.

641 Krossárdalsvegur, 2,84 km.

Óspakseyri, a farm, church and once a trading place named for the robber Óspakur who lived there. The land is that of the settler Þorbjörn bitra, from whom Bitrufjörður takes its name.

Bitrufjörður, a short fjord with little flat land, and small valleys off it.

Guðlaugsvík, a farm. Named after a man, Guðlaugur, who was murdered at Guðlausghöfði according to the *Book of Settlement*.

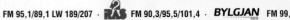

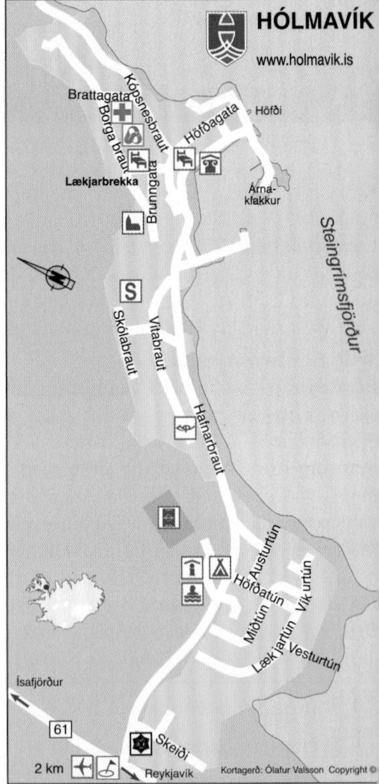

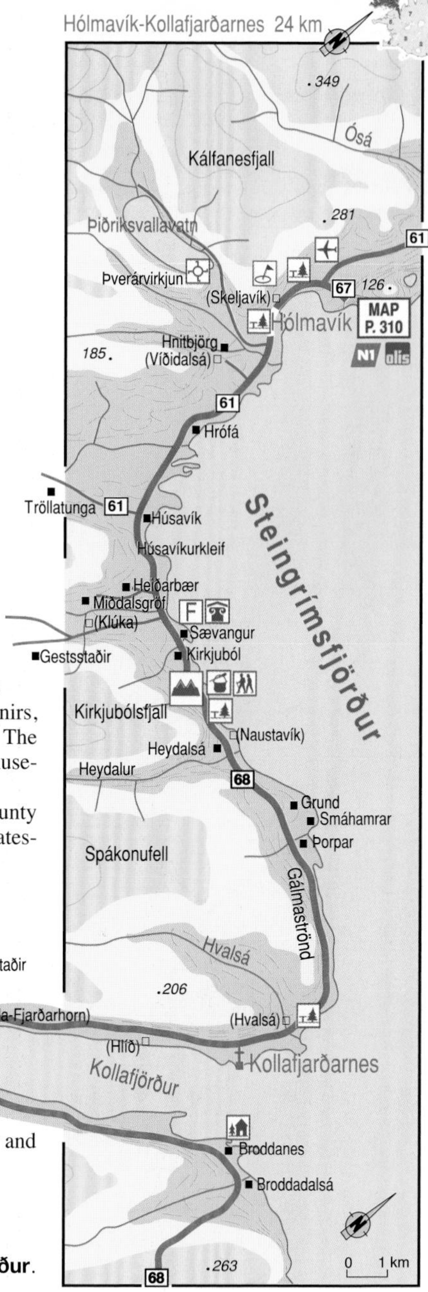

67 **Hólmavíkurvegur,** 1,63 km.

ólmavík, (pop. 391) a village in the land of Kálfanes. Before trading started there in 1895, there was trade at Skipatangi in nearby Skeljavík bay. Now the main trading centre for the district. Fishing and fish-processing. At Hólmavík is a library, church, guesthouse, restaurant, coffe house and an outdoor swimming pool with hot tubs, it is also possible to go deep sea fishing and horse riding. The Museum of Sorcery & Witchcraft in Hólmavík presents the history of witch-hunting in the 17th century Iceland as well as various aspects of magic from younger sources. The museum shop offers souvenirs, books and magical amulets that might assist you in daily strife. The Tourist Information Centre is located in the same building as the museum.

Skeljavík, an abandoned farm where the people of Strandasýsla county erected a monument in 1979 to Hermann Jónasson (1896-1967) statesman and prime minister.

Sævangur, community center. There is an interesting exhibition about the icelandic sheep and sheep farming with special emphasis on the Strandir area. The children can enjoy themselves in their own room, in which are toys and colour books, while the grown-ups can view the exhibition, and the museum also has a small science room where people can taka a look at various things through microscope. One of the main attraction in the Sheep Farming Museum are lambs which the visitors can feed with milk from a bottle. There is also a coffee bar and handicraft- and souvenir store.

Kirkjuból, a farm and the community centre Sævangur.

Heydalsá, a farm, site of a secondary school founded in 1896 and operated for 20 years.

Gálmaströnd, the coast to the south of the mouth of **Steingrímsfjörður**. Much driftwood, to which Skálholt cathedral had the rights.

Kollafjarðarnes, a farm and church.

61 **Djúpvegur,** p. 303
690 **Steinadalsvegur,** p. 282

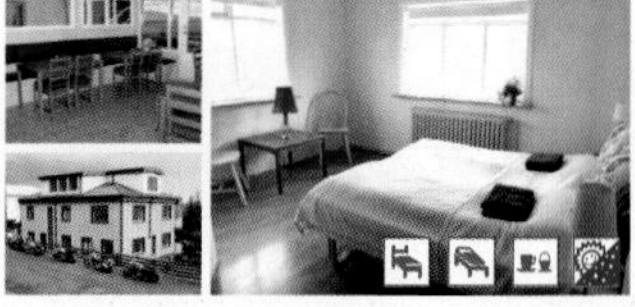

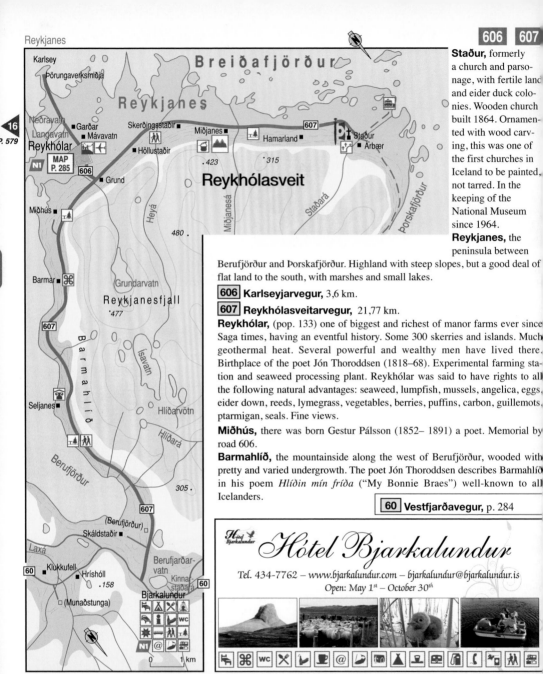

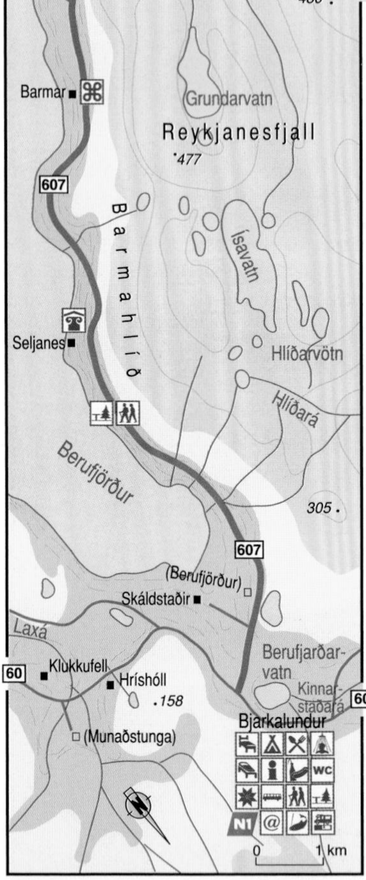

Staður, formerly a church and parsonage, with fertile land and eider duck colonies. Wooden church built 1864. Ornamented with wood carving, this was one of the first churches in Iceland to be painted, not tarred. In the keeping of the National Museum since 1964.

Reykjanes, the peninsula between Berufjörður and Þorskafjörður. Highland with steep slopes, but a good deal of flat land to the south, with marshes and small lakes.

606 Karlseyjarvegur, 3,6 km.

607 Reykhólasveitarvegur, 21,77 km.

Reykhólar, (pop. 133) one of biggest and richest of manor farms ever since Saga times, having an eventful history. Some 300 skerries and islands. Much geothermal heat. Several powerful and wealthy men have lived there. Birthplace of the poet Jón Thoroddsen (1818–68). Experimental farming station and seaweed processing plant. Reykhólar was said to have rights to all the following natural advantages: seaweed, lumpfish, mussels, angelica, eggs, eider down, reeds, lymegrass, vegetables, berries, puffins, carbon, guillemots, ptarmigan, seals. Fine views.

Miðhús, there was born Gestur Pálsson (1852– 1891) a poet. Memorial by road 606.

Barmahlíð, the mountainside along the west of Berufjörður, wooded with pretty and varied undergrowth. The poet Jón Thoroddsen describes Barmahlíð in his poem *Hlíðin mín fríða* ("My Bonnie Braes") well-known to all Icelanders.

60 Vestfjarðavegur, p. 284

16 P. 579

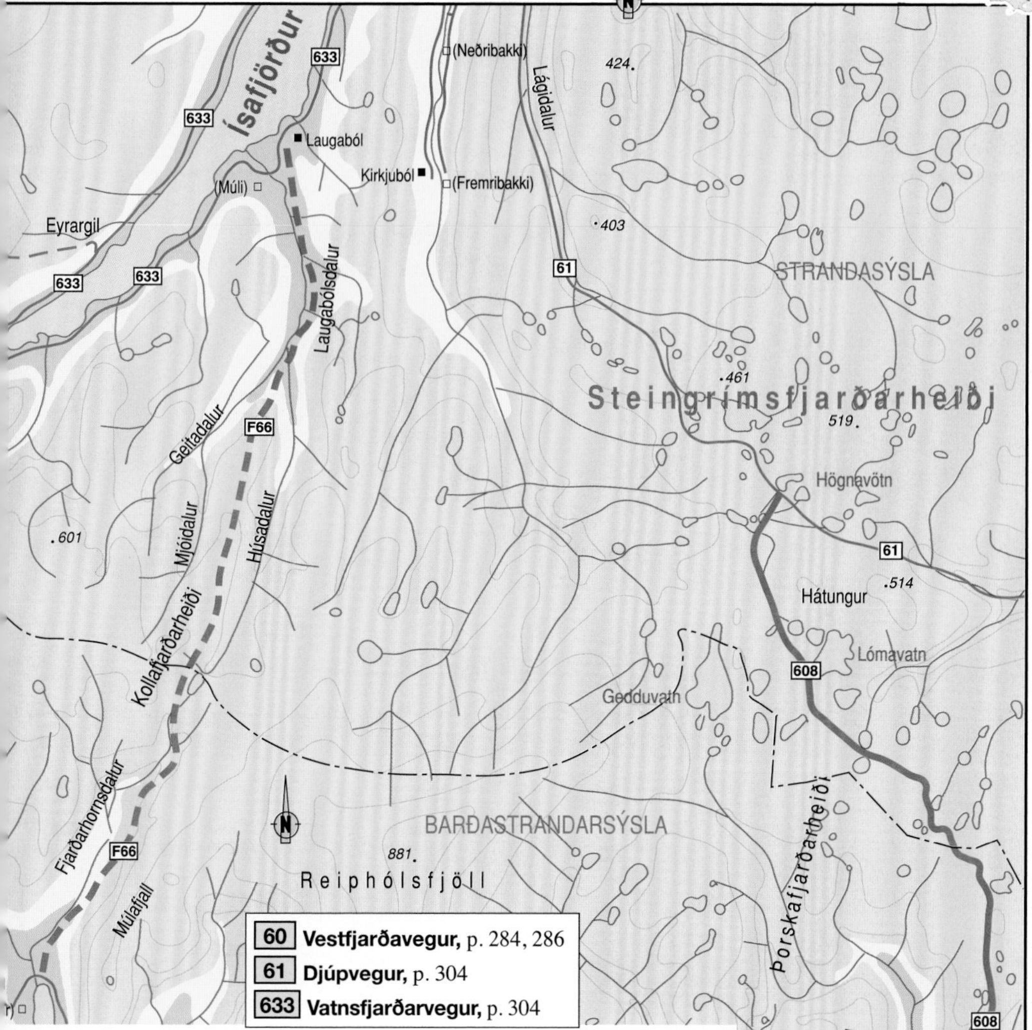

60	**Vestfjarðavegur,** p. 284, 286
61	**Djúpvegur,** p. 304
633	**Vatnsfjarðarvegur,** p. 304

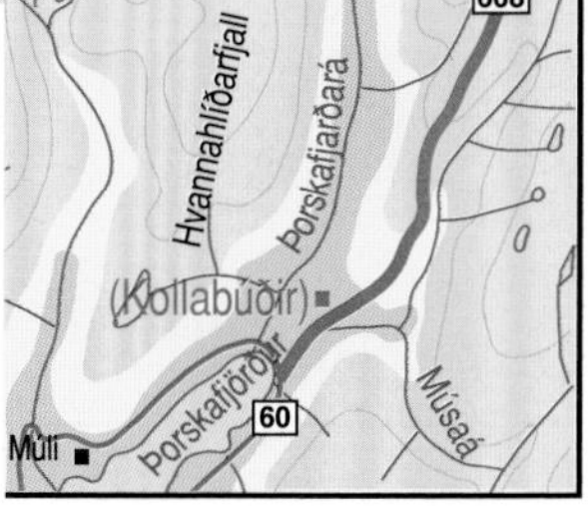

F66 Kollafjarðarheiði, 23 km, a jeep-route.

Fjarðarhorn, the innermost farm in Kollafjörður, now abandoned, from which the jeep-track goes up onto Kollafjarðarheiði moor and down into Laugarbólsdalur.

Kollafjörður, a fjord, 16 km long, with many fords and flats that can be crossed at low tide. At its head lies the route up onto Kollafjarðarheiði moor which was one of the much-travelled routes between Breiðafjörður and the Ísafjarðardjúp fjords. The other two main routes were over Skálmardalsheiði moor and Þorskafjarðarheiði moor. All these moors reach a height of 400-500 m, but the Skálmardalsheiði route offers the shortest distance across the wilderness between farms. It lies up from the head of Skálmarfjörður and comes down via the Gjörvidalur valley at the head of Ísafjörður. The longest route was Þorskafjarðarheiði, going up the valley Kollabúðardalur in Þorskafjörður and coming down Langidalur in Ísafjarðardjúp. The people of Breiðafjörður would travel over these moors to get to Bolungarvík, for winter fishing or to go to Ísafjörður for trade. These routes were in use around 1900 for herding sheep to Ísafjörður. For this they also used a short cut over Hestfjarðarheiði moor and down into Álftafjörður

Þorskafjarðarheiði, (490 m) moor and the mountain road crossing it. The shortest route between Reykjavík and Ísafjarðardjúp, stony and barren. A refuge hut of the Public Roads Administration is located there.

Kollabúðir, an abandoned farm at the head of Þorskafjörður; site of the ancient assembly of the Western fjords district, the Þorskafjarðarþing. In late 19th century the scene of the so-called Kollabúðafundir, meetings held in order to further the cause of the political and cultural independence of Iceland. Ruins of the old booths are visible at Kollabúðareyri on the Músará river. Towards the end of the 16th century Kollabúðir was a German trading place.

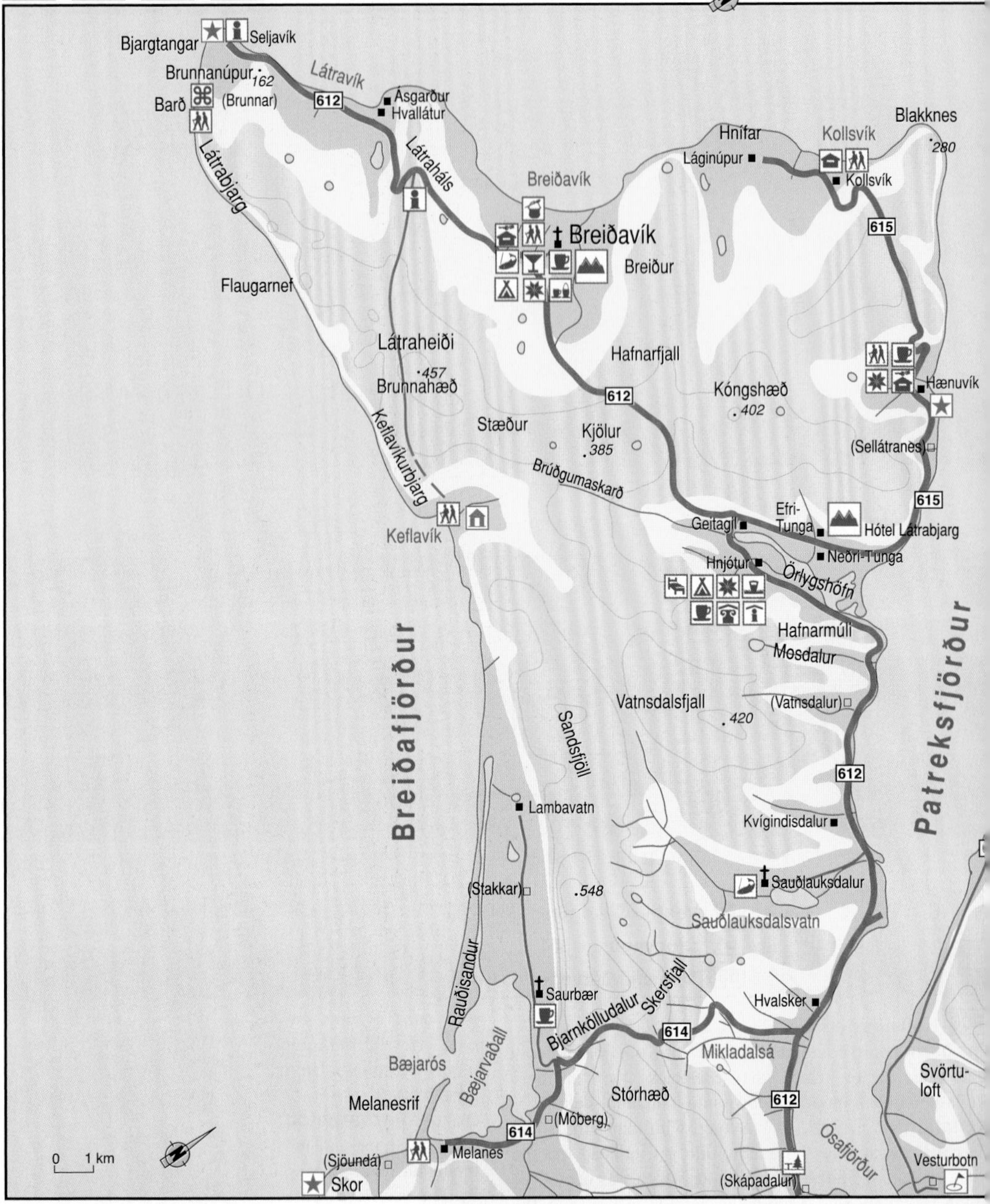

17
P. 580

Bjargtangar
Seljavík
Brunnanúpur 162
Látravík
Barð
(Brunnar)
612
Ásgarður
Hvallátur
Látrabjarg
Látraháls
Hnífar
Kollsvík
Blakknes
280
Láginúpur
Kollsvík
Breiðavík
Breiðavík
Breiður
615
Flaugarnef
Látraheiði
457
Brunnahæð
Hafnarfjall
Kóngshæð
402
Hænuvík
612
Keflavíkurbjarg
Stæður
Kjölur
385
Brúðgumaskarð
(Sellátranes)
615
Keflavík
Geitagil
Efri-Tunga
Hótel Látrabjarg
Hnjótur
Neðri-Tunga
Örlygshöfn
Hafnarmúli
Mosdalur
Breiðafjörður
Patreksfjörður
Vatnsdalsfjall
420
(Vatnsdalur)
Sandsfjöll
612
Lambavatn
Kvígindisdalur
(Stakkar)
548
Sauðlauksdalur
Sauðlauksdalsvatn
Rauðisandur
Saurbær
Skersfjall
Hvalsker
Bjarnkölludalur
614
Mikladalsá
Bæjarós
Bæjarvaðall
Stórhæð
Svörtuloft
Melanesrif
(Móberg)
612
614
Ósafjörður
0 1 km
(Sjöundá)
Melanes
Vesturbotn
Skor
(Skápadalur)

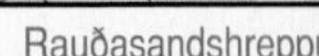

614 **Rauðasandsvegur,** 9,7 km.

ásar in Seljavík bay, between Brunnanúpur and Bjargar-ıngi. There are visible ruins of the walls of the house, the emains of a fence and what was probably a well shelter. It said that the place used to be a farm, abandoned in the 15th entury. If this is true, it was the westernmost place of uman habitation in Iceland and consequently the whole of urope.

eflavík, an abandoned farm and former fishing station. here are some important remains of a fishing station from ng ago. Refuge hut.

aurbær, often called Bær á Rauðasandi, a church and for-ıer home of local leaders, most noted of whom was Eggert annesson (1515-83), local governor. English pirates pil-ged Bær in his day.

auðisandur, ("Red sands") a settled district in an arc etween the Skorarhlíðar slopes and the Látrabjarg cliffs, king its name from the colour of the sand on the coast. narrow area of flat land, cut across by the Bæjarvaðall goon, above which are steep rocky slopes. This is the esternmost township in Iceland and indeed in Europe.

lelanes, the easternmost farm in the Rauðisandur district. ome old soil layers perhaps indicating former grain-grow-g. Just east of there is the abandoned farm **Sjöundá**, scene f a crime early in the 19th century, on which writer Gunnar Gunnarsson's novel *Svartfugl* is based. Bjarni Bjarnason and Steinunn Sveinsdóttir were found guilty of murdering their spouses, and condemned to death.

Skor, west of the mountain Stálfjall along the Skorarhlíðar slopes lay a rough and dangerous route between the Barðaströnd coast and the Rauðisandur district. Lighthouse built 1953 at Skor. Previously a fishing-station, being one of the few landings in the area. Skor is best known in Icelandic history for being the place from which the magistrate and poet Eggert Ólafsson set out on his fatal voyage in the spring of 1768. His wife and all the boat crew perished with him. Eggert is said to have had with him on board the halberd of Gunnar from Hlíðarendi of *Njáls saga*. Memorial plaque to Eggert at Skor (see Road 62, Svefneyjar).

Skersfjall, a mountain where the road reaches a height of 350 m.

615 **Kollsvíkurvegur,** 20 km.

Kollsvík, two farms. In the 19th century a whirlwind tore down the buildings, killing the occupants.

Tunga, there was once a community centre and an elementary school. Now a hotel.

612 **Örlygshafnarvegur,** 46,44 km.

62 **Barðastrandarvegur,** p. 306

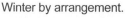

The landing site at Hnjótur.

Memorial at Hnjótur.

Kryppa beneeth Hafnarmúli.

Látrabjarg, a 14 km long cliff, one of the biggest bird-cliffs in Iceland, where eggs have been gathered by absailing. Shipwrecks have occurred there. The highest point (441 m) is at Heiðnakast east of the canyon Saxagjá. It is climbable. In June 2010 a German tourist who was taken pictures from the edge of the cliff fell to his death.

Bjargtangar, the westernmost point of Iceland and also of Europe. The nearest land due south is the Antarctic.

Hvallátur, the westernmost home of Iceland (and thus Europe), just north of Bjargtangar. Formerly a farm and big fishing-station, relics of which are still visible. It was from there that the rescue of the crew of the British trawler *Dhoon* off Látrabjarg in 1947 was organized – one of the boldest rescues off Iceland.

Breiðavík, a church and the westernmost guesthouse in Europe. Good walking routes.

Hnjótur, a farm and a remarkable museum of local objects. This memorial was erected in 1998 in remembrance of rescuers which have saved Icelandic and foreign seamen as well as the memory of those who could not be saved. Al this has been the work of dedicated local man, Egil Ólafsson (1925-1999).

Örlygshöfn, a grassy valley by a sea lagoon.

Hafnarmúli, a landing place between Mosdalur anc Örlygshöfn. Some ruins are still visable, thought be fron the original settlement.

Kryppa, below Hafnarmúli, east of the old landing places It is said that the people there lived in crofts in this place i former times.

Kvígindisdalur, a weather station.

Sauðlauksdalur, a church and former parsonage in a small valley. Sea and sand erosion. Trout lake. The Rev Björn Halldórsson (1724-94) was noted for his horticultura activities. He was the first to grow potatoes in Iceland an the first to begin anti-erosion work, building the Ranglátu wall, still visible.

Frá Básum

The landing site at Básar

619 KETILDALAVEGUR

Ketildalir, the district on the southern shore of Arnarfjörður. Some small valleys, partly grassy, trout streams, seafishing, farms. The valleys: Hvestudalur, Hringsdalur, Bakkadalur, Austmannsdalur, Fífustaðadalur and Selárdalur are separated by steep ridges.

Þórishlíðarfjall, there some fossil and lignite have been found.

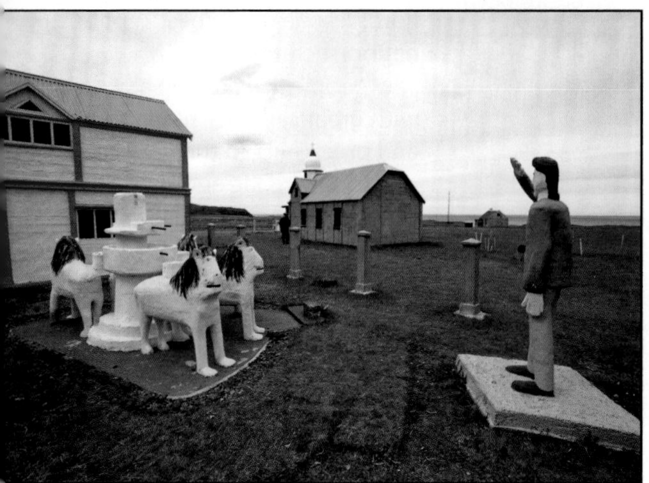

Samúel Jónsson's house and private church in Selárdalur.

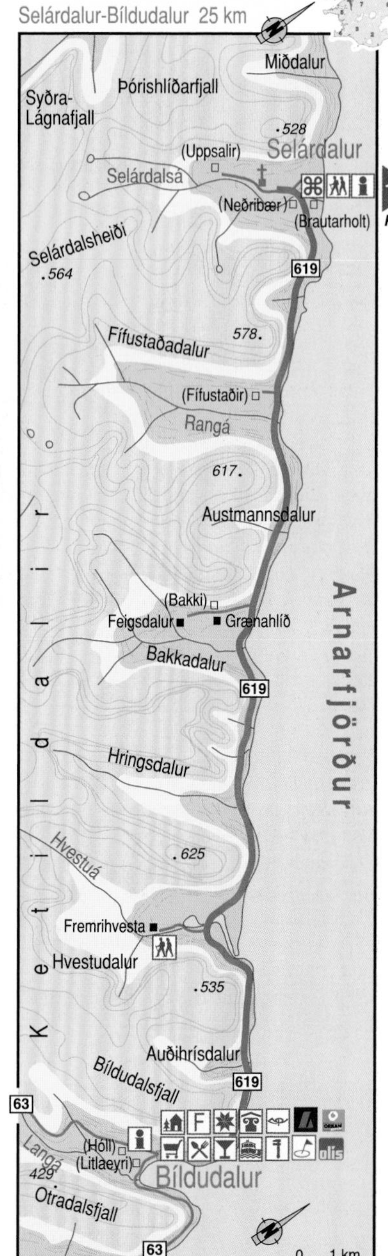

Selárdalur, a church and former parsonage, often mentioned in history. Birthplace of the poet Jón Þorláksson (1744-1899). The most famous pastor there was Páll Björnsson (1621-1706), known as a great scholar but as well; of witchcraft persecution. He was the nephew of Arngrímur the learned and was one of the best educated Icelanders of the 17th century leaving behind many manuscripts. In the winter of 1699 the people of Selárdalur were allegedly targeted by witchcraft. The wife of the Rev. Páll was the principal sufferer and as a result, two men were burned at the stake. Páll was a good speaker and an unusually good linguist e.g. writing verses in Greek. According to a legend, from Páll's time a black sailed schooner was seen off the coast of Selárdalur. People feared that pirates were on board. The pastor went out to the vessel and spoke to the crew in some eastern language and warned them that the district was full of witches. The result was that they exchanged gifts with him and went away. He was an excellent mathematician and studied Oriental mysticism. He was the first Icelander to have built a full decked fishing boat.

Brautarholt, an outlying farm from the Selárdalur parsonage, home of artist Samúel Jónsson (1884-1969). When an altar-piece he wanted to give to Selárdalur church on its centenary was rejected, he built his own church for it. Some of Samúel's statues stand nearby. The altar-piece is now preserved in Listasafn Alþýðu (The Labour Unions' Art Gallery) in Reykjavík.

Bakki, formerly an official trading place, later moved to Bíldudalur. The author Guðmundur Kamban (1888-1945) was brought up there. He was one of the first Icelanders to make motion pictures.

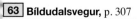

63 Bíldudalsvegur, p. 307

Tyrðilmýri-Hvannadalsá 44 km

18 P. 581

Dalsfjall
Mýrará
Snæfjallaströnd
Æðey
(Tyrðilmýri)
(Lónseyri)
Miðfell
(Unaðsdalur)
Rjúkandi
Dalbær
Dalsá
Bæjarfjall
(Bæir)
Ísafjarðardjúp
635
Flautá
Lóndjúp
(Lónseyri)
Kaldalón
Seleyri
Kaldárvatn
(Ármúli)
Ármúli
Hóp
Skjaldfannardalur
Melgraseyrar-oddar
635
Selá
Melgraseyri
638
Skjaldfönn
Laugarholt
Laugaland
Melgraseyrarmúli
Hraundalsháls
(Hamar)
Borgarey
Bjarnardalsá
Hamars-fjall
61
(Hallsstaðir)
Hallstaðafjall
244
Reykjanes
61
Hafnardalur
Máfavötn
635
Hafnardalsfjall
Nauteyrarós
Hafnardalsá
Ísafjörður
(Nauteyri)
Hafnardalur
Háafell
469
(Arngerðareyri)
Þverá
61
(Rauðamýri)
Langadalsá
Hvannadalsá
Rauðamýrarfjall
Lágadalsá
Tungu-fjall
516
(Neðribakki)
0 1 km

Hvannadalsá-Tyrðilmýri 44 km

Æðey, the biggest island in Ísafjarðardjúp, 1.26 km^2, just off the Snæfjallaströnd coast. One of the main breeding grounds of the eider duck in Iceland, fertile, good landing place, pretty scenery. In 1615 some shipwrecked Spanish sailors settled there. After they had been rather aggressive, Ari Magnússon of Ögur attacked them with a force of men, killing them all dishonourably, some on Æðey, others at Sandeyri on Snæfjallaströnd.

Tyrðilmýri, an abandoned farm. The river Mýrará harnessed to generate electricity.

Unaðsdalur, an abandoned farm and church. Guest accommodation and restaurant facilities are open during the summer in the Dalbær community centre.

Bæir, two abandoned farms; Hærribær and Neðribær ("Upper farm and Lower farm"). Made famous by notorious ghosts, whose activities were recorded by the author Þórbergur Þórðarson (1889-1974). Now a TV relay station.

Snæfjallaströnd, ("Snowy mountains coast") the district between the fjord Kaldalón and the mountain Vébjarnarnúpur.

Kaldalón, a fjord ca. 5 km long, largely full of silt. Off it is a broadish valley of the same name. At the head of the valley there are some grassy islets, then moraine brought by a glacier tongue that descends there.

638 Laugalandsvegur, 3,44 km.

Ármúli, an abandoned farm on the Langadalsströnd coast below a 375 m high mountain of the same name. Formerly a doctor's residence, the last to practice there having been Sigvaldi Kaldalóns, composer (1881-1946) who took his surname from the fjord.

Skjaldfönn, a farm in the **Skjaldfannardalur** valley. From the valley is a beautiful walking route to Hornstrandir.

Laugaland, a farm in the Skjaldfannardalur valley. Birthplace of the poet Steinn Steinarr (1908-58).

Selá, one of the biggest rivers in the Western fjords, coming from the Drangajökull glacier.

Nauteyri, a parsonage.

61 Djúpvegur, p. 300 **634 Reykjanesvegur,** p. 301

lúka, a farm where there is a warm spring, Gvendarlaug, named for ishop Guðmundur góði ("the good") (1160-1237) and a bathing place or centuries. A hotel and swimming pool. There is also the second part of ne Museum of Icelandic Sorcery and Witchcraft, the main exhibition is t Hólmavík, well worth the visit.

akki, there is a green house. Also the house Pöntun from Seyðisfjörður, hich is Norwegian originally.

645 Drangsnesvegur, 34 km.

aldrananes, a farm and church, rich in driftwood, eider duck colonies nd seals.

rímsey, the biggest island in the Strandir district, rather high, used for ay and grazing. Once used for a fox farm. Lighthouse.

rangsnes, (pop. 69) a village and trading place. Fishing and fish rocessing. Just beyond the town there is a rock called **Kerling** (Old oman), with distinct human facial features. According to local tales, this s a troll woman who was turned into stone by the sun near the Malarhorn ountain ridge. A signboard at the site, telling the troll woman´s story in celandic and two other languages.

jarnarfjarðarháls, the ridge between Steingrímsfjörður and jarnarfjörður, across which the road goes. Many lakes and tarns, the biggest being Urriðavatn, where there is trout-fishing. Geothermal heat in jarnarfjörður, used for domestic heating.

elkollusteinn, a stone by **Bassastaðir**, known from the story about uðmundur góði ("the good").

elströnd, ("Seal coast") the northern coast of Steingrímsfjörður. Many les and skerries, eider duck and seal colonies. Geothermal heat in veravík, where there used to be a swimming pool.

taður, a former parsonage in the valley Staðardalur. Its best known clergyman was Jón Árnason (1665-1743), later bishop of Skálholt. In the hurch there is a 240 year old pulpit.

taðardalur, a low, wide, grassy alley at the head of Steingrímsörður.

Klúka-Staðardalur 18 km

16 P. 579

Húnaflói
Grímseyjarsund
Grímsey
Bjarnarfjörður
645
Bakkagerði
Bær
Kaldrananes
Drangsnes
Bæjarvötn
Sæból
Bæjarfell
643
Bjarnarfjarðarháls
(Hafnarhólmur)
Hamarsvötn
(Vík)
Urriðavötn
645
Laugarhóll
Bakki
Oddi
Klúka
Hveravík
Svanshóll
(Kleifar)
(Hella)
Haugsvatn
643
Selströnd
(Sandnes)
MAP P. 310
645
Selkollusteinn
Ós
Hólmavík
61
Bassastaðir
Trékyllisá
Steingrímsfjörður
Selá
643
Hrófberg
.349
Hrófbergsvatn
Stakkanes
Geirmundarstaðir
Fitjavatn
Staðarfjall
Staður
Staðardalur
0 1 km
61

Staðardalur-Klúka 18 km

61 Djúpvegur, p. 302

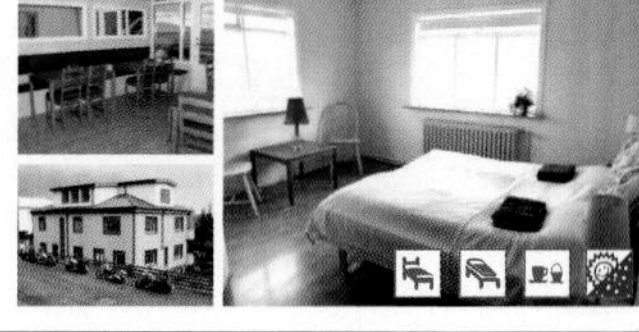

643 STRANDAVEGUR

Norðurfjörður-Klúka 78 km

P. 579

Munaðarnes
(Fell)
Krossnesfjall
646
Kálfatindur
Ófeigsfjörður
(Seljanes)
Seljanes
647
Steintún
(Ófeigsfjörður)
N1
Norðurfjörður
Krossnes
F649
Húnaflói
Urðartindur
Trékyllisvík
358
Ingólfsfjörður
(Eyri)
649
Melar
Reykjarneshyrna
Árnesey
444
643
316
Stóra-Ávík
Litla-Ávík
(Ingólfsfjörður)
Árnes
Finnbogastaðir
(Reykjarnes)
Bær
S
645
(Gíslabali)
Gjögursvatn
Reykjarnes
Glissa
Sætanesfjall
646
634
673
Örkin
Sætrur
Kjörvogur
Gjögur
626
Ónar
643
(Naustavík)
Reykjarfjarðará
(Reykjarfjörður)
Reykjarfjörður
Kambur
548
(Kambur)
(Kúvíkur)
(Kjós)
Djúpavík
Veiðileysa
(Byrgisvík)
Kleifará
(Veiðileysa)
643
744
Byrgisvíkurfjall
Selja
702
Trékyllisheiði
(Kolbeinsvík)
677
776
485
Kaldbaksá
(Kaldbakur)
Kaldbaksvík
(Kleifar)
673
Kaldbakskleif
Kaldbakshorn
689
Balafjöll
(Eyjar)
Fossá
(Goðdalur)
643
495
Þverá
Hólsfjall
Hallardalsá
(Asparvík)
Sunndalur
Balar
(Skarð)
Klúka
Laugarhóll
(Brúará)
Svanshóll
Bakki
(Reykjarvík)
Oddi
Ásmundarnes
0 1 km
643
645

Klúka-Norðurfjörður 78 km

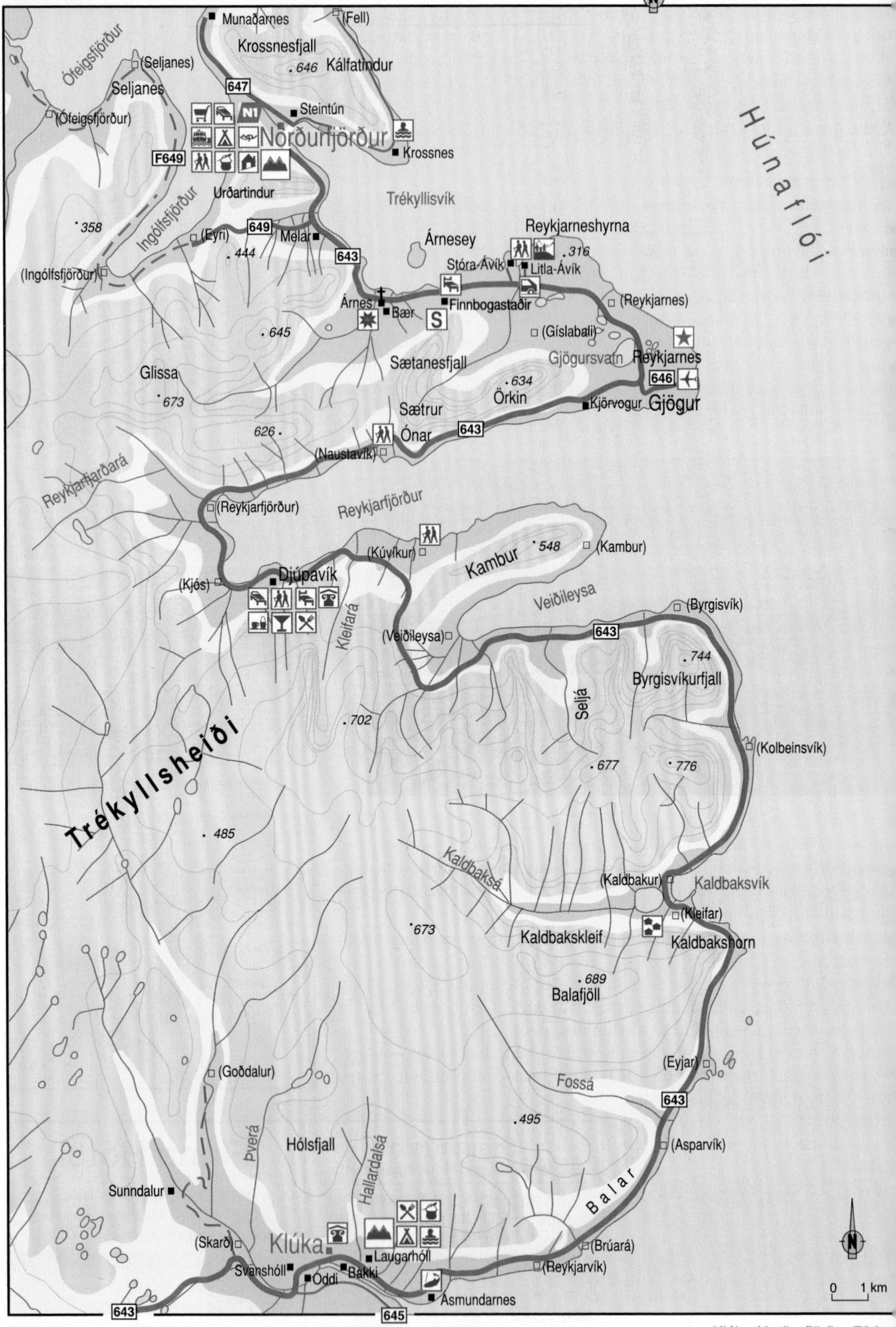

645 **Drangsnesvegur,** p. 319

feigsfjörður, an abandoned farm on a fjord of the same ıme. Some of the richest land in Strandasýsla because eider, seals and driftwood. The last shark-fishing from ere was in 1915 on the boat *Ófeigur*, which is now preserved in the folk museum at Reykir in Hrútafjörður. irthplace of the poet, scholar and painter Jón uðmundsson (1574-1658) who was twice outlawed for rcery.

gólfsfjörður, a long, narrow fjord. In 1942 a herring ctory was built at Eyri on the east of the fjord and run r 10 years. The factory building and other installations n still be seen.

47 Munaðarnesvegur the distance to Munaðarnes 4,5 km. Offers a magnificent view of the bays of feigsfjörður, Eyvindarfjörður and the cove of Drangak and beyond that the magnificent mountain passes of angaskörð.

49 Ófeigsfjarðarvegur 4 km.

649 Ófeigsfjarðarvegur 15,79 km km from Eyri to Hvalá.

orðurfjörður, a trading-place on a fjord of the same ıme, going north from Trékyllisvík bay. **Kálfatindur** 46 m) a mountain at the head of the fjord provides a od viewpoint. A lodge owned by the Icelandic Touring ssociation, Valgeirsstaðir is located in the bottom of ordfjordur, just above a sandy beach. A convenience ore is in 10 minutes walking distance from the house d a swimming pool is located in **Krossnes**, also close .

nes, a church and former parsonage, vicarage, comınity center, museum, and a craft house. Down by the ore are some distinctive rocky crags, called **Árnesapar**.

nnbogastaðir, a children's boarding school.

ékyllisvík, a broad bay with a good deal of flat land. ıe of best farming areas of the northern Strandir disct. A biggish island, **Árnesey**, formerly called Tréllisey, a good breeding-ground for birds. It was off ere that Þórður kakali gathered the crew for his journey at led to the Flóabardagi battle in midsummer 1244. uch driftwood. A former shark-fishing centre.

óra-Ávík and **Litla-Ávík,** a farm where there is a large ne carried by drift-ice from Greenland. At Stóra-Ávík Kistuvogur where people were burned for witchcraft. weather station at Litla-Ávík.

ykjarnes, the peninsula between Reykjarfjörður and ékyllisvík bay, low and marshy with many lakes. The iking mountain Reykjarneshyrna (316 m) to the north. view dial at the foot of the mountain.

646 Flugvallarvegur, 1,75 km.

Gjögur, a hamlet with some fishing. Formerly the biggest shark-fishing centre of the district, involving 15-18 open boats with 7-11 men on each. Lighthouse

Kjörvogur, once a weather station, now it is at Litlu-Ávík.

Sætrafjall, (634 m) a rocky and imposing mountain. Small creeks and skerries below, called **Ónar**, where the Spaniards killed by Ari of Ögur in 1615 had been shipwrecked (see Road 635, Æðey).

Trékyllisheiði, an old moorland riding trail between Steingrímsfjörður and Reykjarfjörður, 300-400 m high.

Kjós, a farm which Símon J. Ágústsson professor (1904–76) came from.

Djúpavík, a village with few inhabitants. Formerly a herring-salting station, and a herring factory was built there in 1934-35, later closed when herring disappeared from the waters north of Iceland. Historical Exhibition in the herring factory.

Kúvíkur, for about 250 years the only trading place in Strandasýsla county. Now abandoned. Home of the poet Jakob Thorarensen (1886-1972), whose grandfather Jakob Thorarensen (1830-1911) ran a store for nearly sixty years.

Reykjarfjörður, a biggish fjord 13-14 km long and 3 km wide at the mouth. Very little flat land.

Veiðileysufjörður, ("Fjord with no fishing") a small fjord enclosed by high, steep mountains.

Byrgisvíkurfjall, (744 m) an imposing rock mountain at Veiðileysufjörður. One of the highest in this area.

Kaldbaksvík, a small bay with two abandoned farms, one being Kaldbakur, the home of the settler Önundur tréfótur ("wooden-leg"), who is said to be buried in the Önundarhaugur mound in the valley Kaldbaksdalur. Summer houses, fishing lake, and geothermal heat at Hveratungur.

Kaldbakshorn, (508 m) a sheer, high mountain ridge. Below it is **Kaldbakskleif** which can be dangerous because of falling rocks, though there have been no known accidents there, perhaps because it was consecrated by bishop Guðmundur góði ("the good") (1160-1237).

Balar, the coast from Bjarnarfjörður to Kaldbaksvík bay. Very little flat land, high and rocky mountains, little grass. The beginning of the northern Strandir district, where mountains are higher, scenery more wild and barren than in the southern Strandir.

Goðdalur, an abandoned farm in a valley of the same name. Destroyed by an avalanche in 1948 in which only the farmer survived.

4 P. 567

Skagaströnd-Blönduós 23 km

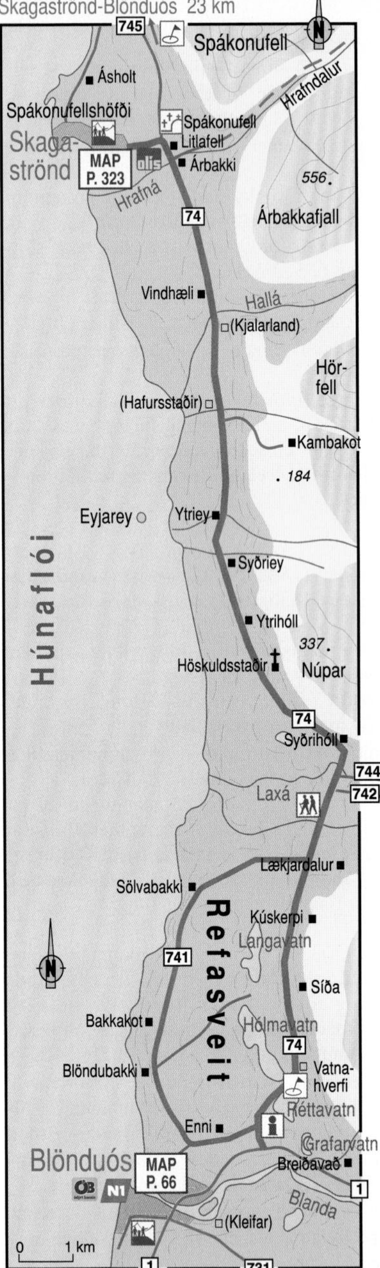

Blönduós-Skagaströnd 23 km

Skagaströnd, (pop. 501) once a trading post run by the Danes with history dating back into the 16th century and, until the 19th century, served a huge region stretching west and east. A village started to gro there in the late 19th century, focusing on the fishing industry. Catches b the freezer trawler Arnar are among the highest in Iceland, but numero smaller boats are also based here and there is a lively fish market. On th other hand, the past few years have seen considerable changes in th business sector. At the biotechnology science hotel BioPol, researche study marine life in Húnaflói bay, seeking innovative options for utilisi ocean resources. Kántrýbær, a restaurant known throughout Iceland, ar the Country Radio of Iceland, FM 96.7, are owned by Iceland's count music king, Hallbjörn Hjartarson. In a beautiful building down by the se Café Bjarmanes opens during the summer months and is popular amo travellers. Each year, over a hundred artists spend a residency at Ne staying there for a month at a time and exercising their creativity in wh used to be a fish freezing plant. The Icelandic Directorate of Labour ope ates a payment office in Skagaströnd for national unemployment benefi The picturesque campground offers plenty of room for camping vehicle caravans and tent trailers. The swimming pool is small but enjoyable, ar has developed a tradition of offering coffee to people in the hot tub. Bu in 1899 and recently restored, Árnes is the village's oldest building ar houses a museum depicting domestic conditions and customs early in th 20th century. The headland Spákonufellshöfði is a popular place for wal ing, with marked trails and information signs about the birds and plan while on clear spring and summer evenings the midnight sun can be se setting over the sea to the north. Towering majestically above the villag Spákonufell mountain also offers a number of marked trails. Brochur on the trails at both Spákonufellshöfði and Spákonufell can be obtained many places in the village. The Museum of Prophecies holds a historic exhibition about a local fortune-teller, cf. Spákonufell. About four kil metres from Skagaströnd, the local golf club's nine-hole course is co sidered scenic and challenging. The main employment is provided the fisheries, light industry, trade and services, and there is a compulso school, church, restaurant, coffee house, community centre, health clin sports hall and swimming pool.

Spákonufell, ("Fortune-teller's fell") a former church, once the home Þórdís spákona ("fortune-teller") mentioned in *Kormáks sag* Spákonufellsborg (646 m) is the most imposing mountain in this area.

Árbakki, a farm at the mouth of the Hrafndalur valley, birthplace archeologist and politician Dr. Valtýr Guðmundsson (1860-1928), w taught at the University of Copenhagen.

Ytriey, a farm where there is a monument to the county girls' school th was there from 1883-1900.

Vindhæli, an old manor farm.

Höskuldsstaðir, a church and parsonage. Home of famous pastors, e Magnús Pétursson (1710-84), writer of annals, and Eggert Ó. Brie (1840-93), a great scholar. Birthplace of the brothers Sigurður Stefánss (1744-98), the last bishop at Hólar, and governor Ólafur Stefánss (1731-1812) (see Viðey, Rvík). A rune-stone from the early 14th centu was found in the churchyard.

Syðri-Hóll, a farm, home of the well-known scholar and writer Magn Björnsson (1889-1963), to whom there is a memorial by the roadside.

741 Neðribyggðarvegur, 8,4 km.

Refasveit, flat country between the rivers Blanda and Laxá. Two ro of farms, Efribyggð and Neðribyggð ("Upper district and Lower d trict"), with roads alongside each. Four small lakes in a row: Grafava Réttavatn, Hólmavatn and Langavatn, counting from the south.

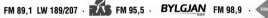

1 Norðurlandsvegur, p, 68

731 Svínvetningabraut, p. 345

742 Mýravegur, p. 348

744 Þverárfjallsvegur, p. 348

745 Skagavegur, p. 349

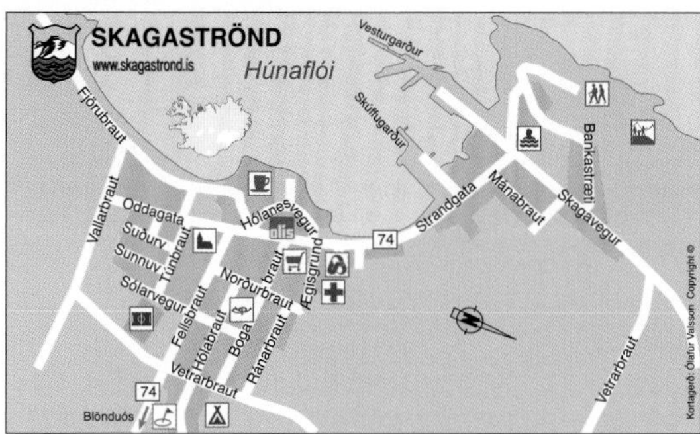

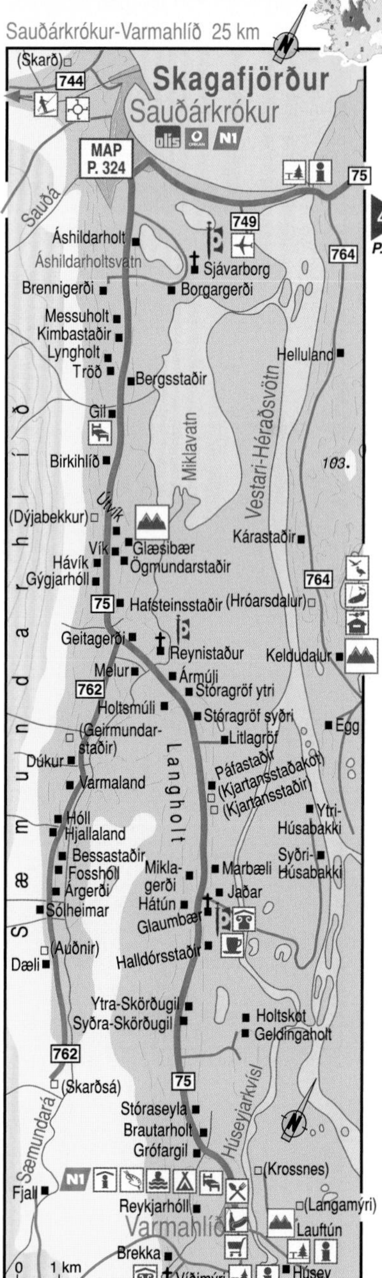

Varmahlíð-Sauðárkrókur 25 km

Sauðárkrókur, (pop. 2,575) a town in Skagafjörður. See p. 326.

Sjávarborg, a tarred wooden church of the older towerless-type was built in 1853. From 1892 its use was secular and in 1975 the building was moved to the northern part of the cliff and turned at the same time. The door now faces south! In the keeping of the National Museum since 1972.

Áshildarholtsvatn, a lake, site of geothermal heat, from where hot water is piped to Sauðárkrókur for domestic heating.

Miklavatn, ("Great lake") 6.18 km², a sanctuary with a great variety of bird life.

762 Sæmundarhlíðarvegur, 8 km.

Sæmundarhlíð, the slopes from Vatnsskarð to Reynistaður. Named after the settler Sæmundur suðureyski. Along the slope is a river called Sæmundará but changes its name by Reynistaður, there is called Reynisstaðará and then it changes again and then its is called Staðará.

Reynistaður, a church and manor farm through the ages. Home of Þorfinnur karlsefni and of his descendants to 1259, also of Earl Gissur Þorvaldsson for a while. Convent from 1295 to 1552. The farmhouse porch (bæjardyrahús) at Reynistaður, one of the few stave structures dating from the 18th century in Iceland, has been restored. In the keeping of the National Museum since 1999.

Holtsmúli, there was born a horse called Hrafn, 802, in the year 1968. This horse is considered one of Icelands greatest horses.

Glaumbær, a farm, church and parsonage. There is a monument by the sculptor Ásmundur Sveinsson in memory of Guðríður Þorbjarnardóttir and her son Snorri Þorfinnsson, the first European born west of the Atlantic. Late in life, Guðríður travelled to Rome, after which she became a nun and hermit in Glaumbær. Guðríður may rightly be considered the greatest Icelandic woman traveller before this century (see Road 574, **Hellnar**). Home of many men of influence. One of Iceland's few remaining turf farms is there, mainly from the 19th century with some older parts, protected and now the site of the Skagafjörður heritage museum. In the keeping of the National Museum since 1947. Not to be missed.

Geldingaholt, the scene in 1255 of the Battle of Geldingaholt, where Oddur Þórarinsson, one of the bravest men in Iceland in his day, was slain.

1 Norðurlandsvegur, p. 70	**744 Þverárfjallsvegur,** p. 348
749 Flugvallarvegur, p. 326	**764 Hegranesvegur,** p. 326

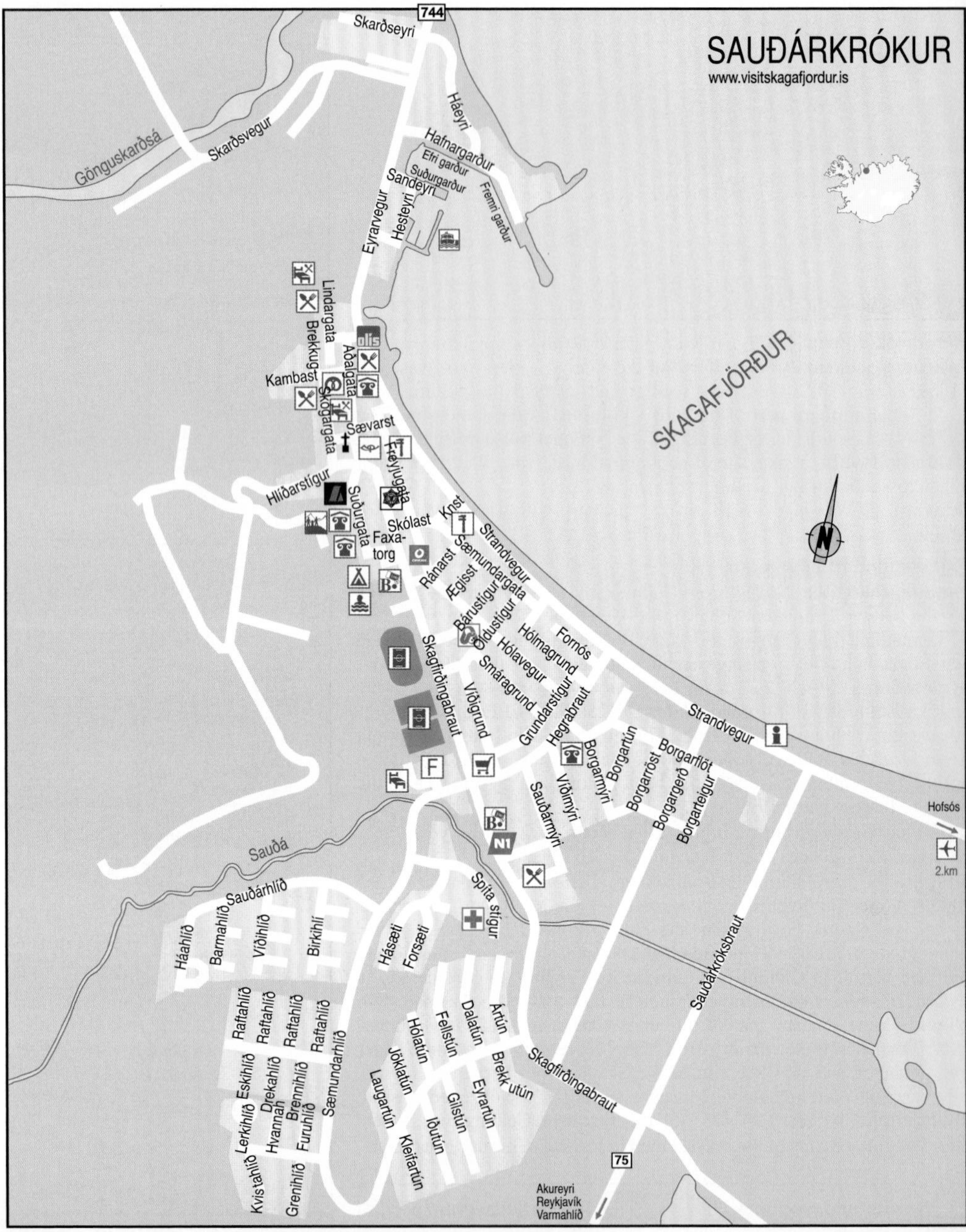

SAUÐÁRKRÓKUR

www.visitskagafjordur.is

Ólafshús
RESTAURANT

Aðalgata 15,
550 Sauðárkrókur
Tel. 453 6454
videosport@simnet.is

Pizzeria, fish,
steak and grill.

All kinds of food.
Popular restaurant
in the heart of town.

Kaupfélag Skagfirðinga

THE SKAGAFJÖRÐUR CO-OP
Ártorg 1 · 550 Sauðárkrókur · Tel. 455-4500 · Fax 455-4501

Skagfirðingabúð:

The department store in Sauðárkrókur.
One of the biggest of its kind outside Reykjavík.

We look forward to seeing you in Skagfirðingabúð.

Auto Repair

Tel. 455 4570
Freyjugata 9
550 Sauðárkrókur

Our campsite and swimming pool are situated in the heart of the town, only a stone´s trow from other services. The Sauðárkrókur Golf Club´s 9-hole golf course, just above the town, is open every day. Visitors are welcome.

Tel. 453 5226

The pool is open:	Summer opening (June 1st -August 31st)
Monday - Friday	07:00 - 22:00
Saturday and Sunday	09:00 - 18:00

EMERGENGY TELEPHONE

112
ONE ONE TWO

POLICE
AMBULANCE
FIREBRIGADE
RESCUE SERVICE

KS Súrmjólk

Soured Milk
Refreshing, light, digestable
For Breakfast, dessert, or just anytime...

Iceland Post

Phone: 580 1200
www.postur.is

Narfastaðir-Sauðárkrókur 15 km

5 P. 568

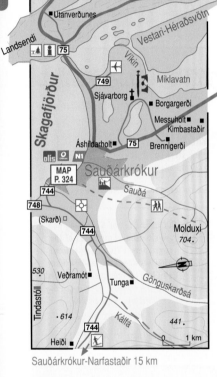

Hegranes, a strip of land between the estuary branches of the riv Héraðsvötn, ca. 15 km long and 5 km wide, with basalt ridges and ste crags but also grassy marshes, lakes and tarns. Sea cliffs at the northern enc

764 Hegranesvegur, 20,6 km. **749 Flugvallarvegur,** 0,49 km

Garður, a farm on Hegranes. The ancient Hegranesþing assembly was held there and bothy ruins ma still be seen.

Geitaberg, (138 m) a beautif view from Lautinantsvörð cairn.

Ríp, a church, a parsona until 1907, where the vers fier Hannes Bjarnason (1776 1838) was pastor. Rögnvald Pétursson of Winnipeg (187 1940), long one of the ma leaders of Canadian Icelander also came from there.

Keldudalur, in 2002 excavation was started the and the site is still beg excavated. An interesting site.

Helluland, a farm in Hegranes, whence came the painter Sigurð Guðmundsson (1833–74) who was a moving spirit in the foundation The National Museum of Iceland and became its first employee. T farmer Sigurður Ólafsson (1856-1942), known for his ingenuity, built t first pulley-ferry to cross the Héraðsvötn rivers.

Héraðsvötn, one of the biggest Icelandic rivers, glacial, rising in t Hofsjökull glacier in many branches. It flows in two main streams, Eyst and Vestari-Jökulsá ("Eastern and Western Jökulsá") north of the highlan and down the valleys of Skagafjörður. After the two streams meet, the riv is called Héraðsvötn, but it again divides at its estuary. The bridge ov Vesturós, built in 1926, is 113 m long. Before the bridge was built, peop would cross the river by ferry; Jón Ósmann (1862-1914) was a ferrym for a long time. A shelter for the ferrymen that used to stand at Furðustranc at the east end of the bridge, has been rebuilt and a sign board put up nea by. There is a resting place just east of the bridge and a footpath leads dov to the shelter. A new bridge a bit to the south of the old bridge, was tak into use in 1994.

Sauðárkrókur, (pop. 2,575) a town at the head of Skagafjörður, authoriz trading place since 1857, obtained its municipal charter in 1947. The ma occupations are trading, fishing and light industry, including a rock wo factory. Community centre. Secondary school serving the northwest the country. At the Heritage House, Exhibitions from The Skagafjord Heritage Museum and Information center. The Tannery Visitor Centre Sauðárkrókur is the only tannery in Europe which makes fishleather. T Visitor Centre provides visitors with an unusual way to experience the ta nery and its products: guided tours of the actual tannery, where fish-sk is expertly processed to make high-quality leather. At the Visitor Cent leather goods made from the tannery's products by outstanding designe and craftspeople are offered for sale, right next door to the tannery whe the leather is made. Leathers and hid can also be purchased there, direct from the tannery, along with fir hand information about the produc Fishleather from Atlantic Leath has caught the imagination of i ernationally-known fashion houses a brands such as Prada, Dior and Nik Hydro-electric power plant on t river Gönguskarðsá. Steadily develo ing harbour construction. Airport Borgarsandur.

Sauðárkrókur-Narfastaðir 15 km

76 Siglufjarðarvegur, p. 327
744 Þverárfjallsvegur, p. 348
748 Reykjastrandarvegur, p. 352

A drawing from the church at Hofsstaðir from 1898 by Johannes Klein. This church was replaced by a new church around 1900, which still stands there.

ʼolkuós, at the mouth of the Kolka river. Once an anchorage and trading lace.

ʼ66 Bakkavegur, 3,6 km.

rimnes, a farm. In the book of Settlers is said that a great forest was t Brimnes. Now there is no forest but some efforts are being made to hange that.

ækur, an abandoned farm in the Viðvíkursveit district. It was there that e tenor Stefán (Guðmundsson) Íslandi (1907-1994), one of Iceland's est-known singers, sang "publicly" for the first time in the winter of 924-25.

Iofstaðasel, a farm. Prinsess Anna stayed there in 2002.

Iofstaðir, a church, where in Catholic times there was a sacred statue of e Virgin Mary. This image was believed to be sacred and attracted many lgrims, who would promise gifts to secure and answer to their prayers. 'his image and the cross at Kaldaðarnes were probably the most sacred nages in catholic Iceland. It is now in the National Museum of Iceland. Iowever, the church was given a replica which still attracts numerous onations. There are many other artefacts worth seeing in the church at Iofstaðir.

verá, a farm, birthplace of Jón Steingrímsson (1728-91), known as the Fire Pastor" (see Kirkjubæjarklaustur, V-Skaft).

rostastaðir, a substantial farm, now and through the ages. Home of heriff Jón Espólín (1769-1836), historiographer and professor at Kongsberg in Norway. Also the birthplace of Þorkell Þorkelsson, chief eteorologist (1876-1921).

Ijaltastaðir, the district girls' school was situated there 1878-80.

lugumýri, a church and manor farm. Home, in the 13th century of the hief Kolbeinn ungi ("the young") and remains of his fort can be seen on hill to the southeast of the farm. Later Earl Gissur Þorvaldsson lived ere for a while. It was during his time there, in 1253, that the lugumýrarbrenna ("the burning of Flugumýri farm") took place, when is foes attempted to kill him. Twenty five people died in the fire, but arl Gissur managed to save his life by hiding in a big cask half-full of our whey (used for storing food), and later took cruel revenge on his nemies. The ecclesiastical conferences of the Hólar bishopric used to be eld there. In the churchyard is a tombstone to the historiographer Jón spólín (1769-1836).

lóðafeykir, (990 m) an impressive mountain, steep and rocky, above 'lugumýri. The story goes that Helga Sigurðardóttir, mistress of the last 'atholic bishop Jón Arason, hid out on this mountain while Danish warhips were in the north in 1551, the summer after Jón was beheaded in the truggles of the Reformation.

1 Norðurlandsvegur, p. 70 | **75 Sauðárkróksbraut,** p. 326

767 Hólavegur, p. 355 | **769 Ásavegur,** p. 355

Sleitustaðir-Syðstagrund 30 km

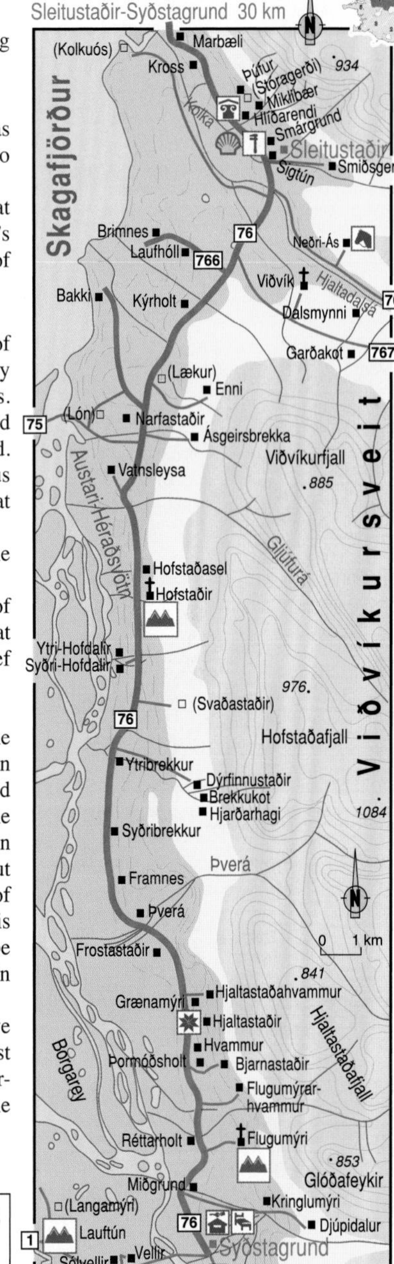

Syðstagrund-Sleitustaðir 30 km

5
P. 568

Höfði-Sleitustaðir 22 km

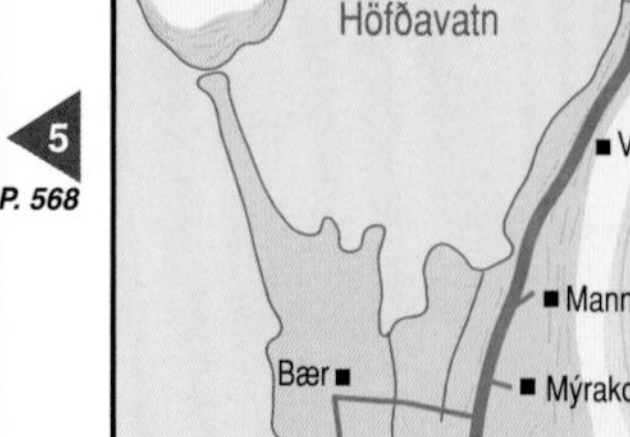

Sleitustaðir-Höfði 22 km

77 **Hofsósbraut,** 2,3 km.

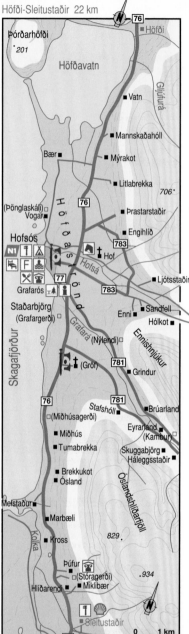

Bær, a substantial farm. There was once a fishing-station at Bæjarklettar **Mannskaðahóll,** ("Loss-of-life hill") where Icelanders are said to hav fought and defeated English robbers in 1431, killing 80 of them, wh were then buried in two mounds near the road. Nearby is Ræningjalá ("Robbers' hollow").

783 **Höfðastrandarvegur,** 6,76 km.

781 **Deildardalsvegur,** 13,4 km.

Hofsós, (pop. 181) one of oldest trading places in Iceland, where there also one of oldest houses in Iceland (1777), Pakkhúsið (Warehouse), i the keeping of the National Museum since 1954. In another old stor built 1910 is the Icelandic Emigration Centre. It was founded in 1996 an dedicated to commemorate Icelandic emigrants to North America and promote connections between their descendants and the people of Icelan The Centre now offers four exhibits in three separate buildings, as well a a genealogical information service, library facilities and more. The exhi bitions combine text, photographs and tableaux to illustrate the condition in Iceland that influenced the decision to emigrate, the journey to th 'New World' and the new way of life they encountered. At Hofsós yo will also find a sewing company that specialises in flag making.

Staðarbjörg, some unusually beautiful columnar basalt on the shore nea Hofsós. It and the columnar basalt at **Dverghamrar** at Síða, his birt place, is thought to have been the inspiration for the distinctive ceiling i The National Theatre in Reykjavík.

Grafará, a river flowing out of the Deildardalur valley. At its mouth wa **Grafarós** where there was a trading station from 1835-1915, for a tim one of two main trading places in the Skagafjörður district.

Gröf, home of Ragnheiður Jónsdóttir (1646-1715) widow of two bishops great patron of art. Turf church with wooden frame of stave constructior believed to date originally from the late 17th century. Considered to be th oldest chapel in the country, all timbers were renewed in 1953. In th keeping of the National Museum since 1939.

Höfðaströnd, the farming district between Óslandshlíð and th Höfðahólar landslip.

Stóragerði, there is a transportation museum, privatly run.

Sleitustaðir, a farm since the original settlement, a small community.

Hofsós

769 **Ásavegur,** p. 355

akki, an abandoned farm.

jall, birthplace of Sölvi Helgason (1820-95) who called himself Sólon slandus. He was a well-known wanderer, and once spent time in prison Copenhagen for passport fraud. Sölvi had artistic talents, was a skilled raughtsman, sketched and painted in water colours. He left many anuscripts with his stories and reflections. Davíð Stefánsson's story *ólon Íslandus* is based on Sölvi. A memorial to Sölvi at Lónkot.

ell, a church and once a parsonage, which has been moved to Hofsós. ome of the famous priest-sorcerer Hálfdan Narfason about 1600. (See **álfdanarhurð**.) Birthplace of Ólafur Davíðsson (1862-1903), folklore pecialist and naturalist.

86 Sléttuhlíðarvegur, 5,2 km.

léttuhlíð, the farming area from the Höfðahólar landslip to the river tafá. Broadish flat land with two hills, Hrolleifshöfði (88 m) by the sea, nd the oval-shaped Fell (173 m), at the east end of which is the lake léttuhlíðarvatn. The **Hrolleifsdalur** valley goes off there, through it ıns the river **Hrolleifsá**, a good fising river.

álmey, an island with steep cliffs off Sléttuhlíð, 2.4 km², max. eight 156 m. Grassy and good pasture for sheep. The farm there was bandoned in 1951. According to legend there is a spell on Málmey so at neither mice nor horses will thrive there and no married couple hould live on the island for longer than twenty years or the wife will isappear and never be seen again. Folk tales tell of just such occurences.

Drangey

rangey, (200 m) a rocky tuff island, grassy on top, difficult to climb. irdhunting and egg-collecting. Uninhabited. Famous from *rettis saga*, as Grettir the strong had a hide-out there, here he and his brother Illugi were slain.

órðarhöfði, (202 m) a headland.

ónkot, guesthouse and restaurant. Site of Iceland's largest community ent, 700 square meters in area and 11 m tall at its highest point. Exhibition here of work of Sölvi Helgason, see **Sléttuhlíð** above.

öfðavatn, a lagoon at the east end of Þórðarhöfði, 9.27 km².

öfði, the outermost farm on Höfðaströnd, originally settled by Höfða-órður. **Höfðahólar**, nearby, formed by landslip.

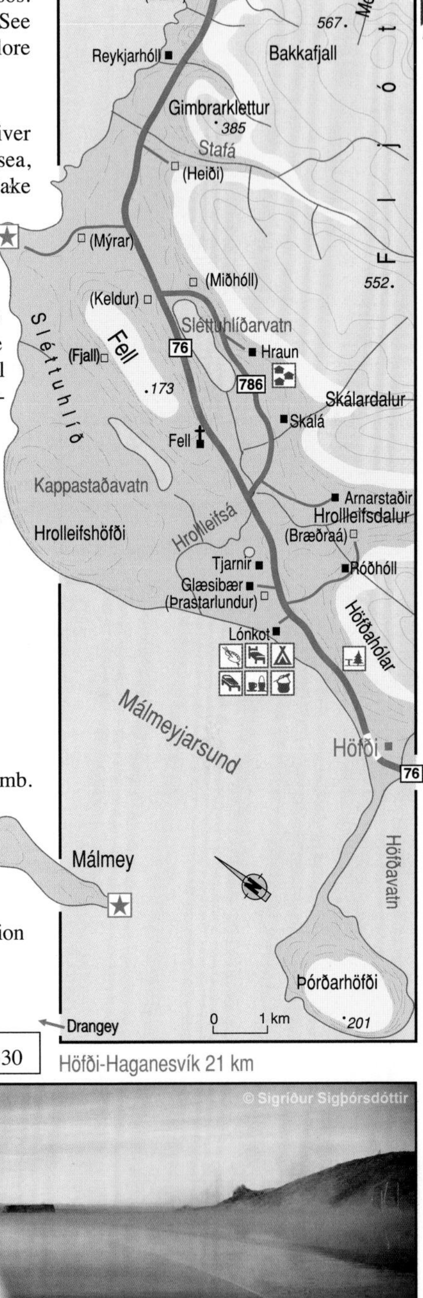

787 Flókadalsvegur, p. 330

© Sigríður Sigþórsdóttir

Hofsós swimming pool

Siglufjörður-Haganesvík 24 km

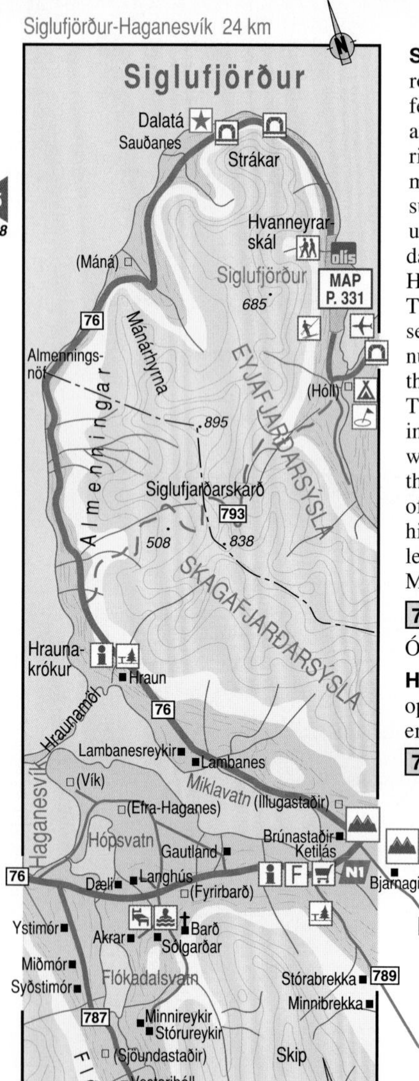

Haganesvík-Siglufjörður 24 km

5 P. 568

Siglufjörður, (pop. 1,190) a fishing town on a fjord of same name, surrounded by steep mountains with little flat land. In 1919 an avalanche fell on Engidalur opposite the town, killing 7 people. Siglufjörður was an important herring centre from 1904 to recent times, when the herring disappeared. Good harbour, school, bank, hospital and a herring museum, which was awarded the Micheletti award in 2004. During summer, the atmosphere of the „Herring Era" is recreated on the museum dock and the locals in vintage costumes salt herring and sing and dance to accordion music. The Folk Music Centre is located in Madame House where the Rev. Bjarni Thorsteinsson lived from 1888 to 1898. The centre brings to life the world of Icelandic folk music. Visitors can see people of all ages chanting rímur, singing the tvísöngur, reciting nursery rhymes, and playing folk instruments such as the langspil and the Icelandic fidla. The centre also depicts the life of the Rev. Bjarni Thorsteinsson and how he collected the folk songs. Excellent skiing ground. Beautiful walking routes. A popular destination for bird watchers. Seven walls have been constructed in the high ground above the town in order to ward off avalanches. Two of them go by the name of Stóri-boli (Big bull), 18 m high, and Litli-boli (Little bull), 14 m high. Together these two walls, completed in 1999, are nearly 1 km in length. There is a beautiful walking route there with an amazing view. Memorial to sailors lost at sea in town.

792 Langeyrarvegur, 2 km. This route leads to the tunnel to Ólafsfjörður, Héðinsfjarðargöng tunnel.

Héðinsfjarðargöng, a tunnel between Siglufjörður and Ólafsfjörður opened in 2010, making the route between these two fjords much shorter and safer to drive.

793 Skarðsvegur, 13 km.

Siglufjarðarskarð, 630 m, a pass between Siglufjörður and Fljót. Used for sightseeing in the summer, not for those who are afraid of height.

Strákar, (676 m) a mountain dropping sheer into the sea. The tunnel Strákagöng, 800 m long, opened in 1967, goes through it.

Almenningar, the coastline north from the farm Hraun to the mountain Mánárhyrna. Boundary between Skagafjarðarsýsla county and Siglufjörður at Almenningsnöf. Úlfsdalir, two valleys between the Fljót district and Siglufjörður, now abandoned.

Hraun, an old manor farm, the northernmost farm in Skagafjarðarsýsla county. The nearest farm to Siglufjarðarskarð pass.

Hraunakrókur, one of the most important fishing places in the Fljót district of old. Ruins of many fishermen's booths can be seen there.

Miklavatn, a good trout lake, 7.43 km^2, also with sea fish. A narrow isthmus, Hraunamöl, separates it from the sea. There are many interesting remains of fishing in days gone by, well worth seeing.

Ketilás, there are crossroads there that lead to Siglufjörður, Ólafsfjörður and Skagafjörður. Community centre.

787 Flókadalsvegur, 6,4 km.

Flókadalur, a large valley upwards of Vestur-Fljót, lies to the south. It is named after Flóki Villgerðarson (Hrafna-Flóki). Who made the valley his home when he came to Iceland for the second time. Flóki is said to be buried at Stóru-Reykjar at the place named Flókasteinar (Flóki´s rocks).

Barð, a church and parsonage. At Sólgarðar at Barð is a school and a swimming pool.

Haganesvík, once a there was a village there.

Fljót, the northernmost district of Skagafjörður, with two valleys, good, broad flat land, with the Haganesvík bay. Formerly much cod and shark fishing. Fertile and grassy, with geothermal heat in places, often snowbound in winter.

82 Ólafsfjarðarvegur, p. 363 **789 Sléttuvegur,** p. 363

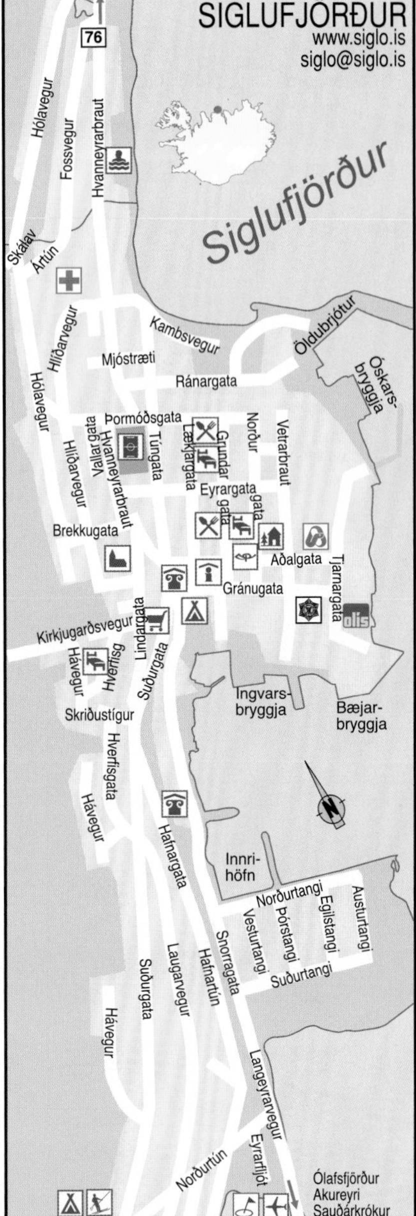

Siglufjörður

Héðinsfjörður Tunnels

5
P. 568

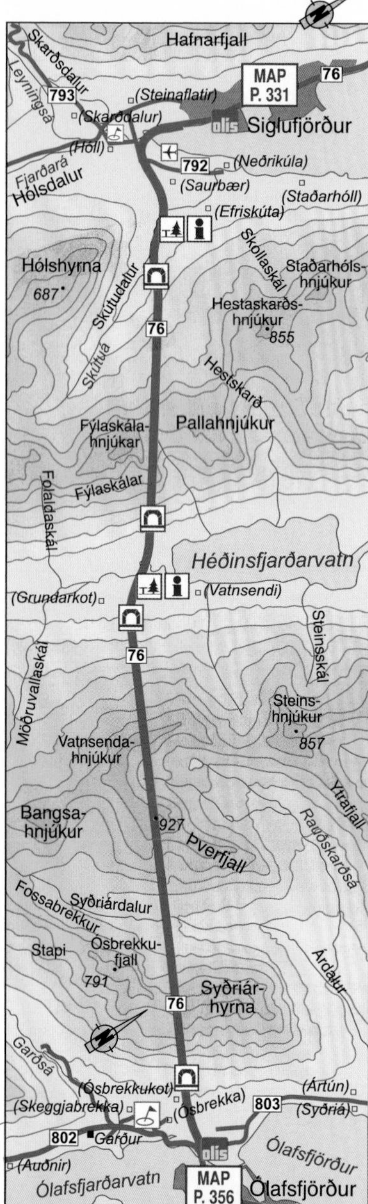

Siglufjörður, see p. 330.

Héðinsfjörður tunnels, lead traffic via a deserted fjord between the se tlements to the west and east. The tunnel east from Siglufjörður is 3.9 k long, while the one west from Ólafsfjörður is 7.1 km. These tunnels ha created wonderful opportunities for the traveller, making a huge area nor of Ring Road No. 1 more accessible, including this area's diverse bird life

Ólafsfjörður, a valley, 15 km long, grassy but narrow, with fine mou tains having jagged peaks at the head of a short (5 km) fjord of the sa name. The fjord opens out between high cliffs, **Ólafsfjarðarmúli** to t south and **Hvanndalabjarg** to the north. There is virtually no flat la on the coast. There are various folktales associated with Ólafsfjörður, e. about the Rev. Hálfdan Narfason, who rode on the Devil with Farmer J from Málmey through Skagafjörður to the Hvanndalir valley in Hvan dalabjarg (see Road 76, Fell and Málmey). In Ódáinsakur ("Field of t undying") in the valley grew a herb that made people immortal.

Ólafsfjarðarvatn, a lake, 2,51 km^2, at the head of the fjord, empties in the sea. Fishing-lake, sometimes with salt-water fish in it.

Ólafsfjörður, (pop. 799) is one of the two villages in Fjallabyggð muni ipality. The fjord and high surrounding mountains, together with a la and estuary, form a magnificent setting. Employment is mostly based fishing or light industry, but plenty of recreation is also on hand for tou ists and outdoor enthusiasts. In the winter, they can choose between sl lom and cross-country skiing, and perhaps try skating, fishing throug the lake ice or zipping over the landscape on a snow scooter. Durin summer, the mountains, lake, estuary and black beach are enchantin Since 2011, North Sailing has offered whale watching from this harbou which is ideally situated by the mouth of the large fjord to the eas Eyjafjörður, near where whales are frequently sighted. A range of hikin routes through valleys and mountains lead to superb panoramas, in th midst of peace and quiet. North of the tunnel going east to Eyjafjörðu the now-abandoned, awe-inspiring road around the Múlinn peninsu climbs to an altitude of 300 m. In fair weather, it provides a terrific vie and the best place to watch the midnight sun in Iceland. Note howev that you cannot walk the whole way around the peninsula, since the roa has started to collapse down the slope. Ólafsfjörður has Iceland's only s jump, as well as a splendid natural history museum displaying one of th country's most diverse bird collections, while sports clubs and other loc organisations put on numerous events. Many of Iceland's leading blu musicians appear at the Blue North Festival in June, and there is also classical music festival in August which prides itself on world-cla opera singers and musicians during the berry-picking season. Children all ages from far and wide take part in a football tournament every Jul Sailors' Day, a few weeks earlier, has a long tradition here, and emph sises entertainment for the entire family and every visitor. The monume in memory of drowned seamen, which was erected by the church 1940, was the first of its kind in Iceland.

82 **Ólafsfjarðarvegur,** p. 362	793 **Skarðsvegur,** p. 330
802 **Garðsvegur,** p. 362	803 **Kleifavegur,** p. 362

From Ólafsfjörður

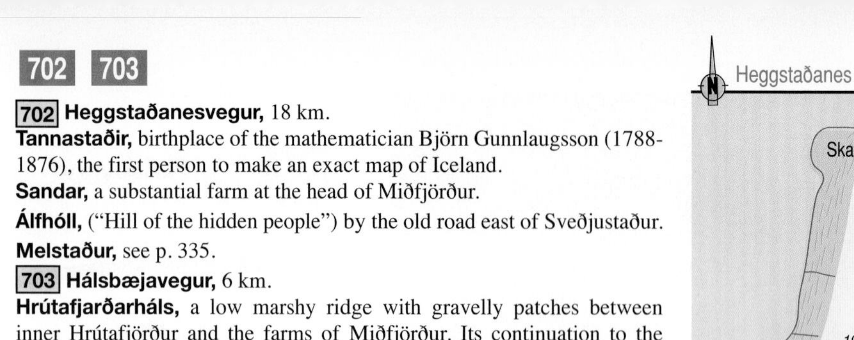

702 Heggstaðanesvegur, 18 km.

Tannastaðir, birthplace of the mathematician Björn Gunnlaugsson (1788-1876), the first person to make an exact map of Iceland.

Sandar, a substantial farm at the head of Miðfjörður.

Álfhóll, ("Hill of the hidden people") by the old road east of Sveðjustaður.

Melstaður, see p. 335.

703 Hálsbæjavegur, 6 km.

Hrútafjarðarháls, a low marshy ridge with gravelly patches between inner Hrútafjörður and the farms of Miðfjörður. Its continuation to the north between the fjords is the peninsula **Heggstaðanes** or **Bálkastaðanes**. The ridge was formerly difficult to cross because of marshes and bogs.

1 Norðurlandsvegur, p. 63
68 Innstrandavegur, p. 309
704 Miðfjarðarvegur, p. 335

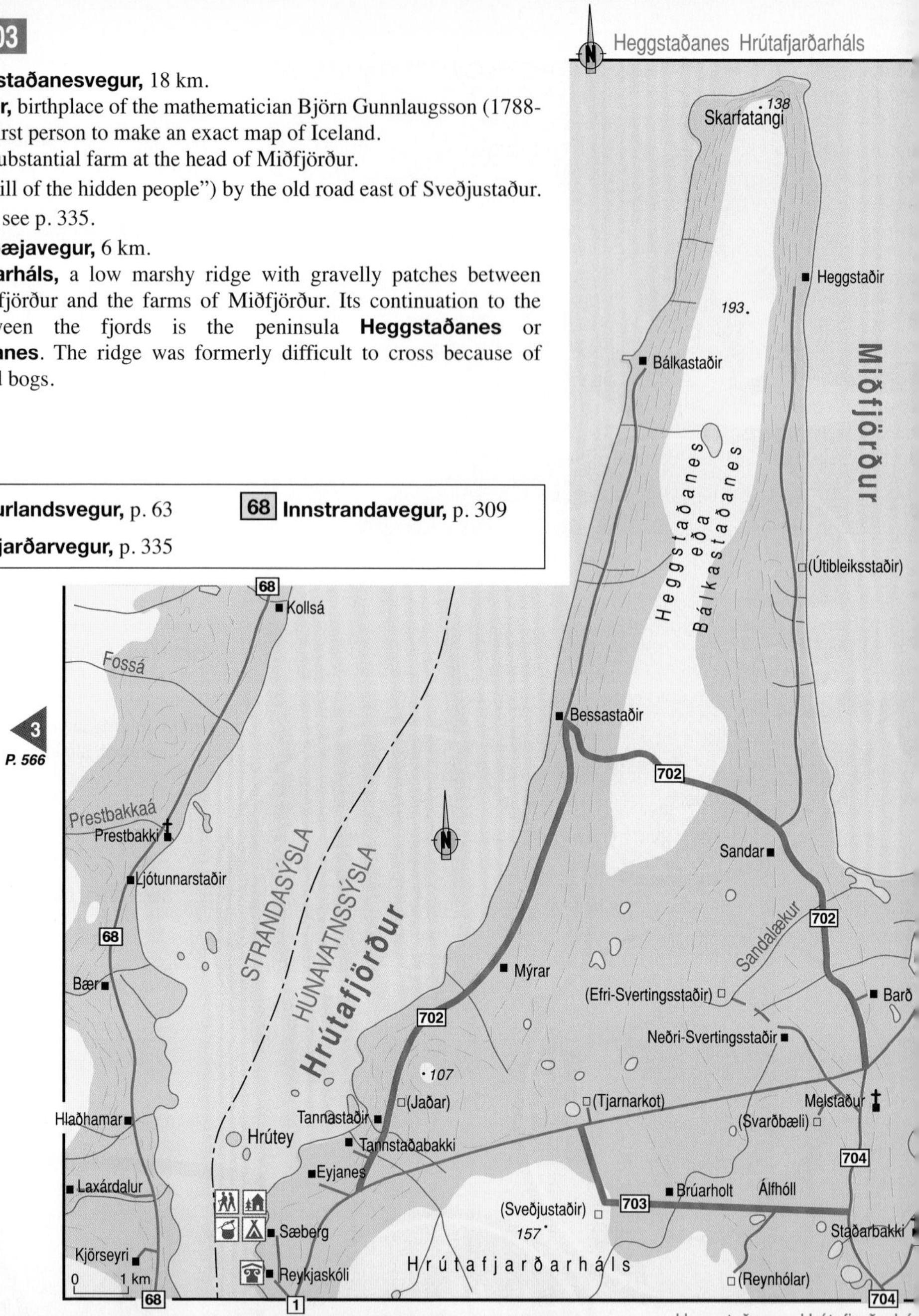

3 P. 566

Heggstaðanes Hrútafjarðarhá

ðalból, riding trails from there south to Arnarvatnsheiði moor.

fri-Núpur, a church. The grave of the poetess Vatnsenda-Rósa (1795-855) is there, with a tombstone erected in 1965 by the women of the istrict. Route from there south to Arnarvatnsheiði moor.

orfastaðavatn, a fishing lake. A jeep track leads there from 'orafastaðir. A fishing licence can be obtained at Haugur.

lúpsdalstunga, in the Núpsdalur valley, the home, in the 10th century, f Steingerður, mistress of Kormákur the poet.

705 Vesturárdalsvegur, 9 km.

lúkur, from where there is a jeep-track over Hrútafjarðarháls ridge to ne farm Brandagil in Hrútafjörður, a very beautiful route in summer.

704 Miðfjarðarvegur, 36 km.

taðarbakki, a church, the nearest farm to Melstaður. Nowhere in celand is there such a short distance between two churches.

rekkulækur, from there came the writer Friðrik Á. Brekkan 1888–1958).

jarg, ("Crag") a farm in Miðfjörður, taking its name from a glacier-roded rock north of the homefield. Fine panoramas from there. Grettir he strong was brought up at Bjarg, and there is a hummock in the omefield called Grettisþúfa, where his head is said to be buried. Memorial to Grettir's mother, Ásdís.

Melstaður, an old manor farm, parsonage and church. Residence in the 0th century of Kormákur the poet and later of Oddur Ófeigsson, menioned in the *Bandamanna saga*. It grew in importance after the introluction of Christianity, and was considered the second richest parsonige in northern Iceland. Residence in the 16th century of Björn Jónsson, on of Bishop Jón Arason of Hólar, and later, 1598-1649, of Arngrímur ónsson the learned, who was a prolific writer. Some interesting old relcs in the church.

eykir, home of Miðfjarðar-Skeggi, who took the sword Sköfnungur rom the burial mound of Hrólfur kraki in *Hrólfs saga*.

augarbakki, a small village, heated from local hot springs, just south f the Miðfjarðará bridge. Ásbyrgi community centre. See p. 63.

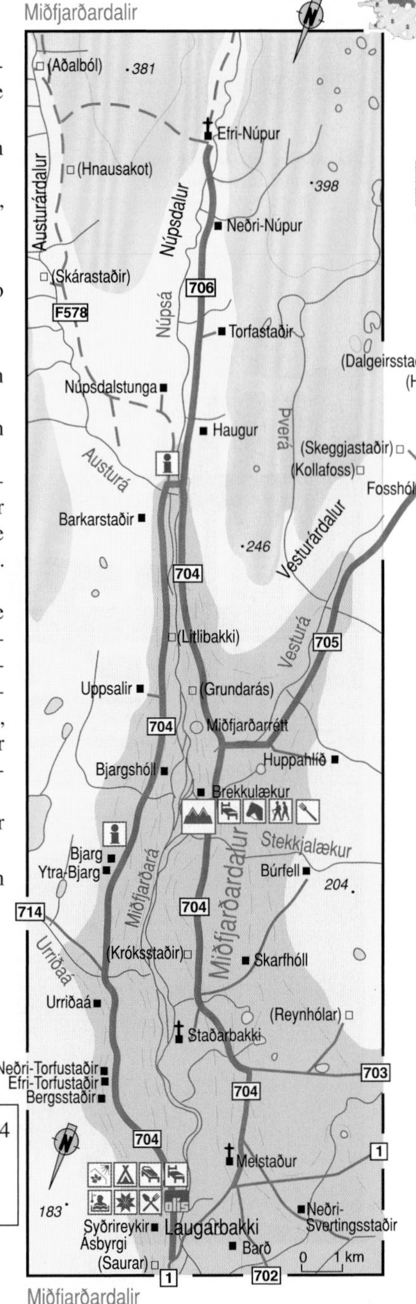

1 Norðurlandsvegur, p. 63
702 Heggstaðanesvegur, p. 334
703 Hálsbæjavegur, p. 334
714 Fitjavegur, p. 341
F578 Arnarvatnsvegur, p. 466-467

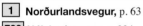

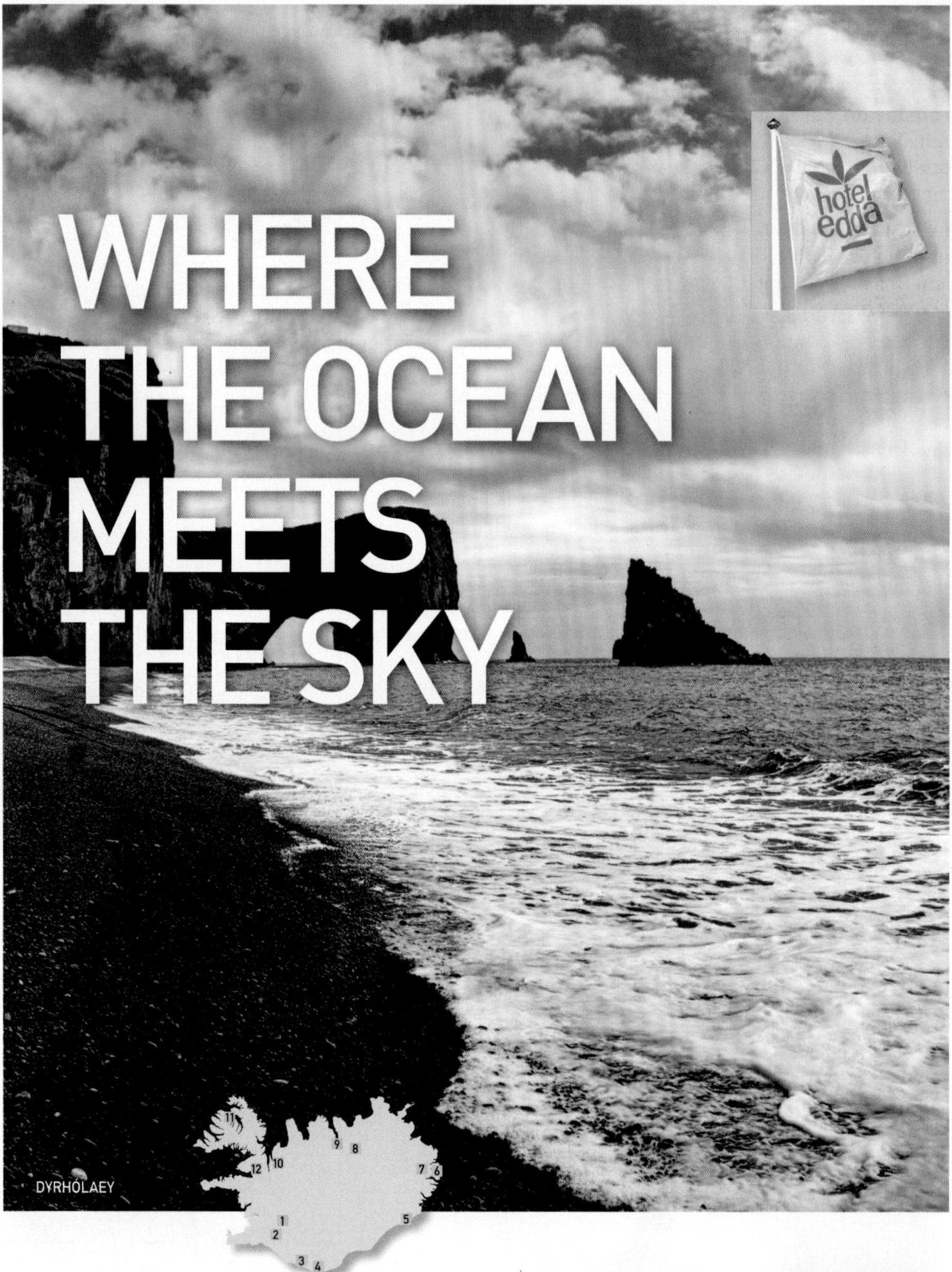

Húnaþing-vestra is an exciting destination for travellers who want to experience Icelandic culture, history and nature at its best. Located at the mid-way point between Reykjavík and Akureyri the area is characterised by unspoilt moors and wetlands, majestic mountains, a vivid coastline and rich fishing rivers and lakes.

Hvammstangi on the Vatnsnes peninsula is the capital of the region and from there and its surrounding areas you can find a wide range of excellent services and restaurants along with accommodation at all levels of comfort and value inviting you to experience all the best that the area has to offer.

A great place to start your trip is at the award winning museum run by The Icelandic Seal Center in Hvammstangi. There you will find an extensive educational exhibit detailing the way of life of Icelandic

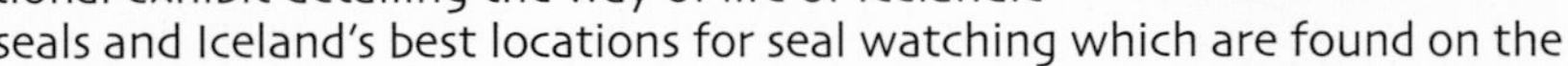

seals and Iceland's best locations for seal watching which are found on the peninsula. The museum building also houses the areas Tourist Information Center where you can learn about everything there is to see and do in Húnaþing-vestra, such as; seal watching boat tours, Iceland´s largest wool factory, horse tours and rental, many unique and interesting museums, quality local handcraft markets, fun and family friendly swimming pool and hot pots, endless nature and wildlife areas and many walking paths to name but a few.

The Vatnsnes peninsula is the undoubted pearl of the region, with Iceland´s largest seal colonies found along its shores and numerous places of interest such as the famous giant rock formation Hvítserkur, Hamarsrétt sheep corral, Illugastaðir with its gruesome history and the unique Borgavirki Viking fort but a selection.

For further information see **www.visithunathing.is** or contact the Tourist Information Center on +354 45 12345 or **info@selasetur.is**

Bergstaðir-Hvammstangi 19 km

3 P. 566

MAP P. 338

Hvammstangi-Bergstaðir 19 km

The church at Kirkjuhvammur

Hamarsrétt, a sheep fold by the ocean.

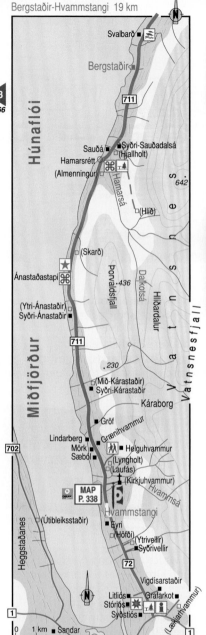

Skarð, houses and greenhouses heated from springs on the shore. A ligh housee built in 1947.

Ánastaðir, a farm where in 1882 thirty-two large whales ran agroun during an intensely cold spring. This was said to have saved the loca people from starvation. Ánastaðastapi is a sharp-pointed rock in the sea.

Káraborg, (476 m) a spectacular crag from which there is a fine view. riding trail goes past the crag to the Vesturhóp district.

Vatnsnes, the peninsula between Miðfjörður and Húnafjörður, with high mountain range, **Vatnsnesfjall**, the highest peak being **Þrælsfe** ("Slave mountain") (906 m).

Hvammstangi, (pop. 546) a village by Miðfjörður fjord: the only tradin village in Vestur-Húnavatnssýsla county, legally recognised for commerc in 1895, with trade starting around 1900. Main industries: agriculture fishing, trade and other services. All of the buildings are heated geother mally, using water piped in from the hot spring at Laugarbakki. While modern church has now replaced the old one at Kirkjuhvammur, the orig inal church is still standing, cared for by the National Museum, with th only operable watermill in Iceland right by it. Health centre, home for th elderly, community centre, museum of commerce, compulsory school an swimming pool. Hvammstangi is also home to the Icelandic Seal Centre which hosts an exhibition on seals around Iceland, both in the present an the past. In the same building, you can visit art shows over the summe and a tourist information centre. The Seal Centre conducts research o both seals and eco-tourism.

HVAMMSTANGI
www.northwest.is

Kortagerð: Ólafur Valsson Copyright ©

711 Vatnsnesvegur, 77 km.

Kirkjuhvammur, wooden church, of younger type with a tower, built in 1882 In the keeping of the National Museun since 1976.

72 Hvammstangavegur, 6 km.

1 Norðurlandsvegur, p. 64
702 Heggstaðanesvegur, p. 334

Bjargaós, estuary of Hópið.

Vesturhóp, a good farming district below the Vatnsnesfjall mountain range and south of the lake Sigríðarstaðavatn.

Sigríðarstaðavatn, a fishing lake, 6 km long, narrow and shallow. East of the lake are 50-80 m high cliffs called Nesbjörg.

Hvítserkur, a 15 m high basalt crag rising from the sea near the farm Súluvellir. The action of the surf has eroded it to make it resemble a three-legged monster. On the way to Hvítserkur seal breeding grounds can be seen unusually close to. There are often hundreds of seals lying on the sands beyond the estuary. One of the most accessible seal breeding grounds in the country.

Síða, a row of farms on the east of the Vatnsnes peninsula alongside Sigríðarstaðavatn.

Krossanes, a farm with good land and many natural advantages. In the 16th century the home of local governor Jón Sigmundsson, who had disputes with Bishop Gottskálk Nikulásson in the last years of his life.

Hindisvík, an abandoned farm on an bay of the same name at the end of the Vatnsnes peninsula. Picturesque landscape and a good view of the Strandir coast. Just east of there is Strandvík, where the brig *Valborg* stranded in 1869 in some of the worst weather to have raged in Iceland. Home for a time of the distinguished and talented poet Rev. Sigurður Norland (1885-1971), who also wrote in English, quatrains following Icelandic rules of metre and alliteration, such as:

She is fine as morn in May
Mild, divine and clever
Like a shining summer day
She'll be mine forever

Katadalur, an abandoned farm. Friðrik Sigurðsson lived there with his parents. He was the last man to be executed along with Agnes Magnúsdóttir for the murders at Illugastaðir, January 12th 1830. See p. 65.

Tjörn, a church and parsonage. Ögmundur Sivertsen (1799-1845), naturalist and poet, was pastor there for a time. Roads lead from Tjörn to the valleys Þorgrímsdalur and Katadalur.

712 Þorgrímsstaðavegur, 8 km.

Illugastaðir, an abandoned farm. The farmer, Natan Ketilsson, and his shepherd Pétur Jónsson were murdered there in 1828 (see **Þrístapar**, A-Hún). Natan got the farm in 1824 and his family has been there since. From Illugastaðir came captain Hrólfur Jakobsson who drowned in 1910 shortly before his departure to the island Jan Mayen where he and another man had intended to put up a hunting camp, hunt for seal and claim the island for Iceland. It was, however, not until 1921 that Norwegians first settled on Jan Mayen and put up a weather station there.

Svalbarð, a farm. There is a marked seal watching location and a parking lot.

Hvítserkur

Neðra-Vatnshorn-Kista 23 km

714 Hrísar
715
Neðra-Vatnshorn 1
715 Víðidalstunga
Storhóll
Dæli
Vatnshóll
711 314
Birkihlíð Sporður Þóreyjarnúpur
Víðigerði
Litla- Stóra- Ásgeirsá Auðunar-staðir
N1
1
Þórukot Galtarnes Urðarbak
161.
Hörgshóll
Vesturhóp
Víðidalsá
716
Böðvarshólar
Lækjamót
(Síða) 711
(Bjarghús)
Þorkelshóll
Núpukot
Grund
(Foss)
Faxalækur
Sólbakki
Breiðabólsstaður
1 Árnes 717
(Litla-Borg)
(Hvoll)
(Klambra)
Borgarvirki
177
Vesturhópsvatn
(Harastaðir)
Stóra-Borg
Þverárrétt
Syðri- Þverá
Neðri- Þverá Efri-Þverá
(Gottorp)
(Vatnsendi)
717
(Ásbjarnarnes)
Þorfinnsstaðir
Vesturhópshólar
470.
(Sigríðarstaðir)
Kista
Hóp
Nesbjörg
Sigríðarstaðasandur
Sigríðarstaðavatn
.387
0 1 km
Ægissíða
711

Kista- Neðra-Vatnshorn 23 km

3 P. 566

Þóreyjarnúpur, a strange rock near a farm of same name. Long the home of the poet Hans Natansson (1816-1887).

Böðvarshólar, a farm, birthplace of Bríet Bjarnhéðinsdóttir (1856-1940) an active champion for women's rights in Iceland, and her brother Prof Sæmundur Bjarnhéðinsson (1863-1936) who did much to cure leprosy.

716 Síðuvegur, 5,8 km.

Breiðabólsstaður, a church and parsonage, where lawspeaker Hafliði Másson lived about 1100. Under his supervision the Icelandic laws were first recorded in 1117. Monument. It was there that Bishop Jón Arason set up his printing-press about 1530. There are now only two books printed there extant: *Passio* and *Guðspjallabók* ("Book of gospels"), both of which have been published in fascimile.

717 Borgarvegur, 13,5 km.

Borgarvirki

Borgarvirki, ("Citadel") (177 m) a group of rocks on the ridges between the Vesturhóp district and the Víðidalur valley, with basalt columns 10-15 m high and a circular depression at the top, open to the east. There a big stone wall has been raised, through which is the entrance. The wall and others nearby were repaired in 1949-50, and in the depression are the ruins of huts and a well. Nobody knows why Borgarvirki was made. One story is that Víga-Barði in *Heiðarvíga saga* intended it as a defence against attack from the people of the Borgarfjörður district, another that it was the work of Finnbogi rammi in *Finnboga saga ramma*. View dial.

Stóra-Borg in Víðidalur, a substantial farm, good salmon-fishing. Home of Finnbogi rammi in Saga times.

Vatnsendi, a farm, for some time home of the well-known poetess Rósa Guðmundsdóttir (Vatnsenda-Rósa) (1795-1855).

Vesturhópsvatn, a fishing-lake, ca. 7 km long and 1-2 km wide, emptying through Faxalækur into the Víðidalsá river.

Ásbjarnarnes, there lived Víga-Barði Guðmundarson (989), farmer, who is mentioned in *Grettir saga* and *Heiðarvíga saga*.

Vesturhópshólar, a church and parsonage till 1851. The former prime minister Jón Þorláksson (1877-1935) came from there.

1 Norðurlandsvegur, p. 64
714 Fitjavegur, p. 341
715 Víðidalsvegur, p. 341

714 Fitjavegur, 15 km.

Hrappsstaðir, once the outermost farm in Víðidalur, from whence there is a jeep-track south to Arnarvatnsheiði moor, road F578.

Bakkabunga, a hill with rocky edges on the west of the valley Víðidalur, where the remains of plants, including alder, have been found in strata dating from late Tertiary or early Quaternary ages.

Kolugljúfur, a 1 km long and 40–50 m deep ravine. Takes its name from a troll called Kola who dug the ravine and lived theres. Beautiful waterfalls in the ravine.

Víðidalstunga, a church and old manor farm between the rivers Fitjá and **Víðidalsá**. Land belonging to the Vídalín family from 15th century until about 1900. The best-known member of this family was Páll Jónsson Vídalín (1667-1727), magistrate, poet and schoolmaster, author along with Árni Magnússon of the *Jarðabók 1702-12,* an Icelandic Domesday book. The *Flateyjarbók,* the largest extant Icelandic vellum manuscript, was written at Víðidalstunga, on the initiative of the farmer Jón Hákonarson (b. 1350).

Víðidalur, a wide, green valley, with low hills on the western side and **Víðidalsfjall** (993 m) on the eastern side. The river Víðidalsá flows through the valley, a good salmon river, coming from Stórisandur, total length 65 km. Another river connects with Víðidalsá, Fitjá, there you can find a great fishing spot called **Kerafossar**.

Víðihlíð, a community in the Auðunarstaðir lands. Community centre, library, school.

Auðunarstaðir, a farm in Víðidalur named after the settler Auðun skökull ("horse's phallus"), to whom the British royal family can trace its family line. Community centre Víðihlíð nearby.

715 Víðidalsvegur, 13,2 km.

Ásgeirsá, a farm opposite Auðunarstaðir. Home of Hrefna, the wife of Kjartan Ólafsson in *Laxdæla saga*.

Lækjamót, a farm at the northern end of Víðidalur. The first missionaries, Þorvaldur víðförli ("Þorvaldur the widely travelled") and Bishop Friðrekur, stayed there for three years towards the end of the 10th century.

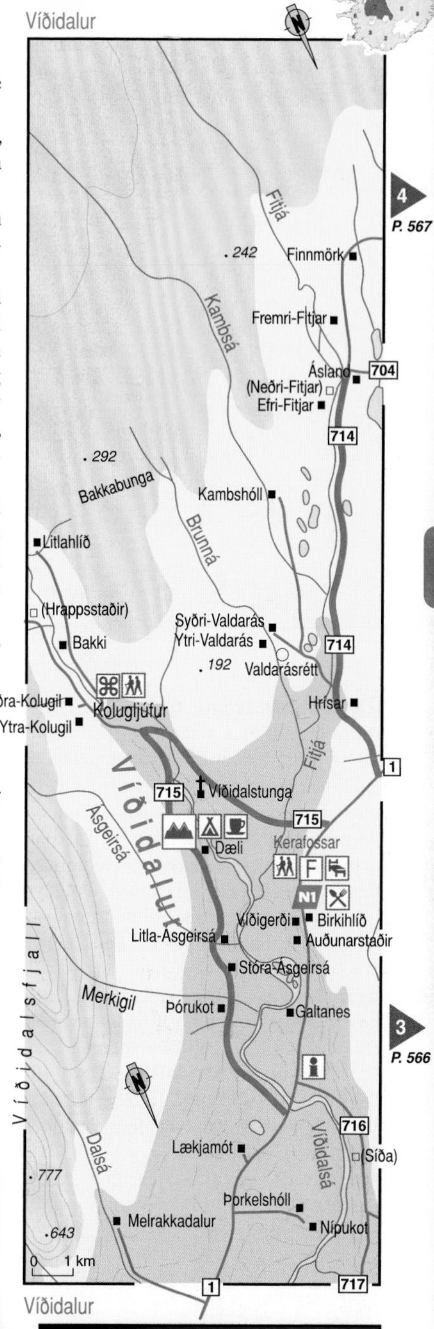

1 Norðurlandsvegur, p. 64

704 Miðfjarðarvegur, p. 335

716 Síðuvegur, p. 340

717 Borgarvegur, p. 340

Kolugljúfur

4
P. 567

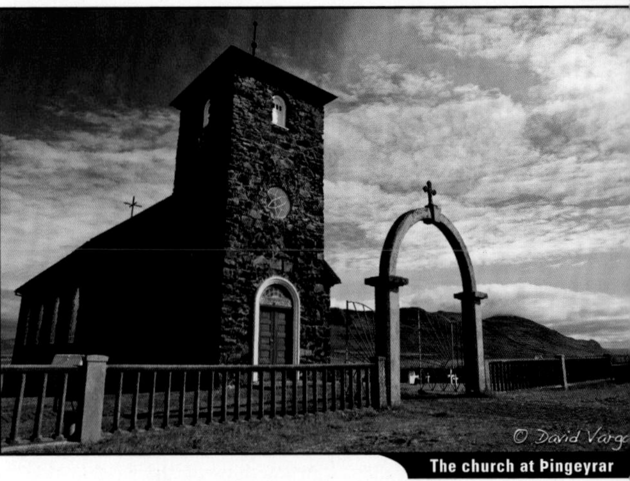

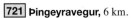

The church at Þingeyrar

721 **Þingeyravegur,** 6 km.

Þingeyrar, a manor farm of great historical importance, the most important in Húnavatnssýsla county, with more land than most other farms in Iceland, meadows and pastures. Salmon and seal. A stone church built 1864-65 by Ásgeir Einarsson, member of parliament, containing many fine relics. An ancient assembly site, and the site of the first monastery in Iceland, Þingeyraklaustur, established 1133. It was one of the foremost educational centres of that time, the place where more Sagas were written down than anywhere else. Many well-known Icelanders have lived there, e.g Hulda Stefánsdóttir, headmistress and author of a four-volume autobiographical work which is considered among the finest of its kind in Iceland (see **Möðruvellir**, p. 357). Birthplace of Björn M. Ólsen (1850-1919), first rector of the University of Iceland, it is also the birthplace of Jón Eyþórsson (1895-1968) meteorologist.

Þingeyrarif, a sand-bar reaching most of the way across the lake Hóp.

Hóp, the fifth largest lake in Iceland, 29-44 km² depending on the tide which affects the water level. Fed by Víðidalsá and Gljúfurá, it empties out through Bjargaós.

Vatnsdalur – Víðidalsfjall

Þing, the plain south and east of Hóp from the rive Gljúfurá and east to Húnavatn Lake and the river Giljaá Grassy and fertile.

Vatnsdalur, a 25 km long valley. On its eastern side i the mountain Vatnsdalsfjall, steep, with rocks and scree the highest peak being **Jörundarfell** (1,018 m). On th west are low ridges up to Víðidalsfjall with many farm in grassy, fertile country.

Sunnuhlíð, the innermost farm in Vatnsdalur on the eastern side. Opposite it are remains of the farm Þórhallastaðir, where Grettir the strong wrestled with th ghost, Glámur, in *Grettis saga*.

Þórormstunga, the home in mid-19th century of Jó Bjarnason, a self-taught mathematician and astronomer who worked out almanacs and eclipses and wrote man works on astronomy and natural science.

Marðarnúpur, a farm. Guðmundur Björnsson (1864-1937) Surgeon General and first President of th National Life-Saving Association of Iceland grew u there.

Hof, an old manor farm on the settlement land o Ingimundur gamli ("the old"), who chose it on advic from the gods. His temple is said to have been a **Goðahóll** just above the farm. A memorial to the settle by the road.

Dyngja, 50 m deep, a grassy hollow north of Hof. Thi spot is considered to be enchanted.

Eyjólfsstaðir, birthplace of Prof. Sigurður Norda (1886-1974), a distinguished scholar for whom one o the research institutes in the University of Iceland ha been named.

Hvammur, a substantial farm. Gedduhryggir, rock layers sloping 40°-50° down into the valley. North o Hvammur is a landslide of boulders, Hvammsurði. Near the farm the stream Fosslækur tumbles over th Hjalli cliffs in a beautiful high waterfall.

1 **Norðurlandsvegur,** p. 65
722 **Vatnsdalsvegur,** p. 343
724 **Reykjabraut,** p. 344

722 VATNSDALSVEGUR

orsæludalur, a farm since the original settlement.

rímstunga, a big sheep farm, church and former parsonage. West of it s a rugged gorge, through which flows the river Álka. The beginning of he old route south via Grímstunguheiði moor to Borgarfjörður, now a eep-track south to the moors and Stórisandur. The home, in the 10th century of Óttar, father of the poet Hallfreður vandræðaskáld.

laukagil, a farm taking its name from the Haukagil gorge, which in turn s said to have got its name from two berserkers who were beaten to leath and their bodies thrown into it. The poet Hallfreður vandræðaskáld vas brought up at Haukagil. A lovely copse of coniferous trees.

ls, a substantial farm. Birthplace of Halldóra Bjarnadóttir (1873-1981), a ioneer of the Icelandic handicrafts industry. The local meeting place is at ısbrekka, a new farm nearby. The witch Ljótunn of *Vatnsdæla saga* is aid to have lived at Ás.

Jndirfell, (also known as Undornfell) a church and former parsonage. 3irthplace of the painter Þórarinn B. Þorláksson (1867-1924). A district irls' school had its beginnings there 1879-83.

Cornsá, a farm below which is **Kattarauga** ("Cat's eye"), a large, deep ool with floating islands. A protected natural feature.

Injúkur, (111 m) the peak of a hill that almost closes off the valley, elow which is farm of the same name. An excellent view of Vatnsdalur rom Hnjúkur.

órdísarlundur, a grove of trees planted by the Húnvetninga Society in Reykjavík in memory of Þórdís Ingimundardóttir, the first person born in /atnsdalur.

/atnsdalshólar, an area of small hills and hillocks at the mouth of /atnsdalur, the debris of a tremendous landslide from Vatnsdalsfjall, covring about 4 km², supposedly uncountable. Other geographical features n Iceland considered to be uncountable are the islands of Breiðafjörður nd the lakes on Arnarvatnsheiði moor.

722 **Vatnsdalsvegur,** 46 km.

/atnsdalsá, a river having its source in numerous streams on Grímstunga noor and at Stórisandur. Further down it is deep and calm, there called Inausakvísl (see below), flowing into Húnavatn. A popular salmon river.

lóðið, a lake near the Vatnsdalshólar hills, created by a landslide in Dctober 1720 that dammed the river. Remains of the landslide can still be een at the farm Bjarnastaðir east of Flóðið.

Inausakvísl, the lowest part of the river Vatnsdalsá, between the lakes lóðið and Húnavatn. Deep and calm, it is an excellent fishing river.

Vatnsdalur

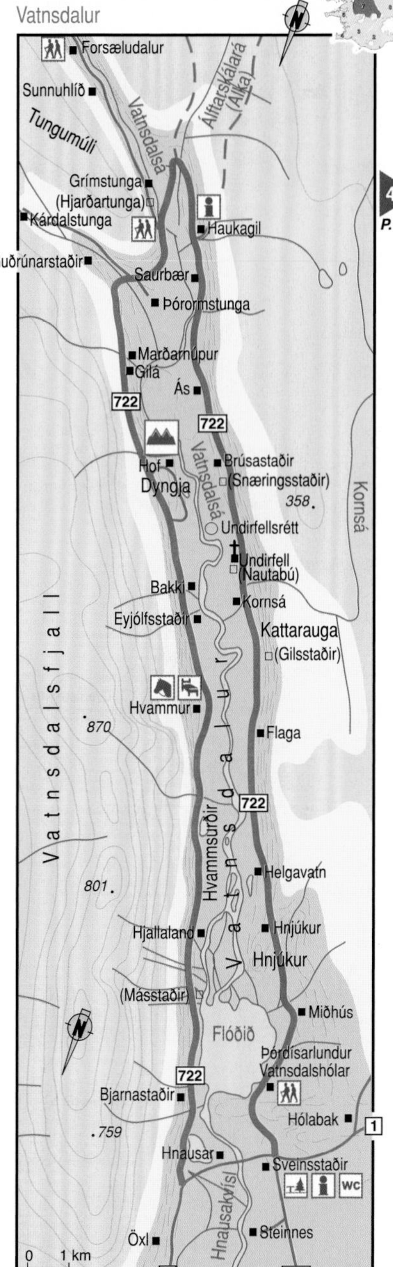

Vatnsdalur

4 P. 567

1 **Norðurlandsvegur,** p. 65 | 721 **Þingeyravegur,** p. 342

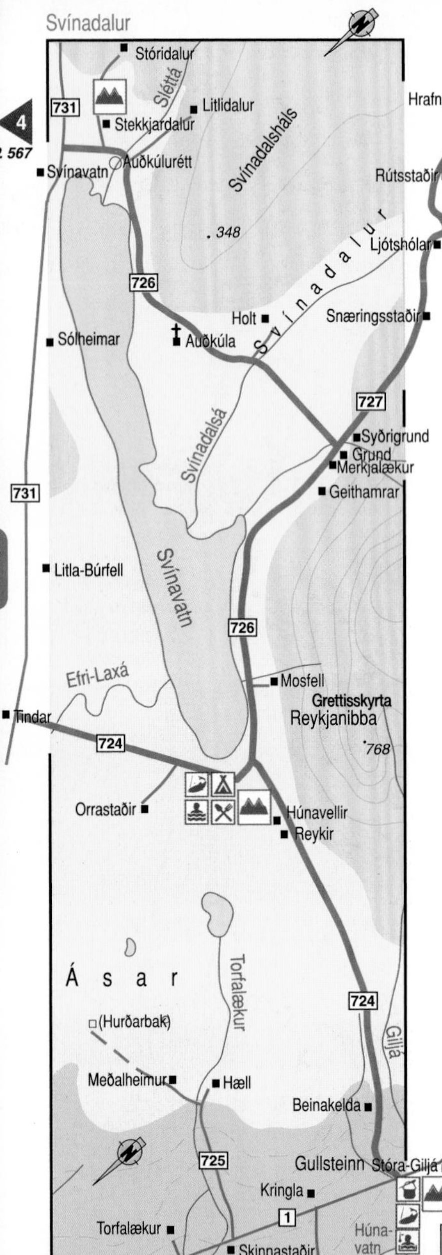

727 Svínadalsvegur, 8,65 km.

Svínadalur, ("Swine valley") a shallow, broad valley, grassy and fertile, the farms scattered but with good land. *Landnámabók* ("The Book of Settlements") says that the valley got its name from the swine of the settler Ingimundur gamli ("the old"). They vanished one year, but were found the following year, their numbers having increased.

726 Auðkúluvegur, 14,6 km.

Stóridalur, a substantial farm through the ages, 250 m above sea level. The same family has lived there since 1792.

Auðkúla, a church, a parsonage until 1952. A substantial farm, which once owned the whole of Auðkúluheiði moor and Kjölur as far south as the lake Hvítárvatn. The residence of local leaders in the 13th and 14th centuries. The unusual church is octagonal, made of timber.

724 Reykjabraut, 12,8 km.

Reykir, a farm on the Reykjabraut road. Geothermal heat, one of oldest swimming schools in Iceland, swimming teaching having started in 1820. Children's boarding school.

Reykjanibba, (769 m) a mountain above Reykir and Mosfell. On its eastern side are two rhyolite caves called **Grettisskyrta** ("Grettir's shirt") where Grettir is said to have put out his shirt to dry. Long ago the mountain split in two and a large part of it subsided towards the lake, Svínavatn.

Sauðadalur, ("Sheep valley") a valley going south between the mountains Vatnsdalsfjall and Svínadalsfjall. The valley is named for the sheep of the settler Ingimundur gamli ("the old").

1 Norðurlandsvegur, p. 67 **725 Miðásavegur,** p. 67
731 Svínvetningabraut, p. 345

731 SVÍNVETNINGABRAUT

ólheimaháls, (329 m) long, low ridges east of the Svínavatn lake. West f the ridge are the small lakes Hafratjörn and Lómatjörn, where divers nd many kinds of duck can often be seen.

úrfell, a farm above which are some basalt columns now called Búrellsfell. Down towards the lake Svínavatn are the "woods" Tindaskógur nd Búrfellsskógur, but all that is now left of these is some dwarf birch.

unnfríðarstaðir, a farm presented to the local forestry association for ee-planting.

agaðarhóll, an imposing farm opposite the southern end of the lake axárvatn. There is a fine view from the Hólsberg rock southeast of the arm.

axárvatn, a long, narrow trout lake, 2.9 km^2. The level of the lake rose y 1.5 m when the Laxá river was harnessed for hydro-electric power in 933. Power 480 kW.

olkumýrar, *the Book of Settlement* says the a man called Þorbjörn kolka ettled there.

akásar, the slopes west of the river Blanda, with a few farms.

lánafoss waterfall the river Laxá. In ie story of orvaldur víðförli 'the widely travlled") it is said that ie name comes om Máni the hristian, who aught so many ılmon under the ılls that he was able prevent a local ımine. Mánafoss is 5-3 m high, but ther difficult to ach because of itches. South of auðanes are the olkumýrar marsh-, grassy pools with w hills in between.

The church at Auðkúla.

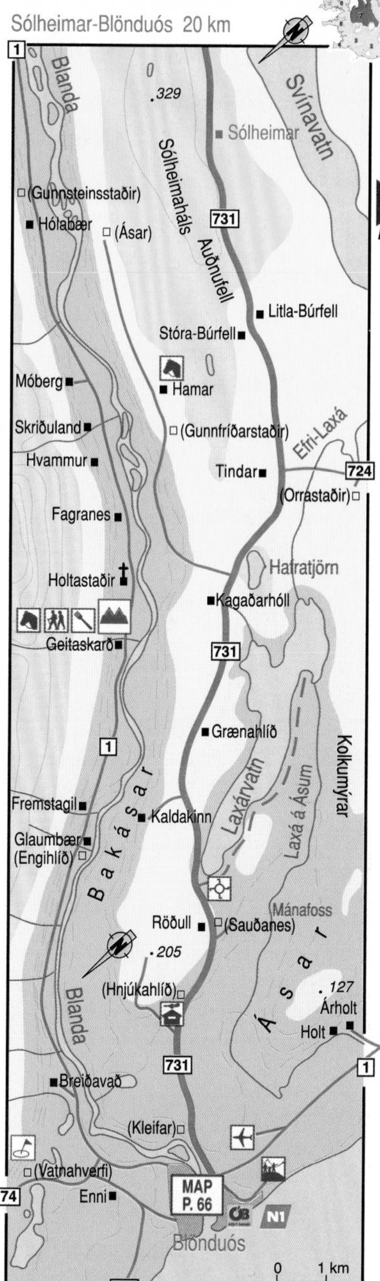

1 Norðurlandsvegur, p. 68	**74 Skagastrandarvegur,** p. 322
724 Reykjabraut, p. 344	**741 Neðribyggðarvegur,** p. 322

4 P. 567

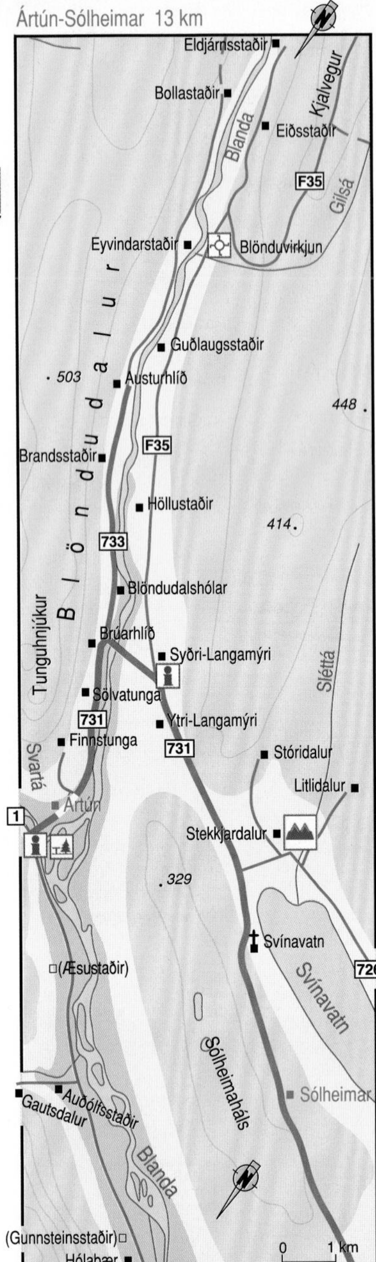

733 Blöndudalsvegur, 10 km.

Eyvindarstaðir, formerly a substantial farm that owned all the land sout to the glaciers.

Blöndustöð, a major hydro-electric power plant on the river Blanda completed 1991. The dams created a huge lake, 30 km^2 on the moors. Th plant itself is underground. Power 150 MW.

Gilsá, a river joining the Blanda south of Guðlaugsstaðir. Beginning c the track to Kjalvegur (F35) south across Auðkúluheiði moor. From Kja vegur there is a jeep-track north of the mountain Sandkúlufell to Stóri sandur sands, from where it is possible to descend to either the Vatnsdalu or Víðidalur valleys, or go west via Arnarvatnsheiði moor to the valley of Borgarfjörður via Kalmanstunga.

Guðlaugsstaðir, a farm where there is a memorial to the professor an doctor, Guðmundur Hannesson (1866-1946), a pioneer in health care an organisation, who was born there. The farm has belonged to the sam family since 1680.

Brandsstaðir, a farm, home of Björn Bjarnason, who wrote the Brands staðir annals covering the years 1783-1858.

Blöndudalshólar, a parsonage until 1880, and church till 1882. Not fa from the bridge over the river Blanda.

731 Svínvetningabraut, 33 km.

Blanda, 125 km, one of the longest glacial rivers in Iceland. It come mainly from the western part of the Hofsjökull glacier, the uppermo sources being below the mountain Blágnípa. Close to the farms it flow through big, wild gorges known as **Blöndugil**. There are only two bridge on the Blanda, one at Blönduós, the other in the lower part of the Blöndu dalur valley.

Svínavatn, a farm and church beside a lake of the same name in th Svínadalur valley (see Road 727). There are fish in the lake, which i 11,78 km^2, but the winter ice is often unsafe and some pastors from Au kúla have been drowned in it. The lake was thought to be haunted.

Interior of the church at Svínavatn.

1 Norðurlandsvegur, p. 69
726 Auðkúluvegur, p. 344
F35 Kjalvegur, p. 456

734 SVARTÁRDALSVEGUR

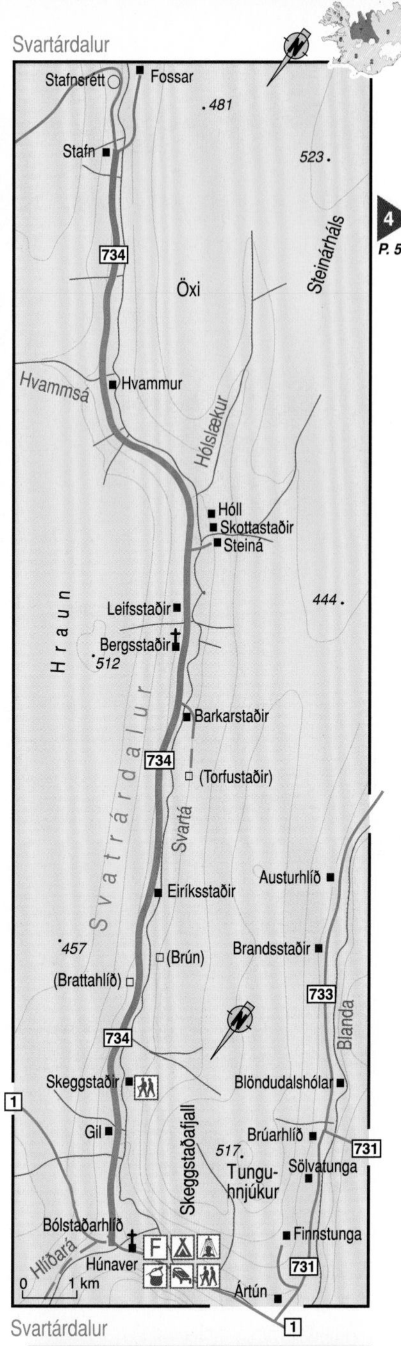

ossar, ("Waterfalls") a farm in the Fossadalur valley, about 2 km south of Stafnsrétt, a sheep-gathering pen at 320 m above sea level. Long the home of moorland shepherds. From there it is possible to go by jeep to the lake Aðalmannsvatn and Álfgeirstungur, also by another track via ossabrekka north of the glacier Hofsjökull. Near Fossar is the abandoned arm **Kóngsgarður**, birthplace of Sigurbjörn Sveinsson (1887-1950), popular author of children's books.

tafn, at a height of 280 m this is one of furthest inland farms in the vartárdalur valley. Nearby is **Stafnsrétt**, one of the biggest sheep-gathering pens in Iceland, always busy in autumn. A jeep-track leads from here over Kiðaskarð pass to Skagafjörður, and another via Eyvindar-staðaheiði moor south to the river Strangakvísl.

ergsstaðir, a church and parsonage until the 20th century.

iríksstaðir, a farm.

rattahlíð, an abandoned farm, was once called Eiríksstaðakot, but was changed to Brattahlíð when the house that still stands there was built in 1905.

rún, an abandoned farm from which came the poet and horseman Sigurður Jónsson (1898-1970), who always added "from Brún" to his name.

vartárdalur, the easternmost of the valleys in this county leading up to the highlands. Shallow, with little flat land but grassy slopes.

vartá, a good fishing river.

únaver, a community centre.

ólstaðarhlíð, a church and substantial farm for centuries. For 300 years, 1528-1825, the home of successive generations of the same family, which produced numerous children, many of whom were famous or influential people in their time. Descendants are still known as the Bólstaðarhlíð family. The mouth of Svartárdalur, where Bólstaðarhlíð stands, is believed by some to be the Ævarsskarð mentioned in the Sagas.

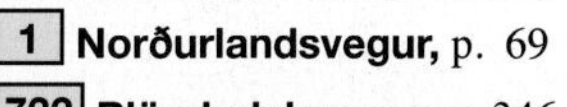
1 **Norðurlandsvegur,** p. 69 | 731 **Svínvetningabraut,** p. 346
733 **Blöndudalsvegur,** p. 346

4
p. 567

744 Þverárfjallsvegur, 39 km.

Norðurárdalur, a pretty side-valley northeast of the mouth of the Laxárdalur valley. There is a road through it, and over the mountain Þverárfjall to Laxárdalur in Skagafjörður.

Laxá, a good fishing-river, coming from Laxárdalur, a long valley extending to near Bólstaðarhlíð. There were once farms all along it, but now there are only four. This river was often dangerous in floods, and a number of people have drowned there.

Mánaskál, a farm where the settler Hólmgöngu-Máni ("Máni of the islet-duels") is said to have built his farm when he moved from Mánavík on Skagi. He is supposed to be buried in the Mánahaugur mound on Illviðrahnjúkur (969 m) in the Laxárdalur mountains. There are indeed signs of a rock-built mound, but it can supposedly bring bad luck to touch it.

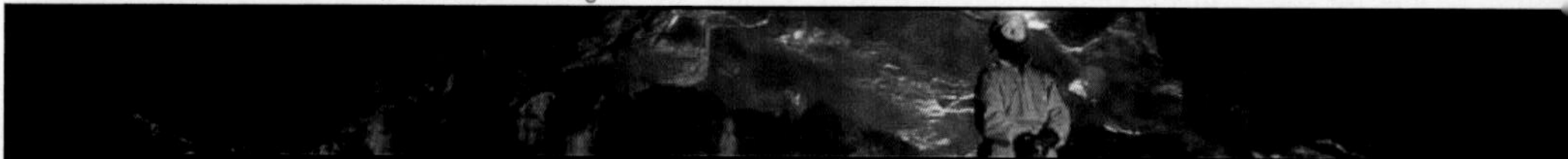

742 Mýravegur, 6 km.

74 Skagastrandarvegur, p. 322
745 Skagavegur, p. 351

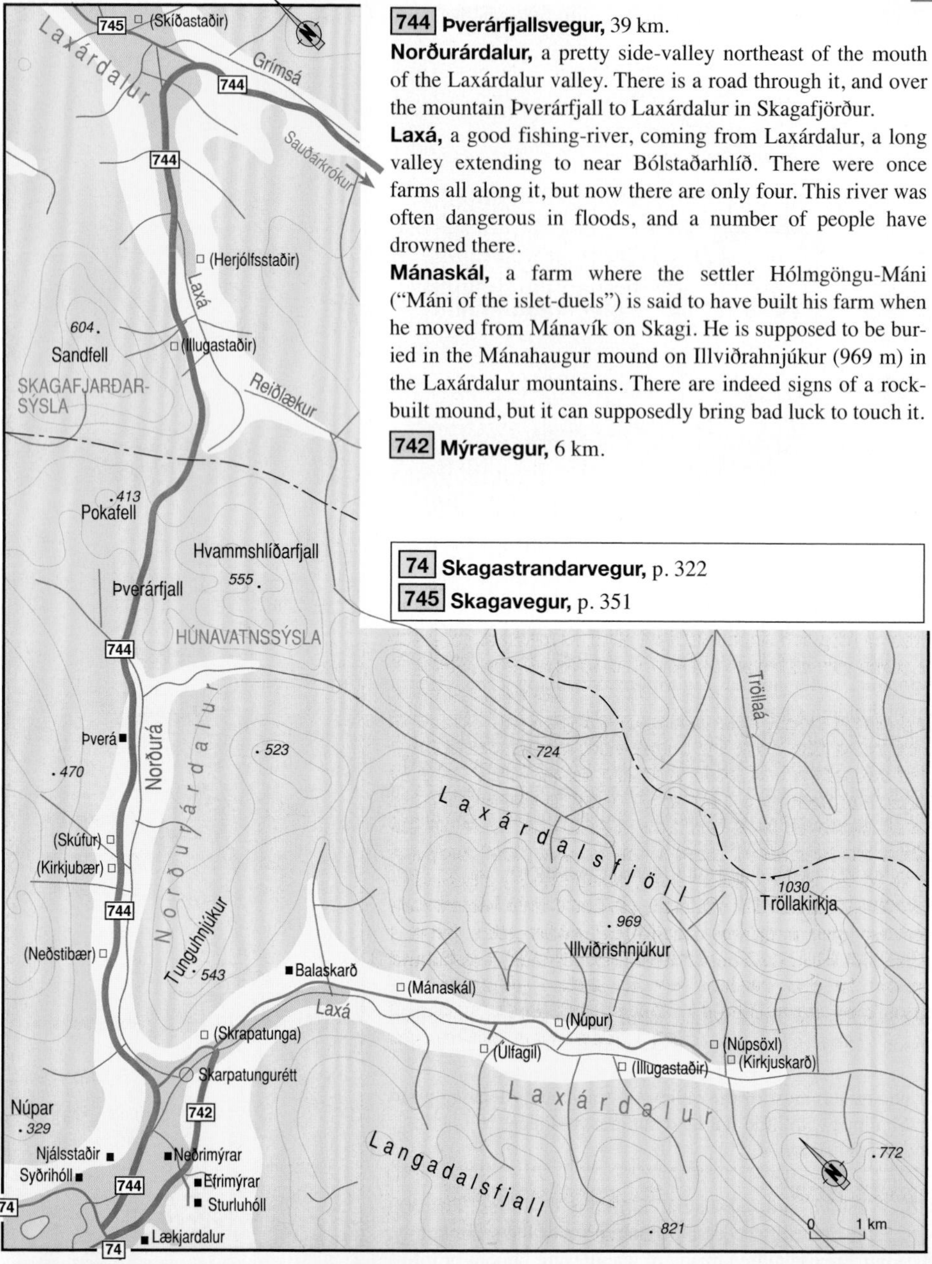

Kyrpingsfjall, (98 m) gravel ridges rising to the north between the Laxá river and the valley Torfdalur. The southernmost and lowest ridge nearest Laxá is called Gullbrekka, below which is Gullkelda, a deep bog into which the farm Gullbrekka is said to have sunk with its occupants at the death of Þorgerður or Þorbjörg kólka of Kólkunes.

Laxá í Nesjum, a small river with some salmon.

The lighthouse in Kálfshamarsvík.

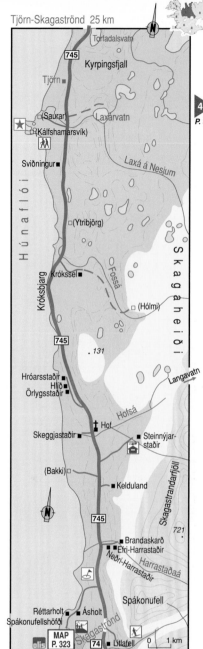

Kálfshamarsvík, a small bay, north of which is Kálfshamarsnes. Around 1900 there was a fishing station there, and a small settlement, but it was finally abandoned around the time of the depression, 1940. Interesting basalt columns. Signposts bearing the names of the buildings and inhabitants and much other information have been put up in various places in Kálfshamarvík. The signs rest on basalt columns.

Fossá, a waterfall falling from a 20 m high cliff, Króksbjarg, straight to the sea. It is best to see the waterfall from the sea. Just north of the waterfall is an unusual cliff, Bjargastapi.

Króksbjarg, 10 km of cliffs, 40-50 m high. At their southern base is a 16 m thick clay layer, on top of which are an 8 m layer of brown sandstone and a thick layer of basalt which has reversed magnetic polarisation.

Örlygsstaðir, a substantial farm on the Skagi peninsula, one of the so-called Brekkubæir. The home, in the 16th century, of Guðmundur Andrésson, one of the men who killed Clerk Kristján and his Danish followers in 1551 in revenge for the execution of the last Catholic Bishop in Iceland, Jón Arason, and his sons (see Road 45, Kirkjuból).

Hof, a farm and church, home of Jón Árnason (1819-88), librarian and important collector of folktales.

74 **Skagastrandarvegur,** p. 322

Tjörn-Skagaströnd 25 km

Skagaströnd-Tjörn 25 km

4 P. 567

Hóll-Tjörn 40 km

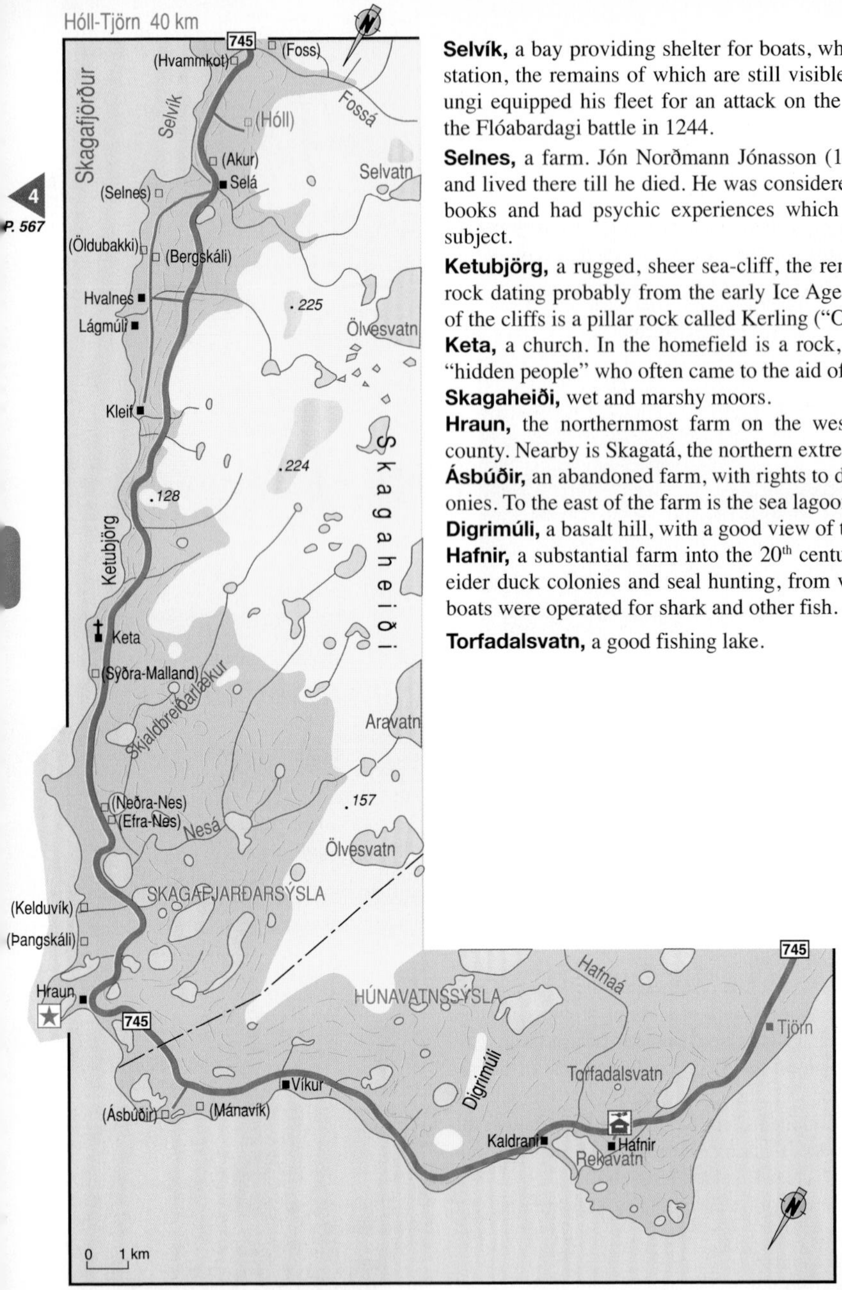

4 P. 567

Selvík, a bay providing shelter for boats, where there was once a fishin station, the remains of which are still visible. It was there that Kolbein ungi equipped his fleet for an attack on the Western fjords, resulting i the Flóabardagi battle in 1244.

Selnes, a farm. Jón Norðmann Jónasson (1898–1976) bought the farn and lived there till he died. He was considered peculiar man, wrote som books and had psychic experiences which he held lectures about th subject.

Ketubjörg, a rugged, sheer sea-cliff, the remains of an old volcano, th rock dating probably from the early Ice Age. Very impressive. Northeas of the cliffs is a pillar rock called Kerling ("Old woman").

Keta, a church. In the homefield is a rock, believed to be the home o "hidden people" who often came to the aid of people in distress.

Skagaheiði, wet and marshy moors.

Hraun, the northernmost farm on the west side of Skagafjarðarsýsl county. Nearby is Skagatá, the northern extremity of Skagi.

Ásbúðir, an abandoned farm, with rights to driftwood and eider duck col onies. To the east of the farm is the sea lagoon Ásbúðavatn.

Digrimúli, a basalt hill, with a good view of the Strandafjöll mountains.

Hafnir, a substantial farm into the 20th century, with rights to driftwood eider duck colonies and seal hunting, from which as many as 20 rowin boats were operated for shark and other fish.

Torfadalsvatn, a good fishing lake.

Tjörn-Hóll 40 km

745 SKAGAVEGUR

auðárkrókur, (pop. 2,575) a town at the head of Skagafjörður, see p. 26.

eðramót, a farm. Home of Haraldur Björnsson (1891-1967), the first celander to become a professional actor, and Björn Sigurðsson MD 1913-1959), a scientist recognised world-wide for being the first to resent theories about slow viral infections, c.f. his PhD thesis, Immunological studies on paratuberculosis" (1955).

eiði, a farm in the Gönguskörð valley, birthplace of botanist Stefán tefánsson (1863-1921), the first headmaster of Menntaskólinn á kureyri (Akureyri Junior College).

önguskörð, a shallow valley or pass at the southern end of the ountain Tindastóll, leading from above Sauðárkrókur to the head f Laxárdalur. On the mountain Tindastóll, near the abandoned rm Breiðsstaðir, about 15 km from Sauðárkrókur, lies a ski slope ith a 1,250 m traction lift. Side valleys lead from it south and est into the mountains and on to Húnavatnssýsla. Excellente ski-g area.

vammur, a church and parsonage.

axárdalur, a fairly long (14 km) grassy but rather narrow alley reaching from the Sævarlandsvík bay to Gönguskörð, the ass behind Tindastóll mountain. Through it flows Laxá, a shing river.

ævarland, the outermost farm in the Laxárdalur valley at e head of the delightful Sævarlandsvík bay. East of it the ountain Tindastóll ends in the wedge-shaped point Landsendi 'Land's end"). The Sævarlandsstapi crag off-shore near there. he islands Drangey and Málmey can be seen in the fjord in the istance.

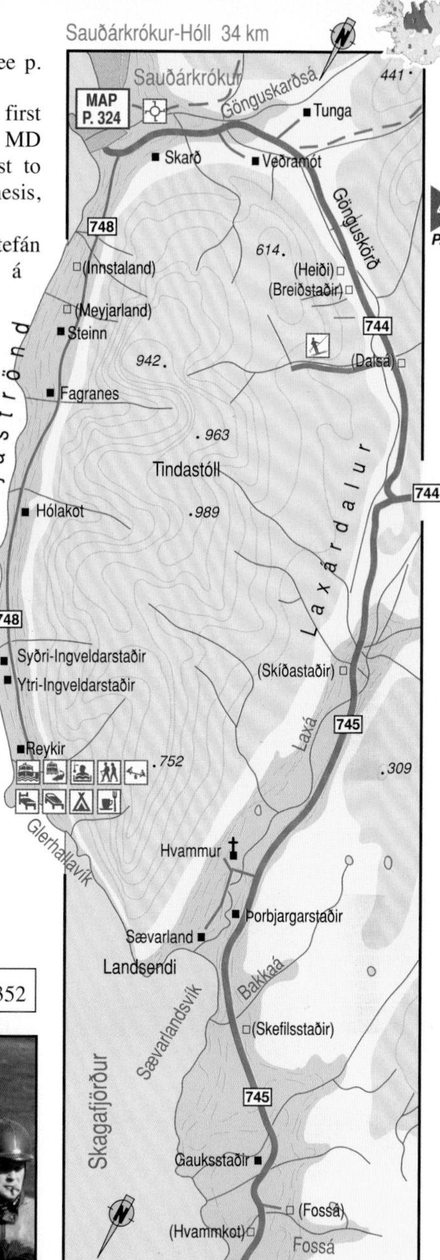

744 **Þverárfjallsvegur,** p. 348 748 **Reykjastrandarvegur,** p. 352

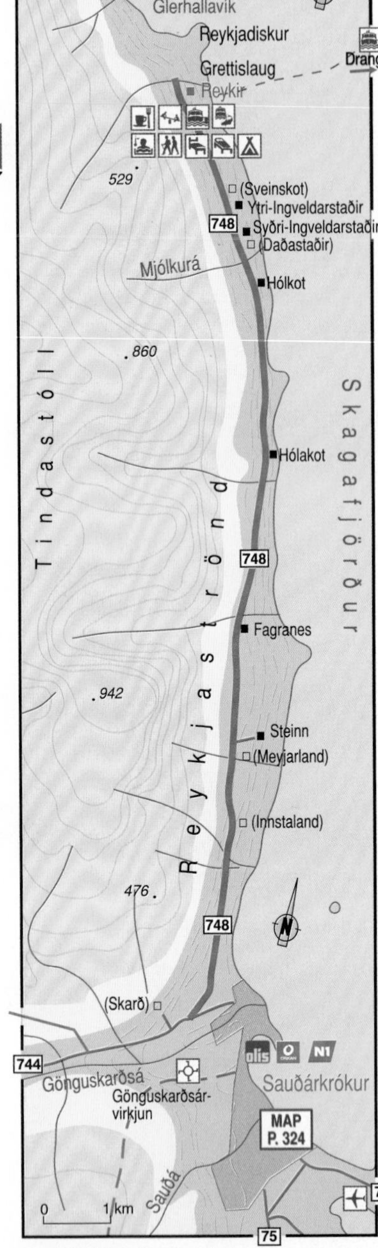

4 P. 567

Glerhallavík, a small bay below high cliffs. Famous for its beautifu stones washed out of the rock and polished by the surf. It is against th law to take stones from this protected area.

Grettislaug.

Reykir, a farm on the Reykjaströnd shore, the farm to which Grettir swa from Drangey to fetch fire. A semicircular point of land there is calle Reykjadiskur, and on its southern side is the spring **Grettislaug,** whe Grettir the strong bathed after swimming from Drangey. Jón Eiríksson **Fagranes**, known as the Earl of Drangey, has had the area of the sprin rebuilt. He has also rebuilt a small boat harbour and fishermen's dwellin as first steps in a programme to develop the area. Boat trips to **Drangey**.

Tindastóll, (989 m) one of the most imposing mountains of Skagafjörðu reaching from the Reykjaströnd coast to the Laxárdalur valley, ca. 20 km Steep and rugged on the east, but more sloping and grassy on the wes Many folktales are connected with it. One is about the wishing-stone be found in a well near Glerhallavík bay. It is said to float up eve Midsummernight. The view from Tindastóll was the poet Matthía Jochumsson's inspiration in his poem about Skagafjörður. Nearby is th cove Baulubás and in it Bauluhellir ("Cow cave"), which got its nam because cows walked through it from Atlastaðir. It used to be the home sea-monsters. Tindastóll was the home of giants and trolls, their king li ing there and his daughter at Glerhallavík. One of the giants kidnapped daughter of the Bishop of Hólar and kept her in his cave.

Reykjaströnd, the coastline north of Sauðárkrókur. A narrow strip of fl land, steep mountainside and rather barren country.

75 **Sauðárkróksbraut,** p. 323 744 **Þverárfjallsvegur,** p. 348

751 Efribyggðarvegur, 12 km. **752 Skagafjarðarvegur,** 36,7 km.

lafgrímsstaðir, there is the base camp for Arctic Rafting river rafting in ökulsá East and West. They offer trips everyday on both rivers from May ɔ September.

/lælifellshnjúkur, (1,138 m) one of the highest and most imposing mounains of Skagafjörður. It is said that 10 counties can be seen from there. A narked walking route.

/lælifell, a church and parsonage, a manor farm of old. The settlement ınd of Vékell hamrammi.

ßakkaflöt, a centre of river rafting for the rivers Austari-Jökulsá and /estari Jökulsá, two rivers that are fed from the glacier Hofsjökull.

ßkíðastaðir, birthplace of Pálmi Hannesson (1898-1956), a well-known aturalist, member of parliament and headmaster of Menntaskólinn í ꞏeykjavík (Reykjavík College, formerly “The learned school”).

Reykjafoss, a sizeable, pretty waterfall in the Svartá river, the biggest ıver of the district. There is a walking path following the fence at /indheimamelar, passing Reykjafoss and a bridge to the Svartá to Foslaug, natural pool.

lúseyjarkvísl, a deep and smooth-flowing river, formed from the Svartá ınd other streams from the western mountains.

lestavígshamar, (“Horse killing crag”) a single crag on the west bank of lúseyjarkvísl. Former assembly site.

754 Héraðsdalsvegur, 7,6 km. **753 Vindheimavegur,** 6,88 km.

ungusveit, the district between the Héraðsvötn lakes to the east and the ıvers Húseyjarkvísl and Svartá to the west. Some high rocky ridges, with ıarsh and moorland. About 200 m high in the north and 350 m in the outh. Known as **Reykjatunga** in the north and **Eggjar** farther south.

ßteinsstaðir, a farm in the Tungusveit district. Birthplace of Sveinn Pálsson, octor and naturalist (1762-1840), who was the first person to make important iscoveries about the movements of glaciers. Geothermal heat on the farm ınd at Steinsstaðalaug pool, where swimming was taught from 1822.

Reykir, church and old manor farm. Much geothermal heat. A swimming ool was built there in 1882. There is so much heat that the churchyard is ctually “cozy”, being probbly the only warm graveyard in ıe world. The farmer, Kristján ɔhannesson, has built a house ı the old style, of turf and stone, /ith a panelled interior, where he as set up his personal collection f old objects.

irkjuhóll, there was one f Icelands most know poet, tephan G. Stephansson (1853–927), born.

1 Norðurlandsvegur, p. 70
75 Sauðárkróksbraut, p. 323

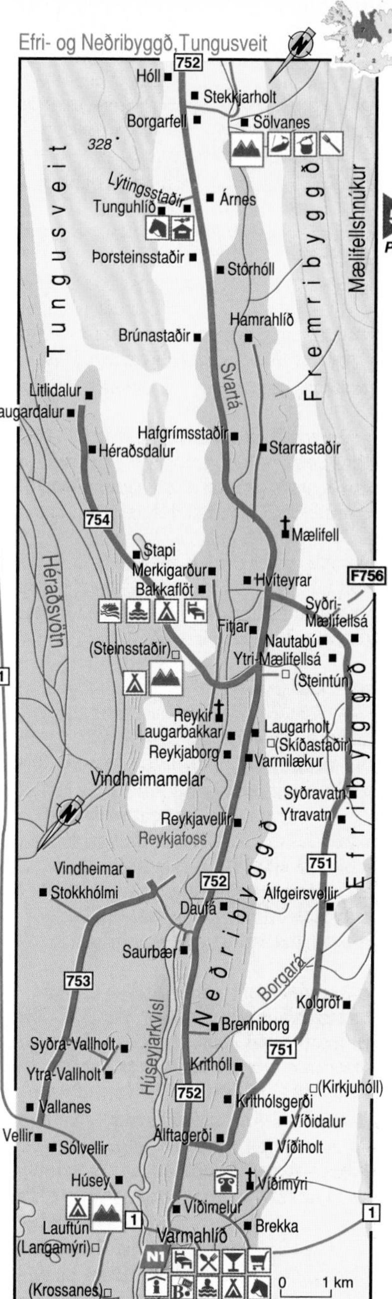

5 P. 568

Skagafjarðadalir-Kjálki

752 Skagafjarðarvegur, 36,7 km.

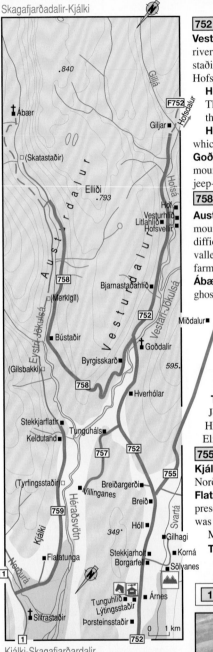

Vesturdalur, a long, narrow valley, down which flows the mostly clea river Hofsá to join the Vestari-Jökulsá river. Several farms. From Þorljóts staðir, abandoned since 1944, there is a jeep-track to Laugafell and th Hofsjökull glacier.

Hof, an old manor farm, the settlement land of Eiríkur Hróaldsson The farm once owned land far into the highlands and gave its name t the glacier Hofsjökull.

Hofsdalur, a narrow valley, uninhabited above Goðdalir, throug which flows the glacial river Vestari-Jökulsá.

Goðdalir, a church, and a parsonage until 1907, an old manor farm. Th mountain above is called **Goðdalakista** ("Goðdalir's chest") (595 m). A jeep-track from there south to the mountains.

758 Austurdalsvegur, 19 km. **759 Kjálkavegur,** 9,8 km.

Austurdalur, a 50 km long valley, narrow but fairly grassy, between hig mountains. The river Eystri-Jökulsá flows down it, often in a deep gorge difficult to cross. There is now a bridge between Merkigil and Ábær. Th valley used to have a large number of inhabitants, now there is only on farm there.

Ábær, a church on farmland that has been abandoned since 1941. A famous ghost, Ábæjar-Skotta, who caused farmers in Skagafjörður all kinds of trouble, came from there. She was said to be seen in company with the ghost of a half-skinned bull calf, Þorgeirsboli, and when she was tired, she would sit on the skin he dragged behind him and let him pull her along.

Merkigil, ("Mark canyon") the only inhabited farm in Austurdalu east of the river Eystri-Jökulsá. Gets its name from the magnificen rocky gorge through which the river runs nearby.

Tunguháls, the outermost farm in Tungusveit. The Rev. Jóna Jónasson (1856-1918), scholar and author, usually associated wit Hrafnagil in Eyjafjörður, was brought up there. Birthplace of the poe Elínborg Lárusdóttir (1891-1973).

755 Svartárdalsvegur, 6,7 km. **757 Villinganesvegur,** 3,8 km

Kjálki, the area along the east of the river Héraðsvötn, from the rive Norðurá to Merkigil in Austurdalur.

Flatatunga, a farm in the Kjálki area. Some very old wood carvings wer preserved there, thought to be a detail from "The Last Judgement", whic was carved in the 11th century in Byzantine style. Now in the Nationa Museum.

Tyrfingsstaðir, an abandoned farm.

Kjálki-Skagafjarðardalir

1 Norðurlandsvegur, p. 72 F752 Skagafjarðarleið, p. 470-471

Laufskálarétt

767 768 769

767 **Hólavegur,** 11 km að Hólum en 13,13 km að Hofi.

ljaltadalur, a rather long, narrow valley, enclosed by high mountains ,000-1,200 m) with passes and side-valleys. Shelterd and grassy.

lof, a farm, the home of the settler Hjalti Þórðarson, for whom a magnif-ent funeral feast was held, according to "The Book of Settlements".

lólar, (pop. 78) the most important historical site in northern Iceland. eople in the North still speak of travelling "home" to Hólar. Bishopric 106-1798, and again from 1986. Cathedral college 1106-1802. Printing ress 1530-1800. Seat of many famous bishops, e.g. Jón Ögmundarson, 106-21, Jón Arason, 1524-50, the last Catholic Bishop in Iceland, and uðbrandur Þorláksson, 1571-1627, whose printing of the first Icelandic ible was crucial to the preservation of the language. The Cathedral, the ldest stone church in Iceland, built of red sandstone from the mountain ólabyrða, consecrated in 1763 and reconsecrated 1988 after extensive novation. Many ancient relics. A turf farmhouse near the top of the field, uilt in 1860, has been in the care of the National Museum since 1956. uðunarstofa, reconstruction of a house built in Hólar in early 14th century hich lasted for 500 years. Traditional Norwegian log-stave house with turf oof. Bishop's office. Houses a collection of old books printed in Hólar and ome of the Cathedral's treasures. Archeological research is being carried ut at Hólar and in **Kolkuós**, the old harbour. Extensive program of con-erts and church services throughout the summer, culminating in the Hólar stival mid August. An agricultural college was established at Hólar in 882 which was the foundation of the present University College, special-ing in equine science, rural tourism, aquatic science, archeology and ultural heritage.

íðines, near Hólar. Site of the 1208 battle between the poet olbeinn Tumason and the forces of Bishop Guðmundur the good, in hich Kolbeinn was slain.

ðvík, a church and at one time a parsonage. In ancient times the home of orbjörn öngull, who killed Grettir the strong. Later the home of Jón Pétursson 733-1801), a doctor famous for his cures and a book on medicine.

68 **Hjaltadalsvegur,** 12,14 km.

eykir, the innermost farm in Hjaltadalur. It has two warm springs, iskupslaug ("Bishop's pool"), a stone-built bathing pool of 42°-43°C here it is said the bishops bathed, and Hjúalaug ("Servants pool"). In 928 they made a turf-built pool at Hjúalaug for teaching swimming.

69 **Ásavegur,** 7 km.

eðri-Ás, ancient home of Þorvaldur Spak-Böðvarsson, the first Ice-nder to build a church at his farm, in 984. The site still bears the name ænhús ("Chapel"). Excavations confirm site of an early church. oadside memorial.

76 **Siglufjarðarvegur,** p. 328

Hjaltadalur

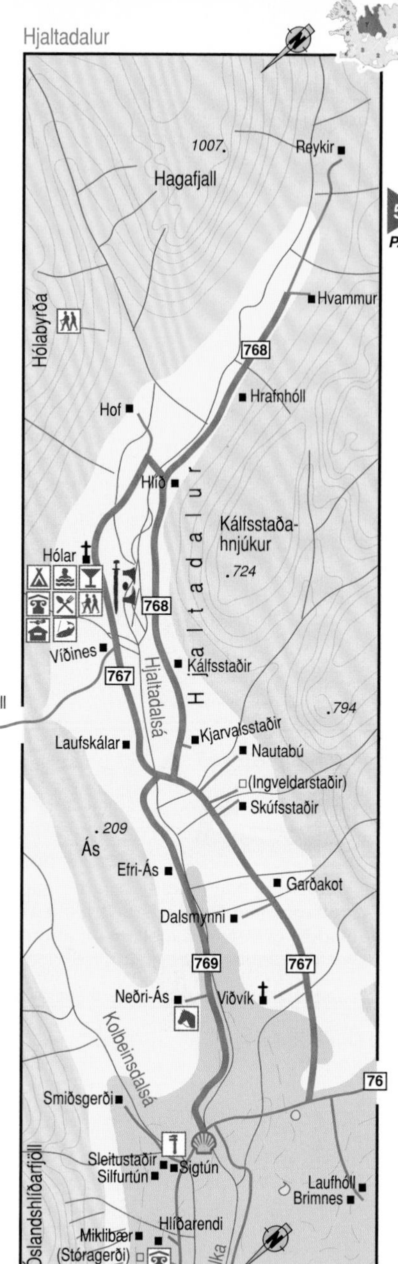

Hjaltadalur

5
P. 568

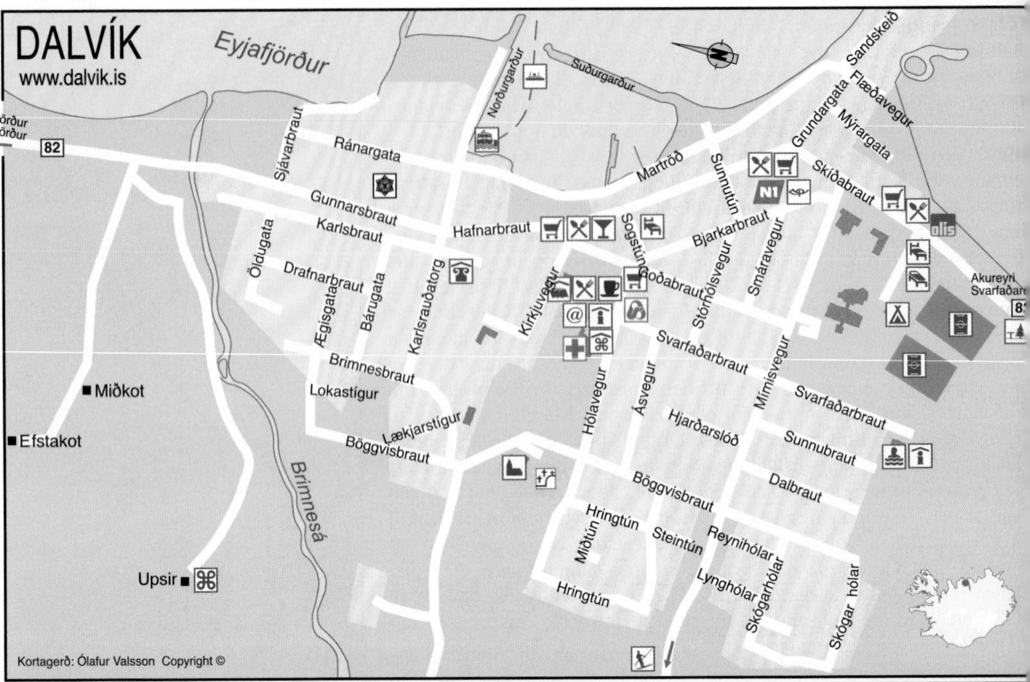

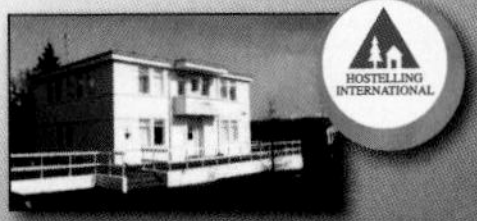

DALVÍK

www.dalvik.is

Eyjafjörður, Siglufjörður, Ólafsfjörður, 82, Ránargata, Sjávarbraut, Norðurgarður, Suðurgarður, Sandskeið, Flæðavegur, Grundargata, Mýrargata, Martröð, Sunnutún, Skíðabraut, Gunnarsbraut, Karlsbraut, Hafnarbraut, Öldugata, Drafnarbraut, Ægisgata, Bárugata, Karlsrauðatorg, Kirkjuvegur, Sogstún, Goðabraut, Bjarkarbraut, Stórhólsvegur, Smáravegur, Akureyri, Svarfaðardalur, Brimnesbraut, Lokastígur, Lækjarstígur, Böggvisbraut, Hólavegur, Ásvegur, Svarfaðarbraut, Mímisvegur, Hjarðarslóð, Sunnubraut, Dalbraut, Miðkot, Efstakot, Brimnesá, Upsir, Hringtún, Miðtún, Steintún, Reynihólar, Lynghólar, Skógarhólar, Skógar hólar

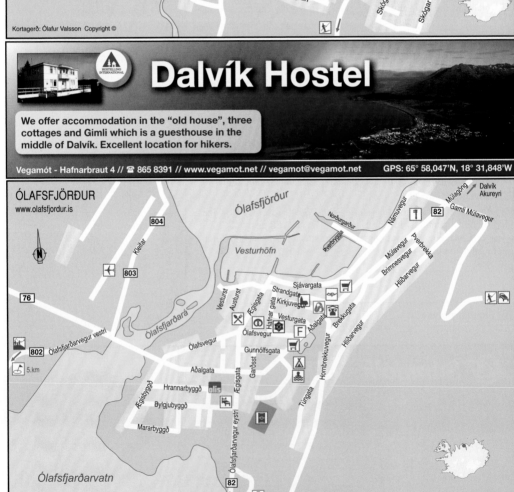

ÓLAFSFJÖRÐUR

www.olafsfjordur.is

Ólafsfjörður, Dalvík, Akureyri, Múlagöng, 82, Gamli Múlavegur, Námuvegur, Norðurgarður, Þverbryggja, Vesturhöfn, 804, Kleifar, 803, Þverbrekka, Múlavegur, Brimnesvegur, Hlíðarvegur, 76, Sjávargata, Strandgata, Kirkjuvegur, Vesturst, Austurst, Ægisgata, Hafnar gata, Vesturgata, Aðalgata, Brekkugata, Ólafsfjarðará, Ólafsvegur, Ólafsfjarðarvegur vestri, 802, 5.km, Gunnólfsgata, Hornbrekkuvegur, Hlíðarvegur, Aðalgata, Garðsst, Hrannarbyggð, Ægisbyggð, Bylgjubyggð, Mararbyggð, Túngata, Ólafsfjarðarvegur eystri, Ólafsfjarðarvatn, 82, Siglufjörður

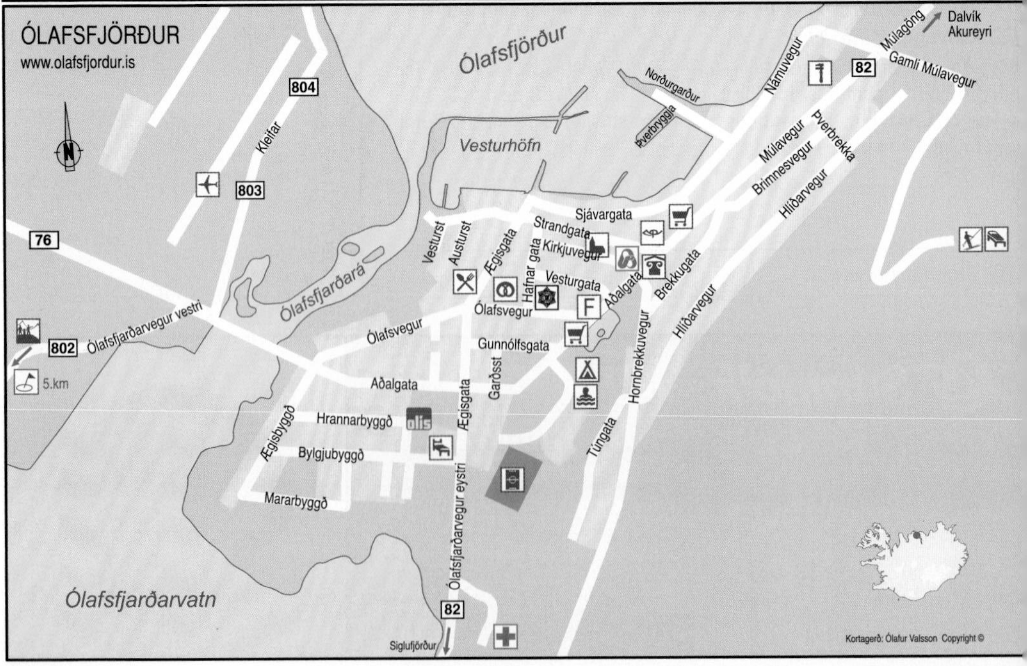

82 ÓLAFSFJARÐARVEGUR

rskógsströnd, the coast from the abandoned farm Hillur north to ámundarstaðaháls ridge. Broad, grassy lowland, many farms and fishg-villages. Árskógsströnd comprises the villages of **Hauganes** and **rskógssandur**, each with a population of under 120. The ferry Sæfari ies between Árskógssandur and the island of Hrísey.

agriskógur, the outermost farm on the section of coast known as almaströnd. The poet and playwright Davíð Stefánson (1895–1964) 'rom Fagriskógur", one of Iceland´s best-loved writers, was from there. onument.

ötlufjall, (964 m) the mountain above Fagriskógur, with many southoping terraces.

rnarnes, a farm. The painter Kristín Jónsdóttir (1888-1959) came from ere.

11 Hjalteyrarvegur, 3 km. **812 Bakkavegur,** 6 km.

jalteyri, (pop. 43) a fishing-village and once a herring processing staon.

vammsfjall, the northernmost of a fine row of peaks reminiscent of ormous house gables. Most of the peaks and the passes between them ke their names from farms: Hofsskarð, Þríklakkar, Þrastarhólmshnjúkur, allgilsstaðahnjúkur, Staðarskarð above Möðruvellir, ending in Fálkaus or Fornhagaöxl (703 m), an imposing rocky saddle.

of, one of outermost farms in the Hörgárdalur valley. Home of the botast and folklorist Ólafur Davíðsson (1862-1903). He drowned in the river örgá.

13 Möðruvallavegur, 3,9 km.

öðruvellir, a substantial farm of great historical importance for many nturies. Church and parsonage. A monastery was founded there in 1296, was the seat of governors 1797–1874, and from 1888 to 1902 a high hool, which was then moved to Akureyri and later became the Junior ollege of Akureyri. The poets Bjarni Thorarensen (1786–1841) and avíð Stefánsson from Fagriskógur (1895-1964) are buried at öðruvellir. Birthplace of Hannes Hafstein (1861–1922), poet and the st Icelandic Minister of State, Jón Sveinsson (Nonni) (1857-1944), thor of many books in Icelandic and German, whose books have been anslated to more than 40 languages, Hulda Á. Stefánsdóttir (1897–989), writer and headmistress, and Steindór Steindórsson (1902–997), writer, naturalist and headmaster. The church, built 1868, is one the biggest country churches in Iceland. There have been more seris fires at Möðruvellir than anywhere else in Iceland.

1 Norðurlandsvegur, p. 76	**809 Hauganesvegur,** p. 358
815 Hörgárdalsvegur, p. 389	**816 Dagverðareyrarvegur,** p. 389

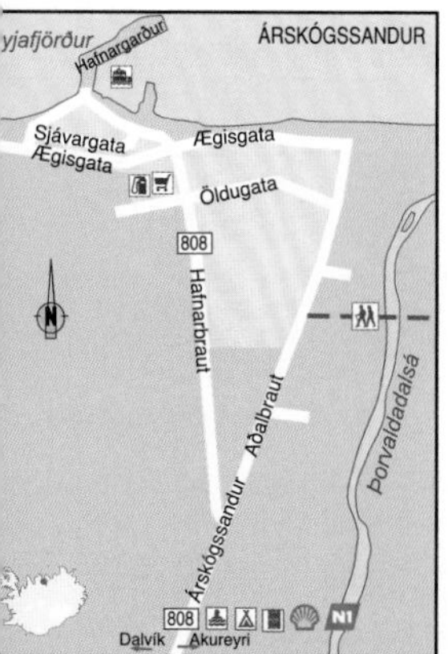

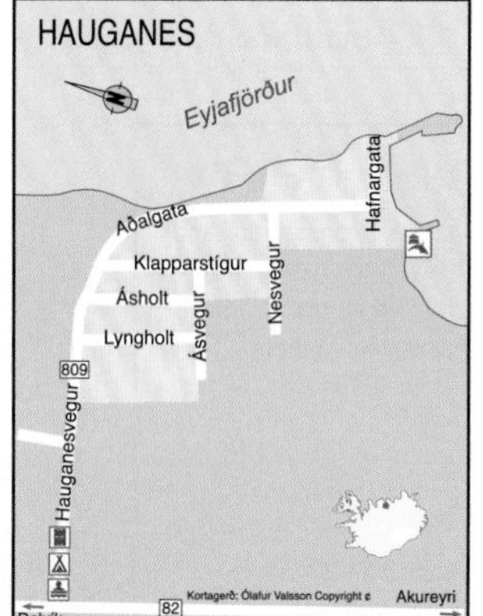

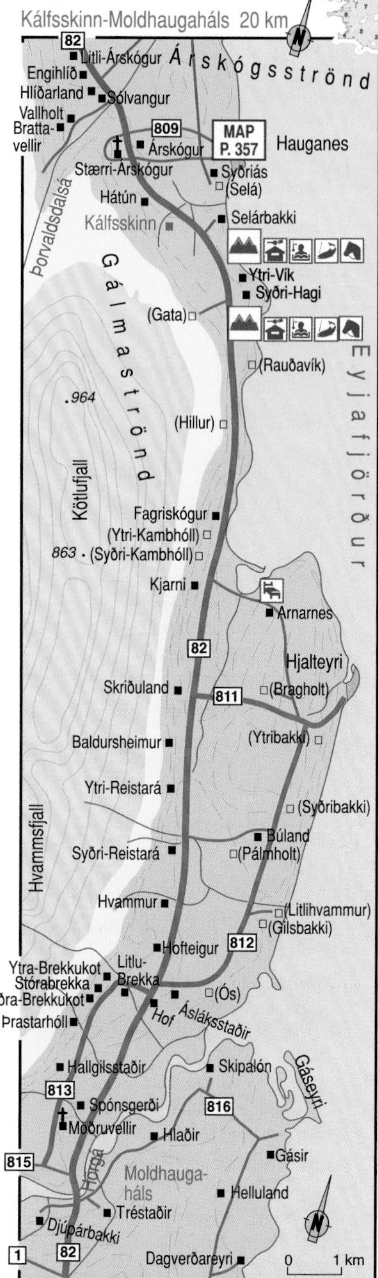

5 P. 568

Dalvík-Kálfsskinn 14 km

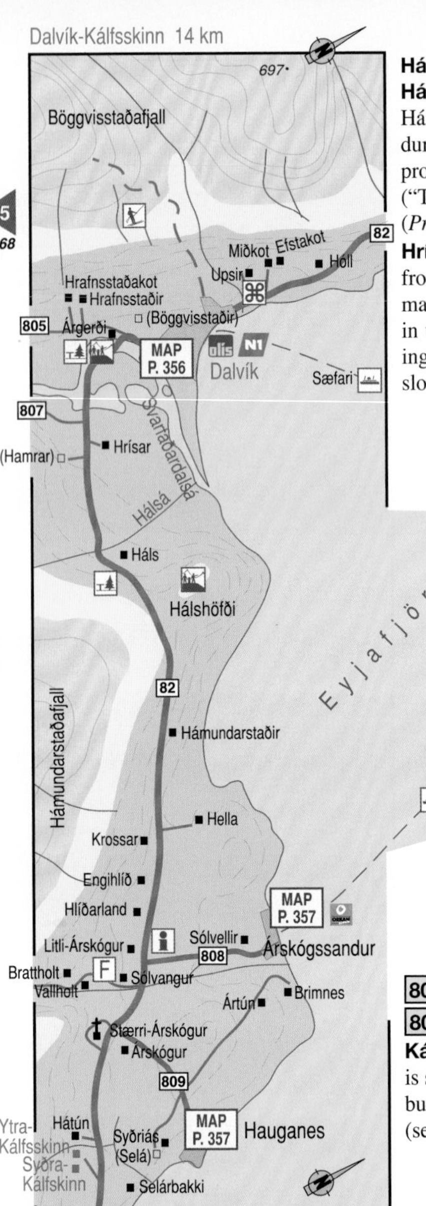

Kálfsskinn-Dalvík 14 km

Hámundarstaðaháls, separates Árskógsströnd and Svarfaðardalur.

Hámundarstaðir, the outermost farm on Árskógsströnd, where the settle Hámundur heljarskinn ("death's hide") and Helgi magri ("the lean") live during their first winter in Eyjafjörður. South of the farm is a mountai probably the Sólarfjall ("Sun mountain") mentioned in *Landnámabó* ("The Book of Settlements") now called Hámundarstaðafjall. Wild primu (*Primula egaliksensis*), found nowhere else in Iceland, grows there.

Hrísey, (pop. 171) the second biggest island off Iceland, 8.0 km², ca. 2 k from Helluhöfði point on Árskógsströnd. Hrísey has a surface of approx mately 11.5 square km. The island is approx. 7 km long and 2.5 km broa in the broadest place. North of the lighthouse is the highest point measu ing 110 m. This highest point is named "Bratti" and from it there are rubb slopes towards the sea. Numerous man made embankments lie all over th island, the longest being almo 3 km long. These embank ments are believed to b very old and some believ that they may have serve as fences in the olden day The" leylines" on the islan are by many considered to be spectacular source of energy an many visitors as well as inhabitan feel that this raw energy of the ear "charges their battery" in a uniqu way. Many birds nest on the island an because of the reservation of the wild fov life the birds are unusually tame, especial the ptarmigan. Visitors must keep to marke walking paths. It is also possible to take tri on a hay cart towed by a tractor around the villag and its surroundings. A village at the southern end the only occupied part. Fishing and fish processing a the main industries. Geothermal heat. Quarantine cent imported pets. **www.hrisey.net**

808 Árskógssandsvegur, 2 km.

809 Hauganesvegur, 2,6 km.

Kálfsskinn, a farm where Hrærekur, king of the Upplendings in Norwa is said to be buried in the mound called **Hrærekshóll**. Two other kings l buried in Iceland, the twin brothers Geirmundur and Hámundur heljarskir (see road 590, Skarð). Monument.

805 Svarfaðardalsvegur, s. 387 **807 Skíðadalsvegur,** s. 388

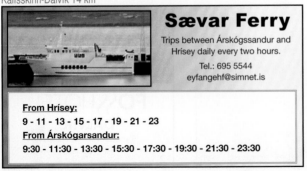

82 ÓLAFSFJARÐARVEGUR

lafsfjarðarmúli, the outermost mountain spur and cliffs between yjafjörður and Ólafsfjörður, ca. 400 m high, steep and with scree. Good ew, the island Grímsey visible in clear weather. Landslides and ava-nches can be expected. Tunnel opened 1991.

álfdanarhurð, a reddish patch on the slopes of Ólafsfjarðarmúli. Asso-ated with the Rev. Hálfdan Narfason and his dealings with giants, trolls ıd the Devil (see Road 76, Fell and Málmey).

ígindi, ("Pissing") a waterfall on Ólafsfjarðarmúli.

auðakot, an abandoned cottage farm. Monument to the last occupants.

arlsá, an abandoned farm on the Upsaströnd coast. Monument to yvindur Jónsson (1678-1746), boatbuilder, said to have been the rst Icelander to build a decked ocean-going ship.

psir, a farm above Dalvík, parsonage until 1851 and church until cently, when it was moved to Dalvík. Birthplace of Bjarni Pálsson 719-79), Surgeon General (See Road 62, Svefneyjar.). The peak Upsi ove the farm.

psaströnd, the coast line from Dalvík to Ólafsfjarðarmúli.

alvík, (pop. 1,359) a town with fishing, fish processing and trading. ood harbour. Community centre, museum, modern swimming pool with ectacular view. Some industry. In the summer of 1934 an earthquake stroyed or damaged most of the houses in the area. Hot spring domestic eating since 1969. The second weekend of August each year, local fish-g and fish processing companies join forces to offer a great feast of sea-od dishes and a programme of entertainment, all for free! The Great sh Day is most certainly a day you do not want to miss. At Dalvík you ay also find the Hvol museum. Quite a uniqe museum that is devided to three main parts including a room that is dedicated to Iceland's tallest an (2,34 m), a polar bear and birds as Dalvik's closest environment mprimises the Svarfaðardalur Nature Reserve is an area of about 8 uare km. of wetland. Within the reserve are dry river-banks as well as arshes with sedge bogs, ditches and fertile ponds with reeds. This natu-l environment provides an excellent habitat for many species of breed-g birds. (More information on www.dalvik.is or www.travel2dalvik. m).

áls, farm and birthplace of Pastor Friðrik Friðriksson (1868–1961) under of the Icelandic YMCA in Reykjavík 1899. Memorial nearby.

803 **Kleifavegur,** p. 362 | 805 **Svarfaðardalsvegur,** p. 387

807 **Skíðadalsvegur,** p. 388

Ólafsfjörður-Dalvík 19 km

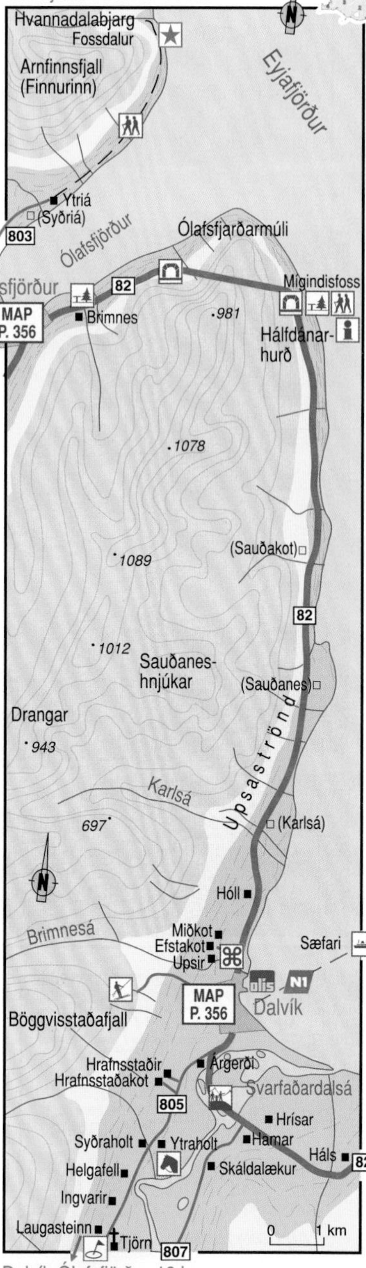

Dalvík-Ólafsfjörður 19 km

Grímsey

Grímsey, (pop. 76) a green island off Iceland's north coast, is the country's northernmost point. Grímsey, with its rich fishing grounds and rich bird life, is probably best known for its geographic position, right on the Arctic Circle. People travel from far and wide simply to step across that line. The island is 5.3 km in area, and its highest point is 105 m above sea level. It lies 41km off the Icelandic mainland.

The islanders are cheerful and energetic. The local economy centres on the fisheries. Grímsey produces especially fine saltfish (salted cod), a delicacy in southern Europe and South America.

Múli, the community centre, houses a primary school, community hall, library, and health-care centre. Health-care services are provided by doctors from Akureyri on the mainland.

Miðgarðar Church was built in 1867, using driftwood (timber was always in short supply in Iceland). Recently renovated and painted in its original colours, the church is a fine building. The pastor of Dalvík now serves the parish.

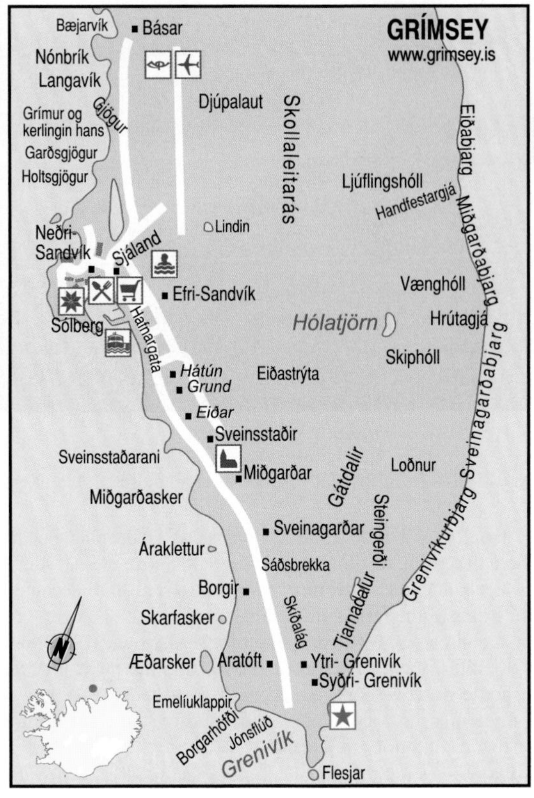

5
P. 568

An excellent swimming pool opened in 1989. Búðin general store serves the islanders' needs, with a wide range of goods. The island has two guesthouses, they are open all year round. In 1998 the crafts gallery Sól was opened by women on the island; it is open in summer on the days when the ferry calls at the island. The Krían restaurant, is open in summer.

The Sæfari ferry sails from Dalvík to Grímsey three days a week all year round. Regular flights are also operated three days a week in winter, and seven days a week in summer.

The islanders have their own "national" festival on November 11th each year, to mark the birthday of Dr. Daníel Willard Fiske, the island's American benefactor. Having seen Grímsey from the sea, Dr. Fiske was impressed that people lived on this remote island, and also by the fact that they were keen chess players! Around 1900, Dr. Fiske gave the Grímsey islanders the largest gift of money that Icelanders have ever received.

It is said that Grímsey (= Grímur's Island) got its name from a certain Grímur, the first settler on the island. Grímur's brother Kolbeinn is also commemorated by an island named after him, Kolbeinsey. Grímur is believed to have built a heathen temple at Kirkjuhóll, and according to folklore he wanted to be buried there, with a view of the sea and land. He is said to be buried with his wife on a cliff top at Sandvíkurgjögur.

Grímsey is said to be the home of many elves or "hidden people," whose church is supposed to be at Nónbrík.

At Prestaskvompa (Priest's Hollow) is a cave that passes under the whole island. Its name comes from the legend that a pastor rowed into the cave with four companions to explore: none of them was ever seen again.

Lágheiði-Ólafsfjörður 19 km

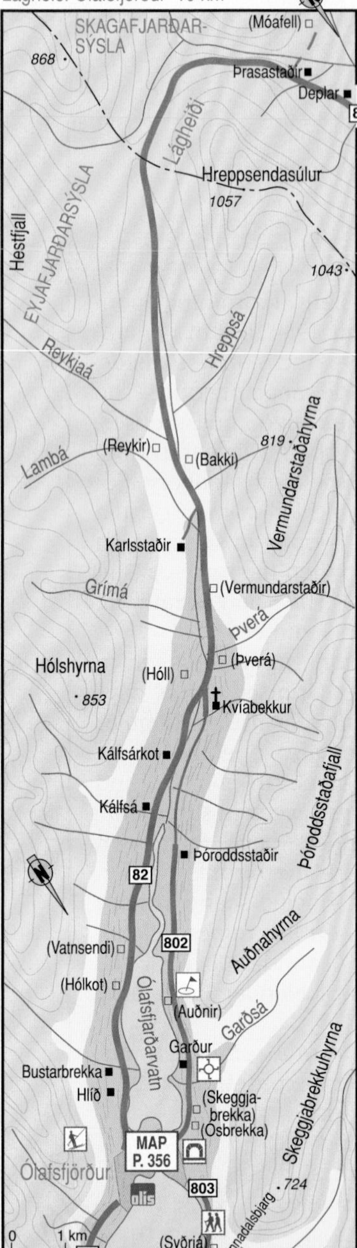

Ólafsfjörður-Lágheiði 19 km

Aurora Borealis over Ólafsfjörður.

Reykir, the innermost farm in Ólafsfjörður, now abandoned. Geotherm heat.

Hvanndalir, there was a field called "Ódáinsakur", meaning deathles meadow, where the eating of some of the vegetation gave eternal life. Th farm there was abandoned when this "curse of eternal life" became to much to bear. Ruins of the farm still remain.

Kvíabekkur, a church and a parsonage until 1914. Around 1330 Láren íus, Bishop of Hólar, founded a sort of old folks home there for retire priests. The home of governors, e.g. Þorkell Fjeldsted (1740-96), wh was one of three men on a committee appointed by the Danish king 1770 to investigate conditions in Iceland.

802 Garðsvegur, 2 km. From there lie the **Héðinsfjarðargöng**, 6,9 k long tunnel, connecting Siglufjörður and Ólafsjörður. Opened in 2010.

803 Kleifavegur, 2,7 km.

Gunnólfsá, a farm on the west of Ólafsfjörður, now a small village calle Kleifar.

Ólafsfjörður, see p. 332.

76 Siglufjarðarvegur, p. 332

Midnight sun in Ólafsfjörður.

tífla, ("Dam") the main valley of the Austur-Fljót district, taking its ame from the Stífluhólar hills which block the valley. They were formed y landslides from the mountain Strengur on the east. A dam was built iere when Skeiðsfoss was harnessed.

'89 Sléttuvegur, 6,7 km.

keiðsfoss, a waterfall in the river Stífluá, harnessed for electricity for ie town of Siglufjörður 1945. Most of the valley went under water.

nappsstaðir, a church on land originally settled by Þórður knappur. he oldest wooden church in Iceland, consecrated 1840.

undur, a farm, birthplace of the novelist Guðrún frá Lundi (1887-1975), ne of Iceland's most prolific and popular writers.

lvarfdalur, a valley.

lreppsendasúlur, (1,057 m) the mountain to the north of the Lágheiði ioor.

ágheiði, (409 m) a moor with a narrow road between the Fljót district nd Ólafsfjörður. Grassy, but snowy in winter and often unpassable.

76 **Siglufjarðarvegur,** p. 330

Ketilás-Lágheiði 19 km

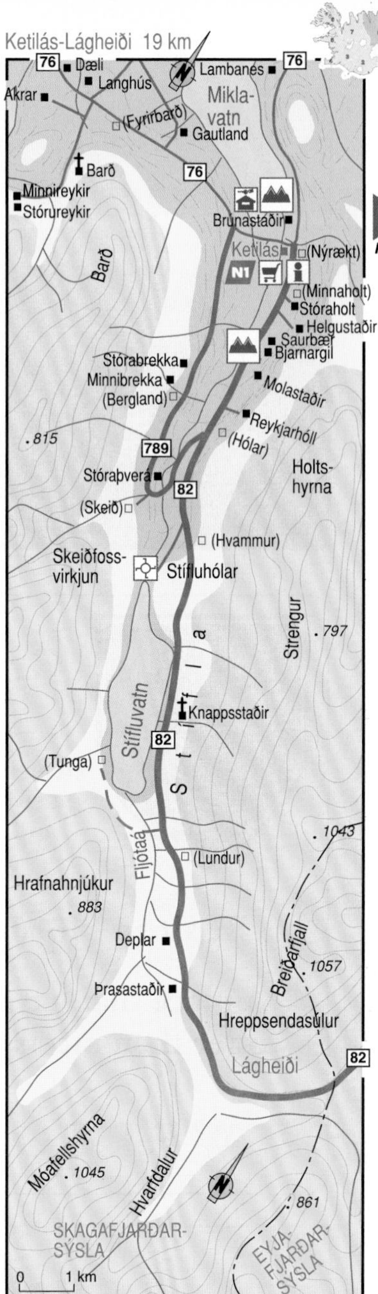

Lágheiði-Ketilás 19 km

In Ólafsfjörður

Grenivík.

Grenivík

Near the elementary school is a swimming pool and a campsite.

Explore Fjörðurnar!

A place that has more to offer then meets the eye.

WELCOME

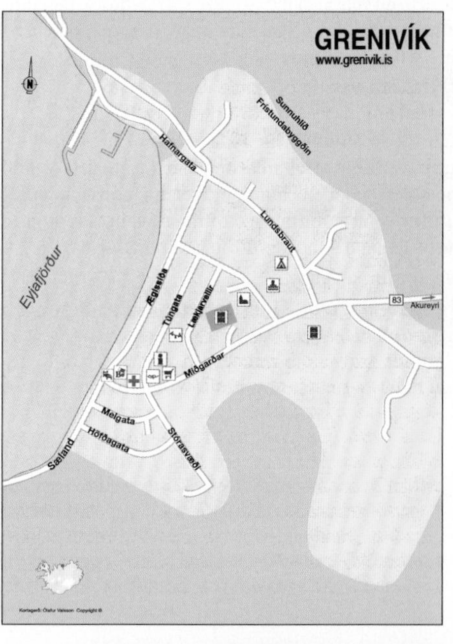

Gljúfurárrétt

átraströnd, the coast of Eyjafjörður north of the village Grenivík, near jögurtá. Steep cliffs below the mountains. Formerly several farms and fishrmen's homes but now all abandoned except one near Grenivík.

aldbakur, (1,167 m) the highest mountain on the Látrarströnd coast and the nost impressive on the east of Eyjafjörður, a striking feature of the view north rom Akureyri.

renivík, (pop. 278, 360 in the Grýtubakkahreppur district) a fishing village nat began to form around 1900. Grenivík includes an elementary school, layschool, community centre, swimming pool, camping area, retirement ome, health clinic, church and accommodations for travellers. There is a hop in the area, a savings bank, post office, hairdresser, dried fish factory, ish factory, garage, boat mechanic, and a pharmaceutical company. There are arious activities in Grýtubakkahreppur, including the Magna Sports Club est. 1915), Þráin Horseback Riding Club, a 9-hole golf course in Hvammur, aldbakur Tours (which takes skiers up Mount Kaldbakur in snow cats), ólarhestar horse rental in Grýtubakki, swimming pool, fitness centre and a our-day hike along the Fjörður region and Látraströnd coast organized by jörðungar. The Grenivíkurgleði festival has become an annual event in renivík, held the third weekend in August. This is a family festival featuring ome of Iceland's great performers along with local acts, as well as grilling, inging, dancing, and a firework show.

31 Höfðavegur, 3,6 km.

öfði, a parsonage until 1890, and church till 1880. A farm since the original ettlement. Early this century the home of Þórður Gunnarsson (1865-1935) ho along with his brothers operated fishing boats and was active in other pheres. These brothers were the most enterprising people on the east side of yjafjörður. There was a fishing centre at **Kljáströnd** and some farms, now bandoned.

engilhöfði, (261 m) a mountain south of Grenivík.

öfðahverfi, a small farming district between the river Fnjóská and the village Grenivík, taking its name from **Þengilhöfði**.

léskógar, late in the 19th century a school for adolescents was set up and un there for several years through the agency of Einar Ásmundarsson from es. Now a guest house.

rtún, a guesthouse and campsite.

aufás, a parsonage and church, and an old farmhouse. Fertile farmland with nany assets. The church was built in 1865 at the instigation of Rev. Björn Hallórsson, who also had the farmhouse built during his priesthood (1853-82). A ery clear example of the northern type of farmhouses where the gables of all ne front buildings face forwards. Behind the entrance building, a passage leads o rear buildings, which are arranged at right angles. The Rev. Björn, who wrote nany good hymns, ran a junior secondary school at Laufás. His son was Bishop órhallur Bjarnason (1846-1916). Birthplace of Tryggvi Gunnarsson (1835-917), the master carpenter who built the church, later a member of parliament, ank director and important entrepreneur. Many other remarkable pastors have erved at Laufás. Laufás has been a vicarage from the earliest Christian times. he last clergyman to live in the old farmhouse, Þorvaldur Þormar, moved into ne new vicarage in 1936 where successive ministers of the Laufás parish lived ntil the year 2000.

1 **Norðurlandsvegur,** p. 86 | 835 **Fnjóskadalsv. eystri,** p. 397
F839 **Leirdalsheiðarvegur,** p. 478

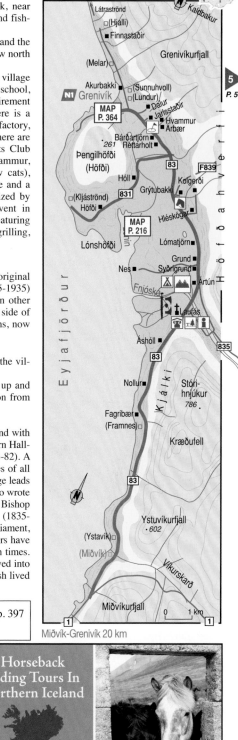

Grenivík-Miðvík 20 km

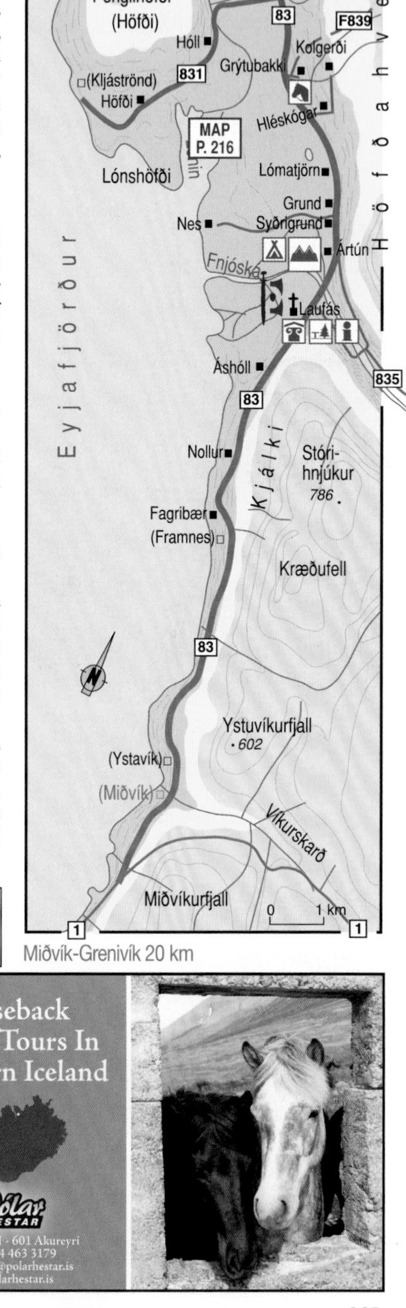

Miðvík-Grenivík 20 km

6 P. 569

Tjörn-Kross 26 km

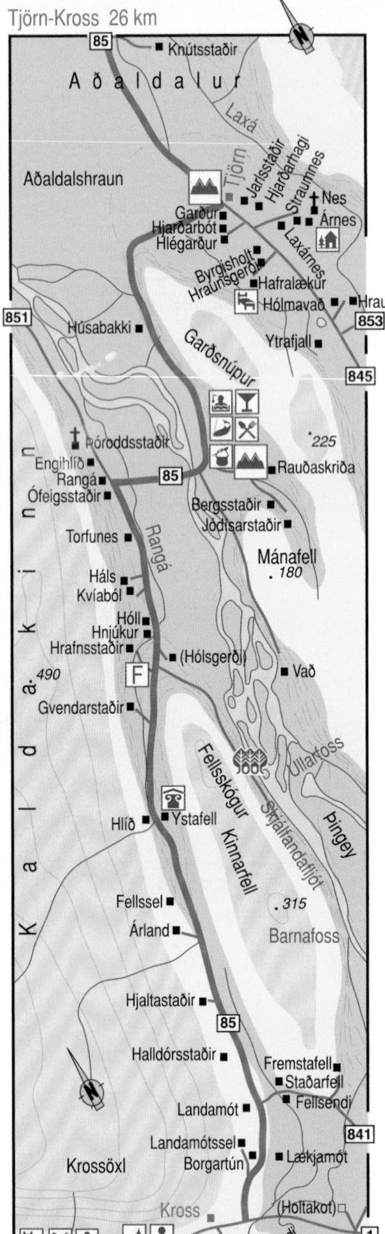

Kross-Tjörn 26 km

Húsavík

Aðaldalur, ("Main valley") a broad lowland area at the head of Skjálfandaflói gulf, between the river Skjálfandafljót and Hvammsheiði moor and then east of Fljótsheiði moor to the lake Vestmannsvatn. It lies largely on the Aðaldalshraun lava field, which comes from the Lake Mývatn area. Widespread birch bushes and strangely beautiful lava formations. Farms along the edge of the lava. Belts of sand along the coast.

Garðsnúpur, the steep northern end of Fljótsheiði ("River moor").

Rauðaskriða, ("Red landslide") a farm since the original settlement, often occupied by powerful Icelanders such as the district governor Hrafn Guðmundsson (d. 1432) and Hrafn Brandsson (15th century). The group of farms near Rauðaskriða is called **Skriðuhverfi**.

Skjálfandafljót, one of largest rivers of northern Iceland, with its source in Vonarskarð and the glaciers Tungnafellsjökull and Vatnajökull, with tributaries from the Ódáðahraun lava field. Flows through Bárðardalur valley. Many waterfalls, among them Aldeyjarfoss, Goðafoss and (near Kinnarfell) Barnafoss and Ullarfoss.

Ljósvetningabúð, community centre at the north end of the mountain Kinnarfell.

Ystafell, a farm, long the home of Sigurður Jónsson (1852-1926), the great cooperative leader and Minister of State. The birthplace in 1902 of the Federation of Icelandic Cooperatives, to which there is a memorial. Part of the protected **Fellsskógur** woods near Kinnarfell. An interesting transport exhibition, with vehicles of all ages and types open to the public.

Fellsskógur, one of the largest birch forests in Iceland, rarely visited. Part of a 22,000 ha nature reserve. Turn east off Highway 85 at Hólsgerði and follow jeep tracks south into the forest. National Forest.

Kaldakinn, the district north of Ljósavatnsskarð pass and west of the river Skjálfandafljót down to the sea. Above are the high Kinnarfjöll mountains (900-1,000 m) with their permanent snows.

1 **Norðurlandsvegur,** p. 88
841 **Fremstafellsvegur,** p. 398
845 **Aðaldalsvegur,** p. 400
851 **Út-Kinnarvegur,** p. 403
853 **Hvammavegur,** p. 400

Ljósavatnsskarð

Húsavík, (pop. 2,228)a fishing village and a perfect centre for individual tourists and groups travelling in the Northeast. Visitors can during their stay in Húsavík choose between a fine hotel, guesthouse and camping. Húsavík is located on the Eastern Shore of Skjálfandi-bay facing the impressive Kinnarfjöll mountains across the bay. Húsavík offers an ample selection of easy hikes through varied landscape for example, along the shores of the bay, up the Húsavík mountain or around the lake **Botnsvatn** where trout fishing is free of charge. Even though fishing and fish processing is the important industry in Húsavík the town is now well known as the whale watching capital of Europe. Whale watching trips from Húsavík harbour on traditional fishing boats and passenger boats are getting increasingly popular. The Husavik Whale Centre is the first and only information centre on whales in Iceland. The Church in Húsavík, built in 1907, is said to be the most beautiful wooden church in Iceland. In the Museum House are a folk museum for the area, a nature museum, art gallery, the library and district archives. A nice all year round heated swimming pool is open for visitors from early morning to late at night. Húsavík being located just south of the Arctic Circle enjoys 24 hours daylight in summer and the romantic midnight sun frequently paints the evening sky with colours beyond imagination. In the winter when the days are short and the nights are long the dark night sky is frequently decorated with millions of stars and flashing Northern Lights (Aurora Borealis). Winter excursions are constantly gaining popularity, the options are many and there is something for everybody. Snow-scooter tours, Super-Jeep safaris, fishing through ice and cross-country skiing are just examples of the various ways one can enjoy the splendour of Northeast Iceland in winter. The contrast of hot springs and geothermal areas against snow, ice and frozen waterfalls give explorers the experience of a lifetime.

Laxamýri, ("Salmon marsh") one of the biggest and wealthiest farms in Iceland, because of good farming land, salmon and eider ducks.

Laxá, a river that flows through an old lava-field with beautiful rock formations and some pseudo-craters; further up the river is the hydroelectric-power station Laxárvirkjun in a beautiful canyon.

Litlu-Núpar, there have some signs of an old settlement.

852 Sandsvegur, 6,49 km.

Sandur, a farm to north of Aðaldalshraun.

Knútsstaðir, a farm by the river Laxá, good fishing. In nearby lava there are strange hollow crater hills, some of which one can stand up in, the best known being **Knútsstaðaborg**.

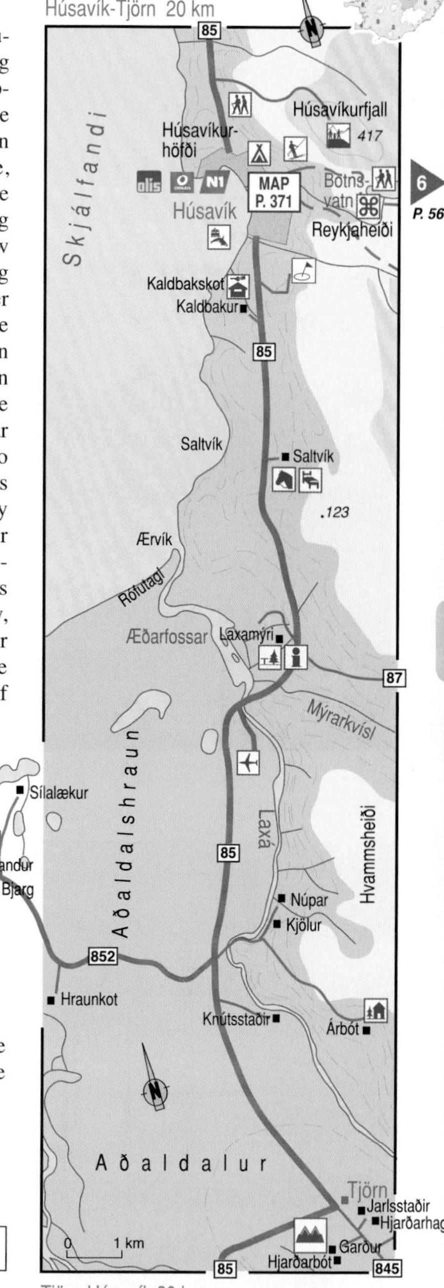

87 Kísilvegur, p. 386 **845 Aðaldalsvegur,** p. 400

Einar Gíslason

Húsavík.

Einar Gíslason

Mærudagar, Húsavík harbor.

Mánáreyjar, two small islands, Háey and Lágey ("High island and Low island"), 9 km off Tjörnes, belonging to the farm Máná.

Tjörnes, the peninsula between the Skjálfandaflói gulf and Öxarfjörður. There is a high mountain range along it, and an old footpath and horse-trail across Tunguheiði moor between the farms Syðri-Tunga and Fjöll in the Kelduhverfi district. On the west and north there is a good deal of flat land with rivers running into the Skjálfandi gulf, as well as some high sandstone ridges by the sea, 400-500 m thick, dating from the Tertiary period and the Ice Age. Towards the south there are alternate shell and lignite layers, showing big changes in sea level. In the southernmost and oldest of these are shells of creatures that now live only in warmer sea along west-European coasts. In younger layers there are cold-sea shells and at Breiðavík arctic shells. During World War I there was a lignite mine on Tjörnes in the land of the farms Hringver and Ytri-Tunga.

Máná, the northernmost farm in Tjörnes.

Mánárbakki, a farm and museum, and a weather station where research into the northern lights has been going on since 1984, financed by the Japanese government.

Breiðavík, a bay and a farm of the same name at the extreme northern point of the Tjörnes peninsula. Thick earth strata from the Ice Age. Excavations have been carried out near Breiðavík at what is thought to be the site of the settlement farm **Böðólfskytja**.

Hallbjarnarstaðir, a farm near which there are layers of shells ofprehistoric origin in the cliffs. Long the home of Kári Sigurjónsson (1875-1949), who with scientists investigated the shells, though the pioneering work was done by Guðmundur G. Bárðarson (1880-1933), geologist.

Layers of shells in Hallbjarnarstaðakambur ridge.

Sólvangur, a community centre.

Ytritunga, a farm from which there is a road down to the sea, this being the best way to approach the prehistoric Tjörnes shell-layers in the cliffs both sides of the river Hallbjarnarstaðaá. There was a lignite mine on the farm land, and on the shore there is a boulder brought by ice from Greenland. Small pier, some fishing.

Kaldakvísl, the southernmost river on the Tjörnes peninsula. New bridge built over the gorge in 1971.

Lundey, ("Puffin island") a 41 m high rocky island, belonging to the farm Héðinshöfði. Grassy on top, huge numbers of puffins breed there. Lighthouse.

Héðinshöfði, a farm, for 20 years the home of sheriff and parliamentarian Benedikt Sveinsson (1826-1899) who was prominent in the fight for independence, after the death of Jón Sigurðsson. His son, the poet Einar Benediktsson (1864-1940), who lies buried in the national cemetery at Þingvellir (see Road 36), was brought up there. Monument.

19 P. 582

6 P. 569

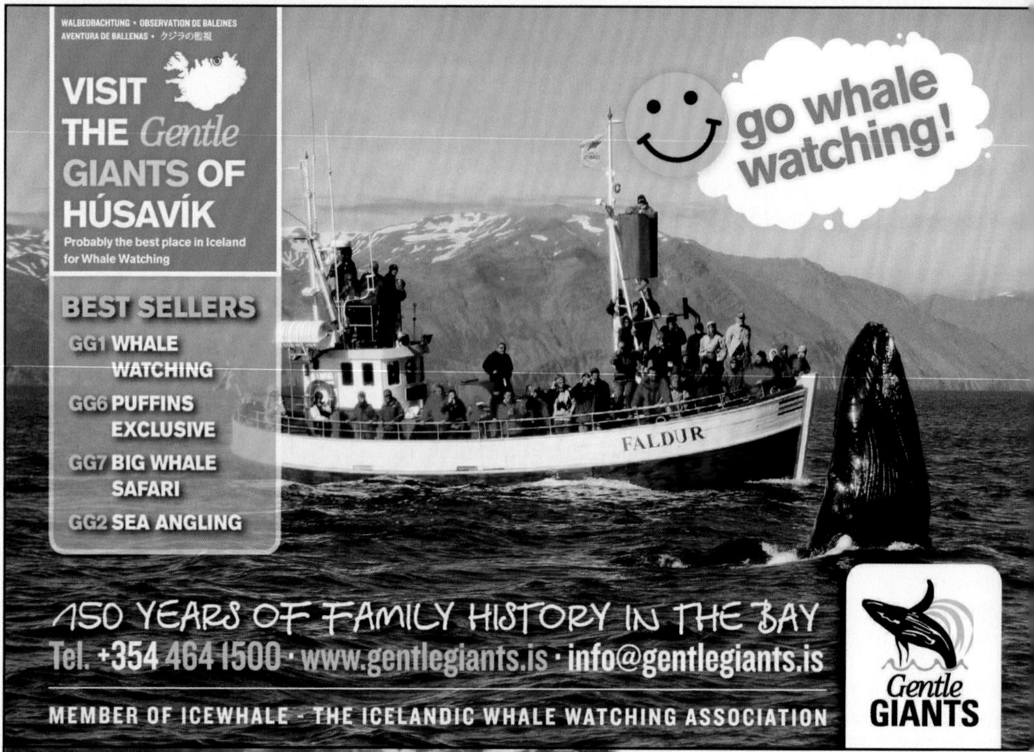

NÁTTFARI
North Sailing
HÚSAVÍK

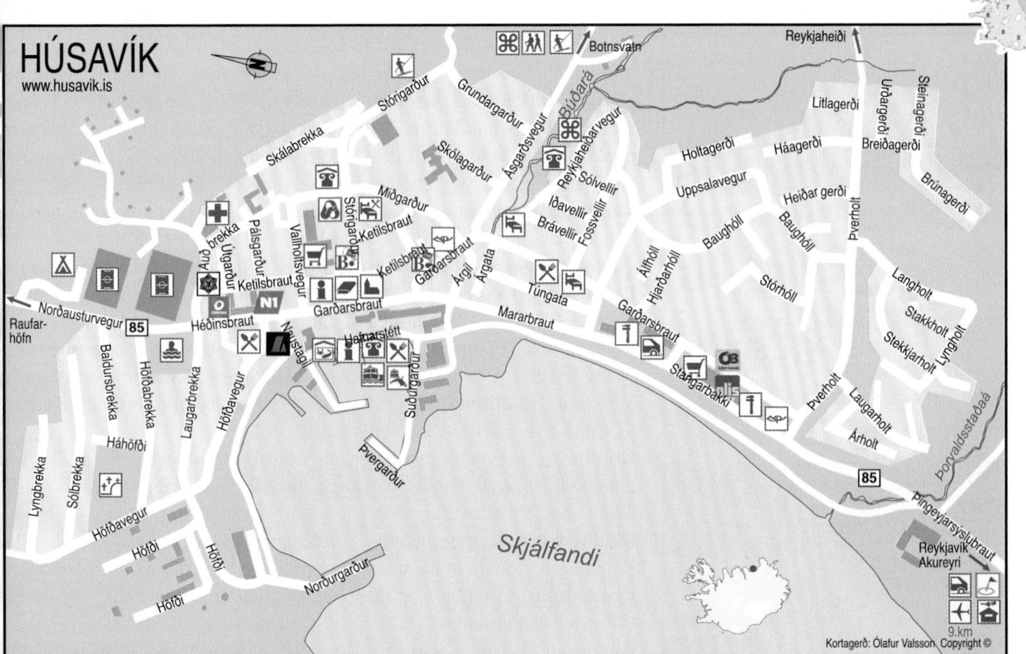
HÚSAVÍK
www.husavik.is
Botnsvatn
Reykjaheiði
Búðará
Stórigarður
Grundargarður
Skálabrekka
Ásgarðsvegur
Reykjaheiðarvegur
Skólagarður
Sólvellir
Miðgarður
Iðavellir
Brávellir
Fossvellir
Ketilsbraut
Auðbrekka
Útgarður
Pálsgarður
Vallholtsvegur
Garðarsbraut
Árgil
Árgata
Túngata
Mararbraut
Héðinsbraut
Norðausturvegur
85
Raufarhöfn
Naustagil
Hafnarstétt
Suðurgarður
Baldursbrekka
Höfðabrekka
Laugarbrekka
Höfðavegur
Háhöfði
Lyngbrekka
Sólbrekka
Höfði
Norðurgarður
Þvergarður
Skjálfandi
Holtagerði
Háagerði
Litlagerði
Urðargerði
Steinagerði
Breiðagerði
Brúnagerði
Uppsalavegur
Heiðar gerði
Baughóll
Álfhóll
Hjarðarhóll
Stórhóll
Þverholt
Langholt
Stakkholt
Lyngholt
Stekkjarholt
Stangarbakki
Laugarholt
Árholt
Þorvaldsstaðaá
Þingeyjarsýslubraut
Reykjavík
Akureyri
9.km
Kortagerð: Ólafur Valsson Copyright ©

19
P. 582

Kelduhverfi, the district at the head of Öxarfjörður between the mountains of Tjörnes and the river Jökulsá. Inland there are many fissures and chasms, difficult and dangerous to cross. At about the time of the volcanic activity by Leirhnjúkur in 1975 (see Road 848) there were repeated earthquakes in the Kelduhverfi district, very frequent and some quite severe in early 1976. There was another series of severe earthquakes in early 1978. The land is thought to be spreading and indeed, many new fissures and cracks have appeared and some older ones have got wider and deeper. These changes can be seen as far north as the sea. At the same time the land has subsided by at least a meter. The greatest changes are in the area between the farms Lindarbrekka and Hlíðargerði, most obviously by the farms Lyngás, Framnes and Hlíðargerði. Warm water has come up in many of the fissures. Down on the flat land called Vestur-Sandur a new lake has appeared, **Skjálftavatn** ("Quake Lake"). This has meant that the course of many rivers have changed radically.

Keldunes, a community of 6 farms near the Keldunes well, a big spring under the lava. Birthplace of High Sheriff Skúli Magnússon (1711-94) (see Viðey, Reykjavík).

Skúlagarður, a community centre, named for High Sheriff Skúli Magnússon, to whom there is a memorial, an eagle on a basalt column.

Krossdalur, birthplace of the poet Kristján Jónsson, called Fjallaskáld ("Poet of the mountains") (1842-69).

Garður, a church, a parsonage until 1872. A farm of the original settlement. The home of Þórir Skeggjason, who had fierce quarrels with Grettir the strong Ásmundarson.

Grásíða, a smoke-curing industry is run there under the name of the farm. Trout and salmon are smoked over fires using animal dung in the way it has been done in Iceland since earliest times.

Víkingavatn, a farm of the original settlement near a fishing-lake of same name. Now a summer house.

Lón, ("Lagoon") named for the sizeable sea-lagoons emptying into the Lónsós estuary. Trout-fishing and nesting islets. Salmon farm.

Rifós, a salmon farm.

Auðbjargarstaðir, the westernmost farm in the Kelduhverfi district.

Imbuþúfa, view dial.

Ásbyrgi

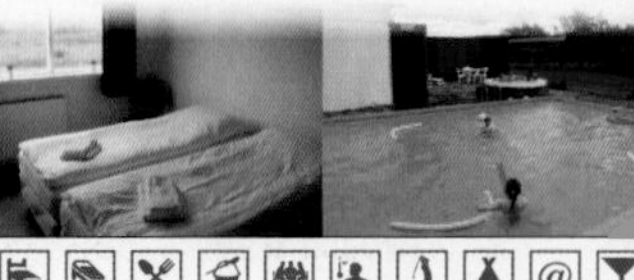

866 Austursandsvegur, 10 km.

Sandá, a river.

Lundur, once a children's boarding school, built 1928, now there is a preschool and an elementary, summer hotel and a swimming pool.

865 Gilsbakkavegur, 4,5 km.

Skinnastaður, a church and parsonage, which according to folklore was the home of powerful priest-magicians, the Rev. Einar galdrameistari ("master magician") and Jón greipaglennir ("wide-hand"). At nearby Þangbrandslækur, the missionary Þangbrandur is said to have baptized the local people in a local stream.

Jökulsá á Fjöllum, one of greatest Icelandic rivers, the second longest at 206 km, and having the largest drainage basin, 8,000 km^2. It comes from Vatnajökull in two main streams, the eastern one being called Kreppa. Jökulsá divides into many forks before emptying into Öxarfjörður, the main one being Bakkahlaup, which flows through Kelduhverfi. Waterfalls: Selfoss, Dettifoss, Hafragilsfoss and Réttarfoss.

Jökulsárgljúfur, a National Park. In Ásbyrgi there is a Visitor Centre. The centre provides comprehensive information about the Park, its surroundings, hiking trails, natural attractions, history, services and recreational options. The Centre is open from May 1st to September 30th. Outside this period, the Centre opens by arrangement. Ásbyrgi is a popular summer holiday destination and is within Vatnajökull National Park. The forest in Ásbyrgi is under the protection of the Forestry Service. See information on Vatnajökull National Park on p. 122.

Ástjörn, a small but deep lake in a wooded dell just east of Ásbyrgi, peaceful and pretty.

Ás, an old manor farm, parsonage till 1816.

861 Ásbyrgisvegur, 3,52 km.

Ásbyrgi, a U-shaped depression about 3.5 km long, surrounded by cliffs up to 90 m high with a huge crag (2 km by 250 m) called Eyjan ("The island") in the open end of the U. Its origin is uncertain. It might have been formed by subsidence, or it could have been formed by floods in the river Jökulsá. There are also signs of sea-water having flowed into it. The legendary explanation is that it is a hoofprint made by Sleipnir, the eight-legged horse belonging to Óðinn, father of the gods, the crag Eyjan having been formed by the frog of his hoof. There is a small lake at the inner end. Vegetation ranges from moorland growth near the open end to thickly growing birch and rowan trees farther in. Ásbyrgi is a popular summer holiday destination and is within Vatnajökull National Park. The forest in Ásbyrgi is under the protection of the Forestry Service.

Klifshagi-Keldunes 23 km

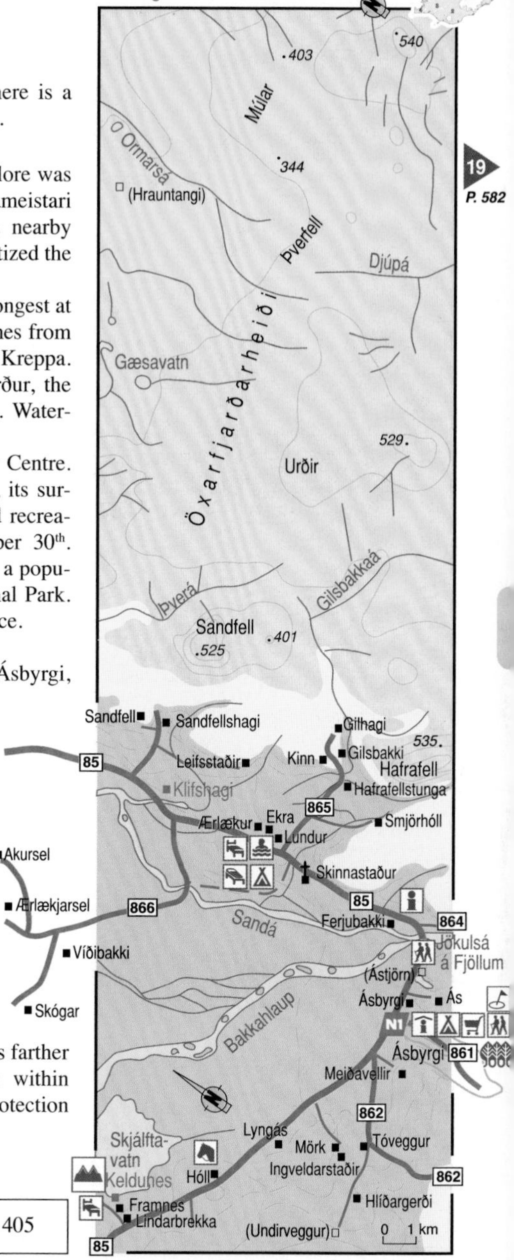

Keldunes-Klifshagi 23 km

19 P. 582

862 Dettifossvegur, p. 480 **864 Hólsfjallavegur,** p. 405

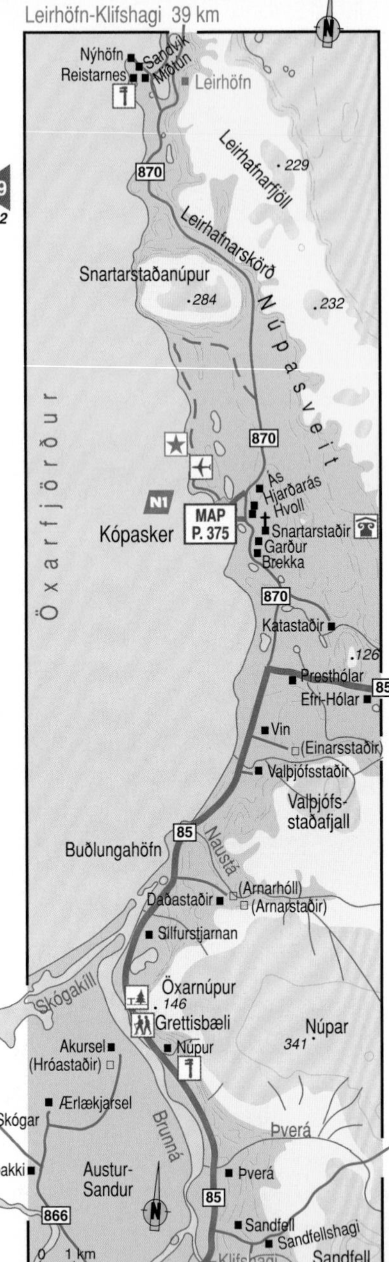

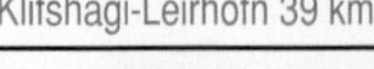

Leirhafnarskörð, a pass between the spur Snartarstaðanúpur (248 m and the Leirhafnarfjöll mountains. Site of a small eruption in 1823.

Leirhöfn, a substantial farm, well-cultivated land. The farmer Helg Kristjánsson (1894-1982) built a private library of about 10 thousan volumes which he gave to the county. It is now kept at Snartarstaðir a Kópasker. An excellent natural harbour, and harbour construction at near by **Nýhöfn** for the many small boats that go fishing from there. Aroun 1950 farms were built there.

Hvallág, a beautiful rest stop by the see at the foot of Snartarstaðarnúpu (284 m).

Núpasveit, the area between the spurs Öxarnúpur and **Snartarstaða núpur**, into the centre of which flowed lava from the Rauðhólar hills o Öxarfjarðarheiði moor.

Öxarfjörður, the area east of the river Jökulsá as far as the Öxarnúpu spur, with the delta Austursandur between the branches of Jökulsá. Gentl slopes with birch-trees merging into dwarf-willows. The river Sandá, a branch of Jökulsá, flows through it and joins Brunná, a mountain strea from the eastern moors. There is a good deal of geothermal energy there.

Snartarstaðir, a church since 1928. Site of official gatherings. Museum county library in Núpasveitarskóli, an old school house built in 1928. Th school operated there until 1983 when a new school was built at Kópasker.

Silfurstjarnan, a fish farm with charr, halibut and turbot ideally situate in an area rich of geothermal water.

Öxarnúpur, (146 m) a sheer crag with scree at the foot, the easternmos spur of the mountain Núpar (341 m). On the crag is Grettisbæli ("Grettir' hide-out"), a rocky stronghold roofed by basalt columns, one of the place where Grettir the strong is said to have stayed for a while.

866 Austursandsvegur, p. 376
870 Sléttuvegur, p. 376

Kópasker.

ópasker, (pop. 122) a village, a legalised port since 879. Pier for oceangoing ships, airstrip. On January 3th 1976 there was a very severe earthquake whose picentre was out in the fjord, about 12 km northwest f the village. There was a great deal of damage, with evere cracks in many houses so that some could no onger be lived in. The water mains were in pieces and he harbour wall split along a fault, the two sides moving in opposite directions. Bridges in the area of Núpur vere destroyed, the lava hills by Presthólar were damged as if by an explosion and boulders fell from)xarnúpur spur.

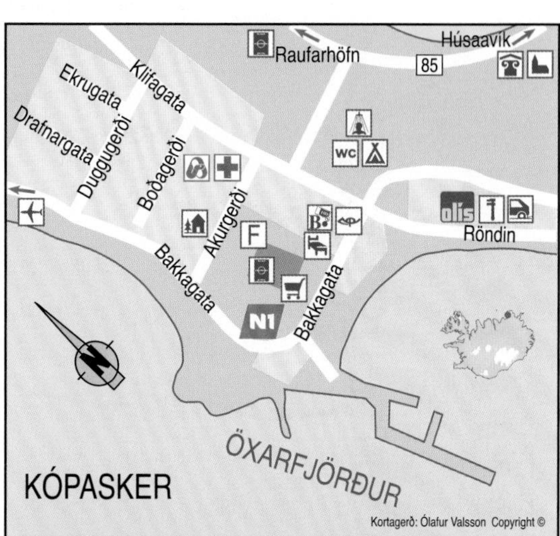

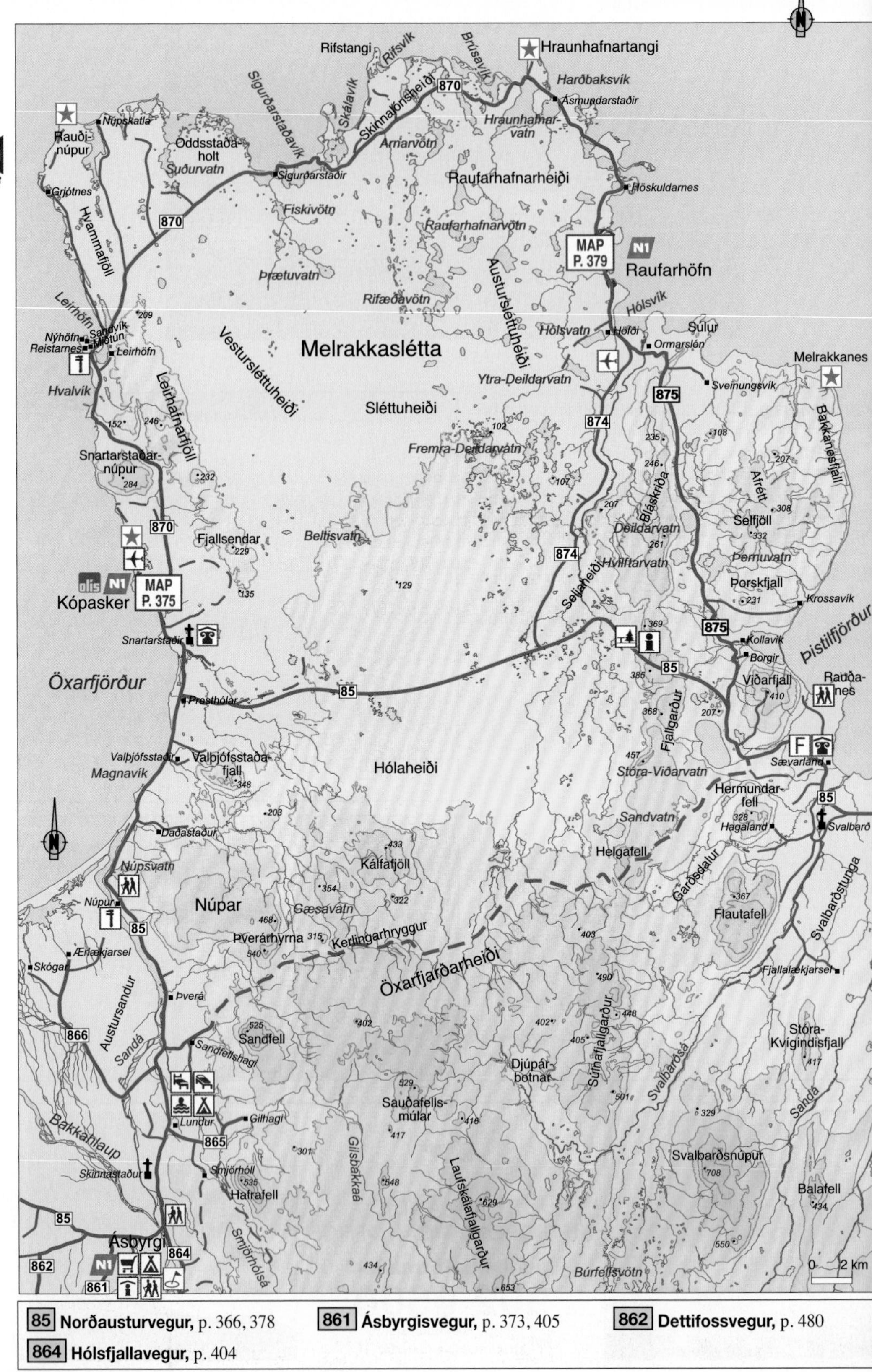

85 **Norðausturvegur,** p. 366, 378	861 **Ásbyrgisvegur,** p. 373, 405
862 **Dettifossvegur,** p. 480	864 **Hólsfjallavegur,** p. 404

20 P. 583

© Björn Hróarsson

70 **Sléttuvegur,** 57,8 km.

leyjarþúfa, ("Virgin's knoll") a small knoll with a staff n the top, between Harðbakur and the lake raunhafnarvatn, 200-300 m south of the road. ccording to legend the whole population of the Slétta rea died of a plague, except for one woman in the eastrn part and one man in the western part. They met up on leyjarþúfa and laid the foundations for a new generaon in the area.

raunhafnartangi, the northernmost point of Iceland, uches the Arctic Circle. Named for Hraunhöfn ("Lava arbour"), a small inlet nearby. An historical place, here *Fóstbræðra saga* tells us Þorgeir Hávarsson was ain and where his burial mound is said to be. ighthouse.

kinnalón, once a manor farm, now abandoned.

ifstangi, long thought to be the northernmost point of eland. The farm **Rif** has been abandoned.

likalónsdalur, a grassy area of subsidence with cliffs ong the edges in many places. It extends far south into e moors, dividing Vesturslétta from Austurslétta, the estern from the eastern part of the Melrakkaslétta ains. The farm Blikalón by the sea.

ddsstaðir, once a manor farm, now abandoned.

úpskatla, a farm beside the lake below the crater auðinúpur. Birthplace of the novelist Guðmundur lagnússon (1887-1918), whose pen-name was Jón rausti. **Rauðinúpur,** (73 m) a high crater at the northwestern tip of the Melrakkaslétta plains, erupted late in the Ice Age. Steep cliffs with many seabirds towards the sea but grassy at the inland end. At the northeastern corner is Karl, a big pinnacle rock, sometimes called Jón Trausti, for the novelist.

Gefla, a distinctive mountain in the northen end of Leirhafnarfjöll. An easy walk up the mountain and a great view of the Plain.

874 **Raufarhafnarvegur,** 20,1 km.

875 **Hálsavegur,** 20 km.

Melrakkaslétta, ("Arctic Foxes' plain") the peninsula between Öxarfjörður and Þistilfjörður between the spur Snartarstaðarnúður and the river Ormarsá. All flat and low except for the mountains Leirhafnarfjöll in the west. The northern and eastern coast is much-indented with coves, nesses and lagoons. Dry in the west but marshy in the east, with many lakes and tarns. Farms, many now abandoned, only along the coast. Much driftwood and trout-fishing, eider duck and seals are often spotted there. Foxes were widespread, hence the name, and polar bears occasionally drifted ashore on ice-floes. Melrakkaslétta boasts a large number of lakes inlets, where cayaking is possible. Information is available at Hotel Norðurljós in Raufarhöfn. Marked walking routes.

Víðinesá-Raufarhöfn 29 km

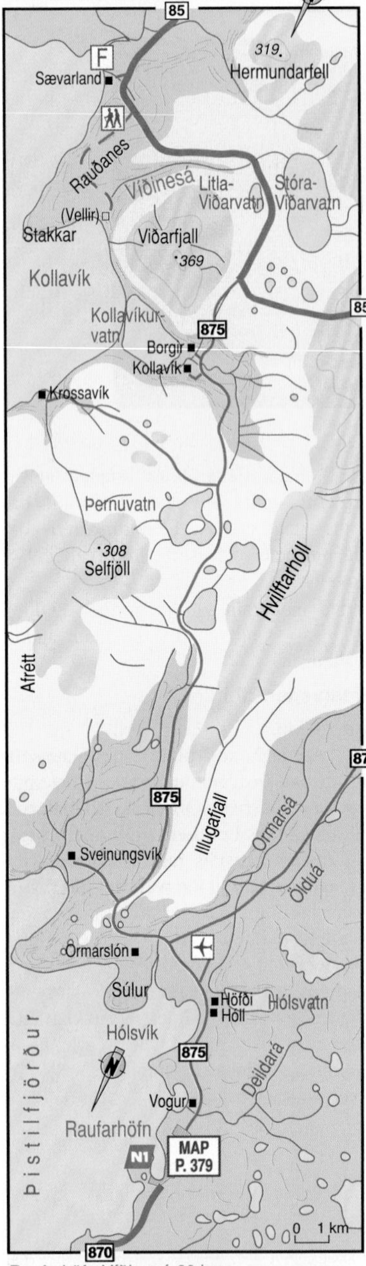

Viðarvatn, actually two lakes, **Stóra-Viðarvatn** and **Litla-Viðarvat** ("Big and Little Viðarvatn"), good for fishing, southwest of Viðarfjall (41 m). From the larger lake the river Víðinesá flows out into Þistilfjörður.

Viðarfjall, (410 m) a mountain below which the shore, Borgarfjörur, is passa ble but dangerous.

Kollavík, a farm on a bay of the same name, a farm since the original settle ment. The fishing-lake Kollavíkurvatn nearby.

Ormarslón, the easternmost farm on the Melrakkaslétta plain.

Ormarsá, a good fishing-river, the biggest on Melrakkaslétta.

Raufarhöfn, (pop. 169) a village which was once one of the biggest herrin ports in Iceland. See town map, p. 379.

Heimskautsgerðið, (The Polar Enclosure) This is where the day is th longest in the summer and shortest in the winter. Around the summer solstic the sun does not set for several solar days. The light there is unique and owin to how low the surrounding landscape is nothing blocks the horizon for a tota of 360°. The spectacular show put on by the interaction between light an shade there prompted men to contemplate how to capture all of this for exploi tation by tourism. The first ideas were to somehow define the three hour peri ods of the solar day with some sort of solar watch and utilize the influence o the midnight sun to magnify the effect. But no matter what configuration wa tried it was obvious that the conditions on the Melrakkaslétta plateau con tained something even more powerful, something that was hidden there Something was needed that could lift this idea to higher flights and intensif the sunset in a potent way. Bit by bit, things began to fall into place. In th end, a circle was formed with a diameter of 54 m, enclosed by a stacked roc wall. On the wall there are four gates with openings to the four cardina points. The lower layer of the wall is about 2.5 m high. On top of it there ar 68 gateways with a continuous rock layer upon them. The visual effect is tha this upper layer floats on the rays of the midnight sun and at sunrise and sun set at other times of the year. In the middle of the circle there is an 8-10 r high pillar resting on four bollards. The spaces between the bollards point t the four gates so that the midnight sun will appear in the north gate. Th spring equinox and fall equinox have also been kept in mind as well as th winter solstice when the sun barely peeks up over the horizon. Around th middle there are four columns, each one unique. Inside the wall there are 6 rocks, the dwarfs, which form a circle. The concept behind the dwarfs is take from the Dwarf Tale in Völuspá. The dwarf concept is well-known throughou Europe where dwarfs and plants associated with the seasons have had the pu pose of ensuring growth and prosperity in nature. With these concepts in min the year circle of the dwarfs is formed inside the big wall circle. Each dwa has his restricted role. The artist, Haukur Halldórsson, has drawn each indi vidual dwarf according to his function. The author, Jónas Friðrik, has simulta neously written a poetic text about them. The cooperation of these two artis has awoken great expectations as they are actually working on designing me chandise for selling as souvenirs about the phenomenon discussed above The Polar Enclosure.

Raufarhöfn-Víðinesá 29 km

Raufarhöfn

RAUFARHÖFN
www.raufarhofn.is

870 **Sléttuvegur,** p. 376

874 **Raufarhafnarvegur,** p. 376

875 **Hálsavegur,** p. 376

A village on the east of the Melrakka-slétta plain. In 1836 Raufarhöfn was officially designated a trading centre, having up to that time been simply a farm, named Reiðarhöfn in the 1703 census.

The rauf, or rift, that gives the village its name is a shallow channel between the Hólmi, which falls steeply to the sea but has a good deal of vegetation towards the top, and the Höfði, which is at the southern end of a fairly wide point of land, south of the so-called Klif. The Höfði, on which there is a lighthouse, has a rich birdlife. It is quite high and an excellent place from which to view the village and its harbour. Good trout-fishing in the area.

The harbour underwent extensive improvements in the beginning of the „herring years" around 1950, and piers were built making it possible to land great amounts of herring. Indeed, Raufarhöfn was for a while one of the main salting and processing centres in Iceland.

Raufarhöfn is the northernmost village in Iceland. There are the darkest winter nights but also the brightest summer nights and for a whole month in the summer the sun doesn't set. There is an airport near the village but no scheduled flights.

The church, designed by Guðjón Samúelsson, was built in 1927 and to a large extent rebuilt in 1979. The pulpit was once in the old church at Ásmundarstaðir, having been given to that church in 1851 by Danish merchants in Raufarhöfn. The altar piece is also from Ásmundarstaðir, painted in 1890 by Sveinungi Sveinungason (1840–1915).

Þistilfjörður

Heimskautsgerði

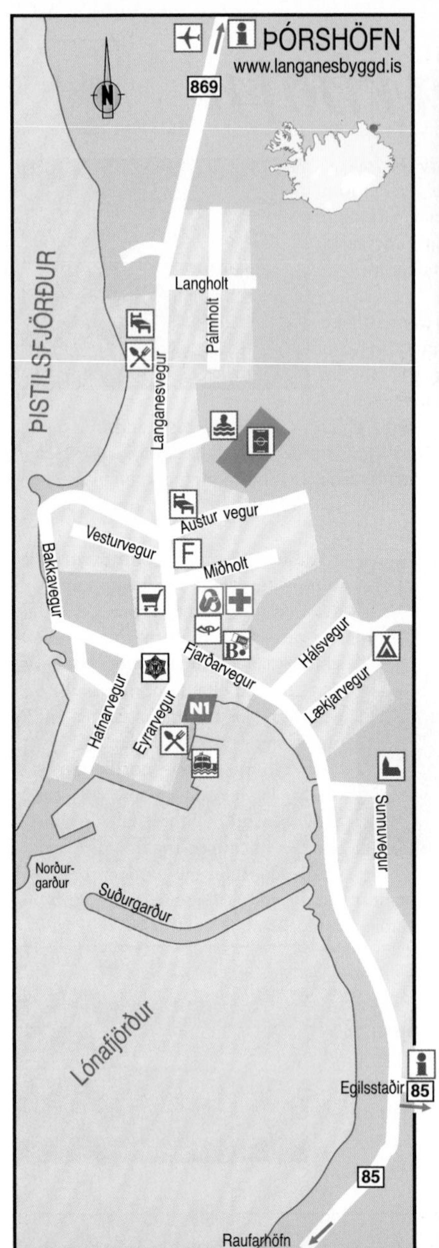

A village on the east side of Lónafjörður, a fjord out of Þistilfjörðu to the southeast. There is a good natural harbour and shelter fron the northeast wind, which is the main sea wind in this part of th country.

Þórshöfn has been the centre for trade in the area for centuries Though it is mentioned in the authorization papers of foreign trader from the 16th century onwards, it only became an authorized tradin post in 1846, when first private, then company-owned ships began t trade there regularly. Trading took place on board the ships until abou 1880, when they built warehouses, the first buildings in Þórshöfn To begin with, trade was in the hands of the Danish company Örun & Wulff, which built a substantial shop-cum-home in Þórshöfn. Afte that, trade was in the hands of various locals, the Langanes Co-op established 1911, having run it the longest, but does no longer excist.

This prosperous community is based on fishing and fish-processing In addition to the traditional processing of various white fish there is factory producing capelin meal and a plant where herring and capeli are processed for the human food market. To make even better use o what the ocean has to offer, the most recent innovation is harvestin and processing mussels.

Rauðanes

órshöfn, (pop. 379) a village with fishing, herring-salting, trading.

afralónsá, the biggest river in Þistilfjörður, coming from Hafralón far p on the moors but with tributaries whose sources are even farther way. Good fishing.

68 Laxárdalsvegur, 3,6 km.

istilfjörður, the bay between the Melrakkaslétta plain and the Langanes eninsula, with farms along its head, where there are low hills and val-ys with many rivers, the main ones being Svalbarðsá, Sandá, Hölkná, axá, and Hafralónsá. All rise in the moors and most have trout and almon. Formerly there were several farms on the extensive moors far-her inland.

auðanes, fairly long peninsula with steep cliffs east of the mountain 'iðarfjall. Many seabird nest there, and there are some picturesque pin-acle rocks, **Stakkar**, in the sea. The end of the peninsula has broken way and is called Stakkatorfa. There are caves under it, accessible by mall boats in good weather. There are also caves in the cliffs. An area of atural beauty well worth seeing with marked walking paths.

valbarð, one of the biggest farms of the district, church, a parsonage ll 1936, an ancient assembly site. On the walls of the church choir pitaphs have been written, believed to be the work of Bólu-Hjálmar (see óla, Skag).

ævarland, a farm which was the birthplace of the painter Gunnlaugur löndal (1893-1962).

xarfjarðarheiði, the moor between Öxarfjörður and istilfjörður. A summer road, highest at Einarsskarð (380 m), 8 km long. Grassy moorland. Farms there now all abandoned.

ttarshnjúkur, a mountain, marked walking routes.

rauntangi, a farm abandoned in 1943, the last farm on Öxar-arðarheiði to be abandoned.

auðhólar, a row of craters from which lava has flowed down to ie farms Presthólar in the Núpasveit district and Ormarslón on ie Melrakkaslétta plain.

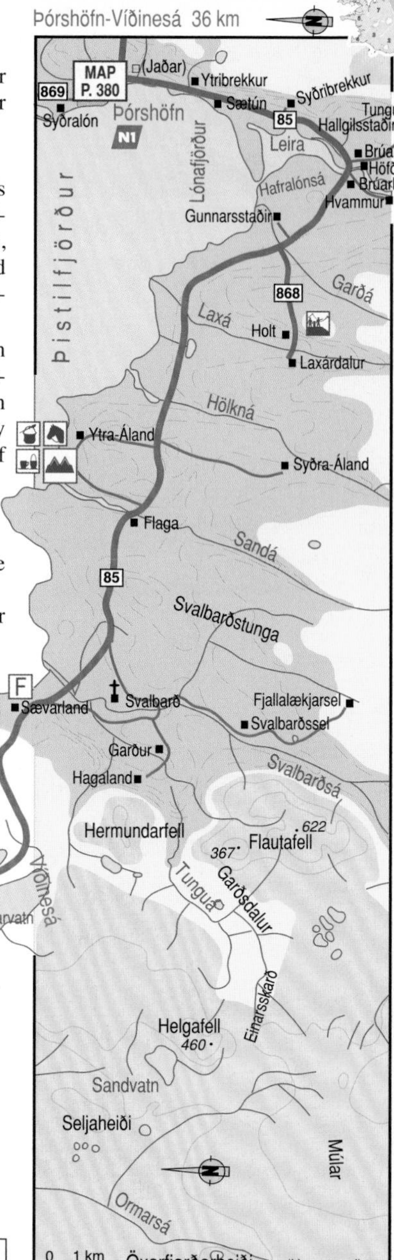

869 Langanesvegur, p. 408

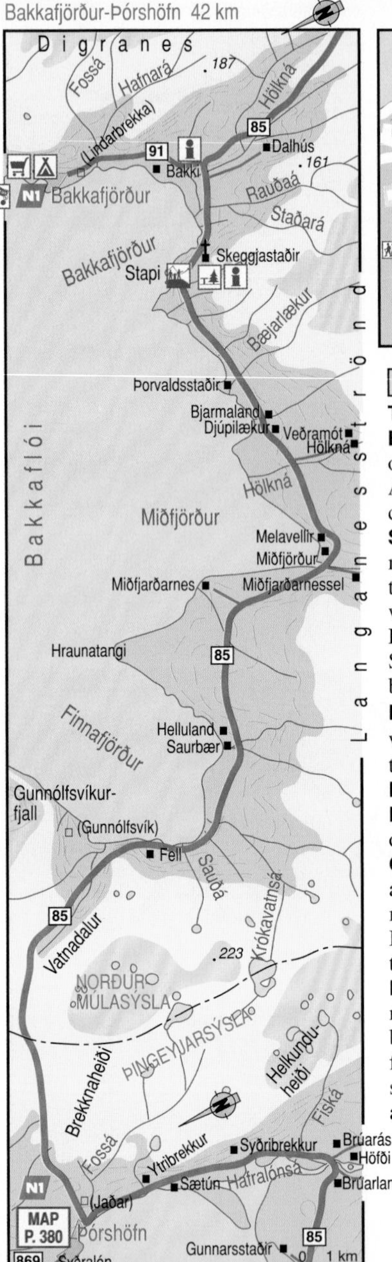

20 P. 583

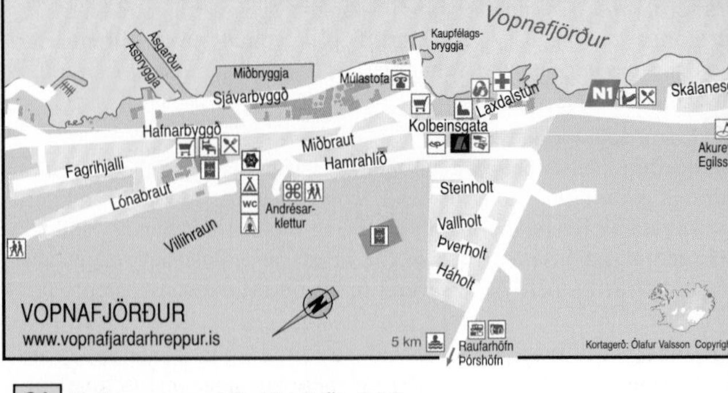

91 Hafnarvegur í Bakkafirði, 4,9 km.

Tóarnef, a point of land near the end of the road at Steintún, good view.

Bakkafjörður, (pop. 78) a village in the land of Höfn which became a official trading place in 1883. Main occupations are fishing and service At Bakkfjörður are elementary school, health care centre, community centre, campsite and a grocery store. Good walking routes in the area.

Skeggjastaðir, a church and parsonage. A little to the west is a strang rock, **Stapi**, rising straight out of the sea. The church was built in 184 the pastor Rev. Hóseas Árnason paying out of his own pocket for all th work, since both the bishop and the local people refused to help. Th Provost at Hof in Vopnafjörður, Rev. Guttormur Þorsteinsson, who owne Skoruvíkurfjörður on the Langanes peninsula, donated driftwood for th building.

Þorvaldsstaðir, a farm where the poet Magnús Stefánsson (1884-1942 whose pen-name was Örn Arnarson, grew up. He was born at Kverká tunga in the same district.

Djúpilækur, birthplace of the poet Kristján Einarsson (1916-94).

Miðfjarðará, the biggest river on the Langanesströnd coast, good salm on-fishing.

Gunnólfsvík, the northernmost farm on the Langanesströnd coast, no abandoned. Once a fishing-station. To north is **Gunnólfsvíkurfjall** (71 m). Good views. This marks the eastern end of the tuff area of norther Iceland, the west end of which is the valley Bárðardalur through whic the river Skjálfandafljót runs (see Road 85).

Langanesströnd, the coast between the peninsulas Langanes and Digra nes east of Bakkafjörður. There are three short fjords on the Bakkafl bay: **Finnafjörður**, **Miðfjörður** and **Bakkafjörður** or Sandvík. Little re flat land, but big, low moors inland, from which run many streams. Simila scenery to that in Þistilfjörður. Farms now only along the coast, formerl also on the moors.

Brekknaheiði, the northern part of moors between Langanesströnd an Þistilfjörður, formerly called **Helkunduheiði**. Low hills alternate wit marshes, small lakes and tarns, mostly below 200 m. There were for merly the boundaries between the 4 parts of Iceland, also between th bishoprics and still between Þingeyjarsýsla and Múlasýsla countie The road reaches a height of 160 m.

869 **Langanesvegur,** p. 408

Vopnafjörður.

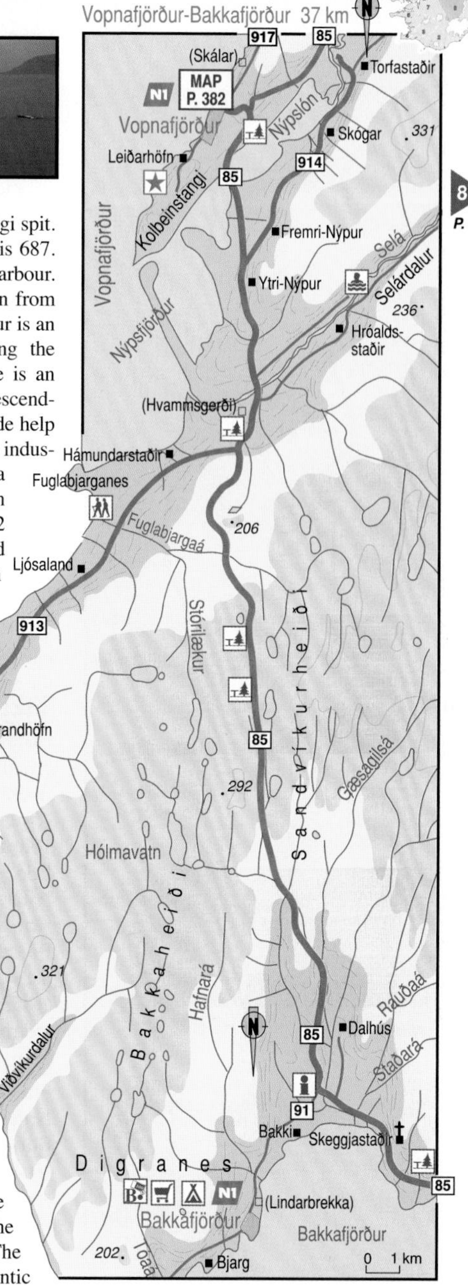

8 P. 571

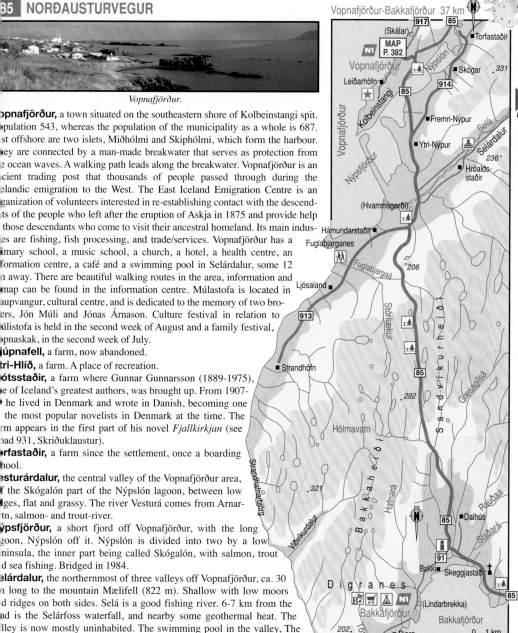

ɔpnafjörður, a town situated on the southeastern shore of Kolbeinstangi spit. ɔpulation 543, whereas the population of the municipality as a whole is 687. st offshore are two islets, Miðhólmi and Skiphólmi, which form the harbour. ıey are connected by a man-made breakwater that serves as protection from ɛ ocean waves. A walking path leads along the breakwater. Vopnafjörður is an ıcient trading post that thousands of people passed through during the ɛlandic emigration to the West. The East Iceland Emigration Centre is an ganization of volunteers interested in re-establishing contact with the descend-ıts of the people who left after the eruption of Askja in 1875 and provide help those descendants who come to visit their ancestral homeland. Its main indus-ɛs are fishing, fish processing, and trade/services. Vopnafjörður has a imary school, a music school, a church, a hotel, a health centre, an formation centre, a café and a swimming pool in Selárdalur, some 12 ı away. There are beautiful walking routes in the area, information and map can be found in the information centre. Múlastofa is located in aupvangur, cultural centre, and is dedicated to the memory of two bro-ers, Jón Múli and Jónas Árnason. Culture festival in relation to úlistofa is held in the second week of August and a family festival, ɔpnaskak, in the second week of July.

úpnafell, a farm, now abandoned.

tri-Hlíð, a farm. A place of recreation.

ótsstaðir, a farm where Gunnar Gunnarsson (1889-1975), ıe of Iceland's greatest authors, was brought up. From 1907- he lived in Denmark and wrote in Danish, becoming one the most popular novelists in Denmark at the time. The ɪm appears in the first part of his novel *Fjallkirkjan* (see ɔad 931, Skriðuklaustur).

rfastaðir, a farm since the settlement, once a boarding hool.

ɛsturárdalur, the central valley of the Vopnafjörður area, f the Skógalón part of the Nýpslón lagoon, between low lges, flat and grassy. The river Vesturá comes from Arnar-tn, salmon- and trout-river.

ýpsfjörður, a short fjord off Vopnafjörður, with the long goon, Nýpslón off it. Nýpslón is divided into two by a low ninsula, the inner part being called Skógalón, with salmon, trout d sea fishing. Bridged in 1984.

ɛlárdalur, the northernmost of three valleys off Vopnafjörður, ca. 30 ı long to the mountain Mælifell (822 m). Shallow with low moors d ridges on both sides. Selá is a good fishing river. 6-7 km from the ad is the Selárfoss waterfall, and nearby some geothermal heat. The lley is now mostly uninhabited. The swimming pool in the valley, The lárdalur swimming pool, is considered by many to be the most romantic ol in Iceland because it has no electricity and therefore relies on moonlight, rora boreales and the stars for light as the day wanes. The dressing rooms ɛ illuminated by candlelight. There is currently one inhabited farm in the lley.

13 Strandhafnarvegur, 12 km.

ri-Hágangur, (923 m) and **Syðri-Hágangur,** (952 m) two imposing ɔuntains west of Sandvíkurheiði moor.

ındvíkurheiði, (275 m) low moors between Bakkafjörður and ɔpnafjörður, marshy with lakes and tarns. any streams originate there.

91 Hafnarvegur, p. 382
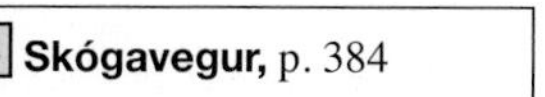
914 Skógavegur, p. 384
917 Hlíðarvegur, p. 384

Bakkafjörður-Vopnafjörður 37 km

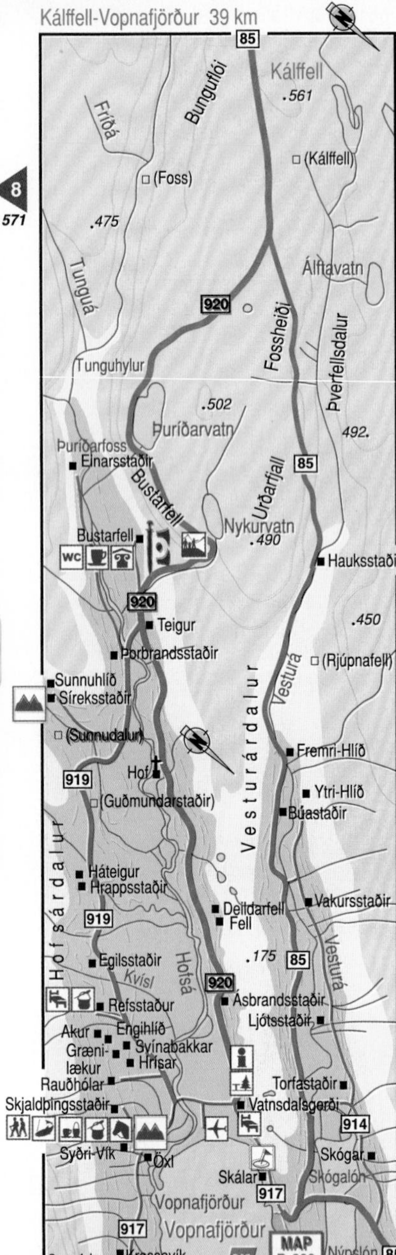

920 Hofsárdalsvegur, 31,86 km

Bustarfell, a manor farm through the ages, with a long history. The far has been in the same family since 1532. This turf house with red gable and grass-grown roof is one of the oldest and best preserved farms of i kind in Iceland. The house preserves much history about Iceland and i people. In 1770, sadly, the original farm burned down, but it was quick rebuilt and was lived in until 1966. Then the family built a new house c Bustarfell which they still live in. Now there is a museum. The Museun i.e. the relics, were given to Vopnafjörður by Elín Methúsalemsdóttir i the year 1982. The houses were sold to the Icelandic nation in 1943 b Methúsalem Methúsalemsson. They are now preserved by the Iceland National Museum. A visit to the Museum at Bustarfell is a journe through the history of farming and changes in lifestyle from the begin ning of the 18th century to the mid-20th century. The Museum show clearly the lifestyle changes that occured from the time it was rebui until the family moved into the "new house". Guests can follow the di ference in the standard for quality, for example when running water an a heating system were lead to the house. Beside Bustarfell Museum i Café Croft placed. It is little but very homelike and cosy where guest can sit down and enjoy coffee, tea or a chocolate along with a tasty trad tional cakes and pies.

Bustarfell, sharp-topped mountain, with two lakes on top, Þuríðarvat and Nykurvatn, good view. View-dial. Below the mountain is a farm the same name.

914 Skógavegur, 7,7 km. 915 Vesturárdalsvegur, 19,8 km

Hofsárdalur, the westernmost and biggest of the Vopnafjörður valley broad at the mouth but narrowing into Fossdalur. **Hofsá** is a good fishin river. To the east is a low ridge, to the west high mountains, **Smjörfjö** ("Butter mountains") (1,251 m). Grassy, fertile farming area.

Teigur, a farm where the poetess Guðfinna Þorsteinsdóttir, pen-nam Erla, (1891-1972) lived for many years. The geologist Dr. Sigurðu Þórarinsson (1912-83), born at Hof, was brought up there.

Hof, a church, parsonage, historically important manor farm. Home Brodd-Helgi and his son Bjarni Brodd-Helgason, mentioned in *Vopn firðinga saga*. Among pastors who served there was Einar Jónsso (1853-1931) one of Iceland's best genealogists. There are a number old ruins on the land of Hof.

919 Sunnudalsvegur, 16 km.

Fjallasíða, the row of farms below the mountains on the eastern side Hofsárdalur.

Sunnudalur, a farm in a valley of the same name, now also calle Hraunfellsdalur. Site of an ancient assembly, mentioned in the Sagas.

Hrappsstaðir, a farm. From there began the path over Smjörvatnshei moor to Fossavellir at Jökulsárhlíð. The route is about 38 km, steep i places and with heavy snow, highest point at 750 m. Once a route ofte travelled.

Refsstaður, a parsonage till 178 and a church till 1812.

917 Hlíðarvegur, p. 423

In the Jökuldalur valley.

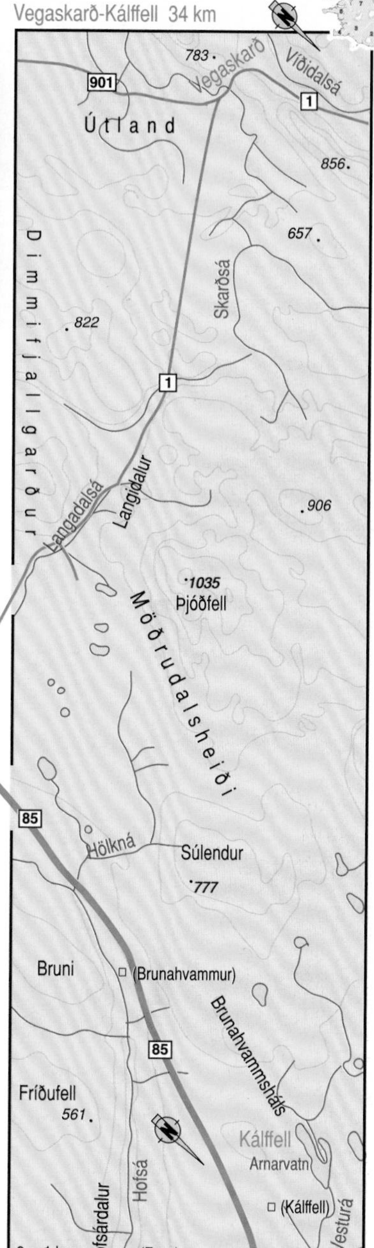

immifjallgarður, ("Dark mountain range") going south from Haugsræfi to Þjóðfell, most of its peaks being 600-900 m high. Formerly there as a route across there between the Hólsfjöll farms and Vopnafjörður, ut it was difficult in winter and there were frequent accidents. In ebruary 1874 two men were lost in a snow storm with their horse and art. Their bodies were found 2 weeks later. The horse stood by them, live but unable to move because its reins were frozen to the ground.

augsöræfi, a mountain range east of Hólsfjöll, up to 1,000 m igh. There is a large lake there called Haugsvatn. An old route, bout 70 km long, went across there between Vopnafjörður and ólsfjöll, Vopnafjörður then being the trading post for the rmers. The mountain range gets its name from one of its eaks, Haugur (965 m).

ökuldalsheiði, extensive moorland southwest of opnafjörður, about 60 km long. It lies in a depression ounded by the mountains Þjóðfell and Súlendur to the est, the ranges Þríhyrningsfjallgarður and Möðrudalsallgarður to the northwest and Jökuldalsfjöll to the east.

angidalur, a narrow valley between the Möðrudalsfjallgarður range and e mountain Þjóðfell.

jóðfell, (1,035 m) a tuff mountain north of the eastern Möðrudalsfjallarður range, Langidalur lying between them. The road to Vopnafjörður southeast of Þjóðfell, called Biskupsáfangar at that point. The area ortheast of Þjóðfell is called Þjóðfellsbungur, and the adjoining area löðrudalsheiði.

úlendur, (804 m) a mountain north of the road.

runahvammur, an abandoned farm in the valley Fossárdalur, named for runi, the mountain opposite. Birthplace of the poet Þorsteinn Valdimarsn (1918-77).

oss, ("Waterfall") an abandoned farm in Hofsárdalur, the next farm yond Burstarfell, named for a waterfall in the river Hofsá across from . The Hofsá has salmon up as far as Foss.

1 Austurlandsvegur, p. 96 **901 Möðrudalsfjallgarðar,** p. 96

Laxamýri-Reykjahlíð 46 km

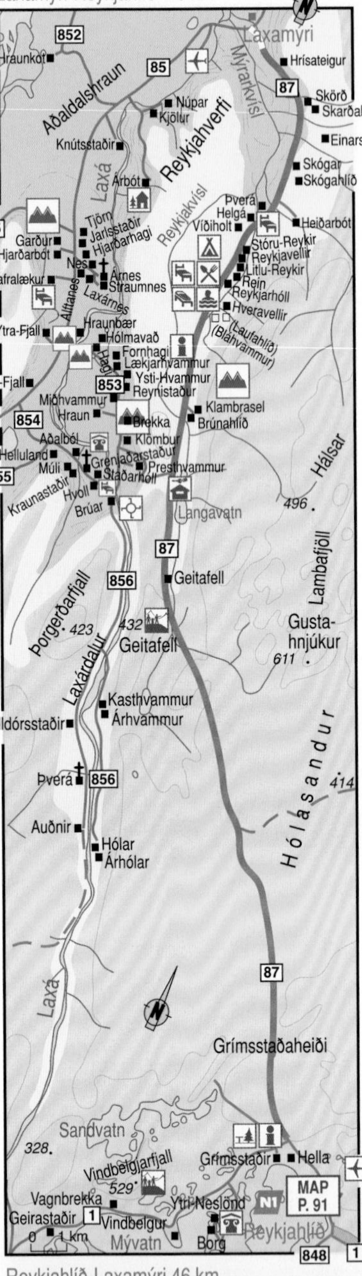

6
P. 569

Grísatungufjöll, (736 m) the southern end of the Tjörnes (see Road 85 mountains.

Reykjaheiði, high moorland between the districts Reykjahverfi an Kelduhverfi. Flattish, but with lava and isolated fells and spur Moorland vegetation. Big volcanic craters. Snowy and stormy, heigh 300-400 m. The Reykjaheiðarvegur route went across these moors, bu was abandoned when the road was built round Tjörnes.

Þeistareykjabunga, (564 m) a shield volcano, always visible fro the Reykjaheiðarvegur road and the Kelduhverfi district. South of it ar the explosion craters Stóra-Víti ("Big Hell") and Litla-Víti ("Littl Hell").

Þeistareykir, an abandoned farm towards the south of Reykjaheiði moo Much geothermal heat and some sulphur mines, which were operated a one time. Good shepherd's hut. South of there is the mountain Bæjarfja (570 m). Jeep-track from the Reykjaheiðarvegur road and Hólasandur.

Reykjahverfi, a farming area between the farms Laxamýri and Geitafe to the south. To the west is the Hvammsheiði moor, and to the east moo rising up towards the Lambafjöll mountains and Reykjaheiði. Heat ha been piped from Reykjahverfi 18 km to Húsavík for domestic heating.

Skörð, a farm in Reykjahverfi. Home of a famous 19th century versifie Skarða-Gísli, whose son was Arngrímur Gíslason málari (1829-87), very artistic self-taught painter. See **Tjörn** in Svarfaðardalur.

Hveravellir, the main hot spring area in Reykjahverfi, with several farm Hothouses, swimming pool and local community centre. The bigge springs are Syðstihver, Uxahver and Baðstofuhver (or Ystihver), one o biggest in Iceland. The river Mýrarkvísl, formed by several streams, flow from there and down near Laxamýri.

Lambafjöll, a large mountain range, the highest peak being Kista (84 m), to the north and east of which is the spur Höfuðreiðarmúli.

Geitafell, (432 m) a mountain and a farm of same name. View-dial on th mountain.

Hólasandur, a sand desert between the Laxárdalur valley and the Lak Mývatn district, formerly a much-travelled route. A major effort is unde way there to reclaim the land. The Kísilvegur road was built acro Hólasandur in 1967. Extensive revegetation work done on behalf of loc conservation group Húsgull and the Soil Conservation.

Sandvatn, a good fishing lake, only accessable by 4x4 cars.

1 **Norðurlandsvegur,** p. 92
845 **Aðaldalsvegur,** p. 400
852 **Sandsvegur,** p. 367
854 **Staðarbraut,** p. 401
856 **Laxárdalsvegur,** p. 401
85 **Norðausturvegur,** p. 367
848 **Mývatnsvegur,** p. 92
853 **Hvammavegur,** p. 401
855 **Fagranesvegur,** p. 401

Reykjahlíð-Laxamýri 46 km

805 SVARFAÐARDALSVEGUR

tlastaðir, the innermost farm in Svarfaðardalur, from where a route ɔes across Heljardalsheiði moor into the valley Kolbeinsdalur.

laufabrekkur, a farm, home of Klaufi, often mentioned in *Svarfdæla ıga*. He earlier lived at Klaufanes, where some ruins of his dwellings ıve been excavated.

rðir, a church and formerly the home of influential men.

reiðarsstaðir, a farm, once the home of Hreiðar heimski ("the fool-h"), known as a great practical joker.

teindyr, ("Stone doorway") on the Þverá river, which emerges from the teindyragil gorge, where there are numerous plants and a pretty water-ıll, **Steindyrafoss**.

akki, a farm. Three brothers, Gísli, Eiríkur and Helgi, the most notori-ıs fools in Icelandic folklore, are supposed to have lived there.

arðshorn ytra, monument to the first settler in the valley, Þorsteinn vörfuður ("Trouble-maker"), source of the name Svarfaðardalur.

rund, the land settled by Þorsteinn Svörfuður. Community cen-e, former assembly site. In the mountain above the farm is **ykurtjörn**, a small lake in which a monster is supposed to have ırked.

örn, a substantial farm and church and a parsonage till 1917, ırthplace of Dr. Kristján Eldjárn (1916-82), 3rd President of Iceland. n the slope directly above the farm there was a cottage farm called ullbringa. In 1884 the artist Arngrímur Gíslason from Sköð in the eykjahverfi district moved in there and built a studio on to the cot-ge. This was probably the first artist's studio in the country. In the)'s the Central Bank of Iceland had the building, known as **Arn-rímsstofa** ("Arngrímur's studio"), restored in memory of Kristján ldjárn, who had written a book about Arngrímur in 1983. In the keep-g of the National Museum since 1953 and is looked after by the family Tjörn.

varfaðardalur, a broad and fertile valley, with many farms and high ıautiful mountains. At the bottom of Skíðadalur valley is the glacier **ljúfurárjökull**. Svarfaðardalur has four beautiful churches, with old tar pieces. Birdland is an exhibition located at Húsabakki. The surro-ıding valley, Svarfaðardalur, is renowned for its diverse bird life, and ıarked trails will lead you from Húsabakki through the Svarfaðardalur ıature Reserve.

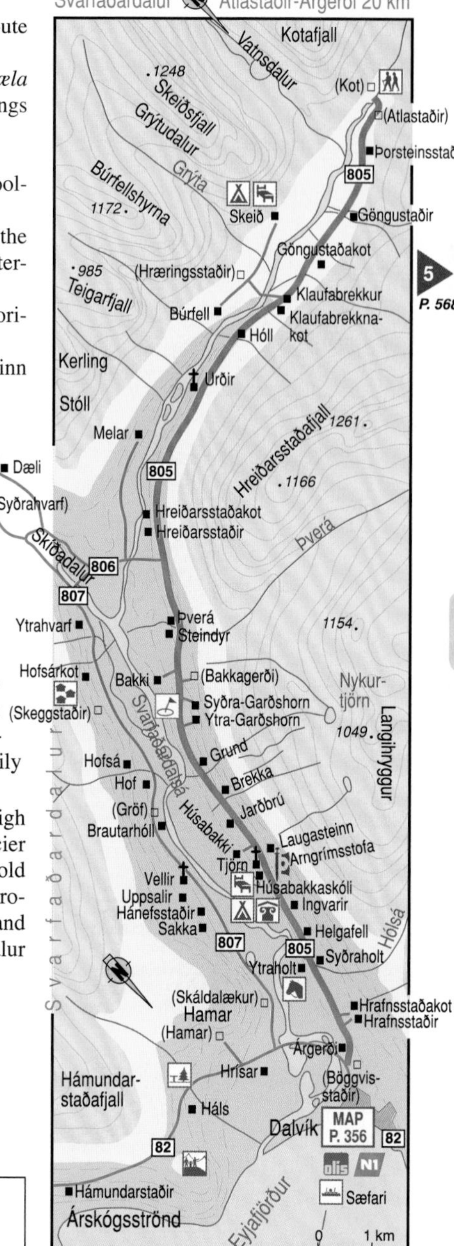

82 Ólafsfjarðarvegur, p. 358

806 Tunguvegur, p. 388

807 Skíðadalsvegur, p. 388

5
P. 568

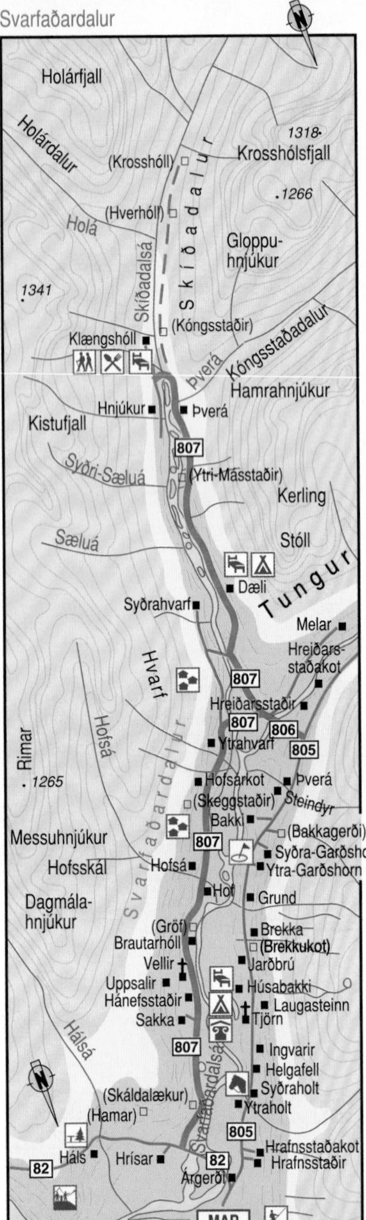

Svarfaðardalur

807 **Skíðadalsvegur,** 19,3 km.

Kóngsstaðir, an abandoned farm where trees have thrived since the land was put under protection. Good bilberry country.

Klængshóll, the innermost occupied farm in Skíðadalur.

Hofsá, a farm where there is a small wood, with a memorial to Soffonías Þorkelsson (1876-1964), a Canadian Icelander who made a handsome gift to promote forestry work there.

Hof, one of the larger farms in the valley. An old landslide from Hofsskál above the farm has formed clear ridges there. The peak **Messuhnjúkur**(1,100 m) above Hofsskál.

Vellir, a church, the home of Valla-Ljótur in Saga-times. The church was built in 1861 and has a 2-ton bell given by the Canadian Icelander Soffonías Þorkelsson (1876-1964), which was until recently the biggest bell in Iceland.

Hánefsstaðir, a farm where Eiríkur Hjartarson (1885-1981) started experimental forestry many years ago, but later gave all the land to the Eyjafjörður Forestry Club, which has since sold the farm but not the woodland. Monument to Eiríkur.

Brekkukot, an abandoned farm where Jóhann K. Pétursson, Jóhann Svarfdælingur (1913–1984), was brought up. He was for a time the tallest man in the world, 234 cm og 163 kg.

Sakka, a farm drawing its name from the marshy land around the farm.

Skáldalækur, a small river and a farm of the same name.

Háls, a farm. Rev. Friðrik Friðriksson (1868–1961), the founder of WMCY in Reykjavík 1899, was born there. A memorial to him and a history sign near the farm.

806 **Tunguvegur,** 1,4 km.

Stóll, ("Seat") a finely formed mountain between valleys, its highest peak, **Kerling** ("Old woman") (1,212 m), giving a fine view.

Tungur, the place where the valleys Svarfaðardalur and Skíðadalur join. Though there are now no trees, *Svarfdæla saga* says the area was so wooded as to provide the material to build an ocean-going ship.

Melar, a farm, where in 1625, at Melaeyrar, the first witch-burning in Iceland took place. Fossils of coniferous trees and cones have been found at a height of 300-350 m in the mountain above.

82 **Ólafsfjarðarvegur,** p. 358 **805** **Svarfaðardalsvegur,** p. 387

315 816

örgárdalur, a 50 km long valley on the west of Eyjafjörður, with many rms near its mouth, enclosed by high mountains with permanent snow-ifts. The Hörgá river, though it has the glacial colour, is a good fishing-ver.

elamörk, the district on the east side of Hörgárdalur from the river ægisá to the sea. Above are high peaks, the highest being **Strýta** ,454 m) and **Kista** (1,447 m), near the **Vindheimajökull** glacier in ıssárdalur. Many farms.

15 Hörgárdalsvegur, 13,58 km.

16 Dagverðareyrarvegur, 10,4 km.

ɔrnhagi, a farm where Víga-Glúmur lies buried, according to the Sagas.

uðbrekka, an old manor farm, birthplace of Þorleifur, father of Björn ‹i ("the rich") (see Road 61, Vatnsfjörður).

ríhyrningur, there grows a very rare mushroom, *Calvatia gigantea*, that .n grow upto 1 m in diameter.

öðruvellir, one of most historical places in northern Iceland. Church ıd parsonage (see Road 82). See road 82, p. 357.

laðir, a farm, the home for many years of the author Ólöf Sigurðardóttir 857–1933). Steindór Steindórsson frá Hlöðum ("from Hlaðir") (1902–97), author of this book, was brought up there and uses the name of the ɾm.

‹ipalón, the outermost farm on the east side of the Hörgárdalur valley. ade famous in the early 19th century by Þorsteinn Daníelsson (1786–82), a builder who was also very enterprising in farming and fishing. ıe buildings he erected at Skipalón are still standing. Lónsstofa, a g built home dating from 1824, now plastered, in the keeping of e National Museum since 1986, and Smíðahús (Smithy), a tarred ɔoden building from 1843, in the keeping of the museum since 85.

ásir, a farm near the estuary of the river Hörgá, which was for any centuries the biggest port in northern Iceland. Silting in the ʼer eventually made it unusable and trade was then moved to Akureyri. rass-grown ruins of the old port.

agverðareyri, a farm where there was for a time herring processing and herring factory. The same family has farmed there since the end of the th century.

‹jaldarvík, once two farms now combined and made into an old peoe's home, founded in 1943 by Stefán Jónsson, owner of the farms. In 65 it was donated to the town of Akureyri, which now runs it. Nearby a relay station of the State Broadcasting Service.

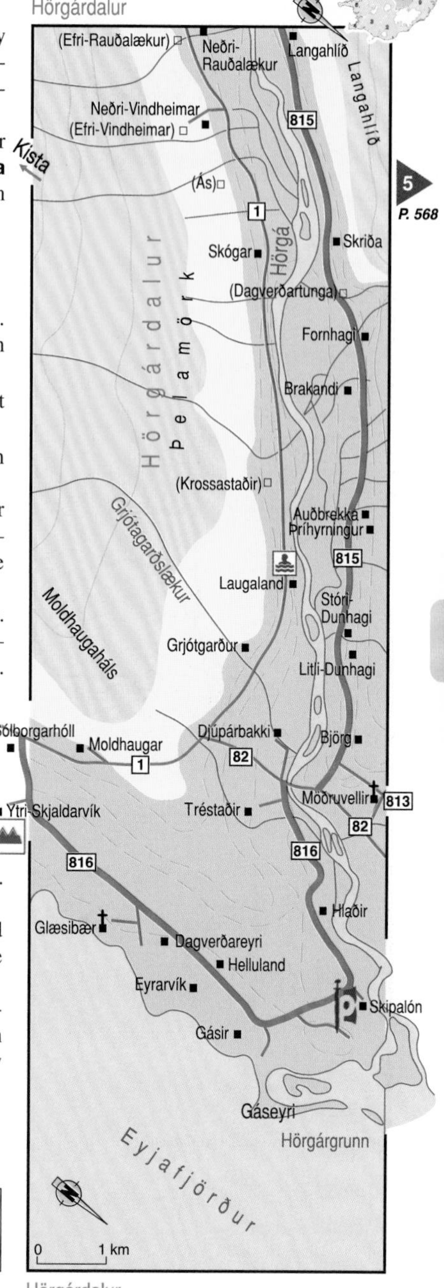

1 **Norðurlandsvegur,** p. 76

82 **Ólafsfjarðarvegur,** p. 357

313 **Möðruvallavegur,** p. 357

Hörgárdalur

5
P. 568

Hraundrangi
719
Staðarbakki
Flöguháls
(Flaga)
814
Myrká
Árhvammur
Auðnir
wc
1068
Myrkárbakki
Bakki
Búðarnes
Myrká
Slembimúli
Steinsstaðir
(Efstalandskot)
Hörgá
(Efstaland)
Baugasel
Gerði
Högg
(Miðland)
Staðartunguháls
Þúfnavellir
Barkárdalur
(Neðstaland)
Öxnadalsá
1
Barká
Bugur
814
Barká
Hörgárdalur
Staðartunga
Syðri-Bægisá
Öxnhóll
815
Ytri-Bægisá
Hallfríðarstaðir
855
Garðshorn
Neðri-Rauðalækur
Langahlíð
1
Lönguhlíðarfjall
(Efri-Vindheimar)
Neðri-Vindheimar
Selhnjúkur
815
Hörgá
Skógar
Skriða
(Dagverðartunga)
Ytri-Tunguá
Fornhagi
(Vaglir)
Brakandi
1
0 1 km

Hörgárdalur

Hjaltadalsheiði, (1,000 m) a moor which was formerly a much-travelle but dangerous route, with mountains (1,200-1,300 m) on both sides.

814 Staðarbakkavegur, 14,28 km.

Myrká, ("Dark river") a farm and a church until 1910 and parsonage till 1850. Connected with one of best known ghost stories of Icelandic folklore, *Djákninn á Myrká* ("The Deacon of Myrká"). It tells how the deacon at Myrká had invited the young woman Guðrún, from another farm, to the Christmas festivities at Myrká. Unfortunately, he drowned in the river Hörgá and was buried at Myrká the week before Christmas. Despite this, he came riding to her farm, where they had not heard of his death, put her behind him on the horse and set off for Myrká. As they rode the moon shone on the back of his head so Guðrún could see his white skull under his hat. She realised she was riding with a dead man, but gave no sign until they reached Myrká, where t deacon tried to drag her into his grave, which he had left open to go on th journey. She managed to get hold of the rope of the lych-gate bell and ri it, and he fell into the grave. The churchyard at Myrká is still well-mai tained, and there is still a bell in the lych-gate, as in the folk-tale.

The church at Grund.

Þúfnavellir, a farm, behind it **Barkárdalur** valley, over 7 km². The river Barká comes from under it which is what gives the Hörgá river its glacial colour. In front of the glacier are the undulating Húðarhólar (475 m).

Barkárjökull, a glacier at the end of the valley.

815 Hörgárdalsvegur, 13,58 km.

Melar, community centre.

Skriða, ("Landslide") an ancient manor farm west of the Hörgá river, fc merly called Langahlíð. The name was changed after it was buried by landslide in 1397, in which 16 people lost their lives, including the farme Hrafn Bótólfsson, local governor. Early in the 19th century it was the hon of Þorlákur Hallgrímsson (1754-1846) of Skriða. He was a pioneer in hor culture and forestry. Some of the trees he planted are still standing.

1 Norðurlandsvegur, p. 75

Samkomugerði-Akureyri 21 km

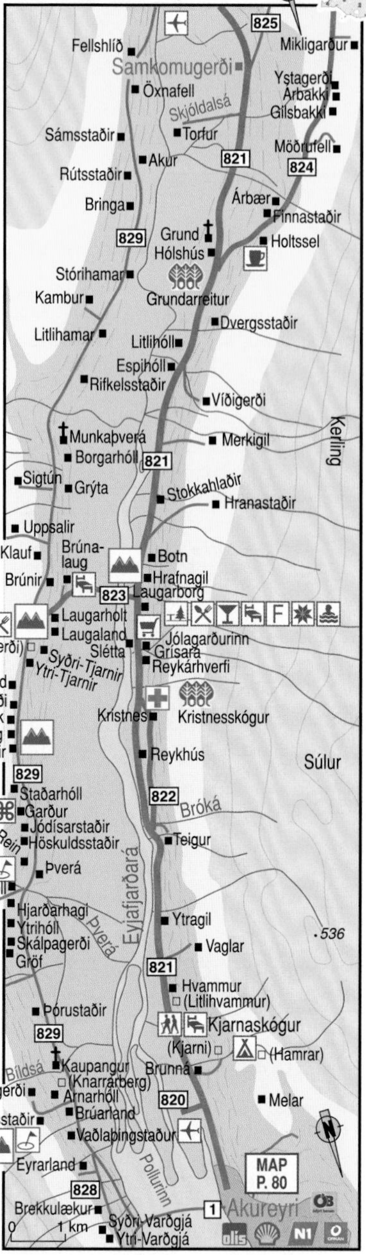

5 P. 568

24 **Finnastaðavegur,** 7 km.

öðrufell, a farm, long the site of a leprosy hospital. The Möðrufell ıvafield and the results of a landslide can be seen.

lofasteinar, an old place of execution in the Möðrufellshraun lavafield.

erling, (1,538 m) the highest mountain in the settled parts of northern eland. A fine view from the top.

rund, one of biggest and most historical manor farms in Eyjafjörður. he home of Sighvatur Sturluson and others of his family in the 13th century. Made famous by Grundar-Helga in 14th century, in connection with e Grundarbardagi ("Battle of Grund"). In the 16th century Þórunn, a aughter of the last Catholic bishop Jón Arason lived there, and the Grund hairs, one of which is now in the National Muesum, date from her time. rund was later the home of Magnús Sigurðsson (1846-1925), who made any improvements and built the present church, one of the finest in eland and now protected, in 1905. Historic forest from 1900, **rundarreitur**. The early origins of forestation. Danish aspen and Swiss ine are common. National Forest.

spihóll, a substantial farm, birthplace of historian Jón Espólín (1760–836). Often mentioned in *Víga-Glúms saga*.

otn, a summer camp for children with special needs.

eykárhverfi, (pop. 254) a small village with a school and a community entre. Some geothermal heat.

ólagarðurinn, (the Christmas Garden), the first of its kind in Iceland.

rafnagil, a manor farm now and in the past, a church till 1862, arsonage till 1919. Þorgils skarði was slain there in 1258. Among amous clergymen who lived there were Bishop Jón Arason and e Rev. Jónas Jónasson (1856-1918), writer and scholar. A school nd the Laugarborg community centre.

23 **Miðbraut,** 2,12 km

22 **Kristnesvegur,** 1,88 km.

ristnes, (pop. 56) land settled by Helgi magri ("the lean"). In 1947 tuberculosis sanatorium was opened there. It was the first large uilding in Iceland to be heated by water from hot springs. It is now geriatric and rehabilitation hospital.

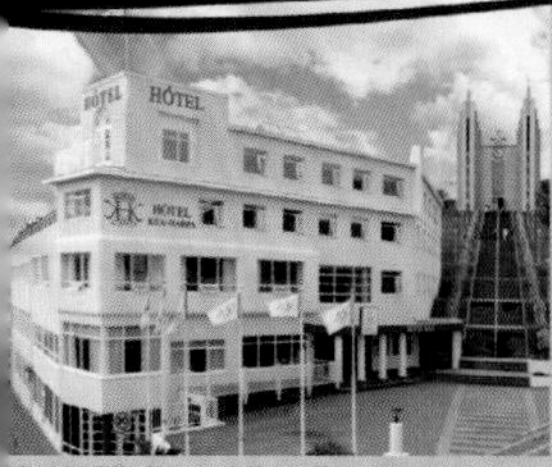

ristnesskógur, diverse possibilities for outdoor recreation. umerous tree species. National Forest.

jarni, formerly a substantial farm, now belonging to Akureyri. Forestry ation since 1946. Kjarnaskógur ("The Kjarni woods"), Akureyri's outdoor ecreation area, is on Kjarni land.

20 **Flugvallarvegur,** 0,19 km.

1 **Norðurlandsvegur,** p. 85 | 825 **Dalsvegur,** p. 392

828 **Veigastaðavegur,** p. 394 | 829 **Eyjafjarðarbr. eystri,** p. 394

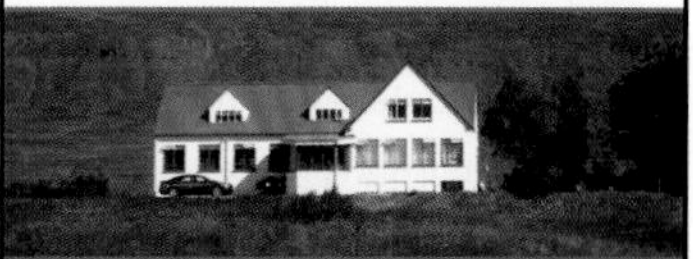

MAP P. 80

Akureyri-Samkomugerði 21 km

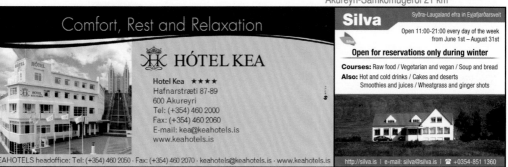

5 P. 568

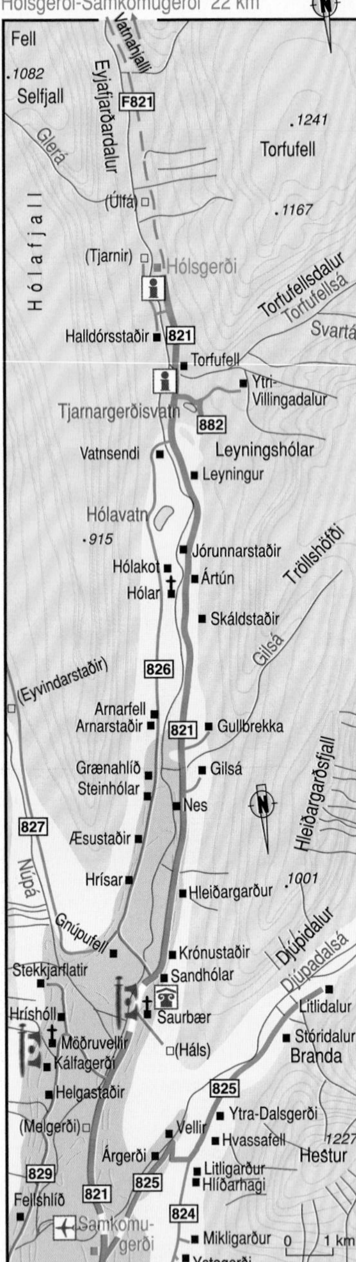

Vatnahjalli, a terrace on the mountain south of the river Hafrá an Ullarvötn (or Urðarvötn) lakes. The traditional route from Eyjafjörður southern Iceland, either via Kjölur or Stórisandur.

Eyjafjarðardalur, a valley. From there lies route F821 to Sprengisandur.

Úlfá, an abandoned farm. An avalanche fell there in 1925.

Tjarnir, now the innermost farm in Eyjafjörður.

Torfufellsdalur, a side-valley going off near Leyningshólar, the norther part being called Villingadalur from which the river **Torfufellsá** flow through a picturesque canyon.

882 Leyningshólavegur, 1,6 km.

Leyningshólar, a hilly area formed by landslide and glacial ridge Nearby are some nice native woods, the only ones worthy of the name i Eyjafjörður and under the protection of the Eyjafjörður district Forestr Association since 1938-39. This is the only place where native birch ha survived in the Eyjafjörður district. Some planting has also taken plac **Tjarnagerðisvatn**, a lake by Leyningshólar.There is a "sibyl's grave mound north of the lake.

Hleiðargarður, a farm for which one of the most notorious and destru tive ghosts in the area, Hleiðargarðsskotta, was named.

Saurbær, a church, a parsonage till 1932. Turf church with timber-fram structure, built in 1858. Iceland's largest turf church. In the keeping of th National Museum since 1961. There was a monastery at Saurbær aroun 1200-1217. The building Sólgarður, by the farmstead, contains the fasc nating trivia collection of Sverrir Hermannsson (1928-2008).

Melgerðismelar, site of an airfield built during World War II, for som years the main airfield in northern Iceland. Now only used for glider There is geological evidence that the Eyjafjörður fjord reached all the wa to Melgerðismelar at the end of the Ice Age.

825 Dalsvegur, 7,4 km.

Djúpidalur, ("Deep valley") narrow and with such high mountains th for nearly half the year the sun can not be seen from the farm **Stóridalu** formerly one of the manor farms of Eyjafjörður and site of one of thre important pagan temples in the district.

Hvassafell, a farm famous at end of 15th century because of th "Hvassafell Case", where an accusation of incest let to a long strugg between secular and clerical powers. The Rev. Jónas Jónasson's nov *Randíður í Hvassafelli* is based on these events.

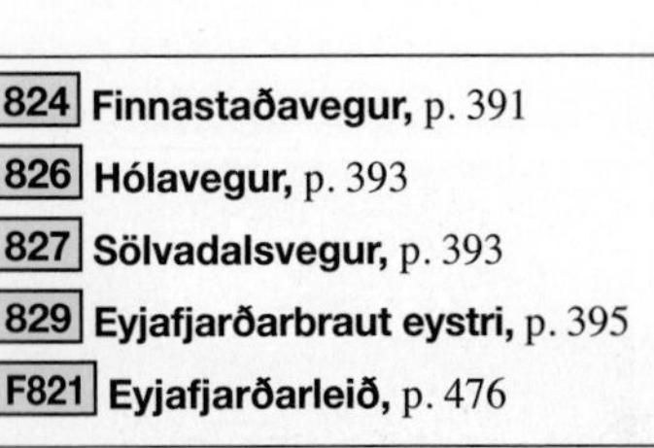
824 Finnastaðavegur, p. 391
826 Hólavegur, p. 393
827 Sölvadalsvegur, p. 393
829 Eyjafjarðarbraut eystri, p. 395
F821 Eyjafjarðarleið, p. 476

The turf church at Saurbær

27 **Sölvadalsvegur,** 11 km.

ıugafell, (892 m) and Laugafellshnjúkur (987 m) mountain peaks ›rtheast of Hofsjökull. Both are visible from far and wide. Between em is the river Hnjúkskvísl, and to the north the river Laugakvísl. On a dge leading northwest from Laugafell there are warm springs 40-50°C, ›m which flows a warm stream. Various kinds of grass flourish at near- Valllendisbrekkur and around the springs although the altitude is over 0 m. In 1948 the Akureyri Tourist Association built a tourist hut there. earby is a rock with a small trough, probably man-made, containing kewarm water. The story goes that Þórunn from Grund (see Road 821) ought her people to stay there in the 15th century during the Black eath, and made the pool.

ólafjall, (1,002 m) the mountain above Hólar, a long spur between yjafjörður and the Sölvadalur valley. A fine view from the top.

ölvadalur, a valley going southeast from Möðruvellir, ca. 25 km long. ›rmerly it had 9 farms but there are now only 3. The valley has often en hard hit by landslides and avalanches, most recently in June, 1995 hen there was a landslide in Hólsfjall, 1 km long and half a km wide. It ırtled over the river Núpsá, filling its 50 m deep gorge and continuing ıto the other bank. Its path lay from 50 to 150 m away from the farm ıildings at Þormóðsstaðir. The climb onto Hólafjall starts at Þormóðs- aðir.

núpufell, a farm across from Saurbær east of the Eyjafjarðará river. lentioned in old tales. Site of one of the main pagan temples in yjafjörður. Bishop Guðbrandur Þorláksson had a printing-press there 589-91.

26 **Hólavegur,** 12 km.

ólar, a farm with remains of a 19th century turf farmhouse. In the care of e National Museum since 1990. A wooden church built in 1853 by the ıme carpenter as built the turf church at Saurbær. Just south of Hólar is **ólavatn**, a fishing-lake and camp for Christian youth.

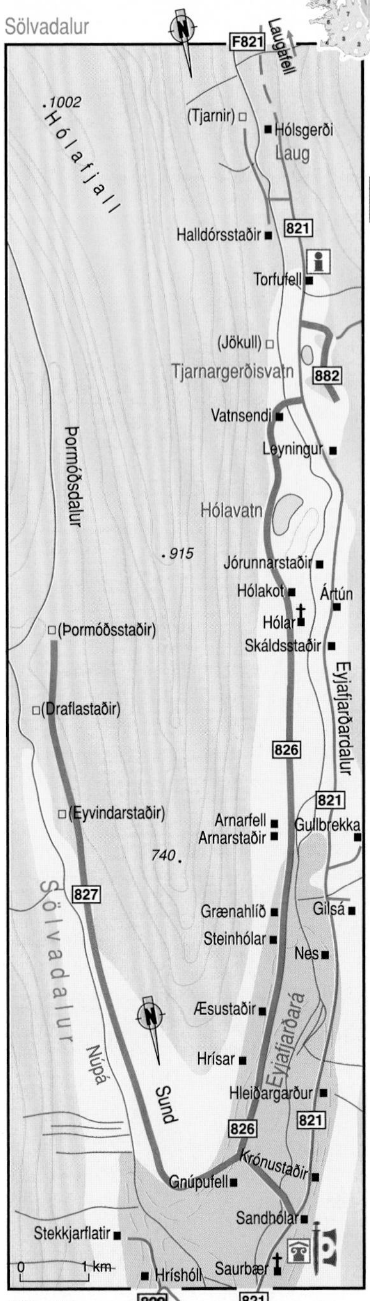

5 P. 568

821 **Eyjafjarðarbraut vestri,** p. 392 **F821** **Eyjafjarðarleið,** p. 466
882 **Leyningshólavegur,** p. 392

5 P. 568

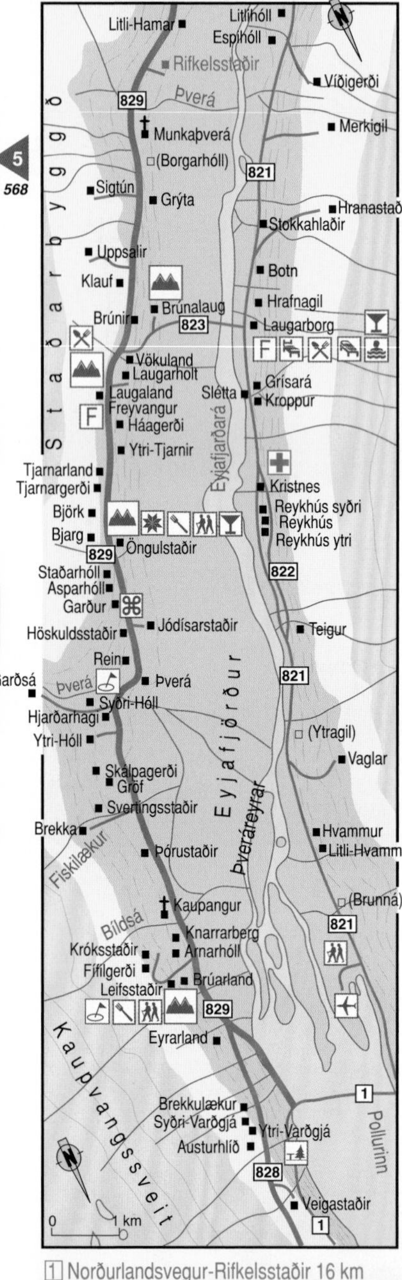

The church at Munkaþverár.

Munkaþverá, ("Þverá of the monks") has always been one of the most important substantial farms of the district. Church. The home, in Saga times, of Víga-Glúmur and a little later of Einar Eyjólfsson Þveræingur ("Of Þverá"), who probably built the first church there. According to *Ólafs saga helga* in *Heimskringla* Einar protested when his brother Guðmundur ríki ("the rich") of Möðruvellir suggested King Ólafur be given the island Grímsey, as he requested. Einar pointed out that the king could support a whole army o Grímsey from where he might then invade and conquer Iceland. His argu ments were accepted and the idea was dropped. A monastery founded i 1155 remained there till the Reformation in 1550, after whic Munkaþverá was long a residence of sheriffs and magistrates. Th Vitaðsgjafi field there never lay fallow. In the churchyard is th Sturlungareitur ("Plot of the Sturlungas"), probably the grave of Sighvatu Sturluson and his sons, who fell in battle at Örlygsstaðir in Skagafjörðu Memorial to the last Catholic bishop Jón Arason, who studied in the mon astery.

Grýta, a small farm near Munkaþverá, believed to be the birthplace c Jón Arason. Memorial garden to him.

Laugaland, a parsonage, school, the community centre Freyvangur. girls' school from 1876 to the end of the 19th century, a school of domes tic science 1937-75.

Þveráreyrar, sandspits north of the river Þverá. Where Eyjólfur ofsi an Hrafn Oddsson fought Þorgils skarða and Sturla Þórðarson in 1255 Eyjólfur was killed. **Staðarbyggð**, between the rivers.

Staðarbyggð, a settlement.

Garðsárgil, rocky gorge in the Þverá river below the farm Garðsá. Wha was formerly a small wood has now grown into a pretty grove.

Kaupangssveit, the district between the farm Kaupangur and the Þver river, off which goes Garðsárdalur.

Kaupangur, a church and substantial farm. Above it is the Bíldsárskar pass over which there was a riding-trail into the Fnjóskadalur valley.

Bíldsá, small tributary just north of Kaupangur. *Landnámabók* ("Th Book of Settlements") states that Helgi magri ("the lean") moored his shi by the river Bíldsá, the fjord having reached that far inland at the time.

828 Veigastaðavegur, 3,9 km.

Litla-Eyrarland, a farm near the site of the ancient Vaðlaþing assembly.

829 EYJAFJARÐARBRAUT EYSTRI

yjafjörður, the collective name for the whole district south of Akureyri, 60 km long valley narrowing towards its head, where it is sometimes alled Eyjafjörður Valley. Fertile and well cultivated, with many prosperus farms. High and imposing mountains, especially on the west. Eyjaarðará is a smooth-flowing, rather deep river but does not have much sh.

löðruvellir, a manor farm now and in the past. The home of Guðmundur ki ("the rich") Eyjólfsson in Saga times. Early in the 15th century the ome of Loftur ríki Guttormsson and later of his descendants. In the hurch there is a fine old altar-piece. In the churchyard there is the only emaining bell-gate of its kind, dating from around 1780. In the keeping f the National Museum since 1962.

löðruvallafjall, the mountain above Möðruvellir, high and steep, but airly grassy.

álfagerði, a farm, home of the 18th century Kálfagerði brothers, guilty f murder and other crimes.

lelgastaðir, a farm, the childhood home of the writer Páll J. Árdal 1857-1930), and birthplace of authoress Kristín Sigfúsdóttir (1876-953).

ellshlíð, a farm, birthplace of Hallgrímur Kristinsson (1876-1923), one f the leaders of the cooperative movement in Iceland.

)xnafell, from there came Margrét J. Thorlacius (1908–1989), wellnown in Iceland for clairvoyance and spiritual healing.

lútsstaðir, a farm, birthplace of the Rev. Helgi Hálfdánarson (1826-894), later the headmaster of the Theological college. He was a respectd writer, historian and hymn-writer. His son was Bishop Jón Helgason 1866-1942) who was born at Garðar on Álftanes near Reykjavík.

lifkelstaðir, a farm, site of one of the local pagan temples, Freyshof "Temple of Freyr"), remains of which are said still to be visible.

821 **Eyjafjarðarbraut vestri,** p. 392 **826** **Hólavegur,** p. 393
827 **Sölvadalsvegur,** p. 393

Möðruvellir-Rifkelsstaðir 13 km

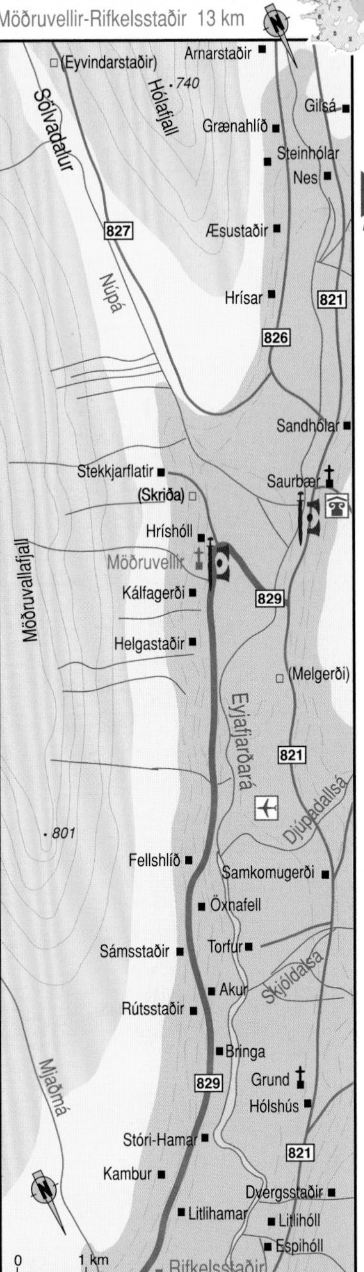

Rifkelsstaðir-Möðruvellir 13 km

5
P. 568

The church and bell-gate at Mörðuvellir

The bell-gate

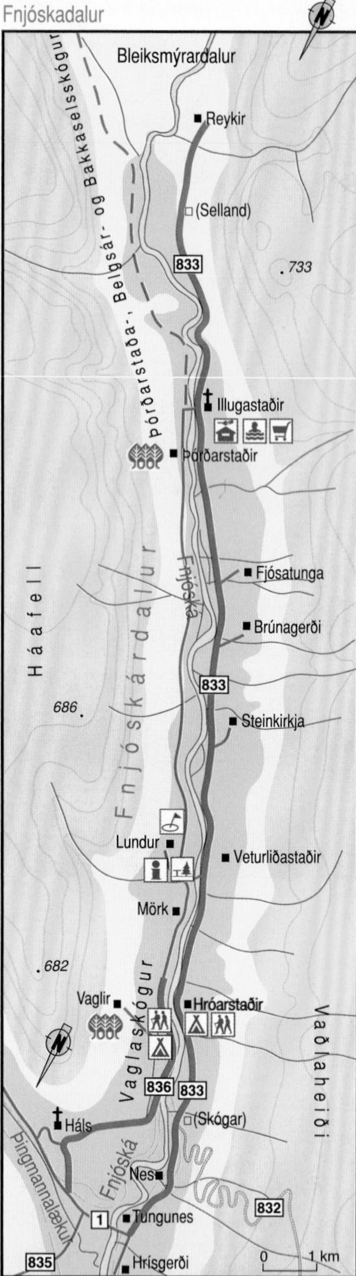

Fnjóskadalur

833 Illugastaðavegur, 20 km. **836 Vaglaskógarvegur,** 5,5 km

Bleiksmýrardalur, a grassy, fertile valley through which flows the river Fnjóská. The last horse-fight in Iceland took place there at Vindhólanes in 1623.

Reykir, a farm in Fnjóskadalur. Geothermal heat and cultivation. Two very rare plants, Ólafur's eyebright and Wall speedwell grow there.

Selland, an abandoned farm where the printer Sigurður O. Björnsson (1901-75) started growing coniferous and birch trees in 1946.

Illugastaðir, an abandoned manor farm and a church in which is an old pulpit. The northern Iceland trade unions have built a number of summer houses there.

Þórðarstaðir, a farm, site of one of the finest birchwoods in Iceland. Home of 19th century scholar and book-collector Jónatan Þorláksson (1825-1906), who took great care of the trees. The woods there, at nearby Belgsá river and Bakkasel and the areas of Lundarskógur and Vaglaskógur form the largest woods in northern Iceland and one of greatest in the whole country. Near Þórðarstaðir is a bridge over the Fnjóská river.

Þórðarstaðaskógur, (incl. **Belgsáskógar** and **Bakkaselsskógar**) birch forest with large trees, also older plantings of Norwegian spruce and black pine. Belgsá and Bakkasel are within Þórðarstaðarskógur forest. A 4WD is required. National Forest.

Lundur, a farm since the settlement, east of the Fnjóská river. Protected woods, in the care of the Forestry Service. Home of versifier Björn Jónsson (1768-1845). A 9 hole golf course.

In the Vaglaskógur woods.

Vaglaskógur, second-largest forest in the country and one of the most beautiful. Popular for outdoor recreation, marked hiking paths. Large and straight birch trees, up to 13 m. Tree collection.National Forest.

Skógar, despite the name there are hardly any trees there. Once a ferry point by Fnjóská.

832 Vaðlaheiðarvegur, 19 km, the old road over Vaðlaheiði, to Fnjóskadalur.

1 Norðurlandsvegur, p. 87 **835 Fnjóskadalsv. eystri,** p. 397

835 Fnjóskadalsvegur eystri, 22,4 km.

Dalsmynni, a deep pass, through which the Fnjóská has forced its way into Eyjafjörður. Steep, high mountains 800-1,000 m on both sides, very little flat land, danger of avalanches and landslides. Now no farms on the south side, but on the north are two prosperous farms, Skarð and Þverá. Some woods nearby.

In the Dalsmynni pass.

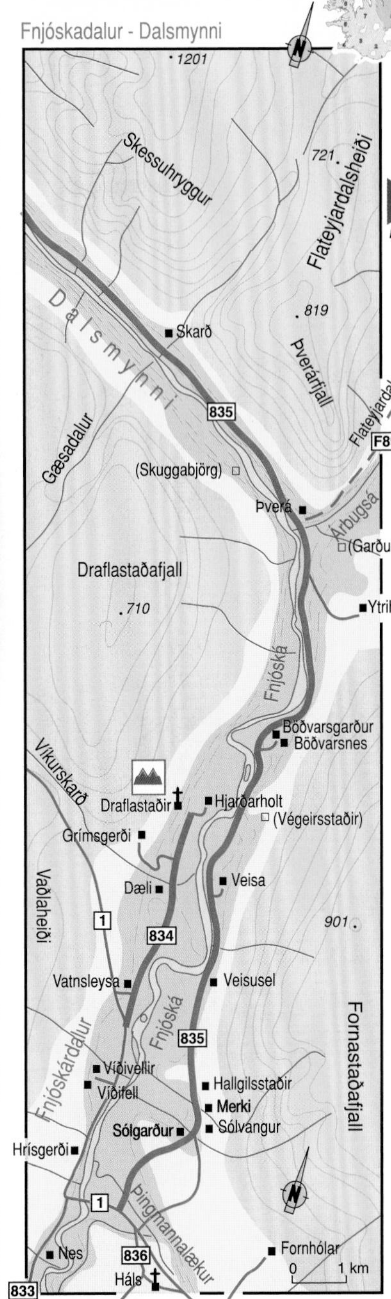

Flateyjardalsheiði, and Flateyjardalur, a continuation of Fnjóskadalur to the sea. The moors are above the valley, but there is good flat land near the sea, where it is grassy and there are fishing-rivers. Formerly there were several farms, the last one abandoned in 1954, but buildings still stand at Brettingsstaðir (once the site of a church) and Jökulsá. Fine scenery. The first part of the Saga of Finnbogi rammi took place in Flateyjardalur.

Garður, an abandoned farm. The first place in Iceland where wild gypsophilia was found.

Végeirsstaðir, an abandoned farm where the landowners planted various trees.

Hallgilsstaðir, a farm where Tryggvi Gunnarsson (1835-1917), later a member of parliament and bank director, started out as a farmer (see Road 83, Laufás).

834 Fnjóskadalsvegur vestri, 4,87 km.

Draflastaðir, a farm and a parsonage.

1 Norðurlandsvegur, p. 87	**833 Illugastaðavegur,** p. 396
836 Vaglaskógarvegur, p. 396	**F899 Flateyjardalsvegur,** p. 478

P. 569

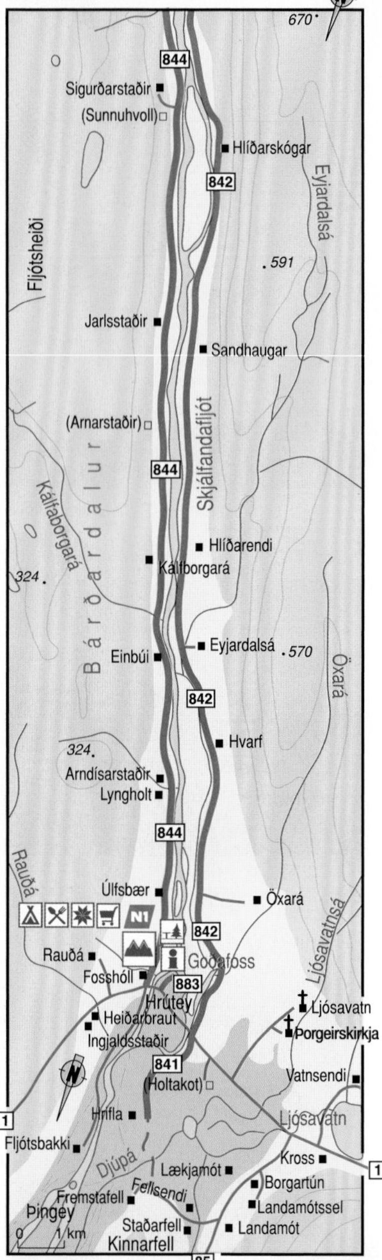

Bárðardalur

844 **Bárðardalsvegur eystri,** 22,6 km.

Bárðardalur, the valley opening between Ljósavatnsskarð pass and Goðafoss and reaching up onto the moors, one of the longest inhabited valleys in Iceland, but rather narrow and shallow. Basalt mountains up to 750 m on the west, Fljótsheiði moors, (528 m) on the east. The river Skjálfandafljót flows through the valley over the Bárðardalshraun lava field that probably came all the way from Trölladyngja in Ódáðahraun north of Vatnajökull more than 7,000 years ago. The valley is dry, mostly grassy, but with some soil erosion on the eastern side. Bushes on the western slopes. Few farms but good sheep pastures.

842 **Bárðardalsvegur vestri,** 37,66 km.

841 **Fremstafellsvegur,** 5,3 km.

Sandhaugar, a farm mentioned in *Grettis saga*. Some woods now in the care of the Forestry Service.

Eyjadalsá, a church and parsonage till 1858. According to *Grettis saga* this is where the housewife at Sandhaugar was going when Grettir the strong carried her across the river Eyjadalsá.

Öxará, a farm since the settlement. The home of Þorkell hákur, with whom Skarphéðinn Njálsson argued at Alþingi and whom Guðmundur ríki slew, as told in the *Ljósvetninga saga*.

Goðafoss, ("Falls of the gods") among the finest in the country, not very high but cut into two horseshoe-shaped falls. Not far above the falls the river Skjálfandafljót divides in two, forming the island **Hrútey**. According to the Sagas Þorgeir of Ljósavatn threw his statues of the gods into the falls when Iceland converted to Christianity in the year 1000, hence the name. Just below Goðafoss is a hole through the lava known as Hansensgat ("Hansen's hole") into which a chemist from Akureyri named Hansen fell but survived unhurt. *Undirheimaförin* ("Journey to the Underworld") by the poet Kristján Jónsson, called Fjallaskáld, commemorates the event.

Hrifla, a farm on the banks of Skjálfandafljót. The birthplace of Jónas Jónsson (1875-1968), one of the most influential politicians of this century, and a great social innovator. He founded the Progressive Party.

Djúpá, ("Deep river") flowing from the lake Ljósavatn into the Skjálfandafljót river. The waterfall Barnafoss at the confluence.

883 **Goðafossvegur,** 0,34 km.

1 **Norðurlandsvegur,** p. 88 **85** **Norðausturvegur,** p. 366

By Ljósavatn

843 Lundarbrekkuvegur, 2,89 km.

Svartárkot, the innermost farm on the east side of the Bárðardalur valley, 400 m above sea level, near the moors and at the edge of the Ódáðahraun lava field. It is on the lake **Svartárvatn** to which farmer Einar Friðriksson brought trout spawn from Lake Mývatn late in the 19th century, a unique event in those days. Good fishing in the lake. The river Svartá, in which is the waterfall **Ullarfoss**, flows out of the lake, is joined by Suðurá, and flows into Skjálfandafljót a little north of the farm Víðiker. Jeep track from Svartárkot to the Dyngjufjöll mountains.

The farm Svartárkot 1897. The river Svartá running from the lake. The mountains Sellandafjall and Bláfjall in the distance.

Víðiker, a farm at the edge of the moors east of the Bárðardalur valley. Birthplace of Hermann Jónasson (1858-1923), headmaster and member of parliament, known for his skill in interpreting dreams.

Lundarbrekka, church and farm east of the Skjálfandafljót river. Originally settled by Gnúpa-Bárður, the first settler in Bárðardalur, who later moved his whole household right across the central highlands to Fljótshverfi near Kirkjubæjarklaustur in the south. No doubt he was the first Icelander to take that route.

842 Bárðardalsvegur vestri, 37,6 km.

Mjóidalur, ("Narrow valley") a deserted valley off the Bárðardalur valley, where a farm of the same name was abandoned in 1894. That was the last home in Iceland of poet Stephan G. Stephansson, who emigrated to Canada (see Road 751).

Íshólsvatn, a trout lake in an uninhabited valley above the farm Mýri. Sprengisandsleið (Road F26) lies along its eastern shore.

Aldeyjarfoss, an impressive waterfall in the Skjálfandafljót river, in a unique setting of basalt columns and rock caves.

Mýri, now the innermost farm in the west of the Bárðardalur valley. Beginning of Sprengisandsleið (Road F26).

Stóruvellir, a substantial farm of old, one of oldest stone houses in rural Iceland, built of Icelandic stone. A rare species of wild corn grows there. Suspension bridge over the river Skjálfandafljót. Nearby community centre and boarding school. Above the farm is the mountain Vallafjall (670 m).

Kiðagil is located in the middle of Bárðardalur on the west side of Skjálfandafljót. It is named after Kiðagil at Sprengisandur which Grímur Thomsen wrote a poem about. Travellers used to rest there and graze their horses before or after crossing the Sprengisandur desert. In 1960 Kiðagil was donated by Páll H. Jónsson (1860-1955) so that a grammarschool could be built in the valley. Now there is a travel service all year. At Kiðagil is an exhibition, Outlaws at Ódáðahraun, myth or reality, that gives good insight to the life of icelandic outlaws. There is also an exhibition about the first journey on cars over Sprengisandur. Kiðagil is also a community centre.

Bárðardalur

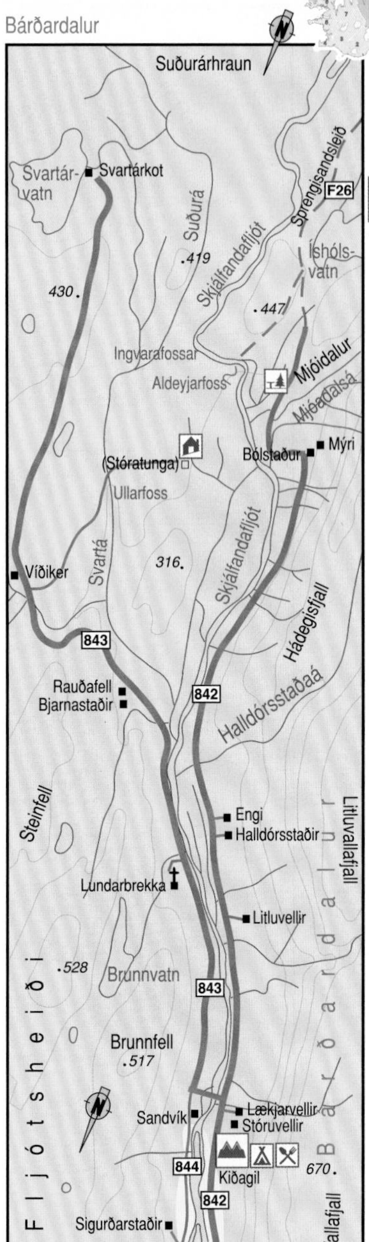

Bárðardalur

844 Bárðardalsvegur eystri, p. 398 **F26 Sprengisandsleið,** p. 432

6
P. 569

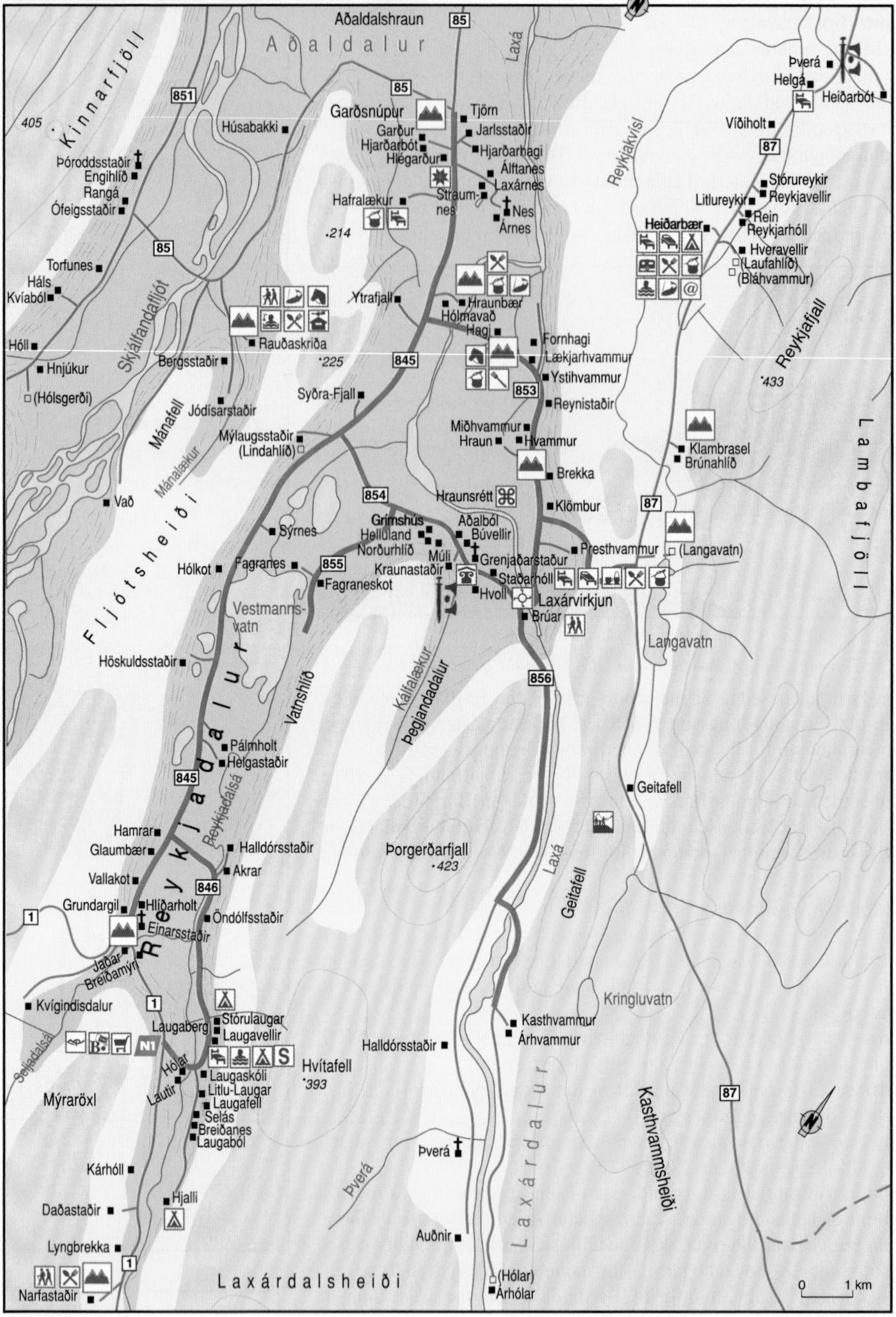

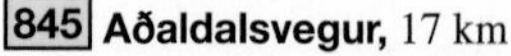

845 Aðaldalsvegur, 17 km.

Nes, a farm and church, parsonage till 1860. Good fishing. Among those serving there was the poet Rev. Einar Sigurðsson of Nes (1538-1626), often associated with Heydalir (S-Múl) in the eastern fjords.

Hólmavað, a farm, birthplace of poet, writer and translator Jakobína Johnson (1883-1977), who for years lived and wrote in Seattle, USA.

Ytra-Fjall, a farm, long the home of writer and scholar Indriði Þorkelsson (1869-1943).

Syðra-Fjall, a farm. Þorkell Jóhannesson (1895-1960), professor, historian and rector of the University of Iceland came from there.

Vestmannsvatn, a fishing-lake, 2.38 km^2, fed by the river Reykjadalsá, emptied by Eyvindarlækur, with a much-indented shore and many grassy islets. To the east is the summer camp of the Church Youth Association the Hólar diocese.

Grenjaðarstaður

atnshlíð, wooded slope to the east of Vestmannsvatn lake.
eykjadalur, a valley starting at Vestmannsvatn lake and eaching on to the moors. Shallow, with low moors on ach side: Fljótsheiði to the west, Laxárdals- and ývatnsheiði to the east. Grassy, several farms.
elgastaðir, a farm of the original settlement, an ancient nanor farm and church till 1872, parsonage till 1907.
inarsstaðir, a substantial farm and a church.

846 Austurhlíðarvegur, 5,8 km.

augar, (pop. 111) a small school and commerce commuity in the eastern part of the Þingeyjar region. See p. 89.
reiðamýri, a community centre and beside it a grove of ees planted some time before 1920.

853 Hvammavegur, 8 km.

agi II, from there came the artist Hringur Jóhannesson 1932–1996).
raunsrétt, a sheep fold, built in 1838.
vammar, several farms east of the river Laxá, north of ower-station. Southernmost is Presthvammur, where the hieftain Áskell of *Reykdæla saga* is thought to have lived.

854 Staðarbraut, 6,9 km.

úli, an old manor farm, church, and parsonage till 1880. lany well-known pastors have served there. In the 15th entury there was Sveinbjörn Þórðarson, known as Barnaveinbjörn ("Sveinbjörn of the children") who fathered 50 hildren to whom he admitted, but it was thought there vere more. Among his descendants were the bishops ón Arason and Guðbrandur Þorláksson. Among other vell-known incumbents were Þorleifur Skaftason (1663-748), and Benedikt Kristjánsson (1824–1903). In the 2th century Oddur Helgason, Stjörnu-Oddi (Star-Oddi), farmhand, lived at Múli. He was known for analysing he movement of the sun, moon and stars.
renjaðarstaður, an ancient manor farm, church and arsonage, considered one of best livings in Iceland.)ne of the large farm houses of the northern type, mostly uilt in the later half of the 19th century. Housed a post ffice in the later half of the 19th century, till around 1900. In the keeping of the National Museum since 1954. A folk museum since 1958.
Laxá, one of best known and most popular salmon rivers in the country. Comes from Lake Mývatn and has an average flow of 40 m^3/sec. Very beautiful with islets, pools and whirlpools. 340 islets with vegetation have been counted in the river, and there are twelve fords.
Laxárvirkjun, a hydro-electric station, near Brúar at the foot of Laxárgljúfur gorge, first built in 1939 but extended twice since. The gorge is deep and in places wild, with the waterfalls Brúarfossar (sometimes called Laxárfossar) at the lower end.

855 Fagranesvegur, 2,3 km.

856 Laxárdalsvegur, 13,76 km.

Laxárdalur, a shallow and fairly narrow valley, 26 km long from Brúar to Helluvað by Lake Mývatn. Laxá runs along it on a lava bed. Luxuriant vegetation.
Kringluvatn, a good fishing lake.
Þverá, a manor farm, mentioned in early history. A church of hewn stone, built 1878, with an altar-piece by Arngrímur Gíslason. The first cooperative in Iceland, Kaupfélag Þingeyinga, was founded at Þverá in 1882 in a turf farm house which is still standing, built in the latest half of the 19th century. In the keeping of the National Museum since 1968.
Auðnir, a farm, long the home of Benedikt Jónsson (1846-1939), prominent in social affairs of the district. His daughter, the writer Unnur Bjarklind, pen-name Hulda, (1881-1946), was born and brought up there.

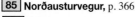

1 Norðurlandsvegur, p. 89 **85 Norðausturvegur,** p. 366
87 Kísilvegur, p. 386 **851 Út-Kinnarvegur,** p. 403

Björg - Þóroddsstaður 13 km

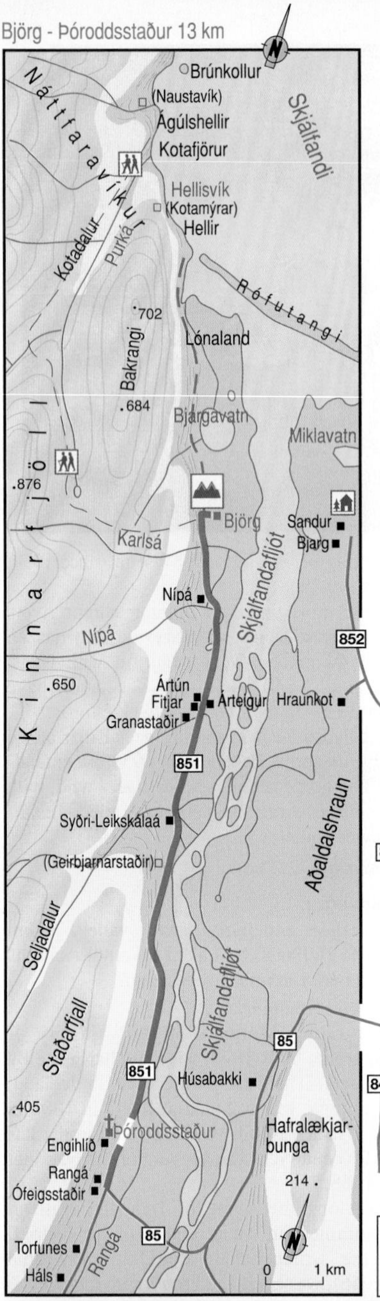

6 P. 569

Náttfaravíkur, bays beneath the Víknafjöll mountains. The Book o Settlements relates how, when Garðar Svavarsson, one of the firs Norsemen to visit Iceland, spent the winter in Húsavík, a boat broke free from his ship, and in it, a man called Náttfari, and a slave and a slave-woman, came ashore. Náttfari settled in Náttfaravíkur for a time later moving to Reykjadalur, from where he was driven when other settlers arrived.

Bakrangi, (702 m) a mountain on the edge of Kaldakinn.

Björg, the northernmost farm in Kaldakinn, with rights to meadows an perquisites. Road 851 ends there, but there is a passable road extending another 5 km to the sea, to a point about an hour's walk from Naustavík To walk north around Litlufjörubjarg and Hellisflös to Hellisvík it was necessary to wait for low tide and a calm sea. There, running south into the sheer cliff is a long cave known as Ágúlshellir or Þinghellir according to a folktale it was the home of a giant named Ágúll, and in the 17th century a magician, Arnór Ólafsson of Sandur in Aðaldalur is supposed to have had friendly dealings with him. It was not known exactly how long the cave was, as it was generally half full of gravel but it was believed that a tunnel deep inside it led into another far bigger cave where Ágúll kept his hoard of gold. Various changes have taken place on the western shore of the Skjálfandaflói bay since 1970 Where it used to be possible to walk on the beach, the sea began eroding the cliffs and many old structural remains on the shore have been washed into the sea. The popular explanation is that there is a connection between this and the volcanic activity in the Þingeyjarsýslur counties during the same years. In 1973 the sea washed all the loose material out of the cave, revealing its floor at a depth of 50 m, but no tunnel to the hoard of gold came to light, and, worse still, the walking route north to Víkur is now completely impassable. A 10 m long tunnel was made leading out of the cave; this solved the problem to begin with, but after a few years the sea advanced so far into the shore from the west that the path is completely impassable. It is to be hoped that this impressive route will be opened up once again, but those intending to travel this way should seek guidance at Björg.

Þóroddsstaður, a farm, church site and vicarage until 1916.

85 **Norðausturvegur,** p. 367
852 **Sandsvegur,** p. 367
845 **Aðaldalsvegur,** p. 400

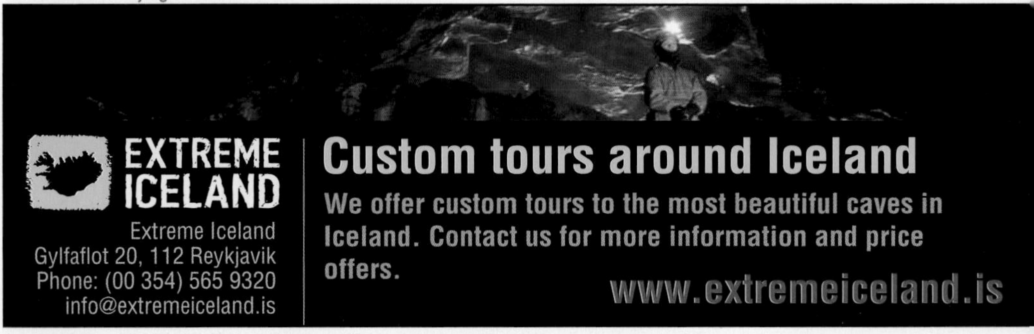

Þóroddsstaður- Björg 13 km

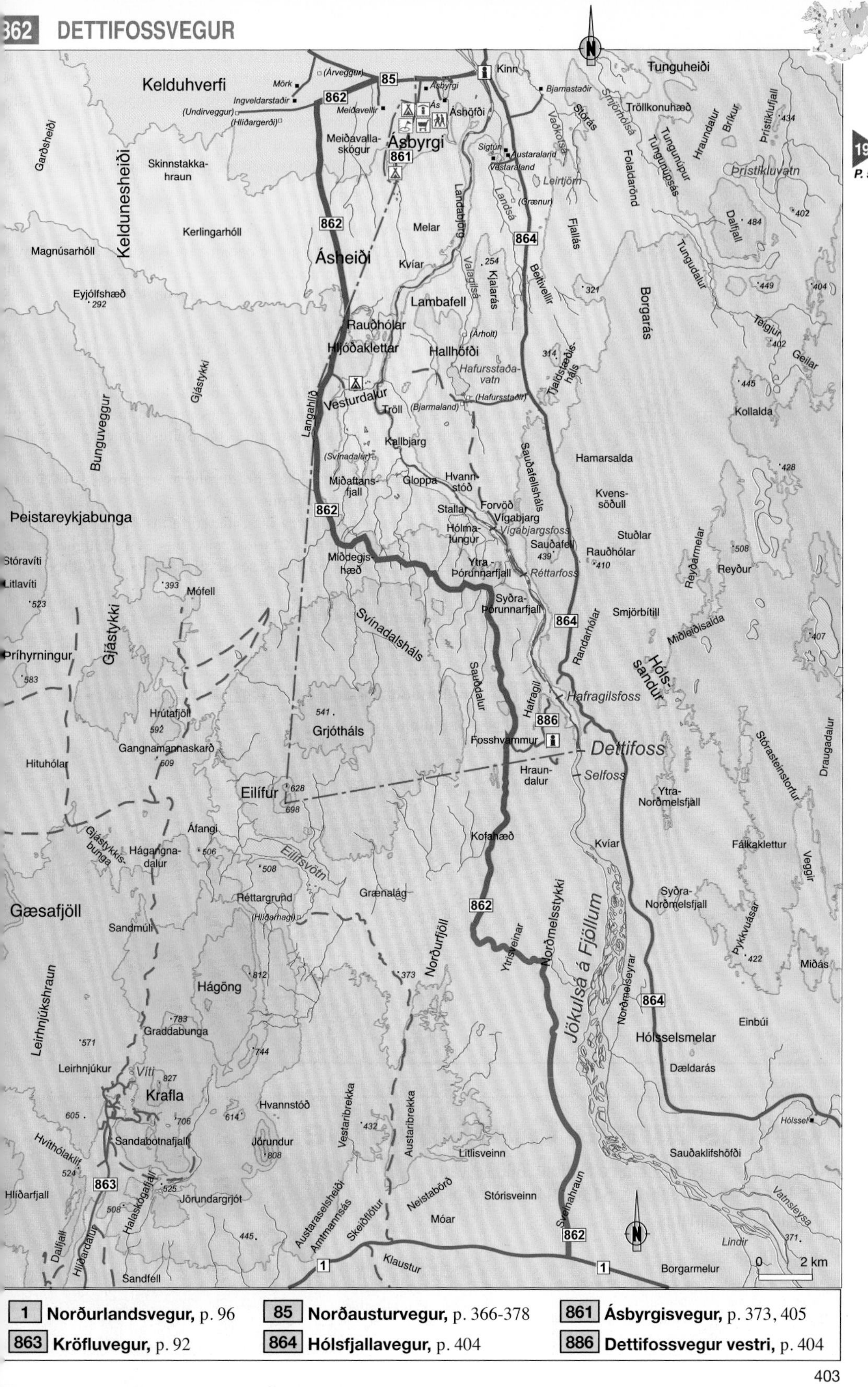
Kelduhverfi
Kelduneshei∂i
Ásbyrgi
Ásheiði
Dettifoss
Jökulsá á Fjöllum
Gjástykki
Krafla
Gæsafjöll
Hólssandur
Hólsselsmelar
Vesturdalur
Hljóðaklettar
Rauðhólar
Lambafell
Hallhöfði
Svínadalsháls
Grjótháls
Eilífur
Hágöng
Leirhnjúkur
Víti
Selfoss
Hafragilsfoss
Réttarfoss
Vígabjargsfoss
Tunguheiði
Kinn
Þeistareykjabunga
Borgarás
Nordurfjöll
Stórisveinn
Klaustur
Borgarmelur
0 2 km
19
P. 582

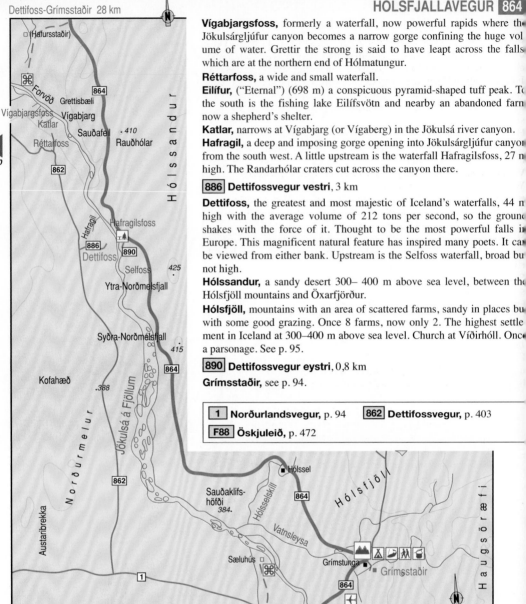

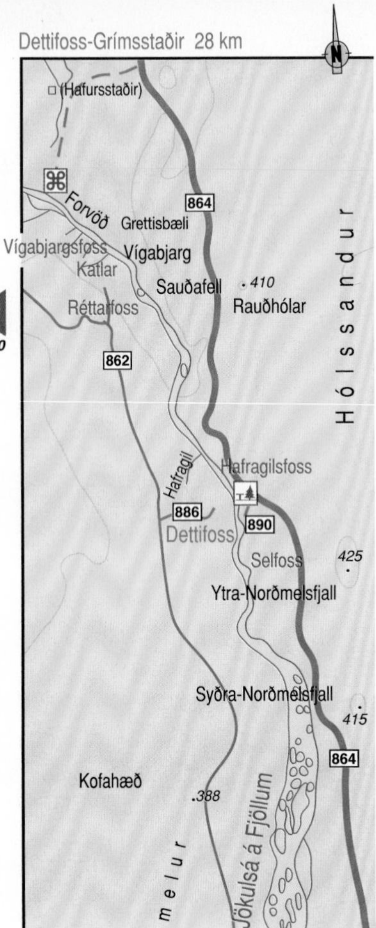

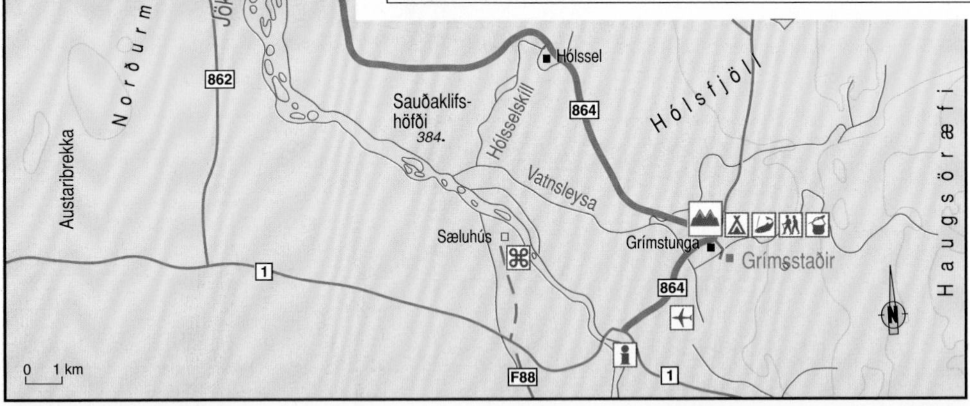

Dettifoss-Grímsstaðir 28 km

7 P. 570

Vígabjargsfoss, formerly a waterfall, now powerful rapids where th Jökulsárgljúfur canyon becomes a narrow gorge confining the huge vol ume of water. Grettir the strong is said to have leapt across the falls which are at the northern end of Hólmatungur.

Réttarfoss, a wide and small waterfall.

Eilífur, ("Eternal") (698 m) a conspicuous pyramid-shaped tuff peak. T the south is the fishing lake Eilífsvötn and nearby an abandoned farn now a shepherd's shelter.

Katlar, narrows at Vígabjarg (or Vígaberg) in the Jökulsá river canyon.

Hafragil, a deep and imposing gorge opening into Jökulsárgljúfur canyo from the south west. A little upstream is the waterfall Hafragilsfoss, 27 n high. The Randarhólar craters cut across the canyon there.

886 Dettifossvegur vestri, 3 km

Dettifoss, the greatest and most majestic of Iceland's waterfalls, 44 n high with the average volume of 212 tons per second, so the groun shakes with the force of it. Thought to be the most powerful falls i Europe. This magnificent natural feature has inspired many poets. It ca be viewed from either bank. Upstream is the Selfoss waterfall, broad bu not high.

Hólssandur, a sandy desert 300– 400 m above sea level, between th Hólsfjöll mountains and Öxarfjörður.

Hólsfjöll, mountains with an area of scattered farms, sandy in places bu with some good grazing. Once 8 farms, now only 2. The highest settle ment in Iceland at 300–400 m above sea level. Church at Víðirhóll. Onc a parsonage. See p. 95.

890 Dettifossvegur eystri, 0,8 km

Grímsstaðir, see p. 94.

1 Norðurlandsvegur, p. 94 **862 Dettifossvegur,** p. 403

F88 Öskjuleið, p. 472

Grímsstaðir-Dettifoss 28 km

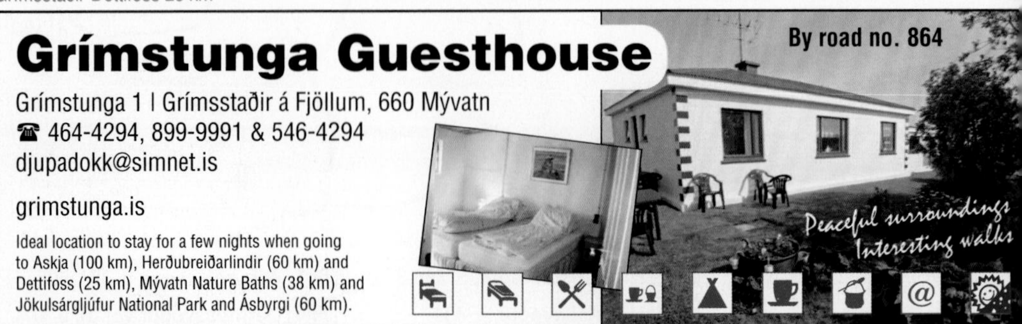

861 **Ásbyrgisvegur,** 3,5 km.

Ásheiði, a broad moor south and east of Ásbyrgi with a lot of low vegetation.

Jökulsárgljúfur, the largest river canyon in Iceland and most spectacular, about 25 km. The upper canyon, between the mountain Þórunnarfjall and Dettifoss, is up to 120 m deep. The land along the western bank up as far as Dettifoss is a National Park of over 120 km^2, established in 1973 and a part of Vatnajökull National Park since 2008. See p. 373.

Hljóðaklettar, ("Echo rocks") a group of rocks by the Jökulsá river that gets its name from strange echoes created by the numerous caves and uncommon rock formation.

Vesturdalur, a small valley south of Hljóðaklettar enclosed by cliffs. Wardens on site during the season.

Karl and **Kerling,** ("Old man" and "Old woman") two rocks in the Jökulsá river about 1 km south of Hljóðaklettar. Across the river is the cave Tröllahellir ("Giants' cave").

Hafursstaðir, an abandoned farm, once the uppermost in the Öxarfjörður district. There a difficult road leads to Forvöð and Skógarbjörg on the river across from Hólmatungur.

Svínadalur, an abandoned farm 250 m above sea level, interesting landscape, e.g. caves.

Hólmatungur, on the west side of the canyon. Many springs and tumbling brooks, woodland, rich in flowers, sheltered from most wind-directions, fine basalt columns. Unusual and beautiful scenery. Just to the south is Réttarfoss and the cliff Réttarbjarg.

Forvöð, opposite Hólmatungur in the Jökulsárgljúfur canyon. Pretty and unusual. A lone rock, Vígabjarg, with a path to **Grettisbæli** ("Grettir's hide-out"), another cave used by the outlaw Grettir the strong, at the top.

85 **Norðausturvegur,** p. 373	**862** **Dettifossvegur,** p. 373
886 **Dettifossvegur vestri** p. 404	**890** **Dettifossv. eystri** p. 404

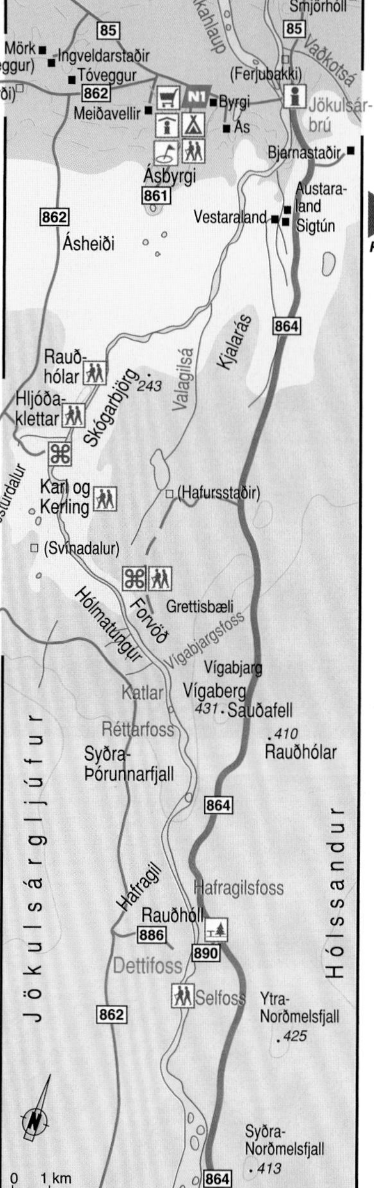

For furher information:

The landscape around Svínadalur is unique and beautiful. One particular aspect worth mention is the cave Gloppuhellir by Jökulsá river. East of Svínadalur the same river falls through a narrow canyon. The vertical cliffs are called Kallbjörg (Calling cliffs). The distance between them is about 80 m, and people used to stand on each side and call out to each other across the river. The poet Jón Magnússon wrote a series of a verses about the last inhabitant of Svínadalur, Páll Jónsson (1870-1956), whose wife died on 15 December 1915, having six days previously given birth to triplets. A blizzard had been raging for days when this ocurred. When the storm allayed the new-born were brought from their birthplace by sled, in a tub used for bathing sheep, to be taken in by households where there was only one child.

Dettifoss

Welcome to the Various Museums in Fjarðabyggð

■ The Icelandic Wartime Museum

Spítalakampur v/Hæðargerði | Reyðarfjörður | Tel: 470 9063 | peturs@fjardabyggd.is

Open 13:00 – 17:00 pm, 7 days a week, from June 1st – August 31st or by arrangement.

Travel back to the days of the 2nd World War and the military occupation of Reyðarfjörður.

■ The East Iceland Maritime Museum

Strandgata 39b | Eskifjörður | Tel: 470 9063 | peturs@fjardabyggd.is

Open 13:00 – 17:00 pm, 7 days a week, from June 1st – August 31st or by arrangement.

Objects and utensils relating to fishing and seafaring in general, local trade, industry, and medicine from times past.

■ Sören and Sigurborg's Stone Collection

Lambeyrarbraut 5 | Eskifjörður | Tel: 476 1177 | www.steinasafn.is

No formal opening hours, but feel free to drop by when Sigurborg is at home or make an appointment.

The museum prides itself of various Icelandic rock formations.

■ The Museum House in Norðfjörður

Egilsbraut 2 | Neskaupstaður | Tel: 470 9063 | peturs@fjardabyggd.is

Open 13:00 – 17:00 pm, 7 days a week, from June 1st – August 31st or by arrangement.

• Tryggvi Ólafsson Art collection

Tryggvi Ólafsson, born in 1940 at Norðfjörður in Fjarðabyggð, is one of Iceland´s best known contemporary artists.

• The Jósafat Hinriksson's Maritime Museum

Interesting objects relating to fishing, iron work, boat building and the old ways of the Icelandic people.

• The East Iceland Museum of Natural History

The best of Icelandic nature; Icelandic mammals, shellfish, birds, insects and a stone collection as well as specimens from the East Icelandic flora.

■ French fishermen in Iceland

Búðavegur 8 | Fáskrúðsfjörður | Tel: 475 1525 / 864 2728 | www.fransmenn.net

Open 10:00 – 17:00 pm, 7 days a week during summer.

The museum tells the story of the French fishermen and the era they spent in Fáskrúðsfjörður. Their heyday in Iceland was from the early nineteenth century until 1914.

■ Petra's Stone Collection

Fjarðarbraut 21 | Stöðvarfjörður | Tel: 475 8834 / 866 3668 | www.steinapetra.com

Open 9:00 – 18:00, 7 days a week.

A large and impressive private collection of stones and rock formations mainly from the mountains around Stöðvarfjörður, a souvenir shop and a unique garden.

ÍSLENSKA/SIA.IS/FJA 46211 05/09

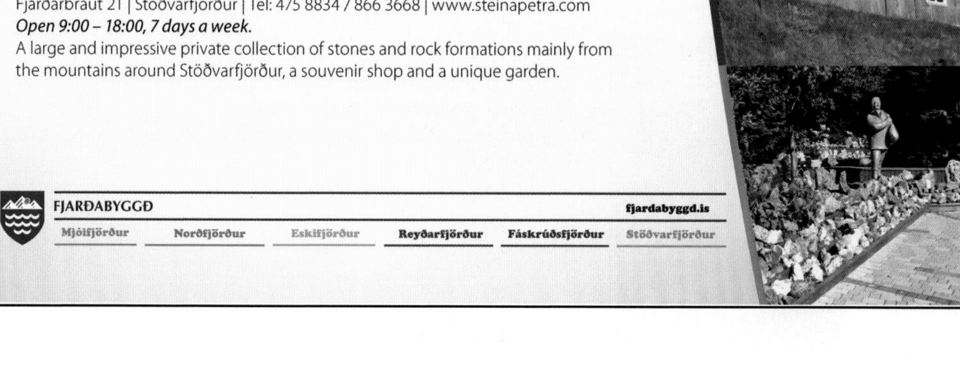

FJARÐABYGGÐ
fjardabyggd.is
Mjóifjörður
Norðfjörður
Eskifjörður
Reyðarfjörður
Fáskrúðsfjörður
Stöðvarfjörður

20
P. 583

Langanes

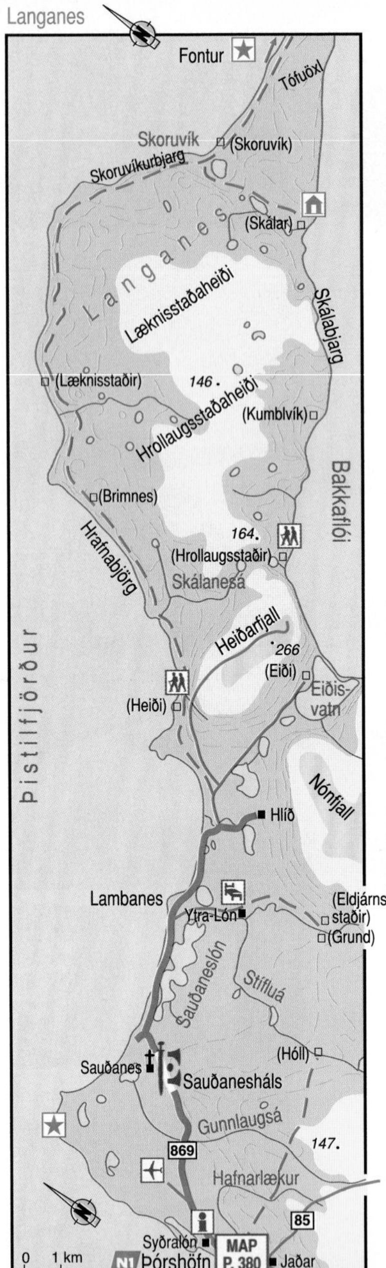

Langanes

Fontur, the outermost point of the Langanes peninsula, with high, sheer cliffs. Many ships had been wrecked nearby, the first lighthouse erected in 1910. Near the lighthouse is a rift in the cliffs, **Engelskagjá** ("The English gorge"), where shipwrecked English sailors are said to have managed to climb up. However, all but the captain died of exposure on way to the nearest farm. A cross marks the spot.

Skálar, a farm, abandoned since 1954. A fishing village grew up there early this century, having a population of 117 in 1924. Many Icelandic and Faroese fishermen went there in summer. Now deserted but remains visible. Churchyard. To the south is Skálabjarg (130 m), a bird-cliff.

Skoruvíkurbjarg, big bird-cliffs, one of the biggest Arctic tern breeding-grounds in Iceland. Easy access by jeep-track to the cliff edge, 33,23 km from Sauðanes. At **Skoruvík,** east of the cliffs is much driftwood.

Heiðarfjall, (266 m) a mountain where there was an American radar station in the second World War, 7,58 km from Sauðanes.

Eldjárnsstaðir, an abandoned farm, where a polar bear drifted ashore on an ice floe in 1918 and almost killed a man, but was itself killed.

Sauðanes.

Sauðanes, a church and parsonge. Rectory built of stone in 1879-81. This rectory, one of the few remaining stone houses in Iceland. The rocks used in its construction are from Brekknafjall and Prestlækjarbot. The doors and doorframes are made of solid redwood which had drifted ashore. In the keeping of the National Museum since 1989 and was formally opened after renovations in the summer of 2003. Fertile land, with an eider duck colony. In the summer time there is a information centre and café in the house.

Syðralón, a substantial farm on whose land is the village Þórshöfn.

Langanes, a large peninsula between Þistilfjörður and Bakkaflói, mountainous in the south but lower in the north but with high cliffs all around it. Breeding-place of gannet. Some flat land on the west, little on the east. Marshy in places. Has a raw, foggy climate. Little habitation, many farms having been abandoned in recent years.

Þórshöfn, (pop. 380) a village with fishing, herring-salting, trading. See road 85, p. 380.

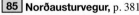

85 **Norðausturvegur,** p. 381

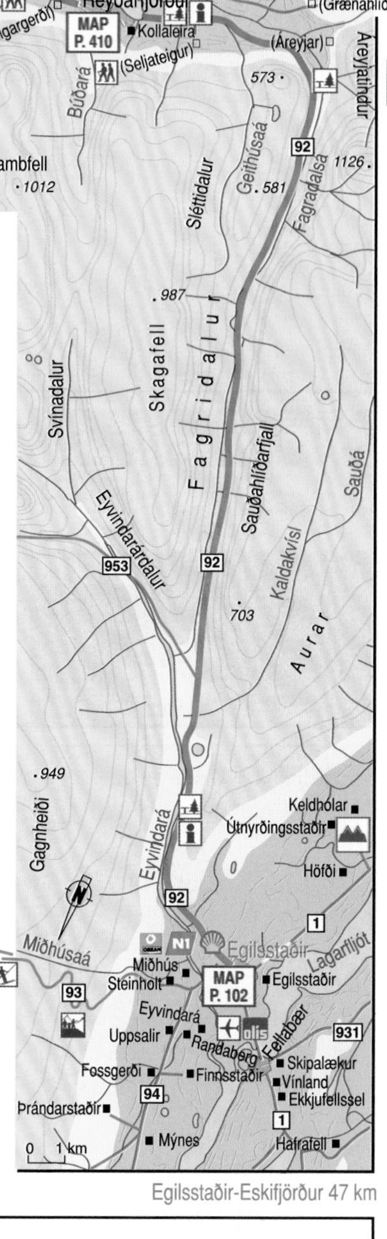

9 P. 572

Eskifjörður, (pop. 1,014) a town since 1978, part of Fjarðabyggð, on the east side of a short fjord of the same name going north out of Reyðarfjörður. Fishing and fish processing. Community centre Valhöll, folk museum, maritime museum and a outdoor swimming pool. Trading started there ca. 1787.

Hólmatindur, (985 m) one of most majestic mountains off Reyðarfjörður, with the spur Hólmaháls ridge reaching onto the Hólmanes peninsula. Hólmanes and part of the ridge have been a nature reserve since 1973. On the mountain side of the road is the location of a cairn said to be the burial ground of a prophetess who stated that she would be the guardian of Reyðarfjörður as long as her bones remained unbroken.

Hólmar, a parsonage until 1930, church till 1909. A very wealthy farm in its time. Disputes in the Hólmar parish in 1880 led to the majority of the parishioners establishing the first Icelandic free-church congregation, which flourished for 50 years.

Sómastaðir, a house built of uncut stone in 1875, with mortar made of glacial clay, an unusual building technique in Iceland. The turf farmhouse, onto which it was built is now long gone. In the keeping of the National Museum since 1989. Now Alcoa Fjarðaál has built a state of the art aluminium smelter near to Sómastaðir.

Hraun, there stands the aluminum smelter of Alcoa Fjarðaál. It was opened in 2007 and produces 350 thousand tons of aluminum a year.

Reyðarfjörður, (pop. 1,152) a town founded at the turn of last century because of herring fishing, is now part of Fjarðarbyggð. After a road was built through the Fagridalur valley in 1909 the village grew larger. Trading, administration and industry. Community centre Félagslundur. A whole golf course, recently made and a bit of a challange. A World War II Museum was opened in 1995 because there was an important military base located east of town. In January 1942 a platoon of British soldiers on winter exercises were caught in a very bad blizzard on the mountain above Eskifjörður. The family at Veturhús farm rescued and housed 48 of them but unfortunately another nine perished. Viw-dial.

Reyðarfjörður, 30 km long, the biggest of the Eastern fjords. Little flat land, but a short valley at the head.

Áreyjatindur, (971 m) an imposing mountain off Reyðarfjörður.

Fagridalur, a valley along which lies the main route from Egilsstaðir to Reyðarfjörður.

1 **Austurlandsvegur,** p. 101
93 **Seyðisfjarðarvegur,** p. 414
94 **Borgarfjarðarvegur,** p. 415
96 **Suðurfjarðavegur,** p. 420
931 **Upphéraðsvegur,** p. 426
953 **Mjóafjarðarvegur,** p. 429
954 **Helgustaðavegur,** p. 412

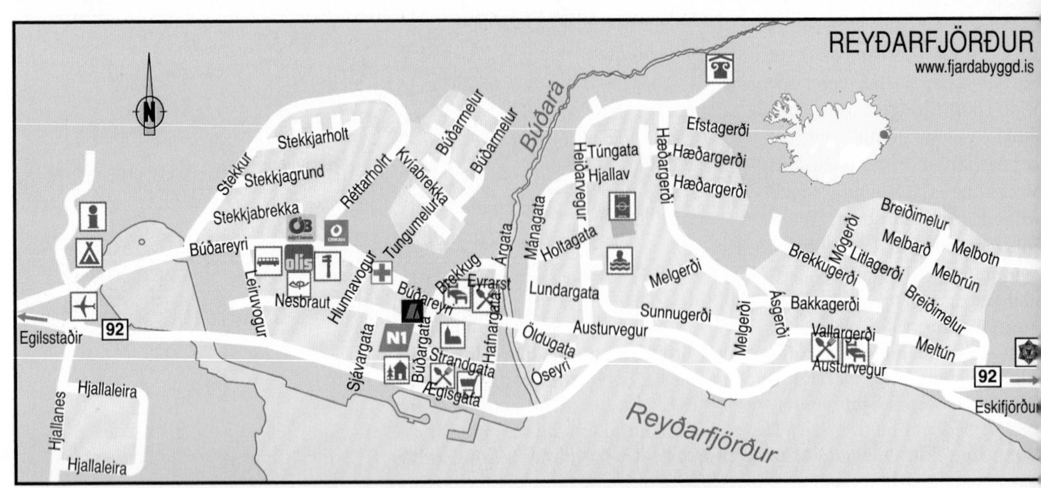
REYÐARFJÖRÐUR
www.fjardabyggd.is
Stekkjarholt
Stekkur
Stekkjagrund
Stekkjabrekka
Búðareyri
Réttarholt
Kvíabrekka
Búðarmelur
Búðarmelur
Búðará
Tungumelur
Leiruvogur
Nesbraut
Hlunnavogur
Brekkug
Búðareyri
Eyrarst
Árgata
Mánagata
Holtagata
Heiðarvegur
Túngata
Hjallav
Hæðargerði
Efstagerði
Hæðargerði
Hæðargerði
Lundargata
Melgerði
Sunnugerði
Austurvegur
Öldugata
Óseyri
Melgerði
Ásgerði
Bakkagerði
Brekkugerði
Mógerði
Litlagerði
Breiðimelur
Melbarð
Melbotn
Melbrún
Breiðimelur
Meltún
Vallargerði
Austurvegur
Sjávargata
Búðargata
Hafnargata
Strandgata
Ægisgata
Egilsstaðir
92
Hjallaleira
Hjallanes
Hjallaleira
Reyðarfjörður
92
Eskifjörður

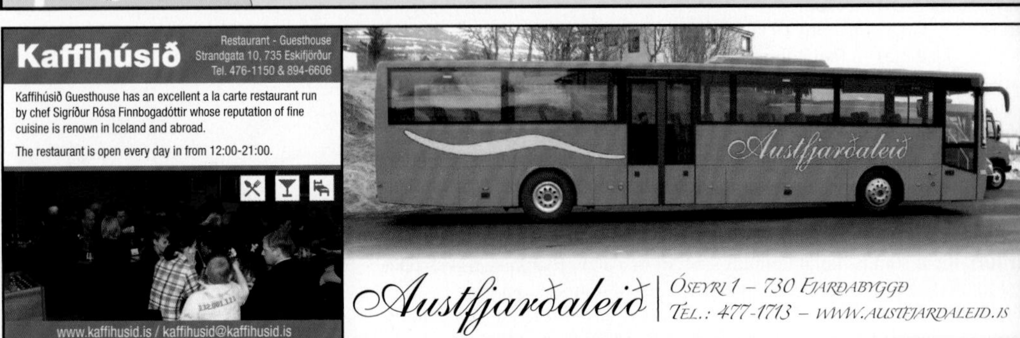
Kaffihúsið
Restaurant - Guesthouse
Strandgata 10, 735 Eskifjörður
Tel. 476-1150 & 894-6606
Kaffihúsið Guesthouse has an excellent a la carte restaurant run by chef Sigríður Rósa Finnbogadóttir whose reputation of fine cuisine is renown in Iceland and abroad.
The restaurant is open every day in from 12:00-21:00.
www.kaffihusid.is / kaffihusid@kaffihusid.is
Austfjarðaleið
Austfjarðaleið
Óseyri 1 – 730 Fjarðabyggð
Tel.: 477-1713 – www.austfjardaleid.is

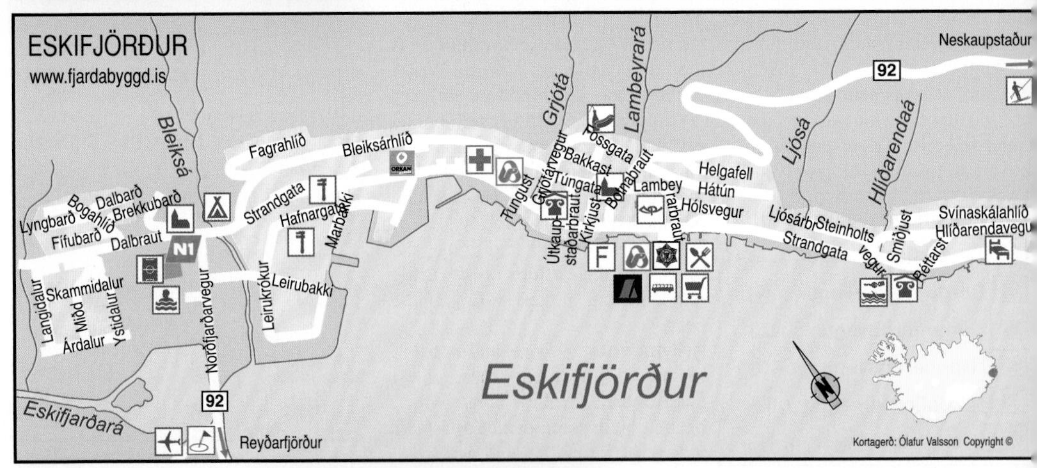
ESKIFJÖRÐUR
www.fjardabyggd.is
Neskaupstaður
92
Bleiksá
Fagrahlíð
Bleiksárhlíð
Grjótá
Lambeyrará
Ljósá
Hlíðarendaá
Lyngbarð
Bogahlíð
Dalbarð
Brekkubarð
Fífubarð
Dalbraut
Strandgata
Hafnargata
Marbakki
Tungust
Grjótárvegur
Bakkast
Pósgata
Túngata
Lambey
Helgafell
Hátún
Hólsvegur
Útkaupstaðarbraut
Kirkjust
Ljósárbr
Steinholtsvegur
Strandgata
Smiðjust
Réttarst
Svínaskálahlíð
Hlíðarendavegur
Skammidalur
Langidalur
Miðd
Ystidalur
Árdalur
Norðfjarðarvegur
Leirukrókur
Leirubakki
Eskifjörður
92
Eskifjarðará
Reyðarfjörður
Kortagerð: Ólafur Valsson Copyright ©

Mjóeyri Travel Service
Strandgata 120
735 Eskifjörður
Tel.: 4771247
www.mjoeyri.is
mjoeyri@mjoeyri.is

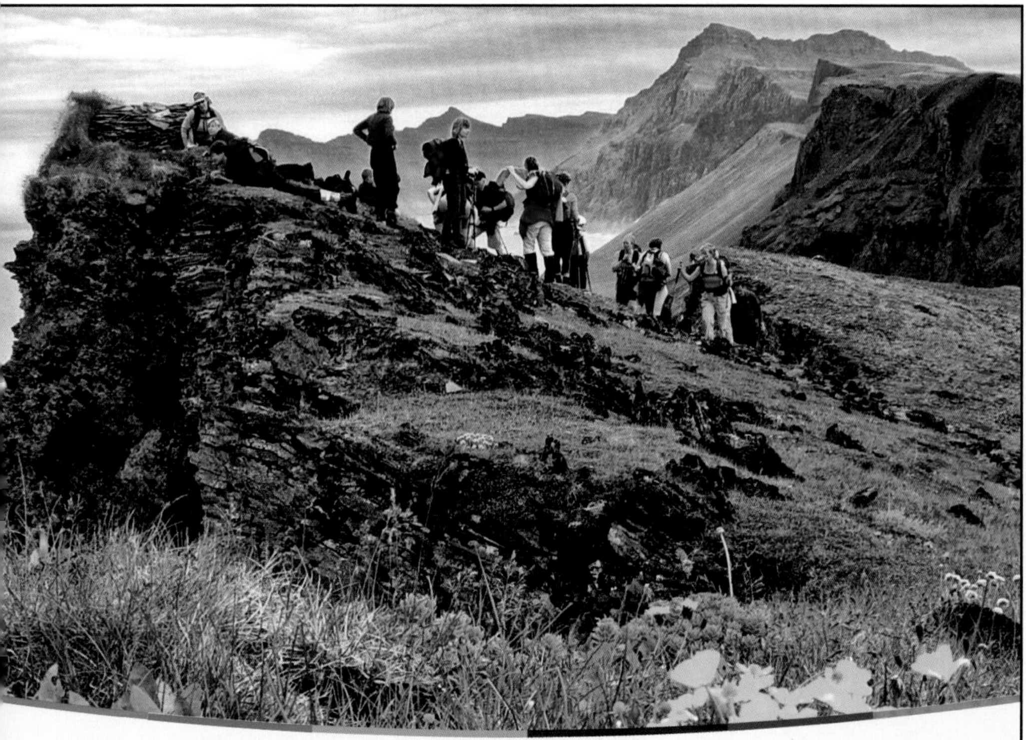

9
P. 572

Neskaupstaður, (pop. 1,466) the 2nd biggest town in eastern Iceland, built on the land of the farm Nes, originally settled by Egill rauði ("the red"). Fishing and allied industries, trading, and some farming. Authorized trading place since 1929, is now part of Fjarðabyggð. Hospital, Trades College, the community centre Egilsbúð and a nice newly renovated outdoor swimming pool. In a distinguished building from 1924, the Museum House, Safnahúsið, houses three separate art, folk and natural science museums, all under the same roof and beautifully situated in the town center next to the port area. Outside the town is a public park, a nature reserve. On December 20th, 1974, an avalanche fell on Neskaupstaður, killing 12.

Skorrastaður, a parsonage until 1894, church till 1896, when the church building was blown down. Now a farm with a ceramic gallery.

Norðfjörður, a short fjord, see p. 495.

Oddsskarð, (632 m) a pass over and through the mountain between Eskifjörður and Norðfjörður, with a 626 m long tunnel. There is a skiing and wintersport centre at Odds skarð.

954 Helgustaðavegur, 11,4 km.

Stóra-Breiðuvík, the trading centre of Reyðarfjörður until the end of the Danish trade monopoly in 1787. Few remains. Possible to drive from there via Víkurheiði moor to Vöðlavík (Road 958).

Helgustaðir, an Iceland spar mine, one of the best in the world, in use from the 17th century until the 20th, remains still visible. The mine and its surroundings are a protected natural feature.

It is against the law to disturb or remove any of the stones.

Svínaskálastekkur, an abandoned farm. Birthplace of Dr. Richard Beck professor, who emigrated to Canada and was a leader among Icelanders there. There was a whaling station there around 1900.

Mjóeyri, a place of the last execution in east Iceland, on September 30th 1786. The burial site can still be seen. Now Mjóeyri is a site of plenty for a tourist with guided tours, boat trips, see angling and accommodation. A beautiful shore line ideal for a pit stop.

958 Vöðlavíkurvegur, p. 494

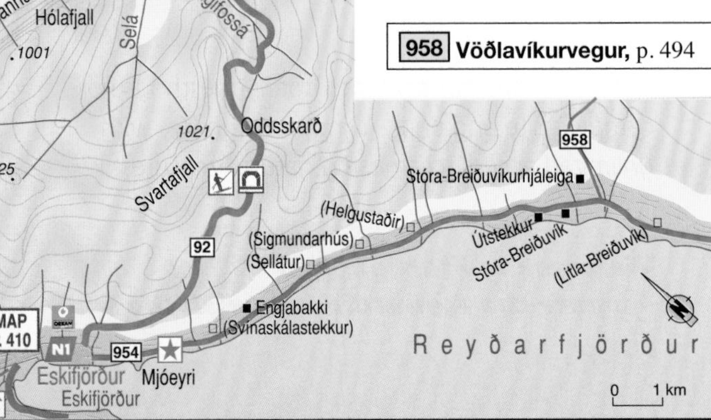

Eskifjörður-Neskaupstaður 25 km

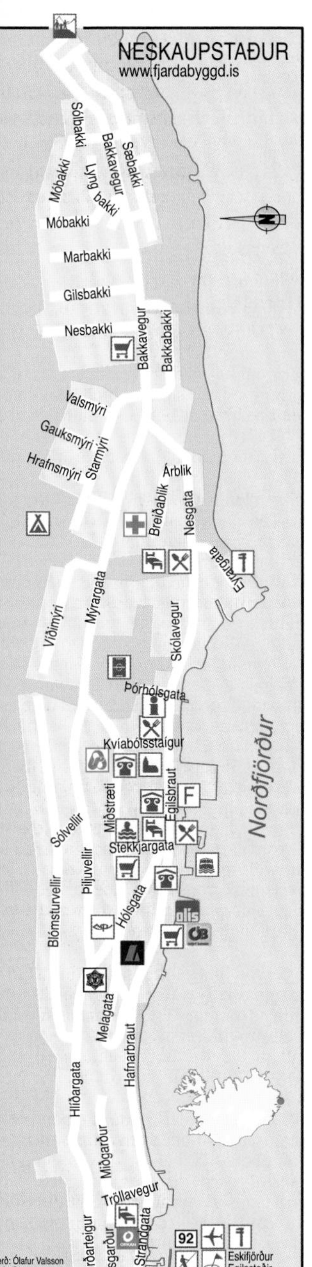

Neskaupstaður.

9
P. 572

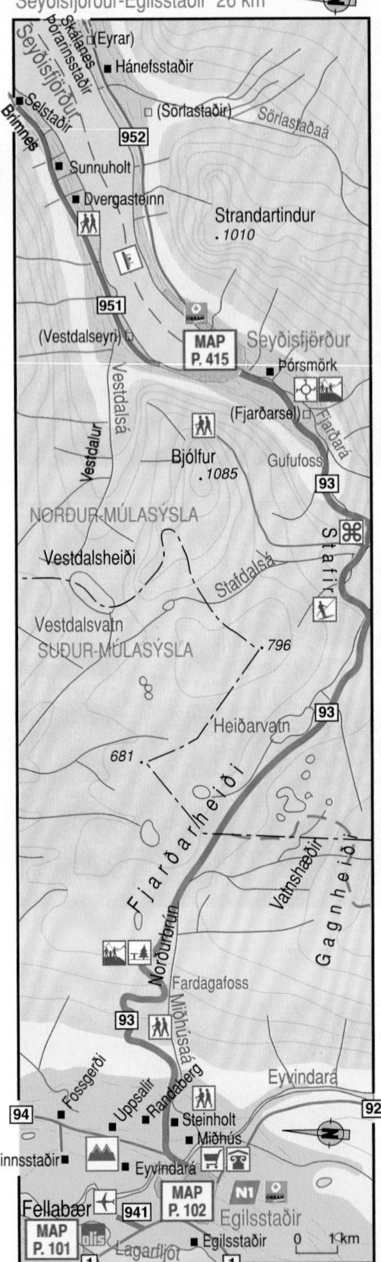

Skálanes, a nature and heritage centre, on the south coast of Seyðisfjörður. In summer the centre provides services to tourists. Skálanesbjarg cliffs are home to thousands of sea birds. 47 different species go through there every year and 40 species nest there annually. At Skálanes there is a major eider duck nesting colony. The Skálanesbjarg cliff is also unique in a geological sense as it contains plutonic rock that has altered the surrounding stone resulting in a veritable flora of zeolite. The most common mammals in the area are reindeer, fox, mink and field mice. Beneath the cliffs are abundant fishing grounds and different whale species can routinely be observed from the edge of the cliff. www.skalanes.com

Þórarinsstaðir, archaeological excavations in recent years have revealed remains of a stave church, dating from 940 -1000.

Hánefsstaðir, trading started there in around 1800. A dairy farm.

952 Hánefsstaðavegur, 7,51 km. **951 Vestdalseyrarvegur,** 8 km.

Brimnes, a historical fishing station and farm on the north shore of the fjord. Barely passable road. Lighthouse.

Dvergasteinn, ("Dwarfs' stone") a farm and a church until the turn of the century, parsonage till 1940. There is a rock by the shore which resembles a house and is called Dvergasteinn. Legend has it that both the church and the rock were once on the south side of Seyðisfjörður. Then the church was moved north to Dvergasteinn and shortly thereafter the rock came sailing across the fjord to the church.

Seyðisfjörður, (pop. 658) municipality by a long and narrow fiord of the same name, surrounded by rugged mountains. The municipality is divided into two parts, called Búðareyri and Alda. Commerce began there in 1843. Main industries now are fishing industry, iron industry and tourism. Posts of the police commissioner, pastor and doctor are there as well as a church, a hospital, an indoor swimming pool and steam bath, the community meeting hall, Herðubreið, the county library and a technology museum. In the vicinity of the technology museum one can visit the oldest mechanics smithy in Iceland in addition to the oldest telegraphy station in the country. The first town in Iceland to have electric street lamps installed. Art exhibitions and numerous events are held the whole year round in Skaftafell, which is the visual art centre for East of Iceland. There are a number of festivals in town during the summer months. Art is flourishing in Seyðisfjörður. The international ferry, Norræna, sails between Iceland and the European continent the whole year and stops at Seyðisfjörður. As a result there is good tourist service in Seyðisfjörður. For exemple you can go sea angling, sightseeing, bird watching, kayaking, diving, paragliding, on a jeep safari or mountain biking. If you want to go hiking there are many marked hiking trails. In the year 1906, a sea telephone cable was laid to Seyðisfjörður from Europe, thus enabling Iceland to commence telecommunication with foreign countries. After the turn of the 19th century Seyðisfjörður was a very prosperous town, due to a good harbor. Otto Wathne (1834-1898), a Norwegian entrepreneur, lived there and a monument was later made in his honor and for Ingi T. Lárusson (1892-1946), the composer. www.seydisfjordur.is

Bjólfur, (1,085 m) a mountain named after the first settler in this fiord. On the highest peak of the mountain there was supposedly a temple in ancient times. Snow and mud avalanches have often fallen from the steep mountainsides that surround the town, sometimes with catastrophic consequences. Now, avalanche protection walls have been built in the Bjólfur mountainside and a snow avalanche inspector is posted in Seyðisfjörður all year round. It is possible to drive up there by a summer road, spectacular view.

Vestdalur, in the pass between Seyðisfjörður and Fljótdalshérað, not far from Vestdalsvatn lake, where archaeologists have uncovered the remains of a woman from around 940, together with about 400 beads. This is thought to be one of Iceland's most remarkable finds of recent decades. Vestdalseyri and the valley of Vestdalur are on the Nature Conservation Register, due to their cultural features and diverse vegetation. **Vestdalseyri,** a trading and fishing post. The village that was built up in the late 19th century was finally abandoned in 1963.

Fjarðará, a river nearby worth visiting. It has 25 waterfalls, Gufufoss being the largest. It was harnessed in 1913.

Fjarðarselsvirkjun is the country's oldest power plant (1913) still being used and the first alternating current power plant. Furthermore, the first high voltage line was laid to Seyðisfjörður from there. Next to the old power plant stands the first high voltage tower in Iceland. This old power plant has provided Seyðisfjörður with light and warmth for almost a century. www.fjardarsel.is

Stafir, the name given to two lines of cliffs, a lower and an upper line (Neðri-Stafur and Efri-Stafur), on the way up to Fjarðarheiði pass. A monument just on top of Neðri-Stafur to Þorbjörn Arnoddsson, a pioneer in winter transportation from Seyðisfjörður. Beside this monument, the river Fjarðará has carved pretty potholes in the basalt rock. The entrance to the skiing area shared by Seyðisfjörður and Fljótsdalshérað is just below Efri-Stafur.

Fjarðarheiði, (620 m) a moor crossed by a paved road steep at both ends. Great views, view-dial on the northern edge. Possible to drive to Gagnheiði moor, site of a TV relay station and magnificent views.

Miðhúsaá, a river that runs from the Fjarðarheiði moor. In the river are some very beautifull waterfalls like Fardagafoss, behind it is a small cave with a guest book. It is said that a troll used to live there with a chest full of gold.

1 Austurlandsvegur, p. 101
92 Norðfjarðarvegur, p. 409
94 Borgarfjarðarvegur, p. 41

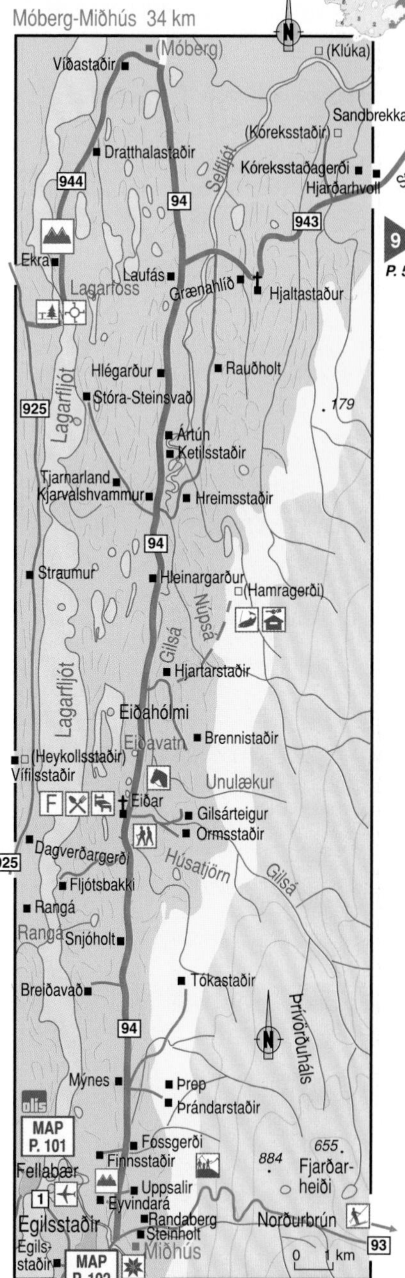

yrfjöll, ("Doorway mountains") (1,136 m) the most impressive of the ountains in the Hérað district, split by the deep, rocky pass called Dyr 'Doorway").

tórurð, west of Dyrfjöll, one of Icelands pearls of nature. Marked walk-g routes.

44 Lagarfossvegur, 10 km.

agarfoss, see p. 425.

943 Hjaltastaðarvegur, 10 km.

jaltastaður, a church and a parsonage till 1919. Community centre, jaltalundur. It was there that the Hjaltastaður Devil, a well-known Ice-ndic ghost, was active in the late 17th century. He would speak to people sultingly for hours on end, challenge them to wrestling matches, bang oors, use bad language and shriek most dreadfully. The community centre jaltalundur is not far from Hjaltastaðir.

iðar, an historically important manor farm. Church, parsonage, swim-ing pool, sport statium, and facilities for large gatherings. Home of elgi Ásbjarnarson of *Fljótsdæla saga*. A farmers' school was establish-l there 1883, changed into a public school 1918. At present, however, o school of any kind is run at Eiðar. A hotel provides accommodation in ummer. Radio relay station, sportsground, community centre. Some oods and walking routes by **Húsatjörn**. A biggish fishing lake, Eiðavatn, ith the lovely wooded island **Eiðahólmi**.

thérað, the district from Eyvindará all the way to the sea, divided in vo settlements, Eiðaþinghá on the south side and Hjaltastaðarþinghá or tmannasveit on the north side. On the east side of the district are high icturesque tuff and basalt mountains. The highest ones are **Beinageitar-all** 1107 m and Dyrfjöll 1136 m.

liðhús, a farm with a good deal of woodland on the river Eyvindará cross from Egilsstaðaskógur woods. In 1990 a store of silver was und there, the largest to have been found in Iceland. Objects from it e in the National Museum in Reykjavík.

1 Austurlandsvegur, p. 101
93 Seyðisfjarðarvegur, p. 414
925 Hróarstunguvegur, p. 425

Dyrfjöll

Njarðvíkurskriður-Móberg 28 km

9
P. 572

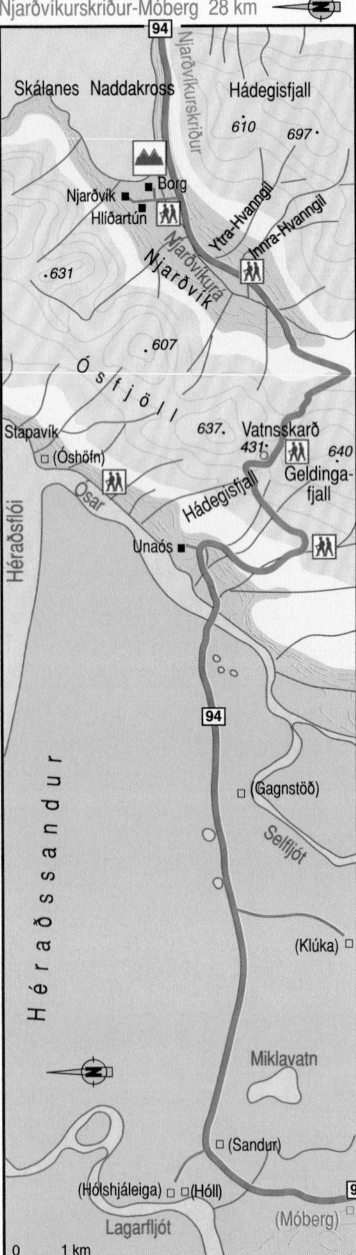

Móberg-Njarðvíkurskriður 28 km

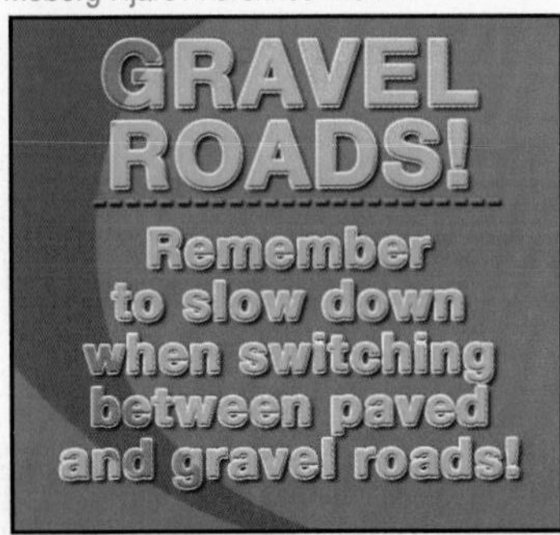

Njarðvíkurskriður.

Njarðvíkurskriður, a very steep scre between the Njarðvík bay and Borgar fjörður. Formerly a very dangerous route where the many accidents that occurre were at one time attributed to an evil spiri named Naddi. He is said to have dwelt i Naddagil ("Naddi's canyon"), at the nort end of scree, where there is a cave in th cliffs at sea level, the cave has now col lapsed. A farmer named Jón Bjarnaso was walking by himself in this place whe he encountered the monster and fogh him, ultimately driving him into the sea He then put up a cross in Skriður, in 1306 as thanks to God for protecting him. Th cross, **Naddakross**, has been regularl renewed ever since, together with th inscription, *Effigiem Christi qui transis pronus honora*, which is to the effec that travellers should pray at the cross before continuing across the scree.

Njarðvík, the northernmost bay on the Eastern fjords, with a grassy wooded valley at its head. A farm of the same name, frequently men tioned in local folklore, near which there is an ancient ruin, **Þorra garður**, said to date from Saga times, also some burial mounds. Þiðrand Geitisson is said to have been slain at **Þiðrandaþúfa** ("Þiðrandi's hil ock") at the farm Borg. Two skerries, called Gunnarssker, in the ba named for Gunnar Þiðrandabani ("Þiðrandi's bane"). There used to be small turf-roofed church in Njarðvík; it was demolished in the middle c the 20th century.

Innra-Hvanngil, a rhyolite canyon with dark basaltic rocks just 200 m walk from the road.

Vatnsskarð, (431 m) a mountain pass, with road, named for a small lak at the north end.

Unaós, the outermost farm in Hjaltastaðarþinghá settlement, at th mouth of the Selfljót river, named for Uni Garðarsson the Dane. Uni wa the son of Garðar Svavarsson, who discovered Iceland and called Garðarshólmi ("Garðar's isle"). Harold Fairhair king of Norway sent Un to Iceland to colonise it, for which he was to receive an earldom. Fror there he went south along the east of Iceland, staying with Úlfljótur i Skaftafell County. Úlfljótur slew Uni at his second attempt to escap after having got his host´s daughter with child. Therefore this firs attempt of a Norwegian king to seize Iceland failed because Uni wa slain by Icelanders.

Selfljót, a rather deep and quiet river. Formed from the Gilsá river, com ing from the lake Vestdalsvatn, and many tributaries from the Úthéra mountains. A landing dock and a storehouse were constructed there i the middle of the 20th century for the benefit of local farmers. Good fish ing. Where it flows into the sea it is called Óshöfn. This has sometime been an anchorage. The sagas tells of a ship that was sailed into the inlet of Unaós and this is supported by the landmark names Ár (Oar), Skipaklettur (Ship Rock), Knörr (a type of ship) and Knarrará (Ship River) just beyond the bridge that stands there today.

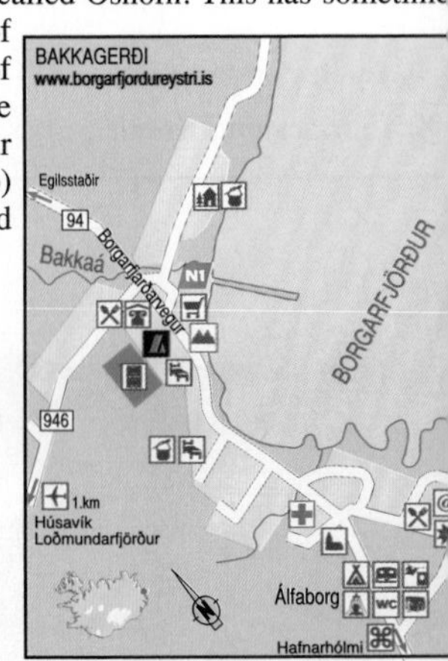

946 Hólalandsvegur, 7,6 km. **947 Desjarmýrarvegur,** 2,9 km.

taðarfjall, a colourful rhyolite mountain with basalt arches above)esjarmýri. The story goes that the giantess Gellivör who lived there was urned to stone and can still be seen in the scree below the mountain.

lfaborg, ("Elves' rock") a picturesque rock, from which the fjord gets ts name. Said to be the home of elves. Public park. Viewdial.

löfn, the outermost farm on the east side of Borgarfjörður with a harour and a small island with a puffin colony. At the island Hafnarhóli is n excellent view for bird watching. www.puffins.is

akki, a substantial farm, now abandoned. Mentioned in a story about ;unnar Þiðrandabani ("Þiðrandi's bane"). Some old relics have been ound in ruins there. Around the turn of the century a great slab of stone vas found during a dig. When it was raised they found a hollow beneath t. It was decided not to go on down into the hollow, the slab was eplaced and a wall built on top of it. It is thought they had found the iiding place of Gunnar Þiðrandabani.

akkagerði, (pop. 100) a village in Borgarfjörður, and a trading post ince 1894. Now fishing, fish processing, trade and farming. A church vith a fine altar piece painted by Jóhannes S. Kjarval (1885-1972), who ;rew up in Borgarfjörður. It shows Christ giving the Sermon on the Aount, standing on Álfaborg with the Dyrfjöll mountains behind him. The Gallery Kjarvalsstofa is located in the Cultural Community Centre. (jarvalsstofa is an exhibition of life of Jóhannes Sveinsson Kjarval. He vas an artist and painted people and nature. He sketched the faces of most of his compatriots in the area in 1926. The exhibition connects them in a inique way to the present. He revolutionized the country's art history, and s most definately the country's most beloved painter. During his adult ife, he spent many summers in the East to paint Mts Dyrfjoll and the colurful landscapes of Borgarfjordur east and its vicinity. He painted the ltarpiece of the Bakkagerdi church in 1914. It was, and still is, the hamet's most precious property. Most visitors of this area pay the church a isit to see it. In the Gallery there is a workshop for children.

orgarfjörður, a short, wide fjord and 10 km long, grassy, fertile valley of he same name. Magnificent, colourful mountains, especially Dyrfjöll and taðarfjall, of rhyolite and basalt. Numerous rare and beautiful stones, minrals and plants are found there The stones can´t be collected unless with permission from landowners. There is a good bird-watching hut on the each by the pier. Most Icelandic birds with beach habitats can be observed rom a hut. Beauiful walking routes. www.borgarfjordureystri.is

eitavík, a farm on a small bay of the same name. Childhood home of rtist Jóhannes S. Kjarval (1885-1972) who painted many pictures of orgarfjörður, for instance, most of his famous "Heads" were painted here in the nineteen-forties. Monument to him.

notrunes, the outermost farm on the west side of Borgarfjörður. Jamed for an elf lady, who had a family in both this world and the hiden world of elves.

F946 Loðmundafjarðarleið, p. 492

Bakkagerði-Njarðvíkurskriður 8 km

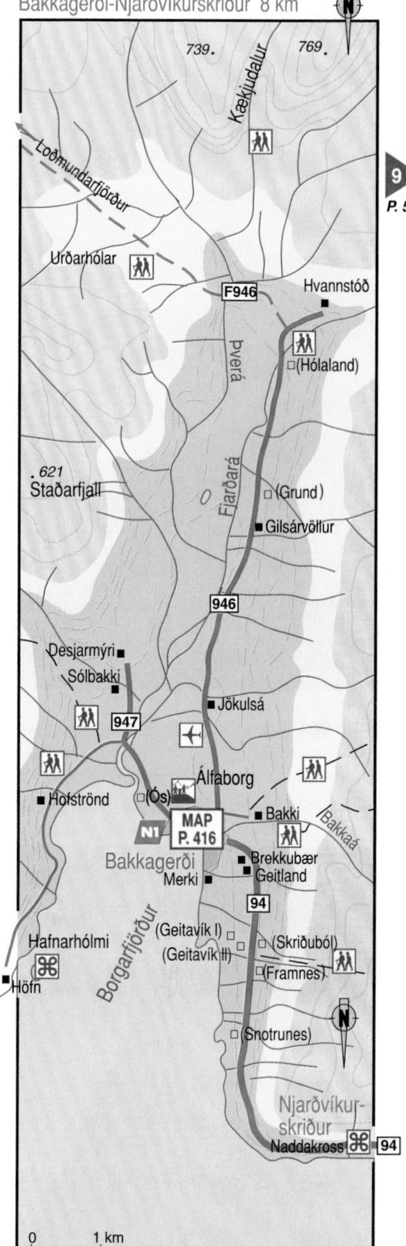

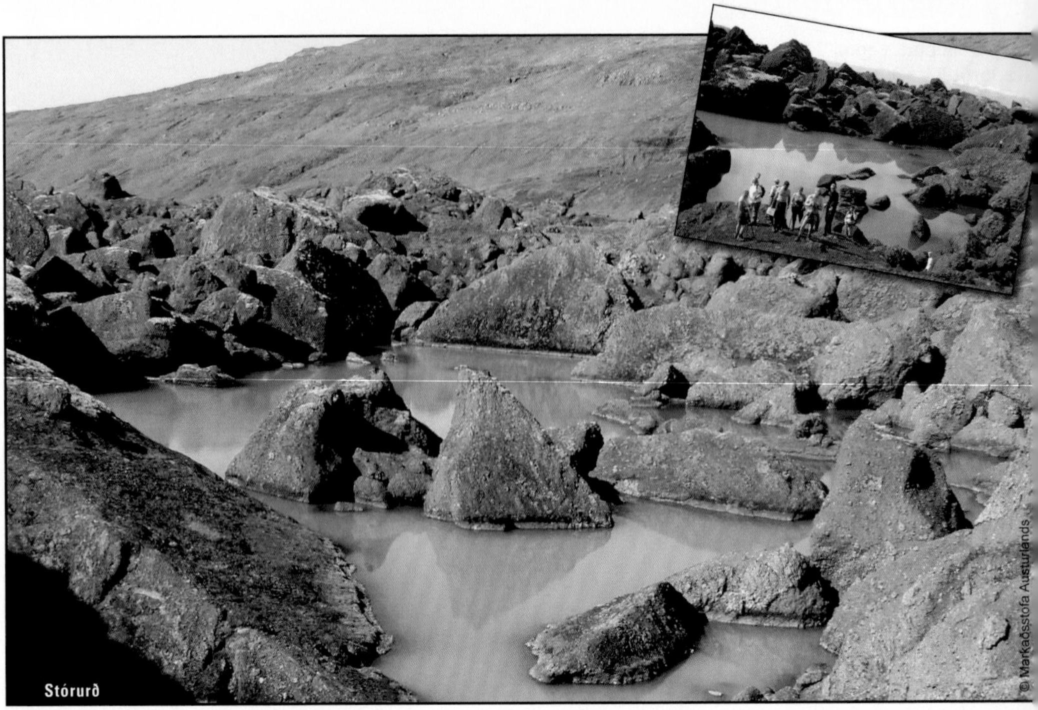

Stórurð

© Markaðsstofa Austurlands

Stórurð, massive rocks, one of East Iceland's most stupendous sights. They are thought to have fallen from the mountain above onto glacial ice, which then carried them farther down the valley before melting. See also p. 415.

Þerribjörg, below Kollumúli mountain (cf. p. 423), consists of magnificent cliffs from a former central volcano. These were exposed in all their colourful beauty by the erosion of ocean breakers.

Þerribjörg

© Markaðsstofa Austurlands

Hafnarnes-Reyðarfjörður 35 km

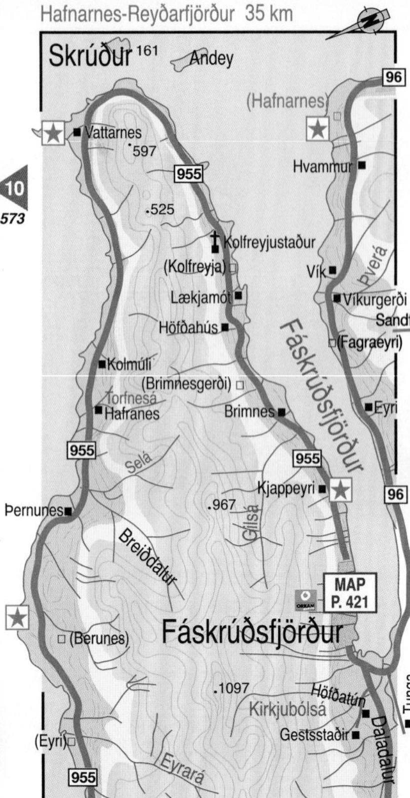

10 P. 573

Skrúður 161, Andey, (Hafnarnes), Vattarnes, 597, 955, Hvammur, 525, Kolfreyjustaður, (Kolfreyja), Vík, Lækjamót, Víkurgerði, Sandfell, Höfðahús, (Fagraeyri), Kolmúli, (Brimnesgerði), Torfnesá, Hafranes, Brimnes, Eyri, Selá, Kjappeyri, Þernunes, 967, Gilsá, Breiðdalur, Fáskrúðsfjörður, (Berunes), 1097, Höfðatún, Tunga, Kirkjubólsá, Gestsstaðir, Daladalur, (Eyri), Eyrará, Hólagerði, Reyðarfjörður, 1105, (Selstaðir), Dalir, Hraun, (Sómastaðagerði), (Framnes), Sómastaðir, 1118, Ljósá, (Teigargerði), 919, 1039, Kollaleira, Slétta, Búðará, (Seljateigur), Sléttuá, Skagafell, (Áreyjar), (Grænahlíð), Kollfell, 92, 936, 96

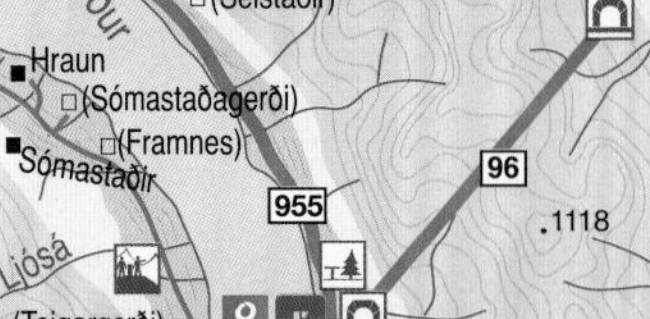

MAP P. 421

MAP P. 410

Reyðarfjörður-Hafnarnes 35 km

Hafnarnes, an abandoned group of farms on the south side of Fáskrúðsfjörður. Formerly a busy fishing centre with 8 farms and a school. The French hospital was moved there from Fáskrúðsfjörður and served as flats and a school.

955 Vattarnesvegur, 49 km.

Víkurheiði, from the farm Vík lies a hiking trail over Víkurheiði to Stöðvarfjörður.

Fagraeyri, a German company built a whaling station here in 1903 and it was run until in1905. Remnants of the station can be seen here still. The station was purchased later by Chr. Salvesen and Co. And moved to the Falkland Islands when whaling commenced in the South Polar Sea. Fishing was carried out from Fagraeyri until 1950.

Sandfell, (743 m) a rhyolite mountain south of Fáskrúðsfjörður. It is a typical laccolith believed to be 600 m thick and one of the best examples of mountains from the tertier period in the northern hemisphere. It can be seen very clearly while travelling up the mountain how the basalt layers have been lifted and turned over on its south side while other layers lie untouched beneath it. This is a nice hiking trail, taking a total of 2-3 hours one way.

Stöðvarskarð, from the farm Merki, where a television station can be found, there is a hiking trail through Stöðvarskarð passage to the farm Stöð in Stöðvarfjörður. This trail follows an old electricity line road for the majority of the way.

Stuðlaheiði, lies between Fáskrúðsfjörður and Reyðarfjörður. Over this heathland is a hiking trail from Dalir in Fáskrúðsfjörður to the abondoned farm Stuðlar in Reyðarfjörður.

Reindalsheiði, from the farm Tunguholt in Tungudalur in Fáskrúðsafjörður there lies a marked hiking trail.

Gilsárfoss, a beautiful waterfall in the river Gilsá. There is a 15 minutes walk to the waterfall from the road.

Fáskrúðsfjarðargöng, a tunnel 5.9 km long through the mountainous land between Fáskrúðsfjörður and Reyðarfjörður. Opened in 2005. The tunnel has made the distance between the two villages shorter by 31 km.

Fáskrúðsfjörður, (Búðir) (pop. 662) a village on a rather long fjord of the same name which has a valley at the head with many wooded areas, the largest at Gestsstaðir, where wild aspen is found. Became part of Fjarðabyggð in 2006. Fishing and fish processing. Trading started ca. 1890. Formerly a base for French fishermen, who had their own hospital, chapel and cemetery. These beautiful old buildings will open in May 2014 after careful restoration as an exclusive hotel and museum dedicated to the French heritage of Fáskrúðsfjörður. Until then you can learn aobut the local French history at the Frenchmen in Iceland Museum. The French used a big rock, which can still be seen in the village, as a bearing for landward sailing. They painted a black cross on it, and joined in prayer there before sailing out to sea. A memorial to Carl D. Tulinius, a merchant, Berg Hallgrímsson, a businessman and Dr. Charcot. Skrúður Community centre. A "French Days" festival is held in the last weekend in July each summer in Fáskrúðsfjörður. During this festival 1999, Foreign Minister Halldór Ásgrímsson unveiled a reproduction of Einar Jónsson´s bust of Dr. Charcot. The Icelandic government donated the bust to commemorate relations between Fáskrúðsfjörður and France. A swimming pool, camping grounds and a 9 hole golfcourse are located just outside the village.

Kolfreyjustaður, a church and parsonage. Among pastors there was Ólafur Indriðason (1796-1861), father of the poets Páll (1827-1905) and Jón (1850-1916) Ólafsson. Birthplace of Jón. Both brothers wrote many poems about the Kolfreyjustaður area. Just east of Kolfreyjustaður is a small peninsula called Hvalnes. There the French vessel Manon stranded in 1924. All the sailors were saved and the flotsam was auctioned away. A part of the old warehouse at Hafnargata 21 was built from Manon´s boards.

Andey, a low, grassy island at the mouth of Fáskrúðsfjörður. Eider duck colony. In Andey you can also find puffins.

Skrúður, (161 m) a high grassy island with cliffs. Many seabirds, including gannet. Famous from a folktale about a giant said to have lived there in a cave, **Skrúðshellir**. He put a spell on the daughter of the pastor at Hólmur in Reyðarfjörður and lured her to Skrúður.

Skrúðshellir, a high, broad cave in the cliffs with a big scree at the back.

Vattarnes, a farm and fishing-station, close to shark-fishing grounds. Between Vattarnes and Kolfreyjustaður the road goes along the scree Vattarnesskriður and Staðarskriður. Farmers at Vattarnes have utilised the island Skrúður and grazed their sheep there all year round.

92 Norðfjarðarvegur, p. 409

936 Þórdalsheiðarvegur, p. 492

eydalir, see p. 106.

97 Breiðdalsvíkurvegur, 1 km.

reiðdalsvík, see p. 106.

næhvammur, the outermost farm on the northern side of the Breiðdalur alley. Late in the 18th century a polar bear was killed right at the front door fter having chased a man who was walking there on his way from Stöðvarörður. Burial mounds have been found near Snæhvammur, with relics at ast 1,000 years old, now kept in the National Museum. In 1940 a mine xploded on the beach nearby, causing damage. The farm was moved many ears ago because of the danger of avalanches, but is now in danger from sand rosion.

úlur, (664 m) interestingly shaped peak above Kambanes peninsula.

töðvarfjörður, (pop. 203) a village on the north side of a small, pleasant ord of the same name, with the short, grassy, wooded valleys Stöðvardalur and fnadalur at its head. Became part of Fjarðabyggð in 2006. Fishing, some rming, and trading since 1896. Home of Petra Sveinsdóttir whose well-known rivate collection of stones is open to the public. Accommodation and tourist rvices are offered in the old church building and no other church building in eland is known to accomodate such activities. Fishing, fish processing and ommerce are the main industies there. The Snærós gallery is run by the the artists Ríkharður Valtingojer and Sigrún Friðriksdóttir. Various art items may be purchased at the gallery.

Saxa, an unusual bottleneck phenomenon just north of the buildings at Lönd, formed by shoreline cliffs which constrict bigger ocean swells until they spout high into the air at Saxa's landward end. Its name refers to slicing or cutting, and fits well with how Saxa chops up quantities of seaweed, hurling the bits onto the cliffs.

Jafnadalur, a north facing valley in Stöðvarfjörður fjord. A good walking path leads through the valley over Stöðvarskarð connecting it to Fáskrúðsfjörður fjord. At the end of the valley is Einbúi „The Hermit", a fairly unique and a solitary rock in otherwise flat surroundings. In Jafnadalur valley is also a beautiful 6 m stone arch, located on Álftafell mountain. Excellent hiking area.

FÁSKRÚÐSFJÖRÐUR
www.austurbyggd.is

1 **Austurlandsvegur,** p. 106
964 **Breiðdalsvegur,** p. 106
966 **Suðurbyggðarvegur,** p. 106

Heydalir-Hafnarnes 34 km

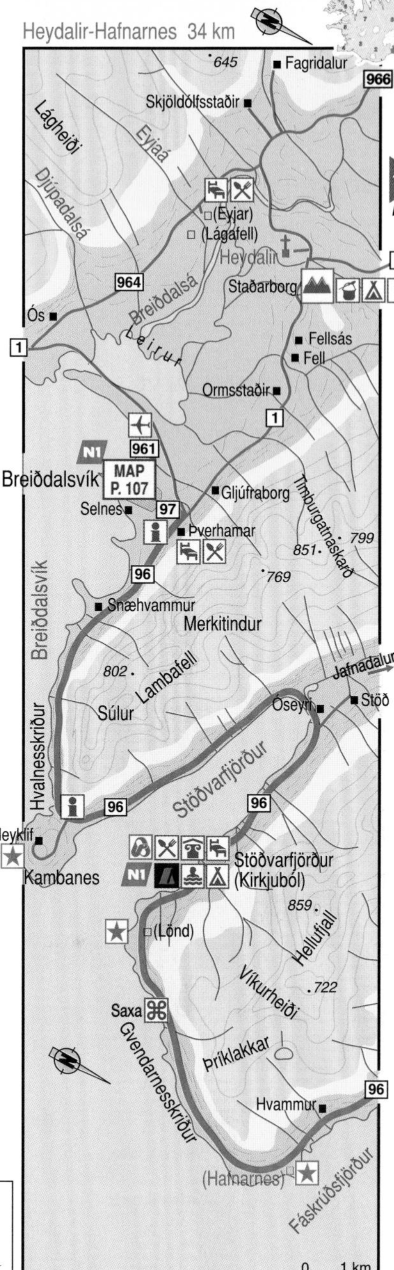

Hafnarnes-Heydalir 34 km

Ketilsstaðir-Jökulsárbrú 35 km

9
P. 572

Jökulsárhlíð.

Ketilsstaðir, the outermost farm in the Jökulsárhlíð distric with seal-hunting, driftwood and other natural advantages. Fro there the road crosses Hellisheiði moor to Vopnafjörður. A 310 hectare area of land between Ketilasstaðir and Hjarðargrund i Jökuldalur has been fenced off and will be kept inaccessible t livestock from the beginning of spring until the first snow. The area wi be divided into sections for forest planting and restoration of barren lan and grazing.

Kaldá, a deepish river in a deep canyon, rising in the Smjörfjöll mou tains and flowing into Jökulsá.

921 Eyjavegur, 5,95 km. **922 Másselsvegur,** 6,74 km.

Sleðbrjótur, ("Sleigh breaker") a church and community centre, a ancient manor farm. Said to be named for an incident when some slave broke their sled on their way from Vopnafjörður. They then met som slaves from the next farm and tried to buy their sled, but were refused. fight broke out in which all the slaves were killed.

Surtsstaðir, a farm in the homefield of which is the rock Drykkjarstein ("Drinking stone"), about 10 m high, with a spring in it.

Fossvellir, the innermost farm in the Jökulsárhlíð district, beside the rive Laxá which there descends in pretty falls. A former assembly site. Ther is an abattoir and freezing-plant at Fossvellir.

Smjörvatnsheiði, ("Butter lake moor") an old mountain rou between Jökulsárhlíð and Vopnafjörður, with a refuge hu about mid-way. Now a jeep-track from Hofteigur in Jökuldalur. Accordin to *Vopnfirðinga saga* the criminal Svartur was outlawed to these moor He was particularly evil in that he stole and killed more sheep than h needed. Brodd-Helgi, a boy of 12 at the time, is said to have slain him i a hard battle, thus winning renown.

Jökulsárhlíð, the district along the east side of Fljótsdalshérað fro Fossvellir. The mountains Smjörfjöll and Hlíðarfjöll beyond. Little fl land, what there is mostly along the Jökulsá river. High cliffs in the nor along the coast. Fine views.

1 Austurlandsvegur, p. 100 **925 Hróarstunguvegur,** p. 425
926 Húseyjarvegur, p. 425

Jökulsárbrú-Ketilsstaðir 35 km

Vatnsdalsgerði-Ketilsstaðir 31 km

The church at Sleðbrjótur.

yðri-Vík, the first land to be settled in Vopnafjörður. The settler was yvindur Vopni of Strind in Norway, and he gave the fjord his name.

rossavík, an ancient manor farm on the east of Vopnafjörður. Home of eitir and his son Þorkell of *Vopnfirðinga saga*. The home around 1800 f sheriff Guðmundur Pétursson (1748-1811), a wealthy and enterprising ıan.

indfell, a farm where lignite is found.

yvindarstaðir, in Böðvarsdalur, scene of a battle between the Hofverjar 'Men of the farm Hof") and Þorkell Geitisson, 4 men on each side being ain, the battle scene is called **Hofsmannaflöt**.

öðvarsdalur, a farm in a valley of the same name. Route from there, assable in summer, over Hellisheiði moor to Ketilsstaðir in the Jökuls- :hlíð district.

mjörfjöll, ("Butter mountains") between Vopnafjörður and Jökulsárhlíð, :eep and rocky on the Vopnafjörður side. Mostly 1,200 m high, the ighest 1,251 m. Little vegetation, rough and much scree, some rhyolite. nowdrifts all summer in many places. Various streams become difficult cross during thaws, though there is usually little water in them at other mes.

agridalur, an abandoned farm and former weather station. Between agridalur and the spur Kollumúli is an uninhabited valley, Kattardalur. Vest of Fagridalur is the mountain **Búr** (416 m), with sheer cliffs escending into the sea and rocky coves below.

ollumúli, (602 m) a spur with high cliffs at the outer end of the eninsula between Vopnafjörður and Héraðsflói. Bjarnarey island ffshore.

ellisheiði, (655 m) a mountain road across the moor between opnafjörður and Jökulsárhlíð, passable for all cars. Not kept open in the inter. Much used as a trade route to Vopnafjörður in former times, and s an emergency route when others were impassable.

Ketilsstaðir-Vatnsdalsgerði 31 km

8 P. 571
MAP P. 382

85 **Norðausturvegur,** p. 384
915 **Vesturárdalsvegur,** p. 384
919 **Sunnudalsvegur,** p. 384

Brú-Gilsá 31 km

Snæfell, (1,833 m) the highest mountain in Iceland after Vatnajökull, co spicuous, with fine views from the top. An old volcano, the peak snov covered. Local people say when it is clear over Snæfell in the evening, yc can depend on good weather the next day. The local touring club has bu a hut near the river Grjótá on the west of Snæfell. It is in this area that th majority of Iceland's wild reindeer are found (see Road F909).

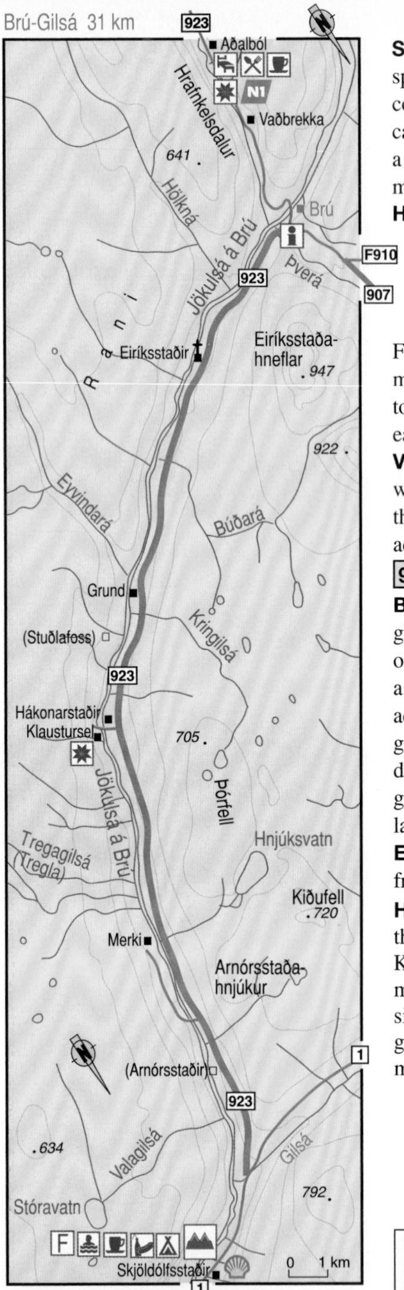

Hrafnkelsdalur, a side-valley from the Jökuldalur valley, long and broa often grassy with bushes. Geothermal heat in places. There are no only the 2 farms Vaðbrekka and Aðalból. Ruins of about 20 Saga ag farms have been found there.

Aðalból, a farm about 80 km from the sea, once the home of Hrafnke Freysgoði of *Hrafnkels saga*. Tracks for vehicles from there to th mountain Snæfell and other highland areas. The route up from the valle to Ytra-Kálfafell is rather steep and difficult, but then becomes relativel easy to the glacier Eyjabakkajökull.

Vaðbrekka, one of two inhabitaded farm in Hrafnkellsdalur. Almost mi way between Vaðbrekka and Aðalból there is a pedestrian bridge acro the river Hrafnkela on the land of Vaðbrekka. It was built to facilita access to sheep sheds at Þórisstaðir.

907 Brúarvegur, frá Hringvegi á Austurleið F910, 21 km.

Brú, ("Bridge") the innermost farm in Jökuldalur, with land in to th glaciers and west to the river Kreppa. There was formerly a natural brid over the Jökulsá river, which is where the name comes from. There is no a man-made bridge there. Four-wheel drive vehicles can be driven we across the moors south of the mountains Þríhyrningur and Mynnisfja garður and on track F905 south from Möðrudalur. It is also possible drive (F910) east of Kreppa as far as the glacier Brúarjökull. Another trac goes from Brú north across Jökuldalsheiði moor to join Highway 1 at th lake Sænautavatn.

Eiríksstaðir, a church, moved there from Brú. There is a magnificent vie from Eiríksstaðahneflar (922 m and 947 m), two peaks above the farm.

Hákonarstaðir, a farm dating to the Settlement Era and situated besi the Jökulsá river, across from **Klaustursel**. The bridge over the Jökulsá Klaustursel farmstead is the oldest in Iceland that is still in use. Special manufactured in the USA, it was imported as parts, riveted together site and erected in 1908. Klaustursel has a small zoo, with reindeer, fo geese and other Icelandic animals, together with a gallery offering item made of reindeer leather.

Gilsá-Brú 31 km

1 Austurlandsvegur, p. 99 | **907 Brúarvegur,** p. 99, 485
923 Jökuldalsvegur, p. 424 | **F910 Austurleið,** p. 490

925 926 927

róarstunga, the area between the rivers Jökulsá á Brú and Lagarfljót :om Ós to Rangá. The southernmost part is the Lágheiði moor, the orthern end of Fljótsdalsheiði. Long and low hills with wet ground, ens and marshes in between, many lakes.

926 **Húseyjarvegur,** 21 km.

úsey, the outermost farm in Hróarstunga in the middle of the flat ınd, near the confluence of the rivers Jökulsá and Lagarfljót. It once ad the greatest amount of seal hunting in the Héraðsflói district.

925 **Hróarstunguvegur,** 42 km. 927 **Brekkubæjarvegur,** 7 km.

itli-Bakki, close to Geirsstaðir. The ruins near Geirsstaðir date from bout 980 and consist of a church, a house, an enclosing wall and some ther remains. A replica of the church has been built there. It is also lanned to rebuild the house and to use it and the church for living unctions with people in Viking period costumes and farm animals on iew to give an idea of life in the early days of Christianity in Iceland.

lallfreðarstaðir, a farm, home for a time of poet Páll Ólafsson (1827-905), who often mentioned the area in his verse. Memorial to him.

kersl, some strange crags north of Kirkjubær, once the dwelling-lace of the giant Þórir and his wife. Every year they put a spell on ither the pastor or the shepherd in Kirkjubær that made them come to kersl. A pastor named Eiríkur managed to change this, and they aited for him in their cave to no avail. In the end Þórir froze fast to ıe ice on Þórisvatn when fishing, and his wife turned into kessusteinn ("Giantess rock").

Kirkjubær, a church and till recently a parsonage.

agarfoss, a waterfall in the river Lagarfljót opposite Kirkjubær, ıe only falls in this river. Lagarfoss is divided in the middle by a rock, here a salmon ladder was built in 1935. It has now been replaced. 'he west branch is rapids, the east branch plunges off a 6 m high ledge. 'otal drop: 11 m. The falls were harnessed for power in 1975, so their ppearance has changed, and there is a bridge on the dam.

altastaðir fram, farm, dating from 1882, with living quarters above ıe cow-house, a storeroom, a kitchen with a stone stove, a pantry and barn. It gives a good impression of how ordinary people in Iceland ved, using their cows as a source of heat. In the keeping of the lational Museum since 1976.

inghöfði, an old assembly site by the river Krakalækur, mentioned in ıe Sagas. Ruins of booths still visible. Site during the 19th century of ational meetings similar to the Kollubúðir meetings in the Western 'jords (see Road 608).

Jrriðavatn, a fishing-lake with warm springs in it, water from which s piped to the towns Egilsstaðir and Fellabær. A farm of the same ame beside the lake.

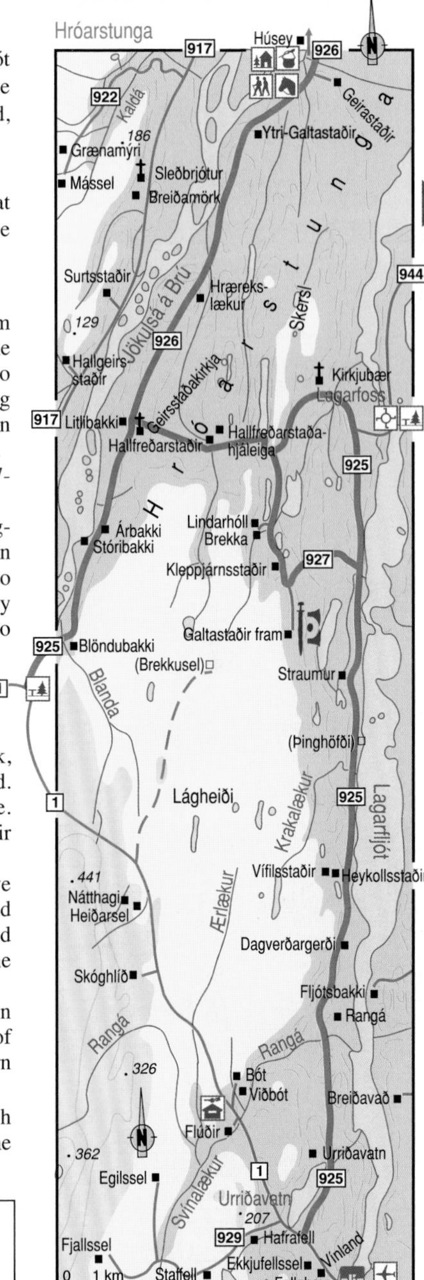

1	**Austurlandsvegur,** p. 101	917	**Hlíðarvegur,** p. 422
922	**Másselsvegur,** p. 422	929	**Hafrafellsvegur,** p. 101
944	**Lagarfossvegur,** p. 415		

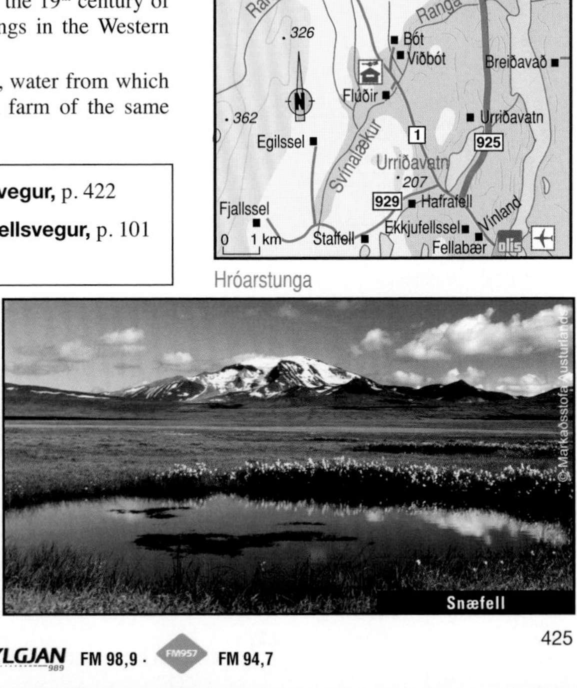

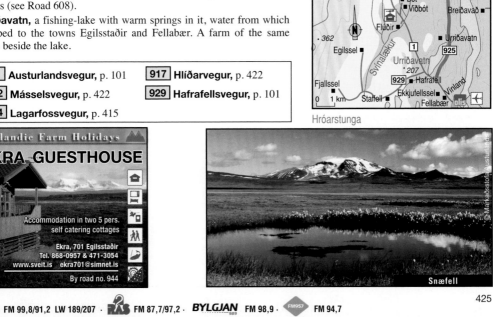

Snæfell

Arnheiðarstaðir-Fellabær 24 km

9 P. 572

Fljótsdalur, the valley district between the rivers Hrafnsgerðisá on th west and Gilsá on the east. The lower part of valley near the Lagarflj river is broad with meadows, and about 10 km from Lagarfljót it divide into the narrow valleys Norðurdalur and Suðurdalur, between which is th mountain spur Múli (642 m).

Fellaheiði, (700 m) the moors above Fell west of the river Lagarfljó Many lakes and tarns, with trout. Continuation to the south int Fljótsdalsheiði moor, where there are also numerous lakes, tarns, stream and brooks. Reindeer often come down there and even to the farm especially if winter pastures are poor.

Ás, a church, a parsonage until 1880.

Meðalnes, an abandoned farm, once the home of the parents of th Icelandic-Canadian writer Jóhann Magnús Bjarnason (1866-1945).

The memorial to Jóhann Magnús from Meðalnes in Fell.

Fell, the farming area along the western side of the river Lagarfljó Rather barren, with many rocks, crags and marshes. Little meadow-lan but good grazing. Several lakes and tarns.

Lagarfljót, a broad river, the inner part of which is a lake extending fro Fljótsdalur to beyond Egilsstaðir. Deep, max. 112 m, average 50.7 m, least 30 km long and 2.5 km at its broadest point, area 53 km². Natur gas in places. A little trout-fishing. There are many stories of a monster i the lake, known as Lagarfljótsormurinn ("The Lagarfljót serpent"). Ne the bridge the lake becomes the river Lagarfljót, mostly quiet-flowin though deep, which marks the boundary between the counties of Norðu Múlasýsla and Suður-Múlasýsla. The summer of 1999 the passanger shi Lagafljótsormurinn began sailing on the river. The tours are very popula The ship carries 130 passangers.

Fellabær, (pop. 416) a village across the bridge from Egilsstaðir. Mai activities trading, service and industry.

941 Flugvallavegur, 0,55 km.

1 Austurlandsvegur, p. 101
92 Norðfjarðarvegur, p. 409
93 Seyðisfjarðarvegur, p. 414
94 Borgarfjarðarvegur, p. 415
925 Hróarstunguvegur, p. 425

Fellabær-Arnheiðarstaðir 24 km

'allanes, a church. Best known of pastors there was the poet Stefán)lafsson (ca. 1619-88). After Hallgrímur Pétursson (see Saurbær, Borg) e was Iceland's greatest poet in the 17th century. He did many translations ıto and from Latin. He was also a song-writer and an astronomer. The ommunity centre Iðavellir nearby. Vallanes today, is one of Iceland's ırgest farms growing entirely organic grains, fruits and vegetables.

ıjóanes, home of Helgi Ásbjarnarson, a Saga age chieftain of the :astern fjords. Fenced to protect the woods from sheep.

'arthús, a sherpherds' hut, famous for the tale of the violent death there f one Parthúsa-Jón, at the hands of a ghost.

lallormsstaður, a manor farm in its time. Church till 1895, parsonage ıll 1880. Domestic science school founded in 1930, still in use, now as n annex of Menntaskólinn á Egilsstöðum (Egilsstaðir College), in ooperation with which they graduate students on the Domestic Science ine. The compulsory level school for the area is also there, and a music chool. Hallormsstaður is the main centre of the Forestry Service. ;irthplace of Guðmundur Magnússon (1741-98), who lived most of his ife abroad and published ancient literature, e.g. the first volume of the *æmundar-Edda*, 1787, in Latin translation, with notes and vocabulary. Ie also translated *Egils saga* into Latin, wrote an Icelandic-Latin ictionary, published a play by Terentius, 1780, and other works. Hotel, ee add p. 103.

lallormsstaðarskógur, ("Hallormsstaður woods") at the turn of the entury considered to be the biggest woods in Iceland. Almost all of the voods protected from grazing animals between 1905 and 1927. Placed ınder nursery protection of the Forestry Service in 1907. The wood itself s now 740 km², and between 1965 and 1980 areas of land on both sides f the woods were brought inside fences along with the wood, the total enced in area now being 1850 hectares (about 4,500 acres). The fence long the river Lagarfljót is 15 km long. In 1903 a nursery area, called Mörkin, was established to grow different kinds of native and foreign rees, and has flourished ever since. It is now possible to see 70 species of oreign trees there. In the Guttormslundur grove, named for Guttormur 'álsson, forester (1884-1964), is the tallest tree in Iceland, one of a ıumber of Russian larches planted in 1938. The **Atlavík** bay on Lagarfljót s the best-known holiday area in Hallormsstaðarskógur, and there are 40 .m of roads in the woods, many of which make excellent walking routes. National Forest.

ìilsá, a river forming the boundary between Norður-Múlasýsla and ;uður-Múlasýsla counties.

Irafnkelsstaðir, a farm in the lower Fljótsdalur valley, named for Irafnkell Freysgoði of *Hrafnkels saga*. A lovely protected birchwood, **Ranaskógur**, nearby.

Úlfsstaðir-Hrafnkelsstaðir 24 km

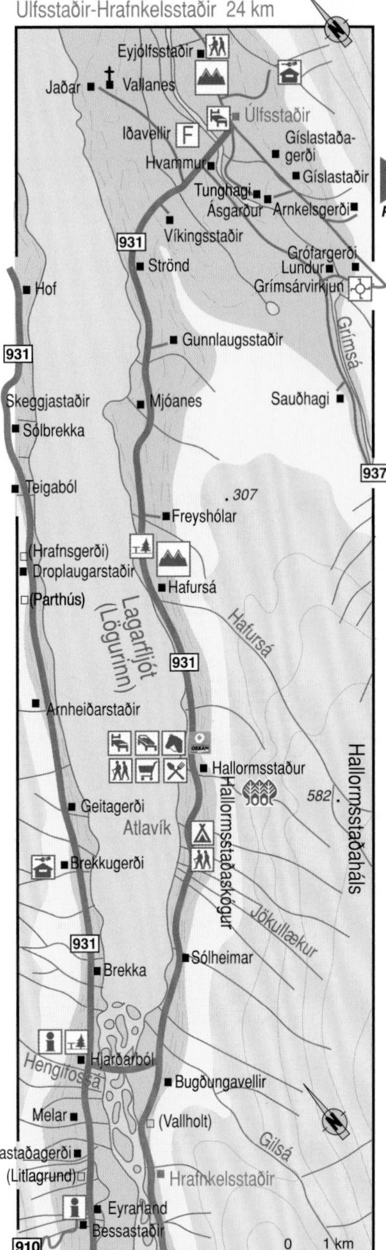

Hrafnkelsstaðir-Úlfsstaðir 24 km

1	**Austurlandsvegur,** p. 101	910	**Austurleið,** p. 490
937	**Skriðdalsvegur,** p. 105	933	**Fljótsdalsvegur,** p. 428

Hrafnkelsstaðir-Arnheiðarstaðir 22 km

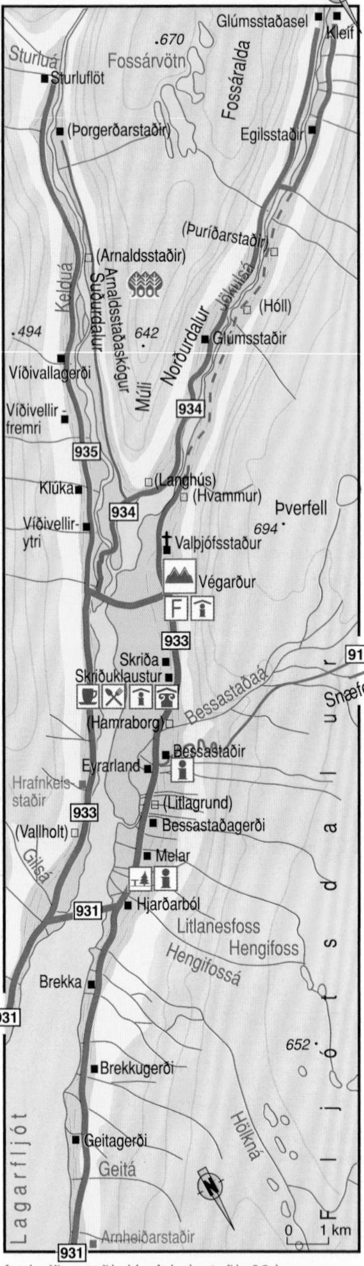

24 P. 587

9 P. 572

Arnheiðarstaðir-Hrafnkelsstaðir 22 km

Arnaldsstaðaskógur, natural birch forest high on a steep mountai slope. Turn southwest from Highway 934 onto tracks north of Keldu river. Steep hiking path. National Forest.

935 Suðurdalsvegur, 12,5 km. **933 Fljótsdalsvegur,** 17 km.

Sturluflöt, a rough track leads from there across the highlands from ther south to Víðidalur í Lóni (see Stafafell, A-Skaft).

Kárahnjúkavirkjun, a power plant, with its generating station situate about 900 m inside Teigsbjarg mountain.

Valþjófsstaður, an ancient manor farm, church and parsonag Community centre Végarður. The famous Valþjófsstaður church door, on of the finest items in the National Museum at Reykjavík, came fro there. The door now on the church is an exact replica. Tröllkonustígu ("Giantess' path") above the farm. Once the home of the Þórarinsso brothers, Þorvarður, one of the most powerful men in Iceland in his da (d. 1297), and Oddur, a great warrior slain in 1255 at Geldingaholt.

Végarður, a Visitor Centre for the Kárahnjúkar hydropower project.

Skriðuklaustur, a substantial farm for centuries, site of a monastery fro 1493 until the Reformation, then a church till 1792. Home of a number c prominent men, e.g. Sheriff Hans Wium (1715-88), who is buried ther In 1939 the author Gunnar Gunnarsson settled at Skriðuklaustur and bui a large, unusual house, which he later presented to the Icelandic natio (see Road 85, Ljótsstaðir). For a time an experimental station for shee breeding and soil cultivation. Now a centre of culture and history, run b the Institute of Gunnar Gunnarsson, with various cultural activities an access to the ruins of the monastery. Klausturkaffi café offers launch an teatime buffet. In 2010 the Snæfell Visitor Centre for the east territory of Vatnajökull National Park was opened at Skriðuklaustur. The centre has an interesting exhibition on the area and the nature and a souvenir shop that focuses on locally produced products.

See information on Vatnajökull National Park on p. 122.

Hengifoss, ("Hanging falls") one of the highest waterfalls in Icelan 128 m, in the river Hengifossá near the farm Brekka. In the gorge ther which is pretty and varied, are lignite and fossils. Another waterfa further downstream, Litlanesfoss, is set in basalt columns. A walking pat leads to Hengifoss from the highway.

934 Múlavegur í Fljótsdal, 13 km. **910 Austurleið,** p. 490

)alatangi, a weather station and lighthouse. One of the irst lighthouses built in Iceland, 1895. In the keeping of he National Museum since 2003.

/ljóifjörður, a long, narrow fjord, surrounded by high nountains and steep cliffs. Today the fjord is largely ininhabited, whereas in its heyday in 1902, there were 112. Became part of Fjarðabyggð in 2006. Some trout in he Fjarðará river. A lot of bilberries and other berries in \ugust. Often good fishing in the fjord in late summer.

3rekkuþorp, an old fishing village. The first icehouse in celand was built there in 1895. Community centre ;ólbrekka.

\sknes, site of a whaling-station built in 1901 by Norwegians. 14 vhaling boats sailed from there in the early years of last century, and ome 300-400 men worked at the station.

:jörður, a farm of the original setlement, formerly the site of a church. t is at the sea end of Fjarðardalur, a pretty, wooded valley with many :liffs and waterfalls.

953 Mjóafjarðarvegur, 46,5 km, accessible to all cars. From ;ólbrekka the road is hard to travel by car, but can easily be accessed by 'oot and is well worth the trip.

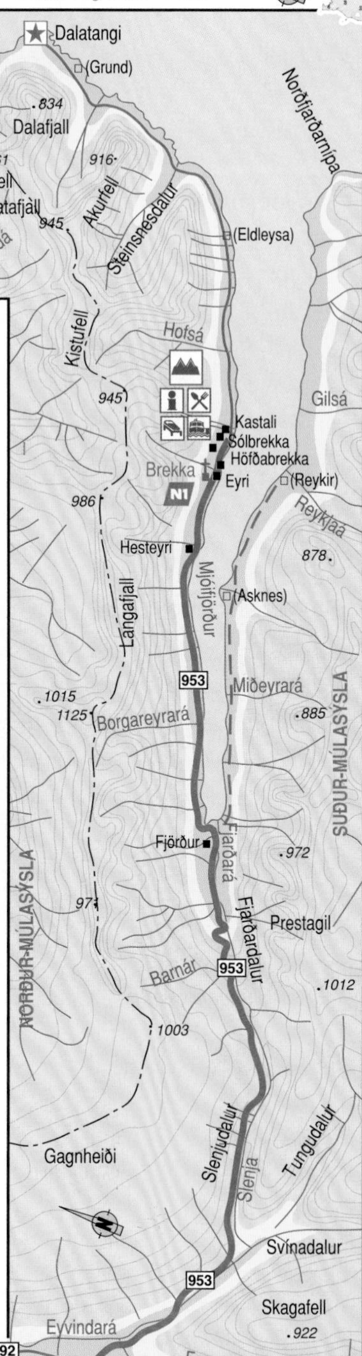

The Klifbrekkufossar waterfalls in Mjóifjörður.

92 Norðfjarðarvegur, p. 409

22
P. 585

14
P. 577

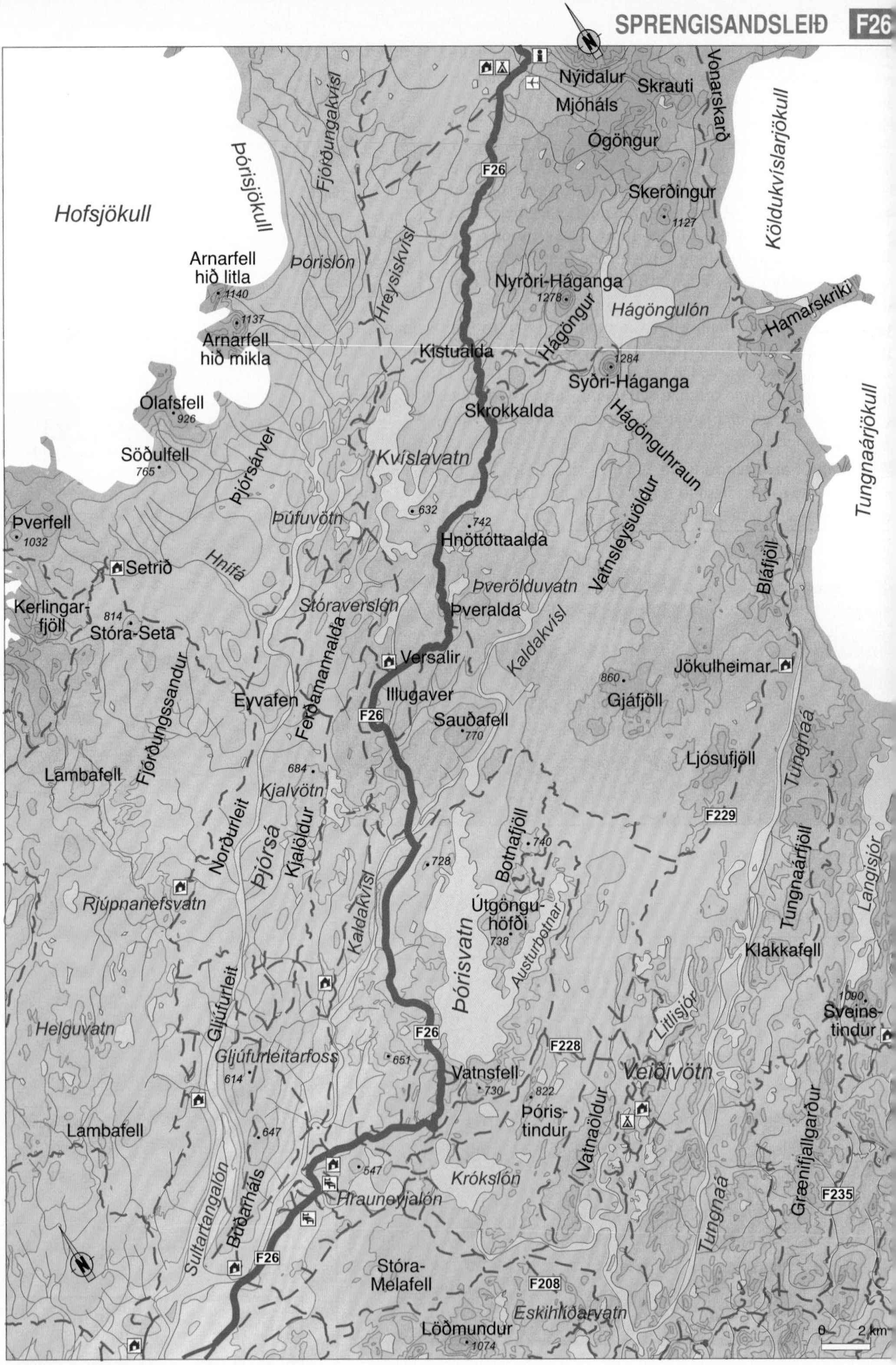

Hofsjökull
Þórisjökull
Fjórðungakvísl
Nýidalur
Skrauti
Mjóháls
Vonarskarð
Ógöngur
Köldukvíslarjökull
F26
Skerðingur
1127
Arnarfell hið litla
1140
Þórislón
Hreysiskvísl
Nyrðri-Háganga
1278
Hágöngulón
Hamarskriki
1137
Arnarfell hið mikla
Kistualda
Hágöngur
1284
Syðri-Háganga
Ólafsfell
926
Skrokkalda
Hágönguhraun
Tungnaárjökull
Söðulfell
765
Þjórsárver
Kvíslavatn
632
Vatnsleysuöldur
Þverfell
1032
Þúfuvötn
742
Hnöttóttaalda
Setrið
Hnífá
Þveröldurvatn
Bláfjöll
Kerlingarfjöll
814
Stóra-Seta
Stóraverslón
Þveralda
Kaldakvísl
Ferðamannalda
Versalir
Jökulheimar
Fjórðungssandur
860
Eyvafen
Illugaver
Gjáfjöll
F26
Sauðafell
770
Tungnaá
Ljósufjöll
Lambafell
684
Kjalvötn
F229
Norðurleit
Þjórsá
Kjalöldur
Botnafjöll
740
728
Tungnaárfjöll
Langisjór
Rjúpnanefsvatn
Kaldakvísl
Útgönguhöfði
738
Austurbotnar
Klakkafell
Þórisvatn
1090
Sveinstindur
Helguvatn
Gljúfurleit
F26
Litlisjór
Gljúfurleitarfoss
651
F228
614
Vatnsfell
730
822
Veiðivötn
Lambafell
647
Þóristindur
Vatnaöldur
Grænifjallgarður
547
Krókslón
Sultartangalón
Búðarháls
Hrauneyjalón
Tungnaá
F235
F26
Stóra-Melafell
F208
Eskihlíðarvatn
Löðmundur
1074
0 2 km

F26 **Sprengisandsleið (Ölduleið)** 107,9 km. A old route betweeen the South and the North. This old route across the interior between the north and south of Iceland is still in use today. Formerly the bishops of Skálholt used it on their way to the east of Iceland, as many place names indicate. Names like **Sveinar**, **Sprengir** og **Beinakerling** (see F752). Then it was more or less lost and out of use until the 18th and 19th centuries. The first trip by car was made in 1933. The oldest route was up from the Þjórsárdalur valley, on the west side of the Þjórsá river and across it at Sóleyjarhöfðavað ford, then north across the sands to the farm Mýri in the Bárðardalur valley, about 240 km (see Road 842). Less frequented was the route up from Galtalækur, along the east of the Þjórsá river to Sóleyjarhöfði, where the two routes came together. With the new power station on the Tungnaá river and bridges across it the **Sprengisandur** route has been moved further east away from Þjórsá, though there are several sideroads to the old route.

Versalir, a guesthouse and a restaurant since 1987. There is a junction just befor Versalir that divides Sprengisandsleið to two routes: **Kvíslaveituvegur** and **Ölduleið**.

Þúfuver, some wet grasslands along the Þjórsá river. Þúfuver and Eyvindarver belong to the broad, marshy grasslands called Þjórsárver. These grasslands are more extensive on the west side of the river and also more isolated and difficult to reach.

Fjórðungakvísl, a river formed by Hagakvísl and Nýjadalsá that come from Tungnafellsjökull. It later joins Bergvatnskvísl and more rivers to make Þjórsá, the longest river in Iceland.

Fjórðungsvatn, a shallow lake that sometimes almost disappears in dry periods.

Eyvindarver, marshlands along the river Þjórsá, rich with bird-life mainly geese and swans. By Lindarbakki there are some ruins of a shelter built by the 18th century outlaw Fjalla-Evindur.

Innrahreysi, there are some ruins of a shelter of the outlaw Fjalla-Eyvindur. Eyvindur and his wife, Halla, were caught there in 1772.

Inn með Öldum, ("In along the ridges") a collective name for the road (or tracks) from the bridge on the Kaldakvísl river to the Nýidalur valley. This country is very barren and rocky. From south to north the four main ridges along the route are, **Þveralda** (728 m), **Hnöttóttaalda** (785 m), **Skrokkalda** (922 m) and **Kistualda** (786 m).

Vonarskarð, ("Hope pass") a mountain pass, really more of a wide valley between the two glaciers Vatnajökull and Tungnafellsjökull, 900 to 940 m above sea level, 15-20 km long and with about 13 km distance between the two glaciers. **Skjálfandafljót** and **Kaldakvísl** come from Vonarskarð.

Mynni þess að norðan er milli Fljótsborgar og Gæsahnjúks eða Tindafells. Skarðið er gróðurlaust að mestu. Jeppafært er um skarðið að hausti, frá Skrokkköldu á F910 norðan við Tungnafellsjökul.

Nýidalur, ("New valley") or **Jökuldalur,** ("Glacier valley") a valley on the southern side of Tungnafellsjökull. Its floor is about 800 m above sea level, yet surprisingly rich in vegetation. Probably the highest area of such vegetation in Iceland. This valley was off the beaten track and was found by three farmers from the north in 1845. Two tourist huts by the west entrance to the valley. The lodges in Nýidalur are just by the highland route over Sprengisandur. A warden is appointed during the summer. From the houses you can view the sout-west side of the glacier Tungnafellsjökull. The glacier can easily be accessed by foot about Mjóháls east of Vonarskarð.

26 **Landvegur,** p. 161 | **F208** **Fjallabaksleið nyrðri,** p. 436 | **F228** **Veiðivatnaleið,** p. 446
F229 **Jökulheimaleið,** p. 447 | **F235** **Langisjór,** p. 443

23 P. 586

22 P. 585

843
Klukku-fjall
Mýri
Aldeyjarfoss
Svartárvatn
Svartárkot
Suðurá
Hádegis-fjall
Suðurárbotnar
Almenningur
Hjalladalsá
Ísólfsvatn
Sandá
Fjallalda
Hrauntunga
Ísólfsdalur
Mjóadalsá
F26
Dyngjufjöll ytri
Askja
Fnjóská
Austurkróksfjall
Þvergil
Skjálfandafljót
Sandmúli
Frambruni
Bleiksmýrardalur
Hraun
Tungufell
Fjallsendi
F910
Æsustaðatungur
Gvendar-hnjúkur
Krókdalur
Öxnadalur
Þríhyrningur
1040
F26
Syðrimúli
Hattalda
Nýjabæjarafrétt
Bleiksmýrardrög
Tröllladyngja
1460
F821
Fljótshnjúkur
Geldingaárdrög
Kiðagilsdrög
Sandbúðir
Jökulfall
Skjálfandafljót
F881
Tjarnardrag
Illviðrahnjúkar
988
F26
Laugafell
879
Gæsa-hnjúkar
1240
F752
Laugafells-hnjúkur
Fjórðungsvatn
Fjórðungsalda
972
F910
Dvergalda
F752
Sprengisandur
Tungnafell
1392
Tindafell
1198
Kvíslarhæð
Vegamótavatn
Tungnafells-jökull
Rauðkúla
1520
Tómasarhagi
Miklafell
1456
Klakkur
Háalda
Fjórðungskvísl
Nýidalur
Vatnajökull
Ógöngur
Vonarskarð
Hofsjökull
F26
Krosshnjúkar
0 2 km

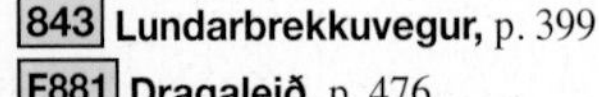
843 **Lundarbrekkuvegur,** p. 399
F881 **Dragaleið,** p. 476

F752 **Skagafjarðarleið,** p. 470
F910 **Austurleið,** p. 488-491

F821 **Eyjafjarðarleið,** p. 476

Gunnar Guðjónsson

Hofsjökull

F26 **Sprengisandsleið (Bárðardalsleið)** 96 km. Passable for all jeeps, but with difficult rivers to cross.

Tómasarhagi, ("Tómas' pasture") a green area (mostly moss) west of the glacier Tungnafellsjökull, first found by Tómas Sæmundsson in 1835. There may possibly have been more vegetation there at that time.

Tungnafellsjökull, (1,540 m) a glacier mountain, 50 km², steep on the south and west sides. The German geologist Hans Reck was the first to do research work on Tungnafellsjökull in 1906. The route lies west of Fjórðungsvatn to Kiðagil.

Fjórðungsvatn, a shallow lake that sometimes almost disappears in dry periods. East of the lake is **Fjórðungsalda**, (969 m) a wide mountain ridge with a fine view from the top.

Sandbúðir, a weather station for some years in connection with plans to lay high-tension power lines across Sprengisandur. Now there is an automatic weather station.

Kiðagil, a narrow canyon about 6 km long going west from the river Skjálfandafljót. In times past this was the first stop to the north of the Sprengisandur desert. The canyon can not be seen from the road.

Kiðagilsdrög, a shallow valley up from Kiðagil.

Fremri-Mosar and **Ytri-Mosar,** some meager grasslands by the road with the stream Mosakvísl flowing north to Mjóadalsá.

Aldeyjarfoss, an impressive waterfall in the Skjálfandafljót river, in a unique setting of basalt columns and rock caves.

Svartárkot, a farm located innermost to the east in the valley of Bárðardalur. It stands on the heath at the edge of Ódáðarhraun, 400 m above sea level. A sizeable lake, named Svartárvatn, close by.

Mjóadalsá, a river by Mýri in the Bárðardalur valley. Formerly an obstacle to travel, bridge built in 1977.

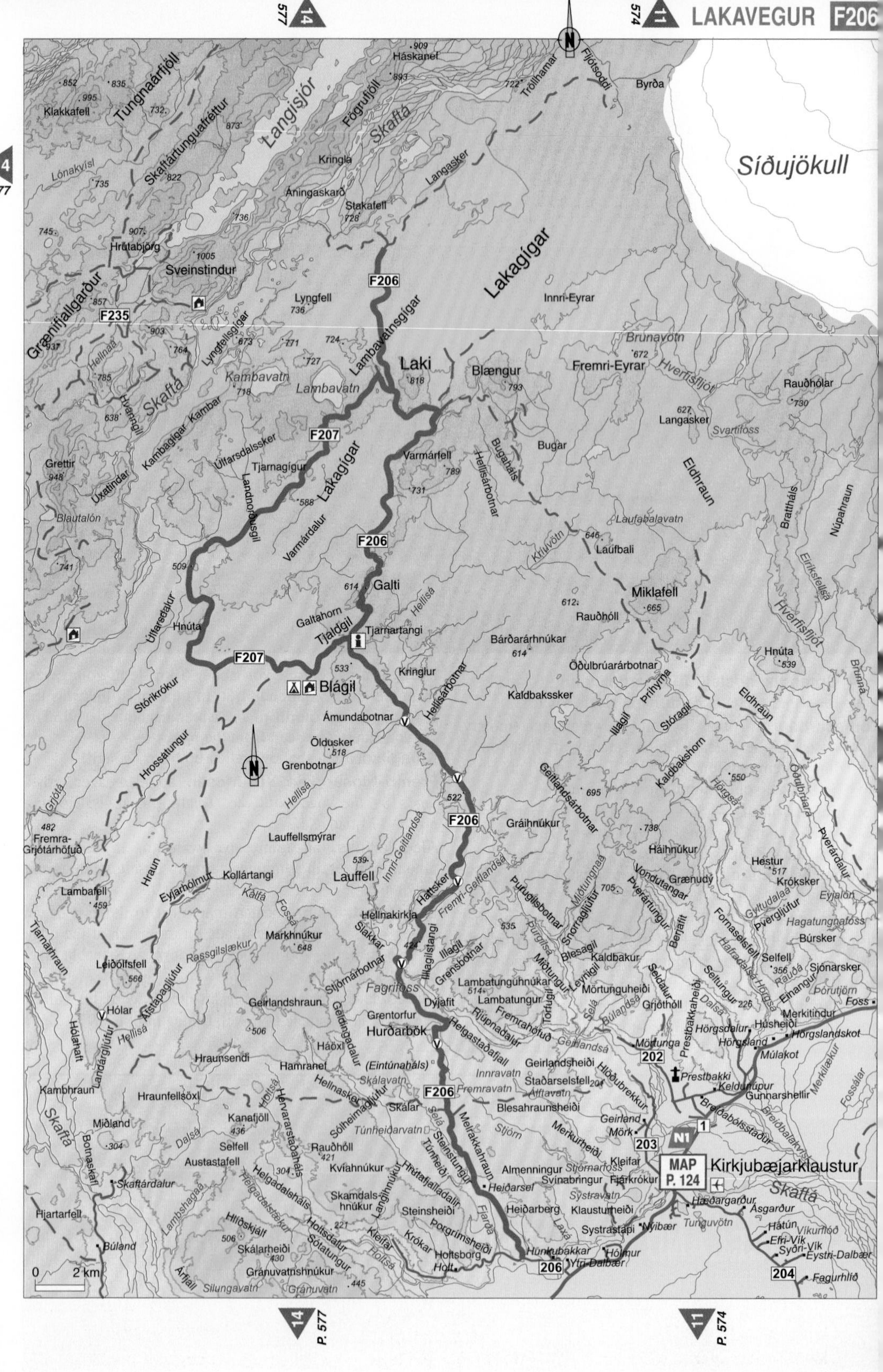

P. 577 14
P. 574 11

Fjaðrárgljúfur

F206 **Lakavegur** 48,8 km to the parking lot at Laki. Passable by all jeeps. On this route two rivers need to be crossed **Geirlandsá** and **Hellisá**.

Fjaðrárgljúfur, a canyon through tuff, 100 m deep, just below the farm Heiðarsel. There is a walking route along the eastern edge, and it is possible to walk up through the canyon, though then one must wade across the river.

Heiðarsel, a deserted farm on the east bank of the river Fjarðará. People lived on the farm until 1980s; it was the home of Þorbjörg Jónsdóttir (born in 1903), wife of the German folklorist Dr. Bruno Schweizer (1897 - 1958), documenting on paper and film some unique discription of the last stages of the Icelandic turf-roofed houses, work, transportation, and many other aspects of daily life in this static time that heralded the end of the ancient Icelandic rural community.

Selárgljúfur, a canyon just above the farm Heiðarsel.

Raflínuvegur ("Linesmen's road") a jeep-track at right angles to the road, leading east to the edge of the moor.

Eintúnaháls, ("One field ridge") an abandoned farm in a grassy, little valley, occupied from the early 19th century to 1934.

Fagrifoss, a waterfall just below the ford. Access is best from the east. The fords on the rivers Geirlandsá and Hellisá are problematic for smaller cars, and can become suddenly impassable when the rivers rise.

F207 **Hringleið** by Laki 23,9 km. Passable by all jeeps.

Laki, (818 m) a tuff mountain in the middle of the Lakagígar row of craters. Panoramic view in good weather.

Lakagígar, a 40 km long row of craters, from the river Skaftá up onto the Vatnajökull glacier. More than 100 craters, some as high as 100 m, now mostly moss-grown. An eruption started in the craters west of Laki in June 1783 and continued there in July, but moved to the eastern craters in the end of July and continued there into the autumn. Source of the Skaftáreldar lava field. Lakagígar are a part of Skaftafell National Park. The area contains some of the world's most remarkable geological formations while the plant and animal life is also of special interest. Because the area is very sensitive to encroachment, the aim of the conservation order is to preserve this unique and extremely sensitive area for future generations.

Galti, a steep mountain giving a good view over the moors.

Blágil, ("Blue canyon") a canyon west of the road near the Hellisá river. Mostly filled with lava from the Skaftáreldar eruptions.

1 **Suðurlandsvegur,** p. 127 — **202** **Prestbakkavegur,** p. 127 — **203** **Geirlandsvegur,** p. 127
204 **Meðallandsvegur,** p. 162 — **206** **Holtsvegur,** p. 128, 163 — **F235** **Langisjór,** p. 443

14
P. 577

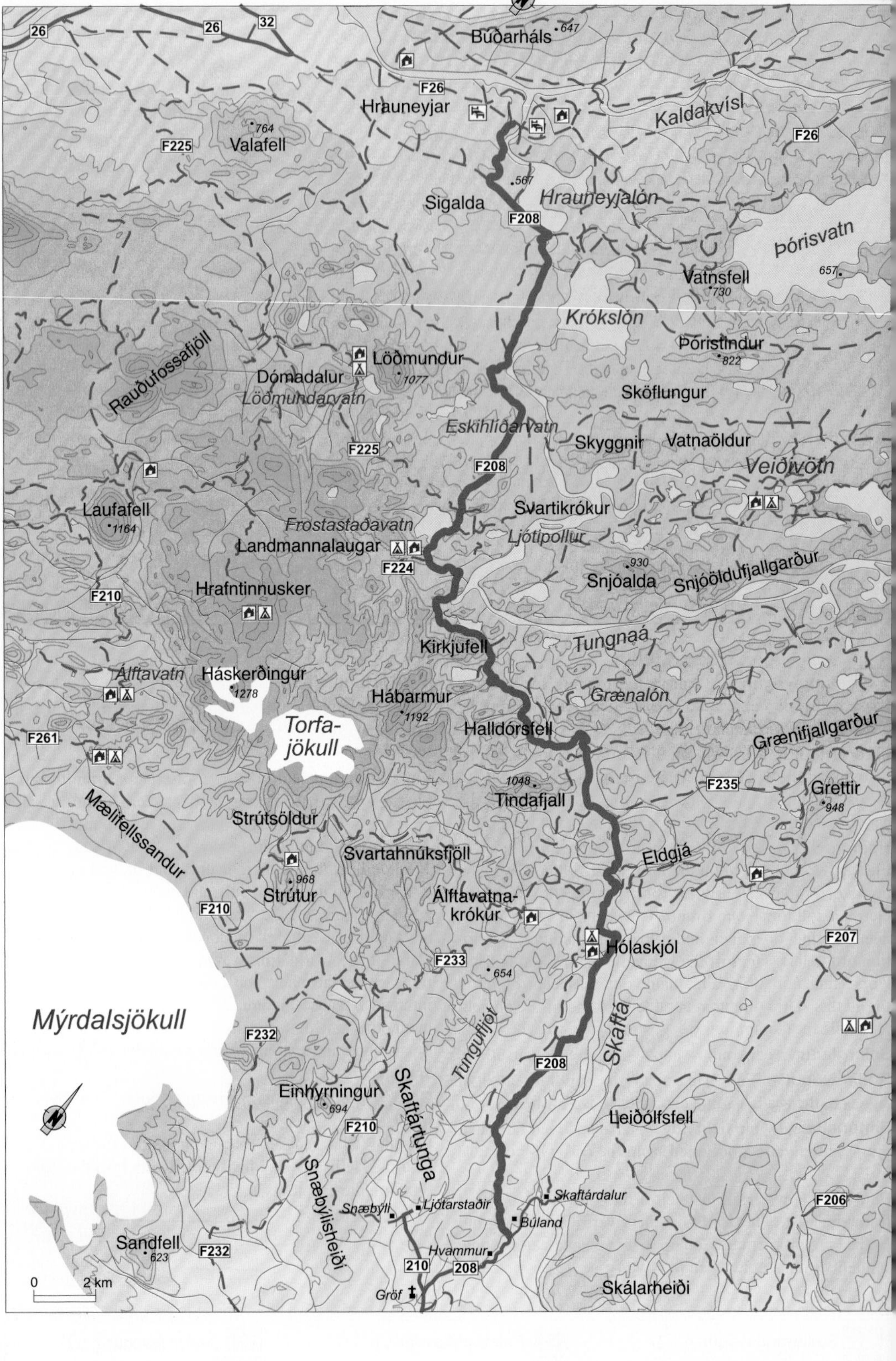

26
26
32
Búðarhals 647
F26
Hrauneyjar
Kaldakvísl
F26
F225
764
Valafell
567
Sigalda
Hrauneyjalón
F208
Þórisvatn
657
Vatnsfell
730
Krókslón
Þóristindur
822
Rauðufossafjöll
Löðmundur
1077
Dómadalur
Löðmundarvatn
Sköflungur
Eskihlíðarvatn
Skyggnir
Vatnaöldur
F225
F208
Veiðivötn
Laufafell
1164
Svartikrókur
Frostastaðavatn
Ljótipollur
Landmannalaugar
F224
930
Snjóalda
Snjóöldufjallgarður
F210
Hrafntinnusker
Kirkjufell
Tungnaá
Álftavatn
Háskerðingur
1278
Hábarmur
Grænalón
1192
Torfa-
jökull
Halldórsfell
Grænifjallgarður
F261
1048
Tindafjall
F235
Grettir
948
Mælifellssandur
Strútsöldur
Svartahnúksfjöll
Eldgjá
968
Strútur
F210
Álftavatna-
krókur
Hólaskjól
F207
F233
654
Mýrdalsjökull
Tungufljót
Skaftá
F232
F208
Einhyrningur
694
Skaftártunga
F210
Leiðólfsfell
Snæbýlisheiði
Skaftárdalur
F206
Snæbýli
Ljótarstaðir
Búland
Sandfell
623
F232
Hvammur
210
208
0
2 km
Skálarheiði
Gröf

F208 Fjallabaksleið nyrðri (Sigölduleið) 85,4 km. Passable by all jeeps. Many small fords on the route.

Frostastaðavatn, a lake surrounded by lava, said to have once had a farm on its shore.

Ljótipollur, an explosion crater with colourful sides and greenish water.

Frostastaðaháls, connects the rhyolite mountains Norður-Námur and Suður-Námur.

Kýlingar, marshy grassland around two inlets from the Tungnaá river.

Kirkjufell, (964 m) an impressive table mountain of rhyolite.

Jökuldalir, valleys surrounded by impressive mountains, the highest being **Tindafjall** (1,048 m). The river Jökuldalakvísl is usually shallow but the riverbed may be soft and not safe to ford. Hut.

Herðubreið (Hörðubreið), ("The broad shouldered") (812 m) a tuff mountain. The view in all directions from the Hörðubreiðarháls ridge just south of the mountain is the finest on these routes. Rain and fog are rather frequent.

Eldgjá, ("Fire canyon") a 40 km long volcanic rift reaching from the Mýrdalsjökull glacier to the mountain Gjátindur. Most impressive at the northern end where it is 600 m wide and 200 m deep. Extensive lava fields have come from Eldgjá and spread over the lowlands of Meðalland, Landbrot and Álftaver. Named by Þorvaldur Thoroddsen, the first geologist to study Eldgjá. He thought there had been only one eruption about 1,100 years ago but later research shows that there have been many eruptions, the lava of Álftaver being the oldest.

Eldgjá

Fremri-Tólfahringar and **Innri-Tólfahringar,** ("Ring of twelve") an area along the Skaftá river where it is said there were once 12 farms, with a church at Réttarfell, and hence the name. Ruins of two farms have been found there.

Svartinúpur, a low mountain and a farm of the same name, abandoned since the eruption of Katla in 1918.

Búland, the northernmost farm in the Skaftártunga district. Above Búland is a canyon, Granagil. There is an old burial cairn, **Granahaugar**, where Grani Gunnarsson was buried.

Skaftárdalur, the western most farm at Síða.

26 Landvegur, p. 160
32 Þjórsárdalsvegur, p. 175
208 Skaftártunguvegur, p. 129
210 Ljótarstaðavegur, p. 129
F26 Sprengisandsleið, p. 430-433
F206 Lakavegur, p. 434
F207 Lakagígavegur, p. 437
F210 Fjallabaksleið syðri, p. 438-441
F224 Landmannalaugavegur, p. 444
F225 Landmannaleið, p. 444
F232 Öldufellsleið, p. 448
F233 Álftavatnskrókur, p. 449
F235 Langisjór, p. 443
F261 Emstruleið, p. 452

14 P. 577

13 P. 576

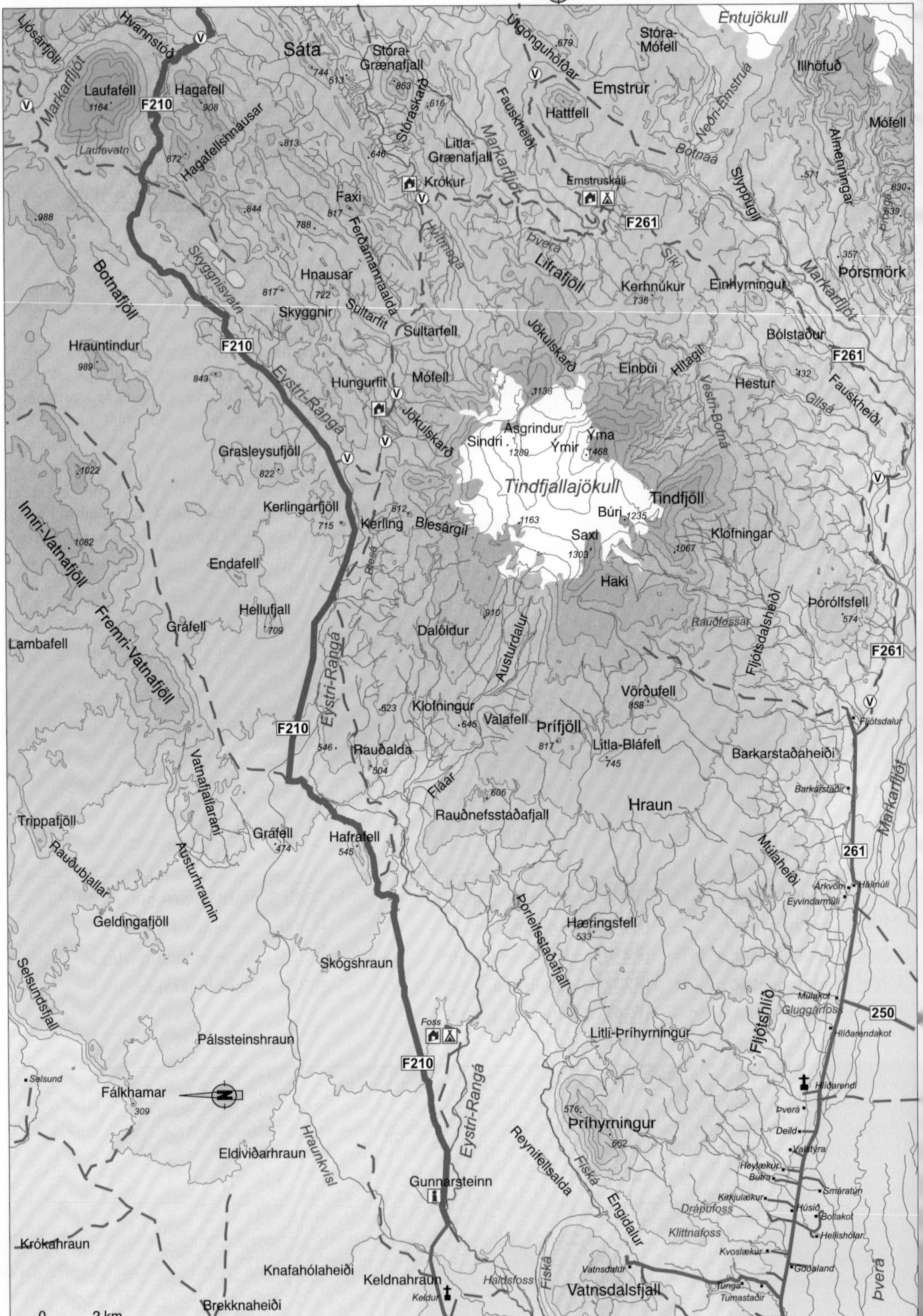

Ljósárfjöll
Hvannstóð
Laufafell
1164
Markarfljót
Laufavatn
Hagafell
908
F210
Hagafellshnausar
872
Sáta
744
513
Stóra-Grænafjall
863
Stóraskarð
616
813
646
Litla-Grænafjall
Krókur
Faxi
817
844
788
988
Ferðamannaalda
Hvítmaga
Útgönguhöfðar
679
Stóra-Mófell
Emstrur
Fauskheiði
Hattfell
Markarfljót
Neðri-Emstruá
Botnaá
Emstruskáli
F261
Þverá
Lifrafjöll
Síki
Entujökull
Illhöfuð
Almenningar
Mófell
Slyppugil
571
830
539
Þröngá
357
Þórsmörk
Markarfljót
Kerhnúkur
736
Einhyrningur
Skyggnisvatn
Botnafjöll
Hnausar
817
722
Skyggnir
Sultarfit
Sultarfell
Hrauntindur
989
F210
843
Eystri-Rangá
Jökulskarð
Bólstaður
F261
Einbúi
Hitagil
Vestri-Botná
Hestur
432
Fauskheiði
Gilsá
Hungurfit
Mófell
1138
Jökulskarð
Ásgrindur
Sindri
1289
Ýmir
Ýma
1468
Grasleysufjöll
822
1022
Tindfjallajökull
Tindfjöll
Kerlingarfjöll
715
Kerling
812
Blesárgil
1163
Búri
1235
Saxi
1303
Klofningar
1067
Innri-Vatnafjöll
1082
Blesá
Endafell
Haki
Hellufjall
709
Gráfell
910
Dalöldur
Austurdalur
Rauðfossar
Fljótsdalsheiði
Þórólfsfell
574
F261
Lambafell
Fremri-Vatnafjöll
Eystri-Rangá
623
Klofningur
645
Valafell
Þríhjöll
817
Vörðufell
858
Litla-Bláfell
745
Fljótsdalur
F210
546
Rauðalda
504
Barkarstaðaheiði
Barkarstaðir
Fláar
606
Rauðnefsstaðafjall
Hraun
Vatnafjallarani
Trippafjöll
Gráfell
474
Hafrafell
545
261
Rauðubjallar
Austurhraunin
Múlaheiði
Árkvörn
Hámúli
Eyvindarmúli
Markarfljót
Geldingafjöll
Þorleifsstaðafjall
Hæringsfell
533
Selsundsfjall
Skógshraun
Múlakot
Gluggafoss
250
Hlíðarendakot
Fljótshlíð
Foss
Pálssteinshraun
Litli-Þríhyrningur
F210
Selsund
Fálkhamar
309
Hlíðarendi
Þverá
Deild
Valstýra
576
Þríhyrningur
662
Eystri-Rangá
Hraunkvísl
Reynifellsalda
Fiská
Eldiviðarhraun
Heylækur
Butra
Smáratún
Gunnarsteinn
Engidalur
Kirkjulækur
Drápufoss
Húsið
Bollakot
Klittnafoss
Hellishólar
Krókahraun
Kvoslækur
Fiská
Vatnsdalur
Goðaland
Knafahólaheiði
Keldnahraun
Haldsfoss
Vatnsdalsfjall
Tunga
Tumastaðir
Þverá
Keldur
Brekknaheiði
0 2 km
Vatnsdalsvatn
Fagrahlíð

Eystri-Rangá, a clear river with its source in Rangárbotnar, running into Þverá near Oddi in Rangárvallasýsla county. Average flow 44 m³/sec.

Langvíuhraun, a lavafield that was very rough and difficult to cross until the 1947 eruption of Hekla filled it with pumice. Water from the river Eystri-Rangá has been diverted to the lava to promote vegetation and hinder erosion.

Hungurfit, grassland on the old Fjallabaksleið ("Behind the mountains") route. Jeep track from there to a bridge over Markarfljót, near Krókur. For mountain vehicles only.

Laufafell, (1,264 m) a majestic mountain, mostly rhyolite. A track, for mountain vehicles only, leads from this route west of Laufafell and Hrafntinnusker and on to Landmannaleið.

Ljósá, a river coming from the Reykjafjöll mountains and running into Markarfljót. South of Reykjadalir are **Ljósártungur**, mostly rhyolite. Lots of geothermal heat thereabout. To the east is **Launfitjarsandur**, probably an old lake-bed.

Torfahlaup, a narrow canyon on the Markarfljót river. Legend has it that a lad named Torfi, jumped over it carrying his sweetheart on his back, to escape from her family, who wanted him killed.

Álftavatn, a deep lake with good fishing. Two cabins built by the Touring Club of Iceland in 1979. The lodges are located in a beautiful spot on the north site of lake Álftavatn. A warden is appointed during the months of June, July and August. The camping site is located by the lake. Route to Torfahlaup along the lake past the mountain Torfatindur.

210 **Ljótarstaðavegur,** p. 129 | 250 **Dímonarvegur,** p. 138, 169 | 261 **Fljótshlíðarvegur,** p. 168, 169
F261 **Emstruleið,** p. 452

14
577

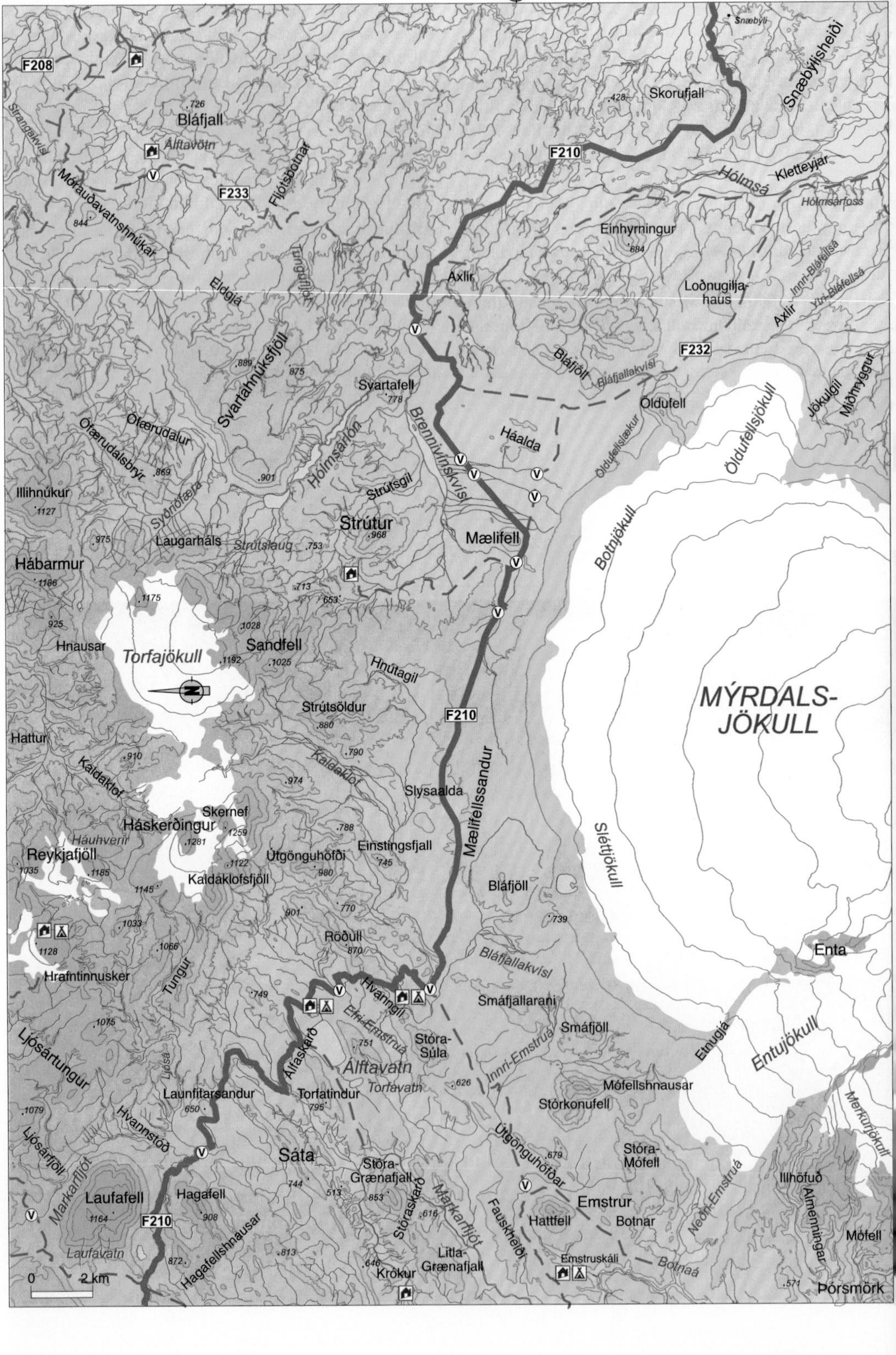

F208
F210
F233
F232
Snæbýli
Snæbýlisheiði
Skorufjall
.428
Bláfjall
.726
Álftavötn
Strangakvísl
Mórauðavatnshnúkar
844
Fljótsbotnar
Hólmsá
Kletteyjar
Hólmsárfoss
Einhyrningur
684
Tungufljót
Eldgjá
Axlir
Loðnugilja-
haus
Innri-Bláfellsá
Ytri-Bláfellsá
Axlir
Svartahnúksfjöll
.889
875
Svartafell
778
Bláfjöll
Bláfjallakvísl
Öldufell
Jökulgil
Mið-hryggur
Ófærudalur
Ófærudalsbrýr
.869
Hólmsárlón
Brennivínskvísl
Háalda
Öldufellsjökull
Öldufellslækur
Illihnúkur
1127
.901
Strútsgil
Syðri-Ófæra
Strútur
.968
Mælifell
Botnjökull
.975
Laugarháls
Strútslaug
.753
Hábarmur
1186
.713
653
.1175
925
.1028
Hnausar
Torfajökull
.1192
Sandfell
.1025
Hnútagil
Strútsöldur
.880
F210
MÝRDALS-
JÖKULL
Hattur
.910
.790
Kaldaklof
Kaldaklof
.974
Slysaalda
Mælifellssandur
Skernef
Háskerðingur
.1259
.788
Háuhverir
.1281
Einstingsfjall
Reykjafjöll
1035
.1185
.1122
Útgönguhöfði
745
980
Sléttjökull
1145
Kaldaklofsfjöll
Bláfjöll
.770
901
.739
.1033
Röðull
870
1128
.1066
Enta
Hrafntinnusker
Tungur
Bláfjallakvísl
.749
Hvanngil
Smáfjallarani
Eyri-Emstrurá
.1075
Ljósártungur
Ljósá
.751
Stóra-
Súla
Smáfjöll
Etnugjá
Álftaskarð
Álftavatn
Innri-Emstrurá
Entujökull
Torfavatn
Launfitarsandur
Torfatindur
795
.626
Mófellshnausar
.1079
650
Stórkonufell
Hvannstóð
Merkurjökull
Ljósárfjöll
Útgönguhöfðar
.679
Stóra-
Mófell
Sáta
Stóra-
Grænafjall
Markarfljót
744
513
853
Illhöfuð
Laufafell
Hagafell
Stóraskarð
.616
Markarfljót
Fauskheiði
Emstrur
Neðri-Emstrurá
Almenningar
1164
908
Hattfell
Botnar
F210
Mófell
Laufavatn
Hagafellshnausar
872
.813
.646
Litla-
Grænafjall
Emstruskáli
Botnaá
0
2 km
Krókur
.571
Þórsmörk

F210 **Fjallabaksleið syðri, Miðvegur (Ljótastaðavegur)** 112,5 km, Ljótastaðavegur is 25 km. The route is passalbe for all jeeps, not small jeeps. Many rivers need to be crossed on this route. It is safer to have two jeeps. The main rivers that need to be crossed are: Markarfljót by Laufafell, Kaldaklofskvísl south of Hvanngil and Hólmsá south of Mælifellssandur.

Hvanngil, a small valley which has been a popular resting place for those travelling between Landmannalaugar and Þórsmörk. Sheperds' hut and accommodation. Good hiking area. A marked walking route (Laugavegur) to Hrafntinnusker and Landmannalaugar to the north and Emstrur and Þórsmörk to the south.

Mælifellssandur, sands between the glaciers Torfajökull and Mýrdalsjökull about 600 m above sea level. Once a much-used route, the western part named Gásasandur. A passable road but care must be taken because of quicksands.

Brytalækir, a short clear stream with its source in Mýrdalssandur, a tributaty of Hólmsá.

Slysaalda, ("Casualty ridge") a sand ridge in the western part of Mælifellssandur. In 1868 four people from Skaftafellssýsla county perished there, their remains not being discovered till ten years later. Memorial.

Mælifell, (791 m) a tuff mountain towards the east of Mælifellssandur. Good views.

Brennivínskvísl, ("The schnaps branch") a clear river, tributary of Hólmsá. The origins of its unusual name are unknown.

Hólmsárbotnar, southeast of the Torfajökull glacier.

Hólmsárlón, a lagoon of unusual beauty, and hot pools, among them **Strútslaug**.

Snæbýli, a farm in Skaftártunga. There Road 210 beginns.

F208 **Fjallabaksleið nyrðri,** p. 436 **F232** **Öldufellsleið,** p. 448 **F233** **Álftavatnskrókur,** p. 449

14
P. 577

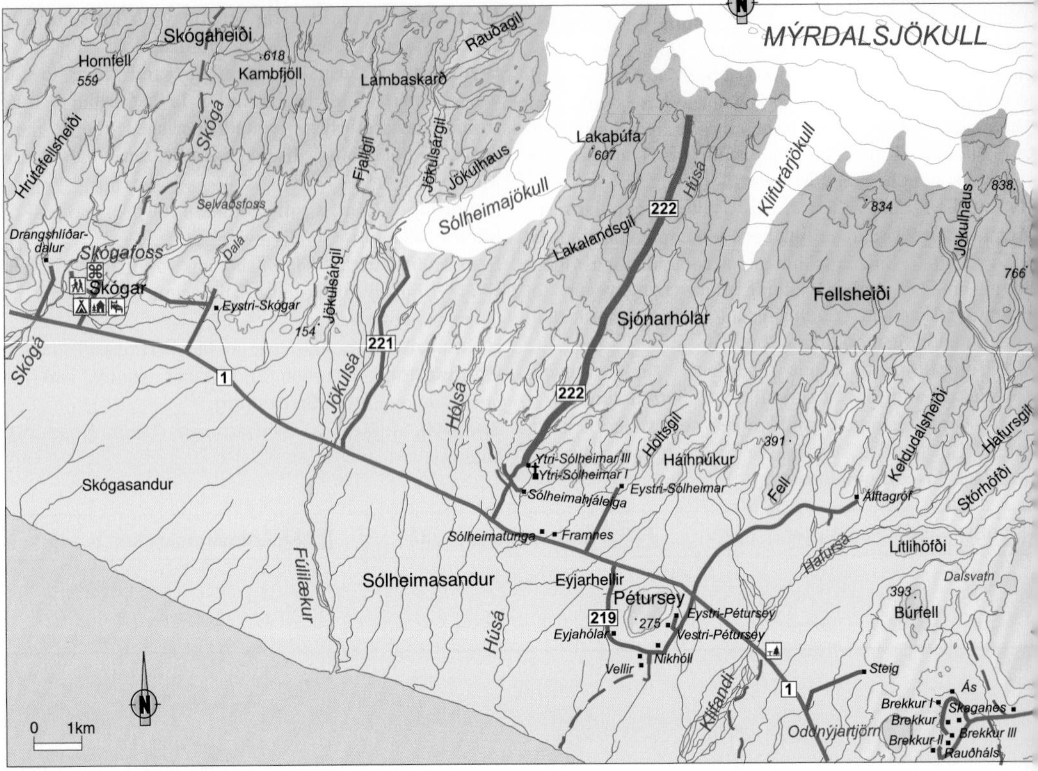

F221 **Sólheimajökulsvegur** 9,4 km. This route is passable for all jeeps. It is possible to take snowmobile tours on the glacier **Sólheimajökull** www.snow.is

F222 **Mýrdalsjökulsvegur** 10 km.

1 **Suðurlandsvegur,** p. 133

219 **Péturseyjarsvegur,** p. 132

Skógarfoss, p. 133

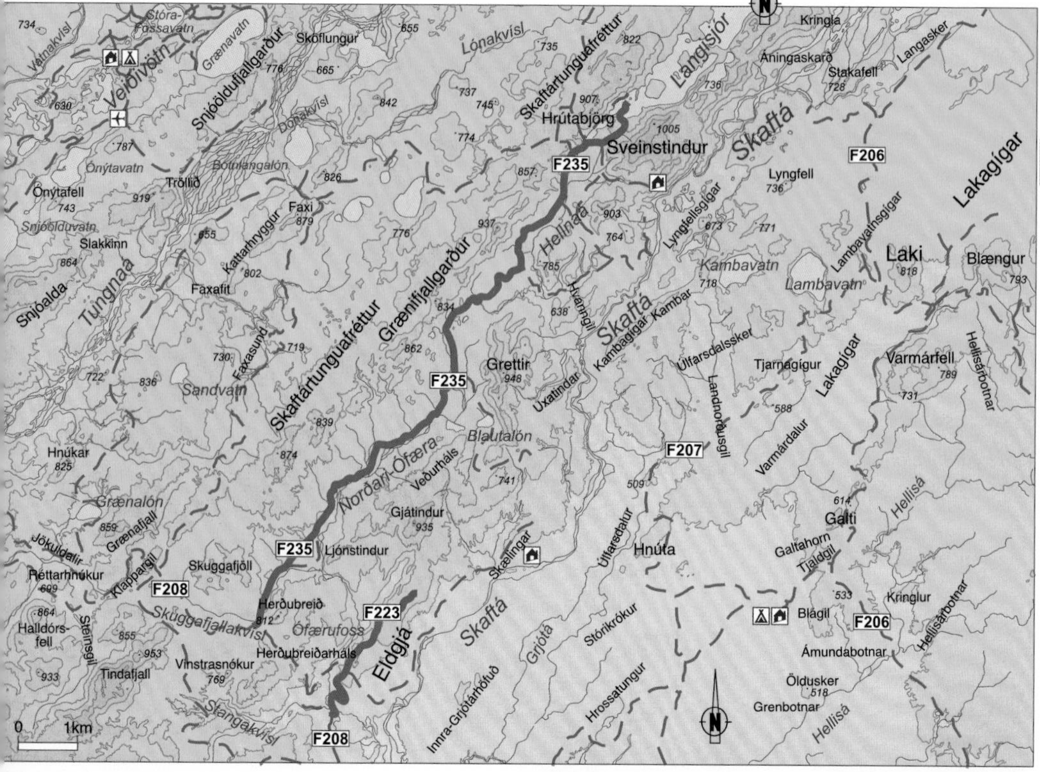

14
P. 577

F235 **Langisjór,** 25,4 km. Passable by all jeeps. A few rivers and creeks need to be crossed. There is a trail west of Herðubreið (Hörðubreið) leading to Langisjór, going over Skuggafjallakvísl and other rivers.

Langisjór, (Skaftárvatn) a lake 20 km long and 2 km wide.

Sveinstindur, (1089 m) mountain on the souths side of Langisjór.

Breiðbakur, (1028 m) mountain. The highest mountain on the west of Langisjór, a jeep track leeds to it. Beautiful view over Langisjór.

F223 **Eldgjárvegur.**

F206 **Lagavegur,** p. 434 | **F207** **Lakagígavegur,** p. 437 | **F208** **Fjallabaksleið nyrðri,** p. 436

14
P. 577

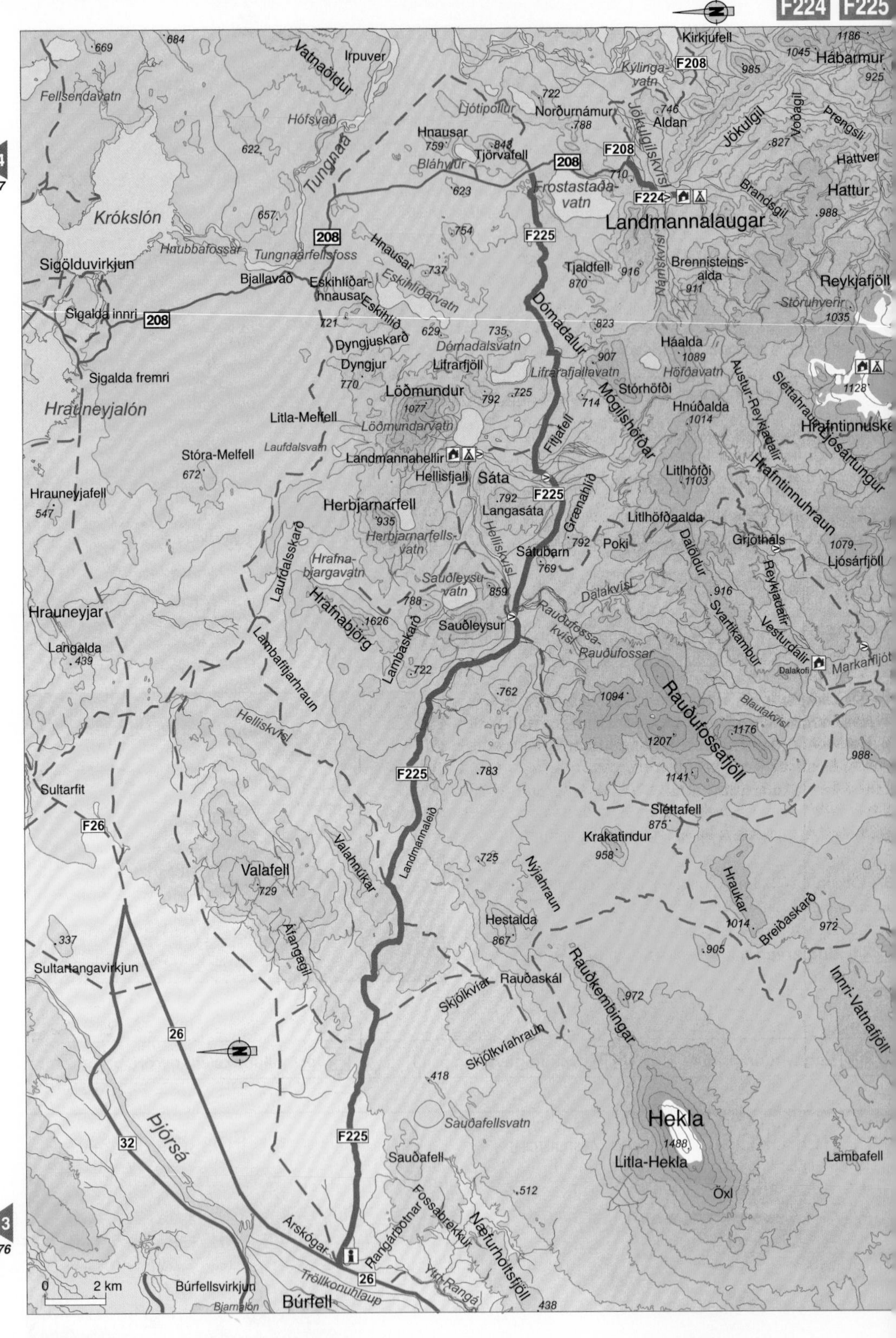

13
P. 576

Landmannalaugar

F224 **Landmannalaugavegur,** 2,5 km. Leeds to F208 that goes to Landmannalaugar. Passable for small jeeps, crossing two small rivers, Námskvísl and Laugalæna. It is possible to leave small cars and walk to Landmannalaugar via walking bridges.

Landmannalaugar, one of Iceland's natural jewels and popular tourist attractions in Iceland. Streams of geothermal and spring water come from under a high wall of lava and mix to make streams and pools of just the right temperature for bathing. Though the altitude is over 600 m, the river banks are covered in grass and flowers. The very colourful rhyolite mountains surrounding it make this area quite unique. The Icelandic Touring Association has operated a mountain lodge in Landmannalaugar since 1951. The lodge is in the altitude of 600 m and is located by the edge of Laugahraun lava field. In walking distance from the lodge is a natural warm geothermal pool that is very popular for bathing. A warden is appointed during most of the year. There begins the popular 4 day trip from Landmannalaugar to Þórsmörk, Laugavegur route. The area around the lodge also offers numerous different hiking possibilities. Campsite. View dial at Bláhnúkur. The site is reasonably accessible in the summer and there are quite good summer roads leading to it.

Laugahraun, a dark rhyolite lava field with some obsidian from the Brennisteinsalda ridge, with steam and sulphur springs.

Jökulgil, a long, narrow valley between colourful rhyolite mountains.

Jökulgilskvísl, the river through the Jökulgil valley. It was a serious hindrance until bridged in 1966.

F225 **Landmannaleið (Dómadalsleið)** 40,9 km, from Landvegur. This route is passable for small jeeps, some small rivers need to be crossed. It is possible to drive to Landmannahellir, 8,5 km.

Sölvahraun, a lava field that was covered with moss, grass and dwarf shrubs until it the 1980 Hekla eruption.

Valagjá, an interesting crater east of Valahnúkur.

Rauðufossafjöll, ("Red falls mountains") (1,230 m) mountains named for the reddish explosion crater on their slopes, down which run the waterfalls Rauðufossar.

Kringla, a grassy plain the floor of which is at 590 m, encircled by mountains mostly around 1,000 m high.

Landmannahellir, a cave, a good place for a break on the old Dómadalur pass. The cave itself was once used as accommodation for those who had to travel through the highland pastures. Today at Landmannahellir there are fine cabins with decent facilitie designed to accommodate tourists and their travel horses.

Löðmundur, (1,077 m) the highest mountain in this area, very impressive.

Dómadalur, a valley with a small lake named Dómadalsvatn.

26 **Landavegur,** p. 158-161 32 **Þjórsárdalsvegur,** p. 175-176 F26 **Sprengisandsleið,** p. 430-433
F208 **Fjallabaksleið nyrðri,** p. 436

14
P. 577

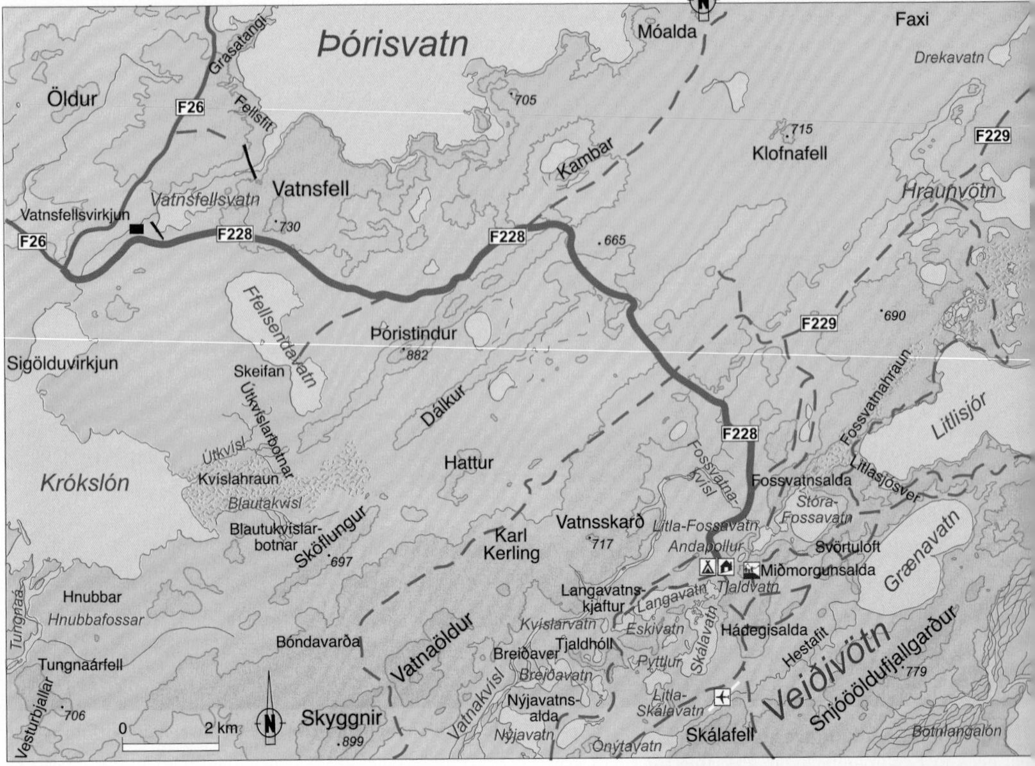

F228 Veiðivatnaleið, 21 km. This route is only passable by jeeps because of two deep fords that need to be crossed. There is a hut by Tjaldavatn. A view dial by Miðmorgunsalda.

© Markaðsstofa Austurlands

F26 Sprengisandsleið, p. 430-433 **F229 Jökulheimaleið,** p. 447

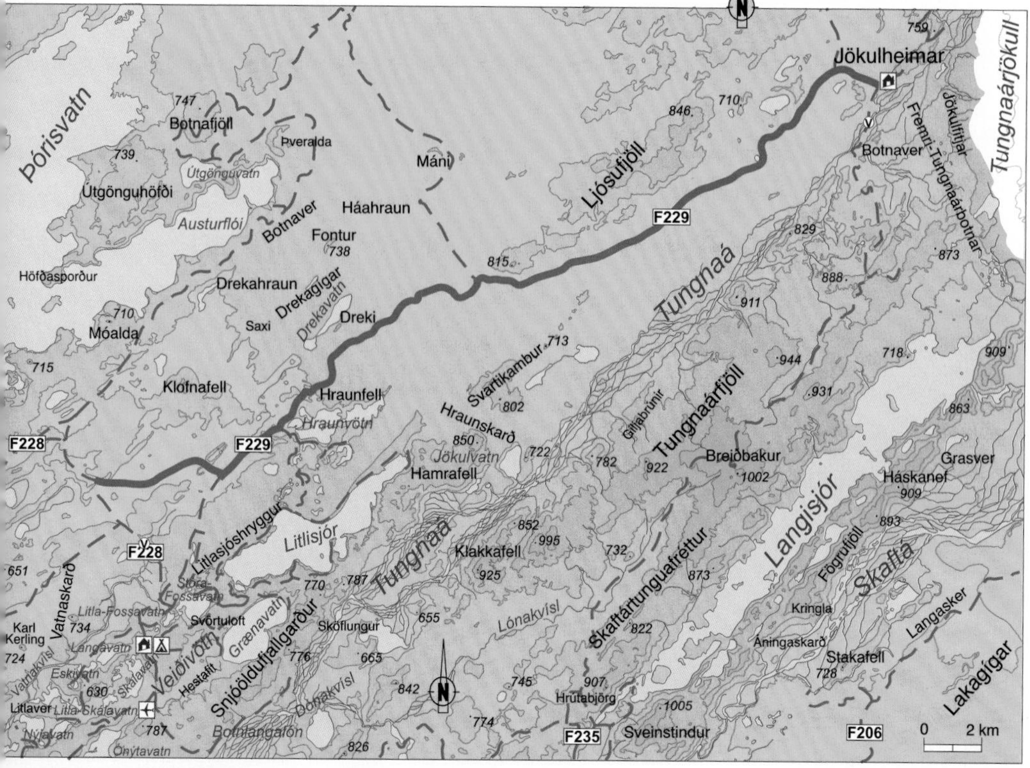

14 P. 577

F229 Jökulheimaleið, 36,1 km. The route lies north of **Veiðivötn** to a cabin at the foot of Tungnaárjökull glacier. The route is passable for all jeeps. North of the cabin is an ill passable route to Vonarskarð called Bárðargata. It is also possible to go to Jökulheimar through a so called Jökulheimastyttingur which lies west of the main route and joins the main route on the south side of Drekavatn lake.

F206 **Lakavegur,** p. 434 F228 **Veiðivatnaleið,** p. 446 F235 **Langisjór,** p. 443

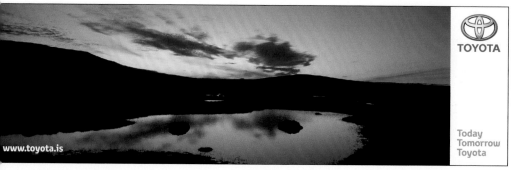

14 P. 577

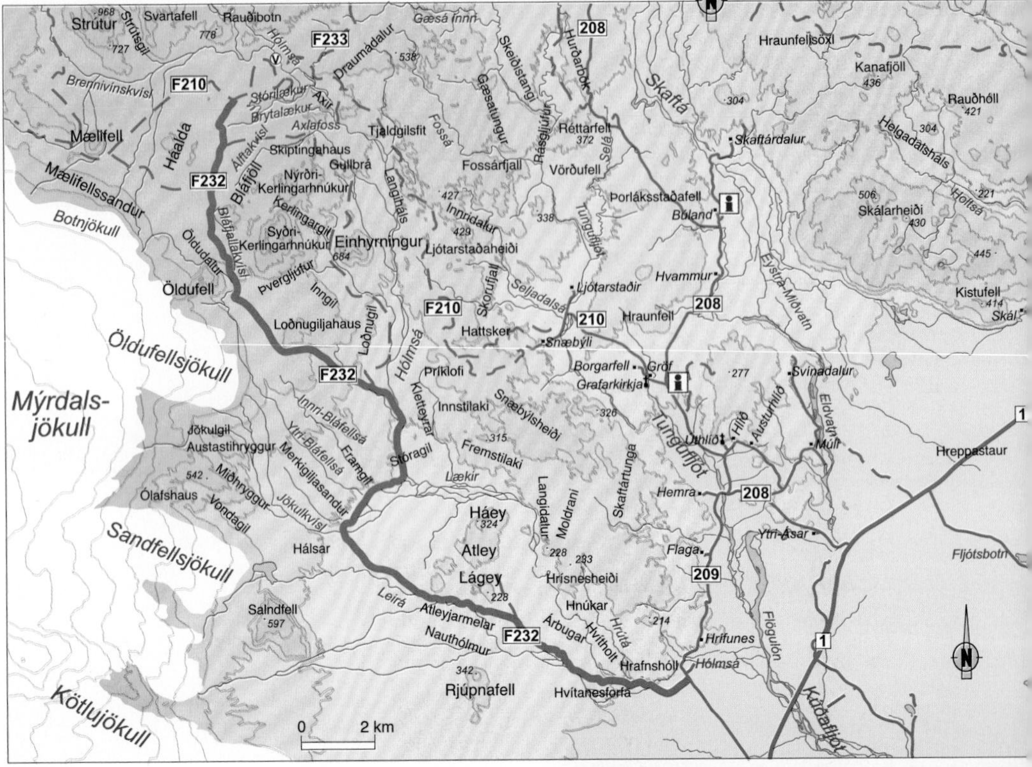

F232 Öldufellsleið 35,7 km. Passable by all jeeps. Considered one of the most beautiful routes of the country. The route lies close to Mýrdalsjökull. One ford needs to be crossed, Bláfjallakvísl.

Hólmsá, a river with its source under the glacier Torfajökull, running into Hólmsárbotnar, along the edge of Mýrdalssandur and into Kúðafljót. Tjaldagilsháls east of Hólmsá with a beautiful view.

1 **Suðurlandsvegur,** p. 129

208 **Skaftártunguvegur,** p. 129

209 **Hrífunesvegur,** p. 129

210 **Ljótarstaðavegur,** p. 129

F208 **Fjallabaksleið nyrðri,** p. 436

F210 **Fjallabaksleið syðri,** p. 438-441

F233 **Álftavatnskrókur,** p. 449

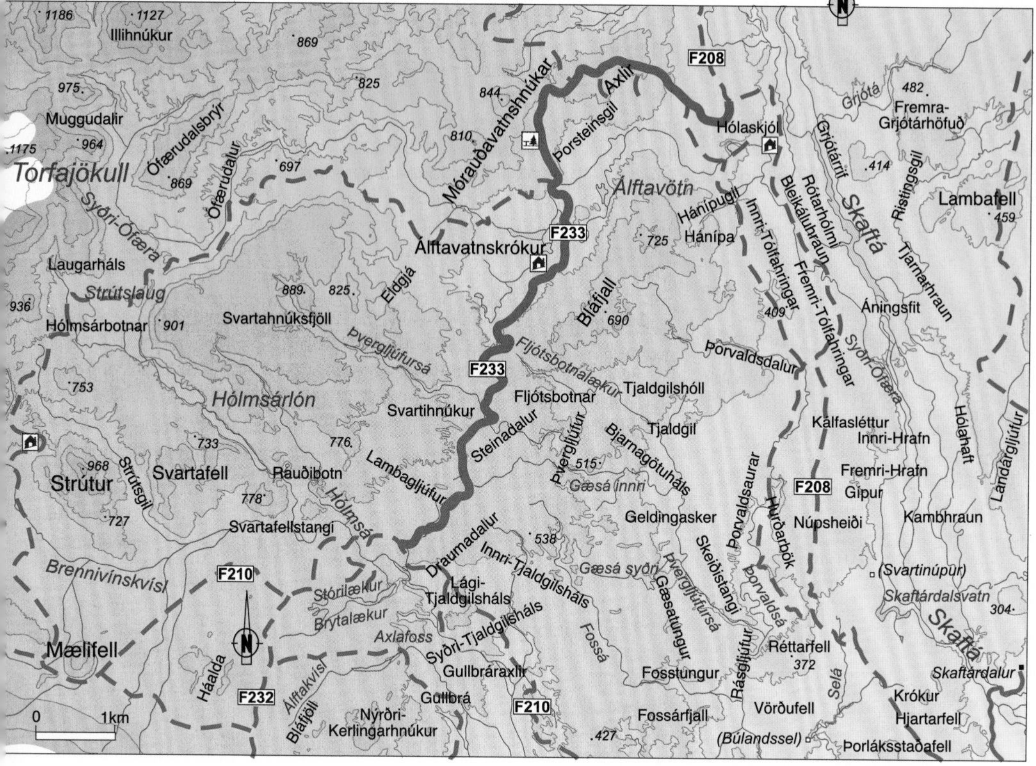

F233 ÁLFTAVATNSKRÓKUR

14 P. 577

233 **Álftavatnskrókur,** 20,7 km going south west of)ute F208. Only passable by jeeps. A ford must be taken ver the Syðri-Ófæra river which can be an obstacle for nall jeeps.

lyrðri-Ófæra and **Syðri-Ófæra,** ("Northern and)uthern impassable") two rivers that flow through the ldgjá canyon and join the Skaftá river. The northern ver enters the rift in two impressive waterfalls, færufoss. A natural bridge across the lower falls)llapsed in 1994. The southern river also plunges in a aterfall into the narrow canyon Hánípugil, just before it)mes down to Hánípufit. a green spot on the west banks f the Skaftá river.

Ófærufoss.

F208 **Fjallabaksleið nyrðri,** p. 436 F210 **Fjallabaksleið syðri,** p. 438-441 F232 **Öldufellsleið,** p. 448

P. 576 13 · P. 577 14 · 13 P. 576

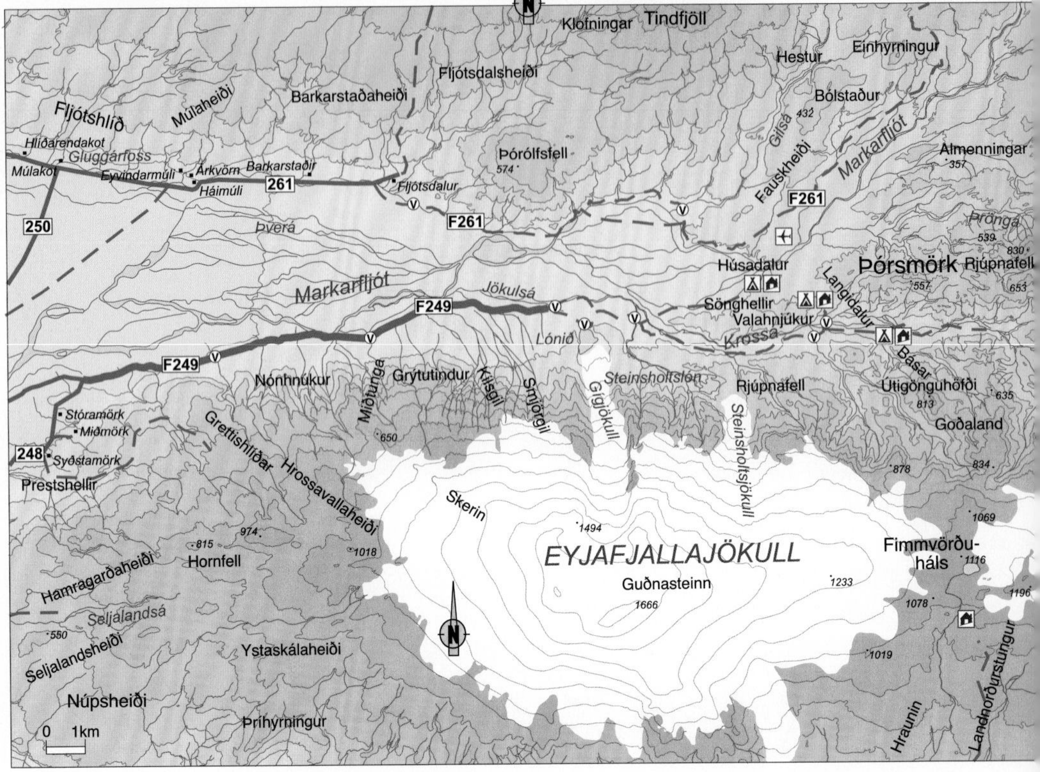

WARNING: Road F249 is not recommended for small cars, only for 4-wheel drive vehicles in convoy, because of dangerous rivers.

F249 Þórsmerkurvegur, 28,9 km. From the old bridge over Markarfljót to Gathillur. Some dangerous glacial rivers need to be crossed.

Nauthúsagil, a canyon by Stóra-Mörk.

Mörk, (Stóra-Mörk, Mið-Mörk and Syðsta-Mörk) the last farms on the way to Þórsmörk. Stóra-Mörk was often mentioned in *Njáls saga*.

Gígjökull, ("Crater glacier") a steep glacier-tongue coming down from the crater of the Eyjafjallajökull glacier, hence the name. The lake Jökullón in front of the glacier is more than 40 m deep and usually has icebergs floating on it. The glacier is getting smaller every year. The river Jökulsá runs from the lagoon to Markarfljót.

Steinholtsjökull, a glacier-tongue coming down from Eyjafjallajökull. In January 1967 a big part of the mountain Innstihaus broke off and fell down on the glacier causing a tremendous flood.

Stakkholtsgjá, a large canyon in the region of Stakkholt, with perpendicular walls up to 100 m high on both sides. The canyon divides in two, the left part ending in a narrow chasm with a lovely waterfall with very clear water. It takes about an hour to go through Stakkholtsgjá, and this must be done on foot.

Þórsmörk, the region west of the Mýrdalsjökull glacie between the rivers Krossá and Markarfljót. Famous fo having a great variety of natural features and goo weather, and therefore a very popular place for outings Protected since 1921, in the care of the Forestry Service National Forest. Cabins in the valleys Langidalur an Húsadalur. Campsites in Langidalur, the Össugil canyo in Húsadalur and the canyon Slyppugil. Skagfjörðsská is located by the roots of Langidalur in Þórsmörk not fa from Krossá river. The lodge has two floors and i accommodates up to 75 people (in bunkers wit mattresses). There are several beautiful hiking route from Skagfjörðsskáli. Most people end thei "Laugarvegur" hike in Langidalur. Landgræsla ríkisins the Soil Conservation Service of Iceland has restore vegetation on barren land in Þórsmörk.

Goðaland, the region on the south side of Kross opposite Þórsmörk, great contrasts in nature with gullie canyons and glaciers. Extensive birchwoods. Cabins c the touring club Útivist and a campsite at Básar.

248 Merkurvegur, p. 166 · **250 Dímonarvegur,** p. 138, 169 · **261 Fljótshlíðarvegur,** p. 168-169

F261 Emstruleið, p. 453, 453

14
P. 577

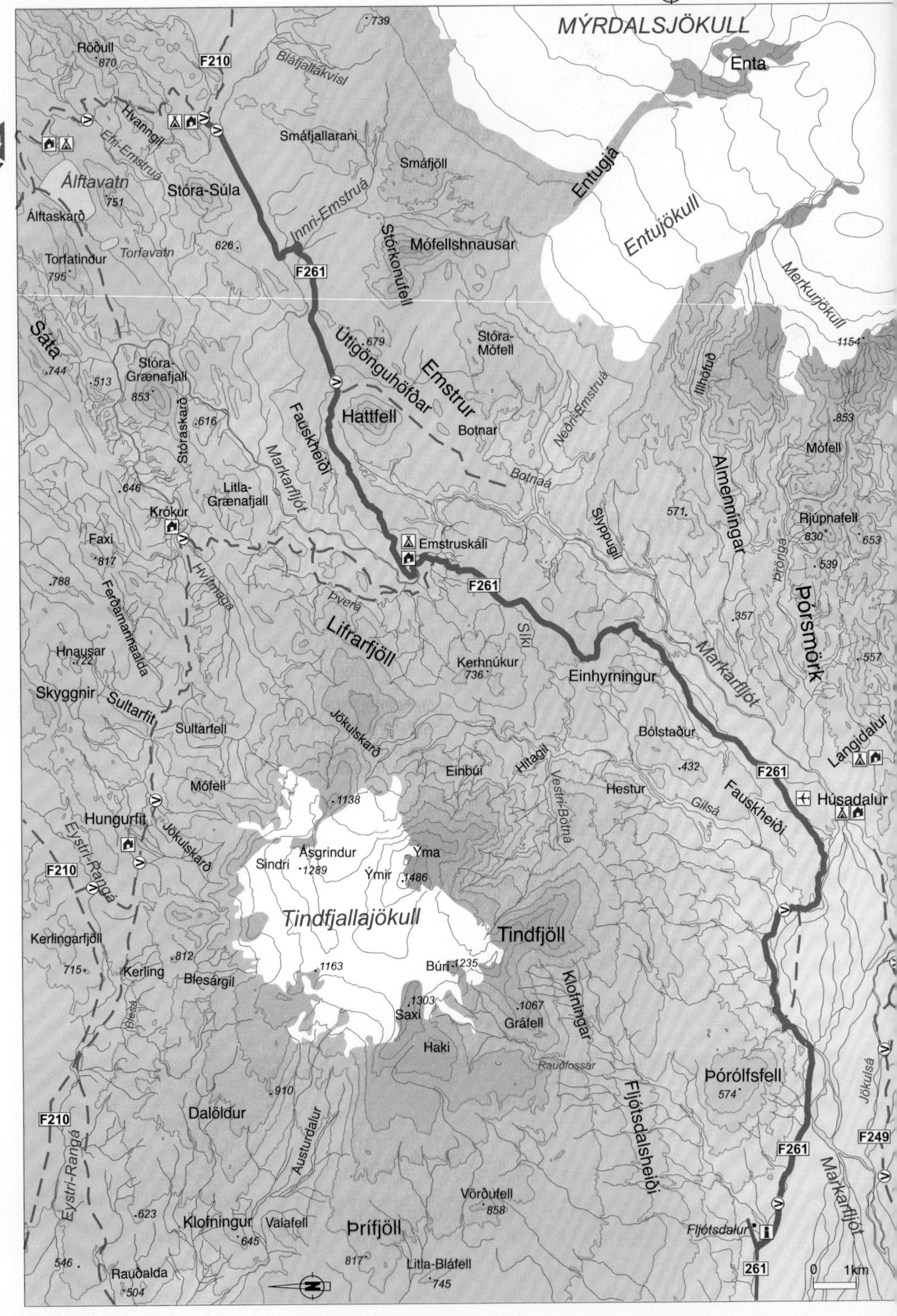

261 **Fljótshlíðarvegur,** p. 168-169 F210 **Fjallabaksleið syðri,** p. 438-441 F249 **Þórsmerkurvegur,** p. 450

261 **Emstruleið** 37,3 km. Passable by all jeeps. The acial river Gilsá needs to be crossed and also the river áfjallakvísl.

ilsá, a river coming from the glacier Tindfjallajökull.

arkarfljótsgljúfur, a rugged canyon, 100 m deep, east Einhyrningur.

arkarfljót, a 100 km long river, its drainage basin out 1,070 km^2, rising in the Reykjardalir valleys but ostly coming from the Mýrdalsjökull glacier. Bridge ar Emstrur (1978), where the remains of an old rope-ay can be seen.

öllagjá, a canyon through which the road goes, a ver bed formed by Markarfljót in a massive débâcle 000-2,500 years ago.

inhyrningur, ("Unicorn") (769 m) a mountain that om some angles resembles a horn. The settlement land Sighvatur rauði is thought to be at its foot.

attfell (Hattafell), (909 m) a conspicuous mountain the Emstrur area. To its southwest is the canyon attfellsgljúfur, an ancient riverbed.

Emstrur, the area north of the river Syðri-Emstruá, between Mýrdalsjökull and Markarfljót. Very little vegetation. Cabin built by the Touring Club of Iceland. The ITA lodges stand close by the river Sydri-Emstruá. A warden is appointed during the months of June, July and August. Close by the Emstrur lodges is the magnificent canyon Markarfljótsgljúfur that is well worth a short hike. A 4x4 path leads to the lodges.

Fremri-Emstruá, a river from under Entujökull, a tongue of the Mýrdalsjökull glacier. Bridged in 1978 by the Touring Club of Iceland then again in 1988 after the first footbridge was swept away in floods.

Innri-Emstruá, a river falling from the Mýrdalsjökull glacier into Markarfljót. Bridged in 1975.

Kaldaklofskvísl, a river that runs from the mountains Kaldaklofsfjöll into Markarfljót. There is a ford a little to the east of the Hvanngil canyon, but it can be dangerous in high water. Footbridge near the ford built by the Touring Club of Iceland in 1985.

21
P. 584

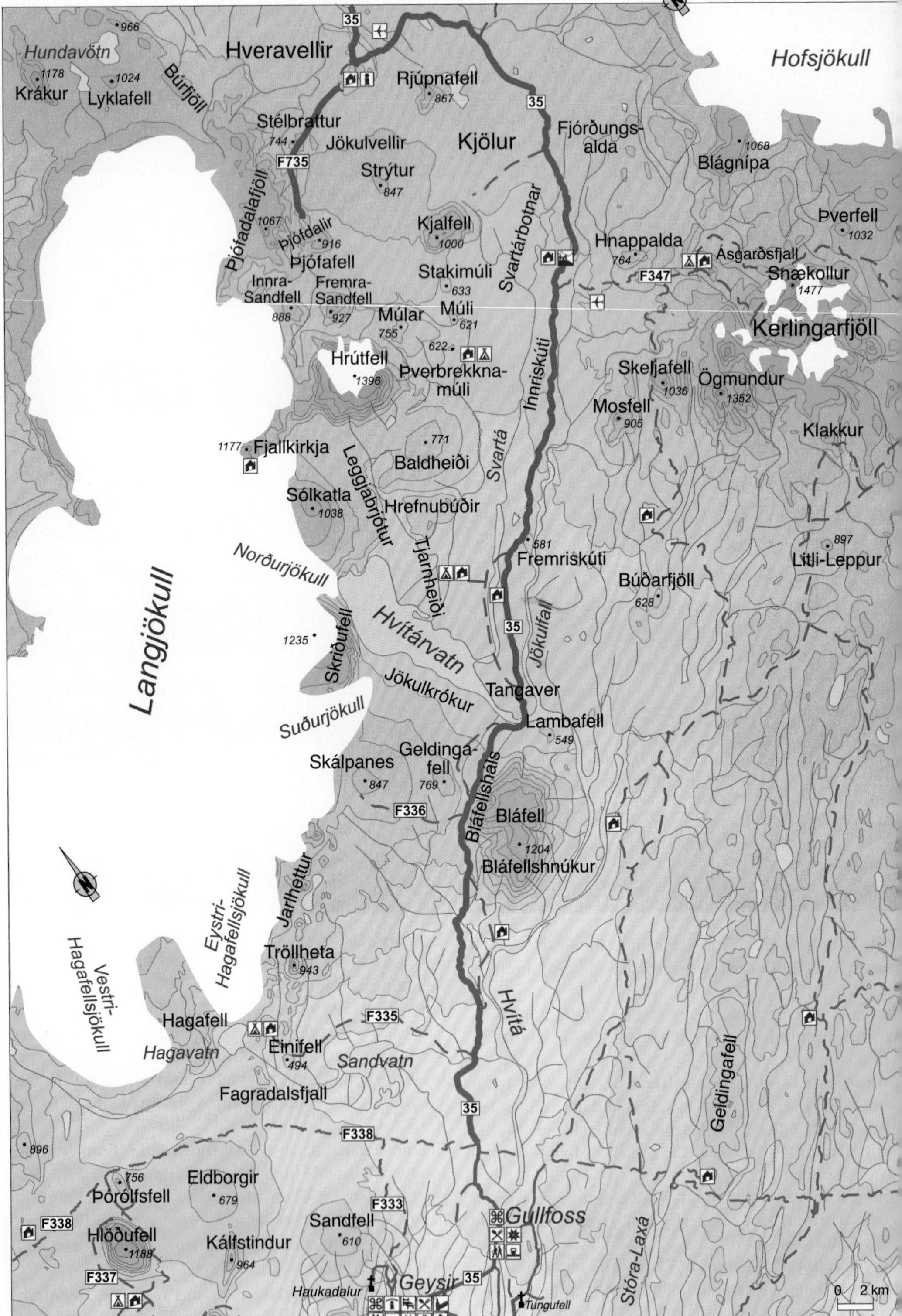

Hundavötn
966
1178
Krákur
1024
Lyklafell
Búrfjöll
35
Hveravellir
Rjúpnafell
867
Hofsjökull
35
Stélbrattur
744
Jökulvellir
Kjölur
Fjórðungs-
alda
1068
Blágnípa
F735
Strýtur
847
Þjófadalafjöll
1067
Þjófdalir
916
Þjófafell
Kjalfell
1000
Svartárbotnar
Hnappalda
764
Þverfell
1032
Ásgarðsfjall
F347
Snækollur
1477
Innra-
Sandfell
888
Fremra-
Sandfell
927
Stakimúli
633
Múlar
755
Múli
621
622
Kerlingarfjöll
Hrútfell
1396
Þverbrekkna-
múli
Innriskúti
Skeljafell
1036
Ögmundur
1352
Mosfell
905
Klakkur
1177
Fjallkirkja
Leggjabrjótur
771
Baldheiði
Svartá
Sólkatla
1038
Hrefnubúðir
581
Fremriskúti
897
Litli-Leppur
Norðurjökull
Tjarnheiði
Búðarfjöll
628
Langjökull
Skriðufell
1235
Hvítárvatn
35
Jökulfall
Jökulkrókur
Tangaver
Suðurjökull
Lambafell
549
Skálpanes
847
Geldinga-
fell
769
Bláfellsháls
F336
Bláfell
1204
Bláfellshnúkur
Jarlhettur
Eystri-
Hagafellsjökull
Vestri-
Hagafellsjökull
Tröllheta
943
Hvítá
Hagafell
F335
Hagavatn
Einifell
494
Sandvatn
Fagradalsfjall
Geldingafell
35
896
F338
756
Þórólfsfell
Eldborgir
679
F333
Gullfoss
Sandfell
610
F338
Hlöðufell
1188
Kálfstindur
964
Stóra-Laxá
F337
Haukadalur
Geysir
35
Tungufell
0 2 km
35
30

F35 **Kjalvegur** ("Keel road") the south section, 88,2 :m from the service centre by Gullfoss to the junction ɔ Hveravellir. From there and north to road 731 are 79 m. This route is passible for all vehicles. Kjalvegur has ılways been a much-used mountain route between the orth and south of Iceland, being easily accessible from Húnavatnssýsla, Skagafjörður and Eyjafjörður. The many grassy areas made this route easier than other inland racks when people travelled on horseback. The old-st track was through the centre of Kjölur, on the east of Kjalfell, but after the incident at Beinahóll in 1780 peo-ple mostly used the western route through Þjófadalir.

F335 **Hagavatnsvegur** 16,7 km to the Icelandic Tour-ng Association hut by Jarlhettur. Passable for allt small eeps to the hut.

Hagavatn, a good-sized lake by the glacier edge. A tour-st hut belonging to the Touring Club of Iceland. A war-len is appointed during the months of July and August.

Farið a river flowing from Hagavatn lake.

F336 **Skálpanesvegur** 7,9 km. The route is passable or all small jeeps to the hut.

Jarlhettur, a row of tuff peaks.

Skálpanes, an old shield volcano with lava flows owards Hvítárvatn and the roots of Bláfell.

Geldingafell, (763 m) a tuff mountain.

Bláfell, (1,204 m) the highest mountain in southwest celand.

Hvítá, a big glacial river coming from Hvítárvatn. There re plans to harness this river by the mountain Bláfell.

Hvítársandar, sands and barren land between Jökulfalla nd Tjarnarheiði south to Hvítá.

Hvítárvatn, a lake 26.6 km^2, 419 m above sea level, 84 n deep. Glacier-coloured, it often has icebergs floating n it.

Karlsdráttur, a place where the glacier flows into Hvít-rvatn lake. Patches with rich vegetation growing at app-oximately 420 - 440 meters above sea level

Hvítárnes, wide, wet and flat grasslands by Hvítárvatn. A tourist hut built 1930, rebuilt and improved since. a mall creek on the north side of Hvítárvatn lake. A tour-st hut built 1930, rebuilt and improved since. It was elieved that a female ghost use to haunt the Hvítárnes rea. On a rock south of the hut is a memorial to Tryggva Magnússon (1896-1943) a pioneer in highland travelling.

Tjarnheiði, an oasis east of Hvítárnes og Fúlakvísl.

Svartá, a river that runs from Kjalhraun lava field.

Hrefnubúðir, (648 m) a mountain on the north of Hvítárnes, with some birch-bushes on the sides. This is about the highest that birch-bushes thrive in Iceland.

Baldheiði, a dolerite dome, 771 m.

Fúlakvísl, a river that runs from Langjökull to Hvít-árvatn lake.

Fremriskúti, (572 m) and **Innriskúti,** (710 m) tuff mountains in southern Kjölur. Marked path from Innri-Skúti to a cabin belonging to the Touring Club of Iceland at Þverbrekkumúli.

Hrútfell, (1,410 m) a table mountain in the southwest area of Kjölur, with a 10 km^2 glacier top. One of the most majestic mountains in the area.

Gránunes, a field named after a mare.

F347 **Kerlingarfjallavegur** 10,5 km. Passable for jeeps. Some small rivers need to be crossed and ford over Blákvísl by Gýgjarfoss.

Árskarð, (also named Ásgarður) a pass or a canyon at the north side of Kerlingarfjöll.

Kerlingarfjöll, a cluster of majestic rhyolite peaks, some of them partially covered by glacier. Lots of geothermal heat in the valleys between the peaks. The highest peaks are **Snækollur** (1,477 m), **Loðmundur** (1,432 m) and **Mænir** (1,335 m). A visitors centre.

Kjalhraun, a lava field in the centre of Kjölur, 450 km^2. Some rocks and pinnacles around the crater **Strýtur** in the centre of the lavafield, otherwise rather flat and easy to cross, with a fair bit of vegetation.

Beinahóll, or Beinabrekka ("Hill of bones") on a low lava ridge on the northeast of Kjalfell. In 1780 four men from Reynistaður in Skagafjörður perished there in bad weather together with a flock of sheep, hence the name.

Blágnípa, (1068 m) a table mountain on the west ridge of Hofsjökull.

Kjalfell, (1000m) a small table mountain with dolerite on top.

Kjölur, the valley between the glaciers Hofsjökull and Langjökull, 25-30 km wide, 600 to 700 m above sea level. Mostly covered by lava and very barren.

Geirsalda, named after Geir G. Zoëga (1885-1959) road administrator. View dial.

Rjúpnafell, (867 m) tuff mountain.

30 **Skeiða- og Hrunamannavegur,** p. 173 | **35** **Biskupstungnabraut,** p. 183 | **F333** **Haukadalsvegur,** p. 461

F337 **Hlöðuvallavegur,** p. 458 | **F338** **Skjaldbreiðarvegur,** p. 460-461 | **F735** **Þjófadalavegur,** p. 456

21 P. 584

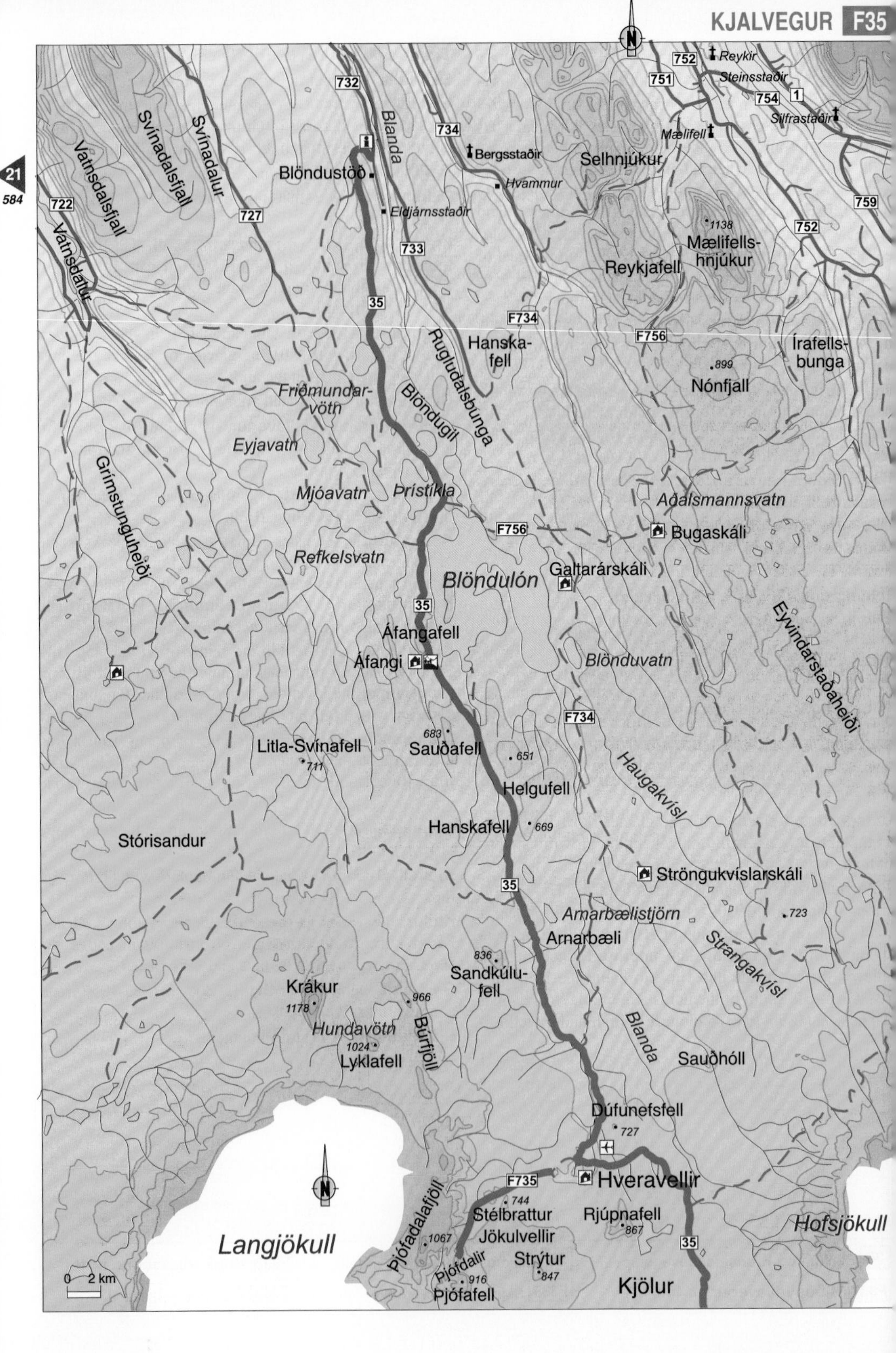
732
734
752
751
754
1
Reykir
Steinsstaðir
Silfrastaðir
Mælifell
Bergsstaðir
Hvammur
Selhnjúkur
Blöndustöð
Eldjárnsstaðir
Blanda
Svínadalsfjall
Svínadalur
Vatnsdalsfjall
Vatnsdalur
722
727
733
759
752
1138
Mælifells-
hnjúkur
Reykjafell
35
F734
F756
Hanska-
fell
Rugludalsbunga
Írafells-
bunga
899
Nónfjall
Friðmundar-
vöth
Blöndugil
Eyjavatn
Grímstunguheiði
Mjóavatn
Þrístikla
Aðalsmannsvatn
F756
Bugaskáli
Refkelsvatn
Blöndulón
Galtarárskáli
35
Áfangafell
Áfangi
Eyvindarstaðaheiði
Blönduvatn
F734
683
Sauðafell
Litla-Svínafell
711
651
Haugakvísl
Helgufell
Hanskafell
669
Stórisandur
Ströngukvíslarskáli
35
Arnarbælistjörn
723
Arnarbæli
Strangakvísl
836
Sandkúlu-
fell
Krákur
1178
966
Hundavötn
Blanda
1024
Lyklafell
Búrfjöll
Sauðhóll
Dúfunefsfell
727
F735
Hveravellir
744
Stélbrattur
Rjúpnafell
867
Þjófadalafjöll
Jökulvellir
Hofsjökull
1067
Langjökull
35
Strýtur
Þjófdalir
916
847
Kjölur
Þjófafell
0 2 km

F35 **Kjalvegur norðurhluti,** 79 km from Hveravellir north to route 731. Passable for all cars.

F735 **Þjófadalsvegur** 12,7km. Passable for all cars to Hveravellir, only for jeeps from Hveravellir to Þröskuldar. From there is an 8-900m walk to a FÍ touring hut in Þjófadalur valley, built in 1939.

Þjófadalir, ("Thieves' valleys") some valleys east of the Langjökull glacier. The story, almost certainly apocryphal, is that 9 students from Hólar hid out there and lived off stolen sheep after having killed a serving woman at Hólar. The area can be reached by jeep-track from Hveravellir. A tourist hut built 1939. You can take several short but joyful hikes from the lodge, e.g. Hrufafell, Fagrahlíð and Jökulkrók by the edge of the glacier Langjökull.

Hveravellir, ("Hot spring plains") a geothermal area to the north of Kjalhraun, about 650 m above sea level, and one of the best known geothermal areas in Iceland. Many beautiful and peculiar hot springs, such as Bláhver, Öskurhólshver, Eyvindarhver, Bræðrahverir etc. Ruins of the shelter of the 18th century outlaw Fjalla-Eyvindur are to be found near the spring Eyvindarhver, where he is said to have boiled his meat. Memorial to the outlaw and his woman raised there in 1998. Tourist huts and other shelters, a bathing basin, and a weather report station. The Touring Club of Iceland built a house at Hveravellir in 1938. The house is heated with hot spring water, there is also a pool, suitable for bathing, just outsite the house. There is also a new and spacious mountain lodge at Hveravellir. **Hveravellir is a protected natural area that should not be spoiled in any way!** See more on Hveravellir, p. 459.

Dúfunefsfell, ("Dove nose mountain") (727 m) a high tuff mountain by the northern boundaries of Kjölur. Flat wasteland south of the mountain is believed to be **Dúfunefsskeið**, mentioned in *Landnámabók* ("The Book of Settlements") as the setting of the horse race between Þórir Dúfunef and the freed slave Örn.

F734 **Svartárdalsvegur (Vesturheiðarvegur-Kjalvegur hinn forni)** 56,9 km. A route from Kjalvegur route by Seyðisá. Goes down to Fossárdalur valley. Only a part of the route is passable for jeeps.

Seyðisá, a big clear river coming from the Búrfjöll mountains and taking in the rivers Þegjandi ("Keeping quiet") and Beljandi ("Roaring") on the way to the Blanda.

Blanda, 125 km, one of the longest glacial rivers in Iceland. It comes mainly from the western part of the Hofsjökull glacier, the uppermost sources being below the mountain Blágnípa.

Áfangi, a campsite and accommodation 40 km north of Hveravellir and 75 km from Blönduós.

Helgufell, (663 m) a prominent mountain in the middle of Auðkúluheiði moor.

Auðkúluheiði, a wide area or moorland with both scattered and continous grasslands between the river Blanda to the east, Grímstunguheiði moor to the west, and Hveravellir to the south. This area is mostly 400 to 500 m above sea level. A good deal of the northern part of the moor is under water since the Blanda was harnessed 1984-88. Among roads built there in connection with the building of the hydro-electric plant is one going over the mountain **Áfangafell**, from which there is a panoramic view. Shelter.

Þrístikla, a good-sized lake, as are the lakes Mjóavatn, Galtaból and Friðmundarvötn to the north of it.

F756 **Mælifellsdalur** 44,7 km. Passable for all jeep and small jeeps.

Mælifellshnjúkur, (1138 m), one of the highest and most imposing mountains of Skagafjörður. It is said that 10 counties can be seen from there. Marked walking route.

Blöndugil, an 18 km long canyon on the river Blanda, 50 to 100 m deep in many places. More info on **Blöndustöð** on p. 346.

Gilsá, a small river running into the Blanda where Kjalvegur comes down to the Blöndudalur valley.

1 **Norðurlandsvegur,** p. 72
722 **Vatnsdalsvegur,** p. 343
727 **Svínadalsvegur,** p. 344
733 **Blöndudalsvegur,** p. 346
734 **Svartárdalsvegur,** p. 347
751 **Efribyggðarvegur,** p. 353
752 **Skagafjarðarvegur,** p. 353-354
754 **Héraðsdalsvegur,** p. 353
759 **Kjálkavegur,** p. 354

Gunnar Guðjónsson
Þjófadalir

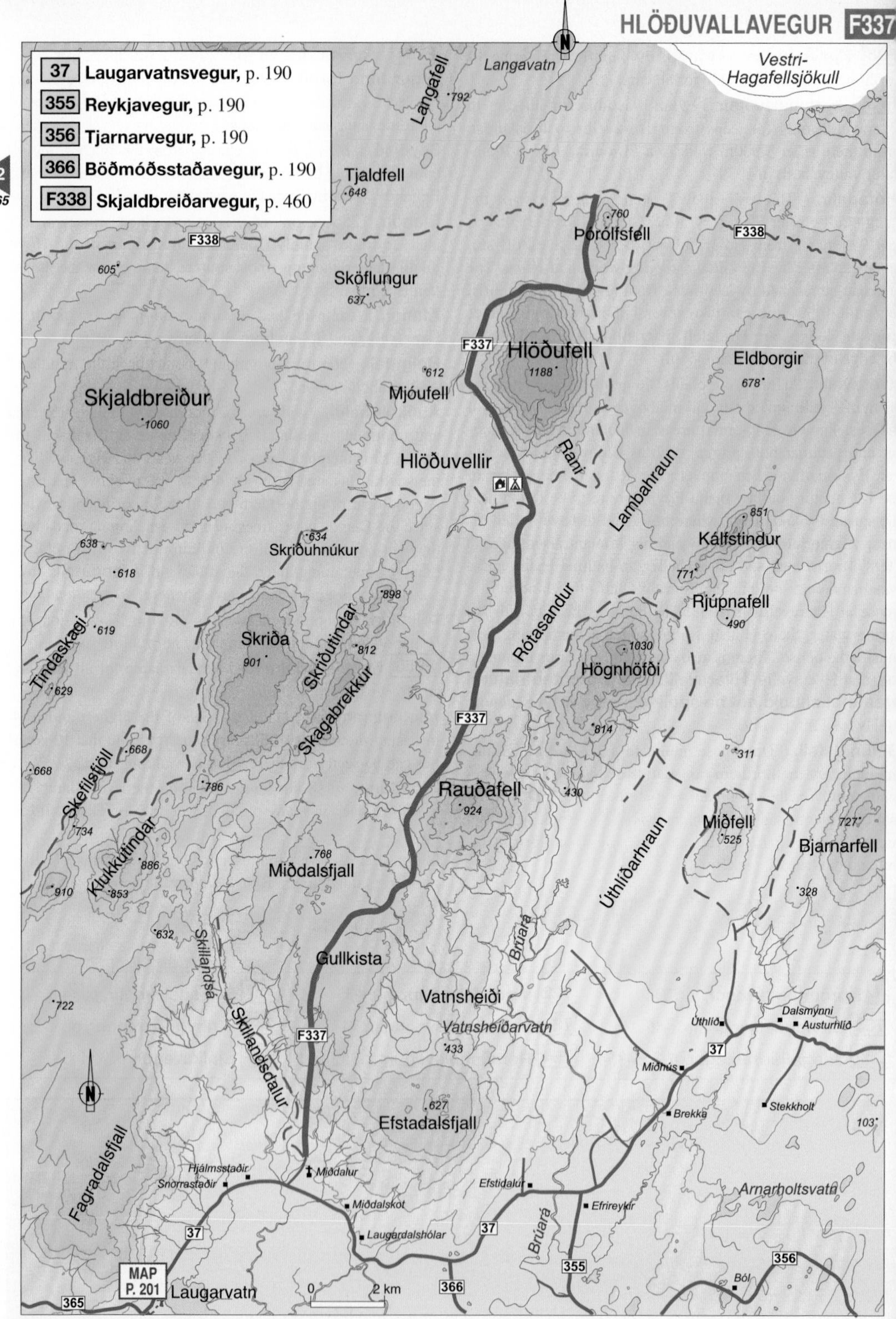

F337 Hlöðuvallavegur, 31,5 km. Route F337 if quite steep going up Miðdalsfjall mountain. This route goes to route F338 to Hlöðuvellir, it doesn´t matter on which side of the mountain the route is driven as it goes around the mountain. The route is fairly rough and can be a nuisance to small jeeps.

Gullkista, („Chest of Gold“) a box shaped peak on the mountain Miðdalsfjall (678 m).

Come to Hveravellir and enjoy!

Hveravellir is one of Iceland's natural wonders popular with travellers in all seasons. The area is surrounded by spectacular landscape with geysers such as Eyvindahver, Öskurhóll and Bláhver.
Eyvindahver derives it names from the famous Icelandic saga about the couple Fjalla – Eyvindur (Mountain – Eyvindur) and Halla. They fled from the law into the highlands shortly after 1760 and spent some 20 years living in the wilderness. Remains from their stay can still be seen at Hveravellir.

To get to Hveravellir you drive Kjalvegur, which is one of the oldest roads in the high lands and lies through the centre of the country. Kjalvegur opens in the middle of June and closes depending on weather conditions. There are also two bus companies that go to Hveravellir every day, SBA and Trex. Hveravellir is open all year.

Hvervellir has been a nature preserve since 1960. A manned metrological observation was in operation from 1965 till the year 2004.

Two Mountain huts are at Hveravellir. The older one built in 1938 and has cooking facilities and accommodates 30 people and has cooking facilities. The other hut is built in 1980 accommodates 15 people and has a restaurant. Sleeping bag accommodations and made up beds are available. A good camping area with showers and bathrooms. Hveravellir operates a small shop and also offers soup, trout and a special icelandic bread, „hverabrauð". Horse trips and glacier excursions.

The huts are heated up with geothermal heating and hot tap water is readily available at all times. Showers and a warm pool are in the area. After a long day in the high lands it's nice to relax in a nature made hot pool situated next to one of the huts and let the tiredness fade a way.

Hveravellir has one of the best facilities for horses and riders in the highland. There are two stables, storage for saddles and restrooms for travellers.

Hay can be bought for the horses but has to be ordered in advance at the same time as the stables.

Daily bus trips to Hveravellir over Kjölur, from middle of June till the end of August, **www.sba.is**. Trips are both from Reykjavík and Akureyri, departure in the morning and arriving in Akureyri or Reykjavik in the evening. Usually you can get to Hveravellir by 4x4 but you better keep an eye on the weather before you take off and check if the roads are open in the wintertime, especially in the springtime when snow is melting. In the summertime the road is open for well equipped cars; note the road is gravel-surfaced.

HVERAVALLAFÉLAGIÐ EHF *Tel: 452-4200 & 894-1293 – www.hveravellir.is – hveravellir@hveravellir.is*

2
P. 565

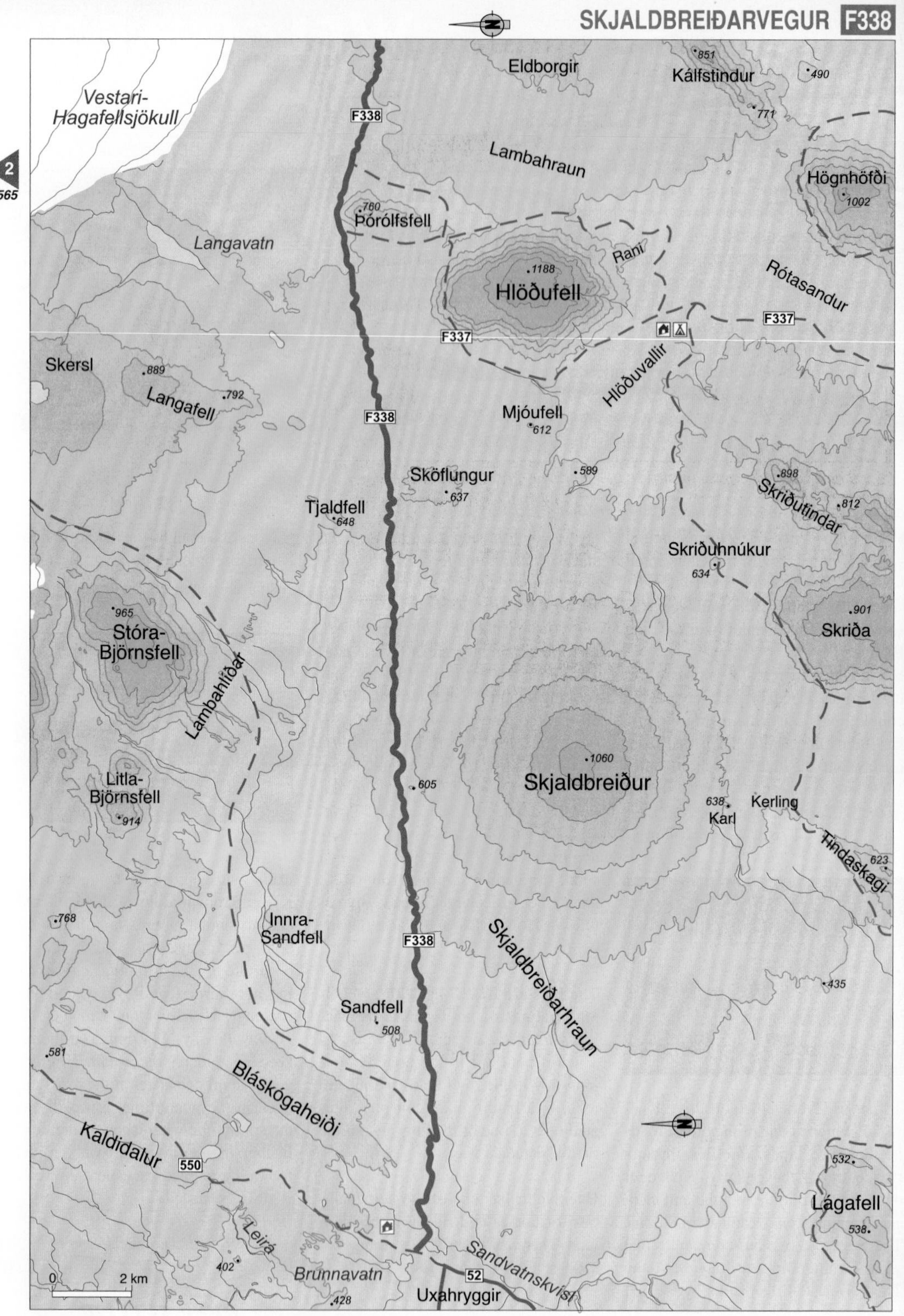

F338 Skjaldbreiðarvegur (Línuvegur), 48 km. Lies between F35 Kjalvegur and F550 Kaldadalsvegur. The route is passable by all jeeps but two fords need to be crossed. This route has a beautiful view to Langjökull.

F333 Haukadalsvegur.

F338 SKJALDBREIÐARVEGUR

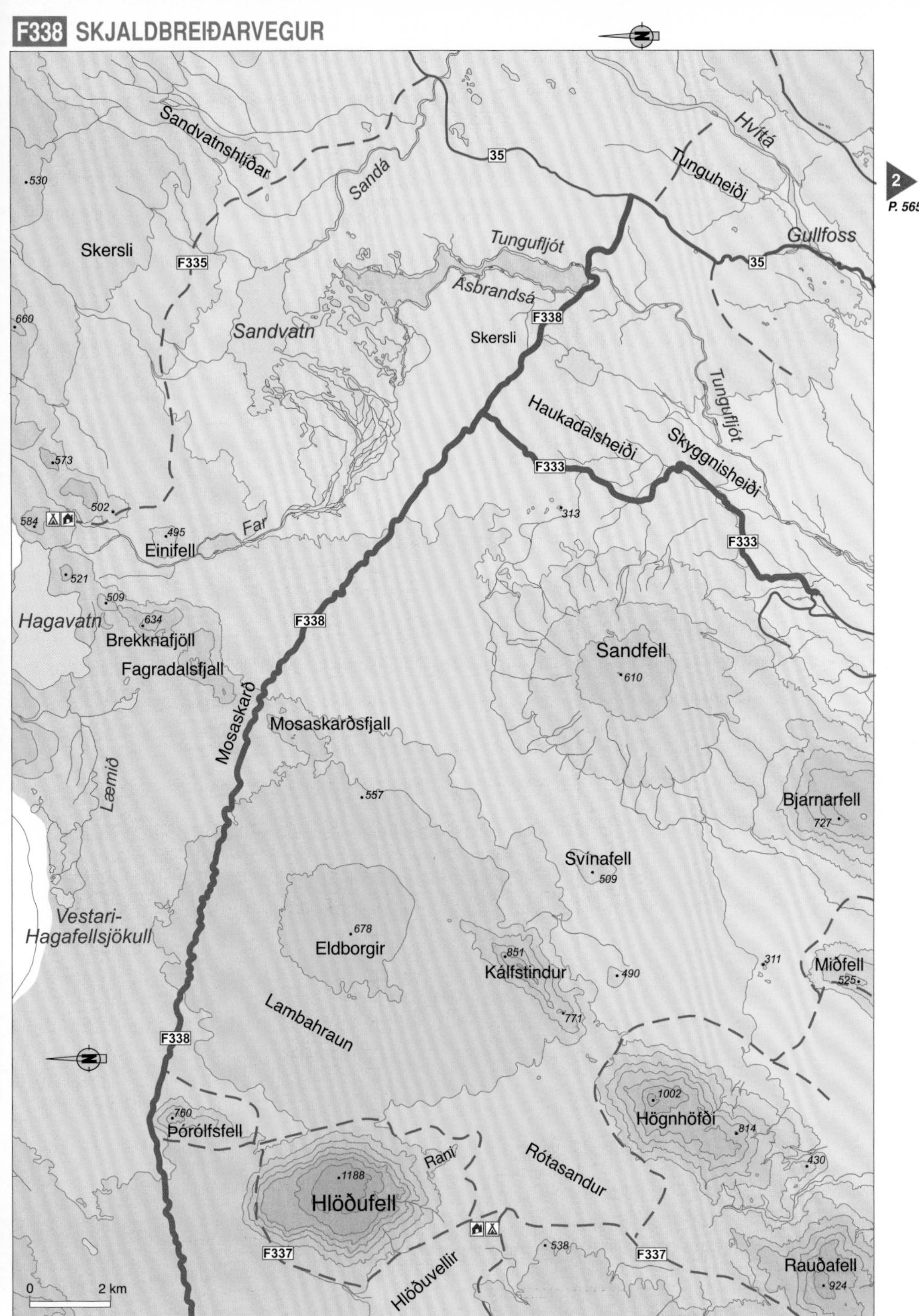

35 **Biskupstungnabraut,** p. 180-184 F335 **Hagavatnsvegur,** p. 455 F337 **Hlöðuvallavegur,** p. 458

2
P. 565

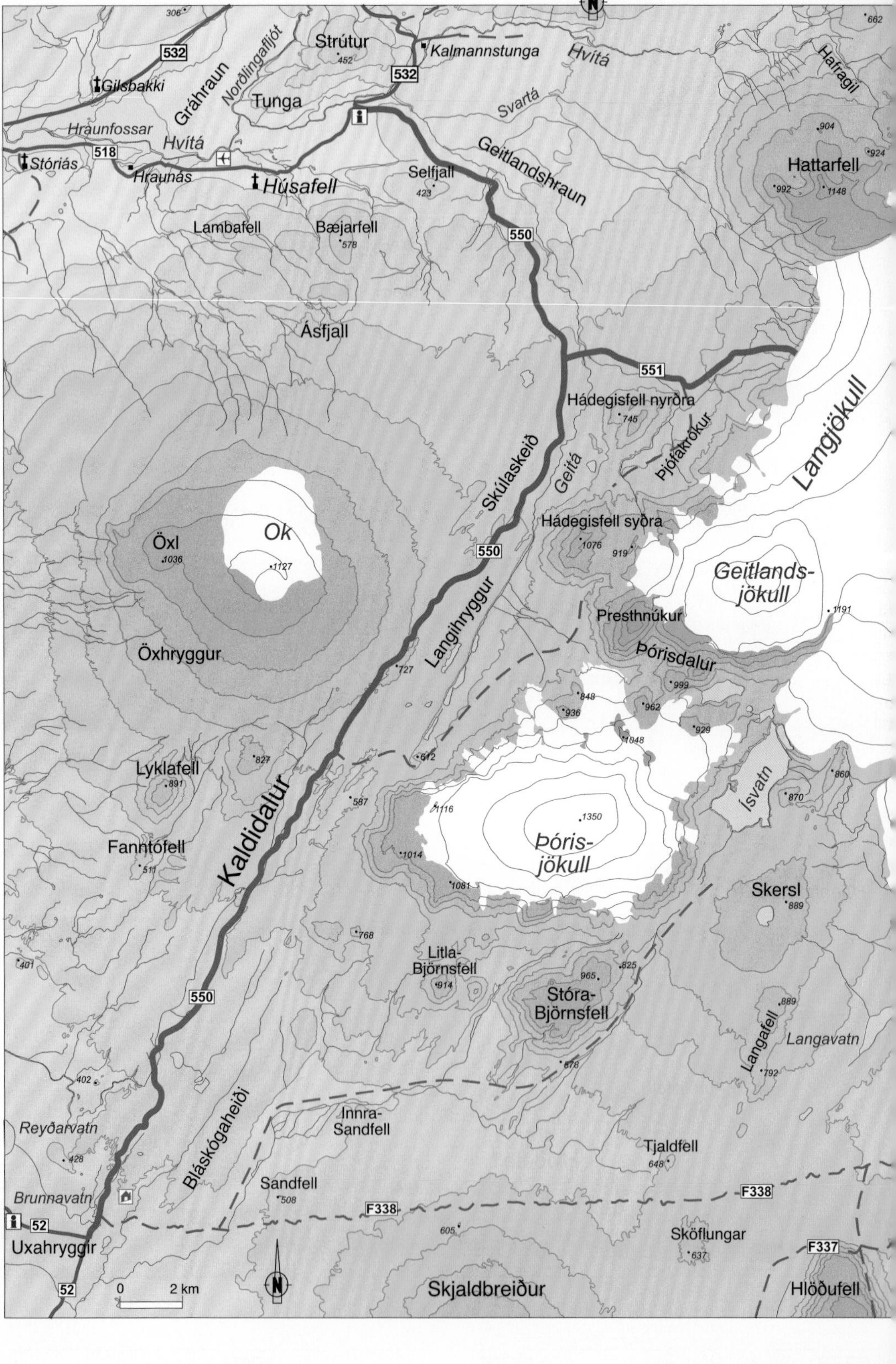

N

306
532
Gilsbakki
Gráhraun
Norðlingafljót
Strútur
452
Tunga
Kalmannstunga
532
Hvítá
Svartá
Hafragil
662
Hraunfossar
Hvítá
518
Stóriás
Hraunás
Húsafell
Selfjall
423
Geitlandshraun
904
924
Hattarfell
992
1148
Lambafell
Bæjarfell
578
550
Ásfjall
551
Hádegisfell nyrðra
745
Þjófakrókur
Langjökull
Skúlaskeið
Geitá
Hádegisfell syðra
1076
919
Öxl
1036
Ok
1127
550
Geitlands-
jökull
Langihryggur
Presthnúkur
1191
Þórisdalur
Öxhryggur
727
999
848
962
936
929
1048
612
Lyklafell
891
827
860
Ísvatn
870
Kaldidalur
587
1116
1350
Þóris-
jökull
Fanntófell
511
1014
1081
Skersl
889
768
Litla-
Björnsfell
914
965
825
Stóra-
Björnsfell
401
550
889
Langafell
Langavatn
792
402
678
Bláskógaheiði
Innra-
Sandfell
Reyðarvatn
Tjaldfell
648
428
Sandfell
508
F338
Brunnavatn
F338
52
605
Sköflungar
637
Uxahryggir
F337
N
52
0 2 km
Skjaldbreiður
Hlöðufell

550 **Kaldadalsvegur,** ("The cold valley route") 62,7 km between Þingvellir and Húsafell, **Kaldidalur** being the valley between Ok and Langjökull. This route is passable for all cars.

Björnsfell, **Stóra-Björnsfell** and **Litla-Björnsfell**, (914 m and 1,050 m) tuff mountains to the south of Þórisjökull.

Þórisjökull, (1350 m) a glacier covered tuff mountain, 33 km^2. Formerly a part of Langjökull but now separated from it by the valley Þórisdalur, well-known from *Grettis saga*.

Egilsáfangi, some grasslands by the road, an important resting place for travellers on horseback.

Beinakerling, ("Bone crone") a cairn by the road, one of the best known of this type of cairn. Travellers were supposed to compose some comment or greeting in verse, put it in a sheep's or cow's leg-bone and leave it in the Beinakerling for the next traveller who came along.

Hrúðurkarlar or **Hrúðurkatlar,** ("Barnacles") a cluster of tuff hills.

Fanntófell, a cone shaped tuff mountain to the south of Ok, the home of giants, according to folk tales.

551 **Langjökulsvegur** 7,7 km, from Kaldadalsvegur north of Hádegisfell to Langjökull. Passable for small jeeps. The route ends at the foot of Langjökull glacier.

Eiríksjökull, (1,675 m) a dome-shaped glacier dominating the view from the northern part of this route.

Hafrafell, (1,167 m) a mountain on the edge of Langjökull.

Geitlandshraun, an area of lava and sand below Geitlandsjökull to the west, between the rivers Geitá and Hvítá. The lava field, in which there are many caves, came from some craters by the glacier. The glacial river Svartá divides Geitland in two.

Geitá, a glacial river coming from the glaciers Geitlandsjökull and Þórisjökull. One of the rivers that join Hvítá in Borgarfjörður. Bridged to the west of Þjófakrókur.

52 **Uxahryggjavegur,** p. 236
518 **Hálsasveitarvegur,** p. 263
F337 **Hlöðuvallavegur,** p. 458
F338 **Skjaldbreiðarvegur,** p. 460

15 P. 578

BREIÐAFJÖRÐUR

Hellissandur
MAP P. 276
Keflavík
Keflavíkurbjarg
Bali
Rif
Björnssteinn
MAP P. 276
575
Ingjaldshóll
Gufuskálavör
(Gufuskálar)
Gufuskálar
Írskrabrunnur
574
Öndverðarnes
Skarðsvík
Fálki
(Írskubúðir)
Bekkjahraun
579
Prestahraun
Breiðidalur
Svöðufoss
(Foss)
Kerlingarfoss
Enni
419
Bæjarfoss
ÓLAFSVÍK
MAP P. 276
Gamlavík
(Haukabrekka)
Sjávarfoss
Fróðárrif
Klettakotsvaðall
Búrfell
232
Hólmkelsá
Dýjadalsvatn
Ennisdalur
Fossdalur
418
Rjúkandi
490
Gufuskálamóður
Neshraun
Saxhólsbjarg
Svörtuloft
Öndverðarneshólar
Stóri-Saxhóll
125
Saxhólahraun
Saxhóll
Klukkufoss
469
Hreggnasi
Skál
556
Hettudalir
570
Gerðubergsdalur
Bugsvatn
Fróða
Hellisfjall
Fróðá
54
Fróðármúli
Tindfell
673
Sauðhóll
110
(Forni-Saxhóll)
(Saxhóll)
Fannhamrar
Miðfell
Bárðarkista
683
Geldingafell vestra
830
Geldingafell
824
Tághálsar
633
Rauðakúla
768
Kambsheiði
Sandkúlur
844
Jökulháls
Hamraendafjall
Lambhagatjarnir
(Garðar)
Svörtutindar
605
Blágilsjökull
Jökulhálsjökull
SNÆFELLSJÖKULL
Norðurþúfa
Miðþúfa
1446
Vesturþúfa
1442
Hyrningsjökull
Hnausahraun
Hnausahryggir
Brennivínskúlur
657
Náttmálahnúkur
Gróf
Hamraendar
Beruvík
279
(Berutóftir)
Beruvíkurlækur
(Litlalón)
Þverlækur
693
Hólatindajökull
Kvíahnúksjökull
Kálfatraðahraun
510
Botnsfjall
Hnausar
(Hólahólar)
Hólahólar
Kvíahnúkur
706
Stagfell
Sönghellir
Kýrskarð
Klifhraun
Breiðavík
Stapafell
432
Sauðá
Stapagil
Eiríksbúð
Arnarfell
Arnarstapi
Beruvíkurhraun
572
Dritvík
Tröllakirkja
(Einarslón)
Purkhólar
145
Merkjahryggur
Dagverðará
Laugarvatn
Bárðarlaug
Lónbjarg
Vatnshellir
Drangahraun
Brekkubær
Gíslabær
Laugarbrekka
(Dagverðará)
Hellnar
Hellnanes
Svalþúfa
(Malarrif)
Malarrif
Lóndrangar

FAXAFLÓI

0 1 km

Stapafell and Snæfellsjökull.

570 **Jökulhálsleið,** 18,5 km. From Stapafell north of Arnarstapi to Ólafsvík. This route is passable by all cars in the summer, but not untill July when all the snow has cleared.

Snæfellsjökull, (1,446 m), a national park, a central volcano and one of the most famous mountains in Iceland. Long thought to be the highest mountain in the country, probably because it stands alone and is the highest mountain rising straight up from the sea. Eggert Ólafsson and Bjarni Pálsson (see Road 62, Svefneyjar) are the first people known to have climbed it (in July 1753). The trip was considered highly dangerous at the time, though travel on the glacier is common today. At the top there is a large crater, 1 km in diameter with cliff-walls up to 200 m high by **Jökulþúfur**, three crags on the crater rim, but open to the west. There have been many eruptions under and around the glacier, though none since settlement times. Craters under the glacier have mostly produced acid (light-coloured) pumice and lava but on the lower land west and southwest of the glacier most eruptions have produced basalt. The most recent eruption was probably about 1,750 years ago, to the northwest of the glacier. Eruptions have often caused enormous flooding, e.g. along the course of the river Móðulækur. Around the turn of last century the glacier was twice the size it is today, then it grew rapidly smaller until about 1960, since when it has remained stable and even grown in places. There are still many moraines that show the former extent of the glacier. To the east and southeast of the ice there are thick layers of pumice, which was mined until 1935 and floated down along Kýrskarð pass in wooden troughs to the Klifhraun lava field, where water was used to pump it aboard freighters. Pumice has been mined there, but is now taken to Ólafsvík. New Age and mystic groups world-wide believe Snæfellsjökull to be a focus of power. It first became famous after the publication in 1864 of Jules Verne's *Journey to the Centre of the Earth*.

Kambsheiði, the moor between the Breiðavík and Fróðársveit districts. Many old routes crossed it, often dangerous and difficult to follow.

54 **Snæfellsnesvegur,** p. 238-250

574 **Útnesvegur,** p. 270–275

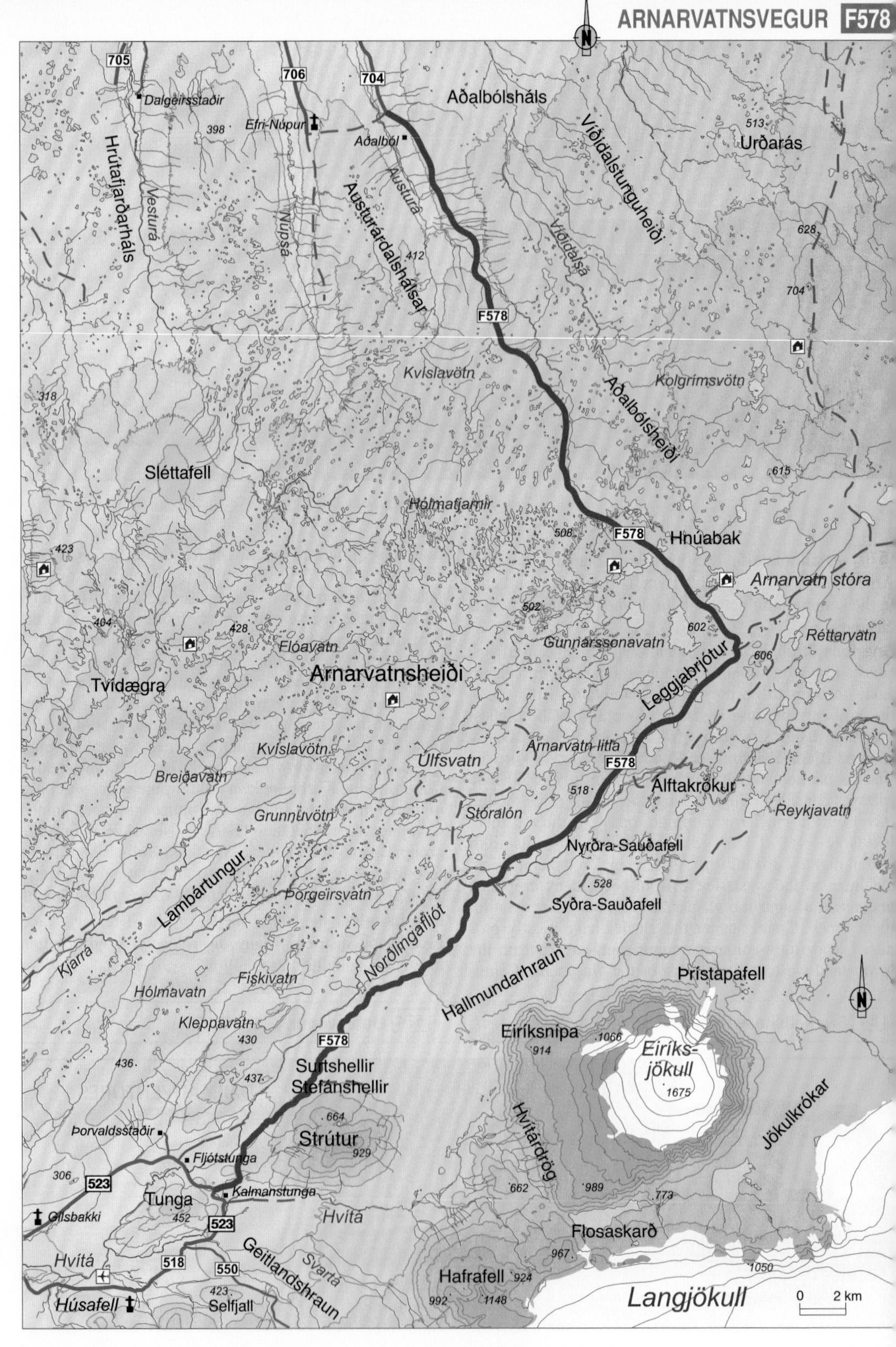
705
706
704
Dalgeirsstaðir
398
Efri-Núpur
Aðalból
Aðalbólsháls
Víðidalstunguheiði
513
Urðarás
Hrútafjarðarháls
Vesturá
Núpsá
Austurárdalshálsar
Austurá
412
Víðidalsá
628
704
F578
Kvíslavötn
Kolgrímsvötn
Aðalbólsheiði
318
Sléttafell
615
Hólmatjarnir
508
F578
Hnúabak
423
Arnarvatn stóra
502
602
404
428
Flóavatn
Gunnarssonavatn
Leggjabrjótur
606
Réttarvatn
Tvídægra
Arnarvatnsheiði
Kvíslavötn
Úlfsvatn
Arnarvatn litla
F578
Breiðavatn
518
Álftakrókur
Grunnuvötn
Stóralón
Reykjavatn
Nyrðra-Sauðafell
Lambártungur
Þorgeirsvatn
528
Syðra-Sauðafell
Kjarrá
Norðlingafljót
Hallmundarhraun
Þrístapafell
Fiskivatn
Hólmavatn
Kleppavatn
430
F578
Eiríksnípa
914
1066
Eiríks-
jökull
1675
436
437
Surtshellir
Stefánshellir
Hvítárdrög
Jökulkrókar
664
Strútur
929
Þorvaldsstaðir
Fljótstunga
306
523
Tunga
Kalmanstunga
662
989
773
Gilsbakki
452
523
Hvítá
Flosaskarð
Hvítá
518
550
Geitlandshraun
Svartá
967
1050
Hafrafell
924
Húsafell
423
Selfjall
992
1148
Langjökull
0
2 km

F578 **Arnarvatnsvegur,** 42 km from Kalmanstungu, by Lake Arnarvatn stóra to Núpsárbrú bridge in Austurárdal valley.

Stórisandur, west of Réttarvatn lake the Skagfirðingavegur route continues to the east to Grettishæð. From there it is possible to drive to Grímstunguheiði in Vatnsdalur valley. This route is very slow with larged rocks on the road. Not passable for small jeeps. By Grettishæð is a route to the south and the east through Krákshraun and east to route F35 Kjalvegur. This part of the route is also slow.

Víðgelmir, a cave down in the lava near the farm Fljótstunga, see p. 264.

Stefánshellir, a cave a little north of Surtshellir, see p. 264.

Hallmundarhraun, a lava field, thought to have been formed at the time of the settlement, coming from craters in Jökulkrókur between the glaciers Langjökull and Eiríksjökull and reaching down to the river Hvítá, where the Hraunfossar falls (see Road 518) come out from under it. The caves there are more numerous, larger and more famous than in any other lava field in Iceland. It is thought to be named for the giant Hallmundur of *Grettis saga*.

Kalmanshellir, a cave east of Eiríksjökull and north of Þrístapafell in Jökulkrókur, about 4 km long. Considered to be Icelands longest cave.

Hallmundarhellir, a cave east of Reykjavatn lake.

Surtshellir, undoubtedly the most famous cave in Iceland. Right by the road just after it goes up onto the lava field. There are four openings, not all of a size for people to get through. The cave is 1970 m long, or 3500 m along with the cave Stefánshellir, which connects up to it, and with interesting side caves. Stone-built walls and bones have been found there. Outlawed thieves, called Hellismenn ("Cave men"), hid out in the caves in the 10th century, but were killed by farmers led by the chieftains of inland Borgarfjörður. According to *Hellismanna saga* the outlaws were sleeping in **Vopnalág** ("Weapon dell") at the southern end of the Þorvaldsháls ridge when the farmers attacked them.

Eiríksjökull, (1,675 m) the greatest mountain in this region, the highest west of the Vatnajökull glacier (apart from the highest point on the Hofsjökull ice cap) and the third-highest mountain in Iceland, outside the ice caps. Tuff with a basalt shield and an ice cap from which glaciers extend towards the north.

Arnarvatnsheiði, ("Eagle lake moor"), the moor north of the river Norðlingafljót, rocky, eroded hills but some vegetation by the many lakes, most of which are good fishing lakes.

Arnarvatnshæðir, hills southwest of the lake Arnarvatn stóra. Peat layers formed from angelica are found on the eastern slopes.

Réttarvatn, a lake to the east of Arnarvatnshæðir.

Tungukollur, (496 m) a small mountain on the road to Miðfjörður, offering a panoramic view of the moors.

Suðurmannasandfell, ("Southern men sand mountain") (718 m) a mountain providing the major landmark along the road to the Víðidalur valley.

Tvídægra, ("Two-day") flat, gently-sloping moors reaching north to Húnavatnssýsla county. A great deal of impassable boggy land with shallow lakes and tarns but with some low bare hills in between. Fishing in most of the lakes. Formerly people often travelled across the moor but it was difficult to find one's way and dangerous in winter and indeed many lost their lives there. To the west of the road to Miðfjörður were the Núpdælir paths south to Kalmanstunga. Even further to the west was another route going south to Borgarfjörður, and it was there that the Heiðarvíg ("Moor murders") took place when Víga-Barði of *Heiðarvíga saga* took revenge on the men of Borgarfjörður for having killed his brother.

Hveraborg, a geothermal area north of Tvídægra. A part of the hot water runs to Síká river, there it is possible to bath. A jeep track leads to Hverborg but the last part travellers need to walk for about an hour. There is a cabin at Hverborgir and it is possible to get a key at Staðarskáli in Hrútarfjörður.

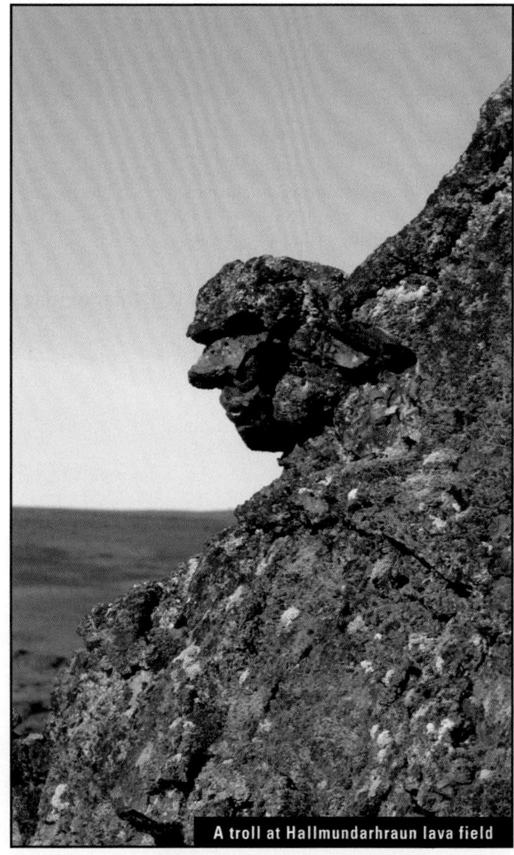

A troll at Hallmundarhraun lava field

518 **Hálsasveitarvegur,** p. 262 | **523** **Hvítársíðuvegur,** p. 263 | **550** **Kaldadalsvegur,** p. 263
704 **Miðfjarðarvegur,** p. 335 | **705** **Vesturárdalsvegur,** p. 335 | **706** **Núpsdalsvegur,** p. 336

2 P. 565

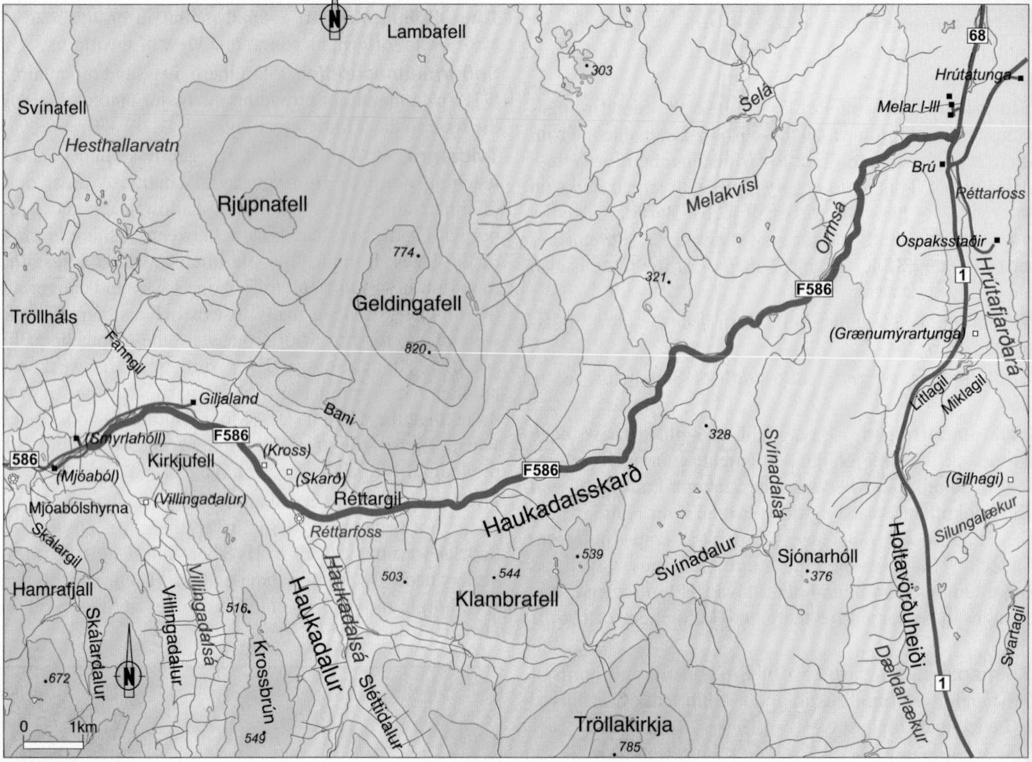

F586 Haukadalsskarðsvegur, 19,8 km. Between Haukadalur and Hrútafjörður, an ok jeep track through Haukadalsskarð. The route is passable for all jeeps, also small jeeps if the route is driven carefully. A small ford needs to be crossed by Haukadalsá.

Haukadalsskarð, a pass that was once an important route from the Haukadalur valley over to Hrútafjörður in the north. Little used now but passable for jeeps in the summer.

1 Vesturlandsvegur, p. 59 **68 Innstrandavegur,** p. 309-312 **586 Haukadalsvegur,** p. 277

22
P. 585

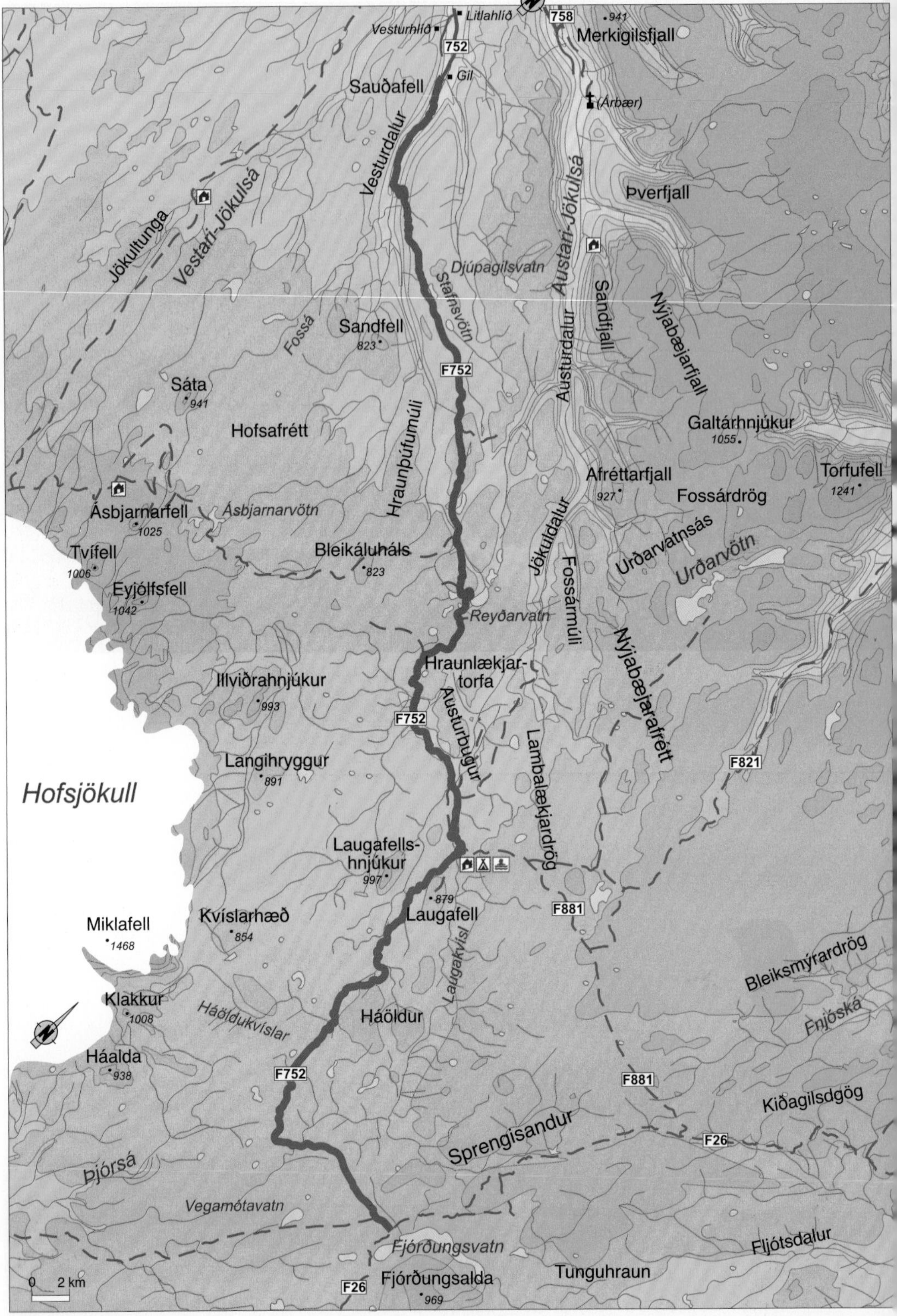

Litlahlíð
Vesturhlíð
758
752
•941
Merkigilsfjall
Sauðafell
Gil
(Árbær)
Vesturdalur
Austari-Jökulsá
Þverfjall
Jökultunga
Vestari-Jökulsá
Djúpagilsvatn
Stafnsvötn
Sandfjall
Nýjabæjarfjall
Fossá
Sandfell
823
Austurdalur
F752
Sáta
941
Hofsafrétt
Hraunþúfumúli
Galtárhnjúkur
1055
Afréttarfjall
927
Torfufell
1241
Fossárdrög
Ásbjarnarfell
1025
Ásbjarnarvötn
Jökuldalur
Urðarvatnsás
Urðarvötn
Tvífell
1006
Bleikáluháls
823
Fossármúli
Eyjólfsfell
1042
Reyðarvatn
Nýjabæjarafrétt
Hraunlækjar-
torfa
Illviðrahnjúkur
993
Austurbugur
F752
Lambalækjardrög
Langihryggur
891
F821
Hofsjökull
Laugafells-
hnjúkur
997
879
Laugafell
F881
Miklafell
1468
Kvíslarhæð
854
Laugakvísl
Bleiksmýrardrög
Klakkur
1008
Háöldukvíslar
Háöldur
Fnjóská
Háalda
938
F752
F881
Kiðagilsdrög
Sprengisandur
F26
Þjórsá
Vegamótavatn
Fjórðungsvatn
Fljótsdalur
0 2 km
F26
Fjórðungsalda
969
Tunguhraun

F752 **Skagafjarðarleið (Forsetavegur)** 30,2 km. he route is passable for all jeeps. There is one obstacle on the way, a ford on the Bergvatnskvísl river. It is easy in drought but the water can rise rapidly during rainy seasons and be dangerous for small jeeps. On the north side on this route is **Beinakerling** („ Bone crone") a cairn by the road, one of the best known of this type of cairn. Travellers were supposed to compose some comment or greeting in verse, put it in a sheep's or cow's leg-bone and leave it in the Beinakerling for the next traveller who came along.

Bergvatnskvísl, a clear river, the northernmost roots of the Þjórsá river, 230 km long, the longest river in Iceland.

Hofsjökull, 1800m) a glacier, 1000 km2. With some steap mountains like **Blágnípa** (1068 m), on the west side, **Arnarfell hið mikla** (1143 m), on the south side and **Miklafell** (1456 m), on the east side.

F752 **Skagafjarðarleið** 28,5 km from Laugafell to Gil in Vesturdalur, passable for all jeeps if there is not much water in the Hnjúkskvísl river.

Laugafell (892 m) and **Laugafellshnjúkur,** (997 m) two mountains which are prominent landmarks, rising as they do from rather flat country. To the northwest of Laugafell there are some geothermal springs 40-50°C, a bathing pool and a good tourist hut built 1948. The story goes that people lived there at one time, and there are some signs of ruins. A pool with changing rooms.

Austari-Jökulsá, a big glacial river collecting many streams and rivers from the Hofsjökull glacier and flowing down to the Austurdalur valley. This river used to be a big obstacle but now there is a bridge at Austurbugur.

Eyfirðingavegur, an old route from Þingvellir to North Iceland.

Strompleið, south of Orravatnsrústir ir a west bound route, passable for all jeeps.

Orravatnsrústir, grasslands around the lakes Reyðarvatn and Orravatn. Mostly wet ground with lots of cottongrass and sedge. This area is extremely marshy with hillocks tens of metres in diameter and up to three metres high, covered with dwarf shrubs. The river outlet for the area is Rústakvísl, later to join Hofsá. In the centre of the area is a small hill, Orrahaugur, where there is a good refuge hut.

Giljamúli, a mountain spur between the valleys Vesturdalur and Giljadalur, its highest point being Stafnsvatnahæð (716 m). There is a very poor road onto it from the abandoned farm Þorljótsstaðir and past the two lakes Stafnsvötn and Langavatn.

Reyðarfell, (802 m) a mountain north of the lake Reyðarvatn.

752 **Skagafjarðarvegur,** p. 353 | 758 **Austurdalsvegur,** p. 354 | F26 **Sprengisandsleið,** p. 433
F821 **Eyjafjarðarleið,** p. 467 | F881 **Dragaleið,** p. 476

7
P. 570

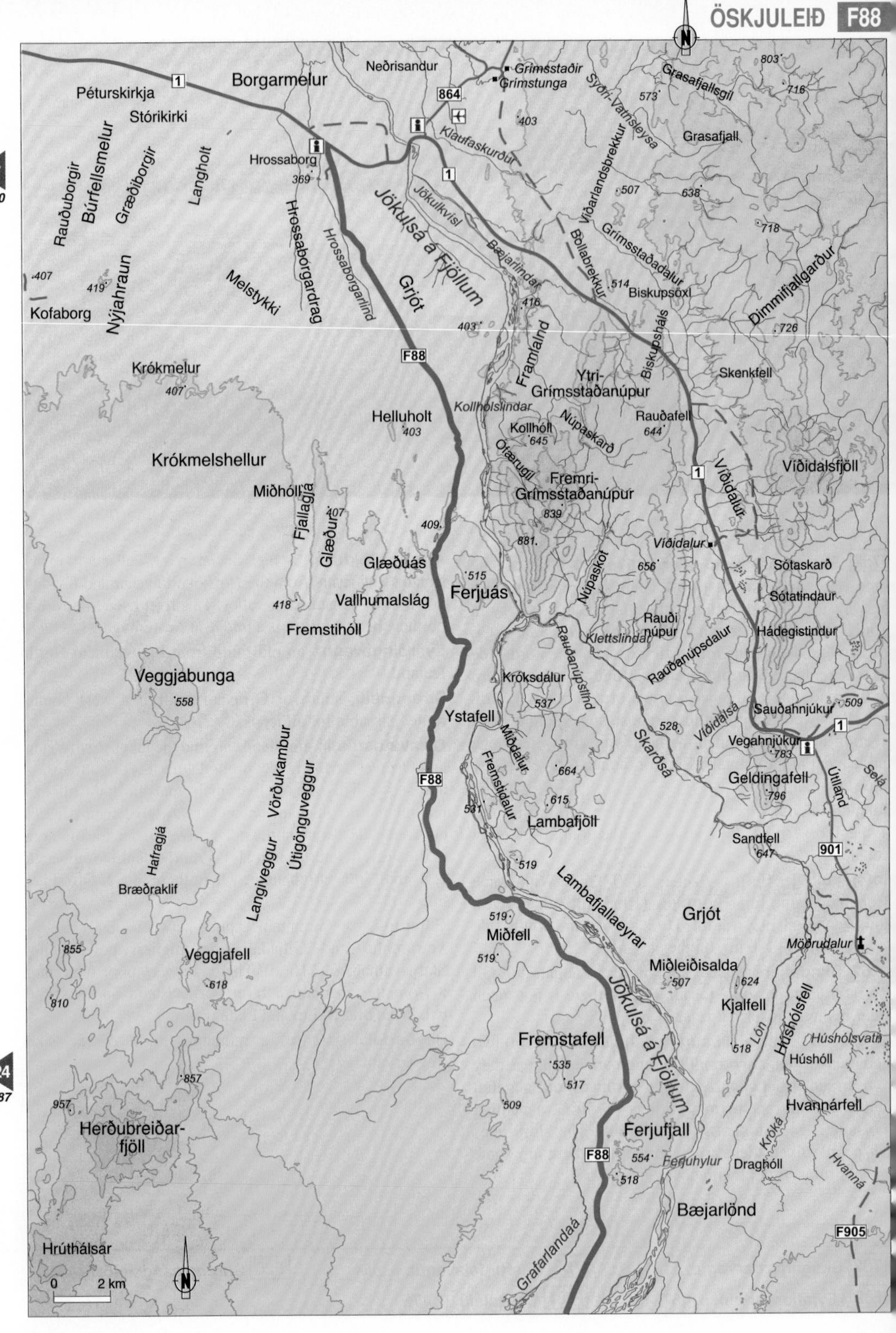

24
P. 587

Herðubreið.

F88 **Öskjuleið,** 79,9 km, from the Ring Road by Hrossaborg. Passable by all jeeps, also small jeeps. A ford in Grafarlandaá and Lindá need to be passed.

Hrossaborg, an old crater, about 500 m long, rising about 40 m above the flat sands around it.

Herðubreiðarfjöll, (1,094 m) tuff mountains. Between them and the mountain **Hrúthálsar**, ridges (1,055 m), to the south is **Eggert** (1,332 m).

Grafarlönd, an area around the river Grafarlandaá with scattered vegetation. A nesting area for geese.

Kollóttadyngja, (1,177 m) a shield volcano with an 800 m wide crater at the top. In the floor of the crater, which is 30 m deep, there is a 70 m deep basin. One of the most regular shield volcanoes in Iceland. At Bræðrafell to the south of Kollóttadyngja there is a cabin belonging to the Touring Club of Akureyri, built in 1960.

Herðubreiðarlindir, an area of rich vegetation 5-6 km northeast of Herðubreið. Many springs appear from under the lava to make one stream or river, Lindaá. A wonderful oasis in the middle of black sands and lava. Ruins of a shelter, **Eyvindarkofi**, made by Fjalla-Eyvindur, the 18th century outlaw. A good tourist hut and a popular camping place. **Protected area**.

Herðubreið, (1,682 m) a table mountain with a crater at its top, rising 1,000 to 1,100 m above the surrounding highlands. One of the most majestic mountains in Iceland, with a nearly round base having a circumference of 8-9 km. The mountain is tuff with a basalt shield and steep screes all around. It was long held to be impossible to climb, the first ascent being in 1908 by Hans Reck and Sigurður Sumarliðason. The easiest route is directly from the west, but even this is difficult and there is always the very real danger of rockfalls.

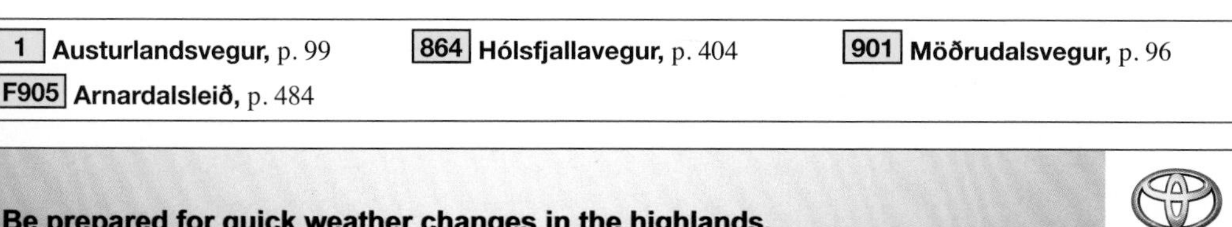

1 **Austurlandsvegur,** p. 99 **864** **Hólsfjallavegur,** p. 404 **901** **Möðrudalsvegur,** p. 96
F905 **Arnardalsleið,** p. 484

Miðdegistindar
F905
504
Bæjarlandalækur
Grafarlandaá
Arnaldseyrar
957
Herðubreiðar-
fjöll
Grafarlönd austari
Fossholar
Grjót
F88
Jökulsá á Fjöllum
Arnardalsá
Hrúthálsar
901
852
Mývatnsöræfi
Lindahraun
Linddaá
Arnardalsmúli
Móraudúvatn
638
Arnardalsalda
Eggert
1232
Herðubreiðarlindir
(Eyvindarkofi)
Þorsteinsskáli
Dyngjuháls
Hrútsrandir
Álftavatn
Kreppulindir
Kreppa
Kollóttadyngja
1177
Herðubreið
1682
656
Þorlákslindur
714
Þorlákslindarhryggur
679
F88
Bræðrafell
892
F910
822
834
Hlaupfell
678
Herðubreiðartögl
1051
856
Dyngjufjallaháls
1057
809
848
849
1073
Svartadyngja
719
605
Upptyppingar
Stórakista
1098
711
Miðfell
738
1077
Kollur
1231
1035
Litlakista
1048
Vikrafell
845
602
925
Lónshnjúkur
852
Eystraskarð
1126
1040
F910
Dyngjufjöll
1125
Höttur
738
F910
Víkursandur
Öskjuop
Kreppulón
Rauðskeggur
F894
Biskup
Svarthöfði
1012
Dreki
Dyngja
Vikraborgir
733
Vaðhnjúkar
F903
Víti
Bátshraun
Drekagil
Askja
776
1112
1053
Jökulsá á Fjöllum
Krepputunga
Kreppuháls
Kreppa
F902
Öskjuvatn
Suður-
botnar
F910
Nautagil
Vaðalda
Askur
1245
916
0
2 km
Dyngjuvatn
Þorvaldsfjall

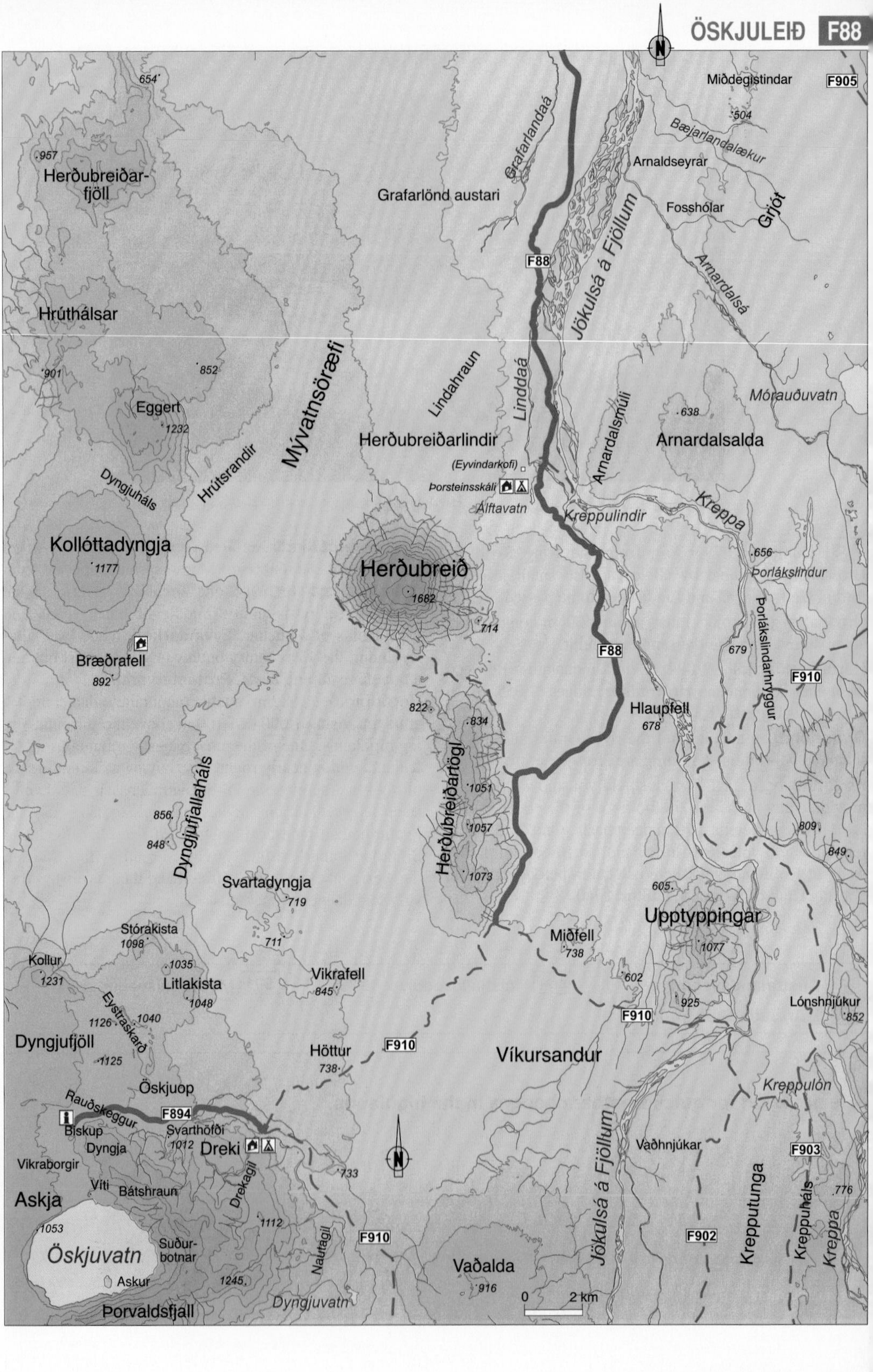

24
P. 587

23
P. 586

F894 **Öskjuvatnsvegur**, 7,8 km, of Austurleið route by Drekagil to Öskjuvatn. Passable for all cars to the parking lot by Öskuvatn.

Askja, a 50 km² caldera in the Dyngjufjöll mountains. The bottom, about 1,100 m above sea level, is mostly covered with rough lava. In the southeast corner, in a smaller caldera is the lake, Öskjuvatn, 217 m deep, and thus the second deepest lake in Iceland. The caldera and the lake were formed in the eruption of 1875, when there was a tremendous explosion in the small crater **Víti** ("Hell") on the northeastern shore of Öskjuvatn. This eruption produced more ash than any other eruption in Iceland, covering much of eastern Iceland, so that many farms had to be abandoned. This was a major cause of the emigrations to North America (see Road 77, Hofsós). There have been many other eruptions in Askja, the latest in 1961 when lava flowed from **Öskjuop**, the craters now named Vikraborgir. In 1907 two Germans, Walther von Knebel and Max Rudloff, were lost, presumed drowned, while doing research at Askja

Dyngjufjöll, a cluster of mountains around the Askja caldera, forming a square about 24 km a side, rising 600-700 m above the surrounding plateau and 100-200 m above the bottom of Askja. Evidence suggests that these mountains are the remnants of a huge volcanic zone from the ice age, that collapsed. There are many younger lava streams, almost no vegetation and geothermal heat in many places. The highest peak is Þorvaldstindur (1510 m) on the south rim, named for the 19th century geologist Þorvaldur Thoroddsen. The main passes into Askja are **Suðurskarð** on the south, **Jónsskarð** on the northwest and Öskjuop on the northeast, where the road-track is.

Dyngjufjöll ytri, (1,000 m) a 20 km long tuff ridge separating the Dyngjufjöll mountains from the Dyngjufjalladalur valley. Its higher end is named **Fjallsendi** ("Mountain's end").

Dyngjufjalladalur, a 15 km long valley through which lies the Gæsavatnaleið road going via Suðurárbotnar to Svartárkot in the Bárðardalur valley. Accessible ONLY to well equipped mountain vehicles. This route was first driven in July 1944.

Drekagil, ("Dragon canyon") in the eastern part of Dyngjufjöll. A cabin called Dreki built by the Touring Club of Akureyri. From here track F910 goes south by Dyngjufjöll, north of Trölladyngja and Tungnafellsjökull, joining Sprengisandsleið (F26) at Tómasarhagi. From Dreki to Tómasarhagi is about 100 km. **This route is only safe with two or more vehicles travelling in tandem.**

Kattbekingur, (1,055 m) a light brown, steep-sided tuff mountain with a sharp crest.

Vatnsfell, (1,308 m) a lone mountain in the Dyngjufjöll range. Originally named Wattsfell for W.L. Watts, an Englishman who, accompanied by the Icelandic guide "Glacier Páll", was the first to walk across Vatnajökull (1875). Excellent views.

F902 **Kverkfjallaleið,** p. 482 **F903** **Hvannalindavegur,** p. 482 **F905** **Arnardalsleið,** p. 484
F910 **Austurleið,** p. 488-491

5
P. 568
22
P. 585

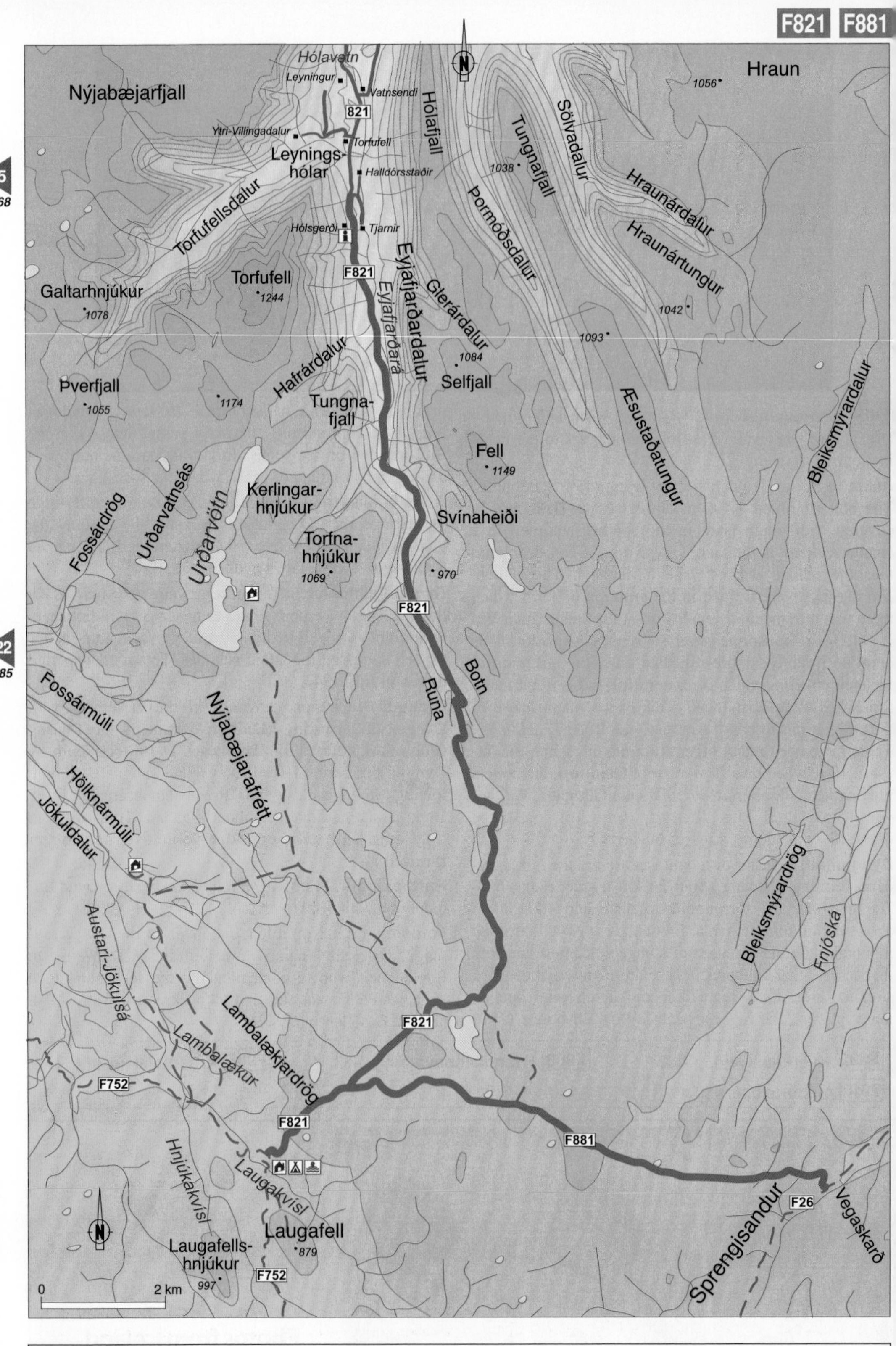

821 **Eyjafjarðarbraut vestri,** p. 392 F26 **Sprengisandsleið,** p. 430-433 F752 **Skagafjarðarleið,** p. 450

F881 **Dragaleið** 18,3 km, Westbound from route F26, ;prengisandsleið to Laugafell. The route is passable for ıll jeeps even small jeeps.

;prengisandur, a wide and extensive desert in the entre of Iceland with indistinct boundaries, but usuılly understood to be between Eyvindarver/**Háumýrar/** **ȷjórsárver** and Kiðagil and between the glaciers Hofsökull and Tungnafellsjökull and the river Skjálfandafljót. ⁄lostly about 700-800 m above sea level and about 30 by '0 km in area. In times past this route was not very much ısed, mostly because of the distance between grasslands. ;ince the road was made it has been used a good deal by notor vehicles in summertime.

F821 **Eyjafjarðarleið** 41,7 km. The route is passable for all jeeps. Many creeks cross the road and it is steep in places.

Nýibær, for some time a weather report station, now abandoned. The present road from Eyjafjörður is up through Runa and by Nýibær to Laugafell.

Hólafjall, a long, narrow mountain between Eyjafjörður and the valley Sölvadalur. A jeep-track, now abandoned, once ran along it, reaching an altitude of 1002 m. The view from Hólafjall is very good. From Þormóðsstaðir is a road on the northern end of Hólafjall, step but accessible for most cars.

Runa, the head of the Eyjafjörður valley.

6
P. 569

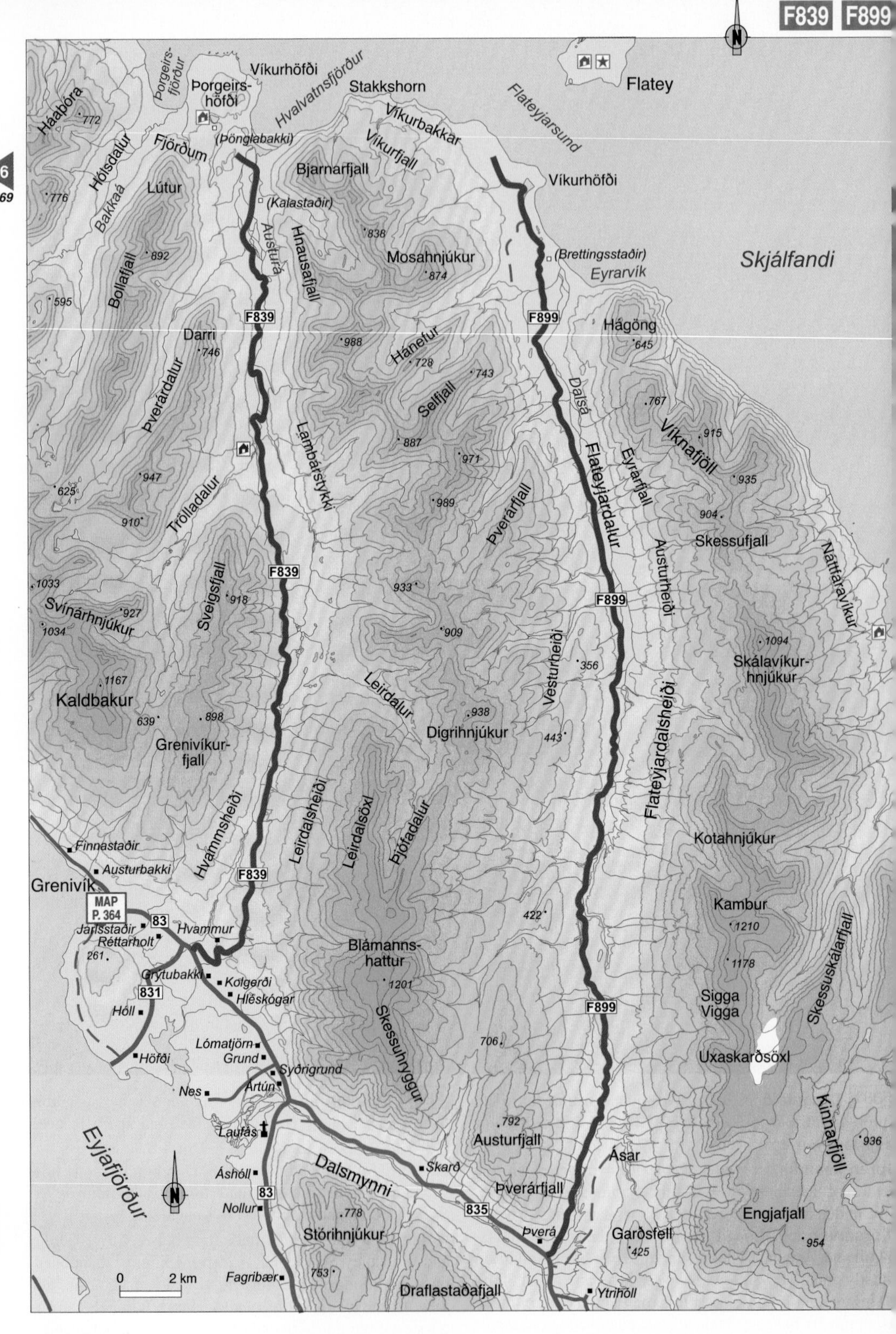
Víkurhöfði
Þorgeirsfjörður
Þorgeirshöfði
Stakkshorn
Hvalvatnsfjörður
Flatey
Flateyjarsund
Háaþóra
772
Fjörðum
(Þönglabakki)
Víkurbakkar
Víkurfjall
Bjarnarfjall
Víkurhöfði
Hólsdalur
Lútur
776
Bakkaá
(Kalastaðir)
Austurá
Hnausafjall
838
Mosahnjúkur
874
(Brettingsstaðir)
Eyrarvík
Skjálfandi
Bollafjall
892
595
F839
F899
Hágöng
645
Darri
746
988
Hánefur
728
743
Þverárdalur
Selfjall
Dalsá
767
Víknafjöll
915
Lambárstykki
887
971
Flateyjardalur
Eyrarfjall
935
947
625
Trölladalur
910
989
Þverárfjall
904
Skessufjall
Austurheiði
Náttfaravíkur
1033
Sveigsfjall
918
933
Svínárhnjúkur
927
1034
909
Vesturheiði
1094
Skálavíkurhnjúkur
356
1167
Kaldbakur
Leirdalur
938
Dígrihnjúkur
639
898
443
Flateyjardalsheiði
Grenivíkurfjall
Leirdalsheiði
Leirdalsöxl
Þjófadalur
Kotahnjúkur
Hvammsheiði
Finnastaðir
Austurbakki
Grenivík
MAP P. 364
83
Kambur
Jarlsstaðir
Réttarholt
Hvammur
422
1210
261
Blámannshattur
1178
Grýtubakki
Kolgerði
1201
831
Hléskógar
Skessuhryggur
Sigga Vigga
Skessuskálarfjall
Hóll
Lómatjörn
706
Uxaskarðsöxl
Höfði
Grund
Syðrigrund
Nes
Ártún
Kinnarfjöll
792
Laufás
Austurfjall
936
Eyjafjörður
Ásar
Áshóll
Skarð
Dalsmynni
Þverárfjall
835
Nollur
778
Engjafjall
Þverá
Garðsfell
Stórihnjúkur
954
425
0
2 km
Fagribær
753
Draflastaðafjall
Ytrihóll

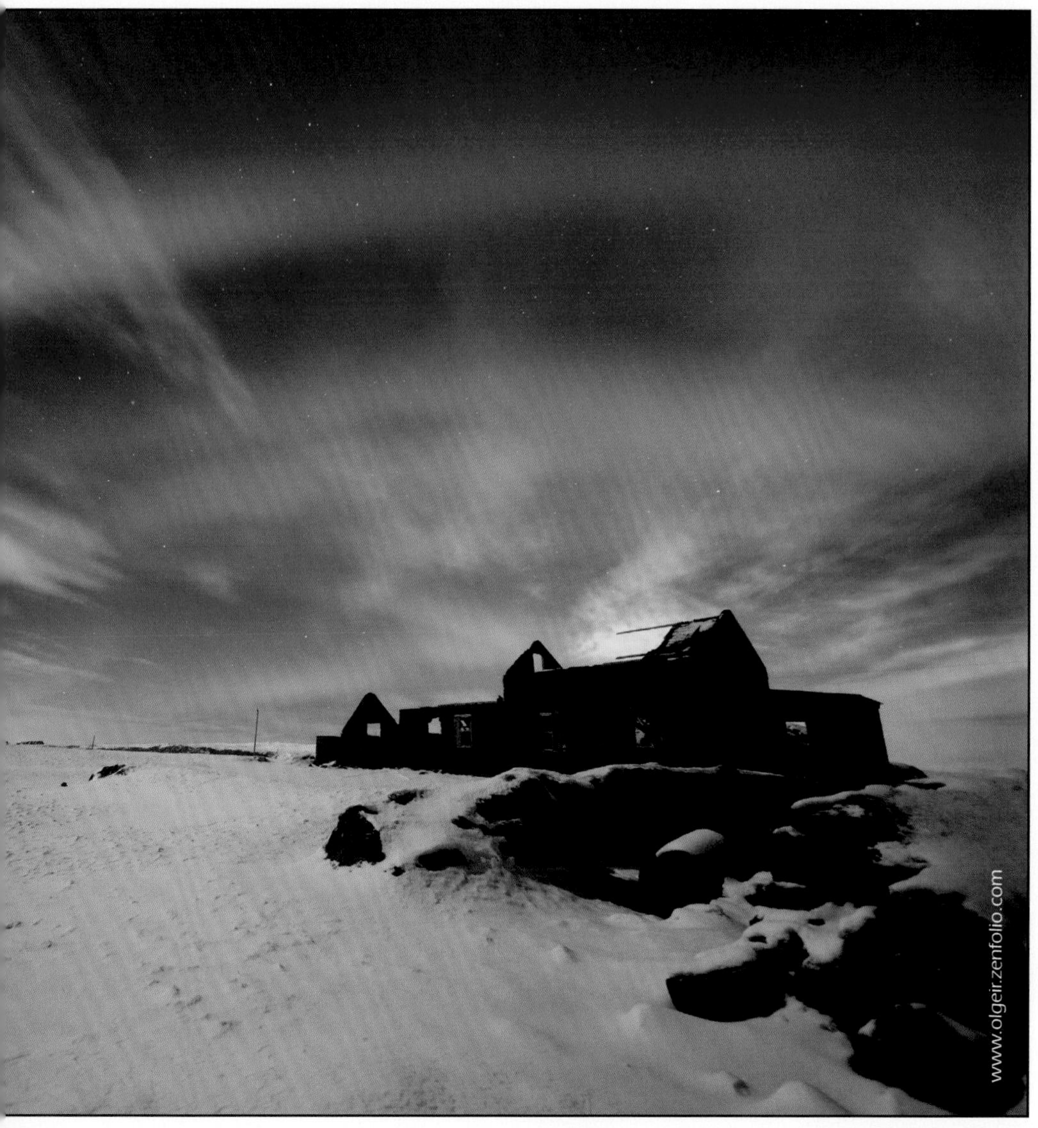

F839 **Leirdalsheiðarvegur** 34,4 km. The route is passable for all jeeps, also small jeeps. Some creeks and small fords need to be crossed. There is a hut at Flateyjardalsheiði heath.

Flateyjardalsheiði and **Flateyjardalur** stretch for 30 km from Fnjóskadalur valley to the sea. The valley is very fertile and colourful with fish in most rivers. In the Flateyjardalur valley where 5 farms, now all abandoned, the last one in 1953, Brettingsstaður. The valley is the scene of the story of Finnbogi rammi.

F899 **Flateyjardalsvegur** 27,5 km. Not passable for small jeeps.

Fjörður, two small fjords, **Hvalvatnsfjörður** and **Þorgeirsfjörður**, on the east of Eyjafjörður. Pleasant grassy valleys at their heads, with good trout streams. A jeep track from there over Leirdalsheiði moor to Grýtubakki in the Höfðahverfi district. A popular walking district.

Flatey (flat island), on Skjálfandi bay. Flatey befits its name by reaching a maximum altitude of only 22 m, in an area of 2.62 km^2. Although the island was inhabited from the 12th century till 1967, it was not until around 1943 that the population peaked at 120. Besides fishing and livestock farming, Flatey residents relied to some extent on driftwood, seals and birds. A cooperative store and primary school came into operation in the early 20th century, and several attractive houses are still maintained by descendents of former residents.

83 **Grenivíkurvegur,** p. 365 **831** **Höfðavegur,** p. 365 **835** **Fnjóskadalsvegur eystri,** p. 397

Weather stations in Iceland

Weather information for 3 weatherstations in Iceland, average values for 1961-1990

	Jan.	Feb.	Mars	April	May	Jun.	Jul.	Aug.	Sept.	Okt.	Nov.	Des.	Year
Reykjavík													
mean temp. °C	-0.5	0.4	0.5	2.9	6.3	9.0	10.6	10.3	7.4	4.4	1.1	-0.2	4.3
max temp. °C	9.9	9.4	13.0	14.7	18.8	19.5	24.3	19.9	18.5	13.6	11.3	10.7	24.3
precipitation mm	75.6	71.8	81.8	58.3	43.8	50.0	51.8	61.8	66.5	85.6	72.5	78.7	798.8
sunshine hours	26.9	51.8	111.1	140.0	192.0	161.3	171.3	154.8	124.8	83.4	38.5	12.1	1268.4
Akureyri													
mean temp. °C	-2.2	-1.5	-1.3	1.6	5.5	9.1	10.5	10.0	6.3	3.0	-0.4	-1.9	3.2
max temp. °C	13.0	13.8	15.0	19.8	24.6	29.4	27.6	27.7	21.8	19.5	17.6	-	29.4
precipitation mm	55.2	42.5	43.3	29.2	19.3	28.2	33.0	34.1	39.1	58.0	54.2	52.8	489.5
sunshine hours	339.6	36.1	407.5	458.8	502.5	176.6	158.2	135.6	417.1	382.7	347.0	333.4	1642.5
Hveravellir													
mean temp. °C	-6.9	-6.3	-6.1	-3.4	0.5	4.9	7.0	6.3	2.4	-1.3	-4.8	-6.3	-1.2
max temp. °C	8.6	6.6	5.7	6.7	15.7	18.5	22.3	21.5	16.8	9.7	7.8	9.1	22.3
precipitation mm	60.3	71.3	60.8	47.3	31.5	60.3	56.9	76.8	57.7	82.5	54.7	66.0	724.4

www.vedur.is

NEW WEATHERFORCASTS:
www.vedur.is

WIND SPEED

m/s	km/hrs	knots	Beaufort number	Description	Specification for estimating speed over land.
0-0.2	< 1	< 1	0	Calm	Smoke rises vertically.
0.3-1.5	1-5	1-3	1	Light air	Direction of wind shown by smoke drift. Flags don´t move.
1.6-3.3	6-11	4-6	2	Light breeze	Wind felt on face; leaves rustle; ordinary waves moved by wind.
3.4-5.4	12-19	7-10	3	Gentle breeze	Leaves and small twigs in constant motion; wind extends light flag.
5.5-7.9	20-28	11-16	4	Moderate breeze	Raises dust and loose paper, small branches are moved.
8.0-10.7	29-38	17-21	5	Fresh breeze	Small trees in leaf begin to sway, crested wavelets form on inland waters.
10.8-13.8	39-49	22-27	6	Strong breeze	Large branches in motion; whistling heard in telegraph wires; umbrellas used with difficulty.
13.9-17.1	50-61	28-33	7	Near gale	Whole trees in motion; inconvenience felt when walking against the wind.
17.2-20.7	62-74	34-40	8	Gale	Breaks twigs off trees; generally impedes progress.
20.8-24.4	75-88	41-47	9	Strong gale	Slight structural damage occurs (chimney-pots and slates removed).
24.5-28.4	89-102	48-55	10	Storm	Seldom experienced inland; trees uprooted; considerable structural damage occurs.
28.5-32.6	103-117	56-63	11	Violent storm	Very rarely experienced; accompanied by widespread damage.
32.7 and over	118 and over	64 and over	12	Hurricane	Hurricane.

© David Varga

23
P. 586

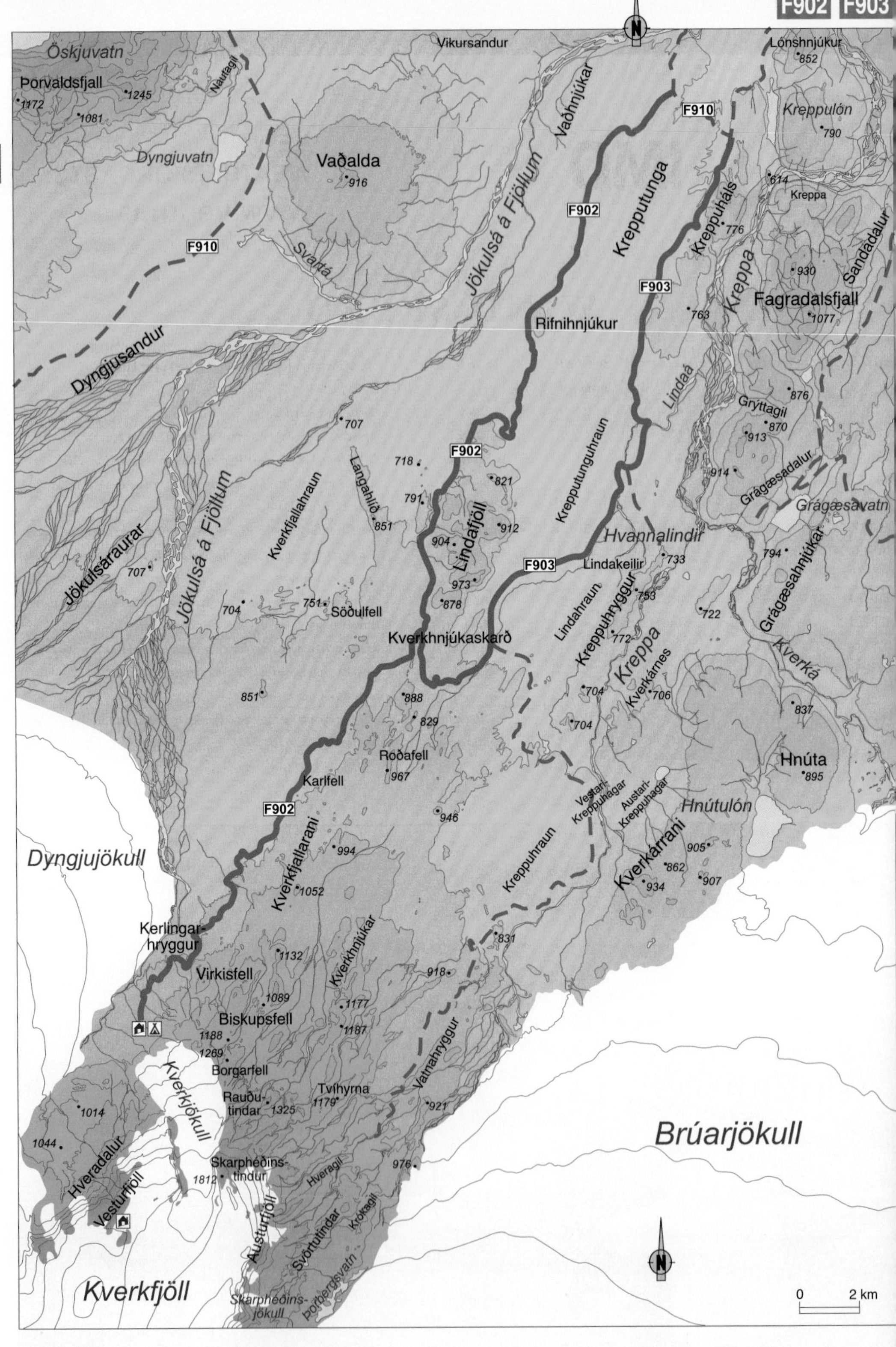
Öskjuvatn
Þorvaldsfjall
Nautagil
Vikursandur
Vaðhnjúkar
Lónshnjúkur
Kreppulón
Dyngjuvatn
Vaðalda
F910
F902
F903
Krepputunga
Kreppuháls
Kreppa
Sandadalur
Svartá
Jökulsá á Fjöllum
Fagradalsfjall
Rifnihnjúkur
Dyngjusandur
Lindaá
Gryttagil
Grágæsadalur
Grágæsavatn
Langahlíð
Kverkfjallahraun
Krepputunguhraun
Lindafjöll
Hvannalindir
Lindakeilir
Grágæsahnjúkar
Jökulsáraurar
Lindahraun
Kreppuhryggur
Sööulfell
Kverkhnjúkaskarð
Kverká
Kverkárnes
Roðafell
Hnúta
Karlfell
Vestari-Krepppuhagar
Austari-Kreppuhagar
Hnútulón
Kverkfjallarani
Dyngjujökull
Kreppuhraun
Kverkárrani
Kerlingar-hryggur
Virkisfell
Kverkhnjúkar
Biskupsfell
Borgarfell
Kverkjökull
Vatnahryggur
Rauðu-tindar
Tvíhyrna
Brúarjökull
Hveradalur
Skarphéðins-tindur
Hveragil
Vesturfjöll
Austurfjöll
Svörtutindar
Krókagil
Kverkfjöll
Skarphéðins-jökull
Þorbergsvatn
0
2 km

Öskjuvatn.

F902 **Kverkfjallavegur** 41,3 km. Accessible by jeeps.

Kverkfjallarani or **Kverkhnjúkarani**, a ridge.

Kverkfjöll, (1,920 m) a magnificent mountain range in northern Vatnajökull. One of the largest geothermal areas in the country on the west side of the mountains, creating many beautiful ice caves in the glacier. A good tourist hut north of Kverkfjöll and another one high in the mountains. Good walking routes.

F903 **Hvannalindavegur** 26,4 km. Accessible by jeeps.

Krepputunga, the district between the rivers Kreppa and Jökulsá á Fjöllum, 50-60 km long.

Hvannalindir, an area where several streams come up from under a lava field, surrounded by grasslands and other vegetation not usually seen at that height (650 m). Lindakeilir is a small cone shaped hill in the western part of the area. Many protected ruins in the lava edge, possibly made by the 18th century outlaw Fjalla-Eyvindur. A warden in the summer.

Fagradalsfjall, (1,022 m) the largest mountain in the Brúaröræfi wilderness.

F910 **Austurleið,** p. 488-491

24 P. 587

F905 **Arnardalsleið** 26,1 km. This route is passable by all jeeps, also small jeeps, though some fords need to be crossed.

Arnardalsfjöll, (679 and 671 m) two small but conspicuous mountains in the middle of Arnardalur.

Arnardalur, a lovely, broad valley west of the Fjallgarðar ranges, with good flat land, spring-fed rivers and areas of vegetation. North of the valley, there are two gravel ledges with a particularly well-formed glacial ridges on the northern one, west of the road. The crossroads at Ytra-Mynni are on the southern one. At the eastern end of the valley, accessible by jeep-track, are the ruins of the farm, **Dyngja**. Þorsteinn jökull was said to have fled to there at the time of the plague, around 1500. From the south of Arnardalur a jeep-track goes along Álftadalsdyngja to Brúarjökull and along Brúardalir east to Jökuldalur.

Grjót, a withered plain by Hvanná.

901 **Möðrudalsvegur,** p. 96 **F88** **Öskjuleið,** p. 472 **F910** **Austurleið,** p. 488-491

F907 BRÚARVEGUR

F907 **Brúarvegur,** 20,7 km. A route between route 1 ınd F910. Passable for all cars.

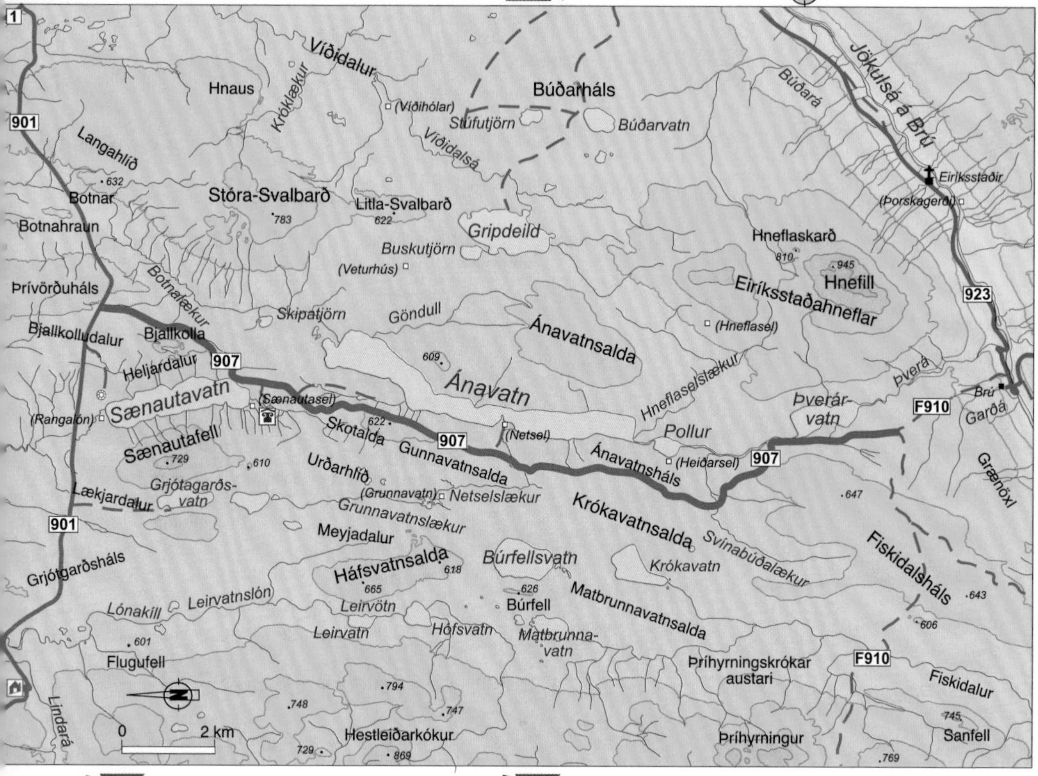

Sænautasel, an abandoned farm (occupied 1843–1943) t the southern end of the lake Sænautavatn ("Sea-monster lake"). It achieved notoriety through the Halldór Laxness' account A Midwinter Night on Jökuldalsheiði Moor. It was renovated in 1992-3 and is considered well vorth a visit. Land reclamation and revegetation.

Jökuldalsheiði, the moor east of the Fjallgarðar ranges ınd west of the Jökuldalur valley. Hilly, with sparse egetation and a number of good fishing lakes, among hem Ánavatn which lies parallel to the road. A number of moorland farms were started there after 1840, some of them continuing into the 1940's. The farms that were inhabited the longest were Rangalón, on the north side of Sænautavatn lake by the main road, 1843-1924, **Ármótasel**, by the main road by Jökuldalur, 1853-1943, Veturhús, on the east side of Ánavatn lake, 1846-1941, **Heiðarsel,** on the west side of Ánavatn lake, 1857-1946, and Sænautasel, on the south side of Sænautavatn lake, 1843-1943.

Grunnavatn, an abandoned moor farm.

Netsel, an old abandoned moor farm where Þorsteinn Jökull from Brú lived for a year trying to avoid the plague.

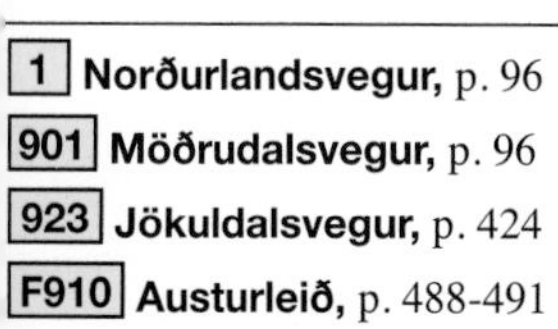

1 **Norðurlandsvegur,** p. 96
901 **Möðrudalsvegur,** p. 96
923 **Jökuldalsvegur,** p. 424
F910 **Austurleið,** p. 488-491

24 P. 587

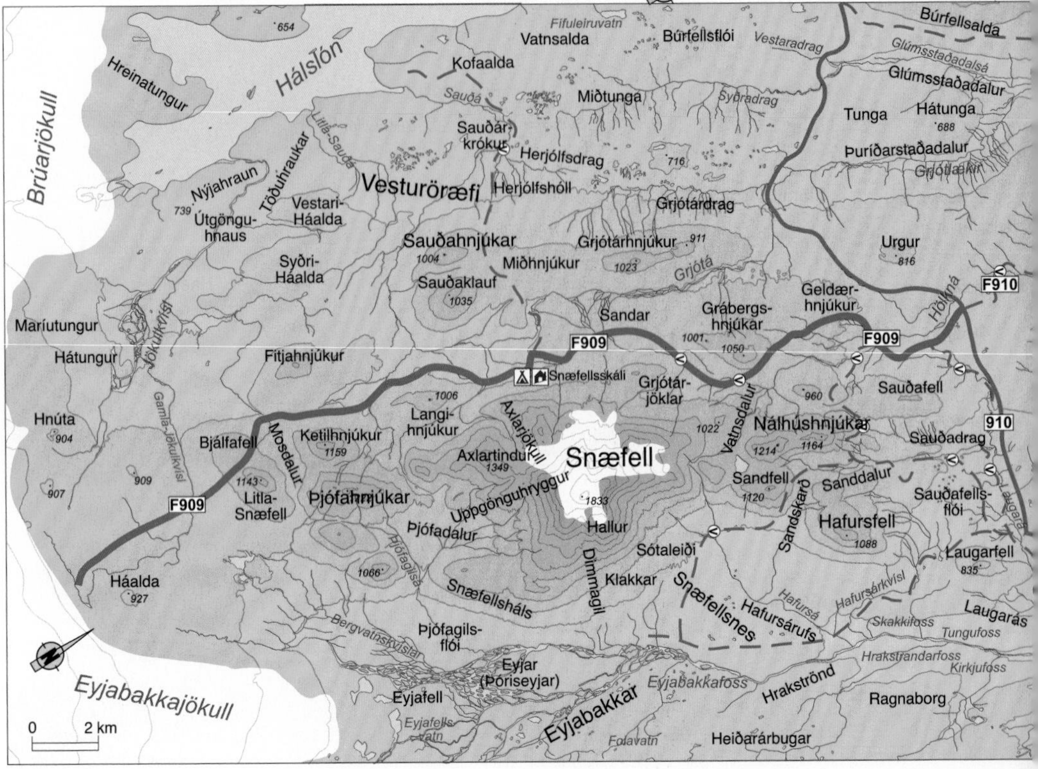

F909 Snæfellsleið 13,7 km. Passable for small jeep though some small creeks need to be passed on the way to the hut by the mountain Snæfell. The route continues for 18,2 km south of the hut towards Maríutungur on the east side of Brúarjökull.

Snæfell, (1,833 m) the highest mountain in Iceland outside the ice-caps. It is a conical central volcano, quite severely weathered by wind and glaciers. It is not clear when it last erupted, since neither lava nor ash-layers can clearly be identified with it. The first person known to attempt to climb the mountain was Sveinn Pálsson in 1794, but it was Guðmundur Snorrason from Bessastaðagerði in Fljótsdalur who first succeeded in conquering it in 1877. To the east of Snæfell the Eyjabakkajökull glacier stretches down onto Eyjabakkar, a marshy area of luxuriant vegetation at a height of 650-680 m soon to becoma a Ramsar-site. Important grazing and calving areas of the reindeer in the east are around Snæfell. Large herds can often be seen in Vesturöræfi, between Snæfell and Hálsalón. The animals are also spread around the highland west north and east of Snæfell and can sometimes be seen in the lowland in late winter. In the first half of the 20th century the reindeer mostly lived in the highland west of Snæfell, in Vesturöræfi and Kringilsárrani, but part of this area was covered by the surging glacier Brúarjökull in 1964. Reindeer have been imported to Iceland from Finnmark in Norway four times. In 1771 they were installed first in the Westman Islands and then in the Rangárvallasýsla county, but they became entirely extinct in the "Móðuharðindin" ("The hardship of the mist") of 1783-4. In 1777 they were imported to Hafnarfjörður near Reykjavík. These animals were the start of the Reykjanes stock which at one time was numbered in the hundreds but died out entirely before 1930. Reindeer that were released on Vaðlaheiði opposite Akureyri in 1784 became the stock of Þingeyjarsýsla county. It grew to more then thousand animals in the mid-19th century but the last of them disappeared in 1936. Finally, reindeer were put ashore in Vopnafjörður in 1787. They lived mostly on the moors from Möðrudalur south to Lón and probably numbered a few thousand in the mid-19th century, but a period of hard weather towards the end of the century reduced their numbers there as elsewhere. By 1940 there were only a few hundred left, the only reindeer in Iceland. Since then their numbers have greatly increased, the population was estimated to be over 54.000 animals during the summer of 2012. They can now be found on moors and mountains from Jökulsá á Fjöllum south to Jökulsá á Breiðamerkursandi. Reindeer that stay close to farms and villages during late winter can cause damage to trees, fences and forestry projects. In later years hunting permits have been given for up to 1200 reindeer each year.

F910 Austurleið, p. 488-491

www.olgeir.zenfolio.com

23 P. 586

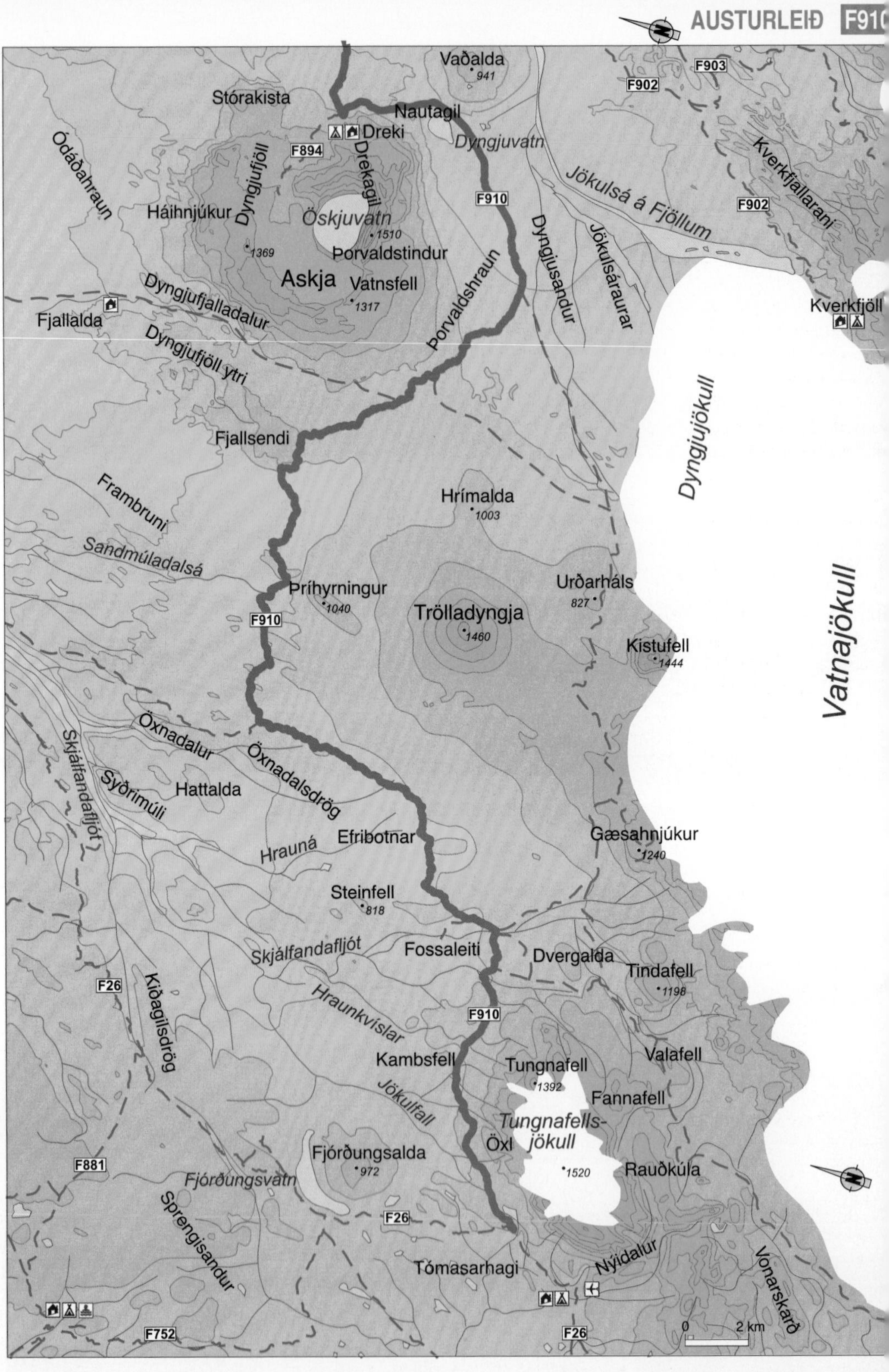

Vaðalda 941
F903
F902
Stórakista
Nautagil
Dreki
Dyngjuvatn
Ódáðahraun
F894
Dyngjufjöll
Drekagil
Kverkfjallarani
Jökulsá á Fjöllum
F910
F902
Háihnjúkur
Öskjuvatn
1510
1369
Þorvaldstindur
Dyngjusandur
Jökulsáraurar
Askja
Vatnsfell
1317
Þorvaldshraun
Dyngjufjalladalur
Kverkfjöll
Fjallalda
Dyngjufjöll ytri
Dyngjujökull
Fjallsendi
Frambruni
Hrímalda 1003
Sandmúladalsá
Þríhyrningur 1040
Urðarháls 827
Trölladyngja 1460
F910
Kistufell 1444
Vatnajökull
Öxnadalur
Öxnadalsdrög
Skjálfandafljót
Syðrimúli
Hattalda
Efribotnar
Hrauná
Gæsahnjúkur 1240
Steinfell 818
Skjálfandafljót
Fossaleiti
Dvergalda
Tindafell 1198
F26
Kiðagilsdrög
Hraunkvíslar
F910
Kambsfell
Tungnafell 1392
Valafell
Jökulfall
Fannafell
Tungnafells-jökull
Öxl
Fjórðungsalda 972
1520
Rauðkúla
F881
Fjórðungsvatn
Sprengisandur
F26
Tómasarhagi
Nýidalur
Vonarskarð
F752
F26
0 2 km

22 P. 585

F910 Austurleið (Trölladyngjuleið) 119,2 km. A difficult and a slow route.

Tungnafell, (1,392 m) a mountain north of Tungnafelljökull. The glacier is named for the mountain.

Jökulfall, one of the source tributaries of the river Skjálfandafljót, coming from Tungnafellsjökull.

Skjálfandafljót, one of largest rivers in the north, falling into the Skjálfandaflói bay. 178 km long and with a drainage area of 3,860 km^2. The bridge there was built in 1986.

Marteinsflæða, an area of vegetation named for Marteinn Þorgrímsson of Lake Mývatn who walked to there in the early 19th century, a considerable feat at that time.

Jökuldælaflæða, an area of vegetation found by men from the Jökuldalur valley in 1834.

Surtluflæða, ("Black ewe marshes") an area of rivers and vegetation discovered in 1880 and named for black shreds of wool found there.

Trölladyngja, (1,459 m) the greatest shield volcano in Iceland, about 10 km in diameter and rising 500-600 m above the surrounding area. The crater is 1,200-1,500 m long, 500 m wide and 100 m deep. Lavaflows are thought to have run down the Bárðardalur valley.

Þríhyrningur, (1,044 m) a prominent tuff crest north of the mountain Trölladyngja.

Ódáðahraun, ("Ill deeds lava field") the largest lava field in Iceland, bounded by Vatnajökull to the south, Skjálfandafljót to the west and Jökulsá á Fjöllum to the east. Its northern boundary is not so clear, but usually considered to be Highway 1 in the Lake Mývatn district. Very much a desert with lava, sands, lot of mountains, cliffs, etc. Hardly any running water is found there, though there is some on the eastern and western edges. This area was unexplored and thus mysterious, giving rise to tales of extensive outlaw settlements. Organized travel and exploration was first begun in the early 19th century.

Holuhraun, ("Pitted lava") a large, sandy lava field north of Vatnajökull. Named in 1884 by Þorvaldur Thoroddsen the geologist.

Svartá, a 5 km long clear river running into Jökulsá á Fjöllum. In it is the waterfall Skínandi. It has a consistent flow of 20 m^3/sec. At the confluence it is, in winter, twice the size of the glacial river, though the latter is much the larger in the summer.

Vaðalda, (941 m) an old shield mountain on the west bank of the river Jökulsá, rising about 250 m above the surroundings.

Dyngjuvatn, a shallow lake. Can reach a length of 6 km during spring thaw but is much smaller later in the summer.

Gæsavatnaleið 59,1 km. A very difficult route and it is not advisable to go on one car.

Gæsavötn, ("Goose lakes") two shallow lakes 920-940 m above sea level. Named by two men who saw geese on the lake in 1880. Ruins of huts nearby but their origin unknown.

Kistufell, (1,446 m) a tuff mountain in northern Vatnajökull. In 1950 an Icelandic aircraft (Geysir) crashlanded on Bárðarbunga in Vatnajökull and the (successful) rescue operation had its headquarters near Kistufell. The crew was saved 6 days after the crash.

Dyngjuháls, (1,000-1,100 m) a volcanic ridge just north of Vatnajökull. Along the length of it run five parallel rows of craters from which both large and small lava flows have run to the north and west.

Vatnajökull, the largest glacier in Iceland and Europe, over 8000 km^2, its highest point being **Bárðarbunga** (2000 m). The highest point in Iceland is **Hvannadalshnjúkur** (2110 m) on the **Öræfajökull** glacier. The biggest glacier coming from Vatnajökull is Brúarjökull. Vatnajökull has been a National Park since 2008..

Urðarháls, (1,025 m) a glaciated, dolerite volcano, its crater about 1,100 m long, 800 m wide and 100 m at its deepest.

Dyngjujökull, one of Iceland's biggest outlet glaciers. Late on warm summer days melt water comes roaring off the glacier creating huge rivers that flow all over the sands east of the volcano Urðarháls. These are called **Síðdegisflæður** ("Evening morasses") and are very dangerous for all motor vehicles.

F26 Sprengisandsleið, p. 430-433 | **F752 Skagafjarðarleið,** p. 470 | **F881 Dragaleið,** p. 476
F894 Öskjuvatnsvegur, p. 474 | **F902 Kverkfjallaleið,** p. 482 | **F903 Hvannalindavegur,** p. 482

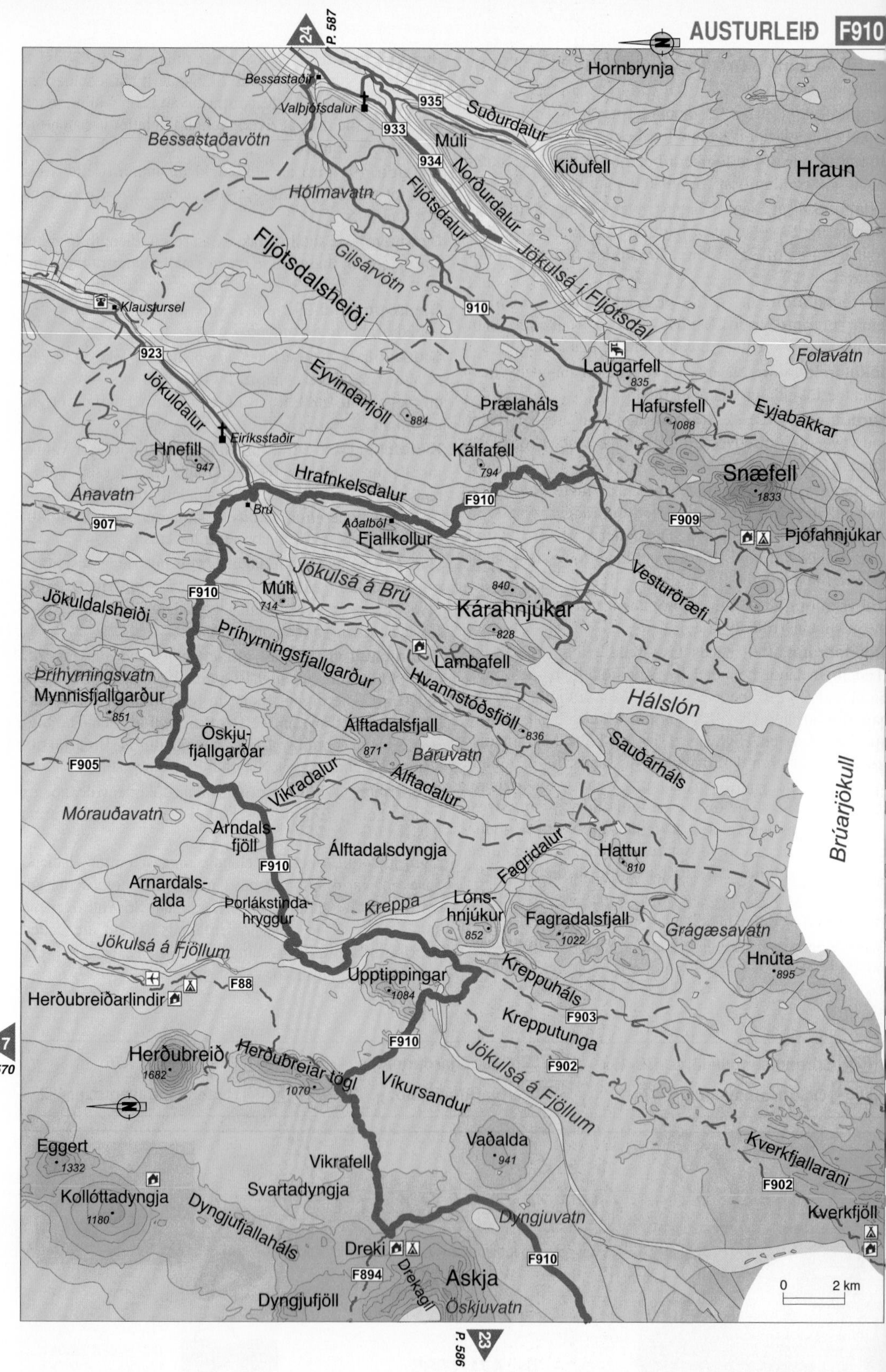
24 P. 587
Hornbrynja
Bessastaðir
Valþjófsdalur
935
933
934
Suðurdalur
Múli
Norðurdalur
Kiðufell
Hraun
Bessastaðavötn
Hólmavatn
Fljótsdalur
Fljótsdalsheiði
Gilsárvötn
Jökulsá í Fljótsdal
Klaustursel
910
923
Folavatn
Laugarfell
835
Eyvindarfjöll
884
Þrælaháls
Hafursfell
1088
Eyjabakkar
Jökuldalur
Eiríksstaðir
Hnefill
947
Kálfafell
794
Snæfell
1833
Hrafnkelsdalur
Ánavatn
Brú
F910
907
Aðalból
Fjallkollur
F909
Þjófahnjúkar
Jökulsá á Brú
840
Vesturöræfi
Jökuldalsheiði
Múli
714
Kárahnjúkar
828
Þríhyrningsfjallgarður
Lambafell
Þríhyrningsvatn
Mynnisfjallgarður
851
Hvannstóðsfjöll
836
Hálslón
Öskju-
fjallgarðar
Álftadalsfjall
871
Báruvatn
Sauðárháls
F905
Vikradalur
Álftadalur
Brúarjökull
Mórauðavatn
Arndals-
fjöll
Álftadalsdyngja
Fagridalur
Hattur
810
Arnardals-
alda
Þorlákstinda-
hryggur
Kreppa
Lóns-
hnjúkur
852
Fagradalsfjall
1022
Grágæsavatn
Jökulsá á Fjöllum
Hnúta
895
Upptippingar
1084
Kreppuháls
F88
Herðubreiðarlindir
F903
Krepputunga
7
P. 570
Herðubreið
1682
Herðubreiðar tögl
1070
F902
Víkursandur
Jökulsá á Fjöllum
Eggert
1332
Vikrafell
Vaðalda
941
Kverkfjallarani
Kollóttadyngja
1180
Svartadyngja
F902
Dyngjufjallaháls
Dyngjuvatn
Kverkfjöll
Dreki
Drekagil
F910
F894
Askja
Dyngjufjöll
Öskjuvatn
0
2 km
23 P. 586

F910 **Austurleið** 148 km (the east section).

Jökulsá á Fjöllum, the largest river in the north, falling into Öxarfjörður, 206 km long with a drainage basin of 7,380 km^2 (1,700 of which is under the glacier). Its lower reaches often called Jökulsá í Öxarfirði. Bridge at Upptyppingar, built 1986.

Upptyppingar, (1,084 and 987 m) two pyramid shaped tuff mountains west of Jökulsá, prominent landmarks. There is a bridge on Jökulsá south of Upptyppingar, built in 1986.

Herðubreiðartögl, (1059 m) an 8 km long tuff ridge to the south of Herðubreið, rising to 450 m above the plateau.

Kreppa, is the name of deep and wide glacial river that has its source in the west part of the glacier Brúarjökull and joining Jökulsá by Herðubreiðarlindir. In August 1999 there was a flood in the rivers Kreppa and Jökulsá á Fjöllum. This flood, believed to be the greatest in the area for almost a hundred years, caused extensive damage to vegetation at Herðubreiðarlindir, cleared a path for a new branch out of Kreppa, and remodelled the landscape in other ways. The swollen rivers breached the road at Grímsstaðir á Fjöllum and Öxarfjörður, and swept the bridge across the river Sandá in Öxarfjörður out to sea.

Hvanná, a river that runs through the Byttuskarð pass between the two mountain ranges Brattifjallgarður and Mynnisfjallgarður.

Fjallgarðar, a series of mountain ranges reaching more or less all the way from the glacier to Melrakkaslétta (see Road 85). The different ranges have different names, such as Öskjufjallgarður, Mynnisfjallgarður, Dimmifjallgarður etc.

Þríhyrningsdalur, a broad dale in between the Fjallgarðar ranges with flat sands and sparse vegetation. The lake Þríhyrningsvatn at its northern end.

Brúaröræfi, (500-700 m) the wilderness from Brú at Jökuldalur, south from Arnardalur to Brúarjökull, between Jökulsá á Fjöllum and Dal.

Fagradalsfjall, (1022 m) the largest mountain in the Brúaröræfi wilderness.

Krepputunga, the district between Jökulsá á Fjöllum and Kreppa, 50-60 km long.

Hrafnkelsdalur, a rather long, broad valley leading off Jökuldalur, quite grassy with birch bushes and some geothermal activity. Ruins of 20 ancient farmsteads have been found there. The road up out of the valley is steep and generally not dependable. The river Hölkná, which has to be forded, is often very swollen.

Fljótsdalsheiði, a broad area of moorland, mostly covered with vegetation, between Jökuldalur and Fljótsdalur. In ages past the main route from Fljótsdalur to Aðalból in Hrafnkelsdalur lay across. A track, only accessable for altered jeeps leads from Kelduá to a mountain hut by Geldingafell.

Eyvindarfjöll, the glacier is named for Eyvindur Bjarnason, whom Hrafnkell Freysgoði killed there. Eyvindur was the brother of Sámur from Leikskálar.

907 **Brúarvegur,** p. 99	**923** **Jökuldalsvegur,** p. 424	**933** **Fljótsdalsvegur,** p. 428
934 **Múlavegur,** p. 428	**935** **Suðurdalsvegur,** p. 428	**F88** **Öskjuleið,** p. 472-475
F894 **Öskjuvatnsvegur,** p. 474	**F902** **Kverkfjallaleið,** p. 482-483	**F903** **Hvannalindavegur,** p. 482-483
F905 **Arnardalsleið,** p. 484	**F909** **Snæfellsleið,** p. 486	

ÞÓRDALSHEIÐARVEGUR F936

1 **Austurlandsvegur,** p. 112
92 **Norðfjarðarvegur,** p. 409-41
96 **Suðurfjarðarvegur,** p. 420
937 **Skriðdalsvegur,** p. 105
938 **Múlavegur,** p. 105

9 P. 572

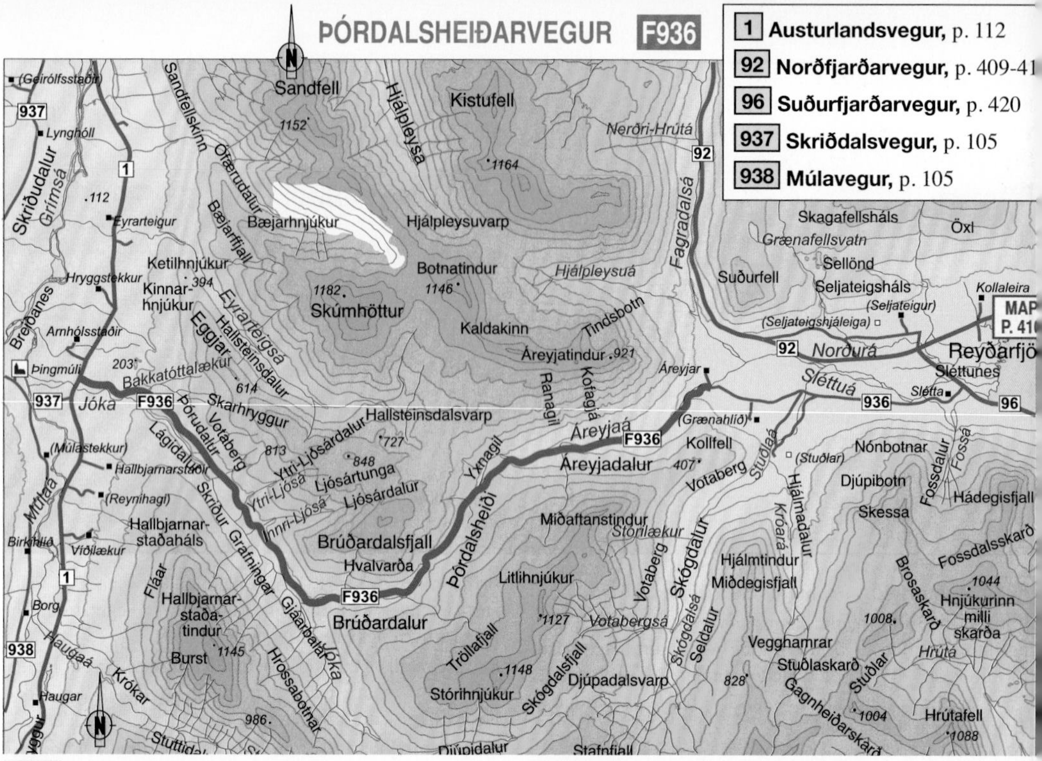

F936 Þórdalsheiði 15,9 km. Passable for small jeeps. The route lies from Skriðudalur through Þórudalur, Þórdalsheiði to Reyðafjörður by Áreyri.

Stafsheiði, a much travelled heath once.

Þórutótt, named after a woman, Þóra, that lived there alone.

Þórudalur, a narrow valley.

LOÐMUNDARFJARÐARVEGUR F946

9 P. 572

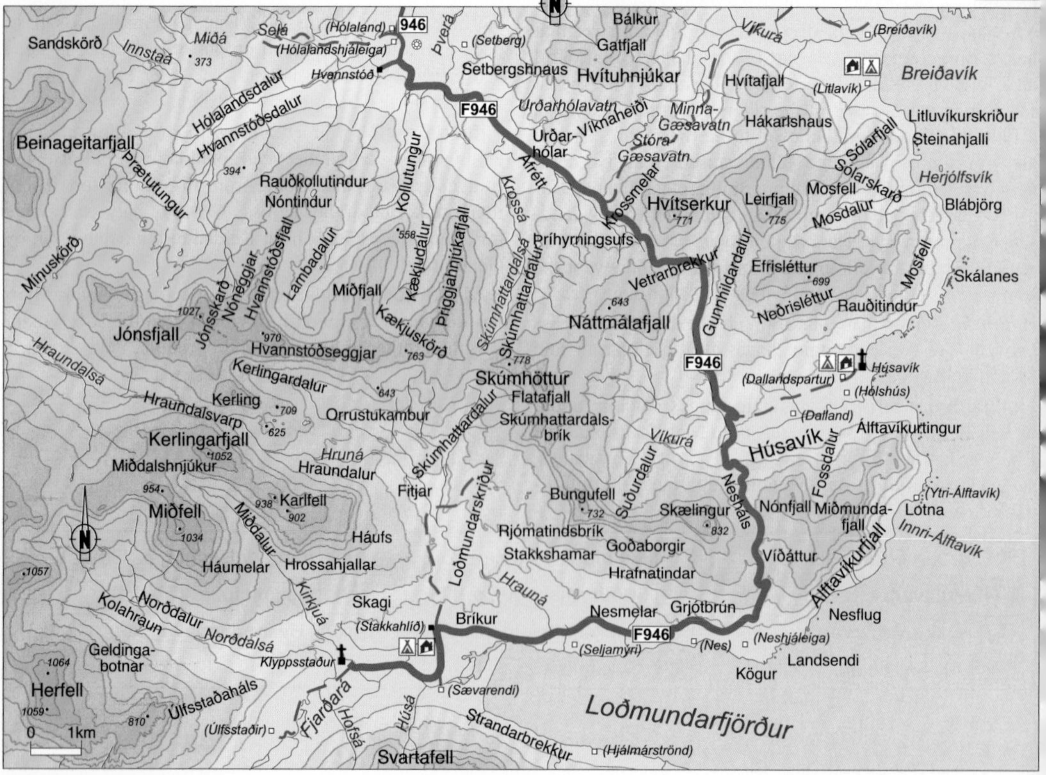

F946 **Loðmundafjörður,** 32,1 km. This route is only for experienced drivers on special jeeps.

Víknaslóðir is the name of the area from Héraðsflói to Seyðisfjörður. Amazing walking routes.

Hvítserkur, (774 m) a ignimbrite mountain northwest of Húsavík bay, with predominant white and pink colours, cut by dark basalt walls and streaks here and there. One of the most distinctive mountains in Iceland, often called Röndólfur ("The streaky one").

Breiðavík, a small and beautiful bay, reminiscent of Borgarfjörður. site of a lodge owned by the Touring Club of Fljótsdalur is located there.

Húsavíkurheiði, a pass over which it is possible to take the jeep-track to Húsavík in dry summer conditions, steep at the Húsavík end. Close to the cross roads to Loðmundarfjörður there is a clear profile of a face in the rock.

Húsavík, a little bay with a wide, short valley at its head. Formerly it had several farms, now all abandoned. The principal farm was Húsavík, a church. Part of the old churchyard has been broken off by the sea. A great variety of stones in the area. A mountain lodge owned by the travel agency of the district of Fljótsdalur is located there.

Álftavíkurtindur, (385 m) a peak well-known for its varied stones and for its spherulites. It is not readily accessible as only a narrow path leads there.

Nesháls, (435 m) a low ridge between Húsavík and Loðmundarfjörður, steep on both sides but with a jeep-track across it.

Skælingur, (832 m) a magnificent mountain with steep rock walls west from Nesháls. Visible from far out to sea. Seafarers call it "The Chinese Temple", the highest peak being reminiscent of a temple with a dome.

Loðmundarfjörður, a 7 km long fjord, rather deep. There is a wide, green valley, marshy in places, at its head, where there were once more than 10 farms, now all abandoned. The valley splits into two, Bárðarstaðadalur and Norðdalur, with the mountain **Herfell** (1,064 m) between them. The fjord is surrounded by a magnificent ring of mountains. An old riding path goes across Hjálmárdalsheiði moor to Seyðisfjörður. In Loðmundarfjörður there were once 10 farm, some of which were homes to two or three families. In 1860 the number of inhabitants was 143; by 1973 human habitation had ceased altogether. However, service is provided to tourists in Stakkahlíð in summer.

Nes, an abandoned farm on the north side of Loðmundarfjörður.

Karlfell, (926 m) an impressive rocky mountain, regular in shape and outstanding among the mountains of Loðmundarfjörður.

Stakkahlíð, formerly a manor farm, the largest in Loðmundarfjörður, abandoned in 1967. The farm buildings are well preserved. The view from there is very good. East of Stakkahlíð is **Stakkahlíðarhraun**, rhyolite screes from the mountain Flatafjall, rough in places. There were once plans to mine and export perlite from the screes. It is not quite clear how Stakkahlíðarhraun was formed and geologists do not agree on the subject. Jeep-tracks up to the screes. Close to the scree is Orrustukambur ("Battle crest") where petrified wood is to be found. The largest petrified trees to have been preserved in Iceland are kept by the Iceland Forestry Service at Hallormsstaður and on private land in Seyðisfjörður.

Sævarendi, an abandoned farm on the south side of Fjarðará. The farmer of Sævarendi was the last person to leave the district (1973).

Klyppsstaður, a farm and a church, formerly a parsonage, now deserted. Though the farm buildings have fallen, the church is still standing as are the crosses in the churchyard. Near the farm is the river **Kirkjuá** with a nice little waterfall. The river often flooded, causing serious damage to the farmlands. In 2009 a hut was built at Stakkahlíð.

9
P. 572

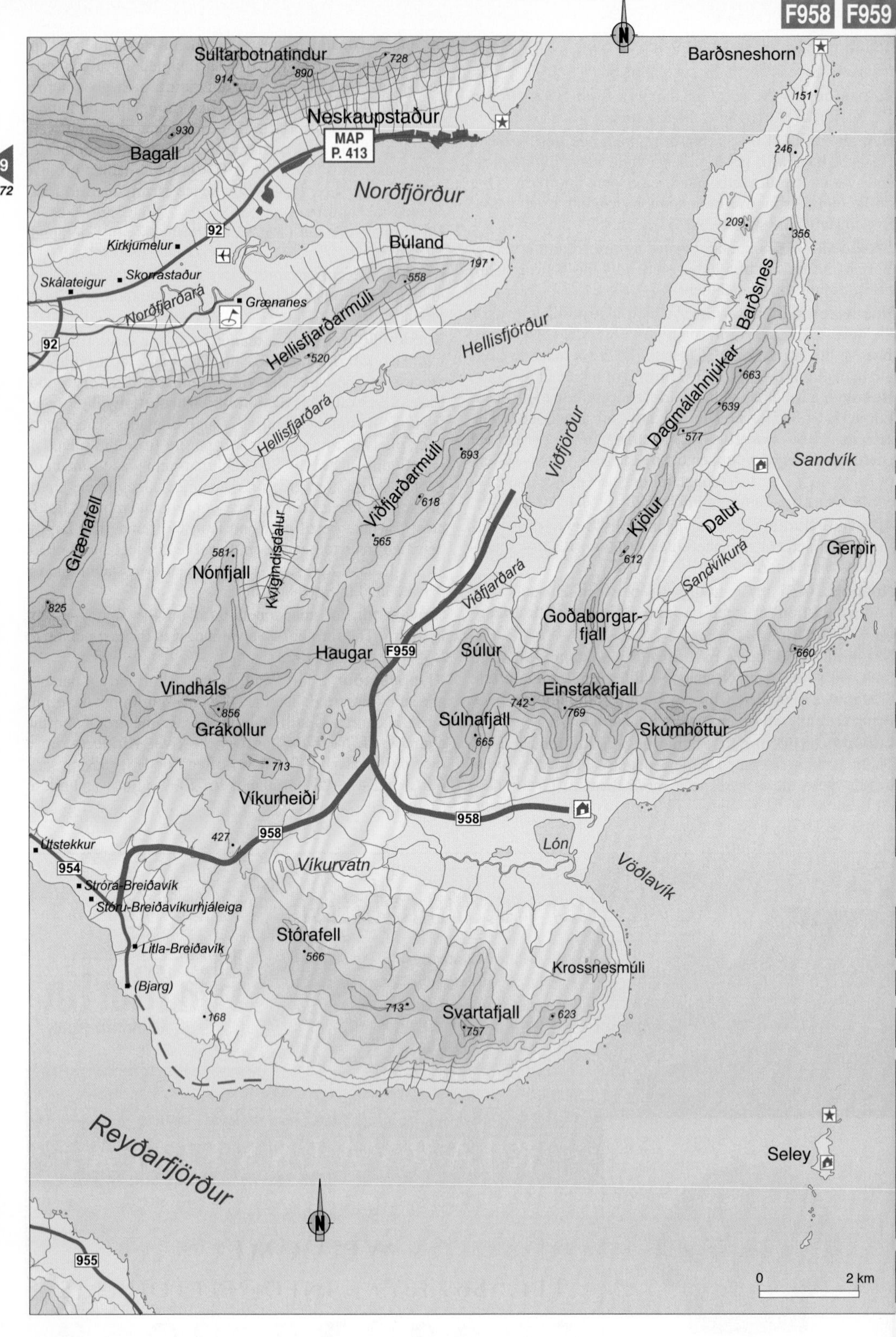
Sultarbotnatindur
728
890
914
Barðsneshorn
151
Neskaupstaður
MAP
P. 413
930
Bagall
246
Norðfjörður
209
356
92
Kirkjumelur
Búland
197
Skálateigur
Skorrastaður
558
Barðsnes
Norðfjarðará
Grænanes
Hellisfjarðarmúli
92
Hellisfjörður
520
Dagmálahnjúkar
663
639
Hellisfjarðará
577
Viðfjörður
693
Sandvík
Viðfjarðarmúli
618
Kjölur
Dalur
565
Kvígindisdalur
581
612
Gerpir
Grænafell
Nónfjall
Sandvíkurá
Viðfjarðará
825
Goðaborgar-
fjall
Haugar
F959
Súlur
660
Vindháls
Einstakafjall
742
856
769
Grákollur
Súlnafjall
Skúmhöttur
665
713
Víkurheiði
958
427
958
Útstekkur
Lón
954
Víkurvatn
Vöðlavík
Stóra-Breiðavík
Stóru-Breiðavíkurhjáleiga
Stórafell
Litla-Breiðavík
566
Krossnesmúli
(Bjarg)
713
Svartafjall
623
168
757
Reyðarfjörður
Seley
955
0
2 km

Barðsneshorn, or Horn, is the outermost point of the highland peninsula Barðsnes. It falls very steeply to the sea, with many sheer cliffs. It and the mountain above it are of rhyolite and are steeply canted to the west. This appears to be the western side of a volcano which has mostly been worn away by the sea. On the west of the peninsula the rhyolite shows itself in Rauðubjörg ("Red cliffs"), which are multicoloured with a reddish gold cast and can be seen from Neskaupstaður. Down near sea level there are carbonated tree trunks 1-3 feet in diameter. These are considered to be the oldest vegetable remains in Iceland, probably about 15 million years old. There are many birds on Barðsnes and a spectacular view. The five farms that once were there have all been abandoned.

Norðfjarðarflói, devides into 3 fjords, **Norðfjörður**, Hellisfjörður and Viðfjörður.

Hellisfjörður, a fjord out of the Norðfjörður bay, with headlands Viðfjarðarmúli (689m) to the south and Hellisfjarðarmúli (558 m) to the north.

Viðfjörður, a fjord stretching south from the Norðfjörður bay where there was a farm of the same name, abandoned since 1955. The same family had lived there since 1750. The farm was said to have been haunted for centuries, the second quarter of the 20th century seeing particularly frequent and violent supernatural activity. Some blame these ghosts for the death by drowning of three brothers in 1936. The author Þórbergur Þórðarson (1889-1974) wrote about these ghosts in *Viðfjarðarundrin* ("The Viðfjörður wonders").

F959 **Viðarfjarðarvegur,** 8,6 km. Only for jeeps.

Sandvík, a bay to the north of the mountain **Gerpir**, the easternmost point of Iceland. Home of the ghost Sandvíkur-Glæsir ("The Sandvík dandy"), who wore a tie and tails and courteously took off his head in greeting.

F958 **Vaðlavíkurvegur,** 12,6 km from road 954. Passible by jeep.

Vöðlavík, a bay where there were two serious accidents. The boat *Bergvík* from the Westman Islands stranded in December 1993 and in January 1994 the salvage vessel *Goðinn* went down while attempting to tow the *Bergvík* away. One member of the crew of the *Goðinn* was lost, but the others were saved in a difficult and daring rescue operation performed by US helicopter crews from the Keflavík naval base.

92 **Norðfjarðarvegur,** p. 409-412 **954** **Helgustaðavegur,** p. 412 **955** **Vattarnesvegur,** p. 420

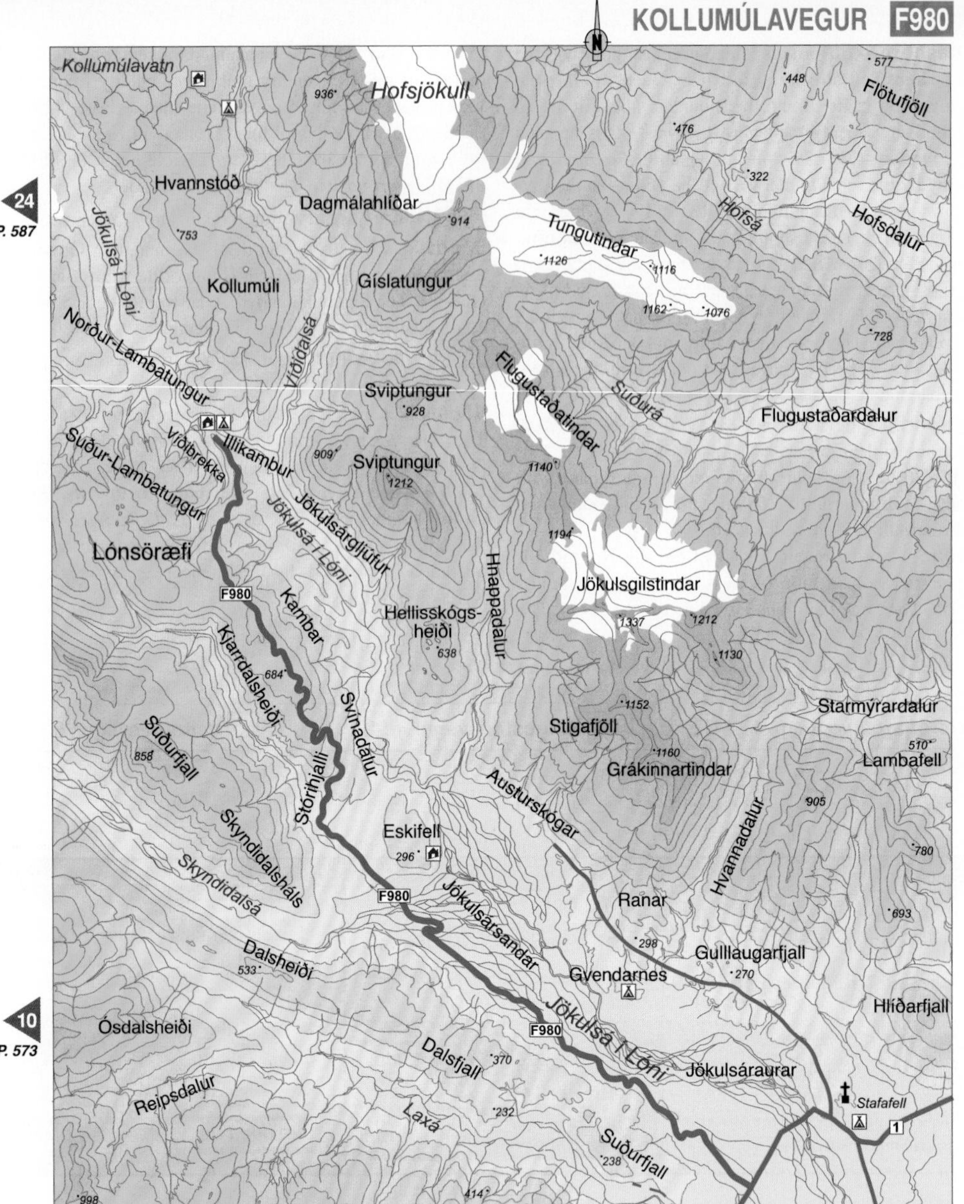

F980 Kollumúlavegur, 24,5 km off the main road by Þórisdalur in Lón to Illikambur. Only for large jeeps, traveling in tandem. **Skyndidalsá** a glacial river, a dangerous obstacle in rainy weather or when sun melts the glaciers. The river bed is soggy and treacherous. Dangerous to cross. Beyond the river is a jeep-track alongside Eskifell and up onto Illikambur by Kollumúli.

Jökulsá í Lóni, a sizeable glacial river having its source in the eastern part of Vatnajökull and flowing along Lón to the sea. Sometimes it flows along canyons, but towards the middle of the Lón district it spreads out along mud flats. A difficult river to ford.

Lónsöræfi, ("The Wilderness Lagoon") a broad unbuilt area east of Vatnajökull. In recent years it has become increasingly popular to walk in this area, huts have been put up and footbridges built on the most difficult rivers. Before the "mini-ice age" of 1600-1900 people travelling between different parts of Iceland often crossed Lónsöræfi, for instance from Þingeyjarsýsla county in the north to Hornafjörður in the southeast. This may explain why both the rivers Jökulsá í Lóni and Víðidalsá have fords called Norðlingavað ("Northerners' ford"). Lónsöræfi is rugged and dramatic countryside, very colourful. The central volcano piled its lava on top of that from the Álftafjarðar volcano by the Þvottá river. The mountains have numerous needles and pinnacles and are scored by canyons, so it is vital to follow designated walking routes carefully. To the north of Lónsöræfi is Hraun, a rocky moorland area of frequent fogs and snows, reaching north to Fljótsdalur. Apart from the glaciers, no place in Iceland has more precipitation. When it rains, rivers in the area can become unpassable torrents without warning.

1 Austurlandsvegur, p. 112

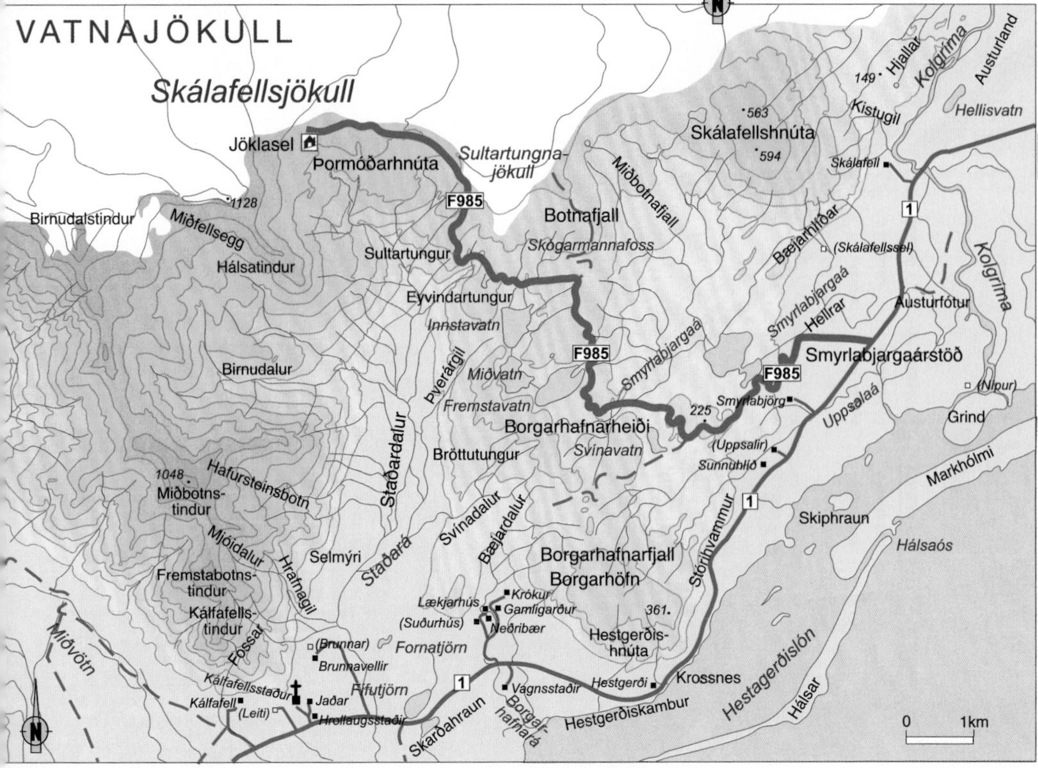

F985 **Jökulvegur,** 16,3 km, Passable by all jeeps, also small jeeps. Steep hills.

1 **Austurlandsvegur,** p. 116

Jöklasel, a centre of glacial activities and a restaurant. The view from Jöklasel is absolutely breathtaking.

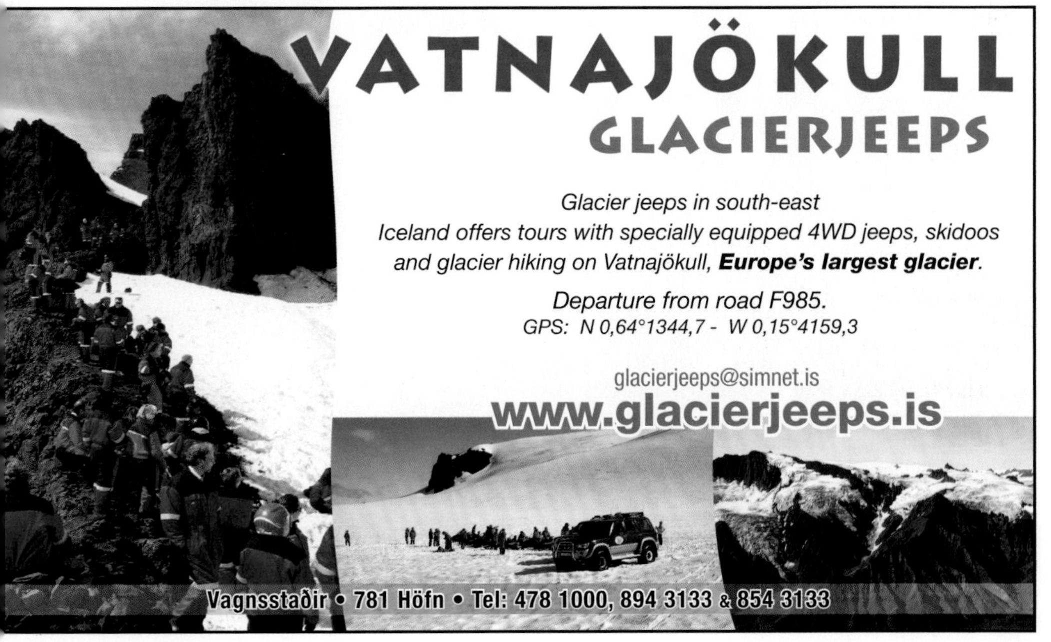

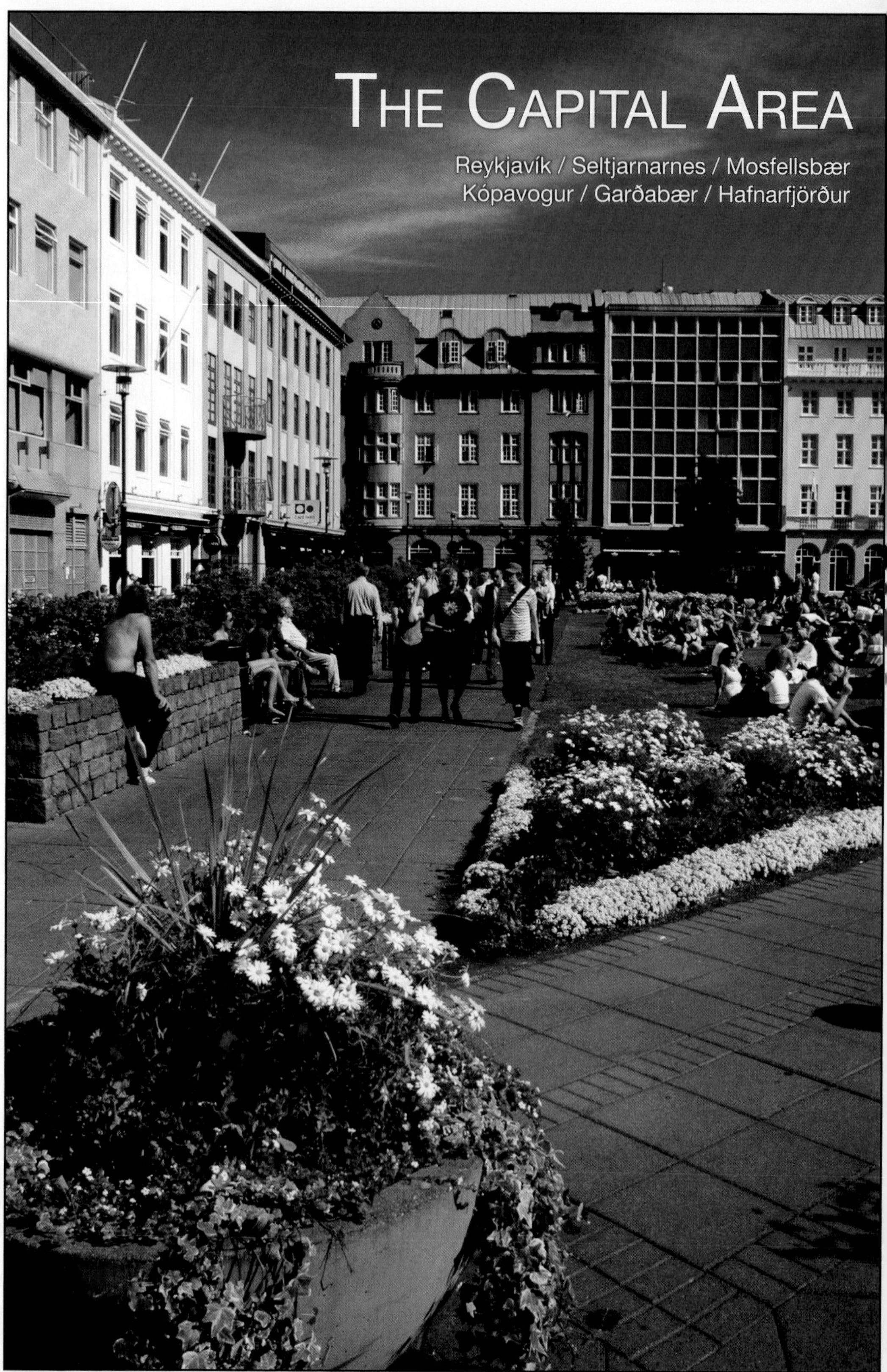

The Capital Area

Reykjavík / Seltjarnarnes / Mosfellsbær
Kópavogur / Garðabær / Hafnarfjörður

1 SUÐURLANDSVEGUR – VESTURLANDSVEGUR

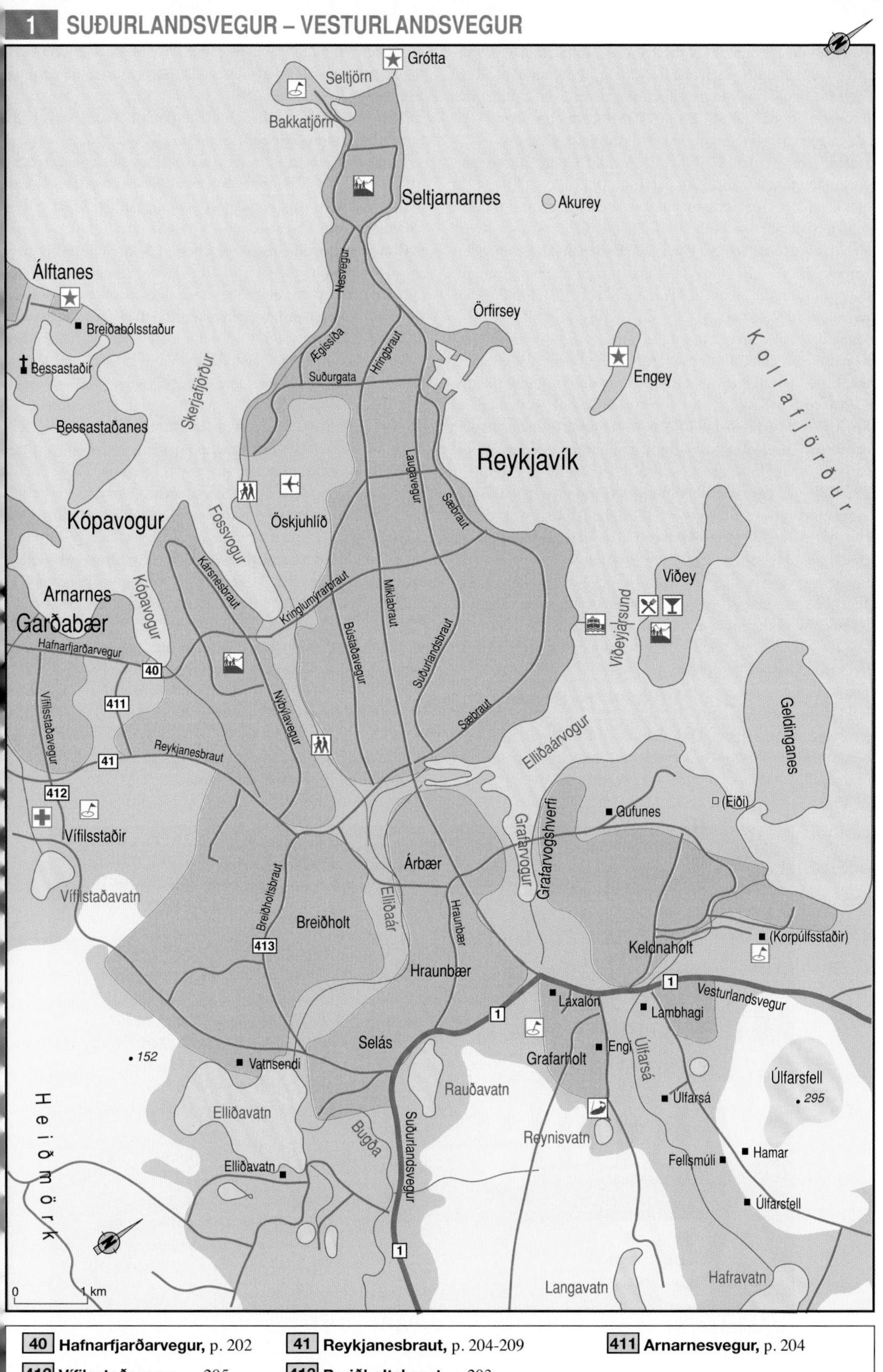

40 **Hafnarfjarðarvegur,** p. 202 | 41 **Reykjanesbraut,** p. 204-209 | 411 **Arnarnesvegur,** p. 204
412 **Vífilsstaðavegur,** p. 205 | 413 **Breiðholtsbraut,** p. 203

Reykjavík, Reykjavík, is the nations capital and by far the largest community in Iceland, with a population of about 200,000. Including the neighbouring towns, the capital area has a total population of about 170,000, which is about 60% of Iceland's population of 300,000 people.

Iceland was settled by Norwegian and Celtic immigrants during the late 9th and 10th centuries A.D. According to the medieval Book of Settlements, Ingólfur Arnarson – the first settler of Iceland – built his farm on the peninsula where Reykjavík stands today. The place was named Reykjavík – "Smoky Bay" - after the columns of steam that rose from the hot springs in the area and made such a profound impression on the original settlers.

Many centuries later, around the middle of the 18th century, a small town started to grow around the farm of Reykjavík, thanks to Royal Treasurer Skúli Magnússon, known as the Father of Reykjavík, who established wool workshops at Reykjavík as part of his efforts to modernise the Icelandic economy. This led to the beginnings of urban development at Reykjavík. Reykjavík received its town charter in 1786.

The Icelandic parliament, Alþingi, was founded in 930 AD at Þingvellir in the southwest. In 1798 the Alþingi was abolished, but in 1845 it was re-established in Reykjavík, where the country's government and administration were now located. In due course, when Iceland won Home Rule and then independence from Danish rule, Reykjavík became the capital of Iceland. With the rapid economic progress of the 20th century, Reykjavík grew steadily, but developed especially fast in the second half of the century.

For a living view of Reykjavík's past, visit the open-air Reykjavík City Museum- Árbæjarsafn, located in the eastern part of the capital. The innovative Reykjavík 871 +/- 2 Settlement Exhibition is located on Aðalstræti in the city centre, allows visitors to view the recently discovered, oldest settlement ruins in Reykjavík and Iceland (possibly those of Ingólfur Arnarson or his descendents), featuring an original Viking age longhouse.

Viðey, is the largest island in Kollafjörður. There are regular ferry connections between Skarfabakki and Viðey. You can say that that island is in fact two islands but connected by an isthmus. The larger section is closer to land and is called Heimaey or Austurey (East island), but the other one is called Vesturey (West island). Viðey is only 3 km long and 800 m at its widest point, or about 1,5 km^2. Viðey is now mostly owned by the City of Reykjavík. Viðeyjarstofa, Viðeyjarkirkja (church) and Viðeyjarskóli (school) have all been restored. A new pier has been made and the island has electricity and running water. Information signs are by the end of the pier, behind Viðeyjarstofa, by Viðeyjarskóli and by the foundations of the houses that once formed a village. Viðeyjarskóli, the school, is on the eastern island. It ran from 1912 till 1941, with 40 students in its prime. Renovations were made between 1989-1993 and today there are good facilities for various occasion in the old school building. There is also a interesting exhibition on the islands history in the building. There are organized walkes around the island during the summer time. There are marked walking paths, a playground for children and a barbeque available for visitors. At Viðeyjarstofa is a restaurant. At Vesturey is a good walking route to the artwork of Richard Serra called Áfangi. On October 9th 2007 the light artwork of Yoko Ono, Imagine Peace Tower, was light for the first time. She dedicated the work to her husband's memory, John Lennon. Every year the Peace Tower is light on John Lennons birthday and turned of on December 8th, the anniversary of his death.

For further information and schedules go to:
www.elding.is or **www.videy.com**

ing world of Icelandic fisheries and coastal culture

Iceland's past, present and future are closely tied to fishing and seafaring, dominating the atmosphere of Icelandic seaside villages and interwined with the character of the nation. Therefore it is impossible to truly get to know Iceland without getting to know its fishing history.

The Maritime Museum´s exhibitions reveal the Icelandic maritime history throughout the ages. The museum´s main exhibitions illustrate the development from rowing boats to modern trawlers, trading vessels and routes and the construction of Reykjavik Harbour. Beside these main exhibitions guests can browse through various visiting exhibitions.

Docked to a special pier is the **Coast Guard Vessel Óðinn.** Óðinn participated in all three Cod Wars against Britain in the latter part of the 20th century. Óðinn was also used effectively as a rescue vessel saving crews of grounded or sinking ships as well as towing nearly 200 vessels to safety.

At the **Museum´s Café**, which offers traditional Icelandic delicacies, guests can sit outdoor and sip their drinks while they gaze at the old harbour. It is only 10 minutes walk from the city center to the museum.

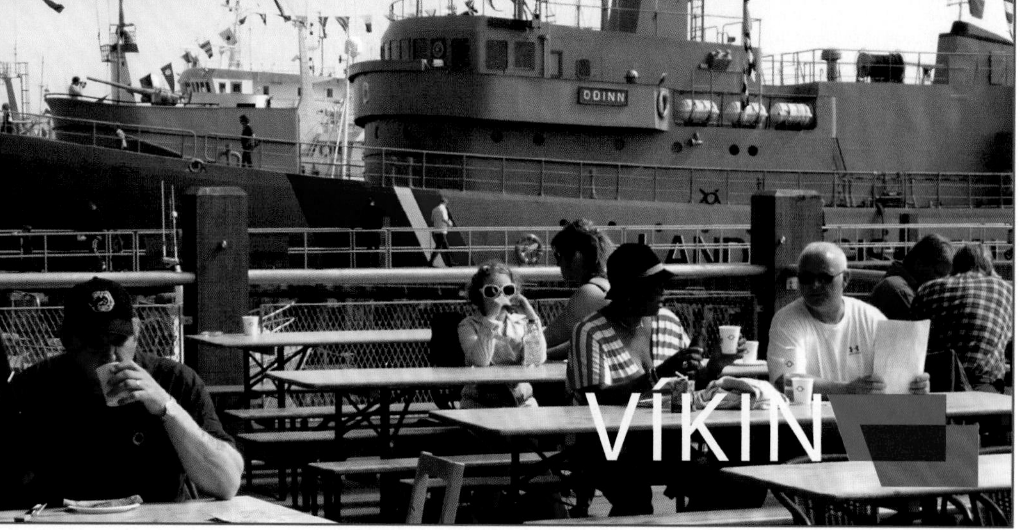

1. **Ráðhúsið, Reykjavík City Hall,** is at the north-western corner of the lake Tjörnin on the corner of Tjarnargata and Vonarstræti. The building was designed by Margrét Harðardóttir and Steve Christer. Offices and meeting rooms are situated on the upper stories while the ground floor, which is open to the public from 8-17 on weekdays and 12-18 on weekends, is devoted to cultural activities of various kinds. In the main hall there is a huge three-dimensional map of Iceland.
2. **Aðalstræti,** ("Main Street") is Reykjavík's oldest street. Ingólfur Arnarson's farm is generally considered to have been situated at the southern end of the street, which must then have been the path he walked along down to the sea. While Reykjavík was small, Aðalstræti was the main street, lined with the homes of influential people, the meeting house and the town's main well, Ingólfsbrunnur ("Ingólfur's well"), outside the present No. 9. One of the oldest buildings in Reykjavík built around 1762, is No. 10, which is from the time of Skúli Magnússon. The Settlement exhibition Reykjavik 871±2 is based on archaeological finds in Reykjavík, well-preserved ruins of a Viking-Age long house from the 10th century and objects and remains of human habitation believed to date from the 9th-century settlement of Reykjavík. The exhibition gives a clear picture of the people and their way of life at this time, and the visitor can view the ruins and the objects connected to them in addition to information in the form of texts, pictures and multimedia designed to provide an extra focus on specific aspects of the history. The Settlement Exhibition is open every day from 10-17 and is located in Reykjavík old centre, on the corner of Aðalstræti and Suðurgata. Regular guided tours around the exhibition.
3. **Tourist Information Centre** – Reykjavík's official Tourist Information Centre, located at Aðalstræti 2, has all you need for a great holiday. Free booking service, tourist information for all parts of Iceland, money exchange, VAT cash refund, maps and brochures, internet and IP phone centre, Reykjavík Welcome Card and friendly staff.
4. **Grjótaþorp,** ("Grjóti village") is the area between Aðalstræti, Túngata, Garðastræti and Vesturgata. It takes its name from the farm Grjóti, a tenant farm of the original farm, Reykjavík. The majority of the houses are from the late 18th century and the streets have not been reorganized, so the "village" has a distinct flavour of times past.
5. **Austurstræti,** ("East Street") was originally a path along the north side of Austurvöllur Green from Aðalstræti to Lækurinn ("The brook"). About 1820 the path was paved with stones and an open drain built alongside it. The path was then called Langastétt ("The long pavement"), or, in Danish, Lange Fortoug. In 1848 when a number of streets in Reykjavík were given names, Langastétt was named Austurstræti in view of the direction it took from Aðalstræti.
6. **Hafnarstræti,** ("Harbour Street") lies east from the northern end of Aðalstræti, north of and parallel to Austurstræti. Originally it was a path along the shoreline from Lækjartorg Square to Vesturgata, but received its present name in 1848. The curve on the street followed the curve of the shoreline. The land north of the street today is all land-fill.
7. **Reykjavík Art Museum - Hafnarhús,** is located between Tryggvagata and Geirsgata. The exhibition halls are located on two floors. It also has a multi-purpose space and an outdoor area in an enclosed courtyard. Its many galleries house the diverse exhibitions of contemporary art and is a permanent residence for the works of Erró. The museum has a shop, a library and restaurant. The Museum is open daily from 10-17. Thursday 10-22. Free entrance.
8. **Alþingishúsið, Parliament House,** was built in 1880-81 to the design of the Danish architect F. Meldahl. Its walls are of basalt which was quarried and cut on the Skólavörðuholt hill east of the Tjörnin Lake. Parliament was first convened in Alþingishúsið on July 1st in 1881. Since then, all its meetings have been held there apart from ceremonial meetings held at Þingvellir.
9. **Reykjavík Harbour,** right up to 1900 ships coming to Reykjavík had been forced to anchor out in the bay, people and goods being ferried to and from land in rowboats. Small piers had been built behind the shops on Hafnarstræti and elsewhere to receive them. Harbour construction started in 1913 and went well, so the first ship was able to dock in Reykjavík in 1915. The material for the harbour was mostly from the hills Skólavörðuholt and Öskjuhlíð. A railway was built between Öskjuhlíð and the harbour, along which a steam engine pulled cars loaded with stone. Various boat tours are available from Reykjavík Marina, including whale watching and sea angling tours. There are also a number of good restaurants located near the marina.
10. **Dómkirkjan, the Cathedral.** When the bishopric was moved from Skálholt to Reykjavík the old church on Aðalstræti was not considered grand enough, so it was decided to build a new one. Work started in 1788 and the cathedral was consecrated in 1796. It contains a number of noteworthy objects, among them a carved marble font by Bertel Thorvaldsen which he gave to the church in 1839. Since it was re-established in 1845, the opening of Parliament has always started with a service in Dómkirkjan.
11. **Arnarhóll,** is the grassy hill between Kalkofnsvegur, Hverfisgata, Ingólfsstræti and the Central Bank of Iceland. The name is thought to come from Landnámabók ("The Book of Settlements") where Ingólfur's high-seat posts are said to have been found "by Arnarhvál below the heath". The statue of Ingólfur Arnarson was unveiled on Arnarhóll on February 24th 1924.
12. **The Culture House,** is a listed building and its use today takes into consideration the building's protected status and historical value. It is a unique venue for promoting Icelandic history and cultural heritage. Exhibitions in the Culture House emphasize in particular the history and culture of Iceland, the country's independence and governance, as well as its ancient and modern literature. In the building there are facilities for exhibitions, meetings, gatherings, lectures, artistic events, public ceremonies and other occasions. The Culture House restaurant and souvenir shop are located on the ground floor.
13. **Þjóðleikhúsið, The National Theatre,** is on Hverfisgata, east of Safnahúsið. Construction started in 1928 to a design by State Architect Guðjón Samúelsson. Inside the theatre the walls are decorated with works by Guðmundur Einarsson from Miðdalur and Ríkarður Jónsson, and there are numerous busts and portraits of people who have influenced Icelandic art and culture over the years.
14. **Alþjóðahúsið, The Intercultural Centre,** is on Laugavegur 37. The primary objective of the Intercultural centre is to provide a forum for a multicultural society in Iceland. In a society that is truly multicultural, there is a dynamic interaction between all peoples of various different origins. In a multicultural society, different cultural groups live together, side by side. They are all equal, showing mutual respect for each other, working together towards the common goal of creating a multicultural society. The Intercultural Centre promotes this dynamic interaction between peoples of different origins and cultural backgrounds. The Intercultural Centre works systematically to prevent prejudice in our society by providing extensive educational programmes, introductions to different societies, cultural events and by creating an inclusive forum where those of Icelandic origin interact with those who have come to Iceland from abroad. The Intercultural Centre is an advocate for the rights of migrants and everyone of non-Icelandic descent.
15. **Lækjartorg,** ("Brook square") is opposite the Government house north of Austurstræti. It has been of importance in the life of Reykjavík from earliest times. Farmers bringing wares to market ended their journey there, and commonly camped on Lækjartorg while they completed their business in town.
16. **Stjórnarráðshúsið, Government House,** on Lækjargata opposite Lækjartorg, was originally built as a prison. Construction began in 1761 and was completed in 1771. When Governor E.C.L. Moltke came to Iceland in 1819 he obtained permission to move into the building and had it extensively renovated. After that it was the home and workplace of the Governor while that post existed. From 1873-1904 it was the residence of the Governor-General, after which it housed the government when a Home Rule Minister was appointed in Reykjavík. It now houses the offices of the Prime Minister. It was on the steps of this building that Iceland was declared a sovereign state on December 1st 1918. On the lawn are two statues by Einar Jónsson: one, put up in 1931, of Hannes Hafstein, the first Icelander to be Home Rule Minister, and the other, from 1915, of King Christian IX of Denmark giving Icelanders their constitution.

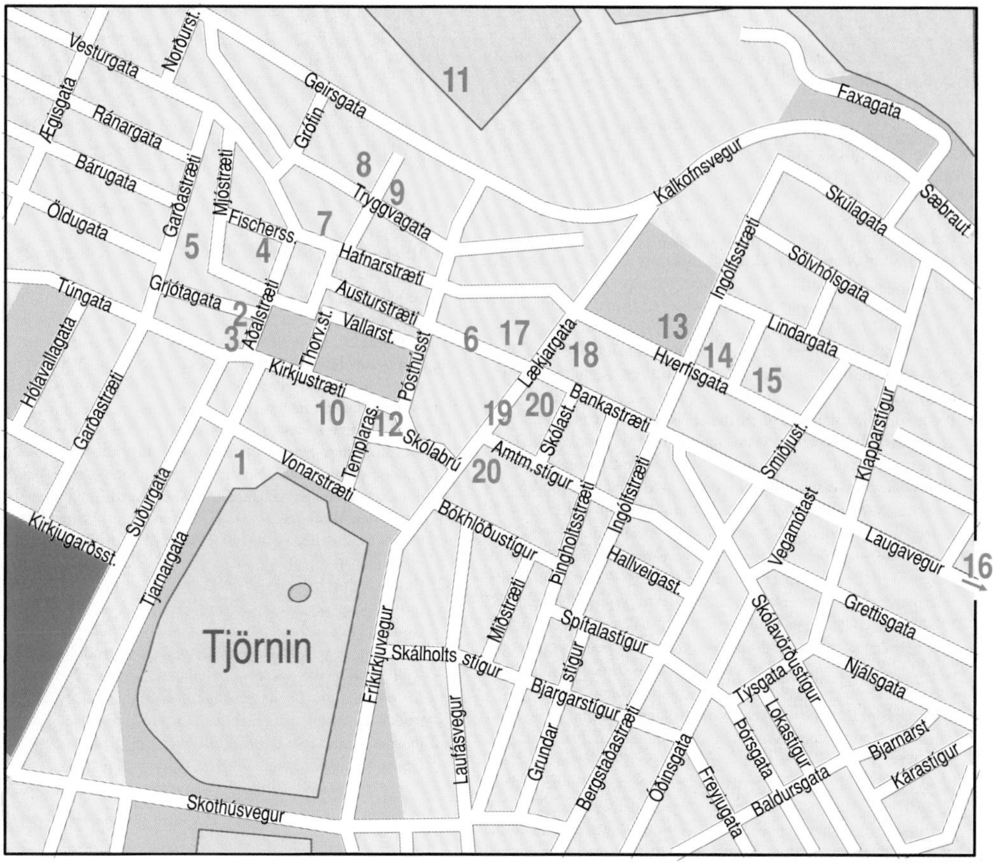

17. Lækurinn, ("The brook") ran from the northeastern corner of the Tjörnin lake to the sea at the foot of the hill Arnarhóll. In 1911 Lækurinn was enclosed and covered and the street widened. Though no longer visible it is still there, and occasionally, when tides are unusually high, sea water flows along it and into the Tjörnin as it did in the past.

18. Bernhöftstorfa, the area between Lækjargata, Bankastræti, Amtmannsstígur and Skólagata, is named for T.D. Bernhöft who ran a bakery at Bankastræti 2. The buildings on Bernhöftstorfa, along with Stjórnarráðshúsið and Menntaskólinn í Reykjavík and Íþaka, form the oldest row of houses in Reykjavík.

19. Menntaskólinn í Reykjavík, The Reykjavík Secondary Grammar School. When the Bessastaðir School was moved to Reykjavík a site "east of Lækurinn" was selected. The building was designed by Danish State Architect Jörgen Hansen Koch, the building materials imported ready-cut from Norway. Construction began in 1844 and teaching in the building in 1846. The full name of the school was then "The Learned School in Reykjavík". South of the main building is the school's library, built in 1866 with money donated by the Englishman Charles Kelsall. It was later named Íþaka in honour of Daniel Willard Fiske of Ithaca, N.Y, who donated a great many books and journals to the library.

20. Tjarnargata, ("Pond Street") is the street along the western bank of the Tjörnin Lake. The northernmost end of it has a very long history indeed, since it is likely that it was a path from Ingólfur Arnarson's farm, Reykjavík, along the shore of Tjörnin to a well southwest of where the City Hall now stands. Most of the houses along the street, built of wood and clad with corrugated iron, are from just after the turn of the century. No. 32 is called Ráðherrabústaðurinn ("The Minister's Residence") and was originally built at Sólbakki in Önundarfjörður and belonged to a Norwegian, Hans Ellefsen. He is said to have either given it to Hannes Hafstein when he became Home Rule Minister in 1904 or sold it to him for 1 krona. It is now used by the Icelandic Government for official receptions.

21. Suðurgata, ("South Street") one of Reykjavík's oldest streets, runs from Túngata south to Skerjafjörður. There is a cemetery on Suðurgata. The cemetery for the church in Reykjavík appears to have originally been at the corner of Aðalstræti and Kirkjustræti, where there is now a little park, but by the early 19th century this was full. The area on Suðurgata was chosen as the new cemetery and the first burial there was in 1838. Many of the most influential Icelanders of the 19th and early 20th centuries are buried there.

22. Útlagar, ("Outlaws") is a statue in bronze at the corner of Suðurgata and Hringbraut. It is a good illustration of the fact that many Icelandic outlaws were seen more as victims than as criminals.

23. Þjóðarbókhlaðan, National and University Library of Iceland, Arngrímsgata 3, combines the National Library (established 1918) and the University Library (established 1940) in one building which was opened on December 1st, 1994. In 1970 Parliament decided that a people´s library should be raised to commemorate the 1100th anniversary of the settlement of Iceland in 1974. Architect Manfreð Vilhjálmsson.

24. Þjóðminjasafn Íslands, The National Museum. On June 16th 1944 a meeting of both houses of Parliament agreed "to raise a building to house the National Museum and to start construction immediately." The building was completed and opened to the public in 1952, and has housed the museum ever since. The National Museum of Iceland is the country´s largest museum of cultural history and nurtures knowledge and innovation while maintaining a wide perspective and a sense of community. The museum's permanent exhibition, Making of a Nation – Heritage and History in Iceland is an exciting journey through time, presenting the nation's cultural history from settlement to present day. Special exhibitions feature highlights from the Museum's collections and archives, and are intended to shed light on particular subjects of cultural history as well as contemporary cultural issues.

25. Háskóli Íslands, The University of Iceland. Established in 1911 when three professional schools, the Theological School, the Law School and the Medical School, were combined. The main university building was built 1936-40 to the design of State Architect Guðjón Samúelsson. Sæmundur á selnum ("Sæmundur riding the seal"), a sculpture by Ásmundur Sveinsson, is on the lawn in front of the main building, and by the Geological Institute there is a memorial by Ríkarður Jónsson to the French scientist Dr. J.B. Charcot, who perished with the ship Pourqui pas? in 1936.

26. Tjörnin, ("The pond") is a lake in the centre of Reykjavík, originally formed by a lagoon inside the reef that used to be where Hafnarstræti now lies. There are two islets in Tjörnin. The one in the southern end is man-made and the one in the northern end, though natural, has been enlarged and turfed over to attract nesting birds. Bird-life is rich and varied on Tjörnin, especially in the spring. 40-50 kinds of birds spend some part of each year there, and 80 different kinds have been seen altogether.

27. Listasafn Íslands, The National Art Gallery, is at Fríkirkjuvegur 11. The building is from just before 1920, when it was an icehouse, called Herðubreið, which used ice taken from Tjörnin in the winter. In 1958 it was made into a night club, called Glaumbær. In 1971 there was a fire in Glaumbær which gutted it. After that the building was extended and renovated with an eye to its new role, and the National Art Gallery opened there in 1988.

28. Sóleyjargata 1, offices of the President of Iceland, Ólafur Ragnar Grímsson. Once home of the first president of Iceland, Sveinn Björnsson, and also, later, the home of Kristján Eldjárn, Iceland's third president.

29. Hljómskálagarðurinn, ("Bandstand Park") reaches from the southern end of the Tjörnin Lake to Hringbraut. In 1922 permission was granted to build the bandstand that still stands on the corner of Sóleyjargata and Skothúsvegur. It was to be, and still is, the headquarters of the Reykjavík City Band.

30. Norræna húsið, Nordic House, stands in Vatnsmýrin ("The water meadow"), east of the main University building. The Nordic Council decided in 1963 to build a Nordic cultural centre whose function was to strengthen the connection between Iceland and the other Nordic countries and to promote knowledge and understanding of the Nordic cultural heritage. The building was designed by the Finnish architect Alvar Aalto.

31. Umferðarmiðstöðin, ("Coach Terminal") at Vatnsmýrarvegur 10, houses the Bus Terminal (BSÍ). The Fly bus departs there to Keflavík International Airport.

32. Örfirisey, or Effersey, ("Ebb island") is to the west of the mouth of the older Reykjavík harbour. The island was once connected to the mainland by a narrow isthmus that went underwater at high tide. The isthmus has now been extended with landfill and is covered with buildings. Reykjavík bought the island in 1906 as part of the preparations for harbour construction. Örfirisey has long been associated with fishing and fish processing and one of the countries most advanced fish freezing and processing plants, now owned by Grandi hf., opened there in 1979.

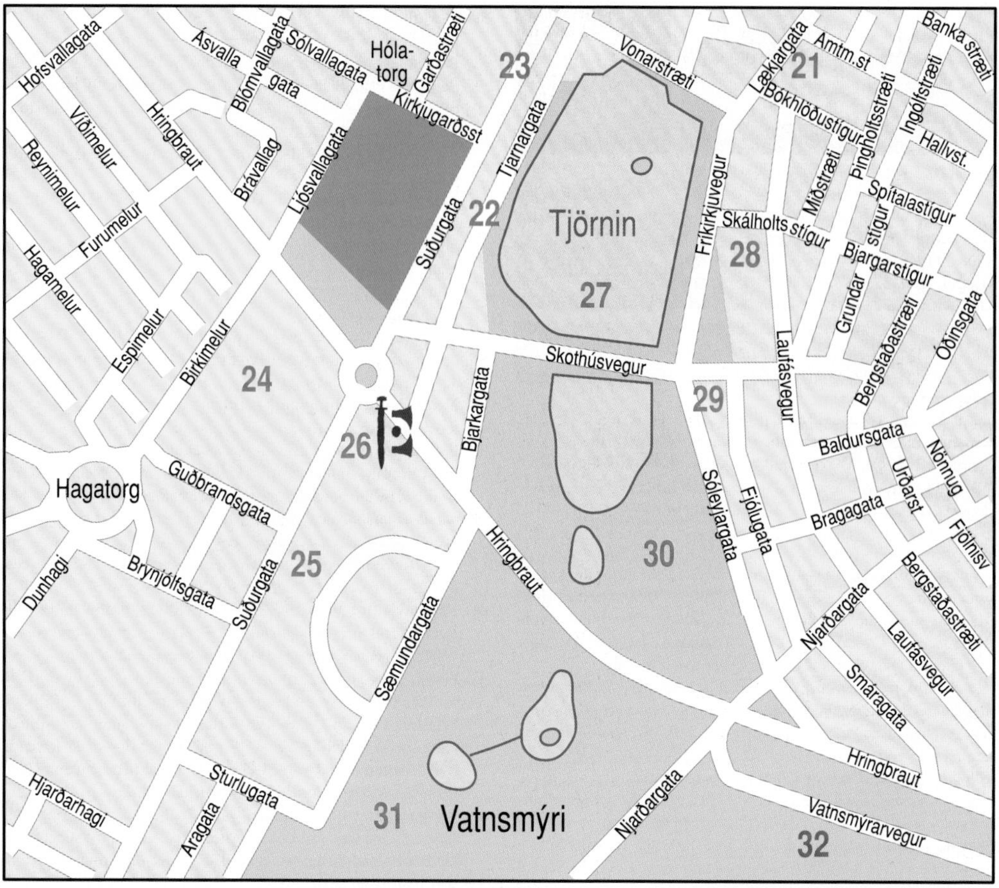

Hofsvallagata
Ásvallagata
Sólvallagata
Hóla-torg
Garðastræti
23
Vonarstræti
Lækjargata
Amtm.st
21
Bankastræti
Blómvallagata
Kirkjugarðsst
Tjarnargata
Bókhlöðustígur
Ingólfsstræti
Þingholtsstræti
Hallvst.
Víðimelur
Reynimelur
Hringbraut
Brávallag
Ljósvallagata
Miðstræti
Spítalastígur
Suðurgata
22
Tjörnin
Fríkirkjuvegur
Skálholtsstígur
Furumelur
Hagamelur
28
Bjargarstígur
27
Grundarstígur
Óðinsgata
Espimelur
Birkimelur
Laufásvegur
Bergstaðastræti
Skothúsvegur
24
29
Bjarkargata
26
Baldursgata
Nönnug
Hagatorg
Guðbrandsgata
Urðarst
Sóleyjargata
Fjólugata
Bragagata
Fjölnisv
30
Dunhagi
Brynjólfsgata
25
Hringbraut
Bergstaðastræti
Sæmundargata
Njarðargata
Laufásvegur
Smáragata
Hjarðarhagi
Sturlugata
Aragata
31
Vatnsmýri
Njarðargata
Hringbraut
Vatnsmýrarvegur
32

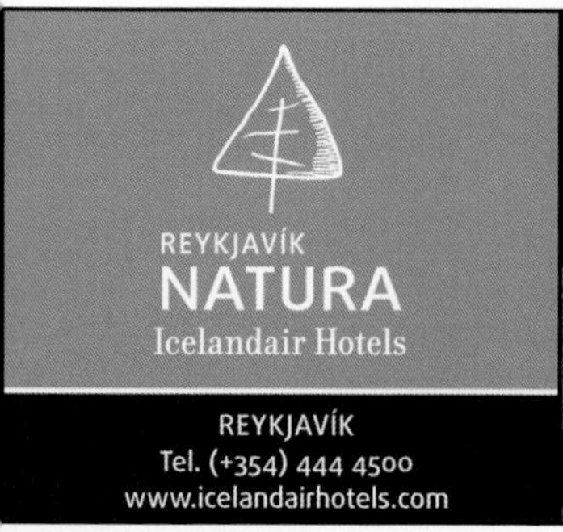

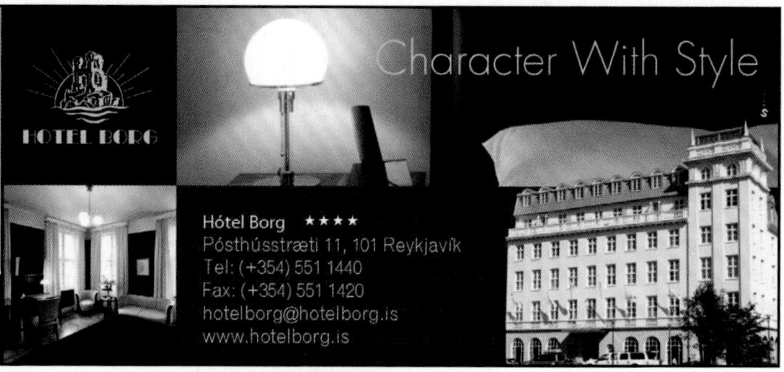

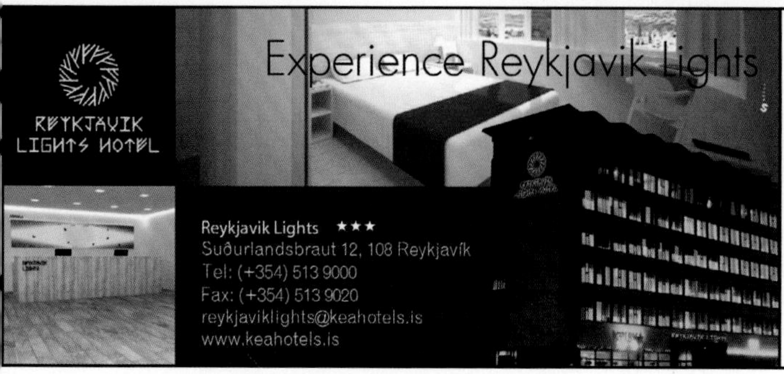

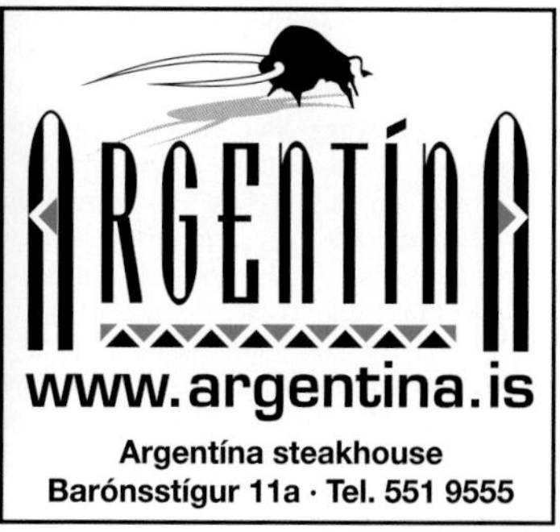

33. Landakot, formerly a tenant farm of the original farm, Reykjavík, was purchased by the Catholic community in 1859, and has since been the site of the headquarters of the Catholic Church in Iceland. Kristskirkja ("Christ's church") of Landakot, designed by State Architect Guðjón Samúelsson, was consecrated in 1929.

34. Kolaportið, Iceland's only flea market. It takes place indoors close to Reykjavík Harbor. In Kolaportið you can buy everything from old records to liquorice and fermented shark. Kolaportið is open during weekends 11-17.

35. Skólavörðuholt, ("School Cairn hill") is the basalt hill rising to the east of Lækjargata and Tjörnin. It was once called Arnarhólsholt. Its present name derives from the fact that when the school at Skálholt was moved to Reykjavík shortly before 1800 the students built a cairn there on the hill by the main road into Reykjavík. The School Cairn was a favourite place for the citizens of Reykjavík to walk to and admire the view until it was torn down in 1931 to make way for the statue of Leifur Eiríksson. There are a number of remarkable buildings at the top of the hill, such as Hallgrímskirkja church and the Einar Jónsson Museum.

36. Hallgrímskirkja, ("The church of Hallgrímur") is at the top of Skólavörðuholt. The idea of building a church in memory of the poet Hallgrímur Pétursson first arose in 1914. The first designs for such a church on Skólavörðuholt were made by State Architect Guðjón Samúelsson. The actual building process extended over many years and the church wasn't finally completed and consecrated until October 28th 1986. The church tower is 74.5 m high and offers a superb view of Reykjavík and the surrounding countryside.

37. Listasafn Einars Jónssonar, The Einar Jónsson Museum, is on Skólavörðuholt on the corner of Eiríksgata and Njarðargata. It was built between 1916 and 1923 by the sculptor Einar Jónsson, who lived in it until his death in 1954. He bequeathed the building to the Icelandic people along with all his works, which are on display there. There are casts of many of his sculptures in the garden surrounding the house.

38. Reykjavíkurflugvöllur, Reykjavík Airport, is in the Vatnsmýri meadow southwest of the Öskjuhlíð hill. The first commercially owned air plane in Iceland was sent to Reykjavík in a box in 1919. It was assembled in a field in Vatnsmýri and took off from there on September 3rd. For the next two decades this imperfect and primitive airstrip was the headquarters of whatever airlines operated there. When the British Army came to Iceland in 1940 they immediately started construction of a proper airport on the same site, and it is still there today. Now domestic flights and flights to Greenland and the Faroe Islands are operated from Reykjavík Airport.

39. Öskjuhlíð/Perlan, ("The Pearl"). Öskjuhlíð is a basalt hill (61m high) north of the Fossvogur inlet. At the end of the ice age, when the sea level was higher than it is today, Öskjuhlíð was an island. Some tide marks and marine eroded rocks are to be found at a height of about 45m. When the hot water heating system was constructed in the 30's storage tanks were built on top of Öskjuhlíð. They have now been replaced by larger ones, on top of which is the viewing platform and restaurant Perlan, which rotates. The Saga Museum located inside one of the tanks, transports you to the Viking Age and brings back to life renowned figures and major events in Icelandic history. Visitors to the museum are guided through the museum's many attractions as well as through a chronological history of the country. In this vibrant, multidimensional museum, both Icelandic and foreign visitors are given an opportunity to learn about Icelandic history in a way that is both educational and fun. The Museum is open every day from 10 -18 from April 1st - September 30th, from 12 -17 the rest of the year.

40. Nauthólvík Geothermal Beach. In Iceland the sea is normally far too cold to tempt swimmers, but at Nauthólsvík a thermal beach has been created, where natural hot water flows out into the sea, and you can frolic in the waves as if you were in the Mediterranean! A beach of golden sand has been made (Icelandic sand is usually black, which is less picturesque for a bathing beach), and by the beach a "pool" has been enclosed, where the water temperature is about 20°C. Refreshments and various services are available at the beach. The geothermal beach is open daily 10-20 in the summer months .

41. Reykjavík Art Museum - Kjarvalsstaðir is located in the Miklatún Park, between Miklabraut and Flókagata. Built in honour of the painter Jóhannes Kjarval (d.1972), it was opened in 1973.

42. Höfði, a large timber house on Borgartún, built 1909 by the French for their consul. Now a hospitality house for the City of Reykjavík. Winston Churchill, the then British prime minister, visited at Höfði in 1941 during his visit to the British forces in Iceland. In 1986 summit talks between President Ronald Reagan and General Secretary Mikhaíl Gorbatsjov were held at Höfði.

43. Laugardalur, ("Hot spring valley") lies between the ridges Laugarás and Grensás, or more precisely between the streets Suðurlandsbraut and Laugarásvegur. The Laugardalsvöllur sports field was built there between 1950 and 1957 and was followed by one building after another. The Laugardalshöll sports stadium, the Laugardalslaug swimming pool, a Skating Rink and then more sports fields and office buildings. Laugardalur is now the main headquarters of all sports in Iceland that are associated with Íþróttasamband Íslands ("The Icelandic Sport Federation"). On August 18th 1961, Reykjavík's 175th birthday, Grasagarður Reykjavíkur ("The Reykjavík Botanical Gardens") was established. It contains examples of most Icelandic plants (about 300-350) as well as thousands of foreign plants. Þvottalaugarnar ("The washing springs") are hot springs where people, especially from Reykjavík, used to come to do their washing in memory of which Ásmundur Sveinsson's statue Þvottakonan ("The washerwoman") has been put up there. In 1928-30 drilling for hot water produced a considerable flow of water at 93°C. Hot water was piped to a number of buildings, first of all to the newly-built Austurbæjarskólinn junior school on Skólavörðuholt. This was the beginning of the massive operations to heat all of Reykjavík with natural hot water. In addition to the Reykjavík Botanical Gardens and the sporting facilities in Laugardalur, there is Húsdýragarðurinn, a Zoo containing all the domestic animals to be found on Icelandic farms, and Fjölskyldugarðurinn, a family fun park with all kinds of facilities and equipment for the amusement of young and old.

44. Reykjavík Art Museum - The Ásmundur Sveinsson Sculpture Museum, is on the corner of Sigtún and Reykjavegur. In 1942 the sculptor Ásmundur Sveinsson set about building this square house with its domed roof. He bequeathed his art gallery and collection to the city of Reykjavík and it was formally opened May 21st 1983.

45. Árbæjarsafn, Árbær Museum. Árbær is an old farm northeast of the Elliðaár Rivers and south of Vesturlandsvegur (Highway 1). In 1957 Reykjavík City Council decided to establish a folk museum to be housed at Árbær, whose old farm buildings formed the core of the museum. Old buildings of historical interest have been moved to Árbær from Reykjavík and elsewhere in the country. Árbær Museum tries to give a sense of the architecture and way of life in Reykjavík and during summer visitors can see domestic animals and lifestyles of the past. There are many exhibitions and events held at the Museum, including craft days, vintage car displays, Christmas exhibitions and much more. Árbær Museum is open every day from 10-17 in June, July and August. From September to May the Museum is open by arrangement and runs guided tours at 1pm Monday, Wednesday and Friday. A great fish restaurant, Gallerý fiskur is located within walking distance of the museum. The restaurant is family friendly, reasonably priced and of course there is fresh fish everyday.

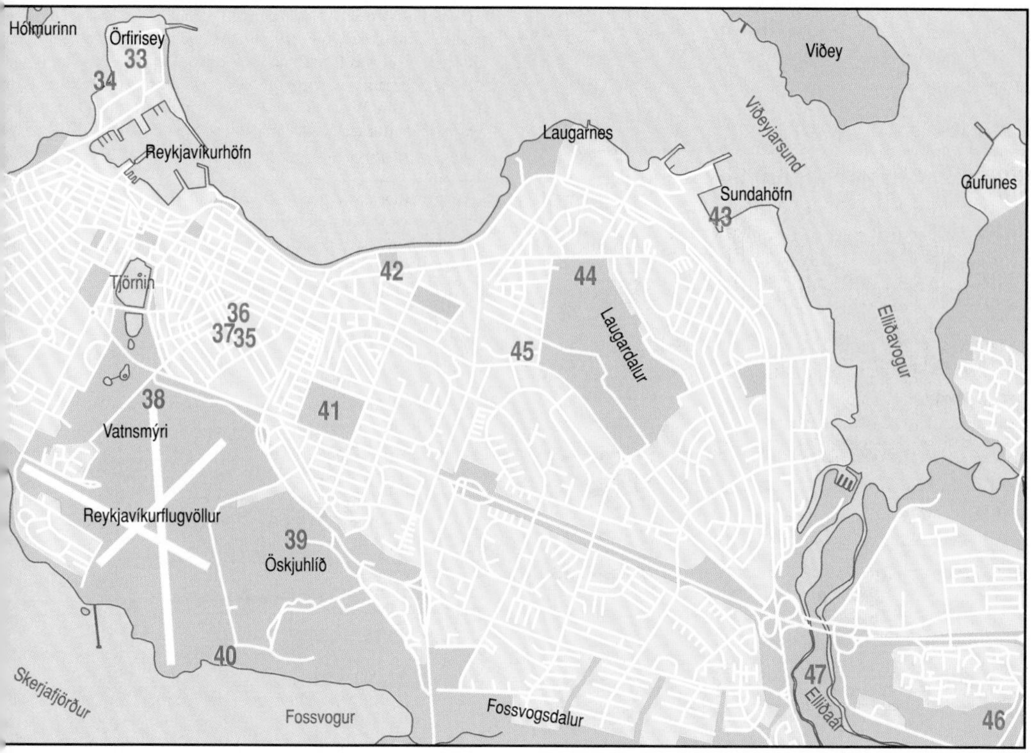

46. Elliðaárdalur, ("The valley of the Elliðaár Rivers"). The Elliðaár Rivers are mentioned as early as in Landnámabók: "Ketilbjörn went to Iceland when there were a number of settlements on the coast. His ship was named Elliði. He came to the Elliðaár estuary below the heath." The hydro-electric plant near the river mouth began operating in 1921, and the rivers now belong to Reykjavík Electricity. Shortly before 1900, Englishmen started using the Elliðaár for angling since when other types of fishing have not been employed there. The rivers are now among the best salmon rivers in the country, and Reykjavík is probably the only capital city in the world to have such a river within its boundaries.

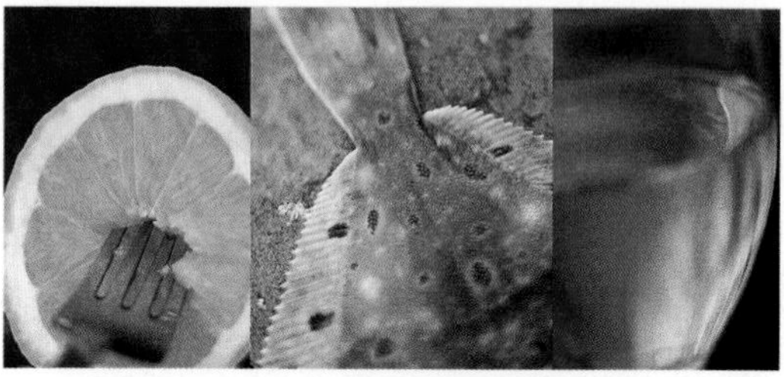

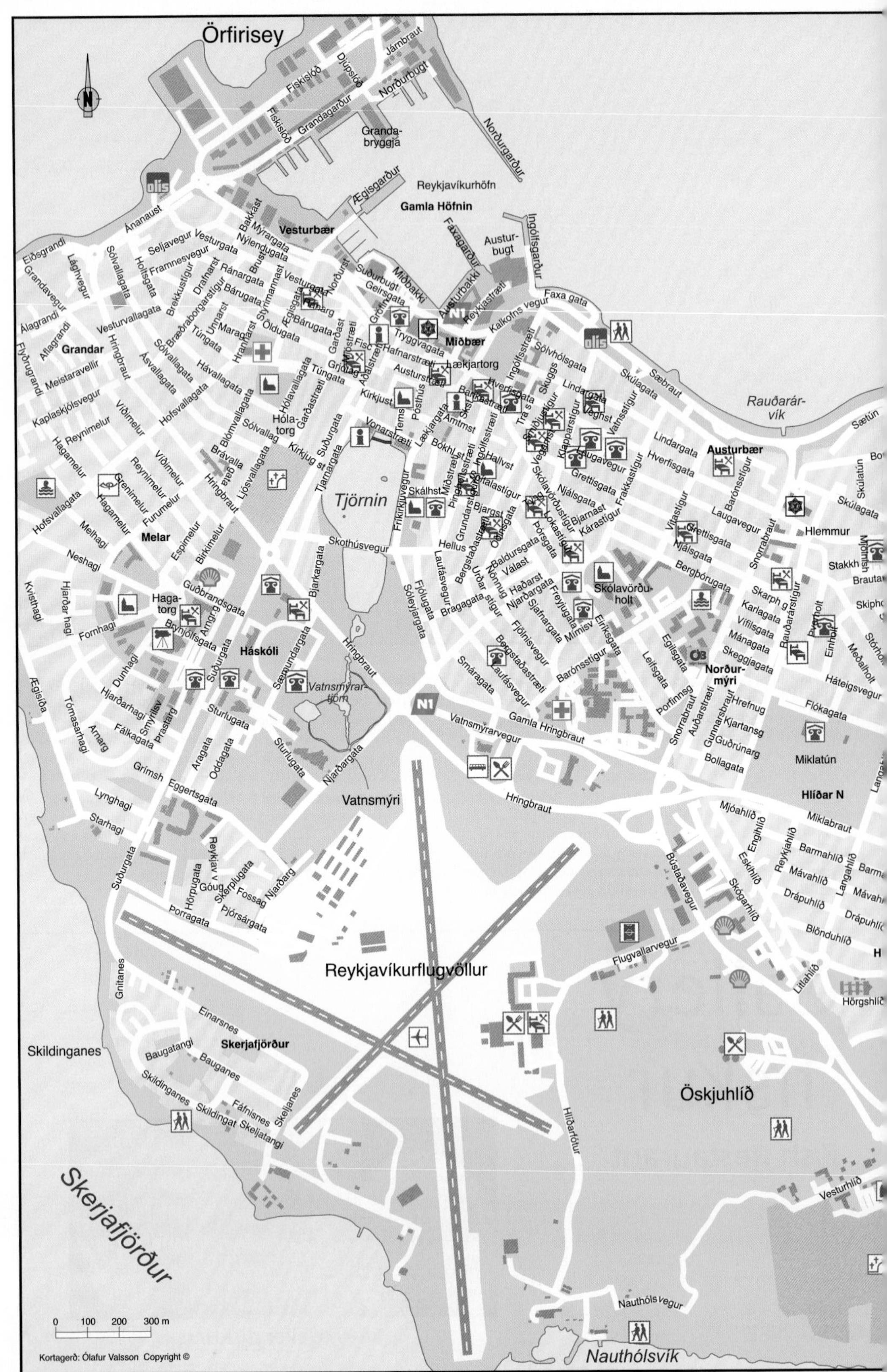
Örfirisey
Reykjavíkurhöfn
Gamla Höfnin
Vesturbær
Miðbær
Grandar
Melar
Tjörnin
Hólatorg
Hagatorg
Háskóli
Vatnsmýrartjörn
Vatnsmýri
Skólavörðuholt
Austurbær
Norðurmýri
Rauðarárvík
Hlemmur
Miklatún
Hlíðar N
Reykjavíkurflugvöllur
Skerjafjörður
Skildinganes
Öskjuhlíð
Nauthólsvík
Skerjafjörður
0 100 200 300 m
Kortagerð: Ólafur Valsson Copyright ©

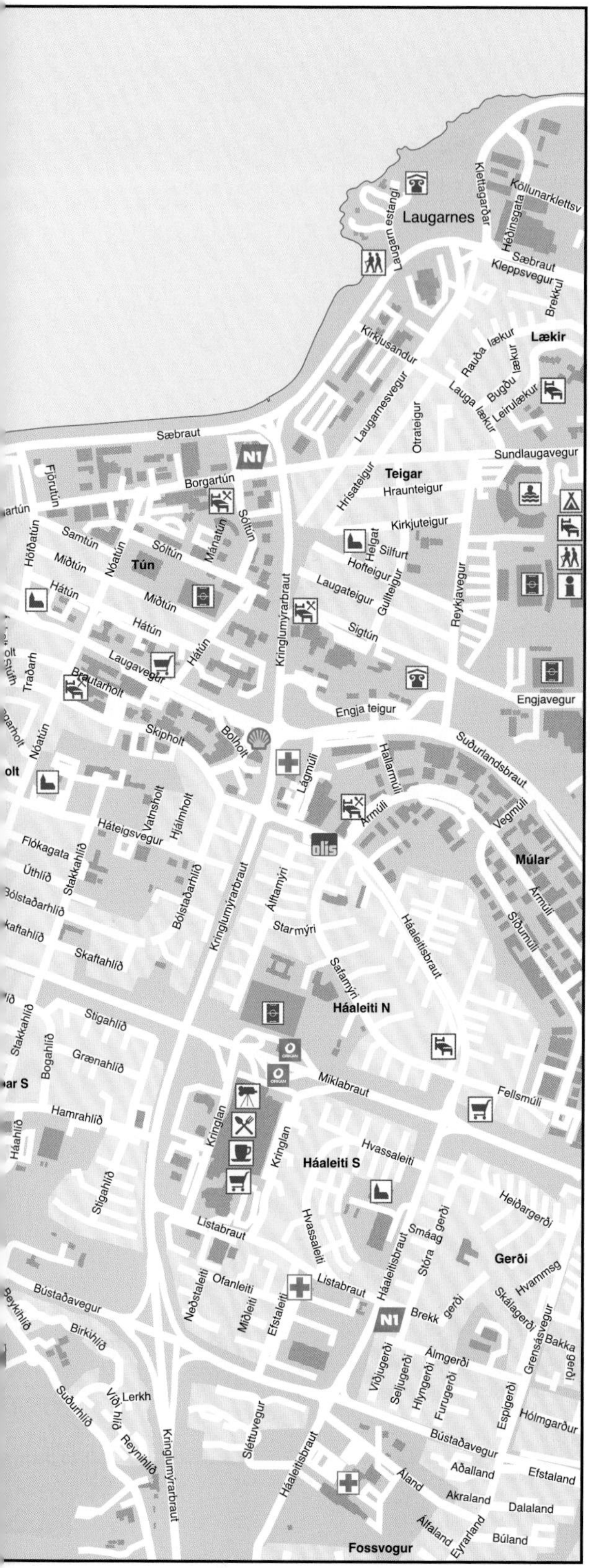

Iceland Post
Phone: 580 1200
www.postur.is

ORKAN

EMERGENGY
TELEPHONE
112
ONE ONE TWO
POLICE
AMBULANCE
FIREBRIGADE
RESCUE SERVICE

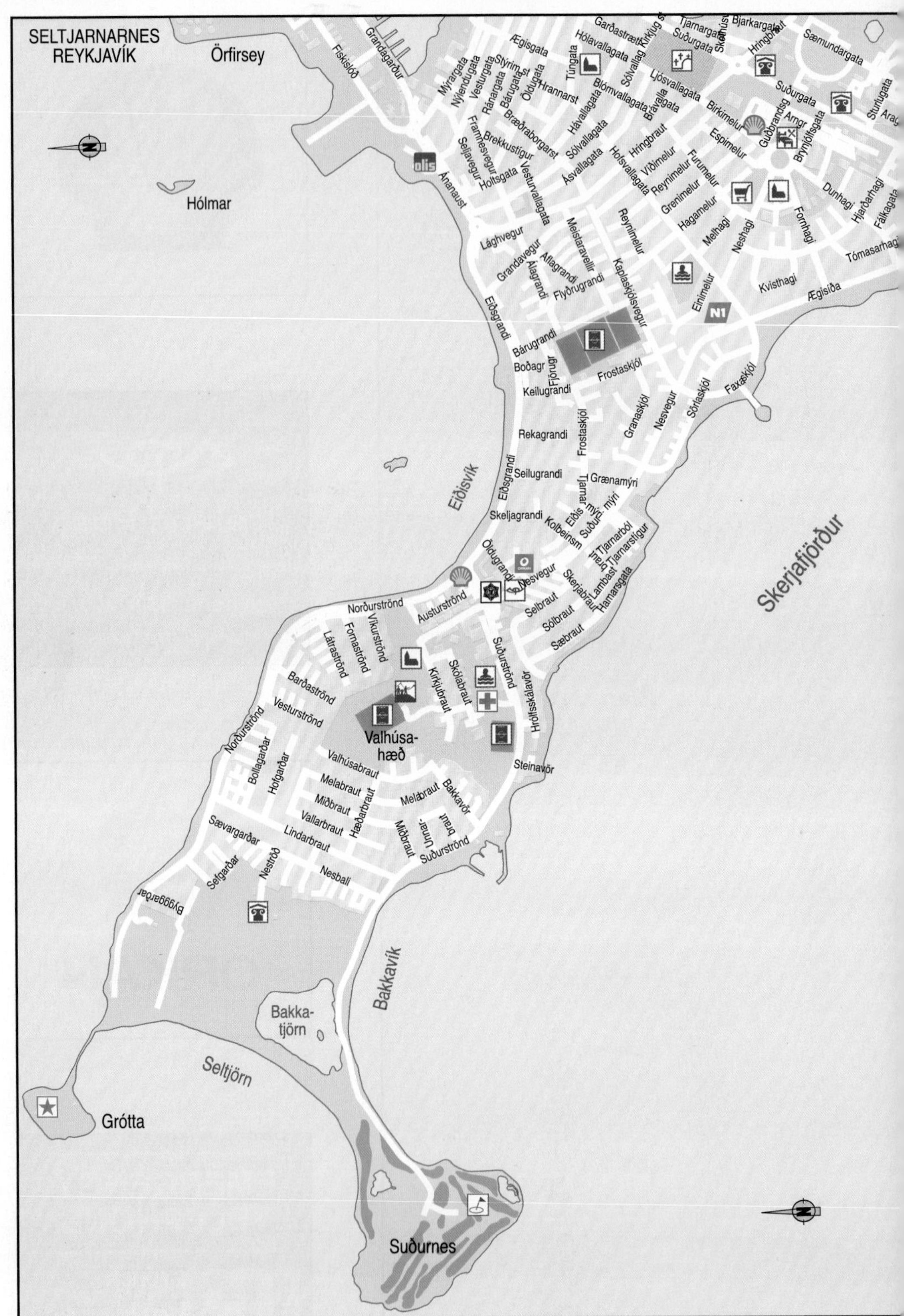
SELTJARNARNES
REYKJAVÍK
Örfirsey
Hólmar
Eiðisvík
Skerjafjörður
Valhúsa-
hæð
Bakkavík
Bakka-
tjörn
Seltjörn
Grótta
Suðurnes
Grandagarður
Fiskislóð
Ægisgata
Túngata
Hólavallagata
Garðastræti
Tjarnargata
Suðurgata
Bjarkargata
Hringbraut
Sæmundargata
Ljósvallagata
Blómvallagata
Hávallagata
Sólvallagata
Ásvallagata
Hofsvallagata
Hringbraut
Víðimelur
Reynimelur
Grenimelur
Furumelur
Hagamelur
Melhagi
Neshagi
Espimelur
Birkimelur
Guðbrandsg
Brynjólfsgata
Dunhagi
Hjarðarhagi
Fálkagata
Fornhagi
Tómasarhagi
Kvisthagi
Ægisíða
Einimelur
Reynimelur
Kaplaskjólsvegur
Meistaravellir
Flyðrugrandi
Aflagrandi
Álagrandi
Grandavegur
Lághvegur
Eiðsgrandi
Bárugrandi
Boðagr
Fjörugr
Keilugrandi
Frostaskjól
Granaskjól
Nesvegur
Sörlaskjól
Faxaskjól
Rekagrandi
Seilugrandi
Skeljagrandi
Grænamýri
Tjarnarból
Tjarnarstígur
Kolbeinsm
Öldugrandi
Nesvegur
Skerjabraut
Hamarsgata
Lambast
Selbraut
Sólbraut
Sæbraut
Norðurströnd
Austurströnd
Víkurströnd
Fornaströnd
Látraströnd
Barðaströnd
Vesturströnd
Norðurströnd
Kirkjubraut
Skólabraut
Suðurströnd
Hrólfsskálavör
Steinavör
Bollagarðar
Hofgarðar
Valhúsabraut
Melabraut
Miðbraut
Vallarbraut
Hæðarbraut
Lindarbraut
Melabraut
Bakkavör
Unnar-
braut
Miðbraut
Suðurströnd
Sævargarðar
Sefgarðar
Neströð
Nesbali
Byggarðar
Mýrargata
Nýlendugata
Vesturgata
Ránargata
Bárugata
Öldugata
Hrannarst
Bræðraborgarst
Brekkustígur
Framnesvegur
Seljavegur
Holtsgata
Vesturvallagata
Ánanaust
olis
N1

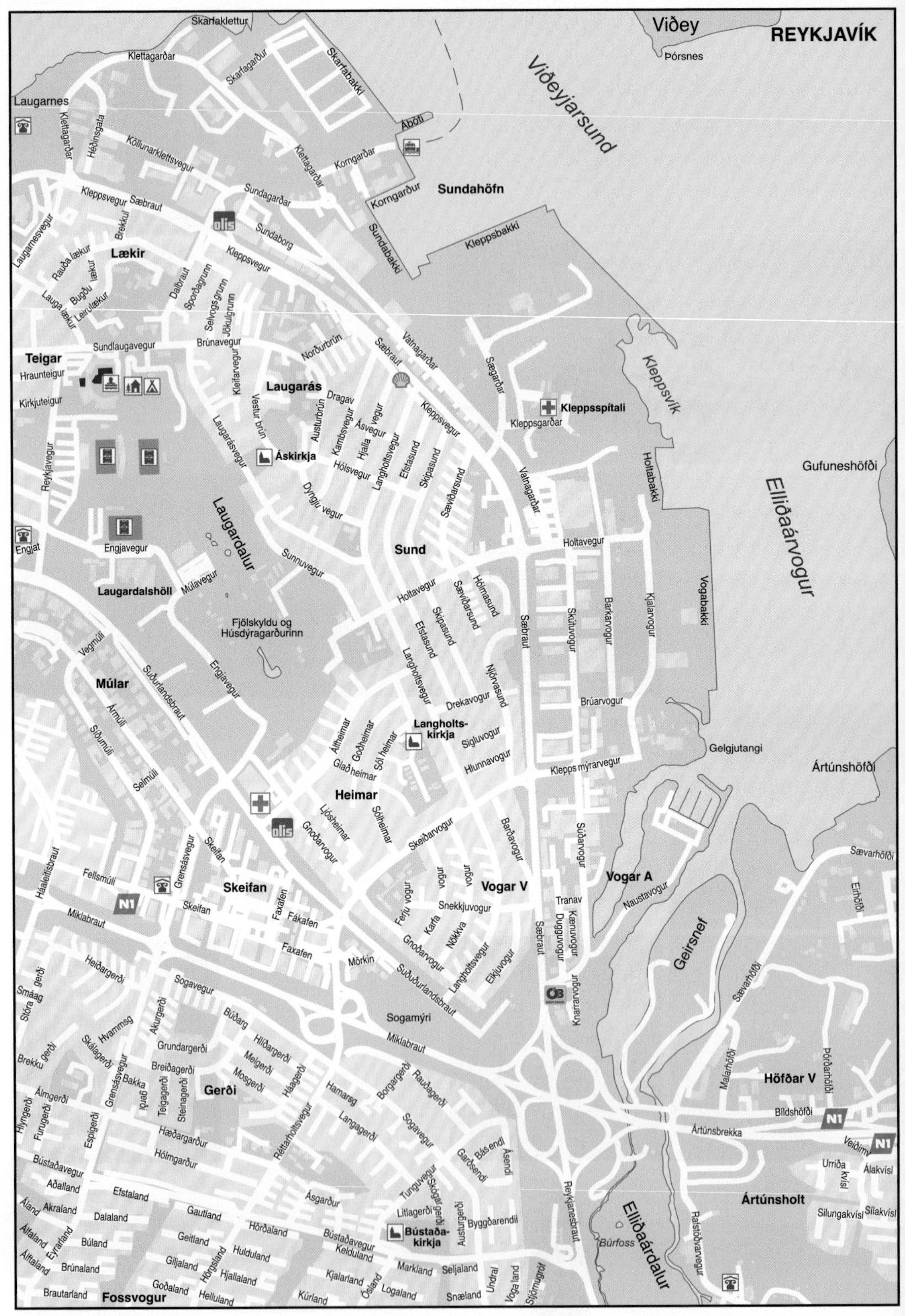
REYKJAVÍK
Viðey
Þórsnes
Viðeyjarsund
Skarfaklettur
Klettagarðar
Skarfagarður
Skarfabakki
Laugarnes
Klettagarðar
Héðinsgata
Köllunarklettsvegur
Kleppsvegur
Sæbraut
Sundagarðar
Korngarðar
Korngarður
Ábóti
Sundahöfn
Sundaborg
Sundabakki
Kleppsbakki
Laugarnesvegur
Brekku
Lækir
Rauða lækur
Bugðu lækur
Laugalækur
Leirulækur
Dalbraut
Sporðagrunn
Selvogsgrunn
Jökulgrunn
Kleppsvegur
Sundlaugavegur
Brúnavegur
Norðurbrún
Vatnagarðar
Sæbraut
Sægarðar
Kleppsvík
Teigar
Hraunteigur
Kirkjuteigur
Kleifarvegur
Vestur brún
Laugarás
Dragav
Austurbrún
Kambsvegur
Ásvegur
Hjalla vegur
Langholtsvegur
Kleppsvegur
Kleppsspítali
Kleppsgarðar
Laugarásvegur
Áskirkja
Hólsvegur
Efstasund
Skipasund
Sæviðarsund
Holtabakki
Gufuneshöfði
Reykjavegur
Dyngju vegur
Vatnagarðar
Elliðaárvogur
Laugardalur
Engjat
Engjavegur
Sunnuvegur
Sund
Holtavegur
Laugardalshöll
Múlavegur
Holtavegur
Sæviðarsund
Hólmasund
Vogabakki
Fjölskyldu og Húsdýragarðurinn
Skipasund
Efstasund
Sæbraut
Skútuvogur
Barkarvogur
Kjalarvogur
Vegmúli
Langholtsvegur
Múlar
Suðurlandsbraut
Engjavegur
Ármúli
Síðumúli
Drekavogur
Njörvasund
Brúarvogur
Álfheimar
Goðheimar
Langholts-kirkja
Sigluvogur
Gelgjutangi
Selmúli
Sól heimar
Glaðheimar
Hlunnavogur
Klepps mýrarvegur
Ártúnshöfði
Heimar
Ljósheimar
Sólheimar
Barðavogur
Súðarvogur
Háaleitisbraut
Gnoðarvogur
Skeiðarvogur
Sævarhöfði
Skeifan
Grensásvegur
Fellsmúli
Skeifan
Vogar V
Vogar A
Naustavogur
Eirhöfði
Faxafen
Tranav
Kænuvogur
Dugguvogur
Miklabraut
Skeifan
Fákafen
Ferju vogur
Snekkjuvogur
Karfa
Nökkva
Sæbraut
Geirsnef
Faxafen
Gnoðarvogur
Heiðargerði
Mörkin
Suðurlandsbraut
Langholtsvegur
Eikjuvogur
Sævarhöfði
Smáag
Stóra gerði
Sogavegur
Akurgerði
Búðarg
Knarrarvogur
Sogamýri
Hvammsg
Skálagerði
Grundargerði
Hlíðargerði
Melgerði
Miklabraut
Brekku gerði
Breiðagerði
Mosgerði
Háagerði
Hamarsg
Borgargerði
Rauðagerði
Malarhöfði
Þórðarhöfði
Höfðar V
Grensásvegur
Bakka gerði
Teigagerði
Steinagerði
Gerði
Ámgerði
Langagerði
Sogavegur
Bíldshöfði
Hlyngerði
Furugerði
Espigerði
Hæðargarður
Réttarholtsvegur
Ártúnsbrekka
Veiðimv
Bústaðavegur
Hólmgarður
Básendi
Ásendi
Garðsendi
Urriða kvísl
Álakvísl
Aðalland
Tunguvegur
Skógargerði
Reykjanesbraut
Ártúnsholt
Áland
Akraland
Efstaland
Dalaland
Gautland
Ásgarður
Litlagerði
Austurgerði
Byggðarendi
Silungakvísl
Sílakvísl
Álfaland
Eyrarland
Búland
Hörðaland
Geitland
Bústaðavegur
Kelduland
Bústaða-kirkja
Elliðaárdalur
Raftóðvarvegur
Búrfoss
Álftaland
Brúnaland
Giljaland
Hörgsland
Hulduland
Hjallaland
Markland
Seljaland
Brautarland
Fossvogur
Goðaland
Helluland
Kjalarland
Ösland
Logaland
Kúrland
Snæland
Undral
Voga land
Sjómugrðr

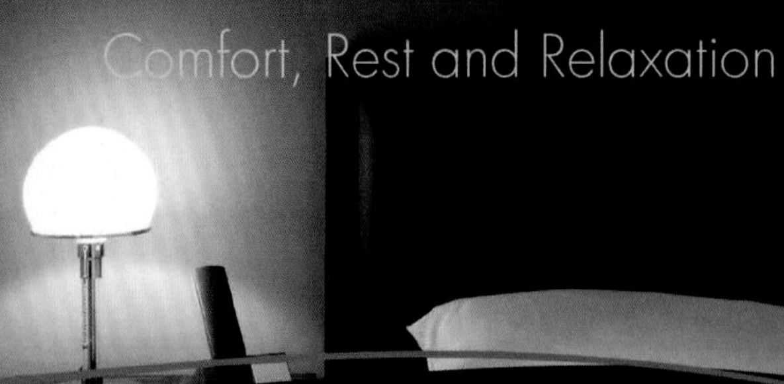

Keahotels welcome you to Iceland. We invite you to share with us all the best of what our country has to offer. Our six hotels are in key locations, granting you a full access to the most attractive places in Iceland. Situated in Reykjavík, Akureyri and by Lake Mývatn, Keahotels are joined in a mutual booking system, providing our clients with professional and efficient service. Computers with high speed internet connections are available to our guests in all our hotels.

Ranging from two up to four stars, our hotels are all fully equipped with hospitality and friendliness.

Headoffice: Hafnarstræti 87-89, 600 Akureyri
Tel: (+354) 460 2050 · Fax: (+354) 460 2070
E-mail: keahotels@keahotels.is
www.keahotels.is

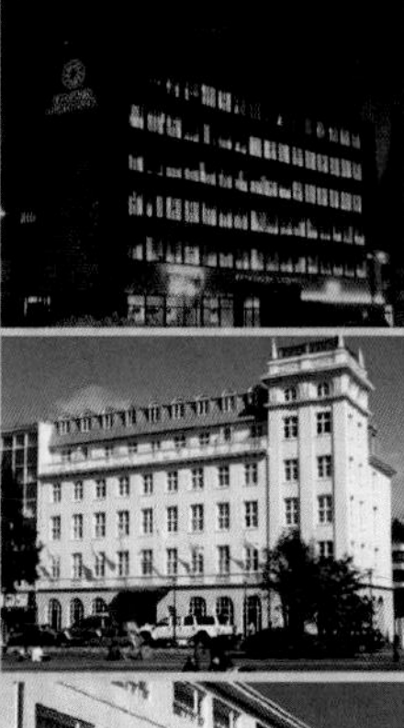

Reykjavik Lights ★★★
Suðurlandsbraut 12
108 Reykjavík

Tel: (+354) 513 9000
Fax: (+354) 513 9020
reykjaviklights@keahotels.is
www.keahotels.is

Hotel Borg ★★★★
Pósthússtræti 11
101 Reykjavík

Tel: (+354) 551 1440
Fax: (+354) 551 1420
hotelborg@hotelborg.is
www.hotelborg.is

Hotel Björk ★★★
Brautarholt 22-24
105 Reykjavík

Tel: (+354) 511 3777
Fax: (+354) 511 3776
bjork@keahotels.is
www.keahotels.is

Hotel Kea ★★★★
Hafnarstræti 87-89
600 Akureyri

Tel: (+354) 460 2000
Fax: (+354) 460 2060
kea@keahotels.is
www.keahotels.is

Hotel Norðurland ★★★
Geislagata 7
600 Akureyri

Tel: (+354) 462 2600
Fax: (+354) 462 2601
nordurland@keahotels.is
www.keahotels.is

Hotel Gígur ★★
Skútustaðir
660 Mývatn

Tel: (+354) 464 4455
Fax: (+354) 464 4279
gigur@keahotels.is
www.keahotels.is

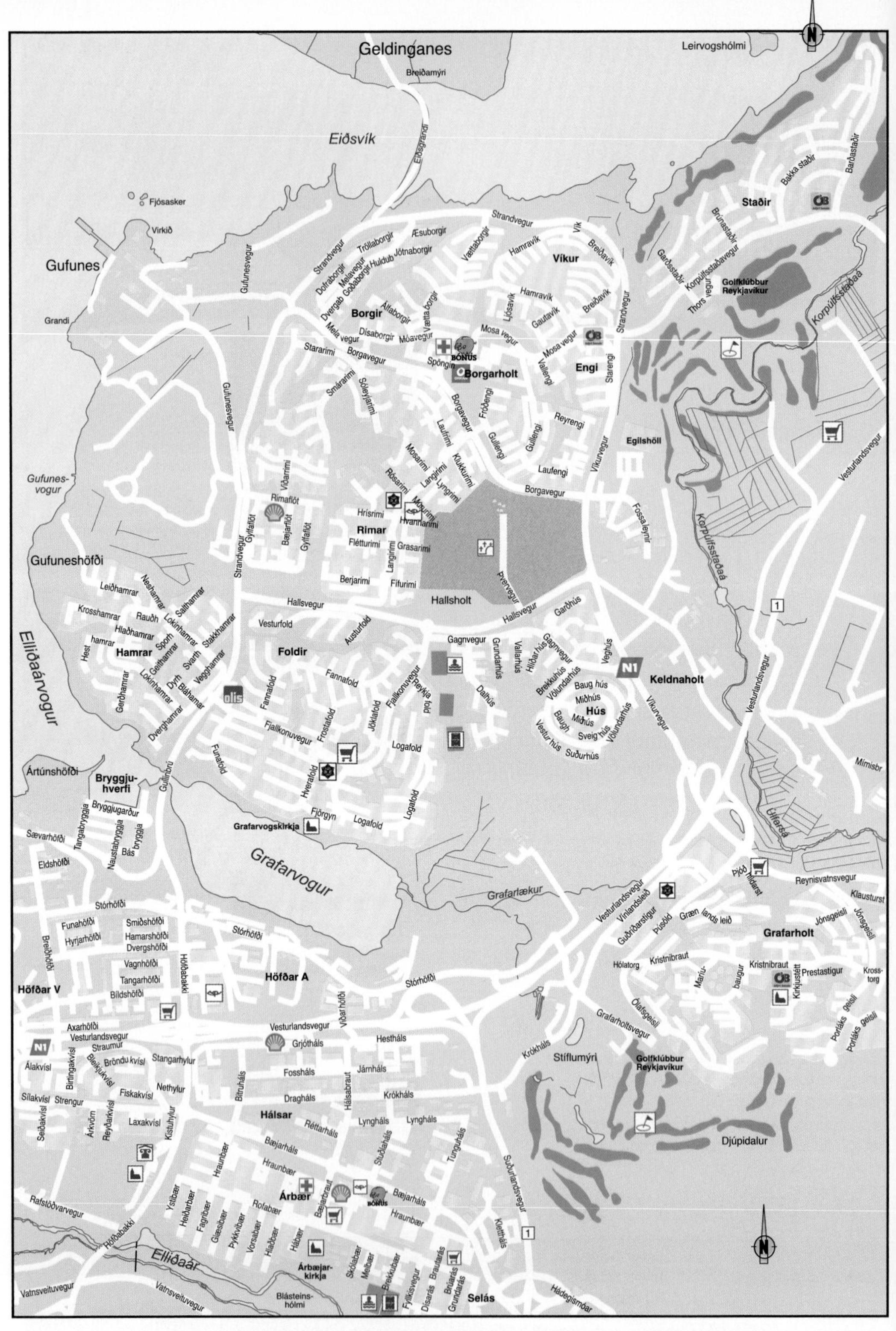

Geldinganes
Leirvogshólmi
Eiðsvík
Gufunes
Grafarvogur
Elliðaárvogur
Foldir
Rimar
Borgir
Víkur
Engi
Staðir
Hamrar
Hús
Keldnaholt
Grafarholt
Höfðar A
Höfðar V
Hálsar
Árbær
Selás
Djúpidalur
Stíflumýri
Egilshöll
Hallsholt
Borgarholt
Gufuneshöfði
Ártúnshöfði
Bryggju-hverfi
Grafarvogskirkja
Árbæjar-kirkja
Golfklúbbur Reykjavíkur
Elliðaár

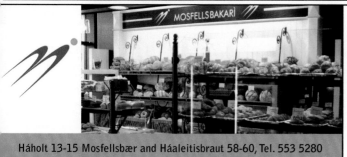

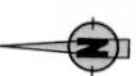

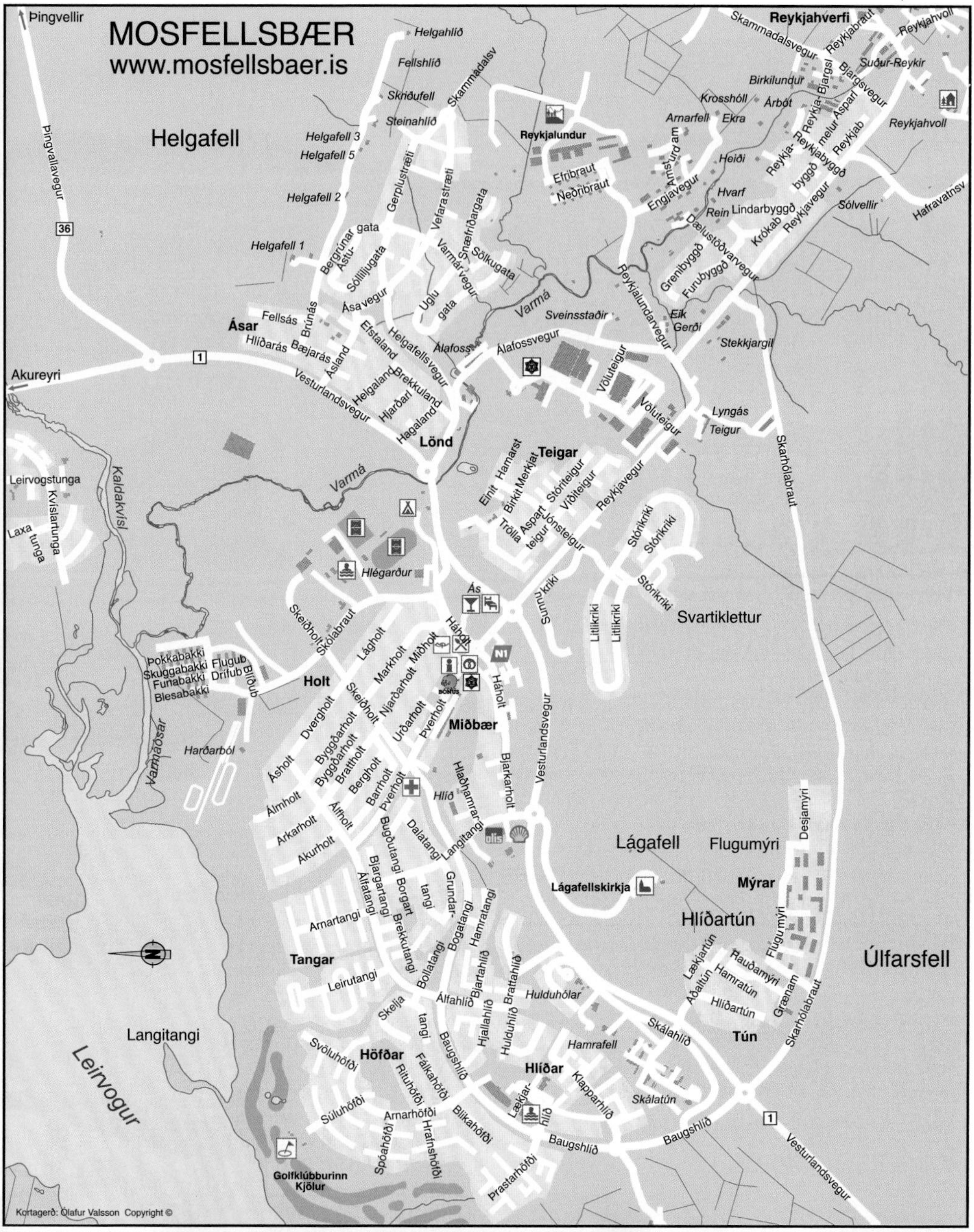

MOSFELLSBÆR
www.mosfellsbaer.is
Þingvellir
Þingvallavegur
36
Helgafell
Helgafell 1
Helgafell 2
Helgafell 3
Helgafell 5
Helgahlíð
Fellshlíð
Skriðufell
Steinahlíð
Skammadalsv
Reykjalundur
Efribraut
Neðribraut
Reykjahverfi
Skammadalsvegur
Reykjabraut
Reykjahvoll
Suður-Reykir
Birkilundur
Krosshóll
Árbót
Arnarfell
Ekra
Heiði
Hvarf
Rein
Lindarbyggð
Sólvellir
Hafravatnsv
Engjavegur
Amsturdam
Krókab
Reykjavegur
Grenibyggð
Furubyggð
Dælustöðvarvegur
Reykjalundarvegur
Eik
Gerði
Stekkjargil
Sveinsstaðir
Varmá
Ásar
Fellsás
Hlíðarás
Brúnás
Bæjarás
Ásland
Ásavegur
Efstaland
Helgafellsvegur
Álafoss
Álafossvegur
Völuteigur
Lyngás
Teigur
Vesturlandsvegur
Helgaland
Brekkuland
Hjarðarland
Hagaland
Lönd
Akureyri
1
Leirvogstunga
Kvíslartunga
Laxatunga
Kaldakvísl
Teigar
Einit
Hamarsteigur
Birkiteigur
Merkiteigur
Stórateigur
Víðiteigur
Jónsteigur
Aspart
Tröllateigur
Reykjavegur
Skarhólabraut
Stórikriki
Sunnukriki
Litlikriki
Svartiklettur
Hlégarður
Ás
Skeiðholt
Skólabraut
Lágholt
Markholt
Miðholt
Háholt
N1
Pokkabakki
Skuggabakki
Funabakki
Blesabakki
Flugub
Drífub
Bllöb
Holt
Harðarból
Varmárósar
Dverholt
Skeiðholt
Njarðarholt
Urðarholt
Þverholt
Miðbær
Ásholt
Byggðarholt
Brattholt
Bergholt
Barrholt
Álmholt
Álfholt
Arkarholt
Akurholt
Hlaðhamrar
Bjarkarholt
Hlíð
Dalatangi
Langitangi
olís
Lágafell
Flugumýri
Desjamýri
Lágafellskirkja
Mýrar
Hlíðartún
Úlfarsfell
Buðutangi
Bjargartangi
Álfatangi
Borgartangi
Grundartangi
Arnartangi
Brekkutangi
Bogatangi
Hamratangi
Tangar
Leirutangi
Bollatangi
Bjartahlíð
Brattahlíð
Álfahlíð
Hulduhólar
Lækjartún
Aðaltún
Hamratún
Rauðamýri
Grænamýri
Hlíðartún
Tún
Skálahlíð
Langitangi
Leirvogur
Skeljatangi
Svöluhöfði
Höfðar
Fálkahöfði
Hjallahlíð
Hulduhlíð
Hamrafell
Hlíðar
Klapparhlíð
Skálatún
Súluhöfði
Arnarhöfði
Rituhöfði
Blikahöfði
Lækjarhlíð
Baugshlíð
Spóahöfði
Hrafnshöfði
Prastarhöfði
Golfklúbburinn Kjölur
Kortagerð: Ólafur Valsson Copyright ©

MOSFELLSBAKARÍ

KFC

Natural History Museum of Kópavogur

The Natural History Museum of Kópavogur is situated in the Cultural Centre of Kópavogur, next to Art Museum Gerðarsafn and Salurinn Concert Hall. It is housed on the first floor in a new, beautiful building along with Kópavogur Public Library.

Exhibition

There are two main exhibition themes, Icelandic fauna, with emphasis on birds and molluscs, and Icelandic rocks and minerals. On display are also mammals, crustaceans, and live fish in small aquariums. Also on view are live „marimos", a large spherical form of green algae, found only in three lakes in the world, including lake Mývatn in northeast-Iceland, which among other things is famous for its bird life.

Outdooractivity

When visiting the museum, it is ideal to pay a visit to Kópavogur Church, situated atop Borgarholt, a rocky hill overlooking the Cultural Centre. The hill is protected as a natural monument as it provides unusually clear evidence of a glacial retreat some ten thousand years ago, with accompanying actions of the ocean and rising of land mass. The hill also provides an excellent view of the capital area and in between rocks one can find many species of wild Icelandic plants.

Research

Research at the institute is conducted mainly in freshwater ecology. Studies include nation-wide lake surveys, local lake monitoring, environmental impact assessments, and biological studies at the species and population level. The institute cooperates closely with research institutes in Iceland, Denmark, Norway and Canada.
For further information on exhibitons and research see www.natkop.is

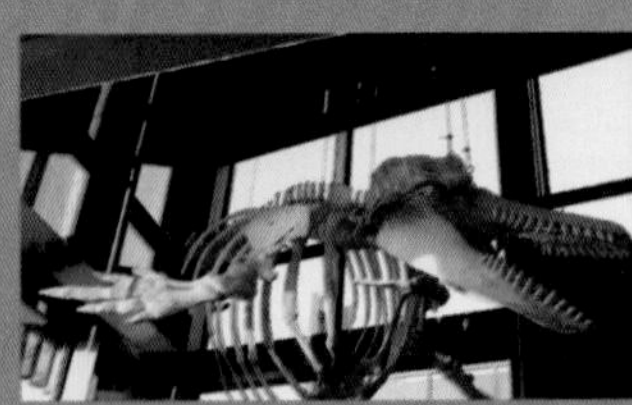

Opening hours
Monday-Thursday: 10:00-19:00
Fridays: 11:00-17:00
Saturday: 13:00-17:00
Free admission.

Natural History Museum of Kópavogur
Hamraborg 6 A, 200 Kópavogur
Phone: 5700430 • Fax: 5700431
www.natkop.is • natkop@natkop.is

Náttúrufræðistofa Kópavogs
Natural History Museum of Kópavogur

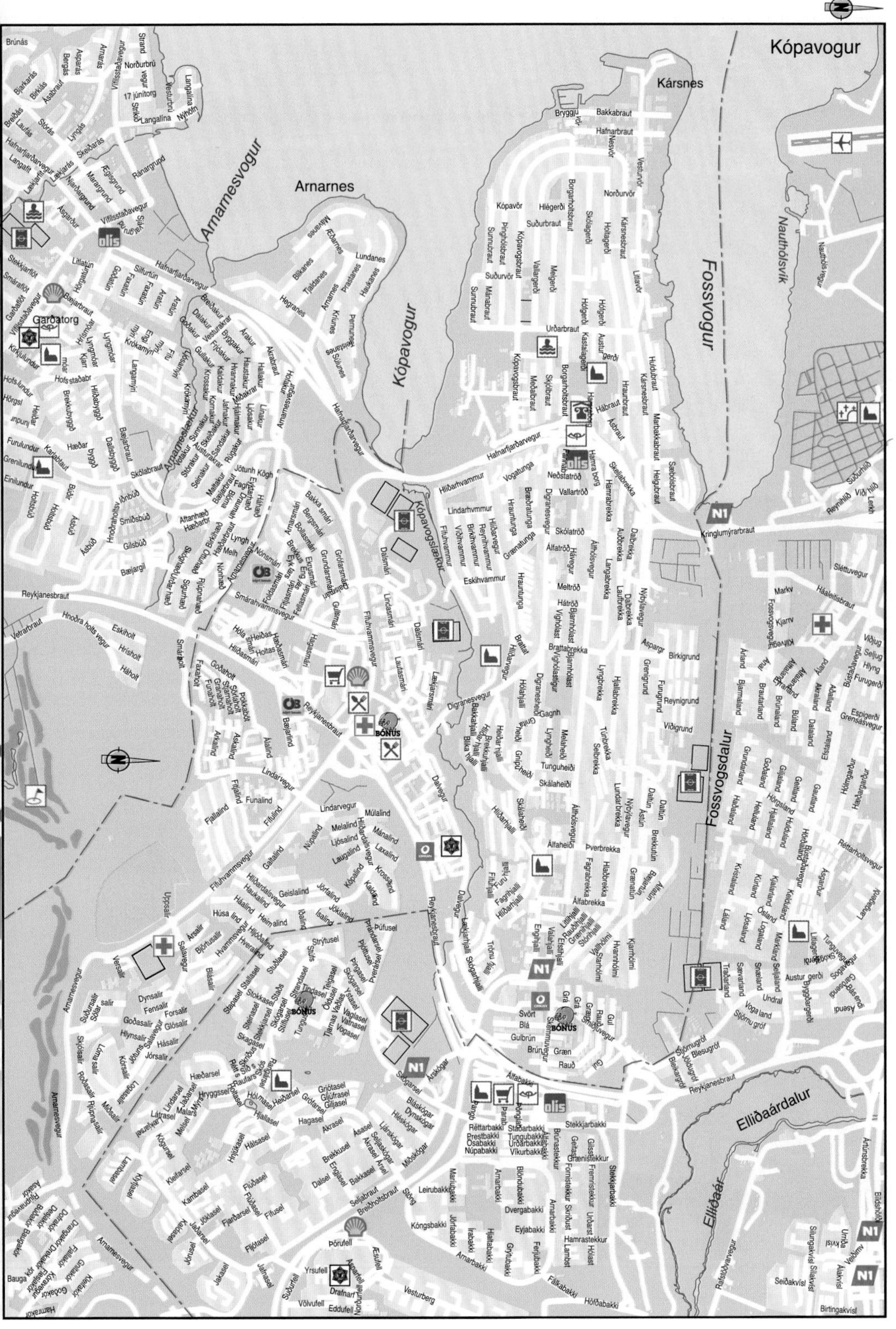

Kópavogur
Kársnes
Arnarnes
Arnarnesvogur
Kópavogur
Fossvogur
Nauthólsvík
Fossvogsdalur
Elliðaárdalur
Elliðaár
Garðatorg
Hafnarfjarðarvegur
Reykjanesbraut
Kringlumýrarbraut
Digranesvegur
Nýbýlavegur
Vesturvör
Bakkabraut
Hafnarbraut
Kópavogsbraut
Borgarholtsbraut
Hamraborg
Smáratorg
Lindarvegur
Fífuhvammsvegur
Arnarnesvegur
Breiðholtsbraut

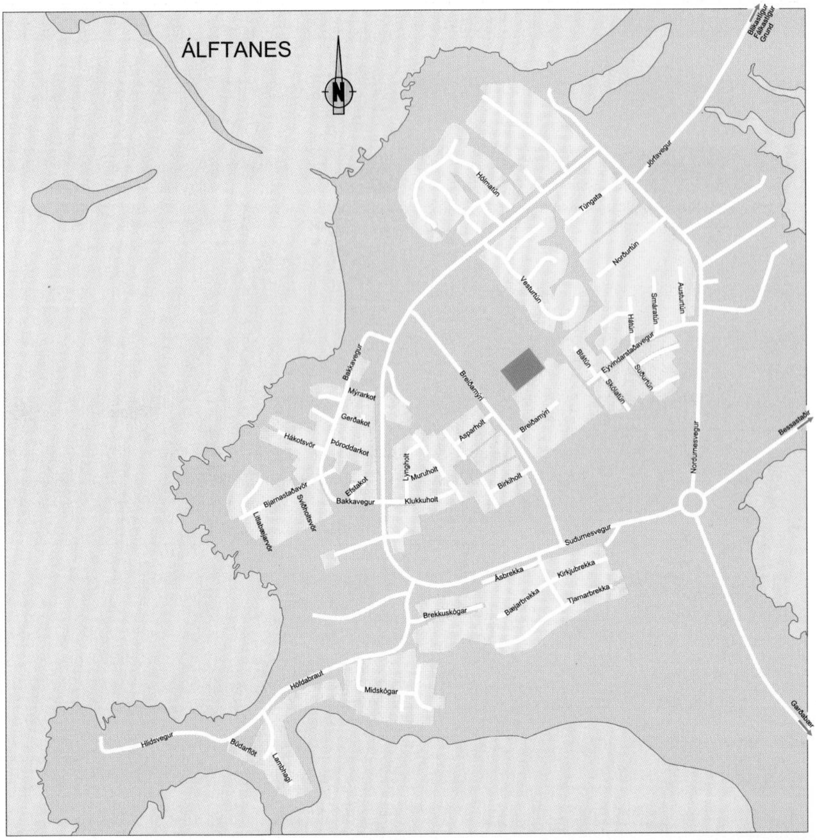

ÁLFTANES

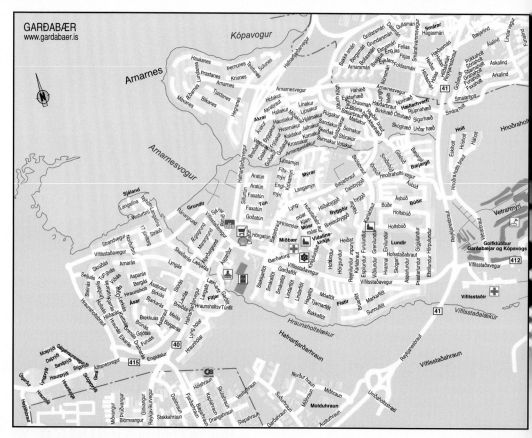

GARÐABÆR
www.gardabaer.is

Garðabær, (pop. 10,909) a municipality in the Greater Reykjavík area and a community rich in unspoiled nature for the enjoyment of outdoor life by its residents. The lava landscape ("Búrfellshraun") is believed to be around 7200 years old and is one of the main natural features surrounding Garðabær. There is ample space for free outdoor activities and many hiking tracks, for example in the outdoor area "Heiðmörk". There are two lakes in the area of Garðabær, "Vífilsstaðavatn" and "Urriðavatn". Vífilsstaðavatn and its surroundings is a nature reserve according to the Nature Conservation act. A fishing license can be purchased for Vífilsstaðavatn in the summers. The outdoor swimming pool in Garðabær (25 m) is located in the sports centre "Ásgarður".

Places of cultural interest are: The Museum of Design and Applied Art, exhibition hall located at Garðatorg. Open from 12-17 Thuesdays till Sundays during exhibitions. The old farm Krókur (built 1923) in Garðaholt is open on Sunday afternoons during summertime. At Garðabær there is olso the Hofsstaðir archeology site located at Kirkjulundur. The house was built in the 9th century. The remains have been preserved and a public garden built around them. You can see the remains in the gardens, where there are also multimedia displays telling the story of Hofsstadir and the lives of those who lived there over a thousand years ago. Hofsstaðir archeology site is open 24 hours. No entrance fee.

Garðabær

Index and more information about Iceland

The Icelandic Horse

The Icelandic horse is rather small, its height usually being about 140 cm. It is sturdy and hardworking and has greater endurance than its foreign cousins. It has a characteristic varied colouring that breeders have attempted to preserve rather than eliminate. As a riding animal, the Icelandic horse is exceptional in that it has five gaits, called fet, skeið, tölt, brokk and stökk in Icelandic. It has become famous internationally for its various gaits and smooth movement. Icelandic horses are considered energetic and ready to run, and they are also admired for their even and friendly disposition. Icelandic farmers have traditionally been interested in the strength and endurance of horses.

Red skewbald

Black

Dark bay

Grey mare with a foal

Red-dun

Light black

Bay-roan

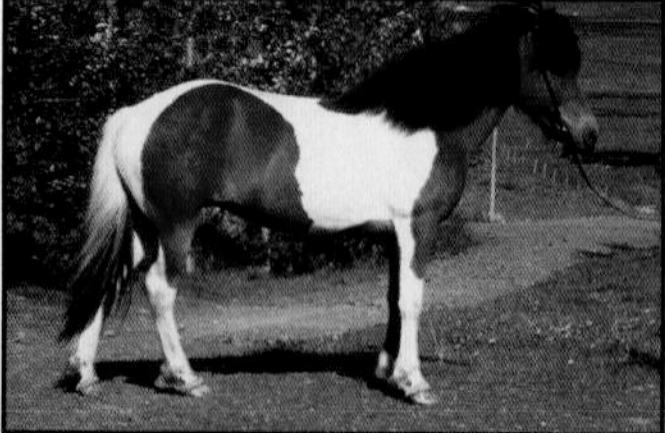

Bay skewbald

Pale dun, dun

Palamino

Buckskin

Blue dun

Silver dapple

Chestnut

Dapple grey

Black skewbald

Silver dapple, skewbald

Yellow dun

Dark roan stud mare
with a foal

Chestnut with white socks

Buckskin, light

The Icelandic Sheep

The Icelandic sheep is special in many ways. For example, leader sheep possessing the qualities of the Icelandic type do not exist anywhere else in the world. There are many stories of how they have rescued both men and other sheep from danger. Icelandic sheep are so-called short-tailed animals, a type which was formerly common in northwestern Europe, but which is now found in only few areas of the world. It is a strong, hardy species that has adapted well to Icelandic conditions. The majority of the national flock has horns, but polled sheep are also common.

White, polled ewe, with tan fibres and a black spot

White, horned ram, with a black cheek

Black, polled ewe

Dark-grey, polled ewe

White, polled ram

Grey, horned ewe

Homozygous grey, polled ewe

Brown, polled ewe lamb

Brown, horned ewe

Grey-brown, horned ram lamb

Black mouflon, horned ewe

Grey mouflon, horned ewe

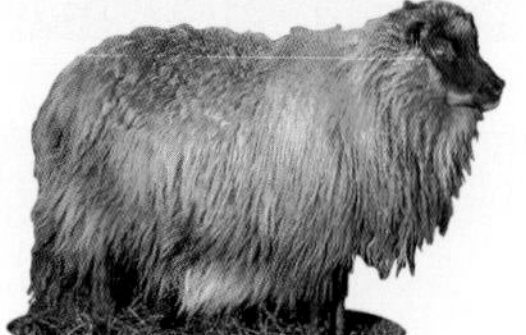

Brown mouflon, polled ewe

Black badgerface, horned ram lamb, with a dark flank spot

Grey badgerface, horned ewe lamb

Brown badgerface, horned ewe

Black piebald, horned ewe, with dark eyerings only

Black piebald, polled ewe, with dark cheeks and a collar

Black piebald, horned ewe, with a hood

Black piebald, horned ewe, with dark outer socks

Black piebald, polled ewe, with patches

Grey piebald, polled ewe, with patches

Brown piebald, polled ewe lamb, with a hood

Brown piebald-mouflon, horned ram lamb, with an eagle head

Black mouflon-piebald, horned leader wether, with a blaze and socks

Black badgerface-piebald, horned ewe lamb

Black fourhorned ewe

Black piebald, fourhorned ram lamb, with patches

Black piebald, horned leader ram, with socks, head and nose spots

Brown piebald, horned leader ewe with black and brown piebald ewe lambs, all with white collars and stockings

Brown piebald polled ram, with a head spot and socks, the high crown showing the presence of the gene for fourhornednes

Black piebald, horned leader ewe, with a blaze, a collar and socks

The Icelandic Cattle

The Icelandic breed of cattle is smaller than cattle in neighbouring countries. It is a hardy and fertile type of cow and produces a great deal of milk. The number of dairy farmers is gradually declining as the productivity of individual farmers increases. There are currently about 1,100 milk farmers in the country. Most milk production and cattle breeding is conducted in the south, west and north-central areas of the country, near the major urban centres.

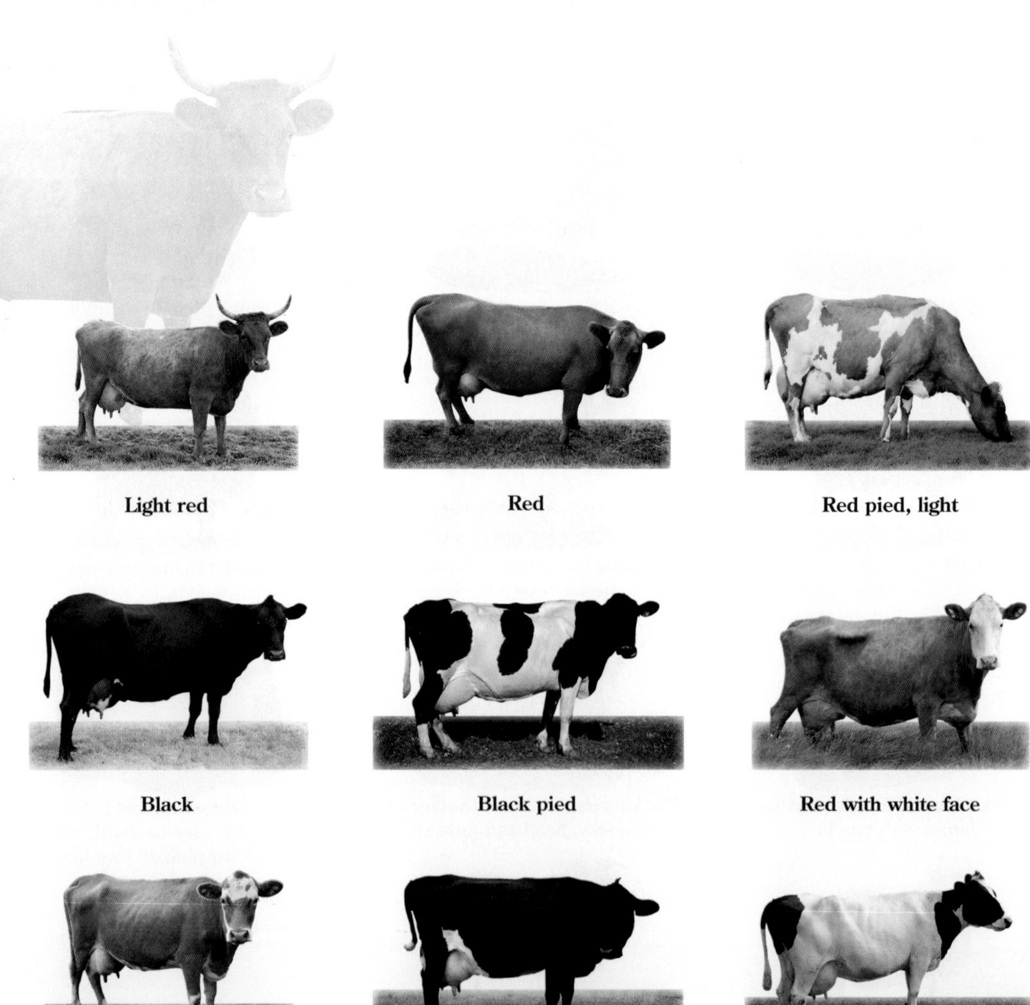

Light red

Red

Red pied, light

Black

Black pied

Red with white face

Red with white face markings

Black, with inguinal region

Black pied, extensive white

Brindle pied

Grey, blue roan

Brown, white face, socks

Grey

Red brindle

Brindle

White

White, red ears and muzzle

Dun, white dorsal line

Brown grey, white inguinal region

Brown, light

Brown, dark

Black sided, homozygous

Dun

Dun, white dorsal line

The Icelandic Dog

The Icelandic Sheepdog has assisted with guarding and hearding horses, cattle and sheep since it was brought here during the original settlement in Iceland. Research has shown that it is of Nordic origin like the Icelandic sheep and goats. Like the Icelandic goat the Icelandic Sheepdog was close to extinction in the mid 20th century. In the last decades some measures have been taken in reversing this process, both in Iceland and abroad. The main characteristics of the Icelandic Sheepdog are its pricked ears and curled tail and its many colours.

Light tan dog with a black mask and white collar

Reddish tan and light tan bitches, both with black masks

Black tricolour dog with a blaze

Tricolour and black masked puppies

Black tricolour dog

Reddish brown dog with a black mask

Black tricolour bitch puppy

Proud mother with her puppy, both light tan with black mask

Reddish tan dog with a white collar with a bitch of the same colour and another light tan bitch with a black mask

Reddish tan dog with a white collar

Light tan three year old bitch

Reddish tan puppies, all with black mask

Two bitches, one light tan, the other reddish tan with a white collar

Puppies, some with a blaze and other with half a white face

Light tan two year old dog

A light reddish tan dog on a winter's day

Reddish tan dog with a black mask and a blaze

Light tan bitch with a half a white face

Brown bitch

Light tan bitch with a white collar

Reddish tan dog with a black mask

Reddish tan bitch with a white collar and blaze

Reddish tan puppy with a black mask, six weeks old

The Icelandic Goat

The Icelandic goat is now a unique breed, because it was brought here over 1100 years ago and no other goats have been introduced to this island since then. However, the stock currently consists of only about 520 animals, a number which undoubtedly puts it at great risk of dying out, compared to other goat breeds internationally.

Goats are thought to be the oldest species of livestock. Even though cow's milk has gained prominence in western farming, this is not usually the case in other parts of the world. Actually, goat milk is better suited to humans, as it is more easily digested and less likely to cause allergy. Above all, it is healthy for babies who are not fed on breast milk.

The largest herd of Icelandic goats now has its home at Háafell, where Jóhanna Þorvaldsdóttir and Þorbjörn Oddsson have raised goats for 23 years. In summer months the population of over a hundred adult animals increases by nearly a hundred kids.

As well as welcoming groups who want to get acquainted with this breed, the farm staff are gathering knowledge about it and utilising its hair, meat and milk, some of which is used for making cheese. The horns are also used for pretty crafted goods such as pocket snuff containers and buttons.

Those interested in learning more about any of these activities should contact Jóhanna, at **haafell@gmail.com**.

Open farms

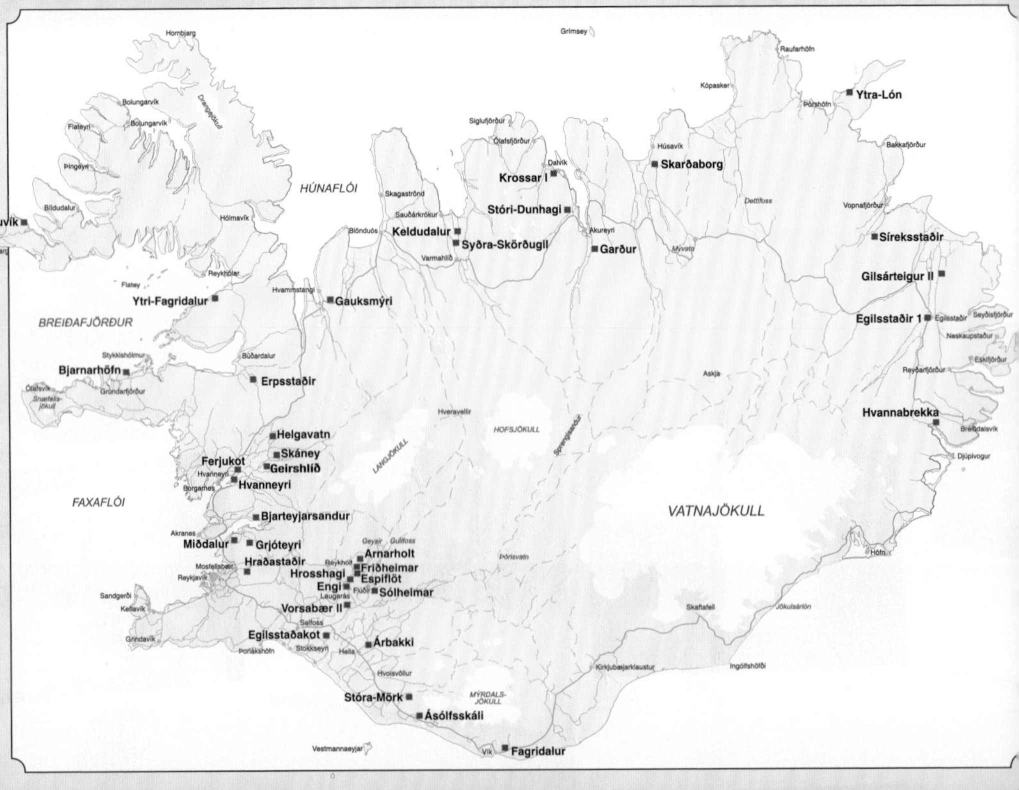

Welcome to the countryside

OPEN FARMS

– A Visit to an Open Farm

Open Farms is an opportunity to visit farms and get familiar with the work done in rural Iceland. Open Farms is a collaboration between the farms and The Farmers Association of Iceland. The farms represent a cross-section of Icelandic agriculture today.
Farmers take a fee for visits. Amounts are different based on the nature and scope of the services. In most cases the farmers only accept cash and visitors are politely asked to keep that in mind.

- More information on Open Farms can be found on **www.bondi.is**
- Have a nice trip, we hope you enjoy visiting the countryside!

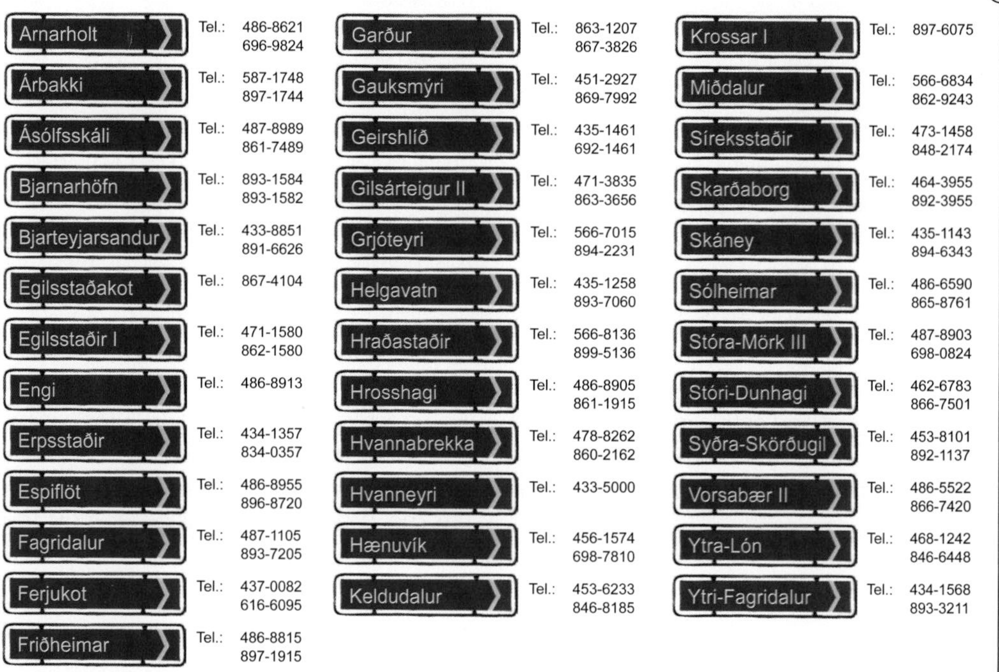

Farm	Tel.:
Arnarholt	486-8621 696-9824
Árbakki	587-1748 897-1744
Ásólfsskáli	487-8989 861-7489
Bjarnarhöfn	893-1584 893-1582
Bjarteyjarsandur	433-8851 891-6626
Egilsstaðakot	867-4104
Egilsstaðir I	471-1580 862-1580
Engi	486-8913
Erpsstaðir	434-1357 834-0357
Espiflöt	486-8955 896-8720
Fagridalur	487-1105 893-7205
Ferjukot	437-0082 616-6095
Friðheimar	486-8815 897-1915
Garður	863-1207 867-3826
Gauksmýri	451-2927 869-7992
Geirshlíð	435-1461 692-1461
Gilsárteigur II	471-3835 863-3656
Grjóteyri	566-7015 894-2231
Helgavatn	435-1258 893-7060
Hraðastaðir	566-8136 899-5136
Hrosshagi	486-8905 861-1915
Hvannabrekka	478-8262 860-2162
Hvanneyri	433-5000
Hænuvík	456-1574 698-7810
Keldudalur	453-6233 846-8185
Krossar I	897-6075
Miðdalur	566-6834 862-9243
Síreksstaðir	473-1458 848-2174
Skarðaborg	464-3955 892-3955
Skáney	435-1143 894-6343
Sólheimar	486-6590 865-8761
Stóra-Mörk III	487-8903 698-0824
Stóri-Dunhagi	462-6783 866-7501
Syðra-Skörðugil	453-8101 892-1137
Vorsabær II	486-5522 866-7420
Ytra-Lón	468-1242 846-6448
Ytri-Fagridalur	434-1568 893-3211

Farm Food Direct

Aided by the Farm Food Direct marketing programme, the production and sale of goods directly to consumers enables farmers to develop a wide range of products which have their origins in Icelandic nature.

More and more, Icelandic farmers are selling home-grown and homemade products, including handicrafts, straight from the farm. This trend is encouraged by increased tourism: consumers demand a greater selection of products that bring out local traits and traditions. Origin labelling attracts ever-increasing interest, together with good old-fashioned personal service.

Farm Food Direct is based on the following principles:

- Utilising historical traditions as well as innovative local techniques
- Preserving cultural heritage and introducing it to future generations
- Nurturing a mutual understanding between producers and consumers, bringing them closer together
- Returning to the original producer a larger part of the proceeds from the sale of goods and services

Another aim of Farm Food Direct is to support rural populations and employment. Finally, the goods sold under this programme are only made on a small scale, i.e. they are not mass-produced.

In early 2013, approximately 100 farms were involved, and their number is growing. These members are either already making or intend to start making Icelandic food products or handicrafts. While some are still developing their products, others have started to sell them. The opposite page lists the Farm Food Direct members when this book went to press.

The quality seal „First-hand"

In 2009, Farm Food Direct adopted a quality seal as a logo on product packaging. To use this seal, each farm must apply for permission, which is only granted if the farm fulfils both the quality requirements and an assessment by Farm Food Direct. The programme ensures that all necessary production licences have been obtained and that the farmstead and its vicinity are clean and tidy. However, programme members are not obligated to adopt this quality seal, although all of them must maintain the prescribed government licences, like any other production company.

An updated member list and information on product offerings and opening hours can be found at www.beintfrabyli.is and in the brochure The Ideal Holiday, available at most tourist facilities.

Farms selling at the farmstead
Distance selling only

The Southwest
- Háls
- Eystri-Leirárgarðar
- Bjarteyjarsandur

The West and Westfjords
- Háafell
- Ystu-Garðar
- Norðtunga 3
- Örnólfsdalur
- Hundastapi
- Grímsstaðir 2
- Brennistaðir
- Bjarnarhöfn
- Suður-Bár
- Álftavatn
- Foss
- Erpsstaðir
- Staður
- Skálholt, Barðaströnd
- Gemlufalli
- Núpur II
- Höfði
- Bræðrabrekka
- Húsavík
- Háibakki
- Ensku húsin, Langá
- Hverinn, Kleppjárnsreykir

The North
- Dæli
- Gil
- Litla - Hlíð
- Stórhóll
- Laugarmýri
- Holtsel
- Garður
- Höfði 1
- Litli – Dunhagi
- Skjaldarvík
- Syðri-Hagi
- Skarðaborg
- Vogafjós / Vogar
- Hella
- Garður 1
- Lón II
- Tjörn
- Þorfinnsstaðir

The East
- Síreksstaðir
- Egilsstaðir
- Vallarnes
- Fljótsbakki
- Möðrudalur
- Klaustursel
- Blöndubakki
- Aðalból
- Miðhús
- Setberg
- Borg, Skriðdalur

The South
- Seljavellir
- Miðsker
- Smyrlabjörg
- Fossnes
- Langamýri
- Akur, Laugarási
- Efstidalur II
- Skálmholt
- Sólheimar
- Egilsstaðakot
- Seljatunga
- Engi
- Langholtskot
- Hrólfsstaðahellir
- Kaldbakur
- Vestra-Fíflholt
- Lágafell
- Smáratún
- Þorvaldseyri
- Nýibær
- Búland

See map p. 538-539

Hornbjarg
Drangajökull
Bolungarvík
Ísafjörður
Flateyri
Núpur 2
Gemlufall
Höfði
Þingeyri
Arnarfjörður
Bíldudalur
Patreksfjörður
Látrabjarg
Skálholt
Brjánslækur
Staður
Reykhólar
Flatey
HÚNAFLÓI
Bakki
Hólmavík
Drangsnes
Húsavík
Miðhús
Hafnir
Skagaströnd
Sauðárkrókur
Gil
Blönduós
Tjörn
Varmahlíð
Þorfinnsstaðir
Bólstaðarh
Jörfi
Hvammstangi
Dæli
Stórhóll
Ytri-Fagridalur
Þurranes
Laugarbakki
BREIÐAFJÖRÐUR
Brekkulækur
Stykkishólmur
Búðardalur
Vatn
Suður-Bár
Bjarnarhöfn
Erpsstaðir
Hellissandur
Ólafsvík
Grundarfjörður
Snæfells-
jökull
Álftavatn
Foss
Hveravelli
Arnarstapi
Ystu-Garðar
Örnólfsdalur
Glitstaðir
Norðtunga 3
Háafell
LANGJÖKULL
Grímsstaðir II
Hundastapi
Ensku húsin
Kleppjárnsreykir
Leirulækur
Borgarnes
FAXAFLÓI
Bjarteyjarsandur
Neðri-Háls
Háls
Akranes
Geysir
Gullfoss
Efsti-Dalur 2
Mosfellsbær
Vegatunga
Langholtskot
Ásgarður
Reykjavík
Engi
Laxárdalur
Akur
Sólheimar
Fossnes
Keflavík
Ormsstaðir
Skaftholt
Hveragerði
Langamýri
Skálmholt
Hrólfsstaðahellir
Egilsstaðakot
Kaldbakur
Grindavík
Seljatunga
Hvolsvöllur
Smáratún
Vestra-Fíflholt
Búland
Lágafell
Nýibær
Þorvaldse
Önundarhorn
Vestmannaeyjar

Grímsey
Raufarhöfn
Kópasker
Þórshöfn
Lón 2
Húsavík
Bakkafjörður
Grenivík
Skarðaborg
Höfði 1
Dettifoss
Vopnafjörður
Skjaldarvík
Akureyri
Hella
Reykjahlíð
Sírekksstaðir
Straumur
Mývatn
Vogafjós
Garður
Borgarfjörður
Garður I
Holtsel
Blöndubakki
Grænahlíð
Fljótsbakki
Möðrudalur
Egilsstaðir 1
Seyðisfjörður
Setberg
Miðhús
Vallanes
Neskaupstaður
Klaustursel
Eskifjörður
Askja
Aðalból 2
Reyðarfjörður
Borg
Fáskrúðsfjörður
Stöðvarfjörður
Breiðdalsvík
Djúpivogur
VATNAJÖKULL
Miðsker
Seljavellir
Höfn
Smyrlabjörg
Skaftafell
Jökulsárlón
Kirkjubæjarklaustur
Ingólfshöfði
BEINT FRÁ BÝLI

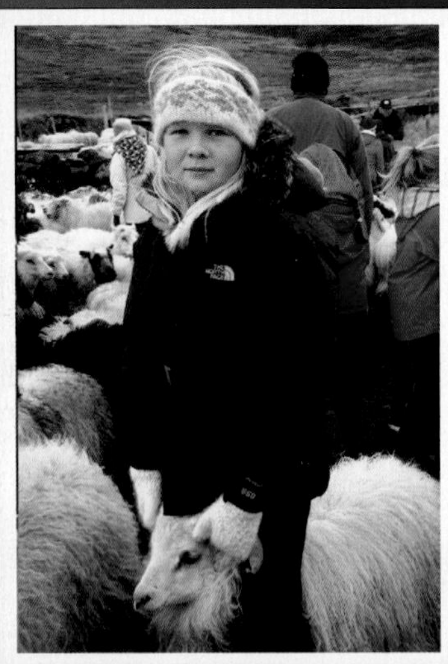

ICELAND
AND AGRICULTURE

There are unique conditions for producing wholesome and unpolluted food products in Iceland and the land is self-sufficient in meat, dairy products, eggs, and to a large extent also in the production of certain vegetables.

At the turn of last century, 73% of Icelanders lived in rural areas and were engaged in farming. By 1940, 32% of the employable population worked in agriculture. At the beginning of the nineties, the percentage had dropped to about 4% and will probably decline even more in coming years.

Icelandic grass is better and more nourishing forage than most other grass grown in Europe. The explanation for this is found in the long hours of daylight during the country´s short, cool summers. These conditions cause grass to grow exceptionally well during bright summers.

Icelandic farmers have relatively large holdings, which include on average 30-50 hectares of cultivated hayfields, the total size of farms often being hundreds of hectares.

One characteristic of Icelandic agriculture is the varied colouring of its native livestock. Horses, cattle and sheep exhibit many colour varieties, no particular variety having been favoured. However, emphasis has been placed on the wool of white sheep being pure white, as this variety is more valuable.

There are about 4000 full-time farmers in Iceland, and their numbers are decreasing, although the number of individuals deriving part of their income from farming is increasing. The majority of Icelandic farmers live on their own land, and holdings have often been in the same family for generations. Most do reasonably well, although very few can be said to belong to a high-income group.

Icelandic food production is based on purity, wholesomeness and sustainability. In Iceland there has been a ban on the use of antibiotics as feed additives and hormone implants as growth promoters, while the use of pesticides and herbicides is in general very restricted.

The move towards organic agriculture in Iceland has not attracted quite the same attention as it has in some other European countries due to the fact that domestic products are already protected by strict regulations.

The Farmers Association of Iceland
Hagatorg 1 107 Reykjavík, tel: 563-0300

www.bondi.is – www.bbl.is

TRADITIONAL ICELANDIC FOOD

Hangikjöt – Smoked lamb

Smoked lamb, leg or shoulder, can be had on the bone, boned or cooked and sliced as luncheon meat. Raw hangikjöt should be boiled in unsalted water at a low heat for about 11/2 hours. In Iceland hangikjöt is traditionally served either hot or cold, with potatoes in a white (béchamel) sauce and green peas (variations according to taste). Popular as a luncheon meat, especially on Icelandic rye pancakes (flatbrauð). A favourite with Icelanders at any time, hangikjöt is traditional Christmas fare.

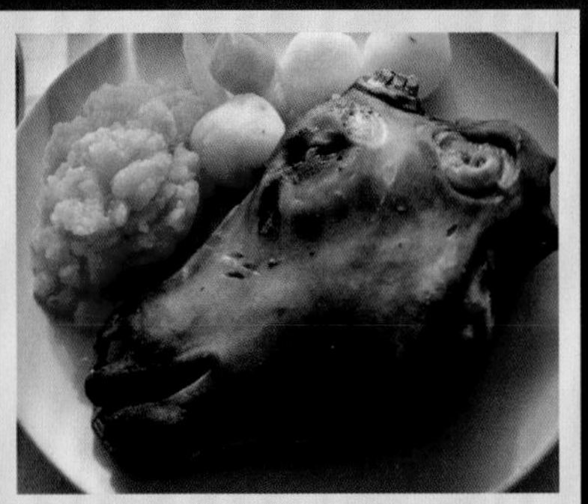

Svið – Singed sheep heads

Singed sheep heads should first be thoroughly rinsed and then boiled in well-salted water for 11/2 to 2 hours. Svið can be eaten hot or cold, with either plain boiled potatoes, mashed potatoes or swede turnips. A popular dish in Iceland, svið are an ideal item for a packed lunch. Also available ready-cooked, tinned or pressed and gelled (sviðasulta).

Saltkjöt – Salted lamb/mutton

Salted lamb/mutton needs to be boiled for 11/2 hours in unsalted water. It is served either hot or cold with potatoes or swede turnips and is frequently accompanied by split pea soup.

Lambakjöt – Lamb

Sheep breeding in Iceland goes back to the time of settlement, which explains the nations high consumption of lamb. In keeping with tradition, sheep are allowed to graze freely in mountain areas over the summer, feeding on the fresh grass and wild herbs that give Icelandic lamb its distinctive flavour.

Slátur – Blood and liver puddings

Slátur is a traditional Icelandic food, prepared every year in the months of September and October when the slaughtering season is at its peak. There are two types of slátur: blóðmör (blood pudding) and lifrarpylsa (liver pudding). Blóðmör consists of sheep´s blood, meal, suet and spices, mixed together and sewn up in sheep stomachs. Lifrarpylsa is quite similar, the difference being that instead of blood minced lamb liver is used. The puddings are boiled for 3 hours and generally served with creamed potatoes or mashed swede turnips. Precooked slátur which only needs to be heated and can also be fried is available at all stores.

Skyr – an Icelandic dairy product

Akin to yogurt and the German Quark, skyr is a dairy product with a very low fat content. Usually eaten with milk or cream, sometimes sprinkled with sugar and often berries when in season; it can of course be eaten plain. Varieties of skyr with added berries and fruits are also available.

Þorramatur – Traditional Icelandic foods

In addition to smoked and salted lamb, singed sheep heads, dried fish and rye pancakes (flatbrauð), traditional Icelandic food includes shark and various pickled foodstuffs, chiefly meat, that have been allowed to stand in whey for 3-4 months. Þorramatur is particularly associated with the period January-March.

Icelandic milk products

Icelandic milk is one of nature's bounties, of which its countrymen are rightly proud. Through the centuries, this delicate product has been handled with respect and now, in recent years, with imaginative flair. The Icelandic dairy industry is subject to strict production control and all products must meet the high level of quality expected by the public.

Nýmjólk
Whole milk, 3.9%
(pasteurised).

Léttmjólk
Low-fat milk, 1.5%
(pasteurised).

Undanrenna
Skimmed
milk, 0.1%
(pasteurised).

Fjörmjólk
Semi-skimmed
milk, 0.3%.
Calcium and
protein-enriched,
fortified with
vitamins A + D
(pasteurised).

Lífræn mjólk
Organic nonhomogenised
Whole milk, 4.1%
(pasteurised).

G-mjólk
Whole milk, 3.9%,
long-life (UHT).

Stoðmjólk
Follow-on milk for
babies aged 6-24
months.

Kókómjólk
Chocolate milk,
low-fat, 2.0%,
long-life (UHT).

Rjómi
Cream, 36%
(pasteurised).

Matreiðslurjómi
Light cream, 15%
(pasteurised).

Kaffirjómi
Coffee cream, 12%,
long-life (UHT).

Sýrður rjómi
Crème fraiche:
5%, 10% or 18%;
spiced/flavoured.

Súrmjólk
Cultured milk,
3.9%.

Mysa
Whey
(pasteurised).

Skyr
Traditional Icelandic
non-fat dairy
product with creamy
texture. Plain or
flavoured with fruit.

Skyr.is
Flavoured non-fat
protein-rich drink,
with creamy texture,
made from the
traditional Icelandic
dairy product skyr.

Skyrdrykkur
A non-fat drink from skyr. No white
sugar, no artificial sweeteners.
Contains agave syrup as
a sweetener. Available with four
different fruit flavours.

Óskajógúrt
Yoghurt – plain,
with fruits or
flavoured, 3.4%,
low-fat 1.3%.

Létt drykkjarjógúrt
Flavoured, low-fat
drinking yoghurt,
1.3%.

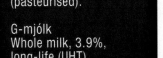

Icelandic meat

Iceland offers a fine variety of meats: lamb, pork, and beef, as well as a limited amount of horse meat and reindeer. Meat display counters are always well stocked with quality fresh meat, handled by top class butchers. Iceland has strict regulations relating to the handling and storage of meat and the use of hormones is strictly forbidden.

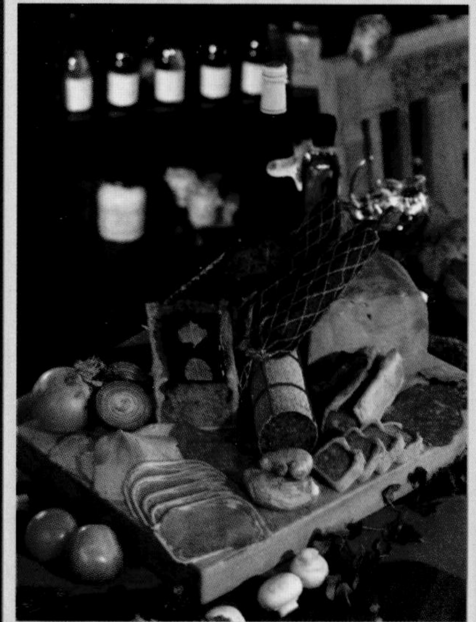

ICELANDIC	ENGLISH
Kjöt	Meat
Lamb	Lamb
Naut	Beef
Svín	Pork
Folald	Horsemeat (Foal)
Hreindýr	Reindeer
Læri	Leg
Lærissneið	Slices of leg
Hryggur	Saddle/rack
Kótilettur/rifjur	Cutlets/chops
Frampartur	Shoulder
Frampartssneiðar	Shoulder slices
Hamborgarhryggur	Smoked saddle of pork
London lamb	Ligthly smoked lamb
Kjötfars	Sausage meat (f. Meatballs)
Kjöthakk	Minced meat
Lundir	Tenderloin
Hryggvöðvi (filé)	Fillet
Smásteik (gúllas)	Boneless stewing meat
Súpukjöt	Pot stew meat (with bones)
Afturhryggsneið (T-bein)	T-bone steak
Hamborgarar	Hamburgers
Rifjasteik	Rib steak
Skinka	Ham
Beikon (flesk)	Bacon
Saltkjöt	Salted meat
Reykt kjöt	Smoked meat
Kálfasneið (schnitzel)	Veal schnitzel
Hangikjöt	Smoked lamb

Geothermal pools

Extensive geothermal activity is one of Iceland's most distinctive features, with geothermal areas covering more of this country than any other. In fact, geothermal heat is known to be present at over 700 Icelandic sites. For geothermal warmth to reach the surface, water needs to bring it there from underneath. For this to happen, precipitation must seep down into the ground to a level at which enough warmth exists for the water to be heated appreciably. The heated water must then find a crack or some other means of leaking to the surface once more.

In general, a certain amount of precipitation does manage to seep through the ground down into bedrock, where the warmth that heats it is thought to stem from magma. Magma is the molten rock that comes up from the earth in volcanic eruptions. In Iceland, an eruption has happened approximately every five years since long before Iceland was settled, meaning that eruptions have occurred about 230 times in the 1100 years since the settlement.

Like ice on a lake, the earth's crust floats on the earth's mantle, and thus has some freedom to move under certain conditions. The force behind such movements is the heat created deep in the earth by the breakdown of radioactive materials. This heat has to be conducted from the earth's core through the mantle and crust before reaching the surface. However, the rock in between is not a sufficiently good heat conductor to be able to bring up the heat that is continuously being created down in the core. Convection currents have thus formed in the mantle to carry this heat upwards. These mantle currents are the cause not only of crust movements and volcanism but also of geothermal activity, since the heat which they carry upwards from the core may warm up water on the way to the surface. The amount of heat thus dissipated is greatest at tectonic plate boundaries, where the plates of the earth's crust meet. One such boundary lies across Iceland and provides cracks for magma to move upwards, heating the nearby crust and in some places creating magma chambers. These magma chambers cause volcanic systems to form at the surface. When a number of such systems are grouped together, they form a volcanic zone. Icelandic volcanism has always been linked to volcanic zones. In a geological sense, hot springs represent leakage from the flowing processes already described, with the leaks occurring because of faults in the bedrock. In fact, if it were not for bedrock fractures and other inconsistencies, the heated water, i.e. geothermal water, would have no upward escape route from its underground system and for the most part would end up flowing laterally until coming out at the bottom of the sea. The most common routes to the top follow dykes and fault lines. Over time, however, the bedrock becomes compressed, which slows down the leakage. Moreover, substances that are dissolved in the water precipitate from it and gradually clog the openings, so that disturbances such as earthquakes are needed in order to maintain geothermal flow to the surface.

Ever since the settlement, Icelanders have used geothermal water for washing and bathing. This is often mentioned in the sagas, with the most famous instance probably being that of Snorri Sturluson at Reykholt, in Borgarfjörður, West Iceland. Snorri, who was a productive saga writer, enjoyed relaxing in the hot water and discussing the topics of the day, just as people still do in hot tubs at modern swimming pools all around Iceland. The island's geothermal activity clearly caught the attention of the early settlers, as they referred to geothermal phenomena in their place names. Thus a great number of the original names include terms such as varm (warm), reyk (smoke/steam) or laug (bathing pool). One of Iceland's first internationally known geologists, Sigurður Þórarinsson, estimated that at least 55 place names, or around 2% of all saga place names, were linked to geothermal activity. The first Icelandic building believed to have been geothermally heated was a house in Mosfellsdalur, just north of Reykjavík. Hot water pipes were laid to it in 1909. However, geothermal steam had been piped a year earlier into a house at Sturlureykir (in the same district as Snorri lived long ago) and used for all of the cooking. Where the people of Reykjavík had traditionally washed their laundry in a hot spring, drilling in 1928 brought up about 15 litres of water per second at 94°C, enough to operate a geothermal heating utility in the growing city. Although in 1930 this utility served only the national hospital, a school and about 60 homes, further developments were rapid. Today, no other nation uses geothermal water for such a large proportion of its energy needs as Iceland, and most people nowadays could not do without geothermal energy in their daily lives.

At several places in Iceland, it so happens that geothermal water collects naturally at comfortable temperatures for bathing. In other places, people have come to nature's assistance to obtain the right temperatures and amount of water. Finally, in modern times many special swimming pools, hot tubs, etc. have been constructed. Therefore, it is often difficult to distinguish which pools are natural and which are not. For instance, there was no geothermal activity at the surface when construction started on the Blue Lagoon. Its water is pumped up out of drill holes and the surroundings are entirely designed by people. Iceland's best-known natural bathing springs include the following:

The Sturlungs' spring, Hnappadalur

(6452174-2217024)

From the route through Hnappadalur valley, take the road which leads west to Rauðháls ridge and then between the lava fields of Rauðhálsahraun and Gullborgarhraun to Syðri-Rauðamelur farm. The farmstead is somewhat south of Syðri-Rauðamelskúla hill (154 m), and the warm spring is in a flat area slightly east of the hill. This pool, which was mentioned in the Saga of the Sturlungs, is built of turf and filled by mineral water at 45°C. Although the water is not always as clear as the most finicky would like, it is wonderfully soothing. The Saga mentions that a certain Aron Hjörleifsson enjoyed these waters in 1222. The spring is located a few hundred metres east of Syðri-Rauðamelur, and a road leads to a drill hole 20-30 metres north of the spring. The pool temperature is generally around 41°C.

Landbrot spring (6449933-2219110)

By Skjálg farm in Hnappadalur valley, at more or less the shortest point between the Rauðhálsahraun and Eldborgarhraun lava fields, a road turns off west past the abandoned farm of Landbrot. Going south, you will find a tiny but very comfortable warm pool just north of Eldborgarhraun. While the water is more than hot enough, at about 42°C, there is hardly space for more than two people.

Hella spring, Vatnsfjörður (6534629-2329571)

Nestled picturesquely below cliffs by the seashore, this pool is located below the old farmstead of Hella, right by Flókalundur. Stones have been cemented together to create a pool which is 4 x 3 m in size and 50-70 cm deep. The water comes from a borehole up on the cliff, close to the older location of the pool, and keeps a temperature of around 38°C.

Grjótagjá (6537581-1652974)

The track here from National Road No. 1, a distance of only two kilometres, is passable for any kind of car. While the pool setting is fabulous, under huge blocks of barren lava, the pure groundwater here has remained too hot to enter since the last period of local volcanic activity, in 1975 to 1984. However, the temperature is gradually returning to a comfortable level. The pool is divided naturally into two chambers, with separate entrances, so men can go in on one side and women on the other, changing clothes inside and keeping them dry on the clean rock surfaces.

Warm stream below Klambragil

(6402897-2113346)

On the edge of the Hellisheiði moor, Klambragil gully begins at Molddalahnúkar peaks and leads towards Hveragerði village. One of the most convenient ways to reach it is to turn off National Road No. 1 by the hut on Hellisheiði. Drive across the small river Hengladalsá just beside the lava field, and continue following the vehicle track to the peaks, which are quite prominent in fair weather. Boiling-hot springs emerge here and there in the gully, adding to the considerable flow of the stream. At the point where the stream bends, a piled-up dam has created a pool with space for up to ten people. Another way to get there is to hike up east of where Djúpagil gully cuts down through the east edge of Hellisheiði. In this case, go through Hveragerði village and past the horse stabling area as far as vehicles can go. Then you cross Hengladalsá river, walk up the Rjúpnabrekkur slopes over the ridge, and descend into Reykjadalur valley, all of which makes for a wonderful hike. The upper part of the valley is divided by Ölkelduhnjúkur peak, with a stream flowing along each side of it. While the eastern stream is only 8°C, the western one is around 70°C. Since the latter flows out of Klambragil gully, the bathing place is generally named after it. The two small streams merge to create one stream which carries a lot of water (some 180 l/sec), and normally measures around 35-40°C. However, the temperature and thus the ideal bathing location can be expected to vary, as these factors are partly influenced by the seasons and the weather. Because the banks are often marshy and therefore sensitive to disturbance, they have been badly damaged in many places by visiting humans and livestock. The water nonetheless remains almost entirely clear, since the finest material immediately gets washed downstream, although some algae does grow on the bottom and along the banks. In spite of previous efforts to deepen bathing pools in the gravelly area below where the small streams join, sediment has virtually filled them up again. The water thus tends to be too shallow for sitting mostly submerged, and it is necessary to keep up efforts to maintain the existing pools. Note that there are no facilities for changing clothes, and nowhere to put them except the banks.

Geothermal streams in Vonarskarð

(6441451-1752887)

In Vonarskarð pass, the bacteria growing on the bed of one geothermal stream make it pink, while a somewhat cooler stream runs into it which also contains some algae. A dam has been piled across the cooler one, just below a small waterfall, and there is another dam below where the two streams join. The water depth hardly reaches half a metre anywhere, however, and these pools will probably fill with sediment during every spring thaw and require some annual maintenance. The one below the waterfall is triangular, with a width of 3 m, a length of 2 m and a temperature of about 37°C.

Laugafell pools (6501669-1819912 and 6501648-1819920)

The landmarks for this site are Laugafell and Laugafellshnjúkur (879 and 997 m), two hyaloclastite mountains located northeast of Hofsjökull glacier, in the highlands above the Eyjafjörður area. The pools associated with Laugafell are situated on a ridge to its northwest. Geothermal springs of up to approximately 50°C feed the three main pools, which in turn feed a warm stream. The huts at Laugafell belong to the Akureyri Touring Club. Northwest of the oldest hut, a shallow depression in the barren, hard ground is fed by a warm spring underneath. This depression is some two metres in length, and wide enough for the average person to be covered by water when lying down. Some people associate this pool with a woman named Þórunn, who according to legend had the depression dug. She is supposed to have brought her household here from the Eyjafjörður area to escape the Black Death, though in fact she was not born until nearly a century after the Black Death came to plague the Icelanders. Stones and turf have been piled up to create the main pool, which measures about 16.5 x 7.2 m. Its depth ranges from 0.4 m at one end to 1.5 m at the point of drainage. Since 50-70 people can bathe at the same time, this pool's size adds to its popularity. Also, its 5 litres per second of 36°C water, mostly coming from one edge of the bank, never cloud up with dirt from the bottom.

Landmannalaugar (6359516-1903713)

These springs emerge from below the towering lava field named after them, Laugahraun. A number of warm and cool springs collect in a tranquil stream that you can relax and even swim in, close to the huts belonging to the Icelandic Touring Association. The pool itself is dammed by rocks, with hot water coming from springs both in the bottom and the bank above. While temperatures of up to 41°C are found, they are lower farther from the geothermal inflow. The pool has a gravel bed and considerable algal growth.

Strútslaug (6352504-1856677)

The river Hólmsá runs out of two gullies southeast of Torfajökull glacier. Along the river's upper section, the flatter land known as Hólmsárbotnar has patches of grass and several geothermal springs. According to a folk tale, a ram (hrútur) drowned at the southernmost spring, which is therefore named Hrútslaug. Going up Hólmsárbotnar past the north end of Hólmsárlón lake will bring you to the largest hot spring, which is known variously as Hólmsárbotnahver, Hitulaug or Strútslaug. The carbonated water has deposited quite a lot of minerals below the spring. The walk here from the hut near Strútur mountain takes about one and a half hours. Located up on the river bank, the pool is divided in two by a piled wall, so that one part measures 6 x 6 m and the other 8.5 x 5 m. The greatest depths of the two sections are about 0.5 and 0.6 m and their temperatures are 43°C and 37°C. Much of the area around the spring stays wet, so that algae and bacteria flourish. The pool itself contains a lot of microorganisms, in addition to the fine bottom material which gets stirred up during bathing.

Hveravellir pool, Kjölur (6451974-1933228)

The geothermal field just southeast of today's weather observation station is not very large. On the other hand, it is thought to be over 6,600 years old. Even though earthquakes are generally needed for the periodic renewal of hot spring activity, as discussed earlier, some of the larger springs here have not changed much over the past few centuries. The ones that are currently active are mostly found on or by two mounds of mineral precipitates. Between these mounds, the ground is lower and marshy. However, some of the hot springs are situated in gravelly or marshy areas outside of the two mounds. While the hot springs total a few dozen, not all are large. About twenty of them are prominent, and some have colourful Icelandic names. Hveravellir's wide variety of geothermal features includes some of Iceland's most beautiful hot springs. These have been little disturbed by humans and, fortunately, scarcely exploited for energy, although hot water has been tapped for the mountain hut, swimming pool and the house for weather observation personnel. The mountain hut, which is east of the geothermal field, was built by the Icelandic Touring Association in 1938. Despite a change in ownership, it is still standing there, just north of the comfortably warm swimming pool. Created in 1950 by piling stones on two sides, this pool receives its hot water from the geothermal field and allows you to relax in comfort at about 630 m above sea level.

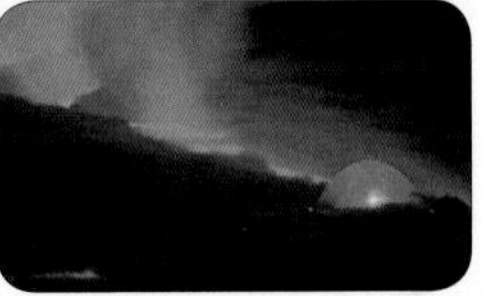

ICELANDIC LAVA CAVES

In Iceland's lava fields, which cover about 11% of the country, there are about 600 known caves. Records tell of people having entered such caves before the year 1000. Surtshellir cave (note that hellir in any Icelandic name below means „cave") was in fact the first lava cave on earth to be mapped, as it was surveyed by the well-known Icelandic natural scientists Eggert Ólafsson and Bjarni Pálsson in 1756. As of 1970, however, fewer than 20 lava caves were known to exist in Iceland. This changed abruptly, because in 1979 the Icelandic speleologist Björn Hróarsson began to seek out, explore and study lava caves. In 1989, he founded the Icelandic Speleological Society and in 1990 published his book Hraunhellar á Íslandi (Lava Caves in Iceland), which described 150 lava caves. The work of the "cavemen" in the Icelandic Speleological Society has since been extremely successful and led to the discovery of a large number of lava caves, as evidenced by Björn Hróarsson's more recent book of 2006, Íslenskir hellar (Icelandic Caves), which lists about 520 lava caves. Thus, about 500 caves were discovered in the last quarter century, stretching to a total length of around 100 kilometres.

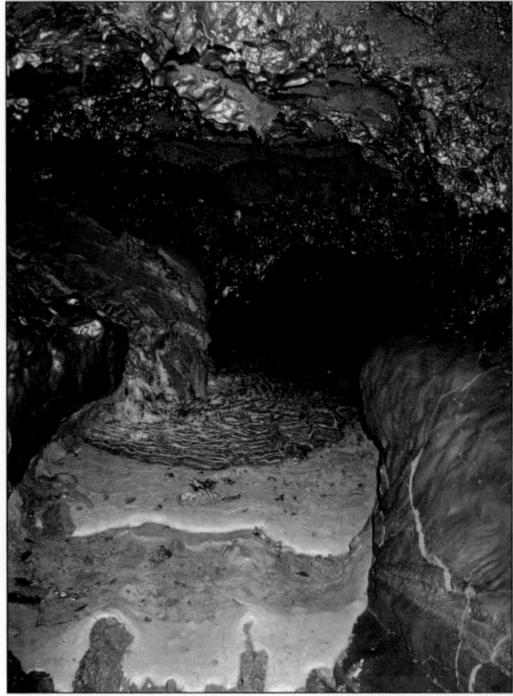

WHAT IS A LAVA CAVE?

There are many ways to define a lava cave, with no one definition being more correct than the others. A completely dark cavity in volcanic rock is one of the definitions used by lava cave experts in recent years. According to it, any hollow space in the lava not reached by any light would be called a lava cave. Others use a longer definition, requiring the hollow space both to be longer than 20 metres and passable to human beings in order to be called a lava cave. Lava caves are divided into a number of categories depending on how they were formed: lava tube caves, craters, blister caves, fissure caves, rootless vent caves, sea caves, erosional caves and, finally, man-made caves.

When we refer to the length of a cave, we mean the total cave length, that is, the length of the main passage together with the lengths of any side passages. The length of the main cavern alone is called the main passage length. Thus, in caves which have many long side passages there is a considerable difference between the total cave length and the main passage length. Where one cave begins and another ends is frequently a topic of debate! What makes a cave, where should the line be drawn between two caves in the same lava tube, and what constitutes a cave system? While it is difficult to give a definitive answer to these questions, certain points should be kept in mind. For instance, a cave is considered the same even if there are several openings where the roof has caved in. Also, a cave can be a single cave without being completely passable everywhere for a person remaining underground. Similarly, there do not need to be accessible connections between all parts of a single cave, so that the Icelandic caves named Hulduhellir, Stefánshellir and Surtshellir are in fact considered as one cave even though it is not possible to travel between them and Hulduhellir is entirely inaccessible. When referring to a cave's height, we mean the ceiling height, i.e. from floor to ceiling. The vertical depth of a cave, in contrast, refers to the difference between the altitudes of the cave floor at each end. Once the cave's depth and length are clear, it becomes possible to calculate its slope

The formation of lava caves

Magma from a volcanic eruption often flows into defined channels and tends to form tunnels through the spreading lava field. When the molten lava inside a tunnel runs out and leaves it empty at the end of an eruption, provided that the tunnel remains hollow while cooling and hardening, a lava tube forms. To describe these processes more exactly, we can say that when a lava stream follows the same course for some distance, it generally forms first a channel, open to the sky, and farther on a tunnel. Under the cover of lava that has already stiffened over the tunnel and may later become fairly smooth and passable for walkers, called pahoehoe lava, the molten stream underneath can flow long distances. Farther on, the molten lava is likely to start coming up here and there through openings to the surface, from where it flows in thin streams that pile together when stiffening and are then called ropy lava. When magma from the eruption stops feeding a tunnel, the tunnel empties to form a chamber. If the roof of this chamber is strong enough to hold itself up after cooling, this chamber will remain as a cave. However, in order for the chamber to become hollow in the first place, the slope of the tunnel must be steep enough for the lava left in it to run down the passage after fresh lava from behind stops pushing it. Flow in the tunnel stops when either the volcanic activity ends or the stream finds another passage. When new lava stops feeding into a tunnel with little slope and no longer pushes the previous lava forward, the lava present will solidify, filling the tunnel and leaving either no cave or one partly filled with lava, as many actually are. Moreover, the roof may be so weak that it collapses to some extent, leaving no cave but rather piles of fallen rubble in the lava channel. The viscosity of the lava, the quantity and speed of its flow and the landscape it crosses are also important in determining whether a lava cave forms.

Conservation

Lava caves are among Iceland's most vulnerable natural features. Damage to them cannot be taken back, but is permanent and irreparable. We need to bear in mind that man alone destroys caves; if no one ever visited them, they would generally remain unchanged and undamaged for thousands of years, or even hundreds of thousands, like many of Korea's largest caves.

Three approaches probably matter most for conserving lava caves. First of all, education; second, directing caving trips to caves which can tolerate the traffic; and third, closing off the most vulnerable caves to any traffic. Education and knowledge about the world of caves is extremely important for protecting them. The goal of visitors is and always must be to leave no traces behind. Nothing may be left except perhaps footprints, nothing may be taken away but photographs, and nothing may be broken. On the other hand, there

are numerous caves which can withstand traffic well, even the passage of whole groups, so long as the proper attitude, a good tour guide and adequate illumination are involved.

Caves are also threatened by the construction of power plants and roads. When lava fields are flooded, as by hydropower reservoirs, any caves there will be lost forever. An absolute demand must be that any caves in the lava fields be studied before being flooded, so as not to show disrespect of both nature and science. Seeing lava fields disappear under the reservoir of Hágöngumiðlun was painful, and the parties involved made no attempt to carry out speleological research. Not only must this neglect of research never be repeated, but other lava fields need protection from flooding. Lava fields and everything they contain are by nature too remarkable to destroy.

In a country where lava covers about 11% of the surface area, it is hardly possible to avoid routing any roads over lava fields, though it should be avoided insofar as possible. Wherever roads are built over lava, speleological research should be conducted on the intended route so that caves in the area can be left unharmed. Nowadays, environmental impact assessments are usually conducted before laying roads, but caves are generally not taken into consideration. This must change. For example, the cave Búri in Leitahraun was discovered on 7 May 2005, constituting one of the greatest cave discoveries in Iceland for centuries. Around the same time, a lava cave

was discovered on the island of Jeju, South Korea. That cave was named Yongchon and is about 2,450 metres long. Like Búri, it is one of the most important lava caves in its home country. As befits civilized societies, societies which take an interest in their natural treasures, Yongchon cave was sealed off within a week of being found. Two sturdy gates were erected at the entrance, with about five metres in between that were monitored by motion sensors directly connected to the nearest police station. All traffic in the cave would have to follow set rules. Within a few months of the discovery, books and pamphlets were published to introduce the cave to the public as well as the international scientific community. Here in Iceland, where nature conservation is unfortunately decades behind the standard in most other countries, nothing was done about the discovery of Búri.

Caring for caves

Most cave formations are very delicate, often unable to bear even the slightest touch without breaking. Usually, caves are completely untouched when discovered, even if five

Icelandic Lava Caves

or ten thousand years have passed since they were formed. A cave's climate stays stable, with similar temperature and humidity year-round, along with silence and an absence of light and life, so that there is almost no erosion. Caves have therefore generally remained unchanged for millennia, until the first humans arrive. As soon as the first rays of light cut through the hitherto permanent darkness, danger threatens.

There has been a disgraceful lack of good conduct in Icelandic lava caves. Throughout much of the twentieth century, most known caves were severely damaged, with lava formations being broken and removed and all sorts of rubbish left behind.

Raufarhólshellir was sheared of its beautiful formations in the first decades of the twentieth century. Stefánshellir was divested of its stalactites and lava straws soon after news of its location got out in the middle of the century. Víðgelmir was damaged and large amounts of trash left there in the 1940s and 1950s. The bones in Surtshellir, thousands of years old, disappeared. Similar stories can be told of most other caves that were known by around the middle of the twentieth century. Waste such as batteries, flares, plastic bags and bottles, clothing, string and the packaging from film, chocolate or drinks were often thrown aside on the spot.

Stalactites and other lava formations in the caves were broken off and removed, only to crumble and gather dust in people's homes, largely forgotten.

Spelunking equipment

Exploring caves rarely requires much special equipment. Illumination is the most important consideration. Two good lights are a must, as well as extra batteries. The light used must enable the spelunker to see well enough to avoid damaging the cave, and the energy source must be sufficient to provide full strength for the entire trip. While either good electric torches or diode lights will suffice, one has to have a backup light along in any case. Sufficient illumination is crucial for not damaging the cave. No open flame must ever be lit in caves, nor any flares or other light sources which cause pollution.

Helmets are very beneficial, for example bicycle helmets. The lack of erosion in caves means that nothing has blunted the edges of stones which have fallen from the ceiling. Bumping into them without a helmet can thus be very painful.

Fortunately, however, material very rarely collapses from a cave ceiling. Mostly, this happens during the first years after the cave is formed, while the lava is still cooling enough to crack and buckle, causing collapses which later become highly unlikely. The temperature in many Icelandic caves is about freezing or up to one to three degrees Celsius. In larger caves it is generally slightly warmer deep in the cave. As long as people keep moving, they tend not to feel the cold much since the air is completely still, but the chill sinks in when sweaty spelunkers sit down for a moment. Also, water is usually leaking from the cave ceiling. Even when the sun is shining brightly overhead and it has not rained for days or weeks, there will still be a steady drip inside the cave. For these reasons, spelunkers must protect themselves from wet as well as cold.

Since clothing often gets soiled and torn when exploring caves, it is wise not to wear expensive garments. It is also advisable to avoid wearing fabrics such as loose wool, which is likely to leave fibres behind in the cave. Gloves or mittens are necessary, but again woollen mittens are not a good choice. Leather or lined rubber gloves are well suited for spelunking.

Strong footwear is important because it is difficult to walk around on sharp, uneven stones. Fairly flexible hiking boots work best. If there is water in the cave, though, rubber boots may well be a better choice. Where ice covers the cave floor, it is often quite slippery, calling for some sort of spikes. In some cases it is necessary to use ropes or ladders to enter and explore the cave. Aluminium or cable ladders will manage in most cases, although some caves require a complete rappelling kit. In any case, a proper attitude towards nature is the most important factor in every cave trip. To leave the cave without a trace is the highest aim of any spelunker.

Dear Traveller

Iceland is unique, with incredible sights to please the eye and nourish the soul. On the other hand, not everyone sees and experiences this island in the same way. The psychic Erla Stefánsdóttir has for instance long been renowned among Icelanders for her visions, since she sees and feels wavelengths which reach far beyond what ordinary human eyes are capable of. We the editors of Iceland Road Atlas were thus curious to know how Erla views our landscape and wanted to give you, our Atlas readers, a chance to partake in this view, for your enlightenment and enjoyment.

Erla Stefánsdóttir

ERLA STEFÁNSDÓTTIR

Dear traveller,

On my journeys around Iceland, I have drawn this country's major energy lines onto maps. Most energy lines are either varying frequencies of yellow, or else violet or blue. The difference between such lines is that the blue ones, if they flow through a place we stay, affect how likely we are to perceive anyone moving between distinct worlds, whereas the violet ones flow between vegetation zones and the elf world, and the yellow ones provide unbelievable energy in many dimensions. If you should be planning to travel around the Ring Road by car, I advise you to drive slowly. Stop here and there, using not only your physical body but also your emotions, and look with your heart too. The earth's energy veil consists at once of the radiation and channels of the life force.

Such energy pathways exist in every dimension, as does indeed all of nature, which is full of life in countless forms, active at various frequencies. Iceland's energy is unique, matched in very few other places. Whether you are heading west or north, south or east, take care to notice especially the mountains, rivers, waterfalls, hay fields and forests. Try comparing two different mountains, or else different valleys or fjords, or lakes or rivers. You can also do special exercises for your senses of feeling, sight and hearing.

ICELAND'S ENERGY CENTRE

The biggest, most powerful energy lines in this country flow through Hofsjökull glacier, which is located in the middle of the island and is its primary energy centre. These lines connect the courses of energy and development for all conscious beings inhabiting Iceland. In addition, these energy lines are the divinity's means of connecting with creation - pathways which give us joy and strength while we explore the island. It is certainly better to return from your trip full of energy and happiness than exhausted. It is possible to read more about energy centres in my book Lífssýn mín ("My vision of life"), which was published in Icelandic in 2003. As emissions of and channels for the life force, energy paths form a grid over the entire earth, doing so in every world, from the physical up to the spiritual world, allowing us to say that the earth's energy system is reflected in God's embrace.

EARTH'S ENERGY LINES

The Chinese call these lines dragon paths and the Australian Aborigines song lines, while the English language also refers to them as ley or force lines. Energy lines are like currents of light flowing within every country as well as between countries. The greatest light currents may be over a hundred metres in height or breadth, whereas the smallest barely reach our ankles and resemble the blue trails left over the centuries by man's domestic animals.

While the largest and brightest energy flows are those between the world's energy centres, there are also very strong pathways between the energy centres inside each country. Thus, not only are there seven energy centres on the earth as a whole, but each country has its own particular seven energy centres.

EXPERIENCE FOR YOURSELF

You should definitely not try to rush through Iceland's largest and strongest life currents in one summer, since you must allow yourself enough time to experience their power. Take at least one month to make the most of each and every one, applying your mind as well as your feelings in many dimensions. Reflect upon your colours and the names of your centres in many worlds, because you will never appreciate their glory and sanctity by hurrying up that challenging slope in the physical realm alone. Instead, pause for a while; close your eyes. By daydreaming, you will bring your inner sight and hearing to play.

Akureyri's hidden worlds - the Angel City of Akureyri

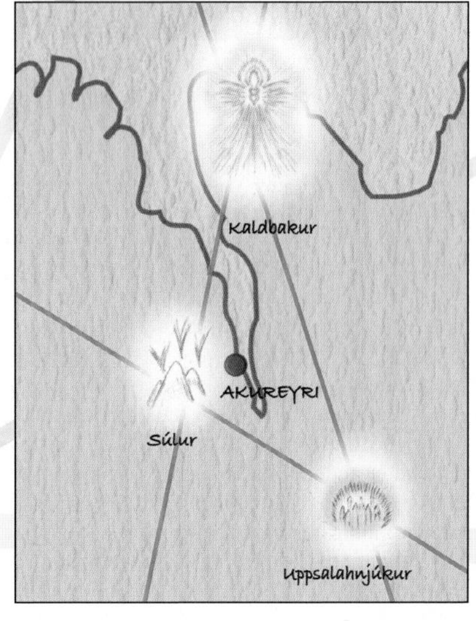

EARTH ENERGY

All types of life are imbued with a life force which has the flow and sound of a beautiful symphony and is the innate form of matter. Mother Earth is a living being, endowed with strength, awareness and life. The circulatory system or energy lines of earth are like a living light that flows between energy points. Whether such energy lines are called ley lines, dragon paths or song lines, they make up a densely woven grid extending throughout the world and linking together major and minor energy centres, vegetation zones and elf worlds. Moreover, these lines lend us, as the earth's inhabitants, power and joy. Iceland itself has seven energy centres, over which the island's brightest mountain gods tower majestically. Hofsjökull glacier is the primary centre, emitting energy currents which have 12 frequencies and range from blue water lines in the highest spheres of the material world and lowest spheres of the mental world, up to yellow lines in the highest spheres of the intuitive world. These currents of light connect the outposts of the island, guarded by those natural beings which are represented in the official Icelandic emblem. To the west is Snæfellsjökull, to the east Snæfell, to the north Kaldbakur, and to the south Mýrdalsjökull, not to mention the Queen of Icelandic Mountains, Herðubreið, and their prince, Hlöðufell.

ENERGY RELATED TO EYJAFJÖRÐUR

The energy line that flows directly north from Hofsjökull glacier fills Eyjafjörður with light and is directed towards Kaldbakur mountain, that is, towards the Goddess who grants us a promise of hope and sanctity. In general, Eyjafjörður's mountains and vegetation are inhabited by Iceland's gentlest supernatural beings: elves, hidden people, dwarves, gnomes, faeries and nymphs. The energy line to Kaldbakur is one of Iceland's strongest, so we should concentrate our inner consciousness on it and relish it. Eyjafjörður is a realm of supernatural beings, an area of true springtime and bliss even during the frosty northerlies of winter. The peaks of Súlur, Kaldbakur and Uppsalahnjúkur transmit soft violet rays one to another, forming a triangle of currents around Akureyri.

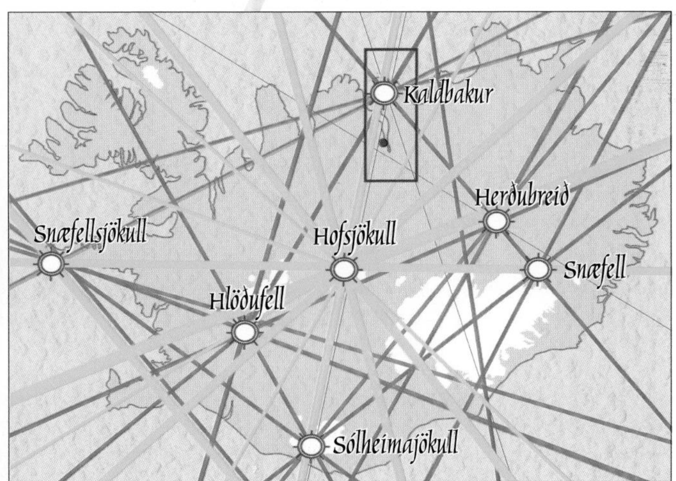

It is interesting to recall that Helgi the Lean, one of the original settlers of Iceland and a protector of this community, believed in the god Thor, whose "heaven" was Uppsalir (included in the name Uppsalahnjúkur). Many travellers make their way to Akureyri and could take advantage of a very interesting map of the "hidden worlds" of Akureyri, which is based on Erla's visions and philosophy and was published by Katrín Jónsdóttir. The Iceland Road Atlas has graciously received permission to publish three of the map's sixteen pages. If you are interested in seeing more of the map, please check in the tourist shops and the Eymundsson bookshop in Akureyri, or at the shops Betra Líf and Gjafir Jarðar in Reykjavík.

Three elf habitations on Vaðlaheiði heath

Sensing the past in the present

By fantasising, we can look forwards and backwards in time and have fun time-travelling around the fjord and valleys of Eyjafjörður, with its churches existing variously in the present or past. They are connected by bands of light which illuminate them like lighthouses, helping them impart their histories of varying length. Some churches date as far back as 1000 or even earlier, since many were built on the ruins of old pagan temples, as is often the case in Iceland. The churches need not be used much today for one to be able to enter and feel the presence of those previously occupying them in happiness or sorrow. The stillness communicates the proper tones, together with other indications of the nation's religious culture. Icelanders of earlier times had the talent of creating a path of light by knocking stones together into cairns, even though it was many kilometres between such cairns. Their horses were then capable of following such a path to the next farm, despite blizzards that blinded people.

ELF VILLAGES

Opposite Akureyri, three villages may be observed on the lower slopes of Vaðlaheiði. Elves live in one, hidden people in another, and a cluster of ten or twelve houses which I believe to represent previous human habitations appears above Festarklettur rock, which is east of and inland from the fjord. The ancient assembly site Vaðlaþing lies above Festarklettur, including a stone circle with sailcloth or skins stretched over it for a roof. Even today one can discern ships of different sizes there, indicating that the fjord once reached farther south, but has since filled with sediment through the ages. Thus it is hardly surprising that sharp-eyed Akureyri residents sometimes notice lights in windows across the fjord, in places without any houses in the physical world.

ORIGINAL EYJAFJÖRÐUR SETTLERS

Pioneers coming from Norway, like Helgi the Lean and his wife, Þórunn Hyrna, would clearly have entered this fjord from the north. The sagas report that they lived near Sólarfjall mountain and even on Hrísey island for their first year here, but later established the farm of Kristnes. Many of those moving here later stopped first at the medieval trading post of Gásir, which was a good place to moor ships and was close to fishing grounds. At Gásir I have seen visions which seem to be up to 1500 years old, involving people who are not Scandinavian, but have darker skin and stiff hair.

An elf residence on Vaðlaheiði

The colours of Akureyri's guardian angel are shades of blue-green, glistening with green and gold energy. These colours reveal the angel as harmonising with Iceland's fertility goddess.

Mount Kaldbakur, silvery blue-green, with thin violet-pink rays, is one of Iceland's greatest energy centres. In the green force emitted, elves and supernatural beings dance in the glow of this mountain goddess. You might meditate on and sound out green notes through the pendant on your necklace, so as to achieve divine harmony.

Our surrounding wealth

The hidden worlds are an inner revelation of nature. Nature, like all creation, is made up of countless spheres, since the creator of all controls everything around us. It is ours to enjoy this wealth, noting how it is truth itself and how you, I, every one of us and all of Iceland, nature and indeed the entire earth are united. Every backyard contains tree sprites, flower fairies, and grass elves, in addition to the inhabitants of possible cliffs, and little gnomes in small houses that look like stones. Walk slowly in the vicinity of your home - you and your family are not the only ones living there!

Tiny grass elves are a joy to see waking up in the spring as the grass turns green. After growing along with the grass, they fall asleep once again in autumn.

Jolly dwarves stay by the University of Akureyri, wearing cheerfully coloured clothes. They smile and wave when shown attention.

Of all the beings around us, the hidden people resemble us most. Usually they dress like 19TH - century Icelanders.

The fertility goddess of Iceland sends off her nymphs to places which are promising for vegetation. Here is one such nymph.

Gnomes are very small, perhaps up to 10 cm tall. Their houses are ornamented and they save their baby cradles and high chairs because upon reaching old age, they will start all over again.

Instructions for the General Public Regarding Natural Disaster in Iceland

Text Color: Green = Precautions – Red = Preventive response

General Instructions

Preventive measures are an important part of dealing with danger

In homes and workplaces, individuals should talk about possible dangers, discuss safety measures, locate exits and know where safety equipment is kept. Knowledge of first aid is very practical and can save lives. The Icelandic Red Cross gives first aid courses for the general public.

You should know how to operate safety equipment.

In homes and in workplaces safety equipment should include:

- Fire extinguisher.
- Smoke detectors.
- Safety ladder or rope to evacuate high buildings.
- Tools such as a hammer, a saw, a screwdriver, an ax, a wrench and a crowbar.

Keep the following equipment in an emergency kit where everyone can find it:

- First-aid medical kit.
- Flashlight.
- Radio with batteries.
- First-aid instruction manual.
- List of important telephone numbers (relatives, service providers etc.).
- Your own emergency plan for the family/ workplace.

Discuss and practice actions to be taken during an emergency situation (emergency plan). Let children participate so they will be prepared to respond appropriately.

General precautions if a dangerous situation develops:

Those who are in or near a town or village when a dangerous situation develops should report to the nearest emergency aid centre or contact the police. Emergency aid centres (Fjöldahjálparstöð) are identified by the logos (see picture) of the Red Cross (Rauði kross Íslands) and the Civil Protection (Almanna-varnir).

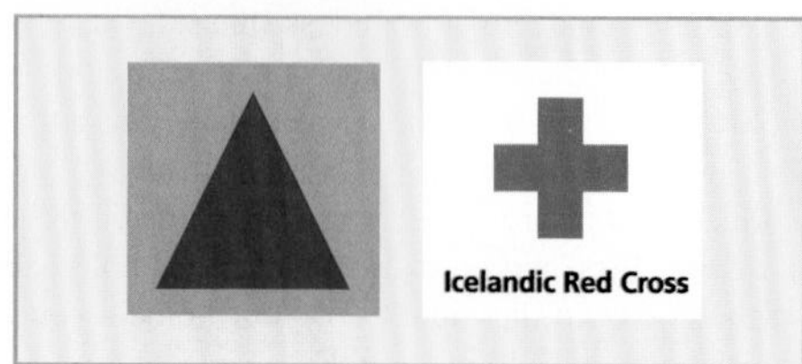

- When an emergency is declared or a dangerous situation develops a SMS message will be sent to connected mobile phones in areas at risk with information and/or instructions of actions.
- If a dangerous situation develops, it is important that families gather together to coordinate their actions.
- If you evacuate your home, keep in mind that emergency aid centers are usually located in schools.
- If an emergency aid center is not nearby, contact the police (112) and notify them of your whereabouts.

Radio FM and LW

Announcements from the Civil Protection are sent to the State Radio (FM and LW) and TV as well as other media. Listen to the radio for announcements and news, and follow any instructions given.

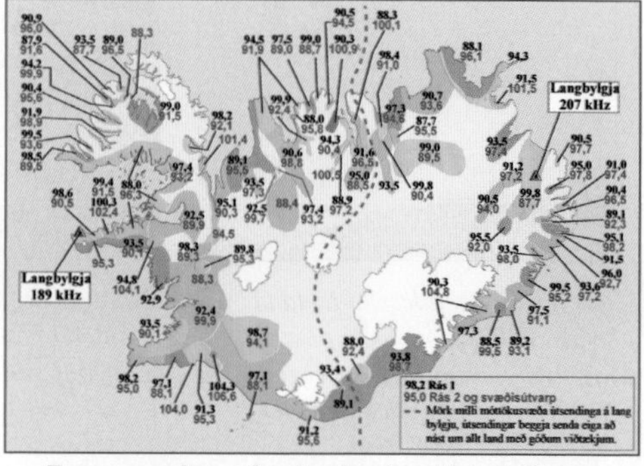

Frequencies of principal radio stations

- Report accidents and request assistance by calling **Emergency alert at 112.** • If you need assistance and the telephones do not work, and you have no other means of communication, put a cloth or a flag out of a window, or at some other noticeable location, outside the house. In case of emergency, flags or signals are a request for assistance.
- Do not use the telephone except for emergency purposes. Keep conversations to an absolute minimum or use text messages, twitter or facebook.
- Announcements from the Civil Protection are sent to the State Radio and TV as well as other media.

If in need for further information after a disaster, contact your Embassy, Consulate, Travel Agency or Tourist Information Centre. If those are not available, contact the Police at Emergency alert 112 or a helpful native.

Volcanic eruptions

Volcanic eruptions can begin without warning, but they are usually preceded by earthquakes that can be detected by seismograph. Eruptions can cause danger by lava flow and ash fall. The ash from a single eruption can fall throughout the country depending upon the weather. The falling ash can be unsafe and hazardous because of poisonous gases and materials. It especially poses a threat to animals. Clouds of ash can cause disturbances to air traffic. Always wear a helmet in the vicinity of eruptions.

- Avoid areas where ash is falling, because of the danger of lightning, and keep in mind that the falling ash may fall so densely as to block out sunlight. If hit by falling ash, take the shortest way out by moving perpendicular to the direction of the wind.
- Wear a dust mask or keep a wet cloth over your nostrils and mouth.
- Stay where the wind blows and do not go into low areas were gas can accumulate. The gas is a lethal poison, which in most cases has no smell and is difficult to detect.
- Shut windows in the path of the eruption and prevent fallen ash from entering the house through the chimney.

Lightning

Lightning is not common in Iceland and because of that people are often not prepared to protect themselves from the danger it poses. If a thunderstorm with lightning passes over, take the following precautions:

Outdoors:

- Avoid water, open and high areas. If you take refuge in a vehicle, keep the doors and window shut. Do not use radio-telephones or other telecommunications equipment.
- Avoid metallic objects which may conduct electricity such as power lines, fences, engines, machines etc.

Dangerous places include small huts, or shelters and areas close to trees. Seek shelter, if possible, in larger buildings or in vehicles

If you think lightning will strike near you, you should:

- Crouch with your feet together. Cover your ears with your hands to reduce the risk of hearing damage.
- Keep at least 5 meters away from the next person.

Indoors:

- Avoid water. Keep away from the buildings outside doors, windows and plumbing.
- Do not use telephones or headphones.
- Keep away from appliances, such as computers, power tools and television sets. Avoid metallic objects which may conduct electricity. Also keep away from antennas.

Electricity does not remain in persons hit by lightning, so necessary assistance can be rendered immediately. Apply first aid and call the Emergency Service 112.

www.almannavarnir.is

Civil Protection Natural Disaster

Instructions for the general public regarding natural disaster in Iceland

Avalanches

The Icelandic Meteorological Office and meteorological observers monitor the probability of avalanches near inhabited areas. If there is a danger of an avalanche, you should depart the affected area in accordance with instructions given.

If that is not possible, you should take the following measures:

- Spend as little time as possible outside and do not go near the avalanche area.
- Stay in that part of the house, which is farthest from the hillside. Close windows and doors tightly. Put shutters on windows facing the hillside.
- Do not stay in a basement unless it is completely underground and has a concrete roof.
- If you live in a remote area, you should establish contact by telephone, or radio, with someone outside the danger zone and communicate with him or her, regularly.

If the Chief of Police gives an evacuation order, you must comply. Local Civil Protection committees open emergency aid centre and maintain a register of people staying there until they are allowed to go back to their homes.

When traveling in mountainous areas where there is a danger of avalanches, for example on skis, snowboards, snowmobiles or motor vehicles, care should be taken not to start an avalanche by cutting the mountain side.

If you get caught in an avalanche you should:

- Keep your head up and use a swimming and rolling motion to stay near the surface
- Cover your face to prevent your mouth and nose from getting filled with snow if you are out of control.
- Move as much as you can to create space to breath when the avalanche is slowing down.
- Keep calm. Do not try to call for help, until you hear the rescuers.

ALWAYS BELIEVE THAT YOU WILL BE RESCUED. THAT WILL INCREASE THE POSSIBILITY OF BEING FOUND ALIVE!

Earthquake

There is seldom advance warning of an earthquake. Therefore, it is important to take security measures ahead of time and to learn how to respond.

Security measures:

- Secure cabinets, shelves and heavy objects to the floor or wall.
- Do not keep heavy objects on top of shelves or on walls.
- Secure heating equipment and radiators. Know where the water main and electric circuit breaker are.
- Secure picture frames and wall light fixtures with closed-loop hangers. Put security latches/child safety latches on cabinet doors.
- Prevent objects from falling on beds.
- Make sure that ceiling panels and raised floors are properly fastened. Cover windows to prevent flying glass in case they are broken. Locate beds and chairs away from windows if there is a danger of an earthquake.
- Announcements from the Civil Protection will be made on the State Radio in case of a natural disaster.

www.almannavarnir.is

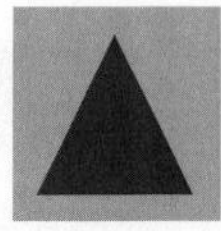

Preventive response:

It is good to remember the words DUCK, COVER, HOLD and how to react in the event of an earthquake. Those who are indoors when a large earthquake occurs should especially avoid:

- Furniture that may move.
- Objects that may fall from shelves and cabinets (especially in kitchens).
- Radiators that may move.
- Broken glass.
- Falling building parts.

Guard against falling objects by:

Ducking in an open doorway, covering the head (with one hand) and holding onto the doorway,

Ducking in the corner of a supporting wall, covering the head and holding on, if possible,

Ducking under a table, covering the head and holding onto a sturdy piece of a furniture

Do not run aimlessly inside or run outside in panic!

Those who are outside should:

- Find an open space and avoid buildings and electric poles. Keep a safe distance from man-made structures that are as tall as or taller than you.
- Duck and cover your head (at least with hands) if you cannot get to an open space.
- Avoid falling rocks and gravel slides in mountainous areas.
- Those who are driving should stop their automobiles in a safe place.

After an earthquake, one should:

- Wear shoes (if debris is on the floor).
- Obtain a first aid kit if needed.
- See if anyone is hurt, and if so, call the Emergency Service at 112. If it is not possible to get help by telephone, mark the place of the accident with a flag.
- Turn off the water and heat if a leak is unmanageable, and shut down the main electrical circuit if the building is damaged.
- See if there is a fire and do not use an open flame if there is danger of a fire starting.
- Leave calmly if you think the building is uninhabitable after an earthquake. Many accidents occur when people run out through debris after an earthquake.
- Dress appropriately for the weather conditions if you leave the building. Remember that the automobile is often the first heated shelter available and it has a radio.
- Remember the emergency shelters in schools.
- Listen after announcements from the Civil Protection that are sent to the Radio.
- Never touch damaged electric poles.

www.almannavarnir.is

Information on mountain roads

Information on the approximate opening date of the principal mountain roads is given in the table;the map below shows the locations of mountain roads. The first two columns of the table show the earliest and latest opening dates of the roads over the past 5 years. The third column shows the average date of opening during this period. More detailed information on the opening of highland roads can be found in maps issued weekly by The Icelandic Roads Administrator and the Environmental and Food Agency during the spring and early summer, and published in the press. Further in formation on the state of the roads is also available on telephone 1777.
www.vegagerdin.is

Mountain ROADS 2008-2012	**Earliest** opening date	**Latest** opening date	**Average** opening date 2008-2012
Lakagígar, F206	5-Jun	28-Jun	15-Jun
Fjallabaksleið nyrðri, F208			
1. Sigalda - Landmannalaugar	31-May	29-Jun	11-Jun
2. Laugar - Eldgjá	7-Jun	26-Jun	17-Jun
3. Eldgjá - Skaftártunga	31-May	29-Jun	19-Jun
Fjallabaksleið syðri, F210			
1. Keldur - Hvanngil	12-Jun	8-Jul	27-Jun
2. Hvanngil - Skaftártunga	12-Jun	8-Jul	8-Jun
Landmannaleið (Dómad.), F225	2-Jun	5-Jul	12-Jun
Emstruleið, F261	12-Jun	1-Jul	24-Jun
Kjalvegur, 35			
1. Gullfoss - Hveravellir	5-Jun	22-Jun	12-Jun
2. Hveravellir - Blönduvirkjun	26-May	22-Jun	6-Jul
Sprengisandur, F26			
1. Hrauneyjar - Nýidalur	10-Jun	5-Jul	24-Jun
2. Nýidalur - Bárðardalur	23-Jun	13-Jul	3-Jul
Skagafjarðarleið, F752	30-Jun	13-Jul	5-Jul
Eyjafjarðarleið, F821	3-Jul	13-Jul	4-Jul
Öskjuleið, F88			
1. To Herðubreiðarlindir	14-Jun	20-Jul	26-Jun
2. Herðubreiðarlindir - Dreki	15-Jun	29-Jun	22-Jun
Öskjuvatnsvegur, F894	15-Jun	20-Jul	1-Jul
Vesturd. (Hljóðaklettar), F862	6-May	25-Jun	31-May
Kverkfjalaleið, F902	14-Jun	29-Jun	20-Jun
Uxahryggjavegur, 52	24-Apr	31-May	16-May
Kaldadalsvegur, 550	20-May	29-Jun	10-Jun

Travel in the highlands of Iceland has increased considerably in recent years; this reflects an increase in leisure time, improvements in vehicles for rough-country travel, and awakening interest in year-round travel.

SENSITIVE ENVIRONMENT
Land which is more than 300 metres above sea level is classified as highland;the climate in the highlands is changeable, and these regions are generally blanketed with snow well into the summer months.

During the spring and early summer, when the snow melts and frozen earth thaws, both roads and vegetation are in a vulnerable state and easily damaged. The greatest risk is due to the impact of premature traffic, especially when vehicles drive off-road to circumvent snowdrifts. Attempts to use snowmobiles in spring, when snowcover is decreasing, can also inflict damage.

The highland summer lasts only a month and a half, and this is the period of growth for highland vegetation, which is thus low-growing and sensitive to any disturbance. Even walkers can inflict permanent damage on vegetation. So all travellers in the highlands should treat the natural environment with care and respect.

OPENING OF MOUNTAIN ROADS
The state of snow cover is the most important factor in deciding when mountain roads can be opened to traffic. Roads are often very wet following the spring melt, and this can also lead to roads remaining closed to traffic.

In cases where mountain roads pass through conservation areas, the roads may not be opened until the area as a whole is in a state to withstand the pressures of visitors, even if the road itself is clear of snow and could withstand traffic.

MOUNTAIN ROAD CONDITIONS
Since 1989, the Public Roads Administration and the Environmental and Food Agency have published maps showing the condition of mountain roads every week during the spring and early summer. The maps are issued each Thursday, for as long as any mountain road remains closed. About 300 copies of the maps are distributed to hotels, the media, travel agencies etc. Up-to-date information on the state of the roads, including mountain roads, is available on telephone 1777.

ENVIRONMENTAL AND FOOD AGENCY

THE ICELANDIC ROADS ADMINISTRATION

www.vegagerdin.is

ATLAS

This edition now includes a detailed 24-page Atlas on a scale of 1:500,000

The road system is according to the latest information from the Icelandic Road Administration.

The Atlas includes symbols which indicate basic services available in the area.

Legend:

	Emergency shelter
	Tourist hut, lodge
	Accommodation
	Camping site
	Tourist information
	Museum, exhibition, cultural centre, visitor centre
	Swimming pool
	Golf course
	Ski area
	Airport, airfields
	Scheduled ferry
	Road tunnel
	Hot spring area
	Ford
	Farm
	Church
	Built-up areas
	Lighthouse
	Paved road
	Gravel road
	Primary gravel road
	Other gravel road
	Highland gravel road
F586 704	Road number
	National park boundaries
	Lava
	River, brook
Hjaltadals-jökull	Glacier
1138	Spot elevation, metres
0 5 10 km	Map is in the scale 1:500 000 1 cm on the map is 5 km on land

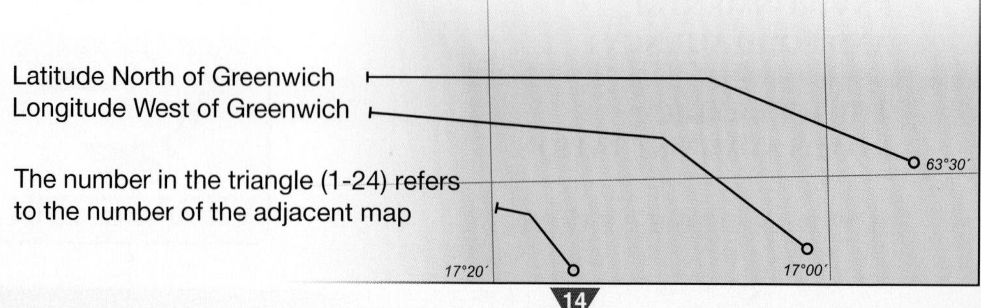

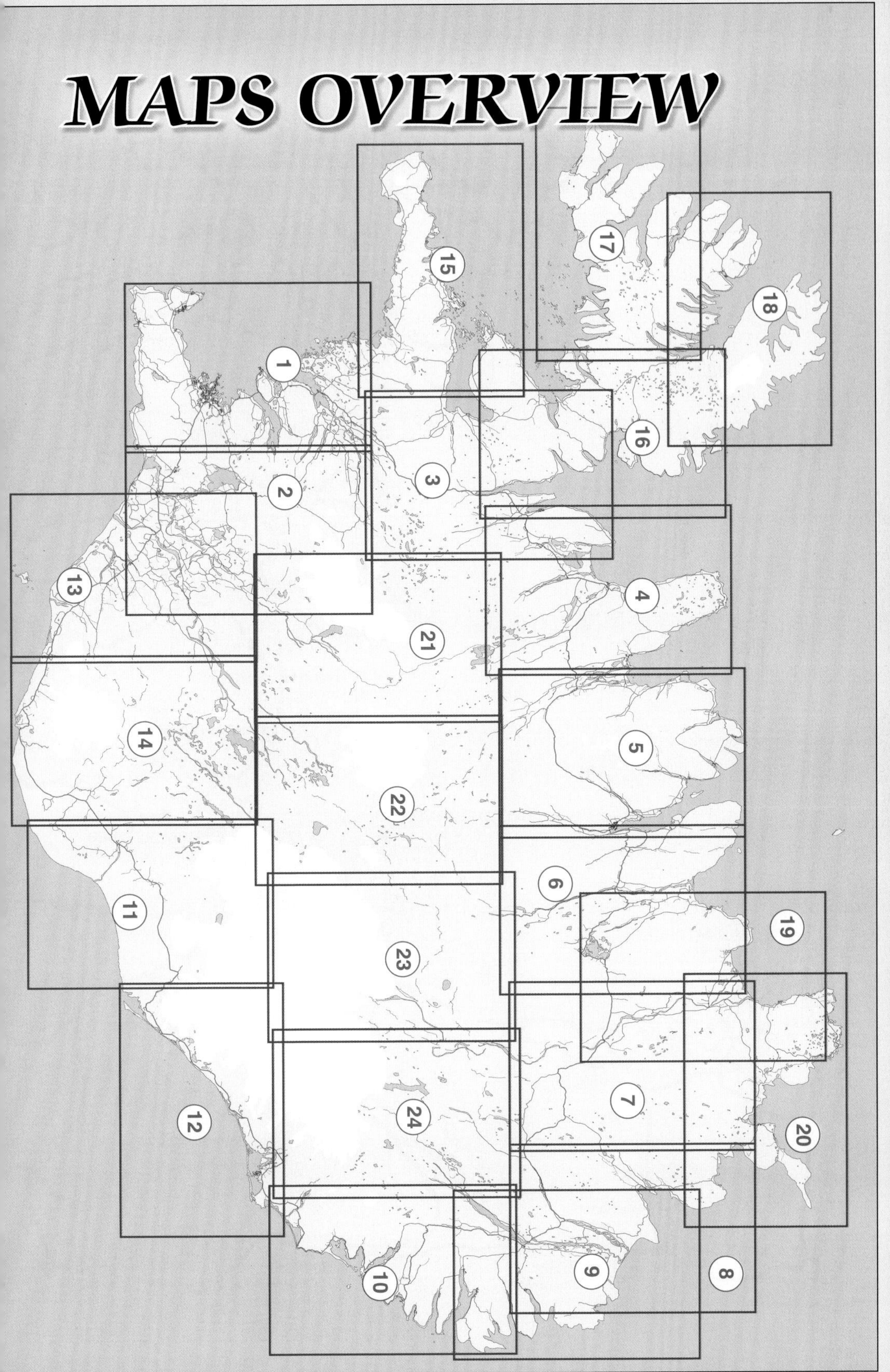
MAPS OVERVIEW
1
2
3
4
5
6
7
8
9
10
11
12
13
14
15
16
17
18
19
20
21
22
23
24

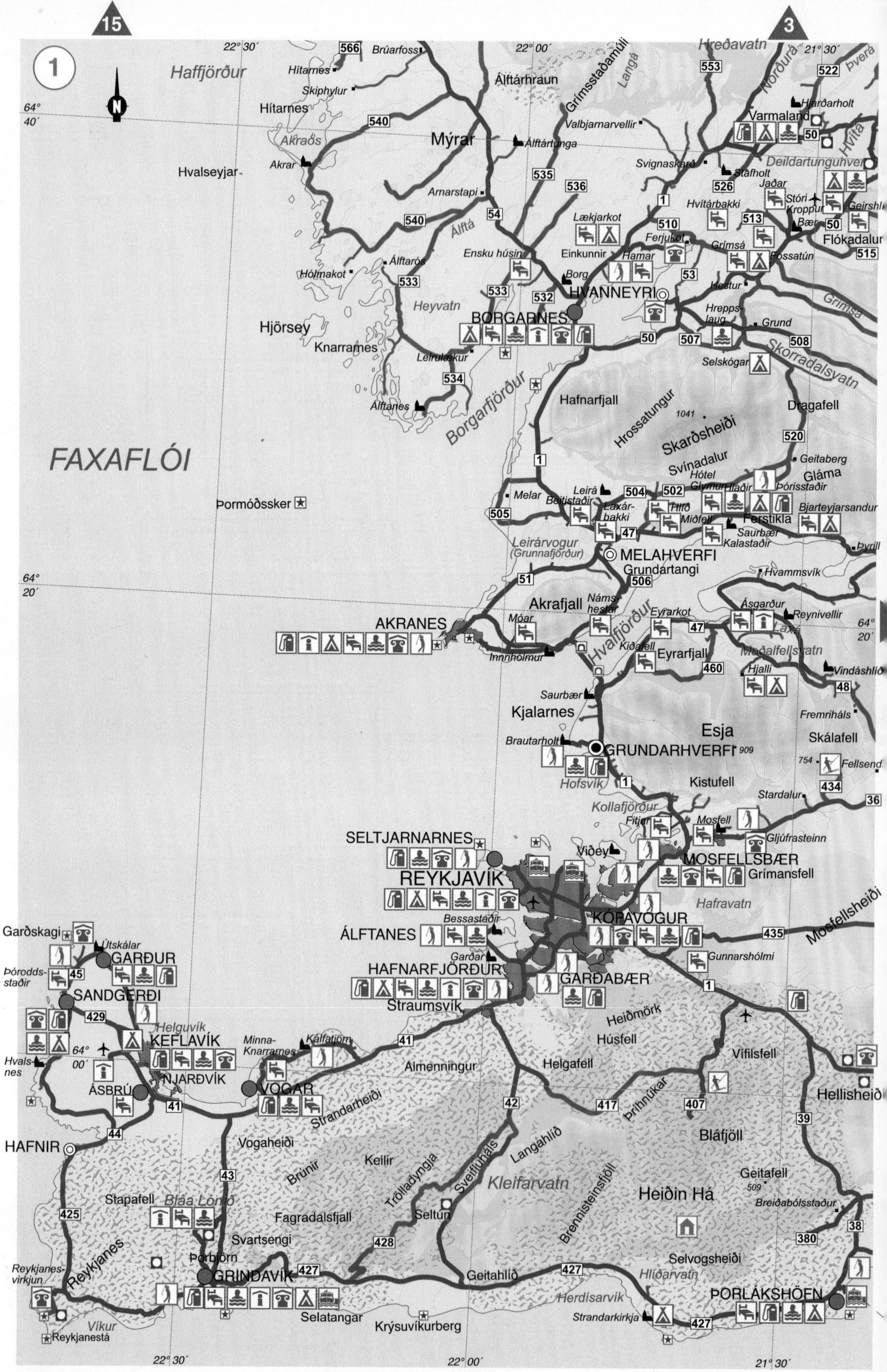

15
3
1
FAXAFLÓI
Haffjörður
Hítarnes
Mýrar
Hvalseyjar
Hjörsey
Knarrarnes
Borgarfjörður
BORGARNES
HVANNEYRI
Varmaland
Deildartunguhver
Flókadalur
Skorradalsvatn
Hafnarfjall
Skarðsheiði
Dragafell
Þormóðssker
Leirárvogur
(Grunnafjörður)
MELAHVERFI
Grundartangi
AKRANES
Akrafjall
Hvalfjörður
Kjalarnes
Esja
GRUNDARHVERFI
Kollafjörður
MOSFELLSBÆR
SELTJARNARNES
REYKJAVÍK
KÓPAVOGUR
ÁLFTANES
HAFNARFJÖRÐUR
GARÐABÆR
Straumsvík
Garðskagi
GARÐUR
SANDGERÐI
KEFLAVÍK
NJARÐVÍK
ÁSBRÚ
VOGAR
HAFNIR
Reykjanes
GRINDAVÍK
Kleifarvatn
Bláfjöll
Heiðin Há
Hellisheiði
ÞORLÁKSHÖFN
Selatangar
Krýsuvíkurberg
Reykjanestá
22° 30´
22° 00´
21° 30´

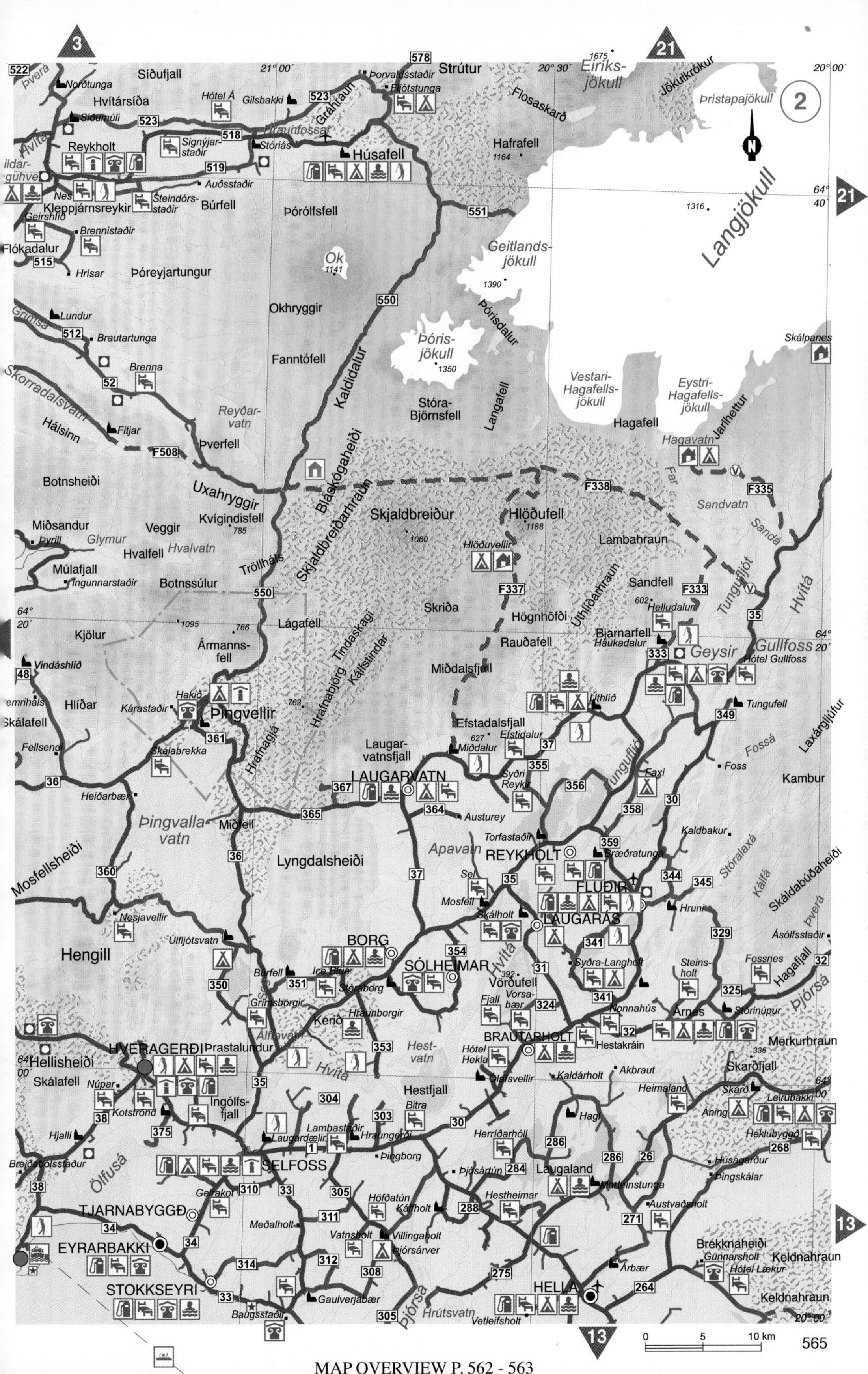

MAP OVERVIEW P. 562 - 563

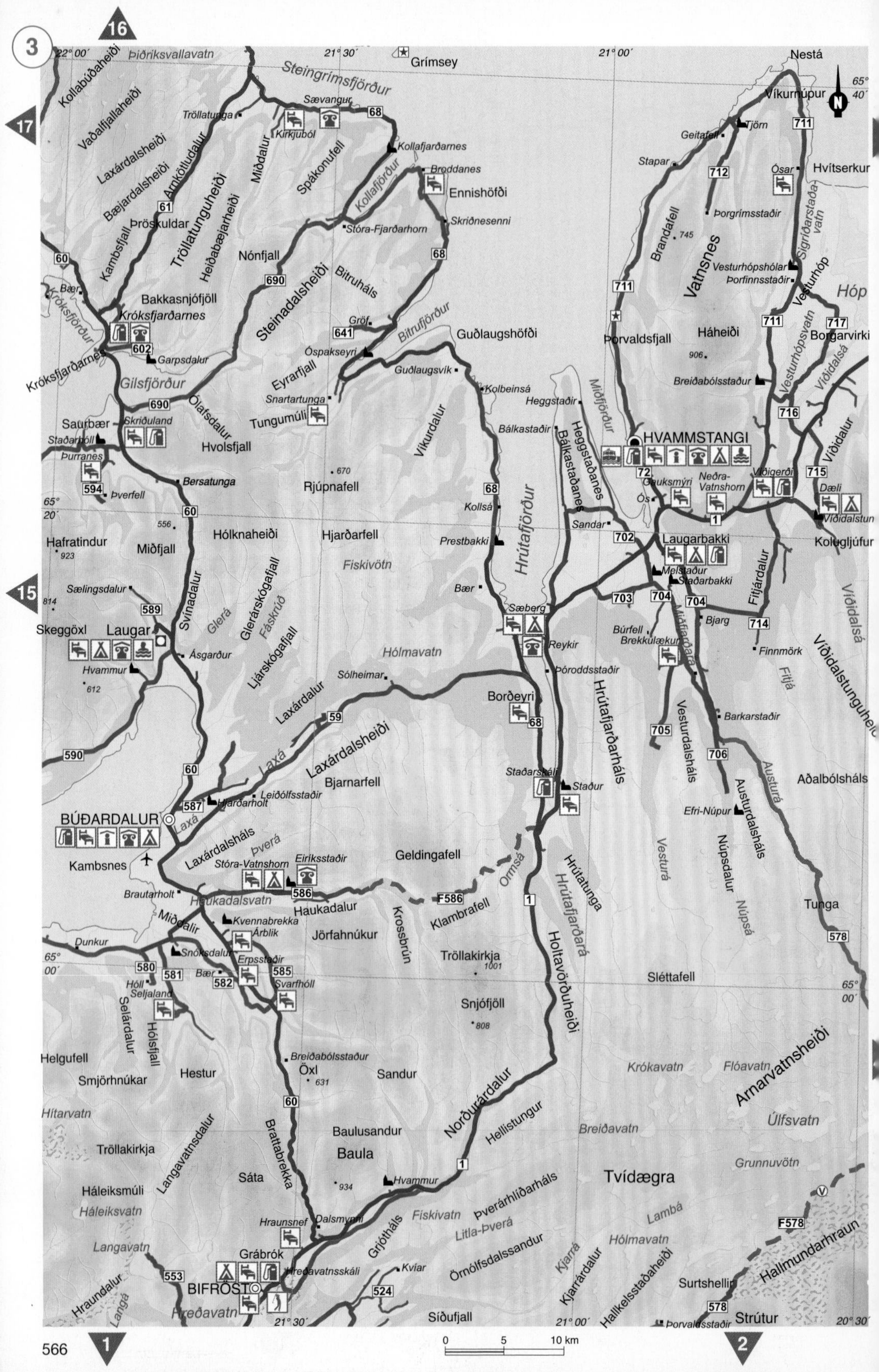
3
16
17
15
1
2
Grímsey
Steingrímsfjörður
Kollafjarðarnes
Broddanes
Ennishöfði
Skriðnesenni
Stóra-Fjarðarhorn
Gilsfjörður
Króksfjarðarnes
Bitrufjörður
Guðlaugshöfði
Hrútafjörður
HVAMMSTANGI
Vatnsnes
Hóp
Laugarbakki
Laugar
BÚÐARDALUR
Hvammsfjörður
Laxárdalsheiði
Haukadalsvatn
Holtavörðuheiði
Norðurárdalur
Baula
BIFRÖST
Grábrók
Tvídægra
Arnarvatnsheiði
Hallmundarhraun
Surtshellir
Strútur
0 5 10 km

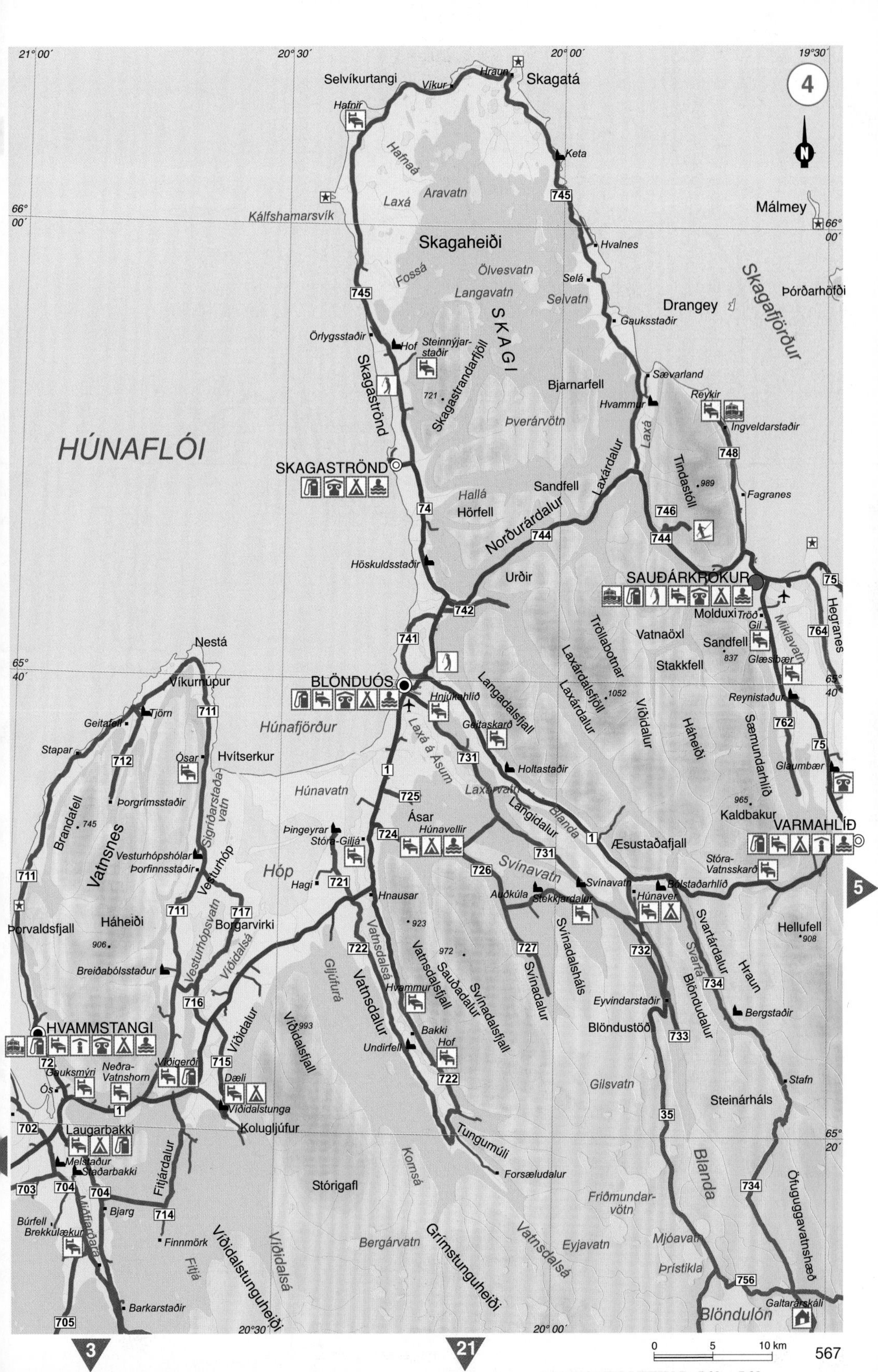

4
21° 00´
20° 30´
20° 00´
19°30´
66° 00´
65° 40´
65° 20´
Selvíkurtangi
Víkur
Hraun
Skagatá
Hafnir
Keta
Hafnaá
Laxá
Aravatn
745
Málmey
Kálfshamarsvík
Skagaheiði
Hvalnes
Fossá
Ölvesvatn
Selá
Langavatn
Selvatn
Skagafjörður
Þórðarhöfði
Drangey
Gauksstaðir
SKAGI
Örlygsstaðir
Hof
Steinnýjarstaðir
Skagaströnd
Skagastrandarfjöll
721
Sævarland
Bjarnarfell
Hvammur
Reykir
Ingveldarstaðir
Þverárvötn
HÚNAFLÓI
Laxárdalur
Tindastóll
748
SKAGASTRÖND
989
Hallá
Sandfell
Fagranes
74
Hörfell
Norðurárdalur
746
744
Höskuldsstaðir
Urðir
SAUÐÁRKRÓKUR
75
742
Molduxi
Tröð
Gil
Miklavatn
Hegranes
Tröllabotnar
Vatnaöxl
741
Sandfell
764
837
Glæsibær
Nestá
Stakkfell
Laxárdalsfjöll
Víkurnúpur
BLÖNDUÓS
Langadalsfjall
1052
Laxárdalur
Víðidalur
Háheiði
Hnjúkahlíð
Reynistaður
Tjörn
711
Geitaskarð
Sæmundarhlíð
762
Geitafell
Húnafjörður
Stapar
Ósar
Hvítserkur
712
731
Laxá á Ásum
Glaumbær
1
Sigríðarstaðavatn
Húnavatn
Laxárvatn
965
Holtastaðir
Þorgrímsstaðir
725
Kaldbakur
Brandafell
745
Ásar
Langidalur
Blanda
VARMAHLÍÐ
Þingeyrar
Húnavellir
Stóra-Giljá
724
Æsustaðafjall
Vesturhópshólar
Vatnsnes
Vesturhóp
731
Þorfinnsstaðir
Hóp
726
Svínavatn
Stóra-Vatnsskarð
Hagi
721
Svínavatn
Bólstaðarhlíð
5
Auðkúla
Hnausar
Stekkjardalur
Húnaver
711
717
Borgarvirki
Þorvaldsfjall
Háheiði
923
Svartárdalur
Hellufell
908
906
Vesturhópsvatn
Víðidalsá
722
Vatnsdalsá
972
727
Svínadalsháls
732
Gljúfurá
Hraun
Breiðabólsstaður
Svartá
734
Vatnsdalur
Sauðadalur
Svínadalsfjall
Svínadalur
Vatnsdalsfjall
Hvammur
716
Bergstaðir
Blöndudalur
Eyvindarstaðir
Víðidalsfjall
993
Víðidalur
HVAMMSTANGI
Bakki
Hof
Blöndustöð
733
Undirfell
72
Gauksmýri
Neðra-Vatnshorn
715
Víðigerði
Dæli
722
Stafn
Gilsvatn
Ós
1
Víðidalstunga
Steinárháls
702
Kolugljúfur
35
Laugarbakki
Tungumúli
Fitjárdalur
Melstaður
Staðarbakki
Forsæludalur
Blanda
703
704
704
Stórigafl
Kornsá
Friðmundarvötn
734
Öfuggavatnshæð
Bjarg
Miðfjarðará
714
Búrfell
Brekkulækur
Finnmörk
Víðidalstunguheiði
Víðidalsá
Bergárvatn
Grímstunguheiði
Vatnsdalsá
Eyjavatn
Mjóavatn
Fitjá
Þrístikla
756
Barkarstaðir
Galtarárskáli
705
20°30´
20° 00´
Blöndulón
3
21
0
5
10 km

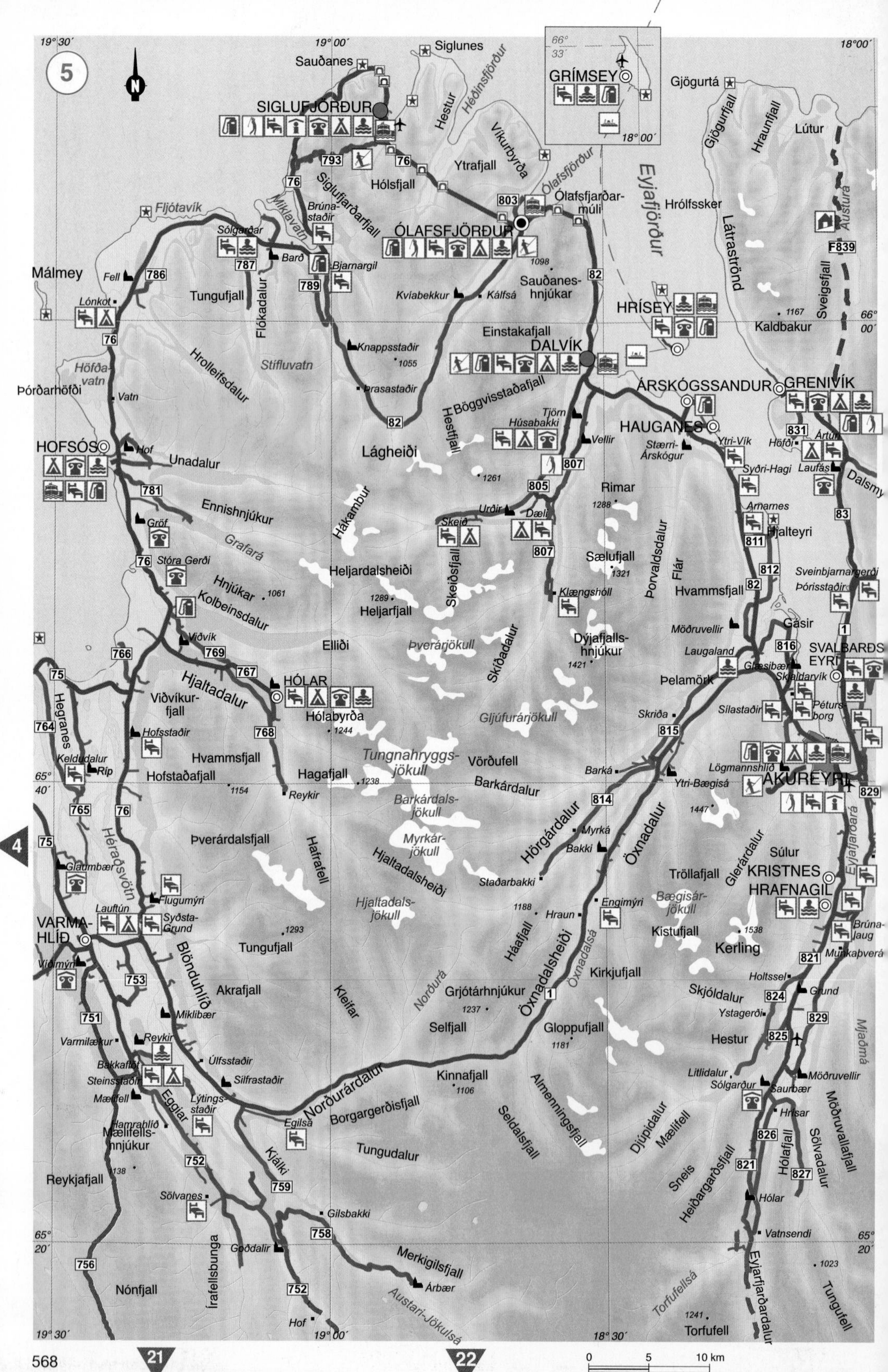
5
19° 30´
19° 00´
18°00´
66° 33´
18° 00´
66° 00´
65° 40´
65° 20´
18° 30´
Siglunes
Sauðanes
Héðinsfjörður
Hestur
SIGLUFJÖRÐUR
GRÍMSEY
Gjögurtá
Gjögurfjall
Hraunfjall
Lútur
Víkurbyrða
Ytrafjall
Hólsfjall
Siglufjarðarfjall
793
76
Fljótavík
Miklavatn
Brúna-staðir
Ólafsfjörður
Ólafsfjarðar-múli
803
ÓLAFSFJÖRÐUR
Eyjafjörður
Hrólfssker
Látraströnd
Austurá
F839
Sólgarðar
787
Barð
789
Bjarnargil
1098
Sauðanes-hnjúkar
82
Málmey
Fell
786
Tungufjall
Flókadalur
Kvíabekkur
Kálfsá
HRÍSEY
Sveigsfjall
1167
Kaldbakur
Lónkot
Einstakafjall
DALVÍK
Stífluvatn
Knappsstaðir
1055
Höfða-vatn
Hrolleifsdalur
Þórðarhöfði
Vatn
Þrasastaðir
Böggvisstaðafjall
ÁRSKÓGSSANDUR
GRENIVÍK
Hestfjall
Tjörn
Húsabakki
HAUGANES
Stærri-Árskógur
Ytri-Vík
831
Höfði
Ártún
HOFSÓS
Hof
Unadalur
Lágheiði
Vellir
807
Syðri-Hagi
Laufás
Dalsmynni
1261
805
Rimar
781
Ennishnjúkur
Hákambur
Urðir
Dæli
1288
Arnarnes
Gröf
Skeið
Hjalteyri
83
Grafará
Skeiðsfjall
Sælufjall
811
Þorvaldsdalur
Flár
812
Sveinbjarnargerði
Stóra Gerði
Heljardalsheiði
1321
Þórisstaðir
Hjnúkar
1061
Kolbeinsdalur
1289
Heljarfjall
Klængshóll
Hvammsfjall
Möðruvellir
Gásir
1
Viðvík
Elliði
Þverárjökull
Dýjafjalls-hnjúkur
816
SVALBARÐS-EYRI
766
769
Skíðadalur
Laugaland
Glæsibær
75
767
1421
Skjaldarvík
HÓLAR
Hjaltadalur
Viðvíkur-fjall
Hólabyrða
Þelamörk
Hegranes
764
Hofsstaðir
768
1244
Gljúfurárjökull
Skriða
Sílastaðir
Pétursborg
815
Keldudalur
Rip
Hvammsfjall
Tungnahryggs-jökull
Vörðufell
Lögmannshlíð
AKUREYRI
Hofstaðafjall
1154
Hagafjall
1238
Barkárdalur
Barká
Ytri-Bægisá
Reykir
829
765
76
Barkárdals-jökull
814
1447
Héraðsvötn
Myrká
Hörgárdalur
Öxnadalur
Eyjafjarðará
75
Þverárdalsfjall
Hafrafell
Myrkár-jökull
Bakki
Glerárdalur
Súlur
4
Glaumbær
Hjaltadalsheiði
Staðarbakki
Tröllafjall
KRISTNES
HRAFNAGIL
Flugumýri
Hjaltadals-jökull
Bægisár-jökull
Engimýri
1188
Hraun
Lauftún
Syðsta-Grund
VARMA-HLÍÐ
1293
Tungufjall
Háafjall
Öxnadalsá
Kistufjall
1538
Brúna-laug
Kerling
Víðimýri
Blönduhlíð
Öxnadalsheiði
821
Munkaþverá
Kirkjufjall
Holtssel
753
Akrafjall
Grjótárhnjúkur
Norðurá
Kleifar
Skjóldalur
Grund
824
Ystagerði
1237
751
Miklibær
Selfjall
Gloppufjall
829
Mjaðmá
Varmilækur
Reykir
1181
Hestur
825
Bakkaflöt
Úlfsstaðir
Steinsstaðir
Silfrastaðir
Kinnafjall
Litlidalur
Möðruvellir
Mælifell
1106
Sólgarður
Saurbær
Lýtings-staðir
Norðurárdalur
Almenningsfjall
Eggjar
Borgargerðisfjall
Seldalsfjall
Djúpidalur
Hrísar
Möðruvallafjall
Hamrahlíð
Mælifells-hnjúkur
Egilsá
Mælifell
826
Sölvadalur
Kjálki
Tungudalur
Hólafjall
752
Reykjafjall
1138
Sneis
821
Heiðargarðsfjall
827
759
Sölvanes
Hólar
Gilsbakki
758
Vatnsendi
Íralfellsbunga
Goðdalir
Merkigilsfjall
756
1023
Árbær
752
Nónfjall
Austari-Jökulsá
Torfufellsá
Eyjafjarðardalur
Tungufell
1241
Torfufell
Hof
21
22
0
5
10 km

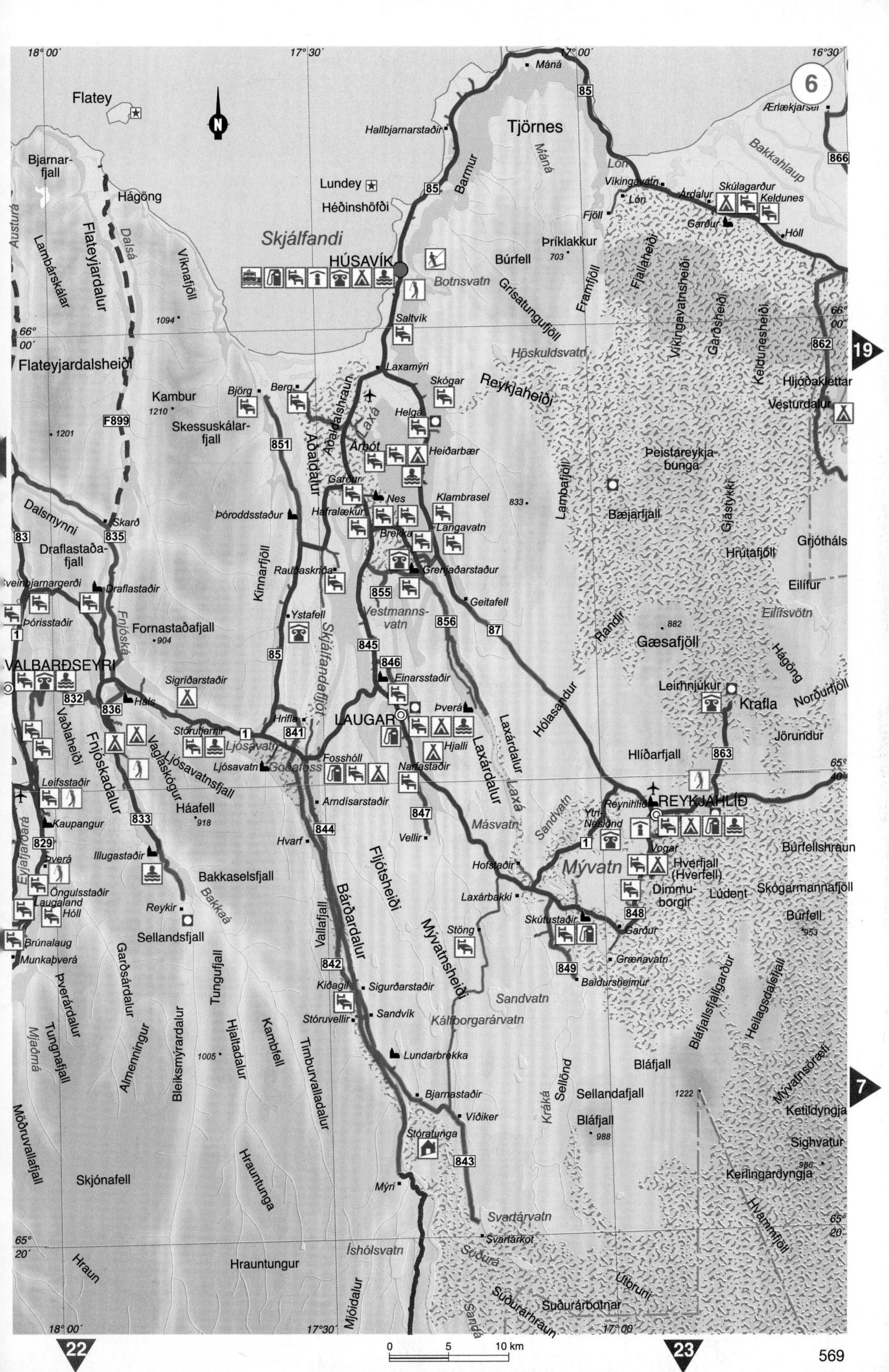

6
Flatey
Tjörnes
Skjálfandi
HÚSAVÍK
Lundey
Héðinshöfði
Hallbjarnarstaðir
Máná
Barmur
Botnsvatn
Saltvík
Laxamýri
Reykjaheiði
Höskuldsvatn
Grísatungufjöll
Búrfell
Þríklakkur
Framfjöll
Fjallaheiði
Víkingavatnsheiði
Garðsheiði
Keldunesheiði
Ærlækjarsel
Bakkahlaup
Víkingavatn
Lón
Fjöll
Árdalur
Skúlagarður
Keldunes
Garður
Höll
Hljóðaklettar
Vesturdalur
Þeistareykjabunga
Bæjarfjall
Lambafjöll
Gjástykki
Hrútafjöll
Grjótháls
Eilífur
Eilífsvötn
Gæsafjöll
Randir
Hágöng
Leirhnjúkur
Krafla
Norðurfjöll
Jörundur
Hlíðarfjall
Hólasandur
REYKJAHLÍÐ
Reynihlíð
Ytri-Neslönd
Vogar
Mývatn
Hverfjall (Hverfell)
Dimmuborgir
Lúdent
Búrfellshraun
Skógarmannafjöll
Búrfell
Garður
Grænavatn
Baldursheimur
Skútustaðir
Laxárbakki
Hofstaðir
Sandvatn
Mývatnsheiði
Kálfborgarárvatn
Sellönd
Kráká
Sellandafjall
Bláfjall
Bláfjallsfjallgarður
Heilagsdalsfjall
Mývatnsöræfi
Ketildyngja
Sighvatur
Kerlingardyngja
Hvammfjöll
Útbruni
Suðurárbotnar
Suðurárhraun
Suðurá
Svartárvatn
Svartárkot
Ísholsvatn
Mjóidalur
Stóratunga
Víðiker
Bjarnastaðir
Lundarbrekka
Stóruvellir
Sandvík
Kiðagil
Sigurðarstaðir
Mýri
Bárðardalur
Fljótsheiði
Vallafjall
Timburvalladalur
Kambfell
Hjaltadalur
Bleiksmýrardalur
Almenningur
Hrauntunga
Hrauntungur
Skjónafell
Möðruvallafjall
Tungnafjall
Hraun
Garðsárdalur
Tungufjall
Sellandsfjall
Reykir
Bakkaá
Bakkaselsfjall
Illugastaðir
LAUGAR
Einarsstaðir
Þverá
Hjalli
Narfastaðir
Fosshóll
Goðafoss
Ljósavatn
Stóratjarnir
Ljósavatnsfjall
Háafell
Vaglaskógur
Fnjóskadalur
Sigríðarstaðir
Hals
Hrifla
Arndísarstaðir
Hvarf
Vellir
Másvatn
Laxárdalur
Laxá
Geitafell
Grenjaðarstaður
Vestmannsvatn
Skjálfandafljót
Ystafell
Rauðaskriða
Brekka
Langavatn
Klambrasel
Hafralækur
Nes
Garður
Árhót
Heiðarbær
Helga
Skógar
Aðaldalshraun
Aðaldalur
Berg
Björg
Kinnarfjöll
Þóroddsstaður
Kambur
Skessuskálarfjall
Flateyjardalsheiði
Flateyjardalur
Víknafjöll
Dalsá
Hágöng
Bjarnarfjall
Lambárskálar
Austurá
Skarð
Dalsmynni
Draflastaðafjall
Draflastaðir
Sveinbjarnargerði
Þórisstaðir
Fornastaðafjall
Fnjóská
VALBARÐSEYRI
Vaðlaheiði
Leifsstaðir
Kaupangur
Eyjafjarðará
Þverá
Öngulsstaðir
Laugaland
Höll
Brúnalaug
Munkaþverá
Þverárdalur
Mjaðmá
0 5 10 km

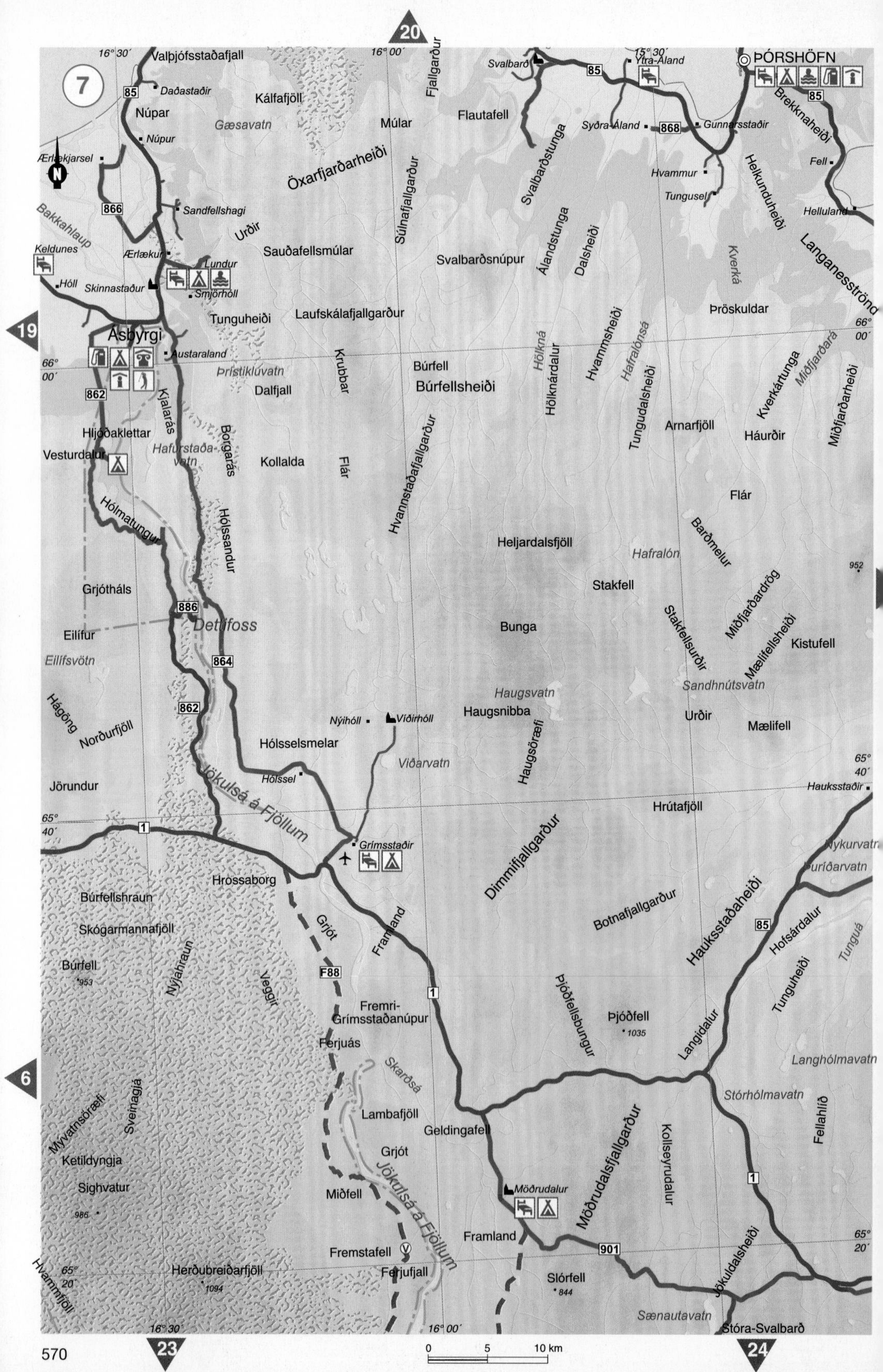
7
20
19
6
23
24
Valþjófsstaðafjall
Daðastaðir
Núpar
Núpur
Ærlækjarsel
Kálfafjöll
Gæsavatn
Múlar
Fjallgarður
Flautafell
Svalbarð
Ytra-Áland
ÞÓRSHÖFN
Brekknaheiði
Syðra-Áland
Gunnarsstaðir
Fell
Hvammur
Tungusel
Helkunduheiði
Helluland
Langanesströnd
Öxarfjarðarheiði
Súlnafjallgarður
Svalbarðstunga
Álandstunga
Dalsheiði
Kverká
Bakkahlaup
Keldunes
Sandfellshagi
Urðir
Sauðafellsmúlar
Svalbarðsnúpur
Ærlækur
Lundur
Höll
Skinnastaður
Smjörhóll
Tunguheiði
Laufskálafjallgarður
Þröskuldar
Ásbyrgi
Austaraland
Þrístiklúvatn
Krubbar
Búrfell
Búrfellsheiði
Hölkná
Hölknárdalur
Hvammsheiði
Hafralónsá
Tungudalsheiði
Kverkártunga
Miðfjarðará
Miðfjarðarheiði
Dalfjall
Kjalarás
Hljóðaklettar
Vesturdalur
Hafurstaðavatn
Borgarás
Kollalda
Flár
Hvannstaðafjallgarður
Arnarfjöll
Háurðir
Hólmatungur
Hólssandur
Heljardalsfjöll
Hafralón
Barðmelur
952
Grjótháls
Stakfell
Miðfjarðardrög
Dettifoss
Eilífur
Eilífsvötn
Bunga
Stakfellsurðir
Mælifellsheiði
Kistufell
Hágöng
Norðurfjöll
Haugsvatn
Sandhnútsvatn
Nýihóll
Víðirhóll
Haugsnibba
Urðir
Mælifell
Hólsselsmelar
Viðarvatn
Haugsöræfi
Jörundur
Hólssel
Jökulsá á Fjöllum
Hauksstaðir
Hrútafjöll
Grímsstaðir
Dimmifjallgarður
Nykurvatn
Þuríðarvatn
Hrossaborg
Búrfellshraun
Skógarmannafjöll
Botnafjallgarður
Hauksstaðaheiði
Hofsárdalur
Tunguá
Grjót
Framland
Búrfell
953
Nýjahraun
Veggir
Tunguheiði
Fremri-Grímsstaðanúpur
Þjóðfellsbungur
Þjóðfell
1035
Langidalur
Ferjuás
Langhólmavatn
Skarðsá
Stórhólmavatn
Mývatnsöræfi
Sveinagjá
Lambafjöll
Geldingafell
Kollseyrudalur
Fellahlíð
Ketildyngja
Grjót
Sighvatur
Miðfell
Möðrudalur
Möðrudalsfjallgarður
986
Framland
Fremstafell
Jökuldalsheiði
Hvammfjöll
Herðubreiðarfjöll
1094
Ferjufjall
Slórfell
844
Sænautavatn
Stóra-Svalbarð
16° 30´
16° 00´
15° 30´
66° 00´
65° 40´
65° 20´
85
866
862
886
864
868
1
F88
901
0
5
10 km

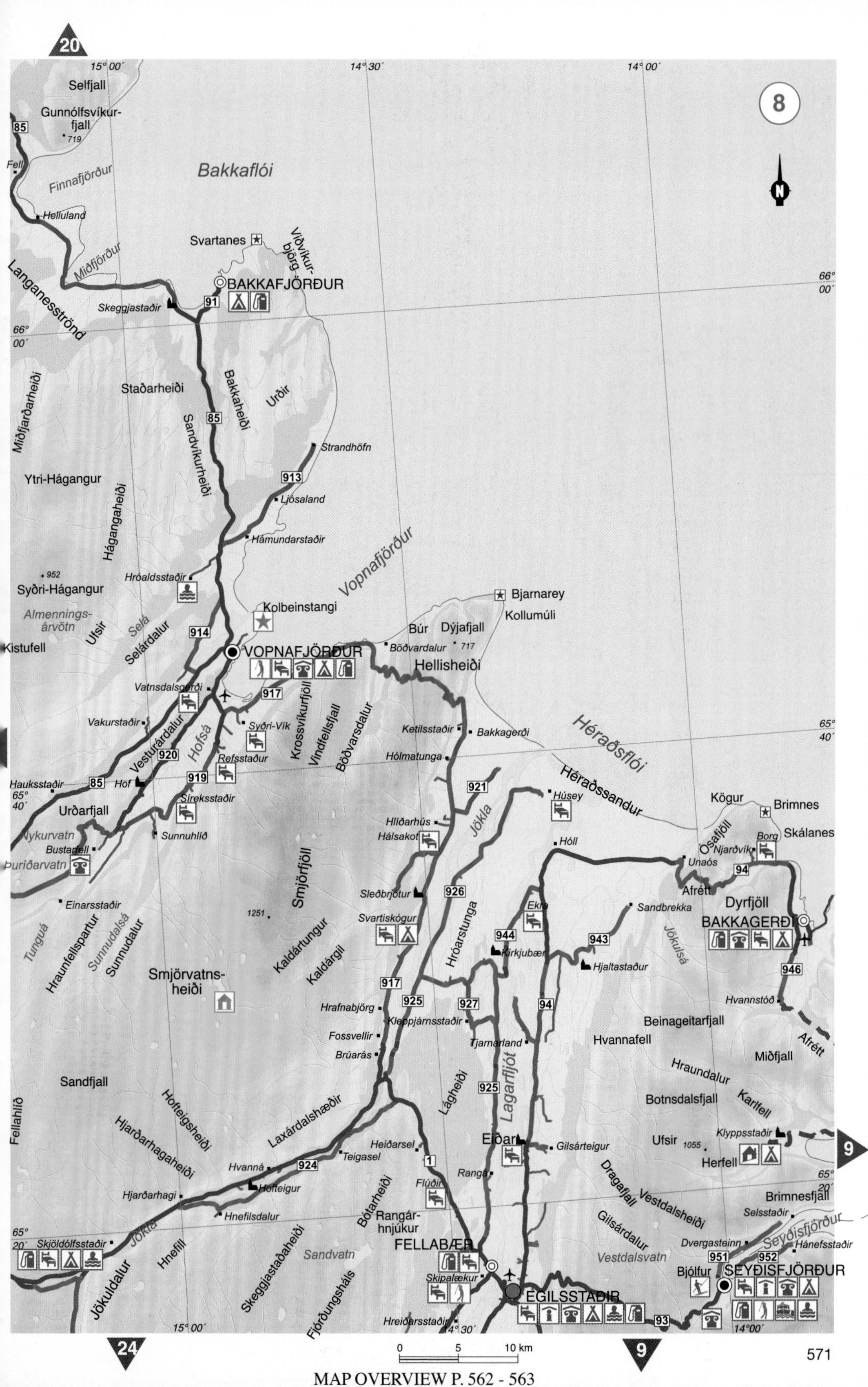

MAP OVERVIEW P. 562 - 563

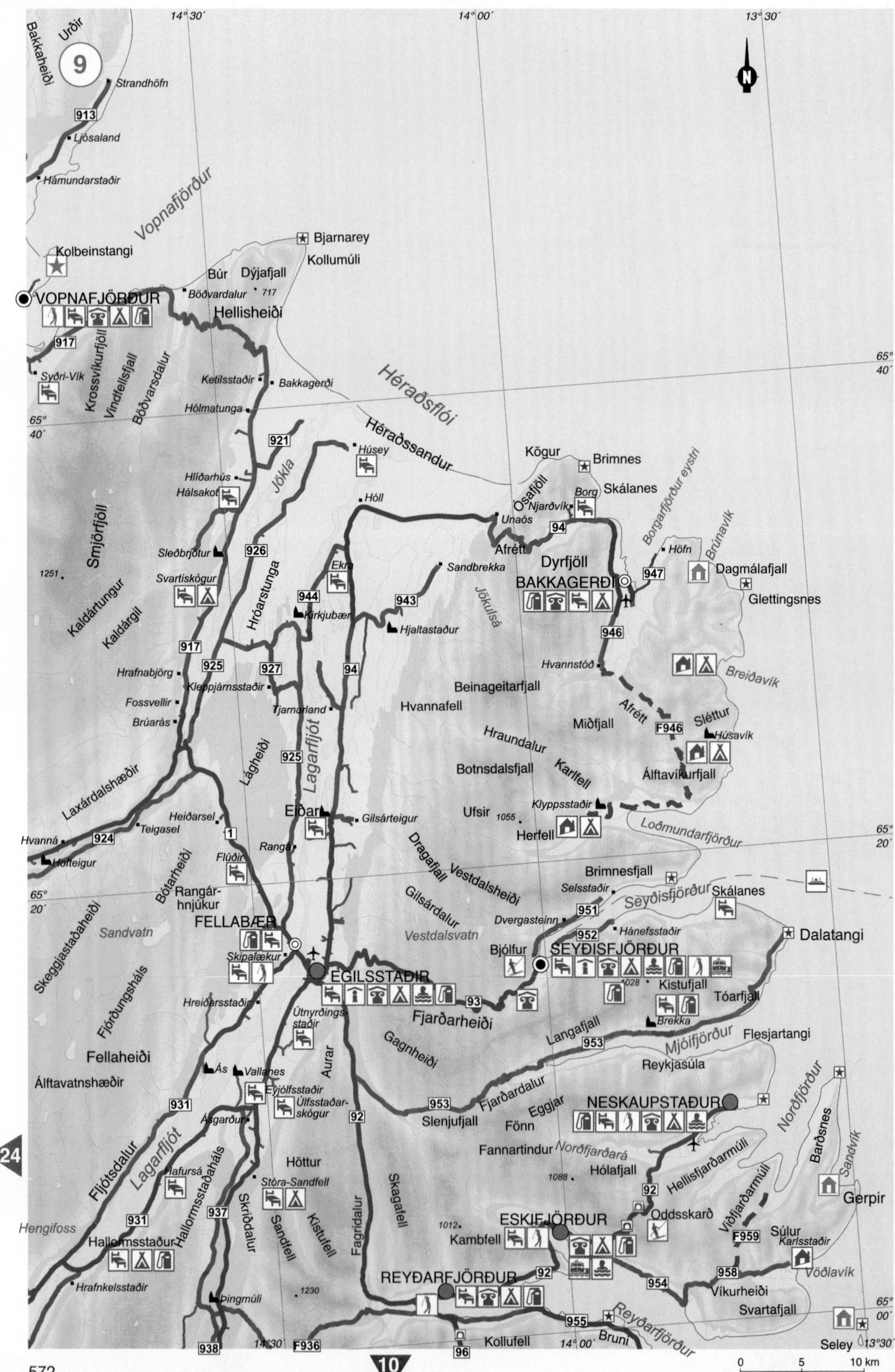

9
8
24
10
Vopnafjörður
VOPNAFJÖRÐUR
Kolbeinstangi
Bjarnarey
Kollumúli
Búr
Dýjafjall
Böðvardalur
717
Hellisheiði
Strandhöfn
Ljósaland
Hámundarstaðir
Syðri-Vík
Krossvíkurfjöll
Vindfellsfjall
Böðvarsdalur
Ketilsstaðir
Bakkagerði
Hólmatunga
Héraðsflói
Héraðssandur
Húsey
Hóll
Hlíðarhús
Hálsakot
Jökla
Smjörfjöll
Sleðbrjótur
Svartiskógur
Hróarstunga
Ekra
Kirkjubær
Sandbrekka
Hjaltastaður
Kaldártungur
Kaldárgil
Hrafnabjörg
Kleppjárnsstaðir
Fossvellir
Brúarás
Tjarnarland
Lagarfljót
Lágheiði
Laxárdalshæðir
Hvanná
Hofteigur
Teigasel
Heiðarsel
Eiðar
Gilsárteigur
Rangá
Flúðir
Bótarheiði
Rangárhnjúkur
FELLABÆR
Skipalækur
Sandvatn
Skeggjastaðaheiði
Fjórðungsháls
Fellaheiði
Álftavatnshæðir
Hreiðarsstaðir
EGILSSTAÐIR
Útnyrðingsstaðir
Ás
Vallanes
Eyjólfsstaðir
Úlfsstaðarskógur
Ásgarður
Aurar
Fljótsdalur
Hafursá
Hallormsstaðaháls
Skriðdalur
Sandfell
Kistufell
Stóra-Sandfell
Höttur
Hengifoss
Hallormsstaður
Hrafnkelsstaður
Þingmúli
1230
Fagridalur
Skagafell
Kögur
Brimnes
Ósafjöll
Borg
Njarðvík
Skálanes
Unaós
Afrétt
Dyrfjöll
BAKKAGERÐI
Borgarfjörður eystri
Höfn
Brúnavík
Dagmálafjall
Glettingsnes
Jökulsá
Hvannstóð
Breiðavík
Beinageitarfjall
Hvannafell
Miðfjall
Sléttur
Húsavík
Hraundalur
Karlfell
Botnsdalsfjall
Álftavíkurfjall
Klyppsstaðir
Ufsir
1055
Herfell
Loðmundarfjörður
Dragafjall
Vestdalsheiði
Gilsárdalur
Vestdalsvatn
Brimnesfjall
Selsstaðir
Seyðisfjörður
Skálanes
Dvergasteinn
Hánefsstaðir
Bjólfur
SEYÐISFJÖRÐUR
Dalatangi
1028
Kistufjall
Tóarfjall
Brekka
Fjarðarheiði
Gagnheiði
Langafjall
Mjóifjörður
Flesjartangi
Reykjasúla
Fjarðardalur
Eggjar
Slenjufjall
Fönn
NESKAUPSTAÐUR
Norðfjörður
Fannartindur
Norðfjarðará
Hólafjall
1088
Hellisfjarðarmúli
Viðfjarðarmúli
Barðsnes
Sandvík
Gerpir
Oddsskarð
1012
Kambfell
ESKIFJÖRÐUR
Súlur
Karlsstaðir
Vöðlavík
REYÐARFJÖRÐUR
Víkurheiði
Svartafjall
Reyðarfjörður
Bruni
Kollufell
Seley
913
917
921
926
944
943
94
947
946
F946
925
927
924
1
951
952
93
953
92
931
937
938
F936
96
955
954
958
F959
14° 30´
14° 00´
13° 30´
65° 40´
65° 20´
65° 00´
0
5
10 km

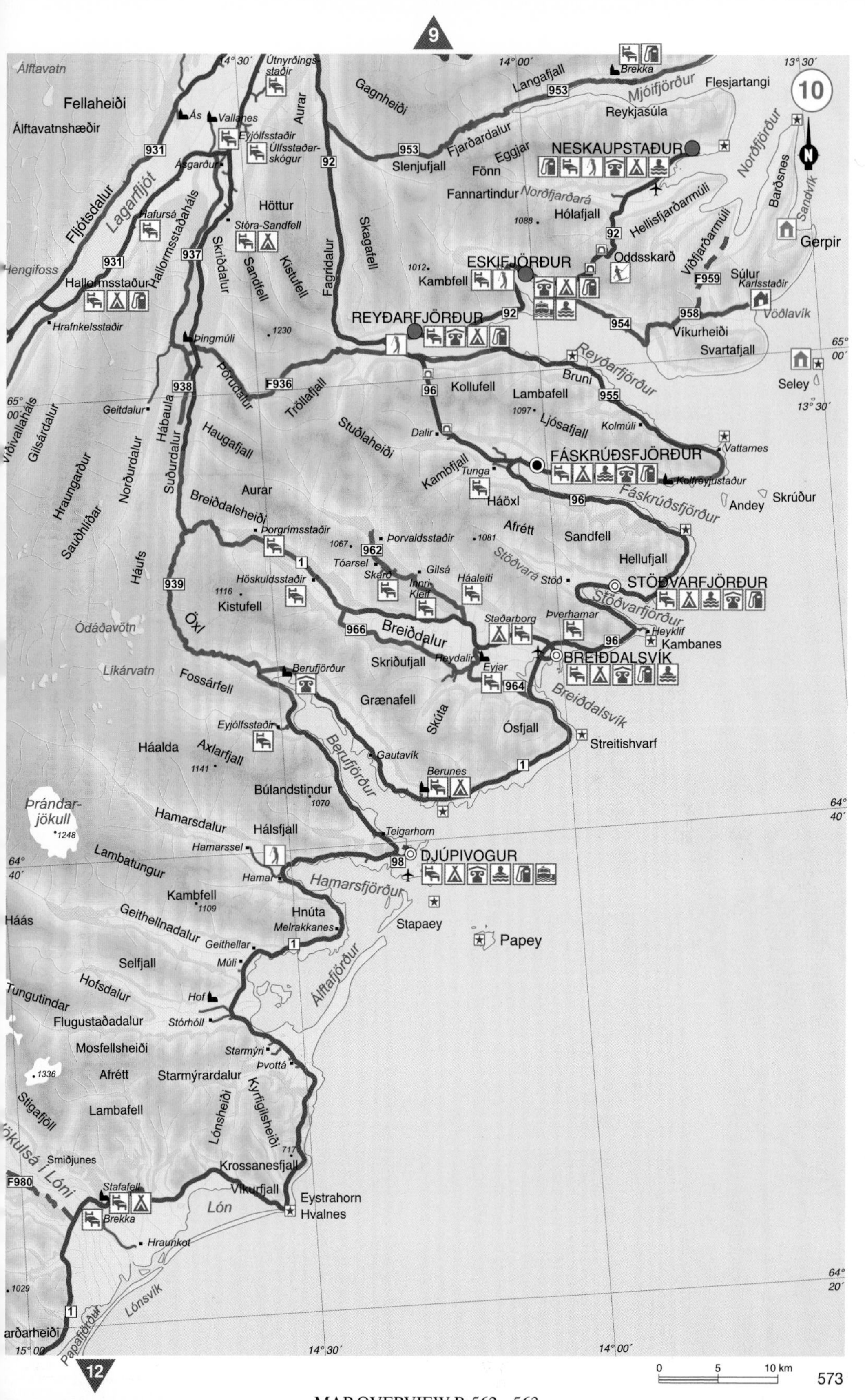

MAP OVERVIEW P. 562 - 563

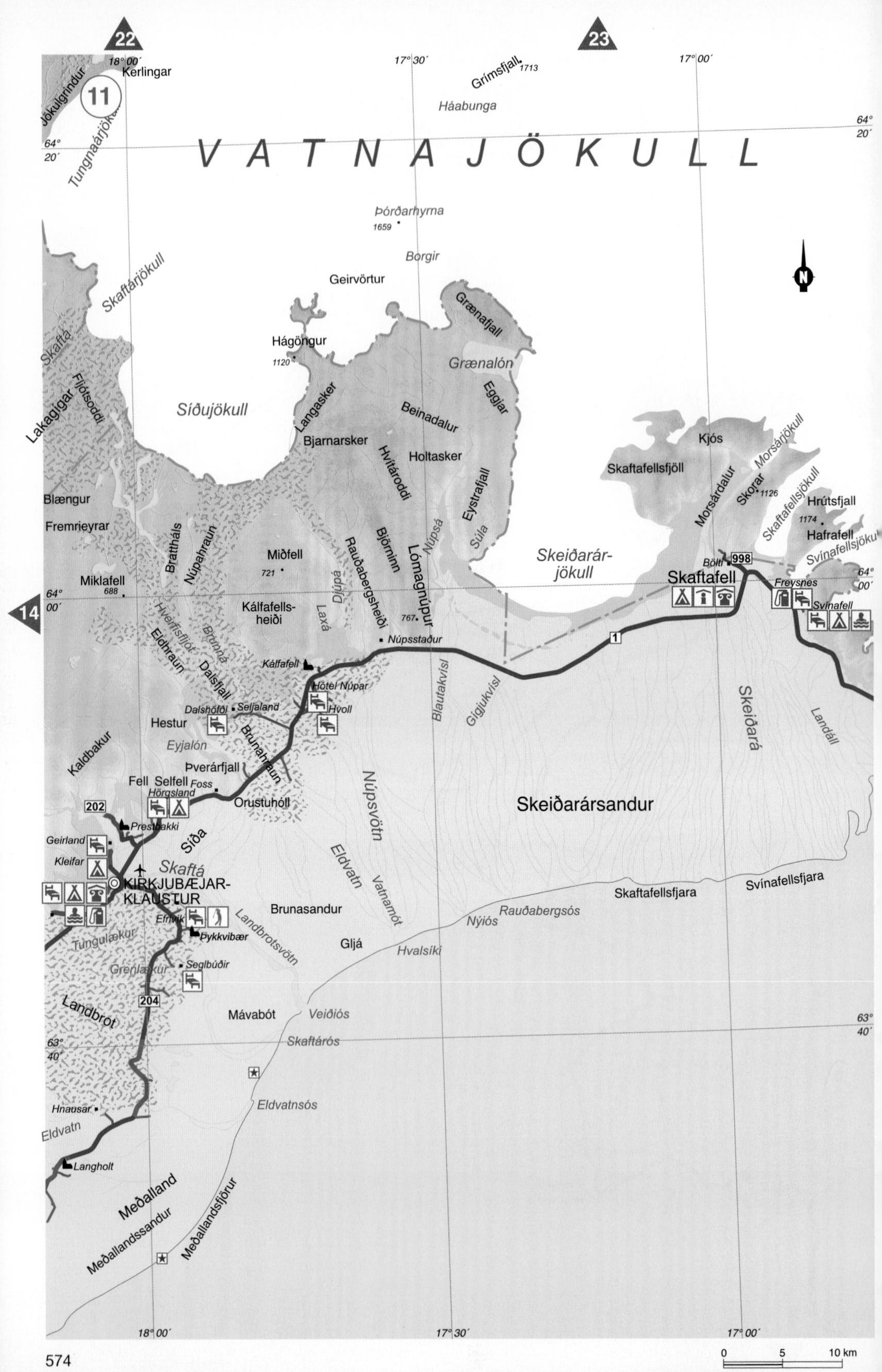
22
23
11
14
VATNAJÖKULL
Grímsfjall 1713
Háabunga
Kerlingar
Jökulgrindur
Tungnaárjökull
Þórðarhyrna 1659
Borgir
Geirvörtur
Skaftárjökull
Grænafjall
Hágöngur 1120
Grænalón
Síðujökull
Skaftá
Fljótsoddi
Lakagígar
Langasker
Beinadalur
Eggjar
Bjarnarsker
Hvítároddi
Holtasker
Kjós
Skaftafellsfjöll
Morsárjökull
Eystrafjall
Morsárdalur
Skorar 1126
Skaftafellsjökull
Hrútsfjall 1174
Hafrafell
Svínafellsjökull
Blængur
Fremrieyrar
Bratthåls
Núpahraun
Miðfell 721
Rauðabergsheiði
Björninn
Lómagnúpur 767
Núpsá
Súla
Skeiðarárjökull
Bölti
998
Skaftafell
Freysnes
Svínafell
Miklafell 688
Kálfafellsheiði
Djúpá
Laxá
Hverfisfljót
Brunná
Eldhraun
Dalsfjall
Núpsstaður
Kálfafell
1
Hótel Núpar
Hvoll
Dalshöfði
Seljaland
Hestur
Eyjalón
Brunahraun
Blautakvísl
Gígjukvísl
Skeiðará
Landáll
Kaldbakur
Þverárfjall
Fell
Selfell
Foss
Hörgsland
Orustuhóll
Núpsvötn
Skeiðarársandur
202
Prestbakki
Geirland
Kleifar
Síða
Skaftá
Eldvatn
KIRKJUBÆJAR-KLAUSTUR
Vatnamót
Landbrotsvötn
Brunasandur
Skaftafellsfjara
Svínafellsfjara
Efrivík
Þykkvibær
Rauðabergsós
Nýjós
Tungulækur
Gljá
Hvalsíki
Seglbúðir
Grenlækur
204
Landbrot
Mávabót
Veiðiós
Skaftárós
Hnausar
Eldvatnsós
Eldvatn
Langholt
Meðalland
Meðallandssandur
Meðallandsfjörur
18° 00´
17° 30´
17° 00´
64° 20´
64° 00´
63° 40´
0
5
10 km

VATNAJÖKULL

Fláajökull
Fláfjall
Viðborðsdalur
Hornafjarðarfljót
Viðborðsfjall
Hótel Vatnajökull
Laxárdalur
Skeggtindar
1029
Lónsvík
Papafjörður
Fjarðarheiði
Rauðaberg
NESJAHVERFI
Seljavellir
Bjarnanes
Almannaskarð
Vestrahorn
Heinabergsfjöll
Heinabergsjökull
Snjófjall
Litlafell
Hafrafell
Mýrar
Lambleiksstaðir
Brunnhóll
Hornafjörður
Árnanes
Hólmur
HÖFN
Skarðsfjörður
Skálafellsjökull
Skálafell
Nýpugarðar
Stokksnes
Austurfjörur
Suðurfjörur
Hvanney
Skinneyjarhöfði
Kálfafellsfjöll
Kálfafellsdalur
Staðarfjall
Snæfell
1383
Esjufjöll
Smyrlabjörg
Brunnavellir
Kálfafellsstaður
Vagnsstaðir
Hestgerðislón
Þverártindur
1113
Steinafjall
Reynivellir
Gerði
Hali
Breiðamerkurjökull
Stemmulón
Morsárjökull
Breiðamerkurfjall
Breiðárlón
Jökulsárlón
Hrollaugseyjar
Skaftafellsjökull
Hrútsfjall
1174
Hafrafell
Öræfajökull
Snæbreið
Fjallsjökull
Svínafellsjökull
2110
Hvannadalshnjúkur
Hrútá
Kvísker
Freysnes
Svínafell
Breiðamerkursandur
Kvíárjökull
Tvísker
Sandfellsheiði
Hof
Hnappavellir
Landáll
Fagurhólsmýri
Öræfi
Leirur
Ingólfshöfði

16° 30´ 16° 00´ 15° 30´ 15° 00´ 64° 20´ 64° 00´
1 99 984 986 F985
11 12
0 5 10 km

MAP OVERVIEW P. 562 - 563

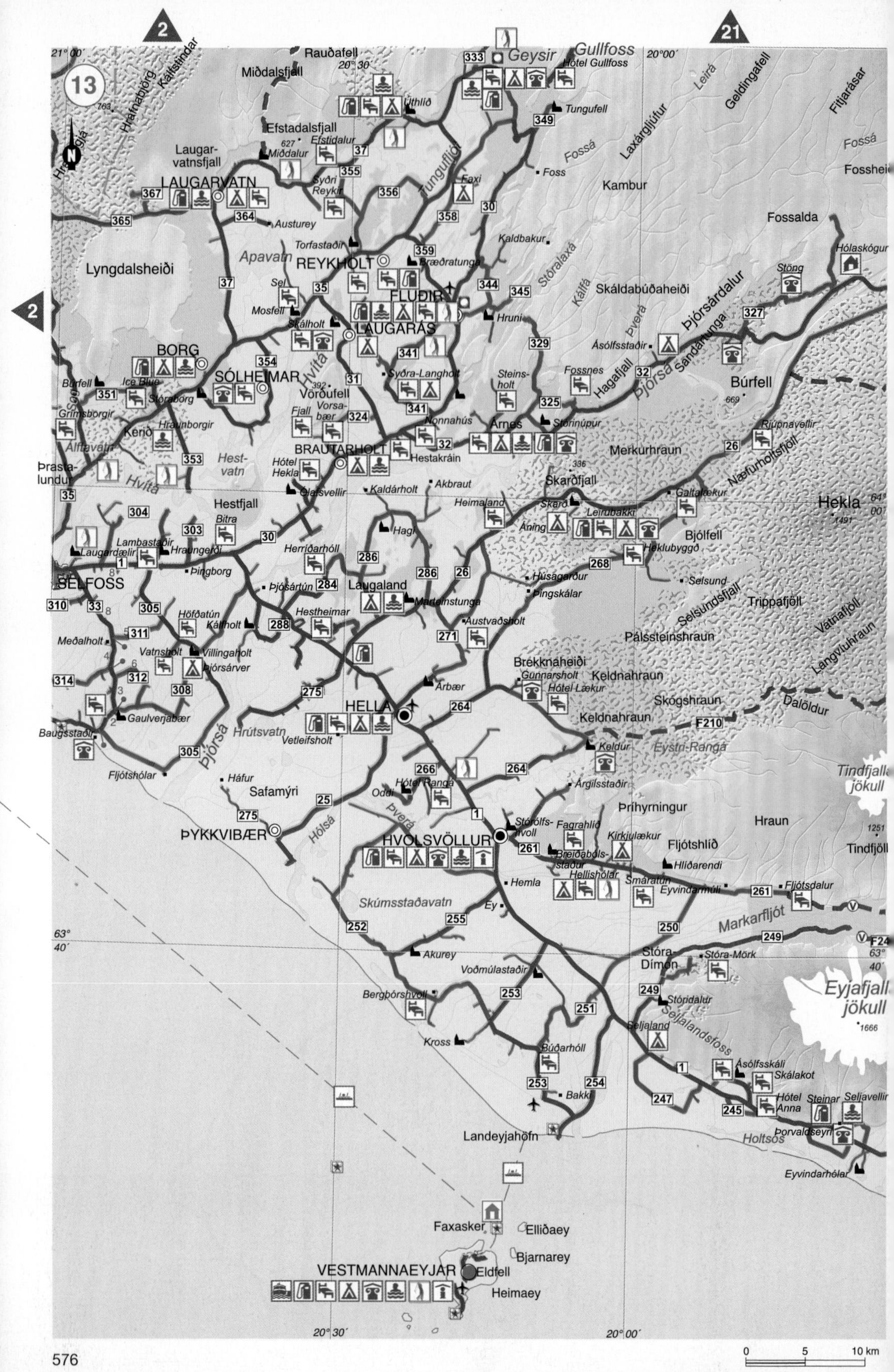
13
2
21
Geysir
Gullfoss
Hótel Gullfoss
Miðdalsfjall
Rauðafell
Efstadalsfjall
Laugarvatnsfjall
LAUGARVATN
Lyngdalsheiði
Apavatn
REYKHOLT
FLÚÐIR
LAUGARÁS
BORG
SÓLHEIMAR
Vörðufell
BRAUTARHOLT
Hótel Hekla
Hestvatn
Hestfjall
SELFOSS
Laugaland
HELLA
Hrútsvatn
Safamýri
ÞYKKVIBÆR
HVOLSVÖLLUR
Skúmsstaðavatn
Kambur
Fossalda
Skáldabúðaheiði
Þjórsárdalur
Búrfell
Merkurhraun
Skarðfjall
Hekla
Bjólfell
Trippafjöll
Pálssteinshraun
Keldnahraun
Skógshraun
Brekknaheiði
Þríhyrningur
Fljótshlíð
Markarfljót
Tindfjallajökull
Tindfjöll
Hraun
Eyjafjallajökull
Stóra-Dímon
Seljalandsfoss
Holtsós
Landeyjahöfn
Faxasker
Elliðaey
Bjarnarey
VESTMANNAEYJAR
Eldfell
Heimaey
20° 30´
20° 00´
21° 00´
63° 40´
0
5
10 km

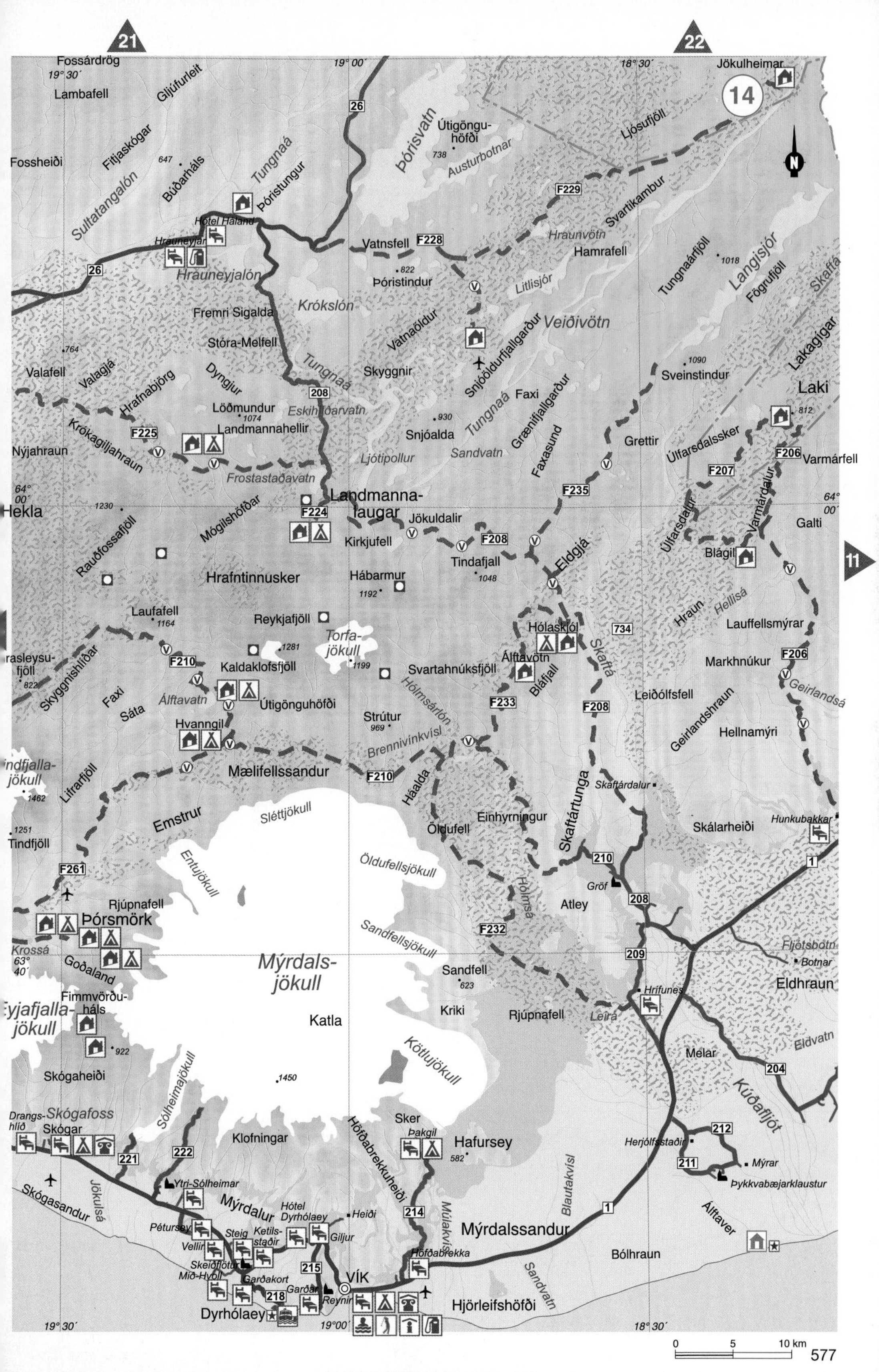

MAP OVERVIEW P. 562 - 563

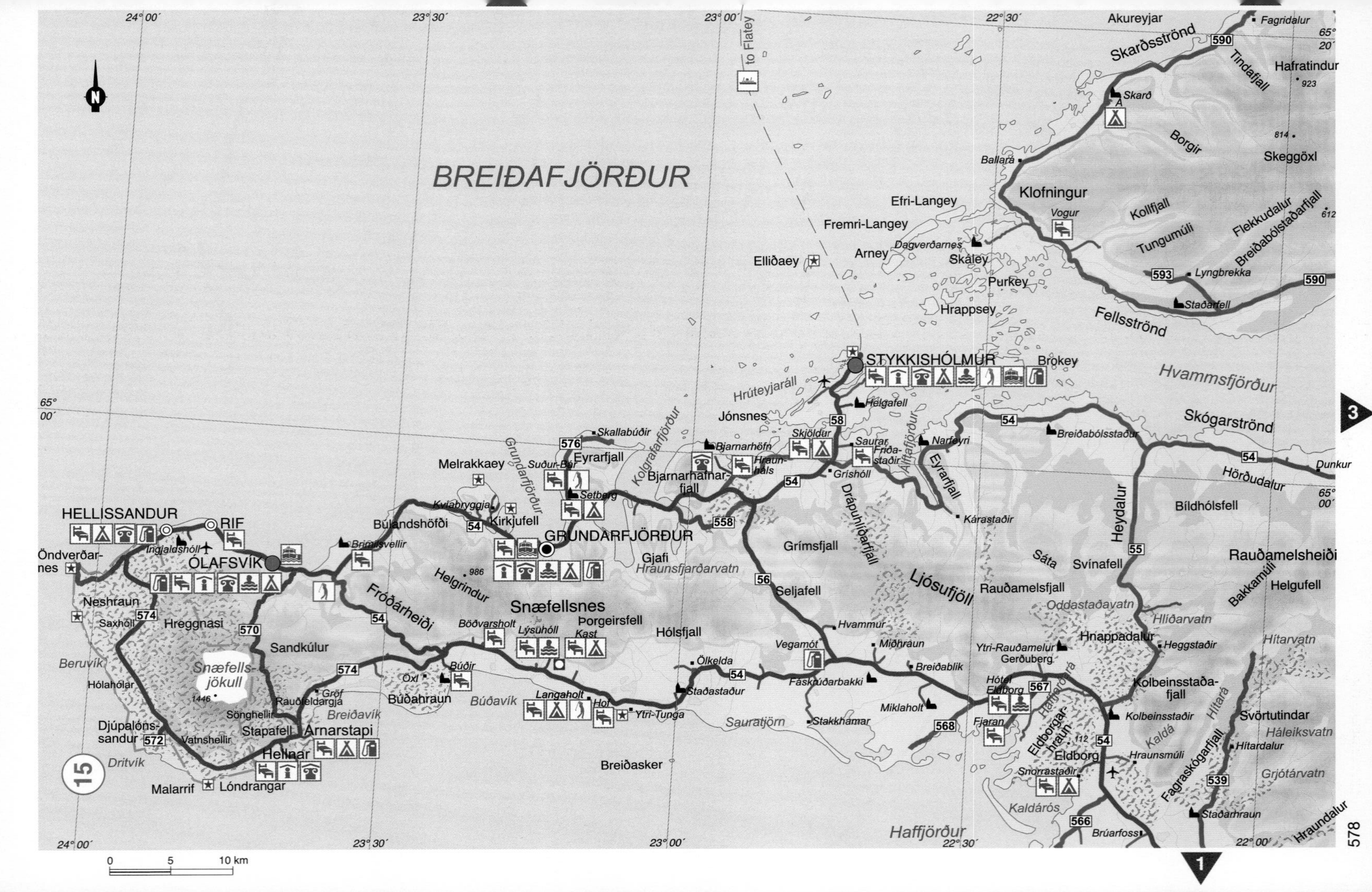

BREIÐAFJÖRÐUR
to Flatey
Akureyjar
Fagridalur
Skarðsströnd
Tindafjall
Hafratindur
923
Skarð
Borgir
814
Skeggöxl
Ballará
Klofningur
Efri-Langey
Fremri-Langey
Vogur
Kollfjall
Flekkudalur
Breiðabólstaðarfjall
612
Tungumúli
Dagverðarnes
Arney
Elliðaey
Skáley
Purkey
Lyngbrekka
Staðarfell
Hrappsey
Fellsströnd
STYKKISHÓLMUR
Brokey
Hvammsfjörður
Hrúteyjaráll
Helgafell
Jónsnes
Skógarströnd
Breiðabólsstaður
Skallabúðir
Grundarfjörður
Kolgrafarfjörður
Bjarnarhöfn
Skjöldur
Saurar
Fróðastaðir
Álftafjörður
Narfeyri
Melrakkaey
Suður-Bár
Eyrarfjall
Hraunháls
Bjarnarhafnarfjall
Grísholl
Eyrarfjall
Dunkur
Hörðudalur
Setberg
Dráputhlíðarfjall
Kárastaðir
Bíldhólsfell
HELLISSANDUR
RIF
Kvíabryggja
Kirkjufell
Búlandshöfði
GRUNDARFJÖRÐUR
Heydalur
Ingjaldshóll
Brimilsvellir
Öndverðarnes
ÓLAFSVÍK
986
Helgrindur
Gjafi
Hraunsfjarðarvatn
Grímsfjall
Sáta
Svínafell
Rauðamelsheiði
Ljósufjöll
Rauðamelsfjall
Seljafell
Bakkamúli
Helgufell
Neshraun
Fróðárheiði
Snæfellsnes
Oddastaðavatn
Hlíðarvatn
Saxhóll
Hreggnasi
Þorgeirsfell
Hólsfjall
Böðvarsholt
Lýsuhóll
Kast
Hvammur
Vegamót
Miðhraun
Ytri-Rauðamelur
Hnappadalur
Heggstaðir
Gerðuberg
Hítarvatn
Sandkúlur
Beruvík
Snæfellsjökull
Ölkelda
Breiðablik
Búðir
Öxl
Hólahólar
Gröf
Rauðfeldargjá
1446
Búðahraun
Búðavík
Langaholt
Hof
Staðastaður
Fáskrúðarbakki
Hótel Eldborg
Kolbeinsstaðafjall
Hítará
Haffjarðará
Miklaholt
Kolbeinsstaðir
Svörtutindar
Sönghellir
Breiðavík
Ytri-Tunga
Sauratjörn
Stakkhamar
Háleiksvatn
Djúpalónssandur
Stapafell
Arnarstapi
Vatnshellir
Fjaran
Eldborgarhraun
112
Kaldá
Hítardalur
Hellnar
Eldborg
Hraunsmúli
Fagraskógarfjall
Dritvík
Breiðasker
Snorrastaðir
Grjótárvatn
Malarrif
Lóndrangar
Staðarhraun
Kaldárós
Hraundalur
Brúarfoss
Haffjörður
24° 00´
23° 30´
23° 00´
22° 30´
22° 00´
65° 00´
65° 20´
0
5
10 km
15
1
3

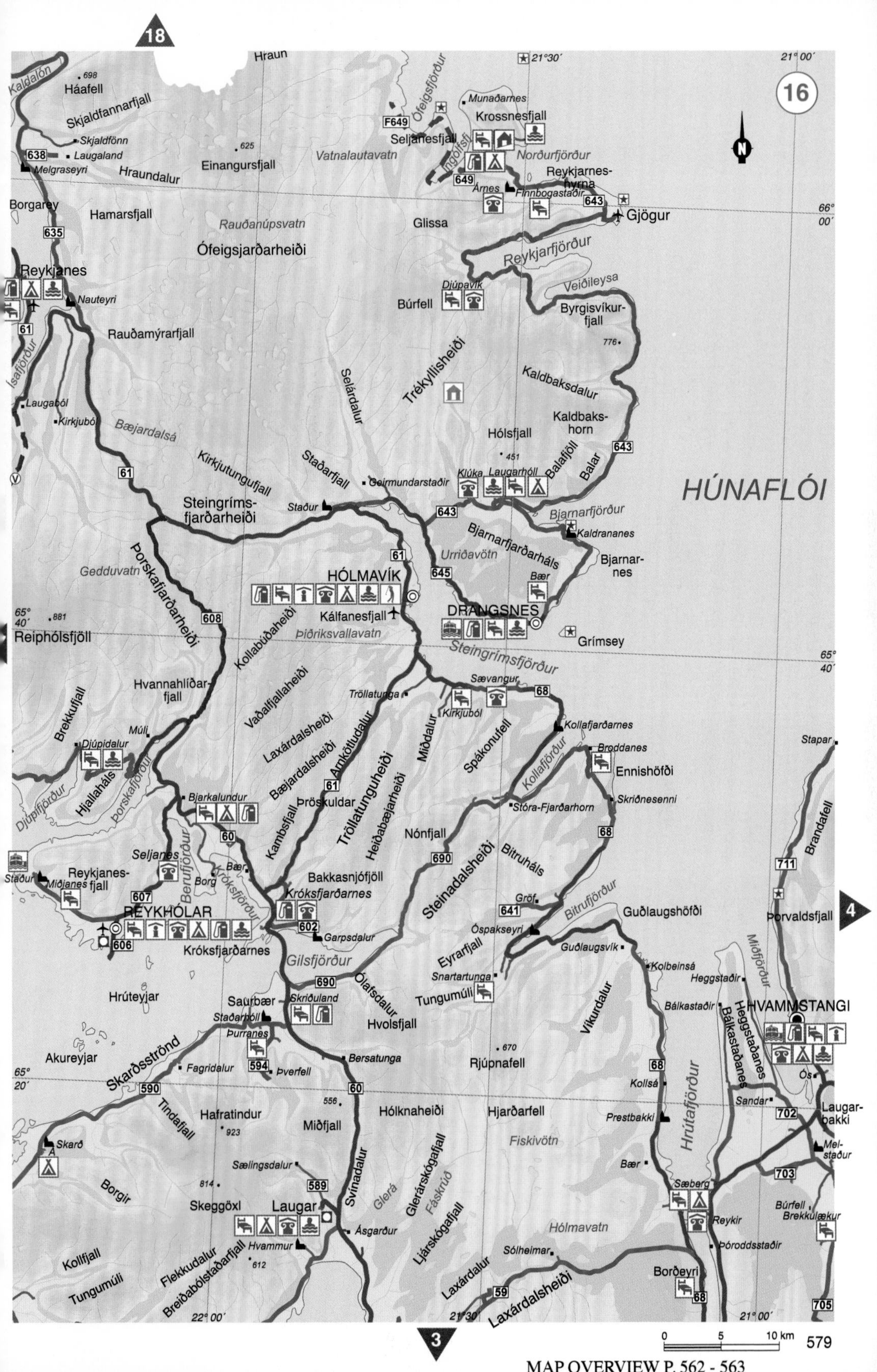

HÚNAFLÓI
HÓLMAVÍK
DRANGSNES
REYKHÓLAR
HVAMMSTANGI
Steingrímsfjörður
Reykjarfjörður
Gjögur
Krossnesfjall
Norðurfjörður
Trékyllisheiði
Steingríms-fjarðarheiði
Þorskafjarðarheiði
Gilsfjörður
Hrútafjörður
Laugar
Borðeyri
Reykjanes
Grímsey
Bjarnarfjörður
Kaldbaksdalur
Ófeigsjarðarheiði

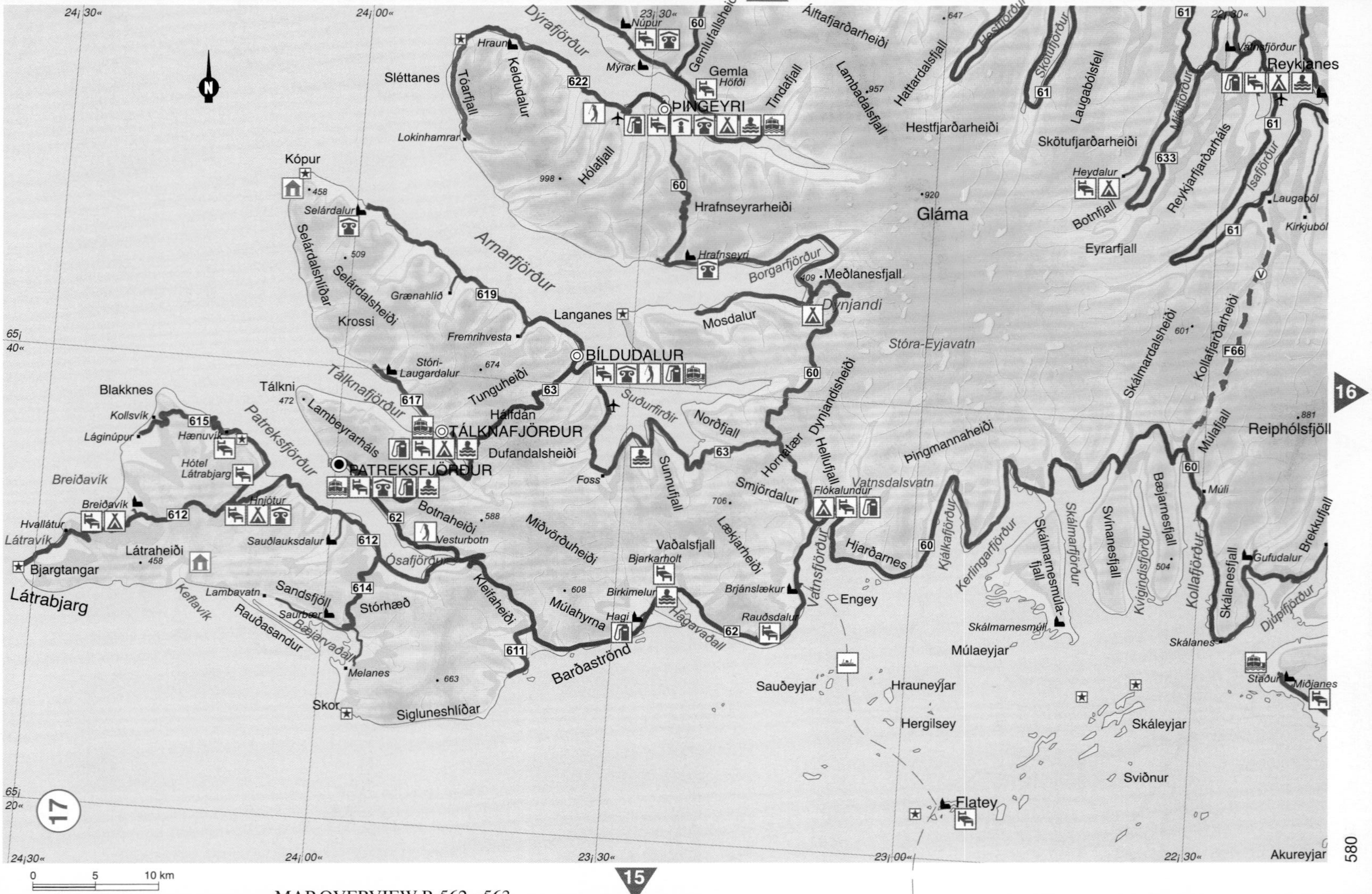
17
Látrabjarg
Bjargtangar
Látravík
Hvallátur
Breiðavík
Látraheiði
458
Keflavík
Lambavatn
Rauðasandur
Sandsfjöll
Saurbær
Bæjarvaðall
Melanes
Skor
663
Sigluneshlíðar
Stórhæð
Blakknes
Kollsvík
Láginúpur
Hænuvík
Hótel Látrabjarg
Hnjótur
Sauðlauksdalur
Patreksfjörður
PATREKSFJÖRÐUR
Botnaheiði
588
Vesturbotn
Ósafjörður
Kleifaheiði
Miðvörðuheiði
608
Múlahyrna
Hagi
Barðaströnd
Birkimelur
Bjarkarholt
Hagavaðall
Vaðalsfjall
Lækjarheiði
Brjánslækur
Rauðsdalur
Tálkni
472
Lambeyrarháls
Tálknafjörður
TÁLKNAFJÖRÐUR
Dufandalsheiði
Hálfdán
Tunguheiði
674
Stóri-Laugardalur
Foss
Sunnufjall
Suðurfirðir
Norðfjall
706
Smjördalur
Hornatær
BÍLDUDALUR
Langanes
Arnarfjörður
Fremrihvesta
Krossi
Grænahlíð
Selárdalsheiði
Selárdalshlíðar
509
Selárdalur
Kópur
458
Mosdalur
Dynjandi
Dynjandisheiði
Hellufjall
Flókalundur
Vatnsdalsvatn
Vatnsfjörður
Engey
Hjarðarnes
Þingmannaheiði
Kjálkafjörður
Kerlingarfjörður
Skálmarnesmúla-fjall
Skálmarnesmúli
Skálmarfjörður
Svínanesfjall
Kvígindisfjörður
Bæjarnesfjall
504
Kollafjörður
Múlaeyjar
Sauðeyjar
Hrauneyjar
Hergilsey
Flatey
Skáleyjar
Sviðnur
Skálanes
Skálanesfjall
Djúpifjörður
Staður
Miðjanes
Gufudalur
Brekkufjall
Múli
Múlafjall
Reipholsfjöll
881
Kollafjarðarheiði
F66
Skálmardalsheiði
601
Stóra-Eyjavatn
Meðlanesfjall
409
Borgarfjörður
Hrafnseyri
Hrafnseyrarheiði
Glàma
920
Sléttanes
Tóarfjall
Keldudalur
Hraun
Lokinhamrar
Dýrafjörður
Mýrar
Núpur
Gemlufallsheiði
Gemla
Höfði
ÞINGEYRI
Hólafjall
998
Tindafjall
Lambadalsfjall
957
Álftafjarðarheiði
647
Hattardalsfjall
Hestfjarðarheiði
Hestfjörður
Skötufjörður
Laugabólsfell
Skötufjarðarheiði
Heydalur
Botnfjall
Eyrarfjall
Mjóifjörður
Reykjarfjarðarháls
Ísafjörður
Laugaból
Kirkjuból
Reykjanes
Vatnsfjörður
Akureyjar
60
61
62
63
611
612
614
615
617
619
622
633
24¡ 30«
24¡ 00«
23¡ 30«
23¡ 00«
22¡ 30«
65¡ 40«
65¡ 20«
0
5
10 km
15
16

MAP OVERVIEW P. 562 - 563

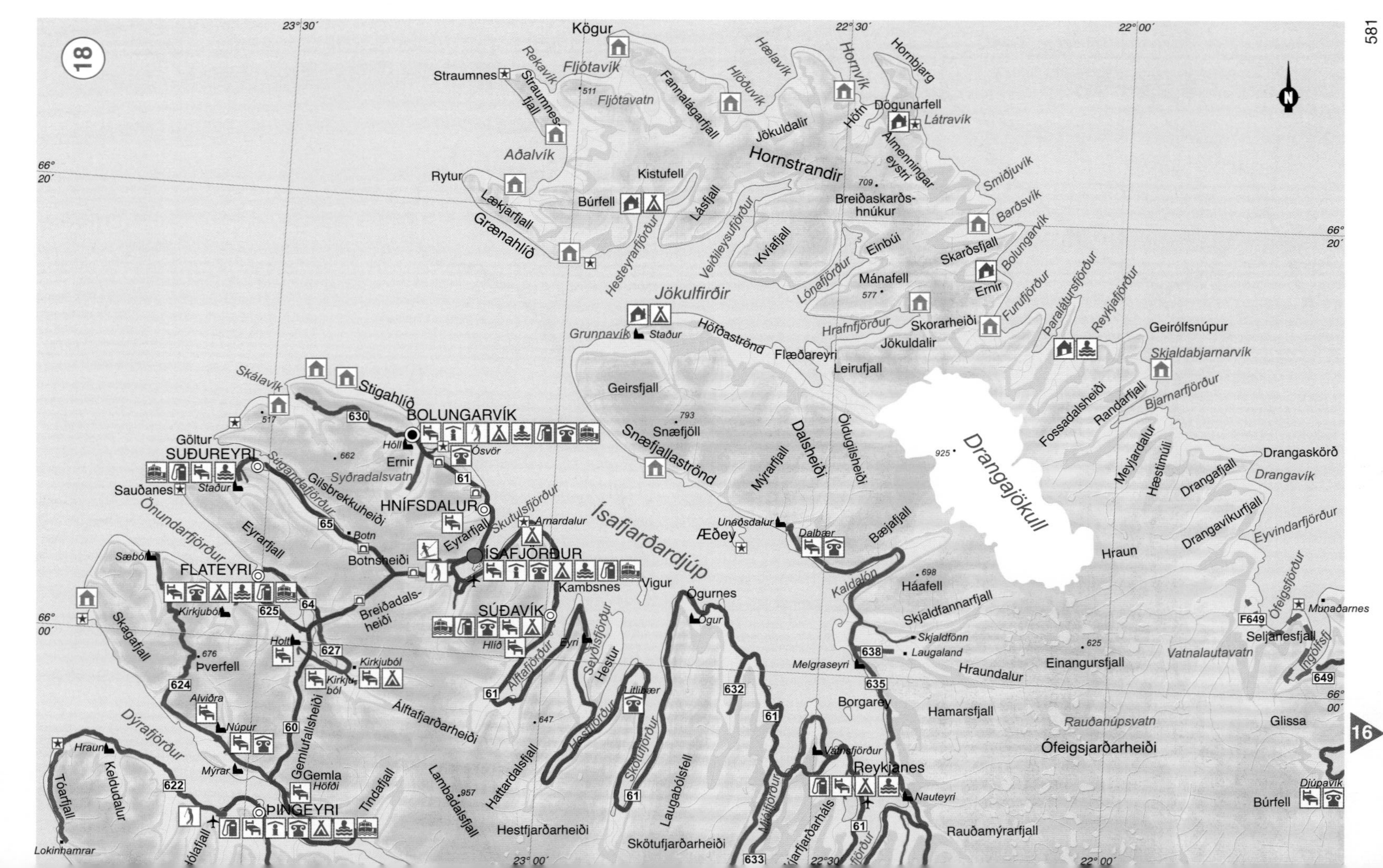

MAP OVERVIEW P. 562 - 563

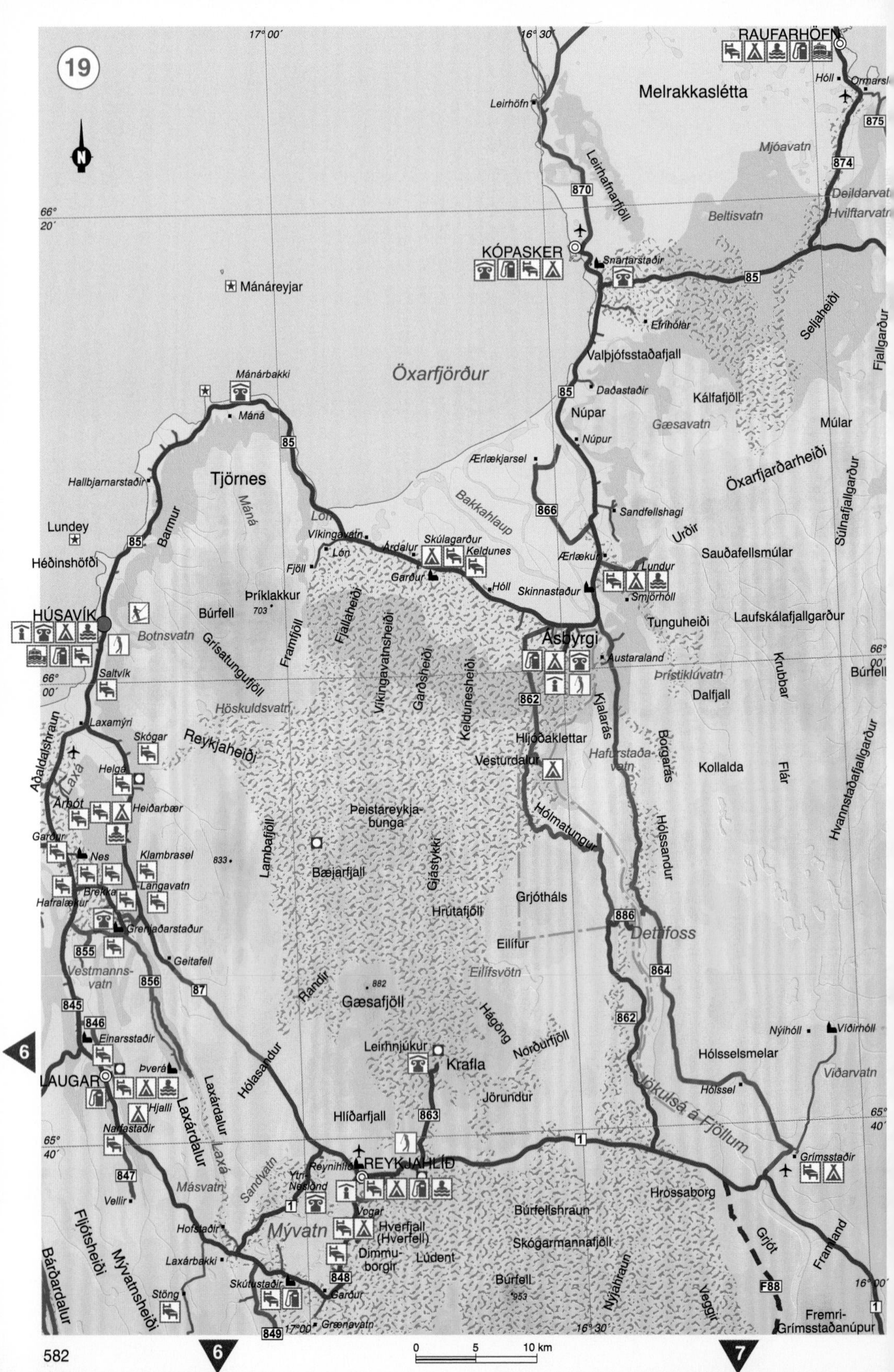
19
RAUFARHÖFN
Melrakkaslétta
Leirhöfn
Leirhafnarfjöll
Mjóavatn
Beltisvatn
KÓPASKER
Snartarstaðir
Mánáreyjar
Efrihólar
Valþjófsstaðafjall
Seljaheiði
Mánárbakki
Öxarfjörður
Daðastaðir
Kálfafjöll
Núpar
Gæsavatn
Múlar
Máná
Núpur
Ærlækjarsel
Öxarfjarðarheiði
Tjörnes
Hallbjarnarstaðir
Bakkahlaup
Sandfellshagi
Lundey
Víkingavatn
Skúlagarður
Keldunes
Urðir
Héðinshöfði
Lón
Árdalur
Sauðafellsmúlar
Fjöll
Garður
Lundur
Skinnastaður
Smjörhóll
Þríklakkur
Hóll
HÚSAVÍK
Búrfell
Tunguheiði
Laufskálafjallgarður
Botnsvatn
Ásbyrgi
Austaraland
Saltvík
Þrístiklúvatn
Dalfjall
Höskuldsvatn
Laxamýri
Skógar
Reykjaheiði
Hljóðaklettar
Vesturdalur
Kollalda
Helga
Árbót
Heiðarbær
Þeistareykjabunga
Hólmatungur
Hólssandur
Nes
Klambrasel
Bæjarfjall
Langavatn
Hafralækur
Brekka
Grjótháls
Hrútafjöll
Grenjaðarstaður
Dettifoss
Eilífur
Geitafell
Eilífsvötn
Vestmannsvatn
Gæsafjöll
Hágöng
Nýjhóll
Víðirhóll
Einarsstaðir
Leirhnjúkur
Krafla
Norðurfjöll
Hólsselsmelar
LAUGAR
Þverá
Víðarvatn
Hjalli
Jörundur
Hólssel
Hlíðarfjall
Jökulsá á Fjöllum
Narfastaðir
Laxárdalur
REYKJAHLÍÐ
Reynihlíð
Grímsstaðir
Sandvatn
Mássvatn
Hrossaborg
Vellir
Vogar
Búrfellshraun
Fljótsheiði
Hofstaðir
Mývatn
Hverfjall (Hverfell)
Skógarmannafjöll
Mývatnsheiði
Laxárbakki
Dimmuborgir
Lúdent
Búrfell
Skútustaðir
Garður
Stöng
Bárðardalur
Grænavatn
Nýjahraun
Veggir
Fremri-Grímsstaðanúpur
85
870
874
875
866
862
886
864
855
856
87
845
846
847
863
1
848
849
F88
6
7
0 5 10 km

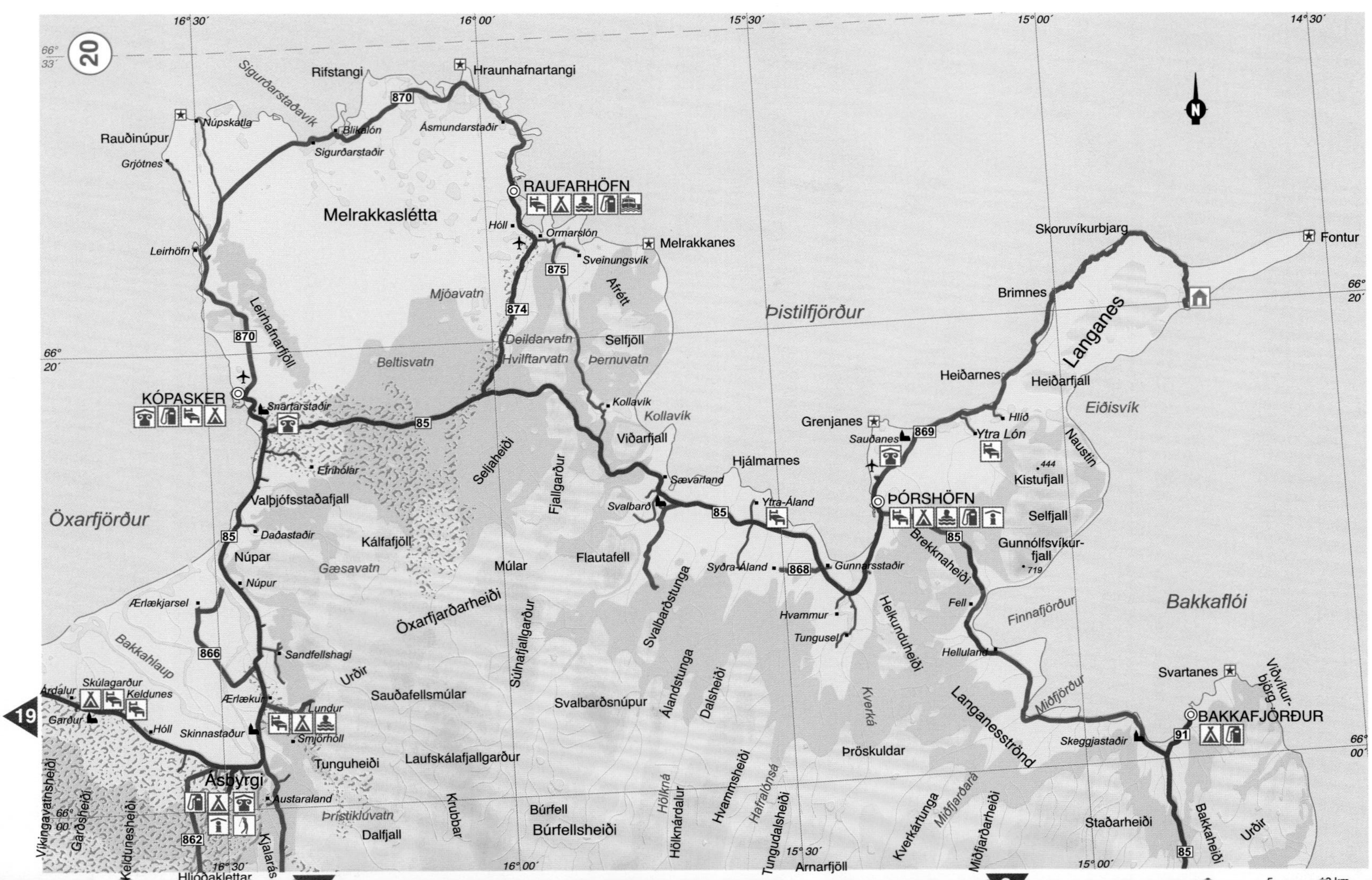

MAP OVERVIEW P. 562 - 563

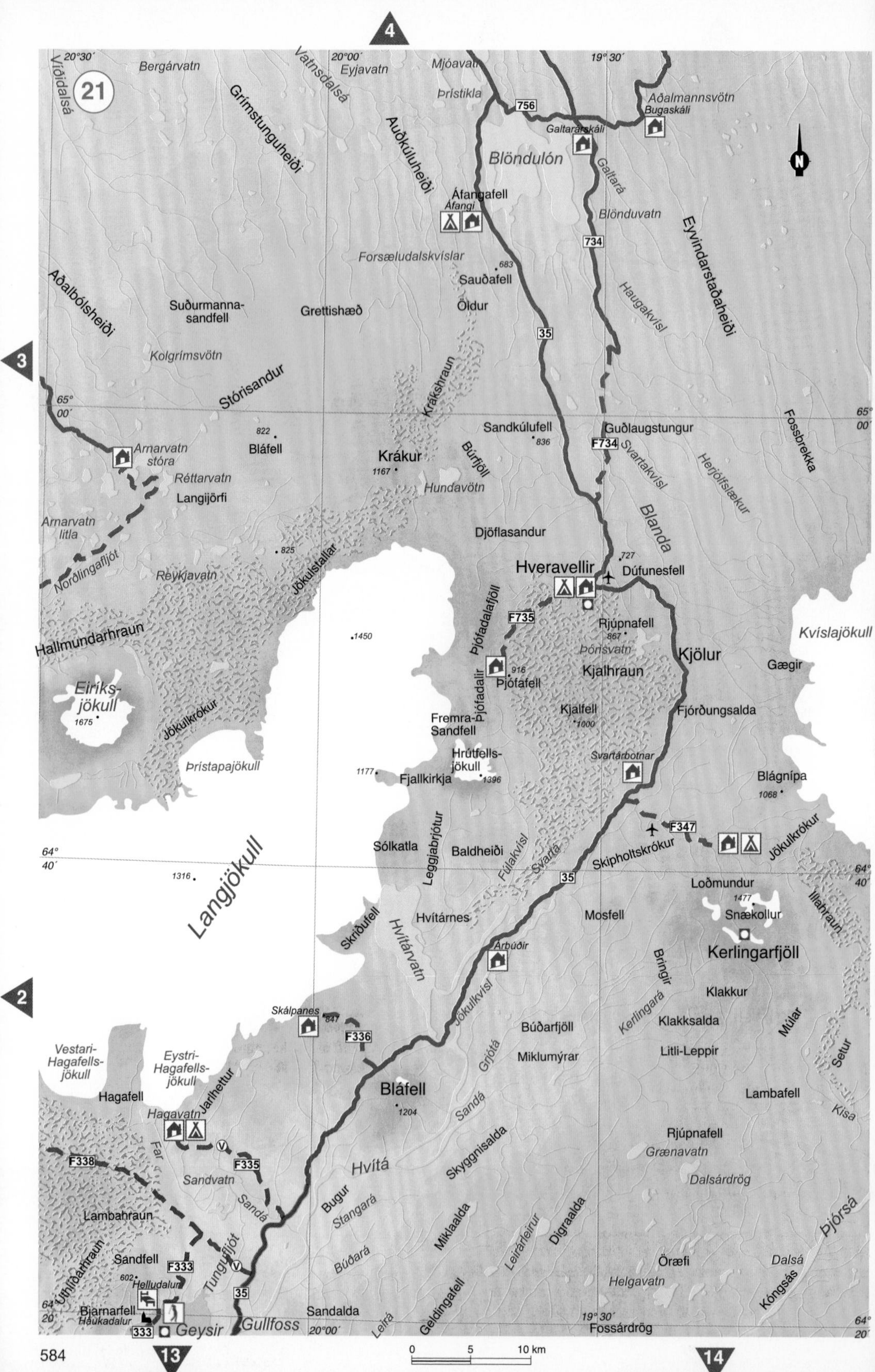
21
Bergárvatn
Víðidalsá
Grímstunguheiði
Vatnsdalsá
Eyjavatn
Mjóavatn
Þrístikla
Auðkúluheiði
Blöndulón
Galtarárskáli
Aðalmannsvötn
Bugaskáli
Galtará
Áfangafell
Áfangi
Blönduvatn
Eyvindarstaðaheiði
Forsæludalskvíslar
Sauðafell
Haugakvísl
Aðalbólsheiði
Suðurmanna-
sandfell
Grettishæð
Öldur
Kolgrímsvötn
Stórisandur
Krákshraun
Sandkúlufell
Guðlaugstungur
Fossbrekka
Arnarvatn
stóra
Bláfell
Krákur
Búrfjöll
Svartakvísl
Herjólfslækur
Réttarvatn
Langijörfi
Hundavötn
Arnarvatn
litla
Djöflasandur
Blanda
Norðlingafljót
Reykjavatn
Jökulstallar
Hveravellir
Dúfunesfell
Hallmundarhraun
Þjófadalafjöll
Rjúpnafell
Kvíslajökull
Þórisvatn
Kjölur
Kjalhraun
Gægir
Eiríks-
jökull
Þjófadalir
Þjófafell
Kjalfell
Fjórðungsalda
Fremra-
Sandfell
Jökulkrókur
Hrútfells-
jökull
Svartárbotnar
Þrístapajökull
Fjallkirkja
Blágnípa
Leggjabrjótur
Sólkatla
Baldheiði
Fúlakvísl
Svartá
Skipholtskrókur
Jökulkrókur
Langjökull
Loðmundur
Snækollur
Illahraun
Skriðufell
Hvítárnes
Mosfell
Hvítárvatn
Árbúðir
Bringir
Kerlingarfjöll
Klakkur
Jökulkvísl
Kerlingará
Klakksalda
Múlar
Skálpanes
Búðarfjöll
Vestari-
Hagafells-
jökull
Eystri-
Hagafells-
jökull
Grjótá
Miklumýrar
Litli-Leppir
Setur
Jarlhettur
Hagafell
Bláfell
Lambafell
Hagavatn
Sandá
Kisa
Rjúpnafell
Grænavatn
Far
Skyggnisalda
Hvítá
Sandvatn
Dalsárdrög
Sandá
Bugur
Stangará
Lambahraun
Miklaalda
Digraalda
Þjórsá
Úthlíðarhraun
Leirárleirur
Sandfell
Tungufljót
Búðará
Öræfi
Dalsá
Helludalur
Helgavatn
Köngsás
Bjarnarfell
Haukadalur
Sandalda
Geldingafell
Geysir
Gullfoss
Leirá
Fossárdrög
756
734
35
F734
F735
F347
F336
F335
F338
F333
333
683
822
836
1167
825
727
1450
867
916
1000
1675
1177
1396
1068
1316
1477
647
1204
602
20°30´
20°00´
19° 30´
65° 00´
64° 40´
64° 20´
3
4
2
13
14
0
5
10 km
N

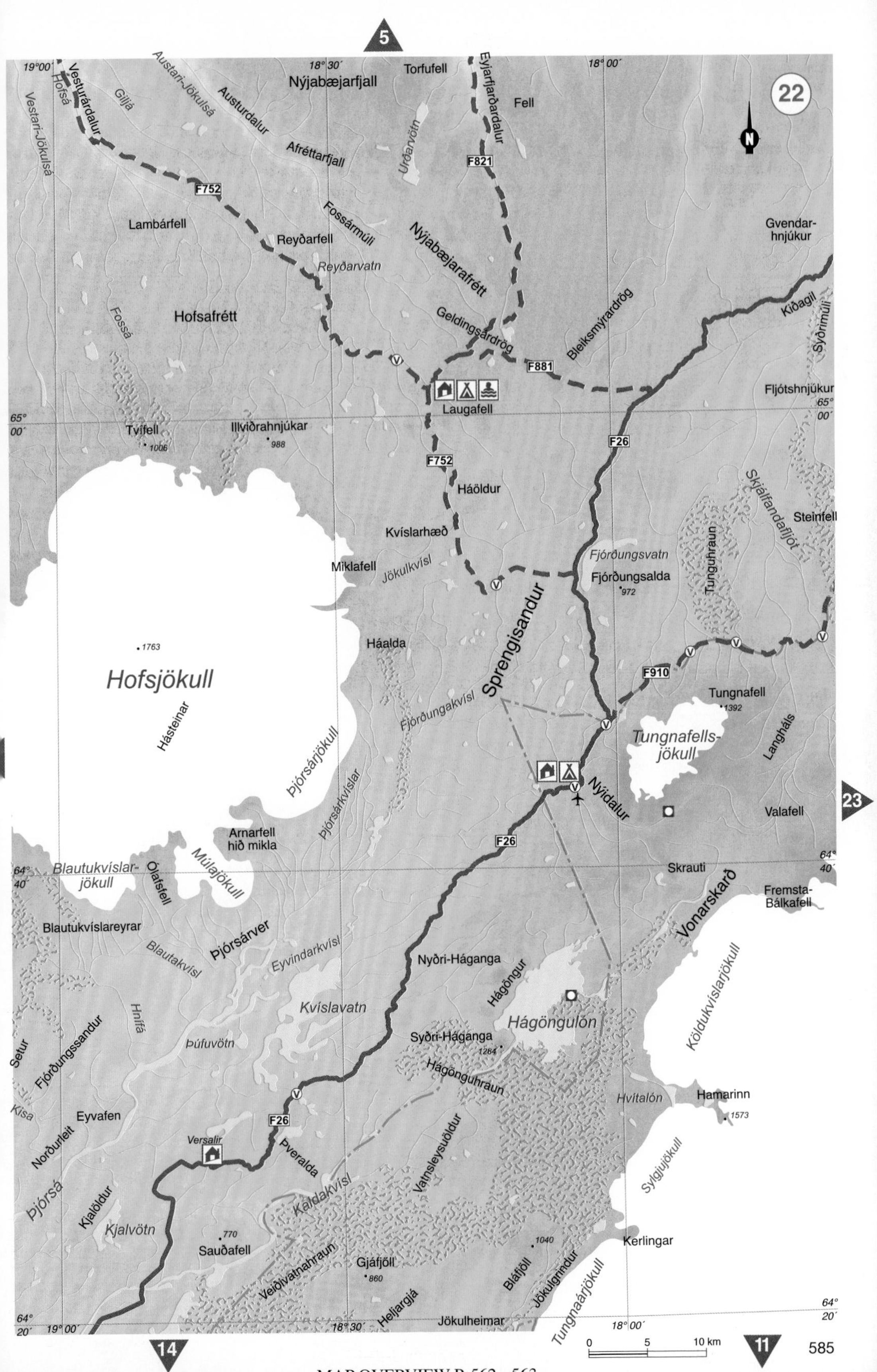

MAP OVERVIEW P. 562 - 563

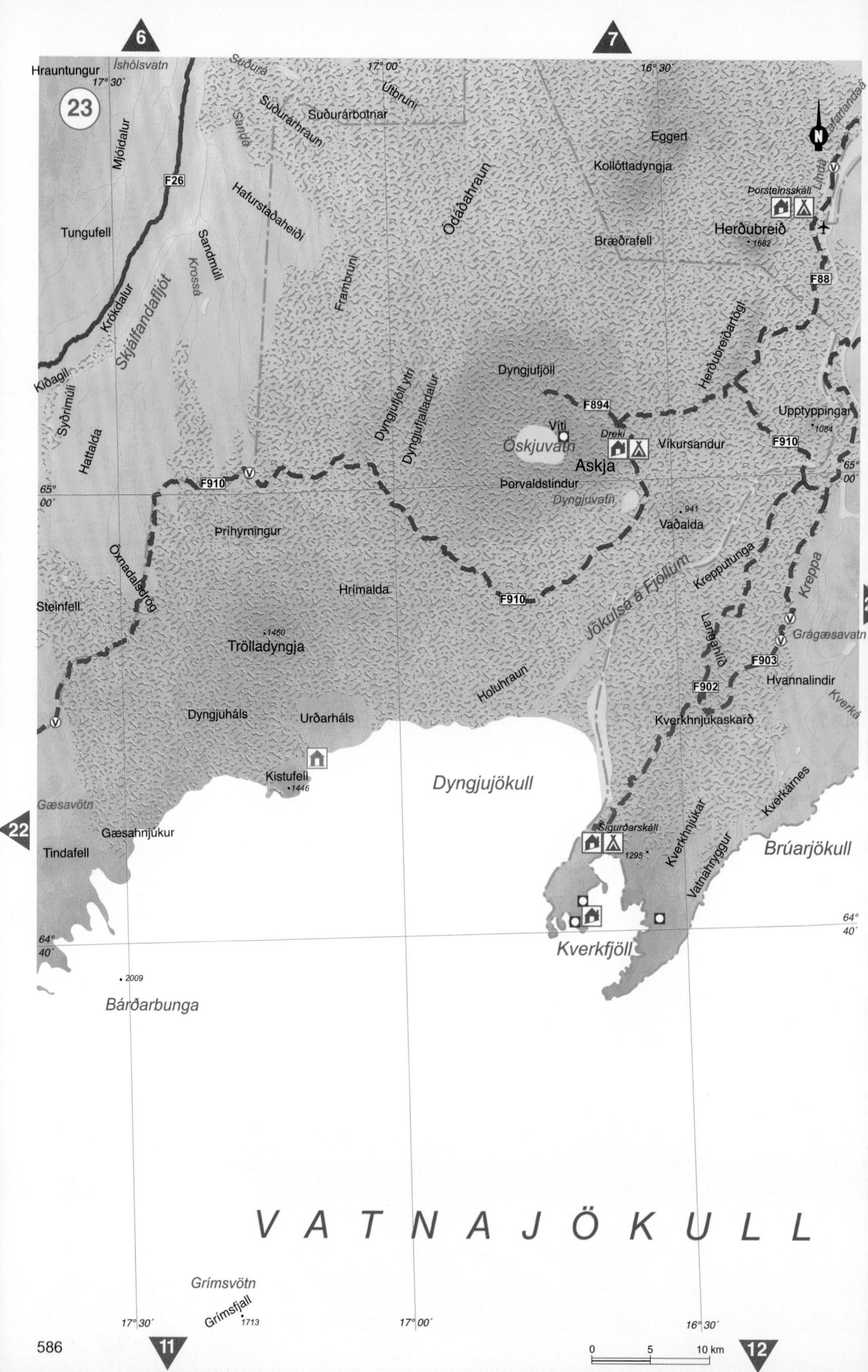
6
7
23
Hrauntungur
Íshólsvatn
Suðurá
Útbruni
Suðurárbotnar
Suðurárhraun
Sandá
Mjóidalur
F26
Eggert
Kollóttadyngja
Þorsteinsskáli
Herðubreið
1682
Bræðrafell
Hafurstaðaheiði
Ódáðahraun
Tungufell
Sandmúli
Krossá
Skjálfandafljót
Krókdalur
Frambruni
F88
Herðubreiðartögl
Kiðagil
Syðrimúli
Hattalda
Dyngjufjöll
F894
Dyngjufjöll ytri
Dyngjufjalladalur
Víti
Öskjuvatn
Dreki
Askja
Víkursandur
Upptyppingar
1084
F910
Þorvaldstindur
Dyngjuvatn
941
Vaðalda
Þríhyrningur
Öxnadalsdrög
Krepputunga
Hrímalda
Jökulsá á Fjöllum
Kreppa
Steinfell
1460
Trölladyngja
Langahlíð
Grágæsavatn
F903
Hvannalindir
Holuhraun
F902
Kverká
Dyngjuháls
Urðarháls
Kverkhnjúkaskarð
Kistufell
1446
Dyngjujökull
Kverkárnes
Gæsavötn
22
Gæsahnjúkur
Tindafell
Sigurðarskáli
1295
Kverkhnjúkar
Vatnahryggur
Brúarjökull
Kverkfjöll
2009
Bárðarbunga
V A T N A J Ö K U L L
Grímsvötn
Grímsfjall
1713
11
12
0
5
10 km

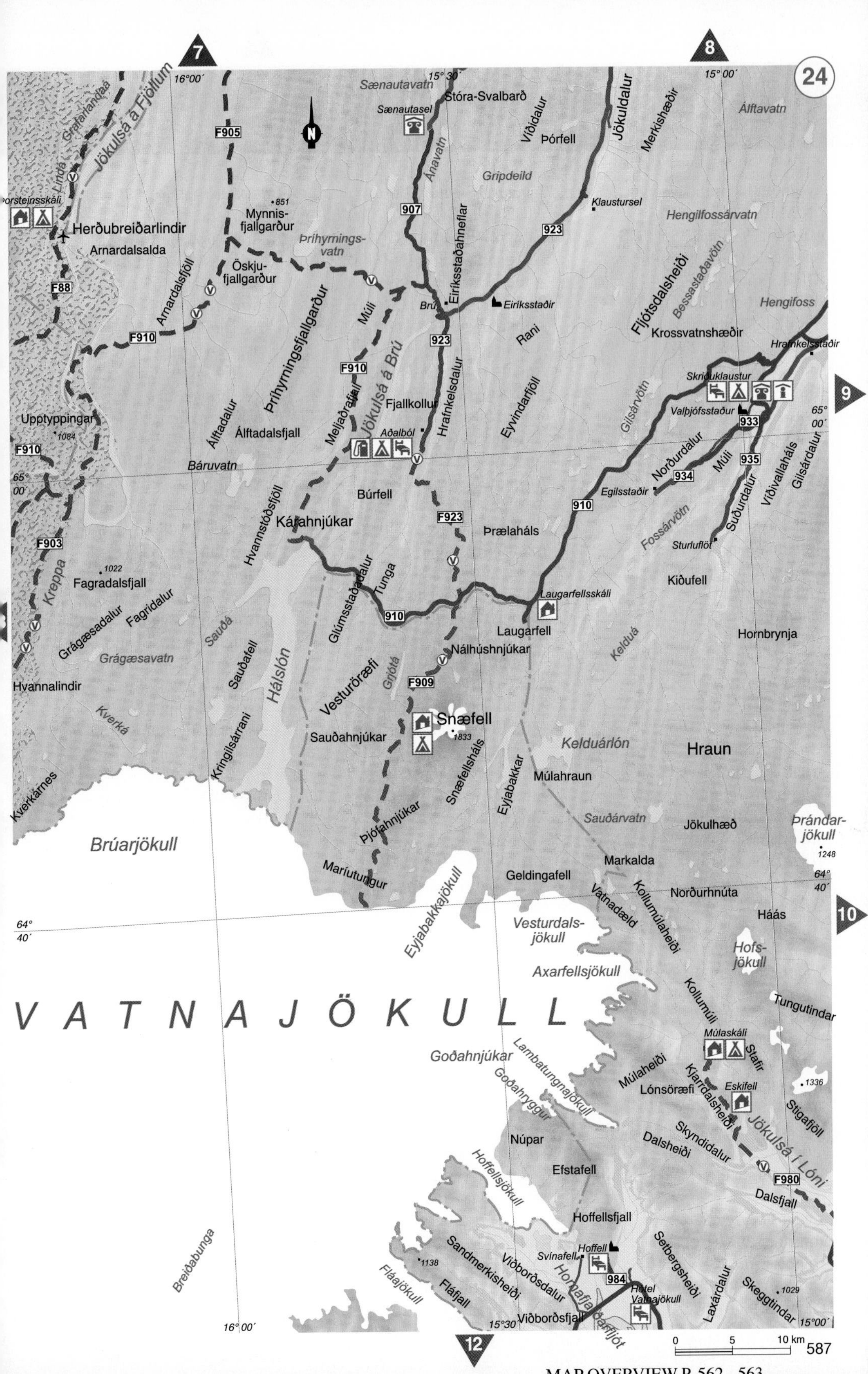

MAP OVERVIEW P. 562 - 563

INDEX

Photo Credit

Björn Jónsson: 61, 161, 240, 241, 248, 263, 264, 278, 283, 309, 349, 385, 395,
Daniel Bruun/Jóhannes Klein: 110, 111, 257, 398, 399
Friðþjófur þorkelsson: Hestar
Fríða Hálfdanardóttir: 175, 183, 189, 236, 468
Hálfdan Örlygsson: 58, 59, 60, 61, 70, 72, 73, 74, 190, 194, 197
Jón Eiríksson, the Icelandic sheep and cow
Jónas Reynir Helgason: 87, 366, 398
Mats Wibe Lund: 138
Olgeir Andrésson: 73, 116, 160, 248, 270, 274, 336
Pálmi Guðmundsson: 86, 95, 169, 230, 231, 244, 345, 346, 396, 422, 426
Peter Lorkowski: 498
Rúnar Gunnarsson: 86, 176, 181, 224, 227, 468, 484, 489, 523
Þjóðminjasafn Íslands: 120, 170, 202, 392
Örlygur Hálfdanarson: 104, 135, 149, 222, 268, 269, 314
The Icelandic Horse :
Reference: "Íslenski hesturinn – litir og erfðir",
Stefán Aðalsteinsson

Safetravel
- For Your Safe Return

Driving in Iceland

Conditions in Iceland are in many ways unusual and often quite unlike what foreign drivers are accustomed to. It is therefore very important to find out how to drive in this country. We know that the landscapes are beautiful, which naturally draws the driver's attention away from the road. But in order to reach your destination safely, you must keep your full attention on driving.

- The speed limit is often 60 km/hr on thruways, but in residential areas it is usually only 30 km/hr.
- The main rule in rural areas is that gravel roads have a speed limit of 80 km/hr, and paved roads 90 km/hr.
- Watch out for single-lane bridges, they are many in Iceland. Slow down when getting close to them.
- Common place for accidents to occcur on rural roads is where a paved road suddenly changes to gravel. Reduce speed to avoid serious accidents.

Highland driving

Driving in the Icelandic highland is quite different from driving in the lowland. The conditions can change fast due to weather, rain and even sometimes snow. Therefore roads can be closed and rivers can be too big to cross.

Before you start your travel you should get information about the area as well as leave your travel plan with someone who can check up on you if needed. You can make your travel plan here.

- Start by checking if the area you are going to visit is open
- Get as much information about the area as you can
- Information centers, rangers and hut wardens can help you get the information needed
- Are you sure that you have the experience and knowledge needed to go the highland?
- If you are driving be on a 4x4 jeep, other cars will only get you into trouble
- If you are no sure how to cross a river skip it or wait for the next car to assist you ove

Get more information on www.safetravel.is

The emergency number in Iceland is 112

Safetravel

- For Your Safe Return

Outdoors

Good preparation is the key for a successful travel. Keep the below points in mind and remember that your first destination should always be **safetravel.is**

- Always leave your travel plan with someone who can react if needed
- Check the weather forecast. In Iceland the weather can change fast
- Remember to bring the right equiptment for the kind of travel you are planning
- Map, kompass and GPS should always be used when travel outside urban areas

Hiking

The first question that comes up for every hiker is where to go and what hiking trail to choose. Is it a well-known marked trail or off the beaten path? Regardless of what is decided, proper trail selection and route planning are essential components to a successful hike.

To ensure a better hike keep this in mind:

- When choosing a hiking trail, hikers should always use themselves as a frame of reference, i.e. their level of fitness and their experience and knowledge of hiking.
- Don't set out to do too much, plan reasonable distances each day.
- Keep in mind that even though a trail may have markers, visibility can be so poor that it is not possible to see from one mark to another.
- Compasses and GPS devices should be brought, alongside the knowledge of how to use them.
- A route plan is an important aid for every hiker. With a route plan you can plot day trips, distance to hike each day, write down accommodation details, a contingency plan if that might be needed, and other things that are important in making a good hike even better.
- The route plan should be left with a trustworthy person. He or she will then have exact information about the trip, in the event that a situation may arise in which it is needed.

Get more information on www.safetravel.is

The emergency number in Iceland is 112

Safetravel

- For Your Safe Return

Nature

The Icelandic nature is one of a kind and we are drawn to it again and again but at the same time travelling in the nature can be dangerous so we should keep the following in mind

- Get good information about the area you are travelling to
- Accidents are common when people get to close to the sea, cliff edges and hot springs.
- Sudden changes in weather are common especially in the highland
- When travelling the highland remember to check where you will find service. Often you have to drive a long way to get oil or food.

Off Road

Off road driving in Iceland is strictly prohibited and you can get very high fund braking those laws. Whilst travelling around the country, the highest respect for the Icelandic environment must be shown. It's good to remember to take nothing besides photographs and leave nothing behind except footprints.

- Check out the road map and see where the roads and trails are.
- Get information about the appropriate routes at visitor centres, and from rangers or staff.
- Find out in advance when mountain roads are likely to be open, along with other related information, at visitor centres.
- Get more information about driving in Iceland at www.safetravel.is
- The emergency number in Iceland is 112

Get more information on www.safetravel.is

The emergency number in Iceland is 112